Contemporary Authors

NEW REVISION SERIES

ISSN 0275-7176

Contemporary Authors

A Bio-Bibliographical Guide to
Current Writers in Fiction, General Nonfiction,
Poetry, Journalism, Drama, Motion Pictures,
Television, and Other Fields

LINDA METZGER
Editor

PETER M. GAREFFA
JAMES G. LESNIAK
DEBORAH A. STRAUB
Associate Editors

NEW REVISION SERIES
volume 14

GALE RESEARCH COMPANY • BOOK TOWER • DETROIT, MICHIGAN 48226

STAFF

Linda Metzger, *Editor, New Revision Series*

Peter M. Gareffa, James G. Lesniak, and Deborah A. Straub, *Associate Editors*

Donna Olendorf and Thomas Wiloch, *Senior Assistant Editors*

Candace Cloutier, Nancy Hebb, Kerry L. Lutz, Joan E. Marecki,
Margaret Mazurkiewicz, Bryan Ryan, Susan Salter,
Michaela Swart Wilson, and Robert T. Wilson, *Assistant Editors*

Jean W. Ross and Walter W. Ross, *Interviewers*

Melissa J. Gaiownik, Timothy Marshall, Allison Payne,
and Mary Alice Rattenbury, *Editorial Assistants*

Frederick G. Ruffner, *Publisher*
James M. Ethridge, *Executive Vice-President/Editorial*
Dedria Bryfonski, *Editorial Director*
Christine Nasso, *Director, Literature Division*
Ann Evory, *Senior Editor, Contemporary Authors*

Library of Congress Catalog Card Number 81-640179
ISBN 0-8103-1943-8
ISSN 0275-7176

Contents

Authors and Media People
Featured in This Volume

Judith Appelbaum—American magazine editor, columnist, and founder and managing director of a publishing consulting firm; her co-authored work *How to Get Happily Published* offers writers advice for achieving successful publication. (Sketch includes interview.)

Harriette Arnow—American novelist whose work depicts the erosion of rural life in the Cumberland hills of Kentucky; Joyce Carol Oates praised *The Dollmaker*, Arnow's best known book, as "our most unpretentious American masterpiece."

Christiaan Barnard—South African surgeon who performed the world's first successful heart transplant operation; his autobiography, *Christiaan Barnard: One Life*, recounts his achievements en route to becoming "the world's most famous surgeon"; also author of the medical novels *The Unwanted* and *In the Night Season*.

Jan and Stan Berenstain—American authors and illustrators of juvenile works; creators of the popular and award-winning juvenile series the "Berenstain Bears" and the feature "It's All in the Family," which currently appears in *Good Housekeeping;* an entry for their son Michael Berenstain also appears in this volume.

Fernand Braudel—French historian who advocates a multidisciplinary approach to the study of the past; among his works in English translation are *The Structures of Everyday Life*, which was nominated for the 1982 *Los Angeles Times* Book Prize, and *The Wheels of Commerce*, which won that award in 1983.

Leonard Cohen—Canadian poet, novelist, singer, and songwriter; his work includes the poetry collections *Let Us Compare Mythologies, Flowers for Hitler*, and *Credo*, the novels *The Favorite Game* and *Beautiful Losers*, and the song "Suzanne."

Joan Didion—American novelist, essayist, and screenwriter; a practitioner of New Journalism, she has won praise for her elegant writing style and distinctive literary voice; Didion's novel *Play It as It Lays* received a National Book Award nomination in 1971, her collection of essays *The White Album* was nominated for a 1980 National Book Critics Circle Prize and a 1980 American Book Award, and her novel *Democracy* garnered a *Los Angeles Times* Book Prize nomination in 1984.

John Gregory Dunne—American novelist, nonfiction writer, and screenwriter; his fiction stems from his own Irish Catholic experience, which he refers to as the "Mother Lode"; his works include the novels *Vegas* and *Dutch Shea, Jr.* and the screenplays, co-authored with his wife, Joan Didion, "Panic in Needle Park," "A Star Is Born," and "True Confessions."

Allan W. Eckert—American author who combines natural history with fiction to create a form some critics call "documentary fiction"; among his best known books are *The Frontiersmen, The Great Auk*, and *Incident at Hawk's Hill*. (Sketch includes interview.)

Ron Galella—American magazine and newspaper photographer who specializes in candid shots of international celebrities; one of his favorite subjects was Jacqueline Kennedy Onassis, who sued the photographer in 1972, charging him with invasion of her privacy. (Sketch includes interview.)

Joanne Greenberg—American novelist and short story writer; under the pseudonym Hannah Green, author of the autobiographical work *I Never Promised You a Rose Garden*, the story of a young girl's battle against schizophrenia.

William Kennedy—American professor, novelist, and author of nonfiction; he is best known for the novels in his "Albany cycle"—*Legs, Billy Phelan's Greatest Game*, and *Ironweed*, which was named one of 1983's best books by the *New York Times Book Review* and won the 1983 National Book Critics Circle Prize and the 1984 Pulitzer Prize.

Dan Kurzman—American journalist, formerly a foreign correspondent for the *Washington Post*, and author of award-winning nonfiction; his books include *Subversion of the Innocents, Miracle of November*, winner of the 1980 Cornelius Ryan Award, and *Ben-Gurion*, which received the 1984 National Jewish Book Award for biography.

Fran Lebowitz—American essayist and former columnist for *Interview* and *Mademoiselle;* her collections of humorous essays, *Metropolitan Life* and *Social Studies*, are bestselling commentaries on the customs and behavior of twentieth-century Americans. (Sketch includes interview.)

Eric Van Lustbader—American novelist who infuses his fiction with Oriental culture and tradition; among his works are the heroic fantasy cycle "The Sunset Warrior" and the suspense thrillers *The Ninja* and its sequel, *The Miko*. (Sketch includes interview.)

Robert K. Massie—American biographer and author of nonfiction; his *Nicholas and Alexandra* relates the story of the last czar of Russia and his family; *Peter the Great*, which won a 1981 Pulitzer Prize, examines the ruler considered to be the architect of modern Russia. (Sketch includes interview.)

Donald McCaig—American novelist, poet, and sheep farmer who writes suspense fiction set primarily in rural communities; his 1984 book, *Nop's Trials*, regarded as a classic "man-and-his-dog" story, catapulted him to commercial and critical success.

Ian McEwan—British novelist and author of short stories, teleplays, film scripts, and radio plays; considered by many critics to be one of the best British writers of his generation, he is known for his use of black comedy; his fiction includes the novels *First Love, Last Rites* and *The Comfort of Strangers*, a 1981 Booker McConnell Prize finalist.

N. Scott Momaday—American professor, poet, novelist, autobiographer, and recounter of Native American tales; his poetry and prose reflect his Kiowa Indian heritage in theme and subject matter; among his works is the Pulitzer Prize-winning novel *House Made of Dawn.* (Sketch includes interview.)

N. Richard Nash—American playwright, screenwriter, television writer, and novelist; best known for his immensely popular play "The Rainmaker," he has concentrated for some years on writing novels, notably *Cry Macho, East Wind, Rain,* and *Radiance.* (Sketch includes interview.)

Larry Niven—Award-winning American author of science fiction; winner of five Hugo Awards and a Nebula Award, he is recognized as a master of the "hard science" school of science fiction; among his works are *Ringworld* and its sequel, *The Ringworld Engineers.*

Judson Philips—American mystery writer who is considered "the old pro of whodunit fiction"; best known for the mystery novels written under the pseudonym Hugh Pentecost, notably those featuring the characters Pierre Chambrun, John Jericho, and Julian Quist. (Sketch includes interview.)

Peter S. Prescott—American book critic and magazine editor, currently with *Newsweek;* among his books are *Soundings,* a collection of his book reviews, and *The Child Savers,* which garnered the 1981 Robert F. Kennedy Book Award. (Sketch includes interview.)

David Pryce-Jones—Austrian-born British novelist, biographer, literary critic, and historian; his biography *Unity Mitford* aroused controversy within British publishing and social circles when the surviving members of the upper-class Mitford family attempted to suppress publication of the book and, failing that, strove to discredit both the book and its author.

Kenneth Rexroth—American poet, essayist, editor, translator, and painter who died in 1982; during a career that spanned over half a century, he experimented with a variety of avant-garde and modernist literary techniques, ranging from those of the Cubists in the 1920s to those of the Beat Generation in the 1950s; among his many collections of poetry are *The Phoenix and the Tortoise, The Signature of All Things, In Defense of the Earth,* and *The Homestead Called Damascus.* (Sketch includes interview with Morgan Gibson, Rexroth's former student.)

Pierre Salinger—American journalist; formerly press secretary to President John F. Kennedy, he is now a foreign correspondent for ABC News; author of *America Held Hostage,* a behind-the-scenes account of the attempts to free American government personnel held prisoner in Iran for fourteen months in 1979 and 1980.

Robert Schuller—Popular American minister, television evangelist, and author; known for his "Hour of Power" television program as well as for establishing the first drive-in church and founding the controversial Crystal Cathedral; author of numerous inspirational books, notably the bestselling *Tough Times Never Last But Tough People Do!* and *Tough-Minded Faith for Tenderhearted People.*

Andrew Sinclair—British novelist, historian, biographer, playwright, filmmaker, and author of film and television scripts; his highly imaginative allegorical novels *Gog* and *Magog* have been hailed by some as the products of genius and by others as unsuccessful attempts at sophisticated satire.

Gilbert Sorrentino—American novelist and poet; adamant in his belief that form is more important than content, he has become known for the innovative structure of his work, especially his unorthodox approach to language in such novels as *Mulligan Stew* and *Blue Pastoral.* (Sketch includes interview.)

Thomas Thompson—American journalist, novelist, and author of nonfiction who died in 1982; among his books are the bestselling *Blood and Money,* an account of the death of a Texas socialite and her husband's subsequent trial, acquittal, and murder, *Serpentine,* a work about the infamous criminal Charles Sobhraj, and the novel *Celebrity,* an examination of what Thompson once labelled "the most appalling condition people can achieve."

Phillippe van Rjndt—Canadian novelist and screenwriter; using a name and identity he assumed in 1974, van Rjndt writes novels based on international crime, politics, and intrigue, which include *The Tetramachus Collection, The Trial of Adolf Hitler,* and *Samaritan.*

John Edgar Wideman—American professor, novelist, short story writer, and memoirist; his fiction is noted for portraying the harsh realities of black ghetto life in a formal, highly literate, and complex style; among his works are the novel *Sent for You Yesterday,* which won the 1984 P.E.N./Faulkner Award for fiction, and his memoirs, *Brothers and Keepers.*

Preface

The *Contemporary Authors New Revision Series* provides completely updated information on authors listed in earlier volumes of *Contemporary Authors* (*CA*). Entries for active individual authors from *any* volume of *CA* may be included in a volume of the *New Revision Series*. The sketches appearing in *New Revision Series* Volume 14, for example, were selected from more than twenty previously published *CA* volumes.

As always, the most recent *Contemporary Authors* cumulative index continues to be the user's guide to the location of an individual author's listing.

Compilation Methods

The editors make every effort to secure information directly from the authors. Copies of all sketches in selected *CA* volumes published several years ago are routinely sent to the listees at their last-known addresses. Authors mark material to be deleted or changed and insert any new personal data, new affiliations, new writings, new work in progress, new sidelights, and new biographical/critical sources. All returns are assessed, more comprehensive research is done, if necessary, and those sketches requiring significant change are completely updated and published in the *New Revision Series*.

If, however, authors fail to reply or are now deceased, biographical dictionaries are checked for new information (a task made easier through the use of Gale's *Biography and Genealogy Master Index* and other volumes in the "Gale Biographical Index Series"), as are bibliographical sources such as *Cumulative Book Index* and *The National Union Catalog*. Using data from such sources, revision editors select and revise nonrespondents' entries that need substantial updating. Sketches not personally reviewed by the biographees are marked with a dagger (†) to indicate that these listings have been revised from secondary sources believed to be reliable, but they have not been personally reviewed for this edition by the authors sketched.

In addition, reviews and articles in major periodicals, lists of prestigious awards, and, particularly, requests from *CA* users are monitored so that writers on whom new information is in demand can be identified and revised listings prepared promptly.

Comprehensive Revision

All listings in this volume have been revised and/or augmented in various ways, though the amount and type of change vary with the author. In many instances, sketches are totally rewritten, and the resulting *New Revision Series* entries are often considerably longer than the authors' previous listings. Revised entries include additions of or changes in such information as degrees, mailing addresses, literary agents, career items, career-related and civic activities, memberships, work in progress, and biographical/critical sources. They may also include the following:

1) **Major new awards**—Fernand Braudel, William Kennedy, and Robert K. Massie are only three of the numerous award-winning authors with updated entries in this volume. The revised sketch for French historian Fernand Braudel notes that *The Structures of Everyday Life* was nominated for the 1982 *Los Angeles Times* Book Prize, an award granted Braudel's *The Wheels of Commerce* in 1983. William Kennedy's bestselling novel *Ironweed* was a 1983 publishing sensation; as indicated in his updated entry, this novel won the 1983 National Book Critics Circle Prize, was named one of the year's best books by the *New York Times Book Review*, and garnered the 1984 Pulitzer Prize for fiction. And biographer Robert K. Massie's listing has been updated to include the Pulitzer Prize and the American Book Award nomination his book *Peter the Great* received in 1981.

2) **Extensive bibliographical additions**—Among the prolific authors with updated entries in this volume are the husband-and-wife writing team Jan and Stan Berenstain, mystery writer Judson Philips, and free-lance author W.E.D. Ross. The revised sketches for Jan and Stan Berenstain include thirty new titles in their popular "Berenstain Bears" juvenile series, as well as five new television scripts based on their successful animal characters. Judson Philips's updated entry lists twenty-five books he has written since his sketch last appeared in *CA,* most of which were published under his well-known pseudonym Hugh Pentecost. W.E.D. Ross writes in several genres, including westerns, gothics, and romances, and signs his work with some

fourteen different pseudonyms; his revised bibliography has been augmented by the addition of thirty-three books not in his original entry.

3) Informative new sidelights—Numerous *CA* sketches contain sidelights, which provide personal dimensions to the listings, supply information about the critical reception the authors' works have received, or both. For example, in sidelights for novelist and essayist Joan Didion, senior assistant editor Donna Olendorf discusses the author's fascination with the minutiae of life, commenting that Didion is, "by her own admission, a non-intellectual writer, more concerned with images than ideas." Didion confided to a college audience that as a younger woman she "kept trying to find that part of my mind that could deal in abstracts. But my mind kept veering inexorably back . . . to the specific, to the tangible, to what was generally considered by everyone I knew, the peripheral." Her obsession with perfecting the details of her writing elicits praise from critics; in the words of John Leonard, "Nobody writes better English prose than Joan Didion. Try to rearrange one of her sentences, and you've realized that the sentence was inevitable, a hologram."

An eclectic and intellectually independent poet, critic, and artist, Kenneth Rexroth participated in many of the important literary, artistic, and political movements of the twentieth century. Assistant editor Nancy Hebb writes in sidelights, "The length and breadth of his career resulted in a body of work that not only chronicles his personal search for visionary transcendence but also reflects the artistic, cultural, and political vicissitudes of more than half a century." Rexroth's forays into such movements as Chicago's "second renaissance," Objectivism, Cubism, West Coast poetry, and the "Beats" and his involvement with Roman Catholicism, Buddhism, mysticism, and communism are examined in the sidelights section of his revised entry.

In much of his fiction, novelist and memoirist John Edgar Wideman draws upon his youthful experiences in a Pittsburgh ghetto, describing that setting in a complex style sometimes compared to that of James Joyce. As assistant editor Joan E. Marecki points out in sidelights, "Wideman's highly literate style is in sharp contrast to his gritty subject matter, and while reviews of his books have been generally favorable from the start of his writing career, some critics initially expressed the opinion that such a formal style was not appropriate for his stories of street life." Wideman's recent works have won both commercial and critical acclaim—his novel *Sent for You Yesterday* captured the 1984 P.E.N./Faulkner Award—but the author takes his success in stride, continuing to focus on the process of writing rather than on sales of his books or awards. A former college basketball star, Wideman draws a parallel between the response to athletic events and his writing. "I'm an old jock," he told one interviewer. "Sometimes the crowd screams, sometimes the crowd doesn't scream."

These sketches, as well as others with sidelights compiled by *CA*'s editors, provide informative and enjoyable reading.

Writers of Special Interest

CA's editors make every effort to include in each *New Revision Series* volume a substantial number of revised entries on active authors and media people of special interest to *CA*'s readers. Since the *New Revision Series* also includes sketches on noteworthy deceased writers, a significant amount of work on the part of *CA*'s editors goes into the revision of entries on important deceased authors. Some of the prominent writers, both living and deceased, whose sketches are contained in this volume are noted in the list on pages 7-8 headed "Authors and Media People Featured in This Volume."

Exclusive Interviews

CA provides exclusive, primary information on certain authors in the form of interviews. Prepared specifically for *CA,* the never-before-published conversations presented in the section of the sketch headed *CA INTERVIEW* give *CA* users the opportunity to learn the authors' thoughts, in depth, about their craft. Subjects chosen for interviews are, the editors feel, authors who hold special interest for *CA*'s readers.

Authors and journalists in this volume whose sketches include interviews are Judith Appelbaum, Allan W. Eckert, Ron Galella, Fran Lebowitz, Eric Van Lustbader, Robert K. Massie, N. Scott Momaday, N. Richard Nash, Judson Philips, Peter S. Prescott, Kenneth Rexroth, and Gilbert Sorrentino.

Contemporary Authors Autobiography Series

Designed to complement the information in *CA* original and revision volumes, the new *Contemporary Authors Autobiography Series* provides autobiographical essays written by important current authors. Each volume contains from twenty to thirty specially commissioned autobiographies and is illustrated with numerous personal photographs supplied by the authors. The range of contemporary writers who will be describing their lives and interests in the new *Autobiography Series* is indicated by the variety of authors who contributed to Volume 1—writers such as Dannie Abse, Vance Bourjaily, Erskine Caldwell, Jerome Charyn, Elizabeth Forsythe Hailey, Marge Piercy, Frederik Pohl, James Purdy, Mary Lee Settle, and Diane Wakoski. Though the information presented in the autobiographies is as varied and unique as the authors, common topics of discussion include their motivations for writing, the people and experiences that shaped their careers, the rewards they derive from their work, and their impressions of the current literary scene.

Autobiographies included in the *Contemporary Authors Autobiography Series* can be located through both the *CA* cumulative index and the *Contemporary Authors Autobiography Series* index, which lists not only personal names but also titles of works, geographical names, subjects, and schools of writing.

CA Numbering System

Occasionally questions arise about the *CA* numbering system. Despite numbers like "97-100" and "112," the entire *CA* series consists of only 54 physical volumes with the publication of *CA New Revision Series* Volume 14. The following information notes changes in the numbering system, as well as in cover design, to help *CA* users better understand the organization of the entire *CA* series.

CA First Revisions
- 1-4R through 41-44R (11 books)
Cover: Brown with black and gold trim.
There will be no further *First Revisions* because revised entries are now being handled exclusively through the more efficient *New Revision Series* mentioned below.

CA Original Volumes
- 45-48 through 97-100 (14 books)
Cover: Brown with black and gold trim.
- 101 through 112 (12 books)
Cover: Blue and black with orange bands.
The same as previous *CA* original volumes but with a new, simplified numbering system and new cover design.

CA New Revision Series
- *CANR*-1 through *CANR*-14 (14 books)
Cover: Blue and black with green bands.
Includes only sketches requiring extensive change; **sketches are taken from any previously published *CA* volume.**

CA Permanent Series
- *CAP*-1 and *CAP*-2 (2 books)
Cover: Brown with red and gold trim.
There will be no further *Permanent Series* volumes because revised entries are now being handled exclusively through the more efficient *New Revision Series* mentioned above.

CA Autobiography Series
- *CAA*-1 (1 book)
Cover: Blue and black with pink and purple bands.
Presents specially commissioned autobiographies by leading contemporary writers to complement the information in *CA* original and revision volumes.

Retaining *CA* Volumes

As new volumes in the series are published, users often ask which *CA* volumes, if any, can be discarded. The Volume Update Chart on page 13 is designed to assist users in keeping their collections as complete as possible. All volumes in the left column of the chart should be retained to have the most complete, up-to-date coverage possible; volumes in the right column can be discarded if the appropriate replacements are held.

Cumulative Index Should Always Be Consulted

The key to locating an individual author's listing is the *CA* cumulative index bound into the back of alternate original volumes (and available separately as an offprint). Since the *CA* cumulative index provides access to *all* entries in the *CA* series, the latest cumulative index should always be consulted to find the specific volume containing a listee's original or most recently revised sketch.

Those authors whose entries appear in the *New Revision Series* are listed in the *CA* cumulative index with the designation **CANR-** in front of the specific volume number. For the convenience of those who do not have *New Revision Series* volumes, the cumulative index also notes the specific earlier volumes of *CA* in which the sketch appeared. Below is a sample index citation for an author whose revised sketch appears in a *New Revision Series* volume.

> Sagan, Carl (Edward) 1934- CANR-11
> Earlier sketch in CA 25-28R

For the most recent information on Sagan, users should refer to Volume 11 of the *New Revision Series*, as designated by "CANR-11"; if that volume is unavailable, refer to *CA* 25-28 First Revision, as indicated by "Earlier sketch in CA 25-28R," for his 1977 listing. (And if *CA* 25-28 First Revision is unavailable, refer to *CA* 25-28, published in 1971, for Sagan's original listing.)

Sketches not eligible for inclusion in a *New Revision Series* volume because the biographee or a revision editor has verified that no significant change is required will, of course, be available in previously published *CA* volumes. Users should always consult the most recent *CA* cumulative index to determine the location of these authors' entries.

For the convenience of *CA* users, the *CA* cumulative index also includes references to all entries in these related Gale literary series: *Something About the Author, Dictionary of Literary Biography, Contemporary Literary Criticism,* and *Authors in the News.*

As always, suggestions from users about any aspect of *CA* will be welcomed.

Volume Update Chart

IF YOU HAVE:	YOU MAY DISCARD:
1-4 First Revision (1967)	1 (1962) 2 (1963) 3 (1963) 4 (1963)
5-8 First Revision (1969)	5-6 (1963) 7-8 (1963)
Both 9-12 First Revision (1974) AND *Contemporary Authors Permanent Series*, Volume 1 (1975)	9-10 (1964) 11-12 (1965)
Both 13-16 First Revision (1975) AND *Contemporary Authors Permanent Series*, Volumes 1 and 2 (1975, 1978)	13-14 (1965) 15-16 (1966)
Both 17-20 First Revision (1976) AND *Contemporary Authors Permanent Series*, Volumes 1 and 2 (1975, 1978)	17-18 (1967) 19-20 (1968)
Both 21-24 First Revision (1977) AND *Contemporary Authors Permanent Series*, Volumes 1 and 2 (1975, 1978)	21-22 (1969) 23-24 (1970)
Both 25-28 First Revision (1977) AND *Contemporary Authors Permanent Series*, Volume 2 (1978)	25-28 (1971)
Both 29-32 First Revision (1978) AND *Contemporary Authors Permanent Series*, Volume 2 (1978)	29-32 (1972)
Both 33-36 First Revision (1978) AND *Contemporary Authors Permanent Series*, Volume 2 (1978)	33-36 (1973)
37-40 First Revision (1979)	37-40 (1973)
41-44 First Revision (1979)	41-44 (1974)
45-48 (1974) 49-52 (1975) ↓ ↓ 112 (1985)	NONE: These volumes will not be superseded by corresponding revised volumes. Individual entries from these and all other volumes appearing in the left column of this chart will be revised and included in the *New Revision Series*.
Volumes in the *Contemporary Authors New Revision Series*	NONE: The *New Revision Series* does not replace any single volume of *CA*. All volumes appearing in the left column of this chart must be retained to have information on all authors in the series.

Contemporary Authors

NEW REVISION SERIES

† *Indicates that a listing has been revised from secondary sources believed to be reliable,
but has not been personally reviewed for this edition by the author sketched.*

ABEL, Ernest L(awrence) 1943-

PERSONAL: Born February 10, 1943, in Toronto, Ontario, Canada; son of Jack (a dressmaker) and Rose (Tarshes) Abel; married Barbara Ellen Buckley (a teacher), September 20, 1971; children: Jason Robert, Rebecca Rosanne. *Education:* University of Toronto, B.A., 1965, M.A., 1967, Ph.D., 1971. *Home:* 106 Ranch Trail W., Williamsville, N.Y. 14221. *Office:* Research Institute on Alcoholism, 1021 Main St., Buffalo, N.Y. 14203.

CAREER: University of North Carolina at Chapel Hill, research associate of drug action program, beginning 1971; Research Institute on Alcoholism, Buffalo, N.Y., acting deputy director, 1983-84, currently supervisor of research.

AWARDS, HONORS: Research fellowship from Medical Research Council of Canada, 1971-73.

WRITINGS: Ancient Views on the Origins of Life, Fairleigh Dickinson University Press, 1973; *Drugs and Behavior,* Wiley, 1974; *The Roots of Anti-Semitism,* Fairleigh Dickinson University Press, 1975; (editor) *The Scientific Study of Marijuana,* Nelson-Hall, 1975; *Moon Madness,* Fawcett, 1976; *The Handwriting on the Wall,* Greenwood Press, 1977; *A Comprehensive Guide to the Cannabis Literature,* Greenwood Press, 1979.

Marijuana: The First Twelve Thousand Years, Plenum, 1980; *A Marihuana Dictionary,* Greenwood Press, 1982; *Alcohol and Reproduction,* Greenwood Press, 1982; *Smoking and Reproduction,* Greenwood Press, 1982; *Marihuana, Tobacco, Alcohol, and Reproduction,* CRC Press, 1983; *Narcotics and Reproduction,* Greenwood Press, 1983; *Drugs and Sex,* Greenwood Press, 1983.

WORK IN PROGRESS: Lead and Reproduction; Psychoactive Drugs and Sex; Fetal Alcohol Effects.

* * *

ABU JABER, Kamel S(aleh) 1932-

PERSONAL: Born March 8, 1932, in Amman, Jordan; married Loretta Pacifico (a teacher), October 5, 1957; children: Linda, Nyla. *Education:* Syracuse University, B.A., 1960, Ph.D., 1965; Princeton University, additional study, 1962-63. *Religion:* Greek Orthodox. *Residence:* Amman, Jordan. *Office:* Center of Strategic Studies, University of Jordan, Amman, Jordan.

CAREER: Jordan Ministry of Interior, Amman, clerical worker and translator, 1952-54; Syracuse University, Syracuse, N.Y., lecturer, 1965; University of Tennessee at Knoxville, assistant professor, 1965-67; Smith College, Northampton, Mass., associate professor, 1967-69; University of Jordan, Amman, associate professor, 1969-71, professor, 1971—, dean of faculty of economics and commerce, 1972-79, director of Center of Strategic Studies, 1984—. Minister of national economy, Jordan Cabinet, 1973.

MEMBER: American Political Science Association, Middle East Institute, Southern Political Science Association, Pi Sigma Alpha.

AWARDS, HONORS: Woodrow Wilson fellowship; Ford Foundation foreign area fellowship for research in Lebanon, Syria, and Jordan, 1963-64.

WRITINGS: (Editor) *Judhur al-Ishtirakiyyah* (title means "Roots of Socialism"), Tal'ah Publishing House, 1964; *The Arab Ba'th Socialist Party: History, Ideology, and Organization,* Syracuse University Press, 1966; (co-author) *Modern Socialism,* Harper, 1968; (contributor) C. Leiden, editor, *The Conflict of Traditionalism and Modernism in the Muslim Middle East,* University of Texas at Austin Press, 1969; (co-author) *The Arab-Israeli Confrontation, 1967,* Northwestern University Press, 1969; (co-author) *Government and Politics of the Contemporary Middle East,* Dorsey, 1970; *United States of America and Israel* (in Arabic), M'had al-Buhuth wa al-Dirasat al-Arabiyyah, 1971; (contributor) J. M. Landua, editor, *Man, State and Society in the Contemporary Middle East,* Pall Mall, 1972; *Israeli Political System* (in Arabic), Ma'had al-Buhuth wa al-Dirasat al-Arabiyyah, 1973; (contributor) *European Business in World Development,* Financial Times, 1977; (co-author) *The Beduens of Jordan: A People in Transition,* Royal Scientific Society Press, 1978; *The Jordanians and the People of Jordan,* Royal Scientific Society Press, 1980; (editor) *Levels and Trends of Fertility and Mortality in Selected Arab Countries of West Asia,* Population Studies Program, University of Jordan, 1980; (contributor) *Women in the Arab World,* International Labor Organization, 1980.

Contributor to *Middle East Journal, Muslim World, Redaktion Bustan, Revista Mexicana de Orientacion,* and numerous other journals.

ADAMS, Eugenia
See OWENS, Virginia Stem

* * *

ADORJAN, Carol (Madden) 1934-

PERSONAL: Surname is pronounced A-*dor*-ian; born August 17, 1934, in Chicago, Ill.; daughter of Roland Aloysius (a salesman) and Marie (Toomey) Madden; married William W. Adorjan (an industrial representative), August 17, 1957; children: Elizabeth Marie, John Martin and Katherine Therese (twins), Matthew Christian. *Education:* Mundelein College, B.A. (magna cum laude), 1956. *Home:* 812 Rosewood Ave., Winnetka, Ill. 60093.

CAREER: Writer. High school English teacher, St. Scholastica High School, Chicago, Ill., 1956-59. Writer-in-residence, National Radio Theatre, 1980, Illinois Arts Council, 1981-82. Corresponding secretary, Off Campus Writers' Workshop, 1967-69.

AWARDS, HONORS: Josephine Lusk Prize from Mundelein College, 1956, for short story, "Coin of Decision"; first prize from *Earplay 1972*, University of Wisconsin, for "The Telephone"; Midwest Professional Playwrights fellowship, 1977; Illinois Arts Council completion grant, 1977-78; first prize, Dubuque Fine Arts Society's National One-Act Playwriting Contest, 1978; Ohio State Award, 1981, for adaptation of *The Sea Wolf*.

WRITINGS—Juveniles: *Someone I Know*, Random House, 1968; *Jonathan Bloom's Room*, J. Philip O'Hara, 1972; (contributor) N. Gretchen Greiner, editor, *Like It Is*, Broadman, 1972; *The Cat Sitter Mystery*, J. Philip O'Hara, 1976; *Big Party*, Children's Press, 1981; *The Electric Man*, Children's Press, 1981; (adaptor) *The Sea Wolf*, National Radio Theatre, 1981. Author of radio plays including "The Telephone," "Friends," "A Safe Place," All Things Even Frisky," and "The Outcasts of Poker Flat." Contributor of short stories and articles to national magazines, including *Today, Woman's Day, North American Review, American Girl, Ingenue*, and *Redbook*, and to newspapers.

WORK IN PROGRESS: A full length and one-act play; a novel.

SIDELIGHTS: Carol Adorjan told *CA:* "I have been writing for as long as I can remember. It was only about ten years ago, however, that I began to think of myself as 'a writer' rather than as 'someone who wrote.' Once I realized that writing defined who I am and not merely what I do, commitment followed. Now I perceive writing as both art and business, and I spend time and energy on both aspects." Adorjan continues: "I am interested in reality and illusion as they affect our individual lives and our relationships with others. My themes grow out of this concern. My continuing goal is to treat my material with compassion and humor."

AVOCATIONAL INTERESTS: Photography.

* * *

ADYTUM
See CURL, James Stevens

AGRANOFF, Robert 1936-

PERSONAL: Born May 25, 1936, in Minneapolis, Minn.; son of Phillip Paul and Rose (Stern) Agranoff; married Zola O. Besco, December 29, 1959; children: Karen, David. *Education:* Wisconsin State University, River Falls (now University of Wisconsin—River Falls), B.A., 1962; University of Pittsburgh, M.A., 1963, Ph.D., 1967. *Politics:* Democratic. *Home:* 2514 Deepwell Ct., Bloomington, Ind. 47401. *Office:* School of Public and Environmental Affairs, Indiana University, Bloomington, Ind. 47405.

CAREER: Northern Illinois University, De Kalb, assistant professor, 1966-72, associate professor, 1972-79, professor of political science, 1979-81, coordinator of mental health and human services program, Center for Governmental Studies, 1972-77, director of Center for Governmental Studies, 1976-80; Indiana University at Bloomington, professor of public affairs, 1981—, chairman of Faculty of Policy and Administration, 1981-85. Campaign director, Minnesota Democratic-Farmer-Labor Party, 1968-69. U.S. member of comparative study group on social planning and human resource administration, International Institute of Administrative Sciences. Consultant in public administration, mental health, and human services to numerous institutions and governmental boards, including Illinois Department of Mental Health, Institute of Politics and Government in Arkansas, National Science Foundation, White House Conference on Aging, 1981, U.S. Conference of Mayors, and International City Management Association. *Military service:* U.S. Navy, 1955-57.

MEMBER: American Political Science Association, American Society for Public Administration (member of executive committee, 1974-77; chairperson of Section on Human Resources Administration, 1975-76), American Public Welfare Association, Association of Mental Health Administrators (chairperson of executive committee, 1973-75), Policy Studies Organization, Academy of Health Administration, Midwest Political Science Association (public relations director, 1972-74; membership chairperson, 1973-74).

AWARDS, HONORS: Mellon fellow, University of Pittsburgh, 1962-64; Maurice and Laura Falk Foundation grant, 1963; National Science Foundation award; University of Michigan, 1965; National Institute of Mental Health award, 1973.

WRITINGS: The New Style in Election Campaigns, Holbrook, 1972; (editor with Arthur Dykstra, Jr.) *Mental Health Administration in Transition*, Association of Mental Health Administrators, 1975; *The Management of Election Campaigns*, Holbrook, 1976; (editor) *Coping with the Demands for Change within Human Services Administration*, American Society for Public Administration, 1977; (with Alex Paltakos) *Dimensions of Services Integration* (monograph), SHARE Monographs, 1979; (editor) *Human Services on a Limited Budget*, International City Management, 1983; (with Valerie Lindsay) *Intergovernmental Problem Solving: The Local Perspective* (monograph), SHARE Monographs, 1983; *Explorations in Intergovernmental Management*, State University of New York Press, 1985.

Contributor: P. Allen Dionisopoulis, editor, *Racism in America*, Northern Illinois University Press, 1971; Ray Hiebert and others, editors, *The Political Image Merchants: Strategy in New Politics*, Acropolis, 1971; Thomas J. Mikulecky, editor, *Human Services Integration*, American Society for Public Administration, 1974; (and editor with Walter Fisher, Joseph Mehr, and Philip Truckenbrod) *Explorations in Competency Module Development: Relinking Higher Education and the Human Services,* Center for Governmental Studies, Northern Illinois University, 1975; H. George Frederickson and Charles Wise, editors, *Public Administration and Public Polity,* Heath, 1977; Wayne Anderson, Bernard Friedan, and Thomas Murphy, editors, *Managing Human Services,* International City Management, 1977; J. Chenautt and Francis Burnford, editors, *Human Services Education,* McGraw, 1978; Wade Silverman, *Community Mental Health,* Wiley, 1981; Thedor J. Litman and Leonard S. Robins, editors, *Health Politics and Policy,* Wiley, 1984.

Principal author of script and technical consultant for film, "Political Parties in America: Getting the People Together," Encyclopaedia Britannica Films, 1976. Contributor to professional journals, including *American Political Science Review, American Behavioral Scientist, Policy Studies Journal, Public Administration Review, Journal of Health and Human Resources Administration,* and *New England Journal of Human Services.* Member of editorial advisory board, *Journal of Mental Health Administrators,* 1975-79; member of editorial board of *Public Administration Review,* 1978-81, *Journal of Health and Human Resources Administration,* 1978—, and *New England Journal of Human Services,* 1980—. Advisory editor, *Human Services Policy and Administration,* 1976—. Editorial consultant to numerous professional journals.

WORK IN PROGRESS: A study of block grants and a study of human services in American cities.

BIOGRAPHICAL/CRITICAL SOURCES: Campaign Insight, March, 1972.

*   *   *

AIMES, Angelica   1943-

PERSONAL: Born December 25, 1943, in Shanghai, China. *Education:* Attended Sorbonne, University of Paris and American University in Beirut. *Office:* 224 East 18th St., New York, N.Y. 10003.

CAREER: Writer, 1977—.

WRITINGS—All historical romance novels; published by Pinnacle Books, except as indicated: *Samantha,* 1978; *Francesca,* 1978; *Daughter of Desire,* 1979; *Divided Heart,* 1981; *So Tender, So True,* Pioneer Books, 1984; *Two Lives, Two Loves,* Pioneer Books, 1984.

WORK IN PROGRESS: A historical romance/family saga, spanning nearly a hundred years and three generations in the life of an early American family.

SIDELIGHTS: Angelica Aimes told *CA:* "My extensive travels, my intense curiosity to discover how people live in other places and other times have drawn me to the realm of historic romance where adventure, fantasy, and wish fulfillment reign supreme and virtually anything is possible."

*   *   *

ALBAUM, Gerald (Sherwin)   1933-

PERSONAL: Born November 2, 1933, in Los Angeles, Calif.; son of Leslie and Edith (Elster) Albaum; married Carol Weinstein, October 10, 1954; children: Marc, Lisa, Daniel. *Education:* University of Washington, Seattle, B.A., 1954, M.B.A.,

1958; University of Wisconsin, Ph.D., 1962. *Religion:* Jewish. *Home:* 720 Fair Oaks Dr., Eugene, Ore. 97401. *Office:* College of Business Administration, University of Oregon, Eugene, Ore. 97403.

CAREER: University of Wisconsin—Madison, instructor in marketing, 1960-62; University of Pittsburgh, Pittsburgh, Pa., assistant professor of marketing, 1962-64; University of Arizona, Tucson, associate professor of marketing, 1964-67; University of Massachusetts—Amherst, associate professor of marketing, 1967-69; University of Oregon, Eugene, associate professor, 1969-72, professor of marketing, 1972—. University of Hawaii, visiting associate professor of marketing, 1968-69, visiting professor of marketing, 1971; visiting professor of marketing, Arizona State University, 1976; University of Texas at Austin, visiting professor of marketing, 1983, senior research fellow, Institute for Constructive Capitalism, 1984—. *Military service:* U.S. Army, 1954-56.

MEMBER: Academy of International Business, American Marketing Association, Association for Consumer Research.

WRITINGS: (Editor with J. H. Westing) *Modern Marketing Thought,* Macmillan, 1964, 3rd edition, 1975; *Price Formulation,* Division of Economics and Business Research, University of Arizona, 1965; (with F.L.W. Richardson) *Human Interaction and Sales Success,* Division of Economics and Business Research, University of Arizona, 1967; (with Gordon E. Miracle) *International Marketing Management,* Irwin, 1970; (editor with M. Venkatesan) *Scientific Marketing Research,* Free Press, 1971; (with Donald S. Tull) *Survey Research: A Decisional Approach,* Intext, 1973; (editor with Gilbert A. Churchill, Jr.) *Critical Issues in Sales Management: State-of-the-Art and Future Research Needs,* Division of Research, College of Business Administration, University of Oregon, 1979.

Contributor of articles to marketing, management, and social science journals.

WORK IN PROGRESS: Studying research methodology; a book on marketing research methods.

*   *   *

ALEXANDER, Marc   1929-
(Marcus Aylward, Mark Ronson)

PERSONAL: Born January 27, 1929; son of Ronald and Marie (Poole) Alexander. *Education:* Wellington Teachers' College, Wellington, New Zealand, graduate. *Home:* Crooks Cottage, Gilsland, Cumbria, England. *Agent:* Rupert Crew Ltd., Kings Mews, London W.C.1, England.

CAREER: Began writing career in New Zealand as sub-editor on *Gisborne Herald;* went to Europe in 1954 and worked as a reporter, then feature writer, for *Reveille; Television Mail,* co-founder, 1959, became editorial director; has also edited *International Broadcast Engineer, Vision, International Sound Engineer,* and *International TV Technical Review.* Director of Pacific Press Ltd. Inaugurated *Vision* Awards, a festival for British documentary films, and *Icarus,* a poetry magazine; organizer of British Television Advertising Awards and World Newsfilm Awards.

WRITINGS: In Ostia, Linden Press, 1959; *Behind the Scenes with a Fishing Fleet* (juvenile), Phoenix House, 1964; *Golden Dollar,* Ward, Lock, 1965; *The Past,* Parrish, 1965, A. Lynn, 1967; *The Water War,* Ward, Lock, 1966; *The Rhineland,* Rand

McNally, 1967; *Hand of Vengeance,* Ward, Lock, 1967; *A Fast Gun for Judas,* Ward, Lock, 1968; *The Sundown Trail,* Ward, Lock, 1968.

(With David Leader) *The Sportsman's Book of Records,* Clipper Press, 1971; *True Adventure Stories: 45 Authentic Stories,* Clipper Press, 1972; *Haunted Inns,* F. Muller, 1973; *Haunted Castles,* F. Muller, 1974; *Phantom Britain: This Spectre'd Isle,* F. Muller, 1975, Transatlantic, 1976; (and photographer) *Legendary Castles of the South,* Pacific Press, 1977; *The Outrageous Queens,* F. Muller, 1977; *The Mist Lizard,* F. Muller, 1977, revised edition, Piccolo Books, 1980; (and photographer) *Ghostly Cornwall,* Pacific Press, 1977; (and photographer) *Legendary Castles of the Border,* Pacific Press, 1977; *Royal Murder,* F. Muller, 1978, *Haunted Churches and Abbeys of Britain,* Arthur Barker, 1978; *To Anger the Devil: An Account of the Work of Exorcist Extraordinary the Reverend Dr. Donald Omand,* N. Spearman, 1978, published as *The Man Who Exorcised the Bermuda Triangle: The Reverend Dr. Donald Omand, Exorcist Extraordinaire,* A. S. Barnes, 1980, revised British edition published as *The Devil Hunter: An Account of the Work of Exorcist Extraordinary the Reverend Dr. Donald Omand,* Sphere Books, 1981; (and photographer) *Legendary Castles of Scotland,* Pacific Press, 1978; *Gilsland,* Griffin Press, 1978.

The Dance Goes On: The Life and Art of Elizabeth Twistington Higgins MBE (also see below), Leader Books, c.1980; *Enchanted Britain: Mystical Sites in Rural England, Scotland and Wales,* Weidenfeld & Nicolson, 1981; *British Folklore, Myths and Legends,* Crescent, 1982; *Haunted Pubs in Britain and Ireland,* Sphere Books, 1984. Also author of *Boats on Wheels,* Macdonald & Janes, and *Haunted Houses You May Visit,* Sphere Books.

Under pseudonym Marcus Aylward: *Harper's Folly,* Arthur Barker, 1984; *Harper's Luck,* Arthur Barker, 1985.

Under pseudonym Mark Ronson: *Bloodthirst,* Hamlyn, 1979; *Ghoul,* Hamlyn, 1980; *Ogre,* Hamlyn, 1980; *Plague Pit,* Hamlyn, 1981; *Haunted Castles,* Beaver, 1982; *Super Ghosts,* Beaver, 1982; *The Dark Domain,* Century, 1984.

Also author of television documentary films "The Dance Goes On," based on his book of the same title, 1981, "Secret Paradise," 1983, and "Return to Eden," 1984. Author of commentary for cinema documentary "Bangladesh, I Love You," 1980. Former editor, *Exploration.*

WORK IN PROGRESS: Not after Nightfall, for Viking, and *The Last Pagan,* for F. Muller; *Harper's Gold,* under pseudonym Marcus Aylward, for Arthur Barker; *Here Be Dragons,* for Beaver, and *Whispering Corner,* for Century, both under pseudonym Mark Ronson.

*　　*　　*

ALLEN, Johannes 1916-1973

PERSONAL: Born May 16, 1916, in Copenhagen, Denmark; died December 14, 1973, of a heart attack; son of Poul and Karen (Schleisner) Allen; married Lise Luetzen, December 12, 1941. *Education:* Oestersoegades Gymnasium, graduate, 1935. *Home:* C.V.E. Knuthsvej 34, Hellerup DK-2900, Denmark. *Agent:* Kurt Michaels, Charlottenlund DK-2920, Denmark.

CAREER: Novelist and playwright. Journalist with *Berlingske Tidende,* Copenhagen, Denmark, 1937-45, and *Politiken,* Copenhagen, 1945-49. Consultant to Danish television, 1965-73.

MEMBER: Danish Journalists' Union, Danish Writers' Association (member of board, 1966-70), Danish Playwrights' Society, P.E.N.

AWARDS, HONORS: Carl Moeller's Humorist Legate, 1944; Antonius Prize, Danish Society for Mental Hygiene, 1951, for the film, "Cafe Paradize."

WRITINGS—Novels, except as indicated: *Det bor i os alle,* Schoenbergske, 1941; *Hinsides alle Droemme,* Schoenbergske, 1942; *Frihed, Lighed og—Louise,* Schoenbergske, 1943; *En letbenet Dame,* Schoenbergske, 1946; *Mennesker ved en Graense* (play; first produced, 1953), Branner & Korch, 1953; *Ung Leg* (also see below), Branner & Korch, 1956, translation by Naomi Walford published as *Young Love,* Hogarth, 1958, Knopf, 1959.

I disse skoenne Tider, Branner & Korch, 1961, translation by Keith Bradfield published as *It's a Swinging Life,* Hogarth, 1966; *Det aerede Medlem,* Branner & Korch, 1963; *Operation Charlie* (play; first produced, 1965), Arena, 1965; *Nu,* Branner & Korch, 1967, translation by Fred Marker published as *Tumult,* Hogarth, 1969, same translation published as *Relations,* World Publishing, 1970; *Data for din Doed,* Branner & Korch, 1970, translation by Marianne Rogers published as *Data for Death,* Hogarth, 1971; *TV-Kuppet,* Winther, 1971; *Manden med Krykkerne,* Branner & Korch, 1973.

Unpublished stage plays: "Vorherres Moerkekammer," first produced, 1947; "Harlekins Tryllestav," first produced, 1951.

Screenplays: "My Name Is Petersen," 1946; "Passenger from London," 1948; "Naalen," 1950; "Cafe Paradize," 1950; (adapter) "Det sande ansigt," 1951; "Vejrhanen," 1952; "Farlig Ungdom," 1953; "Taxa K 1640 efterlyses," 1955; "Ung Leg" (based on his novel of the same title), 1956; "Natlogi betalt," 1957; "Guld og groenne Skove," 1958; "Pigen i Soegelyset," 1959; "Gymnasiepigen," 1960.

Radio plays: "Alt for Marie," 1943; "Hr. Adam smiler," 1953; "Pas paa Bruden," 1954; "For egen Domstol," 1964; "En venlig Hilsen til Gudrun," 1965.

SIDELIGHTS: Johannes Allen traveled in the United States in 1939, 1947, and 1961. His wife Lise Allen told *CA* that her husband "was one of the Danish authors that really won a market in the English speaking countries. . . . His books were translated into twenty-one foreign languages, a number which is nearly [equal] to the amount of translations of the Danish author Hans Christian Andersen.

"[Johannes] was always writing on vital problems in society, how to understand, help, and forgive those who did not fit into the quasi-strong regulations of what you should do . . . to be considered okay. His film about the booze addicts won international fame, and although it was made in 1950, his film 'Cafe Paradise' is still shown . . . and still discussed as the most sober film on alcoholics."

AVOCATIONAL INTERESTS: Playing chess and tennis.

BIOGRAPHICAL/CRITICAL SOURCES: Spectator, July 19, 1969.†

*　　*　　*

ALOTTA, Robert I(gnatius) 1937-

PERSONAL: Born February 26, 1937, in Philadelphia, Pa.; son of Peter Philip (a driver and salesman) and Jean (a secretary; maiden name, Sacchetti) Alotta; married Alice J. Danley, October 1, 1960; children: Peter Anthony, Amy Louise. *Education:* La Salle College, B.A., 1959; University of Pennsylvania, 1980; Temple University, Ph.D. candidate, 1981—. *Politics:* "I vote the man, not the party." *Religion:* "Christian Existentialist." *Office:* Philadelphia Housing Authority, 2012 Chestnut St., Philadelphia, Pa. 19103.

CAREER: Triangle Publications, Philadelphia, Pa., merchandising manager in *Inquirer* division, 1959-63, manager of customer service department in *Inquirer-Daily News* divisions, 1963-66, new business coordinator in *Daily News* division, 1966-67; Penn Central Transportation Co., Philadelphia, manager of special projects, 1967-72; Philadelphia Housing Authority, Philadelphia, director of public information, 1972—.

Has made regular appearances on "Captain Noah Show," on WPVI-Television, 1971-76, and other radio and television programs. President of Delaware Valley department of Council on Abandoned Military Posts, 1970—; member of board of directors and executive committee of Philadelphia Council for International Visitors, 1975—; member of board of directors, Wheels, Inc., 1978—. Philadelphia Area Council for Tourism, member, 1975—, chairman, 1978—. Member of president's council of advisers at La Salle College, 1976—. *Military service:* U.S. Army, Security Agency, 1960-61.

MEMBER: American Association for State and Local History, National Association of Housing and Redevelopment Officials, American Name Society, Organization of American Historians, Company of Military Historians (treasurer of Philadelphia area chapter), Council for Abandoned Military Posts (chapter president, 1970—), Historical Society of Pennsylvania, Shackamaxon Society (president, 1965—), Friends of the Philadelphia Free Library, Alpha Phi Omega, Tau Alpha Pi.

AWARDS, HONORS: Philadelphia Copy Club annual award, 1961; Foundation for Community Health citation, 1963; certificate of excellence from Philadelphia Art Directors' Club, 1965; National Retail Merchants Association gold medal, 1965, silver medal, 1966; George Washington Honor Medal from Freedoms Foundation, 1970, and George Washington Honor Certificate, 1973, both for "A Fort Mifflin Diary"; Valley Forge Honor Certificate, 1974, for "Old Fort Mifflin: The Defenders"; America the Beautiful Award from *Holiday*, 1971; recognized by Pennsylvania House of Representatives, 1972, and by Governor of Pennsylvania, 1974; received awards from Freedoms Foundation, 1973, 1974, 1976, 1978; Legion of Honor from Chapel of the Four Chaplains, 1975; Colonial Dames state award, 1975, and national award, 1976, and Daughters of the American Revolution national bicentennial award, 1976, all for *Street Names of Philadelphia;* Americanism Award from County Detectives Association, 1977.

WRITINGS: Street Names of Philadelphia, Temple University Press, 1975; *Stop the Evil: A Civil War History of Desertion and Murder,* Presidio Press, 1978; *Old Names and New Places,* Westminster, 1979; *Number Two: A Look at the Vice Presidency,* Messner, 1981.

Also author of pamphlets, "Historic Churches of Pennsylvania," 1965, "The Men of Mifflin," 1970, "The Spirit of the Men of Mifflin," 1971, "A Glossary of Fortification Terms," 1972, "A Fort Mifflin Diary," 1973, "Old Fort Mifflin: The Defenders," 1974, "Just Some Girl" (poems), 1974, "Old Fort Mifflin: The Buildings and Structures," 1976, and "Old Fort Mifflin: The Chain of Command."

Author of "Past Prolog" scripts on American history, for WCAU-FM Radio, 1976. Contributor to local and national history journals.

SIDELIGHTS: Robert I. Alotta once wrote *CA:* "I hated history when I was in school, perhaps because I couldn't remember all the dates. So, I decided to write history as I felt it should be written—sort of putting my money where my mouth is. Maybe I've been lucky as a writer."

Alotta's attempts to make history more interesting include his association with the Shackamaxon Society, which he founded to care for Old Fort Mifflin, an abandoned structure in southwest Philadelphia, and his creation of the Old Fort Mifflin Guard, a Revolutionary War re-enactment group for young men and boys. Civic activities of a more light-hearted nature include his W. C. Fields Birthday Party, Philadelphia-New York Hoagie Competition and Eat, and Penn's Landing Celebration. He has also served as a judge for Philadelphia's Mummer's Day Parade. He worked with the Free Library of Philadelphia on a program for school-age children, "Touch the Author."

*   *   *

ALPHONSO-KARKALA, John B.   1923-
(John B. Alphonso Karkala, John A. Karkala, John B. A. Karkala)

PERSONAL: Surname legally changed; born May 30, 1923, in South Kanara, Mysore State, India; son of Anthony (a teacher) and Theresa (Pinto) Alphonso; married Leena Anneli Hakalehto (an assistant professor of German), December 20, 1964; children: Siita Karoliina, Juho Krishna, Uma Maija. *Education:* Bombay University, B.A. (honors), 1950, M.A., 1953; University of London, additional study, 1954-55; Columbia University, Ph.D., 1964. *Politics:* Liberal. *Religion:* "Hindu/Buddhist/Christian (one-third each)." *Home:* 20 Millrock Rd., New Paltz, N.Y. 12561. *Office:* Department of English and World Literature, State University of New York College, New Paltz, N.Y. 12561.

CAREER: State University of New York College at New Paltz, assistant professor, 1964-65, associate professor, 1965-68, professor of literature, 1969—. Visiting lecturer, City College of the City University of New York, 1963; visiting professor, Columbia University, 1969-70. Worked with Indian Foreign Missions in Geneva, Switzerland, London, England, and United Nations, New York, N.Y., 1953-60. Curriculum consultant, UNESCO Associated Schools and Colleges, 1976-77.

MEMBER: International Congress of Orientalists, International Congress of Comparative Literature, Modern Language Association of America (group chairman, 1970), American Oriental Society, Association for Asian Studies, Finnish American Society.

AWARDS, HONORS: Columbia University faculty scholarship, 1962-63; State University of New York faculty research fellowships, 1966-67, 1969-70.

WRITINGS: Indo-English Literature in the Nineteenth Century, Mysore University, 1970; (editor) *Anthology of Indian Literature,* Penguin, 1971; *Comparative World Literature: Seven Essays,* Nirmal, 1974; *Jawaharlal Nehru: A Literary Portrait,* Twayne, 1975.

Under name John B. Alphonso Karkala: *Joys of Jayanagara,* Literary Press, 1981.

Under name John A. Karkala: (Editor with wife, Leena Karkala) *Bibliography of Indo-English Literature, 1800-1966*, Nirmal, 1974.

Under name John B.A. Karkala: *Passions of the Nightless Night* (novel), Hind (New Delhi), 1974; *When Night Falls* (poems), Literary Press, 1980; (editor) *Vedic Vision*, Heinemann, 1980.

Contributor of articles to numerous journals.

WORK IN PROGRESS: Epic Genre in World Literature; Myth, Matrix, and Meaning, with wife Leena Karkala.

SIDELIGHTS: John B. Alphonso-Karkala writes *CA:* "Since the primary bread-and-butter vocation is brain-sharpening, writing is an after-dinner luxury. Even though the vague pressure of publish or perish plagues the members of academia, I try to ignore it, and do my own thing, when I feel like it, more to entertain myself, and keep sanity in an institution that engulfs most faculty members with insane meetings. Writing is a 'sadhana,' a yoking of an individual's energies to reveal the occasional 'darshana' glimpses of strange experiences, aesthetic or otherwise, that ooze out of one's being, during the love-affair with a typewriter, often misunderstood by other members of the family. It demonstrates that writing is a process of fictionalizing the Truth. Truth itself will be too terrible to face or express."

*   *   *

ALPHONSO KARKALA, John B.
See ALPHONSO-KARKALA, John B.

*   *   *

ALTER, Judith (MacBain) 1938-
(Judy Alter)

PERSONAL: Born July 22, 1938, in Chicago, Ill.; daughter of Richard Norman (a physician) and Alice (Peterman) MacBain; married Joel Alter (a physician), May 16, 1964 (divorced August, 1982); children: Colin, Megan, Jamie, Jordan. *Education:* University of Chicago, B.A., 1961; Northeast Missouri State University, M.A., 1964; Texas Christian University, Ph.D., 1970. *Residence:* Fort Worth, Tex. *Office address:* Box 20783, Fort Worth, Tex. 76129.

CAREER: Chicago Osteopathic Center, Chicago, Ill., typist and secretary, 1954-61; Kirksville College of Osteopathic Medicine, Kirksville, Mo., writer and editor in public relations, 1962-64; Fort Worth Osteopathic Hospital, Fort Worth, Tex., secretary, 1965-66, editor of employee publication, 1965-73, public relations consultant, 1971-73; free-lance writer, 1973-75; Texas Christian University, Fort Worth, instructor in English as a second language, 1975-76; Texas College of Osteopathic Medicine, Fort Worth, director of publications, 1972, acting director of public information, 1977-78, associate director of news and information, 1978-80; Texas Christian University, editor of Texas Christian University Press, 1982—.

MEMBER: Western Writers of America (member of board of directors, 1976-77; president, 1985-86), Women in Communications, Inc., Authors Guild, Western American Literature Association, Southwestern American Literature Association.

WRITINGS—Under name Judy Alter: (With Phil Russell) *The Quack Doctor*, Branch-Smith, 1974; *Stewart Edward White* (pamphlet), Boise State University, 1975; *Dorothy Johnson*

(pamphlet), Boise State University, 1975; *After Pa Was Shot* (juvenile), Morrow, 1978; (with Sam Pearson) *Single Again*, Branch-Smith, 1978.

The Texas ABC Book, Branch-Smith, 1981; (with Joyce Roach) *Texas and Christmas*, Texas Christian University Press, 1983; *Luke and the Van Zandt County War*, Texas Christian University Press, 1984.

Author of book reviews and a column, "Along Publishers' Row," for *Roundup*, and "Women's Lit.," a review column in *Fort Worth Star Telegram*, 1974-75.

WORK IN PROGRESS: A juvenile novel; continuing research on Texana.

SIDELIGHTS: Judy Alter comments: "I always wanted to write—I feel as if publication has come after years of paying dues. I am very interested in Texas history as a viable subject for juvenile and adult fiction. I am most grateful to contacts made through Western Writers of America. I see discouragement for the new writer with no contacts, and wish the system could be changed.

"My interest in Western literature grew out of American literature studies in graduate school but gradually I have become more interested in popular literature rather than academic studies. But my writing began as strictly non-fiction, and it was a long, slow transition. For a long time, I thought I simply couldn't write fiction, and lots of short story manuscripts buried in my files seem to support that idea."

She adds: "Now I see myself, both as editor and author, as more and more interested in the undeveloped potential of regional fiction for young adult readers. Both my juvenile novels are rooted in Texas, growing out of actual historical events."

BIOGRAPHICAL/CRITICAL SOURCES: Fort Worth Star Telegram, May 9, 1978.

*   *   *

ALTER, Judy
See ALTER, Judith (MacBain)

*   *   *

AMES, Leslie
See ROSS, W(illiam) E(dward) D(aniel)

*   *   *

AMOSS, Berthe 1925-

PERSONAL: First name is pronounced "beart" (as in "bear"); born September 26, 1925, in New Orleans, La.; daughter of Sumter Davis (a lawyer) and Berthe (Lathrop) Marks; married Walter James Amoss, Jr. (president of Lykes Bros. Steamship Co.), December 21, 1946; children: Jim, Bob, Billy, Mark, Tom, John. *Education:* Tulane University, B.A.; studied art at University of Hawaii, at Kunstschule, Bremen, Germany, and Academie des Beaux Arts, Antwerp, Belgium. *Religion:* Roman Catholic. *Home:* 3723 Carondelet St., New Orleans, La. 70115. *Agent:* Harriet Wasserman, Russell & Volkening, Inc., 551 Fifth Ave., New York, N.Y. 10176.

CAREER: Writer and illustrator of books for children. Instructor of writing and illustrating children's books, Tulane University, beginning 1976.

WRITINGS—Self-illustrated; juveniles, except as indicated: *It's Not Your Birthday*, Harper, 1966; *Tom in the Middle*, Harper, 1968; *By the Sea*, Parents Magazine Press, 1969.

The Marvellous Catch of Old Hannibal, Parents Magazine Press, 1970; *Old Hasdrubal and the Pirates*, Parents Magazine Press, 1971; *The Very Worst Thing*, Parents Magazine Press, 1972; *The Big Cry*, Bobbs-Merrill, 1972; *The Great Sea Monster; or, A Book by You*, Parents Magazine Press, 1975; *The Chalk Cross* (young adult novel), Seabury, 1976; *The Witch Cat*, Preservation Resource Center of New Orleans, 1977; *Secret Lives*, Little, Brown, 1979; *The Loup Garou*, Pelican, 1979.

Illustrator of numerous books, including *The Mysterious Prowler*, Harcourt, 1976.

SIDELIGHTS: Berthe Amoss speaks German and French. The Amoss family has lived in Hawaii, Belgium, and Germany.†

*   *   *

ANDERSEN, Christopher P(eter)   1949-

PERSONAL: Born May 26, 1949, in Pensacola, Fla.; son of Edward Francis (a commander in the U.S. Navy) and Jeanette (Peterson) Andersen; married Valerie Jean Hess (a banker), February 3, 1972; children: Katharine. *Education:* University of California, Berkeley, B.A., 1971. *Home:* 200 East 66th St., New York, N.Y. 10021. *Office: People,* Time & Life Building, New York, N.Y. 10020.

CAREER: *Time,* New York City, correspondent in San Francisco, Calif., 1969-71, staff writer in New York City, 1971-72, and in Montreal, Quebec, 1972-74; *People,* New York City, assistant editor, 1974-75, associate editor, 1975-80, senior editor, 1980—. *Member:* Players Club.

WRITINGS: *The Name Game*, Simon & Schuster, 1977; *A Star Is a Star Is a Star!: The Life and Loves of Susan Hayward*, Doubleday, 1980; *The Book of People*, Putnam, 1981; *Father, the Figure and the Force*, Warner, 1983; *Success over Sixty*, Summit, 1984. Contributor of articles to periodicals, including *New York Times* and *Reader's Digest.*

SIDELIGHTS: Christopher P. Andersen writes: "As a professional journalist since the age of seventeen, I have done stories on thousands of personalities, from presidents to axe murderers to movie stars. Hence my books have all dealt with people—some famous, most not—and what motivates them. In short, how and why we all do what we do. It is a daunting pursuit, but it is hard to think of a more rewarding one."

BIOGRAPHICAL/CRITICAL SOURCES: *Chicago Tribune Book World*, August 23, 1981.

*   *   *

ANDERSON, (Helen) Jean   1931-

PERSONAL: Born October 12, 1931, in Raleigh, N.C.; daughter of Donald Benton (a university vice-president) and Marian (Johnson) Anderson. *Education:* Attended Miami University, Oxford, Ohio, 1947-49; Cornell University, B.S., 1951; Columbia University, M.S., 1957. *Politics:* Independent. *Home:* 1 Lexington Ave., New York, N.Y. 10010. *Agent:* McIntosh & Otis, Inc., 475 Fifth Ave., New York, N.Y. 10017.

CAREER: Iredell County, N.C., assistant home demonstration agent, 1951-52; North Carolina Agricultural Extension Service, Raleigh, woman's editor, 1952-55; *Raleigh Times*, Raleigh, woman's editor, 1955-56; *Ladies' Home Journal*, New York, N.Y., assistant editor, 1957-61, editorial associate, 1961-62, copy editor, 1962, managing editor, 1963; *Venture* (magazine), senior editor, 1964-68, contributing editor, 1968-71; free-lance writer, 1968—.

MEMBER: American Home Economics Association, Home Economists in Business, Les Dames D'Escoffier, New York Women's Culinary Alliance, New York Travel Writers, Gamma Phi Beta, Phi Kappa Phi, Omicron Nu.

AWARDS, HONORS: Pulitzer traveling scholarship, 1957; Southern Women's Achievement Award, 1962; George Hedman Memorial Award, 1971; R. T. French Tastemaker Award for best basic cookbook of the year and best overall cookbook of the year, 1975, for *The Doubleday Cookbook;* R. T. French Tastemaker Award for best specialty cookbook of the year, 1980, for *Half a Can of Tomato Paste and Other Culinary Dilemmas.*

WRITINGS: *Henry the Navigator: Prince of Portugal*, Westminster, 1969; *The Haunting of America: Ghost Stories from Our Past*, Houghton, 1973.

Cookbooks: (With Yeffe Kimball) *The Art of American Indian Cooking*, Doubleday, 1965; *Food Is More than Cooking: A Basic Guide for Young Cooks*, Westminster, 1968; (editor) *Family Circle Illustrated Library of Cooking: Your Ready Reference for a Lifetime of Good Eating*, twelve volumes, Rockville House, 1972; *The Family Circle Cookbook*, Quadrangle, 1974; (with Elaine Hanna) *The Doubleday Cookbook*, Doubleday, 1975; *Recipes from America's Restored Villages*, Doubleday, 1975; *The Green Thumb Preserving Guide: The Best and Safest Way to Can and Freeze, Dry and Store, Pickle, Preserve and Relish Home-Grown Vegetables and Fruits*, Morrow, 1976; *The Grass Roots Cookbook*, Quadrangle, 1977; *Jean Anderson's Cooking*, Morrow, 1979.

(With Ruth Buchan) *Half a Can of Tomato Paste and Other Culinary Dilemmas*, Harper, 1980; *Jean Anderson Cooks*, Morrow, 1982; *Unforbidden Sweets*, Arbor House, 1982; *Jean Anderson's New Processor Cooking*, Morrow, 1983; *Jean Anderson's New Green Thumb Preserving Guide*, Morrow, 1985; (with Elaine Hanna) *The New Doubleday Cookbook*, Doubleday, 1985. Contributor of articles to periodicals, including *Family Circle, Bon Appetit, Gourmet, Food and Wine, Ladies' Home Journal, Better Homes and Gardens*, and *Travel and Leisure.*

WORK IN PROGRESS: *The Portuguese Cookbook*, for Morrow.

SIDELIGHTS: "*Jean Anderson Cooks* has sensible comments on just about everything gastronomic," reports *Time* reviewer Michael Demarest. "Both for literary and culinary satisfaction," he indicates, the work is "one of the most rewarding [cookbook] volumes in years."

BIOGRAPHICAL/CRITICAL SOURCES: *Time*, November 22, 1982.

*   *   *

ANDERSON, Olive M(ary)   1915-

PERSONAL: Born May 2, 1915, in Dakota City, Neb.; daughter of Francis J. (a clergyman) and Olive Angeline (McKenzie) Aucock; married Fred N. Anderson (a clergyman), August 20, 1935; children: Mary Anderson Sarber, Francis Nels. *Education:* Nebraska Wesleyan University, A.B., 1937. *Religion:* Methodist. *Home:* 211 Seventh St., Pecatonica, Ill. 61063.

CAREER: Writer, 1941—.

MEMBER: North American Mycological Association, National Audubon Society, Sierra Club, Michigan Botanical Club, Wisconsin Regional Writers, Upper Peninsula of Michigan Writers, North Country Trail Association, Pecatonica Prairie Path (member of board of directors).

WRITINGS—All nonfiction: *A Wilderness of Wonder,* Augsburg, 1971; *Seeker at Cassandra Marsh,* Christian Herald Books, 1978; *Utopia in Upper Michigan: The Story of a Cooperative Village,* Northern Michigan University Press, 1982; *Pictured Rocks Lakeshore Trail: A North Country Trail Guide,* North Country Trail Association, 1983.

Author of "Lizzie Hawkins Speaking," a column appearing in more than twenty weekly periodicals, 1955-71. Contributor of articles and stories to magazines.

WORK IN PROGRESS: A comprehensive book about Pictured Rocks National Lakeshore, to include geography, geology, botany, wildlife, history, and a guide section.

SIDELIGHTS: Olive Anderson writes: "I began serious nature study after we built our family cabin in the unfamiliar setting of the north woods. The story of this is told in *A Wilderness of Wonder.* My insatiable curiosity about the natural world and my observation of it led to *Seeker at Cassandra Marsh,* where I lived close to the earth and its Creator. My current writing concerns man's relationship to the earth on which he lives."

She adds: "Writing is an exciting occupation which has led me to many new adventures. I recently discovered the thrill of original research as I delved into the history of an 1890s cooperative village for *Utopia in Upper Michigan.* I did my first backpacking two years ago, because it seemed necessary to have that experience to write a trail guide. Who knows what tomorrow may bring?"

AVOCATIONAL INTERESTS: Nature photography, nature study, hiking, camping, books.

*   *   *

ANDERSON, Scarvia (Bateman) 1926-

PERSONAL: Born August 12, 1926, in Baltimore, Md.; married John S. Helmick, 1983. *Education:* Mississippi State University, B.S., 1945; George Peabody College for Teachers, M.A., 1951; University of Maryland, Ph.D., 1955; also attended Oxford University, 1955-56. *Politics:* "Usually Republican." *Religion:* Protestant. *Home:* 145 15th St. N.E., Atlanta, Ga. 30361. *Office:* School of Psychology, Georgia Institute of Technology, Atlanta, Ga. 30332.

CAREER: Worked as a teacher in public schools of Nashville, Tenn., 1945-50; Naval Research Laboratory, Washington, D.C., research psychologist, 1951-55; Educational Testing Service, executive in Princeton, N.J., 1956-73, executive in Atlanta, Ga., 1973-83; Georgia Institute of Technology, Atlanta, adjunct professor, 1983—. Consultant, Human Assessment and Program Evaluation, Educational Testing Service, 1983—.

MEMBER: International Council of Psychologists, American Psychological Association (fellow), American Educational Research Association, National Council on Measurement in Education, Evaluation Research Society, Sigma Xi.

AWARDS, HONORS: Outstanding performance award from Department of the Navy, 1955; Fulbright scholar, 1955-56.

WRITINGS: (With Martin Katz and Benjamin Shimberg) *Meeting the Test,* Scholastic Book Services, 1963; (editor) *Sex Differences and Discrimination in Education,* Charles A. Jones Publishing, 1972; (with Samuel Ball) *The Profession and Practice of Program Evaluation,* Jossey-Bass, 1978; (editor with Ball and Richard Murphy) *Encyclopedia of Educational Evaluation,* Jossey-Bass, 1983; (editor with John S. Helmick) *On Educational Testing,* Jossey-Bass, 1983. Editor-in-chief, *New Directions for Program Evaluation,* 1978—.

SIDELIGHTS: Scarvia Anderson once told *CA* that "the challenge for any writer from a technical background is to communicate to those who don't necessarily have that background—without talking down to them." She adds: "But that's not as great a challenge as moving from technical writing to fiction—the sheer mechanics of trying to get something published or even read."

*   *   *

ANDREWS, Frank M(eredith) 1935-

PERSONAL: Born April 2, 1935, in New York, N.Y.; son of F. Emerson and Edith (Severance) Andrews; married Ann Skilling, July 6, 1962; children: Kenneth, Steven. *Education:* Dartmouth College, B.A. (magna cum laude), 1957; graduate study at University of Sydney, 1958, and New School for Social Research, 1959; University of Michigan, Ph.D., 1962. *Office:* Survey Research Center, Institute for Social Research, University of Michigan, Ann Arbor, Mich. 48109.

CAREER: Russell Sage Foundation, New York, N.Y., study director, 1959; University of Michigan, Ann Arbor, assistant study director of Survey Research Center, Institute for Social Research, 1959-61, study director, 1962-68, senior study director, 1968-71, program director, 1971—, lecturer, 1963-67, assistant professor, 1967-71, associate professor, 1971-76, professor of psychology, 1976—, professor of population planning, 1979—.

Consultant to Republic of Panama, Pan-American Health Organization, UNESCO, U.S. Agency for International Development, National Science Foundation, Korea Development Institute, Philippine Institute for Development Studies, Chinese Academy of Science, and other agencies.

MEMBER: International Sociological Association, American Psychological Association, American Sociological Association, Society for International Development, Society for Social Studies of Science, Population Association of America, American Statistical Association, Phi Beta Kappa, Sigma Xi.

WRITINGS: A Study of Company-Sponsored Foundations, Russell Sage Foundation, 1960; (with Donald C. Pelz) *Scientists in Organizations: Productive Climates for Research and Development,* Wiley, 1966, revised edition, Institute for Social Research, University of Michigan, 1976; (with James N. Morgan, John A. Sonquist and Laura Klem) *Multiple Classification Analysis: A Computer Program for Multiple Regression Using Categorical Predictors,* Institute for Social Research, University of Michigan, 1967, 2nd edition, 1973; (with Godofredo Aranda, Maria Aranda, Abel Centurion, and Edgar Flores) *Barriades de Lima: Dwellers' Attitudes Toward Public and Private Services,* Centro de Investigaciones Sociales por Muestro, Ministerio de Trabajo, Lima, Peru, 1967; (contributor) D. Allison, editor, *The R & D Game,* MIT Press, 1969.

(Contributor) N. K. Denzin, editor, *Sociological Methods: A Sourcebook,* Aldine, 1970; (contributor) B. T. Eiduson and L.

Beckman, editors, *Career Choice and Development in Scientists*, Russell Sage Foundation, 1972; (with Monica D. Blumenthal, Robert L. Kahn, and Kendra B. Head) *Justifying Violence: Attitudes of American Men*, Institute for Social Research, University of Michigan, 1972; (with Robert C. Messenger) *Multivariate Nominal Scale Analysis: A Report on a New Analysis Technique and a Computer Program*, Institute for Social Research, University of Michigan, 1973; (with others) *A Guide for Analyzing Social Science Data*, Institute for Social Research, University of Michigan, 1974, 2nd edition, 1981; (contributor) I. A. Taylor and J. Getzels, editors, *Perspectives in Creativity*, Aldine, 1975; (with Stephen B. Withey) *Social Indicators of Well-Being: Americans' Perceptions of Life Quality*, Plenum, 1976; (editor and contributor) *Scientific Productivity: The Effectiveness of Research Groups in Six Countries*, Cambridge University Press and UNESCO, 1979.

(Co-editor and contributor) *Quality of Life: Comparative Studies*, Sage Publications, 1980; (contributor) F. T. Juster and K. C. Land, editors, *Social Accounting Systems*, Academic Press, 1981; (contributor) E. Roberts and others, editors, *The Development and Dissemination of Biomedical Innovations*, MIT Press, 1981; (editor and contributor) *Research on the Quality of Life*, Institute for Social Research, University of Michigan, in press.

Contributor to professional journals, including *Ekistics, American Sociological Review, Social Indicator Research, Public Opinion Quarterly, Social Science and Medicine*, and *Journal of Creative Behavior*.

* * *

ANGLIN, Douglas G(eorge)   1923-

PERSONAL: Born December 16, 1923, in Toronto, Ontario, Canada; son of George Chambers (a physician) and Ruth Cecilia (Cale) Anglin; married Mary Elizabeth Watson, June 26, 1948; children: Margaret Alice, Deirdre Ruth. *Education:* University of Toronto, B.A. (honors), 1948; Oxford University, B.A., 1950, M.A., 1954, D.Phil., 1956. *Religion:* United Church of Canada. *Home:* 2691 Basswood Crescent, Ottawa, Ontario, Canada K1V 8K2. *Office:* Department of Political Science, Carleton University, Ottawa, Ontario, Canada K1S 5B6.

CAREER: University of Manitoba, Winnipeg, assistant professor, 1951-57, associate professor of political science and international relations, 1957-58; Carleton University, Ottawa, Ontario, associate professor, 1958-65, professor of political science, 1965—. Vice-chancellor, University of Zambia, 1965-69. *Military service:* Royal Canadian Naval Volunteer Reserve, active duty, 1943-45; became lieutenant. *Member:* International Studies Association, Canadian Political Science Association, African Studies Association, Canadian Association of African Studies (president, 1973-74). *Awards, honors:* Rhodes scholar, 1948.

WRITINGS: (Editor with Millar MacLure): *Africa: The Political Pattern*, University of Toronto Press, 1961; *The St. Pierre and Miquelon Affaire of 1941*, University of Toronto Press, 1966, revised edition, 1970; (editor with Carl Widstrand and T. M. Shaw) *Canada, Scandinavia and Southern Africa*, Africana Publishers, 1978; (editor with Widstrand and Shaw) *Conflict and Change in Southern Africa*, University Press of America, 1978; (with Shaw) *Zambia's Foreign Policy: Studies in Diplomacy and Dependence*, Westview, 1979. Contributor

of chapters to several books; contributor to professional journals.

BIOGRAPHICAL/CRITICAL SOURCES: Horizon, November, 1966; *Canadian Journal of Economics and Political Science*, August, 1967.

* * *

APPELBAUM, Judith (Pilpel)   1939-

PERSONAL: Born September 26, 1939, in New York, N.Y.; daughter of Robert C. (an administrator) and Harriet (a lawyer; maiden name, Fleischl) Pilpel; married Alan Appelbaum (a lawyer), April 16, 1961; children: Lynn Stephanie, Alexander Eric. *Education:* Vassar College, A.B. (with honors), 1960. *Residence:* New York, N.Y.; and Danbury, Conn. *Office:* Sensible Solutions, Inc., 14 East 75th St., New York, N.Y. 10021.

CAREER: Harper's Magazine, New York City, editor, 1960-69; John Day Co., New York City, editor, 1970-71; *Harper's Magazine*, editor, 1971-75; *Harper's Weekly*, New York City, managing editor, 1975-76; *Atlas World Press Review*, New York City, senior consultant, 1977; *Publishers Weekly*, New York City, managing editor, 1978-81, contributing editor, 1981-82; Sensible Solutions, Inc. (publishing consulting firm), New York City, founder and managing director, 1979-82; *New York Times*, New York City, columnist for *New York Times Book Review*, 1982-84; Sensible Solutions, Inc., managing director, 1984—. Member of faculty, Publishing Institute, University of Denver, 1981—, New York University Center for Publishing, 1981—, City University of New York education in publishing program, 1982—. Member of advisory board, Coordinating Council of Literary Magazines, 1980—, policy board of Center for Book Research, 1983—, and statistics committee, Book Industry Study Group, 1984—. Lecturer on writing to groups of professional writers.

MEMBER: P.E.N., Society for Scholarly Publishing, Authors League of America, Authors Guild, Committee of Small Magazine/Press Editors and Publishers, Women's Forum, Women's Media Group.

WRITINGS: (Editor with Tony Jones and Gwyneth Cravens) *The Big Picture: A Wraparound Book*, Harper Magazine Press, 1976; (with Nancy Evans) *How to Get Happily Published: A Complete and Candid Guide*, Harper, 1978, 2nd edition, New American Library, 1982.

Also editor of *Publishers Weekly* Special Reports, including "The Question of Size in the Book Industry Today," 1978, "Getting a Line on Backlist," 1979, "Paperback Primacy," 1981, and "Small Publisher Power," 1982.

Book review editor, *Book Research Quarterly*, 1984—; editorial adviser, *Book Industry Study Group Newsletter*, 1980-83. Contributor of articles to *Harper's, Change, Writer*, and other publications.

SIDELIGHTS: In *How to Get Happily Published: A Complete and Candid Guide*, professional editor Judith Appelbaum and her collaborator Nancy Evans address many of the publishing problems facing both amateur and professional writers. Drawing on their own experiences, Appelbaum and Evans offer what *Choice* calls "many 'insider' tips aimed to increase the writer's chances for publication success and satisfaction." While there are numerous "how-to" books on publishing, *How to Get Happily Published* differs from many in its field because it emphasizes steps for authors to take *after* their book has been accepted for publication, suggesting that if promotional prospects look bleak, they should promote the book themselves. And for those who are unable to find an interested publisher, Appelbaum and Evans offer helpful advice on the possibilities of "self-publishing" gathered from years in the trade. *Publishers Weekly* believes the authors "display a real capacity to stimulate the reader as well as explain the nuts and bolts of getting 'happily' published," and the *Antioch Review* finds the authors "helpful in answering just about every question a writer might find necessary to ask." As *Best Sellers* puts it: "Anyone who has ever seriously considered professional writing should find this 'how to' volume very worthwhile."

CA INTERVIEW

CA interviewed Judith Appelbaum by telephone on May 4, 1984, at her home in New York City.

CA: You got an early start in publishing, beginning when you were eighteen with a summer job at what is now Harper & Row and then becoming an editor on Harper's *magazine in 1960. Did your attraction to publishing grow out of a desire to write, or was it the industry itself that interested you?*

APPELBAUM: It wasn't a wish to write. I never really wanted to write, and the reason I write is that I have things I want people to know. My first impulse still is an editor's impulse, to get somebody else to do it. But when I feel very strongly about something or when I think nobody will present it quite the way I want it presented, then I sit and confront blank pieces of paper—or blank computer screens, now. So it was publishing itself that interested me.

CA: Many people who enter publishing get stuck in routine jobs and either stay on one level or get out to try something else. Did you find it a difficult or frustrating field to get started in?

APPELBAUM: No, but I had several advantages, one of which was that *Harper's* magazine, when I joined it, was edited by Jack Fischer, who was an absolutely wonderful man as well as a brilliant editor. One of the things he liked to do best was bring young people along, and that was lucky for me. The other advantage of being at *Harper's* for all those years was that it was a very small place. If you were energetic and you had your eyes open and you were interested in doing more than what you were assigned to do at the moment, there was plenty of opportunity to get in and try your hand at this, try your hand at that. People were willing to let you, and if it worked, they were willing to keep letting you.

CA: The smallness must be a great advantage. Some people seem to get lost in the shuffle at big companies.

APPELBAUM: Yes. Had I been working in the trade book editorial department at Harper, which is the house *Harper's* magazine was part of when I joined it (before it became Harper & Row), I think I would have had much less latitude.

CA: Harper's Weekly *and* How to Get Happily Published *(1978, revised edition 1982) were related. What was the philosophy behind* Harper's Weekly *and how did it lead to* How to Get Happily Published?

APPELBAUM: The philosophy behind it was that a lot of people have something valuable to say and can say it in print

to the benefit of a lot of other people, and they needed a medium they could contribute to. *Harper's Weekly* was a reader-written paper. By and large, the pieces in it were by people who were not writers. We found that their articles worked very well when they were short and when they were based on experience rather than opinion.

The readership was wonderful. And working on the *Weekly* was wonderful because of the communal feeling; we and the readers were all doing this thing together.

One survey showed that the people who subscribed to *Harper's Weekly* were enormously active in their communities and in the wider worlds surrounding those communities. They were people who wanted to make things happen, who cared about what happened to the world, what happened to other people. One of the fascinating things about *Harper's Weekly* was that we would run an article about something that the writer was passionate about, and six months to a year later we'd see a piece on that subject in the *New York Times* or *Newsweek* or some other big national publication. By no means everything that we published surfaced later in the national media, but a lot of things did, because important movements do start with some nut, somebody who just cares desperately.

The *Weekly* worked well editorially and had a good renewal rate, but it had been founded, along with another spin-off of *Harper's* magazine, on the theory that three magazines could function not much more expensively than one. That turned out, not surprisingly, to be false. So it was folded. Nancy Evans had been an editor there and we both felt—all of us who worked on the *Weekly* felt—that its death was a terrible shame. Nancy and I thought that maybe, at the least, we could codify what we had learned about how people who are not writers can break into print and do some good for various segments of the public. So *How to Get Happily Published* was originally conceived as a kind of offshoot of *Harper's Weekly,* as a guide to using the power of print for people who weren't writers.

But almost at once when we began to do our research for the book, we came smack up against the problem that professional writers face over and over again. They too have trouble using the power of print: although they can get their manuscripts bought and set in type, they can't reach the audience they ought to be reaching because of the way book publishing works. So *How to Get Happily Published* came to be a book for professional writers as well as for would-be writers.

CA: Have you had a lot of positive response from people who have been helped by it?

APPELBAUM: Yes. Of the many nice aftermaths of having written that book, that's been the nicest, the response that we get from readers. We get a lot of letters and some phone calls, and when I was at the *New York Times* I got a fair number of personal visits. People generally say, in essence, It works! You know, I tried that stuff you say in chapter two or chapter four or chapter six and it works—both people who have sold books or articles to established publishers and people who have decided to self-publish. And there seem to be more and more people who have decided on the strength of the book to self-publish and who are very glad that they did.

CA: Do you think there is a significant increase in self-publishing?

APPELBAUM: I think so, although it's very hard to document. If you look at the number of publishers, you find that it's zooming. Bowker's list is up to 16,000 or 17,000, and I think a lot of those publishers are probably self-publishers. I don't know any way to pin it down, but my impression is that self-publishing is really on the rise.

CA: You stress in your book the importance of the query letter. Are there instances when it is better to send the whole article, or at least something more than a query letter?

APPELBAUM: I would never say that you should *never* do *anything.* There's always a time for the really bizarre move. But I am a very firm believer in doing things by easy stages. I think sometimes it's even better to have a step that precedes the query letter if you can do that. I mean, if you have a contact whom you know more or less personally, it might be better to phone, say, and talk about how you want to send in this query letter. It's easy to take a phone call. It's relatively easy to look at a query letter and say, Well, yeah, I'll look at your work. It's a little bit harder to look at a whole proposal and it's very hard for an editor to say, Yes, I'll buy this manuscript. So it seems to me that if you start off with things that are easy to say yes to (from the editor's point of view), you get the editor in the habit of saying yes, you get the editor's input and you get the editor feeling, legitimately, that he or she is involved in this thing. Therefore the editor is more reluctant to cut and run.

CA: What do you consider the major pitfalls for writers trying to break into print?

APPELBAUM: If the question must be phrased in terms of major pitfalls, I suppose I would answer in terms of getting lost in the shuffle. But I think the major opportunities—I don't mean to sound like Pollyanna, but I'd like to turn the question around—the major opportunities for writers involve taking hold of the publishing process, the process of connecting with readers, and making it happen better. And I think that gets more possible all the time—not easy, but do-able.

CA: During your work as managing editor of Publishers Weekly *and at the* New York Times *you surveyed major trends in publishing, such as the proliferation of the small publishing houses. Do you think this trend is likely to continue?*

APPELBAUM: Yes. There seem to be more and more of them all the time. And I think they are getting stronger and savvier, many of them, and that writers are more attracted to them. People who try to make a living writing still face some stumbling blocks with small houses, and most of them have to do with the advance. But in many ways small firms can offer better deals than large, old-line houses.

CA: What's your opinion of the health of publishing today?

APPELBAUM: I think it's very healthy. The moaning and groaning that we've heard over the past few years (which has abated noticeably) was traceable to some very severe problems among large, well-established East Coast houses. Those problems haven't gone away, though some of them are on the way to being solved. But it's useful to remember that commentary on publishing comes out of New York, for the most part, and when commentators based in New York tell their national audiences that everything stinks, they're acting like a man with Limburger cheese on his moustache. From their point of view the statement, "Everything stinks," is absolutely accurate. But if you just change your perspective, if you look beyond the Hud-

son, across the country, you see a lot of very encouraging and exciting things.

I think the shakeout that's taken place in New York publishing has been more healthy than unhealthy, and I've heard a lot of New York publishers admit that in the past year or so. Hardcover houses that used to depend on paperback reprinters for their real profits have learned that the industry doesn't work that way anymore and they're trying to regroup and function differently. But they're huge and they're as sluggish as huge things usually are, so it's hard for them to change the way they do things, the way they set up their procedures, the way they think.

CA: What about getting a job in publishing, especially with the instability we hear about in publishing jobs? Any advice for bright young graduates who think they have something to offer the field?

APPELBAUM: I think it makes sense to try to find a smallish house, because at a small house you can have the sort of situation that I had at *Harper's,* where you can learn how the whole process works and try out a lot of things, find out what you're best at and become something of a generalist besides. I think it might make sense to look into the publishing operations of nonpublishing companies. Many, many large businesses have publishing arms which probably don't get approached by as many bright young people as Doubleday and Harper & Row do. I wouldn't rule out the conventional approaches to Harper & Row or Doubleday or whatever, but it seems to me that the learning experience there is not as good as the one smaller houses can offer, and the competition for getting in is much greater.

CA: At the New York Times Book Review *you wrote the "New and Noteworthy" and "Paperback Talk" columns. The* Book Review's *bestseller lists are often attacked on the grounds that they unfairly influence sales and actually hurt sales of books that aren't listed on them. How do you feel about the criticism, and how do the lists seem justified to you?*

APPELBAUM: I think the lists—which were not my responsibility at the *Times* or *Publishers Weekly*—function the way popularity contests of all sorts do. They attract the attention of the public, and since they do boost sales of the books that manage to get on them, they're beneficial to the industry, and possibly to the culture. I don't believe that the sorts of books that don't make the lists would sell better if there were no bestseller rosters; I do believe that the books that get listed sell better as a result.

However, I think that the lists, all of them, could stand a lot of rethinking. For example, it no longer makes sense to run lists broken down by format. We have hardcover lists and trade-paperback lists and mass-market paperback lists even though those divisions don't mean much anymore in terms of marketing or the size of the audience or any of the things that they used to mean a lot in terms of. The current system makes it possible for a book to be on two lists at the same time—at number four, say, on the hardcover list and number eight on the paperback list in the same week. A book that does that must be outselling all the books at number one on every list—and yet it's number four and number eight.

Then you have books with huge sales figures that yet never show up on the lists because they sell relatively slowly and the lists cover only books that sell fast.

And you have booksellers reporting who really have no idea what they're selling. That's happening somewhat less as stores become computerized; the larger, more sophisticated stores do know what they're selling. But a lot of the small ones don't. And when you get to the bottom of the lists, you tend to have virtually identical sales figures. It's really a toss-up which titles get on at the bottom. I could go on. So I think it would be nice if somebody or some group of people would overhaul the lists. But I wouldn't abolish them if I were running the world.

CA: They are *fun to read.*

APPELBAUM: They are, and they do help readers. There are well over half-a-million books in print today, and even an ordinary store has thousands of different titles. You can get paralyzed by that wide a range of choice. The lists provide a way to narrow it and make it manageable.

CA: Tell me something about Sensible Solutions.

APPELBAUM: Sensible Solutions is a consulting firm that Nancy Evans and Florence Janovic and I founded in 1979. It works for publishers and authors and gets involved mostly in the marketing aspects of publishing. Its reason for being was our belief that large trade houses really can't market anything but bestsellers (the system for them, which works most of the time but not always, involves mobilizing other generalists in the book business, including reviewers, booksellers and librarians). When a large trade-book house has a title that isn't supposed to be a bestseller—a book on, say, raising your child—the way to reach its audience is by finding specialists—people who publish newsletters for parents and run parenthood groups and that kind of thing—who will broadcast the book's availability and its worth. That's prohibitively expensive for one book that isn't going to sell a great many copies. If a trade house was willing to specialize in parenting books, it could amortize the cost of making all those connections over many titles, but since trade houses refuse to specialize, they can't do that. Our idea was that an author could do the legwork necessary for setting up a book's marketing network, with guidance and with coordination with the publishing people. That way, the book would have a chance to reach its audience without the publisher having to spend prohibitively large amounts of money.

CA: What are you working on now that you'd like to talk about?

APPELBAUM: I'm about to start selecting books to cover in the book review section of *Book Research Quarterly,* a new journal created by John P. Dessauer, the founder and director of the Center for Book Research at the University of Scranton. Since the Center was launched a year or so ago, I've been on its policy board, and I've felt continually excited about the investigations it's initiating and the reports of those investigations that it will disseminate through its *Quarterly.* Because the book industry has been surprisingly under-researched in the past, publishers, booksellers, librarians and other people who are professionally involved with books have had a hard time figuring out the best ways to run their operations, but in the near future the Center's work should be far enough along to help them function more intelligently.

This summer, I'll be teaching at some of the intensive annual publishing programs for men and women who want to break into the field. I've done that for several years now and I love having the chance to let people in on things I've learned about the business and to learn from them how it strikes newcomers, who may, after all, see opportunities and idiocies much more clearly than those of us who are used to the industry's ways. In the fall, along with other members of the Women's Media Group, I'll be running a new course about the media—with particular emphasis on print—in a New York City public high school.

And one of these days, Nancy Evans and I are going to do a new edition of *How to Get Happily Published.* We have folders full of facts and case studies and stacks of new resources that we're eager to take account of in our book.

BIOGRAPHICAL/CRITICAL SOURCES: Publishers Weekly, November 21, 1977; *Library Journal,* December 15, 1977; *Antioch Review,* spring, 1978; *Best Sellers,* May, 1978; *Choice,* October, 1978.

—*Interview by Jean W. Ross*

*   *   *

APPLEBEE, Arthur N(oble)   1946-

PERSONAL: Born June 20, 1946, in Sherbrooke, Quebec, Canada; born a U.S. citizen; son of Roger K. (a university dean) and Margaret (Aitken) Applebee; married Marcia Lynn Hull (a teacher), June 15, 1968 (divorced); married Judith A. Langer (a university professor), May 23, 1982. *Education:* Yale University, B.A. (cum laude), 1968; Harvard University, M.A.T., 1970; University of London, Ph.D., 1973. *Home:* 24 Delmar, San Francisco, Calif. 94117. *Office:* School of Education, Stanford University, Stanford, Calif. 94305.

CAREER: National Council of Teachers of English, Urbana, Ill., part-time staff assistant, 1964-69; Massachusetts General Hospital, Child Development Laboratory, Boston, research assistant and psychologist, 1969-71; University of Lancaster, Lancaster, England, research associate at International Microteaching Unit, 1973-74; Tarleton High School, Tarleton, England, English and drama teacher, 1974-76; National Council of Teachers of English, staff associate, 1976-80, and associate director of ERIC Clearinghouse on Reading and Communication Skills; Stanford University, School of Education, Stanford, Calif., associate professor of education, 1980—.

MEMBER: International Reading Association, National Conference on Research in English, American Educational Research Association, National Association of Teachers of English (England).

AWARDS, HONORS: Promising researcher award from National Council of Teachers of English, 1974; National Council on Research in English fellow, 1984; recipient of grants from National Institute of Education and National Council of Teachers of English.

WRITINGS—Published by National Council of Teachers of English, except as indicated: *Tradition and Reform in the Teaching of English: A History,* 1974; *The Child's Concept of Story: Ages Two to Seventeen,* University of Chicago Press, 1978; *A Survey of Teaching Conditions in English, 1977,* 1978.

Writing in the Secondary School: Current Practice in English and the Content Areas, 1981; (with others) *Reading, Thinking and Writing: Results from the 1979-80 National Assessment of Reading and Literature,* Education Commission of the States, 1981; *Contexts for Learning to Write: Studies of Secondary School Instruction,* Ablex Publishing, 1984.

Contributor: Martin Nystrand, editor, *Language as a Way of Knowing*, Ontario Institute for Studies in Education, 1977; Leon F. Williams, *Workload Starter Kit for Secondary English Teachers*, 1980; Nystrand, editor, *What Writers Know: The Language, Process, and Structure of Written Discourse*, Academic Press, 1982; Charles R. Cooper, editor, *Researching Response to Literature and the Teaching of Literature*, Ablex Publishing, in press. Also contributor to *Encyclopedia of Educational Research*, Macmillan, 1982, and *Developing Basic Skills Programs in Secondary Schools*, 1982. Contributor to psychology and education journals in England and the United States. Editor, *Research in the Teaching of English*, 1984—.

SIDELIGHTS: Arthur N. Applebee told *CA:* "Early involvement in various projects and activities of the National Council of Teachers of English led to a continuing concern with educational issues and a specific interest in language and language learning. This interest has had diverse manifestations, leading to studies in educational psychology, learning disabilities, educational history, curriculum evaluation, and most recently in various aspects of the teaching of writing. The National Study of Writing in the Secondary School, which I directed, provided a not particularly encouraging portrait of students' experiences as writers in American schools. My work has sought to understand why conditions are so bleak, and to propose some viable alternatives. Writing about writing is itself a learning process; it is never clear exactly what the recommendations will look like until we begin to write them up to share outside of our research group."

*   *   *

ARNCLIFFE, Andrew
    See WALKER, Peter N.

*   *   *

ARNOW, Harriette (Louisa Simpson) 1908-
    (Harriette Simpson)

PERSONAL: Born July 7, 1908, in Wayne County, Ky.; daughter of Elias Thomas (a teacher, farmer, and oil well driller) and Mollie Jane (a teacher; maiden name, Denney) Simpson; married Harold B. Arnow (publicity director for Michigan Heart Association), March 11, 1939; children: Marcella Jane, Thomas Louis. *Education:* Attended Berea College, 1924-26; University of Louisville, B.S., 1931. *Home:* 3220 Nixon Rd., R.R. 7, Ann Arbor, Mich. 48105.

CAREER: Author.

MEMBER: Women's International League for Peace and Freedom, P.E.N., Authors Guild, Authors League of America, American Civil Liberties Union, Phi Beta Kappa (honorary).

AWARDS, HONORS: Friends of American Writers award, runner up for National Book Award, *Saturday Review* national critics' poll co-winner for best novel, Berea College Centennial award, *Woman's Home Companion* Silver Distaff award for "unique contribution by a woman to American life," all 1955, all for *The Dollmaker;* commendation from Tennessee Historical Commission and award of merit of American Association for State and Local History, both 1961, both for *Seedtime on the Cumberland; Tennessee Historical Quarterly* prize for best article of the year, 1962; Outstanding Alumni award, University of Louisville, College of Arts and Sciences, 1979; honorary degrees from Albion College, Transylvania College, and University of Kentucky.

WRITINGS: (Under name Harriette Simpson) *Mountain Path* (novel), Covici-Friede, 1936; *Hunter's Horn* (novel), Macmillan, 1949, reprinted, Avon, 1979; *The Dollmaker* (novel), Macmillan, 1954, reprinted, Avon, 1972; *Seedtime on the Cumberland* (nonfiction), Macmillan, 1960; *Flowering of the Cumberland* (nonfiction), Macmillan, 1963; *The Weedkiller's Daughter* (novel), Knopf, 1970; *The Kentucky Trace: A Novel of the American Revolution*, Knopf, 1974; *Old Burnside* (nonfiction), University Press of Kentucky, 1978.

Also author of short stories in the 1930s, two of them anthologized in *O. Henry Memorial Award Prize Stories*. Contributor of articles and reviews to magazines.

SIDELIGHTS: Harriet Arnow is a Kentucky-born novelist whose best work captures the erosion of rural life in the Cumberland hills. "I was aware that nothing had been written on the Southern migrants, of what was actually happening to them and to their culture, of how they came to the cities for the first time in the 1920s, leaving their families behind," she explained to Barbara L. Baer in the *Nation*. "I began writing during the depression which had sent hill people back home again. And then, as I was still writing during the Second War, I witnessed the permanent move the men made by bringing their wives and children with them to the cities. With that last migration, hill life was gone forever, and with it, I suppose, a personal dream of community I'd had since childhood."

To recapture that sense of community, Arnow spent two decades writing her Kentucky trilogy, a series of novels which begins with a coming-of-age story called *Mountain Path*, continues with a serious adventure novel entitled *Hunter's Horn*, and culminates in *The Dollmaker*, Arnow's best known fiction and, according to Joyce Carol Oates, "our most unpretentious American masterpiece." Over the years, many labels have been attached to these writings, but "whether the books are read today as regional, or realistic or even feminist writing, they are first of all a coherent vision in the best tradition of American fiction," in Baer's opinion. "They tell the stories of men and women who see their dreams of self-sufficiency shrink and their personal freedoms foreclosed by a rapacious industrial society."

In *Mountain Path*, her first and most autobiographical novel, Arnow focuses on a young student teacher from the city and her experiences in a community of feuding mountaineers. Torn between the intellectual existence for which her education has prepared her and the pull of the earthy backwoods culture, the heroine faces a difficult decision, complicated by her love for a mountain man. Unlike earlier novelists who caricatured "hillbillies" or moralized about their violent feuds, Arnow acknowledges the individuality of her characters and the legitimacy of their ways. Even though the book was tagged a "regional" novel and eventually went out of print, it garnered enough attention to establish Arnow as "a writer of considerable talent," Glenda Hobbs reports in the *Dictionary of Literary Biography*.

In *Hunter's Horn*, the second book of her trilogy, Arnow continues her exploration of the conflict between an individual's dreams and society's demands, this time from a male point of view. Nunn Ballew, husband, father, and Kentucky farmer, becomes engrossed in the pursuit of "King Devil," an elusive red fox that has been raiding local farms and destroying livestock. Like Ahab in *Moby Dick*, Ballew will stop at nothing to catch his prey—even though his obsession triggers both personal anguish and the community's ridicule and disdain.

His family also suffers as Ballew invests money that could pay for his 14-year-old daughter Suse's schooling in expensive hunting dogs. No sooner does he kill "King Devil"—which turns out to be a female slowed down because she is carrying pups—than Suse discovers she is pregnant. An independent, high-spirited girl who wants to go north and get an education, Suse is confident that her father will support her decision not to wed.

Instead, in a riveting scene that is played out before the assembled community, Ballew capitulates to the local mores he has always scorned. Asserting that his fire will warm no bastard, he insists that Suse marry the father of the child. As Hobbs reports, "Nunn, nearly frozen with ambivalence and grief wins back the neighbors' approval in exchange for his daughter's back and heart being 'broke to the plow.'"

Reviewers consider it a mark of her excellence that Arnow sustains reader sympathy for Nunn Ballew. "However much we may resent Nunn's improvidence and his betrayal of Suse," writes a *Ms.* reviewer, "it is a testament to Arnow's extraordinary skill at characterization that almost against our will we share his anguish and cheer him on after his four-legged red whale. *Hunter's Horn* manifests Arnow's ability to create male characters as palpable and as complex as her best women. Nunn can't be written off as another hateful man."

In spite of the appeal he exerts, Nunn Ballew pales in comparison to Gertie Nevels, a character Baer describes as "larger than life, a rawboned figure hewn from some matriarchal past" and the protagonist of the third and final volume of the trilogy, *The Dollmaker*. Published at a time when strong women were a rarity in fiction, the 1954 best-seller was a critical as well as a popular success and tied for best novel in the *Saturday Review* national critics' poll. "Perhaps partly because most of the novel is set outside Kentucky, critics were less tempted to call the book 'regional,'" *Dictionary of Literary Biography* contributor Glenda Hobbs explains.

For thirty-one weeks the novel remained on the best-seller lists, and, when Columbia purchased the movie rights, it appeared as though the story would be filmed. But, with the passage of time, the public's interest subsided and movie executives had second thoughts about the novel's commercial appeal. They shelved the project, for reasons which *Chicago Tribune* reporter Eric Zorn details: "In a year when Ernest Hemingway won the Nobel Prize for literature and the public taste was for action, drama and romance they found onscreen in such movies as 'From Here to Eternity' and 'On the Waterfront,' Arnow offered a grim picture of the cultural collision of traditional, rural lifestyles with industrial America. It was not thrilling, uplifting, intellectually ambitious or filled with adventure, suspense or intrigue."

The story instead depicts a Kentucky woman's losing battle to retain her dignity when her family is relocated in Detroit. A simple country woman with a talent for whittling and a love of the land, Gertie Nevels seeks no greater fulfillment than raising her family on a farm of her own. But she gives up her dream to follow her husband Clovis up north when he takes a wartime job in a factory. With her she brings a magnificent block of cherry wood from which she plans to carve a religious figure—Judas, maybe, or the laughing Christ—if, as she explains to a stranger, "I can ever hit on the right face."

In the brutal environment of the Detroit projects, inspiration never comes, and Gertie finds herself sacrificing her artistic integrity to survival. The dolls she once hand-carved for her daughter's pleasure, she now mass-produces to feed her family. And though she ultimately "adjusts," Gertie feels corrupted—her children lost to her, her self-reliance undermined. The book ends with her splintering the beloved cherry wood block so she can manufacture crude dolls for quick money.

While some critics have interpreted this ending as evidence of Gertie's defeat, Dorothy H. Lee offers a brighter interpretation. "The hidden face in the wood is that of Christ: Gertie does not contradict the scrapwood man's assumption that it is," she writes in *Critique*. "Questioned further by the man as to whether or not she could find a face for him, she responds, 'They was so many would ha done; they's millions and millions a faces plenty fine enough—fer him. . . . Why some a my neighbors down there in the alley—they would ha done.' She thus reveals that she retains her vision of Christ's humility. Further, she perceives her neighbors as crucified and, although she would not be able so to verbalize, as scapegoats of the processes of urbanization—of competition, poverty, materialism, and mechanization. She has always had compassion for others, but her vision now is less provincial. She recognizes suffering of a broader scope and understands the unity of all men who share it."

In her *Nation* article, Barbara L. Baer gauges the effect this ending has upon the reader: "In the beautiful last dialogue, as the woodcutter gives Gertie his ax, we learn what Gertie has learned; no individual face can encompass the complexity of human suffering, whether a man's or a woman's, a relative's or a stranger's, a friend's or an enemy's."

Joyce Carol Oates was so moved by the story that she chose to critique it for the *New York Times Book Review* seventeen years after it originally appeared, calling it "one of those excellent American works that have yet to be properly assessed" and rekindling the public's interest. Among the readers whose curiosity was piqued was Jane Fonda, who eventually acquired filming rights and successfully brought the story to television as an ABC-TV movie in 1984.

Though nothing else Arnow has written before or since has come close to achieving *The Dollmaker*'s acclaim, Glenda Hobbs believes that the author has earned a permanent place in American letters. "Arnow alone has rendered Kentucky highlanders fully and fairly," she writes in the *Dictionary of Literary Biography*, "rescuing them from the literary stereotype of the lazy, suspicious, ignorant, manically violent hillbilly. Taking their dignity for granted, Arnow also avoids the passionate yearning for identification with the rural poor that betrays insecurity and condescension. . . . Arnow's unique, obstinate characters, even in the face of economic ruin and spiritual exhaustion, will endure and prevail. With luck and justice, so should Arnow's place in American literature."

BIOGRAPHICAL/CRITICAL SOURCES—Periodicals: *New York Times*, May 28, 1949; *New York Times Book Review*, May 29, 1949, March 22, 1970, January 24, 1971; *New Yorker*, May 1, 1954; *Saturday Review*, November 23, 1963; *New Republic*, August 31, 1974; *Nation*, January 31, 1976; *Critique: Studies in Modern Fiction*, Volume XX, number 2, 1978; *Ms.*, December, 1979; *Georgia Review*, winter, 1979; *Chicago Tribune*, February 10, 1983.

Books: Hariette Arnow, *The Dollmaker*, Macmillan, 1954; Wilton Eckley, *Harriette Arnow*, Twayne, 1974; *Contemporary Literary Criticism*, Gale, Volume II, 1974, Volume VII,

1977, Volume XVIII, 1981; *Dictionary of Literary Biography, Volume VI: American Novelists since World War II,* Second Series, Gale, 1980.

—Sketch by Donna Olendorf

* * *

ASHBROOK, James B(arbour)   1925-

PERSONAL: Born November 1, 1925, in Adrian, Mich.; son of Milan Forest (a minister) and Elizabeth (Barbour) Ashbrook; married Patricia Cober (a social worker), August 14, 1948; children: Peter, Susan, Martha, Karen. *Education:* Denison University, B.A. (with honors), 1947; Colgate Rochester Divinity School, B.D., 1950; Union Theological Seminary and William White Institute of Psychiatry, graduate fellow, 1954-55; Ohio State University, M.A., 1962, Ph.D., 1964. *Politics:* Democrat. *Home:* 1205 Wesley Ave., Evanston, Ill. 60202. *Office:* Garrett-Evangelical Theological Seminary, Northwestern University, 2121 Sheridan Rd., Evanston, Ill. 60201.

CAREER: Clergyman of American Baptist Church; pastor in Rochester, N.Y., 1950-54, and Granville, Ohio, 1955-60; Colgate Rochester Divinity School, Rochester, N.Y., associate professor, 1960-65, professor of pastoral theology, 1965-69, professor of psychology and theology, 1969-81; Northwestern University, Garrett-Evangelical Theological Seminary, Evanston, Ill., professor of religion and personality and adjunct member of graduate faculty, 1982—. Visiting lecturer at Denison University, 1958-60, and Princeton Theological Seminary, 1970-71. Summer clinical pastoral training at Rochester State Hospital, 1949, Bellevue General Hospital, 1950, and Illinois State Training School for Boys, 1951. Consultant and supervisor, Counseling Center, University of Rochester, 1969-75, and Genesee Ecumenical Pastoral Counseling Center, 1975-81; consultant to Chief of U.S. Air Force Chaplains, 1969, to Rochester Board of Education, 1969-73, to Family Court of Monroe County (N.Y.), 1972-74, and to St. Ann's Home for the Elderly, 1972—.

MEMBER: American Association of Pastoral Counselors (diplomate; chairman of centers and teaching committee, 1970-71), American Academy of Religion, Society for the Scientific Study of Religion, American Psychological Association, American Board of Professional Psychology, Phi Beta Kappa.

AWARDS, HONORS: Faculty fellowship, American Association of Theology Schools, 1963-64, 1971-72; postdoctoral fellowship, University of Rochester Center for Community Studies, 1971-73; alumni citation, Denison University, 1972; LL.D., Denison University, 1976.

WRITINGS: (Contributor) Simon Doniger, editor, *The Minister's Consultation Clinic,* Channel Press, 1955; (contributor) Hans Hoffman, editor, *Religion and Mental Health,* Harper, 1961; (contributor) David Belgum, editor, *Religion and Medicine,* Iowa State University Press, 1967.

(Contributor) William Bier, editor, *Psychological Testing for Ministerial Selection,* Fordham University Press, 1970; *Be/Come Community,* Judson, 1971; *In Human Presence: Hope,* Judson, 1971; *Humanitas: Human Becoming and Being Human,* Abingdon, 1973; *The Old Me and a New i: An Exploration of Personal Identity,* Judson, 1974; *Responding to Human Pain,* Judson, 1975; (with Paul W. Walaskay) *Christianity for Pious Skeptics,* Abingdon, 1977; *The Human Mind and the Mind of God: Theological Promise in Brain Research,* University Press of America, 1984.

Member of editorial board, "Ministry Monograph" series, 1965-70. Contributor to psychology and religion journals. Associate editor, *Review of Religious Research;* member of editorial advisory board, d, *Journal of Pastoral Care,* 1965—; consulting editor, *Journal of Counseling Psychology,* 1968-74.

* * *

ASHLEY, Steven
See McCAIG, Donald

* * *

ATKINSON, (Justin) Brooks   1894-1984

PERSONAL: Born November 28, 1894, in Melrose, Mass.; died January 13, 1984, in Huntsville, Ala.; son of Jonathan Henry (a journalist) and Garafelia (Taylor) Atkinson; married Oriana MacIlveen (a writer), August 18, 1926; children: (stepson) Bruce T. MacIlveen. *Education:* Harvard University, A.B., 1917. *Residence:* Huntsville, Ala. 35810.

CAREER: Springfield Daily News, Springfield, Mass., reporter, 1917; Dartmouth College, Hanover, N.H., English instructor, 1917-18; *Boston Evening Transcript,* Boston, Mass., reporter and assistant to drama critic, 1918, 1919-22; *Harvard Alumni Bulletin,* Cambridge, Mass., associate editor, 1920-22; *New York Times,* New York, N.Y., book review editor, 1922-25, drama critic, 1925-42, 1946-60, news correspondent in Chungking, China, 1942-44, news correspondent in Moscow, 1945-46, critic-at-large, 1960-65. *Military service:* U.S. Army, 1918.

MEMBER: New York Drama Critics Circle (first president, 1936), American Academy of Arts and Sciences (fellow), Actors' Equity Association (honorary life member), The Players (New York City).

AWARDS, HONORS: L.H.D. from Williams College, 1941; Pulitzer Prize in journalism, 1947, for series of articles on the Soviet Union; D.H.L. from Adelphi College (now University), 1960; L.L.D. from Pace College (now University), Franklin and Marshall College, Brandeis University, and Clark University, all 1965, from Washington College, 1966, and from Long Island University, 1967; named to Theatre Hall of Fame and Museum, 1972; L.D. from Dartmouth College, 1975; recipient of medal by Theatre Committee for Eugene O'Neill, 1980. Mansfield Theatre renamed Brooks Atkinson Theatre, 1960.

WRITINGS: Skyline Promenades: A Potpourri (nonfiction), Knopf, 1925; *Henry Thoreau: The Cosmic Yankee* (biography), Knopf, 1927; *East of the Hudson* (nonfiction), Knopf, 1931; *The Cingalese Prince* (travel), Doubleday, 1934.

Cleo for Short (nonfiction), Howell, Soskin, 1940; *Broadway Scrapbook* (collected articles), Theatre Arts, 1947, reprinted, Greenwood Press, 1970; *Once around the Sun* (essays), Harcourt, 1951; (author of foreword) *New Voices in the American Theatre* (play anthology), Modern Library, 1955.

Tuesdays and Fridays (collected articles), Random House, 1963; *Brief Chronicles* (collected articles), Coward, 1966; (author of introduction) Marian Spitzer, *The Palace,* Atheneum, 1969; (author of introduction) Norman Nadel, *A Pictorial History of the Theatre Guild,* Crown, 1969; *Broadway* (theatre history), Macmillan, 1970; *This Bright Land: A Personal View,* Natural History Press, 1972; (with Al Hirschfield) *The Lively Years: Reviews and Drawings of the Most Significant Plays since*

1920, Association Press, 1973; Robert G. Lowery, editor, *Sean O'Casey: From Times Past*, Macmillan, 1982.

Editor: Henry David Thoreau, *Walden and Other Writings*, Modern Library, 1937; Ralph Waldo Emerson, *Complete Essays and Other Writings*, Modern Library, 1940; *College in a Yard: Minutes by Thirty-Nine Harvard Men*, Harvard University Press, 1957; *The Pace Report: Thirty-Five Alumni, Faculty Members, and Administrators Describe a College in Transition*, Pace College, 1966; *Sean O'Casey Reader: Plays, Autobiographies, Opinions*, St. Martin's, 1968.

SIDELIGHTS: For thirty-one years the most influential voice in American drama belonged to *New York Times* critic Brooks Atkinson, an opening-night regular on the New York theatre scene between 1925 and 1960. Certainly Atkinson was not only one of the most respected, but one of the most genuinely loved critics in America, as popular with playwrights, directors, and actors as he was with his many readers. In a posthumous profile of the journalist, *Times* writer Richard F. Shepard described Atkinson as a figure who "exemplified the spirit of the Renaissance man with a mind that constantly inquired and fingers that always wrote."

In the same article Arthur Gelb, a *Times* managing editor who was associated with the critic during Atkinson's long career, called him "the conscience of the theater. He rediscovered Off-Broadway in the [1950s] when other critics did not want to bother going off the beaten path. His standards were high, but his criticism was tempered by compassion. . . . He had a compelling sense of courtesy toward the theater and an unfailing sense of optimism about its potential. He was the ideal theater critic for his time."

As much as he loved writing about plays, however, Atkinson was first and foremost a newspaperman. During World War II, after being rejected by the Navy because of his age, Atkinson requested a leave of absence from drama criticism in order to cover war news. "In 1942," Shepard wrote, "the [*Times*] sent him to Chongqing [then known as Chungking], the provisional capital of China. He traveled to front-line areas, bivouacked with Chinese troops and wrote of the exploits of the Flying Tigers. He was the first correspondent to report that Lieut. Gen. Joseph W. Stilwell had been relieved of his post because of his differences with Generalissimo Chiang Kai-shek." Following that assignment, Atkinson began a ten-month stint as a Moscow correspondent, and he continued to report on the political and social conditions of the Soviet Union after his return to New York. A series of these Soviet Union articles earned Atkinson a Pulitzer Prize in 1947.

And while he never won any notable journalistic awards for his years of witty, erudite critical articles, Atkinson was honored by the theatre community in several ways: he was made a life member of Actors' Equity in 1960; the same year saw the Mansfield Theatre renamed the Brooks Atkinson Theatre. In 1972 the critic was one of the first elected members of the Theatre Hall of Fame and Museum. And in 1980, on his eighty-sixth birthday, Atkinson was presented with a medal by the Theatre Committee for Eugene O'Neill (the writer's 1956 review of the Off-Broadway premier of O'Neill's *The Iceman Cometh* brought much-needed critical and commercial attention to the Off-Broadway scene). On this occasion Atkinson, according to Shepard's article, "spoke briefly about the relationship of critic and playwright: 'The important thing was to keep things on the level,' he said. 'Now that I look back on it, I think I did a good job at that.'"

BIOGRAPHICAL/CRITICAL SOURCES: Oriana Atkinson, *Over at Uncle Joe's*, Bobbs-Merrill, 1947; *Newsweek*, December 28, 1959; *New Yorker*, May 14, 1960; *Audubon*, September, 1965; *Saturday Review*, October 8, 1966; *Times Literary Supplement*, January 14, 1983.

OBITUARIES: New York Times, January 15, 1984; *Washington Post*, January 15, 1984; *London Times*, January 16, 1984; *Chicago Tribune*, January 17, 1984; *Time*, January 23, 1984.†

* * *

AUMBRY, Alan
See BAYLEY, Barrington J(ohn)

* * *

AUVERT, Elizabeth

PERSONAL: Born in Maracaibo, Venezuela; daughter of Rodolfo Augusto (a newspaper publisher and merchant) and Albertina (Silva) Auvert; divorced; children: Annabelle, Melissa, Bettina. *Education:* University of Arkansas, Ph.D., 1967. *Home:* Houston, Tex.; and Aptdo. Correos, No. 120, Maracaibo, Venezuela.

CAREER: Former associate professor at various American and Venezualan colleges and universities, including Centenary College, Shreveport, La. Writer.

WRITINGS—All published by Ediciones Albatros: (Editor) Lope de Vega, *El Duque de Viseo* (literary criticism), 1969; *Comparative Historical Chronology of Spain: Twelfth Century B.C. to Twelfth Century A.D.*, 1972; *Ataulfo, el Rey Barbaro* (historical novel; title means "Ataulph, the Barbarian King"), 1983.

* * *

AWOLOWO, Obafemi Awo 1909-

PERSONAL: Born March 6, 1909, in Ikenne, Western Nigeria; son of David Sopulu (a Yoruba farmer) and Mary (Efunyela) Awolowo; married Hannah Idowu Dideolu, December 26, 1937; children: two sons, three daughters. *Education:* Wesley College, Ibadan, Nigeria, graduate, 1927; University of London, B.Com. (with honors), 1944, LL.B., 1946. *Religion:* Protestant. *Address:* 31 Park Lane, P.O. Box 632, Apapa, Nigeria; and Ikenne, Ijebu Remo, Nigeria.

CAREER: School teacher in Ogbe, Abeokuta, Nigeria, 1928-29; stenographer in Lagos, Nigeria, 1930-32; Wesley College, Ibadan, Nigeria, clerk-stenographer, 1932-34; reporter, Nigerian *Daily Times*, 1934-35; Nigerian Motor Transport Union, assistant secretary, 1936-40, general secretary, 1941-44; editor, *Nigerian Worker*, 1939-44; called to the Bar at Inner Temple, 1947; solicitor and advocate of the Supreme Court of Nigeria in Ibadan, 1946-52; Western Region of Nigeria, cabinet minister and leader of government business, 1952-54, premier, 1954-59; leader of the opposition in Federal Parliament, Lagos, Nigeria, 1960-62; elected leader of the Yoruba people, 1966; Government of Nigeria, vice-chairman of the Federal Executive Council and head of the Ministry of Finance, 1967-71; University of Ife, Ile-Ife, Nigeria, chancellor, 1967-75; Ahmadu Bello University, Zaria, Nigeria, chancellor, 1975-78.

Member of Nigerian Youth Movement (leading efforts to reform Ibadan Native Authority Council), 1940-43; co-founder,

Trades Union Congress of Nigeria, 1943; founder of Egbe Omo Oduduwa (Yoruba cultural movement) in London, England, 1945, general secretary, 1948-51; founder of Action Group of Nigeria (a political party), 1951, and Unity Party of Nigeria, 1978; senior advocate of Nigeria.

AWARDS, HONORS: LL.D. from University of Nigeria, 1961, University of Ibadan, 1973, Ahmadu Bello University, 1975, and University of Cape Coast, Ghana, 1976; D.Sc. from University of Ife, 1967; D. Litt. from University of Lagos, 1970; Grand Commander of the Federal Republic of Nigeria.

WRITINGS: Path to Nigerian Freedom, Faber, 1947; *Forward to a New Nigeria,* Western Nigeria Information Services, 1957.

Awo: The Autobiography of Chief Obafemi Awolowo, Cambridge University Press, 1960; *Anglo-Nigeria Defence Pact,* Action Group Bureau of Information, 1960; *Presidential Address Delivered by Chief the Honourable Obafemi Awolowo, Federal President of the Action Group and Leader of the Opposition in the Federal House of Representatives at the Seventh Congress of the Action Group Held at the Abalabi Club, Mushin, on Monday, 19th September, 1960,* African Press, 1960; *Call to Rededication and Reconstruction* (pamphlet), Union Print, 1961; *Forward with Democratic Socialism: A Message by Chief Awolowo from Broad Street Prison, Lagos,* Action Group of Nigeria, 1963.

Thoughts on Nigerian Constitution, Oxford University Press, 1966; *An Address Delivered by Chief Obafemi Awolowo on the Occasion of His Installation as the First Chancellor of the University of Ife at Ile-Ife on Monday, 15 May, 1967,* Ibadan University Press, 1967; *Blueprint for Post-War Reconstruction* (pamphlet), Nigerian Federal Ministry of Information, 1967; *My Early Life* (autobiography), J. West Publications, 1968; *The Path to Economic Freedom in Developing Countries,* University of Lagos, 1968; *The People's Republic,* Oxford University Press, 1968.

The Strategy and Tactics of the People's Republic of Nigeria, Macmillan, 1970; *The Problems of Africa: The Need for Ideological Reappraisal,* Macmillan, 1977; *Awo on the Nigerian Civil War,* J. West Publications, 1981; *Path to Nigerian Greatness,* Fourth Dimension Publishers, 1981; *Voice of Reason, Voice of Wisdom, and Voice of Courage,* Fagbamigbe Publishers, 1981.

Also author of *Action Group Fourteen-Point Programme,* 1959, *African Unity,* 1961, *Africa Must be Economically Independent and Self-Reliant,* 1967, *If We Are United, We Shall Succeed Collectively and Severally,* 1968, *Lecture on the Financing of the Nigerian Civil War and Its Implications for the Future Economy of the Nation,* 1970, and *Memorable Quotes from Awo,* edited by Wunmi Adegbonmire, 1978. Contributor to newspapers. Founder, *Nigerian Tribune,* 1949.

SIDELIGHTS: With considerable financial difficulty, Obafemi Awo Awolowo, whose inherited titles as a descendant of Oduduwo (founder of the Yoruba kingdom) include Ashiwaju of Ijebu-Remo, Losi of Ikenne, Lisa of Ijeun, Apesin of Oshogbo, Odole of Ife, Ajagunla of Ado Ekiti, Odofin of Owo, and Obng Ikpan Isong of Ibibioland, educated himself in Nigeria and later in England. He also has been conferred with Chieftancy titles in other parts of Nigeria. His political activities began while a student in London. His party positions were moderate at first, later moved toward the left in order to accommodate other members of the party and maintain political unity. He was able to visit India in 1952 and 1953 for political discussions with Nehru (whom Awolowo admired) and other Indian leaders, and to study India's system of symbol voting. Later, as premier of Nigeria's Western Region, Awolowo toured England, the United States, West Germany, Italy, and Japan to promote interest in trade and investment operations in Nigeria.

During a dispute with leaders inside his political party, Awolowo and several others were arrested in 1962, Awolowo himself was "detained" and tried for "treasonable felony and conspiracy," convicted, and sentenced to ten years in prison, all in 1962-63. He was imprisoned until 1966, when he was pardoned and released; and whereupon he resumed his political career.

BIOGRAPHICAL/CRITICAL SOURCES: John Gunther, *Inside Africa,* Harper, 1955; *Time,* February 16, 1959; Obafemi Awo Awolowo, *Awo: The Chief Autobiography of Chief Obafemi Awolowo,* Cambridge University Press, 1960; *U.S. News,* July 4, 1960; Edna Mason Kaula, *Leaders of the New Africa* (juvenile), World Publishing, 1966; *The New Africans,* Putnam, 1967; Awolowo, *My Early Life,* J. West Publications, 1968; Adrian A. Roscoe, editor, *Mother Is Gold: West African Literature,* Cambridge University Press, 1971.

*   *   *

AXELL, Herbert (Ernest)   1915-

PERSONAL: Surname is pronounced like "axle"; born July 1, 1915, in Rye, Sussex, England; son of Charles Henry (a photographer) and Bessie May (Rhodes) Axell; married Joan Mary Hamshire, December 5, 1938; children: Roderick Howard. *Education:* Attended elementary school in Rye, England. *Politics:* Conservative. *Religion:* Church of England. *Home:* Suffolk Punch Cottage, Westleton, Saxmundham, Suffolk IP17 3AZ, England. *Office:* Royal Society for the Protection of Birds, The Lodge, Sandy, Bedfordshire SG19 2DL, England.

CAREER: General Post Office, London, England, post office clerk, 1931-46, assistant inspector of postal services, 1946-50; Dungeness Bird Reserve, Kent, England, founder and warden, 1952-59; Minsmere Nature Reserve, Westleton, England, warden, 1959-75; Royal Society for the Protection of Birds, Sandy, England, land use adviser, 1975-80; consultant on bird habitat development and visitor facilities. President, Landguard Bird Observatory; member of board of governors, Lowestoft College of Further Education, 1975. *Military service:* British Army, Royal Horse Artillery, 1940-45; served in Africa and Europe; became lieutenant.

MEMBER: Royal Society for the Protection of Birds, British Trust for Ornithology, Malta Ornithological Society, Suffolk Trust for Nature Conservation, Suffolk Ornithologists Group (president), Suffolk Naturalists' Society, Southwold Archaeological and Natural History Society (president).

AWARDS, HONORS: Member of Order of the British Empire, 1965; Churchill fellowship from Winston Churchill Memorial Trust, 1975 and 1982, for a world tour.

WRITINGS: Minsmere: Portrait of a Bird Reserve, Hutchinson, 1977; *Birds of Britain,* Artus, 1978; (contributor) *Joyce, by Herself and Her Friends,* Macmillan, 1980; (contributor) *Managing Wetlands and Their Birds,* International Waterfowl Research Bureau, 1982; (with Robert Dougall) *Birdwatch Round Britain,* Collins, 1982. Contributor to scientific journals and popular magazines.

WORK IN PROGRESS: An autobiography.

SIDELIGHTS: Herbert Axell writes: ''I am concerned about communication with the public. I wanted to be a journalist and began publishing magazine articles when I was eighteen. Especially since World War II, I have been motivated by the need for painless, exciting, real education of the public in wildlife. Mainly I am involved with birds and their habitats, but necessarily other animals as well (their predators and prey). ''My work includes advising on the making of reserves for birds and birdwatchers in the United Kingdom and overseas. It also includes work on sites much affected by industry and people at leisure. I like to work abroad and have engineered habitats, advised, or lectured in Spain (Coto Donana and Las Tablas de Daimiel reserves for the Spanish government's nature conservancy and on the Costa Brava Nord for the government of Catalonia), [and] Malta (Ghadira National Nature Reserve for Maltese government), [both] in conjunction with the World Wildlife Fund and the International Council for Bird Preservation; Australia; New Zealand; the Philippines; Thailand; Ma-laysia; Singapore; Hong Kong (the Mai Po Nature Reserve for the World Wildlife Fund); Japan; Jamaica; Belgium; and, mostly, the U.S.A., including Hawaii.

''While trying to extol the beauty of wildlife and our need of it and its need of conservation, I know that *Homo sapiens* has to matter most.''

In addition to the countries listed above, Axell has traveled throughout nations of Western Europe and the Persian Gulf and in Kenya, Uganda, Nigeria, India, and Fiji.

AVOCATIONAL INTERESTS: Wildlife photography, ''guiding parties to wildlife areas I know.''

*　　*　　*

AYLWARD, Marcus
    See ALEXANDER, Marc

B

BADASH, Lawrence 1934-

PERSONAL: Surname is pronounced Bay-dash; born May 8, 1934, in Brooklyn, N.Y.; son of Joseph (a statistician) and Dorothy (Langa) Badash; children: Lisa, Bruce. Education: Rensselaer Polytechnic Institute, B.S., 1956; Yale University, Ph.D., 1964. Home: 489 Paso Robles Dr., Santa Barbara, Calif. 93108. Office: Department of History, University of California, Santa Barbara, Calif. 93106.

CAREER: Yale University, New Haven, Conn., instructor, 1964-65; University of California, Santa Barbara, assistant professor, 1966-73, associate professor, 1973-79, professor of history of science, 1979—, director of summer seminar on global security and arms control, 1983.

President of Channel Cities Memorial Society, 1968-69 and 1971-72; member of board of directors, Santa Barbara Chapter of American Civil Liberties Union, 1971-73 and 1978—; member of national board of directors, SANE, 1972-81. Military service: U.S. Navy, naval aviator, 1956-59; became lieutenant.

MEMBER: American Association for the Advancement of Science (fellow), American Physical Society, History of Science Society (member of council, 1974-77), West Coast History of Science Society (co-founder, 1971).

AWARDS, HONORS: NATO postdoctoral fellow, Cambridge University, 1965-66; Guggenheim fellow, 1984-85.

WRITINGS: (Editor) Rutherford and Boltwood: Letters on Radioactivity, Yale University Press, 1969; (editor) Rutherford Correspondence Catalog, American Institute of Physics, 1974; Radioactivity in America: Growth and Decay of a Science, Johns Hopkins University Press, 1979; (editor) Reminiscences of Los Alamos, 1943-1945, D. Reidel Publishing (Netherlands), 1980; Rutherford, Kapitza, and the Kremlin, Yale University Press, 1984.

Contributor to Encyclopaedia Britannica, Encyclopedia Americana, Dictionary of Scientific Biography, Dictionary of American History, Academic American Encyclopedia, and to academic journals.

WORK IN PROGRESS: A biography of Ernest Rutherford.

BADURA-SKODA, Eva 1929-

PERSONAL: Born January 15, 1929, in Munich, Germany; daughter of Karl (a doctor of laws) and Elisabeth (Goette) Halfar; married Paul Badura-Skoda (a concert pianist), September 19, 1951; children: Ludwig, Christina, Elisabeth, Michael. Education: Studied at University of Heidelberg, 1949, Academy of Music, Vienna, 1949-51, and University of Vienna, 1949-52; University of Innsbruck, Ph.D., 1953. Religion: Roman Catholic. Office: Zuckerkandlgasse 14, Vienna A-1190, Austria.

CAREER: International Summer Academy Mozart, Salzburg, Austria, professor of musicology, 1962-63; University of Wisconsin—Madison, Brittingham Guest Professor, 1964, professor of musicology, 1966-74; Council on Intercultural Relations, Vienna, Austria, faculty member, 1973-75; musicologist, writer. Guest professor at Boston University, 1976, Queens University, 1979, and McGill University, 1982. Guest lecturer at Mozart Conference at Stanford University, at University of Amsterdam, and for music academies and societies in the United States, Canada, England, Denmark, Holland, Germany, Austria, Hungary, Israel, Russia, and Japan.

MEMBER: International Musicological Society, American Musicological Society, Music Library Association, and a number of other international and national professional societies.

WRITINGS: (With husband, Paul Badura-Skoda) Mozart—Interpretation, Wancura (Vienna), 1957, translation by Leo Black published as Interpreting Mozart on the Keyboard, St. Martin's, 1962, 2nd edition, 1965; (editor) Musik alter Meister, Volume VII, Akademie Graz, 1959.

Mozart's Klavierkonzert in c-moll, Fink Verlag (Munich), 1972; (contributor) A. Walker, editor, The Chopin Companion: Profiles of the Man and the Musician, Norton, 1973; (editor with Peter Branscombe) Schubert Studies: Problems of Style and Chronology, Cambridge University Press, 1982; (editor) Bericht ueber den Internationalen Joseph Haydn Kongress wein 1982, G. Henle Verlag, 1985; (editor) Mozart Piano Sonatas, Peters-Verlag Leipzig, in press.

Also editor of piano trios by Franz Schubert, three concertos by W. A. Mozart, and of the German opera, "Die reisende

Ceres.'' Contributor to *Musik in Geschichte und Gegenwart, Mozart-Jahrbuch, Grove's Dictionary of Music and Musicians* (6th edition). Also contributor of over ninety articles to various scholarly journals.

SIDELIGHTS: In addition to the English translation, the Badura-Skodas' *Mozart—Interpretation* has been published in French, Italian, Japanese, and Russian. *Avocational interests:* Chess, skiing.

*   *   *

BAILEY, Pearl (Mae)   1918-

PERSONAL: Born March 29, 1918, in Newport News, Va.; daughter of Joseph James (a minister) and Ella Mae Bailey; married John Randolph Pinkett, Jr., August 31, 1948 (divorced, March, 1952); married Louis Bellson, Jr. (a jazz drummer), November 19, 1952; children: Tony Bellson, DeeDee Bellson. *Education:* Attended public schools in Philadelphia, Pa. *Address:* P.O. Box L, Lake Havasu City, Ariz. 86403. *Agent:* William Morris Agency, 1350 Avenue of the Americas, New York, N.Y. 10019.

CAREER: Singer and entertainer, 1933—; vocalist with various popular bands; made Broadway stage debut in ''St. Louis Woman,'' 1946, followed by ''Arms in the Girl,'' 1950, ''Bless You All,'' 1950, ''House of Flowers,'' 1954, ''Hello, Dolly,'' 1967-69; motion pictures include ''Variety Girl,'' 1947, ''Isn't It Romantic,'' 1948, ''Carmen Jones,'' 1954, ''That Certain Feeling,'' 1955, ''St. Louis Blues,'' 1957, ''Porgy and Bess,'' 1959, ''All the Fine Young Cannibals,'' 1960, ''The Landlord,'' 1970, ''Norman, Is That You?,'' 1976, and ''Lost Generation''; television work includes the ''Pearl Bailey Show,'' a musical variety program on American Broadcasting Companies, Inc. (ABC-TV), 1970-71, ''Pearl's Kitchen,'' a cooking show, and guest appearances on several variety programs; night club entertainer in New York, Boston, Hollywood, Las Vegas, Chicago, London; contract recording artist for Coral Records, Decca Records, and Columbia Records. Special representative, United States delegation to United Nations.

AWARDS, HONORS: Donaldson award, 1946, for her performance in ''St. Louis Woman''; Entertainer of the Year award from *Cue* magazine and special Tony award, both 1967, both for ''Hello, Dolly''; March of Dimes Woman of the Year, 1968; U.S.O. Woman of the Year, 1969; citation from Mayor John Lindsay of New York City, 1969; Coretta Scott King Award, American Library Association, 1976, for *Duey's Tale.*

WRITINGS: The Raw Pearl (autobiography), Harcourt, 1968; *Talking To Myself* (autobiography), Harcourt, 1971; *Pearl's Kitchen: An Extraordinary Cookbook,* Harcourt, 1973; *Duey's Tale* (juvenile), Harcourt, 1975; *Hurry Up, America, and Spit,* Harcourt, 1976.

SIDELIGHTS: Pearl Bailey's entertainment career began in 1933 when she won first prize in an amateur night contest at the Pearl Theatre in Philadelphia. She continued in vaudeville, then moved into cabarets, eventually appearing on the stage, in movies, on television, and as one of the most popular night club performers in the United States. Her starring role in the long-running Broadway musical ''Hello Dolly'' earned her a special Tony award and widespread critical acclaim. ''For Miss Bailey this was a Broadway triumph for the history books,'' wrote Clive Barnes in the *New York Times.* ''She took the whole musical in her hands and swung it around her neck as easily as if it were a feather boa. Her timing was exquisite,

with asides tossed away as languidly as one might tap ash from a cigarette, and her singing had that deep throaty rumble that . . . is always so oddly stirring.''

In 1968, Bailey published an autobiographical account of her life entitled *The Raw Pearl.* Although she expressed reservations about her skill with language in the book's foreword, writing ''This is new to me. I don't always have the kind of words I want to express myself,'' many reviewers were charmed with the book. ''Pearl Bailey writes about her life the way she sings,'' observed the *Saturday Review* critic, ''with gusto and warmth and honesty.''

Following the success of *The Raw Pearl,* Bailey penned a second autobiographical account, *Talking to Myself.* According to *Publishers Weekly,* it offers ''affectionate homilies laced with recollections of her life and travels during recent years.'' Jo Hudson acknowledges in *Black World* that the book ''may be criticized from a literary standpoint as being very loosely constructed, a little off-beat, and repetitive in its message. However, if we accept Pearl as being distinctive and truly possessing a style of her own, we will accept *Talking to Myself* in like manner.''

BIOGRAPHICAL/CRITICAL SOURCES—Books: Pearl Bailey, *The Raw Pearl,* Harcourt, 1968; Bailey, *Talking to Myself,* Harcourt, 1971.

Periodicals: *New York Times,* November 13, 1967, November 26, 1967; *Time,* November 24, 1967; *Newsweek,* December 4, 1967; *Ebony,* January, 1968; *Cue,* January 6, 1968; *Saturday Review,* February 22, 1969; *Publishers Weekly,* August 23, 1971; *Black World,* March, 1972.

*   *   *

BAKER, Houston A., Jr.   1943-

PERSONAL: Born March 22, 1943, in Louisville, Ky.; married Charlotte Pierce; children: Mark Frederick. *Education:* Howard University, B.A. (magna cum laude), 1965; University of California, Los Angeles, M.A., 1966, Ph.D., 1968; graduate study at University of Edinburgh, 1967-68. *Office:* Department of English, University of Pennsylvania, Philadelphia, Pa. 19104.

CAREER: Howard University, Washington, D.C., instructor in English, summer, 1966; Yale University, New Haven, Conn., instructor, 1968-69, assistant professor of English, 1969-70; University of Virginia, Charlottesville, associate professor, 1970-73, professor of English, 1973-74, member of Center for Advanced Studies, 1970-73; University of Pennsylvania, Philadelphia, professor of English, 1974—, director of Afro-American Studies Program, 1974-77, Albert M. Greenfield Professor of Human Relations, 1982—. Distinguished visiting professor, Cornell University, 1977; visiting professor, Haverford College, 1983-85. Member of Fulbright-Hays literature screening committee, 1973-74; member of committee on scholarly worth, Howard University Press, 1973—.

MEMBER: Modern Language Association of America, College Language Association, Phi Beta Kappa, Kappa Delta Pi.

AWARDS, HONORS: Alfred Longueil Poetry Award from University of California, Los Angeles, 1966; National Phi Beta Kappa visiting scholar, 1975-76; Center for Advanced Study in the Behavioral Sciences fellow, 1977-78; Guggenheim fellow, 1978-79; National Humanities Center fellow, 1982-83; Rockefeller Minority Group fellow, 1982-83.

WRITINGS: (Contributor) John Morton Blum, general editor, *Key Issues in the Afro-American Experience*, Harcourt, 1971; (editor) *Black Literature in America*, McGraw, 1971; *Long Black Song: Essays in Black American Literature and Culture*, University Press of Virginia, 1972; (editor) *Twentieth-Century Interpretations of Native Son*, Prentice-Hall, 1972; *Singers of Daybreak: Studies in Black American Literature*, Howard University Press, 1974; *A Many-Colored Coat of Dreams: The Poetry of Countee Cullen*, Broadside Press, 1974.

(Contributor) *Contemporary Poets*, St. Martin's, 1975; (editor) *Reading Black: Essays in the Criticism of African, Caribbean, and Black American Literature*, Africana Studies and Research Center, Cornell University, 1976; (editor with wife, Charlotte Pierce-Baker) *Renewal: A Volume of Black Poems*, Afro-American Studies Program, University of Pennsylvania, 1977; (editor) *A Dark and Sudden Beauty: Two Essays in Black American Poetry by George Kent and Stephen Henderson*, Afro-American Studies Program, University of Pennsylvania, 1977; *No Matter Where You Travel, You Still Be Black* (poems), Lotus Press, 1979.

The Journey Back: Issues in Black Literature and Criticism, University of Chicago Press, 1980; *Spirit Run*, Lotus Press, 1981; (editor with Leslie Fiedler) *English Literature: Opening Up the Canon*, English Institute, Johns Hopkins University, 1981; (editor) *Three American Literatures: Essays in Chicano, Native American, and Asian-American Literature for Teachers of "American" Literature*, Modern Language Association of America, 1982; (editor and author of introduction) *Narrative of the Life of Frederick Douglass, an American Slave, Written by Himself*, Penguin Books, 1982; *Blue, Ideology, and Afro-American Literature: A Vernacular Theory*, University of Chicago Press, 1984.

Contributor of about twenty articles and reviews to literature and black studies journals, including *Victorian Poetry*, *Phylon*, *Black World*, *Obsidian*, *Yale Review*, and *Journal of African-Afro-American Affairs*. Member of advisory boards, *Maji*, 1974-76, *Black American Literature Forum*, 1976—, and *Minority Voices*, 1977—.

WORK IN PROGRESS: Contributing to *Research in African Literatures*, edited by Marion Berghahn.

*   *   *

BALFORT, Neil
    See FANTHORPE, R(obert) Lionel

*   *   *

BARBER, Bernard   1918-

PERSONAL: Born January 29, 1918, in Boston, Mass.; son of Albert and Jennie (Lieberman) Barber; married Elinor Gellert, September 25, 1948; children: Leslie Marianne, Christine Ruth, Philip Gellert, John Robert. *Education:* Harvard University, A.B., 1939, A.M., 1942, Ph.D., 1949. *Home address:* Braeside Lane, Dobbs Ferry, N.Y. 10522. *Office:* Department of Sociology, Barnard College, New York, N.Y. 10027.

CAREER: Smith College, Northampton, Mass., instructor, 1948-49, assistant professor of sociology, 1949-52; Barnard College, New York, N.Y., assistant professor, 1952-55, associate professor, 1955-61, professor of sociology, 1961—, chairman of department, 1962-65, 1968—. Member of drug research board of National Academy of Sciences, 1966-70. *Military service:* U.S. Navy, 1942-46; became lieutenant senior grade.

WRITINGS: Science and the Social Order, Free Press of Glencoe, 1952, reprinted, Greenwood Press, 1978; *Social Stratification: A Comparative Analysis of Structure and Process*, Harcourt, 1957; (editor with Walter Hirsch) *The Sociology of Science*, Free Press of Glencoe, 1962, reprinted, Greenwood Press, 1978; (with wife, Elinor G. Barber) *European Social Class: Stability and Change*, Macmillan, 1965; *Drugs and Society*, Russell Sage Foundation, 1967.

(Editor) *L. J. Henderson on the Social System*, University of Chicago Press, 1970; (editor with Alex Inkeles) *Stability and Social Change*, Little, Brown, 1971; (with John Lally, Julia Makarushka, and Daniel Sullivan) *Research on Human Subjects: Problems of Social Control in Medical Experimentation*, Russell Sage Foundation, 1973; (editor) *Medical Ethics and Social Change*, American Academy of Political and Social Science, 1978.

Contributor: *Essays in Sociological Theory*, Free Press of Glencoe, 1949; A. W. Goldner, editor, *Studies in Leadership*, Harper, 1950; Donald Geddes, editor, *An Analysis of the Kinsey Reports*, Dutton, 1954; Hans L. Zetterberg, editor, *Sociology in the United States of America*, UNESCO, 1956; R. A. Cloward and H. D. Stein, editors, *Social Perspectives on Behavior*, Free Press of Glencoe, 1958; E. A. Tiryakian, editor, *Sociocultural Theory, Values, and Sociocultural Change: Essays in Honor of Pitirim A. Sorokin*, Free Press of Glencoe, 1963; Philip Appleman, editor, *Darwin*, Norton, 1970; S. Reiser, A. Dyck, and W. Curran, editors, *Ethics in Medicine*, MIT Press, 1977; Tom L. Beauchamp and LeRoy Walters, editors, *Contemporary Issues in Bioethics*, Dickenson, 1978; Y. Elkana and others, editors, *Toward a Metric of Science*, Wiley, 1978; (contributor) J. Gaston, editor, *The Reward System in British and American Science*, Wiley, 1978.

Contributor to numerous journals, including *American Sociological Review*, *Social Forces*, *Contemporary Psychology*, *Medical Counterpoint*, and *Public Opinion Quarterly*. Advisory editor of *Technology and Culture*. Associate editor of *Social Problems* and *Journal of Health and Social Behavior*.†

*   *   *

BARKEE, Asouff
    See STRUNG, Norman

*   *   *

BARKER, Albert W.   1900-

PERSONAL: Born in 1900; son of Edwin L. (an editor) and Jessie (Wineman) Barker; married Gertrude Rozan (an artist). *Address:* 15 St. Andrews Pl., Yonkers, N.Y. 10705.

CAREER: Writer.

WRITINGS—For young people; published by Messner: *Black on White and Read All Over: The Story of Printing*, 1971; *From Settlement to City*, 1978; *The Spice Adventure*, 1980.

Adult novels: *The Straw Virgin*, Popular Library, 1975.

"Reefe King" series: *Gift From Berlin*, Award Books, 1969; *Apollo Legacy*, Award Books, 1970.

"Hawk Macrae" series; all published by Curtis Books: *If Anything Should Happen to Me*, 1973; *The Big Fix*, 1973; *The Dragon in Spring*, 1973; *The Blood of Angels*, 1974; *The Diamond Hitch*, 1976.

Also author of plays, "Memphis Bound" (musical), "Man on Stilts," "Buckaroo," "Grandma's Diary," "American Holiday."

WORK IN PROGRESS: Moonstruck, a novel; "Few Are Called," a play.

*   *   *

BARKER, Dennis (Malcolm) 1929-

PERSONAL: Born June 21, 1929, in Lowestoft, Suffolk, England; son of George Walter (a company director) and Gertrude Edith (Seeley) Barker. *Education:* Attended grammar schools in High Wycombe and Lowestoft, England. *Residence:* London, England. *Office: Guardian,* 119 Farringdon Rd., London E.C.1, England.

CAREER: Suffolk Chronicle and Mercury, Ipswich, Suffolk, England, reporter, 1947-48; *East Anglian Daily Times,* Ipswich, reporter, feature writer, and theater critic, 1948-58; *Express and Star,* Wolverhampton, Staffordshire, England, estates and property editor, theater critic, and columnist, 1958-63; *Guardian,* London, England, reporter on Midlands staff, Birmingham, 1963-67, reporter, columnist, and feature writer on London staff, 1967—.

MEMBER: National Union of Journalists (chairman of Home Counties district council, 1956-57), Newspaper Press Fund (life member), Writers Guild of Great Britain (associate member).

WRITINGS: Candidate of Promise (novel), Collins, 1969; *The Scandalisers* (novel), Weidenfeld & Nicolson, 1974; *Soldiering On: An Unofficial Portrait of the British Army,* Andre Deutsch, 1981; *One Man's Estate: The Preservation of an English Inheritance,* Andre Deutsch, 1983.

Drafted screenplay of *Candidate of Promise* for Associated British Productions; contributor of scripts and short stories to British Broadcasting Corp. programs. Editorial director and contributor, *East Anglian Architecture and Building Review,* 1955-58.

SIDELIGHTS: Dennis Barker told *CA:* "[I] believe that laughter can lead to serious truths, solemnity to trifling humbug. I believe that that applies in life and in writing: as much to my novels as to my (I hope) essentially human view of the modern British Army or the great estate of a modern English lord struggling against economic and social pressures to keep his home."

Barker's book *Soldiering On: An Unofficial Portrait of the British Army,* according to London *Times* critic Michael Carver, "is a first-class bit of public relations for the Army. Both he and the Army's PR branch, who helped and encouraged him, have earned the Army's gratitude. It is a sympathetic picture that he paints, which should remove many misconceptions about what the Army is like today, based on stories, some true, some exaggerated, of what it was like some time ago."

AVOCATIONAL INTERESTS: Sailing, walking, reading, talking, music.

BIOGRAPHICAL/CRITICAL SOURCES: Times (London), November 29, 1981.

*   *   *   '

BARNARD, Christiaan (Neethling) 1922-

PERSONAL: Born November 8, 1922, in Beaufort West, Cape Province, Republic of South Africa; son of Adam Hendrik (a Dutch Reformed minister) and Maria Elizabeth (De Swardt) Barnard; married Aletta Gertruida Louw, November 6, 1948 (divorced, 1970); married Barbara Maria Zoellner, 1970 (divorced); children: (first marriage) Deirdre Jeanne, Andre Hendrick; (second marriage) one son. *Education:* University of Cape Town, M.B., Ch.B., 1946, M.D., 1953, M.Med., 1953; University of Minnesota, M.S., Ph.D., 1958.

CAREER: Groote Schuur Hospital, Cape Town, Republic of South Africa, intern, 1947; private practice in Ceres, Republic of South Africa, 1948-51; City Fever Hospital, Cape Town, senior resident medical officer, 1951-53; Groote Schuur Hospital, registrar, 1953-55; University of Cape Town, Cape Town, research fellow in surgery, 1953-55; University of Minnesota, Minneapolis, Charles Adams memorial scholar and Dazian Foundation for Medical Research scholar, 1956-58; University of Cape Town, lecturer and director of surgical research, beginning 1958, associate professor, beginning 1963; Groote Schuur Hospital, senior cardiothoracic surgeon, 1958-83, head of cardiothoracic surgery unit, 1961-83. Owner of restaurant chain, 1976—.

MEMBER: South African Medical Association, Society of Thoracic Surgeons, South African Society of Physicians, Surgeons, Gynecologists (founder member).

AWARDS, HONORS: Ernest Oppenheimer Memorial Trust grant, 1960; Dag Hammarskjold International Prize; Kennedy Foundation Award; Milan International Prize for Science; fellowship, American College of Surgeons, 1963, New York Cardiological Society, 1965, and American College of Cardiology, 1967; numerous honorary degrees, foreign orders and awards, honorary citizenships and freedoms.

WRITINGS: (With Velva Schrire) *The Surgery of the Common Congenital Cardiac Malformations,* Harper, 1968; (contributor) *Las greffes du coeur: Interviews du professeur Christiaan Barnard, du Dr. Pierre Grondin et de pluseurs autres,* Editions de l'Homme, Edition Radio-Canada, 1968.

(With Curtis Bill Pepper) *Christiaan Barnard: One Life* (autobiography), Macmillan, 1970; *Heart Attack: You Don't Have to Die,* Delacorte Press, 1971 (published in the Republic of South Africa as *Heart Attack: All You Have to Know about It,* H. Keartland Publishers, 1971); (with Siegfried Stander) *The Unwanted* (novel), Tafelberg (Cape Town), 1974, McKay, 1975; *South Africa: Sharp Dissection,* Books in Focus, 1977; (with Stander) *In the Night Season* (novel), Tafelberg, 1977, Prentice-Hall, 1978 (published in England as *Night Season,* Arrow Books, 1979); *The Best Medicine,* Tafelberg, 1979.

Good Life, Good Death: A Doctor's Case for Euthanasia and Suicide, Prentice-Hall, 1980; (consulting editor) *The Body Machine: Your Health in Perspective,* Crown, 1981 (published in England as *The Body Machine: Latest Medical Perspectives,* Hamlyn Publishing, 1981). Columnist, *Rand Daily Mail* (Johannesburg), beginning 1978. Contributor to medical journals.

Recordings: "Dr. Christiaan Barnard Speaks on the World's First Human Heart Transplant," London Records, 1968.

SIDELIGHTS: On December 3, 1967, Christiaan Barnard, a doctor at the Groote Schuur Hospital in Cape Town, performed the world's first human heart transplant operation. This historic operation made Barnard the "most famous surgeon in the world," George Hackett and Peter Younghusband write in *Newsweek.* Barnard has also performed the world's first double heart transplant and developed the Barnard Valve, an artificial heart valve used in open heart surgery.

Barnard began his career as a general practitioner in the South African countryside. He then worked for a time at the City Fever Hospital in Cape Town, a clinic specializing in cases of tubercular meningitis. In 1956, Barnard went to study at the University of Minnesota, initially studying gastrointestinal pathology, but soon focusing his attention on heart surgery. Some of the pioneering work in heart surgery was then being done at the University of Minnesota, and Barnard was able to see the latest experiments on laboratory animals. When he returned to South Africa, he performed the first successful open heart surgery to be done in that country.

By 1967, the surgical techniques necessary to perform a human heart transplant were known and Dr. Norman Shumway of Stanford University, who had performed successful heart transplants in dogs, announced that the time was near for a human experiment. The major difficulty was in overcoming the human body's natural immunological system. This system rejects all foreign materials which enter the body, protecting it from disease-causing bacteria. As John Lear of *Saturday Review* quotes Barnard explaining: "The difficulty is in how to maintain the existence of a foreign organ in a body wihout it being rejected." Barnard proposed solving this problem by using drugs which neutralize the body's immunological system.

The patient chosen by Barnard to receive the first human heart transplant was Louis Washkansky, a middle-aged grocer with heart disease. Because of his disease, most of Washkansky's heart muscles had deteriorated, an irreversible condition. The donor was a young woman killed in a traffic accident. On December 3, 1967, Barnard performed the operation, removing the woman's heart, freezing it, and implanting it inside of Washkansy. An electric shock caused it to begin beating again. Although the operation was a success ("not a single suture was out of place," Lear states), Washkansky died eighteen days later. The drugs which counteracted his body's natural defenses had left him helpless against infection. In this weakened state, Washkansky contracted pneumonia and died. In later transplant operations, Barnard and other doctors have regulated the drugs used to prevent their patients from reaching such a defenseless state.

When news of the operation reached the rest of the world, Barnard found himself an instant celebrity. He was invited to lecture to doctors in the United States and Europe about his surgical techniques, was featured in newspapers and magazines, and appeared on television talk shows. "Between speaking engagements," Hackett and Younghusband report, "he always found time to pose alongside popes, presidents, and movie stars." In 1970, Barnard published his autobiography, *Christiaan Barnard: One Life,* a book described by P. M. McGrady of *Book World* as "a tickertape parade for the surgeon-hero." Arthur Marshall, writing in the *New Statesman,* finds the book too dramatic, but "the facts themselves are of absorbing interest and [Barnard's] pertinacity and cleverness are remarkable."

Barnard's sudden celebrity status soon led some observers to criticize him. He developed a reputation, Hackett and Younghusband report, "as an egotistical publicity addict." Lear admits that "Barnard is at least as accomplished a showman as he is a surgeon." In defense of his public life, Barnard states in the *New York Times:* "It is the duty of the doctor to serve the public and also to let the public know what is going on. . . .

The practice of withholding information and being secretive belongs to the past."

In the 1970s, Barnard collaborated with Siegfried Stander to write two medical novels based loosely on Barnard's own career. Both *The Unwanted* and *In the Night Season* contain authentic recreations of actual surgeries. Barnard is convinced that such realism was necessary. "Any surgeon," he tells *Publishers Weekly,* "could follow one of the operations in [*The Unwanted*], and reproduce it himself. The details are completely accurate." Speaking of *In the Night Season,* Fitzhugh Mullan writes in the *New York Times Book Review* that Barnard "has done a good job of portraying his physicians as human beings. . . . Barnard's medics offer no shortcuts in their real and readable struggle."

Until 1983, Barnard combined his public life with his work as head of the cardiothoracic surgery unit at Groote Schuur Hospital. In that year his arthritis worsened to the point where he was no longer able to operate as he once had, and Barnard decided to retire. In a farewell press conference held in Cape Town, he announced to the world his plans to leave the practice of medicine. Since 1983, Barnard has raised cattle on a ranch he owns in the Republic of South Africa and run a chain of Italian restaurants. He leaves behind, write Hackett and Younghusband, "an expanded and respected cardiac unit" at Groote Shuur Hospital, as well as his contributions to the advancement of heart surgery.

BIOGRAPHICAL/CRITICAL SOURCES—Books: Peter Hawthorne, *The Transplanted Heart: The Incredible Story of the Epic Heart Transplant Operations by Professor Christiaan Barnard and His Team,* Rand McNally, 1968; Christiaan Barnard and Curtis Bill Pepper, *Christiaan Barnard: One Life,* Macmillan, 1969; L. Edmond Leipold, *Dr. Christiaan Barnard: The Man with the Golden Hands,* Denison, 1971; Donald Zec, *Some Enchanted Egos,* St. Martin's, 1973; Donald Robinson, *Miracle Finders,* McKay, 1976; Lael Wertenbaker, *To Mend the Heart,* Viking, 1980.

Periodicals: *New York Times,* December 6, 1967, February 7, 1968; *Time,* December 15, 1967, February 9, 1968, February 23, 1968, July 20, 1970, April 17, 1978; *National Observer,* January 8, 1968; *Newsweek,* January 8, 1968, June 29, 1970, August 9, 1971, September 5, 1983; *London Observer,* January 14, 1968; *Times Literary Supplement,* April 9, 1970, March 19, 1976; *New Statesman,* May 15, 1970; *Saturday Review,* May 23, 1970; *Book World,* May 31, 1970; *Vogue,* September 15, 1970; *Publishers Weekly,* October 20, 1975; *New York Times Book Review,* November 16, 1975, June 25, 1978; *Saturday Evening Post,* March, 1977; *Maclean's,* January 9, 1978; *People,* April 17, 1978; *Health,* February, 1982.†

—*Sketch by Thomas Wiloch*

*   *   *

BARON, (Joseph) Alexander 1917-

PERSONAL: Born December 4, 1917; son of Barnet Baron and Fanny Levinson; married Delores Salzedo, August 4, 1960. *Education:* Attended grammar school in London, England. *Politics:* None. *Religion:* Jewish. *Home:* 30 Cranbourne Gardens, London NW 11, England. *Agent:* Unna and Durbridge Ltd., 24 Pottery Lane, London W11 4LL, England.

CAREER: Journalist until 1948; free-lance writer, 1948—. *Military service:* British Army, 1939-45. *Member:* P.E.N.

WRITINGS: *From the City, From the Plough,* J. Cape, 1948, reprinted, Lythway Press, 1974; *The Wine of Etna,* Washburn, 1950, published in England as *There's No Home,* J. Cape, 1950, reprinted, Cedric Chivers, 1972; *Rosie Hogarth,* J. Clarke, 1951, reprinted, Cedric Chivers, 1972; *With Hope Farewell,* Washburn, 1952, reprinted, Cedric Chivers, 1973; *The Human Kind: A Sequence,* Washburn, 1953, reprinted, Cedric Chivers, 1973; *The Golden Princess,* J. Cape, 1954, Bantam, 1957; *Queen of the East,* Washburn, 1956; *Seeing Life,* Collins, 1958; *The Lowlife,* A. S. Barnes, 1963, T. Yoseloff, 1964, reprinted, Ian Henry, 1979; *Strip Jack Naked,* Collins, 1966, Yoseloff, 1967.

All published by Macmillan: *King Dido,* 1969; *The In-Between Time,* 1971; *Gentle Folk: A Novel,* 1976; *Franco Is Dying,* 1977.

Also author of many television plays and serials; author of motion picture scripts. Assistant editor, *Tribune,* 1938-39; editor, *New Theatre,* 1946-49.

WORK IN PROGRESS: Two novels; television dramatizations of classic novels for British Broadcasting Corporation.

MEDIA ADAPTATIONS: Carl Forman's screenplay "The Victors" was based on *The Human Kind: A Sequence; The Golden Princess* has been translated into Spanish.

BIOGRAPHICAL/CRITICAL SOURCES: *New York Times Book Review,* April, 1967; *Listener,* May 27, 1971; *Observer,* May 30, 1971, January 25, 1976, October 16, 1977; *Times Literary Supplement,* June 25, 1971, January 23, 1976, December 23, 1977.

*   *   *

BARON, Othello
    See FANTHORPE, R(obert) Lionel

*   *   *

BARRY, Herbert III   1930-

PERSONAL: Born June 2, 1930, in New York, N.Y.; son of Herbert, Jr. (a psychiatrist) and Lucy (Brown) Barry. *Education:* Harvard University, B.A., 1952; Yale University, M.S., 1953, Ph.D., 1957. *Politics:* Democrat. *Home:* 522 North Neville St., Apt. 83, Pittsburgh, Pa. 15213. *Office:* School of Pharmacy, University of Pittsburgh, Pittsburgh, Pa. 15213.

CAREER: Yale University, New Haven, Conn., assistant professor of psychology, 1960-61; University of Connecticut, Storrs, assistant professor of psychology, 1961-63; University of Pittsburgh, School of Pharmacy, Pittsburgh, Pa., associate professor, 1963-70, professor of pharmacology, 1970—. Member of alcohol research review committee, National Institute on Alcohol Abuse and Alcoholism, 1972-76. *Military service:* U.S. Army Reserve, 1951-57; became sergeant.

MEMBER: Society for Cross-Cultural Research (president, 1973-74), Phi Beta Kappa, Sigma Xi.

AWARDS, HONORS: Research Scientist Development Award from National Institute of Mental Health, 1967-77.

WRITINGS: (With Henrik Wallgren) *Actions of Alcohol,* two volumes, Elsevier, 1970; (editor with Alice Schlegel) *Cross-Cultural Samples and Codes,* University of Pittsburgh Press, 1980; (editor with Avraham Yacobi) *Experimental and Clinical Toxicokinetics,* American Pharmaceutical Association, 1984.

Contributor of more than one hundred fifty articles to scientific journals. Managing editor, *Psychopharmacology,* 1974—; consulting editor to several journals on alcohol and pharmacology research, and on cross-cultural comparisons.

WORK IN PROGRESS: *Bio-Medical Statistics,* a textbook; research on effects of drugs, including alcohol and marijuana, on behavior of rats; cross-cultural research comparing child training with other customs; studying birth order and first name as determinants of adult personality and behavior.

SIDELIGHTS: Herbert Barry told *CA:* "I believe that the key to successful writing is a chronic obsession with the project. With this prerequisite, the brain continually creates both the general ideas and the specific phrases, even at times when the conscious thoughts and efforts are elsewhere. Two techniques, which are helpful for most writers, are . . . thorough revisions of what has been written . . . [and] a regular schedule of several consecutive hours at the same time of day devoted to the writing."

*   *   *

BARRY, Joseph (Amber)   1917-

PERSONAL: Born June 13, 1917, in Scranton, Pa.; married Naomi Jolles, 1946 (divorced, 1965); children: Michael Alexander, John Christopher. *Education:* University of Michigan, A.B., 1939, A.B. in L.S., 1940; Sorbonne, University of Paris, graduate study, 1946. *Politics:* "Liberty, equality, fraternity." *Religion:* Humanism. *Address:* 404 Chapel Dr., Syracuse, N.Y. 13219. *Agent:* Robert Lescher, 155 East 71st St., New York, N.Y. 10021.

CAREER: Free-lance writer. New York Public Library, New York City, member of professional staff, 1940-41; *Newsweek,* New York City, manager of Paris edition, 1946-49; *New York Times,* New York City, Paris Bureau chief of Sunday edition, 1949-52; *House Beautiful,* New York City, editorial director, 1952-57; *New York Post,* New York City, Paris columnist, 1958-65; *Village Voice,* New York City, Paris columnist, 1965—. Consultant to UNESCO, Paris, 1975—. *Military service:* U.S. Army, 1941-46; became captain; received Bronze Star.

MEMBER: P.E.N., Author's Guild, Authors League of America, Anglo-American Press Association (Paris), Phi Beta Kappa.

AWARDS, HONORS: *Passions and Politics* was an American Library Association Notable Book in 1974.

WRITINGS: *Left Bank, Right Bank,* Norton, 1951; (editor) *Architecture as Space,* Horizon Press, 1957; *Contemporary American Architecture,* Hawthorn, 1958; *France,* Macmillan, 1965; *The People of Paris,* Doubleday, 1966; *Passions and Politics: A Biography of Versailles,* Doubleday, 1972; *Infamous Woman: The Life of George Sand,* Doubleday, 1977; *George Sand in Her Own Words,* Anchor Press, 1979. Contributor to *Horizon, New Republic, Smithsonian, Holiday,* and other periodicals.

WORK IN PROGRESS: *Couples—France.*

SIDELIGHTS: Joseph Barry told *CA:* "Once you leave your village, you're a world traveler. I left Scranton. Paris, the French, and Gertrude Stein (I was her 'adopted' nephew) were greatest personal influences; Nietzsche, Freud and Marx—psycho-socio-philo-literary influences. May 1968 near revolution in Paris, most stirring event. Two pillars of life, the Freudian pair: *liebe und arbeit*, love and work; love includes the passions of the mind, which are lifelong.''

Infamous Woman: The Life of George Sand has been translated into French, Italian, and Spanish.

BIOGRAPHICAL/CRITICAL SOURCES: Detroit News, July 16, 1972; *The Atlantic,* February, 1977; *New York Times Book Review,* March 27, 1977, January 8, 1978.

* * *

BARTON, Erle
See FANTHORPE, R(obert) Lionel

* * *

BARTON, Lee
See FANTHORPE, R(obert) Lionel

* * *

BATES, Betty
See BATES, Elizabeth

* * *

BATES, Elizabeth 1921-
(Betty Bates)

PERSONAL: Born October 5, 1921, in Evanston, Ill.; daughter of Alexander Willett (a civil engineer) and Elizabeth (a teacher; maiden name, Bragdon) Moseley; married Edwin R. Bates (a lawyer), September 3, 1947; children: Thomas, Daniel, Lawrence, Sarah. *Education:* Attended National Park College, 1939-40, Beloit College, 1940-41, and Katharine Gibbs Secretarial School, 1941-42. *Home:* 5 Milburn Park, Evanston, Ill. 60201.

CAREER: Writer of children's books. Worked as a secretary, 1942-48. Former member of Evanston board of directors of Rehabilitation Institute of Chicago.

MEMBER: Children's Reading Round Table (Chicago), Off-Campus Writers Workshop (Winnetka, Ill.), Garden Club of Evanston (member of board of directors).

WRITINGS—All juveniles; all under name Betty Bates; published by Holiday House, except as indicated: *Bugs in Your Ears* (Junior Literary Guild selection), 1977; *The Ups and Downs of Jorie Jenkins* (Junior Literary Guild selection), 1978; *My Mom, the Money Nut,* 1979; *Love Is Like Peanuts,* 1980; *Picking Up the Pieces,* 1981; *It Must've Been the Fish Sticks,* 1982; *That's What T.J. Says,* 1982; *Call Me Friday the Thirteenth,* 1983; *Herbert and Hortense,* illustrations by John Wallner, Albert Whitman, 1984; *Say Cheese* (Junior Literary Guild selection), 1984.

WORK IN PROGRESS: Nana's Room and *Thatcher Payne,* both children's books.

SIDELIGHTS: Betty Bates told *CA:* ''Recalling how much books meant to me when I was a girl, I feel a need to touch the minds of present-day children. The trick, of course, is to remember the feelings of childhood and to present them truly and honestly.

''I try to present situations with which my young readers can identify and which help them to realize that others have problems similar to theirs. While my themes are serious, I believe humor is essential. In my book for eight-to-eleven-year-olds,

Say Cheese, Christy Hooper deals with both the serious and comic difficulties of being a member of a large, bustling family with limited funds and space.

''A first for me was my book for beginning readers, *Herbert and Hortense,* with which I found the surprise and joy of having my story greatly enhanced by rollicking, amusingly detailed illustrations by John Wallner. I find stimulating challenges in the ever-fascinating world of writing for children, and I keep wondering which will turn up next.''

BIOGRAPHICAL/CRITICAL SOURCES: Evanston Review, September 15, 1977; *North Shore Monthly,* April-May, 1978.

* * *

BATHURST, Sheila
See SULLIVAN, Sheila

* * *

BATTISCOMBE, E(sther) Georgina (Harwood) 1905-
(Gina Harwood)

PERSONAL: Born November 21, 1905, in London, England; daughter of George (a master cotton spinner, and member of Parliament) and Ellen (Hopkinson) Harwood; married Christopher Francis Battiscombe (a lieutenant colonel, Grenadier Guards), October 1, 1932 (died, 1964); children: Aurea (Mrs. George Lawrence Morshead). *Education:* Lady Margaret Hall, Oxford, B.A. (with honors), 1927. *Religion:* Anglican. *Home:* 3 Queen's Acre, King's Rd., Windsor, Berkshire, SL4 2BE, England. *Agent:* A. M. Heath & Co., Ltd., 40-42 William IV St., London WC2N 4DD, England.

CAREER: Writer. County organizer, St. John and Red Cross Hospital libraries, 1948-53.

MEMBER: Royal Society for Literature (fellow), Society of Authors, Church of England Club, Cavalry and Guards.

AWARDS, HONORS: James Tait Black Prize for Biography, 1963, for *John Keble: A Study in Limitations.*

WRITINGS: (Under name Gina Harwood, with A. W. Hopkinson) *The Mantle of Prayer,* Mowbray, 1931; (under name Gina Harwood) *Haphazard,* Mathews & Marrot, 1932; *Charlotte Mary Yonge: The Story of an Uneventful Life,* Constable, 1943; *Two on Safari,* Muller, 1946; *English Picnics,* Harville, 1949; *Mrs. Gladstone: The Portrait of a Marriage,* Constable, 1956, Houghton, 1957.

John Keble: A Study in Limitations, Constable, 1963, Knopf, 1964; *Christina Rossetti* (pamphlet), Longmans, Green for British Council and National Book League, 1965; (editor, with Marghanita Laski, and contributor) *A Chaplet for Charlotte Yonge,* Cresset, 1965; *Queen Alexandra,* Houghton, 1969; *Shaftesbury: A Biography of the Seventh Earl, 1801-1885,* Constable, 1974, published as *Shaftesbury: The Great Reformer, 1801-1885,* Houghton, 1975; *Reluctant Pioneer: The Life of Elizabeth Wordsworth,* Constable, 1978; *Christina Rossetti: A Divided Life,* Constable, 1981.

Contributor of articles and reviews to *Times Literary Supplement, Country Life, Time and Tide, Economist,* other newspapers.

SIDELIGHTS: In her biographies of nineteenth-century English figures, ''Georgina Battiscombe is marvellously immersed in the niceties of Victorian daily life and this gives pleasure in itself,'' writes Michael Ratcliffe in a London *Times* review. Battiscombe's subjects have included English clergyman and poet John Keble, the British reformer Lord Shaftesbury, Queen Alexandra, and the enigmatic poet Christina Rossetti. Of her book *Christina Rossetti: A Divided Life*, Ratcliffe observes: ''She brings to her . . . subject gifts of urbanity and commonsense that particularly suit Christina Rossetti's asperity and caustic wit.''

In the Rossetti biography, writes W. W. Robson in the *Times Literary Supplement*, Battiscombe ''sets out the external, historical facts, such as they are, in a sensible and orderly way; and she handles the poetry with perception and tact. This beautifully produced book is a pleasure to read, from the point of view of presentation, and style, and in every other way.''

In the biography *Queen Alexandra*, another *Times Literary Supplement* reviewer finds that Battiscombe ''has done wonders with her subject. . . . So much of modern biography rests for its success on revelation . . . that we sometimes forget that there is another path to success: a sympathetic understanding of the human character described. Along that difficult path Mrs. Battiscombe moves in triumph.''

AVOCATIONAL INTERESTS: The architecture of the Church of England.

BIOGRAPHICAL/CRITICAL SOURCES: Times Literary Supplement, September 10, 1969, September 4, 1981; *New York Times Book Review*, November 30, 1969; *Times* (London), May 21, 1981; *Washington Post Book World*, January 17, 1982.

*   *   *

BAXTER, Phyllis
    See WALLMANN, Jeffrey M(iner)

*   *   *

BAYLEY, Barrington J(ohn)   1937-
    (Alan Aumbry, P. F. Woods)

PERSONAL: Born April 9, 1937, in Birmingham, England; son of John (a toolmaker) and Clarissa (Love) Bayley; married Joan Lucy Clarke, October 30, 1969; children: Sean, Heather. *Education:* Attended school in Shropshire, England. *Politics:* None. *Religion:* None. *Home:* 48 Turreff Ave., Donnington, Telford, Shropshire, TF2 8HE, England. *Agent:* Scott Meredith Literary Agency, 845 Third Ave., New York, N.Y. 10022.

CAREER: Writer. Has worked in the civil service, in the Australian public service in London, and as a coal miner. *Military service:* Royal Air Force, 1955-57.

WRITINGS—All science fiction; published by DAW Books, except as indicated: *Star Virus*, Ace Books, 1970; *Annihilation Factor*, Ace Books, 1972; *Empire of Two Worlds*, Ace Books, 1972; *Collision Course*, 1973 (published in England as *Collision with Chronos*, Allison & Busby, 1977); *The Fall of Chronopolis*, 1974; *The Soul of the Robot*, Doubleday, 1974; *The Garments of Caean*, Doubleday, 1976; *The Grand Wheel*, 1977; *Star Winds*, 1978; *The Knights of the Limits*, Allison & Busby, 1978; *The Pillars of Eternity*, 1979: *The Seed of Evil* (stories), Allison & Busby, 1979; *The Zen Gun*, 1983.

Contributor of articles and stories, some under pseudonyms Alan Aumbry and P. F. Woods, to British science fiction journals and popular periodicals

WORK IN PROGRESS: A One-Shot Universe; The Rod of Light (sequel to *The Soul of the Robot*); *The Creation of Wealth*, a study in economics.

SIDELIGHTS: ''My primary ambition as a science fiction writer has been to be able to inspire others as I have been inspired,'' Barrington J. Bayley told *CA*. ''A good story is one you carry on thinking about long after you have read it.''

Speaking of *The Pillars of Eternity*, John Clute of the *Washington Post Book World* calls it a ''typical Bayley marriage of space opera and metaphysics.'' Writing of the same book for the *Los Angeles Times Book Review*, Don Strachan agrees: '' 'Pillars' exotically combines a comic-book superhero . . . with intellectually impressive science and philosophy.''

BIOGRAPHICAL/CRITICAL SOURCES: Times Literary Supplement, May 30, 1980; *Los Angeles Times Book Review*, April 25, 1982; *Washington Post Book World*, April 25, 1982.

*   *   *

BEASLEY, Jerry C(arr)   1940-

PERSONAL: Born September 15, 1940, in Nashville, Tenn.; son of Guy E. (a salesman) and Gaynelle (Rucker) Beasley; married Rita M. Shontz, April 6, 1966; children: Amy, Pamela. *Education:* George Peabody College of Vanderbilt University, B.A., 1963; University of Kansas, M.A., 1967; Northwestern University, Ph.D., 1971. *Politics:* Independent. *Home:* 15 Westfield Dr., Newark, Del. 19711. *Office:* Department of English, University of Delaware, Newark, Del. 19716.

CAREER: Alfred I. DuPont School District, Wilmington, Del., English teacher, 1963-64; Nashville City Schools, Nashville, Tenn., English teacher, 1964-65; University of Delaware, Newark, assistant professor, 1969-74, associate professor, 1974-81, professor of English, 1981—.

MEMBER: Modern Language Association of America, American Society for Eighteenth Century Studies, British Society for Eighteenth-Century Studies, Thomas Hardy Society.

WRITINGS: A Check List of Prose Fiction Published in England, 1740-1749, University Press of Virginia, 1972; (editor) *English Fiction, 1660-1800: A Guide to Information Sources*, Gale, 1978; *Novels of the 1740s*, University of Georgia Press, 1982; (editor with Robert Hogan) *The Plays of Frances Sheridan*, University of Delaware Press, 1984.

WORK IN PROGRESS: Editing *The Adventures of Ferdinand Count Fathom; The Works of Tobias Smollett*, for University of Delaware Press; *Tobias Smollett, Novelist*, a critical study; *Politics and the Novel in the Augustan Age*.

SIDELIGHTS: Jerry C. Beasley writes: ''A high-school teacher, Frances Bowen, first inspired me to take the study of literature seriously; later, my love of history and my exciting discovery of Fielding's *Tom Jones* joined to propel me into study of early fiction. I now teach and write about eighteenth- and nineteenth-century English fiction, which (incidentally) has much to teach us about the confusion and disorder of our twentieth-century existence.''

AVOCATIONAL INTERESTS: Organic gardening.

BIOGRAPHICAL/CRITICAL SOURCES: Times Literary Supplement, November 12, 1982.

BEAUSOLEIL, Beau 1941-

PERSONAL: Born September 27, 1941, in the Bronx, N.Y.; son of Frank (an auto mechanic) and Matilda (Jaeske) Beausoleil; children: Connolly. *Education:* Attended secondary school in New Rochelle, N.Y. *Home:* 225 Bennington, San Francisco, Calif. 94110.

CAREER: Radio Corporation of America (RCA), cryptographic technician aboard ship in Pacific Ocean, 1966-68; currently a warehouseman for a publisher. Poet, 1968—. *Military service:* U.S. Army, 1960-65; became sergeant.

WRITINGS—Poetry: Witness, Panjandrum Press, 1976; (contributor of previously unpublished poems) Stephen Vincent, editor, *Five on the Western Edge,* Momo's Press, 1977; *What Happens,* Cloud Marauder Press, 1978; *Red Light with Blue Sky,* Five Trees Press, 1979.

Lascaux, Trike, 1982; *In Case This Way Two Things Fell,* Potes & Poets Press, 1982; *Aleppo,* Sombre Reptiles Press, 1984; *Has That Carrying,* Jungle Garden, 1984. Contributor of poetry to various magazines, including *Beatitude, Abraxas,* and *Berkeley Poetry Review.*

WORK IN PROGRESS: A book of poems, *Lurig,* incorporating research on the first book of the Bible (Genesis), linguistic philosophy, readings in the Kabbalistic traditions, language disorders, and Eastern European and Latin American fiction.

SIDELIGHTS: In her notes on *Witness* Kay Boyle wrote: "The poetry of Beau Beausoleil is that rare quantity that comes unexpectedly out of the unknown. He is a 'you' poet, and in a time when the unhappiness of the 'I' poets is all too prevalent, his work is good to read." Lawrence Fixel commented in his notes on Beausoleil's first book: "What characterizes these poems is the steady level of looking at the self, recording its encounters with others with the phenomenal world. Difficult as this is, the poems retain their shape, their controlled force. Beside the gift of seeing; there is the courage to probe further. Beausoleil's *Witness* is the experience of poems that grow on and beyond the page."

Citing his indebtedness to Federico Garcia Lorca, Beausoleil dedicated the poem "Your Thick Hair" (*Witness*) to the Spanish poet. "It's a poet's poem," Beausoleil told *CA*, "it was written at a point in my writing (after six years) when I knew I had to enter that 'forest of our poems.' Lorca helped me enter it."

Beausoleil added: "More and more I want to wrench something free from the language. I would like my poems to reveal something in the reader's life but not in any sequential order. I have come to feel strongly that the reader is as much text as anything I write. I would like my work to 'read' the one who is reading it. I want a situation where something might possibly happen."

BIOGRAPHICAL/CRITICAL SOURCES: Beau Beausoleil, *Witness,* Panjandrum Press, 1976.

*   *   *

BEEKMAN, E(ric) M(ontague) 1939-

PERSONAL: Born September 25, 1939, in Amsterdam, Netherlands; son of Anton Albert (an engineer) and Geertrui Johanna (van As) Beekman; married Faith L. Foss; children: (previous marriage) Dylan. *Education:* Attended Hope College, 1958-60; University of California, Berkeley, B.A., 1963; University of Ghent, graduate study, 1965-66; Harvard University, Ph.D., 1968. *Politics:* None. *Religion:* None. *Home:* 15 Franklin St., Northampton, Mass. 01060. *Office:* Department of Germanic Languages, University of Massachusetts, Amherst, Mass. 01002.

CAREER: University of Massachusetts at Amherst, assistant professor, 1968-71, associate professor, 1971-80, professor of Germanic languages, 1980—. Visiting scholar at the invitation of the Dutch and Belgian governments, 1976. *Military service:* U.S. Army, 1957-58.

AWARDS, HONORS: Woodrow Wilson fellowship, 1963-64; Fulbright fellowship in Belgium, 1965-66; National Translation Center grant, 1969-70; John Anson Kittredge Fund grant for the arts, 1971; National Endowment for the Humanities grant, 1979-83.

WRITINGS: Homeopathy of the Absurd: The Grotesque in Paul van Ostaijen's Creative Prose, Nijhoff, 1970; *Lame Duck* (novel), Houghton, 1971; *Narcissus: A Poem,* Pennyroyal Press, 1975; *Carnal Lent* (poems), Pennyroyal Press, 1975; *The Killing Jar* (novel), Houghton, 1976; (author of foreword) Paul van Ostaijen, *The First Book of Schmoll,* Bridges Books (Amsterdam), 1982; *The Verbal Empires of Simon Vestdijk and James Joyce,* Editions Rodopi N.V. (Amsterdam), 1983; *Totem* (poems), Pennyroyal Press, 1984.

Editor; all published by University of Massachusetts Press: (And translator and author of notes) *Patriotism Inc. and Other Tales by Paul van Ostaijen,* 1971; (and translator and author of notes) *The Oyster and the Eagle: Selected Aphorisms and Parables of Multatuli,* 1974; (and translator and author of notes) *The Poison Tree: Selected Writings of Rumphius on the Natural History of the Indies,* 1981; (and author of introduction) E. Breton de Nijs, *Faded Portraits,* 1982; (and author of foreword) Multatuli, *Max Havelaar; or, The Coffee Auctions of the Dutch Trading Company,* 1982; (and author of introduction) Robert Nieuwenhuys, *Mirror of the Indies: A History of Dutch Colonial Literature,* 1982; (and author of introduction) Maria Dermout, *The Ten Thousand Things,* 1983; (and author of introduction) A. Alberts, *The Islands,* 1983; (and author of notes) Arthur van Schendel, *John Company,* 1983; (and author of introduction and notes) *Two Tales of the East Indies: "The Last House in the World" by Beb Vuyk and "The Counselor" by H. J. Friedericy,* 1983; E. Du Perron, *Country of Origin,* 1984.

Contributor: L. S. Dembo, editor, *Criticism: Speculative and Analytical Essays,* University of Wisconsin Press, 1968; *New Directions Anthology #24,* New Directions, 1972; Richard Kostelanetz, editor, *In Youth,* Ballantine, 1972; *New Directions #30,* New Directions, 1975; Marc Hanrez, editor, *Les ecrivains et la guerre d'Espagne,* Pantheon (Paris), 1975; Howard Schwartz, editor, *Imperial Messages: One Hundred Modern Parables,* Avon, 1976; Wolfgang Oaulsen and Helmut G. Hermann, editors, *Sinn aus Unsinn: Dada International,* Francke Verlag (Bern), 1982; Thijs Wierema, editor, *Rob Nieuwenhuys: Leven tussen twee vaderlanden,* De Engelbewaarder (Amsterdam), 1982.

Contributor to *Encyclopedia of World Literature in the 20th Century.* Contributor of poems, stories, and articles to *Boston Spectator, Chicago Review, London Magazine, Massachusetts Review, Panache,* and *Dark Horse.*

WORK IN PROGRESS: Editing an anthology.

SIDELIGHTS: E. M. Beekman lived in Indonesia for two years. Some of his works have been translated into French, Italian, Dutch, and Japanese.

*   *   *

BEHRENS, John C. 1933-

PERSONAL: Born February 7, 1933, in Lancaster, Ohio; son of Charles H. and Dorothy M. Behrens; married Patricia Ann Beaty (a therapeutic dietitian), June, 1956; children: Cynthia Sue, Mark Andrew. *Education:* Bowling Green State University, B.S. (journalism), 1955; Pennsylvania State University, M.A., 1956. *Home:* 57 Stebbins Dr., Clinton, N.Y. 13323. *Office:* Department of Journalism, Utica College, Syracuse University, Burrstone Rd., Utica, N.Y. 13502.

CAREER: Lancaster Eagle-Gazette, Lancaster, Ohio, sports editor, 1958-62; Ohio Wesleyan University, Delaware, instructor in journalism, 1962-63; Marshall University, Huntington, W.Va., assistant professor of journalism and member of university public relations staff, 1963-65; Syracuse University, Utica College, Utica, N.Y. 1965—, began as associate professor, currently professor of journalism and coordinator of journalism studies and public relations. Summer or part-time editorial employee of *Columbus Dispatch, Columbus Citizen,* and other newspapers. Curator, Student Press in America Archives, 1968—; publications consultant and editor, Utica School of Commerce, 1970—. Treasurer, Mohawk Valley Council of Churches, 1969-72. *Military service:* U.S. Army, 1956-58; served in Far East; staff writer, *Pacific Stars and Stripes.*

MEMBER: American Society of Journalists and Authors, Authors League of America, Authors Guild, Association for Education in Journalism, American Association of University Professors, College Media Advisers, Sigma Delta Chi, Pi Delta Epsilon, Kappa Tau Alpha. *Awards, honors:* National Council of College Publications Advisers distinguished service award, 1975.

WRITINGS: Magazine Writer's Workbook, Dodrill Press, 1968, 3rd edition, Steffen Publishing, 1983; (editor) *Wood and Stone: Landmarks of the Upper Mohawk,* Central New York Community Arts Council, 1972; *Reporter's Worktext,* Grid Publishing, 1974; *The Typewriter Guerrillas: Closeups of Twenty Top Investigative Reporters,* Nelson-Hall, 1977; *Survey of New York Dailies, 1978-1980,* Utica College, 1978. Correspondent, *Financial Weekly,* 1973-75; author of business column, *Elks,* 1976—; columnist and contributing editor, *American Printer,* 1978—. Contributor of more than 1700 articles to periodicals, including *Writer's Digest, Library Journal, Quill, Radio and TV Weekly, Nieman Reports,* and *Nursing.* Member of editorial board, *College Media Review.*

WORK IN PROGRESS: A book on applied ethics for writers and editors; a text on sports writing and broadcasting; investigations into famous news leaks; "a project involving the history of a space age company that has grown from an abandoned mill to an international complex which provides alloys for NASA: *The Special Metals Story.*"

SIDELIGHTS: John C. Behrens told *CA:* "Motivation and the confidence to reject rejection have been the keys to my success as a writer. I'm a goal-oriented person who starts early each morning (between 6:00 and 6:30 a.m.) and works weekends to accomplish what I want regardless of the hours a project consumes. It's an enjoyable way to earn a living, although by comparison to someone who sells insurance or real estate, you

work more hours and make less money. But I get real satisfaction from fitting the pieces of a story puzzle together. Every non-fiction story is a challenge, an ordeal, and normally a test of my motivation and endurance. To me, there's a sense of worth and accomplishment wth every story I write. However, I also agree with Samuel Johnson's immortal words: 'No man but a blockhead ever wrote except for money.'"

*   *   *

BELL, Thornton
See FANTHORPE, R(obert) Lionel

*   *   *

BENDER, Louis W. 1927-

PERSONAL: Born February 8, 1927, in Graceham, Md.; son of Elmer D. (a minister) and Mildred L. (Walters) Bender; married; wife's name, Elizabeth; children: James Perry, Paul Douglas. *Education:* Moravian College, B.A., 1950; Lehigh University, M.A., 1952, Ed.D., 1965; additional graduate study at Temple University and New York University, 1953-56. *Religion:* Presbyterian. *Home:* 4325 Jackson View Dr., Tallahassee, Fla. 32303. *Office:* Department of Higher Education, Florida State University, Tallahassee, Fla. 32306.

CAREER: English teacher and counselor in Quakertown, Pa., 1951-54; director of guidance in Westwood, N.J., 1954-57; high school dean of boys in Scarsdale, N.Y., 1957-61; high school principal in Tarrytown, N.Y., 1961-62; Bucks County (Pa.) public schools, assistant county superintendent, 1962-65; Pennsylvania Department of Education, Harrisburg, Pa., director of bureau of community colleges, 1965-68, acting assistant commissioner for higher education, 1968-69, assistant commissioner, 1969-70; Florida State University, Tallahassee, professor of higher education, 1970—, and director of State and Regional Higher Education Center.

Evening and summer session instructor, Fairleigh Dickinson University, 1954-60; visiting professor at Lehigh University, 1964, Syracuse University, 1969, North Carolina State University at Raleigh, 1976, Virginia Polytechnic Institute and Commonwealth University, 1980. National lecturer, Nova University, 1972-78. Member, Florida Advisory Council on Military Education, 1982-85, and Florida State Board for Independent Colleges and Universities, 1982-85. Member of advisory board, E.R.I.C. Clearing House for Higher Education, 1975-78; consultant for media systems, Harcourt Brace Jovanovich, Inc., 1976—. *Military service:* U.S. Army, 1945-47.

MEMBER: National Council of State Directors of Community Junior Colleges (life member; chairman, 1968-69), Council of Colleges and Universities (president, 1975-76), American Association of School Administrators, National Education Association, Council of Educational Facility Planners, American Association of Community and Junior Colleges, Phi Delta Kappa.

AWARDS, HONORS: Pennsylvania governor's awards for excellence, 1967, 1968.

WRITINGS: (With James L. Wattenbarger and Norman C. Harris) *A Plan for Community College Education in West Virginia,* West Virginia Board of Regents, 1971; (with Richard C. Richardson, Jr. and Clyde E. Blocker) *Governance of the Two-Year College,* Prentice-Hall, 1972; *Improving Statewide Planning,* Jossey-Bass, 1974; (with Blocker and S. V. Martorana) *The Political Terrain of American Post-Secondary Education*, Nova University Press, 1975.

Federal Regulation and Higher Education, American Association for Higher Education, 1977; (with Benjamin Wygal) *Relating to the Public: Challenge of the Community College*, Jossey-Bass, 1978.

(With Lora Conrad) *Computers and the Small College: A National Study*, Florida State University, Institute for Higher Education, 1982; (with Joan Edwards) *The Role of Women in Community College Foundations*, Florida State University, Institute for Higher Education, 1983; (with Conrad) *Microcomputers and Word Processors in the Small College: A National Study*, Florida State University, Institute for Higher Education, 1983; (contributor) Kenneth Young, editor, *Understanding Accreditation*, Jossey-Bass, 1983.

Also author of education monographs. Contributor to educational journals.

WORK IN PROGRESS: A study of the success of minorities in transferring from two-year colleges and a study of proprietary postsecondary education in Florida.

* * *

BEN-HORIN, Meir   1918-

PERSONAL: Born December 31, 1918, in Koenigsberg, East Prussia (now Kaliningrad, U.S.S.R.); came to United States in 1939, naturalized in 1943; son of Joseph and Dwoira (Polishuk) Schiffman; married Alice Neugebauer, September 15, 1946; children: Judith, David, Gideon. *Education:* Attended Hebrew University, 1937-39; Jewish Theological Seminary of America, B.J.P., 1941; Columbia University, M.A., 1948, Ph.D., 1952. *Home:* 2445 Sittingbourne Ln., Beachwood, Ohio 44122.

CAREER: U.S. Department of the Army, Washington, D.C., investigator, 1946-48; Jewish Cultural Reconstruction, Inc., New York City, field director for western Europe, 1949-50; Hebrew Teachers College, Brookline, Mass., member of faculty and acting registrar, 1951-57; Dropsie University, Philadelphia, Pa., professor of education, 1957-75; Jewish Teachers Seminary, Horace M. Kallen Center for Jewish Studies, New York City, professor of modern Jewish thought and education and vice-president for academic affairs, 1975-78; Cleveland College of Jewish Studies, Cleveland, Ohio, president and professor of modern Jewish thought and education, 1978-81. *Military service:* U.S. Army, 1943-46. U.S. Army Reserve, 1948-74; became colonel (now retired).

MEMBER: American Association of University Professors, National Council for Jewish Education (former vice-president), Civil Affairs Association, Conference on Jewish Social Studies, Conference on Jewish Philosophy (founder), Reserve Officers Association of the United States, Religious Education Association of the United States, Zionist Organization of America, Kappa Delta Pi, Phi Delta Kappa.

WRITINGS: Max Nordau: Philosopher of Human Solidarity, Conference on Jewish Social Studies, 1956; (editor with Bernard Weinryb and Solomon Zeitlin) *Studies and Essays in Honor of Abraham A. Neuman*, Dropsie College Press, 1962; (editor with Judah Pilch) *Judaism and the Jewish School*, Block Publishing, 1966.

Common Faith—Uncommon People: Essays in Reconstructionist Judaism, Reconstructionist Press, 1970; (editor with

Abraham G. Duker) *Emancipation and Counter-Emancipation*, Ktav, 1974; *Solomon Schechter and Mayer Sulzberger: Correspondence of Twenty-five Years*, Conference on Jewish Social Studies, 1985. Contributor to scholarly and literary journals. Managing editor, *Jewish Social Studies*, 1957-69. Member of editorial board, *Judaism* and *Sheviley Ha-Hinnukh*.

WORK IN PROGRESS: Education as Religion; essays in modern Jewish theology; a critique of neo-mysticism; an intellectual biography of Mordecai M. Kaplan, founder of Jewish reconstructionism, entitled *Transnature's God: Mordecai M. Kaplan's Theology.*

SIDELIGHTS: Meir Ben-Horin lists his professional interests as philosophies of education, modern theology, Zionism and Zionist history, nineteenth- and twentieth-century history, history of education, and modern Hebrew literature. He told *CA* that his work "seeks to develop the implications of Jewish religious naturalism which regards Judaism as the Jewish people's evolving civilization of 'the religious.'" He speaks German, Hebrew, and Yiddish, in addition to English, and reads French, Italian, Latin, and Greek.

* * *

BENNETT, Gordon C.   1935-

PERSONAL: Born September 1, 1935, in Philadelphia, Pa.; son of Harold Walter and Agnes (Raff) Bennett; married Ruth Packer, June 8, 1957; children: Brad Alan, Cherry Lynn. *Education:* Dickinson College, A.B., 1957; Temple University, M.A., 1967; Berkeley Baptist Divinity School, B.D., 1960. *Home:* 1743 Russell Rd., Paoli, Pa. 19301. *Office:* Department of Communication Arts, Eastern College, St. Davids, Pa. 19087.

CAREER: Clergyman of American Baptist Convention; minister of churches in Fredericktown, Ohio, 1960-65, and Narberth, Pa., 1965-68; Eastern College, St. Davids, Pa., instructor, 1968-70, assistant professor of speech and drama, 1970—. Actor in and director of church and campus plays; co-founder of King's Players, chancel drama team playing in Philadelphia area.

MEMBER: Religious Speech Communication Association (chairman of religious drama committee), Speech Association of the Eastern States, Fellowship of Reconciliation.

AWARDS, HONORS: Book award, Religious Communication Association, 1976, for *Happy Tales, Fables, and Plays.*

WRITINGS: (With William D. Thompson) *Dialogue Preaching: The Shared Sermon*, Judson, 1969; *God Is My Fuehrer: A Dramatic Interpretation of the Life of Martin Niemoeller*, Friendship, 1970; *Readers Theatre Comes to Church*, John Knox, 1972; *From Nineveh to Now*, Bethany Press, 1973; *Happy Tales, Fables, and Plays*, John Knox, 1975; *S Is for Sloane*, Performance Publishing, 1978; *Solomon Grundy*, Theatre World Publishing, 1978.

Also author of a drama for the Biennial Convention of the American Baptist Churches, 1981, and, with Hugh Pease, of "HMS SinNoMore." Contributor to religion publications.

WORK IN PROGRESS: A theatre handbook for church dramatists.

SIDELIGHTS: Gordon C. Bennett told *CA:* "Sometimes I write plays simply to satisfy the muse that's in me, to let an idea find form for its own sake or simply to entertain with a good story, without attempting to incarnate any profound idea. Other times I make my craft subject to Christ, using drama as a ministry to spark Christian growth, and to awaken the human conscience in terms of promoting peace and social justice. The idolatry of militarism and nuclearism and the importance of peacemaking are common themes in my plays. The real crunch comes with the struggle to avoid writing drama that is too propositional: one has to avoid sermonizing and let the action of the play be the message, as much as possible. Sometimes religious drama makes it as art and sometimes it doesn't, but to me theatre at its best is a temple in which divine truth finds embodiment; thus, both the human spirit and the divine are served. Thornton Wilder's plays are perhaps the best example of this; his major works are a happy combination of excellent workmanship and profound spiritual insight.''

AVOCATIONAL INTERESTS: Playing tennis and softball, camping, writing, amateur acting, gardening, and peace movement work.

*   *   *

BENTLEY-TAYLOR, David 1915-

PERSONAL: Born January 25, 1915, in Liverpool, England; son of Robert Martin (a bank manager) and Winifred (Hughes) Bentley-Taylor; married Jessie Mabel Moore, March 4, 1941; children: Michael Martin and Arthur John (twins), David Andrew, Rupert Paul. *Education:* Oxford University, M.A., 1936. *Religion:* Evangelical Protestant. *Home:* Swandrift, Eardisland, Leominster, Herefordshire HR6 9BU, England.

CAREER: Missionary of China Inland Mission (now Overseas Missionary Fellowship) in China, 1938-44, England, 1944-51, Indonesia, 1952-62, and England, 1962-66; International Fellowship of Evangelical Students, traveling secretary in Africa and West Asia, 1967-74; general secretary of Middle East Christian Outreach, 1974-80.

WRITINGS: The Prisoner Leaps: A Diary of Missionary Life in Java, China Inland Mission Overseas Missionary Fellowship, 1961, revised edition, 1965; *The Great Volcano,* China Inland Mission Overseas Missionary Fellowship, 1965; *The Weathercock's Reward: Christian Progress in Muslim Java,* Overseas Missionary Fellowship, 1967, published as *Java Saga,* 1975; *My Love Must Wait: The Story of Henry Martyn,* Inter-Varsity Press, 1976, 2nd edition, 1978; *Augustine: Wayward Genius,* Hodder & Stoughton, 1980, published as *Augustine, Wayward Genius: The Life of St. Augustine of Hippo,* Baker Book, 1981.

SIDELIGHTS: David Bentley-Taylor told *CA:* ''I became a Christian while a student at Oxford University in England over fifty years ago. Ever since then it has been my faith in Jesus Christ and my desire to make Him known to others that have influenced the way I live. I became a missionary first in China, then in Indonesia, and, later on, . . . in many parts of Africa and the Middle East. As a schoolboy, I imagined I would write books, but I was in my forties before I became an author.

''Living in Java for ten years, speaking Chinese and Indonesian, I found I was in a position to present this marvellous island and the remarkable progress of the gospel there over the past two centuries to my countrymen, few of whom were acquainted with it. Then I was invited to produce a new biography of Henry Martyn, an exceptionally brilliant mathematician and linguist, who lived in the age of Napoleon. Though he died young, his character and his achievement in translating the New Testament into Urdu and Persian had wide influence on

Christian missions as a whole. This led to the still more difficult task of a biography of Augustine of Hippo, written not for theologians but for the general reader. My lifelong interest in him as probably the most influential Christian teacher and author since the days of St. Paul, along with numerous visits to North Africa, made this possible. I was working on it over a five year period, constantly rewriting it and eventually getting two very competent people to read the manuscript and give me their detailed criticisms and suggestions, on nearly all of which I took action.

''I am now in the delightful state of retirement in the splendid English-Welsh borderland where I originated. My main interests are my family (one wife, four sons, four daughters-in-law, and thirteen grandchildren), along with research in history, literature, and the Bible.''

*   *   *

BERBEROVA, Nina (Nikolaevna) 1901-

PERSONAL: Born August 8, 1901, in St. Petersburg, Russia (now Leningrad, Soviet Union), came to the United States in 1951, naturalized in 1959; daughter of Nikolai and Natalia (Karaulova) Berberova; married Vladislav Khodasevich (a poet); married second husband, Nikolai Makeev (a painter). *Education:* Attended Institute of Art History in Russia, and at Sorbonne, University of Paris. *Home:* 46 Stanworth Lane, Princeton, N.J. 08540.

CAREER: Left Soviet Union in 1922; lived in Germany, Czechoslovakia, and Italy; writer, journalist, translator, and editor in Paris, France, 1925-50; worked as a language instructor at the Berlitz School, radio announcer for the ''Voice of America,'' office machine operator, and as editor of a Russian language periodical, 1951-58; Yale University, New Haven, Conn., lecturer, 1958-63; Princeton University, Princeton, N.J., professor of literature, 1963-71. Instructor at Indiana University, summers, 1962, 1963, Columbia University, 1970-71, University of Pennsylvania, fall, 1973, and Princeton University, 1976-77; Katherine McBride Visiting Lecturer, Bryn Mawr College, spring, 1976. Guest at Yaddo, Saratoga Springs, New York, 1964-66.

AWARDS, HONORS: Received honorary degrees from Glassboro Teachers College, 1980, and Middlebury College, 1983.

WRITINGS: (Translator into Russian from the French) Romain Rolland, *Mahatma Ghandi,* Beseda (Berlin), 1924; *Posledenye i pervye* (novel), Povolotzky (Paris), 1929.

Le Symbolisme russe (bound with *Le Symbolisme en France* by Andre Fontainas), Cahiers de la Quinzaine (Paris), 1931; *Povelitelnitsa* (novel), Parabola (Berlin), 1932; *Alexandre Blok et son temps,* Editions du Chene, 1935; *Chaikovskii* (biography), Petropolis (Berlin), 1936; *Borodin,* Petropolis, 1937; *Bez zakata* (novel), Dom Knigi (Paris), 1938; ''Madame'' (play), first produced in Paris, 1938.

Oblegchenie uchasti (stories), YMCA Press, 1949; *Protsess V. A. Kravchenko,* [Paris], 1949; (translator into French with Mina Journot) Jules Margoline, *La Condition inhumaine: Cinq ans dans les camps de concentration sovietiques,* [Paris], 1949; (translator into French) Fiodor Dostoevsky, *Eternel mari,* Editions du Chene, 1949.

(Editor) Vladislav Khodasevich, *Literaturnye stat'i i vospominaniia,* Chekhov Publishing House (New York), 1954; (editor) *Sobranie stikhov Vladislava Khodasevicha,* [Munich], 1959.

(Contributing editor with L. J. Kent) Nikolai Gogol, *Tales and Plays*, translation by Constance Garnett, revised edition, Pantheon, 1964; (editor and author of introduction with Kent) Leo Tolstoy, *Anna Karenina*, translation by Garnett, revised edition, Modern Library, 1965; *The Italics Are Mine* (autobiography), translation by Philippe Radley, Harcourt, 1969, Russian edition, with letters of Kerensky, Gorky, and Bunin, published as *Kursiv Moi*, Fink Verlag, 1972, 2nd edition, Russica Publishing, 1983.

(Contributor) Alfred Appel, Jr. and Charles Newman, editors, *Nabokov: Criticisms, Reminiscences, Translations, and Tributes*, Northwestern University Press, 1970; (author of notes and commentary) Andrey Bely, *The First Encounter*, translation by G. Janacek, Princeton University Press, 1978.

Zheleznaya Zhenshchina, Russica Publishing, 1981, 2nd edition, 1983; (editor) Vladislav Khodasevich, *Selected Prose*, Russica Publishing, 1982; (editor) Zinaida Gippius, *The Petersburg Diaries*, Orpheus Publishing, 1982; *Poems, 1922-1983*, Russica Publishing, 1984; *Russian Free-Masons of the 20th Century*, Russica Publishing, 1985.

Also translator into Russian of works by T. S. Eliot and Constantine Cavafy. Contributor to Russian-language emigre newspapers and magazines in Germany, France, and the United States. Editor of literary sections in several emigre publications.

WORK IN PROGRESS: Researching a book on Free Masons in Russia, 1906-1971.

SIDELIGHTS: Nina Berberova told *CA:* "The Soviet dissident Vladimir Voinovich was visiting me in Princeton and asked: 'For whom do you write?' After a short silence I answered: 'For you, Volodia. You read my book in Moscow? So this makes me happy. And others did, too. And they read me now in Brooklyn and Los Angeles and Chicago and Paris and London.'

"At the age of eleven I knew what I would be—a writer. Because I liked books, perhaps I liked people, too. But mostly I liked writers. I became a writer, and after living and publishing in France, I came to the United States, became a citizen, and have worked as a professor at Yale, Princeton, and other places. I have lectured and written about literature and literary criticism and I also continue to write poetry. It was a surprise to see my writings quoted in some scholarly Soviet publications. But time passes, and things change, and I accept it."

MEDIA ADAPTATIONS: Berberova's book *Chaikovskii* was filmed under the title "Life of Peter Chaikovsky" by Warner Bros. and Sovkino.

BIOGRAPHICAL/CRITICAL SOURCES: Marc Slonim, *Modern Russian Literature*, Oxford University Press, 1953; Gleb Struve, *Russkaya literature za rubezhom*, Chekhov Publishing House, 1956; *New York Times Book Review*, May 25, 1969; *New Yorker*, August 16, 1969; *Spectator*, November 29, 1969; Nina Berberova, *The Italics Are Mine*, Harcourt, 1969.

*   *   *

BERENSTAIN, Jan(ice)

PERSONAL: Daughter of Alfred J. and Marian (Beck) Grant; married Stanley Berenstain (an author and illustrator), April 13, 1946; children: Leo, Michael. *Education:* Attended Philadelphia College of Art, 1941-45. *Residence:* Solebury, Pa.

Agent: Sterling Lord, The Sterling Lord Agency, 660 Madison Ave., New York, N.Y. 10021.

CAREER: Author and illustrator. Creator, with husband, Stan Berenstain, of "It's All in the Family," an illustrated feature first published in *McCall's* and currently in *Good Housekeeping*. Work exhibited in Metropolitan Museum of Art international exhibition of cartoons and in an exhibition of British and American humorous art in London. Works represented in the Albert T. Reid Cartoon Collection at the University of Kansas and the Farrell Library Collection at Kansas State University.

AWARDS, HONORS: School Bell Award, National Education Association, 1960, for distinguished service in the interpretation of education in a national magazine; *Inside, Outside, Upside Down* was named an honor book by the British Book Centre, 1968; award from American Institute of Graphic Arts, 1970, for *The Bear Scouts;* University of Chicago Center for Children's Books named *Bears in the Night* a best book of 1972, and *He Bear, She Bear* a best book of 1974; Philadelphia Library Children's Reading Round Table honor book, 1972, for *Bears in the Night*, 1973, for *The Bears' Almanac: A Year in Bear Country—Holidays, Seasons, Weather, Actual Facts about Snow, Wind, Rain, Thunder, Lightning, the Sun, the Moon, and Lots More*, 1974, for *He Bear, She Bear*, 1976, for *The Bears' Nature Guide*, 1980, for *The Berenstain Bears and the Missing Dinosaur Bone*, 1982, for *The Berenstain Bears Visit the Dentist*, 1983, for *The Berenstain Bears in the Dark, The Berenstain Bears Go to Camp*, and *The Berenstain Bears and the Truth*, and 1984, for *The Berenstain Bears and Too Much TV;* Children's Book of the Year, Child Study Association, 1977, for *The Berenstain Bears' Science Fair*, and 1982, for *The Berenstain Bears Go to the Doctor, The Berenstain Bears Visit the Dentist, The Berenstain Bears and the Sitter*, and *The Berenstain Bears' Moving Day*.

Silver diploma, International Film and Television Festival, Naples, Italy, 1980, for "The Berenstain Bears' Christmas Tree"; silver award, International Film and Television Festival, New York City, 1980, for "The Berenstain Bears' Christmas Tree"; Young Readers' Award, Michigan Council of Teachers of English, 1981, for *Bears in the Night;* Drexel Citation, Drexel University, School of Library and Information Science, 1982, for "contributions to children's literature"; Children's Classic Award, International Reading Association, 1982, for *The Berenstain Bears Go to the Doctor* and *The Berenstain Bears Visit the Dentist*, 1983, for *The Berenstain Bears Get in a Fight, The Berenstain Bears Go to Camp*, and *The Berenstain Bears in the Dark*, and 1984, for *The Berenstain Bears and the Messy Room*, and *The Berenstain Bears and the Truth;* Buckeye Award, Ohio State Library Association, Teachers of English, and International Reading Association, 1982, for *The Berenstain Bears and the Spooky Old Tree*.

WRITINGS—All with husband, Stan Berenstain: *The Berenstain's Baby Book*, Macmillan, 1951, reprinted, Arbor House, 1983; *Sister* (cartoons), Schuman, 1952; *Tax-wise*, Schuman, 1952; *Marital Blitz*, Dutton, 1954; *Baby Makes Four*, Macmillan, 1956; *Lover Boy*, Macmillan, 1958; *It's All in the Family*, Dutton, 1958.

Bedside Lover Boy, Dell, 1960; *And Beat Him When He Sneezes*, McGraw, 1960, published as *Have a Baby, My Wife Just Had a Cigar*, Dell, 1960; *Call Me Mrs.*, Macmillan, 1961; *It's Still in the Family*, Dutton, 1961; *Office Lover Boy*, Dell, 1962; *The Facts of Life for Grown-ups*, Dell, 1963; *Flipsville-*

Squaresville, Dial, 1965; *Mr. Dirty vs. Mr. Clean*, Dell, 1967; *You Could Diet Laughing*, Dell, 1969.

Be Good or I'll Belt You, Dell, 1970; *Education Impossible*, Dell, 1970; *Never Trust Anyone over 13*, Bantam, 1970; *How to Teach Your Children about Sex without Making a Complete Fool of Yourself*, Dutton, 1970; *How to Teach Your Children about God without Actually Scaring Them out of Their Wits*, Dutton, 1971; *Are Parents for Real?*, Bantam, 1972.

"Berenstain Bears" series; published by Random House, except as indicated: *The Big Honey Hunt*, Beginner Books, 1962; *The Bike Lesson*, Beginner Books, 1964; *The Bears' Picnic*, Beginner Books, 1966; *The Bear Scouts*, Beginner Books, 1967; *The Bears' Vacation*, Beginner Books, 1968 (published in England as *The Bears' Holiday*, Harvill, 1969); *Inside, Outside, Upside Down*, 1968; *Bears on Wheels*, 1969.

The Bears' Christmas, Beginner Books, 1970; *Old Hat, New Hat*, 1970; *Bears in the Night*, 1971; *The B Book*, 1971; *C Is for Clown*, 1972; *The Bears' Almanac: A Year in Bear Country—Holidays, Seasons, Weather, Actual Facts about Snow, Wind, Rain, Thunder, Lightning, the Sun, the Moon, and Lots More*, 1973, reprinted as *The Berenstain Bears' Almanac: A Year in Bear Country—Holidays, Seasons, Weather, Actual Facts about Snow, Wind, Rain, Thunder, Lightning, the Sun, the Moon, and Lots More*, 1984; *The Berenstain Bears' Nursery Tales*, 1973; *He Bear, She Bear*, 1974; *The Berenstain Bears' New Baby*, 1974; *The Bears' Nature Guide*, 1975, published as *The Berenstain Bears' Nature Guide*, 1984; *The Bear Detectives*, 1975; *The Berenstain Bears' Counting Book*, 1976; *The Berenstain Bears' Science Fair*, 1977; *The Berenstain Bears and the Spooky Old Tree*, 1978; *Papa's Pizza: A Berenstain Bear Sniffy Book*, 1978; *The Berenstain Bears Go to School*, 1978; *The Bears' Activity Book*, 1979.

The Berenstain Bears and the Missing Dinosaur Bone, 1980; *The Berenstain Bears' Christmas Tree*, 1980; *The Berenstain Bears and the Sitter*, 1981; *The Berenstain Bears Go to the Doctor*, 1981; *The Berenstain Bears' Moving Day*, 1981; *The Berenstain Bears Visit the Dentist*, 1981; *The Berenstain Bears Get in a Fight*, 1982; *The Berenstain Bears Go to Camp*, 1982; *The Berenstain Bears in the Dark*, 1982; *The Berenstain Bears and the Messy Room*, 1983; *The Berenstain Bears and the Truth*, 1983; *The Berenstain Bears and the Wild, Wild Honey*, 1983; *The Berenstain Bears' Soccer Star*, 1983; *The Berenstain Bears Go Fly a Kite*, 1983; *The Berenstain Bears to the Rescue*, 1983; *The Berenstain Bears' Trouble with Money*, 1983; *The Berenstain Bears and the Big Election*, 1984; *The Berenstain Bears and Too Much TV*, 1984; *The Berenstain Bears Shoot the Rapids*, 1984; *The Berenstain Bears and the Neighborly Skunk*, 1984; *The Berenstain Bears and the Dinosaurs*, 1984; *The Berenstain Bears Meet Santa Bear*, 1984; *The Berenstain Bears and Mama's New Job*, 1984; *The Berenstain Bears and Too Much Junk Food*, 1985; *The Berenstain Bears on the Moon*, 1985.

Television scripts: "The Berenstain Bears' Christmas Tree," National Broadcasting Company, 1979; "The Berenstain Bears Meet Bigpaw," NBC, 1980; "The Berenstain Bears' Easter Surprise," NBC, 1981; "The Berenstain Bears' Comic Valentine," NBC, 1982; "The Berenstain Bears Play Ball," NBC, 1983.

SIDELIGHTS: The Berenstain Bears, created by the husband and wife team of Stan and Jan Berenstain, are among the most popular characters in juvenile literature today. Relating the adventures of a human-like bear family, the Berenstain Bears book series has sold over 50 million copies throughout the world. The characters are also featured on television specials, records, and many toy products, as well.

The Berenstain Bears first appeared in the early 1960s when, after many years as free-lance cartoonists, Stan and Jan Berenstain decided that the once-thriving magazine cartoon field was on the wane. As Stan tells Dolly Langdon of *People*, "I could see great cartoonists becoming real estate salesmen." The couple turned their talents to a new field, juvenile books, and in 1962 the first Berenstain Bears book was published. "We wanted a good animal family that could teach things to children painlessly," Jan explains to Langdon.

As magazine cartoonists, the Berenstains had specialized in domestic situation gags, so it is not unusual that their juvenile series revolves around the domestic problems and adventures of a bear family. Papa Bear, Mama Bear, Brother Bear, and Sister Bear are, as G. A. Woods states in the *New York Times Book Review*, very similar to a typical human family. "If," Woods writes, "they didn't have a black olive sitting on the end of their snouts, hairy ankles, and furry hides, you'd swear they're really mom and pop, sis and junior in disguise." Many of the Berenstain Bears' stories are drawn from the real-life experiences of their creators, and include such familiar situations as visiting the doctor, cleaning the house, and buying a Christmas tree.

"Ours is an old-fashioned Mom and Pop operation in which both partners do whatever needs to be done—writing, illustrating, cooking, bottle washing," the Berenstains explain in an article for *Publishers Weekly*. The two of them work on the text of a book together, while Jan usually does the pencil sketches and Stan does the inking. "We do have one rule—a sort of unilateral veto—which has helped us over the humps," the couple write in *Publishers Weekly*. "If one of us strongly objects to some point, project, or approach, it is dropped without argument." After more than twenty years of chronicling the adventures of their bear family, the Berenstains report that they still "find our work (and our bears) tremendously stimulating and enjoyable."

In 1966, Syracuse University established a Stanley and Janice Berenstain manuscript collection.

BIOGRAPHICAL/CRITICAL SOURCES: Newsweek, October 24, 1949; *Times Literary Supplement*, April 2, 1971, October 22, 1971, July 14, 1972; *Christian Science Monitor*, November 11, 1971, November 8, 1972; *New York Times Book Review*, November 25, 1973; *Teacher*, December, 1973; *New Yorker*, December 3, 1973; *Ms.*, December, 1974; *Psychology Today*, January, 1975; *People*, January 22, 1979; *Publishers Weekly*, February 27, 1981; *Parents Magazine*, October, 1982.

*   *   *

BERENSTAIN, Michael   1951-

PERSONAL: Born December 21, 1951, in Philadelphia, Pa.; son of Stanley (an author and illustrator) and Janice (an author and illustrator; maiden name, Grant) Berenstain. *Education:* Attended Philadelphia College of Art, 1969-73, and Pennsylvania Academy of Fine Arts, 1973-74. *Residence:* New Hope, Pa.

CAREER: Random House, Inc., New York, N.Y., designer, 1975; author and illustrator, 1975—.

MEMBER: Authors Guild.

WRITINGS—Self-illustrated juvenile books: *The Castle Book,* McKay, 1977; *The Ship Book,* McKay, 1978; *The Lighthouse Book,* McKay, 1979; *The Armor Book,* McKay, 1979; *The Troll Book,* Random House, 1980; *The Dwarks,* Bantam, 1981; *The Sorcerer's Scrapbook,* Random House, 1982; *The Creature Catalog: A Monster Watcher's Guide,* Random House, 1982.

SIDELIGHTS: A reviewer for *Publishers Weekly* believes that the "extended family of odd little creatures" Michael Berenstain creates for *The Dwarks* "might become as popular as other make-believe characters in the realm of picture books." Noting that Berenstain's parents also write juveniles, the reviewer goes on to state that Michael Berenstain works "in their field but in his own amusing fashion."

BIOGRAPHICAL/CRITICAL SOURCES: New Yorker, December 1, 1980; *Time,* December 21, 1981; *Publishers Weekly,* September 2, 1983.

* * *

BERENSTAIN, Stan(ley) 1923-

PERSONAL: Born September 29, 1923, in Philadelphia, Pa.; son of Harry and Rose (Brander) Berenstain; married Janice Grant (an author and illustrator), April 13, 1946; children: Leo, Michael. *Education:* Attended Philadelphia College of Art, 1941-42, and Pennsylvania Academy of Fine Arts, 1946-49. *Residence:* Solebury, Pa. *Agent:* Sterling Lord, The Sterling Lord Agency, 660 Madison Ave., New York, N.Y. 10021.

CAREER: Author and illustrator. Creator, with wife, Jan Berenstain, of "It's All in the Family," an illustrated feature first published in *McCall's* and currently in *Good Housekeeping.* Work exhibited in Metropolitan Museum of Art international exhibition of cartoons and in an exhibition of British and American humorous art in London. Works represented in the Albert T. Reid Cartoon Collection at the University of Kansas and the Farrell Library Collection at Kansas State University.

AWARDS, HONORS: School Bell Award, National Education Association, 1960, for distinguished service in the interpretation of education in a national magazine; *Inside, Outside, Upside Down* was named an honor book by the British Book Centre, 1968; award from American Institute of Graphic Arts, 1970, for *The Bear Scouts;* University of Chicago Center for Children's Books named *Bears in the Night* a best book of 1972, and *He Bear, She Bear* a best book of 1974; Philadelphia Library Children's Reading Round Table honor book, 1972, for *Bears in the Night,* 1973, for *The Bears' Almanac: A Year in Bear Country—Holidays, Seasons, Weather, Actual Facts about Snow, Wind, Rain, Thunder, Lightning, the Sun, the Moon, and Lots More,* 1974, for *He Bear, She Bear,* 1976, for *The Bears' Nature Guide,* 1980, for *The Berenstain Bears and the Missing Dinosaur Bone,* 1982, for *The Berenstain Bears Visit the Dentist,* and 1983, for *The Berenstain Bears in the Dark, The Berenstain Bears Go to Camp,* and *The Berenstain Bears and the Truth,* and 1984, for *The Berenstain Bears and Too Much TV;* Children's Book of the Year, Child Study Association, 1977, for *The Berenstain Bears' Science Fair,* and 1982, for *The Berenstain Bears Go to the Doctor, The Berenstain Bears Visit the Dentist, The Berenstain Bears and the Sitter,* and *The Berenstain Bears' Moving Day.*

Silver diploma, International Film and Television Festival, Naples, Italy, 1980, for "The Berenstain Bears' Christmas Tree"; silver award, International Film and Television Festival, New York City, 1980, for "The Berenstain Bears' Christmas Tree"; Young Readers' Award, Michigan Council of Teachers of English, 1981, for *Bears in the Night;* Drexel Citation, Drexel University, School of Library and Information Science, 1982, for "contributions to children's literature"; Children's Classic Award, International Reading Association, 1982, for *The Berenstain Bears Go to the Doctor* and *The Berenstain Bears Visit the Dentist,* 1983, for *The Berenstain Bears Get in a Fight, The Berenstain Bears Go to Camp,* and *The Berenstain Bears in the Dark,* and 1984, for *The Berenstain Bears and the Messy Room,* and *The Berenstain Bears and the Truth;* Buckeye Award, Ohio State Library Association, Teachers of English, and International Reading Association, 1982, for *The Berenstain Bears and the Spooky Old Tree.*

WRITINGS—All with wife, Jan Berenstain: *The Berenstain's Baby Book,* Macmillan, 1951, reprinted, Arbor House, 1983; *Sister* (cartoons), Schuman, 1952; *Tax-wise,* Schuman, 1952; *Marital Blitz,* Dutton, 1954; *Baby Makes Four,* Macmillan, 1956; *Lover Boy,* Macmillan, 1958; *It's All in the Family,* Dutton, 1958.

Bedside Lover Boy, Dell, 1960; *And Beat Him When He Sneezes,* McGraw, 1960, published as *Have a Baby, My Wife Just Had a Cigar,* Dell, 1960; *Call Me Mrs.,* Macmillan, 1961; *It's Still in the Family,* Dutton, 1961; *Office Lover Boy,* Dell, 1962; *The Facts of Life for Grown-ups,* Dell, 1963; *Flipsville-Squaresville,* Dial, 1965; *Mr. Dirty vs. Mr. Clean,* Dell, 1967; *You Could Diet Laughing,* Dell, 1969.

Be Good or I'll Belt You, Dell, 1970; *Education Impossible,* Dell, 1970; *Never Trust Anyone Over 13,* Bantam, 1970; *How to Teach Your Children about Sex without Making a Complete Fool of Yourself,* Dutton, 1970; *How to Teach Your Children about God without Actually Scaring Them out of Their Wits,* Dutton, 1971; *Are Parents for Real?,* Bantam, 1972.

"Berenstain Bears" series; published by Random House, except as indicated: *The Big Honey Hunt,* Beginner Books, 1962; *The Bike Lesson,* Beginner Books, 1964; *The Bears' Picnic,* Beginner Books, 1966; *The Bear Scouts,* Beginner Books, 1967; *The Bears' Vacation,* Beginner Books, 1968 (published in England as *The Bears' Holiday,* Harvill, 1969); *Inside, Outside, Upside Down,* 1968; *Bears on Wheels,* 1969.

The Bears' Christmas, Beginner Books, 1970; *Old Hat, New Hat,* 1970; *Bears in the Night,* 1971; *The B Book,* 1971; *C Is for Clown,* 1972; *The Bears' Almanac: A Year in Bear Country—Holidays, Seasons, Weather, Actual Facts about Snow, Wind, Rain, Thunder, Lightning, the Sun, the Moon, and Lots More,* 1973, reprinted as *The Berenstain Bears' Almanac: A Year in Bear Country—Holidays, Seasons, Weather, Actual Facts about Snow, Wind, Rain, Thunder, Lightning, the Sun, the Moon, and Lots More,* 1984; *The Berenstain Bears' Nursery Tales,* 1973; *He Bear, She Bear,* 1974; *The Berenstain Bears' New Baby,* 1974; *The Bears' Nature Guide,* 1975, published as *The Berenstain Bears' Nature Guide,* 1984; *The Bear Detectives,* 1975; *The Berenstain Bears' Counting Book,* 1976; *The Berenstain Bears' Science Fair,* 1977; *The Berenstain Bears and the Spooky Old Tree,* 1978; *Papa's Pizza: A Berenstain Bear Sniffy Book,* 1978; *The Berenstain Bears Go to School,* 1978; *The Bears' Activity Book,* 1979.

The Berenstain Bears and the Missing Dinosaur Bone, 1980; *The Berenstain Bears' Christmas Tree,* 1980; *The Berenstain Bears and the Sitter,* 1981; *The Berenstain Bears Go to the Doctor,* 1981; *The Berenstain Bears' Moving Day,* 1981; *The Berenstain Bears Visit the Dentist,* 1981; *The Berenstain Bears*

Get in a Fight, 1982; *The Berenstain Bears Go to Camp,* 1982; *The Berenstain Bears in the Dark,* 1982; *The Berenstain Bears and the Messy Room,* 1983; *The Berenstain Bears and the Truth,* 1983; *The Berenstain Bears and the Wild, Wild Honey,* 1983; *The Berenstain Bears' Soccer Star,* 1983; *The Berenstain Bears Go Fly a Kite,* 1983; *The Berenstain Bears to the Rescue,* 1983; *The Berenstain Bears' Trouble with Money,* 1983; *The Berenstain Bears and the Big Election,* 1984; *The Berenstain Bears and Too Much TV,* 1984; *The Berenstain Bears Shoot the Rapids,* 1984; *The Berenstain Bears and the Neighborly Skunk,* 1984; *The Berenstain Bears and the Dinosaurs,* 1984; *The Berenstain Bears Meet Santa Bear,* 1984; *The Berenstain Bears and Mama's New Job,* 1984; *The Berenstain Bears and Too Much Junk Food,* 1985; *The Berenstain Bears on the Moon,* 1985.

Television scripts: "The Berenstain Bears' Christmas Tree," National Broadcasting Company, 1979; "The Berenstain Bears Meet Bigpaw," NBC, 1980; "The Berenstain Bears' Easter Surprise," NBC, 1981; "The Berenstain Bears' Comic Valentine," NBC, 1982; "The Berenstain Bears Play Ball," NBC, 1983.

SIDELIGHTS: See *CA* entry for wife, Jan(ice) Berenstain, in this volume.

BIOGRAPHICAL/CRITICAL SOURCES: Newsweek, October 24, 1949; *Times Literary Supplement,* April 2, 1971, October 22, 1971, July 14, 1972; *Christian Science Monitor,* November 11, 1971, November 8, 1972; *New York Times Book Review,* November 25, 1973; *Teacher,* December, 1973; *New Yorker,* December 3, 1973; *Ms.,* December, 1974; *Psychology Today,* January, 1975; *People,* January 22, 1979; *Publishers Weekly,* February 27, 1981; *Parents Magazine,* October, 1982.

*   *   *

BERGER, Andrew J(ohn) 1915-

PERSONAL: Born August 30, 1915, in Warren, Ohio; son of Anton Andrew (a steelworker) and Mary (Rodenberger) Berger; married Edith Grace Denniston, August 13, 1942 (divorced, 1969); children: John D., Diana M. *Education:* Oberlin College, A.B., 1939; University of Michigan, M.A., 1947, Ph.D., 1950. *Politics:* None. *Religion:* None. *Office:* Department of Zoology, University of Hawaii, Honolulu, Hawaii 96822.

CAREER: University of Michigan, School of Medicine, Ann Arbor, instructor, 1950-54, assistant professor, 1954-57, associate professor of anatomy, 1957-64; Maharaja Sayajirao University of Baroda, Baroda, India, senior Fulbright lecturer, 1964-65; University of Hawaii, Honolulu, professor of zoology, 1965-81, professor emeritus, 1981—, chairman of department, 1965-71, acting chairman, 1975-76. Visiting professor at University of California, Los Angeles, summer, 1960; Carnegie visiting professor at University of Hawaii, spring, 1964; visiting professor at University of Minnesota Biological Station, summer, 1974; visiting professor, Cornell University, summer, 1977.

Member of task force of International Biological Program for Hawaii Terrestrial Biology Project, 1967-68; member of governor's committee to prepare program for preservation of scientific areas in Hawaii, 1969-70, and acting chairman of governor's animal species advisory commission, 1970-71; member of advisory committee on land vertebrates of Board of Agriculture, 1970-72; leader, Palila Recovery Team, U.S. Department of the Interior, 1975—; member of Hawaii Forest Birds Recovery Team, 1975—. Honorary associate in ornithology of Bernice P. Bishop Museum, 1965—; honorary member of Laboratory of Ornithology at Cornell University, 1968—; honorary consultant in ornithology to Waimea Arboretum Foundation. Ecology consultant for state and federal agencies and private companies. *Military service:* U.S. Air Force, 1941-46; U.S. Air Force Reserve, 1946-66; became lieutenant colonel.

MEMBER: International Committee for Avian Anatomical Nomenclature, American Association of Anatomists, American Ornithologists Union (fellow), American Society of Zoologists, Association for Tropical Biology, American Association for the Advancement of Science (fellow), Oceanic Institute Alliance, Wilson Ornithological Society (member of council, 1967-70; vice-president, 1971-75; president, 1975-77), Cooper Ornithological Society, Explorers Club (New York), Hawaiian Academy of Science, Conservation Council for Hawaii (member of executive board, 1966-68), Hawaiian Audubon Society (vice-president, 1966-68), Science Research Club (University of Michigan), Senior Research Club (University of Michigan), Sigma Xi, Phi Sigma, Phi Kappa Phi.

AWARDS, HONORS: American Philosophical Society research grant, 1957; McGregor Fund grant, summer, 1958; Guggenheim fellowship, 1963; National Science Foundation grants, 1966-69, 1970-75.

WRITINGS: (With Josselyn Van Tyne) *Fundamentals of Ornithology,* Wiley, 1959, 2nd edition, 1976; (contributor) A. J. Marshall, editor, *Biology and Comparative Physiology of Birds,* Volume I, Academic Press, 1960; *Bird Study,* Wiley, 1961; *Elementary Human Anatomy,* Wiley, 1964; (with J. C. George) *Avian Myology,* Academic Press, 1966; (contributor) Olin Sewall Pettingill, Jr., editor, *Ornithology in Laboratory and Field,* 4th edition, Burgess Publishing, 1970, 5th edition, Academic Press, 1985; (contributor), Pettingill, Jr., editor, *Seminars in Ornithology,* Laboratory of Ornithology, Cornell University, 1972; *Hawaiian Birdlife,* University Press of Hawaii, 1972, 2nd edition, 1981; *The Exotic Birds of Hawaii,* Island Heritage, 1977; (contributor) S. A. Temple, editor, *Endangered Birds: Management Techniques for Threatened Species,* University of Wisconsin Press, 1978; (with Janet Kear) *The Hawaiian Goose: An Experiment in Conservation,* Poyser Ltd., 1980; (contributor) E. S. Reese and Philip Helfrich, editors, *The Natural History of Enewetak Atoll,* Tennessee Department of Energy, 1984.

Contributor to *Merit Student's Encyclopedia, Atlas of Hawaii,* and *Grzimek's Animal Life Encyclopedia.* Contributor of about 145 articles to scientific journals. Assistant editor of *Wilson Bulletin,* 1950-51, and *Auk* (of American Ornithological Union), 1953-54; member of editorial board, *Medical Bulletin* (of University of Michigan), 1961-64; member of editorial committee, East-West Center Press, 1968-70.

*   *   *

BERGER, Evelyn Miller 1896-

PERSONAL: Born November 7, 1896, in Hanford, Calif.; daughter of George Amos (a Methodist bishop) and Margaret (Ross) Miller; married Jesse Arthur Berger, June 16, 1939 (deceased); married C. Maxwell Brown, November 20, 1972. *Education:* Stanford University, A.B., 1921, M.A., 1930; Columbia University, Ph.D., 1932. *Home:* 1830 Alice St., Oakland, Calif. 94612. *Office:* East Bay Psychological Center, 315 14th St., Oakland, Calif. 94612.

CAREER: Teacher in Panama and at high schools in California; Allegheny College, Meadville, Pa., associate professor of Spanish and dean of women, 1932-36; University of Idaho, Moscow, dean of women, 1936-37; San Diego State College (now San Diego State University), San Diego, Calif., dean of women, 1937-38; East Bay Psychological Center, Oakland, Calif., administrative director, beginning 1941.

Teacher and director of Casa Espanola, University of the Pacific, summer sessions, 1929-30. Diplomate in counseling, American Board of Examiners in Professional Psychology; licensed psychologist and marriage and family counselor, State of California; corporate member, American Institute of Family Relations. Conductor of television programs, "Crosswinds" and "It's a Family Affair," KRON-TV, San Francisco. Has also done social service and field work with youth in Chile and Argentina for the Methodist Church. Member of board of directors, Fred Finch Children's Home; trustee, Scarritt College.

MEMBER: American Psychological Association (fellow), American Association of Marriage Counselors (fellow), International Council of Psychologists, National Council on Family Relations, National Vocational Guidance Association, Academy of Religion and Mental Health, American Association of University Women, Western Psychological Association, California State Marriage Counseling Association, California State Psychological Association, California Writers' Club, Family Relations Council of Northern California, Phi Beta Kappa, Kappa Delta Pi, Phi Sigma Iota, Pi Lambda Theta.

AWARDS, HONORS: D.Ph. from University of the Pacific, 1960; received Tower Award from Scarritt College.

WRITINGS: Triangle: The Betrayed Wife, Nelson-Hall, 1971; (with Bonnie Winters) *Social Studies in the Open Classroom: A Practical Guide,* Teachers College Press, 1973; *Writing a Religious Play,* San Leandro Printing Service, 1978; *This One Thing I Do,* Fairway Press, 1984.

Author of books written in Spanish, all published by Methodist Press, Santiago, Chile: *La Huerfana,* 1922; *La Joven,* 1923; *El Hogar social,* 1923. Also author of *Extracurricular Activities for the Spanish Department,* 1932. Author of pamphlets. Contributor of articles on youth and family problems to numerous periodicals.

*   *   *

BERGER, Michael (Louis)   1943-

PERSONAL: Surname is pronounced *Ber*-jer; born February 11, 1943, in Boston, Mass.; son of Clarence Quinn (an educational consultant) and Ethel J. (a social worker; maiden name, Goldberg) Berger; married Linda A. Cannizzo (a speech clinician), October 9, 1976. *Education:* Harvard University, B.A., 1965; Yale University, M.A.T., 1966; Columbia University, Ed.D., 1972. *Home:* Flat Iron Rd., Bates Acres, Great Mills, Md. 20634. *Office:* Division of Human Development, St. Mary's College of Maryland, St. Mary's City, Md. 20686.

CAREER: High school social studies teacher in Englewood, N.J., 1966-69; Marymount College, Tarrytown, N.Y., instructor in education, 1971-72; Fordham University, New York, N.Y., assistant professor of education, 1972-77, director of Institute in Urban Education, 1972-74; St. Mary's College of

Maryland, St. Mary's City, associate professor, 1977-82, professor of education, 1982—, director of teacher education, 1977—, acting chairman of Division of Human Development, 1984—.

Fulbright senior lecturer/research scholar, Universidade de Aveiro, Portugal, 1983. New York State Council on Social Education, president, 1973-74, member of executive committee, 1974-77; member of board of directors of New York State Council for the Social Studies, 1974-76; team leader (chairman) of National Association of State Directors of Teacher Education and Certification accreditation visits, 1977, 1979; coordinator of Maryland Association of Small Teacher Education Programs, 1978-81. Member and chairperson of subcommittee on new areas of certification, professional standards and teacher education advisory board, Maryland State Board of Education, 1978-81; Maryland State Board for Higher Education, member of advisory group, statewide review of education programs, 1979-81, member of advisory task force on higher education and the public schools, 1984—.

MEMBER: American Educational Research Association, American Educational Studies Association, National Council for the Social Studies, Authors League of America, Authors Guild, National Writers Club (professional member), American Association of State and Local History, History of Education Society, History of Science Society, Society for the History of Technology, Society of Automotive Historians, Antique Automobile Club of America, Maryland Association of Teacher Educators (member of executive board, 1979-80), Phi Delta Kappa (former faculty sponsor). *Awards, honors:* Certificate of merit, Phi Delta Kappa, 1976, 1977; Thomas McKean Memorial Cup, Antique Automobile Club of America, 1980, for significant contributions to automotive history.

WRITINGS: Violence in the Schools: Causes and Remedies, Phi Delta Kappa Educational Foundation, 1974; *The Public Education System,* F. Watts, 1977; (contributor) P. R. Baker and W. H. Hall, *The American People,* Sadlier-Oxford, 1977; (contributor) Baker and Hall, *The Growth of a Nation,* Sadlier-Oxford, 1977; *Firearms in American History,* F. Watts, 1979; *The Devil Wagon in God's Country: The Automobile and Social Change in Rural America, 1893-1929,* Archon Books, 1979; *An Album of Aircraft Testing,* F. Watts, 1981. Also author of scripts for three media programs; contributor of chapters to six books. Contributor of approximately forty articles and reviews to professional journals and popular magazines, including *Road & Track, Education Week, Michigan Quarterly Review, Antiques Journal, Hadassah Magazine,* and *Maine Life.*

WORK IN PROGRESS: Selecting and critiquing articles and books for inclusion in *The Automobile: A Reference Guide,* for Greenwood Press.

SIDELIGHTS: Michael Berger told *CA:* "*The Automobile: A Reference Guide* will be the first major attempt to list and describe the impact of the automobile on American history and life. This will be accomplished through a series of bibliographical essays, each devoted to one specific area of the car's influence. As such, it hopefully will prove a powerful reference tool for students of automotive history and will indirectly contribute to additional work in a field that has been somewhat neglected given the pervasiveness of the car in twentieth-century American life.

"Despite an increasing list of credits, I continue to be in sympathy with an observation made, I believe, by Dorothy Parker: 'I do not enjoy writing, but I like having written.'"

AVOCATIONAL INTERESTS: Collecting various artifacts of Americana, gardening.

* * *

BERNABEI, Alfio 1941-

PERSONAL: Born December 23, 1941, in Dovadola, Italy; son of Dante and Maria (Leoni) Bernabei. *Education:* Attended Wallbrook College, 1970-71; University of Reading, B.A., 1974. *Home:* 73 South Hill Park, London N.W.3, England.

CAREER: Free-lance journalist, 1969; Bite Theatre Group, London, England, director, 1975—. *Military service:* Italian Army, 1962-63.

MEMBER: Theatre Writers Union.

AWARDS, HONORS: Italy's National Drama Award, 1962, for ''Incontri.''

WRITINGS—Plays, except as indicated: ''Incontri'' (three-act; title means ''Meetings''), 1962, first produced in Milan, Italy, at Centro Culturale I Rabdomanti, 1963; ''The Jump'' (two-act), first produced in Reading, England, at University of Reading, 1973; ''Gastarbeiter'' (two-act; title means ''Guest Workers''), first produced in Cologne, Germany, at Katz Pott am Bonnerstrasse, 1974, English translation produced as ''Gast,'' in Edinburgh, Scotland, at Edinburgh Festival, 1976; ''The Bite'' (one-act), first produced in London at Institute of Contemporary Art, 1975.

''Grunwicks'' (two-act), first produced in Edinburgh at Edinburgh Festival, 1977; ''In Memory Now,'' first produced in Edinburgh at Edinburgh Festival, 1981; ''Periphery in Mind'' (platform reading), first produced in London at Barbican Centre by Royal Shakespeare Co., 1983; ''Mente Locale,'' first produced for Romagna Province, Italy, 1984.

Also author of ''Avventura,'' for BBC-TV, 1971. Contributor to Italian magazines and newspapers.

WORK IN PROGRESS: A play for Channel 4, ''The Keepers of the Ship.''

SIDELIGHTS: Alfio Bernabei comments: ''I write plays about important social issues, placing them within a historical context. The themes of the plays so far (the insurgence of neo-fascism in parts of Europe, the Chilean coup of 1973, the plight of migrant workers, etc.) indicate the importance I attach to aspects of international politics.''

Most of Bernabei's plays have been written for the Bite Theatre Group which he established in 1975. Bernabei has lived in France and Germany, and traveled in Latin America and Africa.

* * *

BERRIGAN, Edmund Joseph Michael, Jr. 1934-1983 (Ted Berrigan)

PERSONAL: Born November 15, 1934, in Providence, R.I.; died July 4, 1983, in New York, N.Y.; married Sandra Alper; married second wife, Alice Notley; children: Kate, David, Anselm, Edmond. *Education:* University of Tulsa, B.A., 1959, M.A., 1962. *Residence:* New York, N.Y.

CAREER: Editorial assistant, *Art News;* editor and publisher, ''C'' Press and *C* Magazine. Teacher in poetry workshop in St. Mark's Art Project, New York, N.Y., 1966-67; visiting lecturer for Writer's Workshop at University of Iowa, Iowa City, 1968-69; also taught at Yale University, University of Michigan, the Kerouac School, Boulder, Colo., and Essex University, Essex, England. Poet-in-residence, Northeastern Illinois University, 1969-76, and City College of the City University of New York. Member of board of advisors, poetry project of St. Mark's. *Military service:* U.S. Army, 1954-57.

AWARDS, HONORS: Poetry Foundation award, 1964, for *The Sonnets.*

WRITINGS—All under name Ted Berrigan; poetry, except as indicated: *A Lily for My Love: 13 Poems,* privately printed, 1959; (contributor) *Despair: Poems to Come Down By,* F---You Press, c. 1960; *Galileo: Or Finksville* (play), privately printed, 1964; *The Sonnets,* ''C'' Press, 1964, reprinted, Grove, 1967; (with Ron Padgett) *Seventeen* (plays), ''C'' Press, 1965; (with Padgett and Joe Brainard) *Some Things* (drawings and poems), privately printed, 1965; *Living with Chris,* Boke Press, 1966; *Many Happy Returns to Dick Gallup,* Angel Hair, 1967; (with Padgett and Brainard) *Bean Spasms* (poetry and art), Kulchur Press, 1967; *Many Happy Returns: Poems,* Corinth Books, 1969; *Fragment: For Jim Brodey,* Cape Goliard Press, 1969; (with Anselm Hollo) *Doubletalk,* T. G. Miller, 1969; (with Padgett) *Noh,* privately printed, 1969.

(With Tom Clark, Allen Kaplan, and Padgett; in German and English) *Guillaume Apollinaire ist tot: Gedichte, Prosa,* Maerz (Frankfurt), 1970; *In the Early Morning Rain,* Cape Goliard Press, 1970, Grossman, 1971; (with Anne Waldman) *Memorial Day,* Poetry Project, 1971; *Train Ride,* Vehicle Editions, 1971; (with Clark and Padgett) *Back in Boston Again,* Telegraph Books, 1972; *The Drunken Boat,* Adventures in Poetry, 1974; *A Feeling for Leaving,* Frontward Books, 1975; *Red Wagon,* Yellow Press, 1976; *Nothing for You,* Angel Hair, 1977; *Clear the Range,* Adventures in Poetry, 1977; (with Kenneth Koch) *ZZZZZZ,* edited by Kenward Elmslie, 1978; *So Going around Cities: New and Selected Poems, 1958-1979,* Blue Wind Press, 1980.

Editor; published by ''C'' Press, except as indicated: (With Padgett) Tom Veitch, *Literary Days: Selected Writings,* L. and E. Gude, 1964; Kenward Elmslie, *The Power Plant Poems,* 1965; Ron Padgett, *In Advance of the Broken Arm,* 1965; Dick Gallup, *Hinges: Poems,* 1965; Joe Ceravolo, *Fits of Dawn,* 1965; Michael Brownstein, *Behind the Wheel: Poems,* 1967.

Contributor to anthologies, including *Young American Poets,* edited by Paul Carroll, Follett, 1968, *The American Literary Anthology I,* Farrar, Straus, 1968, and *Sparklers,* Random House, 1969. Contributor to *Poetry, Art News, Art and Literature, Angel Hair, Mother,* and *World.*

SIDELIGHTS: In 1980, Alice Smith Haynes commented in *Dictionary of Literary Biography* that Ted Berrigan ''is consciously concerned with form and with his role as the creator; this emphasis is sometimes looked upon as playing 'games with the craft of poetry.' '' According to Haynes, ''when writing a longer poem,'' Berrigan ''sometimes switches lines around once he has finished the initial draft. He may even rearrange the sections of a poem until he achieves an effect that pleases him.'' ''These characteristics of artistic creation place Berrigan loosely within the modern art movement of abstract expressionism,'' Haynes indicated. ''Berrigan, in fact, likens his poetry to the paintings of Willem de Kooning, whose forceful, even violent, brush strokes show his unmistakable presence within his work, a unity of artist and canvas that abstract expressionists seek. In much the same way, Berrigan's presence in his poetry is illustrated by the unusual placement of lines.''

For example, in *So Going around Cities, Los Angeles Times Book Review* critic Peter Clothier pointed out, ''many of the lines or phrases in the sonnets (as in other poems) are interchangeable, repeated in new contexts, an old piece of cloth stitched back into a new quilt. . . . Similarly, large and small chunks of poems from sources as various as Rilke and Rimbaud are picked up and dropped into the text, becoming a part of the texture of the whole.'' Smith concluded that ''the value of [Berrigan's] poetry is defined as much by him as by an audience that appreciates his experiments.''

BIOGRAPHICAL/CRITICAL SOURCES: Hudson Review, summer, 1968; *Yale Review,* June, 1969; *Village Voice,* March 5, 1970; George MacBeth, *Interview with Ted Berrigan,* Ignu Publications, 1971; *Western Humanities Review,* summer, 1971; *Vort,* Number 2, 1972; *Dictionary of Literary Biography,* Volume V: *American Poets since World War II,* Gale, 1980; *Los Angeles Times Book Review,* June 1, 1980.

OBITUARIES: New York Times, July 7, 1983; *Washington Post,* July 9, 1983; *Newsweek,* July 18, 1983.†

*   *   *

BERRIGAN, Ted
See BERRIGAN, Edmund Joseph Michael, Jr.

*   *   *

BERRY, Mary Frances   1938-

PERSONAL: Born February 17, 1938, in Nashville, Tenn.; daughter of George F. and Frances (Southall) Berry. *Education:* Howard University, B.A., 1961, M.A., 1962; University of Michigan, Ph.D., 1966, J.D., 1970. *Office:* Department of History, Howard University, Washington, D.C. 20001.

CAREER: Central Michigan University, Mount Pleasant, assistant professor of history, 1966-68; Eastern Michigan University, Ypsilanti, assistant professor, 1968-70, associate professor of history, 1970; University of Maryland, College Park, associate professor of history, beginning 1969; University of Colorado, Boulder, faculty member, 1976-80; Howard University, Washington, D.C., professor of history and law, 1980—. Adjunct associate professor, University of Michigan, 1970-71. *Member:* American Historical Association, Organization of American Historians, American Society for the Study of Legal History.

WRITINGS: Black Resistance/White Law: A History of Constitutional Racism in America, Appleton, 1971; *Miliary Necessity and Civil Rights Policy: Black Citizenship and the Constitution, 1861-1868,* Kennikat, 1977; *Stability, Security, and Continuity: Mr. Justice Burton and Decision-Making in the Supreme Court,* Greenwood Press, 1978; (with John W. Blassingame) *Long Memory: The Black Experience in America,* Oxford University Press, 1982. Contributor of articles and reviews to history and law journals.

WORK IN PROGRESS: A history of constitutional amendments and the prospects for the Equal Rights Amendment.

*   *   *

BERTRAM, Noel
See FANTHORPE, R(obert) Lionel

BESSER, Gretchen R(ous)   1928-

PERSONAL: Born December 1, 1928, in Brooklyn, N.Y.; daughter of Ben (a businessman) and Sidonya (Menkes) Rous; married Albert G. Besser (an attorney), December 28, 1952; children: James, Neal, Brian. *Education:* Wellesley College, B.A., 1949; Sorbonne, University of Paris, graduate study, 1949-50; Middlebury College, M.A., 1950; Columbia University, Ph.D., 1967. *Home and office:* 227 Tillou Rd., South Orange, N.J. 07079.

CAREER: Fairleigh Dickinson University, Teaneck, N.J., instructor in French, 1955-57; Columbia University, New York, N.Y., preceptor in French, 1957-59, 1963-67; Herbert H. Lehman College of the City University of New York, Bronx, N.Y., assistant professor of French, 1967-70; Rutgers University, Newark, N.J., lecturer in French, 1972-73; National Ski Patrol System, national historian and international liaison in New Jersey, 1980—.

MEMBER: Modern Language Association of America, American Association of Teachers of French, Phi Beta Kappa.

AWARDS, HONORS: Fulbright scholar in France, 1949-50.

WRITINGS: (Translator) Jean Filloux, *The Crossing of the Copula,* Dodd, 1954; *Balzac's Concept of Genius,* Droz (Geneva), 1969; (translator) Gabriel Cousin, *Journey to the Mountain Beyond,* Avon, 1973; (translator) Georges Michel, *Aggression,* Avon, 1973; *Nathalie Sarraute,* G. K. Hall, 1979; *The National Ski Patrol: Samaritans of the Snow,* Countryman Press, 1983.

Contributor to *Columbia Dictionary of Modern European Literature.* Author of ski column for Worrall Publications, 1984—. Contributor of articles and reviews to *French Review, Romantic Review, Nineteenth-Century French Studies, Ski, National Patroller,* and *Eastern Skier.*

WORK IN PROGRESS: A book on the causes, prevention, and treatment of ski injuries; articles on skiing.

SIDELIGHTS: Gretchen R. Besser's involvement with the volunteer winter rescue organization known as the National Ski Patrol began in the late 1960s, when Besser was skiing in Vermont and saw a small boy injured. Though an expert skier, she was powerless to help him, for she had no knowledge of effective rescue techniques. ''I said to myself,'' she told Martta Rose in the *New York Times,* ''Wouldn't it be wonderful to know what to do in such situations?'' Shortly thereafter, Besser joined the National Ski Patrol. Acceptance to the patrol requires skiing competence, completion of courses in advanced first-aid and emergency care (including specialized courses such as frost-bite care and avalanche rescue), and the ability to handle a rescue toboggan, which can weigh as much as three hundred pounds. Duties of the patrol include testing slopes for safety before they are opened to the public, making ''trail sweeps'' for injured skiers after trails close, and promoting skiing safety.

As the National Ski Patrol's historian and international liaison, Besser has travelled to Canada, Australia, France, and Japan; she speaks French, Spanish, German and Italian. Besser described her writing habits to *CA:* ''In the course of writing a book about her, I made the acquaintance of the French novelist, Nathalie Sarraute. . . . Her work habits have strongly influenced my own. She writes every morning from nine to twelve, winter and summer, Sundays and weekdays, without interruption. I try to follow her regimen as nearly as I can, for she has taught me that writing is a ceaseless discipline.''

AVOCATIONAL INTERESTS: Tennis, horseback riding, opera.

BIOGRAPHICAL/CRITICAL SOURCES: Books Abroad, winter, 1971; *New York Times,* February 5, 1984.

* * *

BESSETTE, Gerard 1920-

PERSONAL: Born February 25, 1920, in Sabrevois, Quebec, Canada; son of Jean-Baptiste and Victoria (Bertrand) Bessette; married Irene Bakowski (an attorney, law librarian, and professor), September 3, 1971. *Education:* Externat Classique Sainte-Croix, B.A., 1941; University of Montreal, licence es lettres and M.A., 1946, D.Litt., 1950. *Home:* 270 Frontenac St., Kingston, Ontario, Canada. *Office:* Department of French, Queen's University, Kingston, Ontario, Canada.

CAREER: University of Saskatchewan, Saskatoon, instructor, 1946-49, assistant professor of French, 1949-51; Duquesne University, Pittsburgh, Pa., assistant professor of French, 1952-58; Royal Military College, Kingston, Ontario, associate professor of French, 1958-60; Queen's University, Kingston, professor of French, 1960—.

MEMBER: Royal Society of Canada, Societe des Ecrivains Canadiens.

AWARDS, HONORS: Olympic Games, 1948, bronze medal; Literary Prize of Quebec, 1965, for *L'Incubation;* Governor General's Award, 1966, for *L'Incubation,* and 1972, for *Le Cycle.*

WRITINGS: Poemes temporels, Regain, 1954; *La Bagarre,* Cercle du Livre, 1958; *Le Libraire,* Rene Julliard, 1960, translation by Glen Shortliffe published as *Not for Every Eye,* Macmillan (Toronto), 1962; *Les Images en poesie canadienne-francaise,* Beauchemin, 1960; *Les Pedagogues,* Cercle du Livre, 1960; *L'Incubation,* Librairie Deom, 1965, translation by Shortliffe published as *Incubation,* Macmillan, 1967; *Une Litterature en ebullition,* Editions du Jour, 1968.

Le Cycle, Editions du Jour, 1971; *Trois Romanciers quebecois,* Editions du Jour, 1973; *La Commensale,* Editions Quinze, 1975; *Les Anthropoides,* Editions La Presse, 1977; *Mes romans et moi,* Editions H.M.H., 1979; *Le Semestre,* Editions Quebec/Amerique, 1979; *La Garden-Party de Christophine,* Editions Quebec/Amerique, 1980.

WORK IN PROGRESS: Research on French Canadian literature.

BIOGRAPHICAL/CRITICAL SOURCES: Patricia Smart, editor, *Litterature canadienne-francaise,* University Press of Montreal, 1969; Rejean Robidoux, *Livres et auteurs quebecois,* Editions Jumonville, 1971; Gerard Bessette, *Mes romans et moi,* Editions H.M.H., 1979.

* * *

BHAKTIVEDANTA SWAMI, A. C.
See PRABHUPADA, A. C. Bhaktivedanta

* * *

BHATT, Jagdish J(eyshanker) 1939-

PERSONAL: Born February 17, 1939; came to United States,

1961, naturalized citizen, 1976; son of Jeyshanker Mancharam and Kamala (Jeyshanker) Bhatt; married January 22, 1970; wife's name, Meena; children: Amar Jagdish, Anita Jagdish. *Education:* University of Baroda, B.Sc. (with honors), 1961; University of Wisconsin—Madison, M.S., 1963; further graduate study at University of New Mexico, 1966-67, University of California, Santa Barbara, 1968-69, and Stanford University, 1971-72; University of Wales, Ph.D., 1972. *Home:* 11 Midlands Dr., East Greenwich, R.I. 02818. *Office:* Department of Physics (Geology-Oceanography), Community College of Rhode Island, 400 East Ave., Warwick, R.I. 02886.

CAREER: Jackson Community College, Jackson, Mich., instructor in physics and chemistry, 1964-65; Oklahoma Panhandle State College (now University), Goodwill, instructor in geology and physical sciences, 1965-66; University of Northern Iowa, Cedar Falls, instructor in geology, summer, 1967; Stanford University, Stanford, Calif., research scholar and scientist in geology, 1971-72; State University of New York at Buffalo, assistant professor of oceanography, geology, and environmental sciences, 1972-74; Community College of Rhode Island, Warwick, assistant professor, 1974-79, associate professor, 1979-84, professor of geology and oceanography, 1984—.

Member of Rhode Island Ocean Technology Task Force Committee, 1975-76. Developed courses in oceanography and programs in ocean training and off-shore technology. Geo-Resources and environmental consultant, 1972-80.

MEMBER: International Oceanographic Foundation, Geological Society of America, Oceanic Society.

AWARDS, HONORS: Wolfson doctoral fellowship at University of Wales, 1970-71; nominee, Chancellor's Award for Excellence in Teaching, State University of New York at Buffalo, 1973, Jefferson Award, 1983, and Distinguished Teacher Award, Community College of Rhode Island Foundation, 1984; honored as ''Contemporary Author'' by Archives of Bowling Green State University, 1983.

WRITINGS: Laboratory Manual on Physical Geology, Guymon, 1966; *Laboratory Manual on Physical Sciences,* Guymon, 1966; *Cretaceous History of Himalayan Geosyncline,* Guymon, 1966.

(Contributor) J. G. C. Anderson, A. P. Macmillan, and John Platt, editors, *Mineral Exploitation and Economic Geology,* University of Wales, 1971; *Environmentology: Earth's Environment and Energy Resources,* Modern Press, 1975; *Geochemistry and Petrology of South Wales Main Limestone (Mississippian),* Modern Press, 1976; *Geologic Exploration of Earth* (manual), Modern Press, 1976; *Oceanography: Exploring the Planet Ocean,* with instructor's manual, Van Nostrand, 1978, 2nd edition, Celecom, 1983; *Applied Oceanography: Mining, Energy, and Management,* University Microfilms, 1979.

(Coordinator) *Applied Oceanography Manuals,* Community College of Rhode Island Press, 1983, Volume I: *Mineral Resources and Geologic Processes,* Volume II: *Marine Fisheries,* Volume III: *Sea-Farming,* Volume IV: *Ocean Energy,* Volume V: *Sea Mammals,* Volume VI: *Marine Pollution,* Volume VII: *Underwater Habitat by Man.* Contributor to marine/earth scientific journals in England and the United States.

WORK IN PROGRESS: Trace Elemental Distribution in the Marine Carbonates of the South Wales Main Limestone Series (Lower Carboniferous); Exploring the Earth's History: Laboratory Manual; Pacific Resources Consortium, a research project to be presented at ''Oceans 86'' conference; *Ocean*

Enterprise; Odyssey of the Damned, a science fiction novel; *Odyssey of Perception: Selected Poems.*

SIDELIGHTS: Jagdish J. Bhatt writes that his contributions to the study of geology and oceanography include a demonstration of the role of bacteria in the formation of nodular cherts in marine limestones, explanation of the true geochemical and geological nature of South Wales marine limestones, and development of educational curricula on marine technology. He feels that his books provide a comprehensive treatment of contemporary issues of environmental pollution, energy resources, population, food technology, and global management of earth's resources, and a most comprehensive treatment of theoretical and practical ocean-related matters.

Bhatt told *CA:* "As a writer I have always been driven by the philosophy of local to global cooperation as the best way to fulfill the challenge of freeing ourselves from the earthly drudgeries of energy and food shortages, population and pollution dilemma, and from the rising entropy of stress per capita particularly during the present century.

"I consider that the art of organized-thoughts expression is the main business of writing. Therefore, it is a *sine qua non* that writers aim this art not for their ego-pivoting instrument of fame but use it as a powerful means of circumventing human shortcomings, including eradication of intellectual provincialism. By the same token, the art of creative communication (regardless of the writer's background as a scientist, poet, or philosopher) should consistently be affirmed as a fire of imagination ready to erode the darkness of our superfluous values, artificial barriers, wars, racism, colonialism and various other unproductive madness permanently from the face of the planet before mankind embraces the fascinating virgin terrain of the twenty-first century. At the near end of the present century, I cannot resist the temptation of envisioning mankind's unified gift of a world society relatively free of the above mentioned scars and dilemmas. Perhaps writers, through the power of constructive expression, could significantly contribute in their own significant way. The joy of such a gift remains in the fact that we may redeem all the historic blunders we have ever made since we came to be known as *Homo sapien,* that is, man the wise, with a single mighty stroke of progress!

"Another immediate challenge writers of the world at present are facing is the issue of human rights. Although this issue transcends the planetary spatio-temporal complex of geography and history, let us not ignore equally vital issues of human responsibilities and human obligations. Writers of diversified backgrounds must keep the flame of the above-mentioned trinity in the limelight, particularly in light of the fact that it is a prerequisite for our gift to the younger generations of the next century.

"Finally, writers must make a concerted local to global effort to guard the indispensible values, including the fabric of our society—family unity—against the juggernaut technology. Although technology yields constructive fruits of communication, transportation and myriads of materialistic comforts and pleasures, its latent power of dehumanization must not be taken for granted. Otherwise we have little choice but to drown in the deluge of change.

"I have quickly flashed some of these reflections in the hope that readers of *CA* will become aware of the responsibility and challenge of writing in coming years. The art of writing demands martinet discipline of mind and dedication to one's mission in life, and unfortunately during the process of creative writing beloved ones often suffer a great deal. In the final analysis, it is worth the commitment if the quality of one's work is effective in erasing a fraction of our contemporary shadows."

*　　*　　*

BIBO, Bobette
　　See GUGLIOTTA, Bobette

*　　*　　*

BIEGEL, Paul 1925-

PERSONAL: Born March 25, 1925, in Bussum, Netherlands; son of Herman (a merchant) and Madeleine (Povel) Biegel; married Marijke Straeter (a social worker), September 10, 1960; children: Leonie, Arthur. *Education:* Attended University of Amsterdam. *Home:* Keizersgracht 227, Amsterdam, Netherlands.

CAREER: "De Radiobode" (radio weekly), Amsterdam, Netherlands, editor, 1948-65; Koevesdi (press agency), Amsterdam, editor, 1965-67; Ploegsma (publishing firm), Amsterdam, editor, 1967-69; free-lance writer, 1969—. Text writer for "Marten Toonder Comics." Advisor to Van Holkema en Warendorf (publishing firm), Bussum, Netherlands, 1969—.

MEMBER: Dutch Society of Writers (V.V.L.), Dutch Society of Literature.

AWARDS, HONORS: Best children's book of the year award from Collective Promotion of Dutch Books (CPNB), 1965, for *Het sleutelkruid;* award from Children's Jury of Amsterdam, 1970, for *De tuinen van Dorr;* Golden Pencil award from CPNB, 1972, for *De kleine kapitein;* Silver Pencil award from CPNB, 1972, and prize from Jan Campert Foundation, 1973, for *De twaalf rovers;* State Prize, 1973, for complete works; Silver Pencil awards from CPNB, 1974, for *Het olifantenfeest,* and 1982, for *Haas, eerste boek: Voorjaar.*

WRITINGS—In English translation; originals all published in Haarlem, Holland: *Het sleutelkruid,* 1964, translation by Gillian Hume and the author published as *The King of the Copper Mountains,* F. Watts, 1969; *Ik wou dat ik anders was,* 1967, translation by Hume and the author published as *The Seven-Times Search,* Dent, 1971; *De tuinen van Dorr,* 1969, translation by Hume and the author published as *The Gardens of Dorr,* Dent, 1975.

De twaalf rovers, 1971, translation by Patricia Crampton published as *The Twelve Robbers,* Dent, 1974, Puffin, 1977; *De kleine kapitein,* 1971, translation by Crampton published as *The Little Captain,* Dent, 1971; *Het olifantenfeest,* 1973, translation by Crampton published as *The Elephant Party,* Puffin, 1977; *De kleine kapitein in het land van waan en wijs,* 1973, translation by Crampton published as *The Little Captain and the Seven Towers,* Dent, 1973; *Het stenen beeld,* 1974, translation by Crampton published as *Far Beyond and Back Again,* Dent, 1977.

De kleine kapitein en de schat van schrik en vreze, 1975, translation by Crampton published as *The Little Captain and the Pirate Treasure,* Dent, 1980; *Het spiegelkasteel,* 1976, translation by Crampton published as *The Looking-Glass Castle,* Blackie & Son, 1979; *De dwergjes van Tuil,* 1977, translation by Crampton published as *The Dwarfs of Nosegay,* Blackie & Son, 1978; *De rover Hoepsika,* 1977, translation by Crampton published as *The Robber Hopsika,* Dent, 1978; *Twaaf sloeg de klok,* 1974, translation by Crampton published as *The Clock Struck Twelve,* Glover & Blair, 1979; *De brieven van de generaal,* 1977, translation by Crampton published as *Letters from the General,* Dent, 1979; *De toverhoed,* 1979, translation by Crampton published as *The Tin Can Beast and Other Stories,* Glover & Blair, 1980; *De vloek van Woestewolf,* 1974, translation by Crampton published as *The Curse of the Werewolf,* Blackie & Son, 1981; *Virgilius van Tuil,* 1978, translation by Crampton published as *The Fattest Dwarf of Nosegay,* Blackie & Son, 1980; *Virgilius van Tuil op zoek naar een taart,* 1979, translation by Crampton published as *Virgil Nosegay and the Cake Hunt,* Blackie & Son, 1981.

Virgilius van Tuil overwintert bij de mensen, 1982, translation by Crampton published as *Virgil Nosegay and the Wellington Boots,* Blackie & Son, 1984; *Jiri,* 1981, translation by Crampton published as *Crocodile Man,* Dent, 1982.

In Dutch; published in Haarlem, Holland, except as indicated: *De gouden gitaar* (title means "The Golden Guitar"), 1962; *Het grote boek* (title means "The Great Book"), 1962; *De kukelhaan* (title means "Crow Cockerel"), 1964; *Het lapjesbeest* (title means "Patch-Animal"), 1964; *Kinderverhalen* (title means "Chidren's Stories"), 1966; *De rattenvanger van Hameln* (title means "The Pied Piper of Hamlin"), 1967; *De zeven fabels uit Ubim* (title means "The Seven Fables from Ubim"), 1970; *Sebastiaan Slorp,* 1971; *Reinaart de vos* (title means "Reynard the Fox"), 1972; *Wie je droomt ben je zelf* (title means "You Are the Ones You Dream Of"), Collective Promotion of Dutch Books (CPNB), 1977.

Virgilius van Tuil en de rijke oom uit Zweden (title means "Virgil Nosegay and the rich uncle from Sweden"), 1980; *Haas, eerste boek: Voorjaar* (title means "Hare, first book: Spring"), 1981; *Haas, tweede boek: Zomer* (title means "Hare, second book: Summer"), 1982; *Haas, derde boek: Najaar* (title means "Hare, third book: Autumn"), 1982; *Tante Mathilde en de sterren van de Grote Beer* (title means "Aunt Mathilda and the Stars of Big Dipper"), 1984; *De zwarte weduwe* (title means "The Black Widow"), 1984.

Also author of television series, "De vloek van woestewolf."

WORK IN PROGRESS: Japie en de dingen.

SIDELIGHTS: Paul Biegel told *CA:* "I was born in an estatelike home with a huge garden, two parents, two brothers, six sisters, a German maid, a gardener, and a dog. I remember a lot, but I am convinced it is the memories without words, of the years before a child has words to [his] disposition (Adam before he named the things of paradise) that the source of any one's creative urge lies. And the writer, for the rest of his life, tries in vain to find words for it."

Biegel's award-winning *The Little Captain* is described by a *Times Literary Supplement* critic as "a story told with extreme art, especially in the light yet memorable opening." *Times Literary Supplement* reviewer Cara Changeau indicates that *The Curse of the Werewolf* also "has a strong story line using time-honoured features with a judicious mix of the suitably sinister and downright comic."

BIOGRAPHICAL/CRITICAL SOURCES: Times Literary Supplement, April 28, 1972, March 27, 1981.

*   *   *

BIJOU, Sidney W(illiam)   1908-

PERSONAL: Born November 12, 1908, in Baltimore, Md.;

married Janet R. Tobias, August 31, 1934; children: Robert Keneth, Judith Ann. *Education:* Attended Lehigh University, 1928-30; University of Florida, B.S., 1933; Columbia University, M.A., 1937; University of Iowa, Ph.D., 1941. *Politics:* Democrat. *Home:* 5131 North Soledad Primera, Tucson, Ariz. 84718. *Office:* Department of Psychology and Special Education, University of Arizona, Tucson, Ariz. 84721.

CAREER: Board of Education, New York, N.Y., psychologist, 1936-37; State Mental Hygiene Clinic and Hospital, Farnhurst, Del., psychologist, 1937-39; Wayne County Training School, Northville, Mich., research associate, 1941-42, 1946-47; Indiana University at Bloomington, assistant professor of psychology and director of graduate training clinic, 1946-48; University of Washington, Seattle, associate professor, 1948-51, professor of psychology, 1951-65, director of Gatzert Institute for Child Development, 1948-65; University of Illinois at Urbana-Champaign, professor of psychology, director of Child Behavior Laboratory, and member of Institute for Research on the Exceptional Child, 1965-75; University of Arizona, Tucson, adjunct professor of psychology and special education, 1975—. Associate, Center for Advanced Study, University of Illinois, 1972. Member of mental health study section, National Institutes of Health, 1959-63; member of National Science Advisory Board and National Program on Early Childhood Education. Consultant to American Institute of Research. *Military service:* U.S. Army Air Forces, Office of Air Surgeon, 1942-46; became captain.

MEMBER: International Society for the Study of Behavior Development, American Psychological Association (president of Division of Development Psychology, 1965-66), Psychonomic Society, Society for Research in Child Development, Society for Behavior Therapy and Experimental Psychiatry, American Association of University Professors, Midwestern Psychological Association (member of council, 1976-78), Association of Behavior Analysts (president, 1978).

AWARDS, HONORS: National Institutes of Mental Health senior research fellow, 1961-62; American Association on Mental Deficiency research award, 1974; University of Veracruz (Mexico) certificate of merit, 1974; Fulbright-Hays fellowship at Universidad Central de Venezuela; Japan Society for the Promotion of Science fellowship, 1978; Career Research Award, American Academy of Mental Retardation, 1980; Distinguished Scientist Award, Association of Retarded Citizens, 1980; G. Stanley Hall Award in Developmental Psychology, American Psychological Association, 1981; Edward A. Doll Award in Mental Retardation, American Psychological Association, 1984.

WRITINGS: (With D. M. Baer) *Child Development: A Systematic and Empirical Theory,* Appleton-Century-Crofts, Volume I, 1961, Volume II, 1965; (editor with Baer) *Readings in Experimental Analysis,* Appleton-Century-Crofts, 1967; (editor with Emilio Ribes-Inesta) *Behavior Modification: Issues and Extensions,* Academic Press, 1972; *Child Development: The Basic Stage of Early Childhood,* Prentice-Hall, 1976; (editor with E. Rayek-Zaga) *Analysis de la conducta applicade a ensenanza,* Editorial Trillas (Mexico), 1978; (with D. M. Baer) *Behavior Analysis of Child Development,* Prentice-Hall, 1978; (editor with R. Ruiz) *Behavior Modification: Contributions to Education,* Erlbaum Associates, 1981. Contributor of articles to psychology journals. Editor, *Journal of Experimental Child Psychology,* 1963-72; member of editorial board, *Journal of Behavior Therapy and Experimental Psychiatry, Psychological*

Record, Developmental Review, and *Education and Treatment of Children.*

*   *   *

BIMLER, Richard William   1940-

PERSONAL: Born August 28, 1940, in Hillside, Ill.; son of Arthur M. (a florist) and Mildred (a florist; maiden name Schultz) Bimler; married Hazel J. Reichmann, June 10, 1961; children: Diane, Robert, Michael. *Education:* Valparaiso University, B.A., 1963; Concordia Teachers' College, graduate study, 1965; University of Houston, graduate study, 1967-68; University of Missouri—Kansas City, M.A., 1972. *Religion:* Lutheran Church-Missouri Synod. *Office:* Board for Youth Services, Lutheran Church-Missouri Synod, 1333 South Kirkwood Rd., St. Louis, Mo. 63122.

CAREER: St. Andrew Lutheran Church, Houston, Tex., director of youth, 1963-68; Trinity Lutheran Church, Mission, Kan., director of education and youth, 1968-73; Lutheran Church-Missouri Synod, assistant to the president in youth ministry, social ministry, and evangelism of the Minnesota south district in Minneapolis, 1973-77, assistant executive secretary, Board of Youth Ministry in St. Louis, Mo., 1977-79, executive secretary, Board for Youth Services in St. Louis, Mo., 1979—. Active in inner-city work and a former Big Brother. All-Lutheran Youth Gathering, manager, 1973, Global Village manager, 1976, executive director, 1980, 1983, and 1986.

MEMBER: Lutheran Human Relations Association, Religious Education Association, Lutheran Education Association (former president), Department of Pastors and Christian Educators (president, 1968-72), Lutheran Camping Association.

WRITINGS—Published by Concordia, except as indicated: *Youth Ministry Resources,* 1970; *Pray, Praise, and Hooray!,* 1972; *77 Ways of Involving You in the Church,* 1977; *Lord, I Want to Celebrate,* 1980; *The New You,* 1982; *Grand Opening,* C.S.S. Publishing, 1983; *Youth Group Meeting Guide,* Group Books, 1984.

Contributor to *Issues, Advance, Interaction, Director of Christian Education Journal.*

WORK IN PROGRESS: Youth ministry research; parish organization handbook; a youth prayer book; retreats for youth; youth films.

*   *   *

BITTER, Gary G(len)   1940-

PERSONAL: Born February 2, 1940, in Hoisington, Kan.; son of Solomon and Elvera Bitter; married Kay Burgat (a writer), August 19, 1962; children: Steve, Mike, Matthew. *Education:* Kansas State University, B.S., 1962; Kansas State Teachers College (now Emporia State University), M.A., 1965; University of Michigan, additional study, 1965-66; University of Denver, Ph.D., 1970. *Home:* 8531 East Osborn, Scottsdale, Ariz. 85251. *Office:* College of Education, Arizona State University, Tempe, Ariz. 85287.

CAREER: Teacher of mathematics and science at public high schools in Derby, Kan., 1962-65, and mathematics in public schools in Ann Arbor, Mich., 1965-66; Washburn University, Topeka, Kan., instructor in mathematics education, 1966-67; Colorado College, Colorado Springs, instructor in mathematics and computer education, 1968-70; Arizona State University, Tempe, assistant professor, 1970-72, associate professor, 1973-77, professor of education, 1977—. Professor of mathematics education at University of Northern Colorado, summer, 1973, Montana State University, summer, 1975, Temple University, summer, 1980, and Boston University, summer, 1980. Lecturer at University of Colorado, 1968-70. Reviewer of science education proposals for the National Science Foundation, 1977. Consulting mathematics editor, General Cassette Corp., 1970-75; consultant to Kaman Nuclear Co., and to numerous school systems, government organizations, and corporations.

MEMBER: American Association of University Professors, American Education Research Association, Association of Educational Data Processing (member of national board of directors, 1974-75), Mathematical Association of America, National Council of Teachers of Mathematics, School Science and Mathematics, Association for Development of Instructional Systems, Association for Computing Machinery, Futuristic Society, Arizona Association of Educational Data Systems (president, 1972-74; member of board of directors, 1974-75), Arizona Association of Elementary-Kindergarten-Nursery Education, Arizona Association of Teachers of Mathematics (member of board of directors, 1972-75), California Mathematics Association, Phi Delta Kappa.

AWARDS, HONORS: National Science Foundation fellowships, summers, 1963-65, 1965-66, summers, 1967, 1968, 1970; Outstanding Childrens Book Award, National Science Teachers Association, 1975, 1979, 1981; National Migrant Educator of the Month Award, *Migrant Education News,* 1976.

WRITINGS: (With Lyle Mauland) *Limits: Computer Extended Calculus,* University of Denver Press, 1970; (with Mauland) *Functions: Computer Extended Calculus,* Denver University Press, 1970; (with W. Y. Gateley) *Basic for Beginners,* McGraw, 1970, 2nd edition, 1978; (with W. S. Dorn and D. L. Hector) *Computer Applications for Calculus,* Prindle, 1972; (with Jon Knaupp) *Mathematics Activity Manual,* Addison-Wesley, 1972; (with Gateley) *Basic Fibel,* R. V. Deckers, 1973, 2nd edition, 1980.

(Contributor) N. K. Silvaroli and Lynn Searfoss, editors, *Communications, Reading, and Mathematics,* D. A. Lewis Associates, 1975; (with Charles Geer) *Materials for Metric Instruction,* ERIC, 1975; (with K. Maurdeff and Jerald Mikesell) *Investigating Metric Measure,* McGraw, 1975; (with Mikesell) *Discovering Metric Measure,* McGraw, 1975; (with Tom Metos) *Exploring with Metrics,* Messner, 1975; (with Maurdeff and Mikesell) *Multiplication and Division Games and Ideas,* McGraw, 1976; (with Maurdeff and Mikesell) *Activities Handbook for Teaching the Metric System,* Allyn & Bacon, 1976; (with Maurdeff and Mikesell) *Addition and Subtraction Games and Ideas,* McGraw, 1976; (contributor) *Measurement in School Mathematics Yearbook,* National Council of Teachers of Mathematics, 1976; *Calculator Power* (six workbooks), EMC Corp., 1977; (with Metos) *Exploring with Pocket Calculators,* Messner, 1977; (with Mikesell) *Teachers Handbook of Metric Activities,* Allyn & Bacon, 1977; (with J. Engelhardt and J. Wiebe) *Math H.E.L.P.,* EMC Corp., 1977; (with Engelhardt and Wiebe) *One Step at a Time,* EMC Corp., 1977; *Exploring with Solar Energy,* Messner, 1978.

Activities Handbook for Teaching with the Hand-Held Calculator, Allyn & Bacon, 1980; (with wife, Kay Bitter and A. Kopplin) *Hand Calculator Games,* McGraw, 1981; *Microcomputers in Education,* Arizona State University, 1982; *Emerging Technology and Strategies for Marketing Educational Technology Innovation,* U.S. Department of Education, 1982; *Mi-*

crocomputer *Applications for Calculus,* Prindle, 1983; *Computers in Today's World,* Wiley, 1983; (with N. Watson) *The Apple Logo Primer,* Reston, 1983; (with R. Camuse) *Using a Computer in the Classroom,* Reston, 1983.

Contributor to *Encyclopedia of Computer Science,* 1983. Author of columns published in *Teacher,* 1980-81, *Educational Computer,* 1981—, and *Electronic Learning,* 1982-83. Also contributor to mathematics and education journals. *Two Year Mathematics Journal,* member of editorial board, 1970, editor of section, "The Computer Corner," 1973-79. Member of advisory board, *Teacher,* 1977-79; member of editorial board, *Computers in Science and Mathematics,* 1981, and *Electronic Publishing,* 1981-83. *School Science and Mathematics,* associate editor, 1980-81, editor, 1981—.

*   *   *

BITTON, Davis 1930-

PERSONAL: Born February 22, 1930, in Blackfoot, Idaho; son of Ronald Wayne and Lola (Davis) Bitton; married Peggy Carnell, June 1, 1955 (divorced, 1981); children: Ronald, Kelly, Timothy, Tera, Stephanie. *Education:* Brigham Young University, B.A., 1956; Princeton University, M.A., 1958, Ph.D., 1961. *Religion:* Church of Jesus Christ of Latter-day Saints. *Home:* 1032 East 400 S., Salt Lake City, Utah 84102. *Office:* Department of History, University of Utah, Salt Lake City, Utah 84112.

CAREER: University of Texas at Austin, instructor, 1959-62, assistant professor of history, 1962-64; University of California, Santa Barbara, assistant professor of history, 1964-66; University of Utah, Salt Lake City, associate professor, 1966-71, professor of history, 1971—. *Military service:* U.S. Army, 1953-55. *Member:* American Historical Association, Mormon History Association (president, 1970-71), Sixteenth Century Studies Council, Western Society for French History, Utah State Historical Society.

WRITINGS: The French Nobility in Crisis, 1560-1640, Stanford University Press, 1969; (editor) *The Reminiscences and Civil War Letters of Levi Lamoni Wight: Life in a Mormon Splinter Colony on the Texas Frontier,* University of Utah Press, 1970; *A Guide to Mormon Diaries and Autobiographies,* Brigham Young University Press, 1977; (with Leonard J. Arrington) *The Mormon Experience: A History of the Latter-day Saints,* Knopf, 1979; (with Gary L. Bunker) *The Mormon Graphic Image, 1834-1914,* University of Utah Press, 1983.

WORK IN PROGRESS: Early Modern Historiography; Biblical exegesis.

BIOGRAPHICAL/CRITICAL SOURCES: New York Times Book Review, August 10, 1980.

*   *   *

BIXBY, Ray Z.
See TRALINS, S(andor) Robert

*   *   *

BLACK, Maggie
See BLACK, Margaret K(atherine)

BLACK, Margaret K(atherine) 1921-
(Maggie Black, M. K. Howorth)

PERSONAL: Born September 22, 1921, in London, England; daughter of Humphrey Noel (a civil servant) and Gladys (Lewis) Howorth; married Robert Alastair Lucien Black (a university teacher), May 15, 1943 (deceased); children: Andrew Ian, Christopher James Robert. *Education:* Attended University of Witwatersrand and Sorbonne, University of Paris. *Religion:* Agnostic. *Home:* 167 Putney Bridge Rd., London SW15, England.

MEMBER: Authors Lending and Copyright Society, National Union of Journalists.

WRITINGS: Three Brothers: Two Young Explorers, Acorn Press, 1945; *Three Brothers and a Lady,* Acorn Press, 1947; *The Magic Way Readers,* three books, A.P.B. Bookstore (Johannesburg), 1950; *The Mabunga Family,* Institute of Race Relations, 1954; *The City Built on Gold,* Longmans, Green, 1957; (with others) *Happy Trek Readers,* five books, Longmans, Green, 1957; *A South African Holiday,* Longmans, Green, 1958; (editor with Lionel T. Bennett) *The Golden Journey: Anthologies of English Poetry for High Schools,* three books, A.P.B. Bookstore, 1959.

Johannesburg, Longmans, Green, 1961; (with Molly Brearley) *Honey Family,* three books, Educational Supply Association (London), 1961; *No Room for Tourists* (nonfiction), preface by Angus Wilson, Secker & Warburg, 1965.

Under name Maggie Black: *Waste Not, Eat Well,* M. Joseph, 1976; *Meat Preserving at Home,* International Publications Service, 1976; *One Hundred Ways with Cheese,* Charles Letts, 1976; *A Heritage of British Cooking,* Charles Letts, 1977; *Georgian Meals and Menus,* Kingsmead Reprints, 1977; *Homemade Butter, Cheese, and Yoghurt,* E. P. Publishing, 1977; *Cheesecakes,* Ward, Lock, 1980; (with Pat Havard) *Eating Naturally: Recipes for Food with Fibre,* Faber, 1980; (translator) Louisette Bertholle, *French Cooking for All,* Weidenfeld & Nicolson, 1982; *The Wholesome Food Cookbook,* David & Charles, 1982; *Barbecue with an International Flavour,* Foulsham, 1983.

Under name Maggie Black; editor; all by Isabella Mary Beeton; all published by Bobbs-Merrill; all 1977: *Mrs. Beeton's Favorite Cakes and Breads; Mrs. Beeton's Favorite Sweet Dishes; Mrs. Beeton's Favorite Recipes; Mrs. Beeton's Poultry and Game.* Also editor, with Susan Dixon, of *Mrs. Beeton's Cookery and Household Management,* 1980.

Also author of *The Bennet Readers,* "The Kindly Islands" (play), and of radio plays for children. Contributor of articles to *History Today, Herbalist,* and other magazines.

WORK IN PROGRESS: Food Smoking at Home; Food Folklore; Giving Parties; The Latchkey Kids' Cookbook; The Good Cheese Guide.

*   *   *

BLAKE, Peter (Jost) 1920-

PERSONAL: Born September 20, 1920, in Berlin, Germany; came to United States, 1940; naturalized U.S. citizen, 1944. *Education:* Attended University of London, 1939, Regent Street Polytechnic School of Architecture, and University of Pennsylvania, 1940; Pratt Institute, B.Arch., 1948. *Home:* 55 West 55th St., New York, N.Y. 10019. *Office:* Department of Architecture and Planning, Catholic University of America, Washington, D.C. 20064.

CAREER: Architectural Forum, New York City, writer, 1942-43, associate editor, 1950-54 and 1958-61, managing editor, 1961-64, editor-in-chief, 1964-72; Museum of Modern Art, New York City, curator of architecture and design, 1948-50; *House and Home,* architecture editor, 1955-57; Peter Blake & Julian Neski, Architects, New York City, partner, 1956-60; James Baker & Peter Blake, Architects, New York City, partner, 1964-71; *Architecture Plus,* editor-in-chief, 1972-75; Boston Architectural Center, School of Architecture, chairman, 1975-79; Catholic University of America, Washington, D.C., chairman of department of architecture and planning, 1979—. Member of board of directors of Interior Design Conference (Aspen, Colo.), 1965-70.

MEMBER: American Institute of Architects (fellow), Architectural League (vice-president in architecture of New York branch, 1966-68; president, 1971-72), Regional Planning Association.

AWARDS, HONORS: Citation, 1958, for design of American Architecture Exhibition sent to tour iron curtain countries; grant from Ford Foundation, 1960; Howard Myers Award from *Architectural Journal,* 1960; fellow, Graham Foundation for Advanced Studies in Fine Arts, 1962; Architecture Critics Medal, 1975.

WRITINGS: Marcel Breuer, Architect and Designer, Museum of Modern Art, 1949; (editor) *An American Synagogue for Today and Tomorrow: A Guide Book to Synagogue Design and Construction,* Union of American Hebrew Congregations, 1954; (editor) Breuer, *Sun and Shadow: The Philosophy of an Architect,* Dodd, 1955.

The Master Builders: Le Corbusier, Mies van der Rohe, Frank Lloyd Wright, Knopf, 1960, reprinted, Norton, 1976; *Le Corbusier: Architecture and Form,* Penguin, 1963; (with Robert Osborn) *The Everlasting Cocktail Party: A Layman's Guide to Culture Climbing,* Dial, 1964; *Frank Lloyd Wright: Architecture and Space,* Penguin, 1964; *God's Own Junkyard: The Planned Deterioration of America's Landscape,* Holt, 1964; *Mies van der Rohe: Architecture and Structure,* Penguin, 1964.

The New Forces, Royal Australian Institute of Architects, 1971; *Architecture for the New World: The Work of Harry Seidler,* Wittenborn, 1973; *Our Housing Mess, and What Can Be Done About It,* Institute of Human Relations Press, 1974; *Form Follows Fiasco: Why Modern Architecture Hasn't Worked,* Little, Brown, 1977.

Contributor to architecture journals, to popular magazines, and to newspapers. Contributing editor, *New York,* 1968-76.

*   *   *

BLAMIRES, David (Malcolm)   1936-

PERSONAL: Born May 4, 1936, in Heckmondwike, England; son of Clifford and Amy (Firth) Blamires. *Education:* Christ's College, Cambridge, B.A., 1957, M.A. and Ph.D., both 1963; also studied at Free University of Berlin, 1958. *Religion:* Society of Friends (Quakers). *Home:* 136 Wellington Rd., Manchester M14 6AR, England. *Office:* Department of German, University of Manchester, Manchester M13 9PL, England.

CAREER: University of Manchester, Manchester, England, assistant lecturer, 1960-63, lecturer, 1963-69, senior lecturer, 1969-73, reader in German, 1973—.

MEMBER: International Arthurian Society (member of committee of British branch, 1969-74), Modern Humanities Research Association, Association of University Teachers of German of Great Britain and Ireland, David Jones Society (honorary secretary), Friends' Historical Society.

WRITINGS: An Echoing Death (poems), privately printed, 1965; *Characterization and Individuality in Wolfram's "Parzival",* Cambridge University Press, 1966; *The Bible Half Hour* (essays), Beacon Hill Friends House, 1968.

(Coauthor) *David Jones: Artist and Writer,* Manchester University Press, 1971, 2nd edition, 1978; *Homosexuality from the Inside,* Social Responsibility Council, Religious Society of Friends, 1973; *A History of Quakerism in Liversedge and Scholes,* privately printed, 1973; (translator, with Peter Rickard, Alan Deyermond, Peter King, Michael Lapidge, and Derek Brewer) *Medieval Comic Tales,* D. S. Brewer, 1973; (author of introduction) Gerardus Cambrensis, *South Wales Echo,* Enitharmon Press, 1973; *Schoepferisches Zuhoeren* (title means "Creative Listening"), Religioese Gesellschaft der Freunde (Quaeker), 1974; (coauthor) *Towards a Theology of Gay Liberation,* SCM Press, 1977; *Herzog Ernst and the Otherworld Voyage: A Comparative Study,* Manchester University Press, 1979.

Also author of *Postscript to Homosexuality from the Inside,* Friends Homosexual Fellowship, 1982. Contributor of articles and reviews to religious and literary journals, including *Modern Language Review, German Life and Letters, Anglo-Welsh Review, Poetry Wales, Review of English Literature, Critical Quarterly,* and *Friends Quarterly.*

AVOCATIONAL INTERESTS: Topography (especially Orkney, Shetland, and Yorkshire), travel (Europe, Australia, Canada, and United States).†

*   *   *

BLATT, Burton   1927-

PERSONAL: Born May 23, 1927, in Bronx, N.Y.; son of Abraham W. (a manufacturer) and Jennie (Starr) Blatt; married Ethel Draizen, December 24, 1951; children: Edward Richard, Steven David, Michael Lawrence. *Education:* New York University, B.S., 1949; Columbia University, M.A., 1950; Pennsylvania State University, Ed.D., 1956. *Religion:* Jewish. *Home:* 106 Cedar Heights Dr., Jamesville, N.Y. 13078. *Office:* School of Education, 230 Huntington Hall, Syracuse University, Syracuse, N.Y. 13210.

CAREER: Teacher of special class for mentally retarded, New York, N.Y., 1949-56; Southern Connecticut State College, New Haven, associate professor, 1956-59, professor of special education and chairman of department, 1959-61; Boston University, Boston, Mass., professor of special education and chairman of department, 1961-69; Syracuse University, Syracuse, N.Y., Centennial Professor, director of Division of Special Education and Rehabilitation, and director of Center on Human Policy, 1969-76, dean of School of Education, 1976—.

Assistant commissioner and director, Division of Mental Retardation, Massachusetts Department of Mental Health, 1968-69. Appointed to first Connecticut State Advisory Council on Mental Retardation, 1959; former member of Massachusetts Special Commission on Retarded Children and State of New

York Committee for Children. Past member of national advisory committees, R & D Center for Handicapped Children at University of Indiana, United Cerebral Palsy, and National Society for the Prevention of Blindness; consultant to U.S. Office of Education and other federal and state agencies. *Military service:* U.S. Navy, 1945-46.

MEMBER: American Association on Mental Deficiency (vice-president of education, 1971-73; president, 1976-77), Council for Exceptional Children (president of Connecticut chapter, 1960; president of Teacher Education Division, 1969), Phi Delta Kappa.

AWARDS, HONORS: Outstanding Teacher Award, Boston University, 1965; Massachusetts Psychological Association Annual Award, 1967; Massachusetts Association for Retarded Children Annual Award, 1968; Northeast Region Education Award, American Association on Mental Deficiency, 1973; National Humanitarian Award, American Association on Mental Deficiency, 1974; Newell C. Kephart Memorial Award, Purdue University, 1974; New York Schools Teacher of Mentally Handicapped Bicentennial Award, 1976; L.H.D., Ithaca College, 1974; College of New Rochelle's Council for Exceptional Children Award, 1980; Pioneer Developmental Center Annual Award, 1983; Young Adult Institute of New York City Annual Award, 1983.

WRITINGS: (With Seymour B. Sarason and Kenneth Davidson) *The Preparation of Teachers: An Unstudied Problem in Education,* Wiley, 1962; (with Fred Kaplan) *Christmas in Purgatory: A Photographic Essay on Mental Retardation,* Allyn & Bacon, 1965, second edition, 1966; *The Intellectually Disfranchised: Impoverished Learners and Their Teachers,* Massachusetts Department of Mental Health, 1967.

Exodus from Pandemonium: Human Abuse and a Reformation of Public Policy, Allyn & Bacon, 1970; *Souls in Extremis: An Anthology on Victims and Victimizers,* Allyn & Bacon, 1973; *Revolt of the Idiots,* Exceptional Press, 1976; (with Douglas B. Klein and Robert Bogdan) *An Alternative Textbook in Special Education,* Love Publishing, 1977; (with A. Ozolins and J. McNally) *The Family Papers,* Exceptional Press, 1978; *The Professor,* Exceptional Press, 1978.

Published by University Park Press, except as indicated: *In and Out of Mental Retardation,* 1981; *In and Out of the University,* 1982; *In and Out of Books,* 1984; (editor with R. Morris) *Perspective in Special Education,* Scott, Foresman, 1984.

Contributor: Jerome Hellmuth, editor, *Learning Disorders,* Volume I, Special Child Publications, 1966; Hellmuth, editor, *The Disadvantaged Child,* Volume I, Special Child Publications, 1967; Robert B. Kugel and Wolf Wolfensberger, editors, *Changing Patterns in Residential Services for the Mentally Retarded,* President's Committee on Mental Retardation, 1969; Norman R. Bernstein, editor, *Diminished People: The Problems and Care of the Retarded,* Little, Brown, 1970; Jerome H. Rothstein, editor, *Mental Retardation: Readings and Resources,* Holt, 1971; Don L. Walker and Douglas P. Howard, editors, *Special Education: Instrument of Change in Education for the 70's,* University Press of Virginia, 1972; Robert M.W. Travers, editor, *Handbook of Research on Teaching,* 2nd edition, Rand McNally, 1973.

Author of foreword: Frances Kaplan and Sarason, *The Psycho-Educational Clinic,* Massachusetts Department of Mental Health, 1969; Donald Maietta and Don Sandy, *Baby Learns to Talk,* Stanwix, 1969; and various publications of Division of Special Education and Rehabilitation, Syracuse University.

Project director or co-author of a number of research reports, including *The Educability of Intelligence,* Council for Exceptional Children, 1969. Contributor of more than three hundred articles and reviews to journals. Contributor of a series of short stories to *Journal of Learning Disabilities,* 1983-84. Co-editor of series, "Segregated Settings and the Problem of Change," Division of Special Education and Rehabilitation, Syracuse University, 1972—. Member of editorial staff, *American Journal of Mental Deficiency,* 1957-63; consulting editor, *Mental Retardation,* 1963-72; member of editorial boards, *Seminars in Psychiatry,* 1968-70, *Journal of Learning Disabilities,* 1980—, *Journal* of the Association for the Severely Handicapped, 1980—, and *Teacher Education and Special Education,* 1982—; member of publications committee, Council for Exceptional Children, 1969-72; member of editorial advisory board, *Exceptional Parent,* 1971—; book review editor, *Exceptional Children,* 1972-76.

WORK IN PROGRESS: Ernest, Ruth, and Uncle Waldo.

*   *   *

BLEGVAD, Lenore   1926-

PERSONAL: Born May 8, 1926, in New York, N.Y.; daughter of Julius C. (a mechanical engineer) and Ruth (a teacher; maiden name, Huebschman) Hochman; married Erik Blegvad (an illustrator), September 12, 1950; children: Peter, Kristoffer. *Education:* Vassar College, B.A., 1947; studied art in New York, N.Y. and Paris, France. *Home:* 4 Crescent Mansions, 113 Fulham Rd., London S.W.3, England.

CAREER: Painter and writer. Exhibited abstract paper mache sculpture in London showing, 1975.

WRITINGS—All juveniles; all illustrated by husband, Erik Blegvad: *Mr. Jensen and Cat,* Harcourt, 1965; *One Is for the Sun,* Harcourt, 1968; *The Great Hamster Hunt,* Harcourt, 1969; *Moon-Watch Summer,* Harcourt, 1972; (editor) *Mittens for Kittens and Other Rhymes about Cats,* Atheneum, 1974; (editor) *Hark! Hark! the Dogs Do Bark: And Other Rhymes about Dogs,* Atheneum, 1975; (editor) *This Little Pig-a-wig and Other Rhymes about Pigs,* Atheneum, 1978; (editor) *The Parrot in the Garret and Other Rhymes about Dwellings,* Atheneum, 1982; *Anna Banana and Me,* Atheneum, in press.

SIDELIGHTS: Lenore Blegvad told *CA:* "I divide my time between writing and painting, and which one I do at any given moment is dictated by various things: mood, inspiration, location (we live half the year in London and half in the south of France). I find the creative effort for each equally exciting, arduous, and absorbing. The change from one occupation to the other brings new insights every time and somehow suits me to perfection."

Blegvad has studied under Moses Sayer, Andre Lhote, Fernand Leger, and other artists.

BIOGRAPHICAL/CRITICAL SOURCES: Book World, November 3, 1968, August 31, 1969; Doris De Montreville, editor, *Third Book of Junior Authors,* H. W. Wilson, 1972.

*   *   *

BLUE, Rose   1931-

PERSONAL: Surname originally Bluestone; born 1931, in New York, N.Y.; daughter of Irving (a pharmacist) and Frieda (Rosenberg) Bluestone. *Education:* Brooklyn College (now Brooklyn College of the City University of New York), B.A.; also attended Bank Street College of Education. *Politics:* Democrat. *Home:* 1320 51st St., Brooklyn, N.Y. 11219.

CAREER: Writer. Former teacher in public schools of New York, N.Y.; also taught in Bedford Stuyvesant Headstart program. Lyricist of popular songs. Member of Broadcast Music, Inc.

MEMBER: Authors Guild, Authors League of America, Mensa, Professional Women's Caucus.

AWARDS, HONORS: Best Book of the Year award, National Council of Social Studies, Childrens Book Council, 1979, for *Cold Rain on the Water;* Red Ribbon Award of the American Film Festival, for "Grandma Didn't Wave Back."

WRITINGS—Juvenile; all published by F. Watts, except as indicated: *A Quiet Place,* 1969; *Black, Black, Beautiful Black,* 1969; *How Many Blocks Is the World,* 1970; *Bed-Stuy Beat,* 1970; *I Am Here: Yo Estoy Aqui,* 1971; *Grandma Didn't Wave Back* (also see below), 1972; *A Month of Sundays,* 1972; *Nikki 108,* 1973; *We Are Chicano,* 1973.

The Preacher's Kid, 1975; *Seven Years from Home,* Raintree, 1976; *The Yo Yo Kid,* Raintree, 1976; *The Thirteenth Year,* 1977; *Cold Rain on the Water,* McGraw-Hill, 1979; *My Mother the Witch* (also see below), McGraw-Hill, 1981; *Everybody's Evy,* Berkley, 1983.

Teleplays; based on books of the same titles; produced by Multimedia for National Broadcasting Company, Inc.: "Grandma Didn't Wave Back," 1982; "My Mother the Witch," 1984.

Also author of five books for high-interest, low-reading-level series for Scholastic Press; author of five workbooks and twenty-five leaflets for Day Care Center personnel at Brooklyn College School of Education; also author of *Bright Tomorrow,* for Communications Skill Builders. Also author of lyrics for published and recorded songs, including "Drama of Love," "Let's Face It," "My Heartstrings Keep Me Tied to You," "Give Me a Break," and "Homecoming Party," for artists, including Damita Jo, Jodie Sands, and the Exciters. Feature writer for *Teacher, Day Care,* and *Action.* Contributor of short stories to Magazine Management and Sterling Group. Contributing editor, *Teacher.*

SIDELIGHTS: Rose Blue found available books about children inadequate when she was taking a course in children's literature at Bank Street College of Education, so she wrote *A Quiet Place.* "I feel that more sensitive, perceptive books dealing with realities of life and feelings of children are essential to children's literature," she says. "I have attempted to contribute this in my work."

BIOGRAPHICAL/CRITICAL SOURCES: New York Times Book Review, February 4, 1973.

*   *   *

BLYN, George 1919-

PERSONAL: Born May 2, 1919, in New York, N.Y.; son of Philip E. (a businessman) and Rose (Faiby) Blyn; married Charlotte Lilly (a physician), June 22, 1952; children: Stefany, Roslyn, Corliann. *Education:* Attended City College (now City College of the City University of New York), University of Bridgeport, and Boston University; University of Pennsylvania, B.A., 1951, M.A., 1953, Ph.D., 1961. *Home:* 511 Winding Way, Merion Station, Pa. 19066. *Office:* Department of Economics, Camden College of Arts and Sciences, Rutgers University, Camden, N.J. 08102.

CAREER: Villanova University, Villanova, Pa., instructor, 1954-61, assistant professor of economics, 1961-62; Rutgers University, Camden College of Arts and Sciences, Camden, N.J., assistant professor, 1961-62, associate professor, 1962-69, professor of economics, 1969—, chairman of department of business and economics, 1962-71, 1977-79, chairman of department of economics, 1983—. Rutgers University, chairman and member of numerous committees, college faculty senator, university faculty senator, advisor to student organizations, and member of university research council, 1966. Has presented papers at professional conferences. Research associate, Institute for Economic Development and Cultural Change, 1957-58. Actor in numerous productions at Rutgers University. *Military service:* U.S. Army, 1943-46.

MEMBER: American Economic Association, Association of Asian Studies, Association of American Geographers, Association for Indian Economic Studies, Delaware Valley Geographers Association, Beta Gamma Sigma. *Awards, honors:* Faculty research fellow, American Institute of Indian Scholars, 1965-66.

WRITINGS: Agricultural Crops in India: A Statistical Study of Output and Trends (monograph), National Income Unit, Ministry of Finance, Government of India, 1954; *Agricultural Trends in India, 1891-1947: Output, Availability, and Productivity,* University of Pennsylvania, 1966; (contributor) G. Demko and others, editors, *Population Geography,* McGraw, 1970; (contributor) C. N. Vakil and C. H. Shah, editors, *Agricultural Development in India: Policy and Problems,* Orient Longmans (Bombay), 1979; (contributor) Mahinder Chaudhry, editor, *Contributions to Asian Studies,* Volume XIII, E. J. Brill, 1979; (contributor) M. Dutta, editor, *Studies in United States-Asia Economic Relations,* Acorn Press, 1983. Also contributor of "The Indian Economy," to *Collier's Encyclopedia,* 1981; contributor of numerous articles to economics and geography journals, including *Economic Development and Cultural Change, Indian Journal of Nutrition and Dietetics, Indian Economic Journal, Indian Journal of Agricultural Economics, Indian Economic Review,* and *Indian Geographical Journal.*

WORK IN PROGRESS: Research on economic aspects of Punjab-Haryana farmers, the role of British civil servants in Punjab's rural development, the economic impact of the Ben Franklin bridge, and the economic geography of South Jersey.

SIDELIGHTS: George Blyn told *CA:* "[I] have sought to explain [the] economic transformation of India—in particular, the economic behavior of cultivator families—by integrating interdisciplinary graduate study of the region, economic theory, statistical methodology, and field observation, down to the village level."

*   *   *

BOGART, Leo 1921-

PERSONAL: Born September 23, 1921, son of Jacob (a jurist) and Rachel (Blum) Bogart; married Agnes Cohen, August 8, 1948; children: Michele, Gregory. *Education:* Brooklyn College (now Brooklyn College of the City University of New York), B.A., 1941; University of Chicago, M.A., 1948, Ph.D., 1950. *Home:* 135 Central Park West, New York, N.Y. 10023. *Office:* Newspaper Advertising Bureau, 1180 Avenue of the Americas, New York, N.Y. 10036.

CAREER: Standard Oil Company of New Jersey, New York City, opinion and communications research specialist, 1948-

51; McCann-Erickson, Inc., New York City, vice-president of market planning division, 1952-58; Revlon, Inc., New York City, director of market research, 1958-60; Newspaper Advertising Bureau, New York City, vice-president of market planning and research, 1960-66, executive vice-president and general manager, 1966—. Lecturer, Columbia University, 1953-60. *Military service:* U.S. Army, 1942-46.

MEMBER: World Association for Public Opinion Research (president, 1965-66), International Newspaper Advertising Executives (honorary life member), American Association for Public Opinion Research (president, 1966-67), American Psychological Association (fellow; president, consumer psychological division, 1971-72), American Sociological Association (fellow), Market Research Council (president, 1965-66), Radio-Television Research Council, American Marketing Association.

AWARDS, HONORS: Goldish Award of International Newspaper Promotion Association, 1966; Media/Scope medals, 1967 and 1969; award from American Association for Public Opinion Research, 1977; Market Research Council first achievement award, 1978; American Marketing Association attitude research first achievement award, 1982; International Circulation Managers Association achievement award, 1982.

WRITINGS: Age of Television, Ungar, 1956, revised edition, 1972; *Strategy in Advertising,* Harcourt, 1968, revised edition, Crain Books, 1984; (editor) *Current Controversies in Marketing Research,* Markham, 1969; (editor) *Social Research and the Desegregation of the U.S. Army,* Markham, 1969.

Silent Politics: Polls and the Awareness of Public Opinion, Wiley, 1972, revised edition, Transaction/Society, 1985; *Premises for Propaganda: The Cold War Operating Assumptions of the U.S. Information Agency,* Free Press, 1976; *Press and Public: Who Reads What, Where, When and Why in American Newspapers,* Lawrence Erlbaum, 1981. Contributor of more than one hundred articles to journals in his field.

*   *   *

BOGDANOR, Vernon   1943-

PERSONAL: Surname is accented on first syllable; born July 16, 1943, in London, England; son of Harry (a pharmacist) and Rosa Bogdanor; married Judy Evelyn Beckett (a doctor), July 27, 1972; children: two sons. *Education:* Queen's College, Oxford, B.A. (with first class honors), 1964; Nuffield College, Oxford, M.A., 1968. *Agent:* Caradoc King, A. P. Watt & Son, 26/28 Bedford Row, London WC1R 4HL, England. *Office:* Department of Politics, Brasenose College, Oxford University, Oxford, England.

CAREER: Oxford University, Oxford, England, tutor in politics and fellow of Brasenose College, 1966—, university lecturer in politics, 1967—.

WRITINGS: (Editor and contributor) *The Age of Affluence, 1951-1964,* Macmillan, 1970; (editor) *Disraeli: Lothair,* Oxford University Press, 1975; *Devolution,* Oxford University Press, 1979; *The People and the Party System: The Referendum and Electoral Reform in British Parties,* Cambridge University Press, 1981; (editor) *Liberal Party Politics,* Oxford University Press, 1983; *Multi-Party Politics and the Constitution,* Cambridge University Press, 1983; (co-editor) *Democracy and Elections,* Cambridge University Press, 1983; (editor) *Coalition Government in Western Europe,* Heinemann, 1983; *What Is Proportional Representation?,* Martin Robertson, 1984; (ed-

itor) *Parties and Democracy in Britain and America,* Praeger, 1984. Contributor to British periodicals, including *Spectator, Encounter,* and *Times Literary Supplement.*

WORK IN PROGRESS: A book on democratic government in the modern world.

SIDELIGHTS: Vernon Bogdanor's *Liberal Party Politics* is praised by Stephen Koss in the *Times Literary Supplement* as a collection of "highly intelligent essays." He adds: "The editor and his eleven-man team may be taken to constitute a community of interest in the best sense. Although their perspectives and methodologies differ . . . they refer respectfully and profitably to each other's published writings, and acknowledge mutual debts. All, of course, are recognized authorities."

BIOGRAPHICAL/CRITICAL SOURCES: Times Literary Supplement, June 3, 1983.

*   *   *

BOLES, John B.   1943-

PERSONAL: Born October 20, 1943, in Houston, Tex.; son of B. B. (a farmer) and Mary (McDaniel) Boles; married Nancy Gaebler, September 2, 1967; children: David Christopher, Matthew Thomas. *Education:* Rice University, B.A., 1965; University of Virginia, Ph.D., 1969. *Politics:* Democrat. *Religion:* "Baptist/Lutheran." *Home:* 8514 Prichett, Houston, Tex. 77096. *Office:* Department of History, Rice University, Houston, Tex. 77251.

CAREER: Towson State University, Baltimore, Md., assistant professor, 1969-72, associate professor, 1972-75, professor of history, 1975-77; Rice University, Houston, Tex., visiting associate professor of history, 1977-78; Tulane University, New Orleans, La., associate professor, 1978-80, professor of history, 1980-81; Rice University, professor of history, 1981—.

MEMBER: Southern Historical Association, Maryland Historical Society.

AWARDS, HONORS: National Endowment for the Humanities fellow in anthropology, 1976-77.

WRITINGS: Guide to the Papers of William Wirt (pamphlet), Maryland Historical Society, 1971; *The Great Revival, 1787-1805: The Origins of the Southern Evangelical Mind,* University Press of Kentucky, 1972; *Guide to the Papers of John Pendleton Kennedy* (pamphlet), Maryland Historical Society, 1972; (editor) *America: The Middle Period: Essays in Honor of Bernard Mayo,* University Press of Virginia, 1973; *Religion in Antebellum Kentucky,* University Press of Kentucky, 1976; (editor) *Maryland Heritage: Five Baltimore Institutions Celebrate the American Bicentennial,* Maryland Historical Society, 1976.

Black Southerners, 1619-1869, University Press of Kentucky, 1983; (editor) *Dixie Dateline: A Journalistic Portrait of the Contemporary South,* Rice University Studies, 1983.

Contributor of articles and reviews to history journals. Editor, *Maryland Historical Magazine,* 1974-77; managing editor, *Journal of Southern History,* 1983—.

WORK IN PROGRESS: Researching culture and religion in the Antebellum South; co-editing a series of historiographical essays for a book entitled *Interpreting Southern History;* a single-volume interpretive history of the U.S. South.

BONANSEA, Bernardino M(aria) 1908-

PERSONAL: Born September 27, 1908, in Pinerolo, Turin, Italy; came to United States, 1950; son of Giuseppe and Giuseppina (Savino) Bonansea. *Education:* Attended Studio Liceale, 1924-27, and Studio Teologico, 1927-28; Collegio Internazionale Sant' Antonio, B.A., 1931; Catholic University of America, M.A., 1952, Ph.D., 1954. *Home:* Franciscan Monastery, 1400 Quincy St. N.E., Washington, D.C. 20017.

CAREER: Roman Catholic priest of Order of Friars Minor (Franciscan; O.F.M.); missionary in China, 1931-48; Catholic Middle School, Changsha, Hunan, China, professor of English, religion, and music, 1933-48; Siena College, Loudonville, N.Y., assistant profssor of philosophy, 1955-57; Catholic University of America, Washington, D.C., instructor, 1957-58, assistant professor, 1958-60, associate professor, 1960-64, professor of philosophy, 1964-74, senior lecturer, 1974-75, professor emeritus, 1974—; Villanova University, Villanova, Pa., professor of philosophy, 1975-81. Superintendent of Catholic schools, Archdiocese of Changsha, 1940-48; superintendent, Catholic Hospital (Changsha), 1945-48; professor of English, Catholic Nursing School (Changsha), 1946-48; professor of Italian, Hunan Province Music School, 1946-47; secretary, Hunan Province Catholic Relief Committee, 1945-48. Visiting professor of philosophy, St. John's University, Jamaica, N.Y., 1968; ad interim secretary, Apostolic Delegation (Washington, D.C.), 1954, 1960.

MEMBER: Societas Internationalis Scotistica, American Catholic Philosophical Association (constituent member), Renaissance Society of America.

AWARDS, HONORS: Named Lector Generalis by Order of Friars Minor, 1960; Distinguished Service Award, Catholic University of America, 1974.

WRITINGS: Sangue nella Cina Rossa, Gattiglia, 1950; *The Theory of Knowledge of Tommaso Campanella: Exposition and Critique*, Catholic University of America Press, 1954; (contributor) John K. Ryan, editor, *Studies in Philosophy and the History of Philosophy*, Volumes I, II, III, IV, and V, Catholic University of America Press, 1961; (editor and translator) Efrem Bettoni, *Duns Scotus: The Basic Principles of His Philosophy*, Catholic University of America Press, 1961; (contributor) John Clover Monsma, editor, *Science and Religion*, Putnam, 1962; (contributor) Ryan, editor, *Twentieth-Century Thinkers*, Alba House, 1965; (editor with Ryan, and contributor) *John Duns Scotus: 1265-1965*, Catholic University of America Press, 1965; *Tommaso Campanella: Renaissance Pioneer of Modern Thought*, Catholic University of America Press, 1969.

(Editor and translator) Gabriel M. Allegra, *My Conversations with Teilhard de Chardin on the Primacy of Christ: Peking, 1942-1945*, Franciscan Herald Press, 1971; *God and Atheism: A Philosophical Approach to the Problem of God*, Catholic University of America Press, 1979; *Man and His Approach to God in John Duns Scotus*, University Press of America, 1983.

Contributor to *Encyclopedia Americana, Encyclopedia of Philosophy*, and *New Catholic Encyclopedia;* contributor to *New Scholasticism, Franciscan Studies, Antonianum, Catholic Biblical Quarterly*, and other philosophy and theology publications.

SIDELIGHTS: Bernardino M. Bonansea told *CA:* "In my work, *God and Atheism*, the whole problem of God's existence is subjected to a careful analysis, with a view to answering the objections of those philosophers who either deny or question the existence of God or challenge the very possibility of a rational approach to the issue itself. The work contains the most extensive treatment of the classical arguments for God's existence.

"In my latest book, *Man and His Approach to God in John Duns Scotus*, an attempt has been made to present the main philosophical positions of the chief representative of the Franciscan school, whom Charles S. Peirce has called one of 'the greatest speculative minds of the middle ages' and one of 'the profoundest metaphysicians that ever lived.' It is hoped that the work will help to restore the figure of the great medieval master to its true dimension by dissipating the persistent misunderstandings and distortions of his thought."

Bonansea speaks French, Chinese, Latin, German, and Spanish, in addition to his native Italian. He has also studied Greek and Hebrew.

AVOCATIONAL INTERESTS: Classical music.

*　　　*　　　*

BOND, Ruskin 1934-

PERSONAL: Born May 19, 1934, in Kasauli, India; son of Aubrey Alexander (in Royal Air Force) and Edith (Clerke) Bond. *Education:* Attended Bishop Cotton School, Simla, India, 1943-50. *Home:* Ivy Cottage, Landoor, Mussoorie, Uttar Pradesh, India.

CAREER: Worked at one period for Cooperative for American Relief Everywhere (CARE), but has been a full-time writer since the age of twenty-two.

AWARDS, HONORS: John Llewellyn Rhys Memorial Prize for the most memorable work of 1957 by a writer under thirty, for *The Room on the Roof.*

WRITINGS: The Room on the Roof (novel), Deutsch, 1956, Coward, 1957; *The Neighbour's Wife and Other Stories*, Higginbotham (Madras), 1967; *Grandfather's Private Zoo*, India Book House, 1967; *Panther's Moon*, Random House, 1969; *The Last Tiger*, Publications Division (New Delhi), 1970; *Angry River*, Hamish Hamilton, 1972; *The Blue Umbrella*, Hamish Hamilton, 1974; *Once upon a Monsoon Time*, Longman, 1974; *The Cherry Tree*, Hamish Hamilton, 1980; *A Flight of Pigeons*, India Book House, 1980; *The Young Vagrants*, India Book House, 1980.

Published by Julia MacRae (London): *The Road to the Bazaar*, 1981; *Flames in the Forest*, 1982; *Tales and Legends from India*, 1983; *Earthquake*, 1984; *Tigers Forever*, 1984; *Getting Granny's Glasses*, 1985.

Contributor to *World's Best Contemporary Stories*, Ace Books, *Cricket's Choice*, Open Court, and *Young Winter's Tales 1970*, Macmillan. Contributor of short stories and articles to *Reader's Digest, Christian Science Monitor, Lady, Cricket, Short Story International, New Renaissance, Blackwood's*, and other publications.

WORK IN PROGRESS: Short stories; a children's book.

SIDELIGHTS: Ruskin Bond's books deal with life in his native India. Bond writes: "My interests (children, mountains, folklore, nature) are embodied in [these books]. . . . Once you have lived in the Himalayas, you belong to them, and must come back again and again. There is no escape.''

*   *   *

BOOM, Alfred B. 1928-

PERSONAL: Born September 6, 1928, in London, England; married Winifred Brown (a teacher), May 7, 1955; children: Steven, Catherine, Neil. *Education:* Goldsmiths' College, London, Teacher Certificate, 1957; University of Manchester, Dip.Ed., 1963. *Home:* 16 Warren Rd., Woodley, Reading, Berkshire RG5 3AR, England. *Office:* Bulmershe College of Higher Education, Reading, Berkshire, England.

CAREER: Eltham Green School, London, England, teacher, 1957-62; West Suffolk County Council, Bury St. Edmunds, England, remedial adviser, 1962-64; Bulmershe College of Higher Education, Reading, Berkshire, England, lecturer in education, 1965—. President, Joint Council for the Education of Handicapped Children, 1969-70; chairman, Voluntary Service Council for Reading. Toured India in 1969 and 1976 as an adviser on the teaching of retarded children.

MEMBER: National Council for Special Education.

WRITINGS: (With J. Uncles, K. Devereux, and S. Segal) *Backward Children in the USSR*, Edward Arnold, 1965; (editor) *Studies on the Mentally Handicapped Child*, Williams & Wilkins, 1968; *Health Matters*, West Berkshire Community Health Council, 1978; (editor and author of introduction) *Healthy Play—Healthy Children*, Bulmershe College of Higher Education and West Berkshire Community Health Council, 1981.

Also editor of *Housing for the Handicapped*, 1983, and *Handicapped and Elderly: Their Housing Needs*, 1984. Also contributor to *Educating Mentally Handicapped Children*, edited by A. F. Laing, 1972.

SIDELIGHTS: Alfred B. Boom has traveled widely in the United States, the Soviet Union, and Europe, observing special education methods.

*   *   *

BORCHERT, Gerald L(eo) 1932-

PERSONAL: Born March 20, 1932, in Edmonton, Alberta, Canada; son of Leo F. and Lillian (Bucholz) Borchert; married Doris Ann Cox (an instructor), May 23, 1959; children: Mark Gerald Leo, Timothy Walter. *Education:* Attended University of Calgary, 1951-52; University of Alberta, B.A., 1955, LL.B., 1956; Eastern Baptist Theological Seminary, M.Div. (summa cum laude), 1959; Princeton Theological Seminary, Th.M. (first class), 1961, Ph.D. (cum laude), 1967; postdoctoral study, Albright Institute of Archaeological Research, Jerusalem, 1974, Duke University, 1981, and Southwestern Baptist Theological Seminary, 1985. *Home:* 10410 Falling Tree Way, Louisville, Ky. 40223. *Office:* Southern Baptist Theological Seminary, 2825 Lexington Rd., Louisville, Ky. 40280.

CAREER: Ordained clergyman by Baptist Union of Western Canada, 1959. Princeton Theological Seminary, Princeton, N.J., teaching fellow and lecturer in Greek, 1960-62; North American Baptist Seminary, Sioux Falls, S.D., associate professor, 1963-68, professor of New Testament, 1968-77, academic vice-president and dean, 1970-77; Northern Baptist Theological Seminary, Lombard, Ill., professor of New Testament and dean, 1977-80; Southern Baptist Theological Seminary, Louis-

ville, Ky., professor of New Testament interpretation, 1980—, chairman of department, 1983—.

Participant, Baptist-Lutheran Dialogue for the Baptist World Alliance, 1978-82, Lutheran-Evangelical/Conservative Dialogue, 1979-82, and Consultation on World Evangelization, 1980. Treasurer, Sioux Empire Drug Education Committee and Awareness House, Sioux Falls, 1970-77; Baptist Joint Committee on Public Affairs for the United States and Canada, secretary, 1972-74, vice-president, 1975-76. Television teacher, ''Hidden Treasures of the Bible: Studies in the Gospel of John,'' produced by Chicago Sunday Evening Club, 1977-78. *Wartime service:* Civilian retreat master for U.S. Army, 1968-69.

MEMBER: Studiorum Novi Testamenti Societas, American Academy of Religion, Society of Biblical Literature and Exegesis, American Schools of Oriental Research, American Institute of Holy Land Studies in Jerusalem (director, 1971-74, 1984—), Commission on Cooperative Christianity of the Baptist World Alliance (secretary, 1968-75), Sioux Falls Kiwanis Club (director, 1970-76, president, 1974-75).

WRITINGS: Great Themes from John, Baptist Life Association Press, 1966; *The Dynamics of Pauline Evangelism*, Roger Williams Press, 1969; *Today's Model Church*, Roger Williams Press, 1971; (contributor) R. Longnecker and M. Tenny, editors, *New Dimensions in New Testament Study*, Zondervan, 1974; (contributor) J. L. Garrett, editor, *Baptist Relations with Other Christians*, Judson, 1974; *Dynamics of Evangelism*, Word Books, 1976.

(Contributor) W. J. Boney and G. A. Ingleheart, *Baptists and Ecumenism*, Judson, 1980; *Paul and His Interpreters*, Inter-Varsity Press, 1984; (co-editor) *Spiritual Dimensions of Pastoral Care*, Westminster, 1985.

Author of column, ''Forum,'' in *Baptist Herald*, 1969-77. Contributor of articles to numerous periodicals, including *Journal of Ecumenical Studies, Covenant Quarterly, Review and Expositor, Christianity Today, Evangelical Quarterly*, and *Dictionary of Christian Ethics.*

WORK IN PROGRESS: Consultant for revision of *The Living Bible;* preparation of a work on apostasy and security in the New Testament, for Broadman; other research on the resurrection pericopes in the gospels and on Paul and the Western conscience.

*   *   *

BOURDEAUX, Michael 1934-

PERSONAL: Born March 19, 1934, in Praze, Cornwall, England; son of Richard Edward (a master baker) and Lillian (a teacher; maiden name, Blair) Bourdeaux; married Gillian Davies, August 27, 1960 (died,1970); married Lorna Waterton (a research assistant), September 8, 1979; children: (first marriage) Karen Jane, Mark David. *Education:* St. Edmund Hall, Oxford, B.A. (with honors in Russian and theology), 1959; attended Moscow State University, 1959-60; Oxford University, M.A., 1961, B.D., 1968. *Home:* 34 Lubbock Rd., Chislehurst, Kent BR7 5JJ, England. *Agent:* Edward England, 12 Highlands Close, Crowborough, East Sussex TN6 1BE, England. *Office:* Keston College, Heathfield Rd., Keston, Kent BR2 6BA, England.

CAREER: Ordained priest in Episcopalian Church, 1960; Enfield Parish Church, Enfield, England, assistant curate, 1960-64; Centre de Recherches, Geneva, Switzerland, research associate, 1965-68; University of London, London School of Economics and Political Science, London, England, research fellow, 1968-70; Keston College, Keston, England, founder and director, 1969—. Visiting professor, St. Bernard's Seminary, Rochester, N.Y., 1969; research fellow, Royal Institute of International Affairs, 1970-72; Kathryn C. Davis Professor of Slavic Studies, Wellesley College, 1981. Committee member, New Philharmonic Chorus, 1961—. *Military service:* Royal Air Force, 1952-54; became flight lieutenant.

MEMBER: American Association for the Advancement of Slavic Studies, British Tennis Umpires Association.

AWARDS, HONORS: Risen Indeed: Lessons in Faith from the U.S.S.R. was named a Book of the Year by *Church Times;* Templeton Prize for Progress in Religion, 1984.

WRITINGS: Opium of the People: The Christian Religion in the U.S.S.R., Faber, 1965, Bobbs-Merrill, 1966, 2nd edition, Mowbray, 1977; *Religious Ferment in Russia: Protestant Opposition to Soviet Religious Policy,* St. Martin's, 1968; (contributor) *URSS: Dibattito nella communita cristiana,* Jaca Book (Milan), 1968; (contributor) Donald R. Cutler, editor, *The Religious Situation in 1969,* Beacon Press, 1969; (author of introduction) Rosemary Harris and Xenia Howard-Johnston, editors, *Christian Appeals from Russia,* Hodder & Stoughton, 1969; (contributor with Peter Reddaway) Max Hayward and W. C. Fletcher, editors, *Religion and the Soviet State,* Pall Mall, 1969.

(Editor) *Patriarch and Prophets: Persecution of the Russian Orthodox Church Today,* Praeger, 1970; (editor) *Religious Minorities in the Soviet Union, 1960-70,* Minority Rights Group, 1970, revised edition, 1984; (contributor) George Schoepflin, editor, *The Soviet Union and Eastern Europe: A Handbook,* Anthony Blond, 1970; (editor with Howard-Johnston) *The Evidence That Convicted Aida Skripnikove,* David Cook, 1971; *Faith on Trial in Russia,* Harper, 1972; *Land of Crosses: The Struggle for Religious Freedom in Lithuania, 1939-1978,* Augustine Publishing, 1979; *Risen Indeed: Lessons in Faith from the U.S.S.R.,* Darton, Longman, Todd, 1983.

Contributor to *Church Times, Christian Century, Tablet, Church of England Newspaper, Problems of Communism, Survey,* and *Russian Review.* Editor and founder, *Religion in Communist Lands* (journal), 1973—, *Keston News Service* (information service on religion in Communist countries), 1975—, and *The Right to Believe* (news sheet), 1976—.

WORK IN PROGRESS: General editor of "Keston Books."

SIDELIGHTS: The suppression of religion in the Soviet Union and other Communist countries is the continuing study of Episcopalian priest Michael Bourdeaux. His books on the subject document the struggles of religious dissidents behind the Iron Curtain, relating eyewitness accounts of church closings, the arrest and imprisonment of clergymen, and the protests of Christians against the authorities.

Perhaps Bourdeaux's most unexpected discovery about religion in the Soviet Union is that it has persisted at all. "After several decades of ruthless persecution," writes J. Sapiets of the *Tablet,* "when thousands of priests and believers were shot or sent to concentration camps and most of the churches were desecrated, destroyed or turned into warehouses, a new generation has arrived—young men and women who are disillusioned with the official Marxist-Leninist ideology and have found their way back to the Church." Several reviewers see much that Western believers can learn from the hardships endured by their Russian

counterparts. Speaking of the Lithuanian Catholics whose history is presented in *Land of Crosses: The Struggle for Religious Freedom in Lithuania, 1939-1978,* J. Derek Holmes of the *Catholic Herald* writes that the story of these people "ought to prove an example to the rest of the world and an inspiration which must leave its mark on the religious history of the twentieth century."

In 1969, Bourdeaux founded Keston College, the only research center in England devoted to the study of religion in Communist countries. It is from the extensive research conducted by the college that Bourdeaux documents his books. "The main aim of my work and of Keston College," Bourdeaux told *CA,* "is to provide factual data on major religious developments in the Communist world. We wish to inform churches and universities objectively and thus to build up a sympathetic world public opinion in favor of religious freedom under Communism. My motivation—learning at first hand about the persecution of religion in Russia. Having, I hope, established an academic method for the study of the persecuted church, I have tried more and more in recent years to popularize my writing. I want the world to know and to care: the surviving church in Russia is now a reviving church—and it has lessons to teach the world."

BIOGRAPHICAL/CRITICAL SOURCES: Times Literary Supplement, July 22, 1965, March 7, 1968, October 23, 1970; *America,* March 12, 1966, May 4, 1968, November 20, 1971; *Economist,* February 24, 1968, May 23, 1970; *Christian Century,* July 8, 1970, November 24, 1971; *Catholic Herald,* January 4, 1980; *Church Times,* January 18, 1980, February 4, 1983; *Tablet,* March 19, 1983.

*   *   *

BOXMAN
   See CHAMBLISS, William J(oseph)

*   *   *

BOYD, Sue Abbott   1921-

PERSONAL: Born August 31, 1921, in Cedar Rapids, Iowa; daughter of Calvin Eugene and Rose Lillian (Schultz) Abbott; married Arnold Boyd, August 28, 1943 (divorced March, 1954); children: Walter Stanley. *Education:* Attended New School for Social Research, 1949-50. *Home:* 2406 South S St., Ft. Smith, Ark. 72901. *Office:* South & West, Inc., 2601 Phoenix, Ft. Smith, Ark.

CAREER: South & West, Inc., Fort Smith, Ark., founder, president, and editor, 1962—; poet. Founder of Fort Smith Affiliation of Arts, 1963. *Military service:* Women's Army Corps, 1943-45.

MEMBER: United Poets Laureate International (member of international hall of fame), Poetry Society of America, National Federation of State Poetry Societies (chancellor, 1964-68).

AWARDS, HONORS: Hatshakers Award, 1967; Litt.D. from University of Free Asia, 1968; gold plaque from Poetry Society of Oklahoma, 1968.

WRITINGS—Poems; published by South & West, except as indicated: *Decanter: Poems, 1952-1962,* 1962; *The Sample Stage,* 1964; *Fort Smith and Other Poems,* Border Press, 1965; *How It Is: Selected Poems, 1952-1968,* Olivant, 1968; (contributor) Jo McDougall, editor, *The New Look Trio,* 1970; (editor) *Poems by Blacks,* 1972; (editor) *Poems by Poets,* 1973;

A Portion of the Fort Roots Poems: Volume I, Act I, 1973; *Aftermaze,* Pioneer Press, 1977.

Also author of *Of Sun and Stone,* 1959. Contributor of poetry and book reviews to numerous periodicals. Publisher of *Discourses on Poetry,* 1965, 1966, 1967, 1968, and 1970; founder of *Voices International,* 1966—; guest editor of *Poet* (international magazine from India), 1967; founder and adviser to *Tulsa Poetry Quarterly,* 1968—.

SIDELIGHTS: Sue Abbott Boyd is particularly interested in working in prisons.†

* * *.

BRADLEY, R. C. 1929-

PERSONAL: Born August 29, 1929, in Windsor, Mo.; son of Beecher Floyd and Zella Fern (Morgan) Bradley; married Marilyn Elizabeth Brown, June 3, 1962; children: R. C., Jr., Danny Ray. *Education:* Central Missouri State College (now University), B.S., 1950, M.S., 1955, Educational Specialist Degree, 1962; University of Missouri, Ed.D., 1963. *Religion:* Baptist. *Home:* 2032 Houston Pl., Denton, Tex. 76201. *Office:* Elementary Division, Education Building, North Texas State University, Denton, Tex. 76203.

CAREER: Public schools of Clinton, Mo., elementary school teacher, 1950-57, principal, 1957-59; University of Missouri—Columbia, Laboratory School, instructor, 1959-63; North Texas State University, Denton, professor of elementary education, 1963—. Lecturer on education throughout the U.S. Member of board of directors, Reading and Adult Literacy Council, Denton, 1964—.

MEMBER: National Education Association (life member), International Reading Association, Association for Supervision and Curriculum Development, American Association of University Professors, Texas Association for Supervision and Curriculum Development (member of board of directors, 1969—), Texas Elementary Principals and Supervision Association, Aero-Space Educational Council, Phi Delta Kappa.

WRITINGS—Published by University Press (Wolf City, Tex.), except as indicated: *The Education of Exceptional Children,* 1970, revised edition, 1975; *Parent-Teacher Interviews: A Modern Concept of Oral Reporting,* 1971; *Improving Instruction of the Experienced Teacher,* 1974; *The Beginning Elementary School Teacher in Action,* 1974.

Jesus: The Greatest Master Teacher of Us All, 1976; *The Role of the School in Driving Little Boys Sane,* Bassi Association, 1976; *Instructional Design and Strategies for Increasing Teaching Power,* 1977; *Schools as Joyous Places,* 1979; *Teenagers!: How Would You Like to Make Tomorrow the Greatest Day in Your Life?,* 1979; *How to Handle Stress before Distress Mis-Handles You,* 1981; *You Can Make a Difference,* 1983.

Also author of monographs. Contributor of more than two hundred articles to education journals. Editor of Texas Elementary Principals and Supervisors Association *Journal,* 1970—, and Texas Association for Supervision and Curriculum Development *Journal,* 1970—.

WORK IN PROGRESS: Brain Research, for Bassi Association.

SIDELIGHTS: R. C. Bradley told *CA:* "What prompts my delving into educational issues? The belief that schools can be better than they are. No teacher gets up in the morning and goes to school with the intent of harming anybody. But even

well-meaning persons can unwittingly, unconsciously, and unknowingly affect people in negative ways. Consequently, I believe that my work invites the teacher to look at the positive side of teaching, and by so doing, simply knowing certain data and information causes her/him to change because he is moved to really want to. What education needs is more teachers who do what they ought rather than what they want. Educators must change."

* * *

BRADY, Nicholas
See LEVINSON, Leonard

* * *

BRANCH, Melville C(ampbell) 1913-

PERSONAL: Born February 16, 1913, in Richmond, Va.; son of Melville C. and Martha (Bowie) Branch; married Hilda S. Rollman, 1951. *Education:* Princeton University, B.A. (with high honors), 1934, M.F.A., 1936, Ecole des Beaux-Arts, Fountainbleau, France, Diplome, 1934; Cranbrook Academy of Art, independent research in planning, 1937-38; Harvard University, Ph.D. (first doctorate granted in field of planning), 1949. *Home:* 1505 Sorrento Dr., Pacific Palisades, Calif. 90272. *Office:* University of Southern California, Los Angeles, Calif. 90007.

CAREER: Norman Bel Geddes & Co. and George Wittbold, Inc., New York, N.Y., head of urban planning section for General Motors Futurama at New York World's Fair, 1938-39; Executive Office of the President, Washington, D.C., research assistant for National Resources Planning Board, 1939-41; Princeton University, Princeton, N.J., director of Bureau of Urban Research, 1941-43; University of Chicago, Chicago, Ill., associate professor of planning, 1947-51; U.S. Government, Los Angeles, Calif., civil servant, 1951-54; Thompson Ramo Wooldridge, Inc., Los Angeles, corporate associate for planning and member of senior staff, 1954-62; University of California, Los Angeles, lecturer in planning, College of Engineering, 1962-66; University of Southern California, Los Angeles, professor of planning, 1966—. Director of "The City" exhibit, Baltimore Museum of Art, 1940-41; planning consultant, Douglas Aircraft Co., 1962-64. Los Angeles City Planning Commission, member, 1961-70, vice-president, 1964-65, president, 1965-66. *Military service:* U.S. Naval Reserve, active duty, 1943-46, became lieutenant.

MEMBER: American Society of Planning Officials (member of board of directors, 1966-69), American Institute of Planners (trustee, California chapter scholarship fund, 1963-69), Institute of Management Sciences (vice-president of College of Planning, Los Angeles, 1961-62), American Association for the Advancement of Science (fellow), Operations Research Society of America, American Society of Photogrammetry.

AWARDS, HONORS: Social Science Research Council demobilizaiton award, 1946-47; Ford Foundation grant, 1969-70; National Endowment for the Arts grants, 1976, 1977; Samuel H. Kress Foundation grant, 1977; Irvine Co. grant, 1978; Robert G. and Maude Morgan Cabell Foundation grant, 1978.

WRITINGS: (Editor) *Federal Aids to Local Planning,* National Resources Planning Board, 1941; *Aerial Photography in Urban Planning and Research,* Harvard University Press, 1948.

(Contributor) Harvey Perloff, editor, *Planning and the Urban Community,* Carnegie Press and University of Pittsburgh Press,

1960; *The Corporate Planning Process*, American Management Association, 1962; *Planning: Aspects and Applications*, Wiley, 1966; *Selected References for Corporate Planning*, American Management Association, 1966.

Comprehensive Urban Planning: A Selective Annotated Bibliography with Related Materials, Sage Publications, 1970; *City Planning and Aerial Information*, Harvard University Press, 1971; (contributor) Ira M. Robinson, editor, *Decision-Making in Urban Planning: An Introduction to New Methodologies*, Sage Publications, 1972; *Air Pollution and City Planning: Case Study of a Los Angeles District Plan, Findings-Recommendations-Explanation*, Environmental Science and Engineering, University of California, 1972; *Urban Air Traffic and City Planning: Case Study of Los Angeles County*, Praeger, 1973; (contributor) *Manual of Remote Sensing*, Volume II, American Society of Photogrammetry, 1975; *Planning Urban Environment*, Dowden, 1975; (editor) *Urban Planning Theory*, Dowden, 1975; *Comparative Urban Design, Rare Engravings, 1830-1840*, Arno, 1978.

Continuous City Planning, Integrating Municipal Planning and City Planning, Wiley, 1981; *Comprehensive Planning, General Theory and Principles*, Palisades, 1983; *Comprehensive City Planning, Introduction and Explanation*, American Society of Planning Officials, 1985.

Other publications: *Photographic Identification and Analysis of Japanese Antiaircraft Defences*, U.S. Navy Department, 1945; *Toward City Planning of Ocean Environment* (booklet), Department of Engineering, University of California, 1964, also special publication of American Society of Planning Officials, 1964; *Outdoor Noise and the Metropolitan Environment: Case Study of Los Angeles with Special Reference to Aircraft*, Los Angeles Department of City Planning, 1970; *Continuous City Planning*, American Society of Planning Officials, 1973; and other research and technical reports. Contributor to *Planning*, 1965, and to other planning, management, and engineering journals. Advisory editor, *Journal of AIP* (American Institute of Planners), 1958-62, 1975—.

*　　*　　*

BRANFIELD, John (Charles) 1931-

PERSONAL: Born January 19, 1931, in Burrow Bridge, Somerset, England; son of Allan Frederick (a civil servant) and Bessie (Storey) Branfield; married Kathleen Elizabeth Peplow, 1955; children: Susan, Frances, Stephen, Peter. *Education:* Queens' College, Cambridge, M.A., 1956; University of Exeter, M.Ed., 1972. *Home:* Mingoose Villa, Mingoose, Mount Hawke, near Truro, Cornwall, England. *Agent:* A. P. Watt & Son, 26/28 Bedford Row, London WC1R 4HL, England.

CAREER: Camborne Grammar School, Cornwall, England, English teacher and head of department, 1961-76; teacher, Camborne Comprehensive School, 1976-78.

AWARDS, HONORS: Walter Hines Page Scholar, 1974; Arts Council Writers' Award, 1978; nominated by Library Association for Carnegie Gold Medal, 1980.

WRITINGS: A Flag in the Map, Eyre & Spottiswoode, 1960; *Look the Other Way*, Eyre & Spottiswoode, 1963; *In the Country*, Eyre & Spottiswoode, 1966; *The Poison Factory* (juvenile), Harper, 1972 (published in England as *Nancekuke*, Gollancz, 1972); *Why Me?* (juvenile), Harper, 1973 (published in England as *Sugar Mouse*, Gollancz, 1973).

The Scillies Trip, Gollancz, 1975; *Castle Minalto*, Gollancz, 1979, Atheneum, 1982; *Brown Cow*, Gollancz, 1983; *Thin Ice*, Gollancz, 1983. Also author of television script, "The Day I Shot My Dad," produced by British Broadcast Corp., 1975.

AVOCATIONAL INTERESTS: Walking, sailing.

*　　*　　*

BRANLEY, Franklyn M(ansfield) 1915-

PERSONAL: Born June 5, 1915, in New Rochelle, N.Y.; son of George Percy and Louise (Lockwood) Brantley; married Margaret Genevieve Lemon (an elementary school teacher), June 26, 1938; children: Sandra Kay (Mrs. Edward C. Bridges), Mary Jane (Mrs. Robert Day). *Education:* State Normal School (now State University of New York College at New Paltz), lifetime license, 1936; New York University, B.S., 1942; Columbia University, M.A., 1948, Ed.D., 1957. *Religion:* Unitarian. *Home:* 4 London Ct., Woodcliff Lake, N.J. 07680. *Office:* American Museum of Natural History, Hayden Planetarium, 81st St. and Central Park W., New York, N.Y. 10024.

CAREER: Teacher in Spring Valley, N.Y., 1936-42, Nyack, N.Y., 1942-44, and New York City, 1944-54; Jersey State Teachers College (now Jersey City State College), Jersey City, N.J., associate professor of science, 1954-56; American Museum of Natural History, Hayden Planetarium, New York City, director of educational services, 1956—, associate astronomer, 1956-63, astronomer, 1963—, chairman, 1968—.

Part-time instructor at Columbia University, 1945, Alabama State Teachers College (now Alabama State University), 1947, Southwest Louisiana College, 1949, and New York University, 1962. National Science Foundation, referee, 1960—, advisor to Teacher Education Project, 1961; advisor to U.S. Science Exhibit of Century 21 Exposition, World's Fair, Seattle, Wash., 1962; advisor or director of various conferences and institutes sponsored by National Science Foundation and other scientific organizations.

MEMBER: American Astronomical Society (director, Program of Visiting Professors in Astronomy, 1958—; director, Committee on Education in Astronomy, 1958—), National Science Teachers Association, American Association for the Advancement of Science (fellow), Royal Astronomical Society (fellow), Authors Guild, Authors League of America.

AWARDS, HONORS: Edison Award for outstanding children's science book of 1961, for *Experiments in Sky Watching;* named Outstanding Citizen, Newburgh, N.Y., 1965.

WRITINGS—All juveniles; published by Harper, except as indicated: *Lodestar, Rocket Ship to Mars: The Record of the First Operation Sponsored by the Federal Commission for Interplanetary Exploration, June 1, 1971* (science fiction), 1951; *Experiments in the Principles of Space Travel*, 1955, revised edition, 1973; *Mars*, 1955, published as *Mars: Planet Number Four*, 1962, revised edition, 1966; *Exploring by Satellite: The Story of Project Vanguard*, 1957; *Solar Energy*, 1957; *A Book of Satellites for You*, 1958, 2nd edition, 1971; *Man Moves toward Outer Space*, Saga Press, 1958; (contributor) Lawrence M. Levin, editor, *The Book of Popular Science, 1958 Edition*, Grolier Society, 1958; (contributor) Clarence W. Sorenson, *A World View* (social studies textbook), Silver Burdett, 1958; *A Book of Moon Rockets for You*, 1959, 3rd edition, 1970; *Experiments in Sky Watching*, 1959, revised edition, 1967.

A Guide to Outer Space, Home Library Press, 1960; *The Planets and Their Satellites*, Science Materials Center, 1960; *A Book of Planets for You*, 1961, revised edition, 1966; *Exploring by Astronaut: The Story of Project Mercury*, 1961; (editor) *"Reader's Digest" Science Reader* (stories and articles), three volumes, Reader's Digest Services, 1962-64; (author of preface) *The Natural History Library*, American Museum of Natural History and Doubleday, 1962; *A Book of Astronauts for You*, 1963; *Exploration of the Moon*, published for American Museum of Natural History by Natural History Press, 1963, revised edition, 1966; *Apollo and the Moon*, published for American Museum of Natural History-Hayden Planetarium by Natural History Press, 1964; (with Milton O. Pella and John Urban) *Science Horizons*, two volumes, Ginn, Grade 7: *The World of Life*, 1965, Grade 8: *The Physical World*, 1965; *A Book of the Milky Way Galaxy for You*, 1965; *The Christmas Sky*, 1966; *A Book of Stars for You*, 1967; *A Book of Mars for You*, 1968; *The Mystery of Stonehenge*, 1969; *A Book of Venus for You*, 1969.

A Book of Outer Space for You, 1970; *Man in Space to the Moon*, 1970; (editor with Roma Gans) Philip Balestrino, *The Skeleton Inside You*, 1971; *Pieces of Another World: The Story of Moon Rocks*, 1972; *Think Metric!*, 1973; *A Book of Flying Saucers for You*, 1973; *The End of the World*, 1974; *Shakes, Quakes, and Shifts: Earth Tectonics*, 1974; *A Book of Planet Earth for You*, 1975; *Energy for the Twenty-first Century*, 1975; *From Rainbows to Lasers*, 1977; *Color: From Rainbows to Lasers*, 1978; *Age of Aquarius: You and Astrology*, 1979.

Feast or Famine?: The Energy Future, 1980; *Sun Dogs and Shooting Stars: A Skywatcher's Calendar*, Houghton, 1980; *The Planets in Our Solar System*, 1981; *Jupiter: King of the Gods, Giant of the Planets*, Dutton, 1981; *Space Colony: Frontier of the 21st Century*, Dutton, 1982; *Water for the World*, 1982; *Dinosaurs, Asteroids, and Superstars*, 1982; *Saturn: The Spectacular Planet*, 1983; *Halley: Comet 1986*, Dutton, 1983; *Mysteries of the Universe*, Dutton, 1984.

Juvenile books with Nelson Frederick Beeler; all published by Crowell: *Experiments in Science*, 1947, revised and enlarged edition, 1955; *Experiments with Electricity*, 1949; *More Experiments in Science*, 1950; *Experiments in Optical Illusion*, 1951; *Experiments in Chemistry*, 1952; *Experiments with Airplane Instruments*, 1953; *Experiments with Atomics*, 1954; *Experiments with Light*, 1957; *Experiments with a Microscope*, 1957.

Juvenile books with Eleanor K. Vaughan; all published by Harper: *Mickey's Magnet*, 1956; *Rusty Rings a Bell*, 1957; *Timmy and the Tin Can Telephone*, 1959.

"Exploring Our Universe" series; all published by Harper: *The Nine Planets*, 1958, revised edition, 1978; *The Moon: Earth's Natural Satellite*, 1960, revised edition, 1971; *The Sun: Star Number One*, 1964; *The Earth: Planet Number Three*, 1966; *The Milky Way: Galaxy Number One*, 1969; *Comets, Meteoroids and Asteroids: Mavericks of the Solar System*, 1974; *Black Holes, White Dwarfs, and Superstars*, 1975; *The Electromagnetic Spectrum: Key to the Universe*, 1979.

"Let's Read and Find Out" series; all published by Harper: *The Moon Seems to Change*, 1960; *Big Tracks, Little Tracks*, 1960; *What Makes Day and Night*, 1961; *Rockets and Satellites*, 1961, revised edition, 1970; *Sun: Our Nearest Star*, 1961; *The Air Is All Around You*, 1962; *The Big Dipper*, 1962; *What the Moon Is Like*, 1963; *Rain and Hail*, 1963, reprinted, Harper, 1983; *Snow Is Falling*, 1963; *Flash, Crash, Rumble, and Roll*, 1964, published as *Flash, Crash, Rumble, and Roll: Alphabet Teaching Book*, 1966; *North, South, East, and West*, 1966; *High Sounds, Low Sounds*, 1967; *Floating and Sinking*, 1967; *Gravity Is a Mystery*, edited by R. Gans, 1970; *Oxygen Keeps You Alive*, 1971; *Weight and Weightlessness*, 1972; *The Beginning of the Earth*, 1972; *Eclipse: Darkness in Daytime*, 1973; *Sunshine Makes the Seasons*, 1974; *Light and Darkness*, 1975; *Roots Are Food Finders*, 1975; *The Sky Is Full of Stars*, 1981.

"Young Math" series; all published by Crowell: *Measure with Metric*, 1975; *How Little and How Much: A Book about Scales*, 1976.

Adult books: *Science, Seven and Eight* (textbook), Saga Press, 1945; (editor) *Scientist's Choice: A Portfolio of Photographs in Science*, Basic Books, 1958; (editor) *Earth, Air and Space* (symposium on International Geophysical Year, September 12, 1957), American Museum of Natural History-Hayden Planetarium, 1958; *Astronomy* (college textbook), Crowell, 1975. Also author of introduction to *Astro-Murals*, Astro-Murals (Washington, D.C.), 1960. Contributor of weekly article to *Young America*, 1942-46; contributor to *Grade Teacher Magazine, Curator, New York Times Magazine, Natural History, Elementary School Science Bulletin, Nature and Science*, and other periodicals. First chairman of editorial board, Natural History Press, 1962—; advisor, *Science and Children*, 1963, and *Nature and Science*, 1963-69.

SIDELIGHTS: Franklyn M. Branley told *CA* there is a "need for accurate, readable material for young people. They are the nation's most important resource, and any investment in them will be repaid many fold." He first noticed the tremendous dearth of science education books for children while teaching grade school in New York, and has been helping to fill the gap ever since. S. V. Keenan of the *Wilson Library Bulletin* writes that Branley's own education began after his mother's death in 1918, when he was boarded with his brothers and sister at Plattekill, N.Y., "listening to the recitations of the other classes in a country school which had a 'woodshed, outhouse, water pail and dipper, double desks, pot-belly stove.'" Keenan also notes that Branley believes "children's ability to understand, study, and persevere is terribly underrated by adults. . . . We throw away a tremendous potential when we delay the exposure of young people to the excitement of science until they have become cynical sophisticates—say twelve years old."

In *Books Are By People*, Lee Bennett Hopkins calls Branley a man with "tremendous foresight," mentioning that *Exploring by Satellite* was published the day after the Soviet Union launched Sputnik (October 4, 1957). He quotes the scientist as saying: "'To write is to accept a challenge. You have to find out what children really want to know, assess yourself, and determine what skills you have to give them. Each book should be important, interesting, contain an element of surprise for *every* reader, whether it is about the sonic boom or honeybees or how a baby is conceived. Actually, a good book for children is also a good book for adults.'"

AVOCATIONAL INTERESTS: Oil painting, scuba diving, fishing, gardening, boating.

BIOGRAPHICAL/CRITICAL SOURCES: Wilson Library Bulletin, September, 1961; *Young Reader's Review*, December, 1966; Lee Bennett Hopkins, *Books Are By People*, Citation, 1969; *New York Times Book Review*, September 7, 1969; *Nat-*

ural History, December, 1970; *Contemporary Literary Criticism*, Volume XXI, Gale, 1982.

*　　　*　　　*

BRAUDEL, Fernand (Paul) 1902-

PERSONAL: Born August 24, 1902, in Lumeville, Meuse, France; son of Charles (a school principal) and Louise (Falet) Braudel; married Paule Pradel, September 14, 1933; children: Marie-Pierre, Francoise. *Education:* University of Paris, Sorbonne, qualified as teacher, 1923, received doctorate in literature, 1947. *Home:* 59 rue Brillat-Savarin, 75013 Paris, France. *Office:* Maison des Sciences de l'Homme, 54 boulevard Raspail, 75270 Paris, France.

CAREER: High school history teacher in Algiers, Algeria, 1924-32, and Paris, France, 1932-35; University of Sao Paulo, Sao Paulo, Brazil, professor of history of civilization, 1935-37; Ecole Pratique des Hautes Etudes, Paris, director of studies in fourth section, 1937-39, and in sixth section (economic and social sciences), beginning 1947, president of sixth section, beginning 1956; College de France, Paris, professor of modern history, 1949-72, honorary professor, 1972—; Maison des Sciences de l'Homme, Paris, administrator, 1963—. Visiting professor at University of Chicago, 1968. *Military service:* French Army, 1939-45; prisoner of war in Germany, 1940-45; became lieutenant.

MEMBER: Haut Comite de la Langue Francaise, Commission des Archives Diplomatiques, British Academy, American Philosophical Society, Polish Academy of Science, Academy of History (Spain), Academy of History (Argentina), Bavarian Academy of Sciences, Belgrade Academy of Science, Heidelberg Academy of Science.

AWARDS, HONORS: Officier de la Legion d'Honneur; Commandeur de L'Ordre National du Merite; honorary doctorates from universities of Oxford, Sao Paulo, Brussels, Cologne, Geneva, Madrid, Warsaw, Padua, Chicago, Florence, Cambridge, London, Hull, Leiden, East Anglia, and St. Andrews; the Fernand Braudel Center for the Study of Economies, Historical Systems, and Civilizations was established at the State University of New York at Binghamton in 1977; *Los Angeles Times* Book Prize, nominee, 1982, for *The Structures of Everyday Life*, winner, 1983, for *The Wheels of Commerce*.

WRITINGS: La Mediterranee et le monde mediterraneen a l'epoque de Philippe II, Colin, 1949, two-volume revised edition, 1966, translation by Sian Reynolds published as *The Mediterranean and the Mediterranean World in the Age of Philip II*, Harper, Volume I, 1972, Volume II, 1974, 2nd edition, 1976; (with Ruggiero Romano) *Navires et merchandises a l'entree du port de Livourne, 1547-1611* (title means "Vessels and Merchandise Entering the Port of Leghorn, 1547-1611"), Colin, 1951.

(With Suzanne Baille) *Le Monde actuel* (title means "The Contemporary World"), Belin, 1963; (editor) A. Jara and others, *Temas de historia economica hispano-americana* (essays; title means "Themes in the Economic History of Spanish America"), Mouton, 1965; *Civilisation materielle et capitalisme, XVe-XVIIIe siecle*, Colin, 1967, three-volume revised edition, 1979, translation of original edition by Miriam Kochan published as *Capitalism and Material Life, 1400-1800*, Harper, 1973, revised translation by Reynolds published as *Civilization and Capitalism, 15th-18th Century*, Volume I: *The Structures of Everyday Life: The Limits of the Possible*, 1982, Volume

II: *The Wheels of Commerce*, 1983, Volume III: *The Perspective of the World*, 1984; *Ecrits sur l'histoire* (title means "Writings on History"), Flammarion, 1969, translation published as *On History*, University of Chicago Press, 1980; (author of preface) *Conjoncture Economique, Structure Sociales: Hommage a Ernest Labrousse*, Mouton, 1974; *Afterthoughts on Material Civilization and Capitalism* (translation by Patricia M. Ranum of lectures delivered at 1976 Johns Hopkins Symposium in Comparative History), Johns Hopkins Press, 1977.

Editor of *Annales*, 1956-68, and co-editor, with Ernest Labrousse, of *Histoire economique et sociale de la France*, Presses Universitaires de France, four volumes, 1970-81.

WORK IN PROGRESS: A history of France, *Identite de la France*, to be published by Flammarion.

SIDELIGHTS: Fernand Braudel is recognized as one of the most important of contemporary historians. He has been immensely influential, not only as a writer and teacher, but as leader of the school of historical thought associated with the French history journal *Annales*. This school emphasizes a multidisciplinary approach to historical study, combining knowledge and methods from such diverse fields as economics, geography, psychology, and folklore to create a "total" history. "The *Annales* group," write Keith Thomas in the *New York Review of Books*, "is the world's most productive and dynamic school of historians." Braudel himself is judged by Hugh Trevor-Roper, writing in the *New York Times Book Review*, to be "one of the greatest living historians."

Braudel began his career in 1924 as a school teacher in Algiers. It was during this time that he began to work on his doctoral thesis, a project that would take him over twenty years to complete. Braudel chose as his doctoral theme the Mediterranean policy of Philip II of Spain, a sixteenth-century ruler whose reign saw military conflict with the Turkish empire for control of the Mediterranean Sea. In the course of his research, Braudel made use of the government archives at Simancas, Spain, where thousands of documents concerning fifteenth- and sixteenth-century life were stored. Scholars had long known of the archives, but the sheer mass of material available, all of it haphazardly organized, and the reluctance of authorities to allow outsiders to examine it, had prevented any extensive use of the archives for historical research. Braudel was the first to overcome this problem. He used an old movie camera to take still pictures of documents, pictures he could examine later with the aid of a film projector. He was soon taking two or three thousand pictures a day.

The approach Braudel used in his thesis was a nontraditional one. He had long been critical of the academic histories in which a few great men are depicted as having influenced the course of nations. Braudel stressed the need to examine the cultural, economic, and geographic forces at work in human history. The ideas of the French history journal *Annales* further influenced his outlook. *Annales* had been founded in 1929 by Lucien Febvre and Marc Bloch to express their impatience with traditional academic historiography and their demands for a new approach. History, they believed, was not the biography of a few great men; nor was it a steady progress toward some kind of social or spiritual millenium. Rather, it was an endless struggle between man's intentions and the limitations imposed by his environment and by his own nature. The *Annales* group called for historians to make use of new technologies and the methods of other disciplines in their historical research, so that a deeper and more complete understanding of history might be gained. The study of climates and the use of aerial photography were just two innovations of the *Annales* group.

A disciple and then a close friend of Febvre, Braudel adopted the *Annales* approach in his research for his thesis, widening the scope of his investigation as the years went by, so that at times it seemed as if the work would never be completed. He sifted through the records of fifteenth- and sixteenth-century shipping schedules, diplomatic papers, crop records, and court documents, using every available bit of information to form as complete and accurate a picture of the time and place as possible. His aim was to present not the history of King Philip II's reign, but a history of how the nature of Spain and the Mediterranean region at that time influenced the policies Philip adopted. Accordingly, Braudel's thesis, writes Naomi Blivenin in the *New Yorker*, "is about geography, economics, politics, and war; it is about the daily life—agricultural, urban, and maritime—of the rich and poor; it is gossip and description and anecdote; it is about endings—the ending of the Mediterranean world's domination of Western civilization—and it is about continuities and parallels."

When at last Braudel was finished with his research and about to write his thesis, World War II intervened. Braudel was called to serve as lieutenant in the French Army, was captured by the Nazis, and spent the war years as a prisoner in Germany. During his imprisonment, he wrote his long-delayed thesis. Without a single note, document, or book—relying entirely upon his formidable memory—Braudel wrote his thesis in a series of school copy books which, one by one, he mailed out to safety. "I had to believe that history, destiny, was written at a much more profound level," *Time* quotes Braudel as saying of this period. "So it was that I consciously set forth in search of a historical language in order to present unchanging, or at least very slowly changing, conditions which stubbornly assert themselves over and over again."

At war's end, Braudel returned to France and, in 1947, successfully defended his thesis to receive his doctorate degree from the Sorbonne. In 1949, his thesis was published in two volumes as *La Mediterranee et le monde mediterraneen a l'e-poque de Philippe II*. In 1972, it was translated into English and published in the United States. The first volume is a geo-history of the entire Mediterranean area. "Braudel's book," writes J. H. Plumb in the *New York Times Book Review*, "is geographically based—the huge Mediterranean basin with its mountains, deserts, alluvial plains, its forests and marshes, the problems of its boundaries, its routes and villages, its climates and weather are investigated and described in the historical context which Braudel has chosen—the age of Philip II." Braudel shows how geographic and other factors gave rise to the embattled empires of Spain and Turkey. "Politics," Braudel relates, "merely follows the outlines of an underlying reality. These two Mediterraneans, commanded by warring rulers, were physically, economically, and culturally different from each other." In the second volume, Braudel examines how the failure of agriculture to keep pace with a massive increase in the Mediterranean population, and the widening gulf between rich and poor, east and west, led the two empires inevitably into the political and military conflict in which Philip II played a prominent role. The *Choice* critic believes that "the depth, scope, and erudition of the earlier [volume] are maintained in the probing of the tangled web of personalities, diplomatic maneuvers, battles, and religious conflicts."

The massive study has received the highest praise from reviewers throughout the world. It is "one of the few great histories of our times," a critic for the *Economist* believes. Writing in *Encounter*, John Bossy describes the book as "a great work of historical art, indeed of art simply, a triumph of the constructive and concrete imagination, something to redeem the time." "This is evocative history at its best," writes J. H. Elliott of the *New York Review of Books*, "pursued with such richness of detail and example over space and time that it dazzles as well as illuminates." Elliott believes that it "will doubtless stands as one of the crowning achievements of twentieth-century historical craftsmanship." In similar terms, Michael Ratcliffe of the London *Times* calls the book "a masterpiece of French liberal humanism revitalized by the new technology of twentieth century scholarship." Ratcliffe also believes that "few other works of scholarship or the imagination bring us so close to the living presence of our ancestors or reconstruct so brilliantly the resources and world view available to, and shared by, the heroes of both statesmanship and art."

In later works, Braudel has continued to write extremely detailed histories using a multidisciplinary approach. *Capitalism and Material Life, 1400-1800* examines the history of the world during the period immediately preceding the era of capitalism. It shows how the population explosion that began in the sixteenth century outstripped the supply of food and other goods, leading in many parts of the world to the same sort of extreme disparity between the living standards of rich and poor that Braudel had already noted in *La Mediterranee*. He goes on to analyze staple diets, housing, and clothes throughout the world, then turns his attention to the three major factors in the growth of the industrial revolution—the spread of technology, the development of sophisticated monetary and credit systems, and the rise of the city. Braudel concludes that the "capitalist spirit" of certain medieval towns in northern Europe gave birth to the era of "pre-capitalism, which is the source of all the economic creativeness in the world," as well as "all the most burdensome exploitation of man by man."

Capitalism and Material Life, Trevor-Roper believes, "is a marvelously Braudelian book. It has all the genial erudition, the profusion and variety of illustration, the stimulating (and sometimes paradoxical) suggestions, the delightfully unacademic vitality of his great work [*La Mediterranee*]." Although Thomas finds several weaknesses in the book, chief among them Braudel's "inability to take adequate account of ideas, religion, mental attitudes [and] cognitive structures," he nonetheless finds that "all criticisms of the achievement of Fernand Braudel are disarmed by the sheer status of the man, the brilliance of the writing, the range of the erudition, the largeness of the vision, the passionate interest in human life."

Perhaps Braudel's most important work in recent years is the three-volume *Civilization and Capitalism*, an expanded study of the same period already covered in *Capitalism and Material Life*. It covers the economic and social evolution of medieval and modern Europe until the industrial revolution. The three volumes deal with three different aspects of the development of capitalism: the daily life of the people, the rise of market economies, and finally, the creation of an international economic community.

The first volume, *The Structures of Everyday Life: The Limits of the Possible*, is "the most remarkable picture of human life in the centuries before the human condition was radically changed by the growth of industry that has yet been presented," Plumb writes in the *Washington Post Book World*. It is, according to Richard Holmes of *Harper's*, "a book that has no obvious compeer either in scope of reference or level of accessibility to the general reader. [It presents] in vivid, ceaseless detail the daily condition of our ancestors' lives. . . . Their population numbers and their health; their diets and household budgets; their food, drink, clothes, and furniture; their transport, technologies, and inventions; their money and their banking systems; and above all their great cities.'' Holmes calls Braudel's approach ''a new kind of historical vision, both more universal and more mundane.'' By focusing his attention on the particulars of life, Braudel is seeking, John Leonard of the *New York Times* argues, ''the 'everyday' that is 'concealed' in those histories preoccupied by the 'unusual.'''

Having defined the essential conditions of life in the period under discussion, Braudel moves in the second volume of *Civilization and Capitalism* to a discussion of how the technologies and knowledge of the time were put to use. Braudel, writes Paul Stuewe in *Quill and Quire,* ''takes the vast quantity of information available and from it deduces plausible hypotheses about how people carried on the basic activities of everyday life. The results are historic tapestries far richer than those produced by scholars who emphasize personages and events.'' In writing about the beginnings of capitalism, Braudel ''tells in almost incredible detail,'' John Kenneth Galbraith states in the *Washington Post Book World,* ''who these merchants were, whence they came and where they operated, how much money they made, their place in the social and political hierarchy of the time, and of the world of peddlers, fairs, elementary retail shops, currency and stock exchanges, merchant companies and shipping routes in which they participated.''

The Perspective of the World, the third volume in the study, focuses on the rise of Europe to domination over world trade. The role of city-states in the expansion of trade is one of Braudel's primary concerns. He traces how first one, then another, European city came to dominate the economy of the region. Braudel's account of the rise and fall of Amsterdam as an economic power ''has never been better told,'' according to Lawrence Stone of the *New Republic.* ''The scope [of the book] is gigantic,'' Stone continues, ''both in space and time, and it is full of recondite information. . . . There are very many serious defects in this work, . . . but it does make an important new contribution to our understanding of the serial capture by city after city of commercial capitalist hegemony in the early modern world.'' The reviewer for *Publishers Weekly* judges it ''a dazzling economic history'' and ''a magesterial work.''

BIOGRAPHICAL/CRITICAL SOURCES: Journal of Economic History, November, 1950; *Journal of Modern History,* December, 1950, December, 1972; *Times Literary Supplement,* February 15, 1968, January 21, 1983.

New York Times Book Review, December 31, 1972, June 2, 1974, November 10, 1974, May 18, 1975, June 1, 1975, December 7, 1975, May 16, 1982, July 10, 1983; *Saturday Review,* February 27, 1973, February, 1982; *Virginia Quarterly Review,* spring, 1973; *Encounter,* April, 1973; *New Statesman,* June 15, 1973, January 15, 1982; *Economist,* November 10, 1973; *Washington Post Book World,* November 11, 1973, March 7, 1976, June 20, 1982, April 10, 1983; *Observer,* November 11, 1973; *Nation,* February 16, 1974; *History Today,* April, 1974; *New Yorker,* April 1, 1974, July 15, 1983; *History,* June, 1974, February, 1982; *Journal of the History of Ideas,* January, 1977; *Time,* May 23, 1977; *Times Higher Education Supplement,* December 9, 1977.

Newsweek, March 3, 1980; *Times* (London), January 22, 1981, June 21, 1984; *Harper's,* May, 1982; *American Journal of*

Sociology, May, 1982; *New York Times,* May 20, 1982; *Los Angeles Times Book Review,* June 27, 1982, August 14, 1983; *Quill and Quire,* July, 1983; *Publishers Weekly,* August 17, 1984; *New Republic,* October 1, 1984.

—*Sketch by Thomas Wiloch*

*   *   *

BRETT, Leo
    See FANTHORPE, R(obert) Lionel

*   *   *

BREWER, Garry Dwight   1941-

PERSONAL: Born October 2, 1941, in San Francisco, Calif.; son of Dwight C. and Querida (Colson) Brewer; married Saundra Tonsager (a lawyer), December 3, 1962 (divorced, 1975); married Shelley Marshall, May 11, 1976; children: (first marriage) Gabrielle, Gregory (second marriage) Matthew. *Education:* Attended U.S. Naval Academy, 1959-61; University of California, Berkeley, A.B., 1963; San Diego State College (now University), M.S., 1966; Yale University, M.Phil., 1968, Ph.D., 1970. *Politics:* Independent. *Religion:* Presbyterian. *Home:* Wingate Rd., Guilford, Conn. 06437. *Office:* School of Organization and Management, Yale University New Haven, Conn. 06520.

CAREER: Rand Corp., Santa Monica, Calif., staff member, 1970-72, senior staff member, 1972-74; University of California, Berkeley, assistant professor of political science, 1970-71; University of California, Los Angeles, lecturer in political science, 1971; University of Southern California, Los Angeles, lecturer in public administration, 1972-73; Rand Graduate Institute of Policy Studies, Santa Monica, faculty member, 1973-75; Yale University, New Haven, Conn., associate professor of organization and management, 1975-78, professor of organization and management, forestry and environmental studies, and political science, 1978—.

Consultant to Rand Corp., 1969-70, 1974-79, Ford Foundation, 1972—, Russell Sage Foundation, 1974-76, Resources for the Future, 1978—, Science Applications, Inc., 1980—, Woods Hole Oceanographic Institution, 1981—, and other institutions. Member of board of directors of Children's Research Institute of California, 1974-79, and Policy Science Center, 1984—. Summer research fellow, Office of Secretary of Defense, Advanced Research Projects Agency, 1967; fellow, Center for Advanced Study in the Behavioral Sciences, 1974-75. Research director and associate producer of a television documentary, ''What Do We Do Now?,'' 1976. *Military service:* U.S. Navy, 1963-66; became lieutenant. U.S. Naval Reserve, 1966-70.

MEMBER: American Political Science Association, American Association for the Advancement of Science, Society for Values in Higher Education. *Awards, honors:* Research grants from Rand Corp., 1974-75, Fleischman Foundation, 1973-75, Russell Sage Foundation, 1975-76, and Bureau of Education for the Handicapped, 1976-77.

WRITINGS: (With R. Brunner) *Organized Complexity: Empirical Theories of Political Development,* Free Press, 1971; (with M. Shubik and E. Savage) *Gaming Literature Review: A Critical Survey of Literature on Gaming and Allied Topics,* Rand Corp., 1971; *Politicians, Bureaucrats and the Consultant: A Critique of Urban Problem Solving,* Basic Books, 1973; (with Shubik and Savage):*A Partially Annotated Bibliography of Urban Models,* Datum, 1973; (with Brunner) *Political Development and Change: A Policy Approach,* Free Press, 1975.

(With J. S. Kakalik): *Handicapped Children: Strategies for Improving Services,* McGraw-Hill, 1979; (with Shubik) *The War Game: A Critique of Military Problem Solving,* Harvard University Press, 1979; (with P. deLeon) *The Foundations of Policy Analysis,* Dorsey, 1983; (with M. Greenberger and others) *Caught Unawares: The Energy Decade in Retrospect,* Ballinger, 1983.

Contributor: Joseph La Palombara, editor, *Bureaucracy and Political Development,* Princeton University Press, 1967; Robert O. Tilman, editor, *International Biographical Directory of Southeast Asian Specialists,* Interuniversity Southeast Asia Committee of the Association of Asian Studies, 1969.

Arthur I. Siegel, editor, *Symposium on Computer Simulation as Related to Manpower and Personnel Planning,* Bureau of Naval Personnel, 1971; T. R. LaPorte, editor, *Organized Social Complexity: Challenge to Politics and Policy,* Princeton University Press, 1974; H. D. Lasswell and D. Lerner, editors, *Values and Development: Appraising Asian Experience,* MIT Press, 1974; W. D. Hawley and D. Rogers, editors, *Improving the Quality of Urban Management,* Sage Publications, 1974; C. E. Sherrick, editor, *1980 Is Now,* John Tracy Clinic, 1974; B. Famighetti and others, editors, *Education Yearbook 1974-1975,* Macmillan Educational, 1975.

T. Robinson and N. Choucri, editors, *Forecasting in International Relations,* W. H. Freeman, 1977; A. Straszak and J. W. Owsinski, editors, *New Trends in Mathematical Modeling,* Ossolineum and Polish Academy of Sciences, 1978; Saul I. Gass, editor, *Utility and Use of Large-Scale Mathematical Models,* National Bureau of Standards, 1979; Adrian R. Tieman, editor, *The 1978 Energy Update Series,* General Electric Corp., 1979.

William C. Potter, editor, *Verification and SALT,* Westview Press, 1980; Francis Hoole and others, editors, *Marine Policy Papers,* Westview Press, 1982; Kim Cameron and David Whetten, editors, *Organizational Effectiveness,* Academic Press, 1983; Edward Zigler and others, editors, *Children, Families, and Government,* Cambridge University Press, 1983; Jay Chambers and William Hartman, editors, *Special Education Policies,* Temple University Press, 1983; Brian J. Rothschild, editor, *Global Fisheries,* Springer-Verlag, 1983; Aaron Wildavsky and Robert Golembiewski, editors, *The Costs of Federalism,* Transaction Books, 1984.

Also author of numerous papers and research reports. Contributor to *U.S. Naval Institute Proceedings,* 1967, and proceedings of American Political Science Association, 1971, and Military Operations Research Society, 1973. Contributor of reviews and articles to *Air University Review, Military Review, Yale Alumni Magazine, Policy Sciences, Public Policy, Science, Journal of Conflict Resolution,* and other periodicals. Editorial associate, *Public Policy,* 1973-79, *Policy and Politics,* 1977-79, *Policy Studies Review Annual,* 1977-81, *Journal of Conflict Resolution,* 1981—, and *Journal of Accounting and Public Policy,* 1981—; editor of *Policy Sciences,* 1974-76, and *Simulation & Games,* 1977—; member of editorial board of Redaktion *TRANSFER,* 1975—, *Policy Sciences,* 1977—, *Policy & Politics,* 1977—, and *Policy Studies Annual Review,* 1977—.

WORK IN PROGRESS: Three books: *Political Analysis for Managers, The Use and Misuse of Policy Analysis,* and *Natural Resource Policy: Defining the Problem.*

AVOCATIONAL INTERESTS: Fishing, golf.

*   *   *

BREWER, Jeutonne P. 1939-

PERSONAL: Born May 5, 1939, in Enid, Okla.; daughter of William Louis (a barber) and Ila (a hairdresser; maiden name, Sturgeon) Patten; married Chris Edward Brewer (an engineer), June 30, 1962. *Education:* Harding College, B.A., 1960; University of North Carolina, M.A., 1971, Ph.D., 1974. *Home address:* P.O. Box 115, Jamestown, N.C. 27282. *Office:* Department of English, University of North Carolina, Greensboro, N.C. 27412.

CAREER: Junior high school English teacher in Dover, N.J., 1960-62; Warner-Chilcott Pharmaceutical Co., Morris Plains, N.J., control analysis clerk in advertising, 1962-63; junior high school English teacher in Bloomfield, N.J., 1963-64; elementary school teacher at American dependents' school in Kerpen, Germany, and instructor at Berlitz School in Dueren, Germany, 1966-67; North Carolina Agricultural and Technical State University, Greensboro, workshop director of Education Professions Development Act Institute, 1970-72; Greensboro College, Greensboro, N.C., instructor in English, 1972-73; University of North Carolina at Greensboro, instructor, 1973-75, assistant professor, 1975-79, associate professor of English, 1979—, assistant dean of College of Arts and Sciences, 1980—. Participant in seminar on folk tradition in Southern ethnic literature, University of North Carolina at Chapel Hill, 1976; guest lecturer, University of South Carolina at Columbia, 1976, and University of North Carolina at Charlotte, 1981; has presented numerous papers at professional conferences.

MEMBER: Linguistic Society of America, Linguistic Association of the United States, Modern Language Association of America, American Dialect Society (secretary of South Atlantic Region, 1980-85), American Name Society, Association for Computational Linguistics, Association for Computers and the Humanities, American Association of University Professors, South Atlantic Modern Language Association, Southeastern Conference on Linguistics (member of executive committee, 1977-79, 1980-82; vice-president, 1978-79, president, 1979-80), North and South Carolina Association of Linguists, Philological Association of the Carolinas.

AWARDS, HONORS: Research Council grants, University of North Carolina at Greensboro, 1975-76, and 1980-81; North Carolina Humanities Committee grant, 1976; Excellence Fund and summer fellowship, 1979.

WRITINGS: (With Paul D. Brandes) *Dialect Clash in America: Issues and Answers,* Scarecrow, 1977; *Anthony Burgess: A Bibliography,* Scarecrow, 1980; *A Manual for Holding SECOL Spring Meetings,* Southeastern Conference on Linguistics, 1982.

Contributor: David L. Shores and Carole P. Hines, editors, *Papers in Language Variation,* University of Alabama Press, 1977; Bates Hoffer, Susan Penfield Jasper, and Guillermo Bartelt, editors, *Essays in Native American English,* Trinity University Press, 1982; Sarah K. Burton and Douglas D. Short, editors, *Sixth International Conference on Computers and the Humanities,* Computer Science Press, 1983; Michael Montgomery and Guy H. Bailey, Jr., editors, *Language Variety in the South: Perspectives in Black and White,* University of Alabama Press, in press. Contributor of articles and reviews to professional journals, including *American Speech, Orbis: Bulletin International de Documentation Linguistique,* and *SECOL Bulletin.*

WORK IN PROGRESS: A book on language myths; a revised edition of Anthony Burgess: A Bibliography; an article contrasting George Orwell's predictions for language in 1984 with those of Anthony Burgess in 1985; continuing research on slave narratives; research on naming practices for microcomputers and microcomputer programs and on the use of regional vocabulary in Lumbee Indian oral history tapes.

SIDELIGHTS: Jeutonne P. Brewer has studied German, Arabic, Swahili, and Shona. She told CA: "My linguistic patchwork-quilt background in Oklahoma, Texas, Arkansas, New Jersey, North Carolina, and Germany spurred my interest in regional and social dialects. . . . Travel is a major source of enjoyment. I like to travel to other countries and learn about other cultures and languages. Being an 'outsider' in a new environment is a good way to maintain a reasonable and balanced view of cultural and linguistic differences."

Of her work, Brewer said: "I write articles and books in order to understand and to share information about language use and language structure. My focus is on varieties of English that differ from the standard; I describe these nonstandard varieties and compare them with the standard within the framework of a general theory of language. Although my main interest remains sociolinguistics, I have studied university administration as well as linguistics since 1980. This has been study through practical application as the assistant dean of the College of Arts and Sciences at the University of North Carolina at Greensboro. One thing I have learned is that each part of my current appointment—administration and teaching-research—has its own piper, each having his own tune and his own tempo. Each day is challenging and different."

AVOCATIONAL INTERESTS: The out-of-doors, camping, fishing, reading, microcomputers and personal computers, travel.

*   *   *

BRIDGES, Howard
   See STAPLES, Reginald Thomas

*   *   *

BRODY, Baruch A(lter)   1943-

PERSONAL: Born April 21, 1943, in Brooklyn, N.Y.; son of Lester and Gussie (Glass) Brody; married Dena Grosser, August, 1965; children: Todd Daniel, Jeremy Keith, Myles Seth. Education: Booklyn College of the City University of New York, B.A., 1962; Princeton University, M.A., 1965, Ph.D., 1967. Religion: Jewish. Home: 4315 Breakwood, Houston, Tex. 77096. Office: 304 Lovett Hall, Rice University, Houston, Tex. 77001; and Texas Medical Center, Houston, Tex. 77001.

CAREER: Massachusetts Institute of Technology, Cambridge, assistant professor, 1967-73, associate professor of philosophy, 1973-75; Rice University, Houston, Tex., associate professor, 1975-77, professor of philosophy, 1977—, chairman of department, 1975-82, chairman of legal studies program, 1976—; Baylor College of Medicine, Waco, Tex., professor of medicine and community medicine, 1982—. Member of Jewish Community Council of Boston, 1971-73; member of board, Jewish Federation of Houston, 1977—. Former member of Town Meeting, Brookline, Mass.

MEMBER: American Philosophical Association.

AWARDS, HONORS: Franzheim-Fuller Award, 1984.

WRITINGS: (Editor with Nicholas Capaldi) Science: Men, Methods, and Goals, W. A. Benjamin, 1968; (editor) Thomas Reiday Essays, M.I.T. Press, 1969; (editor) Moral Rules and Particular Circumstances, Prentice-Hall, 1970; (editor) Readings in the Philosophy of Science, Prentice-Hall, 1970; (editor) Readings in the Philosophy of Religion, Prentice-Hall, 1973; Logic: Theoretical and Applied, Prentice-Hall, 1973; Abortion and the Sanctity of Human Life, M.I.T. Press, 1975; Beginning Philosophy, Prentice-Hall, 1976; (editor) Mental Health, Reidel, 1978; Identity and Essence, Princeton University Press, 1980; Ethics and Its Applications, Harcourt, 1983.

Contributor to Journal of Philosophy, Monist, Philosophy of Science, American Philosophical Quarterly, and other publications. Member of editorial board, Journal of Medicine and Philosophy and Social Philosophy and Policy.

WORK IN PROGRESS: Beyond Autonomy and Paternalism; The Redistributive Budget.

BIOGRAPHICAL/CRITICAL SOURCES: Times Literary Supplement, January 30, 1981.

*   *   *

BROME, (Herbert) Vincent

PERSONAL: Born in London, England; son of Nathaniel Gregory and Emily Brome. Education: Attended schools in Streatham, England; also privately educated. Religion: None. Home and office: 45 Great Ormond St., London W.C.1, England.

CAREER: Daily Chronicle, London, England, feature writer, 1930-35; editor of Menu (magazine), 1935-39; Ministry of Information, London, journalist, 1942-44; Medical World, London, assistant editor, 1944-46; writer, 1946—. Member of British Library Advisory Committee.

WRITINGS: Europe's Free Press: The Underground Newspapers of Occupied Lands Described as Far as the Censor Permits, Feature Books, 1936; Clement Attlee, Lincolns, Prager, 1949; H. G. Wells, Longmans, Green, 1951, reprinted, R. West, 1979; The Way Back: The Story of Lieutenant Commander Pat O'Leary, Cassell, 1953, 2nd edition, 1957, Norton, 1958; Aneurin Bevan, Longmans, Green, 1953; Acquaintance with Grief (novel), Cassell, 1954; The Last Surrender (novel), A. Dakers, 1954; Six Studies in Quarrelling, Cresset Press, 1958, reprinted, Greenwood Press, 1973; Sometimes at Night, Cassell, 1959; Frank Harris, Cassell, 1959, published as Frank Harris: The Life and Loves of a Scoundrel, T. Yoseloff, 1960.

We Have Come a Long Way (nonfiction), Cassell, 1962; The Problem of Progress, Cassell, 1963; Love in Our Time, Cassell, 1964; Four Realist Novelists: Arthur Morrison, Edwin Pugh, Richard Whiting, and William Pett Ridge, Longmans, Green, 1965; The International Brigades: Spain, 1936-39 (nonfiction), Heinemann, 1965, Morrow, 1966; The World of Luke Simpson, Heinemann, 1966; The Embassy (novel), Cassell, 1967, published as The Ambassador and the Spy, Crown, 1973; Freud and His Early Circle: The Struggle of Psychoanalysis, Heinemann, 1967, Morrow, 1968; The Surgeon, Cassell, 1967; "Man at Large" (three-act play), first produced in Edinburgh, Scotland, at Princess Theatre, 1967; The Operating Theatre (novel), Simon & Schuster, 1968; The Revolution (novel), Cassell, 1969.

Confessions of a Writer, Hutchinson, 1970; The Brain Operators, Cassell, 1971; Reverse Your Verdict: A Collection of

Private Prosecutions, Hamish Hamilton, 1971; *The Day of Destruction*, Cassell, 1974; *Jung: Man and Myth*, Atheneum, 1978; *Havelock Ellis: Philosopher of Sex*, Routledge & Kegan Paul, 1979; *Ernest Jones: Freud's Alter Ego*, Caliban Books, 1982, published as *Ernest Jones: A Biography*, Norton, 1983; *The Day of the Fifth Moon* (novel), Gollancz, 1984.

Also author of *The Imaginary Crime*, 1969, *London Consequences*, 1972, *The Happy Hostage*, 1975, and *Diary of a Revolution*, 1978. Author of seven television and radio plays. Contributor to British periodicals, including *New Society*, *Encounter*, and *Spectator*, and to U.S. periodicals, including *Washington Post*, *New York Times*, and *Nation*.

WORK IN PROGRESS: A play, "Take This Thy Victim"; a novel.

SIDELIGHTS: In *Jung: Man and Myth* Vincent Brome explores the life and career of one of the most controversial figures in the field of twentieth-century psychiatry. "In these pages we find a complex personality, a powerful intellect and, perhaps most surprisingly, a man whose compassion for his patients came clearly from his own experience in suffering and breakdown, his weaknesses and his drives," according to *Los Angeles Times* critic Robert Kirsch. He continues: "One bonus of Brome's biographical method is that [the author] accepts change as part of the process of evoking the whole man. This would seem to be a truism about biography, yet apart from the obvious differences between infancy, youth and old age, many biographers . . . often see character as static and consistent, rather than functioning along a chronological line." Jung, however, "never lost his streak of vanity, nor that quality of perception which some people thought an ultimate openness about the mantic and occult, the mystic and spiritual, and others a kind of naivete. Brome brings alive the complexities of the man and the roots of his myth."

BIOGRAPHICAL/CRITICAL SOURCES: Los Angeles Times, November 21, 1978; *New York Times Book Review*, December 24, 1978; *Times Literary Supplement*, May 6, 1983.

*   *   *

BROOKS, H(arold) Allen 1925-

PERSONAL: Born November 6, 1925, in New Haven, Conn.; son of Harold A. and Mildred (McNeill) Brooks. *Education:* Dartmouth College, B.A., 1950; Yale University, M.A., 1955; Northwestern University, Ph.D., 1957. *Religion:* Protestant. *Residence:* Toronto, Ontario, Canada. *Office:* Department of Fine Art, University of Toronto, Toronto, Ontario, Canada M5S 1A1.

CAREER: W. J. Negin Construction Co., Naugatuck, Conn., apprentice, 1950-52; University of Illinois at Urbana-Champaign, assistant professor of architecture, 1957-58; University of Toronto, Toronto, Ontario, lecturer, 1958-61, assistant professor, 1961-64, associate professor, 1964-71, professor of fine art, 1971—. Mellon Professor at Vassar College, 1970-71. Visiting professor at Dartmouth College, 1969, and Architectural Association School of Architecture, London, England, annually, 1977-82; guest lecturer at schools in the United States, Canada, England, France, Germany, Scotland, the Netherlands, and Switzerland; fellow of Victoria University.

MEMBER: International Committee on Monuments and Sites, Society for the Study of Architecture in Canada, Canadian Association for American Studies, Society of Architectural Historians (president, 1964-66; former member of board of directors), Society of Architectural Historians of Great Britain.

AWARDS, HONORS: Canada Council fellowships, 1962-63, 1975-76, 1977-79; Guggenheim fellowship, 1973; Alice Davis Hitchcock Book Award from Society of Architectural Historians, 1973, for *The Prairie School: Frank Lloyd Wright and His Midwest Contemporaries;* D.Eng., Technical University of Nova Scotia, 1984.

WRITINGS: (Contributor) *Studies in Western Art: Acts of the Twentieth International Conference of the History of Art*, Volume IV, Princeton University Press, 1963; (contributor) H. D. Bullock and Terry B. Norton, editors, *The Pope-Leighey House*, National Trust for Historic Preservation, 1970; *The Prairie School: Frank Lloyd Wright and His Midwest Contemporaries*, University of Toronto Press, 1972, 2nd edition, 1975, Norton, 1976.

(Editor) *Prairie School Architecture: Studies from the "Western Architect,"* University of Toronto Press, 1975; (contributor) Paul E. Sprague, *Guide to Frank Lloyd Wright and Prairie School Architecture in Oak Park*, privately printed, 1976; (editor and contributor) *Writings on Wright: Selected Comment on Frank Lloyd Wright*, MIT Press, 1981; (contributor) Helen Searing, editor, *In Search of Modern Architecture*, MIT Press, 1982; *Frank Lloyd Wright and the Prairie School*, Braziller, 1984.

General editor and contributor, *The Le Corbusier Archive*, thirty-two volumes, Garland Publishing, 1982-84. Contributor to *Encyclopedia of World Art*. Contributor of articles and reviews to art and architecture journals.

WORK IN PROGRESS: Charles Edouard Jeanneret: The Formative Years; editing a book of essays on the architecture and urbanism of Le Corbusier, for Garland Publishing.

SIDELIGHTS: H. Allen Brooks writes: "I am especially concerned with the psychological importance of architecture (and our built environment) as it affects our mental health and well-being. Too many people, I believe, take architecture for granted and are not sufficiently aware of the impact which it has upon us. These concerns surface more frequently in my lectures than in my publications."

AVOCATIONAL INTERESTS: The outdoors, skiing, canoeing.

*   *   *

BROOKS, Terry 1944-

PERSONAL: Born January 8, 1944, in Sterling, Ill.; son of Dean O. (a printer) and Marjorie (Gleason) Brooks; married Barbara Groth, April 23, 1972; children: Amanda Leigh, Alexander Stephen. *Education:* Hamilton College, B.A., 1966; Washington & Lee University, LL.B., 1969. *Home:* 1310 Sinnissippi Rd., Sterling, Ill. 61081.

CAREER: Besse, Frye, Arnold, Brooks & Miller, P.C. (attorneys), Sterling, Ill., partner, 1969—; writer.

MEMBER: American Bar Association, Trial Lawyers of America, Illinois Bar Association, Whiteside County Bar Association.

WRITINGS—Fantasy novels: *The Sword of Shannara*, Random House, 1977; *The Elfstone of Shannara*, Ballantine/Del Rey, 1982; *The Wishstone of Shannara*, Ballantine/Del Rey, 1985.

WORK IN PROGRESS: Additional books in the "Shannara" series; a new fantasy novel.

SIDELIGHTS: "When a new myth-making talent comes along and it's coupled to a free-rolling ability to tell a grand story, delight at this occurence tends to override any shortcomings you may observe in the initial work," says Frank Herbert, author of *Dune*, in his *New York Times Book Review* article on Terry Brooks's *The Sword of Shannara*. Herbert continues: "The Sword of Shannara is a distinctly split work; the first half runs a poor second when compared with the last half. [The author] spends about half of this book trying on J. R. R. Tolkien's style and subject matter. The debt to Tolkien is so obvious that you can anticipate many of the developments. In spite of that, you're held by the numerous hints at what will happen if and when Brooks reverts to his own style. This he does somewhere around Chapter 20."

What the author presents in *The Sword of Shannara*, the first of a fantasy series, is "a marvelous exposition of why the idea is not the story," according to Herbert. "Because of the popular assumption . . . that ideas form 99 percent of a story, writers are plagued by that foolish question, 'Where do you get your ideas?' Brooks demonstrates that it doesn't matter where you get the idea; what matters is that you tell a rousing story. He appears to discover this for himself around the middle of the book." Noting that stories dealing with myth and legend inevitably include a "strong mixture of allegory," Herbert finds that Brooks "adds his own leavening. It's as though he were unwilling to leave out any element of our long mythic history, not even the specialized developments of the movies and science fiction. This goes far beyond the usual fantasy, and the marvel is that he makes these elements essential to his story."

BIOGRAPHICAL/CRITICAL SOURCES: New York Times Book Review, April 10, 1977: *Atlantic*, May, 1977; *Washington Post Book World*, May 1, 1977.

*　　　*　　　*

BROWN, Raymond Lamont
See LAMONT-BROWN, Raymond

*　　　*　　　*

BROWN, Rosellen 1939-

PERSONAL: Born May 12, 1939, in Philadelphia, Pa.; daughter of David H. and Blossom (Lieberman) Brown; married Marvin Hoffman (a teacher), March 16, 1963; children: Adina, Elana. *Education:* Barnard College, B.A., 1960; Brandeis University, M.A., 1962. *Religion:* Jewish. *Home:* 1401 Branard, Houston, Tex. 77006. *Agent:* Virginia Barber Literary Agency, Inc., 353 West 21st St., New York, N.Y. 10011. *Office:* Creative Writing Program, University of Houston, Houston, Tex. 77004.

CAREER: Writer. Tougaloo College, Tougaloo, Miss., member of English and American literature faculty, 1965-67; Bread Loaf Writer's Conference, Middlebury, Vt., member of fiction staff, summer, 1974; Goddard College, Plainfield, Vt., member of creative writing faculty, 1976; Boston University, Boston, Mass., visiting professor of creative writing, 1977-78; University of Houston, Houston, Tex., associate professor in Creative Writing Program, 1982—. Has also participated in poets-in-the-schools programs and writing workshops.

AWARDS, HONORS: Woodrow Wilson fellow, 1960; Howard Foundation grant, 1971-72; National Endowment for the Humanities creative writing grant, 1973-74 and 1981-82; Radcliffe Institute fellow, 1973-75; Great Lakes Colleges new writers award, 1976, for *The Autobiography of My Mother;* Guggenheim fellow, 1976-77.

WRITINGS: Some Deaths in the Delta and Other Poems, University of Massachusetts Press, 1970; (with husband, Marvin Hoffman, Martin Kushner, Philip Lopate, and Sheila Murphy) *Whole World Catalog*, Teachers and Writers Collaborative, 1972; *Street Games* (stories), Doubleday, 1974; *The Autobiography of My Mother* (novel), Doubleday, 1976; *Cora Fry* (poems), Norton, 1977; *Tender Mercies* (novel), Knopf, 1978; *Civil Wars* (novel), Knopf, 1984.

Contributor to anthologies, including *O. Henry Prize Stories*, 1972, 1973, 1976, and *Best American Short Stories*, 1975 and 1979. Contributor of poems and stories to magazines, including *Ms., Atlantic,* and *Hudson Review.*

SIDELIGHTS: Rosellen Brown's *The Autobiography of My Mother* is the story of two women, Gerta Stein, a well-known civil-rights lawyer, and her daughter, Renata. The novel opens with Renata, a former Haight-Ashbury flower-child, returning home to her mother's Upper-West-Side New York apartment with her infant daughter, born out of wedlock in California. The two women have not seen each other in eight years, and the book is filled with tension as they try to readjust to living together. As Laurie Stone explains in the *New York Times Book Review*, "Gerta and Renata cannot stop judging one another by the opposing standards that have made of each of their lives, in its way, a suffocating and dead-ended half-life."

Anatole Broyard, in a *New York Times* review, complains that although "Brown's book raises a number of interesting questions, . . . it is part of the complacency of some modern novelists to believe that they need only ask interesting questions—no answers are required. Answer may be too strong a word. A novel need not give us answers, but it should, perhaps, question the questions until they bleed a little. The main trouble with 'The Autobiography of My Mother' lies in the fact that Gerta is monolithic and Renata is, well, mononucleotic. Larger than life and smaller than life—that is the way they strike me. One gives me agoraphobia with her abstractions, and the other makes me feel claustrophobic inside her narrow egoism." Stone, however, compares Brown's novel to the work of the highly regarded Grace Paley, stating that both authors have "a talent for writing the things that very intelligent people say and think when they are slowly going crazy." Stone concludes that *The Autobiography of My Mother* "is a bitter, funny, stringently unsentimental novel of rare merit. Rosellen Brown's strength lies in the steady but often dazzling accumulation of facts and details. She writes with great candor and ease, never retreating for one moment from her conviction that family is an accident from which the victims can never recover. That they try to, nevertheless, is what makes this novel dramatic and even hopeful."

Brown's next novel, *Tender Mercies*, is an "intense and challenging" book, in which "some recognizable contemporary themes are reworked with rough imaginative power," according to *Chicago Tribune Book World* reviewer Bruce Allen. He finds *Tender Mercies* to be "a truly radical portrayal of what Chaucer called 'wo that is in marriage'; specifically, of the subjection of women by men—self-contained creatures who're unable to understand what they've done, and must be educated in suffering." The action of the novel as described by Allen: "Laura Sturrock, a well-bred 'intellectual' Boston girl, virtually loses her life for having fallen in love with a free-spirited outdoorsman Dan Courser, 'a young, dark-haired, good-looking man who had taken the tiller of a boat he couldn't manage, far from home, and had cut his wife in two.' The result of that hideous accident (of which we gradually learn the details) is that Laura Courser, paralyzed by a broken neck, is in effect a quadriplegic, her body useless except for grotesque twitchings and laboriously mastered small motions.'' She spends a year in a rehabilitation institute, trying to learn to adjust to her new physical limitations, then Dan brings her home to their house in New Hampshire, and the bulk of the book deals with their readjustment to each other.

Carole Horn, in the *Washington Post Book World,* states that ''for the quadraplegic, every simple act of living becomes perilous, fraught with danger, and Brown skillfully conveys the awkwardness and desperation of the untrained person, however loving and well-meaning, trying to deal with these problems for the first time.'' The point-of-view in the novel shifts between Dan, presented as third-person narrative, and Laura, in the form of first-person sequences that Horn calls monologues. ''Uncanny, sometimes brilliant,'' she writes, ''those interior monologues drift from present to past, from reality into dreams. . . . Reading them is scary, and it is moving, and it is probably as close as any of us would want to come to a firsthand understanding of what it means to be a quadraplegic.'' And Joyce Carol Oates, writing in the *New York Times Book Review,* maintains that *Tender Mercies* is ''a haunting novel, as successful in its own way as 'The Autobiography of My Mother.' If the earlier novel is more immediately appealing, this novel, re-read, gives forth small astonishing gems. The virtuoso passage in which poor Laura, totally paralyzed, strives to move a single finger—unfortunately too long to be quoted here, and it would have to be quoted completely—contains prose as masterful, and as moving, as any being written today. And there are many such passages, most of them Laura's, in this fine book.''

Brown's third novel, *Civil Wars,* features the Carlls, Teddy and Jessie, and their two children. Teddy is described by *Time* reviewer John Skow as ''an idealistic white Mississippian, . . . a hero of the civil rights marches of the 60's'' who, unlike many former activists, has maintained his ideological stance, in his case, by ''living as virtually the only whites in a black development in Jackson.'' But through the years, the attitude of the other residents toward their white neighbors has changed, and, writes a *Newsweek* reviewer, ''thievery, vandalism and threatening phone calls late at night make Jessie think it's time to move.'' Teddy, however, remains determined to stay; his life as a traveling textbook salesman is given meaning only because he believes he is still a vital part of an active civil rights campaign. Living in a predominantly black neighborhood is his only remaining ideological statement.

The conflict is resolved when Teddy's sister and her husband, both virulent racists, are suddenly killed in an automobile accident, and, to the Carlls' surprise, they are named in the wills as guardians of two surviving children: a boy, eight, and a girl, thirteen, budding racists in their own right. With the increased space requirements of the household, the issue of whether or not to stay in the old house is settled as the Carlls move to larger quarters in a white, middle-class neighborhood. Here, notes John Skow in a *Time* article, the focus of the novel shifts from Teddy's civil rights ideology to ''Jessie's desperate efforts to stabilize her in-laws' children at some workable level of sanity and racial tolerance.'' Also crucial at this point, states Elaine Kendall in the *Los Angeles Times,* is ''the developing relationship among the [four] children,'' who all have many adjustments to make. Surprisingly, ''there is no explosion; all

goes more smoothly than anyone could have hoped. [The boy] is young enough to be responsive and resilient; [the girl] seems remarkably self-contained, her secret diary the only outlet for her anguish.''

In his *Chicago Tribune Book World* review, Howard Frank Mosher writes: ''Anyone who's discouraged by the reams of contemporary fiction about dull men and women engaged in the grim modern hobby of endless self-examination couldn't do better than to read this fine, new novel. . . . 'Civil Wars' is a fascinating story about serious people dealing with the kinds of serious human problems that make reading fiction fun and worthwhile. . . . In its rich, authentic detailing of the textures of everyday (and not so everyday) family life, 'Civil Wars' reminds me of [Judith Guest's] 'Ordinary People.' Yet Brown's novel ranges well beyond the Carlls' own ups and downs to reflect much of the recent history of the South and any number of people who live there. It is an important story.'' Kendall adds that ''though Brown's concerns are deep and abiding, she can be a witty and aphoristic writer. She gives most of the best lines to Jessie, subtly reminding us that our sympathies should rest with the pragmatic beleaguered woman locked in dubious battle with the escapist romantic man. The pace is leisurely, like the actual pace of the South. The sensational conclusion is not too apocalyptic for a novel dealing with centuries, decades, and years of apocalyptic events; all of them happened first in the public world, then reverberated in the private one.'' Concludes Lynne Sharon Schwartz in the *New York Times Book Review:* ''Any work so clearly of the heart and spirit takes immense risks, this one particularly. It dares to be about ideals and the perils awaiting those committed to them, and it dares to dwell on the most quotidian of matters, with critical scenes taking place in the kitchen and the family car. It directly confronts the sorely ambivalent position of a white family enmeshed in the fight for black people's rights. At a time when fiction by women seems perversely misunderstood, one can only hope that 'Civil Wars' will be recognized as a brave and fine work.''

BIOGRAPHICAL/CRITICAL SOURCES: New York Times, May 26, 1976, November 24, 1978; *New York Times Book Review,* June 20, 1976, December 10, 1978, May 6, 1984; *Chicago Tribune Book World,* November 5, 1978, April 22, 1984; *Washington Post Book World,* November 18, 1978; *Time,* April 30, 1984; *Los Angeles Times,* May 22, 1984; *Newsweek,* May 28, 1984.

—*Sketch by Peter M. Gareffa*

*   *   *

BROWNE, Robert S(pan)   1924-

PERSONAL: Born August 17, 1924, in Chicago, Ill.; son of William H., Jr. (a civil servant) and Julia (Barksdale) Browne; married Huoi Nguyen, April 6, 1956; children: Mai, Alexi, Marshall. *Education:* University of Illinois, B.A., 1944; University of Chicago, M.B.A., 1947; City University of New York, graduate study, 1963-66. *Home:* 214 Tryon Ave., Teaneck, N.J. 07666. *Office:* Howard University, 2400 Sixth St. N.W., Washington, D.C. 20059.

CAREER: U.S. Foreign Aid Program, Cambodia and Vietnam, economist, 1955-61; Phelps Stokes Fund, New York City, project director, 1963-64; Fairleigh Dickinson University, Teaneck, N.J., assistant professor of economics, 1965-70; Black Economic Research Center, New York City, director, 1969-79; executive director of African Development Fund, 1980-

82; Howard University, Washington, D.C., senior research fellow, 1982—. Member of board of directors, Emergency Land Fund and Twenty First Century Foundation. *Military service:* U.S. Army Air Forces, 1944-46; became sergeant.

MEMBER: American Economic Association, National Economic Association, Society for International Development, Council on Foreign Relations, Club of Rome (American association).

WRITINGS: Race Relations in International Affairs, Public Affairs Press, 1961; (editor with Charles V. Hamilton, Howard E. Freeman, Jerome Kagan, and A. Kimball Romney) *The Social Scene,* Winthrop, 1972; *The Lagos Plan of Action vs. the Berg Report,* African Studies Center, Howard University, 1984.

Contributor of articles to academic journals and popular magazines, including *Esquire, Ramparts, New Republic, Ebony, Business and Society Review,* and *New York Times Magazine,* and to newspapers. Editor emeritus, *Review of Black Political Economy;* editorial consultant, *Africa Today;* member of editorial board, *World Policy Journal.*

SIDELIGHTS: Robert S. Browne told *CA:* "Although I derive great satisfaction from encountering beautiful usage of the language, my own writing is almost entirely of a practical rather than a literary nature. My life is committed to expanding the domain of social justice in the world—specifically, to the fighting of economic and social injustice—and my writing emerges as a fruit of the pursuit of this objective."

*　　*　　*

BUCCO, Martin 1929-

PERSONAL: Born December 3, 1929, in Newark, N.J.; son of Mario and Ann (De Salvo) Bucco; married Edith Erickson, 1956; children: Tamara Lisa. *Education:* Attended Rutgers University, 1948-49; Highlands University, B.A., 1952; Columbia University, M.A., 1957; University of California, Berkeley, additional graduate study, 1957-58; University of Missouri, Ph.D., 1963; Yale University, Ph.D., 1977. *Politics:* Independent. *Home:* 140 Circle Dr., Fort Collins, Colo. 80524. *Office:* Department of English, Colorado State University, Fort Collins, Colo. 80523.

CAREER: Junior high school English teacher in Las Vegas, N.M., 1954-55; high school English teacher in Raton, N.M., 1955-56; North Dakota State Teachers College, Valley City, instructor in English, 1958-59; University of Missouri, Columbia, instructor in English, 1959-63; Colorado State University, Fort Collins, assistant professor, 1963-67, associate professor, 1967-71, professor of English, 1971—, honors professor, 1975. Visiting professor, Northern Arizona University, 1962, and University of the Pacific, 1980-81. *Military service:* U.S. Naval Reserve, 1947-49, U.S. Army, 1952-53.

MEMBER: Western Literature Association (member of executive council, 1976—; president, 1982; executive secretary, 1983—), Rocky Mountain Modern Language Association (member of editorial board, 1984—).

AWARDS, HONORS: National Humanities Foundation summer grants, 1968, 1977; recipient of numerous faculty research grants.

WRITINGS: The Voluntary Tongue (poems), Wurlitzer Foundation, 1957; (author of introduction) Thomas Bulfinch, *The Age of Fable,* Harper, 1966; *Frank Waters,* Steck, 1969; *Wilbur Daniel Steele,* Twayne, 1972; *An American Tragedy* (study guide), Cliff's Notes, 1974; *E. W. Howe,* Boise State University, 1977; *Rene Wellek,* G. K. Hall, 1981; *Western American Literary Criticism,* Boise State University, 1984.

Contributor of poems, short stories, and criticism to numerous periodicals, including *Journal of Comparative Literature and Aesthetics, Wordsworth Circle, Twentieth-Century Western Writers, Western Humanities Review,* and *Western American Literature.* Assistant editor, *Ceramic Age,* 1953-54, *Western American Literature,* assistant editor, 1966-74, member of editorial advisory board, 1974—, member of executive council, 1976—.

WORK IN PROGRESS: Critical Essays on Sinclair Lewis, for G. K. Hall.

SIDELIGHTS: Martin Bucco told *CA* that he "began writing at age sixteen—journalism in high school, poetry and stories in college, and criticism in graduate school. . . . My teaching and my writing, my work and my play, form a whole, an outgrowth of my passion for literature and for literary studies."

BIOGRAPHICAL/CRITICAL SOURCES: World Literature Today, spring, 1982; *Comparative Literature,* summer, 1983.

*　　*　　*

BUCHANAN, George Wesley 1921-

PERSONAL: Born December 25, 1921, in Denison, Iowa; son of George (a laborer) and Helen (Kral) Buchanan; married Gladyce Dyer, February 14, 1947; married second wife, Harlene Bower (a high school history teacher), January 10, 1970; children: (first marriage) George Wesley, Jr., Mary Colleen. *Education:* Attended Tabor College, 1940-42; Simpson College, B.A., 1947; Garrett Theological Seminary, M.Div., 1951; Northwestern University, M.A., 1952; Hebrew Union College, postgraduate study, 1957-60; Drew University, Ph.D., 1959. *Home:* 11404 Newport Mills Rd., Silver Springs, Md. 20902. *Office:* Wesley Theological Seminary, Washington, D.C. 20016.

CAREER: Farmer in Denison, Iowa, 1942-44; high school English and science teacher in Kiron, Iowa, 1943-44; clergyman of United Methodist Church and pastor in Iowa, Illinois, Wisconsin, New Jersey, and Ohio, 1944-59; Wesley Theological Seminary, Washington, D.C., professor of New Testament, 1959—.

MEMBER: Society of Biblical Literature, Catholic Biblical Society, Studiorum Novi Testamenti Societas, American Association of University Professors, Middle Atlantic States Society for Biblical Literature (president, 1965-66).

AWARDS, HONORS: Bollingen grant to participate in archaeological excavation at Shecham, Jordan, summer, 1957; Hebrew Union College, Horowitz fellow, 1957-58, Scheuer fellow, 1959-60; American Association of Theological Schools grant for research in Lebanon, Syria, and Jordan, summer, 1966; Hebrew Union College Biblical and Archaeological Schools fellowship for research in Israel, 1966-67; Litt.D., Simpson College, 1973; Rosenstiel fellow at University of Notre Dame, 1973; Association of Theological Schools fellow, and Claremont Society of Biblical Literature fellow, both 1980-81.

WRITINGS: (Contributor) John Monroe Vayinger and Newman S. Cayer, Jr., editors, *Casebook in Pastoral Counseling,* Abingdon, 1962; (author of introduction) R. H. Charles, *Eschatology: The Doctrine of a Future Life in Israel, Judaism and Christianity,* Schocken, 1963; (contributor) Jacob Neusner, editor, *Religions in Antiquity,* E. J. Brill, 1968.

The Consequences of the Covenant, E. J. Brill, 1970; (translator and author of introduction) H. S. Reimarus, *The Goal of Jesus and His Disciples,* E. J. Brill, 1970; (author of commentary) *To the Hebrews,* Doubleday, 1972; (contributor) Neusner, editor, *Christianity, Judaism, and Other Greco-Roman Cults,* Part I, E. J. Brill, 1975; *Revelation and Redemption,* Mercer University Press, 1978; *The Prophet's Mantle in the Nation's Capital,* University Press of America, 1978.

(Contributor) Hubert R. Johnson, editor, *Who Then Is Paul?,* University Press of America, 1980; (contributor) Joel Delobel, editor, *Logia,* University Press of America, 1982; (contributor) W. R. Farmer, editor, *New Synoptic Studies,* Mercer University Press, 1983; *Jesus: The King and the Kingdom,* Mercer University Press, 1984; (contributor) H. O. Thompson, editor, *The Answers Lie Below,* University Press of America, 1984. Contributor to *International Standard Biblical Encyclopedia;* contributor of more than fifty articles and reviews to *Christian Home, Christian Century, Catholic Biblical Quarterly,* and other religious and scholarly journals. Member of editorial board, *Biblical Archaeology Review, Bible Review;* member of advisory board, *Arts and Humanities Citation Index.*

WORK IN PROGRESS: A commentary on the *Book of Revelation; The Gospel as a Literary Form; Kingdom Eschatology; Sin and Sectarianism.*

SIDELIGHTS: George Wesley Buchanan told *CA:* "Research and writing for me is not easy, but necessary. I would not do it if there were not important questions to answer which others are not even asking or are not answering adequately. I only offer the answers that are obvious, and only then after it is clear that these are correct and that no one else is going to give them. Most of my research deals with ancient history that has important implications for twentieth century ethics. My research begins by assuming ancient texts mean just what they seem to say against their own background, deprived of complex European and American philosophical, sociological, psychological, and theological interpretations. To find the correct analysis, I constantly study ancient languages, literature, archaeology, and geography. I publish mostly for scholars but also for clergy and lay reading publics as well. My strongest concerns and motivating ideals are involved with the church and world peace. Although I frequently grow weary, it is no easier for me to leave an important research project than for a good hound dog to leave a hot trail. It is unlikely, however, that I will live long enough to complete the many projects in which I am now engaged."

Buchanan works "with different degrees of facility" in German, French, Spanish, Latin, Hebrew, Greek, Aramaic, Coptic, Syriac, Ethiopic, and Arabic.

* * *

BUCKNALL, Barbara J(ane)   1933-

PERSONAL: Surname is pronounced *Buck*-nall; born June 8, 1933, in Teddington, England; daughter of Eric Herbert (a metallurgist) and Mary (Macaulay) Bucknall. *Education:* Lady Margaret Hall, Oxford, B.A., 1955, M.A., 1958, University of London, Diploma of Librarianship, 1958; Northwestern University, graduate study, 1960-62, Ph.D., 1966. *Politics:* "Vague and uninformed but democratic." *Religion:* Religious Society of Friends. *Home:* 160 Highland Ave., St. Catharines, Ontario,

Canada. *Office:* Department of French, Brock University, St. Catharines, Ontario, Canada.

CAREER: University of Illinois at Urbana-Champaign, instructor, 1962-66, assistant professor of French, 1966-69; Brock University, St. Catharines, Ontario, assistant professor, 1969-71, associate professor of French, 1971—.

MEMBER: Modern Language Association of America.

AWARDS, HONORS: Canada Council fellow, 1974-75.

WRITINGS: The Religion of Art in Proust, University of Illinois Press, 1969; (contributor) Dick Riley, editor, *Critical Encounters: Writers and Themes in Science Fiction,* Ungar, 1978; *Ursula K. LeGuin,* Ungar, 1981; (contributor) *Femimite Subversion Ecriture,* Editions du Remue-Menage, 1983; (contributor) Langdon L. Faust, editor, *American Women Writers: A Critical Guide from Colonial Times to Present,* Ungar, 1983. Also author of a novel. Contributor to *Encyclopedia of World Literature in the Twentieth Century.* Contributor of articles to *Humanities Association Review* and other scholarly journals.

WORK IN PROGRESS: An *Anthology of Proust Criticism;* revision of a manuscript on Proust and three of his literary friends; a study on Rimbaud and science fiction; a book of children's stories.

SIDELIGHTS: Barbara Bucknall writes *CA,* "The struggle between Proust and my other interests continues."

* * *

BURCHFIELD, Robert William   1923-

PERSONAL: Born January 27, 1923, in Wanganui, New Zealand; son of Frederick (an electrician) and Mary (Blair) Burchfield; married Ethel May Yates, July 2, 1949 (divorced, 1976); married Elizabeth Austen Knight, November 5, 1976; children: (first marriage) Jennifer Catherine, Jonathan Robert, Elizabeth Jane. *Education:* Attended Wanganui Technical College, 1934-39; Victoria University College, Wellington, New Zealand, M.A., 1948; Magdalen College, Oxford, B.A., 1951, M.A., 1955. *Religion:* Protestant. *Home:* The Barn, 14 The Green, Sutton Courtenay, Oxfordshire OX14 4AE, England. *Office:* Oxford English Dictionary, 37a St. Giles, Oxford OX1 4AE, England.

CAREER: Oxford University, Oxford, England, junior lecturer in English language and literature at Magdalen College, 1952-53, lecturer in English language and literature at Christ Church, 1953-57, lecturer, 1955-63, fellow and tutor in English language and literature, 1963-79, senior research fellow at St. Peter's College, 1979—. *Military service:* Royal New Zealand Artillery, 1941-46; served in Italy; became sergeant.

MEMBER: Early English Text Society (honorary secretary, 1955-68; member of council, 1968-80), American Academy of Arts and Sciences (foreign honorary member).

AWARDS, HONORS: Rhodes scholarship, 1949-51; Commander, Order of the British Empire, 1975; D.Litt., University of Liverpool, 1978; Lit.D., Victoria University of Wellington (New Zealand), 1983.

WRITINGS: (With C. T. Onions and G.W.S. Friedrichsen) *The Oxford Dictionary of English Etymology,* Oxford University Press, 1966; (contributor) *Pocket Oxford Dictionary,* Oxford University Press, 1969; (editor) *A Supplement to the Oxford English Dictionary,* Oxford University Press, Volume I: *A-G,* 1972, Volume II: *H-N,* 1976, Volume III: *O-Scz,* 1982;

The Spoken Word, British Broadcasting Corp. Publications, 1981; (editor) William Cobbett, *Grammar of the English Language,* Editions Rodopi, 1984. Also author of *The English Language,* 1985. Chief editor, "Oxford English Dictionaries," Oxford University Press, 1971—. Contributor to *Medium Aevum, Essays and Studies, Notes and Queries,* and other journals. Co-editor, *Notes and Queries,* 1959-62.

WORK IN PROGRESS: Editing *A Supplement to the Oxford English Dictionary,* Volume IV: *Se-Z;* writing a grammar of the English language.

AVOCATIONAL INTERESTS: Rugby (member of New Zealand Army team in Italy, 1945), travel in the United States, the Far East, Australia, and New Zealand.

BIOGRAPHICAL/CRITICAL SOURCES: Rising Generation (Tokyo), January 1, 1973, February 1, 1973, March 1, 1973; *The Incorporated Linguist,* summer, 1984.

* * *

BURKE, Carol 1950-

PERSONAL: Born February 12, 1950, in Tahawus, N.Y.; daughter of Raymond and Grace (a teacher; maiden name, Sayer) Burke; married Jerome Christensen (a college professor), August 17, 1974. *Education:* Attended University of Durham, 1968, and Simmons College, 1968-69; Earlham College, B.A. (honors), 1972; Cornell University, M.F.A., 1974. *Office:* Department of English, Purdue University, West Lafayette, Ind.

CAREER: Cornell University, Ithaca, N.Y., instructor in English and women's studies, 1973-75; Purdue University, West Lafayette, Ind., instructor in English, 1975—. Instructor at State University of New York College at Cortland, 1975. Poet-in-residence of Indiana Arts Commission, 1975—. Has given readings from her own works.

WRITINGS: Close Quarters (poems), Ithaca House, 1975; (editor) *Do You Have to Listen to Everything* (writing ideas for teaching creative writing), PITS Press, 1976; (editor with Martin Light) *Back in Those Days: Reminiscences and Stories of Indiana,* Indiana Writers, 1978; (editor) *An Atlanta Tradition,* Wimmer Brothers, 1982; (editor) *Plain Talk,* Purdue University Press, 1983. Contributor of poems to literary journals, including *Hiram Review, Remington Review, North Stone Review, Epoch, Rapport,* and *Penny Dreadful.* Associate editor, *Indiana Writes,* 1976—.

WORK IN PROGRESS: A book on teaching creative writing; editing an anthology of children's writing.

SIDELIGHTS: Carol Burke once wrote *CA:* "As an undergraduate I attended a Quaker college, one which convinced me to change from a pre-med student to an English major. Despite such a change, the human body has remained an important source of imagery for my poems (as it is for many women poets)."

AVOCATIONAL INTERESTS: Travel (Europe, Northern and Western Africa).†

* * *

BURKE, W. Warner 1935-

PERSONAL: Born May 12, 1935; son of Alfred Vernard (a sales manager) and Ruby Inez (Gilbert) Burke; married Roberta Luchetti, October 5, 1974; children: Donovan, Courtney, Brian.

Education: Furman University, B.A., 1957; University of Texas, M.A., 1961, Ph.D., 1963. *Home:* 235 Pelhamdale Ave., Pelham, N.Y. 10803. *Office address:* Box 24, Teachers College, Columbia University, New York, N.Y. 10027.

CAREER: University of Texas, Main University (now University of Texas at Austin), instructor in psychology, 1962-63; University of Richmond, Richmond, Va., assistant professor of psychology, 1963-66; National Training Laboratories Institute, Center for Organization Studies, Washington, D.C., director, 1966-74; executive director, Organization Development Network, 1967-75; free-lance consultant in organization and management, 1974-76; Clark University, Worcester, Mass., professor of management and chairperson of department of management, 1976-79; Columbia University, Teachers College, New York, N.Y., professor of psychology and education, 1979—. Diplomate in industrial/organizational psychology, American Board of Professional Psychology. *Military service:* U.S. Army Reserve, 1953-64.

MEMBER: American Psychological Association, Academy of Management, American Society for Training and Development.

WRITINGS: (Editor with W. B. Eddy, V. A. Dupre, and O. P. South) *Behavioral Science and the Manager's Role,* N.T.L. Learning Resources Corp., 1969, revised edition (with Eddy), University Associates, 1980; (editor with R. Beckhard) *Conference Planning,* N.T.L. Learning Resources Corp., 1970; (with H. A. Hornstein, B. A. Bunker, M. G. Gindes, and R. J. Lewicki) *Social Intervention: A Behavioral Science Approach,* Free Press, 1971; (editor with Hornstein) *Social Technology of Organization Development,* University Associates, 1972; (editor) *Contemporary Organization Development: Approaches and Interventions,* University Associates, 1972; (editor) *Current Issues and Strategies in Organization Development,* Human Sciences Press, 1977; (editor) *The Cutting Edge: Current Theory and Practice in Organization Development,* University Associates, 1978.

(With S. R. Michael, F. Luthans, G. S. Odiorne, and S. Hayden) *Techniques of Organizational Change,* McGraw, 1981; *Organization Development Principles and Practices,* Little, Brown, 1982; (with M. S. Plovnick and R. E. Fry) *Organization Development Exercises: Cases and Readings,* Little, Brown, 1982; (editor with L. D. Goodstein) *Trends and Issues in Organization Development,* University Associates, 1982.

Also contributor to book chapters. Contributor to journals. Editor, *Organizational Dynamics.*

WORK IN PROGRESS: A book chapter, "On Empowerment"; a book on leadership and management.

* * *

BURNS, Thomas (Jr.) 1928-

PERSONAL: Born May 6, 1928, in Arena, Wis. *Education:* University of Wisconsin—Madison, B.B.A., 1950; University of Michigan, M.B.A., 1957; University of Minnesota, Ph.D., 1963. *Office:* Department of Accounting, Ohio State University, Columbus, Ohio 43210.

CAREER: Certified public accountant in Wisconsin and Illinois. Lawrence University, Appleton, Wis., assistant professor of accounting, 1952-55; University of Michigan, Ann Arbor, lecturer in accounting, 1955-57; Southern Illinois University at Carbondale, assistant professor of accounting, 1957-58; University of Minnesota, Minneapolis, instructor in accounting, 1958-63; Ohio State University, Columbus, 1963—, began as associate professor, currently professor of accounting, chairperson of department, 1977-81, director of doctoral program in accounting, 1965-71, 1974—, moderator, accounting research colloquium, 1967—. Visiting associate professor, Stanford University, 1964; visiting professor of accounting, Harvard University, 1964, University of Chicago, 1965, University of California, Berkeley, 1972-73.

MEMBER: American Accounting Association (chairman, committee on Accounting Hall of Fame, 1974; director, 1981-83), Beta Alpha Psi (national president, 1978-79).

WRITINGS: Accounting Trends I, McGraw, 1967, 18th edition, 1984; (with H. S. Hendrickson) *The Accounting Sampler*, McGraw, 1967, 4th edition, 1985; *The Use of Accounting Data in Decision Making*, Ohio State University, 1967; *Academic Careers in Accounting*, Beta Alpha Psi, 1969, revised edition, 1984; *The Behavioral Aspects of Accounting Data for Peformance Evaluation*, Ohio State University, 1969, revised edition, 1971.

(With J. L. Livingstone) *Income Theory and Rate of Return*, Ohio State University, 1971; (with Hendrickson) *The Accounting Primer: An Introduction to Financial Accounting*, McGraw, 1972; *Behavioral Experiments in Accounting*, Ohio State University, 1972; *Accounting in Transition*, Ohio State University, 1974; *Doctoral Programs in Accounting*, American Accounting Association, 1984. Book review editor, *Accounting Review*, 1977-81.

*   *   *

BURROWS, E(dwin) G(ladding)   1917-

PERSONAL: Born July 23, 1917, in Dallas, Tex.; son of Millar (a scholar) and Irene (Gladding) Burrows; married Gwen Lemon (divorced, 1972); married Beth Elpern (a teacher), December 7, 1973; children: Edwin Gwynne, Daniel William, David John. *Education:* Yale University, B.A., 1938; University of Michigan, M.A., 1940. *Home:* 20319 92nd Ave. W., Edmonds, Wash. 98020.

CAREER: WUOM-Radio, Ann Arbor, Mich., manager, 1948-70; University of Wisconsin, Madison, director of National Center for Audio Experimentation, 1970-73; WUOM-Radio, executive producer, 1973-82; writer. *Military service:* U.S. Navy, 1943-46. *Member:* National Association of Educational Broadcasters (chairman of board of directors, 1967).

AWARDS, HONORS: Major Hopwood Award from University of Michigan, 1940; Ohio State Award, 1953, for "Radio Guild Theater," 1954, for "They Fought Alone," 1955, for "A Gallery of Women" and "Red Man in Michigan," 1956, for "Tales of the Valiant," 1971, for "The Tree Plumber," and 1974, for "Properties"; fellow of Yaddo Foundation, 1963, 1966; Borestone Mountain Poetry Award, 1964, for "The Day Grandmother Died."

WRITINGS—Poetry: The Arctic Tern, Grove, 1957; *Man Fishing*, Sumac Press, 1970; *The Crossings*, New Moon, 1976; *Kiva*, Ithaca House, 1976; *On the Road to Baily's*, Fallen Angel Press, 1979; *The House of August*, Ithaca House, 1984.

Plays: "All Night Store," produced by National Center for Audio Experimentation at University of Wisconsin, Madison, 1971; "Six Ecodramas," National Center for Audio Experimentation, 1971; "Circe," Canadian Broadcasting Corp., 1972;

"Visiting Hours," Radio Nederland, 1972; *Properties: A Play for Voices* (produced by Earplay, Madison, Wis., 1974), Quarterly Review of Literature, 1978.

Contributor to anthologies, including *Accent Anthology, Best Poems of 1964, Good Company: Poets at Michigan, The Hopwood Anthology: Five Decades of American Poetry*, and *SPR: A Decade of Poems*. Contributor of poems to magazines, including *American Poetry Review, Epoch, Paris Review, Poetry Northwest*, and *Sumac*.

*   *   *

BURTON, John A(ndrew)   1944-

PERSONAL: Born April 2, 1944, in London, England; son of Andrew (a portrait painter) and Edna (Ede) Burton. *Education:* Educated in public schools in London, England. *Religion:* Atheist. *Home:* 28A Filmer Rd., London S.W.6, England. *Agent:* Murray Pollinger, Murray Pollinger Ltd., 4 Garrick St., London WC2E 9BH, England. *Address:* Old Mission Hall, Sibton Green, Saxmundham, Suffolk.

CAREER: British Museum of Natural History, London, England, assistant information officer, 1963-69; assistant editor, *Birds of the World*, 1969-71, and *Animals*, 1971-72; editor, *Birds International* (journal of British section of International Council for Bird Preservation), 1972-75; Fauna Preservation Society, London, assistant secretary, beginning 1975. Director of Foe Publicity. Natural history consultant to Friends of the Earth Ltd.

MEMBER: International Union for the Conservation of Nature and Natural Resources, British Ornithological Union, Society for the Study of Amphibians and Reptiles, Mammal Society, Linnean Society (fellow), Otter Trust (council member), Tetrapods Club.

WRITINGS: The How and Why of Extinct Animals, Transworld, 1972, Wonder, 1974; *Birds of the Tropics*, Crown, 1973; (editor) *Owls of the World: Their Evolution, Structure, and Ecology*, Dutton, 1973, revised edition, 1980; *Naturalist in London*, David & Charles, 1974; *The How and Why Book of Fossils*, Transworld, 1974, Grosset, 1976; (with D. H. S. Risdon) *The Love of Birds*, Octopus Books, 1975; (with John Sparks) *Worlds Apart: Nature in the City*, Doubleday, 1976; *Musical Instruments from Odds and Ends*, Carousel, 1976; (with E. N. Arnold and Denys Ovenden) *A Field Guide to Reptiles and Amphibians of Europe*, Collins, 1978; (with Bruce Pearson) *Wild Animals*, Collins, 1980; (editor) *Guinness Book of Mammals*, Guinness, 1982. Contributor to science magazines and conservation journals, including *New Scientist* and *Birds International*.

WORK IN PROGRESS: Research on wildlife and wildlife conservation.†

*   *   *

BUSH, William (Shirley, Jr.)   1929-

PERSONAL: Born July 21, 1929, in Plant City, Fla.; son of William Shirley (an auto dealer) and Vera (Crews) Bush; married Mary Sutcliffe (a teacher of French), April 2, 1959; children: Anastasia, James, John, Andrew. *Education:* Stetson University, A.B., 1950; University of South Dakota, M.A., 1953; Universite de Paris, docteur de l'universite, 1959. *Religion:* Greek Orthodox. *Home:* 81 Wychwood Park, London, Ontario, Canada N6G 1R4. *Office:* Department of French, University of Western Ontario, London, Ontario, Canada N6A 3K7.

CAREER: Duke University, Durham, N.C., instructor, 1959-62, assistant professor, 1962-65, associate professor of Romance languages, 1965-66; University of Western Ontario, London, associate professor of Romance languages, 1966-67, professor of French, 1967—.

MEMBER: American Maritain Association, American Weil Society, Amitie Charles Peguy, Fellowship of S. Alban and S. Sergius (president, 1967-69; secretary, 1971-72 and 1973-77).

AWARDS, HONORS: Fulbright awards, 1956-57 and 1957-58; Duke University summer fellowships, 1963 and 1966; Canada Council leave fellowship, 1972-73 and 1979-80; Canada Council research grant, 1983-84, for *The Evolution of Bernanos' Creative Vision.*

WRITINGS: Souffrance et expiation dans la pensee de Bernanos, Lettres Modernes (Paris), 1962; *L'Angoisse du mystere,* Minard (Paris), 1966; *Georges Bernanos,* Twayne, 1970; (editor) *Regards sur Baudelaire,* Lettres Modernes, 1974; *Genese et structures d' "Un Mauvais Reve,"* Lettres Modernes, 1982; (author of preface, notes, and new text conforming to original manuscript) Georges Bernanos, *Sous le soleil de Satan,* Plon (Paris), 1982; (author of preface) Michel Bernanos, *Ils ont dechire Son image . . . : Conte fantastique,* Pensee Universelle (Paris), 1982; (author of preface) M. Bernanos, *Au-devant de Vous: Poemes,* Cahiers Bleus (Troyes-en-Champagne), 1984.

Contributor to *A Critical Bibliography of French Literature;* contributor of articles to *Etudes Bernanosiennes, Prism,* and *Concern.* Member of editorial advisory council, *Twentieth-Century Studies.*

WORK IN PROGRESS: A novel, *The Seventh Summer; Morality and Poetic Structure: Essay on "Les Fleurs du mal";* *The Evolution of Bernanos' Creative Vision; Genese et structures de "Sous le soleil de Satan"; Genese et structures de "Dialogues des Carmelites"; To Quell the Terror,* a historical account of the guillotining of the sixteen Carmelites of Compiegne in 1794.

*   *   *

BUTCHER, James Neal   1933-

PERSONAL: Born November 20, 1933, in Bergoo, W.Va.; son of Lionel Glenn (a coal miner) and Georgia (Neal) Butcher; married Carolyn Williams; children: Sherry, Jay, Neal, Holly. *Education:* Guilford College, B.A., 1960; University of North Carolina at Chapel Hill, M.A., 1962, Ph.D., 1964. *Home:* 9800 Edgewood Rd., Bloomington, Minn. *Office:* Department of Psychology, University of Minnesota, Minneapolis, Minn. 55455.

CAREER: University of North Carolina at Chapel Hill, instructor in psychology, 1960-61; Raleigh Mental Health Center, Raleigh, N.C., psychology trainee, 1961-62; Veterans Administration Hospital, Durham, N.C., psychology intern, 1962-63; University of North Carolina at Chapel Hill, instructor in psychology, 1963-64; University of Minnesota—Minneapolis, assistant professor, 1964-67, associate professor, 1967-70, professor of psychology, 1970—. Visiting instructor in psychology, North Carolina College, 1963-64. *Military service:* U.S. Army, Airborne Infantry, 1951-54; served in Korea, 1952-53.

MEMBER: American Psychological Association (fellow), Guilford Scholarship Society.

WRITINGS: (Editor) *MMPI: Research Developments and Clinical Applications,* McGraw, 1969; *Abnormal Psychology,* Brooks-Cole, 1971, 6th edition (with James C. Coleman) published as *Abnormal Psychology and Modern Life,* Scott, Foresman, 1980, 7th edition, 1984; *Objective Personality Assessment: Changing Perspectives,* General Learning Press, 1971; (editor) *Objective Personality Assessment: Changing Perspectives,* Academic Press, 1972; (with Paolo Pancheri) *Handbook of Cross-National MMPI Research,* University of Minnesota Press, 1976; (editor) *New Developments in the Use of the MMPI,* University of Minnesota Press, 1979; (with Charles D. Spielberger) *Advances in Personality Assessment,* Lawrence Erlbaum, 1983.

WORK IN PROGRESS: Research on cross-cultural objective personality assessment, personality characteristics associated with college adjustment, crisis intervention therapy, psychotherapy, and computerized personality assessment.

C

CAIDEN, Gerald E(lliot)   1936-

PERSONAL: Born June 2, 1936, in London, England; son of Morris and Rosa (Silverman) Caiden; married Naomi Joy Solomons (a university researcher); children: Miriam Hannah, Rachel Debra. *Education:* London School of Economics and Political Science, B.Sc., 1957, Ph.D., 1959. *Home:* 10614 Cushdon Ave., Los Angeles, Calif. 90064. *Office:* School of Public Administration, University of Southern California, Los Angeles, Calif. 90089-0041.

CAREER: West London College of Commerce, London, England, lecturer, 1957-58; University of London, London School of Economics and Political Science, London, tutor, 1958-59; Carleton University, Ottawa, Ontario, Canada Council fellow, 1959-60; Australian National University, Canberra, research fellow, 1961-66; Hebrew University of Jerusalem, Jerusalem, Israel, professor of political science, 1966-68; University of California, Berkeley, visiting professor of political science, 1968-71; University of Haifa, Haifa, Israel, professor of political science, 1971-75, chairman of department, 1972-74; University of Southern California, Los Angeles, professor, School of Public Administration, 1975—.

Visiting professor, Yonsei University (Seoul, Korea), 1982, and London School of Economics and Political Science, 1983. Guest lecturer at Indian Institute of Public Administration, Delhi, and Hebrew University of Jerusalem, 1964, and at other universities and institutes in Canada, England, Israel, and United States. Fellow of National Institute of Law Enforcement and Criminal Justice, 1976. Has done field work in comparative public administration in the Philippines, Hong Kong, India, Israel, Greece, Italy, and France. Consultant to governments of Australia and Israel, American Bar Association, National Institute of Public Administration, National Science Foundation, and several other agencies.

MEMBER: Royal Institute of Public Administration, American Society for Public Administration, Australian Political Science Association.

AWARDS, HONORS: Canada Council fellowship, 1959-60; research grant from Institute of Personnel Administration, Melbourne, Australia, 1963; Storey Memorial Award of Australian Institute of Management, 1964.

WRITINGS: The Federal Civil Service of Canada, [London], 1960; *Career Service: An Introduction to the History of Personnel Administration in the Commonwealth Public Service of Australia, 1901-1961,* Melbourne University Press, 1965; *The A.C.P.T.A.: A Study of White Collar Public Service Unionism in the Commonwealth of Australia 1885-1922,* Department of Political Science, Australian National University, 1966; *The Superannuation Act, 1922-1965,* A.C.O.A. (Sydney), 1966; *The Commonwealth Bureaucracy,* Melbourne University Press, 1967; *Assessing Administrative Performance: A Case Study of Israel's Administrative Culture,* Department of Political Science, University of California, Berkeley, 1968; *Administrative Reform,* Aldine, 1969.

Industrial Relations in the Australian Public Sector, Institute of Industrial Labor Relations, University of Michigan Press, 1971; *Israel's Administrative Culture,* Institute of Governmental Studies, University of California, 1970; *The Dynamics of Public Administration,* Holt, 1971; *Public Employment Compulsory Arbitration in Australia,* Institute of Labor and Industrial Relations, University of Michigan-Wayne State University, 1971; *The Dynamics of Public Administration: Guidelines to Current Transformations in Theory and Practice,* Holt, 1971, 2nd edition, Palisades, 1982; *Politics and Administration: The History of an Untenable Dichotomy,* Department of Political Science, Haifa University, 1973, revised edition published as part of *The Discipline of Public Administration: The Paradigmatic Debate in Perspective,* School of Public Administration, University of Southern California, 1978; *Political Penetration of the Israeli Bureaucracy,* Department of Political Science, Haifa University, 1973, revised edition published as *Toward Depoliticization in a Dominant Party Competitive System: Israel's Experience,* 1974.

Administrative Reform Strategy in Venezuela, United Nations Development Program, 1975; *Towards a More Efficient Government Administration,* Australian Government Publishing Services, 1975; *To Right Wrong: The Ombudsman Experience in Israel,* Institute of Governmental Studies, University of California, 1975, revised edition published as *To Right Wrong: The Initial Ombudsman Experience in Israel,* Ashdown, 1980; *Police Revitalization,* Lexington Books, 1977; *The Search for an Apolitical Science of American Public Administration, 1886-1946,* School of Public Administration, University of Southern California, 1978.

(Editor) *Administrative Reform and Public Policy*, Public Policy Organization, 1981; (editor with Heinrich Siedentopf) *Strategies for Administrative Reform*, Lexington Books, 1982; (with wife, Naomi Caiden) *Administrative Corruption*, Ashdown Press, 1982; (editor) *An International Handbook of the Ombudsman*, Volume I: *Evolution and Present Function*, Volume II: *Country Surveys*, Greenwood Press, 1982; (with Richard Lovard and others) *A Select Bibliography of American Public Administration*, Garland, 1983; (editor with Geraldo Caravantes) *Development: A Reader*, McGraw, 1983; (editor) *Reforming American Bureaucracy*, Policy Studies Organization, 1983; (with H. Alexander) *Public Policy Studies*, Volume V: *Public Policy and Political Institutions: Domestic Reform*, JAI Press, 1984.

Contributor: D. C. Corbett and B. B. Schaffer, editors, *Decisions*, Cheshire, 1965; P. Lengyel, editor, *Approaches to the Science of Socioeconomic Development*, Paris UNESCO, 1971; G. R. Curnow and R. N. Spann, editors, *Public Policy and Administration in Australia*, Wiley, 1975; A. Leemans, editor, *The Management of Change in Government*, Martinis Nijhoff, 1975; Y. Chapel, editor, *Administrative Management for Development*, IIAS (Brussels), 1977; D. Gould, editor, *Administrative Reform in Zaire*, University of Zaire Press, 1978; (with W. Bjur) S. K. Sharma, editor, *Dynamics of Development: An International Perspective*, Volume I, Concept Publishing (New Delhi), 1978; (with H. Hahn) R. Baker and F. Meyer, editors, *Evaluating Alternative Law Enforcement Policies*, Lexington Books, 1979; L. N. Ahmed, editor, *Pemikiran baru: bagi pentadbiran awam Malaysia*, Kementerian Pelajaran Malaysia, 1979.

M. M. Khan, editor, *Bureaucratic Self-Preservation: The Failure of Major Administrative Reform Effort in the Civil Service of Pakistan*, Dacca University Press, 1980; Kahn, editor, *Administrative Reform: Theoretical Perspective*, Dacca University Press, 1981; Siedentopf, editor, *Administrative Reform*, Speyer, 1981; F. Lane, editor, *Current Issues in Public Administration*, St. Martin's, 1982; Changsoo Lee, editor, *The Modernization of Korea and the Impact of the West*, University of Southern California Press, 1982; K. Tummula, editor, *Administrative Systems Abroad*, University Press of America, 1982; Siedentopf, editor, *Strategies for Administrative Reform*, Lexington Books, 1982; D. Rosenbloom, editor, *Public Personnel Policy: The Politics of Civil Service*, Kennikat, 1983; J. Bowman and J. Rabin, editors, *Politics and Administration*, Dekker, 1983; O. Dwividi and W. Kernaghan, editors, *Ethics in the Public Service: Comparative Perspectives*, IIAS, 1983.

Contributor of more than one hundred articles to periodicals, including *Public Administration, Australian Quarterly, International Review of Administrative Sciences,* and *State Audit.* Editorial consultant to several journals, including *Public Personnel Review, Public Administration in Israel and Abroad, Administration and Society, Journal of Public Administration, Southern Review of Public Administration,* and *Public Administration Review.*

SIDELIGHTS: *Administrative Reform* has been published in a Hebrew-language edition.

*   *   *

CALTER, Paul (William) 1934-

PERSONAL: Born June 18, 1934, in New York, N.Y.; son of Arthur and Frances Calter; married Margaret Carey, May 13, 1959; children: Amy, Michael. *Education:* Cooper Union, B.S.,

1962; Columbia University, M.S., 1966. *Home:* 33 South Pleasant St., Randolph, Vt. 05060. *Office:* Department of Mathematics, Vermont Technical College, Randolph, Vt. 05061.

CAREER: Columbia University, New York, N.Y., senior research assistant, Heat and Mass Flow Analyzer Laboratory, 1952-57, 1959-60; Kollsman Instrument Corp., Elmhurst, N.Y., development engineer, 1960-65; Intertype Co., Brooklyn, N.Y., senior project engineer, 1965-68; Vermont Technical College, Randolph, 1968—, began as associate professor, currently professor of mathematics. Independent consultant in the design of optical and mechanical instruments and apparatus. *Military service:* U.S. Army, 1957-59.

MEMBER: Volunteers for International Technical Assistance, Optical Society of America, American Society of Mechanical Engineers, Authors Guild, University Club.

WRITINGS: *Problem Solving with Computers*, McGraw, 1973; *Graphical and Numerical Solution of Differential Equations*, Educational Development Center, 1977; *Magic Squares* (novel), Thomas Nelson, 1977; *Outline of Technical Mathematics*, McGraw, 1978; *Fundamentos di Matematica*, McGraw, 1980; *Technical Mathematics*, Prentice-Hall, 1983; *Practical Math Handbook for the Building Trades*, Prentice-Hall, 1983; *Technical Mathematics with Calculus*, Prentice-Hall, 1984; *Practical Math for Electricity and Electronics*, McGraw, 1984.

Contributor to *Review of Scientific Instruments* and *Journal of Engineering Graphics.*

WORK IN PROGRESS: *Place of Oaks*, a novel; *Mathematics for the Computer*, a textbook.

AVOCATIONAL INTERESTS: Painting, sculpture, mountaineering.

*   *   *

CAMERON WATT, Donald   1928-

PERSONAL: Surname originally Watt; surname changed c. 1964; indexed in some sources under Watt; born May 17, 1928, in Rugby, England; son of Robert Cameron (a schoolmaster) and Barbara (Bidwell) Watt; married Marianne Ruth Grau, December 28, 1951 (died, 1962); married Felicia Cobb Stanley, December 29, 1962; children: (first marriage) Ewen; (second marriage) Cathryn (stepdaughter). *Education:* Oriel College, Oxford, B.A., 1951, M.A., 1954. *Agent:* A. D. Peters & Co., 12 Buckingham St., London WC2N 6BU, England. *Office:* London School of Economics and Political Science, University of London, Houghton St., London WC2A 2AE, England.

CAREER: Assistant editor in British Foreign Office, 1951-54; University of London, London School of Economics and Political Science, London, England, assistant lecturer, 1954-56, lecturer, 1956-62, senior lecturer, 1962-66, reader, 1966-72, titular professor of international history, 1972-82, Stevenson Professor of International History, 1982—. *Survey* editor for Royal Institute of International Affairs, 1962-71; official historian for Cabinet Office; secretary-treasurer of International Commission for the History of International Relations. Member of advisory committee of British National Film Archive; historical adviser to British Broadcasting Corp. television series, "The Mighty Continent." *Military service:* British Army, Intelligence Corps, 1946-48.

MEMBER: International Institute of Strategic Studies, Royal Historical Society (fellow), Association of Contemporary Historians (chairman), Royal Institute of International Affairs, Royal United Services Institute, Greenwich Forum (chairman, 1974-84), Friends of the Royal Academy, Anglo-German Group of Historians, Players Theatre Club.

AWARDS, HONORS: Rockefeller fellow at Institute for Advanced International Studies (Washington, D.C.), 1960-61.

WRITINGS: (Editor with J. B. Donne) *Oxford Poetry, 1950,* Blackwell (Oxford), 1950; *Britain and the Suez Canal,* Oxford University Press, 1956; (editor and author of introduction) *Documents on the Suez Crisis,* Oxford University Press, 1957.

Britain Looks to Germany, Oswald Wolf, 1965; *Personalities and Policies: Studies in the Formulation of British Foreign Policy in the Twentieth Century,* University of Notre Dame Press, 1965; (editor) *Documents on International Affairs, 1961-63,* three volumes, Oxford University Press, 1965-71; (editor) *Survey of International Affairs, 1961-63,* three volumes, Oxford University Press, 1966-77; (editor with Kenneth Bourne) *Studies in International History,* Longmans, Green, 1967; (with Frank Spencer and Neville Brown) *A History of the World in the Twentieth Century,* Hodder & Stoughton, 1967, Morrow, 1968; (editor and author of introduction) *Hitler's "Mein Kampf,"* Hutchinson, 1969; (editor) *Contemporary History in Europe,* Allen & Unwin, 1969.

(Editor with James Mayall) *Current British Foreign Policy, 1970-72,* three volumes, Temple Smith, 1971-73; *Too Serious a Business: European Armed Forces and the Coming of the Second World War,* University of California Press, 1976; (editor) *Greenwich Forum V, the North Sea: A New International Regime?; Records of an International Conference at the Royal Naval College, Greenwich, 2, 3, and 4 May 1979,* Westbury House, 1980; (editor with Bourne) *British Documents on Foreign Affairs: Reports and Papers from the Foreign Office Confidential Print; Russia, 1859-1914,* six volumes, University Publications of America, 1983; *Succeeding John Bull: America in Britain's Place, 1900-1975,* Cambridge University Press, 1984.

Project director of *The Tokyo War Crimes Trial* (transcripts), with index and guide, 1981; editor of *The Soviet Union, 1917-1939,* Volumes I-III, 1984; author of material for "War and Society," for Open University television. Contributor to academic journals in England, Italy, France, Germany, and the United States. Editor of newsletter of European Association of American Studies, 1962-66; member of editorial board of *Political Quarterly,* 1969—, *Marine Policy,* 1978—, and *International History Review.*

WORK IN PROGRESS: How War Came, covering the years 1938-39; *British Images of the Soviet Union, 1930-1950; International Relations, 1945-1975;* "Studying Britain and the sea in the contemporary world."

SIDELIGHTS: Donald Cameron Watt's main interests are American foreign policy, Germany, the Middle East, and maritime affairs; he has visited Switzerland, Austria, Canada, France, Germany, the Netherlands, Belgium, Denmark, Italy, Japan and United States. *Avocational interests:* Cats, exploring London.

*　　　*　　　*

CAMPBELL, George F(rederick)　1915-

PERSONAL: Born July 27, 1915, in England; son of Joseph (a shipwright) and Edith McSorley (Jones) Campbell; married

Elizabeth L. Knox (a copywriter), August 29, 1942; children: Roger, Isabel, Roy. *Education:* Birkenhead Institute of Technology, national certificate in naval architecture, 1937. *Politics:* Liberal. *Religion:* Church of England. *Home:* 35 Camelford St., Brighton, England.

CAREER: Royal Mail Lines, London, England, assistant naval architect, 1939-55; London County Council, London, naval architect, 1955-61; Elliot Automation, Rochester, England, technical illustrator, 1961-63; Art Model Studios, Mt. Vernon, N.Y., ship model maker, 1963-65; Chemplant Designs, New York City, model maker, 1965-67; American Museum of Natural History, New York City, diorama designer and maker, 1967—. Designer-consultant for "Cutty Sark" Preservation Society; consultant to maritime museums and organizations, including World Ship Trust and "Wavertree" Ship Restoration Project, Manhattan.

MEMBER: Royal Institution of Naval Architects.

WRITINGS: (With Prosper Dowden) *Ships of the Royal Mail Lines,* Adlard Coles, 1953; *China Tea Clippers,* Adlard Coles, 1955, revised edition, McKay, 1974; *Jackstay,* Model Shipways, 1962; (with E. W. Petrejus) *Ships of All Ages,* De Esch, 1970; *The Neophyte Ship Modeller's Jackstay,* Model Shipways, 1975. Contributor to *Sea Breezes* and *Ship & Boat Builder.*

WORK IN PROGRESS: Research on Elizabethan and seventeenth-century English shipbuilding techniques for *Sovereign of the Seas;* research on the ancient city of Alexandria with special reference to sea frontage and the lighthouse, Pharos; studying marine paintings of historical ships; a book on a new theory about the "Mary Celeste" mystery; painting specialised subjects of ships by commission in oil and watercolour.

SIDELIGHTS: George F. Campbell once wrote *CA* that he has had a "close and active association with shipbuilding and shipping since childhood through family connections, as second best to a seagoing career thwarted by polio. An understanding of the technicalities of shipbuilding, and of the aesthetic expression of the designers of ships, past and present, inspires me to present these men on a level with the more universally acclaimed civil architects; and to achieve this end by writing, illustrating and painting in the traditional manner, whereby the truth of the subtlety of ship shapes can be shown and their beauty appreciated."

China Tea Clippers is being translated into Russian.

*　　　*　　　*

CANTOR, Eli　1913-
(Gregory A. Douglas)

PERSONAL: Born September 9, 1913, in Bronx, N.Y.; son of Sol M. (a typographer) and Bertha (Seidler) Cantor; married Beatrice Mink (a consultant in audio-speech disabilities), October 4, 1942; children: Ann, Fred. *Education:* New York University, B.S., 1934, M.A., 1935; Harvard University, J.D., 1938. *Politics:* "All systems need gadflies, but with age I've come to deplore rebels without proper cause." *Religion:* "All formal religions tend to be manipulative; mine is private." *Home and office:* 15 West 81st St., New York, N.Y. 10024. *Agent:* Paul Gitlin, 7 West 51st St., New York, N.Y. 10019.

CAREER: Columbia Broadcasting System, New York City, member of legal staff, 1938-39; *Esquire,* Chicago, Ill., member of editorial staff, 1940-41; Research Institute of America, New York City, editor-in-chief of *Research Institute Report,*

1941-60; Photo-Composing Room, Inc., New York City, president, 1961-65; Composing Room, Inc., New York City, chairman of board of directors, 1965-71; Royal Composing Room, New York City, chairman emeritus, 1971—; writer and consultant on management, printing, and publishing, 1971—. Chairman of board of directors of Printing Industries of Metropolitan New York, 1970-72; chairman of research-technical committee of Graphic Arts Technical Foundation, 1971—; chairman of board of directors of Printing Industries of America, 1973-74; graphics panelist for National Endowment for the Arts, 1973—; has represented his industry before the U.S. Congress. Member of Yaddo Development Committee; director of Gallery 303, 1961-78. Lecturer at colleges and universities, including Harvard University, California State Polytechnic College, New York University, Yale University, and Pratt Institute. Worked for Office of War Information.

MEMBER: Chamber Music America (member of board of directors), Authors Guild, Authors League of America, Harvard Club. *Awards, honors:* Awards from the graphics industry for design and leadership; O'Brien Award for best short stories, 1940; the Eli Cantor Fellowship for literature was established at Yaddo, 1984.

WRITINGS: Enemy in the Mirror (novel), Crown, 1977; *Love Letters* (novel), Crown, 1979; (under pseudonym Gregory A. Douglas) *The Rite,* Zebra Books, 1979; (under pseudonym Gregory A. Douglas) *The Nest,* Zebra Books, 1980.

Plays: "Old Lady" (three-act), first produced in New York City at Oscar Serlin Workshop, 1943; "Our Secret Weapon" (television play), first produced in 1943; "Candy Store" (three-act), first produced in New York City at New York City Drama Festival, 1948; "The Golden Goblet" (two-act), first produced in New York City at Theatre 13, 1960; "Yes, There Are Buffalo in Italy" (one-act), first produced at Institute for Advancement of Theatre Arts, 1965. Also author of seven plays for "Armstrong Circle Theatre," 1951-52.

Contributor to anthologies, including *Anthology of Magazine Verse for 1936,* edited by Alan Pater, *O'Brien Best Short Stories,* 1940, and *100 Radio Plays,* edited by Kozlenko, 1941. Contributor of stories, poems, and articles to popular and literary magazines, including *Story, Accent,* and *Poetry.*

WORK IN PROGRESS: A novel about "two misfits who help each other find their authenticity."

SIDELIGHTS: Eli Cantor writes: "The generational swinging of the social pendulum is my main subject. It gives some people a free, exciting ride; others it slices to pieces. Whether it 'advances' Hegelianly as it swings no one knows. My writing is concerned with the impact on individuals, for good or bad; and I am fundamentally concerned with how society is affected by the dynamics of psychological growth (or arrest) in infancy and childhood and in modern family life."

The Eli Cantor Papers were established at the Columbia University Library in 1984.

AVOCATIONAL INTERESTS: Painting, playing chamber music ("on the Cremona violin I am fortunate enough to own"), travel.

BIOGRAPHICAL/CRITICAL SOURCES: Publishers Weekly, January 2, 1978.

*   *   *

CARLSON, Loraine   1923-

PERSONAL: Born May 6, 1923, in Los Angeles, Calif.; daughter of Leon W. (a finance corporation administrator) and Belle (Fowles) Cumings; married Cecil Spencer, November 2, 1946 (divorced, 1951); married Neil Carlson (a graphic artist), December 18, 1958. *Education:* University of Redlands, B.A., 1944; University of Southern California, graduate study, 1950-53. *Office address:* Upland Press, P.O. Box 7390, Chicago, Ill. 60680.

CAREER: Hughes Aircraft Co., Culver City, Calif., technical writer and publications supervisor, 1953-58; TRW Systems, Redondo Beach, Calif., technical writer in Research Division, 1964-66; publisher with husband, Neil Carlson, Upland Press, Chicago, Ill.; has also worked as elementary school teacher, journalist, and travel agent.

WRITINGS—With maps and illustrations by husband, Neil Carlson: *Mexico: An Extraordinary Guide,* Rand McNally, 1971; *The TraveLeer Guide to Mexico City,* Upland Press, 1978, 2nd edition, 1981; *The TraveLeer Guide to Yucatan and Guatemala,* Upland Press, 1980; *The TraveLeer Guide to Yucatan,* Upland Press, 1982.

*   *   *

CARR, Edward Hallet   1892-1982

PERSONAL: Born June 28, 1892, in England; died November 3, 1982, in Cambridge, England. *Education:* Attended Trinity College, Cambridge. *Home:* Dales Barn, Barton, Cambridgeshire, England. *Office:* Trinity College, Cambridge University, Cambridge, England.

CAREER: British Foreign Office, temporary clerk, 1916, attached to delegation to Paris Peace Conference, Paris, France, 1919, temporary secretary at British Embassy, Paris, 1920-21, third secretary, 1922-25, second secretary at British Legation, Riga, Lithuania, 1925-29, staff member in London, England, 1929-30, assistant adviser for League of Nations affairs, 1930-33, first secretary, 1933-36; University College of Wales, Aberystwyth, Wilson Professor of International Politics, 1936-47; Ministry of Information, director of foreign publicity, 1939-40; *The Times,* London, England, assistant editor, 1941-46; Oxford University, Balliol College, Oxford, England, tutor in politics, 1953-55; Cambridge University, Trinity College, Cambridge, England, fellow, 1955-82.

MEMBER: British Academy (fellow), Oxford Club, Cambridge Club.

AWARDS, HONORS: Commander of the Order of the British Empire, 1920; honorary fellow of Balliol College, Oxford University, 1966; Litt.D., University of Manchester, 1964, Cambridge University, 1967; LL.D., University of Groeningen, 1964.

WRITINGS: Dostoevsky, 1821-1881: A New Biography, Houghton, 1931, reprinted, Barnes & Noble, 1962, and Folcroft, 1977; *The Romantic Exiles: A Nineteenth-Century Portrait Gallery,* Gollancz, 1933, reprinted, MIT Press, 1981; *Karl Marx: A Study in Fanaticism,* Dent, 1934; *International Relations since the Peace Treaties,* Macmillan, 1937, new enlarged edition, 1940, published as *International Relations between the Two World Wars, 1919-1939,* St. Martin's, 1947, reprinted, 1969; *Michael Bakunin,* Macmillan, 1937, revised edition, Octagon, 1975; *Britain: A Study of Foreign Policy from the Versailles Treaty to the Outbreak of War,* Longman's Green, 1939; *Propaganda in International Politics,* Farrar & Rinehart, 1939; *The Twenty Years' Crisis, 1919-1939: An Introduction to the Study of International Relations,* Macmillan

(London), 1939, 2nd edition, St. Martin's, 1946, reprinted, Harper, 1964, and Humanities, 1981.

The Future of Nations: Independence or Interdependence?, Kegan Paul & Co., 1941; *Conditions of Peace*, Macmillan, 1942; *Nationalism and After*, St. Martin's, 1945; *The Soviet Impact on the Western World* (lectures), Macmillan (London), 1946, Macmillan (New York), 1947, reprinted, Fertig, 1973; *The Moral Foundations for World Order*, University of Denver Social Science Foundation, 1948.

A History of Soviet Russia, St. Martin's, Part I: *The Bolshevik Revolution, 1917-1923*, three volumes, 1950-53, Part II: *The Interregnum, 1923-1924*, 1954, Part III: *Socialism in One Country, 1924-1926*, three volumes, Volume III in two parts 1958-1964, Part IV: *Foundations of a Planned Economy, 1926-1929*, three volumes, 1969-78, Volume I, with R. W. Davies, in two parts, Volume III, in three parts; *Studies in Revolution*, Macmillan, 1950, revised edition, F. Cass, 1962; *The New Society*, Macmillan (London), 1951, St. Martin's, 1957, new edition, Beacon Press, 1957; *German-Soviet Relations between the Two World Wars, 1919-1939*, Johns Hopkins University Press, 1951, reprinted, Arno Press, 1979.

What Is History?, St. Martin's, 1961; *The October Revolution: Before and After*, Knopf, 1969 (published in England as *1917: Before and After*, Macmillan, 1969).

The Russian Revolution: From Lenin to Stalin, 1917-1929, Free Press, 1979; *From Napoleon to Stalin and Other Essays*, St. Martin's, 1980; *Twilight of the Comintern, 1930-1935*, Pantheon, 1983. Also author, with others, of *Human Rights: Comments and Interpretations*. Author of published lectures and addresses.

SIDELIGHTS: Edward Hallett Carr's "14-volume history of the Soviet Union from 1917-29 is considered the most comprehensive political study of the Bolshevik's consolidation of power," according to a *Los Angeles Times* reporter. Alec Nove writes in the *Times Literary Supplement* that "these fourteen volumes, representing some thirty years of meticulous research, most certainly constitute a great achievement. For anyone who desires to know what happened in Russia between 1917 and 1929 they are and will be essential works of reference. Students of the subject will be reading Carr when the reviewer's grandchildren have graduated. Of course the presentation raises controversial issues, and one can disagree with the author about emphasis and interpretation."

The criticism most frequently made about Carr's work was that he was "ever strong upon the stronger side," a London *Times* reviewer reports, "when he seemed to turn, over the years, from a respect for the power of Hitler's Germany to a greater respect for the power of Stalin's Russia." In the words of *New Yorker* critic William Pfaff, throughout Carr's career, many found fault with his inclination "to demonstrate by his history, tautologically, that those who were successful were right, as is proved by their success; history is going somewhere, and those who make it go are justified in whatever they have to do to accomplish it; those who get in the way deserve what happens to them." Thus, his tendency to downplay Stalinist excesses and dissident reactions until late in the fourteen-volume project seemed first to lend the work an apologetic tone, and, later, an inconsistency. Pfaff maintains that Carr delineated his outlook in his 1961 book *What Is History?*, which Pfaff describes as "an attack upon all those who had lost their sense of a world in motion, regarding change 'not as achievement, as opportunity, as progress, but as an object of fear.'

[Carr] defended 'the possibility of unlimited progress—or progress subject to no limits that we can need or envisage—towards goals which can be defined only as we advance towards them, and the validity of which can be verified only in a process of attaining them.' By implication, the verdict is not yet in on Stalin (or Hitler, one then must add; and Carr in 1939 was an appeaser). This belief is at the core of the controversy over his work.''

Commenting on *A History of Soviet Russia*, however, Nove points out that "any critical remarks must be seen in the context of admiration: an enormous task has been carried out with immense professional skill. Carr is incapable of dullness, and writes with enviably elegant style and clarity." He calls it "a masterwork full of good things. Criticisms of this or that interpretation of events there must be, and this perhaps inevitably occupies much of this review. Yet the overriding impression of any reader of Carr's great study must be one of ungrudging admiration: what a colossal scholarly achievement!''

Several of Carr's works have been translated into foreign languages.

BIOGRAPHICAL/CRITICAL SOURCES: Observer, January 26, 1969, September 7, 1969, December 12, 1971, November 14, 1976, December 31, 1978; *Times Literary Supplement*, January 30, 1969, December 4, 1969, December 3, 1971, January 11, 1980, June 10, 1983; *Listener*, March 12, 1970; *New York Review of Books*, January 22, 1976; *New York Times Book Review*, December 30, 1979, May 29, 1983; *Los Angeles Times Book Review*, April 3, 1983; *New Yorker*, November 21, 1983.

OBITUARIES: Essays in Honor of E. H. Carr, Archon Books, 1974; *Times* (London), November 5, 1982; *Washington Post*, November 6, 1982; *Los Angeles Times*, November 10, 1982; *Time*, November 15, 1982; *AB Bookman's Weekly*, January 31, 1983.†

*   *   *

CARR, Pat M(oore)   1932-
(Pat M. Esslinger)

PERSONAL: Born March 13, 1932, in Grass Creek, Wyo.; daughter of Stanley (an oil camp supervisor) and Bea (Parker) Moore; married Jack H. Esslinger, June 4, 1955 (divorced July, 1970); married Duane Carr (a professor and writer), March 26, 1971; children: Stephanie, Shelley, Sean, Jennifer. *Education:* Rice University, B.A., 1954, M.A., 1955; Tulane University, Ph.D., 1960. *Home:* Pinnacle Star Route, Box 147, Elkins, Ark. 72727.

CAREER: Texas Southern University, Houston, Tex., instructor in English, 1956-58; Dillard University, New Orleans, La., assistant professor of English, 1960-61; Louisiana State University in New Orleans (now University of New Orleans), assistant professor of English, 1961-62, 1965-69; University of Texas at El Paso, assistant professor, 1969-72, associate professor, 1972-78, professor of English, 1978-79.

MEMBER: Phi Beta Kappa, Phi Kappa Phi.

AWARDS, HONORS: South and West short fiction award, 1969; Mark IV Award from Library of Congress, 1970, for *Beneath the Hill of the Three Crosses;* National Endowment for the Humanities grant, 1973; Iowa School of Letters short fiction award, 1977; Texas Institute of Letters short story award, 1978.

WRITINGS: (Under name Pat M. Esslinger) *Beneath the Hill of the Three Crosses* (stories), South & West, 1970; *The Grass*

Creek Chronicle (novel), Endeavors in Humanity, 1976; *Bernard Shaw*, Ungar, 1976; *The Women in the Mirror*, University of Iowa Press, 1977; *Mimbres Mythology*, Texas Western Press, 1978. Work appears in *Best American Short Stories*. Contributor to *Encyclopedia of World Literature*. Contributor of articles and stories (before 1971, under name Pat M. Esslinger) to *Southern Review*, *Yale Review*, *Arizona Quarterly*, and *Western Humanities Review*.

WORK IN PROGRESS: The Village of Women, a novel about *la violencia* in South America; a collection of Indian myths; a collection of stories set during the Civil War.

SIDELIGHTS: Pat M. Carr once wrote *CA:* "Every place I've lived has marked my work, but probably my Wyoming childhood and my years in South America and New Orleans have provided my favorite settings. I've been exceedingly fortunate in that my generation has been able to experience a wide range of conflicts and emotions from the most silent to the most articulate and has possibly come to Matthew Arnold's conclusion that 'Ah, love, let us be true to one another.' All of my own themes, at least, lead there."

*   *   *

CARRICK, Malcolm 1945-

PERSONAL: Born June 23, 1945, in Cardiff, Wales; son of John (a publisher) and Jane (a lecturer; maiden name, Perkins) Carrick. *Education:* Attended Beckenham Art College, 1961-62, Ravens-bourne Art College, 1962-63, and Chelsea Art College, 1963-66. *Home:* 4 Palace Grove, Fox Hill, Upper Norwood SE19 2X10, England.

CAREER: Musician, composer, artist, writer.

WRITINGS—Children's books; self illustrated, except as indicated: *The Wise Men of Gotham*, Collins, 1973, Viking, 1975; *All Sorts of Everything* (not self-illustrated), Heinemann, 1973; *Mr. Pedagouge's Sneeze*, Deutsch, 1974; *The Extraordinary Hatmaker*, Transworld, 1974; *The Fairy Tale Book*, Evans Brothers, 1974; *The Farmer's Wish*, Transworld, 1975; *Make and Do*, Evans Brothers, 1975; *Splodges*, Collins, 1975, Viking, 1976; *Once There Was a Boy and Other Stories* (not self-illustrated), Penguin, 1975; *Making Magic*, Carousel, 1976; *See You Later Alligator*, Deutsch, 1976; *Tramp*, Harper, 1977; *Higgelty Pigglety*, E.M.I. Ltd., 1977; *Today Is Shrew's Day*, Harper, 1978; *Science Experiments*, Carousel, 1978; *I Can Squash Elephants!: A Masai Tale about Monsters*, Viking, 1978; *Horror Costumes and Makeup*, Transworld, 1978; *The Year of Mr. Nobody*, Harper, 1978.

Making Masks, Transworld, 1980; *You'll Be Sorry, You'll Be Sorry When I'm Dead*, Harper, 1980; *Mr. Tod's Trap*, Harper, 1980; *I'll Get You!*, Harper, 1980. Also author of *Scaredy Cat*. Author of stories for BBC radio children's series, "Listen with Mother"; author and illustrator of "Springboard" filmstrip series, and of teleplays with music, including "A Little Black Magic," 1975, and "Walkabout," 1976. Contributor of teleplays to British Broadcasting Corp., series including "Play School," "Blue-Peter," and "For My Next Trick." Composer for "Pop It Goes," 1977.

WORK IN PROGRESS: Work on a BBC-TV children's series, "Jackanory"; illustrations for J.R.R. Tolkien's stories.

SIDELIGHTS: Malcolm Carrick told *CA:* "Interestingly, I had thought of giving up writing books for children as all the work I wanted to do was considered too graphic, too thoughtful, and

introspective for English publishers and audiences. So I went to New York and found a much better reception for my particular fantasy world tinged with autobiography—as in *Tramp*—and my hard graphic style of illustrating—as in *I Can Squash Elephants!* I really consider myself an American author as only there can the full range of styles and genres I use be fulfilled.

"Apart from books, I'm now working in radio ('Listen with Mother') and doing another four folk tales for my 'Springboard' series. Outside of work, I hope to become involved in my great love—adventure playgrounds—again. I've set up many in London over the years and am building a library of children's books for a children's hospice in Oxford.

"For myself, I live and work in the house I grew up in. It's very old, built in 1860; bits of it fall off from time to time. At the very top of the house I have a studio with the original sloped attic shape, a north window, and a view over a field where I used to play football when I was about seven. I used to look over to my house to see if I could wave to my mother before being dragged back to school, which I hated. School seems to be better these days. When children come to visit me in my attic, read my new stories, and talk, they all seem to like school, so something's changed for the better. The view from my window hasn't changed since I've been here. For over thirty years I've been looking out of this window; perhaps I'm part of the view by now. This is the place I describe in my novel, *I'll Get You!*

"I hope to write about another phase of my life soon: the swinging sixties, when we were all 'Jack the Bad' and spent our time wandering around Soho listening to the bands—the Stones, the Animals. Teenagers seem very interested in the sixties these days. It's very odd, they seem nostalgic about something they never knew; I call it *ostalger*—other people's nostalgia, other people's windows."

*   *   *

CARROLL, Anne Kristin
See GALES, Barbara J.

*   *   *

CARTER, Nick
See WALLMANN, Jeffrey M(iner)

*   *   *

CARVER, (Richard) Michael (Power) 1915-

PERSONAL: Born April 24, 1915, in Blechingley, England; son of Harold Power (a merchant) and Winifred Anne Gabrielle (Wellesley) Carver; married Edith Lowry-Corry, November 22, 1947; children: Susanna, Andrew, Alice Carver Walters, John. *Education:* Attended Winchester College and Royal Military College, Sandhurst, 1933-34. *Politics:* None. *Religion:* Church of England. *Home:* Wood End House, Wickham, Fareham, Hants PO17 6J2, England. *Agent:* David Higham Associates Ltd., 5-8 Lower John St., London W1R 4HA, England.

CAREER: British Army, career officer, 1935-76, in Royal Tank Corps, 1935, general staff officer in Seventh Armored Division, 1942, commanding officer of First Royal Tank Regiment, 1943, commander of Fourth Armored Brigade, 1944, technical staff officer in Ministry of Supply, 1947, assistant quartermaster-general of Allied Land Forces in Central Europe, 1951, colonel with general staff of Supreme Headquarters, Allied Powers, Europe, 1952, deputy chief of staff in East Africa, 1954, chief of staff in East Africa, 1955, director of plans in War Office, 1958-59, commander of Sixth Infantry Brigade, 1960-62, general officer commanding Third Division, 1962-64, commander of Joint Truce Force in Cyprus and deputy commander of United Nations Force in Cyprus, 1964, director of army staff duties for Ministry of Defence, 1964-66, commander of Far East Land Forces, 1966-67, commander-in-chief in the Far East, 1967-69, general officer commander-in-chief of Southern Command, 1969-71, chief of general staff, 1971-73, commandant of Royal Electrical and Mechanical Engineers, 1966-76, Royal Tank Regiment, 1968-72, Royal Armoured Corps, 1974-76, aide-de-camp (general), 1969-72, chief of defense staff, 1973-76, retiring as field marshal; writer, 1976—.

MEMBER: Anglo-Belgian Club.

AWARDS, HONORS—Military: Military Cross; companion of the Distinguished Service Order, with bar; commander of the Order of the British Empire; Companion of the Bath, Knight Commander, Knight Grand Cross; cited as a Baron, 1977.

WRITINGS: El Alamein, Batsford, 1962; *Tobruk,* Batsford, 1964; (editor) *The War Lords,* Little, Brown, 1976; *Harding of Petherton,* Weidenfeld & Nicolson, 1978; *The Apostles of Mobility,* Weidenfeld & Nicolson, 1979; *War since 1945,* Putnam, 1981; *A Policy for Peace,* Faber, 1982; *The Seven Ages of the British Army,* Weidenfeld & Nicolson, 1984.

SIDELIGHTS: In his long military career, Michael Carver has earned many honors and written several books on military history and strategy. One of these books, *War since 1945,* is a compendium of selected international conflicts summarized and examined by the author. In a *Times Literary Supplement* review of the work, Edward N. Luttwak has criticism for Carver's brevity in covering certain wars: "[The author's] accounts are in fact outlines of theatre-strategy with a few tactical observations thrown in, and some political commentary. India's wars with China and Pakistan, and French colonial warfare in Indochina and Algeria are somewhat more usefully treated than Korea, Vietnam and the Arab-Israeli wars, but on the whole Lord Carver's text is too prolix and short of detail to serve for quick reference, and much too scant for proper military history."

However, adds Luttwak, "the reader will feel sufficiently rewarded by the first hundred pages to forgive the rest. In these, Lord Carver reviews the small and very small wars of the British Empire in devolution: Palestine, Malaya, Kenya, Cyprus, Aden and Borneo. Here brevity serves a positive use instead of prohibiting a serious study since the conjoint treatment it allows offers the illuminating perspective of one episode on another, without preventing the author from examining the different dimensions that demand attention, from the tactical to the political, since all these wars were so small in scale." And Otto J. Scott, writing about *War since 1945* in the *Los Angeles Times Book Review,* finds that while Carver "does not philosophize, does not draw any grand conclusions," nevertheless he "has provided the most succinct and understandable descriptions of these conflicts that is available. From his descriptions and his brilliant clarity, readers are, at last, provided with the information they need to draw their own conclusions about the post-colonial era, with its multitude of horrifying racial and religious divisions and collisions."

A "thoroughly intelligent and honest contribution to the great nuclear debate," is the way Wolf Mendl characterizes Carver's book *A Policy for Peace* in another *Times Literary Supplement* article. "From the start," continues Mendl, "Carver takes his position somewhere between the total abolitionists and those who want the West to be at least the equal and if possible the superior of the Soviet Union in every kind of nuclear weaponry. He recognizes that in discussions of nuclear war 'there is no proof that one idea is better than another. One can only fall back [on] reason and logic, and one has to admit that at the heart of nuclear deterrent strategy there lies a paradox that is not susceptible to a logical solution.'"

The author "skillfully walks the tightrope between nuclear pacifists and nuclear warriors," Mendl observes. "He understands those who think the world has gone mad as they contemplate the forty thousand or more nuclear warheads the West and the Soviet Union share between them. He sees through much of the nonsense of strategic nuclear sophistry and he asks the basic question that many thoughtful people are asking everywhere: 'In this situation, is war during the rest of the twentieth century, and in the twenty-first, likely to be effective and acceptable as "a continuation of state policy by other means"?'"

BIOGRAPHICAL/CRITICAL SOURCES: Times Literary Supplement, March 20, 1981, November 19, 1982; *Los Angeles Times Book Review,* March 29, 1981; Michael Carver, *A Policy for Peace,* Faber, 1982.

* * *

CASTLE, Mort 1946-

PERSONAL: Born July 8, 1946, in Chicago, Ill.; son of Sheldon H. (in sales) and Lillian (a nutritionist; maiden name, Marcus) Castle; married Jane Potts (a high school French teacher), July 4, 1971. *Education:* Illinois State University, B.S.E., 1968. *Politics:* "Staunch Democrat." *Religion:* Jewish. *Home and office:* 402 Stanton Lane, Crete, Ill. 60417. *Agent:* Mary T. Williamson, Midwest Literary Agency, P.O. Box 26117, Indianapolis, Ind. 46226.

CAREER: Entertainer (singer, musician, comedian, and hypnotist, including television and radio work), 1965-68; Crete-Monee High School, Crete, Ill., English teacher, 1968-80; editorial associate, Writer's Digest School, 1983—. Educational consultant in language arts; public lecturer.

WRITINGS: Mulbray (short stories), Samisdat Associates, 1976; *The Deadly Election* (novel), Major Books, 1976; *Fiction for the Fellows: A Guide to Writing Stories for Men's Magazines* (nonfiction), Pamphlet Publications, 1980; *The Strangers* (novel), Dorchester Publishing, 1984.

Writer of advertising copy, musical continuity, and cartoon captions. Contributor of more than one hundred stories, poems, and articles to popular and literary journals, including *Cavalier, Twilight Zone, Mike Shayne Mystery Magazine, Oyez Review, Nitty-Gritty,* and *True Story.*

WORK IN PROGRESS: The Diakka, a horror novel; numerous short stories and humorous articles.

SIDELIGHTS: Mort Castle writes: "I was fortunate to have been friends with Bill Wantling, one of our most gifted poets, during our undergrad days. I was a jerky suburban kid, dreaming of being show biz boffo, and he was a genuine writer! It was good to sit on his living room floor, ugly central Illinois wind growling outside, strumming guitar, trying to look/sound like Bob Dylan, while Wantling made poems happen. Initial inspiration, experiences that made me think I might someday toss a line in literary waters? I think so. Thanks Bill, and thanks to Miss Ryan, my kindergarten teacher, who kept telling me someday I'd be writing for television.

"I became serious about writing in 1971, at age twenty-five, with certain intimations about my own mortality clobbering me. My first submitted story sold to a men's magazine, *Mr.*—thanks, Everett Myers, editor—and I figured I had it made. Write it up, send it out, get the money. *Hubris*. One hundred fifty rejections later, I had the realization it might not be that easy. It still isn't. One persists and hopes and dreams.

"I resigned my teaching position . . . to work full time as a writer but surprisingly I've found myself doing as much teaching as ever as a consultant in language arts, public lecturer, writer-in-residence, workshop leader, etc. I greatly enjoy meeting people who want to learn about 'wordsmithing,' and, in the past few years, I've made about 400 presentations to groups ranging in age from pre-school to senior citizens.

"But always, there's the writing, the writing, the writing. And that writing can continue to happen only because of the unfailing support of my wife, Jane, and the encouragement of loving family and friends. The writer as a 'loner'? Forget it. It's cliche time—but people *do* need people. I'm blessed—my people are *with* me—and I bless them and plan to dedicate a book to each and every one of them in the years to come."

BIOGRAPHICAL/CRITICAL SOURCES: Chicago Sun-Times, March 1, 1977; *Suburban Tribune,* June 10, 1977, March 3, 1982; *Star-Tribune,* September 25, 1977, July 12, 1984; *Chicago Times,* January 4, 1982.

*   *   *

CATANESE, Anthony James (Jr.)   1942-

PERSONAL: Born October 18, 1942, in New Brunswick, N.J.; son of Anthony James, Sr. (an engineer), and Josephine (Barone) Catanese; married Sara Phillips, October 23, 1968; children: Mark Anthony, Mark Alexander, Michael Scott. *Education:* Rutgers University, B.A., 1963; Rider College, certificate in real estate, 1963; University of Washington, certificate in Computer Applications to Urban Analysis, 1964; New York University, M.U.P. (with honors), 1965; University of Wisconsin, Ph.D., 1968. *Office:* Center for Planning and Development, Georgia Institute of Technology, Atlanta, Ga. 30332-0155.

CAREER: Rutgers University, New Brunswick, N.J., assistant to director, Rutgers Planning Service and Campus Planning Office, 1961-62; Middlesex County Planning Board, New Brunswick, planning assistant, 1962-63, senior planner, 1964-66; New Jersey Department of Conservation and Economic Development, Division of State and Regional Planning, Trenton, N.J., senior planner, 1963-64; Georgia Institute of Technology, School of Architecture, Atlanta, Ga., assistant professor, 1967-68, associate professor of city planning, director of Urban Systems Simulation Laboratory, 1968-73; University of Miami, Coral Gables, Fla., James A. Ryder Professor, 1973-77; University of Wisconsin—Milwaukee, dean of School of Architecture and Urban Planning, 1975-82; provost, Pratt Institute, 1982-84; Georgia Institute of Technology, Center for Planning and Development, director, 1984—.

State planning consultant, Wisconsin Department of Resource Development, Madison, Wis., 1966-67; president, A. J. Catanese & Associates, Atlanta, 1967—; vice-president for management, MRC Realty Joint Venture, 1968—; executive vice-

president, PP&C Properties, 1970—. Lecturer on state planning at New York University, New York, N.Y., 1964; visiting lecturer at Clark College, Atlanta, 1968; visiting professor of urban and regional studies, Virginia Polytechnic Institute, Blacksburg, Va., 1969.

MEMBER: International Platform Association, American Academy of Political and Social Sciences, American Association of University Professors, American Institute of Planners, American Institute of Urban and Regional Affairs, American Society of Planning Officials, Association for Computing Machinery, Association of Collegiate Schools of Planning, National Association of Housing and Redevelopment Officials, National Urban Coalition, Urban America, Inc., Urban and Regional Information Systems Association, Regional Science Association, National Geographic Society, Association of Wisconsin Planners, Georgia Planning Association, Regional Plan Association (New York-New Jersey-Connecticut region), City Planners Section, Georgia Municipal Association, Wisconsin Alumni Union, New York University Planners Organization, Organization of Rutgers Planning, University of Wisconsin Planning Club.

AWARDS, HONORS: American Institute of Planners Contributions to the Profession Award, 1973, service award, 1974, 1978; named citizen of the year, Walnut Area Improvement Council, 1981; named to American Heritage Hall of Fame, 1981; Man of the Year, Pompeii Club, 1982; distinguished service award, Wisconsin Society of Architects, 1982; Research Client Award, *Progressive Architecture,* 1983; distinguished service award, Wisconsin Planning Association, 1983.

WRITINGS: The Alternatives of the Horizon Planning Concept, New Jersey Division of State and Regional Planning, 1964; *A Statewide Planning Analysis of Utility Services in New Jersey,* New Jersey Division of State and Regional Planning, 1964; *The Residential Development of New Jersey: A Regional Approach,* New Jersey Division of State and Regional Planning, 1964; (editor) *The Myths and Realities of the Image of Greenwich Village: A Workshop Model of a Planning Process,* Graduate School of Public Administration, New York University, 1966; *Data Processing for State Planning,* Wisconsin Department of Resource Development, 1967; *The Economy of Northwestern Wisconsin,* Wisconsin Department of Resource Development, 1967; *Comprehensive Plan for Cordele, Georgia,* Keck & Wood, 1969; *Alpharetta Plans for the Future,* Keck & Wood, 1969; *Systemic Planning: An Annotated Bibliography and Literature Guide,* Council of Planning Librarians (Monticello), 1969.

Scientific Methods of Urban Analysis, University of Illinois Press, 1970; *Structural and Socioeconomic Factors of Commuting,* Clearinghouse for Federal Scientific and Technical Reports, 1971; (editor) *New Perspectives on Transportation Research,* Heath, 1972; *Planners and Local Politics: Impossible Dreams,* Sage Publications, 1973; *Urban Transportation in South Florida,* University of Miami, 1974; *Planners and Local Politics: Impossible Dreams,* Sage Publications, 1974, published as *Impossible Dreams: Planners and Local Politics,* Sagemark, 1977; (editor with P. Farmer) *Personality, Politics, and Planning: How City Planners Work,* Sage Publications, 1978; (editor with James C. Snyder) *Introduction to Urban Planning,* McGraw, 1979; (editor with Snyder) *Introduction to Architecture,* McGraw, 1979; *The Politics of Planning and Development,* Sage Publications, 1984.

With others: *A Plan for Manasquan, New Jersey,* Rutgers University, 1963; (with Alan Walter Steiss) *Commercial Land Use in New Jersey,* New Jersey Division of State and Regional Planning, 1964; *The Stottsburg Plan: A Model of Growth and Factors Affecting Development,* Graduate School of Public Administration, New York University, 1965; *Wisconsin Development Plan,* Wisconsin Department of Resource Development, 1967; (editor with John L. Gann and Leo Jakobson) *Explorations into Urban Functions, Spatial Organization, and Environmental Form,* University of Wisconsin Board of Regents, 1967; (with Richard G. Poirier) *Planning for Recreation: A Methodology for Functional Planning,* Department of Planning and Economic Development (Honolulu), 1968; *A Survey of Student Planning Organizations,* American Institute of Planners, 1968; (with Roger J. Budke) *Urban Transportation: Problems and Potentials,* Atlanta Chamber of Commerce, Leadership Development Foundation, 1969; *An Information System for Fulton County, Georgia,* Fulton County Manager's Office, 1969; (with James B. Grant and Edward N. Kashuba) *Application of Computer Graphics to Urban and Regional Planning,* School of Architecture, Georgia Institute of Technology, 1969.

(With Steiss) *Systemic Planning: Essays on Theory and Application,* Heath, 1970; *Hawaii State Growth Policies Plan: 1974-1984,* State of Hawaii, 1974; (with Steiss) *Managing Hawaii's Coast,* State of Hawaii, 1976; (with E. Alexander and D. Sawicki) *Urban Planning: Guide to Information,* Gale, 1978; (with J. C. Snyder) *Federal-State Institutions for Cooperative Planning and Management,* Federal-State Land Use Planning Commission for Alaska, 1979.

Contributor: Michael Sumichrast, editor, *What's Ahead in 1966?,* National Association of Homebuilders, 1965; *Proceedings of Midwest Seminar on Urban and Regional Research,* University of Wisconsin Board of Regents, 1967; *The Recreation Element of the General Plan Revision Program: State of Hawaii,* Donald Wolbrink & Assoc. (Honolulu), 1967.

Handerworterbuch der Raumforshung und Raumordnung, Gebruder Janecks Verlag, 1970; James J. Murray, editor, *Urban and Regional Ground Transportation,* High Speed Ground Transportation Journal, Inc., 1973; H. Patton and R. H. Slavin, editors, *State Issues,* Council of State Governments, 1973; (with Howard Harrenstien) *Proceedings of Governor's Conference on Development of Mass Transit Statewide,* Hawaii Department of Transportation, 1974; T. R. Kitsos, editor, *Land Use in Colorado: The Planning Thicket,* University of Colorado, 1974; (with D. Hinds and B. O'Neil) M. Golden and R. Schumacher, editors, *Proceedings of the Institute of Management Science,* TIMS, 1975; (with Hinds and O'Neil) S. Elmagraby, editor, *Handbook of Operations Research,* Van Nostrand, 1978; Naomi W. Lede, editor, *Strengthening Organizational Capabilities for Transportation Management,* Government Printing Office, 1978.

I. Stollman and others, editors, *The Practice of Local Government,* International City Management Association, 1980; J. C. Snyder, editor, *Architectural Research,* Van Nostrand, 1984.

Contributor of articles to periodicals, including *Jersey Plans, New Jersey Economic Review, Journal of Housing, Les annales de l'economie collective,* and *Traffic Quarterly.*

WORK IN PROGRESS: A book on values for planning.

*   *   *

CAUDILL, Harry M(onroe)   1922-

PERSONAL: Born May 3, 1922, in Whitesburg, Ky.; son of

Cro Carr and Martha V. (Blair) Caudill; married Anne Frye, December 15, 1949; children: James, Diane, Harry Frye. *Education:* University of Kentucky, B.L., 1948. *Politics:* Democrat. *Home address:* Box 727, Whitesburg, Ky. 41858. *Office:* Department of History, University of Kentucky, Lexington, Ky. 40506.

CAREER: Admitted to Bar of State of Kentucky, 1948; lawyer in private practice, 1948-76; University of Kentucky, Lexington, professor of Appalachian studies, 1977—. Member of Kentucky State legislature, 1954-60. Has presented lectures to numerous universities and colleges, and served on many conferences on public affairs throughout the U.S. *Military service:* U.S. Army, Infantry, World War II.

MEMBER: American Bar Association, Soil Conservation Society of America, Sierra Club, Audubon Society, Kentucky State Historical Society, Omicron Delta Kappa, Phi Delta Phi.

AWARDS, HONORS: Friends of American Writers award of merit, 1963, for *Night Comes to the Cumberlands: A Biography of a Depressed Area;* Kentucky Statesman award, 1968; Tom Wallace Forestry award, 1976; American Library Association notable book citations, for *Night Comes to the Cumberlands, My Land Is Dying,* and *Watches of the Night.* Honorary degrees from Tusculum College, 1966, Berea College, 1971, and University of Kentucky, 1971.

WRITINGS: Night Comes to the Cumberlands: A Biography of a Depressed Area, Atlantic-Little, Brown, 1963; *Dark Hills to Westward: The Saga of Jennie Wiley,* Atlantic-Little, Brown, 1969.

My Land Is Dying, Dutton, 1971; *The Senator from Slaughter County,* Atlantic, 1974; *A Darkness at Dawn,* University Press of Kentucky, 1976; *Watches of the Night,* Atlantic, 1976; *The Mountain, the Miner, and the Lord, and Other Tales from a County Law Office,* University Press of Kentucky, 1980; *Theirs Be the Power: The Moguls of Eastern Kentucky,* University of Illinois Press, 1983.

Contributor of articles to periodicals including *Senior Citizen, Reader's Digest, Inter-play, Intellectual Digest, Defenders of Wildlife,* and others.

SIDELIGHTS: Harry M. Caudill has devoted much of his career to chronicling the colorful characters, dramatic events, and often desperate situations that have evolved in the Appalachian region of eastern Kentucky. Caudill, in fact, is "the closest the region has come to having a spokesman with national visibility, impeccable cultural credentials and a strong social conscience," according to Eliot Wigginton in the *Washington Post.* Reviewing Caudill's *The Mountain, the Miner, and the Lord, and Other Tales from a County Law Office,* Wigginton goes on to note that "at first glance, the pages seem peopled by a rogue's gallery of mountain moonshiners, murderers, thieves, bigamists and other ignorant, disreputable 'Deliverance' types. . . . But Caudill knows what he's doing. The fact that these stories have been singled out from the thousands he must have heard [the author is a lawyer and a university professor of Appalachian studies] demands a closer look."

Much of *The Mountain, the Miner, and the Lord* deals with the plight of perhaps America's most abused working group, the coal miners. Expanding on that theme, the author produced *Theirs Be the Power: The Moguls of Eastern Kentucky.* The latter is "a passionate but well-documented chronicle of the rise of King Coal," says *Washington Post Book World* critic Dan E. Moldea, who adds that the work "exhibits how unregulated free enterprise led to the devastation of thousands of human lives. Caudill's [book] is nothing less than an indictment against the coal moguls—names such as Camden, Delano, Forbes, Morgan, Pepper, Rockefeller, Roosevelt, Watson, and Whitfield. From the 1880s on, they poured into the picturesque mountain state, primarily from their homes in New England, exploiting the region's people and destroying their land. Subsequent floods and coal mining disasters have only served to intensify the gloom and depression that the moguls and their plutocracy brought to the area.''

Summarizes Wigginton: ''Those who may be tempted to accuse Caudill of glorifying Appalachian people best left forgotten will be missing several important points [of the author's work]. The men and women [he portrays] do not represent or symbolize the Appalachian personality per se. Every culture and every community has parallel tales. More importantly, they celebrate people who have a magnetism, a tenacity, a personal vision, an independence and a self-sufficiency that elude most of us today. It is almost as though they represent traits and styles of action that are being bred out of the race.''

BIOGRAPHICAL/CRITICAL SOURCES: New Republic, July 20, 1963; *Saturday Review*, August 31, 1963; *New York Times Book Review*, July 13, 1969; *Washington Post*, January 19, 1981; *Washington Post Book World*, January 29, 1984.

*   *   *

CAULFIELD, Malachy Francis 1915-
(Max Caulfield; Max Halstock, Malachy McCoy, pseudonyms)

PERSONAL: Born May 10, 1915, in Belfast, Northern Ireland; son of Malachy (a civil servant) and Julia Mary (Campion) Caulfield; married Mary Mitchell McCoy, September 14, 1943; children: Janet Mary (Mrs. Jean Nicholas), Claire Frances (Mrs. David Howell). *Education:* Earned B.A. from Queen's University, Belfast, Northern Ireland. *Politics:* ''Idiosyncratic.'' *Religion:* ''Latin Catholic.'' *Home:* 7, Paines Cl., Paines Ln., Pinner, Middlesex HA5 3PE, England.

CAREER: Reporter and rewriter for *Irish News*, Belfast, Northern Ireland; reporter for *Daily Mirror*, London, England; news editor of *Sunday Chronicle*, London; associate foreign editor of *Daily Express*, London; chief news editor and head of news department, of Independent Television News, London; assistant editor of *Daily Mail* group, London; editor for *John Bull*, London. Notable assignments include coverage of nuclear development in Britain, the Suez Canal, the Irish Republican Army, and interviews with Brendan Behan, Richard Nixon, Charles de Gaulle, Clark Gable, and Ingrid Bergman. Has appeared on British, Irish, and Canadian television and radio programs. *Member:* Press Club (London).

WRITINGS—Under name Max Caulfield, except as indicated: *The Black City* (fiction), J. Cape, 1952, New American Library, 1954; *Night of Terror* (nonfiction), Muller, 1958; *Tomorrow Never Came* (nonfiction), Norton, 1959; (with Ellen Field) *Twilight in Hong Kong*, Muller, 1960; *The Easter Rebellion* (nonfiction), Holt, 1963.

(With Joan Paisnel) *The Beast of Jersey*, R. Hale, 1972; *The Irish Mystique* (nonfiction), Prentice-Hall, 1973; (with Winifred Young) *Obsessive Poisoner*, R. Hale, 1973; (under pseudonym Malachy McCoy) *Steve McQueen* (biography), Regnery, 1974; (with Ivor Spencer) *Pray Silence*, R. Hale, 1975; (with Linda Lee) *The Life and Tragic Death of Bruce Lee*, Star

Books, 1975; *Mary Whitehouse* (biography), Mowbray, 1975; *Bruce Lee Lives?* (thriller), Star Books, 1975, Dell, 1976; (with James Galway) *James Galway*, Chappel & Co., 1978, Coronet, 1979; (with Denys Webster) *The Danger Game* (nonfiction), R. Hale, 1978; (under pseudonym Max Halstock) *Rats* (nonfiction), Gollancz, 1981; (with Ian Fraser) *Escape from Al-Ould* (nonfiction), Miller, 1983. Also author, under pseudonym Malachy McCoy, of *Kodiak!* (fiction), 1976, and, with Dom Robert Petitpierre, of *Exorcism* (nonfiction), 1977. Contributor to *Illustrated Guide to Britain, Reader's Digest,* and *Route.* Author of celebrity column, *TV Times* (London), 1960-70.

SIDELIGHTS: Malachy Francis Caulfield told *CA:* ''I decided to be a writer when I was about six or seven. By the age of eight I had read *The Count of Monte Cristo, Quo Vadis, The Last Days of Pompeii,* and the entire *Three Musketeers* oeuvre. I devoured everything in sight—boys' magazines and annuals and books of all kinds, and by sixteen had read Tolstoy, Dostoevsky, Rabelais, Boccaccio, Chaucer, Wells, Belloc, Waugh, etc., plus masses of English and Irish poetry. I had also steeped myself in history, particularly Roman history and had read Tacitus, Suetonius, and Gibbon. I had read all the great Irish epic sagas (*Deirdre of the Sorrows, Cuchulainn, Fionn MacCumhail,* etc.). Also Homer, Herodotus, etc. I was particularly attracted by humour, especially American humour and lapped up Damon Runyon, Benchley, Thurber, and Perelman.

''I played the following sports: Gaelic football and hurling, soccer, rugby, cricket, golf, tennis, bowls. I was a fair middle-distance runner and a good swimmer. I spent an inordinate amount of time from the age of twelve to twenty-eight playing poker, solo, and bridge. I have always been a film buff and until recently, attended the cinema two or three times a week. I have only two languages besides English: Latin and Gaelic. I learned to drive a car when aged five.

''I decided the best way to learn to be a writer was to become a newspaper reporter first. While acting as a staff reporter, sub-editor (rewrite man in the U.S.), theatre and film critic and parliamentary reporter in Belfast, I began writing feature articles for my own and other newspapers and magazines.

''Once [I was] in Fleet Street and working for people like Lord Beaverbrook, writing became a wholly professional activity. I nurtured the desire to become a 'creative writer,' of course, and wrote my first book, about Belfast between the wars, while I was associate foreign editor of the *Daily Express.* Thereafter writing became a way of life and remains so.

''I tend to see myself mainly as an expert on Irish affairs—particularly Irish history and topography. I am uniquely positioned to write about Northern Ireland, for instance, because I am a Belfast Catholic whose parents were both born in Southern Ireland and whose paternal family still resides there, and because I am married to a Belfast Protestant and have lived for almost fifty years in England, thus enabling me to be reasonably objective.

''I have, however, a great love for the landscape and history of England and Wales, a fascination reinforced in a most detailed way by my work on two illustrated guide books to Britain. For these two publications, I covered very considerable areas of England and all of Wales, dealing in some detail with the principal towns, villages, architectural, archaeological, historical features, plus the best routes up mountains, the best lakes and rivers and what and where to fish, plus myths and legends.

"I am, to use a hackneyed phrase, widely-travelled. I have enjoyed brief interludes as a foreign correspondent in Italy, Paris, and India. Leaving aside the Polar regions, the only continent I have not visited is Australasia.

"As a young man, I was an avid coarse fisherman. Since then I have fished for shark off Cornwall and gone on *shikari* (a tiger shoot) while a guest of my old friend, the late Maharajah of Cooch-Behar.

"Apart from literature, my main interests are history (with some emphasis on military history), travel, and music (classical only). I play the piano, of course. My principal form of recreation at the moment is *boule*. I still retain a keen interest in foreign affairs."

*   *   *

CAULFIELD, Max
See CAULFIELD, Malachy Francis

*   *   *

CHAIKIN, Miriam   1928-

PERSONAL: Born December 8, 1928, in Jerusalem, Palestine (now Israel); brought to the United States in 1929; daughter of Abraham and Leah (Tikochinsky) Chaikin. *Education:* Attended high school in Brooklyn, N.Y. *Politics:* Democrat. *Religion:* Jewish. *Home:* 107 Waverly Pl., New York, N.Y. 10011.

CAREER: Anna M. Rosenberg Associates, New York City, in public relations, 1957-60; World Publishing Co., Cleveland, Ohio, subsidiary rights director, 1961-66; Bobbs-Merrill Co., Inc., New York City, editorial director, 1969-73; Holt, Rinehart & Winston, Inc., New York City, editorial director, 1973-81; free-lance writer, 1982—.

MEMBER: International P.E.N.

AWARDS, HONORS: P.E.N.-National Endowment for the Humanities Contest award, 1983, for short story "The Samovar."

WRITINGS—All juveniles; fiction; published by Harper, except as indicated: *Ittki Pittki* (picture book), Parents' Magazine Press, 1971; *The Happy Pairr* (picture book), Putnam, 1972; *Hardlucky* (picture book), Lippincott, 1973; *I Should Worry, I Should Care*, 1979; *Finders Weepers*, 1981; *Getting Even*, 1982; *How Yossi Beat the Evil Urge*, 1983; *Lower! Higher! You're a Liar!*, 1984; *Yossi Asks the Angels for Help*, 1985.

Nonfiction; published by Clarion Books, except as indicated: *The Seventh Day: The Story of the Jewish Sabbath*, Doubleday, 1979; *Light Another Candle: The Story and Meaning of Hanukkah*, 1981; *Joshua in the Promised Land*, 1982; *Make Noise, Make Merry: The Story and Meaning of Purim*, 1983; *Shake a Palm Branch: The Story and Meaning of Sukkot*, 1984.

Contributor of adult stories, haiku, and other poetry to a number of periodicals, including *Good Housekeeping, Woman's Day,* and *Midstream*.

WORK IN PROGRESS: The Prophets.

AVOCATIONAL INTERESTS: Walking, cooking, swimming, yoga, belly dancing.

*   *   *

CHAMBLISS, Bill
See CHAMBLISS, William J(oseph)

CHAMBLISS, William J(oseph)   1933-
(Bill Chambliss, Boxman, a pseudonym)

PERSONAL: Born December 12, 1933, in Buffalo, N.Y.; son of Joseph H. (a realtor) and Jean (an actress and poet; maiden name, Ferguson) Chambliss; married Betty Lou Biggs, 1956 (marriage ended); children: Jeff, Kent, Lauren. *Education:* University of California, Los Angeles, B.A., 1955; Indiana University, M.A., 1960, Ph.D.,1962; postdoctoral study at University of Wisconsin—Madison, 1966-67. *Home address:* R.D. 2, Heritage Village, #B-5, Landenberg, Pa. 19350. *Office:* Department of Sociology, University of Delaware, Newark, Del. 19711.

CAREER: University of Washington, Seattle, assistant professor of sociology, 1962-66; University of Wisconsin—Madison, visiting lecturer in sociology, 1966-67; University of California, Santa Barbara, associate professor of sociology, 1967-73; University of Oslo, Oslo, Norway, professor of sociology, 1974-75; University of Stockholm, Stockholm, Sweden, professor of sociology, 1975-76; University of Delaware, Newark, professor of sociology, 1976—. Honorary professorial fellow, Faculty of Law, University College, Cardiff, Wales, 1977; visiting professor, University of Badan (Nigeria), 1969-70, and London School of Economics and Political Science, 1970-71; visiting distinguished scholar at University of Missouri, 1978. *Military service:* U.S. Army, 1956-58.

MEMBER: International Sociological Association, American Sociological Association, Society for the Study of Social Problems, Law and Society Association.

AWARDS, HONORS: National Institute of Mental Health grants, 1962-63, 1965-66; Russell Sage Foundation residency, 1966-67.

WRITINGS: Crime and the Legal Process, McGraw, 1969; (with Robert B. Seidman) *Law, Order and Power*, Addison-Wesley, 1971, 2nd edition, 1984; *Boxman: A Professional Thief's Journey*, Harper, 1972; *Criminal Law in Action*, Wiley, 1975, 2nd edition, 1984; (with Tom Ryther) *Sociology: The Discipline*, McGraw, 1975; (with Milton Mankoff) *Whose Law? What Order?*, Wiley, 1975; *On the Take: From Petty Crooks to Presidents*, Indiana University Press, 1978; *Organizing Crime*, Elsevier, 1982.

Contributor to law and sociology journals. Editor of *Contemporary Crises;* member of editorial board of *British Journal of Law and Society;* contributing editor of *Crime and Social Justice.*

WORK IN PROGRESS: A History of Piracy and Smuggling.

SIDELIGHTS: William J. Chambliss's *On The Take: From Petty Crooks to Presidents* is the result of a decade's research into the recorded crimes of one city, Seattle, Washington. "But the value of [the author's] work," notes *Washington Post* critic Colman McCarthy, "derives from its persuasive refutation of the standard explanation for American crime—'It's the Mafia.' Organized crime, he writes, 'really consists of a coalition of politician, law-enforcement people, businessmen, union leaders and (in some ways least important of all) racketeers.'"

Citing the fact in *On the Take* that some eighty percent of arrests involve the poor and uneducated, those most generally unable to obtain expensive legal defense, McCarthy also states that "it is known . . . that six times more money is stolen from banks by bankers than by street hoodlums. [The *Wall Street Journal*] reads like a crime log, with its three- or four-paragraph stories on convictions or indictments of price-fixers, embezzlers, stock cheats or other crimes of the pen.'' Remarks Chambliss in his work: ''Relying on police and other law enforcement agencies for our information may lead to an overemphasis on the role of those who fit the stereotype of the 'criminal' and a corresponding deemphasis on the importance of businessmen, politicians and law enforcers as institutionalized components of America's political and economic system, which creates and perpetuates syndicates that supply the vices in our major cities.''

''Chambliss would have had a more compelling book if his final chapter on possible reforms 'was stronger,'' concludes McCarthy. ''He did the hard work of penetrating the underworld so well and bravely that he seems to have coasted at the end. His investigation into the nature of the criminal networks is likely to endure longer than his theories.''

BIOGRAPHICAL/CRITICAL SOURCES: William J. Chambliss, *On the Take: From Petty Crooks to Presidents*, Indiana University Press, 1978; *Washington Post*, October 19, 1978.

*   *   *

CHANDOLA, Anoop C. 1937-

PERSONAL: Born December 24, 1937, in Rawatgaon, Pauri, India; son of Satya Prasad and Kishori (Ghildiyal) Chandola; married July 14, 1963; wife's name, Sudha; children: Manjul (son). *Education:* Allahabad University, B.A., 1954; Lucknow University, M.A. (Hindi literature), 1956; University of California, Berkeley, M.A. (linguistics), 1961; University of Chicago, Ph.D., 1966. *Politics:* ''Philosophy of Mahatma Gandhi.'' *Religion:* Hindu. *Home:* 6041 North Calle de la Culebra, Tucson, Ariz. 85718. *Office:* Department of Oriental Studies, University of Arizona, Tucson, Ariz. 85721.

CAREER: Sardar Vallabh Bhai Vidyapeeth University, Vallabh Vidyanagar, India, tutor, 1956-57, lecturer in Hindi, 1957-58; Maharaja Sayajirao University of Baroda, Baroda, India, lecturer in Hindi literature, 1958-59; University of Arizona, Tucson, assistant professor, 1963-66, associate professor, 1967-71, professor of linguistics, Hindi, and Sanskrit, 1971—. Visiting summer assistant or associate professor at University of Wisconsin, 1965, University of California, Berkeley, 1967, 1968, and University of Washington, Seattle, 1969, 1970; visiting professor at University of Texas at Austin. *Member:* American Anthropological Association, Linguistic Society of America, Association for Asian Studies (member of literature and language development committee of South Asia Regional Council, 1972—), Linguistic Society of India.

WRITINGS: (With Norman Zide, Collins Masica, and K. C. Bahl) *A Premchand Reader*, East-West Cultural Center, 1965; (contributor) F. Robert Paulsen, editor, *Changing Dimensions in International Education*, University of Arizona Press, 1969; *A Systematic Translation of Hindi-Urdu into English*, University of Arizona Press, 1970; *Folk Drumming in the Himalayas: A Linguistic Approach to Music*, AMS Press, 1977; *Situation to Sentence: An Evolutionary Method for Descriptive Linguistics*, AMS Press, 1979; (editor) *Mystic and Love Poetry of Medieval Hindi*, Today's and Tomorrow's Publishers, 1982. Contributor of short stories, articles, and reviews in English and Hindi to journals in the United States and India.

CHANG, Lee
See LEVINSON, Leonard

*   *   *

CHARD, Judy 1916-
(Lyndon Chase, Doreen Gordon)

PERSONAL: Born May 8, 1916, in Gloucester, England; daughter of Thomas (an army officer) and Dorothy Isabel (Juan) Gordon; married Maurice Noel Chard (a field manager), July 26, 1941. *Education:* Educated in England. *Religion:* Church of England. *Home:* Morley Farm, Highweek, Newton Abbey, Devon, TQ12 6NA, England.

CAREER: Writer. Has worked as a typist and personal secretary in Birmingham, London, and Wolverhampton, England. Tutor in creative writing, Workers Educational Association and Devon County Council, both Devon, England.

MEMBER: Crime Writers Association, Society of Women Writers and Journalists, Westcountry Writers Association, Romantic Novelists Association.

WRITINGS—Novels; all published by R. Hale: *Through the Green Woods*, 1974; *The Weeping and the Laughter*, 1975; *Encounter in Berlin*, 1976; *The Uncertain Heart*, 1976; *The Other Side of Sorrow*, 1977; *In the Heart of Love*, 1978; *Out of the Shadows*, 1978; *All Passion Spent*, 1979; *Seven Lonely Years*, 1980; *The Darkening Skies*, 1981; *Haunted by the Past*, 1982; *When the Journey's Over*, 1983; *Where the Dream Begins*, 1983; *Rendezvous with Love*, 1984. Author, under pseudonym Lyndon Chase, of *Tormentil*; also author of *Murder Casebook*.

Author of nonfiction works *Along the Lemon, Along the Dart, Along the Teign, Devon Mysteries, The South Hams, About Widecombe*, and *My Devon Life*. Also author of several radio broadcasts based on her nonfiction.

Contributor of short stories, sometimes under pseudonym Doreen Gordon, to periodicals, including *Argosy, Woman's Realm, My Weekly, Story World, London Mystery Magazine, Edgar Wallace Mystery Magazine*, and *Lady*. *Devon Life*, columnist, 1972—, editor, 1981—.

WORK IN PROGRESS: Two serials for Thomson; a sequel to *Devon Mysteries*.

SIDELIGHTS: Judy Chard told *CA:* ''It may be of interest to note that I started to write when I was fifty and into the last ten years I have crammed a lifetime of work and living, meeting new people, and, in fact, my whole life has changed as a result. Most important of all has been my teaching role for the Workers Educational Association, which has opened up a whole new world of helping people who are deeply interested in writing, giving them, too, a new interest.''

*   *   *

CHASE, Glen
See LEVINSON, Leonard

*   *   *

CHASE, Lyndon
See CHARD, Judy

CHASINS, Abram 1903-

PERSONAL: Surname rhymes with "patience"; born August 17, 1903, in New York, N.Y.; son of Saul and Elizabeth (Hochstein) Chasins; married Julia Haberman, 1935 (divorced, 1946); married Constance Keene (a concert pianist and teacher), April 22, 1949. *Education:* Attended Ethical Culture School, 1914-18, Columbia University, 1919-21, Juilliard School, 1918-25, and Curtis Institute of Music, 1926-28. *Home:* 200 East 78th St., New York, N.Y. 10021; and 10717 Wilshire Blvd., Los Angeles, Calif. 90024.

CAREER: Composer and concert pianist. WQXR-Radio (radio network of *New York Times*), New York, N.Y., music director, 1942-65; University of Southern California, Los Angeles, musician-in-residence, 1972—, artistic director of KUSC-Radio (radio station of University of Southern California), 1972-77. Member of Faculty of Curtis Institute of Music, 1926-35, and Tanglewood, 1940-41; lecturer at American universities. Consultant to governments of Canada and Israel; music expert in court cases involving copyright infringements.

AWARDS, HONORS: U.S. Treasury Department awards, 1944, 1945, for meritorious and patriotic services; Mahler Society Award, 1958; String Teachers' Guild award, 1959; Peabody Award, 1960, for radio projects on behalf of musical education; honored by the City of Los Angeles, 1977, for work on RUCA-Radio and National Public Radio network; honored by University of Southern California, 1984, for work in establishing KUSC-Radio.

WRITINGS: Speaking of Pianists, Knopf, 1957, revised edition, 1962, reprinted, Da Capo Press, 1983; *The Van Cliburn Legend,* Doubleday, 1959; *The Appreciation of Music,* Crown, 1965; *Music at the Crossroads,* Macmillan, 1972; *Leopold Stokowski: A Profile,* Hawthorn, 1979, 2nd edition, Dutton, 1982. Composer of "Three Chinese Pieces," "Two Piano Concertos," "Period Suite for Orchestra," "Twenty-four Preludes for Piano," and many works for two pianos. Contributor of articles to national magazines, including *Saturday Review, Saturday Evening Post, McCall's, Ladies' Home Journal,* and *Hi-Fidelity,* and to *New York Times.*

WORK IN PROGRESS: Memoirs, tentatively entitled *Now That I Think of It.*

SIDELIGHTS: Abram Chasins told *CA:* "I write books because it is as necessary a form of expression to me as the need to compose, perform, teach, and broadcast music. Words also enable me to pass on to others some of the fruits of my unusual opportunities to associate and study with truly great people."

One of the great people Chasins studied with was the conductor Leopold Stokowski, who serves as the subject of Chasins' 1979 biography *Leopold Stokowski: A Profile.* As Samuel Lipman notes in a *Times Literary Supplement* article, Chasins, "the distinguished American critic, pianist, and composer has written . . . [an] account of Stokowski, drawing on his own personal and musical association with the conductor. As a composer and pianist Mr. Chasins was the soloist with Stokowski (and the Philadelphia Orchestra) in his own Second Piano Concerto in 1933; as a young instructor he was a colleague of Stokowski in the late 1920s at the Curtis Institute of Music in Philadelphia; in the early 1930s he worked with Stokowski on a study of musical acoustics at the University of Pennsylvania."

Leopold Stokowski: A Profile, says Lipman, "is chatty and eminently readable. Its aim is to evoke not only Stokowski but also his success."

BIOGRAPHICAL/CRITICAL SOURCES: New York Times, April 14, 1972; *Washington Post,* December 13, 1979; *New York Times Book Review,* January 20, 1980; *Times Literary Supplement,* March 7, 1980.

*   *   *

CHAYES, Abram 1922-

PERSONAL: Born July 18, 1922, in Chicago, Ill.; son of Edward and Kitty (Torch) Chayes; married Antonia Handler, December 24, 1947; children: Eva, Abigail, Lincoln, Sarah Prudence, Angelica. *Education:* Harvard University, A.B., 1943, LL.B., 1949. *Home:* 3 Hubbard Park, Cambridge, Mass. 02138. *Office:* 404 Griswold Hall, Harvard Law School, Cambridge, Mass. 02138.

CAREER: Admitted to the Bar of Connecticut, 1950, District of Columbia, 1953, and Massachusetts, 1958; legal adviser to the governor of Connecticut, 1949-50; general counsel for U.S. President's Materials Policy Commission, 1950-51; legal clerk to Supreme Court Justice Felix Frankfurter, 1951-52; Covington & Burling (law firm), Washington, D.C., associate attorney, 1952-55; Harvard University, Cambridge, Mass., assistant professor, 1955-58, professor of law, 1958-61; legal adviser to the assistant secretary, U.S. Department of State, 1961-64; Gingburg & Feldman (law firm), Washington, D.C., associate attorney, 1964-65; Harvard University, professor of law, 1965—. Guest scholar, Brookings Institution, 1977-78. Staff director of Democratic Platform Committee, 1960; director of foreign policy task force of Democratic campaign, 1972. Chairman, International Nuclear Fuel Cycle Evaluation Committee, 1977-78. *Military service:* U.S. Army, field artillery, 1943-46; became captain; received Bronze Star.

MEMBER: American Academy of Arts and Sciences (fellow), American Society of International Law, American Law Institute, Phi Beta Kappa.

AWARDS, HONORS: Carnegie Corp. grant, 1965-66.

WRITINGS: Closed Corporation Seminar Materials, Harvard Law School, c. 1958; (editor) Patricia M. Wald, *Law and Poverty, 1965,* U.S. Government Printing Office, 1965; (editor with R. R. Baxter) *Materials for the Carnegie-Harvard Seminar, 1966,* [Cambridge, Mass.], 1966; (compiler with Thomas Ehrlich and Andreas F. Lowenfeld) *International Legal Process: Materials for an Introductory Course,* two volumes, Little, Brown, 1968-69; (editor with Jerome B. Wiesner) *ABM: An Evaluation of the Decision to Deploy an Anti-Ballistic Missile System,* introduction by Edward M. Kennedy, Harper, 1969.

(With others) *Satellite Broadcasting,* Oxford University Press, 1973; *The Cuban Missile Crisis,* Oxford Univeristy Press, 1974; (with G. W. Rathjens and J. P. Ruina) *Nuclear Arms Control Agreements: Process and Impact,* Carnegie Endowment for International Peace, 1974; (editor with W. Bennett Lewis) *International Arrangements for Nuclear Fuel Reprocessing,* Ballinger, 1977. Contributor of articles to legal journals.†

*   *   *

CHEN, Anthony 1929-
(Tony Chen)

PERSONAL: Born January 3, 1929, in Kingston, Jamaica,

West Indies; came to United States, 1949; naturalized citizen, 1956; son of Arthur (a merchant) and Maud Marie (Ho Pow) Chen; married Pura DeCastro (a nurse supervisor), March 2, 1957; children: Richard, David. *Education:* Attended Art Career School, 1949-51; Pratt Institute, B.F.A. (cum laude), 1955. *Religion:* Roman Catholic. *Home:* 53-51 96th St., Corona, N.Y. 11368.

CAREER: Writer and illustrator of children's books. *Newsweek*, New York, N.Y., art director, 1961-72; Nassau Community College, Garden City, N.Y., instructor in art, 1972-73. Painter and sculptor, with one-man shows in New York. *Awards, honors:* Awards from Society of Illustrators and from Creativity '71; American Institute of Graphic Arts book award, 1972; Society of Illustrators Award of Excellence, 1972; Creativity Award from *Art Direction* magazine, 1972; *Honshi* was selected as a Children's Book Showcase title, 1973.

WRITINGS—Under name Tony Chen; self-illustrated children's books: *Run, Zebra Run*, Lothrop, 1972; *Little Koala*, Holt, 1979.

Illustrator: Helen E. Buckley, *Too Many Crackers*, Lothrop, 1962; Isabelle Chang, *Tales from Old China*, Random House, 1969; Herbert H. Wong and Matthew F. Vessel, *Pond Life: Watching Animals Find Food*, Addison-Wesley, 1970; Hannah Johnson, *Hello, Small Sparrow*, Lothrop, 1971; Edith Hurd, *The White Horse*, Harper, 1971; Ruth Dale, *Do You Know a Cat?*, Singer, 1971; Doris Evans, *Breakfast with the Birds*, Putnam, 1972; Aline Glasgow, *Honshi*, Parents' Magazine Press, 1972; *Dakota Sons*, Harper, 1972; Seymour Simon, *The Rockhound Book*, Viking, 1973; Laurence Pringle, *Follow a Fisher*, Crowell, 1973; Applebaum and Cox, *A Not So Ugly Friend*, Holt, 1973; Charlotte Pomerantz, *The Princess and the Admiral*, Addison-Wesley, 1974; *Many Friends Cooking*, UNICEF, 1980; Sandol Stoddard, *The Doubleday Illustrated Children's Bible*, Doubleday, 1983; *In the City of Paris*, Doubleday, 1984.

SIDELIGHTS: Much of Anthony Chen's painting and sculpture is in private collections. *Avocational interests:* Collecting art, especially animal sculpture from diverse cultures.

BIOGRAPHICAL/CRITICAL SOURCES: American Artist, May, 1972; *New York Times Book Review*, May 7, 1972, March 14, 1984; *Publishers Weekly*, May 22, 1972.

*   *   *

CHEN, Tony
See CHEN, Anthony

*   *   *

CHEW, Ruth 1920-
(Ruth Silver)

PERSONAL: Born April 8, 1920, in Minneapolis, Minn.; daughter of Arthur Percy (a writer) and Pauline (Foucar) Chew; married Aaron B. Z. Silver (a lawyer), April 18, 1948; children: David, Eve (Mrs. Hugh Hamilton Sprunt, Jr.), George, Anne (Mrs. Mark Gloekler), Helen. *Education:* Attended Corcoran School of Art, 1936-40, and Art Students League of New York, 1973—. *Religion:* None. *Home:* 305 East Fifth St., Brooklyn, N.Y. 11218.

CAREER: Writer and illustrator. Artist for *Washington Post*, Washington, D.C., 1942-43, Grey Advertising Agency, New York, N.Y., 1944-46, and Kresge-Newark Department Store, Newark, N.J., 1946-48.

AWARDS, HONORS: Four Leaf Clover Award for Author of the Yaer, Lucky Book Club, 1976-77; *Witch in the House* was nominated for Colorado Children's Book Award; *The Witch's Buttons* was nominated for Arizona Young Readers' Award.

WRITINGS—All self-illustrated books for children; published by Scholastic Book Services, except as indicated: *The Wednesday Witch*, 1969; *Baked Beans for Breakfast*, 1970, published as *The Secret Summer*, 1974; *No Such Thing as a Witch*, 1971; *Magic in the Park*, 1972; *What the Witch Left*, 1973; *The Hidden Cave*, 1973, published as *The Magic Cave*, Hastings House, 1978; *The Witch's Buttons*, 1974; *The Secret Tree House*, 1974.

Witch in the House, 1975; *The Would-Be Witch*, 1976; *The Trouble with Magic*, 1976; *Summer Magic*, 1977; *Witch's Broom*, Dodd, 1977; *The Witch's Garden*, 1978; *Earthstar Magic*, 1979; *The Wishing Tree*, Hastings House, 1980; *Secondhand Magic*, Holiday House, 1981; *Mostly Magic*, Holiday House, 1982; *The Magic Coin*, 1983; *The Witch at the Window*, 1984.

Illustrator: Carol Morse, *Three Cheers for Polly*, Doubleday, 1967; E. W. Hildick, *The Questers*, Hawthorn, 1970; Val Abbott, *The Mystery of the Ghost Bell*, Dodd, 1971; Ann McGovern, *Shark Lady*, Scholastic Book Services, 1978.

AVOCATIONAL INTERESTS: Travel (especially to England and France).

BIOGRAPHICAL/CRITICAL SOURCES: New York Times, May 22, 1977; *Flatbush Life*, May 30, 1977.

*   *   *

CHILDS, David (Haslam) 1933-

PERSONAL: Born September 25, 1933, in Bolton, England; son of John Arthur (an industrial worker; mayor of Bolton) and Ellen (Haslam) Childs; married Monir Pishdad, June, 1964; children: Martin, Julian. *Education:* London School of Economics and Political Science, B.Sc., 1956, Ph.D., 1962; University of Hamburg, graduate study, 1956-57. *Office:* Department of Politics, University of Nottingham, Nottingham NG7 2RD, England.

CAREER: School teacher in London, England, until 1961; television scriptwriter on documentary films, 1961-64; school teacher and teacher in further education courses, 1964-66; University of Nottingham, Nottingham, England, lecturer to senior lecturer, 1966-76, reader in politics, 1976—. Candidate for Parliament, 1964.

MEMBER: Association of University Teachers, Association for Study of German Politics (chairman, 1981—), University Association for Contemporary European Studies, European Movement.

WRITINGS: From Schumacher to Brandt: The Story of German Socialism, 1945-1964, Pergamon, 1966; *East Germany*, Praeger, 1969; *Germany since 1918*, Harper, 1971; *Marx and the Marxists: An Outline of Practice and Theory*, Benn, 1973; (contributor) Roger Tilford, editor, *The Ostpolitik and Political Change in Germany*, Lexington Books, 1975.

Britain since 1945, Benn, 1979; (editor) *The Changing Face of Western Communism*, Croom Helm, 1980; (contributor) James Riordan, editor, *Sport under Communism: The U.S.S.R., Czechoslovakia, the G.D.R., China, Cuba*, Hurst & Co., 1981; (with Jeffrey Johnson) *West Germany: Politics and Society*, Croom Helm, 1981; *The G.D.R.: Moscow's German Ally*,

Allen & Unwin, 1983; (editor) *Honecker's Germany*, Allen & Unwin, 1985. Also contributor to *Collier's Encyclopedia*. Contributor to *Times Literary Supplement, Times Higher Educational Supplement, Guardian, Contemporary Review, World Today*, and other periodicals.

SIDELIGHTS: David Childs is, according to the *Times Literary Supplement*, ''an acknowledged expert'' on East Germany. Reviewing Childs' *The G.D.R.: Moscow's German Ally* in the *Times Literary Supplement*, Timothy Garton Ash states, ''It is an extremely comprehensive, fact-packed short survey, drawing on a wide range of sources for illustration.''

BIOGRAPHICAL/CRITICAL SOURCES: Times Literary Supplement, January 10, 1971, June 8, 1984.

*   *   *

CHITTUM, Ida 1918-

PERSONAL: Born April 6, 1918, in Canton, Ohio; daughter of Harry A. (a farmer) and Ida (Klingaman) Hoover; married James R. Chittum (a tool designer), August 26, 1936; children: Rosalind (Mrs. Thomas Lawrence), James H., Thomas W., Edith Irene, Samme R. *Education:* Attended school through eighth grade in Illinois and Missouri. *Residence:* Findlay, Ill. *Agent:* Ruth Cantor, 156 Fifth Ave., New York, N.Y. 10010.

CAREER: Writer of books for children.

MEMBER: National League of American Pen Women, Authors Guild, Children's Reading Round Table, Friends of Libraries, American Legion Auxiliary.

AWARDS, HONORS: Lewis Carroll Shelf Award of University of Wisconsin for *Farmer Hoo and the Baboons;* certificate of appreciation from Mobile Media, 1975; award of recognition from Central Missouri State University for outstanding contribution to children's literature, 1977.

WRITINGS—Children's books: *Farmer Hoo and the Baboons*, Delacorte, 1971; *The Hermit Boy*, Delacorte, 1972; *Clabber Biscuits*, Steck, 1973; *A Nutty Business*, Putnam, 1973; *The Empty Grave*, American Educational Publications, 1974; *The Secrets of Madam Renee*, Independence Press, 1975; (contributor) *The Princess Book*, Rand, 1975; *The Ghost Boy of El Toro*, Independence Press, 1978; *The Cat's Pajamas*, Parents Magazine Press, 1980; *The Thing without a Name*, Herald House, 1981; (contributor) *A Chilling Collection*, Elsevier-Nelson, 1983. Contributor of short stories and articles to magazines.

SIDELIGHTS: Ida Chittum told *CA:* ''Before I became a writer I was a storyteller and still tell stories to children in many schools and libraries.'' *Avocational interests:* Trees, birds, and all living things; collecting books, especially old ones; people, sunshine.

*   *   *

CHIU, Hungdah 1936-

PERSONAL: Born March 23, 1936, in Shanghai, China; son of Han-ping (a lawyer) and Min-non (Yang) Chiu; married Yuan-yuan Hsieh, May 14, 1966; children: Wei-hsueh (son). *Education:* National Taiwan University, LL.B., 1958; Long Island University, M.A. (with honors), 1962; Harvard University, LL.M., 1962, S.J.D., 1965. *Home:* 6168 Devon Dr., Columbia, Md. 21044. *Office:* 210 University of Maryland Law School, 500 West Baltimore St., Baltimore, Md. 21201.

CAREER: National Taiwan University, Taipei, Taiwan, Republic of China, associate professor of international law, 1965-66; Harvard University, School of Law, Cambridge, Mass.; research associate in law, 1966-70, 1972-74; National Chengchi University, Taipei, professor of law, 1970-72; University of Maryland, School of Law, Baltimore, associate professor, 1974-77, professor of law, 1977—. Research fellow, Institute of International Relations, Mucha, Taipei, 1967-73; International Law Association delegate to United Nations conference on law of the sea, 1976-82. *Military service:* Chinese Army (Republic of China), 1958-60; became second lieutenant; public defender in Judge-Advocate Office, 1959-60.

MEMBER: International Law Association (Taiwan branch), British Institute of International and Comparative Law, Chinese Society of American Law (member of executive council), American Society of International Law (member of Panel on China and International Order, 1969-73), Association for Asian Studies, American Association for Chinese Studies (vice-president, 1982—).

WRITINGS—In English: *The Capacity of International Organizations to Conclude Treaties*, Nijhoff (The Hague), 1966; (with D. M. Johnston) *Agreements of the People's Republic of China, 1949-67: A Calendar*, Harvard University Press, 1968; *The People's Republic of China and the Law of Treaties*, Harvard University Press, 1972; (with S. C. Leng) *Law in Chinese Foreign Policy*, Oceana, 1972; (editor and contributor) *China and the Question of Taiwan: Document and Analysis*, Praeger, 1973; (co-author) *People's China and International Law: A Documentary Study*, two volumes, Princeton University Press, 1974.

(Co-editor) *Legal Aspects of U.S.-Republic of China Trade and Investment*, School of Law, University of Maryland, 1977; (editor and contributor) *Normalizing Relations with the People's Republic of China: Problems, Analysis, and Documents*, School of Law, University of Maryland, 1978; (editor and contributor) *China and the Taiwan Issue*, Praeger, 1979; *Agreements of the People's Republic of China: A Calendar of Events 1966-80*, Praeger, 1981; (co-editor and contributor) *Multi-system Nations and International Law: The International Status of Germany, Korea and China*, School of Law, University of Maryland, 1981; (editor and contributor) *Chinese Yearbook of International Law and Affairs*, Occasional Papers, Volume I, 1981, Volume II, 1982; (co-editor and contributor) *China: 70 Years after the 1911 Hsin-hai Revolution*, University Press of Virginia, 1984; (co-author) *Criminal Justice in Post-Mao China*, State University Press of New York, 1985.

In Chinese: *Hsien-tai Kuo-chi fa wen-t'i* (title means ''Selected Problems of Modern International Law''), New Century Publishing Co. (Taipei), 1966; *Chung-Kuo Kuo-chi-fa wen-t'i O lun-chi* (title means ''Essays on Chinese International Law Problems''), Taiwan Commercial Press (Taipei), 1968; (editor) *Hsien-tai Kuo-chi fa (ts'an-k'ao wen-chien)* (title means ''Modern International Law, Reference Documents''), San-Min Book Co. (Taipei), 1972; (editor) *Hsien-tai Kuo-chi fa* (title means ''Modern International Law''), San-Min Book Co., 1973.

Kuan-yu Chung-kuo ling-tu ti kuo-chi wen-t'i lun chi (title means ''Collected Essays on International Law Problems Concerning Chinese Territory''), Taiwan Commercial Press, 1975; (co-editor and contributor) *Chung-kuo t'ung-i yu Kuo-kung ho-t'an wen-t'i yen-chiu lun-wen-chi* (title means ''Essays on the

Question of Reunification of China and Nationalist-Communist Negotiation''), World Journal, 1981; Chung-mei kuan-hsi lun-chi (title means ''Essays on Sino-American Relations''), Time Cultural Publishing, 1979; Hsien-tai kuo-chi-fa chi-pen wen-chien (title means ''Basic Documents of International Law'') San-Min Book Co., 1984.

Contributor to professional journals, including American Journal of International Law, Asian Survey, Journal of Asian Studies, China Quarterly and Ocean Development and International Law.

*   *   *

CHOUCRI, Nazli 1943-

PERSONAL: Born April 1, 1943, in Cairo, Egypt; came to the United States in 1962, naturalized citizen, 1969; daughter of Mustafa Choucri; married John Osgood Field (a researcher), 1969; children: Allyson. Education: American University, Cairo, Egypt, B.A. (high honors), 1962; Stanford University, M.A., 1964, Ph.D., 1967. Office: Department of Political Science, Massachusetts Institute of Technology, E53-490, Cambridge, Mass. 02139.

CAREER: Queen's University, Kingston, Ontario, assistant professor of political science, 1967-69; Massachusetts Institute of Technology, Cambridge, assistant professor, 1969-72, associate professor, 1972-78, professor of political science, 1978—, research associate at Center for International Studies, 1969, associate director of technology adaptation program, 1976—. Co-chairman of National Academy of Science Middle East Workshop, 1973; member of International Social Science Documentation Committee, 1976—. Consultant to United Nations, U.S. Department of State, Agency for International Development, and Inter-American Development Bank.

MEMBER: International Political Science Association, International Peace Research Society, International Committee for Social Science Information, International Studies Association, American Political Science Association, Council on Foreign Relations, American Association for the Advancement of Science.

AWARDS, HONORS: Fulbright fellow, 1962-63; National Science Foundation grants, 1972-75, 1972-76; National Institute of Mental Health grant, 1978-81.

WRITINGS: (With Michael Laird and Dennis Meadows) Resource Scarcity and Foreign Policy: A Simulation Model of International Conflict (monograph), Center for International Studies, Massachusetts Institute of Technology, 1972; Population Dynamics and International Violence: Propositions, Insight and Evidence, Heath, 1974; Energy Interdependence (monograph), Center for International Studies, Massachusetts Institute of Technology, 1974; Population Dynamics and Local Conflict: A Cross-National Study of Population and War—A Summary (monograph), Center for International Studies, Massachusetts Institute of Technology, 1974; (with W. Parker Mauldin, Frank W. Notestein, and Michael Teitelbaum) A Report on Bucharest: The World Population Conference and the Population Tribune (monograph), Population Council, 1974.

(With Robert C. North) Nations in Conflict: National Growth and International Violence, W. H. Freeman, 1975; (with Vincent Ferraro) The International Politics of Energy Interdependence, Heath, 1976; The Pervasiveness of Politics: Political Definitions of Population Issues (monograph), Institute of Society, Ethics and the Life Sciences, 1976; (editor with Thomas

W. Robinson and contributor) Forecasting in International Relations: Theory, Methods, Problems, Prospects, W. H. Freeman, 1978.

(With David Scott Ross) Energy Exchange and International Relations: A Model of Price, Exchange, and Control, MIT Press, 1982; Energy and Development in Latin America, Heath, 1982; (editor) Multidisciplinary Perspectives on Population and Conflict, Syracuse University Press, 1984.

Contributor: Bruce Russett, editor, Peace, War, and Numbers, Sage Publications, 1972; Michael Haas, editor, International Systems: A Behavioral Approach, Chandler Publishing, 1974; James N. Rosenau, editor, In Search of Global Patterns, Free Press, 1976; The Population Debate: Papers of the World Population Conference, Volume II, United Nations, 1976; Dennis Clark Pirages, editor, The Sustainable Society, Praeger, 1977. Contributor of more than a dozen articles to political science and international studies journals.

WORK IN PROGRESS: Continuing research on international relations and international political economy, public policy in developing areas, and politics of international trade in natural resources.

*   *   *

CHRISTIAN, Henry A(rthur) 1931-

PERSONAL: Born August 22, 1931, in Jersey City, N.J.; son of Henry Arthur (a physician) and Anne V. (Kotyuka) Christian; married Ann L. Quinn, 1951; children: Carolyn, Judith, Peter. Education: Yale University, B.A., 1953, M.A., 1954; Brown University, Ph.D., 1967. Home: 435 Wyoming Ave., Millburn, N.J. 07041. Office: Department of English, Rutgers University, Newark, N.J. 07102.

CAREER: Hopkins Grammar School, New Haven, Conn., instructor in English, 1954-58; Yale University, New Haven, assistant director, American studies for foreign students, 1955; Fulbright lecturer in Denmark, 1958-59; Rutgers University, Newark, N.J., instructor, 1962-67, assistant professor, 1967-72, associate professor of English, 1972—, chairman of department, 1975-78, 1981-84; director of Program in American Studies, 1974-77. Member of Fulbright Regional Interviewing Committee, State of Connecticut, 1959-61, State of New Jersey, 1962—; member of organizing committee and panel moderator, Conference on Literature and the Urban Experience, Rutgers University, 1980. Millburn Short Hills Volunteer First Aid Squad, trustee, 1968-71, crew chief, 1968-76, president, 1975.

MEMBER: Modern Language Association of America, American Studies Association, Immigration History Group of American Historical Association, British-American Alumni Association of English Speaking Union (member of founding committee), Society for Slovene Studies.

AWARDS, HONORS: Citation from U.S. Department of State, 1959, and U.S. Department of Health, Education, and Welfare, Teacher Exchange Section, 1971; Plaque of the City, Ljubljana, Yugoslavia, 1981.

WRITINGS: (Editor) Louis Adamic: A Checklist, Kent State University Press, 1971; (editor) Izbrana pisma Louisa Adamica (title means ''Selected Letters of Louis Adamic''), Cankarjeva Zalozba, 1981; (with Motto, Sonn, and Watts) The City and Literature: An Introduction, Conference on Literature and the Urban Experience, Rutgers University, 1983. Also contributor to Dictionary of Literary Biography, Gale. Contributor of articles to *Fulbright Monitor, Twentieth Century Literature, Fitzgerald Newsletter, Menckeniana,* and *Zbornik Obcine Grosuplje.*

WORK IN PROGRESS: A biography of Louis Adamic; research on Upton Sinclair, Frank Lloyd Wright, and other American figures in literature, art, and architecture.

SIDELIGHTS: Henry A. Christian told *CA* that his primary field is American civilization and he is "interested in literary style and artistic design and the interrelationships therein. I believe in publishing research that is primarily new and otherwise untouched. I believe biography is the key to the truth of the twentieth century in America, about which we have said much but really know little decade by decade, especially in respect to the 1930's. I received my early research and writing training from the late Hemingway scholar, Charles A. Fenton; my faith in scholars from Hyatt H. Waggoner. I have found my greatest satisfaction both in reestablishing Louis Adamic as a literary figure in the United States and in the opportunities for exchanges of information and mutual understanding my research and writing have generated between me and scholars in Yugoslavia, Adamic's country of origin."

*   *   *

CHRISTY, Joe
   See CHRISTY, Joseph M.

*   *   *

CHRISTY, Joseph M.   1919-
   (Joe Christy)

PERSONAL: Born July 17, 1919, in Lawton, Okla.; son of Joseph B. and Bess (Prickett) Christy; married Rene Van Cleave. *Education:* Attended University of Kansas. *Politics:* "Goldwater Republican." *Home:* 1705 Northwest 44th St., Lawton, Okla. 73501.

CAREER: Oklahoma Air Associates, Tillman County Oklahoma Airport, Okla., president, 1961-63; Sports Car Press, Ltd., East Norwalk, Conn., editor of aviation division, beginning 1962; Conde Nast Publications, New York, N.Y., contributing editor, *Air Progress* magazine, 1965-68, *Air Trails* magazine, beginning 1970; Tab Books, Inc., Blue Ridge Summit, Penn., senior aviation editor, 1977—.

MEMBER: American Aviation Historical Society, Air Force Association, Aviation/Space Writers Association, OX-5 Club of America.

AWARDS, HONORS: Aviation/Space Writers Association award for best nonfiction aviation book of 1970, *Summon the Stars.*

WRITINGS: (With Clay Johnson) *Your Pilot's License,* Crown, 1960, revised edition, Sports Car Press, 1965; *Beechcraft Guide: Bonanza, Debonair, Musketeer,* Crown, 1962, published as *Single-Engine Beechcrafts,* Sports Car Press, 1970; (with Page Shamburger) *Command the Horizon: A Pictorial History of Aviation,* A. S. Barnes, 1968; (with Shamburger) *Summon the Stars,* A. S. Barnes, 1970; (with Shamburger) *The Hawks,* Wolverine Publications, 1971; *The P-Thirty-Eight Lightning at War,* Ian Allen, 1977; *P-Forty Hawks at War,* Ian Allen, 1980; *B-Fifty-two Stratofortress in Action,* Ian Allen, 1982.

Published by Sports Car Press: *Racing Planes Guide,* 1963; (with Roy Wieden) *Lightplane Engine Guide,* 1963; (with Shamburger) *Aces and Planes of World War I,* 1968; *Curtiss*

P-Thirty Six to P-Forty, 1970; *The Single-Engine Cessnas,* 1971; *Used Plane Buying Guide,* 1975; *Engines for Home-Built Aircraft,* 1976.

Published by Tab Books: *Learjet,* 1978; *Synthetic Aircraft Fabrics,* 1979; *Refinishing Metal Aircraft,* 1979; *Pilot's Reference Manual,* 1980; *Low Cost Private Flying,* 1980; *Low Cost Aircraft Hangars,* 1981; *U.S. Navy and Japanese Combat Aircraft of WWII,* 1982; *Luftwaffe Planes and Aces,* 1982; *American Airpower: First Seventy-five Years,* 1983; *Aircraft Inspection and Repair,* 1983; *Aerospace Facts,* 1984; *Ultralights,* 1984; *High Adventure,* 1984. Contributor of articles and stories to several periodicals, including *Argosy, Adventure, Flying,* and *Air Facts.*

WORK IN PROGRESS: Air Recreation Vehicles, for Tab Books.

*   *   *

CHURCH, Peter
   See NUTTALL, Jeff

*   *   *

CIPLIJAUSKAITE, Birute   1929-

PERSONAL: Born April 11, 1929, in Kaunas, Lithuania; daughter of Juozas (a professor of medicine) and Elena (Stelmokaite) Ciplijauskas. *Education:* Lycee Lithuanien (Tuebingen), diploma of maturity, 1948; University of Montreal, M.A., 1956; Bryn Mawr College, Ph.D., 1960. *Office:* Department of Spanish, University of Wisconsin, Madison, Wis. 53706.

CAREER: University of Wisconsin—Madison, instructor, 1960-61, assistant professor, 1961-64, associate professor, 1964-68, professor of Spanish literature, 1968-73, John Bascom Professor of Spanish Literature, 1973—. Visiting professor, State University of New York at Stony Brook, 1978, and Siegen University, 1983. Member, Institute for Research in the Humanities, 1974—.

MEMBER: Association for Advancement of Baltic Studies (vice-president, 1982-84).

AWARDS, HONORS: Guggenheim fellow, 1967-68; Institute for Research in the Humanities, Madison, Wis., fellow, 1971-72.

WRITINGS: La soledad y la poesia espanola contemporanea, Insula (Madrid), 1962; *El poeta y la poesia: Del romanticismo a la poesia social,* Insula, 1966; (editor) Luis de Gongora, *Sonetos completos,* Castalia (Madrid), 1968; *Deber de plenitud: La poesia de Jorge Guillen,* SepSetentas (Mexico), 1972; *Baroja: Un estilo,* Insula, 1973; (editor) *Jorge Guillen,* Taurus, 1976.

Los noventayochistas y la historia, Porrua Turanzas (Madrid), 1981; (editor) de Gongora, *Sonetos,* Hispanic Seminary of Medieval Studies (Madison, Wis.), 1981; (translator) Juan Ramon Jimenez, *Sidabrinukas ir as,* [Madison], 1982; *La mujer insatisfecha,* Edhasa (Barcelona), 1984.

WORK IN PROGRESS: The Fictional I in Contemporary Feminine Novel (1970-1985).

BIOGRAPHICAL/CRITICAL SOURCES: Books Abroad, winter, 1970.

CLARK, F(rederick) Stephen   1908-1977
(Clive Dalton)

PERSONAL: Born May 21, 1908, in Gravesend, Kent, England; died, 1977; son of Frederick George (an army officer) and Mabel (Dalton) Clark; married Agnes Staples, September 25, 1937; children: Anne (Mrs. John Sheppard), Richard. *Education:* Attended army-operated schools in various parts of the world. *Religion:* Church of England.

CAREER: Malay Mail, correspondent in London, England, 1936-39; *British Malaya,* London, sub-editor, 1936-39; writer. *Military service:* British Army, Royal Artillery, 1939-45; became sergeant.

WRITINGS: (With Spencer Brown) *Kicks and Ha'pence,* Low, 1937; (with Herman Quist) *Congo Devil: Being an Account of Hickory Quist on Sea and Land,* Low, 1938; (with Christopher Johnson) *I Lived Dangerously,* Low, 1939.

Under pseudonym Clive Dalton: *White Pagan,* Grayson, 1933; *Valiant Journey,* S. Paul, 1935; *Once to Every Man,* S. Paul, 1935; *Malay Canoe,* Coward, 1960; (contributor) *The Decorative Arts of the Mariner,* Cassell, 1966.

Published by Eldon: *Always Afternoon,* 1933; *Island Spell,* 1934; *Child in the Sun* (autobiography), 1937; *Jesting Fates,* 1938; *Spacious Days,* 1939; *Men of Malaysia,* 1942.

Published by Brockhampton Press, except as indicated: *Malay Boy,* 1961; *Malay Island,* 1962; *Malay Cruise,* 1964; *Malay Schooner,* 1965, Chilton, 1966; *Malay Treasures,* 1967; *Malay Pirate,* 1972.

SIDELIGHTS: F. Stephen Clark stated, "All my writing stems from a childhood spent in the Malay islands, in close association with Malay children." His books have been translated into German and Polish; *Malay Cruise* has been issued as a school reader in Australia. *Avocational interests:* Swimming, boating, music.

BIOGRAPHICAL/CRITICAL SOURCES: Clive Dalton, *Child in the Sun,* Eldon, 1937.†

* * *

CLARKE, Austin C(hesterfield)   1934-

PERSONAL: Born July 26, 1934, in Barbados, West Indies; son of Kenneth Trothan (an artist) and Gladys Clarke; children: Janice, Loretta, Mphahlele. *Education:* Harrison College, Barbados, West Indies, Oxford and Cambridge Higher Certificate, 1950; additional study at University of Toronto. *Agent:* Harold Ober Associates, 40 East 49th St., New York, N.Y. 10017.

CAREER: Canadian Broadcasting Corp., Toronto, Ontario, producer and free-lance broadcaster, beginning 1963; Brandeis University, Waltham, Mass., Jacob Ziskind Professor of Literature, 1968-69; Williams College, Williamstown, Mass., Margaret Bundy Scott Professor of Literature, 1971-72; Barbados Embassy, Washington, D.C., cultural and press attache, 1974-75; currently affiliated with Caribbean Broadcasting Corp., St. Michael, Barbados. Visiting professor of Afro-American literature and creative writing, Yale University, 1968-71. Member of board of trustees, Rhode Island School of Design, Providence, 1970-75.

MEMBER: Writers Guild, Canadian Union of Writers, Yale Club (New Haven).

AWARDS, HONORS: Canada Council senior arts fellowships, 1968, 1970, 1974; University of Western Ontario President's Medal for best story, 1965; Belmont Short Story Award, for "Four Stations in His Circle"; Casa de las Americas Literary Prize, 1980.

WRITINGS—Novels, except as indicated: *The Survivors of the Crossing,* McClelland & Stewart, 1964; *Amongst Thistles and Thorns,* McClelland & Stewart, 1965; *The Meeting Point,* Macmillan, 1967; *When He Was Free and Young and He Used to Wear Silks* (short stories), Anansi, 1971, Little, Brown, 1974; *Storm of Fortune,* Little, Brown, 1973; *The Bigger Light,* Little, Brown, 1975; *The Prime Minister,* General Publishing, 1977; *Growing Up Stupid under the Union Jack* (autobiographical novel), McClelland & Stewart, 1980.

Author of *Short Stories of Austin Clarke,* 1984; also author of "Myths and Memories," "African Literature," and other filmscripts, for Educational Television (ETV), Toronto, 1968—.

WORK IN PROGRESS: A study of the symbolism in Richard Wright's story, "The Man Who Lived Underground"; research concerning the position of black women in the Black American Revolution.

SIDELIGHTS: Austin C. Clarke's childhood in colonial Barbados and his experiences as a black immigrant to Canada have provided him with the background for most of his fiction. His writing is almost exclusively concerned with the cultural contradictions that arise when blacks struggle for success in a predominately white society. Clarke's "one very great gift," in the words of a *New Yorker* critic, is the ability to see "unerringly into his characters' hearts," and this ability is what makes his stories memorable. Martin Levin writes in the *New York Times Book Review:* "Mr. Clarke is plugged into the fixations, hopes, loves and dreams of his characters. He converts them into stories that are charged with life."

Clarke's autobiographical novel, *Growing Up Stupid under the Union Jack,* is an example of the author's typical theme and style. The narrator, Tom, is a young man from a poor Barbadan village. Everyone in the village is proud that Tom is able to attend the Combermere School, for it is run by a "real, true-true Englishman"—an ex-British Army officer who calls his students "boy" and "darky" and who flogs them publicly. The students eagerly imitate this headmaster's morals and manners, for to them, he represents "Mother England"; they are unaware that in England, he would be looked down upon as a mere working-class soldier. The book is "a personal, captivating, provoking and often humorous record of ignorance, inhumanity and lowly existence under colonial imperialism in World War II Barbados. . . . With its major emphasis on education and childhood, *Growing Up Stupid under the Union Jack* continues to draw attention to one of the chief preoccupations of the anti-colonial Anglo-Caribbean novel," writes Robert P. Smith in *World Literature Today.* The theme is well-rendered in what Darryl Pinckney calls in the *New York Review of Books* Clarke's "tender, funny, unpolemical style."

Clarke's best-known work is a trilogy detailing the lives of Barbadan blacks who immigrate to Toronto hoping to better their lot. In these novels, *The Meeting Point, Storm of Fortune,* and *The Bigger Light,* "it is as if the flat characters of a Dickensian world have come into their own at last, playing their tragicomic roles in a manner which owes much to Clarke's extraordinary facility with the Barbadan dialect," writes Diane Bessai in *Canadian Literature.* Bessai also expresses eagerness for Clarke to "continue to create his Brueghel-like canvasses with their rich and contrasting detail and mood." "The sense of defeat among the poor islanders is enlivened by the humour of the characters and their glowing fantasies about the presumed wealth of relatives and friends who make it big in the fatlands of the United States or Canada," writes John Ayre in *Saturday Night.*

The first two novels dwell mostly on Bernice Leach, a live-in maid at a wealthy Toronto home, and her small circle of fellow immigrants. Martin Levin writes in the *New York Times Book Review:* "Mr. Clarke is masterful at delineating the oppressive insecurities of Bernice and her friends, and the claustrophobic atmosphere that envelops such a mini-minority" as the Caribbean blacks in Toronto. The third novel, *The Bigger Light,* explores the life of Boysie, the most successful of this immigrant group, and his wife, Dots. Boysie has at last realized the dream that compelled him to leave Barbados: he owns a prosperous business and his own home. However, in the process of realizing his goals, he has become alienated from his wife and his community. Now he searches for a greater meaning to his life—a "bigger light." "*The Bigger Light* is a painful book to read," writes David Rosenthal in *The Nation.* It is "a story of two people with many things to say and no one to say them to, who hate themselves and bitterly resent the society around them. . . . Certain African novelists have also dealt with the isolation of self-made blacks, but none with Clarke's bleak intensity." A *New Yorker* writer praises the book further, citing Clarke's strong writing skill as the element that lifts the book beyond social comment: "The universal longings of ordinary human beings are depicted with a simplicity and power that make us grateful for all three volumes of this long and honest record."

BIOGRAPHICAL/CRITICAL SOURCES: Saturday Night, October, 1971, June, 1975; *New York Times Book Review,* April 9, 1972, December 9, 1973, February 16, 1975; *Canadian Literature,* summer, 1974; *New Yorker,* February 24, 1975; *The Nation,* November 1, 1975; *Contemporary Literary Criticism,* Volume VIII, Gale, 1978; *The Listener,* June 15, 1978; *New York Review of Books,* May 27, 1982; *World Literature Today,* winter, 1982.

*　　*　　*

CLELAND, Charles C(arr) 1924-

PERSONAL: Born May 15, 1924, in Murphysboro, Ill.; son of Homer W. (a merchant) and Stella (Carr) Cleland; married Betty Lou Woodburn (a realtor), July 18, 1948. *Education:* Southern Illinois University, B.S. in Ed., 1950, M.S. in Ed., 1951; University of Texas, Ph.D., 1957. *Religion:* Presbyterian. *Home:* 3427 Monte Vista, Austin, Tex. 78731. *Office:* Education Bldg. 408-A, University of Texas, Austin, Tex. 78712.

CAREER: Has worked as salesman, coal miner, and surveyor's assistant. Brown Schools for Exceptional Children, Austin, Tex., The Oaks, assistant director, 1951-52; Austin State School, Austin, psychologist, 1952-55; Lincoln State School, Lincoln, Ill., chief psychologist, 1956-57; Austin State School, chief of psychology, education, and research, 1957-59; Abilene State School, Abilene, Tex., superintendent, 1959-63; University of Texas at Austin, lecturer, 1963-64, associate professor, 1964-68, professor of special education and educational psychology, 1969—.

Lecturer in management, Illinois Wesleyan University, 1956-57; member of cooperative graduate faculty, James Millikin

University, 1956-57. Member, Texas Board of Psychological Examiners, 1961; member of task force on residential care, Texas Plan to Combat Mental Retardation. Chairman of board of directors, Brown Schools for Exceptional Children; president of board of directors, Austin Child Guidance Center. *Military service:* U.S. Army, 1943-46; served in Pacific theater.

MEMBER: Interamerican Society of Psychology, American Psychological Association (fellow), International Association for Scientific Study of Mental Deficiency, American Academy on Mental Retardation, American Association on Mental Deficiency (fellow; member of executive board, Southwest region, 1962; representative of national association to White House Conference on Aging, 1971), Southwestern Psychological Association (secretary-treasurer, 1963-65), Texas Psychological Association (president, 1961-62), Phi Kappa Phi, Phi Delta Kappa, Psi Chi.

AWARDS, HONORS: Grants from Illinois Psychiatric Research Board, 1956, Brown Foundation, 1969, 1971, and Hogg Foundation for Mental Health, 1971; Education Award, American Association on Mental Deficiency, 1978; Texas Psychological Association award, 1980.

WRITINGS: (With Jon D. Swartz) *Mental Retardation: Approaches to Institutional Change,* Grune, 1969; (contributor) A. A. Baumeister and E. C. Butterfield, editors, *Mental Retardation,* Aldine-Atherton, 1970; (with Swartz) *Administrative Issues in Institutions for the Mentally Retarded,* Hogg Foundation for Mental Health, 1972; *Mental Retardation: A Developmental Approach,* Prentice-Hall, 1978; *The Profoundly Mentally Retarded,* Prentice-Hall, 1979; (with Swartz) *Exceptionalities Through the Lifespan,* Macmillan, 1982.

Also contributor to *Mental Retardation: Theory and Research,* edited by Richard Eyman and George Tarjan, American Association on Mental Deficiency. Contributor of more than 250 articles and reviews to journals.

WORK IN PROGRESS: Editing, with Jon D. Swartz and Albert Shafter, *Readings in Institutional Management;* research and writing on the profoundly retarded.

SIDELIGHTS: Charles C. Cleland told *CA:* "When bored or mentally 'constipated' for ideas or hypotheses, I digress and indulge in writing satirical works. This pastime helps to augment serious efforts."

*　　*　　*

CLERC, Charles 1926-

PERSONAL: Surname is pronounced Clair; born March 16, 1926, in Pocatello, Idaho; son of Clemence Clerc; married Virginia Willson, 1946 (divorced, 1949); married Maria Labriola, February 18, 1966 (divorced, 1974); married Sjaan VandenBroeder Fries, 1977; children: (first marriage) Kim (son); (second marriage) Claudette, Caroline, Rebecca. *Education:* Idaho State College (now University), B.A., 1949, B.A., 1955; University of Utah, M.A., 1957; University of Iowa, Ph.D., 1963. *Residence:* Stockton, Calif. *Office:* Department of English, University of the Pacific, Stockton, Calif. 95211.

CAREER: Has worked as shipyard steamfitter, ranch hand, railroad worker, seaman, construction worker, newspaper reporter, radio news and sports director, announcer, correspondent, advertising writer, and factory worker; University of Iowa, Iowa City, instructor in English, 1962-63; University of the Pacific, Stockton, Calif., assistant professor, 1963-66, associate professor, 1966-70, professor of English, 1970—, acting chairman of department, 1968-69, chairman of department, 1982—. Director, National Defense Education Act (NDEA) Institute in Modern Literary Critical Methods, 1968; distinguished visiting professor, U.S. Air Force Academy, 1980-81. Has also lectured on television in central California, 1967. *Military service:* U.S. Merchant Marine Cadet Corps, 1944-46; served in Okinawa; received citation. U.S. Army, 1951-53; became lieutenant.

MEMBER: Modern Language Association of America.

AWARDS, HONORS: Faculty study grant, 1967, and research grants, 1971, and 1974; named to roll of honor, *Best American Short Stories,* for ''The Rake's Progress,'' 1968; Spanos Distinguished Teaching Award, University of the Pacific, 1980.

WRITINGS: (Editor with Louis H. Leiter) *Seven Contemporary Short Novels,* Scott, Foresman, 1969, 3rd edition, 1982; ''The Pillar'' (play), first produced by Delta College Theater, 1972; (editor and contributor) *Approaches to ''Gravity's Rainbow,''* Ohio State University Press, 1983. Also author of two novels, *Cool Fire,* 1975, and *King Life,* 1977, and of a short story collection, *Seesaw,* 1984.

Contributor of articles and short stories to magazines and literary journals, including *Modern Fiction Studies, English Journal, Pacific Review, The Explicator, Daedelus* and *San Jose Studies.*

WORK IN PROGRESS: Gems: 50 Brief Stories, a textbook-anthology; ''Medusa,'' a screenplay; a critical study of the modern American novel; two novels, *Nino* and *Clara America.*

SIDELIGHTS: Charles Clerc told *CA:* ''As a writer, teacher, and critic, I've always liked to work back and forth between imaginative and scholarly writing. They're not all that different from each other—you can be inventive and creative at both. However, the processes differ. The difference is roughly akin—forgive the cliche but it's serviceable—to switching hats. One hat you put on is academic, the other artistic. It's very challenging and satisfying to work at varying kinds of writing, not to mention distinct genres like fiction and drama.''

* * *

COBB, Vicki 1938-

PERSONAL: Born August 19, 1938, in New York, N.Y.; daughter of Benjamin Harold (a labor arbitrator) and Paula (Davis) Wolf; married Edward S. Cobb (a psychology professor), January 31, 1960 (divorced, 1983); children: Theodore Davis, Joshua Monroe. *Education:* Attended University of Wisconsin, 1954-57; Barnard College, B.A., 1958; Columbia University, M.A., 1960. *Home:* 910 Stuart Ave., Mamaroneck, N.Y. 10543.

CAREER: Scientific researcher in Rye, N.Y., at Sloan-Kettering Institute and Pfizer & Co., 1958-61; science teacher in high school in Rye, 1961-64; Teleprompter Corp., New York City, hostess and principal writer of television series, ''The Science Game,'' beginning 1972; American Broadcasting Co., New York City, writer for ''Good Morning America,'' 1976; public relations director, Scott Publishing Co., 1978-83; currently vice-president, Pinwheel Publishers; lecturer.

MEMBER: Authors Guild, Authors League of America, Writers Guild.

AWARDS, HONORS: Cable television award for best educational series, 1973, for ''The Science Game''; Children's Book Council-NSTA Outstanding Science Trade Books for Children award, 1975, for *Supersuits,* 1980, for *Bet You Can't! Science Impossibilities to Fool You,* 1981, for *Lots of Rot,* and 1982, for *The Secret Life of Hardware;* Child Study Children's Book Committee book of the year award, 1979, for *Truth on Trial: The Story of Galileo Galilei;* Library of Congress Children's Book selections, 1979, for *More Science You Can Eat,* 1981, for *How to Really Fool Yourself: Illusions for All Your Senses,* and 1983, for *The Monsters Who Died: A Mystery about Dinosaurs;* International Reading Association-Children's Book Council Children's Choice selection, 1980, for *More Science You Can Eat;* Children's Science Book Award, New York Academy of Sciences, 1981, for *Bet You Can't! Science Impossibilities to Fool You;* American Library Association notable book citation, 1982, for *How to Really Fool Yourself: Illusions for All Your Senses;* Washington Irving Children's Book Choice award, 1984, for *The Secret Life of School Supplies: A Science Experiment Book.*

WRITINGS—For juveniles, except as indicated: *Logic,* F. Watts, 1970; *Gases,* F. Watts, 1970; *Making Sense of Money,* Parents' Magazine Press, 1971; *Sense of Direction: Up, Down and All Around,* Parents' Magazine Press, 1972; *Science Experiments You Can Eat,* Lippincott, 1972; *How the Doctor Knows You're Fine,* Lippincott, 1973; *The Long and Short of Measurement,* Parents' Magazine Press, 1973; *Heat,* F. Watts, 1973; *Arts and Crafts You Can Eat,* Lippincott, 1974; *Supersuits,* Lippincott, 1975.

Magic . . . Naturally, Lippincott, 1977; *More Science Experiments You Can Eat,* Lippincott, 1979; *Truth on Trial: The Story of Galileo Galilei,* Coward, 1979; (with Kathy Darling) *Bet You Can't! Science Impossibilities to Fool You,* Lothrop, 1980; *How to Really Fool Yourself: Illusions for All Your Senses,* Lippincott, 1981; *Lots of Rot,* Lippincott, 1981; *The Secret Life of School Supplies: A Science Experiment Book,* Lippincott, 1981; *Fuzz Does It,* Lippincott, 1982; *The Secret Life of Hardware: A Science Experiment Book,* Lippincott, 1982; *Gobs of Goo,* Lippincott, 1983; *Brave in the Attempt: The Special Olympics Experience* (adult nonfiction), Pinwheel, 1983; *The Monsters Who Died: A Mystery about Dinosaurs,* Coward, 1983; (with Darling) *Bet You Can! Science Possibilities to Fool You,* Avon, 1983; *Chemically Active! A Science Experiment Book,* illustrated by son, Theo Cobb, Lippincott, 1985. Author of column, ''Cobb's Corner on Science,'' *Instructor.* Editor, ''McGraw-Hill Text Films'' series, Elementary Science Study Prints section, 1970.

WORK IN PROGRESS: The Secret Life of Cosmetics: A Science Experiment Book, for Lippincott.

SIDELIGHTS: Vicki Cobb told *CA:* ''It's my guess that most nonfiction books, both juvenile and adult, are read by people who are, for one reason or another, already interested in the subject matter. If you have already invested time in learning about a subject, almost any book on that subject will have some entertainment value for you, regardless of how badly it is written. Most people find that reading what they already know is usually entertaining.

''I try to write for the uninitiated, the person who must read a book for an assignment or as an introduction to a subject. I feel a tremendous obligation to make my subject matter approachable. I often use a slightly irreverent tone and I constantly relate content to what I presume we all know is true of life and nature. My personality and 'voice' is very much a part of my work. I try and communicate my enthusiasm for the subject matter to my reader and elicit similar feelings. It is my intention that if my book is the first book on a subject that is read, it will definitely not be the last."

BIOGRAPHICAL/CRITICAL SOURCES: Science Books, December, 1972, March, 1974, May, 1977; *Childhood Education,* January, 1975; *School Library Journal,* November, 1975, November, 1976, March, 1977; *Children's Literature Review,* Volume II, Gale, 1976; *Science and Children,* October, 1981; *Daily World,* October 14, 1981; *Appraisal,* spring-summer, 1982.

* * *

CODER, S(amuel) Maxwell 1902-

PERSONAL: Born March 25, 1902, in Straight, Pa.; son of Emmanuel Miller (a machinist) and Abbie (Bailey) Coder; married Elizabeth Maria Dieterle, February 20, 1932; children: Margaret Elizabeth (deceased), Maxine Joyce (Mrs. T.C.B. Howard IV), Donald Maxwell. *Education:* Temple University, B.S. in Ed., 1938; Evangelical Theological College (now Dallas Theological Seminary and Graduate School of Theology), Th.B., 1938, Th.M., 1940. *Politics:* Republican. *Home:* 1860 Sherman Ave., Evanston, Ill. 60201. *Office:* Moody Bible Institute, Chicago, Ill.

CAREER: Businessman, 1928-32; ordained to Presbyterian ministry, 1938; pastor at Grace Church, Camden, N.J., 1935-38, Chelsea Church, Atlantic City, N.J., 1938-43, and Evangel Church, Philadelphia, Pa., 1944-45; Moody Bible Institute, Chicago, Ill., member of faculty, 1945-69, editor-in-chief of Moody Press, 1945-46, vice-president and dean of education, 1947-69, dean emeritus, 1969—. Speaker at Bible and missionary conferences throughout the world.

AWARDS, HONORS: D.D., Bible Theological Seminary of Los Angeles, 1949.

WRITINGS—Published by Moody, except as indicated: *Dobbie: Defender of Malta,* 1946; *Youth Triumphant* (correspondence course), three volumes, 1946; *God's Will for Your Life,* 1950; (editor) *Our Lord Prays for His Own,* 1950; (editor) *The World to Come,* 1954; *Jude: The Acts of the Apostates,* 1955; *The Bible Science and Creation,* 1965; (with William Evans) *Great Doctrines of the Bible,* 1974; (editor) *Nave's Topical Bible,* 1975; *Israel's Destiny,* 1978; *Christian Workers New Testament,* 1980; *The Final Chapter,* Tyndale House, 1984. Also editor, with Wilbur M. Smith, of "Wycliffe Series of Christian Classics," Moody, 1946—.

WORK IN PROGRESS: James; The Comfort of the Scriptures; Peter, two volumes; *Bible Books in Brief.*

SIDELIGHTS: S. Maxwell Coder told *CA:* "My primary reason for writing is that 'necessity is laid upon me; yea, woe is unto me if I preach not the gospel' through the printed page (I Cor. 9:26). A second reason is that much theological or religious writing is phrased in language which obscures the meaning it is intended to convey, creating a great need for clarity and simplicity."

* * *

COHEN, Leonard (Norman) 1934-

PERSONAL: Born September 21, 1934, in Montreal, Quebec, Canada; son of Nathan B. and Marsha (Klinitsky) Cohen; children: Adam, Lorca. *Education:* McGill University, B.A., 1955; graduate study, Columbia University. *Residence:* Montreal,

Quebec, Canada, and Greece. *Office:* Stranger Music, Inc., 1501 Broadway, New York, N.Y. 10036.

CAREER: Poet, novelist, singer, and composer. Currently associated with Stranger Music, Inc., New York, N.Y.; has given concerts in the United States, Canada, and Europe.

AWARDS, HONORS: McGill Literary Award, 1956; Canada Council grant, 1960-61; Quebec Literary Award, 1964; LL.B., Dalhousie University, 1971.

WRITINGS: The Favorite Game (novel), Viking, 1963; *Beautiful Losers* (novel), Viking, 1966; *Songs of Leonard Cohen,* Macmillan, 1969; "The New Step" (play), produced in London, England, 1972; "Sisters of Mercy: A Journey into the Words and Music of Leonard Cohen" (play), produced at Niagara-on-the-Lake, Ontario, and in New York, N.Y., 1973. Also author of video production, "I Am a Hotel."

Poetry; published by McClelland & Stewart, except as indicated: *Let Us Compare Mythologies,* Contact Press, 1956; *The Spice Box of Earth,* 1961, Viking, 1965; *Flowers for Hitler,* 1964; *Parasites of Heaven,* 1966; *Selected Poems, 1955-1968,* Viking, 1968; *The Energy of Slaves,* 1972, Viking, 1973; (with Jurgen Jaensch) *Credo,* Garuda Verlag, 1977; *Death of a Lady's Man* (includes journal entries), 1978, Viking, 1979; *Book of Mercy,* Random House, 1984.

Recordings; produced by Columbia, except as indicated: *Songs of Leonard Cohen,* 1968; *Songs from a Room,* 1969; *Songs of Love and Hate,* 1971; *Leonard Cohen: Live Songs,* 1973; *New Skin for the Old Ceremony,* 1974; *Death of a Lady's Man,* Warner Brothers, 1977; *Recent Songs,* 1979; *Various Positions,* 1984.

Contributor to many anthologies, including *The Penguin Book of Canadian Verse,* edited by Ralph Gastafson, Penguin, 1967, *How Do I Love Thee: Sixty Poets of Canada (and Quebec) Select and Introduce Their Favourite Poems from Their Own Work,* edited by John Robert Colombo, M. G. Hurtig, 1979, and *Five Canadian Poets,* edited by Eli Mandel, Holt-Rinehart (Toronto), 1970. Contributor of poetry to magazines.

Cohen's work has been translated into Hebrew, Spanish, and French.

SIDELIGHTS: Leonard Cohen gained international popularity as a coffeehouse singer with his songs of love and protest in the 1960s and 1970s. "His image is a touchstone . . . for an entire student generation. As poet, novelist and, above all, as a composer/lyricist/singer, . . . he embodies the dreams of many young people," wrote a *Times Literary Supplement* reviewer in 1970. His work has continued to appeal to students, and today, state Pamela Andriotakis and Richard Bulahan in *People,* his followers "often are teenagers, the children of his early admirers."

Cohen began his career as a poet. His first collection, *Let Us Compare Mythologies,* won the 1956 McGill Literary Award. The prize was a plane ticket to the city of Cohen's choice. He elected to travel to Jerusalem but stopped in London, where friends encouraged him to discipline his writing. With their support, he remained in England and completed the first draft of a novel, *The Favorite Game,* in eight months. In 1960 Cohen moved to the Greek island of Hydra, which was his home for the next six years. During that time he published three books of poetry and two novels. He also wrote songs but made no attempt to sell them.

Critics received his first books favorably. Samuel I. Bellman writes of *The Favorite Game* in *Congress Bi-weekly:* "[F.

Scott] Fitzgerald is most strongly evoked here. . . . With the compassion of Philip Roth in *Letting Go* (1962), an intricate study of parent-child relationships, Cohen has given his itinerant, fatuous and self-alienated young poet a moment of greatness.'' Calvin Bedient in the *New York Times Book Review* credits Cohen's early poems as showing ''a splashy imaginative energy that, combined with a hard attitude and frequent candor, [makes] them challenging.'' And a *Times Literary Supplement* reviewer writes of Cohen's second novel, *Beautiful Losers,* ''like the early work of another all-embracing non-stylist, Thomas Wolfe, it has the fascination of its untamed energy.''

The books received critical acclaim, but, their author told Tom Chaffin in *Canadian Forum,* ''I really couldn't meet any of my own bills.'' That situation was unexpectedly remedied in 1966 when, while visiting New York, Cohen was introduced to singer Judy Collins. She asked to hear his songs and was so impressed by them that she introduced several of them on her next album. They were hits, and soon other singers were eager to record Cohen's works. ''Suzanne,'' ''Sisters of Mercy,'' ''The Story of Abraham and Isaac,'' and ''Stories of the Street'' were all successes for various recording artists. In 1968, Cohen decided to cut his own album, although he tells Chaffin: ''Sometimes I think my voice is very bad. I can almost make myself cry with it very early in the morning.'' Chaffin writes, ''While Cohen's fluid, opulently lyric guitar work is of studio musician calibre, his voice is deep, untrained, often off-pitch, sometimes unmercifully rasping—and somehow the perfect foil for his soft Debussy-like melodies.'' The public liked his first album, *Songs of Leonard Cohen,* and subsequent records also sold well. Concert tours were faithfully attended, and the Canadian poet had taken a major step toward becoming what Andriotakis and Bulahan call an ''undisputed cult figure.''

Cohen's fame caused some literary critics to examine his later poetry in relation to his popular songs. David Lehman in *Poetry,* for example, writes: ''The real tension in Cohen's work is due . . . to a clash between poetry and the elements of songwriting which Cohen superimposes on it.'' ''His poems have a randomness which betrays the lack of any sustained vision,'' writes a *Times Literary Supplement* reviewer. ''They are, in short, the poems of a songwriter who is able to convince a semi-literate public that his talent goes deeper simply because his lyrics possess an apparent concern with deeper issues and avoid the more honest banalities of 'moon/June.''' James Healy's *Prairie Schooner* review also suggests that Cohen's real talent lies in songwriting, not poetry: ''*The Energy of Slaves* (Viking Press) is a painful disappointment. . . . Cohen's music *is* his best weapon and maybe he will come to realize this.''

Leslie Fielder, however, states in *Running Man* that this sharp division between pop artist and literary artist is unrealistic and unnecessary. Today's poet works in ''the new post-Modernist world in which the old distinctions between low and high art, mass culture and *belles-lettres* have lapsed completely.'' Reviewing *Death of a Lady's Man* in *Saturday Night,* Eli Mandel suggests that Cohen's work defies categorization and calls the book ''wildly energetic, threatening to fly apart in any one of the thousand directions to which it is attracted, a witty, moving, despairing book, lyrical, dramatic, musical, endlessly entertaining, often boring, even terribly self-centered—further revelations of a mind and personality that will continue to baffle our best critics and to entrance and offend an audience he cultivates and seduces.'' Cohen himself ''reacts caustically to critics who have suggested that his recent celebrity has blunted his powers on the printed page,'' writes Chaffin. ''He also rejects the notion of any tension between his roles as a solitary

poet and public performer.'' Of his simple style, Cohen told Chaffin, ''I like austerity. . . . I like it as a style.''

In Mandel's opinion, Cohen's work has a ''magical luminosity'' that accounts for his great success and popularity. ''Cohen's method is without doubt surrealistic, what Robert Bly recently called 'leaping poetry,' the sudden alteration that occurs when something more than mere association develops in the poetic connection. It's enough to take you by the heart and shake you as if you were in a great windstorm or encountering for the first time one of those huge ships of imagination that Fellini or Rilke saw. Or, to use Bly's example, it's as if the poet suddenly leapt from one brain to another . . . Cohen is capable of those great leaps of imagination; that is why he remains one of [Canada's] best, most loved poets.''

BIOGRAPHICAL/CRITICAL SOURCES: Congress Bi-Weekly, December 20, 1963; *Canadian Literature,* winter, 1965; Guy Sylvestre and others, editors, *Canadian Writers,* revised edition, Ryerson, 1966; *New York Times,* April 4, 1966; *New York Review of Books,* April 28, 1966; *New York Times Book Review,* May 8, 1966, February 18, 1973; *New Leader,* May 23, 1966; *Canadian Forum,* July, 1967, September, 1970, August-September, 1983; *Saturday Night,* February, 1968, November, 1978; *Life,* June 28, 1968; *National Observer,* September 9, 1968; *Time,* September 13, 1968; *Beloit Poetry Journal,* winter, 1968-69; *McCall's,* January, 1969; *Running Man,* July-August, 1969; Michael Ondaatje, *Leonard Cohen,* McClelland & Stewart, 1970; *Times Literary Supplement,* April 23, 1970, September 18, 1970, January 5, 1973; *Jewish Quarterly,* autumn, 1972; *Prairie Schooner,* summer, 1973; *Poetry,* December, 1973; *Contemporary Literary Criticism,* Volume III, Gale, 1975; Michael Gnarowski, *Leonard Cohen: The Artist and His Critics,* McGraw, 1976; *People,* January 14, 1980; *Globe & Mail* (Toronto), April 21, 1984.

—*Sketch by Joan E. Marecki*

*   *   *

COLETTA, Paolo Enrico 1916-

PERSONAL: Born February 3, 1916, in Plainfield, N.J.; son of Alberto Sisto (a tailor) and Maria (Rappoli) Coletta; married Alicevelyn Warner, January 15, 1940 (died, 1967); married Maria Bellina Boyer, September 5, 1967; children: (first marriage) Dana Maria (Mrs. Lawrence Murphy); (stepchildren) Bernarr Boyer, Paula Maria. *Education:* Junior College of Connecticut, A.A., 1936; University of Missouri, B.S., 1938, M.A., 1939, Ph.D., 1942. *Home:* 1519 Riverdale Dr., Winchester-on-Severn, Annapolis, Md. 21401.

CAREER: University of Missouri—Columbia, instructor in history, 1940-42; Stephens College, Columbia, Mo., instructor in social science, 1942-43; South Dakota State College (now University), Brookings, instructor in history, 1946; University of Louisville, Louisville, Ky., instructor in social science, 1946; U.S. Naval Academy, Annapolis, Md., 1958-83, associate professor, 1958-63, professor of history, beginning 1963, and lecturer in sea power and national policy, beginning 1971; became Distinguished Meritorious Professor. Visiting professor, University of Maryland Extension, 1959-62; Fulbright lecturer, University of Genoa, 1971; visiting summer professor at University of Nebraska, 1949, 1952, 1953, and at Colorado College, 1963. *Military service:* U.S. Navy, 1943-46. U.S. Naval Reserve, 1951-73; retired as captain.

MEMBER: American Historical Association, U.S. Naval Institute, American Military Institute, Society of Historians for

Foreign Relations, Organization of American Historians, National Geographic Society, Pacific Historical Society, Southern Historical Association, Naval Reserve Association, Nebraska State Historical Society, Phi Delta Kappa.

WRITINGS: (Contributor) W. W. Jeffries, editor, *Geography and National Power*, U.S. Naval Institute, 1953, 4th edition, 1968; (with Gerald E. Wheeler) *An Outline of World Naval History*, Annapolis Academy Press, 1956; (contributor) H. Wayne Morgan, editor, *The Gilded Age*, Syracuse University Press, 1963; *William Jennings Bryan*, University of Nebraska Press, Volume I: *Political Evangelist, 1860-1908*, 1964, Volume II: *Progressive Politician and Moral Statesman, 1909-1915*, 1969, Volume III: *Political Puritan, 1915-1925*, 1969.

(Contributing editor) *Threshold to American Internationalism: The Foreign Policies of William McKinley*, Exposition Press, 1970; (contributor) Arthur M. Schlesinger, Jr., editor, *History of Presidential Elections*, Chelsea House, 1971; (contributor) Schlesinger, editor, *History of U.S. Political Parties*, Chelsea House, 1972; *William Howard Taft*, University Press of Kansas, 1973; (contributor) Alexander DeConde, editor, *Encyclopedia of American Foreign Policies*, Scribner, 1978; *The U.S. Navy and Defense Unification, 1947-1953*, University of Delaware Press, 1979; *Admiral Bradley A. Fiske and the American Navy*, Regents Press of Kansas, 1979; *Bowman Hendry McCalla: A Fighting Sailor*, University Press of America, 1979.

French Ensor Chadwick: Scholarly Warrior, University Press of America, 1980; (contributing editor) *American Secretaries of the Navy*, Naval Institute Press, 1980; (contributor) Gerald K. Haines and J. Samuel Walter, editors, *American Foreign Relations: A Historiographical Review*, Greenwood Press, 1981; *A Bibliography of American Naval History*, Naval Institute Press, 1981; (editor-in-chief) *U.S. Navy and Marine Corps Bases*, two volumes, Greenwood Press, 1985; *An Annotated Bibliography of U.S. Marine Corps History*, University Press of America, 1985; *A Survey of U.S. Naval Affairs, 1865-1917*, University Press of America, 1985. Contributor to encyclopedias. Contributor of more than seventy-five articles and reviews to history journals.

WORK IN PROGRESS: A biography of Vice-Admiral Patrick N. L. Bellinger of the U.S. Navy.

*   *   *

COLINVAUX, Paul (Alfred) 1930-

PERSONAL: Born September 22, 1930, in St. Albans, England; son of Flora Kingsman (a banker); married Llewellya W. Hillis (a professor), June 17, 1961; children: Catherine Martha, Roger Paul. *Education:* Jesus College, Cambridge, B.A., 1956, M.A., 1960; Duke University, Ph.D., 1962. *Home:* 319 South Columbia Ave., Columbus, Ohio 43209; and 20 Brooks Rd., Woods Hole, Mass. 02543. *Agent:* Murray Curtin and C & J Wolfers Ltd., 3 Regents Square, London WC1H 8H2, England. *Office:* College of Biological Sciences, Ohio State University, 484 West 12th Ave., Columbus, Ohio 43210.

CAREER: Canadian Government, research officer attached as pedologist to Soil Survey of New Brunswick, 1956-59; Queen's University of Belfast, Belfast, Northern Ireland, postdoctoral fellow, 1962-63; Yale University, New Haven, Conn., postdoctoral research fellow, 1963-64; Ohio State University, Columbus, assistant professor, 1964-67, associate professor, 1967-71, professor of zoology, 1971—. Distinguished visiting professor, University of Washington, spring, 1972. Field work in

Portugal, 1954, Nigeria, 1955, Alaska, 1960, 1963, 1965, 1978, Jamaica, 1962, 1969, Bermuda, 1963, Galapagos, 1966, 1969, 1971, Peru, 1977, and Ecuador, 1978-84. Chairman of sponsoring institutions of the Institute of Ecology (TIE), 1978-80; member of advisory subcommittee for ecological sciences of the National Science Foundation, 1979-82. *Military service:* British Army, Royal Artillery, 1949-51; served in Germany; became lieutenant.

MEMBER: INQUA (International Quaternary Association; member of U.S. National Commission), American Society of Naturalists, American Society of Limnology and Oceanography, Ecological Society of America (treasurer, 1984), American Quaternary Association, American Association for the Advancement of Science, Arctic Institute of North America, American Association of University Professors, Authors League of America, Authors Guild, Society of Authors, Ohio Academy of Sciences, Phi Beta Kappa, Sigma Xi.

AWARDS, HONORS: North Atlantic Treaty Organization postdoctoral fellowship, 1962-63; outstanding or distinguished teaching awards at Ohio State University from Student Council, College of Biological Sciences, 1970, Ohio State University Alumni Association, 1971, and College of Arts and Sciences, 1972; Guggenheim fellowship in London, 1971-72; Ohioana Book Award in field of science, 1978.

WRITINGS: The Environment of Crowded Men, MSS Educational Publishing, 1970; *Introduction to Ecology*, Wiley, 1973; *Why Big Fierce Animals Are Rare and Other Essays*, Princeton University Press, 1978; *The Fates of Nations: A Biological Theory of History*, Simon & Schuster, 1980; *Basic Ecology*, Wiley, 1985. Author of twenty-part television series, "What Ecology Really Says," broadcast on WOSU, Columbus, 1974, 1976, and 1978; also author of column, "Science in Review," in *Yale Review*, 1972-75. Contributor to *Science, Nature, Ecology,* and other journals. Contributing editor, *Quarterly Review of Archaeology*.

WORK IN PROGRESS: A sequel to *The Fates of Nations: A Biological Theory of History* based on continued studies on the natural selection of human learning; a history of the environment of the Amazon rain forest and the high Andes since the last ice age; research in Far Eastern Siberia through an arrangement with a member of the U.S.S.R. Academy of Sciences directed at reconstructing the flora and fauna of the old Bering land bridge.

SIDELIGHTS: Paul Colinvaux writes: "I like classes many hundreds strong [about six hundred are enrolled in his classes] and to these I orate. This form of unfashionable teaching has won me every teaching prize available at my university. . . . I have been able to enjoy writing because my student days were pleasantly and totally immune from the instruction of English literature departments. This history also gives me the chance to enjoy reading. It is my passionate belief that science is so intrinsically interesting that it only has to be written about beautifully for everybody to understand all about it.

"My sports are rowing and beagling. At Cambridge I acquired a certain facility with hounds, an expertise at running expeditions to remote places, and a degree in agriculture. Also some useful education. . . . In my first Canadian winter I read all of Gibbons' *Decline and Fall* in Joe's diners. I believe this to be a record."

BIOGRAPHICAL/CRITICAL SOURCES: New York Times Book Review, October 19, 1980; *Times Literary Supplement*, January 2, 1981.

COLLIAS, Joe G. 1928-

PERSONAL: Born April 25, 1928, in East St. Louis, Ill.; son of George Nick (a cleaner) and Martha L. (Vanbuskirk) Collias; married Majorie M. Piel (a publisher), October 1, 1960. *Education:* Washington University, St. Louis, Mo., M.E., 1956. *Politics:* Independent. *Religion:* Lutheran. *Residence:* Crestwood, Mo. *Office:* Boise Cascade Corp., Hazelwood, Mo. 63042.

CAREER: Bemis Bag Co., St. Louis, Mo., design engineer, 1951-61; Boise Cascade Corp., Hazelwood, Mo., art director, 1961—. *Military service:* U.S. Army, 1946-49; became sergeant.

WRITINGS: Last of Steam, Howell-North Books, 1960; *Search for Steam,* Howell-North Books, 1972; *MoPac Power,* Howell-North Books, 1978; *Frisco Power,* MM Books, 1984.

WORK IN PROGRESS: Two books on southwestern railroads.

SIDELIGHTS: Joe G. Collias told *CA:* "My first writing was born of enthusiasm and the excitement conveyed to me by a remarkably human-like machine, the railroad steam locomotive. I now write to preserve in print the same machine, its operations and mechanics and my own experiences in observing it firsthand. Such records are rare and need to be shared with others through the medium of the printed book. Along with the facts come a little of America and its history and a lot of photographs that, though not yet appreciated outside of the railroad-minded fraternity, should be considered as valuable as those of Ansel Adams."

AVOCATIONAL INTERESTS: Art (paints in oils), photography.

*   *   *

COLLINS, Desmond 1940-

PERSONAL: Born May 28, 1940, near Reading, England; son of Harold Kennedy (a company director) and Ivy Kathleen A. Collins; married Ann Alen (a teacher), December 20, 1965; children: Simon Alen. *Education:* Cambridge University, B.A. (with honors), 1962. *Politics:* "Liberal Social Democrat, eugenicist and idealist." *Home:* The Old Rectory, Clayhanger, Tiverton, Devon, England.

CAREER: University of London, London, England; lecturer, 1963-1972, senior lecturer in extramural studies, 1972-81; University of Exeter, Exeter, England, lecturer in extramural department, 1981—. Member of board of directors of Abington Finance Trust Ltd. and John Kennedy Investments Ltd., 1956—. *Member:* Society of Antiquaries of London (fellow), Current Anthropology (associate). *Awards, honors:* M.A. from Cambridge University.

WRITINGS: (With Ruth Whitehouse, Martin Henig, and David Whitehouse) *Background to Archaeology,* Cambridge University Press, 1972; (editor and contributor) *The Origins of Europe,* Allen & Unwin, 1975, Apollo, 1976; *The Human Revolution,* Dutton, 1976; *Early Man in West Middlesex: The Yiewsley Palaeolithic Sites,* H.M.S.O., 1978; *Palaeolithic Europe,* Junction Books, 1985.

SIDELIGHTS: Desmond Collins, who has done field work in Spain, Germany, Israel, and Britain, has recently excavated at West Heath, Hamstead, England. He told *CA:* "My main interest is solving general problems related to human emergence; especially the Neanderthal problem. I am the originator of the theory of evolution of Neanderthal man into Cro-Magnon man by neoteny—the chief selective mechanism being the difficulty of childbirth of big-brained Neanderthal infants."

*   *   *

COLODNY, Robert G. 1915-

PERSONAL: Born August 5, 1915, in Phoenix, Ariz.; son of Omar I. (a scholar) and Pauline (Shenberg) Colodny; married Dorothy Newman, June 15, 1946 (died, 1968); children: Robert Richard. *Education:* University of California, Berkeley, B.A., 1947, M.A., 1948, Ph.D., 1950. *Politics:* Independent. *Religion:* "Scientific Humanism." *Office:* Department of History, University of Pittsburgh, Pittsburgh, Pa. 15260.

CAREER: Has worked as a research chemist and journalist; University of Kansas, Lawrence, 1957-59, became professor of history; University of Pittsburgh, Pittsburgh, Pa., associate professor, 1958-67, professor of history and philosophy of science, 1967—. *Military service:* Spanish Republican Army, 1937-38. U.S. Army, 1941-46; became staff sergeant; received Hans Beimler Medal. *Member:* American Historical Association, History of Science Society, American Association for the Advancement of Science.

WRITINGS: The Struggle for Madrid, Paine-Whitman, 1959; *The Scientific Revolution of the Seventeenth Century,* University of Pittsburgh Press, 1963; *Spain: The Glory and the Tragedy,* Humanities, 1971; *El Asedio de Madrid* (title means "The Siege of Madrid"), Ruedo Iberico, 1971; *Biographies of Twelve Great Chemists,* McGraw, 1972; (author of introduction) *Spain: The Unfinished Revolution,* Camelot, 1972; *The Decline and Fall of Modern Europe,* University of Pittsburgh Press, 1972; (editor) V. V. Nalimov, *In the Labyrinths of Language: A Mathematician's Journey,* ISI Press, 1981; (editor) Nalimov, *The Faces of Science,* ISI Press, 1981; (editor) Nalimov, *Realms of the Unconscious: The Enchanted Frontier,* ISI Press, 1983; *Diary of the Twentieth Congress of Communist Party of the Soviet Union,* Lawrence Hill, 1984.

Editor of "Philosophy of Science" series, University of Pittsburgh Press, Volume I: *Frontiers of Science and Philosophy,* 1962, Volume II: *Beyond the Edge of Certainty,* 1965, Volume III: *Mind and Cosmos: Essays in Contemporary Science and Philosophy,* 1966, Volume IV: *The Nature and Function of Scientific Theories,* 1970, Volume V: *Paradigms and Paradoxes: The Philosophical Challenge of the Quantum Domain,* 1972, Volume VI: *Logic, Laws and Life: Some Philosophical Complications,* 1977. Contributor to professional journals.

WORK IN PROGRESS: History of Modern Scientific Achievements.

SIDELIGHTS: Robert G. Colodny writes *CA* that he believes that "the world uncovered by science and other scholarly endeavors must be made understandable for the common man."

*   *   *

COLYER, Penrose 1940-

PERSONAL: Born September 12, 1940, in Kettering, Northamptonshire, England; daughter of Cecil Frederick (a designer and craftsman) and Ruth (Reddaway) Colyer. *Education:* St. Clare's Hall, London, B.A., 1961. *Home:* Flat 3, 1 Mandeville Pl., London W1M 5LB, England.

CAREER: Teacher of Spanish in private school, and of English to foreign students, 1961-62; teacher of English and French in Beirut, Lebanon, 1962-63; Mary Glasgow Publications, Ltd., London, England, head of French department and secretary of advisory panel, 1963-67; free-lance writer and editor, 1967-68; assistant head of publishing division, Linguaphone Institute, Ltd., 1968-69; Macdonald Educational, London, arts editor, 1969-70; free-lance writer and editor, 1970-72; Brooking School of Ballet and General Education, London, headmistress, 1972—.

MEMBER: Society of Authors, National Trust, National Union of Teachers, Youth Hostels Association, Players Theatre, Mensa, League of Friends of Middlesex Hospital.

WRITINGS: Les Cahiers rouges (title means "The Little Red Books"), Mary Glasgow Publications, 1965; *Les Cahiers verts* (title means "The Little Green Books"), Mary Glasgow Publications, 1967; *Les Aventures d'Auguste* (comic strips; title means "The Adventures of Augustus"), Mary Glasgow Publications, c. 1967; *French for Fun!*, Sonodisc, 1968; *Le Voyage du Jericho* (title means "The Journey of the Jericho"), Longmans, Green, 1969.

I Can Read French, Peter Lowe, 1972, F. Watts, 1974; (translator) Jane Carruth, *Parlez Francais avec Dougal* (title means "Speak French with Dougal"), Hamlyn, 1973; *Book of Numbers*, Mary Glasgow Publications, 1973; *Famous and Fabulous Animals*, Peter Lowe, 1973; *Catherine Verneuil: Danseuse* (title means "Catherine Verneuil: Dancer"), Longman, 1973.

(Editor) *Jeg kan laese engelsk: Min forste dansk-engelske ordbog*, Gyldendal, 1974; *Who Works Here?*, Hamlyn, 1975; *Who Plays Here?*, Hamlyn, 1975; *Who Lives Here?*, Hamlyn, 1975; *Who Was Here?*, Hamlyn, 1975; *Lost in London*, European Schoolbooks, 1976; (editor) *I Can Read German: My First English-German Word Book*, Peter Lowe, 1976; (editor) *I Can Read Spanish: My First English-Spanish Word Book*, F. Watts, 1976; (with Claire Andree Roe) *La France*, Longman, 1977; *Voyage en Normandie*, Longman, 1977.

(Editor) *I Can Read Italian: My First English-Italian Word Book*, Peter Lowe, 1980, F. Watts, 1983; *Passeport pour la France*, Thomas Nelson, 1983.

Also author of books for Longman, *Pierre Leroy: Sous-chef de Gare* (title means "Pierre Leroy: Assistant Station-Master"), *Marium Masse: Forestier* (title means "Marius Masse: Forester"), *Monique et Marie-Claire: Infirmieres* (title means "Monique and Marie-Claire: Nurses"), and *Robert: Boulanger* (title means "Robert: Baker"), 1975.

Also writer of French teaching materials for Mary Glasgow Publications, 1963-65, and for Longman, 1973-75, including "Histoire de France" (title means "French History"), "La Vie en France" (title means "Life in France"), and "Le Pays de France" (title means "The Land of France").

Contributor of articles to *Cherwell, Dundee Evening Courier, Guardian,* and *Punch,* and of book reviews to *New Era.*

SIDELIGHTS: Penrose Colyer once told *CA:* "When teaching I find all too often that published material is difficult, condescending, and distinctly unfunny. To teach via material which is comprehensible, entertaining, and interesting is the aim of my educational writing."

AVOCATIONAL INTERESTS: Dress-making, theatre, flower arranging, cooking, jewelry-making, swimming, riding, brass-rubbing, tennis, international travel.†

COMINS, Jeremy 1933-

PERSONAL: Born May 8, 1933, in Ohio; son of Harry L. (a writer) and Edith (a psychologist) Comins; married Eleanor Fishman (a teacher), February 11, 1959; children: Aaron, Daniel. *Education:* New York University, B.S., 1954, M.A., 1956. *Home:* 1776 East 19th St., Brooklyn, N.Y. 11229.

CAREER: Sculptor and artist (one-man exhibitions in New York area and group exhibitions at galleries and museums, including Museum of Modern Art, Cooper Union Museum, and Philadelphia Museum). Art teacher in public schools in New York, N.Y., 1955—. *Awards, honors:* Photography prizes, 1971-72, for color slide transparencies.

WRITINGS—All self-illustrated with drawings and photographs; published by Lothrop, except as indicated: *Getting Started in African Crafts*, Bruce Books, 1971; *Latin American Crafts and Their Cultural Backgrounds*, 1974; *Art from Found Objects*, 1974; *Eskimo Crafts and Their Cultural Backgrounds*, 1975; *Totems, Decoys, and Covered Wagons: Cardboard Constructions from Early American Life*, 1976; *Slotted Sculpture from Cardboard*, 1977; *Chinese and Japanese Crafts and Their Cultural Backgrounds*, 1978; *Vans to Build from Cardboard*, 1978. Contributor to *School Arts.*†

*   *   *

CONANT, Ralph W(endell) 1926-

PERSONAL: Born September 7, 1926, in Hope, Me.; son of Earle Raymond (a business executive) and Margaret (Long) Conant; married Audrey Karl (a teacher), August 27, 1950; children: Beverlie Elaine, Lisa Audrey, Jonathan Arnold. *Education:* University of Vermont, B.A., 1949; University of Chicago, M.A., 1954, Ph.D., 1959. *Politics:* Democrat. *Religion:* Unitarian. *Address:* Box 2200, North Vassalboro, Me. 04962.

CAREER: Staff associate, National Municipal League, 1957-59; director, Citizens for Michigan, 1959-60; University of Denver, Denver, Colo., assistant professor, 1960-62; Massachusetts Institute of Technology and Harvard University, Joint Center for Urban Studies, Cambridge, Mass., assistant to director, 1962-66; Brandeis University, Lemberg Center for the Study of Violence, Waltham, Mass., associate director, 1967-69; University of Houston, Houston, Tex., professor of political science and director of Institute for Urban Studies, 1969-75; Rice University, Houston, professor of urban studies and president of Southwest Center for Urban Research, 1969-75; Shimer College, Mt. Carroll, Ill., president, 1975-78; Unity College, Unity, Me., president, 1978-81; president of Public Research, Inc., 1981—. Member of Regional Health Advisory Committee, U.S. Department of Health, Education and Welfare. *Military service:* U.S. Army, 1943-45, 1951-53. U.S. Army Reserves, 1945-68; became major.

MEMBER: American Political Science Association.

WRITINGS: (Editor) Milton Greenburg and Sherrill Cleland, *State Constitutional Revision in Michigan,* [Detroit], 1960; *Politics of Regional Planning in Greater Hartford,* Greater Hartford Chamber of Commerce, 1964; (editor) *The Public Library and the City,* MIT Press, 1965; *The Politics of Community Health,* Public Affairs Press, 1968; *Civil Disobedience, Rioting and Insurrection,* Lincoln Filene Center for Citizenship and Public Affairs, 1968; (editor with Molly Apple Levin) *Problems in Research on Community Violence,* Praeger, 1969.

The Prospects for Revolution: A Study of Riots, Civil Disobedience and Insurrection in Contemporary America, Harper's Magazine Press, 1971; *The Metropolitan Library*, MIT Press, 1972; (with Alan Shank) *Urban Perspectives: Politics and Policies*, Holbrook, 1975.

The Conant Report: A Study of the Education of Libraries, MIT Press, 1980; (with T. Easton) *The Small Business Guide to Consultants*, Probus, 1985. Contributor to *American Scholar, Urban Affairs Quarterly, Library Journal, Wilson Library Bulletin, A.L.A. Bulletin, International Journal of Health Education, American Behavioral Scientist*, and other journals.

WORK IN PROGRESS: Cutting Loose: Transitions from Employee to Entrepreneur, for Probus.

AVOCATIONAL INTERESTS: Mountain climbing, skiing, European travel.

BIOGRAPHICAL/CRITICAL SOURCES: Nation, June 14, 1971.

* * *

CONKLIN, John E(van) 1943-

PERSONAL: Born October 2, 1943, in Oswego, N.Y.; son of Evan Nelson (an insurance salesman) and Susan (Brenner) Conklin; married Sarah Belcher; children: Christopher Perry, Anne Tiffany, Lydia Catherine. *Education:* Cornell University, A.B. (cum laude), 1965; Harvard University, Ph.D., 1969. *Home:* 10 Cottage St., Lexington, Mass. 02173. *Office:* Department of Sociology, Tufts University, Medford, Mass. 02155.

CAREER: Harvard University, Center for Criminal Justice, Cambridge, Mass., research associate, 1969-70; Tufts University, Medford, Mass., assistant professor, 1970-76, associate professor, 1976-81, professor of sociology, 1981—, chairman of department, 1981—.

MEMBER: American Sociological Association, Law and Society Association, National Council on Crime and Delinquency, Phi Beta Kappa.

WRITINGS: Robbery and the Criminal Justice System, Lippincott, 1972; (editor) *The Crime Establishment*, Prentice-Hall, 1973; *The Impact of Crime*, Macmillan, 1975; *"Illegal But Not Criminal": Business Crime in America*, Prentice-Hall, 1977; *Criminology*, Macmillan, 1981; *Sociology: An Introduction*, Macmillan, 1984. Contributor of articles to scholarly journals.

*WORK IN PROGRESS: The second edition of *Criminology*, for Macmillan.

* * *

CONRAN, Anthony 1931-

PERSONAL: Born April 7, 1931, in Kharghpur, India; son of Denzil Arthur Stewart and Clarinda Wynne (Jones) Conran. *Education:* University of Wales, University College of North Wales, B.A. (with honors), 1953, M.A., 1956. *Home:* 1 Frondirion, Bangor, Gwynedd, Wales. *Agent:* A. D. Peters, 10 Buckingham St., London WC2N 6BU, England. *Office:* Department of English, University College of North Wales, University of Wales, Bangor, Gwynedd, Wales.

CAREER: University of Wales, University College of North Wales, Bangor, research assistant, 1957-66, tutor in English, 1966—.

MEMBER: Yr Academi Gynreig (English section).

AWARDS, HONORS: Prize from Welsh Arts Council, 1960, for *Formal Poems*.

WRITINGS—Poetry, except as indicated: *Formal Poems*, Christopher Davies, 1960; *Metamorphoses*, Dock Leaves Press, 1961, revised edition, Tern Press, 1979; *Icons: Opus 6*, privately printed, 1963; *Asymptotes: Opus 7*, privately printed, 1963; *A String of Blethers: Opus 8*, privately printed, 1963; *Sequence of the Blue Flower*, privately printed, 1963; *The Mountain*, privately printed, 1963; *For the Marriage of Gerard and Linda*, privately printed, 1963.

Stelae and Other Poems, Opus 9, Clive Allison, 1965; *Guernica*, Gee & Son, 1966; *Collected Poems*, Volume I, Clive Allison, 1966, Volumes II-IV, Gee & Son, 1966-68; (editor and translator) *The Penguin Book of Welsh Verse*, Penguin, 1967; *Claim, Claim, Claim: A Book of Poems*, Circle Press, 1969.

The Margaret Book of Anthony Conran, Deiniol Press, 1973; *Spirit Level*, Christopher Davies, 1974; *Poems, 1951-1967*, Deiniol Press, 1974; (translator) *Eighteen Poems by Dante Alighieri*, Tern Press, 1975; *Cost of Strangeness*, Gomer Press, 1975; *Life Fund*, J. D. Lewis, 1979; *On to the Fields of Praise: Essays on the English Poets of Wales* (essays), Planet Press, 1979.

WORK IN PROGRESS: Research on folksongs.

SIDELIGHTS: Born in India and at first alien to Wales, Anthony Conran has become deeply involved in Welsh culture and custom and is well-known for his translations from the Welsh.

BIOGRAPHICAL/CRITICAL SOURCES: Poetry Wales, spring, 1967.†

* * *

CONSTANTINE, Larry L(eRoy) 1943-

PERSONAL: Born February 14, 1943, in Minneapolis, Minn.; son of Philip Francis (a mechanic) and L. Loraine (a secretary and newspaper writer; maiden name, Hack) Constantine; married Joan Marie Kangas (a family therapist), March 7, 1964; children: Joy Marie, Heather Ellen. *Education:* Massachusetts Institute of Technology, S.B., 1967, graduate study, 1967-68; Boston Family Institute, certificate in family therapy, 1973. *Religion:* "Humanist." *Home:* 22 Bulette Rd., Acton, Mass. 01720.

CAREER: C-E-I-R, Inc., Washington, D.C. (and Boston, Mass.), programmer and analyst, 1963-67; Information & Systems Institute, Inc., Cambridge, Mass., president, 1967-69; International Business Machines, Systems Research Institute, New York, N.Y., adjunct member of faculty, 1968-72; Tufts University, School of Medicine, Boston, Mass., assistant clinical professor of psychiatry, 1973-80; University of Connecticut, Storrs, assistant professor of human development and family relations, 1983—. Family therapist in private practice in Acton, Mass., 1973—. Member of board of directors of Groves Conference on Marriage and the Family. Member of National Council on Family Relations. Independent consultant in general systems theory applied to systems design, 1968-76.

MEMBER: American Orthopsychiatric Association (fellow), Society for Family Therapy and Research.

WRITINGS: (With wife, Joan M. Constantine) *Group Marriage: A Study of Contemporary Multilateral Marriages,* Macmillan, 1973; (with Ed Yourdon) *Structured Design: Fundamentals of a Discipline of Computer Program and Systems Design,* Yourdon Press, 1975, revised edition, Prentice-Hall, 1978.

(With J. M. Constantine) *Treasures of the Island: Children in Alternative Families* (monograph), Sage Publications, 1976; (with Alvin K. Swonger) *Drugs and Therapy: The Psychotherapist's Handbook of Psychotropic Drugs,* Little, Brown, 1976; (editor with Floyd Martinson) *Children and Sex: New Findings and Perspectives,* Little, Brown, 1979; *Family Paradigms: The Practice of Theory in Family Therapy,* Guilford Press, in press.

Also composer of musical works, including "Concerto Grosso No. 1 in G-minor," 1981, "No Hidden Meanings: A Choral Fantasy on the Writings of Sheldon Kopp," 1982, and contemporary settings for children's choir of Psalms 46 and 134, 1984.

Editor, *Lifestyles,* Human Sciences, 1983—.

Contributor of more than fifty articles to family counseling journals and popular magazines, including *Penthouse Forum.*

SIDELIGHTS: Larry L. Constantine writes: "I never considered becoming a writer until my freshman humanities professor, Emmett Larkin, pronounced me hopelessly illiterate and incapable of construcitng a coherent sentence. With the tenacity of scum in a bathtub, I clung to this challenge, determined to learn to write a readable, informative sentence. I advanced to striving for interesting sentences and hope someday to graduate to writing short paragraphs.

"Technical themes were my first literary drills, and my first technical article was published during my sophomore year. I wrote at first to give permanence to otherwise fleeting technical notions and out of unabashed careermanship. Alas, my theories and techniques were largely ignored during my tenure in information sciences, becoming recognized and accepted only after I switched my allegiance to family studies and human relations. There I found the purpose absent in my first career.

"I write not to write but to reach. Writing still does not come easily for me, consisting largely of repeated revision and self-inflicted editing. The work is only the vehicle for the idea, which is, in turn, the servant of the intent, for all my writing is intentioned, part of my drive to be cause, to contribute substantively to human progress. Will evolution's forward thrust outrun the forces of decay or our potential for self-destruction? I know not, but only that I wish to be on one side and not the other.

"In this epoch, human survival will depend on the continued evolution of social forms to fit accelerating conditions of change in a universe of new rules, new constraints, new potentials. We need tolerance of differences, support of variation, and expanded self-understanding if the necessary social innovations are to emerge. Alternatives must be allowed to flourish and to fail freely, to be sifted for new institutions, values, and lifestyles to supplant those which once served us well but now lead us to the very edge of oblivion.

"Social change and alternatives pervade my life. My own family is open, egalitarian, a place of generous freedom and easy affection. We are staunch supporters of the Equal Rights Amendment and advocates of children's rights."

AVOCATIONAL INTERESTS: "I do not readily call myself a composer, but music is the 'other side' of my expressive side: the urgent, gushing, all-absorbing side. Anthony Burgess, who rightfully calls himself both writer and composer, sees literature and music as isomorphic. Certainly for me they have the same wellspring. Despite amateur status and inadequate time to compose, I have had the extraordinary good fortune to have had several major works commissioned and performed: 'Concerto Grosso No. 1 in G-minor' (1981), 'No Hidden Meanings: A Choral Fantasy on the Writings of Sheldon Kopp' (1982), and contemporary settings for childrens' choir of Psalms 46 and 134 (1984). When I need a break from all this creative toil (an almost daily need), I cook, especially Mexican and Italian cuisine, which I do brilliantly."

*   *   *

CONTRERAS, Heles 1933-

PERSONAL: Born August 1, 1933, in Victoria, Chile; son of Domingo and Frieda (Weibel) Contreras; married Gladys Gaete, January 15, 1955 (divorced, 1977); married Karen T. Zagona, December 23, 1983; children (first marriage): Patricio, Moyra, Sandra, Carmen, Leticia. *Education:* University of Conception, Chile, professor de Estado, 1957; Indiana University, M.A., 1959, Ph.D., 1961. *Home:* 2324 Northeast 103rd St., Seattle, Wash. 98125. *Office:* Department of Linguistics GN-40, University of Washington, Seattle, Wash. 98195.

CAREER: University of Concepcion, Concepcion, Chile, professor of linguistics, 1961-64; University of Washington, Seattle, visiting assistant professor, 1964-65, assistant professor, 1965-67, associate professor, 1967-77, professor of linguistics, 1977—.

AWARDS, HONORS: Fulbright scholar, 1958-59; American Philosophical Society research grant, 1982-83.

WRITINGS: (With Sol Saporta) *A Phonological Grammar of Spanish,* University of Washington Press, 1962; (editor) *Los fundamentos de la gramatica transformacional,* Siglo XXI, 1971; *A Theory of Word Order with Special Reference to Spanish,* North-Holland Publishing, 1976; (editor with Jurgen Klausenburger) *Proceedings of the Tenth Anniversary Symposium on Romance Languages,* Volume III, Supplement 2: *Papers in Romance,* Department of Romance Languages, University of Washington, 1980; (with Conxita Lleo) *Aproximacion a la fonologia generativa,* Anagrama, 1982.

*   *   *

COOK, Don(ald Paul) 1920-

PERSONAL: Born August 8, 1920, in Bridgeport, Conn.; son of Paul J. (a schoolteacher) and Nelle Brown (Reed) Cook; married Cherry Mitchell, October 31, 1943 (deceased March 19, 1983); children: Christopher, Jennifer, Adrienne, Deborah, Caron, Danielle, Dominique. *Education:* Attended schools in Pennsylvania. *Religion:* Protestant. *Home:* 4 Allee Jose Roland, L'Etang la Ville, France 78620. *Agent:* Brandt & Brandt, 1501 Broadway, New York, N.Y. 10036. *Office: Los Angeles Times,* 73, Ave. des Champs-Elysees, Paris 75008, France.

CAREER: Began newspaper work at eighteen; *New York Herald Tribune,* New York, N.Y., member of staff, Washington bureau, 1943-45, foreign correspondent, London, England, 1945-49, Germany, 1949-52, roving European correspondent based in Paris, France, 1952-55, chief of London bureau, 1956-60, chief European correspondent, 1960-65; *Los Angeles Times,*

Los Angeles, Calif., Paris correspondent, beginning 1965, European diplomatic correspondent, 1983—.

MEMBER: International Institute for Strategic Studies (London), Authors League of America, Anglo-American Press Association of Paris, Association of American Correspondents in London (former president), Garrick Club (London), Century Association (New York).

AWARDS, HONORS: William the Silent Award for Journalism (The Netherlands), 1956; English-Speaking Union Award, 1958; Overseas Press Club citation, 1966.

WRITINGS: Floodtide in Europe, Putnam, 1965; (contributor) Michael Carver, editor, *The War Lords: Military Commanders of the Twentieth Century,* Little Brown, 1976; *Ten Men and History,* Doubleday, 1981; *Charles de Gaulle: A Biography,* Putnam, 1983. Contributor to *Saturday Evening Post, Reporter, Harper's, Look, Reader's Digest, Atlantic Monthly, Saturday Review,* and *Fortune.*

SIDELIGHTS: Of Don Cook and his book *Charles de Gaulle: A Biography,* Drew Middleton writes in the *New York Times* that "no one has done a better job in painting the real de Gaulle, and no one will be able to write about the general and his troubled times without resorting to this biography." According to *Chicago Tribune Book World* critic Alden Whitman, "the extent to which [de Gaulle] prepared himself for his destiny as both the savior and ruler of his nation is the heart of Don Cook's impressively wrought biography, which presents de Gaulle as a study in power." *Time* reviewer Donald Morrison writes that, as Cook "points out in this robust, unsentimental biography, Charles de Gaulle never deviated from the idea that animated his entire career. As he once summed it up, 'France cannot be France without greatness.'"

"Cook makes the most of the relevant de Gaulle material," Whitman indicates, praising "his newspaperman's eye for significant detail." However, Walter Lord relates in the *New York Times Book Review,* "this book does not rely on headline-making interviews or freshly mined archival material but rather on long firsthand experience. . . . Cook has covered the European political beat for 38 years. Like William Shirer on Hitler's Germany or Robert Donovan on Harry Truman's Washington, he is a seasoned authority on de Gaulle's France." Lord reports that Cook "rightly devotes most of his book to World War II," and in the words of Peter Loewenburg in *Los Angeles Times,* "the story of how Gen. Charles de Gaulle built the Free French movement out of nothing but his will and historical necessity is one of the great sagas of modern history." "The author presents a panorama of World War II's critical events," comments Loewenburg, "the fall of France, the disastrous defeat at Dakar, the North African landings, D-Day in Normandy, the liberation of Paris. The events are thrilling, the pace is fast."

De Gaulle's later career is also covered, Lord reports. Middleton comments that "the author is fair to the early triumphs of de Gaulle's presidency, and he is just in his estimate of the handling of the Algerian crisis. He also points out de Gaulle's errors: the French withdrawal from military integration in the North Atlantic Treaty Organization and his veto against British membership in the Common Market." According to Douglas Porch in *Washington Post Book World,* Cook "catalogues what he sees as de Gaulle's vendetta against *"les anglo-saxons"* during this second period in power, and his often absurd appeal to *"la gloire"* over political reality. Yet, with time, many of de Gaulle's views appear to owe less to the prejudices of a

confirmed Anglophobe and more to a balanced assessment of French interests." *New York Review of Books* critic Robert O. Paxton points out that "while Cook reports de Gaulle's life with evident good intentions of fairness and accuracy," his "American perspective" prevents a well-rounded image of the man Paxton describes as "the boldest and most unsentimental practitioner of traditional national-interest diplomacy" in modern European history. "Nevertheless," Porch indicates, "for anyone attempting to understand de Gaulle, this book offers an excellent starting point." As Middleton concludes, "Don Cook has done all interested in the history of this strident century a great service."

BIOGRAPHICAL/CRITICAL SOURCES: New York Times, January 3, 1984; *Los Angeles Times,* January 22, 1984; *New York Times Book Review,* January 22, 1984; *Washington Post Book World,* February 26, 1984; *New Yorker,* February 27, 1984; *Chicago Tribune Book World,* March 4, 1984; *Time,* March 5, 1984; *Times* (London), April 5, 1984; *New York Review of Books,* April 26, 1984.

*   *   *

COOK, Mark 1942-

PERSONAL: Born December 6, 1942, in Sandown, Isle of Wight; son of Samuel Astbury (a civil servant) and Beatrice (Rawlins) Cook; married Janette McLeod, December 29, 1969. *Education:* Oxford University, B.A., 1965, M.A., 1970, D.Phil., 1971. *Home:* 10 Woodlands Ter., Swansea, Wales. *Office:* Department of Psychology, University College of Swansea, Singleton Park, Swansea, Wales.

CAREER: University of Aberdeen, Aberdeen, Scotland, assistant lecturer in psychology, 1968-69; Oxford University, Oxford, England, research officer in psychology, 1969-73; University College of Swansea, Swansea, Wales, lecturer in psychology, 1973—. Director of research, Psychological Consultancy Services, Ltd., 1981—.

WRITINGS: Interpersonal Perception, Penguin, 1971; (with Michael Argyle) *Gaze and Mutual Gaze,* Cambridge University Press, 1976; *Love and Attraction,* Pergamon, 1977; (with Robert McHenry) *Sexual Attraction,* Pergamon, 1978; *Perceiving Others,* Methuen, 1979; (with Kevin Howells) *Adult Sexual Interest in Children,* Academic Press, 1981; *Bases of Human Sexual Attraction,* Academic Press, 1982; *Levels of Personality,* Holt, 1984; *Issues in Person Perception,* Methuen, 1984.

WORK IN PROGRESS: Productivity and Personnel Selection, for Wiley.

AVOCATIONAL INTERESTS: History of transport, driving cars, collecting government survey maps.

*   *   *

COOKE, William 1942-

PERSONAL: Born December 27, 1942, in Stoke-on-Trent, Staffordshire, England; son of William (a builder) and Ann Maria (Docksey) Cooke. *Education:* University of Leeds, B.A., 1964, M.A., 1966, Ph.D., 1969. *Home:* 17 Stuart Ave., Trentham, Stoke-on-Trent, Staffordshire ST4 8BG, England.

CAREER: Thistley Hough School, Stoke-on-Trent, England, teacher, 1968-70; City of Stoke-on-Trent Sixth Form College, Stoke-on-Trent, tutor of English literature, 1970-79; lecturer in communication, Cauldon College of Further Education, 1979—.

WRITINGS: Edward Thomas: A Critical Biography, 1878-1917, Faber, 1970; *Edward Thomas: A Portrait,* Hub Publications, 1978; (editor) *Anvil,* privately printed, 1979; *Builder,* Yorkshire Arts, 1980; *Small Ads,* Start Press, 1980. Also author of *The Happiest Daze of Your Life,* 1984.

Contributor: Peter Porter and Charles Osborne, editors, *New Poetry I,* Arts Council of Great Britain, 1975; Norman Hidden, editor, *Over to You,* English Speaking Borad, 1975; Patricia Beer and Kevin Crossley-Holland, editors, *New Poetry II,* Arts Council of Great Britain, 1976; Derwent May and Alexis Lykiard, editors, *New Stories 2,* Arts Council of Great Britain, 1977; Fleur Adcock and Anthony Thwaite, editors, *New Poetry 4,* Arts Council of Great Britain, 1978; Alfred Bradley, editor, *The Northern Drift,* Blackie & Son, 1980; Lorna Downman, editor, *The Hitchhiker and Other Short Stories,* Almqvist & Wiksell, 1981; Dominic Hibberd, editor, *The Poetry of the First World War,* Macmillan, 1982.

BIOGRAPHICAL/CRITICAL SOURCES: Spectator, February 14, 1970; *Observer,* February 15, 1970; *Times Literary Supplement,* April 30, 1970, November 23, 1979; *London Magazine,* June, 1970.

* * *

CORAM, Christopher
See WALKER, Peter N.

* * *

CORBIN, Charles B. 1940-

PERSONAL: Born October 20, 1940, in Toledo, Ohio; son of Don E. (a school principal) and D'Esta June (Wolford) Corbin; married Mary Catherine Milligan, June 12, 1964; children: Charles, Jr., John David, William Robert. *Education:* University of New Mexico, B.S., 1960, Ph.D., 1965; University of Illinois, M.S., 1962. *Religion:* Protestant. *Home:* 1427 East Northshore, Tempe, Ariz. 85283. *Office:* Department of Health and Physical Education, Arizona State University, Tempe, Ariz. 85287.

CAREER: Albuquerque (N.M.) public schools, teacher, 1960-61; assistant professor of health and physical education at College of Santa Fe, Santa Fe, N.M., 1964-65, and University of Toledo, Toledo, Ohio, 1965-67; Texas A & M University, College Station, associate professor of health and physical education, 1967-71, and director of health and physical education research laboratory; Kansas State University, Manhattan, professor of physical education, 1971-82, head of department, 1971-75, director of motor development research lab, beginning 1975; Arizona State University, Tempe, professor of physical education and exercise science, 1982—.

MEMBER: American Alliance for Health, Phsyical Education and Recreation, American College of Sports Medicine, American Academy of Physical Education (fellow), National College Physical Education Association, North American Society for Psychology of Sport and Physical Activity, Phi Epsilon Kappa, Phi Delta Kappa.

WRITINGS: (With Linus Dowell and Carl Landiss) *Concepts and Experiments in Physical Education,* Kendall/Hunt, 1968; *Becoming Physically Educated in the Elementary School,* Lea & Febiger, 1969, 2nd edition, 1976; (with Dowell, Homer Tolson, and Ruth Lindsey) *Concepts of Physical Education,* W. C. Brown, 1970, 5th edition (with Lindsey) published as

Concepts of Physical Fitness, 1985; *Inexpensive Games Equipment,* W. C. Brown, 1973; *A Textbook of Motor Development,* W. C. Brown, 1974, 2nd edition, 1980; *The Athletic Snowball,* Human Kinetics, 1977.

(With Lindsey) *Fitness for Life,* 2nd edition, Scott, Foresman, 1983; (co-author) *Choosing Good Health,* Scott, Foresman, 1983; *The Ultimate Fitness Book,* Leisure Press, 1984. Creator of record albums in physical education for Education Activities, Inc. Contributor to professional journals and magazines. Associate editor, *Physical Educator;* member of editorial board, *Journal of Sport Psychology.*

WORK IN PROGRESS: Third editions of *A Textbook of Motor Development* and *Fitness for Life.*

SIDELIGHTS: Charles B. Corbin told *CA:* "Physical fitness is too often perceived as being something for those with good physical skills: the athletes of the world. A major goal of my writing is to convince people that exercise is for everyone. No matter who you are you can enjoy the benefit of exercise and good physical fitness. . . . It is never too late to begin. Regardless of age, sex or ability there is some form of activity that can be done to help you look your best, enjoy life, and benefit your health."

* * *

CORNGOLD, Stanley Alan 1934-

PERSONAL: Born June 11, 1934, in Brooklyn, N.Y.; son of Herman and Estelle (Bramson) Corngold; married Marie Josephine Brettle, July 26, 1961 (divorced, 1969); children: Isabel Anna. *Education:* Columbia University, A.B. (with honors), 1957; additional study at University of London, 1957-58, and Columbia University, 1958-59; Cornell University, M.A., 1963, Ph.D., 1969; University of Basel, additional study, 1965-66. *Home:* 20 Erdman Ave., Princeton, N.J. 08540. *Office:* Department of German, Princeton University, Princeton, N.J. 08544.

CAREER: University of Maryland, European Division, Heidelberg, Germany, instructor in English, 1959-62; Princeton University, Princeton, N.J., assistant professor, 1966-72, associate professor of German, 1972-81, associate professor of comparative literature, 1979-81, professor of German and comparative literature, 1981—. Visiting professor, Bryn Mawr College, 1983-84. *Military service:* U.S. Naval Reserve, 1951-55. U.S. Army, 1955-57.

MEMBER: Nietzsche Society of North America, Goethe Society of North America, Kafka Society of North America (member of executive board), Modern Language Association of America, Phi Beta Kappa.

AWARDS, HONORS: American Council of Learned Societies fellowship, 1965; grant-in-aid for research, Princeton University, 1967, 1972; National Endowment for the Humanities fellowship, 1973; Guggenheim fellowship, 1977; Academy of Literary Studies award, 1983.

WRITINGS: (Editor, and author of introduction, notes, and vocabulary) *"Ausgewaehlte Prosa" by Max Frisch,* Harcourt, 1968; (translator, editor, and author of introduction, notes, and critical apparatus) Franz Kafka, *The Metamorphosis,* Bantam, 1972; *The Commentators' Despair: The Interpretation of Franz Kafka's "Metamorphosis,"* National University Publications, 1973; (editor) *Aspekte der Goethezeit,* Vandenhoeck & Ruprecht, 1977; *The Fate of the Self: Seven German Thinkers,* Columbia University Press, 1985.

Contributor: Willis Barnstone, editor, *Modern European Poetry*, Bantam, 1966; R. G. Collins and Kenneth McRobbie, editor, *New Views of the European Novel*, University of Manitoba Press, 1972; (and editor with Richard Ludwig) *Thomas Mann, 1875-1975*, Princeton University Press, 1975; James Rolleston, editor, *Twentieth-Century Interpretations of "The Trial,"* Prentice-Hall, 1976; Angel Flores, editor, *The Problem of "The Judgment": Eleven Approaches to Kafka's Story*, Gordian Press, 1977; Flores, editor, *The Kafka Debate: New Perspectives for Our Time*, Gordian Press, 1977; Maria Luise Caputo-Mayr, editor, *Franz Kafka—Ein Symposium*, Agora Verlag, 1978; William Spanos, editor, *Martin Heidegger and the Question of Literature: Toward a Post-modern Literary Hermeneutics*, Indiana University Press, 1979.

(With Howard Stern) *Yearbook of Comparative and General Literature*, University of Indiana, 1980; Jonathan Arac and others, editors, *The Yale Critics: Deconstruction in America*, University of Minnesota Press, 1983; *Franz Kafka: Homenaje en su centenario (1833-1924)*, [Buenos Aires], 1983. Contributor to professional journals, including *European Judaism, Critical Inquiry, Literary Review, Newsletter of the Kafka Society of America*, and *Modern Language Studies*.

*   *   *

CORSON-FINNERTY, Adam Daniel   1944-
(Adam Daniel Finnerty, Daniel John Finnerty; A. Daniel McKenna, pseudonym)

PERSONAL: Born May 27, 1944, in Chautauqua, N.Y.; son of John Charles (in U.S. Air Force) and Frances (a teacher; maiden name, Mapes) Finnerty; married Susan Marie Corson (an editor); children: Susan Mapes. *Education:* University of Pennsylvania, B.A., 1967, M.A., 1968; Bryn Mawr College, M.S.S., 1972. *Religion:* Quaker. *Home:* 120 West Mt. Airy, Philadelphia, Pa. 19119. *Office:* American Friends Service Committee, 1501 Cherry St., Philadelphia, Pa. 19102.

CAREER: Horizon House, Philadelphia, Pa., assistant group work supervisor, 1968-69; Horizon House-Jefferson Community Mental Health Center, Philadelphia, group work specialist, 1969-70; City of Philadelphia, intern under deputy health commissioner, 1970-71; Eagleville Drug and Alcohol Rehabilitation Center, Eagleville, Pa., member of school consultation team, 1971-72; Kirkridge Retreat Center, Bangor, Pa., assistant to program director, 1973-74; Shakertown Pledge Group, Philadelphia, director, 1974-75; free-lance writer and consultant, beginning 1975; American Friends Service Committee, Philadelphia, director of material aids program and assistant secretary, International Division, 1979—. Staff director of Liberty to the Captives; co-director of Krowten Associates (consultants). Assistant to director of Montgomery County Opportunity Board, 1966; member of Churchmouse Collective, 1974-77; counselor for dying patients and their families, Albert Einstein Hospital, 1978-79. Chairman, American Christians for the Abolition of Torture. Conducts workshops and seminars.

MEMBER: Mental Health Advocacy Association (founder and president, 1970-72).

AWARDS, HONORS: World Citizen: Action for Global Justice won second place in the 1983 Catholic Book Awards.

WRITINGS: (With Charles Funnell, under name Daniel John Finnerty) *Exiled: A Draft Counselor's Handbook for the Draft-Age Emigrant*, Resistance Press, 1968; (under name Adam Daniel Finnerty) *No More Plastic Jesus: Global Justice and Christian Lifestyle*, Orbis, 1977; *World Citizen: Action for Global Justice*, Orbis, 1982.

Contributor to magazines, including *Fellowship, Win, Friends Journal*, and *National Guardian*. Editor of *Mental Health Advocacy Newsletter*, 1970-72, *Shakertown Pledge Newsletter*, 1974-75, *Creative Simplicity*, 1974-75, and *I. D. Bulletin*, 1979—.

WORK IN PROGRESS: O'Ryan, M.A., a "thriller-spoof," under pseudonym A. Daniel McKenna; "Henry the Last," a comic play; "Melody," a biographical play.

SIDELIGHTS: Adam Daniel Corson-Finnerty wrote: "I guess I have to identify myself as very much the 'sixties' activist. I first got involved in social change by going to participate in the Selma to Montgomery march in 1965. From there, I became involved in the Civil Rights and Peace movements—primarily in the Philadelphia area. Concern about Vietnam led me into a deeper understanding of Third World problems. Seeing that many Third World nations cut their own throats by jailing some of their most creative people (often with help from the United States in the form of training and military aid to the dictators), I have recently been most concerned with human rights.

"I started off at age eighteen as an 'Air Force brat' (father was a career enlisted man) who expected to go into corporate management. Then I hit the big city (Philadelphia), got 'radicalized' by the war in Vietnam, and haven't yet recovered. My religious journey has taken me from mainstream Protestantism into a Jesus-freak phase, then an 'esoteric' phase, then a renewal of interest in my Catholic heritage and a discovery that I think like a Quaker (and enjoy silent worship). I finally 'joined up' with the Society of Friends in 1981.

"My nonfiction is all directed at a concerned-but-not-too-well-informed Middle American audience—in other words *me*, before I started research in any particular field. My fiction is much crazier, free-wheeling, and immoral—a release for that side of my personality."

BIOGRAPHICAL/CRITICAL SOURCES: Chestnut Hill Local, December 16, 1982.

*   *   *

COSTIGAN, Daniel M.   1929-

PERSONAL: Born February 13, 1929, in Orangeburg, N.Y.; son of John E. (an artist) and Ida (Blessin) Costigan; married Dorothy Knopczyk, September 15, 1956; children: Drew, Christopher. *Education:* R.C.A. Institutes, graduate, 1950; New York University, B.S., 1964. *Religion:* Protestant. *Home:* 8 Wyndmoor Way, Edison, N.J. 08820. *Agent:* Patricia Lewis, 133 West 72nd St., Room 601, New York, N.Y. 10023. *Office:* CSO, Inc., Piscataway, N.J. 08854.

CAREER: Worked as a radio technician, 1948-61; free-lance writer, 1955—; Bell Laboratories, Holmdel, N.J., engineer in micrographic and electronic information systems development, beginning 1961; CSO, Inc., Piscataway, N.J., currently engineer in micrographic and electronic information systems development. Chairman, National Microfilm/Electronic Industries Association Microfilm-Facsimile Standards Committee, 1971-82. *Military service:* U.S. Army, 1951-53.

MEMBER: Institute of Electrical and Electronic Engineers, National Micrographics Association (member of publications committee, 1978-80), Association for Information and Image

Management, Telephone Pioneers of America, Kappa Tau Alpha.

AWARDS, HONORS: Certificate of appreciation, National Microfilm Association, 1972; plaque of appreciation, National Micrographics Committee, 1980.

WRITINGS: FAX: The Principles and Practice of Facsimile Communication, Chilton, 1971; *Micrographic Systems,* National Micrographics Association, 1975, 2nd edition, 1980; *Electronic Delivery of Documents and Graphics,* Van Nostrand, 1978. Contributor to numerous periodicals, including *Radio Electronics, Popular Electronics, Medical Times, Journal of Micrographics, World Car Guide,* and *Road & Track.*

WORK IN PROGRESS: Trials and Triumphs of an American Artist, a book-length biography of John E. Costigan.

SIDELIGHTS: Daniel M. Costigan told *CA:* "As an aspiring writer of both fiction and fact, my principal idol had been the late Nevil Shute, the noted British romantic engineer/novelist. Though I have not exactly followed his formidable example, his achievement has convinced me that the engineer's clinical mentality need not necessarily deter him from a literary career."

AVOCATIONAL INTERESTS: Amateur stereo photography, music, electronics, historic preservation.

*   *   *

COTTER, Richard V(ern)   1930-

PERSONAL: Born June 27, 1930, in Long Prairie, Minn.; son of Vernon M. and Edith Cotter; married Carolyn Van Duyn Clark, June 12, 1976. *Education:* Lewis and Clark College, B.S., 1952; University of Oregon, M.S., 1963, Ph.D. (with honors), 1965. *Home address:* P.O. Box 14042, Reno, Nev. 89507. *Office:* College of Business Administration, University of Nevada, Reno, Nev. 89557.

CAREER: Oregon Journal Publishing Co., Inc., Portland, Ore., newsboy and station manager, 1942-43; Oregonian Publishing Co., Inc., Portland, newsboy, branch captain, clerk, night-and-weekend-office manager, 1944-48, district manager, 1948-53; Fairbanks Publishing Co., Inc., Fairbanks, Alaska, business manager, 1953-58; self-employed newspaper distributor and consultant, Portland, 1958-61; Oregon State System of Higher Education, Portland Continuation Center, Portland, instructor in business administration, 1962; University of Oregon, Eugene, instructor in finance, 1963-64; University of Nevada, Reno, assistant professor, 1965-67, associate professor, 1967-71, professor of managerial science, 1971—, associate dean for graduate studies, 1971-78. Visiting professor at University of Oregon, 1967, University of Newcastle, Newcastle, Australia, 1973, University of Western Australia, 1978 and 1983, and University of Hawaii, 1980. *Military service:* Oregon National Guard, 1953-56.

MEMBER: American Finance Association, Academy of International Business, Association for Business Simulation and Experiential Learning, Financial Management Association, Western Finance Association, Western Economic Association, Phi Kappa Phi, Beta Gamma Sigma.

*WRITINGS—*All published by Prentice-Hall: *The Business Policy Game,* 1973; (co-author) *Commercial Banking,* 1976, third edition, 1984; *Modern Business Decisions,* 1985; *The Business Policy Game,* 1985. Contributor to *AACSB Bulletin, Nevada Business Review, Journal of Financial and Quantitative Analysis,* and *National Banking Review.*

AVOCATIONAL INTERESTS: Amateur musician, church choir.

*   *   *

COULETTE, Henri Anthony   1927-

PERSONAL: Born November 11, 1927, in Los Angeles, Calif.; son of Robert Roger and Genevieve (O'Reilly) Coulette; married Jacqueline Meredith, December 27, 1950. *Education:* Los Angeles State College (now California State University, Los Angeles), B.A., 1952; University of Iowa, M.F.A., 1954, Ph.D., 1959. *Politics:* Democrat. *Home:* 485 Madeline Dr., Pasadena, Calif. 91105. *Office:* California State University, 5151 State College Dr., Los Angeles, Calif. 90032.

CAREER: Former high school teacher of English; University of Iowa, Iowa City, instructor at writer's workshop, 1957-59; California State University, Los Angeles, 1959—, currently professor of English. Has given poetry readings at universities and museums. *Military service:* U.S. Army, 1945-46.

MEMBER: International P.E.N., American Federation of Teachers.

AWARDS, HONORS: Lamont Poetry Award from Academy of American Poets, 1965; James D. Phelan Award for Poetry, 1966; John Simon Guggenheim memorial fellowship, 1976.

WRITINGS: (Contributor) *New Poets of England and America,* Meridian, 1957; (contributor) *Poetry for Pleasure,* Doubleday, 1960; (editor, with P. Engle, and contributor) *Midland: Twenty-five Years of Fiction and Poetry from Writing Workshops of the State University of Iowa,* Random House, 1961; (contributor) *Poet's Choice,* Dial, 1962; (editor) *The Unstrung Lyre: Interviews with Fourteen Poets,* National Endowment for the Arts, 1965; *The War of the Secret Agents and Other Poems,* Scribner, 1966; (editor with Philip Levine) *Character and Crisis: A Contemporary Reader,* McGraw, 1966; *The Family Goldschmitt* (poems), Scribner, 1971. Also author of *The Attic* (poems), 1959. Contributor to *Paris Review, New Yorker,* and *Hudson Review.*

SIDELIGHTS: Henri Anthony Coulette is "a poet to watch," writes Dudley Fitts in the *New York Times Book Review.* Discussing the title poem in Coulette's collection *The War of the Secret Agents and Other Poems,* Fitts claims to be "frustrated throughout [this poem] by opacities of allusion and reference." However, he also praises it: "Isolated passages show power. The poem is skillfully written." And Mother Mary Anthony writes in *Western Humanities Review* that *The War of the Secret Agents and Other Poems* is "work of a high order—disciplined originality and strong patterning, layered irony and powerful understatement."

BIOGRAPHICAL/CRITICAL SOURCES: New York Review of Books, April 14, 1966; *New York Times Book Review,* April 17, 1966; *Poetry,* November, 1966; *Books Abroad,* autumn, 1967; *Western Humanities Review,* winter, 1967.†

*   *   *

COURTHION, Pierre (Barthelemy)   1902-

PERSONAL: Born January 14, 1902, in Geneva, Switzerland; son of Louis (a journalist) and Elisa (Bocquet) Courthion; married Pierrette Karcher, April 26, 1927; children: Sabine (Mrs. Tristan d'Oelsnitz). *Education:* Attended University of Geneva, 1920, Ecole des Beaux Arts, Paris, 1921, and Ecole du Louvre, 1923. *Home:* 11 rue des Marronniers, 75016 Paris, France.

CAREER; L'Eclair, Paris, France, editor, 1923-25; League of Nations, International Institute for Intellectual Cooperation, Geneva, Switzerland, joint chief of arts section, 1928-32; Cite Universitaire de Paris, Paris, director of Swiss foundation, 1933-39; director of literary collections "Le Cri de la France," 1940-45, and "Les Grandes Artistes racontes par euxmemes et leurs amis," 1940-46; Association Internationale des Critiques d'Art, Paris, vice-president, 1945-61, member of administrative council, 1962; Syndicat de la presse artistique de France, Paris, vice-president, 1965-78.

Archaeologist for Valais canton, 1933-37; director of Archaeological Museum of Valere, 1933-37; member of international jury for the Auschwitz monument, 1959, and jury of International Guggenheim Prize, 1960; lecturer at Princeton University, Yale University, New York University, and other American universities; director of missions under direction of French ministries of culture and foreign affairs to Brazil, 1963, Venezuela, 1965, the United States, 1967, Canada, 1969, and Japan and the Republic of Korea, 1973. Producer of films on art and artists, "Ingres peintre du nu," "Ingres portraitiste," and "Georges Rouault."

WRITINGS—In English: (Author of introduction) *Gauguin (1848-1903),* Volume II, Faber, 1949; (editor with Pierre Cailler) *Manet raconti par lui-meme et par ses amis,* two volumes, Cailler, 1953, translation by Michael Ross published as *Portrait of Manet by Himself and His Contemporaries,* Roy, 1960; *Montmartre,* Skira, 1955, translation by Stuart Gilbert published under same title, Skira, 1956; *Paris d'autrefois: De Fouquet a Daumier,* Skira, 1957, translation by James Emmons published as *Paris in the Past: From Fouquet to Daumier,* Skira, 1957; *Paris des temps nouveaux: De l'impressionisme a nos jours,* Skira, 1957, translation by Gilbert published as *Paris in Our Time: From Impressionism to the Present Day,* Skira, 1957; *La Peinture flamande, de Van Eyck a Bruegel,* Somogy, 1958, translation by Jonathan Griffin published as *Flemish Painting,* Thames & Hudson, 1958.

Le Romantisme, Skira, 1961, translation by Gilbert published as *Romanticism,* Skira, 1961; *Georges Rouault,* Flammarion, 1962, translation published under same title, Abrams, 1962; *Edouard Manet,* Abrams, 1962; *Georges Seurat,* Editions Cercle d'art, 1969, translation by Norbert Guterman of original French manuscript published under same title, Abrams, 1968; *Impressionism,* translated by John Shepley from original French manuscript, Abrams, 1972, abridged edition, 1977.

Other works: *La Vie de Delacroix* (title means "The Life of Delacroix"), Gallimard, 1927; *Panorama de la peinture contemporaine* (title means "Panorama of Contemporary Painting"), Kra, 1927; *Nicolas Poussin,* Plon, 1929; *Courbet,* two volumes, Floury & Cailler, 1931; *Claude Lorrain,* Floury, 1932; *Henri Matisse,* Rieder, 1934; *Geneve; ou, Le Portrait des Toepffer,* Grasset, 1936; *Delacroix,* Skira, 1940; *Henri Rousseau: Le Douanier,* Skira, 1944; *Bonnard: Peintre du merveilleux,* Marguerat, 1945; *Gericault,* Cailler, 1947; *Peintres d'aujourd'hui* (title means "Painters of Today"), Cailler, 1952; (with Maurice Herzog and others) *La Montagne* (title means "The Mountain"), Librairie Larousse, 1956; *L'Art independant: Panorama international de 1900 a nos jours* (title means "Independent Art: International Panorama from 1900 to Our Time"), Albin-Michel, 1958.

Leon Zack, G. Fall, 1961; *Autour de l'impressionnisme,* Nouvelles Editions Francaises, 1964; *Paris: De sa naissance a nos jours* (title means "Paris: From Her Birth to Our Time"), Somogy, 1966; *Paris: Histoire d'une ville* (title means "Paris: History of a City"), Somogy, 1966; *Elisabeth Kaufmann,* Kossodo, 1967; *Debre,* G. Fall, 1967; *Utrillo et Montmartre,* Fabbri, 1967; *Charles Rollier,* Editions Ides et Calendes, 1969; (author of introduction) *Felice Filippini,* I.L.T.E., 1971; *Soutine peintre du dechirant,* Denoel, 1973; *Pablo Gargallo,* Vingtieme Siecle, 1973; *Artigas et la ceramique d'aujourd'hui* (title means "Artigas and Ceramics Today"), Poligrafa, 1977; *La Peinture flamande et hollandaise,* Nathan, 1983; *Les Primitifs, Naissance de la peinture europeenne,* Nathan, 1985. Writer and compiler of a text with slides, *L'Ecole de Paris, de Picasso a nos jours.*

WORK IN PROGRESS: Vision d'un demi-siecle (memoirs; title means "Vision of Half a Century"); *Bizarreries.*

SIDELIGHTS: Pierre Courthion's study of painter Georges Rouault is "the latest chapter in a running hagiography that [the author] started with an article printed in Paris in 1927," according to Tom Phillips in the *Times Literary Supplement.* Writing in *Publishers Weekly,* a critic describes *Georges Rouault* as a "full-bodied critical appreciation . . . a treasurable experience."

BIOGRAPHICAL/CRITICAL SOURCES: Publishers Weekly, September 26, 1977; *Times Literary Supplement,* February 17, 1978.

*   *   *

COURTINE, Robert   1910-
(La Reyniere, Savarin)

PERSONAL: Born May 16, 1910, in Paris, France; son of Benjamin (a manufacturer's agent) and Marthe (Julien) Courtine; married Elisabeth Mauron, November 10, 1936. *Education:* Attended public schools in Paris, France. *Home:* 49 rue Raspail, 92270 Bois-Colombes, France.

CAREER: Journalist, writer, and composer. Gourmet columnist for French newspapers and magazines, including *Le Monde,* beginning 1949, *La Vie francaise,* beginning 1960, *Depeche du Midi,* beginning 1961, and *Vogue.*

MEMBER: Societe des gens de lettres, Academie Rabelais, Societe des auteurs, compositeurs et editeurs, Association des critiques de music-hall, Academie Malt Whisky.

AWARDS, HONORS: Prize from International Association of Gourmet Journalists, 1954, for *Le Plus doux des peches;* Prix Rabelais, 1960; Prix Epicure, 1977; Officier du merite agricole, 1978; member of various other orders of knighthood, including Commanderie des cordons bleus, Commanderie du Bontemps, and Jurade de Saint-Emilion.

WRITINGS—In English: (Under pseudonym La Reyniere) *Cent Merveilles de la cuisine francaise,* Seuil, 1971, translation by Derek Coltman published as *The Hundred Glories of French Cooking,* Farrar, Straus, 1973; (compiler under pseudonym La Reyniere) *Mes Repas les plus etonnants,* Laffont, 1973, translation by Jane Guicharnaud published as *Feasts of a Militant Gastronome,* recipes translated by Madelaine Damman, Morrow, 1974; (under pseudonym La Reyniere) *Le Cahier de recettes de Madame Maigret,* preface by Georges Simenon, Laffont, 1974, translation by Mary Manheim published as *Madame*

Maigret's Recipes, illustrations by Nikolaus E. Wolff, Harcourt, 1975; *Guide Courtine: Bon Appetit a Paris,* Lyle Stuart, 1976, translation by Rose L. H. Finkenstaedt published as *Guide Courtine: A Guide to Paris Restaurants,* Lyle Stuart, 1976.

Other works: *Un Gourmand a Paris,* B. Grasset, 1959; *Un Nouveau savoir manger,* Grasset, 1960; (under pseudonym Savarin) *La Vraie Cuisine francaise simple et anecdotique, avec quelques-unes des meilleures recettes etrangeres,* Collection Marabout, 1960, new edition, 1967; *Les Dimanches de la cuisine,* La Table ronde, 1962; (under pseudonym Savarin) *La Cuisine du monde entier,* Gerard, 1963; *Goncourt a table,* Fayard, 1963; *Quatre Cent Cinquante Recettes originales a base de fruits,* Editions de la Pensee moderne, 1963; *Mangez-vous francais?,* SEDIMO (Paris), 1965; (with Henry Clos-Jouve) *Ou manger quoi,* Hachette, 1967; *Toutes les boissons et les recettes au vin,* Larousse, 1968; *L'Assassin est a votre table,* La Table ronde, 1969; *Cinq Mille Recettes, cuisine de France et du monde entier,* Centre national du livre familial, 1969; *La Cuisine des fleurs,* illustrations by Henri Samouilov, D. Halevy, 1969.

(With Jean Desmur) *Anthologie de la litterature gastronomique,* Trevise, 1970; (with Desmur) *Anthologie de la poesie gourmande,* Trevise, 1970; *La Gastronomie,* Presses universitaires de France, 1970; (with Francoise Condat) *Guide de l'homme arrive,* illustrations by Jean-Denis Malcles, La Table ronde, 1970; (with Celine Vence) *La Cuisine au fromage,* Denoel, 1971; *Les Vacances dans votre assiette,* Fayard, 1971; (with Vence) *Les Fruits de mer,* Denoel, 1972; *Dictionnaire des fromages,* Larousse, 1972, new edition published as *Larousse des fromages,* Larousse, 1973; (with Vence) *Les Poissons de mer,* Denoel, 1972; *Poulardes et poulets,* Denoel, 1972; (with Pierre Jean Vaillard) *L'Escargot est dans l'escalier,* La Table ronde, 1972; (with Vence) *La Cuisine au vin,* Denoel, 1972; (compiler with Vence) *Les Grands maitres des la cuisine francaise du Moyen Age a Alexandre Dumas,* Bordas, 1972; (with Vence) *Grillades et barbecue,* Denoel, 1972; (with Vence) *Les Salades,* Denoel, 1972; *Un Cognac, un cigare, une histoire,* illustrations by Alde, Editions de la Pensee moderne, 1973; (editor with Maurice Edmond Suilland) *Cuisine et vins de France,* new edition, Larousse, 1974; *Deux Cent Recettes des meilleurs cuisiniers de France,* Michel, 1976; *Balzac a Table,* Laffont, 1976; *Zola a Table,* Laffont, 1978; (with Vence) *The Grand Masters of French Cuisine: Five Centuries of Great Cooking,* Putnam, 1978.

Le Grand Jeu de la cuisine, Larousse, 1981; *Il etait une fou de recettes,* Flammarion, 1984; *Au cochon bleu,* Le Pre aux clercs, 1984; *La Vie parisienne,* Perrin, 1984; *Larousse gastronomique,* Larousse, 1984.

Also author of introductions to cookbooks and *Le Plus doux des peches,* 1952.

SIDELIGHTS: When Robert Courtine, France's leading gourmet, began his career as a political writer, he discovered he was more interested in describing what the politicians ate than what they had to say, according to Sanche de Gramont in *New York Times Magazine.* He had found his *metier.*

It is Courtine's conviction that "only gourmets can be great novelists," he told de Gramont. "Balzac, Proust, and Simenon prove that the greatest novelists are the greatest eaters, for the mind's roots are in the stomach." He chose the pseudonym La Reyniere in honor of Grimod de la Reyniere, the eighteenth-century French gourmet.

Courtine's style of writing has been called "vitriolic." Reviewing *The Hundred Glories of French Cooking,* Phyllis Hanes wrote: "It is a knowledgeable, opinionated, and thoroughly entertaining book. Although it is organized by menu, I found the reading better than the recipes."

BIOGRAPHICAL/CRITICAL SOURCES: *New York Times Magazine,* July 6, 1967; *Saturday Review,* November 20, 1973; *Christian Science Monitor,* December 27, 1973; *Time,* January 1, 1979.

*   *   *

COX, Jack
See COX, John Roberts

*   *   *

COX, John Roberts 1915-1981
(Jack Cox; David Roberts, a pseudonym)

PERSONAL: Born January 15, 1915, in Worsley, Lancashire, England; died June 27, 1981; son of Frank Clarkson (a local educational official) and Elizabeth (Roberts) Cox; married Kitty Margaret Forward, August 26, 1943; children: David John, Martin Andrew, Lindsay Robert. *Education:* University of Geneva, traveling scholar, 1936; Manchester University, B.A., 1941. *Religion:* Anglican/Methodist. *Home:* 43 Hill View Rd., Llandrhos, Llandudno, Gwynedad LL30 1SL, North Wales.

CAREER: *Manchester Guardian,* Manchester, England, news and feature reporter, 1937-40; Lutterworth Press, London, England, editor of *Boy's Own Paper,* 1946-67, managing editor, Lutterworth Periodicals, Ltd., 1953-63; Purnell Group/B.P.C., London, editor of *Family Pets,* 1964-67, general editor of book department, 1966-68, editor of *Boy's Own Annual,* 1959-76, editor of *Boy's Own Anthology,* beginning 1977; International Publishing Corp., Hamlyn Group, London, managing editor of Practical Books Division, 1968-71; consultant editor and author, 1971-81. Geographer. *Military service:* British Army, 1940-46, served in Royal Engineers; became captain.

MEMBER: National Union of Journalists, British Society of Authors, Association of Radio Writers, London Press Club, Guildsman (London), Sports Writers Club, Manchester University Convocation (treasurer, 1948-58; chairman, 1958-68; vice-president, beginning 1969), Wasps Rugby Football Club (vice-president, 1951), Surrey University Rugby Club (vice-president, 1966).

WRITINGS—Nonfiction, except as indicated: *Camping for All,* Ward, Lock, 1951; *Ideas for Rover Scouts,* Jenkins, 1953, 5th edition, 1959; *Ideas for Scout Troops,* Jenkins, 1954, 8th edition, 1963; *The Outdoor Series,* Lutterworth, 1954, 7th edition, 1975; *Dangerous Waters* (young adult fiction; based on a British Broadcasting Corp. radio serial), Lutterworth, 1955; *Camp and Trek,* foreword by Lord Hunt, Lutterworth, 1956, 3rd new and revised edition, 1971; *Portrait of B-P.: The Life Story of Lord Baden-Powell,* Lutterworth, 1957; *Calamity Camp* (young adult fiction), Lutterworth, 1957; *Majorca Moon* (young adult fiction), Lutterworth, 1960; *The Hike Book,* Lutterworth, 1960, 3rd revised edition, 1968; (under pseudonym David Roberts) *The Mushroom God* (young adult fiction), Parrish, 1961; *Don Davies: "An Old International"* (biography), Hutchinson, 1962; *Camping in Comfort,* Lutterworth, 1963; *The Rugby Union Football Book,* Purnell, Volume I, 1968, Volume II, 1970; *Modern Camping,* Hutchinson, 1968; *The World of Rugby,* two volumes, Purnell, 1970-72; *Lightweight Camping,* Lutterworth, 1971; *Fun and Games Outdoors,* Pan Books, 1971; *Fun and Games Indoors,* Pan Books, 1973; *The Outdoor Cookbook,* Lutterworth, 1976; *Camping Skills,* Wolfe Publishing, 1977; *The Outdoor Handbook,* Hamlyn, 1977; *Take a Cold Tub, Sir!: Story of the Boy's Own Paper,* Lutterworth, 1982.

Editor: *World Rover Moot Handbook,* Munro Press, 1939; *The Boy's Book of Popular Hobbies,* Burke, 1954, revised edition, 1968; *The Boy's Own Book of Hobbies,* Lutterworth, 1957, revised edition published as *The Boy's Book of Hobbies,* 1966, 2nd revised edition, 1968; (and contributor) Frank Showell Styles, *Getting to Know Mountains,* George Newnes, 1958; *The Boy's Own Companion,* Volumes I-V, Lutterworth, 1959-64; *Serve by Conserving: A Study of Conservation,* UNESCO [Paris], amended edition by Arco Publications, 1959; *The Boy's Own Book of Outdoor Hobbies,* Lutterworth, 1960, revised edition, 1968; *They Went to Bush: Forestry in Ghana,* MacGibbon & Kee, 1961; *Fred Buller's Book of Rigs and Tackles,* Purnell, 1967; (and reviser) Stuart Petre Brodie Mais, *An English Course for Everybody,* 5th edition, Frewin Publishers, 1969; *The Motorists Touring Maps & Gazetteer,* Hamlyn, 1970; Douglas Gohn, *Tropical Fish: Aquaria,* Hamlyn, 1970; *Quotations for Speakers & Writers,* Hamlyn, 1970; Gilbert Salteritwaite, *Encyclopedia of Astronomy,* Hamlyn, 1970.

Editor of books by Gilbert Davey; all published by Kaye & Ward, except as indicated: *Fun with Radio,* 1957, 6th edition, 1978; *Fun with Short Wave Radio,* 1960, 3rd edition, 1979; *Fun with Electronics,* 1962, revised edition, 1972; *Fun with Transistors,* 1964, revised edition, 1971; *Fun with Hi-Fi,* 1965, revised edition, 1974; *Scout Camping,* Scout Association, 1973; *Fun with Silicone Chips in Modern Radio,* 1982.

Also author of "Richard Hakluyt" (an Elizabethan play for schools), 1937. Editor, with Enid Blyton, of the "Children's Library of Knowledge" series, published by Odhams Books, 1957-60. Author of radio and television scripts, and documentaries for BBC and I.T.A. programs, including two educational series in geography. Author of weekly columns for children in the *Daily Graphic* (Kemsley), 1946-59, *Sunday Graphic,* 1959-61, *Birmingham Weekly Post,* 1957-58, and *Manchester Evening News,* beginning 1975. Also author of column on adult leisure for *Manchester Evening News,* beginning 1977, and of monthly feature *Outdoors with Jack Cox* (official journal of the Scout Association), beginning 1975. Author of *The Scout's Pathfinder Annual,* Purnell, 1980. Contributor of sport and recreation articles, book reviews, and interviews to the *Sunday Times* (London), 1951-68, *Daily Telegraph,* 1956-72, *The Guardian,* 1960-72, *Smith's Trade News,* and various periodicals.

WORK IN PROGRESS: A series of practical books based on conservation in practice for youth groups of all kinds.

SIDELIGHTS: John Cox once wrote *CA:* "I hope to influence young people especially, to whose welfare and interests I have largely devoted my life, along the lines of worthwhile endeavour in outdoor leisure, recreation and achievement. I try always to encourage youngsters and get them to learn from their own mistakes and the mistakes of others, including myself. Conservation of natural resources is all-important today in all parts of the world and I do my utmost to get young people conservation-minded and really active. Enthusiasm then comes naturally. Achievement follows." To aspiring authors he gives this advice: "Young writers: do not be discouraged by rejects. Keep trying to find your niche; have confidence in your own thing once you have found what it is; build on that and you

will impress others through your skill and enthusiasm. Never be afraid to ask for advice or to learn from others."

AVOCATIONAL INTERESTS: Music of all kinds; playing the piano; conservation, ornithology, gardening and outdoor interests.

[Sketch verified by wife, Kitty M. Cox]

*   *   *

CRABB, Lawrence J(ames), Jr. 1944-

PERSONAL: Born July 13, 1944, in Evanston, Ill.; son of Lawrence J. (in sales) and Isabel (an occupational therapist; maiden name, Craigmile) Crabb; married Rachel Lankford, June 18, 1966; children: Keplen, Kenton. *Education:* Ursinus College, B.A., 1965; University of Illinois, M.A., 1969, Ph.D., 1970. *Religion:* "Conservative Evangelical Protestant." *Office:* Grace Theological Seminary, 200 Seminary Dr., Winona Lake, Ind. 46590.

CAREER: University of Illinois at Urbana-Champaign, assistant professor of psychology and staff psychologist at Psychological Counseling Center, 1970-71; Florida Atlantic University, Boca Raton, director of Psychological Counseling Center, 1971-73; private practice of clinical psychology in Boca Raton, 1973-82; Grace Theological Seminary, Winona Lake, Ind., chairman of department of Biblical counseling, 1982—.

MEMBER: American Psychological Association.

WRITINGS: Basic Principles of Biblical Counseling, Zondervan, 1975; *Effective Biblical Counseling: A Model for Helping Caring Christians Become Capable Counselors,* Zondervan, 1977; (with father, Lawrence J. Crabb, Sr.) *The Adventures of Captain Al Scabbard No. 1,* Moody, 1981; (with L. J. Crabb, Sr.) *The Adventures of Captain Al Scabbard No. 2,* Moody, 1981; *The Marriage Builder: A Blueprint for Couples and Counselors,* Zondervan, 1982; *Encouragement: The Key to Caring,* Zondervan, 1984. Contributor of articles and reviews to religious magazines and psychology journals.

SIDELIGHTS: Lawrence J. Crabb, Jr., writes: "Motivated by a desire to see a clear and thorough Biblical view of counseling developed, I have written and intend to continue writing books which integrate conservative evangelical Christianity with psychological concern and to think through the role of the local church in meeting the needs of the people. I am committed to a theistic world view in which an infinite personal God is the Supreme Being and has revealed Himself in Scripture and in His Son, Jesus Christ. To the best of my awareness, I endeavor to . . . reflect this world view in my writings."

*   *   *

CRAIG, David 1932-

PERSONAL: Born July 10, 1932, in Aberdeen, Scotland; son of John (a doctor) and Margaret (Simpson) Craig; married Gillian Stephenson (a doctor), October 7, 1957 (divorced, 1978); children: Marian, Peter, Donald, Neil. *Education:* University of Aberdeen, B.A. (with first class honors), 1954; Cambridge University, Ph.D., 1958. *Politics:* Communist. *Religion:* None. *Home:* Hill House, Main St., Burton, Carnforth, Lancashire, England. *Office:* University of Lancaster, Bailrigg, Lancaster, England.

CAREER: University of Ceylon, Peradeniya, lecturer in English, 1959-61; Workers' Educational Association, Richmond,

Yorkshire, England, organizing tutor, 1961-64; University of Lancaster, Lancaster, England, senior lecturer in literature and creative writing, 1964—.

WRITINGS: Scottish Literature and the Scottish People: 1680-1830, Chatto & Windus, 1961; (editor) *Moderne Prosa und Lyrik der Britischen Inseln*, Aufbau-Verlag, 1968; (editor) Alan Silitoe, *Saturday Night and Sunday Morning*, Longmans, Green, 1968; (editor) Charles Dickens, *Hard Times*, Penguin, 1969.

(Editor with John Manson) Hugh MacDiarmid, *Selected Poems*, Penguin, 1970; *The Real Foundations*, Chatto & Windus, 1973; (editor) *Marxists on Literature*, Penguin, 1975; (editor with Margot Heinemann) *Experiments in English Teaching*, Edward Arnold, 1976; *Latest News* (poems), Journeyman, 1978; (with Nigel Gray) *The Rebels and the Hostage* (novel), Journeyman, 1978; (with Michael Egan) *Extreme Situations*, Macmillan, 1979; (contributor) *New Writing and Writers*, Calder, 1979; (contributor) *New Stories: An Arts Council Anthology*, Hutchinson, 1980 and 1983; *Homing* (poems), Platform, 1980.

Contributor of poetry to anthologies, including *Young Commonwealth Poets*, edited by P. L. Brent, Heinemann, 1968, and *Doves for the Seventies*, edited by Peter Robins, Corgi, 1969 and 1972. Contributor to *New Statesman, New York Review of Books, Spectator, Times Literary Supplement, Times Higher Education Supplement, New Left Review, Scotsman, New Poetry, Tribune, Mosaic, Marxism Today*, and *Essays in Criticism*. Co-founder and editor, *Fireweed*, 1975-78.

WORK IN PROGRESS: Finnbarr's Wilderness, a novel.

* * *

CRAIG, Robert D(ean)   1934-

PERSONAL: Born April 16, 1934, in Hamilton, Ohio; son of Orville and Leona (Thomas) Craig; married Judith Blackwelder (divorced, 1983); children: Larry, Lisa, Tim, Cathy, David, Jenny. *Education:* University of Cincinnati, B.A., 1962, M.A., 1964; further graduate study at University of Innsbruck, 1964; University of Utah, Ph.D., 1966. *Home:* 14432 Southeast 17th St., Bellevue, Wash. 98007.

CAREER: Atomic Energy Commission, Cincinnati, Ohio, office manager, 1952-58; Texas A&M University, Bryan, assistant professor, 1966-67; Brigham Young University—Hawaii Campus, Laie, professor of history, 1967-81, David O. McKay Lecturer, 1969; affiliated with University of Guam, 1981-83. *Military service:* U.S. Army, 1956-58; became sergeant.

MEMBER: American Historical Association, Mediaeval Academy of America, Cincinnati Historical Association, Phi Alpha Theta.

AWARDS, HONORS: Poetry awards include award from National Canticle Society, 1964, for "My Sunday Walk."

WRITINGS: Revolutionary Soldiers in Hamilton County, Ohio, Ohio Historical Association, 1965; *An Old-French Workbook*, Brigham Young University—Hawaii Campus Press, 1965, 2nd edition, 1978.

The Life of St. Alexis, Gallic Press, 1975; (translator) Edmond de Bovis, *Tahitian Culture Before the Arrival of the Europeans*, Brigham Young University—Hawaii Campus Press, 1976; *Index au Bulletin de la Societe des Etudes Oceaniennes* (title means "Index to Bulletin of the Society of Oceanic Studies"), Brigham Young University—Hawaii Campus Press, 1977; *Captain Cook in the Pacific*, Brigham Young University—

Hawaii Campus Press, 1978; (editor) Robert Thomson, *The Marquesas: Their Description and Early History*, Brigham Young University—Hawaii Campus Press, 1978; *Historical Dictionary of Oceania*, Greenwood Press, 1981.

Also author of *History of Tahiti* and *Polynesian Mythology*. Editor of *Pacific Studies: A Journal Devoted to the Pacific—Its Islands and Adjacent Countries*.

SIDELIGHTS: Robert D. Craig writes: "I have had extensive travel in Europe, researching materials in the British Museum, Bibliotheque Nationale, and others. I am interested in Classical and Medieval studies as well as Polynesian culture and have presented numerous talks before various groups on genealogical research, as a result of the 'Roots' phenomenon. I have contributed poetry to various groups and have won national poetry awards."

* * *

CRENSHAW, James L.   1934-

PERSONAL: Born December 19, 1934, in Sunset, S.C.; son of B. D. (a minister) and Bessie (Aiken) Crenshaw; married Juanita Rhodes, June 10, 1956; children: James Timothy, David Lee. *Education:* North Greenville Junior College, A.A., 1954; Furman University, B.A. (magna cum laude), 1956; Southern Baptist Theological Seminary, B.D., 1960; Hebrew Union College, graduate study, 1963; Vanderbilt University, Ph.D., 1964; additional study at Heidelberg University, 1972-73, and Oxford University, 1978-79. *Home:* 3807 Brighton Rd., Nashville, Tenn. 37205. *Office:* Vanderbilt University Divinity School, Nashville, Tenn. 37240.

CAREER: Clergyman of Baptist Church; Atlantic Christian College, Wilson, N.C., assistant professor of religion, 1964-65; Mercer University, Macon, Ga., associate professor of religion, 1965-69; Vanderbilt University Divinity School, Nashville, Tenn., 1969—, began as associate professor, currently professor of Old Testament. Visiting scholar at Columbia University, summer, 1967; National Endowment for the Humanities lecturer at University of Indiana, summer, 1978; instructor at Iliff School of Theology, summer, 1978.

MEMBER: Colloquium for Biblical Research (former president), Society of Biblical Literature (president of Southern Section, 1968-69), Section of Israelite and Early Christian Wisdom (chairman, 1977—), American Academy of Religion, Catholic Biblical Association, American Association of University Professors.

AWARDS, HONORS: Society for Religion in Higher Education cross-disciplinary fellowship, 1972-73; National Endowment for the Humanities, summer fellowship in Annecy, France, 1974; Association of Theological Schools in the United States and Canada grant, 1978-79; American Council of Learned Societies grant, summer, 1980; Guggenheim fellowship, 1984.

WRITINGS: Prophetic Conflict, De Gruyter, 1971; (editor with John T. Willis) *Essays in Old Testament Ethics*, Ktav, 1974; *Hymnic Affirmation of Divine Justice*, Scholars Press, 1976; *Studies in Ancient Israelite Wisdom*, Ktav, 1976; *Samson: A Secret Betrayed, a Vow Ignored*, John Knox, 1978; *Gerhard von Rad*, Word, Inc., 1978; (editor and contributor) *The Divine Helmsman*, Ktav, 1980; *Old Testament Wisdom: An Introduction*, John Knox, 1981; (editor and contributor) *Theodicy in the Old Testament*, Fortress, 1983; *Proverbs, Ecclesiastes, Song of Songs*, Volumes I and II, Graded Press, 1983; *A Whirlpool of Torment: Israelite Traditions of God as an Oppressive Presence*, Fortress, 1984.

Contributor: J. Hayes, editor, *Old Testament Form Criticism*, Trinity University, 1974; *The Interpreters Dictionary of the Bible*, supplementary volume, Abingdon, 1976; *The New English Bible: Oxford Study Edition*, Oxford University Press, 1976; *Tradition and Theology in the Old Testament*, Fortress, 1977; *Israelite Wisdom: Samuel Terrien Festschrift*, Fortress, 1979; B. Long, editor, *Images of Man and God: The Old Testament Short Story in Literary Focus*, Almond Press, 1981; J. Crossan, editor, *Gnomic Wisdom*, Scholars Press, 1981; D. Knight and G. Tucker, editors, *The Hebrew Bible and Its Modern Interpreters*, Scholars Press, in press; *The Encyclopedia of Religion*, Free Press, in press.

Also co-author of *Semitics* and *The Old Testament and Form Criticism;* contributor to *Structuralism*, edited by S. Wittig and Pickwick, 1976. Contributor of about thirty articles and numerous reviews to journals. Society of Biblical Literature monograph series, associate editor, 1974-78, editor, 1978—; member of editorial board, *Religious Studies Review*, 1974—, and *Perspective in Religious Studies*.

WORK IN PROGRESS: Books on the rhetoric of wisdom and on riddles in the Old Testament; essays on the revolution within wisdom research.

SIDELIGHTS: James L. Crenshaw told *CA:* "A single conviction underlies everything I write: the belief that ancient thinkers struggled to understand the human dilemma in the same way we do, and they therefore blazed a trail for us. The task that I set for myself is to clarify the questions and answers that occupied the thinking of those adventurers. If I have concentrated on the problem of evil, it is because I think this fundamental issue facing modern intellectuals links past and present."

* * *

CRONE, (Hans-) Rainer 1942-

PERSONAL: Born July 6, 1942, in Hamburg, Germany; son of Arnold (a doctor of medicine) and Erica (Schottmueller) Crone. *Education:* Studied at Universities of Hamburg, Berlin, Freiburg, Bonn, and Paris; Free University of Berlin, Ph.D., 1974. *Home:* Loehrsweg 2, Hamburg 20, West Germany. *Office:* Department of Art History, Columbia University, New York, N.Y. 10027.

CAREER: Has held several positions in the field of art including, assistant to director, Werner Haftmann, National galerie, Berlin, Germany, 1968, assistant film director to Rosa Von Praunheim on the movie "Berliner Bettwurst," released in West Germany, 1973; guest curator of the Stedelijk Museum, Amsterdam, for the first continental retrospective of British painter Peter Blake, 1973; curator of the first retrospective show of drawings by Andy Warhol, 1976; University of Washington, Seattle, visiting professor, 1974-75; Yale University, New Haven, Conn., assistant professor of the history of art, 1976-79; American Film Institute, Los Angeles, Calif., director's fellow, 1979-80; Free University of Berlin, West Berlin, lecturer, 1983; Columbia University, New York, N.Y., associate professor of art history, 1984—.

AWARDS, HONORS: Federal Republic of Germany film award, for "The Art of Michael Heizer"; *A Golden Picture Show by the Artist Andy Warhol* was judged as one of the most beautiful books of 1976 in the Federal Republic of Germany.

WRITINGS: Andy Warhol, Hatje Verlag, 1970, translation by John William Gabriel published under same title, Praeger, 1970; *Die revolutionaere Aesthetik Andy Warhols*, Melzer Verlag, 1971; *Numerals 1924-1977*, Yale University Art Gallery, 1978; *Francesco Clemente: Watercolors*, Edition Eischofberger (Zurich), 1982; *Francesco Clemente: "Il viaggitore napoletano,"* Verlag Gerd de Vries (Koln), 1982; *Francesco Clemente: Pastelle 1974-1984*, Prestel Verlag (Munich), 1984.

Author and producer, "The Art of Michael Heizer" (monographical film), shown on German television, 1972; author of "Orange Monument: Christo's Valley Curtain," shown on German television, 1974. Also author of catalogue to the Warhol exhibition, *A Golden Picture Show by the Artist Andy Warhol*, 1976. Contributor of several articles to periodicals.

WORK IN PROGRESS: A book on the meaning of abstract art and its origins; monographs on Francesco Clemente and Enzo Cucchi.

* * *

CRUZ, Victor Hernandez 1949-

PERSONAL: Born February 6, 1949, in Aguas Buenas, P.R.; son of Severo and Rosa Cruz; children: Ajani. *Education:* Attended high school in New York, N.Y.

CAREER: Poet. Guest lecturer at University of California, Berkeley, 1969; San Francisco State University, San Francisco, Calif., instructor, 1973—.

AWARDS, HONORS: Creative Artists public service award, 1974, for *Tropicalization.*

WRITINGS: Snaps (poems), Random House, 1969; (editor with Herbert Kohl) *Stuff: A Collection of Poems, Visions and Imaginative Happenings from Young Writers in Schools—Open and Closed*, Collins & World, 1970; *Mainland* (poems), Random House, 1973; *Tropicalization* (poems and prose), Reed, Cannon, 1976; *By Lingual Wholes*, Momo's, 1982. Also author of *Papo Got His Gun*, 1966. Editor, *Umbra.*

WORK IN PROGRESS: A novel, for Random House.

SIDELIGHTS: Victor Hernandez Cruz writes: "My family life was full of music, guitars and conga drums, maracas and songs. My mother sang songs. Even when it was five below zero in New York she sang warm tropical ballads." He adds: "My work is on the border of a new language, because I create out of a consciousness steeped in two of the important world languages, Spanish and English. A piece written totally in English could have a Spanish spirit. Another strong concern in my work is the difference between a tropical village, such as Aguas Buenas, Puerto Rico, where I was born, and an immensity such as New York City, where I was raised. I compare smells and sounds, I explore the differences, I write from the center of a culture which is not on its native soil, a culture in flight, living half the time on memories, becoming something totally new and unique, while at the same time it helps to shape and inform the new environment. I write about the city with an agonizing memory of a lush tropical silence. This contrast between landscape and languages creates an intensity in my work."

Nancy Sullivan writes in *Poetry* magazine: "Cruz allows the staccato crackle of English half-learned, so characteristic of his people, to enrich the poems through its touching dictional inadequacy. If poetry is arching toward the condition of silence as John Cage and Susan Sontag suggest, perhaps this mode of inarticulateness is a bend on that curve. . . . I think that Cruz is writing necessary poems in a period when many poems seem unnecessary."

BIOGRAPHICAL/CRITICAL SOURCES: *Christian Science Monitor,* August 7, 1969; *Poetry,* May, 1970; *New Republc,* November 21, 1970; *Bilingual Review,* September-December, 1974.†

*　　*　　*

CUMMINGS, Betty Sue 1918-

PERSONAL: Born July 12, 1918, in Big Stone Gap, Va.; daughter of Howard Lee and Hattie (Bruce) Cummings. *Education:* Longwood College, B.S., 1939; University of Washington, Seattle, M.A., 1949. *Residence:* Titusville, Fla. *Agent:* Virginia Kidd, 538 East Harford St., Milford, Pa. 18337.

CAREER: Teacher of English at public schools in Norton, Va., 1939-41, Richmond, Va., 1941-42, Buckingham, Va., 1945-46, Thermopolis, Wyo., 1950-57; Brevard County Schools, Titusville, Fla., teacher of English, 1957-73. Writer, 1973—. *Military service:* U.S. Coast Guard, SPARS, 1942-45; became ensign.

MEMBER: National League of American Pen Women, Writers-in-Company.

AWARDS, HONORS: Award from Rollins College Writers' Conference, 1973, for short story "Three Days"; plaque from Writers-in-Company, 1977; National Book Award nominee, for *Hew Against the Grain;* listed on *Horn Book's* "Fanfare Page," for *Let a River Be.*

WRITINGS—Published by Atheneum, except as indicated: *Hew Against the Grain,* 1977; *Let a River Be,* 1978; *Now, Ameriky,* 1979; *Turtle,* 1981; *Say These Names (Remember Them),* Pineapple Press, in press.

SIDELIGHTS: Betty Sue Cummings told *CA:* "In my lifetime I have known many brave women, young and old, and I have a strong need to *record* their courage, both historically and contemporarily speaking. My first book concerned a brave young woman in Civil War days, my second a brave old woman fighting river pollution today, my third a young Irish woman who comes alone to America to earn passage for her family, my fourth an old woman who seeks her lost turtle, my fifth a Miccosukee woman who struggles to save the children in the second Seminole War and to save the memory of their dead villages.

"Nowadays I am concerned with old women and their plight in today's culture. I write about this, knowing that this subject is not necessarily commercially adequate for today's readers. My approach to writing: go from a vision to research to writing. The research must be in such depth that suddenly the story begins to write itself."

*　　*　　*

CUMMINS, D. Duane 1935-

PERSONAL: Born June 4, 1935, in Dawson, Neb.; son of Delmer H. (a businessman) and Ina Z. (Arnold) Cummins; married Darla Sue Beard, October 6, 1957; children: Stephen, Cristi, Caroline. *Education:* Philips University, B.A., 1957; University of Denver, M.A., 1965; University of Oklahoma, Ph.D., 1974. *Politics:* Democrat. *Religion:* Christian. *Home:* 12760 Shady Creek Lane, St. Louis, Mo. 63141. *Office:* Division of Higher Education, Christian Church (Disciples of Christ), 119 North Jefferson, St. Louis, Mo. 63103.

CAREER: History teacher at high school in Denver, Colo., 1957-67, chairman of department, 1959-67; Oklahoma City University, Oklahoma City, Okla., assistant professor, 1967-71, associate professor of history, 1972-74, Darbeth-Whitten Professor of American History, 1974-78, chairman of department, 1969-72, director of Robert A. Taft Institute of Politics and Government, 1970-78, director of Division of Continuing Education, 1971-72, curator of George H. Shirk Oklahoma History Collection, 1977; Christian Church (Disciples of Christ), Division of Higher Education, St. Louis, Mo., president, 1978—. *Military service:* U.S. Army, Infantry, 1955-57.

MEMBER: American Historical Association, Organization of American Historians, Western History Association, Oklahoma Association of History Professors (vice-president, 1970).

WRITINGS: *William Robinson Leigh, Western Artist,* University of Oklahoma Press, 1980; *A Handbook for Today's Disciples in the Christian Church (Disciples of Christ),* Bethany Press, 1981; (editor with Daryl Hohweiler) Joseph Richardson Ward, Jr., *An Enlisted Soldier's View of the Civil War: The Wartime Papers of Joseph Richardson Ward, Jr.,* Belle Publications, 1981. Editor of series of history transparencies published by Keuffel & Esser Corp.

"Inquiries into American History" series; published by Benziger, except as indicated: (With William G. White) *The American Revolution,* 1968, revised edition, Glencoe, 1980; (with White) *The American Frontier,* 1968, revised edition, Glencoe, 1980; (editor) *The Federal Period,* 1971; (with White) *Origins of the Civil War,* 1971, revised edition, Glencoe, 1979; (editor) *Our Colonial Heritage,* 1972; (editor) *Industrialism: The American Experience,* 1972; (editor) *American Foreign Policy,* 1972; (with White) *Contrasting Decades,* 1972, revised edition published as *Contrasting Decades: The 1920's and 1930's,* Glencoe, 1980; *Consensus and Turmoil,* 1972; *Consensus and Conflict,* 1978; (with White) *Combat and Consensus: The 1940's and 1950's,* Glencoe, 1980.

AVOCATIONAL INTERESTS: Photography, travel, literature, poetry.

*　　*　　*

CUPITT, Don 1934-

PERSONAL: Surname is pronounced *Kew*-pit; born May 22, 1934, in Lancashire, England; son of Robert and Norah (Gregson) Cupitt; married Susan Marianne Day (a teacher), December 28, 1963; children: John Robert Gregson, Caroline Mary, Sarah Anne. *Education:* Trinity Hall, Cambridge, B.A., 1955, M.A., 1958; also attended Westcott House, Cambridge, 1957-59. *Religion:* Church of England. *Home:* 62 Humberstone Rd., Cambridge CB4 1JF, England. *Office:* Emmanuel College, Cambridge University, Cambridge CB2 3AP, England.

CAREER: Cambridge University, Cambridge, England, fellow, dean, and director of studies in theology and philosophy, 1966—, university assistant lecturer, 1968-73, lecturer in the philosophy of religion, 1973—. Television writer and presenter for British Broadcasting Corp., "Who Was Jesus," 1976, and "The Sea of Faith" series, 1984.

WRITINGS: *Christ and the Hiddenness of God,* Westminster, 1971, 2nd edition, S.C.M. Press, 1985; *Crises of Moral Authority,* Westminster, 1972, 2nd edition, S.C.M. Press, 1985; (contributor) S. W. Sykes and J. P. Clayton, editors, *Christ, Faith and History,* Cambridge University Press, 1972; *The Leap of Reason,* Westminster, 1976, 2nd edition, S.C.M. Press,

1985; *The Worlds of Science and Religion*, Seabury, 1976; (contributor) John Hick, editor, *The Myth of God Incarnate*, Westminster, 1977; (with Peter Armstrong) *Who Was Jesus?*, British Broadcasting Corp., 1977; *The Nature of Man*, Seabury, 1979; *Jesus and the Gospel of God*, Lutterworth, 1979; *The Debate about Christ*, S.C.M. Press, 1979; (editor) *Explorations in Theology 6*, S.C.M. Press, 1979; (contributor) Michael Goulder, editor, *Incarnation and Myth*, S.C.M. Press, 1979.

Taking Leave of God, Crossroad Publishing, 1980; *The World to Come*, S.C.M. Press, 1982; (contributor) Brian Hebblethwaite and Stewart Sutherland, *The Philosophical Frontiers of Christian Theology*, Cambridge University Press, 1982; *The Sea of Faith*, British Broadcasting Corp., 1984; *Only Human*, S.C.M. Press, 1985. Contributor to theology journals, including *Anglican Theological Review*, *Theology*, and *Journal of Theological Studies*.

WORK IN PROGRESS: Research on philosophical thoelogy.

BIOGRAPHICAL/CRITICAL SOURCES: Times Literary Supplement, December 5, 1980, May 28, 1982.

*   *   *

CURL, James Stevens   1937-
(Adytum, E. B. Keeling, Parsifal)

PERSONAL: Born March 26, 1937, in Belfast, Northern Ireland; son of George Stevens (a businessman) and Sarah (McKinney) Curl; married Eileen Elizabeth Blackstock (a psychiatrist), January 1, 1960; children: Astrid, Ingrid. *Education:* Attended Campbell College, Belfast, 1946-54, and Queens University and Belfast College of Art, 1954-58; Oxford School of Architecture, Dipl. Arch., 1964, Dip. T.P., 1967; University College, London, Ph.D., 1981. *Home:* 5 Clifton Ter., Winchester, Hampshire S022 5BJ, England.

CAREER: Architect and planner, Oxford, England, 1963-69; Oxford School of Architecture, Oxford, tutor in history of architecture, 1967-73; architect to the Scottish contribution to European Architectural Heritage Year, 1973-75; Hertfordshire County Council, Planning Department, Hertfordshire County, England, principal architect-planner, 1975-78; senior lecturer in history of architecture and course leader in architectural conservation, Leicester School of Architecture, 1978—.

MEMBER: Royal Town Planning Institute, Royal Institute of British Architects, Society of Antiquaries of London (fellow), Society of Antiquaries of Scotland (fellow), Royal Incorporation of Architects in Scotland, Oxford Civic Society (chairman, 1969-72), Leicestershire Club.

AWARDS, HONORS: Sir Charles Lanyon Prize for measured drawings; traveling scholarship to Germany, 1962; British Academy research award, 1982 and 1983; Society of Antiquaries of London research award.

WRITINGS: European Cities and Society, Leonard Hill, 1970; *The Victorian Celebration of Death: Architecture and Planning of the 19th Century Necropolis*, David & Charles, 1972; *The Egyptian Revival: An Introductory Study of a Recurring Theme in the History of Taste*, Allen & Unwin, 1972; (contributor) *Encyclopedia of Town Planning*, McGraw, 1973; *City of London Pubs*, David & Charles, 1973; *Victorian Architecture*, David & Charles, 1973; *The Erosion of Oxford*, Oxford Illustrated Press, 1977; *English Architecture: An Illustrated Glossary*, David & Charles, 1977; *A Celebration of Death*, Scrib-

ner, 1980; *The Life and Work of Henry Roberts (1803-76), Architect*, Phillimore, 1983.

Contributor of articles, some under pseudonyms Adytum, E. B. Keeling, and Parsifal, to periodicals, including *Country Life*, *Connaissance des Arts*, *Progressive Architecture*, *Official Architecture and Planning*, *Guardian*, and *Spectator*. Architectural specialist contributor, *Survey of London*, 1970-73.

WORK IN PROGRESS: The Londonderry Plantation, 1609-1914: The History, Architecture, and Planning of the Estates of the City of London and Its Livery Companies in Ulster.

SIDELIGHTS: James Stevens Curl told *CA:* "As an historian I try to ferret out aspects of fact that have not been aired or have been misunderstood. For example, my work on *The Egyptian Revival* was subtitled *An Introductory Study of a Recurring Theme in the History of Taste*, for I became fascinated about how much design motifs derived from Ancient Egyptian art and architecture permeated our civilisation. Nobody had covered this ground before in such a thorough way. Similarly, the architecture of death is something that most commentators have left alone, but I found a whole field was there just for the taking, and I wrote *A Celebration of Death* . . . because nobody had taken the landscapes of cemeteries or the design of monuments and mausolea seriously as real architecture. . . . I have recently made a television programme about death and its monuments, and I have been lecturing on the subject ever since.

"I think there is no point in writing yet another book about someone who has been flogged to death by other writers. I chose Henry Roberts as the subject of my first biography because he is of great importance in the history of housing reform. I was amazed by parrot-like comments of other writers over the years which referred to Henry Roberts as 'obscure' or 'otherwise unknown.' In fact there is a great deal known about him, and I found out a lot more which I incorporated in the book. Roberts was born in Philadelphia, for example, and everyone assumed he was a Londoner because he worked with Lord Shaftesbury and the Prince Consort.

"My current work deals with the estates of the City of London in Ulster, and again I chose the subject because nobody else has done it and because the records from 1609 to 1914 are beautifully preserved in the halls of the London Livery Companies, including marvellous seventeenth-century drawings. It is a fascinating story, and one that sheds a lot of light on the current problems of Northern Ireland, a place that suffers more than anywhere else from ill-informed commentary and wilful ignorance, notably in England and America. I am interested in facts rather than mythology, and I regard facts as my legitimate quarry from which I can fashion my studies. . . . I care deeply about truth above all else, and I regard it as my duty to tell the truth in my writings."

AVOCATIONAL INTERESTS: Travel, opera, music, photography, food, humor.

*   *   *

CURRAN, Charles E.   1934-

PERSONAL: Born March 30, 1934, in Rochester, N.Y. *Education:* St. Bernard's Seminary and College, Rochester, N.Y., B.A.; Gregorian University, Rome, Italy, S.T.B., 1957, S.T.L., 1959, S.T.D., 1961; Academia Alfonsiana, Rome, Italy, S.T.D., 1961. *Office:* Department of Theology, Catholic University of America, Washington, D.C. 20017.

CAREER: Ordained Roman Catholic priest, 1958. St. Bernard's Seminary, Rochester, N.Y., professor of moral theology, 1961-65; Catholic University of America, Washington, D.C., assistant professor, 1965-67, associate professor, 1967-71, professor of moral theology, 1971—. Senior research scholar, Kennedy Center for Bioethics, Georgetown University, 1972.

MEMBER: American Society of Christian Ethics (president, 1971-72), American Theological Society, Catholic Theological Society of America (vice-president, 1968-69; president, 1969-70), College Theology Society.

WRITINGS: Christian Morality Today: The Renewal of Moral Theology, Fides, 1966; *A New Look at Christian Morality,* Fides, 1968; (editor) *Absolutes in Moral Theology?,* Corpus Books, 1968; (with others) *The Responsibility of Dissent: The Church and Academic Freedom,* Sheed, 1969; (editor) *Contraception: Authority and Dissent,* Herder & Herder, 1969; (with Robert E. Hunt and others) *Dissent in and for the Church,* Sheed, 1970; *Contemporary Problems in Moral Theology,* Fides, 1970; (editor with George J. Dyer) *Shared Responsibility in the Local Church,* Catholic Theological Society of America, 1970; *Catholic Moral Theology in Dialogue,* Fides, 1972; *The Crisis in Priestly Ministry,* Fides, 1972; *Politics, Medicine and Christian Ethics: A Dialogue with Paul Ramsey,* Fortress, 1973; *New Perspectives in Moral Theology,* Fides, 1974.

Ongoing Revision: Studies in Moral Theology, Fides, 1975; *Themes in Fundamental Moral Theology,* University of Notre Dame Press, 1977; *Issues in Sexual and Medical Ethics,* University of Notre Dame Press, 1978; *Transaction and Tradition in Moral Theology,* University of Notre Dame Press, 1979; (editor with Richard A. McCormick) *Moral Norms and Catholic Tradition,* Paulist/Newman, 1979; (editor with McCormick) *The Distinctiveness of Christian Ethics,* Paulist/Newman, 1980; *Moral Theology: A Continuing Journey,* University of Notre Dame Press, 1982; *American Catholic Social Ethics: Twentieth-Century Approaches,* University of Notre Dame Press, 1982; (editor with McCormick) *The Use of Scripture in Moral Theology,* Paulist/Newman, 1984; *Critical Concerns in Moral Theology,* University of Notre Dame Press, 1984.

Contributor: S. H. Miller and G. E. Wright, editors, *Ecumenical Dialogue at Harvard,* Harvard University Press, 1964; James E. Biechler, editor, *Law for Liberty,* Helicon, 1967; Harvey Cox, editor, *The Situation Ethics Debate,* Westminster, 1968; William Jerry Boney and Lawrence E. Molumby, editors, *The New Day,* John Knox, 1968; Gene H. Outka and Paul Ramsey, editors, *Norm and Context in Christian Ethics,* Scribner, 1968. Contributor to *Jurist, Commonweal, Homiletic,* and other journals.

WORK IN PROGRESS: Articles and monographs on medical ethics, Roman Catholic social ethics in the United States, and questions of fundamental moral theology.

SIDELIGHTS: In April 1967, Charles E. Curran became a *cause celebre* for priestly academic freedom when he was fired by Catholic University of America, supposedly (although the university gave no reasons for the dismissal) for his liberal views on birth control. The popular teacher chose to fight the ouster, and the Catholic University faculty voted 400 to 18 not to hold classes until he was reinstated. The boycott closed the university for three days before Curran was rehired with the announcement that he would be promoted from assistant to associate professor the following semester.

In the summer of 1968, Curran was, he told *CA,* "the organizer and chief spokesman of a group of American Catholic theologians, ultimately totalling about 600, who dissented from the papal encyclical *Humanae Vitae,*" which reaffirmed the church's traditional stand against artificial birth control. "The day after the encyclical was issued in Rome, I spoke for 89 Roman Catholic theologians . . . indicating that one could be a loyal Roman Catholic and still disagree with this particular teaching. This dissent was widely carried in the newspaper and television accounts of those days. . . . These events are recorded in . . . *Dissent in and for the Church.*"

BIOGRAPHICAL/CRITICAL SOURCES: National Observer, April 24, 1967, May 1, 1967; *Christian Century,* August 27, 1969.

*   *   *

CURTIN, Patricia (W.) Romero   1935-
   (Patricia W. Romero)

PERSONAL: Born July 28, 1935, in Columbus, Ohio; daughter of Warren Arthur Watkins (a farmer); married Philip D. Curtin; children: Stephen, Arthur, Jeffrey. *Education:* Central State College (now University), B.A., 1964; Miami University, Oxford, Ohio, M.A., 1965; Ohio State University, Ph.D., 1971. *Politics:* Democrat. *Religion:* Episcopalian. *Home:* 3831 Fenchurch Rd., Baltimore, Md. 21218.

CAREER: Central State University, Wilberforce, Ohio, instructor in history, 1964-65; Association for the Study of Negro Life and History, Washington, D.C., research associate, 1965-68; United Publishing Corp., Washington, D.C., editor-in-chief, 1968-70; Association for the Study of Negro Life and History, research associate, 1970-72; Outdoor Books, Nature Series, Inc., Baltimore, Md., president, 1982—. Visiting lecturer, Findlay College, 1969, and University of South Florida, Tampa, 1972-74.

MEMBER: American Historical Association, Organization of American Historians, African Studies Association, Association for the Study of Negro Life and History, Southern Historical Association, Phi Alpha Theta.

AWARDS, HONORS: Negro history research grant, Southern Historical Association, 1965-66; Ford Foundation grant, 1969.

WRITINGS—Children's books, published by Outdoor Books: *Michael Shows Off Baltimore,* 1982; *Tippet Shows Off Washington,* 1983.

Under name Patricia W. Romero: (With Charles H. Wesley) *Negro Americans in the Civil War,* Publishers, 1967; (editor) *I, Too, Am America,* Publishers, 1968, revised edition, 1970; (editor) *In Black America,* United Publishing, 1969; *In Pursuit of African Culture,* United Publishing, 1972. Associate editor, *Negro History Bulletin,* 1966-68; research editor, *Negro Life and History,* ten volumes, International Library.

WORK IN PROGRESS: E. Sylvia Pankhurst: Portrait of a Radical, for Weidenfeld & Nicolson; *Cultural History of Lamy from 1873-1960.*

*   *   *

CURTIS, Richard Hale
   See LEVINSON, Leonard

*   *   *

CUTTER, Tom
   See WALLMANN, Jeffrey M(iner)

CZERNIAWSKI, Adam 1934-

PERSONAL: Born December 20, 1934, in Warsaw, Poland; son of Emil Jerzy (a military officer and civil servant) and Maria (Tynicka) Czerniawski; married Ann Christine Daker (head teacher at a high school), July 27, 1957; children: Irena Christine, Stefan Mark Emil. *Education:* University of London, B.A., 1955, B.A., 1967; University of Sussex, M.A., 1968; Oxford University, B.Phil., 1970. *Home:* 6 Tylney Ave., London SE19 1LN, England.

CAREER: U.S. Information Agency, Munich, Germany, broadcaster, 1955-57; Northern Assurance Co., London, England, assistant superintendent, 1957-65; Medway College of Design, Rochester, England, lecturer in philosophy and literature, 1970-74; Thames Polytechnic, London, lecturer in philosophy, 1974-77, senior lecturer and acting head of philosophy division, 1977-78, senior course tutor, 1980-81.

MEMBER: Royal Institute of Philosophy, Polish Society of Arts and Sciences Abroad, Trinity College Oxford Society, United Oxford and Cambridge University Club.

AWARDS, HONORS: Second prize for young writers, Union of Polish Writers Abroad (London), 1954; Abraham Woursell Foundation grant, University of Vienna, 1965, 1970; poetry prize, Union of Writers Abroad, 1967; poetry award, Koscielski Foundation, 1971; Sulkowski prize for literary criticism, Poet's & Painter's Press, 1971; L'ordre du ''Merite Culturel,'' Polish government, 1975; Translators' Award, Arts Council of Great Britain, 1976; Polish Writers' Union Translators' Prize (Warsaw), 1977.

WRITINGS: Polowanie na jednorozca (poetry; title means ''Hunting the Unicorn''), Poets' & Painters' Press (London), 1956; *Topografia wnetrza* (poetry; title means ''Topography of the Interior''), Institut Litteraire (Paris), 1962; *Czesci mniejszej calosci* (short stories; title means ''Parts of a Smaller Whole''), Poets' & Painters' Press, 1964; (editor) *Ryby na piasku* (poetry; title means ''Fish on the Strand''), Swiderski (London), 1965; *Sen cytadela gaj* (poetry; title means ''A Dream, a Citadel, a Grove''), Institut Litteraire, 1966; *Liryka i druk* (literary criticism; title means ''Poetry and Print''), Poets' & Painters' Press, 1972; *Widok Delft* (poetry; title means ''A View of Delft''), Wydawnictwo Literackie (Krakow, Poland), 1973; *Akt* (short stories), Poets' & Painters' Press, 1975; *Wiersz Wspolczsny* (literary essays; title means ''The Contemporary Poem''), Poets' & Painters' Press, 1977; *Wiek zloty 1969-1981* (poetry; title means ''Golden Age'') Institut Litteraire, 1982; *Wladza najwyzsza* (poetry; title means ''Supreme Authority''), Wydawnictwo Literackie, 1982.

Translator: Tadeusz Rozewicz, *Faces of Anxiety*, Rapp & Whiting (London), 1969; Rozewicz, *The Card-Index and Other Plays*, Calder & Boyars (London), 1969; Rozewicz, *The Witnesses and Other Plays*, Calder & Boyars, 1970; W. Tatarkiewicz, *History of Aesthetics*, Mouton, 1970; Rozewicz, *Selected Poems*, Penguin, 1976; Artur Sandauer, *Bialoszewski*, Authors' Agency, 1979; Leon Stroinski, *Window*, Oasis Books, 1979; Rozewicz, *Conversation with the Prince and Other Poems*, Anvil Press, 1982; Leopold Staff, *An Empty Room*, Bloodaxe Books, 1983; Rozewicz, *Mariage Blanc and the Hunger Artist Departs*, Marion Boyars, 1983; Jerzy Szaniawski, *Professor Tutka Stories*, BBC Publications, 1983; Rozewicz, *The Trap*, City University of New York, 1984.

Contributing translator: E. Ordon, editor, *Ten Contemporary Polish Stories*, Wayne State University Press, 1958; P. Mayewski, editor, *Antologia wspolczesnej poezji brytyjskiej i amerykanskiej* (title means ''Anthology of Contemporary British and American Poetry''), Criterion, 1958, 2nd edition, 1965; June Oppen Degan and others, editors, *San Francisco Review Annual*, New Directions, 1963; A. Gillon and L. Krzyzanowski, editors, *Introduction to Modern Polish Literature*, Twayne, 1964; *Polish Writing Today*, Penguin, 1967; Krzeczkowski, Sito, and Zulawski, editors, *Poeci jezkyka angielskiego* (title means ''Poets of the English Language''), [Warsaw], Volume I, 1969, Volume III, 1974; A. N. Bold, editor, *The Penguin Book of Socialist Verse*, Penguin, 1970; J. Harrell and A. Wierzbianska, editors, *Aesthetics in Twentieth-Century Poland*, Bucknell University Press, 1973; Jon Silkin, editor, *Poetry of the Committed Individual*, Penguin, 1973; Jan Krok-Paszkowski, editor, *Portrait of Poland*, Thames & Hudson, 1982; George Theiner, editor, *They Shoot Writers, Don't They?*, Faber, 1984.

Contributor to anthologies, including *Opisanie z pamieci*, edited by Andrzej Lam, PIW (Warsaw), 1965; *Anthologie de la poesie polonaise*, edited by Constantin Jelenski, Editions du Seuil (Paris), 1965; *Neue polnische Lyrik*, edited by Karl Dedecius, Moderner Buch-Club (Darmstadt), 1965; *Explorations in Freedom*, edited by L. Tyrmand, Free Press, 1970; *Kolumbowie i wspolczesni*, edited by A. Lam, Czytelnik (Warsaw), 1972, 2nd revised edition, 1976; *Modern Poetry in Translation*, Volume XXIII-XXIV, edited by B. Czaykowski, [London], 1975; *Modern Slavic Literatures*, Volume II, edited by Czaykowski and others, [New York], 1976; *Een Gevecht om Lucht*, edited by Jan-Willem Overeem and Ewa Dijk-Borkowska, Corrie Zelen, 1979; *Introduction to Modern Polish Literature*, edited by Gillon and others, Hippocrene, 1982; *Modern Poetry in Translation: 1983*, edited by D. Weissport, [London], 1983; *Glosow zbieranie*, edited by A. Mierzejewski and others, Pax, 1983.

WORK IN PROGRESS: Editing *The Burning Forest: An Anthology of Polish Poetry*, for Bloodaxe Books; translating and writing introduction for Roman Ingarden's *The Work of Music and the Problem of Its Identity*.

BIOGRAPHICAL/CRITICAL SOURCES: Kultura (Paris), July, 1957; *Kontynenty* (London), April-June, 1962; T. Terlecki, editor, *Literatura polska na obczyznie 1940-1960*, [London], 1964; J. Brzekowski, *Wyobraznia wyzwolona*, [London], 1966; C. Milosz, *The History of Polish Literature*, Macmillan, 1969; T. E. Bird, editor, *Queens Slavic Papers*, [New York], Volume I, 1973; Karl Dedecius, *Uberall ist Polen*, Suhrkamp Verlag, 1974; *Tygodnik Kulturalny* [Warsaw], September 21, 1975; L. M. Bartelski, editor, *Polscy pisarze wspolczesni*, [Warsaw], 1977.

D

DACEY, Philip 1939-

PERSONAL: Born May 9, 1939, in St. Louis, Mo.; son of Joseph and Teresa (McGinn) Dacey; married Florence Chard, May 25, 1963; children: Emmett Joseph, Fay Pauline Teresa, Austin Warren. *Education:* St. Louis University, B.A., 1961; Stanford University, M.A., 1967; Iowa University, M.F.A., 1970. *Address:* Box 346, Cottonwood, Minn. 56229. *Office:* Southwest State University, Marshall, Minn. 56258.

CAREER: Peace Corps Volunteer in Eastern Nigeria, 1963-65; University of Missouri—St. Louis, instructor, 1967-68; Southwest State University, Marshall, Minn., 1970—, began as associate professor, currently professor of literature.

AWARDS, HONORS: Yankee Poetry Prize for "Storm," 1968; Poet and Critic Prize for "For the Poet's Father, On His Taking Up Gardening Late in Life," 1969; Borestone Mountain Poetry Award, 1974; Discovery Award, 1974; National Endowment for the Arts fellowship, 1975, 1980; Minnesota State Arts Council fellowship, 1975, 1983; first prize, G. M. Hopkins Memorial Sonnet Competition, 1977; first prize in poetry, *Prairie Schooner,* 1977; Bush fellowship, 1977; Pushcart Prize, 1977, 1982; Loft McKnight fellowship, 1984.

WRITINGS: The Beast with Two Backs (a small pamphlet collection of poetry), Gunrunner Press, 1969; (editor with Gerald Knoll) *I Love You All Day: It Is That Simple* (an anthology of modern poetry), Abbey Press, 1970; *Fish, Sweet Giraffe, The Lion, Snake, and Owl* (a small pamphlet collection of poetry), Back Door Press, 1970; *Four Nudes* (a small pamphlet collection of poetry), Morgan Press, 1971.

How I Escaped from the Labyrinth and Other Poems, Carnegie-Mellon University Press, 1977; *The Condom Poems,* Ox Head Press, 1979; *The Boy under the Bed,* Johns Hopkins University Press, 1981; *Gerard Manley Hopkins Meets Walt Whitman in Heaven and Other Poems,* Penmaen Press, 1982; *Fives,* Spoon River Poetry Press, 1984; (editor with David Jauss) *Strong Measures: Contemporary American Poetry in Traditional Forms,* Harper & Row, 1985.

Poems in many anthologies, including: *American Poetry Anthology,* edited by D. Halpern, Avon, 1975; *Heartland II: Poets of the Midwest,* edited by L. Stryk, Northern Illinois University Press, 1975; *Ardis Anthology of New American Poetry,* edited by D. Rigsbee, Ardis, 1977; *A Geography of Poets,* edited by Field, Bantam, 1979; *Walt Whitman,* edited by Perlman, Holy Cow, 1981; *Leaving the Bough,* edited by Gaess, International Publishers Co., 1982; *Poetspeak,* edited by Janeczko, Bradbury, 1983.

Contributor of poetry to *Esquire, New York Quarterly, Poetry Northwest, Nation, Paris Review, American Review, Partisan Review, Hudson Review, Shenandoah,* and other periodicals; editor, *Crazy Horse,* 1971-76.

WORK IN PROGRESS: The Movie: A Book of Poems.

BIOGRAPHICAL/CRITICAL SOURCES: Shenandoah, winter, 1971; *Minnesota Daily,* August 8, 1977; *Great River Review,* fall, 1977; *Tar River Poetry,* spring, 1979; *Parnassus: Poetry in Review,* fall/winter, 1981; *Poet Lore,* winter, 1981-82.

*   *   *

DALTON, Clive
See CLARK, F(rederick) Stephen

*   *   *

DALY, Edith Iglauer
(Edith Iglauer)

PERSONAL: Born in Cleveland, Ohio; daughter of Jay and Bertha (Good) Iglauer; married Philip Paul Hamburger, December 24, 1942 (divorced, 1966); married John Heywood Daly (a commercial salmon troller), March 1, 1976 (died February 18, 1978); children: (first marriage) Jay Philip, Richard Shaw. *Education:* Attended Zimmern School, Geneva, Switzerland, 1937; Wellesley College, B.A., 1938; Columbia University, M.S., 1939. *Politics:* Democrat. *Religion:* None. *Home address:* P.O. Box 116, Garden Bay, British Columbia, Canada V0N 1S0. *Office: New Yorker,* 25 West 43rd St., New York, N.Y. 10036.

CAREER: Princeton University, Princeton, N.J., writer and editor for local government survey, 1939-40; *McCall's,* New York, N.Y., writer for national defense section, 1940-41; Office of War Information, Washington, D.C., writer and editor in radio newsroom in charge of religious and Scandinavian desks, and White House press conference representative for Eleanor Roosevelt, 1941-44; *Cleveland News,* Cleveland, Ohio, war correspondent in Mediterranean theater, 1945; free-lance writer, 1945—.

MEMBER: Authors Guild, Authors League of America, American Civil Liberties Union, Writers Union of Canada, Federation of British Columbia Writers, Cosmopolitan Club.

AWARDS, HONORS: Cleveland Arts Prize, 1983, for creative achievement in literature.

WRITINGS—All under name Edith Iglauer: *The New People: The Eskimo's Journey into Our Time,* Doubleday, 1966, updated edition published as *Inuit Journey,* University of Washington Press, 1979; *Denison's Ice Road,* Dutton, 1975; *Seven Stones: A Portrait of Arthur Erickson, Architect,* University of Washington Press, 1981. Contributor of numerous articles to major magazines and newspapers, including *Saturday Night, New Yorker, Harper's, Atlantic,* and *Maclean's.*

WORK IN PROGRESS: "I am now completely involved in writing about my experience of fishing with my late husband, John Daly, who was a commercial fisherman."

SIDELIGHTS: Edith Iglauer Daly told *CA:* "My first two books were both about the Canadian North, where I went in 1961 to report on the development of the first Eskimo cooperatives for the *New Yorker* magazine. I was lucky enough to be present at the second meeting of the first cooperative, which was in a community hall which the Eskimos had built in a lonely spot near the mouth of Ungava Bay. The Eskimos then lived in tents in the surrounding area which is now a thriving community called Port Nouveau-Quebec. In adding an introduction and epilogue to the 1979 edition, renamed *Inuit Journey,* I made an assessment of the cooperative experiment after twenty years, and told what had happened to the people in my book."

She continues: "I was led by my curiosity about the western Arctic to Yellowknife, in the Northwest Territories. There I met John Denison who was building ice roads to mines in uninhabited areas. After I had been in Yellowknife for some weeks, I did a *New Yorker* story on the opening of the ice road between Yellowknife, on Great Slave Lake, and Port Radium, on Great Bear Lake. I drove the 325 miles in trucks with the crew that annually builds this ice highway. My story was later greatly expanded to become my second book.

"Since then I have written a number of pieces about Canada, including a profile of former Prime Minister Trudeau. I have also written two pieces on air pollution, one of which resulted in a law requiring the New York power companies to change to a relatively sulfur-free oil in the fuel they use."

Daly concludes, "My latest magazine article, for the Canadian publication *Saturday Night,* was about the great Haida Indian artist, Bill Reid, and his work."

*   *   *

DAMOR, Hakji
    See LESSER, R(oger) H(arold)

*   *   *

DANA, Rose
    See ROSS, W(illiam) E(dward) D(aniel)

*   *   *

DANIEL, Julie Goldsmith   1949-
    (Julie Goldsmith Gilbert)

PERSONAL: Born July 21, 1949, in New York, N.Y.; daughter of Henry (a publisher) and Janet (an actress; maiden name, Fox) Goldsmith; married John L. Weisman (employed by a magazine), July 7, 1973 (divorced); married Francis Daniel (a recording engineer). *Education:* Attended Boston University, 1965-67. *Politics:* Democrat. *Religion:* Jewish. *Home:* 201 West 89th St., New York, N.Y. 10024. *Agent:* Robbins & Covey Associates, 2 Dag Hammarskjold Plaza, Suite 403, 866 Second Ave., New York, N.Y. 10017.

CAREER: Professional actress (on stage and in film, commercials, soap opera and dinner theater), 1967-72; writer, 1972—.

MEMBER: Writers Guild of America, Actors Equity, Screen Actors Guild, American Federation of Television and Radio Artists.

AWARDS, HONORS: Fellow of Bread Loaf Writers Conference, 1972; *Ferber: A Biography* was nominated for a National Book Critics Circle Award.

WRITINGS—All under name Julie Goldsmith Gilbert: *Umbrella Steps,* Random House, 1972; *Ferber: A Biography,* Doubleday, 1978; "Honey I'm Home" (play), first produced in New York City at Theater Off Park, November, 1984. Also author of "Abracadabra" (three-act play), first produced as a staged reading, 1973; author of the screenplay version of *Umbrella Steps.*

WORK IN PROGRESS: A novel, *Building* (tentative title); a play, "Spring Killing."

SIDELIGHTS: Of Julie Goldsmith Daniel's *Ferber: A Biography,* Katherine Evans writes in the *Washington Post Book World* that, as the first biography of Edna Ferber ever written, the book "brings good news and bad. The good news first: it is juicy with stories about Ferber and her circle—Robert Sherwood, Alfred Lunt, Mike Todd, Richard Rodgers, Leland Hayward, Moss Hart, and other bright lights of Hollywood and Broadway." According to Howard Teichmann in *New York Times Book Review,* Ferber sold 25 of her works to Hollywood. Her novel *Show Boat* provided the basis for the Oscar Hammerstein II and Jerome Kern musical, and she collaborated with George S. Kaufman on eight plays. Other Ferber novels include *Giant, Cimarron,* and *So Big,* which won the Pulitzer Prize in 1924. Her work was marketable and timely, often characterized by a staunch feminism and social consciousness.

In writing Ferber's biography, Daniels, who is Ferber's great-niece, was able to draw from the writer's notebooks and diaries, and family anecdotes, as well as two autobiographical works by Ferber; notes Teichmann: "With the aid of these documents [Daniels] is able to draw her portrait in the round, reveal her subject not only as a hugely successful American author . . . but also as a petty person who could and often did crack down hard on relatives, friends, waiters and taxi drivers." "The book is written with flair," concludes Teichmann. However, reports Evans, "the bad news is that reading this book can scramble your brain, because [Daniels] has told Ferber's story backwards. Yes, *backwards.* Edna Ferber's life reels dizzily in reverse chronological order: from death back to old age back to maturity, to youth, to birth. . . . Even so, some of the fascination and force of Ferber shines through."

BIOGRAPHICAL/CRITICAL SOURCES: New York Times Book Review, May 7, 1972, March 5, 1978; *Washington Post Book World,* February 12, 1978; *Saturday Review,* February 18, 1978; *Ferber: A Biography,* Doubleday, 1978.

DANIEL, Pete 1938-

PERSONAL: Born November 24, 1938, in Rocky Mount, N.C.; son of Peter Edward and Stella (Hunt) Daniel; married Bonnie Sullivan, June 11, 1961 (divorced, 1972); children: Elizabeth Anne, Laura Elaine. *Education:* Wake Forest College (now University), B.A., 1961, M.A., 1962; University of Maryland, Ph.D., 1970. *Home:* 521A Second St. N.E., Washington, D.C. 20002. *Office:* 5035 National Museum of American History, Smithsonian Institution, Washington, D.C. 20560.

CAREER: University of North Carolina at Wilmington, instructor in history, 1963-66; University of Maryland, College Park, assistant editor of Booker T. Washington papers, 1969-70; University of Tennessee, Knoxville, assistant professor, 1971-73, associate professor, 1973-77, professor of history, 1978; U.S. Senate, Washington, D.C., legislative aide, 1979-80; Smithsonian Institution, National Museum of American History, Washington, D.C., curator, 1982—. Visiting professor, University of Massachusetts, 1974-75.

MEMBER: American Historical Association, Organization of American Historians, Southern Historical Association.

AWARDS, HONORS: Louis Pelzer Prize, Organization of American Historians, 1970, for "Up from Slavery and Down to Peonage: The Alonzo Bailey Case"; National Endowment for the Humanities fellowship, 1970-71, 1978-79, stipend, 1974; American Philosophical Society grant, 1975; Woodrow Wilson International Center for Scholars fellowship, 1981-82.

WRITINGS: The Shadow of Slavery: Peonage in the South, 1901-1969, University of Illinois Press, 1972; (assistant editor with others) Louis R. Harlan, senior editor, *The Booker T. Washington Papers,* Volume II, University of Illinois Press, 1972; (with Raymond Smock) *A Talent for Detail: The Photographs of Miss Frances Benjamin Johnston, 1889-1910,* Harmony, 1974.

Deep'n As It Come: The 1927 Mississippi Flood, Oxford University Press, 1977; (contributor) James C. Cobb and Michael Namorato, editors, *The New Deal and the South,* University Press of Mississippi, 1984; *Breaking the Land: The Transformation of Cotton, Tobacco, and Rice Cultures since 1880,* University of Illinois Press, 1984. Member of board of editorial advisors, Booker T. Washington papers. Contributor of articles to history journals.

AVOCATIONAL INTERESTS: Photography.

*   *   *

DANIELOU, Alain 1907-

PERSONAL: Born October 4, 1907, in Neuilly-sur-Seine, France; son of Charles (a writer and politician) and Madeleine (an educator and founder of religious order; maiden name, Clamorgan) Danielou. *Education:* Educated in France, India, and the United States. *Religion:* Hindu. *Home:* Colle Labirinto, Zagarolo, 00039 Rome, Italy.

CAREER: Hindu University, Benares, India, research professor of Sanskrit literature on music, 1949-54; International Institute for Comparative Music Studies, Venice, Italy, and Berlin, Germany, director, 1962-79. *Member:* French Institute of Indology, Ecole Francaise d'Extreme-Orient. *Awards, honors:* Chevalier Legion d'honneur, 1967; Chevalier Arts et Lettres, 1970; Officier Merite National, 1975.

WRITINGS: Le Betail des dieux (also see below; title means "The Cattle of the Gods"), Buchet-Chastel, 1962; *Hindu Polytheism,* Princeton University Press, 1964; (translator) Ilango Adigal, *Shilappadikaram: The Ankle Bracelet,* New Directions, 1965; *Inde du nord: Collection "Les Traditions Musicales"* (title means "Musical Traditions of Northern India"), Buchet-Chastel, 1966; *Semantique musicale* (title means "Musical Semantics"), Hermann, 1967; *The Ragas of Northern Indian Music,* Barrie & Rockliff, 1968.

Histoire de l'Inde (title means "History of India"), Fayard, 1971, revised edition, 1983; *Situation de la musique et des musiciens dans les pays d'orient,* Olschki, 1971, translation by the author published as *Music and Musicians in the Countries of the Orient,* Olschi, 1971; *Yoga: Methode de reintegration,* L'Arche, 1973, revised edition, 1982, translation by the author published as *Yoga: The Method of Reintegration,* University Books, 1973.

La Sculpture erotique hindoue (title means "Erotic Hindu Sculpture"), Buchet-Chastel, 1975; *Les Fous de dieu: Contes gangetiques* (also see below; title means "God's Madmen"), Buchet-Chastel, 1976, revised edition, 1984; *Les Quatre Sens de la vie: La Structure sociale de l'Inde traditionnelle* (title means "The Four Aims of Life: Social Structures of Traditional India"), Buchet-Chastel, 1976, revised edition, 1984; (translator) *Theatre de Harsha* (title means "The Plays of Harsha"), Buchet-Chastel, 1977; *Le Temple hindou* (title means "The Hindu Temple"), Buchet-Chastel, 1977; *Shiva et Dionysos: Mythes et rites d'une religion pre-aryenne,* Fayard, 1979.

Le Chemin du Labyrinthe (autobiography), Laffont, 1982; *Le Betail des dieux et autres contes gangetiques* (contains *Le Betail des dieux* and *Les Fous de dieu: Contes gangetiques*), Buchet-Chastel, 1983. Also author of *La Musique dans la societe et la vie de l'Inde,* and translator of *Le Shiva Svarodaya-Ancien traite de presages et premonitions d'apres le Souffle Vital.* Editor of UNESCO collection of Oriental and traditional music recordings.

WORK IN PROGRESS: Le Destin de l'homme, secret texts of Shivaism.

SIDELIGHTS: Alain Danielou told *CA* that his "main interest is explaining Hindu traditional civilization, religion and culture to the outside world." He continued: "Hinduism especially in its oldest, Shivaite form, never destroyed its past. It is the sum of human experience from the earliest times. Non-dogmatic, it allows every one to find his own way. Ultimate reality being beyond man's understanding, the most contradictory theories or beliefs may be equally inadequate approaches to reality. Ecological (as we would say today), it sees man as part of a whole where trees, animals, men and spirits should live in harmony and mutual respect, and it asks everyone to cooperate and not endanger the artwork of the creator. It therefore opposes the destruction of nature, of species, the bastardisation of races, the tendency of each one to do what he was not born for. It leaves every one free to find his own way of realization human and spiritual be it ascetic or erotic or both. It does not separate intellect and body, mind and matter, but sees the Universe as a living continuum. It refuses the absurdity of seeing in man a unique being entitled to enjoy and destroy the world for his own benefit as do most of the modern creeds that lead mankind towards its doom.

"I believe any sensible man is unknowingly a Hindu and that the only hope for man lies in the abolition of the erratic, dogmatic, unphilosophical creeds people today call religions."

Danielou speaks English, Hindi, and Italian.

AVOCATIONAL INTERESTS: Painting, playing Western and Indian music.

BIOGRAPHICAL/CRITICAL SOURCES: Alain Danielou, *Le Chemin du Labyrinthe,* Laffont, 1982; *Le Figaro,* January 6, 1984.

* * *

DARROW, Whitney (Jr.) 1909-

PERSONAL: Born August 22, 1909, in Princeton, N.J.; son of Whitney (a publisher) and May Temperance (Barton) Darrow; married Betty Waldo Parish, 1938 (divorced); married Mildred Lois Adkins, October 23, 1942; children: (second marriage) Whitney Barton, Linda Ann. *Education:* Princeton University, A.B., 1931; also attended Art Students League of New York City. *Politics:* Independent. *Home and office:* 331 Newtown Turnpike, Wilton, Conn. 06897.

CAREER: Cartoonist, book illustrator, and advertising artist, 1931—. Work also represented in private art collections.

MEMBER: Dutch Treat Club (New York).

WRITINGS: You're Sitting on My Eyelashes (cartoons), Random House, 1943; *Please Pass the Hostess* (cartoons), Random House, 1949; *Hold It, Florence* (cartoons), Dell, 1953; *Stop, Miss!* (cartoons), Random House, 1957; *Give Up? A New Cartoon Collection,* Simon & Schuster, 1966.

Illustrator: Julian Leonard Street, *Need of Change,* Dodd, 1934; George Jean Nathan, *Beware of Parents: A Bachelor's Book for Children,* Farrar, Straus, 1943; Corey Ford, *Office Party,* Doubleday, 1951; Whitney Darrow, Sr., *Princeton University Press: An Informal Account of Its Growing Pains, Casually Put Together at the Point of a Gun for the Intimate Friends of the Press,* Princeton University Press, 1951; B. M. Atkinson, *What Dr. Spock Didn't Tell Us,* Simon & Schuster, 1959.

Jean Kerr, *The Snake Has All the Lines,* Doubleday, 1960; Art Linkletter, *Kids Sure Rite Funny,* Geis, 1962; Louise Armstrong, *A Child's Guide to Freud,* Simon & Schuster, 1963; Irene Kampen, *Europe without George,* Norton, 1965; Johnny Carson, *Happiness Is . . . a Dry Martini,* Doubleday, 1965; Carson, *Misery Is . . . a Blind Date,* Doubleday, 1967; Robert Kraus, *Whitney Darrow, Jr.'s Unidentified Flying Elephant,* Windmill Books, 1968; Kraus, *Whitney Darrow, Jr.'s Animal Etiquette,* Windmill Books, 1969; Samuel Levenson, *Sex and the Single Child,* Simon & Schuster, 1969, also published as *A Time for Innocence: A Kid's-eye View of the Facts of Life,* 1969.

Kerr, *Penny Candy,* Doubleday, 1970; Enzo Lunari, *Pierino Viaggia in LSD* (title means "Little Peter's Travels on LSD), Ferro (Milan), 1970; Marie Winn, *Shiver, Gobble, and Snore,* Simon & Schuster, 1971; Winn, *The Thief-Catcher,* Simon & Schuster, 1972; Nancy Stahl, *Jelly Side Down,* Fawcett, 1972; Winn, editor, *The Fireside Book of Fun and Game Songs,* Simon & Schuster, 1974; Joanna Cole, *Fun on Wheels,* Scholastic Book Services, 1975; Holly and John Peterson, *Terry's Treasure Hunt,* Scholastic Book Services, 1976; Frances W. Zweifel, *Bony,* Harper, 1977; Peter Schwed, *Hanging in There,* Houghton, 1977; Rose Wyler and Eva-Lee Baird, *Nutty Number Riddles,* Doubleday, 1977; Shirley Gordon, *Grandma Zoo,* Harper, 1978; Joan Kahn, *Hi, Jock, Run around the Block,* Harper, 1978; Nathaniel Benchley, *Walter, the Homing Pigeon,* Harper. Regular contributor of cartoons to *New Yorker,* 1933—; contributor of cartoons to periodicals, including *Judge, Collier's, Ballyhoo, Saturday Review of Literature, College Humor,* and *Saturday Evening Post.* Former art editor, *Princeton Tiger.*

AVOCATIONAL INTERESTS: Golf, bowling, swimming.

BIOGRAPHICAL/CRITICAL SOURCES: Time, October 11, 1943; *Saturday Review of Literature,* January 1, 1944; *New York Herald Tribune Book Review,* December 4, 1949; *Library Journal,* January 1, 1950; *American Artist,* February, 1950; *Art in America,* winter, 1956-57.

* * *

DaSILVA, Leon
See WALLMANN, Jeffrey M(iner)

* * *

DAVIAU, Donald G(eorge) 1927-

PERSONAL: Born September 30, 1927, in West Medway, Mass.; son of George (a spinner) and Jennie (Burbank) Daviau; married Patricia Edith Mara (a teacher), August 20, 1950; children: Katherine Ann, Robert Laurence, Thomas George, Julie Marie. *Education:* Clark University, B.A., 1950; University of California, Berkeley, M.A., 1952, Ph.D., 1955; also attended University of Vienna, 1953-54. *Politics:* Independent. *Religion:* Congregationalist. *Home:* 184 Nisbet Way, Riverside, Calif. 92507. *Office:* Department of Literatures and Languages, University of California, Riverside, Calif. 92521.

CAREER: University of California, Riverside, instructor, 1955-56, assistant professor, 1957-63, associate professor, 1964-70, professor of German, 1971—, head of department of German and Russian, 1969-75. *Military service:* U.S. Naval Reserve, active duty, 1945-46.

MEMBER: International Arthur Schnitzler Research Association (president, 1978—), Modern Language Association of America, American Association of Teachers of German, American Council for the Study of Austrian Literature (president, 1981—), Western Association of German Studies, Austrian P.E.N.

AWARDS, HONORS: Fulbright scholarship for study in Vienna, 1953-54; Ehrenkreuz fuer Wissenschaft und Kunst from Government of Austria, 1977.

WRITINGS: (Editor with Jorun B. Johns) *The Correspondence of Arthur Schnitzler and Raoul Auernheimer: With Raoul Auernheimer's Aphorisms,* University of North Carolina Press, 1972; (translator) Reinhard Urbach, *Arthur Schnitzler,* Ungar, 1973; (with George J. Buelow) *The "Ariadne auf Naxos" of Hugo von Hofmannsthal and Richard Strauss,* University of North Carolina Press, 1975; (editor) *The Letters of Arthur Schnitzler to Hermann Bahr,* University of North Carolina Press, 1978.

(Editor with Ludwig Fischer) *Das Exilerlebnis,* Camden House, 1982; (editor with Johns and Jeffrey B. Berlin) *The Correspondence of Stefan Zweig with Raoul Auernheimer and Richard Beer-Hofmann,* Camden House, 1983; *Hermann Bahr: Der Mann von Uebermorgen,* Oesterreichischer Bundesverlag, 1984; (editor) *Stefan Zweig/Paul Zech: Briefwechsel 1908-1942,* Greifenverlag, 1984; *Herman Bahr,* Twayne, 1985; (editor with Fischer) *Exilliteratur—Wirkung und Wertung,* Camden House, 1985. Contributor to professional journals. Editor of *Modern Austrian Literature,* 1971—.

WORK IN PROGRESS: Editing *Der Briefwechsel zwischen Stefan Zweig und Felix Braun,* with Johns; editing a collection of essays on major living Austrian authors tentatively entitled *Major Figures of Contemporary Austrian Literature;* a critical biography of the German writer Paul Zech; translating Zech's *Deutschland, dein Taenzer ist der Tod.*

* * *

DAVID, Lester 1914-

PERSONAL: Born October 26, 1914, in New York, N.Y.; son of William and Regina (Roth) David; married Irene Neer (a teacher and former journalist), November 30, 1947; children: Margery Ellen (Mrs. Baran S. Rosen), Susan Helen (Mrs. Robert Lewin). *Education:* New York University, B.S., 1934; Columbia University, M.A., 1935. *Office:* 946 Carol Ave., Woodmere, N.Y. 11598.

CAREER: Brooklyn Eagle, Brooklyn, N.Y., editor and reporter, 1936-49; professional writer, 1949—. *Military service:* U.S. Army, 1942-46; managing editor, *Stars and Stripes,* Paris edition, 1944-45.

MEMBER: Society of Magazine Writers (former vice-president).

AWARDS, HONORS: Journalism awards from American Dental Association, 1963, American Medical Association, 1964, Family Service Association, 1966, and Arthritis Foundation, 1969.

WRITINGS: Slimming for Teenagers, Pocket Books, 1966; *Ted Kennedy: Triumphs and Tragedies,* Grosset, 1971; *Ethel: The Story of Mrs. Robert F. Kennedy,* World Publishing, 1971; *Joan: The Reluctant Kennedy,* Funk, 1974; (with Jhan Robbins) *Jackie and Ari: The Inside Story,* Pocket Books, 1976; (with Robbins) *Richard and Elizabeth,* Crowell, 1977; *The Lonely Lady of San Clemente: The Story of Pat Nixon,* Crowell, 1978; (with Charlotte Sanford) *Second Sight: A Miraculous Story of Vision Regained,* M. Evans, 1979.

(With wife, Irene David) *Ike and Mamie: The Story of the General and His Lady,* Putnam, 1981; (with I. David) *The Shirley Temple Story,* Putnam, 1983. Contributor of nearly a thousand articles to national magazines, including *Reader's Digest, Good Housekeeping, Today's Health,* and *This Week.*

BIOGRAPHICAL/CRITICAL SOURCES: Washington Post, July 2, 1971, August 31, 1978; *Detroit Free Press,* September 19, 1978; *New York Times Book Review,* November 12, 1978.

* * *

DAVIDSON, Jessica 1915-

PERSONAL: Born October 3, 1915, in New York, N.Y.; daughter of Israel and Carrie (Dreyfuss) Davidson. *Education:* University of Wisconsin, A.B., 1936; Columbia University, LL.B. (since converted to J.D.), 1939; Danbury State College (now Western Connecticut State University), M.S., 1963. *Politics:* Independent. *Home:* No. 154, R.F.D. 3, Route 39, New Fairfield, Conn. 06812.

CAREER: U.S. Department of Labor, opinions attorney in Washington, D.C., and regional offices, 1943-53; Middle School, Newtown, Conn., sixth-grade teacher, 1957-72, eighth-grade teacher of mathematics, 1972-77.

WRITINGS: (With William G. Martin) *Mind in a Maze,* Prentice-Hall, 1969, published as *Mind-Boggling Brain Benders,* Pren-

tice-Hall, 1974; *Using the Cuisenaire Rods* (photo-text for teachers), Cuisenaire Co., 1969.

What I Tell You Three Times Is True (introduction to semantics for young teenagers), McCall Books, 1970; *The Square Root of Tuesday* (introduction to logic for young teenagers), McCall Books, 1971; *Is That Mother in the Bottle?* (introduction to linguistics for young teenagers), F. Watts, 1972; *2, 4, 6, 8, Let's Start to Calculate,* Cuisenaire Co., 1976; *How to Improve Your Spelling and Vocabulary,* F. Watts, 1980; *How to Improve Your Grammar,* F. Watts, 1980. Work has been anthologized in "Language of Man" series, McDougal, Littell.

WORK IN PROGRESS: A book of mystery stories to be solved by mathematics, tentatively entitled *X Marks the Spot;* revising articles for *The New Book of Knowledge;* preparing test materials for reading competency tests used by the New York school system.

SIDELIGHTS: Jessica Davidson commented to *CA:* "The public is often aroused about the education of children, and the clamor seesaws betwen demands for 'open' education and 'relevant' subject matter on the one hand to 'back to basics!' on the other. I have found myself outside this battleground, believing strongly that the most important lesson—logical thinking for humanitarian ends—cannot really be taught in the classroom, though, now and then, it may be learned there. The best education is that which is freely sought, so my hope is to reach, through my books, young people interested in educating themselves."

AVOCATIONAL INTERESTS: Photography, water sports, gardening, carpentry, reading, making up crossword puzzles for the *New York Times.*

* * *

DAVIS, Dorothy Salisbury 1916-

PERSONAL: Born April 26, 1916, in Chicago, Ill.; daughter of Alfred Joseph (a farmer) and Margaret Jane (Greer) Salisbury; married Harry Davis (an actor), April 25, 1946. *Education:* Barat College, A.B., 1938. *Politics:* Democrat. *Home:* Snedens Landing, Palisades, N.Y. 10964. *Agent:* McIntosh & Otis, Inc., 475 Fifth Ave., New York, N.Y. 10017.

CAREER: Writer. Swift & Co., Chicago, Ill., research librarian and editor of *The Merchandiser,* 1940-46. Member of board of directors, Palisades Free Library, 1967-71.

MEMBER: Author's League of America, Mystery Writers of America (president, 1955-56; executive vice president, 1977-78; member of board of directors).

AWARDS, HONORS: Five nominations for "best mystery novel of the year"; two nominations for "best mystery short story."

WRITINGS—Mysteries, except as indicated; all published by Scribner: *The Judas Cat,* 1949; *The Clay Hand,* 1950; *A Gentle Murderer,* 1951; *A Town of Masks,* 1952; *Men of No Property* (novel), 1956; *Death of an Old Sinner,* 1957; *A Gentleman Called,* 1958; *Old Sinners Never Die,* 1959; *The Evening of the Good Samaritan* (mainstream novel), 1961; *Black Sheep, White Lamb,* 1963; *The Pale Betrayer,* 1965; *Enemy and Brother* (mainstream novel), 1966; (with Jerome Ross) *God Speed the Night,* 1968; *Where the Dark Streets Go,* 1969; *Shock Wave,* 1972; *The Little Brothers,* 1973; *A Death in the Life,* 1976; *Scarlet Night,* 1980; *Lullaby of Murder,* 1984.

Editor: *A Choice of Murders*, Scribner, 1958; *Crime without Murder*, Scribner, 1970; *Tales for a Stormy Night: Collected Crime Stories*, Countryman Press, 1984.

SIDELIGHTS: Dorothy Salisbury Davis told *CA:* "I believe the mystery [form] in which I have worked largely, to be a medium highly reflective of its time, morals, social attitudes." In an interview with *Publishers Weekly*, she stated: "I'm not ashamed of being a mystery writer, although I would like to have succeeded as a mainstream novelist. Any art is contrived; the degree of artistry lies in how you conceal that contrivance. You are guaranteed to have to write in a bizarre fashion for mysteries. Something violent has to happen, something that is not expected, something that is showy. Being bizarre means color, too, and I like that."

MEDIA ADAPTATIONS: Film rights to *God Speed the Night* were sold to Herb Alpert in 1968. In 1970, Otto Preminger and Frank Sinatra, as co-producers, announced the filming of *Where the Dark Streets Go*.

BIOGRAPHICAL/CRITICAL SOURCES: *Times Literary Supplement*, February 23, 1967, August 14, 1970; *Spectator*, November 3, 1967; *Back Stage*, September 15, 1968, November 9, 1968; *Variety*, June 11, 1969, July 1, 1970; *Show Business*, July 5, 1969, July 11, 1970; *National Observer*, January 5, 1970, July 15, 1972; *Newsday*, December 12, 1970; *New York Times*, July 22, 1972; *Saturday Review*, September 9, 1972; *Publishers Weekly*, June 13, 1980.

*   *   *

DAVIS, Gordon
See LEVINSON, Leonard

*   *   *

DEACON, Richard
See McCORMICK, (George) Donald (King)

*   *   *

DEAN, Anabel 1915-

PERSONAL: Born May 24, 1915, in Deming, N.M.; daughter of Orlee Eugene and May (Wheeler) Stephenson; married William O. Hummel, March 10, 1933; married second husband, Edward M. Dean (an accountant), September 3, 1949; children: (first marriage) David; (second marriage) Stephen Mason, Denise. *Education:* Humboldt State Teachers College (now Humboldt State University), B.A., 1959; further study at California State University, Chico and University of California. *Home:* 2993 Sacramento Dr., Redding, Calif. 96001.

CAREER: Enterprise Elementary Schools, Redding, Calif., teacher, 1960—.

MEMBER: National Education Association, California Teachers Association, Enterprise Elementary Teachers Association.

AWARDS, HONORS: *Submerge! The Story of Divers and Their Crafts* (1976) and *Up! Up! and Away! The Story of Ballooning* (1980) were chosen outstanding science books by the National Association of Science Teachers.

WRITINGS—Juvenile: *About Paper*, Melmont, 1968; *Willie Can Not Squirm*, Denison, 1971; *Willie Can Ride*, Denison, 1971; *Willie Can Fly*, Denison, 1971; *Men under the Sea*, Harvey House, 1972; *The Pink Paint*, Denison, 1972; *Bats, the Night Flyers*, Lerner, 1974; *Animals That Fly*, Messner,

1975; *Strange Partners: The Story of Symbiosis*, Lerner, 1976; *Submerge! The Story of Divers and Their Crafts*, Westminster, 1976; *How Animals Communicate*, Messner, 1977; *Plants That Eat Insects: A Look at Carnivorous Plants*, Lerner, 1977; *Fire! How Do They Fight It?* (Junior Literary Guild selection), Westminster, 1978; *How Animals Defend Themselves*, Messner, 1978; *Up! Up! and Away! The Story of Ballooning*, Westminster, 1980; *Wind Sports*, Westminster, 1982; *Going Underground: All About Caves and Caving*, Dillon Press, 1984.

Published by Benefic: *Exploring and Understanding Oceanography*, 1970; *Exploring and Understanding Heat*, 1970; *Hot Rod*, 1972; *Destruction Derby*, 1972; *Drag Race*, 1972; *Road Race*, 1972; *Stock Race*, 1972; *Indy 500*, 1972; *Junior Rodeo*, 1975; *High Jumper*, 1975; *Harness Race*, 1975; *Steeple Chase*, 1975; *Ride the Winner*, 1975; *Saddle Up*, 1975; *Motorcycle Scramble*, 1976; *Motorcycle Racer*, 1976; *Baja 500*, 1976; *Safari Rally*, 1976; *Grand Prix Races*, 1976; *Le Mans Race*, 1976; "Emergency Squad" series, six books, 1978.

AVOCATIONAL INTERESTS: Sports, travel.

*   *   *

DEBUS, Allen G(eorge) 1926-

PERSONAL: Born August 16, 1926, in Chicago, Ill.; son of George Walter William (a manufacturer) and Edna Pauline (Schwenneke) Debus; married Brunilda Lopez-Rodriguez, August 25, 1951; children: Allen Anthony George, Richard William, Karl Edward. *Education:* Northwestern University, B.S., 1947; Indiana University, A.M., 1949, additional study, 1950-51; University College, London, graduate study, 1959-60; Harvard University, Ph.D., 1961. *Residence:* Deerfield, Ill. *Office:* Social Sciences 209, University of Chicago, 1126 East 59th St., Chicago, Ill. 60637.

CAREER: Abbott Laboratories, North Chicago, Ill., research and development chemist, 1951-56; University of Chicago, Chicago, Ill., assistant professor, 1961-65, associate professor, 1965-68, professor of history of science, 1968-78, Morris Fishbein Professor of the History of Science and Medicine, 1978—, director of Morris Fishbein Center for the Study of the History of Science and Medicine, 1971-77. Visiting distinguished professor, Arizona Center for Medieval and Renaissance Studies, 1984. Member of Institute for Advanced Study, Princeton, 1972-73. Member of international advisory, Institute for the History of Science and Ideas, Tel-Aviv University, and Center for the History of Science and Philosophy, Hebrew University of Jerusalem. Holder of chemical patents.

MEMBER: Internationale Paracelsus Gesellschaft, Academie Internationale d'Histoire de la Medicine, Academie Internationale d'Histoire des Sciences (corresponding member), Societe Internationale d'Histoire de la Medicine, History of Science Society (member of council, 1962-65; program chairman, 1972), American Institute of the History of Pharmacy, American Chemical Society (associate; member of executive committee, History of Chemistry Division, 1969-72), American Association for the Advancement of Science (fellow; chairman of electorate nominating committee, Section L, 1974), American Assoiation for the History of Medicine, British Society for the History of Science, Society for the Study of Alchemy and Early Chemistry (member of council, 1967—), Midwest Junto for the History of Science (president, 1983-84), Society of Medical History of Chicago (member of council, 1969-77; secretary-treasurer, 1971-72; vice-president, 1972-74; president, 1974-76).

AWARDS, HONORS: Social Science Research Council and Fulbright fellow in England, 1959-60; Guggenheim fellow, 1966-67; overseas fellow, Churchill College, Cambridge University, 1966-67, 1969; National Endowment for the Humanities fellow at Newberry Library, 1975-76; fellow, Institute for Research in the Humanities, University of Wisconsin—Madison, 1981-82. Research grants from American Philosophical Society 1961-62, National Science Foundation, 1961-63, 1971-74, National Institutes of Health, 1962-70, and American Council of Learned Societies, 1966, 1974-75, 1977-78. Edward Kremers Award, American Institute of the History of Pharmacy, 1978; Pfizer Book Award, History of Science Society, 1978, for *The Chemical Philosophy.*

WRITINGS: The English Paracelsians, Oldbourne, 1965, F. Watts, 1966; (with Robert P. Multhauf) *Alchemy and Chemistry in the Seventeenth Century,* William Andrews Clark Memorial Library, 1966; (author of introduction) Elias Ashmole, *Theatrum Chemicum Britannicum,* Johnson Reprint, 1967; *The Chemical Dream of the Renaissance* (lecture at Churchill College, Cambridge University), Heffer, 1968, Bobbs-Merrill, 1972; (editor) *World Who's Who in Science from Antiquity to the Present,* Marquis, 1968; *Science and Education in the 17th Century: The Webster-Ward Debate,* American Elsevier, 1970; (editor and contributor) *Science, Medicine and Society in the Renaissance: Essays in Honor of Walter Pagel,* two volumes, Neale Watson, 1972; (with Brian A. L. Rust) *The Complete Entertainment Discography, 1898-1942,* Arlington House, 1973; (editor and contributor) *Medicine in Seventeenth Century England,* University of California Press, 1974.

(Author of introduction) John Dee, *The Mathematicall Praeface to the Elements of Geometrie of Euclid of Megara,* Science History Publications, 1975; *The Chemical Philosophy: Paracelsian Science and Medicine in the Sixteenth and Seventeenth Centuries,* two volumes, Science History Publications, 1977; *Man and Nature in the Renaissance,* Cambridge University Press, 1978; *Robert Fludd and His Philosophical Key,* Science History Publications, 1979; *Science and History: A Chemist's Appraisal,* University of Coimbra, 1984.

Editor, "History of Science and Medicine" series, University of Chicago Press. Annotator of three record set, *Music of Victor Herbert,* Smithsonian Institution, 1979. Contributor of about seventy articles to professional journals.

WORK IN PROGRESS: Editing, with Ingrid Merkel, *Hermeticism and the Renaissance,* for Folger Books; *Chemistry and Medicine in the Age of Reason.*

*　　*　　*

de FOX, Lucia Ungaro
　　See LOCKERT, Lucia (Alicia Ungaro Fox)

*　　*　　*

De GREENE, Kenyon B(renton)

PERSONAL: Born in Kansas City, Mo.; son of Charles Arthur (a lawyer) and Leona Helen (Pool) De Greene; married Maria Theresia Haltmeyer; children: Karola Alexandra, Kenyon Brenton, Jr., Erika Krystal, Kenyon David Michael. *Education:* University of California, Los Angeles, A.B., 1946, M.A., 1949, Ph.D., 1953. *Home:* 4345 Chaumont Rd., Woodland Hills, Calif. 91364. *Office:* Institute of Safety and Systems Management, University of Southern California, Los Angeles, Calif. 90089-0021.

CAREER: Montana State University (now University of Montana), Missoula, assistant professor of psychology, 1953-54; University of California, Far East Program, Tokyo, Japan, lecturer in psychology, 1954-55; System Development Corp., Santa Monica, Calif., human factors scientist, 1956-61; Northrop Corp., Hawthorne, Calif., human factors engineer and scientist, 1961-63; Aerospace Corp., El Segundo, Calif., human factors scientist and manager, 1963-65; University of Southern California, Institute of Safety and Systems Management, Los Angeles, 1965—, began as associate professor, currently professor of systems management and human factors.

MEMBER: Society for General Systems Research, American Psychological Association, Human Factors Society, American Association for the Advancement of Science, Institute of Electrical and Electronics Engineers, American Association of University Professors, Sierra Club, Sigma Xi.

WRITINGS: (Editor and contributor) *Systems Psychology,* McGraw, 1970; *Sociotechnical Systems: Factors in Analysis, Design, and Management,* Prentice-Hall, 1973; (contributor) Harriet H. Werley and others, editors, *Health Research: A Systems Approach,* Springer, 1976; *The Adaptive Organization: Anticipation and Management of Crisis,* Wiley, 1982; (contributor) Harold Chestnut, editor, *Supplemental Ways for Improving International Stability,* Pergamon, 1984; (contributor) Joseph Zeidner, editor, *Human Productivity Enhancement,* Praeger, 1985.

Contributor to *International Encyclopedia of Psychiatry, Psychology, Psychoanalysis, and Neurology,* edited by Benjamin Wolman, Van Nostrand, 1977, 1984, and *Encyclopedia of Professional Management,* edited by Lester Bittel, McGraw, 1978, 1985. Contributor of over fifty articles to *Ergonomics, Human Factors, Organization and Administrative Sciences, Behavioral Science, IEEE Transactions on Systems, Man, and Cybernetics, Progress in Cybernetics and Systems Research,* other scholarly journals, and national and international conference proceedings.

SIDELIGHTS: Kenyon B. De Greene comments: "In all my writings I have tried to break with the past, with tradition, with the firmly established, with the tried-and-true. I see myself as part of a revolution in human thinking, an emerging new paradigm as so aptly described by Thomas Kuhn. I have attempted to explain the complexities of systems science in such a way that principles can be applied to the management of sudden new crises, challenges, and opportunities in the world today."

AVOCATIONAL INTERESTS: International travel, conservation, nature study, mountain and water sports.

*　　*　　*

DEISS, Joseph Jay　1915-

PERSONAL: Surname is pronounced "dice"; born January 25, 1915, in Twin Falls, Idaho; son of Joseph John (a rancher) and Charlotte (Neilson) Deiss; married Catherine Dohoney, August 3, 1937; children: John Casy (deceased), Susanna (Mrs. Eric Chivian). *Education:* University of Texas, B.A., 1934, M.A., 1935. *Home:* Thoreau House, Wellfleet, Mass. 02667; and Rte. 2, Box 528, Gainesville, Fla. 32601 (winter).

CAREER: U.S. Government, Washington, D.C., editor and writer, 1936-44; *Executives' War Digest,* New York City, editor, 1944-46; free-lance writer, 1947-50; Medical & Pharmaceutical Information Bureau (public relations), New York City, partner, 1950-54; free-lance writer, 1954—. Vice-director, American Academy in Rome, 1965-69; writer-in-residence, Currier House, Harvard-Radcliffe, 1975.

MEMBER: Authors Guild, Authors League of America, Archaelogical Institute of America, Thoreau Society, Phi Gamma Delta.

AWARDS, HONORS: Distinguished Alumnus Award, University of Texas, 1970; Cavalier, Order of the Star of Solidarity of Italy, 1971.

WRITINGS: A Washington Story (novel), Duell, Sloan & Pearce, 1950; *The Blue Chips* (novel), Simon & Schuster, 1957; *The Great Infidel: Frederick II of Hohenstaufen* (biographical novel), Random House, 1963; *Captains of Fortune—Profiles of Six Italian Condottieri*, Gollancz, 1966, Crowell, 1967; *Herculaneum: Italy's Buried Treasure*, Crowell, 1966, new edition, 1985; *The Roman Years of Margaret Fuller*, Crowell, 1969; *The Town of Hercules: A Buried Treasure Trove* (juvenile), Houghton, 1974; *1980 Year Book* (supplement to *Collier's Encyclopedia*), Collier, 1979. Contributor to national magazines, including *Mademoiselle, Cosmopolitan, Harper's, Reader's Digest, American Heritage,* and *Holiday.*

SIDELIGHTS: Reviewing Joseph Jay Deiss' *Herculaneum: Italy's Buried Treasure* in the *New York Times,* Thomas Lask writes: "With concrete evidence from the Roman city all around him, Mr. Deiss has no trouble summoning up the smallest detail (though not all of them) of first-century imperial existence." Describing Deiss as an "artful guide," Lask finds *Herculaneum* "enticing reading: it is also a spirited [introduction] to the inundated city, to the methods of restoration, to the work still to be done and to the obstacles that prevent it." According to Iola Haverstick in the *New York Times Book Review,* Deiss' *The Roman Years of Margaret Fuller* "[restores] a measure of humanity to the historical flesh and blood woman. [The author believes] previous biographies of Margaret have overstressed her American years and neglected the 'dramatic Roman crisis of her life,' which for her was both a public and a private event. To prove his point," she continues, "he has unearthed a variety of unpublished material, the most important of which are the letters written to Margaret by the Italian republican patriot, Giuseppe Mazzini, and Margaret's correspondence with her lover, the Marchese Giovanni Angelo Ossoli." *Library Journal* reviewer Walter Harding calls the book "a vivid, exciting, and authentic account."

Deiss' books have been translated into twenty-one languages. He has travelled extensively in Latin America and Europe. He told *CA:* "For me, the big bang comes on receiving such an unsolicited letter as the following [from scholar Sir Julian Huxley] about *Herculaneum:* 'This book is wonderful. I find it vivid and historically important. It will be one of my treasured permanent possessions.'"

AVOCATIONAL INTERESTS: Swimming, rowing.

BIOGRAPHICAL/CRITICAL SOURCES: Time, November 23, 1966; *New York Times,* February 4, 1967; *Natural History,* April, 1967; John Bainbridge, *Another Way of Living,* Holt, 1968; *Library Journal,* August, 1969; *New York Times Book Review,* November 30, 1969; *New England Quarterly,* March, 1971; *American Literature,* May, 1970; *Virginia Quarterly Review,* summer, 1970; *American Historical Review,* December, 1970; Eleanore C. Hibbs, *Writing: Fact and Imagination,* Prentice-Hall, 1971; *Psychology Today,* January, 1975; *Social Education,* March, 1975.

De LAGE, Ida 1918-

PERSONAL: Born July 16, 1918, in New York, N.Y.; daughter of Joseph Patrick (a teacher) and Mary Catherine (Sheridan) McCourt; married Maurice Francois De Lage (a papermaker), June 9, 1946; children: Patrick Joseph, Marie Louise. *Education:* Attended New York State Teachers College (now State University of New York College at New Paltz). *Home:* 253 Edison St., Clifton, N.Y. 07013.

CAREER: Writer for children.

WRITINGS—Juveniles; all published by Garrard: *The Farmer and the Witch,* 1966; *Weeny Witch,* 1968; *The Witchy Broom,* 1969; *The Old Witch Goes to the Ball,* 1969.

The Old Witch and the Snores, 1970; *What Does a Witch Need?,* 1971; *Hello, Come In,* 1971; *Beware! Beware! A Witch Won't Share,* 1972; *Pink, Pink,* 1973; *Good Morning Lady,* 1974; *The Old Witch and the Wizard,* 1974; *A Bunny Ride,* 1975.

Bunny School, 1976; *The Old Witch's Party,* 1976; *ABC Firedogs,* 1977; *ABC Halloween Witch,* 1977; *ABC Pigs Go to Market,* 1977; *ABC Pirate Adventures,* 1977; *The Squirrel's Tree Party,* 1978; *Am I a Bunny?,* 1978; *The Old Witch and the Magic Basket,* 1978; *The Old Witch and the Ghost Parade,* 1978; *ABC Christmas,* 1978; *ABC Santa Claus,* 1978; *ABC Easter Bunny,* 1979; *Frannie's Flower,* 1979; *The Old Witch and the Dragon,* 1979; *The Old Witch Finds a New House,* 1979.

The ABC Triplets at the Zoo, 1980; *The Pilgrim Children on the Mayflower,* 1980; *The Pilgrims Come to Plymouth,* 1981; *The Old Witch Gets a Surprise,* 1981; *The Old Witch and the Crows,* 1983.

*   *   *

DEMETZ, Peter 1922-

PERSONAL: Born October 21, 1922, in Prague, Czechoslovakia; came to United States in 1952, naturalized in 1958; son of Hans and Anna (Brod) Demetz; married Hana Mueller, April 21, 1950; children: Anne-Marie Bettina. *Education:* Charles University, Dr.Phil., 1948; Columbia University, M.A., 1954; Yale University, Ph.D., 1956. *Office:* Department of German, 2978 Es, Yale University, New Haven, Conn. 06520.

CAREER: Radio Free Europe editor, 1950-52; Yale University, New Haven, Conn., instructor, 1956-58, assistant professor, 1958-60, associate professor of German, 1960-62, professor of German and comparative literature, 1962—, chairman of department, 1963-69.

MEMBER: Modern Language Association of America, American Association of Teachers of German, P.E.N., Berliner Akademie der Kuenste.

AWARDS, HONORS: Yale Morse fellow, 1959-60; Guggenheim fellow, 1965-66; Golden Goethe Medal, Federal Republic of Germany, 1971.

WRITINGS: Goethes "Die Aufgeregten": Zur Frage der politischen Dichtung in Deutschland, F. Nowack, 1952; *Rene Rilkes Prager Jahre,* E. Diederichs, 1953; (compiler) *Neviditelny domov: Verse exulantu, 1948-53,* Sokolova, c. 1954; *Marx, Engels, und die Dichter: Zur Grundlagenforschung des Marxismus,* Deutsche Verlags-Anstalt, 1959, translation of revised and enlarged edition by Jeffrey L. Sammons published as *Marx, Engels, and the Poets: Origins of Marxist Literary Criticism,* University of Chicago Press, 1967.

(Editor and author of introduction) *Brecht: A Collection of Critical Essays,* Prentice-Hall, 1962; *Formen des Realismus: Theodor Fontane, Kritische Untersuchungen,* C. Hanser, 1964; (editor and author of documentation) Gotthold Ephraim Lessing, *Nathan der Weise,* Ullstein, 1966; (editor with W. T. H. Jackson) *An Anthology of German Literature, 800-1750,* Prentice-Hall, 1968; (editor with Thomas Greene and Lowry Nelson, Jr.) *The Disciplines of Criticism: Essays in Literary Theory, Interpretation, and History,* Yale University Press, 1968.

Kitsch, Belletristik, Kunst: Theodor Fontane, Akademie der Kuenste, 1970; *Postwar German Literature: A Critical Introduction,* Pegasus, 1970; (editor and author of introduction) Karl Ferdinand Gutzkow, *Liberale Energie: Eine Sammlung seiner kritische Schriften,* 1974; (editor with Hans Dieter Zimmerman) *Arsenal: Beitrage zu Franz Tumler,* Piper, 1977; (editor and author of introduction) Walter Benjamin, *Reflections: Essays, Aphorisms, Autobiographical Writings,* Harcourt, 1978; (editor) Theodor Fontane, *Short Novels and Other Writings,* Continuum, 1982. Contributor to articles to professional journals.

SIDELIGHTS: Marx, Engels, und die Dichter has been translated into Spanish and Japanese.†

*   *   *

de MILAN, Sister Jean
   See JEAN, Gabrielle (Lucille)

*   *   *

De MILLE, Nelson
   See LEVINSON, Leonard

*   *   *

DENNY, M(aurice) Ray 1918-

PERSONAL: Born November 5, 1918, in Terre Haute, Ind.; son of Maurice R. and Marie C. (Williams) Denny; married Audrey Deeks, August 22, 1942; married second wife, Ruth Wehner, June 12, 1964; children: (first marriage) Michael, Richard, Douglas. *Education:* University of Michigan, B.S., 1942, M.A., 1943; University of Iowa, Ph.D., 1945. *Home:* 4565 Hawthorne Lane, Okemos, Mich. 48864. *Office:* Department of Psychology, Michigan State University, East Lansing, Mich. 48823.

CAREER: University of Oklahoma, Norman, instructor in psychology and counselor, 1945-46; Michigan State University, East Lansing, assistant professor, 1946-53, associate professor, 1953-57, professor of psychology, 1957-83, professor emeritus, 1983—. Research consultant, Plymouth State Hospital and Training School, 1967-69.

MEMBER: American Psychological Association, American Association for the Advancement of Science, Psychonomic Society, Midwestern Psychological Association (president, 1973-74), Michigan Psychological Association (president, 1958, 1959), Sigma Xi, Psi Chi, Phi Sigma.

WRITINGS: (Contributor) Harvey A. Stevens and Rick Heber, editors, *Mental Retardation: A Review of Research,* University of Chicago Press, 1964; (with S. C. Ratner) *Comparative Psy-*

chology: *Research in Animal Behavior,* Dorsey, 1964, revised edition, 1970; (contributor) F. R. Brush, editor, *Aversive Conditioning and Learning,* Academic Press, 1971; (contributor) Howard Kendler and Janet Spence, editors, *Essays in Neobehaviorism: A Memorial Volume to Kenneth W. Spence,* Appleton, 1971.

(Editor) *Comparative Psychology,* John Wiley, 1980; (with R. H. Davis) *Understanding Behavior,* Paladin Press, 1981; (editor with D. Kendrick and M. Riling) *Theories of Animal Memory,* Erlbaum, in press. Contributor to *Psychological Review, Intelligence, Journal of Experimental Analysis of Behavior,* and other publications.

WORK IN PROGRESS: Research on learning (avoidance learning) and experimental extinction.

*   *   *

DENOON, Donald (John Noble) 1940-

PERSONAL: Born July 29, 1940, in Scotland; son of Alexander (an engineer) and Elspeth (a secretary; maiden name, Noble) Denoon; married Pamela Bavin Tod (a sociologist), January 8, 1966; children: Louise, Alexander, Gordon. *Education:* University of Natal, B.A. (honors), 1961; Cambridge University, Ph.D., 1965. *Office:* Research School of Pacific Studies, Australian National University, Canberra, Australia.

CAREER: Makerere University, Kampala, Uganda, lecturer in history, 1966-72; University of Papua New Guinea, Port Moresby, professor of history, 1972-81; Australian National University, Canberra, senior research fellow, 1982—.

WRITINGS: A Grand Illusion, Longman, 1972; *Southern Africa since 1800,* Longman, 1972; (editor) *A History of Agriculture in Papua New Guinea,* Institute of Papua New Guinea Studies, 1981; (editor) *Oral Tradition in Melanesia,* Institute of Papua New Guinea Studies, 1981; *Settler Capitalism,* Oxford University Press, 1983.

WORK IN PROGRESS: A biography of Ulli Beier; *Medical and Social History of the Pacific.*

SIDELIGHTS: Donald Denoon told *CA:* "My concern is to understand the interaction of race, class, and gender in colonial contexts."

*   *   *

DESCARGUES, Pierre 1925-

PERSONAL: Born September 22, 1925, in Montrouge, France; son of Etienne and Alice (Schaub) Descargues; married Catherine Valogne (a painter and writer), April 22, 1950; children: Olivier. *Education:* Attended Lycee Louis le Grand, Paris, and Sorbonne, University of Paris. *Home:* 6 Rue Boris-Vilde, 92 Fontenay-aux-Roses, France.

CAREER: Arts (weekly), Paris, France, art critic, 1946-50; *Les Lettres Francaises* (weekly), Paris, art critic, 1950—; *Tribune de Lausanne* (daily newspaper), Lausanne, Switzerland, correspondent, 1954-69; Radiodiffusion-Television Francaise, Paris, art critic, 1970-73; Radio-France, Paris, producer of program "les Apres-Midi de France Culture," 1973—. *Plaisir de France* (monthly periodical), art critic, 1970-75.

MEMBER: International Association of Art Critics.

AWARDS, HONORS: Prix Descartes from French-Holland Association, 1967.

WRITINGS: Durer, Somogy, 1954; *Fernand Leger,* Cercle d'Art, 1955; *Picasso,* Editions Universitaires, 1956, new edition, Felicie, 1974; *Le Siecle d'or de la peinture hollandaise,* Somogy, 1956, translation by Stuart Hood published as *Dutch Painting,* Thames & Hudson, 1959; *Le Cubisme,* Somogy, 1956; *La Peinture allemande du XIVeme aux XIVeme siecle,* Somogy, 1958, translation by Stuart Hood published as *German Painting from the 14th to the 16th Centuries,* Thames & Hudson, 1958; *Bernard Buffet* (includes *Bernard Buffet, peintre ou temoin?* by Pierre de Boisdeffre), Editions Universitaires, 1959.

Lucas Cranach, l'aine, translation by Helena Ramsbotham published as *Lucas Cranach, the Elder,* Oldbourne, 1960, and as *Cranach,* Abrams, 1962; *Le Musee de L'Ermitage,* Somogy, 1961, translation by Katharine Delavenay published as *The Hermitage Museum, Leningrad,* Abrams, 1961, revised edition published as *Art Treasures of the Hermitage,* 1972 (translation published in England as *The Hermitage,* Thames & Hudson, 1961, revised edition, 1967); *Rembrandt et Saskia a Amsterdam,* Payot, 1965; *Vermeer,* published in French and in English translation by James Emmons, Skira (Geneva), 1966; (with Kynaston McShine and Pierre Restany) *Yves Klein* (exhibition catalogue), Jewish Museum, Jewish Theological Seminary of America, 1967; *Hals,* published in French and in English translation by James Emmons, Skira, 1968.

Rebeyrolle, Maeght, 1970; (with Francis Ponge) *Georges Braque,* Draeger, 1971, English translation published under same title, Abrams, 1971; *Julio Gonzalez,* Musee de Poche, 1971; *Joan Gonzalez,* Musee de Poche, 1971; *Robert Muller,* La Connaissance (Brussels), 1971; *Le Douanier Rousseau: Etude biographique et critique,* Skira, 1972; *Picasso de Draeger,* Draeger, 1974; *Vincent van Gogh,* Cercle d'Art, 1975; *Goya,* Alfieri & Lacroix, 1976; *Perspective,* Abrams, 1977; *Hartung,* Rizzoli, 1977.

Booklets in "Collection Artistes de ce temps" series, published by Presses Litteraires de France: *Bernard Buffet,* 1949; *Y. Alde,* 1950; *Vieira de Silva,* c. 1950; *Volti,* 1950; *Piaubert,* 1950; *Gili,* 1951; *Rebeyrolle,* 1951; *Bertholle,* 1952; *Gabriel Zendel,* 1952; *J. Dewasne,* 1952.

Other short works and texts of exhibition catalogues: *Jean Aujame,* Galerie de Berri, 1949; *Amedeo Modigliani, 1884-1920,* Braun, 1951; *Bourdelle,* Hachette, 1954; *Jacobsen: Sculptures, 1961-1962,* Galerie de France, 1963; *Niki de Saint-Phalle: Nanas* (text translated by Frances Frank), Iolas Gallery (New York), 1966; *Francois Fiedler,* Maeght, 1967; *Dessins et Traites d'anatomie,* J. L. Binet, 1980; *Gravites malignes et autres causes de pervision de l'harmonie des spheres dans l'oeuvre de Pol Bury,* Daily-Bul, 1980.

WORK IN PROGRESS: Fragonard.

BIOGRAPHICAL/CRITICAL SOURCES: Best Sellers, July 1, 1968; *Time,* December 20, 1971.

*   *   *

De WAAL, Ronald Burt 1932-

PERSONAL: Born October 23, 1932, in Salt Lake City, Utah; son of Jack and Marjorie (Burt) De Waal; married Gayle Lloyd, November 7, 1963; children: Les. *Education:* University of Utah, B.S., 1955; University of Denver, M.A., 1958. *Politics:* Republican. *Religion:* Unitarian Universalist. *Home:* 5020 Hogan Dr., Fort Collins, Colo. 80521. *Office:* Colorado State University Library, Fort Collins, Colo. 80525.

CAREER: University of New Mexico, Albuquerque, special collections librarian, 1958-59; New Mexico Military Institute, Roswell, head librarian, 1959-60; Sperry Utah Co., Salt Lake City, Utah, head librarian, 1961-64; Westminster College, Salt Lake City, head librarian, 1964-66; Colorado State University Library, Fort Collins, humanities librarian and exhibits coordinator, 1966—.

MEMBER: College Art Association of America, Music Educators National Conference, Music Library Association, National Sculpture Society, Baker Street Irregulars, Praed Street Irregulars, Sherlock Holmes Society of London.

AWARDS, HONORS: John H. Jenkins Award for best bibliography, 1974; Two-Shilling Award from Baker Street Irregulars, 1984.

WRITINGS: The World Bibliography of Sherlock Holmes and Dr. Watson: A Classified and Annotated List of Materials Relating to Their Lives and Adventures, 1887-1972, New York Graphic Society, 1974; *The International Sherlock Holmes,* Mansell, 1980; *The Universal Sherlock Holmes,* Greenwood Press, 1985. Contributor to literary journals.

WORK IN PROGRESS: A second edition of the Holmes bibliographies, collected into three volumes and entitled *The Sherlock Holmes Bibliography.*

SIDELIGHTS: Discussing Ronald Burt De Waal's *The International Sherlock Holmes* in the *Spectator,* Benny Green remarks upon the book's "terrifying thoroughness," a comment suggesting the magnitude of the bibliographic task the author has undertaken in his three volumes on the famous detective. As Pauline Greene points out in the *American Book Collector,* "From his inception, there has always been an interest in Sherlock Holmes. The popularity of other literary figures has diminished with time, but this is *not* the case with Holmes. The 1970s saw this interest become almost phenomenal."

In addition to scholarly writings on Holmes, Watson, and Arthur Conan Doyle, De Waal has also cataloged a vast variety of materials that can be classified as "Sherlockiana," including greeting cards, plaques, poems, and bookplates. "Although bibliographies are intended to be works of reference rather than books to be read," writes Green, "there is no question that to even the most desultory [Holmes fan], Mr. De Waal's . . . book contains hundreds of the sort of items which imbue the reader with an anti-social tendency to read them aloud to whoever is in earshot." Greene describes *The International Sherlock Holmes* as a "worthy companion" to De Waal's previous volume *The World Bibliography of Sherlock Holmes and Dr. Watson,* and finds it a "must for all Sherlockians and devotees of the mystery genre. These bibliographies," she continues, "with their enormous lists of material and numerous categories, make it possible to develop individual and unique collections within the field that may still keep one in the collecting game without putting one too greatly out of pocket." De Waal, concludes Greene, "has cast down a weighty gauntlet."

De Waal himself has extensive collections on Holmes and Beethoven, as well as one on Ronald Reagan. He is trying to "collect everything relating to *the* master detective and *the* master composer." The Beethoven collection includes more than one hundred pieces of sculpture as well as books, records, prints, and paintings.

AVOCATIONAL INTERESTS: Classical music, ballroom dancing, running, weight lifting, mountain climbing, coaching Little League baseball.

BIOGRAPHICAL/CRITICAL SOURCES: Baker Street Journal, June, 1972; *American Libraries,* January, 1973; *Los Angeles Herald Examiner,* February 23, 1975; *Punch,* June 18, 1975; *Spectator,* September 27, 1980; *American Book Collector,* November-December, 1980; *Baker Street Miscellany,* fall, 1980; *Baker Street Chronicle,* May-June, 1984.

* * *

DIAMOND, Jay 1934-

PERSONAL: Born January 25, 1934, in New York; son of Charles (a retailer) and Helen (a retailer; maiden name, Klar) Diamond; married Ellen Clements (an artist), June 1, 1958; children: Sheri, Caryn, David. *Education:* City College (now City College of the City University of New York), B.B.A., 1955; New York University, M.A., 1965. *Home:* 3780 Greentree Dr., Oceanside, N.Y. 11572. *Office:* Department of Marketing-Retailing, Nassau Community College, Stewart Ave., Garden City, N.Y. 11530.

CAREER: Helen Diamond (retail chain), Brooklyn, N.Y., partner and buyer, 1955-64; New York Community College, Brooklyn, instructor in retailing and marketing, 1964-65; Nassau Community College, Garden City, N.Y., assistant professor, 1965-67, associate professor, 1967-70, professor of marketing and retailing, 1970—, chairman of department, 1969—. Adjunct instructor at City College of the City University of New York and Pratt Institute, 1955-64.

MEMBER: National Retail Merchants Association (associate member).

WRITINGS—All with Gerald Pintel: *The Mathematics of Business,* with workbook, Prentice-Hall, 1970, 3rd edition, 1984; *Retailing,* with workbook, Prentice-Hall, 1971, 3rd edition, 1983; *Principles of Marketing,* with study guide, Prentice-Hall, 1972, 2nd edition, 1980; *Basic Business Mathematics,* Prentice-Hall, 1972, 3rd edition, 1984; *Introduction to Contemporary Business,* with study guide, Prentice-Hall, 1975; *Retail Buying,* Prentice-Hall, 1976; *Successful Selling,* Reston, 1980.

AVOCATIONAL INTERESTS: Tennis, travel.†

* * *

DIDION, Joan 1934-

PERSONAL: Born December 5, 1934, in Sacramento, Calif.; daughter of Frank Reese and Eduene (Jerrett) Didion; married John Gregory Dunne (a writer), January 30, 1964; children: Quintana Roo (daughter). *Education:* University of California, Berkeley, B.A., 1956. *Residence:* Los Angeles. *Agent:* Lois Wallace, Wallace & Sheil Agency, Inc., 177 East 70th St., New York, N.Y. 10021.

CAREER: Writer. *Vogue,* New York, N.Y., 1953-63, began as promotional copywriter, became associate feature editor. Visiting regents lecturer in English, University of California, Berkeley, 1976.

AWARDS, HONORS: First prize, *Vogue*'s Prix de Paris, 1956; Bread Loaf fellowship in fiction, 1963; National Book Award nomination in fiction, 1971, for *Play It as It Lays;* Morton Dauwen Zabel Award, National Institute of Arts and Letters, 1978; National Book Critics Circle Prize nomination in nonfiction, 1980, and American Book Award nomination in nonfiction, 1981, both for *The White Album; Los Angeles Times* Book Prize nomination in fiction, 1984, for *Democracy.*

WRITINGS: Run River (novel), Obolensky, 1963; *Slouching Towards Bethlehem* (essays), Farrar, Straus, 1968; *Play It as It Lays* (novel; also see below), Farrar, Straus, 1970; *A Book of Common Prayer* (novel), Simon & Schuster, 1977; *The White Album* (essays), Simon & Schuster, 1979; *Salvador* (nonfiction), Simon & Schuster, 1983; *Democracy* (novel), Simon & Schuster, 1984.

Screenplays; with husband John Gregory Dunne: "Panic in Needle Park" (based on a James Mills book of the same title), Twentieth Century-Fox, 1971; "Play It as It Lays" (based on Didion's book of the same title), Universal, 1972; (and others) "A Star Is Born," Warner Bros., 1976; "True Confessions" (based on Dunne's novel of the same title), United Artists, 1981.

Author of column, with Dunne, "Points West," *Saturday Evening Post,* 1967-69, and "The Coast," *Esquire,* 1976-77; former columnist, *Life.* Contributor of short stories, articles, and reviews to numerous magazines, including *Vogue, Saturday Evening Post, Holiday, Harper's Bazaar,* and the *New York Times Book Review.* Former contributing editor, *National Review.*

SIDELIGHTS: An elegant prose stylist and one of the most celebrated of the new journalists, Joan Didion possesses a distinct literary voice, widely praised for its precision and control. She is, by her own admission, a non-intellectual writer, more concerned with images than ideas and renowned for her use of the telling detail. In addition to being "a gifted reporter," Didion, according to *New York Times Magazine* contributor Michiko Kakutani, "is also a prescient witness, finding in her own experiences parallels of the times. The voice is always precise, the tone unsentimental, the view unabashedly subjective. She takes things personally." For years, Didion's favorite subject was her native California, a state that seemed to supply ample evidence of the disorder in society, confirming her suspicion that "things fall apart; the center cannot hold," to quote the poet W. B. Yeats as Didion does. Though her theme has not changed, in recent years she has broadened her perspective, turning to the troubled countries of Central America and Southeast Asia for new material.

Since 1963, Didion has published four short novels *(Run River, Play It as It Lays, A Book of Common Prayer,* and *Democracy),* two collections of magazine essays *(Slouching Towards Bethlehem* and *The White Album)* and a slim volume of journalism called *Salvador.* Her output would be greater if she were not so obsessed with perfection. "I'm not much interested in spontaneity," she admitted to Digby Diehl of the *Los Angeles Times.* "What concerns me is total control."

In addition to writing novels and essays, Didion sometimes collaborates on screenplays with her husband, the novelist John Gregory Dunne. These projects provide considerable income and the chance to work closely with other artists but Didion finds them restrictive, like being "copilot on an airplane," to use her husband's words. In a *New York Review of Books* article, Dunne writes that a screenwriter must "cede to the director certain essential writer's functions—pace, mood, style, point-of-view, rhythm, texture," and Didion has acknowledged that this is her opinion, too.

In her quest for controlled perfection, Didion revises her writing repeatedly, working and reworking the exact placement of important details. *Newsweek*'s Peter S. Prescott says she is "able to condense into a paragraph what others would take three pages to expound. Unerringly, she seizes the exact phrase that not only describes but comments on a scene.'' According to *New York Times* reviewer John Leonard, ''nobody writes better English prose than Joan Didion. Try to rearrange one of her sentences, and you've realized that the sentence was inevitable, a hologram.''

Didion's emphasis on image and detail reflects ner perceptual orientation. She has often said that she is not the least bit intellectual and, in a lecture she delivered at her alma mater, she explained the way her mind works: ''During the years I was an undergraduate at Berkeley, I . . . kept trying to find that part of my mind that could deal in abstracts. But my mind kept veering inexorably back like some kind of boomerang I was stuck with—to the specific, to the tangible, to what was generally considered by everyone I knew, the peripheral. I would try to think about the Great Dialectic and I would find myself thinking instead about how the light was falling through the window in an apartment I had on the North Side. How it was hitting the floor.''

In many of her novels, Didion's starting point has been an image not unlike a shaft of light, a scene that has ''a shimmer around the edges'' and that she builds her story around. ''For my first novel, 'Run River,' it was a detailed picture of a man and a woman in a house on the Sacramento River,'' she told Digby Diehl in the *Los Angeles Times*. ''For 'Play It as It Lays,' it was a starlet being paged at the Riviera Hotel in Las Vegas at one o'clock in the morning. For . . . 'A Book of Common Prayer,' it was the picture of an American woman in an airport coffee shop in Central America. I find that when I explore these pictures, they each contain the essential story for the novels they generated.''

Though she often builds a whole book around a single ''picture,'' Didion's writing can seem fragmented, her chapters short and disjointed, her images unexplored. ''Everything depends on the selection and placement of details,'' notes *Newsweek*'s Walter Clemons, who calls it ''a perilous method. At her worse Didion sounds supercilious, an uncommitted connoisseur of fragments, a severe snob.''

Didion knows her concerns are not the standard ones and in one of her better-known essays, ''In the Islands,'' she describes herself as ''a woman who for some time now has felt radically separated from most of the ideas that seem to interest other people.'' Though she once listed herself a ''republican,'' she has long since abandoned such allegiances, telling *New York Times Book Review* contributor Sara Davidson, ''I never had faith that the answers to human problems lay in anything that could be called political. I thought the answers, if there were answers, lay someplace in man's soul.'' In 1972, she wrote a piece called ''The Women's Movement,'' dismissing feminism as a ''curious historical anomaly'' which had been trivialized by people who did not understand its Marxist roots. Feminists were not amused. In a long and highly critical *Nation* essay, Barbara Grizzuti Harrison attacks Didion's attitude as a pose: ''What interests me more than her trivial and trivializing essay on women's liberation is that she sometimes expresses notions that would not be at all alien to the staunchest of feminists: 'Women don't ever win. . . . Because winners have to believe they can affect the dice.' If that is not a tacit admission that women are relatively powerless, what is? . . . Still, for Didion to have any sympathy with anyone who aligns herself with any cause, any movement, is too much to hope for. . . . Like Grace in *A Book of Common Prayer,* she is *de afuera*—the outsider: 'I have been *de afuera* all my life.' I think she wears that

singularity like a badge. *I am different* translates into *I am superior.*''

''I have a theatrical temperament,'' Didion explained to Michiko Kakutani. ''I'm not interested in the middle road—maybe because everyone's on it. Rationality, reasonableness bewilder me. I think it comes out of being a 'daughter of the Golden West.' A lot of the stories I was brought up on had to do with extreme actions—leaving everything behind, crossing the trackless wastes, and in those stories the people who stayed behind and had their settled ways—those people were not the people who got the prize. The prize was California.''

Born to a family that settled in the Sacramento Valley in the 1800s, Didion hails from a long line of pioneers. Her great-great-great grandmother, Nancy Hardin Cornwall, was originally a member of the 1846 Donner party, but she avoided the disaster that befell that group (trapped in a mountain pass by an early blizzard, they resorted to cannibalism to stay alive) by splitting off from them early to head north through Oregon. Cornwall's own forebears had followed the frontier westward, and this pioneer heritage has exerted a strong influence on Didion, ingraining her with what Kakutani calls ''a kind of hard-boiled individualism'' or, as Didion puts it, an ''ineptness at tolerating the complexities of postindustrial life.''

Though her home life was stable, Didion was a skittish child, frightened of everything from atom bombs to rattlesnakes and convinced that the bridge over the Sacramento River would collapse if she ventured there. To redirect her daughter's energies, Didion's mother gave her a notebook and suggested that she ''stop whining'' and start writing. Her first story, written at age five, concerns a woman who imagines she is freezing to death in the Arctic, only to awaken and discover that she is burning in the desert sun.

During Didion's grade school years, World War II erupted, and the family followed her father from one Army base to another for the duration of the war. Afterwards, the Didions returned to Sacramento, but the experience left its mark on Joan, who turned increasingly to books instead of people for company. By the time she was a teenager, she was recopying passages from Ernest Hemingway and Joseph Conrad to find out the way sentences were put together.

After high school, Didion enrolled at the University of California at Berkeley, where she majored in English literature and published her first short story in *Occident,* a campus magazine. In her senior year, 1955, she entered *Vogue*'s Prix de Paris contest with an article on William Wilson Wurster, the father of the San Francisco style of architecture. It won first prize. In lieu of a trip to France, Didion accepted a cash award and a job at *Vogue*'s New York office, where she remained for eight years, rising from promotional copywriter to associate feature editor. During this period, she met John Gregory Dunne and, after several years of friendship, they married, becoming not just matrimonial partners but literary collaborators as well.

While she was still at *Vogue,* Didion began writing her first novel, *Run River* (published to what she calls ''deafening disinterest''). The book's long descriptive passages about the Sacramento landscape were Didion's way of dealing with her homesickness. In 1964, she gave in to her longing and moved back to the West Coast with Dunne, determined to earn a living as a free-lance reporter. Working together on a series of magazine columns about California for the *Saturday Evening Post,* the couple earned a meagre $7,000 in their first year of what Digby Diehl facetiously calls ''the Good Life in Los Angeles.''

But their writing did attract widespread attention, and when Didion's columns were collected and published in a separate volume called *Slouching Towards Bethlehem,* her reputation as an essayist soared.

The book takes its theme from Yeats's poem "The Second Coming," which reads: "Things fall apart; the center cannot hold; / Mere anarchy is loosed upon the world." For Didion those words sum up the chaos of the sixties, a chaos so far-reaching that it affected her ability to perform. Convinced "that writing was an irrelevant act, that the world as I had understood it no longer existed," Didion, as she states in the book's preface, realized, "If I was to work again at all, it would be necessary for me to come to terms with disorder." She went to Haight Ashbury to explore the hippie movement and out of that experience came the title essay, "Slouching Towards Bethlehem."

Most critics praise it highly. Dan Wakefield, for instance, expresses hope in the *New York Times Book Review* that the collection will be recognized "not as a better or worse example of what some people call 'mere journalism,' but as a rich display of some of the best prose written today." Writing in the *Christian Science Monitor,* Melvin Maddocks suggests, "Her melancholy voice is that of a last survivor dictating a superbly written wreckage report onto a tape she doubts will ever be played." And while *Best Sellers* reviewer T. O'Hara argues that "the devotion she gives to America-the-uprooted-the-lunatic-and-the-alienated is sullied by an inability to modulate, to achieve a respectable distance," most critics applaud her subjectivity. "Nobody captured the slack-jawed Haight-Ashbury hippies any better," states *Saturday Review* contributor Martin Kasindorf. Or, as Wakefield puts it, Didion's "personality does not self-indulgently intrude itself on her subjects, it informs and illuminates them."

In 1970, Didion published *Play It as It Lays,* a best-selling novel that received a National Book Award nomination and, at the same time, created enormous controversy with its apparently nihilistic theme. The portrait of a woman on what *New York Times Book Review* contributor Lore Segal calls a "downward path to wisdom," *Play It as It Lays* tells the story of Maria Wyeth's struggle to find meaning in a meaningless world. "The setting is the desert; the cast, the careless hedonists of Hollywood; the emotional climate, bleak as the surroundings," Michiko Kakutani reports in the *New York Times Magazine.* Composed of eighty-four brief chapters, some less than a page in length, the book possesses a cinematic quality and such technical precision that Richard Shickel remarks in *Harper's* that it is "a rather cold and calculated fiction—more a problem in human geometry . . . than a novel that truly lives."

"The trouble with this book is the nothing *inside* Maria," according to Lore Segal, who adds that the "book feels as if it were written out of an insufficient impulse by a writer who doesn't know what else to do with all that talent and skill." *New York Review of Books* critic D.A.N. Jones finds himself unmoved: "Although she seems to be in hell, and although every event is charged with misery, *Play It as It Lays* cannot be honestly called depressing. The neat, cinematic construction, the harsh wit of the mean, soulless dialogue stimulate a certain exhilaration, as when we appreciate a harmonious and well-proportioned painting of some cruelly martyred saint in whom we do not believe."

John Leonard in the *New York Times,* on the other hand, expresses a far different view: "While the result is not exactly pleasant, it seems to me just about perfect according to its own austere terms," he writes in his review of the novel. "So long as novels are permitted to be about visions, to explore situations, to see truths beyond individual manipulation, then Miss Didion need not equip Maria with a Roto-Rooter or a dose of ideological uplift. The courage to say 'Why not?' to Nothingness is more than enough."

A Book of Common Prayer, Didion's third novel, continues her theme of social disintegration with the story of Charlotte Douglas, a Californian "immaculate of history, innocent of politics." Until her daughter Marin abandoned home and family to join a group of terrorists, Charlotte was a typically naive American, one who "understood that something was always going on in the world but believed that it would turn out all right," according to the story's narrator, Grace Strasser-Mendana. When things fall apart, Charlotte takes refuge in Boca Grande, a fictitious Central American country embroiled in its own domestic conflicts. There she idles away her days at the airport coffee shop, futilely waiting for her daughter to surface and eventually losing her life in a military coup.

In a *New York Times Book Review* interview with Sara Davidson, Didion discussed the texture she was trying to achieve in the novel: "I wrote it down on the map of Central America. 'Surface like a rainbow slick, shifting, fall, thrown away, iridescent.' I wanted to do a deceptive surface that appeared to be one thing and turned color as you looked through it." Didion originally got the story idea during a 1973 trip to Cartagena, Colombia, when her plane stopped over in the Panama airport for an hour. "My experience of that airport was very vivid, super-real," Didion told Digby Diehl in the *Saturday Review.* "I could see the opening scene of a woman having a contretemps with a waitress in the coffee shop about boiling her water twenty minutes for a cup of tea. I started to think about what she was doing there and the novel began to unfold."

Because Charlotte's story is told by Grace, an American expatriate and long-time Boca Grande resident, the book presented several technical problems. "The narrator was not present during most of the events she's telling you about. And her only source is a woman incapable of seeing the truth," Didion explained to Digby Diehl.

In her *New York Times Book Review* article, Joyce Carol Oates speculates that Didion employs this technique because Grace "allows Joan Didion a free play of her own speculative intelligence that would have been impossible had the story been told by Charlotte. The device of an uninvolved narrator is a tricky one, since a number of private details must be presented as if they were within the range of the narrator's experience. But it is a measure of Didion's skill as a novelist that one never questions [Grace's] near omniscience in recalling Charlotte's story."

"Grace appears to debunk Charlotte, to expose her pathetic delusions, but the tenderness she brings to bear on the case serves o redeem the other woman—until she becomes an instance of a sort of gallant particularity for which no science can ever account," writes Frederick Raphael in the *Saturday Review.* Christopher Lehmann-Haupt, on the other hand, maintains in the *New York Times* that Didion "simply asks too much of Charlotte, and overburdened as she is by the pitiless cruelty of the narrator's vision, she collapses under the strain."

Margot Hentoff believes that the book would have more impact if Didion had accurately interpreted "the actual state of the union. We are not dead souls," she writes in the *Village Voice,* "the edge of the abyss was not even close, and we Americans have fallen from grace and lost our innocence so many times that by now the supply of both seems inexhaustible. Let me say that I think Joan Didion is one of our very best writers." She continues. "Didion writes more movingly of time and loss than any other writer of my generation. In her essays. Not in the novels. She has the capacity, I think, to be the Chekhov of our time, but her novels do not come alive because they are insufficiently distanced from her own anxiety—too relentlessly ironic in tone, too emotionally controlled, as if the form itself were the bars of a cell."

After *A Book of Common Prayer*, Didion published *The White Album*, a second collection of magazine essays, similar in tone to *Slouching Towards Bethlehem*, but wider in scope, more tentative and less absolute. "I don't have as many answers as I did when I wrote 'Slouching,'" Didion explained to Michiko Kakutani. She·called the book *The White Album* in consideration of a famous Beatles album that captured for her the disturbing ambience of the sixties. "I am talking here about a time when I began to doubt the premises of all the stories I had ever told myself," Didion writes in the title essay. "This period began around 1966 and continued until 1971." During this time, says Didion, "all I knew was what I saw: flash pictures in variable sequence, images with no 'meaning' beyond their temporary arrangement, not a movie but a cutting-room experience."

Diagnosed at this time as "fundamentally pessimistic, fatalistic, and depressive," Didion includes not only such personal data as her psychiatric profile, but also public news about incidents, including the Charles Manson murders and Robert Kennedy's death. "At times, it seems Didion's own fear and malaise run parallel like train tracks to those of the era," observes Hillary Johnson in the *Christian Science Monitor*. *New York Times Book Review* contributor Robert Towers calls her title essay, "the best short piece (37 pages) on the late 1960's that I have yet read," attributing its success in large part to "the use to which personal neurosis has been put. Joan Didion makes no bones about the seriousness of the neurosis, but she gives the impression of having refined it to the point where it vibrates in exquisite attunement to the larger craziness of the world. . . . It is her nerve-frayed awareness of the gap between the supposedly meaningful 'script' by which we try to live and the absurdities by which we are bombarded that has brought her vision to its preternaturally sharp focus and has helped make her the extraordinary reporter she is."

In her later work, Didion has broadened her perspective while retaining her subjective approach. "I had certain questions about California," she explained to Martin Kasindorf in the *Saturday Review*. "I didn't answer the questions. But I got tired of asking them. I would like to ask some other questions, I think."

Among those questions was one about the differences between North America and its southern neighbors. First surfacing in *A Book of Common Prayer* with its fictitious Central American setting, this question is journalistically addressed in *Salvador*, a nonfiction book. Based on Didion's experiences and written with the assistance of her husband's notes, *Salvador* chronicles the two weeks that Didion and Dunne spent in the war-torn country of El Salvador in June, 1982. "Alternately detached and compassionate, this slim essay is many things at once," observes Carolyn Forche in the *Chicago Tribune Book World:* "a sidelong reflection on the limits of the now-old new journalism; a tourist guide manque; a surrealist docu-drama; a with-

ering indictment of American foreign policy; and a poetic exploration in fear." What the book is not is a panacea—*Salvador* neither offers solutions nor supports any political regime.

While the book has been highly acclaimed for its literary merits, *Salvador* has been criticized on other grounds. *Newsweek* critic Gene Lyon, for example, allows that "Didion gets exactly right both the ghastliness and the pointlessness of the current killing frenzy in El Salvador" but then suggests that "ghastliness and pointlessness are Didion's invariable themes wherever she goes. Most readers will not get very far in this very short book without wondering whether she visited that sad and tortured place less to report than to validate the Didion world view." Others question Didion's credentials as a historian: "Let me get this straight," writes one reader in a letter to the *Los Angeles Times*. "Joan Didion spends two weeks in El Salvador and suddenly becomes a bigger expert on this country than anyone who has previously covered it? How can this be?" And Leonel Gomez Videz, former deputy director of the Agrarian Reform Institute in El Salvador, faults the book for mystifying a subject that desperately needs to be understood. "What she provides is a horrific description of atrocity: 'The dead and pieces of the dead turn up in El Salvador everywhere, every day, as taken for granted as in a nightmare, or a horror movie,'" he writes, quoting *Salvador* in the *New Republic*. "What point is Didion making? Such lurid details make for compelling prose, but in the absence of any analysis of why such murders occur, they seem at best to bolster her thesis of mindless terror and at worst to suggest a penchant for gratuitous special effects."

Juan M. Vasquez, on the other hand, defends Didion's approach. "Didion's book is not for the seekers of solutions, those who would feed the contents of El Salvador into a computer and expect a tidy answer to emerge—pressed, neat, ready for consumption," he writes in the *Los Angeles Times Book Review*. "It is, rather, for those who can subscribe to the foolishness of such notions and who can appreciate that the way some people live—the way some countries live—is not always believable, but it is all too crushingly real." Moreover, Forche maintains that "Didion achieves in this slender volume what she seldom does in her fiction: a consummate political artwork. For the otherwise powerless artist, the tenacious pursuit of reality and the past, in countries where both are constantly thrown into doubt, constitutes the most meaningful act of defiance."

One year after *Salvador* was published, Didion brought out *Democracy*, an enigmatic novel over six years in the making, which features Joan Didion, the author, in a central role. Begun, she writes in the novel, "at a time in my life when I lacked certainty, lacked even that minimum level of ego which all writers recognize as essential to the writing of novels," the book was to have been the story of a family of American colonialists whose interests were firmly entrenched in the Pacific when Hawaii was still a territory. She tells us she abandoned this story because she "lost nerve." But one of the family members continued to haunt her. That was Inez Christian, the daughter, whose fate became entwined for a time with the fate of the nation and whose story Didion ultimately tells.

In the spring of 1975—at the time the United States completed its evacuation of Vietnam and Cambodia—Inez's father is arrested for a double murder with political and racial overtones. "The Christians and their in-laws are the emblems of a misplaced confidence," according to John Lownsbrough in the *Toronto Globe and Mail*, "the flotsam and jetsam of a Manifest Destiny no longer so manifest. Their disintegration as a family in the spring of 1975 . . . is paralleled by the fall of Saigon a bit later that year and the effective disintegration of the American expansionist dream in all its ethnocentric optimism.'' Somehow, her family's tragedy enables Inez to break free of her marriage to a self-serving politician and escape to Malaysia with Jack Lovett, a free-lance C.I.A. agent and the man she has always loved. Though he dies abruptly, Inez holds on to her freedom, choosing to remain in Kuala Lumpur where she works among the Vietnamese refugees.

The story is gradually revealed in a series of short imagistic chapters that segue back and forth through time, reminding *New York Times Book Review* contributor Mary McCarthy of ''a jigsaw puzzle that is slowly being put together with a continual shuffling and re-examination of pieces still on the edges or heaped in the middle of the design.'' The confusion is heightened by Didion's curious mixing of fact and fiction. She says, for instance, that she first met Inez Christian in 1960 when they were both working for *Vogue.* Didion's employment is an easily verified matter of record, but those who go searching for substantiation of Inez's career come up with a blank. To Mary McCarthy this ''raises the question 'What are we supposed to believe here?' . . . What is a live fact—Joan Didion—doing in a work of fiction?''

Some critics argue that the author's presence is intrusive and narcissistic, attracting unnecessary attention to itself. But *New York Times* reviewer Christopher Lehmann-Haupt maintains it ''is actually not a bad strategy on Miss Didion's part—this thrust and parry with the reader, this breaking into the narrative with remarks such as . . . 'Let the reader be introduced to Joan Didion, upon whose character and doings much will depend of whatever interest these pages may have.' It creates the illusion that journalism instead of fiction is going on in the pages of 'Democracy,' and this is good because . . . Miss Didion has always been more sure-footed as a reporter.''

New York Review of Books critic Thomas R. Edwards believes *Democracy* ''finally earns its complexity of form. It is indeed 'a hard story to tell' and the presence in it of 'Joan Didion' trying to tell it is an essential part of its subject. Throughout one senses the author struggling with the moral difficulty that makes the story hard to tell—how to stop claiming what Inez finally relinquishes, 'the American exemption' from having to recognize that history records not the victory of personal wills over reality . . . but the 'undertow of having and not having, the convulsions of a world largely unaffected by the individual efforts of anyone in it.''' At the story's end, ''when the retreat from Vietnam is finished and Inez is alone in Kuala Lumpur, a penitent working with the refugees democracy has created, we feel that along with the novelist and her characters, we too have learned something about the importance of memory,'' writes Peter Collier in the *Chicago Tribune Book World.* ''We also note that Didion, who has earlier compared the writer to the aerialist, is still on the high wire, a little shaky perhaps, but in no real danger of falling.''

BIOGRAPHICAL/CRITICAL SOURCES—Books: Joan Didion, *Slouching Towards Bethlehem,* Farrar, Straus, 1968; Alfred Kazin, *Bright Book of Life: American Novelists and Storytellers from Hemingway to Mailer,* Little, Brown, 1973; *Contemporary Literary Criticism,* Gale, Volume I, 1973, Volume III, 1975, Volume VIII, 1978, Volume XIV, 1980; *Authors in the News,* Volume I, Gale, 1976; Didion, *A Book of Common Prayer,* Simon & Schuster, 1977; *Dictionary of Literary Biography,* Volume II: *American Novelists since World War II,* Gale, 1978; Didion, *The White Album,* Simon & Schuster,

1979; Mark Royden Winchell, *Joan Didion,* Twayne, 1980; *Dictionary of Literary Biography Yearbook: 1981,* Gale, 1982; Didion, *Democracy,* Simon & Schuster, 1984; Ellen G. Friedman, editor, *Joan Didion: Essays and Conversations,* Ontario Review Press, 1984.

Periodicals: *Christian Science Monitor,* May 16, 1968, September 24, 1970, July 9, 1979; *Best Sellers,* June 1, 1968, August 1, 1970; *National Review,* June 4, 1968, August 25, 1970, October 12, 1979; *New York Times Book Review,* July 21, 1968, August 9, 1970, April 3, 1977, June 17, 1979, March 13, 1983, April 22, 1984; *Book World,* July 28, 1968; *Commonweal,* November 29, 1968.

Times Literary Supplement, February 12, 1970, March 12, 1971, July 8, 1977, November 30, 1979, June 24, 1983; *New York Times,* July 21, 1970, October 30, 1972, March 21, 1977, June 5, 1979, March 11, 1983, April 6, 1984, September 14, 1984; *Harper's,* August, 1970, December, 1971; *Newsweek,* August 3, 1970, December 21, 1970, March 21, 1977, June 25, 1979, March 28, 1983, April 16, 1984; *Time,* August 10, 1970, March 28, 1977, August 20, 1979, April 4, 1983, May 7, 1984; *Saturday Review,* August 15, 1970, March 5, 1977, September 15, 1979, April, 1982; *New York Review of Books,* October 22, 1970, May 10, 1984; *New York Magazine,* February 15, 1971, June 13, 1979; *Los Angeles Times,* May 9, 1971, July 4, 1976; *Harvard Advocate,* winter, 1973; *Miami Herald,* December 2, 1973.

Ms., February, 1977; *Village Voice,* February 28, 1977, June 25, 1979; *Atlantic,* April, 1977; *San Francisco Review of Books,* May, 1977; *New Yorker,* June 20, 1977, April 18, 1983; *Sewanee Review,* fall, 1977; *New York Times Magazine,* June 10, 1979; *Chicago Tribune,* June 12, 1979; *Washington Post Book World,* June 17, 1979, March 13, 1983, April 15, 1984; *Chicago Tribune Book World,* July 1, 1979, April 3, 1983, April 15, 1984; *Detroit News,* August 12, 1979; *Nation,* September 26, 1979.

Chicago Tribune Magazine, May 2, 1982; *Los Angeles Times Book Review,* March 20, 1983; *Washington Post,* April 8, 1983; *New Republic,* June 6, 1983; *Toronto Globe and Mail,* April 28, 1984.

                              —*Sketch by Donna Olendorf*

*   *   *

DIETZ, Marjorie (Priscilla) J(ohnson) 1918-

PERSONAL: Born May 15, 1918, in New Haven, Conn.; daughter of George M. (a teacher and writer) and Marjorie (Thatcher) Johnson; married William E. Dietz, March 1, 1956 (deceased). *Education:* Attended Temple University, 1939-40.

CAREER: Flower Grower, New York City, editor, 1961-67; *Home Garden,* New York City, editor, 1967; *Plants and Gardens,* Brooklyn, N.Y., associate editor, 1968—.

WRITINGS: Concise Encyclopedia of Favorite Flowering Shrubs, Doubleday, 1963; *Concise Encyclopedia of Favorite Wildflowers,* Doubleday, 1965; *Landscaping and the Small Garden,* Doubleday, 1973.

Editor: Roy E. Biles, *Complete Illustrated Book of Garden Magic,* J. G. Ferguson, 1969; *Ten Thousand Garden Questions Answered,* 3rd edition (Dietz was not associated with earlier editions), Doubleday, 1974, 4th edition, 1982; *The Complete Guide to Successful Gardening,* W. H. Smith, 1979; Montague Free, *All about House Plants: Their Selection, Culture, and*

Propagation and How to Use Them for Decorative Effect, Doubleday, 1979; *Growing Food and Flowers: Your Questions Answered,* Doubleday, 1981; F. A. Boddy, *Garden Flowers,* Floraprint, 1981; Leslie Johns, *Patio and Window Box Gardening,* Floraprint, 1981; Johns, *Indoor Gardening,* Floraprint, 1981; Benjamin Levell, *Greenhouse Gardening,* Floraprint, 1981; Keith Mossman, *Vegetable Growing,* Floraprint, 1981; Violet Stevenson, *Gardening for Beginners,* Floraprint, 1981; Brian Walkden, *Feeding, Pruning, and Pest Control,* Floraprint, 1981; Roy Genders, *Fruit Growing,* Floraprint, 1982.

Contributor to magazines.†

*   *   *

DILLARD, J(oey) L(ee)   1924-

PERSONAL: Born June 26, 1924, in Grand Saline, Tex.; son of Marvin L. (a wholesaler of produce) and Thelma (Aly) Dillard; married Jane Reed Montgomery, December 28, 1958 (divorced, 1961); married Margie Ivey (an editor), December 22, 1972 (died June 7, 1981); children: (first marriage) Kenneth Joseph. *Education:* Southern Methodist University, B.A. (with highest honors), 1946, M.A., 1951; University of Texas, Ph.D., 1956. *Politics:* Liberal Democrat. *Religion:* Episcopalian. *Office:* Department of Language Arts, Northwestern State University, Natchitoches, La. 71497.

CAREER: Southern Methodist University, Dallas, Tex., instructor in English, 1949-51; Texas College of Arts and Industries (now Texas A & I University), Kingsville, associate professor of English, 1955-59; Inter-American University, San German, Puerto Rico, Teacher of English to Speakers of Other Languages (TESOL) program, director, 1959-60; U.S. Agency for International Development, Yaounde, Cameroon, descriptive linguist, 1963-64; Lamar State College of Technology (now Lamar University), Beaumont, Tex., associate professor of English, 1965-66; Trinity College, Washington, D.C., lecturer in dialectology, 1966-67; Universite Officielle de Bujumbura, Bujumbura, Burundi, Fulbright lecturer in TESOL program, 1967-68; Yeshiva University, Ferkauf Graduate School of Humanities and Social Sciences, New York, N.Y., visiting lecturer in linguistics, 1968-71; Northwestern State University of Louisiana, Natchitoches, 1975—, began as assistant professor, currently professor of English.

Visiting professor of sociolinguistics, Georgetown University, 1967; visiting professor of English, State University of New York College at Potsdam, summer, 1968; visiting professor of linguistics, University of Southern California, summer, 1969, and Linguistics Institute, University of North Carolina, summer, 1972. Fulbright lecturer, Universidad Central del Ecuador, Quito, Ecuador, 1959-60. Director of urban language study for District of Columbia, 1966-67. *Military service:* U.S. Navy, 1943-45.

MEMBER: American Name Society, Linguistic Society of America, Phi Beta Kappa.

AWARDS, HONORS: American Council of Learned Societies grant, University of Texas, summer, 1960.

WRITINGS: (With W. P. Lehmann) *The Alliteration of the Edda,* Department of Germanic Languages, University of Texas, 1954; *Afro-American Vehicle and Other Names,* Institute of Caribbean Studies, 1965; (contributor) E. B. Atwood and A. A. Hill, editors, *Language, Literature, and Culture of the Middle Ages and Later,* University of Texas at Austin, 1969.

(Contributor) John Szwed and Norman Whitten, editors, *Afro-American Anthropology: Current Perspectives,* Free Press, 1970; (contributor) Dell Hymes, editor, *Pidginization and Creolization of Language,* Cambridge University Press, 1971; *Black English: Its History and Usage in the United States,* Random House, 1972; *All-American English,* Random House, 1975; (editor) *Perspectives on Black English,* Mouton, 1975; *American Talk: Where Our Words Came From,* Random House, 1976; *Lexicon of Black English,* Seabury, 1977.

(Editor) *Perspectives on American English,* Mouton, 1980; (with Albert Marckwardt) *American English,* Oxford University Press, 1981; *Toward a Social History of American English,* De Gruyter, 1985.

Contributor to *Linguistic-Cultural Differences and American Education,* 1969. Contributor of about thirty articles and reviews to academic journals, including *Language Learning, Caribbean Studies, Names,* and *Nueva Revista.*

WORK IN PROGRESS: How to Score with English; research on maritime contact languages, history of American English, and Afro-American language and culture.

*   *   *

DINITZ, Simon   1926-

PERSONAL: Born October 29, 1926, in New York, N.Y.; son of Morris and Dinah (Schulman) Dinitz; married Mildred H. Stern, August 20, 1949; children: Jeffrey, Thea, Risa. *Education:* Vanderbilt University, B.A. (magna cum laude), 1947; University of Wisconsin, M.A., 1949, Ph.D., 1951. *Politics:* Democratic. *Religion:* Jewish. *Home:* 298 North Cassady, Columbus, Ohio 43209. *Office:* Department of Sociology, Ohio State University, Columbus, Ohio 43210.

CAREER: Ohio State University, Columbus, instructor, 1951-55, assistant professor, 1956-59, associate professor, 1959-63, professor of sociology, 1963—, research associate in psychiatry, 1957-74, chairman of Research Council, 1969-70, senior fellow, Academy for Contemporary Problems, 1975—. Visiting professor for individual terms at University of Southern California, 1968, University of Wisconsin, 1969, University of Tel Aviv, 1970, 1971, 1973, University of South Florida, 1980, 1981, and University of Haifa, 1982; George J. Beto Visiting Professor of Criminal Justice, Sam Houston State University, 1983. Summer lecturer, University of Wisconsin, 1951, 1952. Member of Columbus Urban Community Task Force, 1969, and Ohio Governor's Task Force on Corrections, 1971. Member of international advisory board, University of Tel Aviv, 1970—. Consultant and advisor to numerous symposia and public and private groups, including United Nations Social Defence Research Institute, Ohio Penal Industries, Eleventh Congress on Crime Prevention and Treatment of Offenders, Buckeyes Boys' Ranch, and Columbus Community Mental Health Center. Editorial consultant, Ohio State University Press, 1978—. *Military service:* U.S. Navy, 1945-46.

MEMBER: American Sociological Association (council member of section on criminology, 1968-71), American Society of Criminology (president, 1970-71), American Psychopathological Association, Society for the Study of Social Problems, Institute of Social and Behavioral Pathology, American Correctional Association, National Council on Crime and Delinquency, Academy of Criminal Justice Sciences, American Association of University Professors, American Association of Professors for Peace in the Middle East, North Central Sociological Association (president, 1982-83), Ohio Correction Association, Ohio Valley Sociological Association (vice-president, 1968-69), Phi Beta Kappa (honorary member), Phi Kappa Phi (honorary member).

AWARDS, HONORS: National Institute of Mental Health research grants, 1958-59, 1959-61, 1963-66, 1966-70; with Benjamin Pasamanick and Frank Scarpitti, Hofheimer Prize for research from American Psychiatric Association, 1967, for *Schizophrenics in the Community: An Experiment in the Prevention of Hospitalization;* State of Ohio research grants, 1969-70, 1970-72; awards from Ohio State University, 1969-70, 1970, 1979; Sutherland Award from American Society of Criminology, 1974; Lilly endowment, 1975-78, 1979-80; Nemzer Award, 1980; *Defensor Pacem* medal from Sam Houston State University, 1983; teaching awards from various universities.

WRITINGS: (With Russell Dynes, Alfred C. Clarke, and Iwao Ishino) *Social Problems: Dissensus and Deviation,* Oxford University Press, 1964; (with Benjamin Pasamanick and Frank Scarpitti) *Schizophrenics in the Community: An Experiment in Prevention of Hospitalization,* Appleton-Century-Crofts, 1967; (editor with Reckless) *Critical Issues in the Study of Crime: A Book of Readings,* W. C. Brown, 1968; (with Shirley Angrist, Mark Lefton, and Pasamanick) *Women after Treatment: A Comparison of Treated Mental Patients and Their Normal Neighbors,* Appleton-Century-Crofts, 1968; (with Clarke and Dynes) *Deviance: Studies in the Process of Stigmatization and Societal Reaction,* Oxford University Press, 1969, 2nd edition, 1975.

(With Reckless) *Experimenting with Delinquency Prevention,* Ohio State University Press, 1972; (with Reckless) *The Prevention of Delinquency: An Experiment,* Ohio State University Press, 1972; (with Pasamanick and Ann I. Davis) *Schizophrenics in the New Custodial Community,* Ohio State University Press, 1974; (with Ferracuti and Acosta de Brenes) *Delinquents and Nondelinquents in the Puerto Rico Slum Culture,* Ohio State University Press, 1975; (with Clarke and Dynes) *Deviance: Studies in Definition, Management and Treatment,* Oxford University Press, 2nd edition, 1975; (with Bartollas and Miller) *Juvenile Victimization: The Institutional Paradox,* Halsted, 1976; (with John P. Conrad) *In Fear of Each Other,* Lexington Books, 1977; (with Joseph E. Scott) *Criminal Justice Planning,* Praeger, 1977; (with Hamparian, Schuster, and Conrad) *The Violent Few,* Lexington Books, 1978; (with Steven Van Dine and Conrad) *Restraining the Wicked: The Incapacitation of the Dangerous Criminal,* Lexington Books, 1979; (with Stuart J. Miller and Conrad) *Careers of the Violent: The Dangerous Offender and Criminal Justice,* Lexington Books, 1982.

Contributor: Charles L. Newman and Reckless, editors, *Interdisciplinary Problems of Criminology: Papers of the American Society of Criminology,* American Society of Criminology, 1965; Paul Hoch and Joseph Zubin, editors, *Psychopathology of Schizophrenia,* Grune, 1966; Alfred M. Freedman and Zubin, editors, *The Psychopathology of Adolescence,* Grune, 1970; Reckless, *American Criminology: New Directions,* Appleton-Century-Crofts, 1973; Paul M. Roman and Harrison M. Trice, editors, *Sociological Perspectives on Community Mental Health,* F. A. Davis, 1974; Israel Drapkin and Emilio Viano, editors, *Victimology: A New Focus,* Volume V, Lexington Books, 1974.

Viano, editor, *Victims and Society,* Visage Press, 1976; S. Landu and L. Sebba, editors, *Criminology in Perspective: Essays in Honor of Israel Drapkin,* Lexington Books, 1977; Harry

E. Allen and Nancy J. Beran, *Reform in Corrections,* Praeger, 1977; William Curry, Charles Petty, and Louis McGarry, editors, *Modern Legal Medicine, Psychiatry and Forensic Science,* F. A. Davis, 1980; David Shichor and Delos Kelly, *Critical Issues in Juvenile Delinquency,* Lexington Books, 1980; Cleon Faust and D. Robert Webster, *An Anatomy of Criminal Justice,* Lexington Books, 1980; Daniel J. Safer, *School Programs for Disruptive Adolescents,* University Park Press, 1982; Herbert Edelhertz and Thomas Overcast, *White Collar Crime: An Agenda for Research,* Lexington Books, 1982; S. Giora Shoham, editor, *The Many Faces of Crime and Deviance,* Sheridan, 1983; Gordan Whitaker and Charles Phillips, editors, *Evaluating Performance of Criminal Justice Agencies,* Sage Publications, 1983.

Also author of research reports. Contributor of 150 articles and reviews to journals. Editor, *Criminologica* (now *Criminology*), 1966-69; member of national editorial board, *Excerpta Criminologica,* 1966-68; associate editor, *American Sociological Review,* 1968-71, *Justice Quarterly,* 1983—; member of editorial board, *Journal of Criminal Law and Criminology,* 1972—; editorial consultant, *Journal of Research in Crime and Delinquency,* 1977—.

BIOGRAPHICAL/CRITICAL SOURCES: Chicago Tribune, February 18, 1968; Israel Barak-Glantz and C. Ronald Huff, *The Mad, the Bad and the Different: Essays in Honor of Simon Dinitz,* Lexington Books, 1981.

*　*　*

DOBBS, Farrell   1907-1983

PERSONAL: Born July 25, 1907, in Queen City, Mo.; died October 31, 1983, in Pinole, Calif.; son of Isaac T. (a mechanic) and Ora L. (Smith) Dobbs; married Marvel S. Scholl (a writer), April 23, 1927; children: Carol Elinor (Mrs. Clifton DeBerry), Mary Lou (Mrs. Paul Montauk), Sharon Buch. *Education:* Educated in public schools of Minneapolis, Minn. *Politics:* Marxist/Socialist. *Religion:* None. *Office:* Pathfinder Press, 410 West St., New York, N.Y. 10014. *Agent:* George Weissman, Monad Press, 410 West St., New York, N.Y. 10014.

CAREER: Strutwear Knitting Co., Minneapolis, Minn., dyer, 1925; reaper and thresher in harvest fields of North Dakota, 1926; Western Electric Co., Minnesota, Iowa, and Nebraska, telephone central office equipment installer, 1926-29, foreman of installation crew, 1930-31, planning engineer, 1931-32; Pittsburgh Coal Co., Minneapolis, Minn., yardman, 1933-34; International Brotherhood of Teamsters, General Drivers local unions 574 and 544, Minneapolis, Minn., secretary-treasurer, 1934-38; Socialist Workers Party, New York City, national labor secretary, 1940-43; *Militant,* New York City, editor, 1943-48; Socialist Workers Party, national chairman, 1949-53, national secretary, 1953-72; was also affiliated with Monad Press, New York City.

WRITINGS—All published by Monad: *Teamster Rebellion,* 1972; *Teamster Power,* 1973; *Teamster Politics,* 1975. Also author of *Teamster Bureaucracy,* Monad.

WORK IN PROGRESS: Volume I of a three-volume series, *A History of the Socialist Workers Party.*

SIDELIGHTS: Farrell Dobbs, who was once labeled by Jimmy Hoffa the ''architect'' of the modern Teamster union, began his career as a laborer in Minnesota, Iowa, and Nebraska before he became associated with Teamster politics as a representative of long-distance truck drivers. As a union spokesman, Dobbs "was a principal leader of a long and bitter truckers' strike in Minneapolis in 1934, attended by violence and a call-up of the National Guard," according to Wolfgang Saxon in his *New York Times* obituary of Dobbs.

Continued Saxon: "Dobbs left the teamsters in 1939 to become national labor secretary of the Socialist Workers Party, which had been founded in 1928. He drew national attention in 1941 when he and 17 other party leaders were convicted in Federal Court in Minneapolis of advocating the overthrow of the government by force and violence [in violation of the Smith Act of 1940]. He served a 16-month prison term in Sandstone Federal Prison, Minnesota." Between 1948 and 1960, Dobbs was the Socialist Workers Party candidate in four Presidential elections.

OBITUARIES: Los Angeles Times, November 3, 1983; *New York Times,* November 3, 1983; *Newsweek,* November 14, 1983.†

*　　*　　*

DOCKRELL, William Bryan   1929-

PERSONAL: Born January 12, 1929, in Manchester, England; son of James (an electrical engineer) and Elizabeth (Slater) Dockrell; married Ann Cirilla (a psychologist), June 12, 1954; children: Julia, Helen, Richard, Catherine, Martin, Mark. *Education:* University of Manchester, B.A., 1950; University of Edinburgh, M.Ed., 1952; University of Chicago, Ph.D., 1963. *Home:* The Coachhouse, Inveresk, Musselburgh, Midlothian, Scotland. *Office:* Scottish Council for Research in Education, 15 St. John St., Edinburgh, Scotland.

CAREER: Education Authority, Manchester, England, psychologist, 1955-58; University of Alberta, Edmonton, assistant professor of educational psychology, 1958-67; Ontario Institute for Studies in Education, Toronto, professor of special education, 1967-71; Scottish Council for Research in Education, Edinburgh, Scotland, director, 1971—. *Military service:* British Army, 1956-57.

MEMBER: American Psychological Association, American Educational Research Association, British Psychological Association.

AWARDS, HONORS: Senior Imperial Relations fellow, London, 1966-67; fellow, Educational Institute of Scotland, 1980.

WRITINGS: (Editor) *On Intelligence,* Methuen, 1971; (with P. M. Broadfoot) *Pupils in Profile,* Hodder & Stoughton, 1977; (editor with W. Dunn and A. Milne) *Special Education in Scotland,* Scottish Council for Research in Education, 1978; (editor with D. Hamilton) *Rethinking Educational Research,* Hodder & Stoughton, 1980; (with H. D. Black) *Diagnostic Assessment in Secondary Schools,* Hodder & Stoughton, 1982; (with Hamilton) *Nuevas Reflexions sobre la investigacion educativa,* Narcea (Madrid), 1983; *An Attitude of Mind,* Scottish Council for Research in Education, 1984.

*　　*　　*

DONLEY, Marshall O(wen), Jr.   1932-

PERSONAL: Born March 20, 1932, in Christiana, Pa.; son of Marshall Owen (a radio-television shop owner) and Edna (Detwiler) Donley; married Margaret T. Reagan, September 18, 1971; children: Marshall Owen III, Susan Reagan. *Education:*

Pennsylvania State University, B.A., 1954; University of Southern California, graduate study, 1954-55; American University, M.A., 1965, Ph.D., 1971. *Politics:* Democrat. *Religion:* Protestant. *Home:* 10365 May Wind Court, Columbia Md. 21044. *Office:* 1625 L St. N.W., Washington, D.C. 20036.

CAREER: Lancaster Intelligencer Journal, Lancaster, Pa., reporter, 1950-52; writer for WGAL-Radio and Television, Lancaster, Pa., 1953; National Education Association, Washington, D.C., assistant editor of *Today's Education,* 1958-70, editor of *NEA Reporter,* 1970-79; Airline Pilots Association, Washington, D.C., director of publications and communications, 1980-81; editor of *The Public Employee,* American Federation of State, County, and Municipal Employees, AFL-CIO, 1981—. Instructor at State University of New York at Buffalo, summers, 1964-65. Has worked as a free-lance musician. *Military service:* U.S. Naval Reserve, 1949-54; U.S. Army, linguist for Security Agency, 1955-58.

MEMBER: Educational Press Association (president of local chapter, 1962), National Education Association (staff organization president, 1961; management organization board member, 1976-77), Phi Kappa Phi, Phi Delta Kappa, Phi Sigma Kappa, Sigma Delta Chi.

AWARDS, HONORS: More than thirty national awards from Educational Press Association and International Labor Communication Association.

WRITINGS: Handbook for Education Editors, World Confederation of Organizations of the Teaching Profession, 1969; *NEA Launches a New Decade of Action,* National Education Association, 1970; *NEA: Vital Force for Action,* National Education Association, 1971; *Power to the Teacher: How America's Educators Became Miliant,* Indiana University Press, 1976; *The Future of Teacher Power in America,* Phi Delta Kappa, 1977. Contributor to professional journals and newspapers.

WORK IN PROGRESS: A History of American Public Employees; two novels.

SIDELIGHTS: Marshall O. Donley, Jr., writes: "Most of my writing has been related to my interest in the history of education, specifically the history of the organization of teachers in the United States into teacher unions and associations. My trips to other countries, e.g., the Soviet Union, have been tied to an interest in the teaching profession in those nations. As a linguist, I have been interested in Korean, French, and Russian. . . ."

AVOCATIONAL INTERESTS: Classical music (has played oboe), eighteenth-century British fiction, contemporary science fiction.

*　　*　　*

DORNER, Peter Paul   1925-

PERSONAL: Born January 13, 1925, in Luxemburg, Wis.; son of Peter (a farmer) and Monica (Altmann) Dorner; married Lois Hartnig, December 26, 1950; children: Cathy, Greg, Paul, Sara, Carrie. *Education:* University of Wisconsin, B.S., 1951; University of Tennessee, M.S., 1953; Harvard University, Ph.D., 1959. *Home:* 541 Woodside Ter., Madison, Wis. 53711. *Office:* International Studies and Programs, University of Wisconsin, Madison, Wis. 53706.

CAREER: Harvard University, Cambridge, Mass., instructor in agricultural economics and economics, 1957-58; University of Wisconsin—Madison, professor of agricultural economics, beginning 1959, dean of international studies and programs, 1980—. Professor of agricultural economics, University of Chile, Santiago, 1963-65. Senior staff economist, Council of Economic Advisors, Washington, D.C., 1967-68. Consultant to the Commission on Rights, Liberties, and Responsibilities of the American Indians, AID Washington, D.C. and field missions in Latin America, President's Panel on the World Food Supply, United Nations and UNDP, Harvard Development Advisory Service in Ethiopia, and U.S. Department of Labor. *Milit~~ ~~ervice:* U.S. Army, Pacific Theater, 1944-46.

MEMBER: International Association of Agricultural Economists, American Economic Association, American Agricultural Economic Association, Association for Evolutionary Economics.

WRITINGS: (Editor and contributor) *Land Reform in Latin America: Issues and Cases,* University of Wisconsin, 1971; *Land Reform and Economic Development,* Penguin, 1972; (editor and contributor) *Cooperative and Commune: Group Farming in the Economic Development of Agriculture,* University of Wisconsin Press, 1977; (co-editor and contributor) *Resources and Development: Natural Resource Policies and Economic Development in an Interdependent World,* University of Wisconsin Press, 1980; (editor and contributor) *World without War: Political and Institutional Challenges,* University of Wisconsin—Madison, 1984.

Contributor of research articles to *Yale Review, Journal of Land Economics, Inter-American Economic Affairs, American Journal of Agricultural Economics,* and other professional journals; also contributor of book reviews to periodicals. Member of editorial council, *Land Economics,* 1961—, and *American Journal of Agricultural Economics,* 1968-71.

WORK IN PROGRESS: Research on economic development, international interdependence, security through cooperation.

*   *   *

DORSET, Ruth
    See ROSS, W(illiam) E(dward) D(aniel)

*   *   *

DOUGLAS, George H(alsey)   **1934-**

PERSONAL: Born January 9, 1934, in East Orange, N.J.; son of Halsey M. (a journalist) and Harriet (Goldbach) Douglas; married Rosalind Braun (an artist), June 19, 1961; children: Philip. *Education:* Lafayette College, A.B., 1956; Columbia University, M.A., 1966; University of Illinois, Ph.D., 1968. *Home:* 1514 Grandview, Champaign, Ill. 61820. *Office:* Department of English, English Building, University of Illinois, 608 South Wright St., Urbana, Ill. 61801.

CAREER: Bell Telephone Laboratories, Whippany, N.J., technical writer, 1958-59; University of Illinois at Urbana-Champaign, Urbana, technical writer at Agricultural Experiment Station, 1961-66, instructor, 1966-68, assistant professor, 1968-77, associate professor of English, 1977—.

MEMBER: Modern Language Association of America, American Society for Aesthetics, American Studies Association, Popular Culture Association.

WRITINGS: H. L. Mencken: Critic of American Life, Archon Books, 1978; *Rail City: Chicago U.S.A.,* Howell-North Books,

1981; *Edmund Wilson's America,* University Press of Kentucky, 1983; *Skyscraper Odyssey,* Hastings House, 1984. Contributor to numerous academic journals and magazines. `

WORK IN PROGRESS: A book on the early history of radio broadcasting in the U.S., entitled *Cat's Whisker;* a book on prominent American women of the 1920s.

SIDELIGHTS: George H. Douglas writes: "I am mainly interested in American culture and American life. My chief concerns are with shifts in style and ways of doing things. I write both nostalgically and critically about the American past and its relation to the present. My great interest is popular culture—railroads, local history, old-time radio, movies, maps, printing, ferry boats, and maritime history."

*   *   *

DOUGLAS, Gregory A.
    See CANTOR, Eli

*   *   *

DOUGLASS, Amanda Hart
    See WALLMANN, Jeffrey M(iner)

*   *   *

DOYLE, Don H(arrison)   **1946-**

PERSONAL: Born February 23, 1946, in Long Beach, Calif.; son of Leo Walter (a physician) and Barbara (Ferron) Doyle; married Marilyn Dunn (a health administrator), 1967; children: Caroline Ruth, Kelly Lynn. *Education:* University of California, Davis, B.A., 1968; Northwestern University, Ph.D., 1973. *Home:* 3942 Woodlawn Dr., Nashville, Tenn. 37205. *Office:* Department of History, Vanderbilt University, Nashville, Tenn. 37235.

CAREER: University of Michigan, Dearborn, assistant professor of history, 1971-74; Vanderbilt University, Nashville, Tenn., assistant professor, 1974-79, associate professor of history, 1979—.

MEMBER: Organization of American Historians, Southern Historical Association.

AWARDS, HONORS: Woodrow Wilson fellowship, 1970; American Philosophical Society grant, 1977-78; American Council of Learned Societies grant, 1978, fellow, 1982-83; National Endowment for the Humanities research grant, 1980-84; Charles Warren Center fellow, 1982-83.

WRITINGS: The Social Order of a Frontier Community: Jacksonville, Illinois, 1825-70, University of Illinois Press, 1978; (contributor) Vernon Burton and Robert C. McMath, editors, *Southern Communities in the Nineteenth Century,* Greenwood Press, 1979; *Nashville in the New South,* University of Tennessee Press, 1985; *Nashville since the 1920s,* University of Tennessee Press, 1985.

WORK IN PROGRESS: New Men, New Cities, New South: Atlanta, Nashville, Charleston, Mobile, 1865-1915.

SIDELIGHTS: Don H. Doyle told *CA:* "My interest in frontier community building derived to a large extent from my family's background in California, which goes back to the Gold Rush days. Jacksonville's founding and its struggle for urban success seems to embody a fundamental recurring theme in American culture—the effort to build a community amid a society that exalts individualism, mobility, egalitarianism. My current work in the South explores the rise of an urban middle class after the Civil War.''

* * *

DRATH, Viola Herms 1926-

PERSONAL: Born February 8, 1926, in Duesseldorf, Germany (now West Germany); came to the United States in 1947, naturalized citizen, 1949; daughter of Ernst (a jurist and banker) and Annemarie Herms; married Francis S. Drath (a professor), February 5, 1947; children; Constance Drath Dwyer, Francesca. *Education:* Attended Leipzig Art Academy; University of Nebraska, M.A., 1952. *Politics:* Independent. *Religion:* ''In favor, but not practising.'' *Home and office:* 3206 Q St. N.W., Washington, D.C. 20007.

CAREER: Peter Publications, editor, 1952-65; correspondent, *Madame* magazine, 1956—; free-lance contributor to national magazines, 1965-70; *Vorwaerts*, Bonn, West Germany, White House correspondent, 1970-75; free-lance writer for German and U.S. periodicals, 1975—; American University, Washington, D.C., lecturer, 1976—. Guest lecturer at University of Southern California, University of Nebraska, American University, and Washington College, Chestertown, Md. Moderator of television programs for University of Nebraska educational television network and for National Education Television Council for Higher Education.

MEMBER: International P.E.N., State Department Correspondents Association, National Press Club, Altrusa, Lincoln Artists' Guild (president, 1958-60), Young Women's Christian Association (Lincoln; member of board of directors, 1963-67).

WRITINGS: Leb Wohl, Isabell (three-act play; title means ''Farewell, Isabel''; first produced in Straubing, Germany, at Municipal Theatre, February, 1946), Desch, 1947; *Kein Verlass auf eine Frau* (three-act play; title means ''No Reliance upon a Woman''; first produced in Munich, Germany, at Junge Buehne, April, 1948), Menge, 1948; (with Harold von Hofe) *Kultur und Alltag* (title means ''Culture and Everyday''), Scribner, 1973; *Willy Brandt: Prisoner of His Past* (biography), Chilton, 1975; *Germany in World Politics*, Cyrco Press, 1979.

Textbooks: *Reporter in Deutschland: A Reader for Beginners,* Holt, 1959; *Typisch deutsch?* (title means ''Typically German?''), Holt, 1961, 2nd edition, 1969; *The Complicated Germans*, Ginn, 1967; (editor) Kurt Hoffman, Heinz Pauck and Guenter Neumann, *Wir Wunderkinder* (filmscript; title means ''Aren't We Wonderful''), Ginn, 1969; *Was Wollen die Deutschen?* (title means ''What Do the German's Want?''), Macmillan, 1970; *Engagement und Provokation* (anthology; title means ''Commitment and Provocation''), Macmillan, 1973; (with Jack Moeller) *Noch dazu!*, Houghton Mifflin, 1980. Contributor of articles and reviews to journals in the United States and abroad, including *Commentary, Harper's, National Observer, Prairie Schooner,* and *Chicago Tribune.*

WORK IN PROGRESS: Hollywood East (tentative title), a novel about the power structure of Washington, D.C.

SIDELIGHTS: Viola Herms Drath writes: ''Being born in Germany and married to an American my interests focus basically on German-American relations, their political and cultural ramifications.''

BIOGRAPHICAL/CRITICAL SOURCES: Lincoln Journal, September 17, 1965, February 23, 1976; *Women's Wear Daily,* December 11, 1975; *Philadelphia Bulletin,* February 9, 1976.†

DRUCKER, Malka 1945-

PERSONAL: Born March 14, 1945, in Tucson, Ariz.; daughter of William Treiber (a clothing manufacturer) and Francine (a writer; maiden name, Epstein) Chermak; married Steven Drucker (a certified public accountant), August 20, 1966; children: Ivan, Max. *Education:* University of California, Los Angeles, B.A., 1967; University of Southern California, teaching credential, 1968. *Home:* 863 Manning Ave., Los Angeles, Calif. 90024. *Agent:* Curtis Brown Ltd., 575 Madison Ave., New York, N.Y. 10022.

CAREER: Writer, 1975—.

MEMBER: Society of Children's Book Writers, Association of Jewish Librarians, P.E.N., California Council on Literature for Children and Young People.

AWARDS, HONORS: Jewish Book Award nominations, 1982, for *Passover: A Season of Freedom,* 1984, for *Shabbat: A Peaceful Island;* award for excellence in a series from Southern California Council on Literature for Children and Young People, 1982, for ''Jewish Holidays'' series.

WRITINGS—Published by Holiday House, except as indicated: (With Tom Seaver) *Tom Seaver: Portrait of a Pitcher* (juvenile; *Sports Illustrated* Book-of-the-Month Club alternate selection), 1978; *The George Foster Story* (juvenile), 1979; (with Elizabeth James) *Series TV: How a Television Show Is Made*, Clarion, 1983.

''Jewish Holidays'' series: *Hanukkah: Eight Nights, Eight Lights,* 1980; *Passover: A Season of Freedom,* 1981; *Rosh Hashanah and Yom Kippur,* 1981; *Sukkot: A Time to Rejoice,* 1982; *Shabbat: A Peaceful Island,* 1983; *Celebrating Life: Jewish Rites of Passage,* 1984.

WORK IN PROGRESS: Eliezer Ben-Yehuda: The Reviver of Hebrew, for Dutton.

SIDELIGHTS: A critic for the *New York Times Book Review* praised Malka Drucker's biography of Tom Seaver for providing the reader with insights into Seaver's home life and the adjustments that the family of a major league baseball player must make. Although *Tom Seaver: Portrait of a Pitcher* does recount some of Seaver's better games and keeps track of the baseball records that Seaver has set, the same reviewer felt that ''this is a fairly flat portrait. . . . There is more both to the athlete and to the man than is recounted here.''

The majority of reviews, however, were positive. A commentator for *Booklist* described *Tom Seaver* as an ''exciting sports biography'' filled with fascinating anecdotes. ''The play-by-play accounts of key moments in Seaver's career are well done—not boringly detailed—while most of the author's fictionalization is realistic enough not to threaten the book's credibility,'' he observed.

Describing the genesis of her writing career for *CA*, Malka Drucker writes: ''When I was fourteen, my pet parakeet died and I was miserable. I picked up my old diary, long abandoned, and wrote of my grief. The words healed me, and I developed a new respect for the power I possessed with words. Also, both my parents are writers. Can anyone influence me more strongly?

''I like to write about those things that have interested me since childhood . . . going to baseball games and celebrating Jewish holidays are both vivid, sweet memories for me. When you're a Jewish kid in New York, baseball and religious ceremonies are the most important things in your life, so why not write about them?'' She explains her purpose in writing *Tom Seaver:* "This was not to be a book about baseball; it was to be about a man who happened to play the game and what the game meant to him. I sympathize with the struggle every child has in making sense of the world. I remember my own and it serves as my creative mine.''

BIOGRAPHICAL/CRITICAL SOURCES: New York Times Book Review, April 30, 1978; *Kirkus Reviews,* June 1, 1978; *Best Sellers,* June, 1978; *Booklist,* July 1, 1978.

* * *

DRUMMOND, Maldwin Andrew Cyril   1932-

PERSONAL: Born April 30, 1932, in London, England; son of Cyril Augustus (a soldier) and Mildred (Humphreys) Drummond; married Susan Cayley, August 21, 1955; married second wife, Gillian Turner Laing; children: (first marriage) Frederica, Annabella; (second marriage) Aldred. *Education:* Attended Royal Agricultural College; University of Southampton, certificate in environmental science (with distinction), 1972. *Religion:* Church of England. *Home and office:* Manor of Cadland, Fawley, Southampton, England. *Agent:* Anthony Sheil Associates Ltd., 2-3 Morwell St., London WC1B 3AR, England.

CAREER: Manor of Cadland, Cadland Farms, Fawley, England, owner, 1956—. Director of Newtown Oyster Co. and Rothesay Seafoods; senior partner of Inland and Waterside Planners. Member of New Forest District Council, 1958-67, Hampshire County Council, 1967-75, and Southampton Harbour Board, 1967-73; chairman of Hamble River Management Committee, 1973-75; verderer of New Forest, 1961—. Member of council of Maritime Trust (vice-chairman, 1971-78; chairman, 1978—); member of management committee of Royal National Life-Boat Institution, 1971—. *Military service:* British Army, Rifle Brigade, 1950-52, Queen's Royal Rifles, 1952-64; became captain.

MEMBER: Geologist Association, Palaeontographical Association, Marine Biological Association, Brackish Water Association, Solent Protection Society (chairman, 1969-71), Society for Environmental Improvement (member of council, 1974—), Royal Yacht Squadron, Royal Cruising Club, Royal Ocean Racing Club.

WRITINGS: (Editor) *The Secrets of George Smith, Fisherman* (self-illustrated), Ilex Press, 1973; *Conflicts in an Estuary,* Ilex Press, 1973; (editor) *Esturine Pollution,* University of Southampton Press, 1974; *Tall Ships,* Angus & Robertson, 1976; *Salt-Water Palaces,* Debrett's Peerage, 1979; (with Paul Rodhouse) *The Yachtman's Naturalist,* Angus & Robertson, 1980; *The Riddle,* Nautical Books, 1985. Yachting correspondent for *Field,* 1964-69.

WORK IN PROGRESS: A novel concerning sailing, curses, and the West Coast of Scotland.

SIDELIGHTS: Maldwin Andrew Cyril Drummond writes briefly: "The sea provides my main motivation, though I am interested and worried about the effects of man on other environments. My books have been devoted to salt water.''

DUCORNET, Erica   1943-
(Rikki; Rikki Ducornet)

PERSONAL: Born April 19, 1943, in Canton, N.Y.; daughter of Gerard and Muriel De Gre; married Guy Ducornet (a painter and potter); children: Jean-Yves. *Education:* Bard College, B.A., 1962. *Home:* 49260 Le Puy-Notre Dame, Maine-et-Loire, France.

CAREER: Writer and illustrator. Drawings have been exhibited widely, notably in Czechoslovakia, 1966, Museum of West Berlin, 1969, 1972, Museum of Lille (France), 1973, Museum of Fine Arts (Belgium), 1974, International Surrealist Exhibition, Chicago, 1977, Museo de Bellas Artes (Mexico), 1979, Centre Culturel Francaise (Sweden), 1982, and Centre Culturel du Mexicaine, (Paris), 1984. With husband, creator of game "Le Nouveau Jeu de Loto,'' 1975.

WRITINGS—Fiction: (Adapter and illustrator) D'Aulnoy, *The Blue Bird* (juvenile), Knopf, 1970; (with husband, Guy Ducornet) *Shazira Shazam and the Devil* (juvenile; Junior Literary Guild Selection), Prentice-Hall, 1970; (under name Rikki) *The Butcher's Tales,* Intermedia, 1978; (under name Rikki Ducornet) *The Stain* (novel), Grove, 1984.

Poetry; self-illustrated; under name Rikki: *From the Star Chamber,* Fiddlehead, 1974; *Wild Geraniums,* Actual Size Press, 1975; *Weird Sisters,* Intermedia, 1976; *Knife Notebook,* Fiddlehead, 1977; *The Illustrated Universe,* Aya Press, 1978.

Illustrator: Paris Leary and Muriel De Gre, *The Jack Spratt Cookbook,* Doubleday, 1965; G. Ducornet, *Silex de l'avenir* (poems), Pierre Jean Oswald, 1966; Mme. Leprince de Beaumont, *Beauty and the Beast* (translated from the French by P. H. Muir), Knopf, 1968; G. Ducornet, *Trophees en selle* (poems), Traces, 1970; (under name Rikki; with G. Ducornet) *Bouche a bouche* (erotic game book), Soror, 1975; (under name Rikki) Susan Musgrave, *Gullband,* J. J. Douglas, 1975; (under name Rikki) Matt Cohen, *The Leaves of Louise,* McClelland & Stewart, 1978; Robert Coover, *Spanking the Maid,* Bruccoli Clark, 1981; *Tlon, Vqbar, Orbis Tertius,* The Porcupine's Quill, 1983.

Work represented in anthologies, including: *The Stonewall Anthology,* University of Iowa Press, 1974, *Minute Fictions,* 1976, 1977, *La Domaine internationale du surrealisme,* Le Puits de l'Ermite, 1978, *Magic Realism,* Aya Press, 1980, *Illusion I,* Aya Press, 1983, and *Shoes and Shit,* Aya Press, 1984. Contributor of short stories and poetry to *Canadian Fiction, Arsenal, Phases, Mundus Artium, Iowa Review, Free Spirits, Malahat Review,* and other periodicals.

WORK IN PROGRESS: A novel, *Entering Fire,* for Chatto & Windus.

SIDELIGHTS: Reviewing Erica Ducornet's *The Stain* in the *Guardian,* Robert Nye remarks: "This is the most brilliant first novel that I have read in years, a beginning which has much about it to excite the keenest expectations.'' Nye asserts that the novel is an "accomplished, and memorable one by any standards. Imagine Cold Comfort Farm revamped by Ronald Firbank, or Clochemerle sent up rotten by Angela Carter after a night on the sloe gin, and you may have some small notion of its outrageous flavour.'' Calling *The Stain* a "highly disciplined extravaganza'' in the *Times Literary Supplement,* Jayne Pilling focuses on the novel as a new facet of the author's work: "Illustration and short story writing have in common a technique of concentration within spatial constraints; but Ducornet's first novel is a promising demonstration of her talent for the longer form. And the writing itself is highly impressive; the grim humour has the verbal spontaneity of a natural idiom, and the prose, however polished, never seems strained.''

BIOGRAPHICAL/CRITICAL SOURCES: Guardian, February 2, 1984; *Times Literary Supplement,* March 2, 1984.

* * *

DUCORNET, Rikki
See DUCORNET, Erica

* * *

DUFF, Maggie
See DUFF, Margaret K.

* * *

DUFF, Margaret K.
(Maggie Duff)

PERSONAL: Born in Walton, Ind.; daughter of Harvey Edward and Dulcie (Crim) Kapp; married Cloyd E. Duff (a musician), October 26, 1940; children: Jonathan Kapp, Barbara Duff Anderson. *Education:* Butler University, A.B., 1937; Case Western Reserve University, M.L.S., 1966; also attended Cleveland Institute of Art. *Home:* 1009 Green Mountain Dr., Livermore, Colo. 80536.

CAREER: Cuyahoga County Public Library, children's librarian in Solon Branch, Ohio, 1966-70, specialist in children's work in Cleveland, Ohio, beginning 1970. Has exhibited paintings and sculptures in Cleveland and Indiana and in private exhibits. Member of board of trustees, Cleveland Orchestra Women's Committee, 1960-65, and Cleveland Institute of Music Women's Committee, 1970-74.

MEMBER: American Library Association (member of Caldecott committee, 1985), Mu Phi Epsilon, Pi Beta Phi.

AWARDS, HONORS: Rum Pum Pum was named a best book, 1978, by *School Library Journal.*

WRITINGS—Under name Maggie Duff: *Jonny and His Drum,* Walck, 1972; *Rum Pum Pum,* Macmillan, 1978; *The Princess and the Pumpkin,* Macmillan, 1980; *Dancing Turtle,* Macmillan, 1981. Also author of over 60 puppet shows for children. Contributor to *Top of the News* and to library journals.

SIDELIGHTS: Maggie Duff's book *The Princess and the Pumpkin* is based on a Majorcan folktale about an unhappy princess who must be made to laugh. The reviewer for *Horn Book* finds that the story "has a familiar pattern but its own individuality of style and flavor."

BIOGRAPHICAL/CRITICAL SOURCES: Booklist, September 15, 1980; *Horn Book,* October, 1980.

* * *

DUGAN, Michael (Gray)   1947-

PERSONAL: Born October 9, 1947, in Melbourne, Australia; son of Dennis Lloyd (a journalist) and June (Wilkinson) Dugan. *Education:* Educated in Melbourne, Australia. *Home:* 2/192 Union Rd., Surrey Hills, 3127 Victoria, Australia.

CAREER: Writer. Vice-president of Children's Book Council of Victoria, 1977—.

MEMBER: International P.E.N., Fellowship of Australian Writers, Melbourne Cricket Club.

AWARDS, HONORS: Commendation from Australian Visual Arts Foundation, 1975.

WRITINGS: Missing People (poetry), Sweeney Reed, 1970; *Returning from the Prophet* (poetry), Contempa, 1972; (editor) *The Drunken Tram* (poetry), Stockland, 1972; (editor with John Jenkins) *The Outback Reader* (prose), Outback Press, 1975; *Clouds* (poetry), Outback Press, 1975; *Publishing Your Poems,* Second Back Row Press, 1978.

(Editor) *The Early Dreaming* (prose), Jacaranda, 1980; (with Josef Szwarc) *"There Goes the Neighborhood!": Australia's Migrant Experience* (history), Macmillan, 1984. Also author of other works on Australian immigration, most of them on Australian statutory authority, for the Australian Institute of Multicultural Affairs.

Juvenile: *Travel and Transport,* Oxford University Press, 1968; *Stuff and Nonsense,* Collins, 1974; *Weekend,* Macmillan, 1976; *Nonsense Places,* Collins, 1976; *Mountain Easter,* Macmillan, 1976; *My Old Dad,* Longmans-Cheshire, 1976; *The Race,* Macmillan, 1976; *The Golden Ghost,* Macmillan, 1976; *True Ghosts,* Macmillan, 1977; *A House in a Tree,* Lion Press, 1978; *Goal,* Macmillan, 1978; *Dragon's Breath,* Gryphon, 1978; *Hostage,* Hodder & Stoughton, 1978; *Nonsense Numbers,* Thomas Nelson, 1978.

Dingo Boy, Penguin, 1980; (editor) *The Puffin Funbook,* Penguin, 1980; (editor) *More Stuff and Nonsense,* Collins, 1980; *Billy,* Penguin, 1981; (editor) *The Moving Skull,* Hodder & Stoughton, 1981; *The Great Overland Riverboat Race,* Penguin, 1982; *Growing Up in the Goldrush,* Kangaroo, 1983. Also author of series "Australian Factfinders," "Famous Australians," and "People in Australia," all Macmillan, 1974-84. Book reviewer for *Age* and *Reading Time.* Editor of *Australian Puffin Club Magazine.*

WORK IN PROGRESS: Various books.

SIDELIGHTS: Michael Dugan writes: "My best memories of childhood are of my first eight years which were spent in the country near Melbourne. When my family moved to the suburbs of Melbourne, I took some time to adjust to the change, and it was during this period that I began to write, mainly poems and stories about the country and about my teddy bears and other toys.

"My father was a journalist and my mother wrote occasional articles and poems, so it was not surprising that I grew up wanting to be a writer. My most successful books for children have been collections of nonsense poetry and a novel for young teenagers, *Dingo Boy.*

"I live and write in a flat near Melbourne, and often I escape to the country or the coast for a few days."

* * *

DUMAS, Claire
See Van WEDDINGEN, Marthe

* * *

DUNKLING, Leslie Alan   1935-

PERSONAL: Born June 24, 1935, in London, England; son of William Joseph George and Ethel (Johnson) Dunkling; married

Nicole Germaine Tripet, December 30, 1961; children: Stephen, Catherine, Laurence. *Education:* University of London, teaching certificate, 1961, B.A. (with honors), 1965; University of Stockholm, M.A., 1967. *Home:* 32 Speer Rd., Thames Ditton, Surrey KT7 0PW, England.

CAREER: Teacher of English and French at Bordestsone Secondary School in Hanwell, England, 1961-62; University of Stockholm, Stockholm, Sweden, lecturer in English, 1965-67; associated with British Broadcasting Corp. (BBC), 1971—, senior producer of "English by Radio," 1977—. Public lecturer; guest on television and radio programs.

WRITINGS: When They Were Young, Svenska Bokforlaget, 1967; *English House Names,* Names Society, 1971; *Kate and the Clock,* Longman, 1971; *The Battle of Newton Road,* Longman, 1972; *The Guinness Book of Names,* Guinness Superlatives, 1974; *First Names First,* Universe Books, 1977; *Scottish Christian Names,* Johnston & Bacon, 1978; *The Loch Ness Monster,* Longman, 1978; *What's in a Name?,* Ventura, 1978; *Seven Sketches,* Longman, 1979; *The Nightmare,* Newbury House, 1979; *Our Secret Names,* Prentice-Hall, 1982; *Everyman's Dictionary of Christian Names,* Dent, 1984; *London,* Longman, 1984; *Mike's Lucky Day,* Longman, 1984; *Journey to Universe City,* Collins, 1985.

Author of about five hundred radio plays, including two full-length plays, and sixty-six television scripts, including "Off We Go," a series to teach English to German children.

Author of "The Names Game," a column syndicated by Central Press Features to about fifty periodicals, 1974-78. Editor of *VIZ.* (journal of Names Society), 1969-71.

WORK IN PROGRESS: A Dictionary of Pub Names; Naming the Day, a dictionary of personal name quotations.

SIDELIGHTS: Leslie Alan Dunkling writes: "I am committed at the moment to the study of personal names; I also write in the field of teaching English as a foreign language."

BIOGRAPHICAL/CRITICAL SOURCES: Times Literary Supplement, March 10, 1972, August 5, 1977.

*   *   *

DUNLOP, Eileen (Rhona) 1938-

PERSONAL: Born October 13, 1938, in Scotland; daughter of James and Grace (Love) Dunlop; married Anthony Kamm, 1979. *Education:* Moray House College of Edinburgh, teacher's diploma, 1959. *Religion:* Presbyterian. *Home:* 46 Tarmangie Dr., Dollar FK14 7BP, Scotland.

CAREER: Eastfield Primary School, Penicuik, Scotland, assistant mistress, 1959-62; Abercromby Primary School, Tullibody, Scotland, assistant mistress, 1962-64; Sunnyside School, Alloa, Scotland, assistant mistress, 1964-70, assistant headmistress, 1970-79; Dollar Academy, Dollar, Scotland, headmistress of preparatory school, 1980—.

MEMBER: International P.E.N. (Scottish Centre).

WRITINGS—For children: Robinsheugh, Oxford University Press, 1975, published as *Elizabeth Elizabeth,* Holt, 1976; *A Flute in Mayferry Street,* Oxford University Press, 1976, published as *The House on Mayferry Street,* Holt, 1977; *Fox Farm,* Oxford University Press, 1978, Holt, 1979; *The Maze Stone,* Oxford University Press, 1982, Coward, McCann & Geohegan, 1983; *Clementina,* Oxford University Press, 1985.

With husband, Antony Kamm; published by Drew, except as indicated: *Edinburgh,* Cambridge University Press, 1982; *The Story of Glasgow,* 1983; *Kings and Queens of Scotland,* 1984; *Scottish Heroes and Heroines of Long Ago,* 1984; *A Book of Old Edinburgh,* Macdonald Publishers, 1984; *Traditional Scottish Rhymes,* 1984; *Scottish Homes through the Ages,* 1985.

SIDELIGHTS: Eileen Dunlop writes: "In my writing I have tried to place my characters in settings which are meaningful to me, where I have myself been aware of the 'spirit of place.' I like to imagine the working of that spirit on the minds and hearts of my characters—the effect of the past on the present. Although I have travelled in Europe, moving from place to place does not mean much to me; I am concerned with 'rootedness,' with the continuity of human experience, and the power of the historical imagination. This is summed up for me in the first lines of "Burnt Notions" in T. S. Eliot's *Four Quartets:*

> 'Time present and time past
> Are both perhaps present in time future.
> And time future contained in time past.
> If all time is eternally present
> All time is unredeemable.
> What might have been is an abstraction
> Remaining a perpetual possibility
> Only in a world of speculation.'"

AVOCATIONAL INTERESTS: Reading, going to the theater, gardening.

*   *   *

DUNNAHOO, Terry 1927-
(Margaret Terry)

PERSONAL: Born December 8, 1927, in Fall River, Mass.; daughter of Joseph Alfred (a mill worker) and Emma (Dolbec) Janson; married Thomas William Dunnahoo (a cinematographer), September 18, 1954; children: Kim, Sean, Kelly. *Education:* Attended parochial schools in Massachusetts. *Politics:* "I vote for the man—or the woman." *Religion:* Roman Catholic. *Home:* 4061 Tropico Way, Los Angeles, Calif. 90065. *Agent:* Evelyn Singer Agency, P.O. Box 163, Briarcliff Manor, N.Y. 10510.

CAREER: Writer. Has worked in a civilian capacity for U.S. Navy on Guam and as a teacher of creative writing in the gifted program, Los Angeles Public Schools. Lecturer to private groups, writer's conferences, and seminars, colleges, and schools. Consultant to See Hear Industries, Asselin Television Productions. Consultant to California Arts Commission.

MEMBER: International P.E.N. (president, Los Angeles Center, 1975-77; member of board of directors), Authors Guild, Authors League of America, Society of Children's Book Writers, California Writer's Guild (member of board of directors), Southern California Council on Literature for Children and Young People.

AWARDS, HONORS: Southern California Council on Literature for Children and Young People's nonfiction award, for *Before the Supreme Court.*

WRITINGS: Emily Dunning, Reilly & Lee, 1970; *Nellie Bly,* Reilly & Lee, 1970; *Annie Sullivan,* Reilly & Lee, 1970; *Before the Supreme Court: The Story of Belva Ann Lockwood,* Houghton, 1974; *Who Cares about Espie Sanchez?,* Dutton, 1976; *This Is Espie Sanchez,* Dutton, 1976; *Who Needs Espie Sanchez?,* Dutton, 1977; *Break Dancing,* F. Watts, 1985.

Under pseudonym Margaret Terry: *The Last of April,* Bouregy, 1981; *Love for Tomorrow,* Bouregy, 1983.

Contributor of reviews to *Los Angeles Herald-Examiner.* Children's book editor, *West Coast Review of Books.*

SIDELIGHTS: Terry Dunnahoo told *CA:* "When I speak to groups of hopeful writers, I tell them I'm the exception to the writer's unwritten rules. As a child, I wasn't an avid reader. I worked my way through high school and business school, which left little time to read. I never had a strong desire to write. No particular incident influenced me. No teacher encouraged me. Writing was something I suddenly decided to do. And, for awhile, I couldn't imagine doing anything else. However, now I've branched out in different areas related to writing. I speak at writers' conferences throughout the United States, I teach creative writing, I review books, I do manuscript analysis, and I've become active in writer's organizations. Each gives me a feeling of helping others. But none gives me more satisfaction than meeting my audience during lecture tours, especially the young people who take Espie Sanchez, one of my fictional characters, so seriously that they believe she's a real person."

* * *

DUNNE, John Gregory   1932-

PERSONAL: Born May 25, 1932, in Hartford, Conn.; son of Richard Edwin (a physician) and Dorothy (Burns) Dunne; married Joan Didion (a writer), January 30, 1964; children: Quintana (daughter). *Education:* Princeton University, A.B., 1954. *Residence:* Los Angeles, Calif. *Agent:* Lynn Nesbit, International Creative Management, 40 West 57th St., New York, N.Y. 10019 (literary); Ziegler Associates, 8899 Beverly Blvd., Los Angeles, Calif. (films).

CAREER: Free-lance writer. Former staff writer, *Time* magazine.

WRITINGS: Delano: The Story of the California Grape Strike, Farrar, Straus, 1967, revised edition, 1971; *The Studio* (nonfiction), Farrar, Straus, 1969; *Vegas: A Memoir of a Dark Season* (novel), Random House, 1974; *True Confessions* (novel; Book of the Month Club selection; also see below), Dutton, 1977; *Quintana and Friends* (essays), Dutton, 1978; *Dutch Shea, Jr.* (novel), Simon & Schuster, 1982.

Screenplays; with wife, Joan Didion: "Panic in Needle Park" (based on a James Mills book of the same title), Twentieth Century-Fox, 1971; "Play It as It Lays" (based on Didion's book of the same title), Universal, 1972; (and others) "A Star Is Born," Warner Bros., 1976; "True Confessions" (based on Dunne's novel of the same title), United Artists, 1981.

Author of column, with Didion, "Points West," *Saturday Evening Post,* 1967-69, and "The Coast," *Esquire,* 1976-77. Contributor to numerous publications, including *Life, Holiday, New Republic, National Review, Harper's,* and *New York Review of Books.*

SIDELIGHTS: John Gregory Dunne is a successful novelist who began his career as a writer at *Time* magazine. After five years in a staff position, Dunne was restless for new opportunities, and he and writer Joan Didion moved to the West Coast to become freelancers shortly after marrying in 1964. During the next ten years, Dunne and Didion collaborated on a series of magazine columns and several screenplays, and Dunne also completed two nonfiction books on his own. While

Delano: The Story of the California Grape Strike and *The Studio* received decent reviews, critical acclaim eluded him, and, at thirty-five, Dunne became so disenchanted with what he was producing that he was unable to write. Not until he secluded himself in a Las Vegas hotel room and began experimenting with fiction did he realize that his own background provided ample material. "When I was doing *Vegas* . . . I realized what I had in my own Irish Catholic experience," he told Didion when she interviewed her husband for the *Washington Post Book World.* "I had the Mother Lode." Since then, Dunne's success has solidified. No longer referred to as "Joan Didion's husband," Dunne has become a respected novelist in his own right, creating books that explore the Irish Catholic experience in graphic language and carefully rendered detail.

Though he is no longer a staff writer, Dunne still utilizes his journalistic skills. "Hating to ask questions and never trusting the answers has defined the type of reporting I do," he wrote in the introduction to *Quintana and Friends,* a collection of his magazine essays. "What I do is hang around. Become part of the furniture. An endtable in somebody's life. It is the art of the scavenger: set a scene, establish a mood, get the speech patterns right." Now that his emphasis has shifted to fiction, Dunne employs these same techniques in the service of novels. In fact, he believes that "the problem with a lot of fiction writers is that they begin to live isolated lives and they begin to feed off themselves. When Dickens or Balzac wanted to know how something worked," Dunne told Digby Diehl in the *Chicago Tribune Magazine,* "they stepped outside the door." And so, when Dunne needed an insider's view of the legal system for *Dutch Shea, Jr.,* the story of a down-and-out lawyer, he got it from the courts. And his realistic rendering of a morgue scene in several articles and his "True Confessions" screenplay is based on his visits to a morgue.

The sleazy characters Dunne creates are as remote from his own privileged family as his slummy settings are from the posh West Hartford neighborhood where he was raised. They resemble more closely the old Irish ghetto where his immigrant grandfather lived—an environment to which Dunne is drawn. "Everything I think and everything I am comes from that old part of Hartford," he told Didion in their *Washington Post Book World* interview. "I get a strong sense of who I am down there. I don't get it in West Hartford, where I actually grew up. I don't get it from anyplace connected with my own sort of upper-middle-class Princeton-West-Hartford background."

Nor is Dunne at ease with his religious heritage. No longer a practicing member of the church, he finds his whole view colored by his Catholic upbringing. "Once a Catholic, always a Catholic," he confessed to Digby Diehl. "It's like being a Jew. I am not a practicing Catholic; I am an avowed Catholic. The way I describe [the character] Dutch Shea, Jr. is how I'd describe myself. In the book I wrote: 'In general, he felt about God as he felt about the Kennedy assassination conspiracy theories: He was willing to believe.' I am willing to believe . . . and hedge my bets."

When Dunne moved out to California, he severed his ties with the cultural heritage of the northeast. "I became an instant Westerner," he told *National Observer* contributor Bruce Cook, "with this difference—I found that the California that interested me most was eastern California. You hear so much about the difference between northern and southern California, but differences in the state are even more pronounced between east and west.''

Dunne's first exposure to the California of farms and orchards came in 1966 when Cesar Chavez began organizing migrant grape pickers for a strike. Dunne was so intrigued that he decided to expand a magazine article he had written on the subject into a full-length book. The result was *Delano: The Story of the California Grape Strike,* an effort that garnered critical praise for its unbiased point of view, but which did not sell especially well. Writing in *America,* Philip A. Carey calls *Delano* ''one of the most appealing stories of contemporary American social history,'' while *New York Times Book Review* contributor Gladwin Hill describes it as ''an exceptionally incisive report on the anatomy of the strike; a colorful, perceptive examination of its impact on the community; and an analysis of actions of both employers and labor so realistic as to make it important reading for current students of economics and public policy.''

The inspiration for *The Studio,* Dunne's second book, was also a magazine piece—this time, a story about Twentieth Century-Fox mogul Richard Zanuck that Dunne wrote for the *Saturday Evening Post.* Though the article was never published, Dunne told *CA:* ''It gave me just the taste I needed. I wanted to do a book, and so I saw Dick Zanuck and told him my plan—to see how a studio operated from top to bottom, and get it down in the book just that way.''

For nearly a year, Dunne checked in periodically at the studio, making himself so much a part of the woodwork that people eventually forgot he was there. In the book, his presence is also undiscernable. According to Cook, Dunne ''did little formal interviewing, but listened very intently. . . . And the result—there to be read in the quick, shifting cinematic scenes of *The Studio*—is simply devastating. Mr. Dunne manages to say more about the Hollywood lunacy by implication and suggestion than any several writers have by direct statement.'' *Newsweek* reviewer Paul D. Zimmerman believes that ''the real contribution of Dunne's book lies in its nicely honed portrait of the Hollywood ethos, that gothic mix of greed, hypocrisy, shrewd calculation, mad hoopla and boundless optimism that shapes American films,'' while *Saturday Review* contributor Robert M. Strozier concludes that *The Studio* ''is probably the best nonfiction book that's ever been written about Hollywood.''

Dunne, however, initially hated the book. ''I thought it was a job of just putting together notes,'' he told *CA.* ''There was no act of creation involved.'' He was so dissatisfied with the manuscript that he didn't want it published and refused to read the galleys (Didion proofread them for him). Dunne had signed a contract with his publisher to write the same kind of book about Las Vegas, but as Martin Kasindorf reports in the *Saturday Review,* ''he couldn't bring himself to complete the research for something so similar to *The Studio.* For a dispiriting eighteen-month period he had writer's block. The Malibu beach house the Dunnes had bought with script fees from *Play It as It Lays* was under messy renovation. Dunne would go on long, senseless drives. The couple came close to a breakup. 'We had a very small child, we had no money and no house, she was working very hard. I wasn't working at all,' recalls Dunne. 'It was simply a difficult time.'''

During one of his drives, Dunne spotted a billboard advising ''Visit Las Vegas before your numbers up.'' Knowing that his Malibu home would not be finished for several more months and hoping to make use of the writer's block he was coming out of, Dunne decided that the city would be the perfect place to spend that summer. He told *CA* that he ''tried desperately'' to get Random House to call the book he produced a novel, but the publisher considered *Vegas: A Memoir of a Dark Season* too autobiographical to pass as fiction. They compromised by calling it a fictionalized memoir which, as Dunne explains in the preface, ''recalls a time both real and imagined.''

The book relates Dunne's experiences with three characters— a lounge comic, a private detective, and a poetry-writing prostitute—whose composites were drawn from real people Dunne encountered there. His interweaving of fact and fiction left readers confused, but critics were appreciative. ''The book,'' writes Peter Straub in the *New Statesman* ''is bitter and touching at once, utterly compulsive reading. The dialogue is from the bottom of the world, spoken by people who hustle by reflex and have passed caring that the hustle is all they've got.'' Jonathan Yardley calls it ''a fine, wry, perceptive, graceful book,'' in his *New York Times Book Review* critique and concludes that *Vegas* ''does as much for the dark side of the American funhouse as Hunter Thompson's 'Fear and Loathing in Las Vegas' did for the manic side.''

Though it never reached bestsellerdom, *Vegas* remains Dunne's favorite, ''not because I think it is my best,'' he explained to Digby Diehl in the *Chicago Tribune Magazine,* ''but because it is the book that taught me how to write.'' It is also the first book in which Dunne mines what he now routinely refers to as the ''Mother Lode''—his Irish American heritage.

That heritage figures prominently in *True Confessions,* Dunne's first bestseller and, according to *New York Times* reviewer Christopher Lehmann-Haupt, ''the book he was born to write.'' Loosely patterned after the 1947 Black Dahlia murder case, *True Confessions* is a murder mystery in which the solution to the murder doesn't matter at all. Instead, Dunne emphasizes the relationship between two Irish Catholic brothers who get involved in the case—Tom Spellacy, a police lieutenant, and Des Spellacy, an ambitious priest. When the victim's severed head turns up in a seedy urban parking lot, Tom launches an investigation that implicates not only the most prominent member of his brother's parish, but his brother Des as well.

''The book is not a suspense novel or murder mystery in the ordinary sense,'' notes *New York Review of Books* contributor Robert Towers. ''Rather, it is concerned with tracing—interestingly and deftly—the 'ripple effect' which the case has upon the racketeers, contractors, blarneying lawyers, glad-handling undertakers, whores, and the variously tainted members of the police force and clergy who populate this crowded work.'' John B. Breslin writes in the *Washington Post Book World* that ''what Dunne wants to explore are the ironies that shape people's lives, sometimes tragically but just as often providentially. . . . When Tom decides, in a moment of justifiable rage, to pull down the whole house of cards by arresting the kingpin, who, he knows, did not kill the girl, he is fully aware that Desmond will fall as well. What he doesn't know, couldn't know because Des barely understands it himself, is that he is doing his brother the greatest favor of his life: 'You were my salvation, Tommy.' And so Dunne's fundamental irony proves to be providential rather than tragic.''

Despite the book's widespread popularity (hardcover sales of more than 50,000 copies, more than a million paperback sales, and a movie spin-off), some critics, such as *Newsweek*'s Raymond Sokolov believe that "Dunne does not quite fulfill the potential of his material. He lets the whodunit side of his story slip too far from view during the long passages of parochial intrigue. His canvas is overcrowded with distracting vignettes of scheming priests and laymen." *Saturday Review* contributor Robert M. Strozier believes "there's just too much smart banter, too much plot, too much gratuitous weirdness, too much cuteness. . . . The book has energy and substance, but unfortunately there's just too, too, too much of everything." For this reason, *Times Literary Supplement* critic Anthony Bailey regards the novel as a promise for the future: "*True Confessions* has a muscle-bound, dirty-talking strength which suggests that Mr. Dunne—stretching his wings a little and looking at the glories as well as the detritus of creation—has it in him to write a first-rate Irish American novel."

Some believe that Dunne fulfilled that promise with *Dutch Shea, Jr.*, his subsequent novel, which also explores the theme of corruption in an Irish Catholic mileau. Shea, a divorced lawyer who represents the kind of clients no one else will touch—pimps, muggers, arsonists—is a disillusioned man drifting through life passively. "The drift is interrupted by the death of Shea's much-loved only child, Cat, an adopted daughter who is the random victim of an IRA bomb in a London restaurant," according to Thomas M. Gannon in *America*. "As he mourns Cat's death, Shea's own life edges toward a crisis, for he, like his father before him and for similar, imprudently well-intentioned reasons, is an embezzler." The story climaxes when Shea's crime is discovered and he is forced to face the consequences of his acts.

Because Shea spends so much time among criminals and degenerates, the book is full of foul-mouthed language and graphic sexual scenes. This emphasis reflects Dunne's knowledge that "he can safely float a novel on a tide of racist slurs, ethnic jokes and what, in more fastidious days, were thought to be irregular sexual connections—and that he can collect the benefits of such ornamentation at the cash register—without actually opening himself to charges of bad taste," according to *Newsweek*'s Peter S. Prescott. But Adam Mars-Jones finds the emphasis disturbing. "Even when there is no obvious occasion for revulsion, no severed nipple, no shredded baby, Dunne finds ways of letting the corruptible body know just what he thinks of it," he writes in the *Times Literary Supplement*. "John Gregory Dunne isn't exposing the spiritual emptiness of modern life. . . . He is turning disgust into another cheap thrill, and fetishizing what he claims to denounce."

Not everyone shares this opinion. *New York Times* reviewer Christopher Lehmann-Haupt, for instance, thinks "the unlikely combination of gags, social satire and personal tragedy hold together even better than it did in Mr. Dunne's earlier novel 'True Confessions.'" And on the front page of the *New York Times Book Review*, contributor George Stade says "Dutch Shea's examinations and cross-examinations of cops and whores, of Myron Mandel, super-pimp, of Packy Considine, jailbird and fence, of Roscoe Raines, burglar . . . , of Robert Beaubois, torch, are all funny, often chastening, sometimes ghastly, and always deftly handled by Dutch Shea and Mr. Dunne."

In the opinion of *National Review* contributor Jeffrey Brodrick, "Dunne presents not so much a plot that unfolds as a character that unravels. Once the bomb goes off we do little more than

follow the vibrations, the shudders, through Dutch's head. Dutch doesn't blow up, he collapses inward for the remaining 352 pages of the novel. Dutch Shea, Jr. is broken from page one. He's a cooked bird and he doesn't even care."

Why does one go on reading when Shea's ultimate demise is so predictable? "Because we hope against hope that Dunne's bright, witty, sad and entirely sympathetic hero will *not* do what we dread he *might* do," according to Evan Hunter in the *Washington Post Book World*, "and because the novel is so rich in character and detail that we are compelled to turn the pages as rapidly as our fingers can move." Hunter concludes by noting that "Dunne has written a fine novel that examines and dissects a unique individual whom we come to know—and indeed love and admire—as the story unfolds toward its tragic end. By so movingly bringing to life this troubled and complicated man, he has illuminated our own human condition—and that, in the long run, is what good fiction is all about."

BIOGRAPHICAL/CRITICAL SOURCES—Books: John Gregory Dunne, *Vegas: A Memoir of a Dark Season*, Random House, 1974; Dunne, *Quintana and Friends*, Dutton, 1978; *Dictionary of Literary Biography Yearbook: 1980*, Gale, 1981; *Contemporary Literary Criticism*, Volume XXVIII, Gale, 1984.

Periodicals: *New York Times Book Review*, November 12, 1967, February 3, 1974, October 16, 1977, January 28, 1979, March 28, 1982; *New Republic*, December 2, 1967, May 10, 1969, March 9, 1974; *America*, January 13, 1968, July 5, 1969, July 31, 1982; *Commonweal*, February 9, 1968; *Yale Review*, summer, 1968; *New York Times*, May 7, 1969, January 10, 1974, September 2, 1977, October 11, 1977, January 25, 1979, September 25, 1981, April 1, 1982; *New Leader*, May 26, 1969; *Time*, June 27, 1969, November 7, 1977, March 29, 1982; *National Review*, December 16, 1969, August 6, 1982; *National Observer*, March 8, 1971; *Newsweek*, January 21, 1974, October 10, 1977, April 19, 1982; *New Yorker*, March 11, 1974, April 24, 1978, May 24, 1982; *New Statesman*, November 1, 1974; *Times Literary Supplement*, December 27, 1974, February 8, 1980, April 21, 1978, September 17, 1982; *Washington Post Book World*, October 23, 1977, March 28, 1982; *Saturday Review*, October 29, 1977, February 17, 1979, April, 1982; *New York Review of Books*, January 26, 1978, June 10, 1982; *Atlantic*, February, 1978; *Washington Post*, January 11, 1979, April 30, 1982; *Chicago Tribune Book World*, January 21, 1979; *Horizon*, January, 1981; *Los Angeles Times Book Review*, April 18, 1982; *Chicago Tribune Magazine*, May 2, 1982.

—*Sketch by Donna Olendorf*

*   *   *

DUNNE, Mary Collins 1914-
(Mary Jo Dunne, Regina Moore)

PERSONAL: Born January 15, 1914, in County Down, Ireland; daughter of George William (a calker) and Brigid (Byrne) Collins; married Stephen John Dunne (a teamster), January 11, 1937 (died, 1983); children: Nancy, Mary Anne, Bernadette, Christine. *Education:* Attended University of San Francisco, University of California, San Francisco City College, and California State University, San Francisco (now San Francisco State University). *Politics:* Democrat. *Religion:* Roman Catholic. *Home:* 266 Jules Ave., San Francisco, Calif. 94112.

CAREER: Writer.

MEMBER: Society of Children's Book Writers, California Writers' Club.

WRITINGS—Juveniles: *Alaskan Summer,* Abelard-Schuman, 1968; *Reach Out, Ricardo,* Abelard-Schuman, 1970; *Gregory Gray and the Brave Beast,* Childrens Press, 1972; *The Secret of Captives Cave,* Putnam, 1976; *Hoby and Stub,* Atheneum, 1980; *Here Comes Kary,* Simon & Schuster, 1983.

Adult novels; all published by Bouregy: *Nurse of the Midnight Sun,* 1973; *Standby Nurse,* 1974; *Cruise of the Coral Queen,* 1975; *Nurse of the Vineyards,* 1975; *Nurse of Crystalline Valley,* 1977; *The Secret of Cliffsedge,* 1979; *Return to Timberlake,* 1981.

Contributor of articles and short stories (some under pseudonym Regina Moore) to numerous periodicals.

WORK IN PROGRESS: A children's novel.

SIDELIGHTS: Mary Collins Dunne told *CA:* "I had an unsettled, but not unhappy, childhood. I came to writing when my four daughters started growing up. When I got published I found to my surprise that now I had an identity of my own. I especially like writing for young people because they are so responsive. I can identify with kids in stories who are unsure, lonely, uprooted, moved around, in both rural and urban settings. No reward is more gratifying than hearing from some far away kid who liked the book, and wants to know when my next one is coming out."

AVOCATIONAL INTERESTS: Gardening, swimming, spectator baseball, travel.

BIOGRAPHICAL/CRITICAL SOURCES: New York Times Book Review, July 19, 1981.

*   *   *

DUNNE, Mary Jo
    See DUNNE, Mary Collins

*   *   *

DUNNER, Joseph   1908-1978
(Germanicus, Alexander Roth)

PERSONAL: Born May 10, 1908, in Fuerth, Germany; died August 24, 1978; son of Samuel (a government official) and Ella (Laske) Dunner; married Ada Bier, December 24, 1935; married Ruth Anita Bevan (a political scientist), January 29, 1971. *Education:* Attended University of Berlin, 1927-30; University of Frankfurt am Main, M.A., 1932; University of Basel, Ph.D., 1934. *Politics:* Republican. *Religion:* Jewish. *Home:* 630 Shore Rd., Long Beach, N.Y. 11561. *Office:* Yeshiva University, 500 West 185th St., New York, N.Y. 10033.

CAREER: Research fellow at International Institute of Social Research, 1930-35, and Brookings Institution, Washington, D.C., 1936-37; United Jewish Appeal, American Joint Distribution Committee, New York City, consultant on refugee problems and lecturer, 1937-42; New York University, New York City, research fellow, 1942-43; Harvard University, Cambridge, Mass., lecturer at School of Overseas Administration, 1943-44; U.S. Office of War Information, chief of Intelligence Section, London, England, 1944-45, and of Press Control Section, Munich, Germany, 1945-46; Grinnell Col-

lege, Grinnell, Iowa, professor of government, 1946-63, chairman of department of political science and director of Institute of International Affairs, 1946-58; Yeshiva University, New York City, David Petegorsky Professor of Political Science and International Relations, 1964-74, professor emeritus, 1974-78. Visiting professor, Hebrew University of Jerusalem, 1950; Fulbright professor, University of Freiburg, West Germany, 1963-64. Trustee, Institute for Mediterranean Affairs; member of board of directors, American Council for World Freedom and American Friends of the Hebrew University.

MEMBER: International Political Science Association, American Political Science Association, American Society of International Law, American Academy of Political and Social Science.

AWARDS, HONORS: Decorated by Government of France; Americanism Medal of Jewish War Veterans; Order of Quissam Alaouite Cherifien from Sultan of Morocco, 1954.

WRITINGS: Die Gewerkschaften im Arbeitskampf, Philographischer Verlag, 1934; *If I Forget Thee . . . ,* Dulane Press, 1937; (contributor) C. J. Fredrich, editor, *American Experiences in Military Government in World War II,* Rinehart, 1948; (contributor) Stuart G. Brown, editor, Internationalism and Democracy, Syracuse University Press, 1949; *The Republic of Israel: Its History and Its Promise,* McGraw, 1950; (contributor) Arnold J. Zurcher, editor, *Constitutions and Constitutional Trends since World War II,* New York University Press, 1951; *Democratic Bulwark in the Middle East,* Grinnell College Press, 1952; *Baruch Spinoza and Western Democracy,* Philosophical Library, 1955; *Links-und Rechtsradikalismus in der Amerikanischen Politik,* Athenaum Verlag, 1964; *Zu Protokoll Gegeben* (autobiography), Deusch Verlag, 1971; *Israel and the People's Republic of China: Communist Expansion in Indochina,* American Friends of Vietnam, 1972.

Editor: *Major Aspects of International Politics,* Grinnell College Press, 1948; *Dictionary of Political Science,* Philosophical Library, 1964; *Hand Book of World History,* Philosophical Library, 1967; *Case Studies on Human Rights and Fundamental Freedoms,* Foundation for the Study of Plural Societies, 1975.

Also co-author of *The Palestine Refugee Problem,* 1959, and editor of *Leftist and Rightest Radicalism in American Politics,* 1964. Contributor, under pseudonyms Germanicus and Alexander Roth, to the Swiss press and *Deutsche Freiheit,* 1933-35; also contributor to newspapers and magazines, including *Des Moines Register, Nation,* and *University Bookman.*

SIDELIGHTS: Joseph Dunner was fluent in French, and had some competence in Spanish and modern Hebrew.

BIOGRAPHICAL/CRITICAL SOURCES: Leo Schwartz, *The Redeemers,* Farrar, Straus, 1953; Joseph Dunner, *Zu Protokoll Gegeben,* Desch Verlag, 1971.†

*   *   *

DURKA, Gloria   1939-

PERSONAL: Born October 12, 1939, in Buffalo, N.Y.; daughter of Chester and Estelle (Godlewski) Szustak; married Paul E. Bumbar, August 3, 1974. *Education:* Medaille College, B.A., 1968; Fordham University, M.A., 1969; New York University, Ph.D., 1973. *Religion:* Roman Catholic. *Home:* 153 Fawn Hill Rd., Tuxedo Park, N.Y. 10987. *Office:* Keating Hall, Fordham University, Bronx, N.Y. 10458.

CAREER: W. H. Sadlier, Inc., New York, N.Y., consultant to Seminar Service, 1971-73; Boston College, Chestnut Hill, Mass., assistant professor of theology, 1973-76, academic director of Institute for the Study of Religious Education and Service, 1973-76; Barry College (now University), Miami, Fla., associate professor of religious education and chairman of Department of Religious Studies and Philosophy, 1977-78; Fordham University, Bronx, N.Y., associate professor of religious education, 1978—. Chairperson of religious education committee at Boston Theological Institute.

MEMBER: Religious Education Association, Association of Professors and Researchers in Religious Education (member of executive committee), American Academy of Religion, College Theology Society, Association of Directors of Graduate Religious Education, Pi Lambda Theta.

AWARDS, HONORS: Founder's Day Award from New York University, 1974.

WRITINGS: Sexuality: Suggested Guidelines for a Four-Year High School Catechesis, Fordham University, 1968; (with husband, Paul E. Bumbar) *Faith: Becoming True and Free,* William Sadlier, 1980.

Editor with Joanmarie Smith: *Emerging Issues in Religious Education,* Paulist Press, 1976; *Modeling God: Religious Education for Tomorrow,* Paulist Press, 1976; *Aesthetic Dimensions of Religious Education,* Paulist Press, 1979; *Family Ministry,* Winston Press, 1980.

Author of instructional cassette tapes on religious education topics, including "Basic Guidelines for Creative Religious Education" series; co-author of "Media, Morality and Youth: A Teacher Training Kit." Contributor to theology and religious education journals. Member of editorial board of *Living Light* and *Religious Education.*

WORK IN PROGRESS: Several articles, including a series for *Today's Parish,* and chapters for books.

SIDELIGHTS: Gloria Durka once wrote *CA:* "I am interested in exploring the ramifications of process philosophy and theology for the educational enterprise as a whole."

*   *   *

DVORETZKY, Edward 1930-

PERSONAL: Born December 29, 1930, in Houston, Tex.; son of Max (a salesman) and Anna Lea (Greenfield) Dvoretzky; married Charlotte Silversteen, August 1, 1953; children: Toban. *Education:* Rice University, B.A., 1953; Harvard University, M.A., 1954, Ph.D., 1959. *Home:* 2035 Ridgeway Dr., Iowa City, Iowa 52240. *Office:* Department of German, University of Iowa, Iowa City, Iowa 52242.

CAREER: Rice University, Houston, Tex., instructor, 1956-59, assistant professor, 1959-64, associate professor of German, 1964-67; University of Iowa, Iowa City, professor of German, 1967—, chairman of department, 1969-79.

MEMBER: Modern Language Association of America, American Association of Teachers of German, Lessing Society, American Goethe Society, P.E.N., Midwest Modern Language Association (chairman of German section, 1970-71), Autorenkreis Plesse, Phi Beta Kappa, Delta Phi Alpha.

AWARDS, HONORS: Fulbright fellowship in Germany, 1953, 1958; Old Gold research fellowship, 1968.

WRITINGS: (Translator and author of introduction) Gotthold Ephriam Lessing, *Emilia Galotti,* Ungar, 1962, Mary S. Rosenberg, 1979; *The Enigma of "Emilia Galotti,"* Nijhoff, 1963; *The Eighteenth-Century English Translations of "Emilia Galotti,"* Rice University Press, 1966; *Lessing: Dokumente zur Wirkungsgeschichte, 1755-1968,* Kuemmerle, Volume I, 1971, Volume II, 1972; (translator and author of introduction) Lessing, *Philotas,* Akademischer Verlag, 1979; *Lessing Heute—Beitrage zur Wirkungsgeschichte,* Akademischer Verlag, 1981; *Der Teufel und sein Advokat—Gedichte und Prosa,* Stoedtner Verlag, 1981; *Tief im Herbstwald,* Graphikum, 1983; (co-author) *Windfusse—The Feet of the Wind,* Im Verlag Zum Halben Bogen, 1984. Contributor of poetry and translations to anthologies. Contributor of articles, poems, translations, and reviews to language and other journals.

*   *   *

DYER, William G(ibb) 1925-

PERSONAL: Born October 4, 1925, in Portland, Ore.; married Bonnie Hansen, January 2, 1952; children: five. *Education:* Attended University of Oregon, 1943, and Washington State University, 1944; Brigham Young University, B.A., 1950, M.A., 1951; University of Wisconsin, Ph.D., 1955. *Home:* 3077 Mojave Lane, Provo, Utah 84601. *Office:* 776 TNRB, Brigham Young University, Provo, Utah 84601.

CAREER: Iowa State University, Ames, instructor in sociology, 1953-55; Brigham Young University, Provo, Utah, assistant professor, 1955-59, associate professor, 1959-63, professor of sociology, 1963—, chairman of department of organizational behavior, 1971-75, dean of School of Management, 1979-84. Visiting professor at University of California, Utah State University, and University of Utah. National Training Laboratories, training consultant, 1959-60, program director of National Training Laboratory for Applied Behavioral Science, 1966-70, member of board of directors, 1967-70, fellow of National Training Laboratories Institute. Senior associate, Leadership Resources, Inc. Organization development consultant to Danish Technological Institute, 1969, and Danish Agricultural Development Organization, 1969-70. *Military service:* U.S. Army Air Forces, 1943; became second lieutenant.

MEMBER: International Association of Applied Social Sciences, Academy of Management, Beta Gamma Sigma.

WRITINGS: (Editor) *Training Designs for Human Relations Laboratories: 1959-60,* National Training Laboratories, 1960; (contributor) Arthur B. Shostak and William Gomberg, editors, *Blue Collar World,* Prentice-Hall, 1964; (with Evan T. Peterson) *Family Centered Nursing Care: A Social Science Perspective,* College of Nursing, University of Utah, 1966; *An Outline of Basic Principles of Sociology Using a Social System Frame of Reference,* Brigham Young University Press, 1967; (contributor) Robert F. Winch and Louis Goodman, editors, *Selected Studies in Marriage and the Family,* Holt, 1968; (contributor) Robert V. Guthrie, editor, *Psychology in the World Today,* Addison-Wesley, 1969; (contributor) J. K. Haddon and M. L. Borgatta, editors, *Marriage and Family,* F. E. Peacock, 1969; (contributor) J. N. Edwards, editor, *The Family and Change,* Knopf, 1969.

(Contributor) Fleming Balveg, editor, *Organization Development*, L.O.K. Publication (Denmark), 1970; (editor) *Modern Theory and Method in Group Training*, Van Nostrand, 1972; *The Sensitive Manipulator: The Change Agent Who Builds with Others*, Brigham Young University Press, 1972, revised edition published as *Insight to Impact: Strategies for Interpersonal and Organizational Change*, 1976; *Creating Closer Families: Principles of Positive Family Interaction*, Brigham Young University Press, 1975; *Team Building: Issues and Alternatives*, Addison-Wesley, 1977.

Contemporary Issues in Management and Organization Development, Addison-Wesley, 1983; *Strategies for Managing Change*, Addison-Wesley, 1984. Also contributor to *Organizational Dynamics*, 1984. Contributor of numerous articles and reviews to sociology and education journals.

E

EAMES, Edwin 1930-

PERSONAL: Born March 7, 1930, in New York, N.Y.; son of Morris and Anna (Korn) Eisenberg; married Phyllis Edelstein (a teacher), September 9, 1951; children: Mona, David, Lori. *Education:* City College (now City College of the City University of New York), B.S.S., 1951; Lucknow University, graduate study, 1953-54; Cornell University, Ph.D., 1965. *Politics:* Democrat. *Religion:* Jewish. *Home:* 309 Florence Ave., Jenkintown, Pa. 19046. *Office:* Department of Anthropology, Bernard M. Baruch College of the City University of New York, 17 Lexington Ave, New York, N.Y. 10010.

CAREER: Temple University, Philadelphia, Pa., instructor, 1956-62, assistant professor, 1962-66, associate professor of anthropology, 1966-70; Bernard M. Baruch College of the City University of New York, New York, N.Y., associate professor, 1970-75, professor of anthropology, 1975—.

MEMBER: American Anthropological Association (fellow), American Association for the Advancement of Science, Philadelphia Anthropological Society (member of council), Phi Beta Kappa, Sigma Xi, Cornell Club of Philadelphia.

WRITINGS: (With Judith Goode) *Urban Poverty in a Cross Cultural Context*, Free Press, 1973; *Anthropology of the City*, Prentice-Hall, 1977; (with P. Saran) *The New Ethnics: East Indians in the United States*, Praeger, 1980; (with E. Cohen) *Cultural Anthropology*, Little, Brown, 1982.

Contributor to anthropology and sociology journals. Consulting editor, *International Journal of Contemporary Sociology*, 1971—.

WORK IN PROGRESS: A guide to guide dog schools; research on the blind and computers.

*   *   *

EARHART, H(arry) Byron 1935-

PERSONAL: Born January 7, 1935, in Aledo, Ill.; son of Kenneth Harry and Mary (Haack) Earhart; married Virginia Margaret Donaho, September 2, 1956; children: Kenneth Clark, David Charles, Paul William. *Education:* Attended Knox College, 1953-56; University of Chicago, B.D. and M.A., 1960, Ph.D., 1965; also attended Columbia University, 1962, and

Tohoku University, 1962-65. *Home:* 3814 Stonegate Rd., Kalamazoo, Mich. 49007. *Office:* Department of Religion, Western Michigan University, Kalamazoo, Mich. 49001.

CAREER: Vanderbilt University, Nashville, Tenn., visiting assistant professor of religion, 1965-66; Western Michigan University, Kalamazoo, assistant professor, 1966-69, associate professor, 1969-75, professor of religion, 1975—. Instructor, International Summer School in Asian Studies, Ewha Womans University, Seoul, South Korea, 1973. Advisor on Far Eastern religion to *Encyclopaedia Britannica*.

MEMBER: Association for Asian Studies, American Academy of Religion, American Society for the Study of Religion.

AWARDS, HONORS: Fulbright fellowship to Japan, 1962-65, and to Korea, 1973; National Endowment for the Humanities grant, summer, 1969, senior grants, summer, 1978 and summer, 1983; American Council of Learned Societies and Social Science Research Council joint grant on East Asia, summer, 1970; Japan Society for the Promotion of Science travel and maintenance grant for study in Japan, 1979-80; distinguished faculty scholar award, Western Michigan University, 1981; distinguished faculty award, Michigan Association of Governing Boards, 1982.

WRITINGS: (Contributor) *Studies of Esoteric Buddhism and Tantrism*, Koyasan University, 1965; (contributor) J. M. Kitagawa and others, editors, *The History of Religion: Essays on the Problems of Understanding*, University of Chicago Press, 1967; *Japanese Religion: Unity and Diversity*, Dickenson, 1969, 3rd edition, Wadsworth, 1982; *The New Religions of Japan: A Bibliography of Western-Language Materials*, Sophia University Press, 1970, 2nd edition, Center For Japanese Studies, University of Michigan, 1983; *A Religious Study of the Mount Haguro Sect of Shugendo: An Example of Japanese Mountain Religion*, Sophia University Press, 1970; *Religion in the Japanese Experience: Sources, Interpretations, and Illustrations*, Dickenson, 1973; (contributor) *Religious Ferment in Asia*, University Press of Kansas, 1974.

(Contributor) *The Mountain Spirit*, Overlook Press, 1979; (translator from the Japanese) Shigeyoshi Murakami, *Japanese Religion in the Modern Century*, Tokyo University Press, 1980; (contributor) *Abingdon Dictionary of Living Religions*, Abingdon, 1981; (editor with Hitoshi Miyake) *Dentoteki shukyo no saisei: Gedatsu-kai no shiso to kodo* (essays in Japanese; title means "The Revival of Traditional Religion: The Thought and Practice of Gedatsu-kai"), Meicho, 1983; *Religions of Japan: Many Traditions within One Sacred Way,* Harper, 1984. Editor of "Religious Traditions of the World" series for Harper. Contributor to *Encyclopedia of Japan;* also contributor to history of religions and Asian studies journals. Editor, *Religious Studies Review,* 1976-79.

WORK IN PROGRESS: Religion in Contemporary Japan: Gedatsu-kai; a study of Mount Fuji as a symbol of Japanese cultural and religious identity; research on the Japanese new religions.

SIDELIGHTS: H. Byron Earhart told *CA:* "Almost all my published writing has been on aspects of Japanese religion, but my first serious interest in the study of religion began when I was a student at Knox College, and John Collier, Sr., introduced me to the richness of the vision of the American Indians. During graduate school at the University of Chicago I continued this interest while studying under Mircea Eliade, and wrote an M.A. thesis on the world view of the Zuni Indians. But I was attracted to the study of Japanese religion, because it featured both active folk religion and more highly organized world religions. Study of Japanese language under Edwin McClellan, Japanese Buddhism under Shoson Miyamoto, and Japanese religion under Joseph M. Kitagawa prepared me for dissertation research in Japan under the supervision of Ichiro Hori. While in Japan from 1962 to 1965, I did additional language work and read Japanese materials on Shugendo, a highly syncretistic folk religious movement, and observed all the surviving rituals of the Shugendo headquarters around Mount Haguro in northeast Japan.

"Since completion of my doctoral dissertation in 1965, I have been teaching in the general area of East Asian religions, but almost all my research and writing has been concerned with Japanese religion. The fascination for the never-ending variety of Japanese religion that first attracted me to this subject still holds my attention. This subject includes elaborate shrine and temple rituals, as well as simple rice-transplanting celebrations, the national religion of Shinto as well as the Indian import of Buddhism and the Chinese imports of Confucianism and Taoism, a rich and varied tradition of several thousand years, as well as dynamic new movements.

"My first work in this area focused on the earlier historical period and the broad sweep of Japanese religious history, but increasingly my attention has been directed to the 'new religions' that have become conspicuous during the past hundred years. I collected information on the Japanese new religions during a 1969 trip to Japan, and gathered comparative information while observing Korean new religions during a 1973 trip to Korea.

"I am now completing a book on one particular new religion, Gedatsu-kai, viewing the movement as a microcosm to interpret religion in contemporary Japan. Much of my time during the next few years will be spent editing nine volumes for the 'Religious Traditions of the World' series, of which I am series editor. One partially completed manuscript to which I hope to return some day is a collection of anecdotes of experiences and reflections on life and study in Japan, tentatively titled *To Japan and Back.* My next major project is a long-term study of Mount Fuji as a symbol of cultural and religious identity in Japan.

"Much of my writing is 'scholarly' or 'didactic' in the sense of closely documented research or teaching texts, and for this reason tends to be rather serious. In a lighter vein, I joke with my colleagues and students that in my research, teaching, and writing, I am actually a kind of travel agent, arranging 'travel time' so that students in my classes and people who read my writing can travel outside their own space and time to the space and time of Japanese religion. My own life has been enriched by the opportunity to observe and live within the richness and variety of Japanese religion, and my hope is that others who experience Japanese religion vicariously through my writings will also realize that enrichment. I count myself lucky to be able to work full time in a field that I enjoy, and to write on topics of my own choice."

          *   *   *

EASTMAN, Ann Heidbreder   1933-
(Margaret Ann Heidbreder)

PERSONAL: Born August 31, 1933, in Minneapolis, Minn.; daughter of H. Willis (in life insurance) and Margaret (Hislop) Heidbreder; married Arthur M. Eastman (head of English department, Virginia Polytechnic Institute and State University), 1973. *Education:* University of Michigan, B.A. (with honors), 1955; additional study at Columbia University, 1956-57, and New York University, 1957-59. *Religion:* Episcopalian. *Home:* 716 Burruss Dr. N.W., Blacksburg, Va. 24060; and R.R. 1, Box 89, Mayhew Turnpike, Bristol, N.H. 03222 (summer).

CAREER: Macmillan Co., Inc., New York City, in sales promotion and editorial assistant, 1955-56; Alfred A. Knopf, Inc., New York City, promotion director and editorial assistant, 1956-57; Holt, Rinehart & Winston, Inc., New York City, assistant social studies editor, 1957-59; McGraw-Hill Book Co., New York City, promotion assistant in children's book department, 1959; Henry Z. Walck, Inc., New York City, school and library consultant, publicity director, and sales promotion manager, 1959-63; Random House, Inc., New York City, school and library consultant, 1963-64; Association of American Publishers, New York City, senior associate for education and library services, research director of National Book Committee, coordinator of Educational Media Selection Centers Program, program director of National Library Week Program, 1964-71; Harcourt Brace Jovanovich, New York City, director of education and library services, 1972-73; Chatham College, Pittsburgh, Pa., director of admissions, 1975-77; freelance marketing, library, and conference consultant, 1977-79; Virginia Polytechnic Institute and State University, Blacksburg, director of public affairs programs, College of Arts and Sciences, staff officer, University Faculty Book Publishing Committee, 1979—.

Organizer and officer, Publishers Library Promotion Group; organizer of Executive Women's Council of Pittsburgh. Member of advisory committee of the White House Conference on Library and Information Services, 1977-79. Public information director, Patrick County Project, 1980-82. Project Coordinator, Books Make a Difference Project, Center for the Book, Library of Congress, 1980—. Virginia lay delegate to White House Conference on Library and Information Services Taskforce, 1984.

MEMBER: International Reading Association, Women's National Book Association (past vice-president; president of New York chapter, 1971-73; organizer of Pittsburgh chapter, 1975; national president, 1976-80), American Library Association,

Literacy Volunteers of America (co-founder; board member, 1978-83), Modern Language Association of America, Society for Scholarly Publishing, Women in Scholarly Publishing, National Citizen's Committee for Public Libraries, Center for the Book, Library of Congress, American Association of School Librarians, Association for Supervision and Curriculum Development, National Council of Teachers of English, American National Standards Institute, League of Women Voters, Virginia Library Association, Zonta, Phi Beta Kappa, Phi Kappa Phi, Delta Gamma.

AWARDS, HONORS: Appointed by governor of Virginia to Equal Employment Opportunity Committee of Commonwealth of Virginia, 1983.

WRITINGS: (With Grant Lee) *Education for Publishing,* Association of American Publishers, 1976; (editor) *Constance Lindsay Skinner, Author and Editor: Sketches of Her Life and Character, with a Checklist of Her Writings, and the "Rivers of America" Series,* Women's National Book Association, 1980; (contributor) Robert D. Stueart, editor, *Information in the 80's,* Jai Press, 1982; (contributor) Kathleen K. Rummel and Esther Perica, editors, *Persuasive Public Relations for Libraries,* American Library Association, 1983; (with Roger Parent) *Great Library Promotion Ideas,* American Library Association, 1984.

Under name Margaret Ann Heidbreder: (Editor) *The Buck Hill Falls Report: The School and Library Market,* Association of American Publishers, 1967; (with John Rowell) *Educational Media Selection Centers: Identification and Analysis of Current Practices,* American Library Association, 1971; (with C. P. Bomar and C. A. Nemeyer) *Guide to the Development of Educational Media Selection Centers,* American Library Association, 1972.

Contributor to library and education journals, including *Publishers' Weekly, Library Journal, School Libraries, The Bookwoman, Library of Congress Bulletin,* and *School Media Quarterly.*

WORK IN PROGRESS: With husband, Arthur M. Eastman, editing an autobiography of John Wrenshall.

*　　*　　*

EBEL, Suzanne
　　See GOODWIN, Suzanne

*　　*　　*

EBERSOLE, A(lva) V(ernon), Jr.　1919-

PERSONAL: Born June 27, 1919, in Liberal, Kan.; son of Alva V. (a civil servant) and E. Lucia (Cash) Ebersole; married Carmen Iranzo (a writer), September 24, 1949. *Education:* Mexico City College, B.A., 1949, M.A., 1951; University of Kansas, Ph.D., 1957. *Home:* Calle America, 3, Real de Montroy, Valencia, Spain. *Office:* Department of Romance Languages, University of North Carolina, Chapel Hill, N.C. 27514.

CAREER: Pacific School of Languages, San Diego, Calif., instructor in Spanish, 1951-52; University of Illinois, Urbana, instructor in Spanish, 1957-59; University of Massachusetts— Amherst, assistant professor, 1959-61, associate professor of Spanish, 1961-62; Adelphi University, Garden City, N.Y., professor of Spanish and chairman of department, 1962-68; University of North Carolina at Chapel Hill, professor of Span-

ish, 1968—, director, UNC-at-Seville Program, 1973—. *Military service:* U.S. Marine Corps, 1937-41. U.S. Naval Reserve, 1944-45.

MEMBER: American Association of Teachers of Spanish and Portuguese, Modern Language Association of America, Asociation Internacional de Hispanistas, American Association of University Professors, Sigma Delta Pi, Pi Delta Phi.

WRITINGS: El ambiente espanol visto por Juan Ruiz de Alarcon, Castalia, 1959; (editor) Calderon de la Barca, *La desdicha de la voz,* Castalia, 1963; (editor) Juan Ruiz de Alarcon, *Obras completas,* Castalia, 1966; (editor) Guillen de Castro, *El Narciso en su opinion,* Taurus, 1968; *Cinco cuentistas contemporaneos,* Prentice-Hall, 1969.

Seleccion de comedias del Siglo de Oro espanol, Castalia, 1974; (editor) Juan Ruiz de Alarcon, *La verdad sospechosa,* Catedra, 1976; *Disquisiciònes sobre El burlador de Seville,* Almar, 1978; *Perspectivas de la Comedia,* Siglo de Oro, 1979; *Perspectivas de la Comedia, II,* Albatros, 1980; *Perspectivas de la novela,* Albatros, 1981; *Sontos Diaz Gonzalez, Censor,* Albatros, 1983; *Los Sainetes de Ramon de la Cruz: Nuero examem,* Albatros, 1983. Contributor to journals. Founder and editor, *Hispanofila,* 1957—; editor, *Estudios de Hispanofila* and *Coleccion Siglo de Oro.*

WORK IN PROGRESS: A study of the complete works of Comella.

AVOCATIONAL INTERESTS: Music (presents concerts, with wife, specializing in Spain's Golden Age).

*　　*　　*

ECKARDT, A(rthur) Roy　1918-

PERSONAL: Born August 8, 1918, in Brooklyn, N.Y.; son of Frederick William (an electrician) and Anna (Fitts) Eckardt; married Alice Lyons (a writer and professor), September 2, 1944; children: Paula Jean, Stephen Robert. *Education:* Brooklyn College (now Brooklyn College of the City University of New York), B.A., 1942; Yale University, M.Div., 1944; Columbia University, Ph.D., 1947. *Politics:* Democrat. *Home:* Beverly Hill Rd., Box 619A, Coopersburg, Pa. 18036. *Office:* Department of Religion Studies, Maginnes Hall, Lehigh University, Bethlehem, Pa. 18015.

CAREER: Clergyman of United Methodist Church; Hamline University, St. Paul, Minn., assistant professor of philosophy and religion, 1946-47; Lawrence College, Appleton, Wis., assistant professor of religion, 1947-50; Duke University, Durham, N.C., assistant professor of religion, 1950-51; Lehigh University, Bethlehem, Pa., associate professor, 1951-56, professor of religion, beginning 1956, head of department, 1951-80, professor emeritus, 1980—. Visiting professor of Jewish studies, City University of New York, 1973; visiting scholar at the Oxford centre for post-graduate Hebrew studies, 1982-83. Member of Committee of Church and Jewish People, World Council of Churches, 1964—; member of board of directors, National Committee on American Foreign Policy; member of international committee, Institute for Contemporary Jewry, Hebrew University of Jerusalem. Special advisor, United States Holocaust Memorial Commission.

MEMBER: American Academy of Religion (president, 1956), Phi Beta Kappa, Pi Gamma Mu.

AWARDS, HONORS: Ford Foundation fellow at Harvard University, 1955-56; Distinguished Alumnus Award of Brooklyn College, 1963; Lilly Foundation fellow at Cambridge University, 1963-64; National Foundation for Jewish Culture fellow, 1968-69; L.H.D., Hebrew Union College—Jewish Institute of Religion, 1969; Rockefeller fellow, University of Tuebingen, 1975-76; Jabotinsky Centennial Medal, 1980. Recipient with wife, Alice L. Eckardt, of Human Relations Award of American Jewish Committee of Philadelphia, 1971, Myrtle Wreath Achievement Award of Allentown chapter of Hadassah, 1971, and of Achievement Award of Eastern Pennsylvania Hadassah, 1975.

WRITINGS: Christianity and the Children of Israel, Kings Crown Press, 1948; *The Surge of Piety in America,* Association Press, 1958; *Elder and Younger Brothers: The Encounter of Jews and Christians,* Scribner, 1967; (editor) *The Theologian at Work,* Harper, 1968; (with wife, Alice L. Eckardt) *Encounter with Israel: A Challenge to Conscience,* Association Press, 1970; *Your People, My People,* Quadrangle, 1974; (with A. L. Eckardt) *Long Night's Journey into Day,* Wayne State University Press, 1982; *Jews and Christians,* Indiana University Press, in press.

Contributor: Harold E. Fey and Margaret Frakes, editors, *The Christian Century Reader,* Association Press, 1962; Gregory Baum, editor, *Ecumenical Theology Today,* Paulist Press, 1964; George A. F. Knight, editor, *Jews and Christians,* Westminister, 1965; Gerald H. Anderson, editor, *Christian Mission in Theological Perspective,* Abingdon, 1967; *The Anatomy of Peace in the Middle East,* American Academic Association for Peace in the Middle East, 1969.

James E. Wood, Jr., editor, *Jewish-Christian Relations in Today's World,* Baylor University Press, 1971; Harold Hart, editor, *Punishment,* Hart Publishing, 1972; Alvin H. Rosenfeld and Irving Greenberg, editors, *Confronting the Holocaust,* Indiana University Press, 1978.

Norma H. Thompson and Bruce K. Cole, editors, *The Future of Jewish-Christian Relations,* Character Research, 1982; Richard W. Rousseau, editor, *Christianity and Judaism,* Ridge Row Press, 1983. Also contributor, with A. L. Eckardt, to annals of the American Academy of Political and Social Science, 1981.

Editor of booklet, *Christianity in Israel,* American Academic Association for Peace in the Middle East, 1971. Contributor to more than fifteen scholarly journals. Editor, *Journal of American Academy of Religion,* 1961-69.

WORK IN PROGRESS: For Righteousness' Sake.

SIDELIGHTS: A. Roy Eckardt told *CA:* "Reinhold Niebuhr has had a profound influence on my thought and theological viewpoint. He brought together an understanding of human nature in the individual and society with a keen perception of how political and social institutions must be devised to protect and foster both."

BIOGRAPHICAL/CRITICAL SOURCES: Alan Davies, *Anti-Semitism and the Christian Mind,* Herder & Herder, 1964; *New York Times Book Review,* April 7, 1968; *Christian Century,* April 24, 1968, March 10, 1971; *Commentary,* June, 1968; *Western Humanities Review,* summer, 1968; Frank E. Talmage, *Disputation and Dialogue,* Ktav, 1975.

ECKARDT, Alice L(yons) 1923-

PERSONAL: Born April 27, 1923, in Brooklyn, N.Y.; daughter of Henry Egmont (an executive) and Almira (Palmer) Lyons; married A. Roy Eckardt (a professor and writer), September 2, 1944; children: Paula Jean, Stephen Robert. *Education:* Oberlin College, B.A., 1944; Lehigh University, M.A., 1966. *Politics:* Democrat. *Religion:* Protestant. *Home:* Beverly Hill Rd., Box 619A, Coopersburg, Pa. 18036. *Office:* Department of Religion Studies, Maginnes Hall, Lehigh University, Bethlehem, Pa. 18015.

CAREER: Time, Inc., New York, N.Y., personnel interviewer and supervisor of office staff, 1944-46; Wisconsin Telephone Co., Appleton, commercial representative, 1947-48; Lehigh University, Department of Religion Studies, Bethlehem, Pa., lecturer, 1972-75, assistant professor, 1976—. Visiting scholar at the Oxford center for post-graduate Hebrew studies, 1982. Research associate for Rockefeller Foundation project in West Germany and Great Britain, 1975-76. Member of Executive board of Zachor: Holocaust Resource Center, 1978—; Christian Study Group on Judaism and the Jewish People, chairman, 1979-81, member, 1981—; member of national board, National Institute on the Holocaust, 1981—; member of international committee of the Institute for Contemporary Jewry, Hebrew University of Jerusalem, 1982. Special consultant, President Carter's Commission on the Holocaust, 1979; special advisor, United States Holocaust Memorial Commission, 1981—.

MEMBER: American Academy of Religion, American Professors for Peace in the Middle East, Lehigh University Women's Club (president, 1960-61), Wednesday Club.

AWARDS, HONORS: Recipient with husband, A. Roy Eckardt, of Human Relations Award of American Jewish Committee of Philadelphia, 1971, Myrtle Wreath Achievement Award of Allentown chapter of Hadassah, 1971, and of Achievement Award of Eastern Pennsylvania Hadassah, 1975; Achievement Award of Southern New Jersey Hadassah, 1979.

WRITINGS: (With husband, A. Roy Eckardt, and illustrator) *Encounter with Israel: A Challenge to Conscience,* Association Press, 1970; (contributor) Donald McEvoy, editor, *Christians Confront the Holocaust,* National Conference of Christians and Jews, 1980; (contributor) Michael A. Ryan, editor, *Human Responses to the Holocaust,* Edwin Mellon, 1981; (contributor) *Issues in Teaching the Holocaust: A Guide,* Yeshiva University, 1981; (contributor) Norma H. Thompson and Bruce K. Cole, editors, *The Future of Jewish-Christian Relations,* Character Research, 1982; (with A. Roy Eckardt) *Long Night's Journey into Day,* Wayne State University Press, 1982; (editor and contributor) *Jerusalem: City of the Ages,* University Press of America, 1984; (contributor) Israel Charney, editor, *Toward the Understanding of Genocide,* Westview Press, 1984.

Also contributor, with A. R. Eckardt, to annals of the American Academy of Political and Social Science, 1981. Contributor to *Christian Century, Midstream, Shoah, Judaism, Journal of the American Academy of Religion, Journal of Ecumenical Studies, Evangelische Theologie,* and other periodicals.

WORK IN PROGRESS: An introductory essay for *Stepping Stones II,* edited by Helga Croner, for Stimulus Books.

SIDELIGHTS: Alice L. Eckardt told *CA:* "Nothing is more true than the familiar observation that the most important aspect of writing is the application of the seat of the pants to the seat of the chair. But even once so situated, one can still engage in procrastination, for example, filling out forms for *Contemporary Authors*. Real engagement with a subject is the best antidote, and then one can lose track of time and other responsibilities totally. The next problem to overcome is an infatuation with the sound of one's own words and phrases in order to be able to delete, reorder, and otherwise revise for the ultimate good of the finished product.

AVOCATIONAL INTERESTS: British history, English churches, brass rubbing, birds, wildflowers, gardening.

BIOGRAPHICAL/CRITICAL SOURCES: Christian Century, March 10, 1971; Frank E. Talmage, *Disputation and Dialogue,* Ktav, 1975.

*   *   *

ECKERT, Allan W.   1931-

PERSONAL: Born January 30, 1931, in Buffalo, N.Y.; son of Edward Russell and Ruth (Roth) Eckert; married Joan Dowling, May 14, 1955 (divorced May, 1975); married Gail Ann Hagemann Green, April, 1976 (divorced June, 1978); married Nancy Cross Dent, 1978; children: (first marriage) Julie Ann, Joseph Matthew. *Education:* Attended University of Dayton and Ohio State University. *Politics:* Uncommitted. *Religion:* Agnostic. *Home and office address:* 209 Riverside Dr., P.O. Box 211, Everglades, Fla. 33929. *Agent:* Don Congdon, Don Congdon Associates, Inc., 177 East 70th St., New York, N.Y. 10021.

CAREER: Writer. Prior to 1955 worked as postman, private detective, fireman, plastics technician, cook, dishwasher, laundryman, salesman, chemist's assistant, trapper, commercial artist, draftsman, and at perhaps fifteen types of factory work and farming; National Cash Register Co., Dayton, Ohio, associate editor of *NRC Factory News,* 1955-56; *Dayton Journal-Herald,* Dayton, at various times outdoor editor, nature editor, police reporter, columnist, feature writer, 1957-60. Consultant to LaSalle University and Writer's Digest, Inc., Cincinnati, Ohio. Member of board of trustees, Dayton Museum of Natural History, 1964-65; founder and board chairman of Lemon Bay Conservancy (now Allan Eckert Conservancy); member of board of directors of Charlotte County (Florida) Civic Association. *Military service:* U.S. Air Force, 1948-52, became staff sergeant.

MEMBER: Outdoor Writers Association (board member, 1962—), Society of Magazine Writers, Authors League of America, Authors Guild.

AWARDS, HONORS: Pulitzer Prize nominations, 1964, 1965, 1967, 1968, 1970; Ohioana Book Award, 1968, for *The Frontiersmen;* Friends of American Writers Award, 1968, for *Wild Season* and *The Frontiersmen;* Newbery-Caldecott Honor Book award from American Library Association, 1972, recognition of merit from George C. Stone Center for Children's Books, 1975, and Austrian Juvenile Book of the Year award, 1977, all for *Incident at Hawk's Hill.*

WRITINGS—Published by Little, Brown, except as indicated: *The Writer's Digest Course in Article Writing,* Writer's Digest, 1962; *The Great Auk* (*Reader's Digest* Condensed Book Club selection), 1963; *The Silent Sky: The Incredible Extinction of the Passenger Pigeon,* 1965; *A Time of Terror: The Great Dayton Flood,* 1965; *The Writer's Digest Course in Short Story*

Writing, Writer's Digest, 1965; *Wild Season* (nature study), 1967; *Bayou Backwaters* (nature study), Doubleday, 1968; *The Crossbreed* (nature novel; *Reader's Digest* Condensed Book Club selection), 1968; *The Dreaming Tree* (novel), 1968; *The King Snake* (nature novel), 1968; *Blue Jacket: War Chief of the Shawnees,* 1969.

In Search of a Whale (nonfiction), Doubleday, 1970; *Incident at Hawk's Hill* (novel; *Reader's Digest* Condensed Book Club selection), 1971; *The Court-Martial of Daniel Boone* (historical novel), 1973; *Tecumseh!* (play), 1974; *The Owls of North America: All the Species and Subspecies Described and Illustrated,* illustrations by Karl E. Karalus, Doubleday, 1974, new edition, 1975; *The HAB Theory* (science fiction), 1976; *The Wading Birds of North America: All the Species and Subspecies Described and Illustrated,* illustrations by Karalus, Doubleday, 1979; *Savage Journey* (novel), 1979.

Song of the Wild (novel), 1980; *Whattizzit? Nature Pun Quizzes,* Landfall Press, 1981; *Johnny Logan: Shawnee Spy,* 1983; *The Scarlet Mansion* (novel), 1985.

"Winning of America" series; all historical narratives: *The Frontiersmen,* 1967; *Wilderness Empire,* 1969; *The Conquerors,* 1970; *The Wilderness War,* 1978; *Gateway to Empire,* 1983.

"Mesmerian Annals" series: *The Dark Green Tunnel,* 1984; *The Wand,* 1985.

Author of over 200 television scripts for "Wild Kingdom," and of screenplays, "The Legend of Koo-Tan," 1971, "Wild Journey," 1972, "The Kentucky Pioneers," 1972, "George Rodgers Clark," 1973. Contributor of over 200 articles to magazines.

WORK IN PROGRESS: A sixth book in the "Winning of America" series, entitled *Twilight of Empire; 2500 Gem, Mineral and Rock Collecting Sites in North America, North of Mexico.*

SIDELIGHTS: Allan W. Eckert has chosen in large part to work within literary genres of his own making, combining both history and natural history with fiction in a fashion peculiarly his own. Eckert's ability to craft popular narratives from subject matter usually reserved for more scholarly texts has placed him in an uncommon middle ground between academic and popular writers. While the author has sometimes drawn fire from academic critics for his use of novelistic techniques, he has also frequently been praised for rendering the detailed nuances of natural science and history in a manner both intelligible and fascinating to readers. A number of writers employ the phrase "documentary fiction" to describe the two major types of writing that make up the bulk of Eckert's output: historical narrative and nature study.

Discussing the former in *Library Journal,* H. E. Smith writes: "Eckert aims to bridge a gap between scholarly history and historical fiction; he uses a lot of dialogue, but it is authentic, derived from diaries and other contemporaneous accounts." The essence of Eckert's approach to historical writing is reflected in his "Winning of America" series, an ongoing collection of books tracing the gradual conquest of the American frontier by settlers and explorers. *New York Times Book Review* critic Walter Havighurst has described the author's methods in *The Frontiersmen,* the first book in the series: "Using the voluminous Draper manuscripts and other firsthand accounts of the winning of the West, Eckert has followed the frontiersmen from the first wondering exploration of the Ohio valley in the 1770's to the crushing of the final Indian resistance in the War of 1812. His book is a panoramic frontier history, crammed with incident, with savages and pioneers.''

Eckert has become widely known for his use of what he has called ''hidden dialog,'' working with highly researched but nevertheless invented conversation to provide the narrative flow in his books. James Nelson Goodsell, speaking in the *Christian Science Monitor,* believes Eckert's ''brand of history takes some getting used to. It reads very like fiction, but is actually fact dressed up in the style of a novel. He leans heavily on dialog to tell his story, making ample use of whatever historical conversation remains in archives but also adopting the practice of [using hidden dialog]—putting quotation marks around material not initially recorded as dialog but recorded as having been said or heard or thought after an event.'' While Goodsell expresses some trepidation about the use of such methods, in a different article in the same publication he asserts, ''If anything, the use of 'hidden dialog' enhances the story and one puts the book down feeling that this concession to the novel has not hurt the story one whit.''

Criticism of Eckert's historical narratives has centered on their relative value as history and as fiction and the part played by his use of ''hidden dialog'' in such a distinction. Historians have sometimes faulted his methods, while at the same time confessing their attraction. Helen Hornbeck Tanner, reviewing *Gateway to Empire* in the *Washington Post,* remarks, ''Readers of Eckert's historical novels always ask if it's 'really true.' His history is often inspired, but not uniformly dependable.'' And professor Irwin Polishook, discussing *Wilderness Empire* in the *New York Times Book Review,* believes the ''author's use of extrapolated 'dialogue' in an effort to make his book more lively and the absence of interpretation limit the value of the account.'' In a *Library Journal* review of Eckert's *Time of Terror: The Great Dayton Flood,* Robert H. Donahugh offers a different perspective: ''Purists may object to [his] liberal use of invented dialogue and stream-of-consciousness, but the result is a vividness and immediacy that will capture and hold readers of all ages.'' A *Kirkus Reviews* critic echoes Donahugh in an article on *Wilderness Empire,* observing how ''contemporary materials have been . . . converted . . . into permissable dialogue, giving the account fictional virtues without destroying its historical values.''

In addition to his historical works, Eckert, working in a detailed, informed, and highly realistic idiom, has authored a body of ''nature novels'' unique in their approach, among them *The Great Auk, Wild Season, Bayou Backwater,* and *Incident at Hawk's Hill.* Drawing on his experiences as a fisherman, trapper, explorer, and versatile outdoorsman, as well as his role as the scriptwriter for over two hundred episodes of the television series ''Wild Kingdom,'' he combines a naturalist's eye for detail with the storyteller's art.

The Great Auk, Eckert's chronicle of the decline of an entire species of bird now extinct, was the author's first published work to treat the natural world, and its characteristic use of fictional methods to portray actual events in the natural environment set a pattern for subsequent works. Marian Sorenson, reviewing *The Great Auk* in the *Christian Science Monitor,* describes the unusual plot of a book intended to be read as a novel, ''In a powerful and poetic flow [Eckert] traces the brief life of a single great auk from its hatching on Edley Island in the North Atlantic until its fatal return two years later to the same island, where it and its mate represent the last two great auks on earth.'' *Best Sellers* critic Oscar A. Bouise finds the term ''novel'' entirely appropriate for *The Great Auk,* remarking; ''The author calls it a novel and rightly so: a more powerful or tragic plot can hardly be matched by anything in the mind of a great writer. Eckert is masterful when describing incidents and places. . . . His descriptions are vivid, palpable, intensely real.''

In a *Best Sellers* article, Ralph C. Baxter explores the difficulties faced by Eckert in *The Great Auk* and in the work on a similar theme which followed it (*The Silent Sky: The Incredible Extinction of the Passenger Pigeon*): ''[He] experienced several essential literary problems in both 'Great Auk' and 'Silent Sky': how to tell the stories of auks and pigeons to adult humans; how to inform about bird behavior and yet create 'novel-story' quality; how to make a conservation message both subtle and compelling.'' Having said which, Baxter asserts, ''Eckert didn't completely solve these problems.'' In the opinion of *New York Times Book Review* critic Robert Murphy however, Eckert fully overcomes the difficulties inherent in writing an extended novel from the point of view of a bird in *The Silent Sky.* He states: ''It is so well provided with details of the bird's existence, ingeniously invented incidents to point up man's extraordinary and wasteful brutality, and the bird's inability to adapt to it, that the melancholy story is made plain. One follows it with a sort of horrified fascination.''

Incident at Hawk's Hill may be said to combine both of the major preoccupations of Eckert's writing career in its tale of a frontier boy adopted by a female badger after he becomes lost in the woods. Writers such as *Christian Science Monitor* critic Jennifer Farley Smith criticize the book for its depiction of violence in the natural world, but other reviewers are quick to point out that the story had been derived from an actual event recorded in Canadian history. ''The truth of the basic outline of the tale adds, of course, enormously to its interest,'' says a critic in *Books and Bookmen,* ''and a great deal of fascinating information is given about badgers and their habits. It is told vividly and convincingly.'' A *Times Literary Supplement* writer finds ''the author's observation of wild life . . . very fine indeed, and the adventure is wonderfully strange.''

While Eckert's writing career has centered on historical subjects and the natural environment, he has also authored plays, short stories, and in recent years several contemporary novels, including his 1976 work of science fiction, *The HAB Theory.* Eckert would prefer to be seen as a writer of diverse abilities, telling *CA:* ''I do not care to be categorized as a writer of only this or that type of writing. What motivates me? Actually it is more a matter of obsessiveness than mere motivation. I *must* write. What constitutes a writer? First he must be a *reader.* He must have something to say and a desire to express it in a way that is better and different than anyone else has said it previously. And he must have the tenacity to go on in the face of repeated rejection. Most important, he must believe in himself and in his ability to express well what he wishes to say.''

Eckert's works have been translated twenty-seven times into thirteen languages.

AVOCATIONAL INTERESTS: Exploring uncharted areas of jungle or wilderness; collecting butterflies, moths, beetles, and other insects (collection includes over twenty-five thousand specimens), as well as fossils, mineral specimens, and other nature objects; collecting rare books (collection exceeds fifteen thousand volumes); observing nature; fishing.

CA INTERVIEW

CA interviewed Allan W. Eckert by telephone on April 13, 1984, at his home in Everglades, Florida.

CA: You've talked about writing for twelve years, through more than a thousand rejection slips . . .

ECKERT: Eleven hundred and forty-seven rejection slips, to be exact.

CA: What kept you going emotionally?

ECKERT: I had to write; it was never really a choice. I cannot remember a time when I was not writing. I think I came out of the womb with a pencil in my hand, because I have always written, and it's a compulsion with me. My work day is usually anywhere from fourteen to eighteen to twenty hours a day, sitting either at the typewriter or at the computer doing my writing.

CA: Was there any encouragement during that long time?

ECKERT: No. In fact, there was quite a great deal of *discouragement.* One of the things that sticks out in my mind was the very first book I wrote. It was a horrible thing. I think I had titled it *Unlawful.* Anyway, it was very bad, a cops-and-robbers shoot-up type of thing. I was in the service at the time. My commanding officer read it and he liked it, and he said, "I have a friend who is an agent and a bookseller, so I'll give it to him and see what he says." I said OK. So he gave it to him and I received a communication from this man—Charles McLean, his name was. He said, "Dear Corporal Eckert: I have to say first-off that I wish you'd stop wasting your time, my time, and everybody else's time, because you are not a writer now, you will never be a writer, you do not have it. Please stop wasting everybody's time." That was the sum and substance of the letter. It was with some gratification that, not many years after that, I saw he was selling my books in his book store. I never pointed out to him what he had written about me.

Yes, there were a great many discouragements, and for perhaps ten of those twelve years the rejection slips were plain, ordinary printed rejection slips—not even a personal note. It was very disheartening. But I couldn't stop writing. Then eventually I began getting little personal notes jotted here and there on the rejection slips, or even personal rejection letters. And I began to realize that it was not the fault of the editors, but my own fault; I was not writing what people wanted to read. I was writing what *I* wanted to read. That's a big mistake that many new writers make.

CA: Many of your early published articles and books were about nature, which you obviously care a great deal about. Did your parents nurture that concern with nature in you, as you have tried to do with your children?

ECKERT: Not at all! Actually, my mother was not a nature lover per se. She was petrified at snakes and spiders and all the other things. My father died when I was a very small child. I lived in the slums of Chicago, which is hardly conducive to the study of nature. Yet I remember as a little boy four and five years old crawling between the areaways of buildings and looking under piles of junk at the mice nesting under there, or sometimes seeing spiders or sometimes a rare snake, and studying the bugs that would turn up when I turned over a board or a sign. So that love has always been there.

CA: In your historical writing especially you have a reputation for doing extensive and thorough research. Have you run into any particularly difficult research problems in researching for the "Winning of America" series?

ECKERT: Oh, sure. Every now and then you come across problems. Unfortunately, one of the things you cannot do in a factual work is embroider or make things up or bridge the gap. Very often you get so frustrated, because you can trace a person's career to such and such a point and then suddenly there's a blank of four or five or maybe ten years. You have no idea what happened during this period, and there's no documentation for it whatsoever. That's how it must remain; you simply cannot make things up. Now, I have written two historical novels in which I have attempted to bridge this gap. One was a novel called *Blue Jacket,* the story of Marmaduke Van Swearingen and how he became a Shawnee Indian by being captured by them and then rising to become their war chief. There were a lot of gaps in his entire history, but there was enough scattered throughout his career that it was relatively easy, knowing the character of the person, to fill in these gaps as he *would have* acted according to what was known by how he *did* act. So that's what I did with him, and I did the same thing just recently with his counterpart, Johnny Logan, who was an Indian captured by the whites and raised by them for a while. There were so many gaps in both their lives that I could not write them as history; they had to be done as historical novels.

CA: In his review of Gateway to Empire (American History Illustrated, *December 1983), Paul A. Hutton, of Utah State University, speculated that despite the research and documentation, "academic historians will probably never recognize Eckert's books as history because of the novelistic techniques he employs." You've noted that some of your books are used in high school and college courses. Do you think they have cleared the hurdle, or will there always be academic critics?*

ECKERT: I think there will always be that sense of antagonism between myself and the "academic historians," part of the reason being plain and simple jealousy. My books are popular. I do tell history in a way that—as I stress it does—takes the better elements of the novel form and blends them with history in such a way that the historical accuracy is not impaired, and yet it can read like a novel so that people can enjoy it and get the real feel and sense of history. At one time, when I was signing books in Columbus, Ohio—it was midday, and I was at Lazarus Department Store, and four or five gentlemen came in at the same time. The question came up of why they were here, why were they not at work. One of them explained that they were instructors at Ohio State University. My wife asked what they taught, and they said history. Then my wife kind of chuckled and said, "You mean you like Allan Eckert books?" They loved them! She pointed out that I get a lot of flack from academic historians, and one of the men said, 'That's all just sour grapes." I don't say I don't make mistakes; I don't think there's anyone writing history anywhere in the world who doesn't make mistakes. But they are honest, legitimate mistakes. I don't make mistakes from copying from previous historians who have copied from previous historians, etc. That's where I find a lot of errors are promulgated throughout the ages, and we come up with an erroneous idea of what history is really all about. My effort is to go back to the original documents and to look at these not just from the angle or concerning the individual I'm interested in primarily, but to get a general feeling of the age, of all sides of any particular issue, what is going on and who is saying what. Everybody who wrote at any time, whether it's in letters or diaries or journals or whatever, had his own particular bias. One must take that into consideration. Therefore, when you get all of these things and put them together in chronological order and begin to feel the sense of what was going on, you see who blew things up, who changed things, who lied, who cheated; you get a much more comprehensive and much better idea of what actually occurred than you do by simply concentrating on an individual or an event from one side.

I get a great deal of mail from historians, especially younger historians, degreed historians who are either teaching or writing. They are almost universally thrilled with the "Winning of America" series and the way I do my research. It is mostly from the old guard that I encounter criticism. One of the worst reviews I ever had was in the *New York Times*. It was written by a historian of the Great Lakes area. He just took *The Frontiersmen* to pieces, but without just cause. This is really sad. Another case in point is where people do not really sense what's going on. For example, in the *Kirkus Reviews* I have been lambasted a couple of times for having dialogue that sounds like a B-grade movie. Unfortunately, this dialogue they were talking about was lifted from the historical record, and that's how they talked. How do you combat this?

CA: Are there writers who have been inspirations to you in any way?

ECKERT: Not so much living writers, although there are a few, but I was very much influenced at a younger age by John Steinbeck, whom I considered to be *the* American writer. I also was influenced by the work of Dickens, Rudyard Kipling, Jack London, and a number of others. These people all had an influence to some extent upon me. I think I felt strongest toward John Steinbeck because of his feel for people and for a situation in its grand scheme as it related to the individual.

CA: Are you still writing scripts for the television series "Wild Kingdom"?

ECKERT: Yes, I've done more than two hundred at this point, and I still do them. They send them down to me every now and then. I refuse now to write any of what we call the mechanical or technical shows, where we're working with a lot of scientists and equipment and so on, banding animals and that kind of thing. I'm really not interested in that kind of show. I still do their species shows, where there are no people involved and we are simply telling the story of how a particular animal lives within its environment.

CA: And that's what some of your books have grown out of?

ECKERT: Right.

CA: In your books about animals, you are particularly good at conveying the relative intelligence of the species you're writing about—dealing with such things as memory or lack of it, and instinctive as opposed to learned behavior. Have you done intensive studies in animal behavior?

ECKERT: Quite a bit—on my own, nothing academic. On my own, I find myself at odds with a lot of scientists who adhere

to the belief that there is no intelligence, that everything is instinctive. I really can't buy this, because I've witnessed too many cases of learned behavior that changes an animal's life and causes it to do something totally apart from its genetic memories, so to speak. It's an interesting subject, and I do take a little criticism in this respect. I have never been accused of anthropomorphism, which I assiduously avoid because I dislike anthropomorphism. I do not give, or tend to give, the feelings, the emotions, the reasoning powers of a human being to an animal. But I cannot believe that animals do not communicate with one another. I've seen too many evidences of it—all my life. I cannot believe that animals cannot reason; I have seen animals reason with great skill in the wild in obtaining their food, protecting their young, and other ways. Yes, I definitely believe that there is a reasoning process that goes on, even down to the smallest creature. Tell me ants can't reason. Follow a line of ants working to some point, and disturb it, and see what happens. Watch how they reason, how they rise to meet the emergency. I think there is definitely reason among virtually all life, including plant life, which may throw some people for a spin.

CA: You are deeply concerned about endangered species. Do you work in any public way for this cause, besides your writing?

ECKERT: I used to. I don't anymore. I founded the Lemon Bay Conservancy in Florida, which is still active and which I understand they have renamed the Allan Eckert Conservancy. In this way we saved an estuarial system, a bay that was endangered, eleven islands in that bay on which a series of trailer camps was going to be built with no sewage facilities. At one time I was greatly involved in trying to help species now and bring awareness to those that we had destroyed. But I find in my later years that my writing has taken different directions. I don't write about nature as much as I used to, nor am I as concerned with crusading as I used to be in my younger years. I simply have other things that I want to do more.

CA: Your travels, especially your jungle explorations, have figured a lot in your writing. Do you still find time to travel extensively?

ECKERT: Not as much as I would like to. I get out occasionally, and of course I live down here in the Everglades now, which is pretty remote, and I go out whenever possible into the very farthest back reaches of the country. I'm a constant source of amusement to the natives—"crackers," as they call themselves—who find it very mysterious that I can go out into areas that they don't know, and find my way around and lead *them* in and out.

CA: Your books cross a lot of boundaries and don't fall easily into categories, which baffles a lot of people.

ECKERT: And which bothers my publishers no end, because I'm always coming up with ideas for something totally different. He says, "You can't do it." My first two books dealt with vanished species—the great auk and the passenger pigeon—and I was very rapidly becoming known as a writer about extinct birds. Well, you've got to realize there's not much of a future in that, so I had to break the mold in a hurry. And each time I have broken the so-called mold, my publisher has gotten pretty antsy and even reticent about taking a flyer on it. But it's worked out well, and by now they realize that I can write almost anything I set my mind to writing.

CA: I think a good example of the boundary crossing with your books is the "adult" book Incident at Hawk's Hill *(1971), which won three big awards for juvenile literature. Does this keep any of your work from having as wide a readership as it should?*

ECKERT: It probably does. I frequently get a call or a letter from somebody who says, "I have all your books; I'm your greatest fan." And it turns out that the person has the "Winning of America" books but has never heard of the others, or has two or three or four of the nature books and has never heard of the "Winning of America" series. It does hurt in that respect. But I really don't consider that my problem. I write what I need and have to write.

I have just embarked now on two different kinds of writing projects that I'm working on full-tilt. One of these is the first of a ten- or eleven-book series, probably, that first one dedicated to the memory of C. S. Lewis, who wrote the children's fantasies entitled the "Chronicles of Narnia." Mine are called the "Mesmerian Annals," and they have much of the flavor of the "Chronicles of Narnia" but a more contemporary setting and different kinds of problems. Little, Brown got the first one and went absolutely berserk over it. They're making it one of their big publishing events of this year and have hired a tremendous artist to do the art work for it. This will be out in May. It's called *The Dark Green Tunnel*. I've already written the second one, *The Wand*, which they think is better than the first one. That will be out about a year from now. So I'm going great guns in that direction.

Right at this moment I'm working on a massive novel, which I think is going to be my tour de force so far as novel writing is concerned. This deals with the activities of a mass murderer in Chicago at the turn of the century and with the detective from Philadelphia who ultimately tracked him down. It goes very deeply into human emotions; it is not a sensation book per se. The man committed something like 130 murders and did various and sundry horrid crimes, but the main thing is looking into the characters, into their emotions and their own justifications of themselves and what they're doing. It will be called *The Scarlet Mansion*. I'll have it done probably by October or November.

CA: Your books are translated into at least thirteen languages now. Do you get more fan mail from any one particular country?

ECKERT: Oddly enough, I get a lot of mail from England and a lot of mail from Australia, some mail from Germany, occasionally a letter from Japan. Once in a while I get a letter from Portugal or Sweden or Denmark or Italy. But it's from all over, and the big ones seem to be the English-speaking countries.

CA: You are interested in collecting rare books and manuscripts. What subjects are important in your collection?

ECKERT: I have a marvelous collection of old volumes, particularly dealing with American history—mostly west of the Mississippi but a good bit of it east of the Mississippi as well. One of these days I think I'm probably going to donate these books to a large library somewhere, possibly Boston University, who collects my papers, simply because I live now in an area where hurricanes do happen, and overnight this beautiful library could be destroyed. I would hate to see that happen, because there are so many irreplaceable volumes in it.

CA: Is there something you haven't done that you'd like to try?

ECKERT: Well, I'm always trying new things that I haven't done before. To me, to be categorized in any particular field is really terrible; and I guess I am the type of person who loves a challenge, and once the challenge has been met, I want to move on to something else. This has been the way of my life since I was a small child. I used to take a lot of flak from my mother in this respect, because I would get keenly interested in a project, and she anticipated that once I had excelled in that project, this would be my forte and I would continue. But at that point I would begin to lose interest and want to go on to different things.

CA: Are there any screenplays in the works?

ECKERT: I do not have any in the works. Oddly enough, I was contacted this morning by a lady in Indiana who wants me to do another outdoor drama similar to *Tecumseh*. I'm constantly getting queries and interest in my works, either for screenplays by somebody else or for me to do them. I field them as they come along. I've done three full-length features for the producers of "Wild Kingdom." I did a half-hour movie for *Encyclopaedia Britannica*. I've written a screenplay and actually a miniseries screenplay for *The Frontiersmen* in eight parts. This is being negotiated. It's been negotiated for so long that I don't know if it'll ever appear, but at least it's in the works.

BIOGRAPHICAL/CRITICAL SOURCES: Christian Science Monitor, October 31, 1963, October 23, 1969, May 13, 1971; *Best Sellers,* November 1, 1963; *Library Journal,* March 15, 1965; August, 1967; *New York Times Book Review,* October 31, 1965, June 4, 1967, September 17, 1967, March 3, 1968, June 30, 1968, November 16, 1969, May 23, 1971, April 7, 1974; *New Yorker,* November 11, 1965; *New York Review of Books,* December 9, 1965; *New York Times,* April 29, 1967; *Times Literary Supplement,* November 3, 1972; *Books and Bookmen,* February 2, 1973; *Washington Post,* November 12, 1979, February 11, 1983; *Contemporary Literary Criticism,* Volume XVII, Gale, 1981; *American History Illustrated,* August, 1983.

—*Sketch by Robert T. Wilson*

—*Interview by Jean W. Ross*

*   *   *

ECKSTEIN, Otto   1927-1984

PERSONAL: Born August 1, 1927, in Ulm, Germany (now West Germany); died of cancer, March 22, 1984, in Boston, Mass.; married Harriet Mirkin, 1954; children: Warren, Felicia, June. *Education:* Princeton University, A.B., 1951; Harvard University, A.M., 1952, Ph.D., 1955. *Office:* Department of Economics, Littauer Center, Harvard University, Cambridge, Mass. 02138.

CAREER: Harvard University, Cambridge, Mass., instructor, 1955-57, assistant professor, 1957-60, associate professor, 1962-63, professor of economics, beginning 1963, Paul M. Warburg Professor of Economics, 1975-84. Data Resources, Inc., founder, 1968, president, 1969-81. Technical director, Joint Economic Committee, U.S. Congress, 1959-61; member of President Lyndon Johnson's Council of Economic Advisers, 1964-66. White House and government advisor. *Military service:* U.S. Army, 1946-47.

MEMBER: American Economic Association, Econometric Society.

AWARDS, HONORS: Guggenheim fellow, 1960.

WRITINGS: Water Resource Development: The Economics of Project Evaluation, Harvard University Press, 1958; (with J. V. Krutilla) *Multiple Purpose River Development: Studies in Applied Economic Analysis,* Johns Hopkins Press, 1958; *Trends in Public Expenditures in the Next Decade,* Committee for Economic Development, 1959; (with others) *Staff Report on Employment, Growth, and Price Levels,* U.S. Government Printing Office, 1959; *Public Finance: Budgets, Taxes, Fiscal Policy* (textbook), Prentice-Hall, 1963, 4th edition, 1979; (with others) *Economic Policy in Our Time: An International Comparison,* three volumes, North-Holland, 1964; (editor) *Studies in the Economics of Income Maintenance,* Brookings Institution Studies of Government Finance, 1967; (editor) *Parameters and Policies in the U.S. Economy,* North-Holland, 1976; *The Great Recession,* North-Holland, 1978; *Core Inflation,* Prentice-Hall, 1981; *The DRI Model of the U.S. Economy,* McGraw, 1983; (with others) *The DRI Report on U.S. Manufacturing Industries,* McGraw, 1984. Also author of articles on taxation, government expenditures, wages and prices, employment problems, economic development, forecasting, and econometric models.

SIDELIGHTS: A prominent American economist, Otto Eckstein was chiefly interested in inflation—its causes, measurement, and the methods of controlling it, relates J. Y. Smith in the *Washington Post.* Eckstein is credited with originating the term "core inflation" to describe basic price fluctuations within the economy after abstracting such temporary factors as increases in produce prices due to unexpected crop damage. And he became nationally known, indicates a *Los Angeles Times* writer, "for his rule for gauging productivity: Each percentage point drop in productivity adds two points to the inflation rate. Thus, he reasoned, increasing productivity would decrease inflation." Eckstein emphasized that federal tax and spending policies could be used to affect the direction of the economy. "As a member of the Council of Economic Advisers," indicates Karen W. Arenson in the *New York Times,* "Mr. Eckstein was responsible for wage-price guidepost policies and helped develop some of the programs of the Great Society."

He also founded Data Resources, Inc. (D.R.I.), the largest economic advisory service in the country, which was purchased by McGraw-Hill in 1979 for $103 million. A *Time* reporter indicated in 1977 that, at D.R.I., Eckstein "has built by far the world's largest bank of economic statistics—more than 3.5 million *series* of figures about the U.S. and 127 other countries. These data are constantly updated by his staff of 250 economists and analysts from the huge mass of numbers put out free by governments, associations and corporations. Then the figures are fed into the most capacious computer that Burroughs has ever sold." According to Smith, "Eckstein and his associates created an econometric model of the U.S. economy and used it both to analyze and forecast economic activity. The model—a set of mathematical equations describing past relationships, such as changes in wages and prices, or the level of interest

rates in connection with housing construction—became steadily more detailed over the years and was the subject of 'Core Inflation.'"

Eckstein thought his greatest influence was as a teacher, however. As Arenson reports, he "left his mark on generations of Harvard students, both economics majors and others. While some professors spurned undergraduate courses whenever possible, Mr. Eckstein made a point of teaching undergraduates. So closely was he identified with the introductory economics course, long known as Economics 10 (and now labeled Social Analysis 10), that he was sometimes referred to as Otto Ec-10, instead of Otto Eckstein."

BIOGRAPHICAL/CRITICAL SOURCES: Time, September 26, 1977; *Euromoney,* December, 1980.

OBITUARIES: Los Angeles Times, March 23, 1984; *New York Times,* March 23, 1984; *Washington Post,* March 23, 1984; *Chicago Tribune,* March 24, 1984; *Times* (London), March 26, 1984; *Newsweek,* April 2, 1984; *Time,* April 2, 1984.†

*   *   *

EDMUND, Sean
   See PRINGLE, Laurence P.

*   *   *

EDWARDS, Gerald (Kenneth Savery) Hamilton
   See HAMILTON-EDWARDS, Gerald (Kenneth Savery)

*   *   *

EELLS, George   1922-

PERSONAL: Born January 20, 1922, in Winslow, Ill.; son of Clark V. (a teacher) and Martha (Hardle) Eells. *Education:* Attended Northwestern University, 1940-43, and Columbia University, 1945. *Politics:* Democrat. *Home:* 514 North Rodeo Drive, Beverly Hills, Calif. 90210. *Agent:* Gloria Safier, Inc., 244 East 53rd St., New York, N.Y. 10022.

CAREER: Parade, New York City, entertainment editor, 1945; *Look,* New York City, 1946-60, entertainment editor, 1948-60; *Theatre Arts,* New York City, editor, 1962; *Signature* (Diners Club magazine), New York City, editor, 1963-67; writer. *Member:* Writers Guild of America, Authors Guild, Authors League of America. *Awards, honors:* National Theater Conference fellowship, 1947; *New York Times'* outstanding non-fiction list, 1967, for *The Life That Late He Led; Reader's Digest'*s most unforgettable characters anthology includes *The Short Profile of Cole Porter,* 1968; first annual Deems Taylor Award of American Society of Composers, Authors, and Publishers ($300), 1968; *New York Times* notable book list, 1981, for *High Times, Hard Times.*

WRITINGS: The Life That Late He Led: A Biography of Cole Porter, Putnam, 1967; *Hedda and Louella* (biographies of Hedda Hopper and Louella Parsons), Putnam, 1972; *Ginger, Loretta, and Irene WHO?,* Putnam, 1976; (with Ethel Merman) *Merman,* Simon & Schuster, 1978, published as *Merman: An Autobiography,* Berkley Publishing, 1979; (with Stanley Musgrove) *Mae West: A Biography,* Morrow, 1982; (with Anita O'Day) *High Times, Hard Times,* Putnam, 1981; *Robert Mitchum,* F. Watts, 1984. Also author of scripts for "This Is Your Life" television series, 1971-72 and 1984. Contributor to magazines.

SIDELIGHTS: "In honor of George Eells, I hereby invent a literary genre—the popcorn book," *Newsweek* critic Walter Clemons writes. "One reads it at a clip, is ashamed of having such a good time and must retrieve one's dignity by putting down the author for having gratified an appetite for gossip about movie stars." A celebrity biographer, George Eells has built his reputation on books about entertainers' lives. His subjects have ranged from musicians (Cole Porter) to gossip columnists (Hedda Hopper and Louella Parsons) to Broadway stars (Ethel Merman), but his best known book to date remains a publication he co-authored with Stanley Musgrove entitled *Mae West: A Biography.*

Published in 1982, two years after the star had died, the book recounts the important events in Mae West's life, her climb from vaudeville to Broadway to the silver screen, and her relentless pursuit of the limelight. The portrait that emerges is not flattering. Manipulative, self-centered, "she seems not to have had a kind bone in her body," *Washington Post Book World* reviewer Jonathan Yardley reports. "Absolutely nothing—moral piety, racial prejudice, private emotions or attachments—stood between Mae West and the advancement of her legend." Writing in the *Chicago Tribune Book World,* Gerald Weales describes her as "completely ruthless, willing to sacrifice anyone who might try to share her spotlight. 'Nobody gets laughs in my pictures but me,' she is supposed to have told Henry Hathaway, insisting that he cut from 'Personal Appearance' (1936) a shot of a bulldog wiggling like the star."

West was equally calculating in her attitude toward men, regarding them as sexual objects to be used and then discarded. "As long as they serve my purpose, they're fine,"she once said. "But if they take up too much of my time, I eliminate them—see what I mean? I never permit myself to get absorbed in anything else. I'm not going to stop being Mae West for any man."

Caught up in the making of her own legend, West appears to have experienced little private life, and critics, therefore, find it understandable that she does not emerge as a human being even in her biography. "The great joy of her life must have been the ease with which her public and private characters coalesced," reports the *Times Literary Supplement.* "Indeed, there was virtually no difference between them." While praising the book as "a fine, honest account of a narcissist's life," *Ms.* magazine concludes that the biography is "sad. At her core, the juice remained unsqueezed." Yardley concludes his review on a brighter note: "She was no angel, but in her unique and original fashion she soared. She gets her just desserts in this perceptive, funny and candid book."

MEDIA ADAPTATIONS: Robert Wise Productions purchased *The Life That Late He Led: A Biography of Cole Porter* for filming.

BIOGRAPHICAL/CRITICAL SOURCES: Washington Post Book World, April 2, 1972, March 14, 1982; *New York Times Book Review,* April 23, 1972, May 21, 1978, June 13, 1982, July 1, 1984; *Newsweek,* February 21, 1977; George Eells and Stanley Musgrove, *Mae West: A Biography,* Morrow, 1982; *New York Times,* March 15, 1982; *Los Angeles Times,* March 18, 1982; *New Yorker,* April 12, 1982; *Ms.,* June, 1982; *Chicago Tribune Book World,* June 13, 1982; *Times Literary Supplement,* June 15, 1984.

EFIRD, James M(ichael) 1932-

PERSONAL: Born May 30, 1932, in Kannapolis, N.C.; son of James R. (in textiles) and I. Z. (Christy) Efird; married Joan Shelf, June 30, 1951 (divorced November, 1971); married Vivian Poythress, March 7, 1975; children: (first marriage) Whitney Michelle. *Education:* Davidson College, A.B., 1954; Louisville Presbyterian Seminary, B.D., 1958; Duke University, Ph.D., 1962. *Religion:* Presbyterian. *Home:* 2609 Heather Glen Rd., Durham, N.C. 27712. *Office:* Duke University Divinity School, Durham, N.C. 27706.

CAREER: Ordained minister of Presbyterian Church, 1958; Duke University Divinity School, Durham, N.C., assistant professor, 1962-68, associate professor of Biblical studies, 1968—, director of academic affairs, 1971-75.

MEMBER: Society of Biblical Literature and Exegesis, Phi Beta Kappa.

WRITINGS: (Editor and contributor) *The Use of the Old Testament in the New and Other Essays,* Duke University Press, 1972; *These Things Are Written: An Introduction to the Religious Ideas of the Bible,* John Knox, 1978; *Daniel and Revelation: A Study of Two Extraordinary Visions,* Judson, 1978; *Jeremiah: Prophet under Siege,* Judson, 1979; *The New Testament Writings: History, Literature, and Interpretation,* John Knox, 1980; *Christ, the Church, and the End: Studies in Colossians and Ephesians,* Judson, 1980; *The Old Testament Writings: History, Literature, and Interpretation,* John Knox, 1982; *The Old Testament Prophets Then and Now,* Judson, 1982; *Biblical Books of Wisdom,* Judson, 1983; *How to Interpret the Bible,* John Knox, 1984.

WORK IN PROGRESS: Marriage, Divorce, and the Bible, for Abingdon; *Four Portraits of Jesus: A Study of the Gospels; Introduction to New Testament Greek.*

*   *   *

EHRLICH, Amy 1942-

PERSONAL: Born July 24, 1942, in New York, N.Y.; daughter of Max (an author) and Doris (Rubenstein) Ehrlich; children: Joss. *Education:* Attended Bennington College, 1960-62, 1963-65. *Home:* 379 6th St., Brooklyn, N.Y. 11215. *Office:* Dial Books for Young Readers, 2 Park Ave., New York, N.Y. 10016.

CAREER: Early jobs for short periods included teacher in day care center, fabric colorist, and hospital receptionist; Dial Books for Young Readers, New York, N.Y., executive editor, 1978—.

WRITINGS—For young people: Zeek Silver Moon, Dial, 1972; (adaptor for young readers) Dee Brown, *Wounded Knee* (originally published as *Bury My Heart at Wounded Knee*), Holt, 1974; *The Everyday Train,* Dial, 1977; (adaptor) Hans Christian Andersen, *Thumbelina,* Dial, 1979.

(Adaptor) Andersen, *The Wild Swans,* Dial, 1981; *Leo, Zack, and Emmie,* Dial, 1981; *Annie and the Kidnappers,* Random House, 1982; *Annie Finds a Home,* Random House, 1982; *Annie: The Storybook Based on the Movie,* Random House, 1982; (adaptor) Andersen, *The Snow Queen,* Dial, 1982; (editor) *The Random House Fairy Tale Treasury,* Random House, 1985; *Bunnies All Day Long,* Dial, 1985; *Bunnies and Their Grandma,* Dial, 1985; *The Legend of Eldorado,* Dial, 1986.

SIDELIGHTS: Amy Ehrlich told *CA:* "As a child, I was an avid reader. Books were my escape, a private world that I could retreat to. But I also learned history, geography, psychology, and ethics from the experiences of characters in fiction. When I work on my books, I go back into my own childhood and try to recreate the vividness of life to me at that time. And now that I have my own child, I see it all over again through his eyes. Writing for children is not easy, but it's a wonderful responsibility.''

* * *

EICHNER, Maura 1915-
(Sister Maura)

PERSONAL: Born May 5, 1915, in Brooklyn, N.Y.; daughter of Andrew and Mary (Doyle) Eichner. *Education:* College of Notre Dame of Maryland, A.B., 1941; Catholic University of America, M.A., 1942; additional study at Johns Hopkins University, 1944, University of Notre Dame, 1955, University of London, 1961, and University of Minnesota, 1966. *Home and office:* College of Notre Dame of Maryland, Baltimore, Md. 21210.

CAREER: Roman Catholic nun, member of School Sisters of Notre Dame (S.S.N.D.); teacher at Catholic junior high school in Annapolis, Md., 1936-38, and at Notre Dame Preparatory School, Baltimore, Md., 1938-41; College of Notre Dame of Maryland, Baltimore, instructor, 1942-48, assistant professor, 1948-53, associate professor, 1953-67, professor of English, 1967—, chairperson of department, 1954-74. Participant, Maryland Poetry-in-the-Schools program. Member of advisory committee, Maryland Arts Council.

MEMBER: National Council of Teachers of English, College English Association, Association of Departments of English, Maryland English Association.

AWARDS, HONORS: Awards for distinguished teaching from Catholic School Press Association, 1956, Freedoms Foundation, 1960, and Lindback Foundation, 1961; Amita Achievement Award, 1979; teacher of the year award from Maryland Council of Teachers of English, 1982; achievement award from Maryland Writers Council, 1984; three awards from *Lyric* (magazine).

WRITINGS—Poems; under name Sister Maura: *Initiate the Heart*, Macmillan, 1946; *The Word Is Love*, Macmillan, 1958; *Bell Sound and Vintage*, Contemporary Poetry, 1966; *Walking on Water*, Paulist/Newman, 1972; *What We Women Know*, Sparrow, 1980; *A Word, a Tree: Christmas Poems*, Franciscan Graphics, 1980. Also author of booklets, *Come Christmas*, 1950, *Christmas Convocation*, 1961, and *The Fall of a Sparrow*, 1966. Poems have been recorded for collections at Lamont Library, Harvard University, and at Library of Congress. Contributor of poetry to periodicals, including *America, Accent, Commonweal, New York Times, Poetry,* and *Yale Review;* contributor of articles and reviews to *Critic, Renascence, Spirit,* and *Thought.*

WORK IN PROGRESS: The Secret Waking, poems.

SIDELIGHTS: Maura Eichner writes: "Teaching is, for me, one of the greatest works to which a person can be called. I am grateful to be a teacher. The real pull in my life is toward teaching, and writing has been supportive of it. You teach writing skills and techniques better, I think, if you work at these yourself."

EISENHOWER, John S(heldon) D(oud) 1922-

PERSONAL: Born August 3, 1922, in Denver, Colo.; son of Dwight David (General of the Army and 34th President of the United States) and Mamie Geneva (Doud) Eisenhower; married Barbara Jean Thomas, June 10, 1947; children: Dwight David II, Barbara Anne (Mrs. Fernando Echavarria-Uribe), Susan Elaine (Mrs. Alexander Hugh Bradshaw), Mary Jean. *Education:* U.S. Military Academy, B.A., 1944; Columbia University, M.A., 1950; U.S. Army Command and General Staff College, graduate, 1955. *Politics:* Republican. *Home address:* P.O. Box 278, Kimberton, Pa. 19442.

CAREER: U.S. Army, cadet, 1941-44, regular officer, 1944-63 (resigned commission as lieutenant colonel, 1963), reserve officer, 1963—, with present rank of brigadier general; spent 1965-69 writing his book on World War II; U.S. Ambassador to Belgium, Brussels, 1969-71. Served with Army of Occupation in Europe, 1945-47; instructor in English at U.S. Military Academy, West Point, N.Y., 1948-51; battalion and division officer in Korea, 1952-53; battalion commander at Fort Benning, Ga., 1953-54; instructor in infantry tactics at Fort Belvoir, Va., 1955-57; member of War Plans Division, Army General Staff, Washington, D.C., 1957-58; assistant staff secretary at the White House, Washington, D.C., 1958-61; researched and did editorial work for his father's memoirs, *The White House Years,* in Gettysburg, Pa., 1961-64. Chairman, Pennsylvania Citizens for Nixon, 1968, and President's Advisory Committee on Refugees, 1975—. Trustee of Eisenhower College, Seneca Falls, N.Y., and of Eisenhower fellowships.

MEMBER: Army-Navy Country Club (Arlington, Va.).

AWARDS, HONORS—Military: Legion of Merit; Bronze Star; Combat Infantryman's Badge; Belgium Order of the Crown Grand Cross. Academic: L.H.D., Northwood Institute, 1970; Chungmu Distinguished Service medal.

WRITINGS: The Bitter Woods: A Comprehensive Study of the War in Europe, Putnam, 1969; *Strictly Personal* (memoir), Doubleday, 1974; *Allies: Pearl Harbor to D-Day,* Doubleday, 1982.

WORK IN PROGRESS: A study of the Mexican-American War, 1846-1848, entitled *Gringo.*

SIDELIGHTS: Reviewing John S. D. Eisenhower's *The Bitter Woods: A Comprehensive Study of the War in Europe* in the *Saturday Review,* Robert Leckie declares the author a "top-flight military historian." Drawing on personal experience as well as German and American sources, Eisenhower chronicles the events leading up to and following the Battle of the Bulge, Adolf Hitler's last great attempt to turn the course of the war in Germany's favor. According to Leckie, "few writers on either side of the conflict are better qualified to tell this story. Himself a staff officer of that First Army against whose units the attack was launched, son of the Supreme Commander, who met in the Bulge the crisis of both his 'crusade' and his career, John Eisenhower reveals in this study not only his intimacy with the members of the Allied High Command but great diligence in consulting German archives and interviewing those German officers who are still living. [This work] may stand as the definitive account of the critical battle of the European Theater.''

Gordon A. Craig, however, writing in the *New York Times Book Review,* feels that the book "suffers in comparison with previous books on the subject. . . . It is too long; the author is slow in getting down to his subject; he is, particularly in the early pages, repetitive.'' Despite these criticisms, Craig credits Eisenhower with ''[reconstructing] a complex series of events that involved simultaneous attacks by six German corps along a 70-mile front with a clarity and attention to detail that are a tribute both to his hard and careful work in the sources and to his personal examination of the terrain. He has made the battle his own—and, particularly when he is dealing with small-unit actions, his account conveys an excitement that is hard to resist.'' ''With an amazing . . . grasp of detail,'' says Charles Poore in the *New York Times*, ''[Eisenhower] tells us what was happening everywhere, at almost every level, within the German as well as the Allied lines. In short, he has bitten off an awful lot, and he chews it into the suburbs of infinity.''

Eisenhower's recent work *Allies: Pearl Harbor to D-Day* is based on a manuscript given the author by his father, Dwight D. Eisenhower, before the latter's death. The work examines, in the words of a critic for the *New York Times Book Review*, ''the personalities who shaped the Allied cause during World War II,'' including such figures as Churchill, Stalin, Marshall, and de Gaulle. ''John Eisenhower,'' the critic asserts, ''has expanded [his father's] monograph into a lengthy, chatty and satisfying history that is at once colorful and clear.''

AVOCATIONAL INTERESTS: Airplane piloting.

BIOGRAPHICAL/CRITICAL SOURCES: New York Times, January 23, 1969; *Saturday Review,* January 25, 1969; *New York Times Book Review,* February 9, 1969, October 24, 1982; *Times Literary Supplement,* January 15, 1970; *Philadelphia Inquirer,* April 6, 1975.

*   *   *

EISNER, Lotte (Henriette)   1896-1983

PERSONAL: Born March 6, 1896, in Berlin, Germany; died November 25, 1983, in Paris, France. *Education:* Attended University of Berlin, 1920, University of Freiburg, 1921-23, University of Munich, 1923; University of Rostock, Dr. phil., 1924. *Home:* 5 rue des Dames Augustines, 92 Neuilly 1, France.

CAREER: Berliner Tageblatt, Berlin, Germany, reporter, 1926; *Literarische Welt,* Berlin, Germany, book reviewer and art critic, 1926-27; *Film Kurier,* Berlin, Germany, film and theatre critic, 1927-33; Cinematheque Francaise, Paris, France, curator, 1945-68, curator honorifique, beginning 1968.

AWARDS, HONORS: Prix Armand Tallier, 1965, for *F. W. Murnau;* Chevalier des Arts et Lettres, 1967; named Chevalier of the French Legion of Honor, 1983.

WRITINGS: L'Ecran demoniaque: Influence de Max Reinhardt et de l'expressionisme, Andre Bonne, 1952, revised edition, 1965, translation by Roger Greaves published as *The Haunted Screen: Expressionism in the German Cinema and the Influence of Max Reinhardt,* University of California Press, 1969; (editor with Heinz Friedrich) *Film, Rundfunk, Fernsehen* (title means ''Film, Broadcasting, Television''), Fischer Buecherei, 1958; *F. W. Murnau,* Terrain Vague, 1965, translation published under same title, University of California Press, 1973; *Fritz Lang,* Oxford University Press, 1976; (editor) *Die daemonische leinwand,* Kommunales Kino, 1978.

Contributor to film periodicals, including *Die Kritik, World Film News, Revue du Cinema, Cahiers du Cinema, Sight and Sound, Film Culture.*

WORK IN PROGRESS: Her autobiography.

SIDELIGHTS: Calling Lotte Eisner ''one of the best-known European film critics,'' a London *Times* writer noted in her obituary that since Eisner was born three days before the Lumiere Cinematographe made its London debut, ''her life was exactly contemporary with the cinema itself.'' Eisner joined the staff of Germany's film daily, *Film Kurier,* in 1927, becoming Germany's first woman cinema critic. With the rise of Adolf Hitler's regime in the early 1930s, Eisner emigrated to France, where she would resume her writing career and live the rest of her life. The *Times* writer remarked on Eisner's ''series of classic books on German cinema,'' including *L'Ecran demoniaque: Influence de Max Reinhardt et de l'expressionisme,* translated as *The Haunted Screen: Expressionism in the German Cinema and the Influence of Max Reinhardt,* which ''analyzed German Expressionism with the insights of a great art historian,'' according to the article.

OBITUARIES: New York Times, November 29, 1983; *Washington Post,* November 29, 1983; *Chicago Tribune,* November 30, 1983; *Times* (London), December 3, 1983; *Newsweek,* December 12, 1983.†

*   *   *

EKMAN, Paul   1934-

PERSONAL: Born February 15, 1934, in Washington, D.C. *Education:* Attended University of Chicago, 1949-52; New York University, B.A., 1954; Adelphi University, M.A., 1955, Ph.D., 1958. *Home:* 3811 16th St., San Francisco, Calif. 94114. *Office:* Department of Psychology, University of California, 402 Parnassus Ave., San Francisco, Calif. 94143.

CAREER: University of California, School of Medicine, San Francisco, research psychologist at Langley Porter Neuropsychiatric Institute, 1960-72, professor of psychology, 1972—. *Military service:* U.S. Army, Medical Corps, 1958-60; became first lieutenant.

MEMBER: American Psychological Association (fellow), American Association for the Advancement of Science (fellow), Federation of American Sciences.

AWARDS, HONORS: National Institute of Mental Health research scientist awards, 1966, 1970, 1977.

WRITINGS: (With Wallace V. Friesen and Phoebe Ellsworth) *Emotion in the Human Face,* Pergamon, 1972, 2nd edition, Cambridge University Press, 1982; *Darwin and Facial Expression,* Academic Press, 1973; *Unmasking the Face,* Prentice-Hall, 1975; (with Friesen) *Facial Action Coding System: A Technique for the Measurement of Facial Movement,* Consulting Psychologists Press, 1978.

Face of Man: Universal Expression in a New Guinea Village, Garland Publishing, 1980; (editor and contributor with K. Scherer) *Handbook of Methods in Nonverbal Behavior Research,* Cambridge University Press, 1982; (editor with Scherer) *Approaches to Emotion,* Lawrence Erlbaum, 1984; *Clues to Deceit in the Marketplace, Marriage, and Politics,* Norton, 1985.

*   *   *

El-AYOUTY, Yassin   1928-

PERSONAL: Born April 14, 1928, in Kanayat, Sharkia, Egypt; son of Shaikh El-Sayed Mohammad (a teacher and farmer) and Aziza El-Sayed Ahmad (El-Shareef) El-Ayouty; married Grace A. Lasser (a teacher), June 17, 1970; children: Youssef. *Ed-*

ucation: Teachers Institute, Zeitoun, Cairo, Egypt, Diploma, 1948; Trenton State College, B.S., 1953; Rutgers University, M.A., 1954; New York University, Ph.D., 1966. *Religion:* Muslim. *Home:* 2 Peter Cooper Rd., New York, N.Y. 10010. *Office:* Secretariat, United Nations, New York, N.Y. 10017.

CAREER: Teacher of social studies in Cairo, Egypt, 1948-52; United Nations Secretariat, New York, N.Y., staff member, 1958—, currently principal officer in department of public information; St. John's University, Jamaica, N.Y., adjunct associate professor, 1966-72, adjunct professor of African and Middle Eastern studies, 1972-73; State University of New York at Stony Brook, professor of political science, 1972—. Member of board of directors, GEMCO National, 1981—. Public speaker and commentator on topics dealing with Africa and the Middle East. Consultant to several colleges, universities, and other institutions; consultant on international affairs to *Forbes* magazine.

MEMBER: American Political Science Association, African Studies Association (fellow), Middle East Studies Association (fellow of North American branch), Egyptian Society of Political Science, Pan-African Pugwash.

AWARDS, HONORS: Fulbright fellow, 1952-54; Louis Bevier Fellowship for Social Sciences, Rutgers University, 1954-55; Founders Day Award, New York University, 1966.

WRITINGS: Dajjal fi Karia (novel), [Cairo], 1948; (editor with Hugh Brooks) *Refugees South of the Sahara: An African Dilemma,* Negro Universities Press, 1970; (contributor) *Report from Vienna: An Appraisal of the International Peace Academy 1970 Pilot Projects,* IPAC (New York), 1970; *The United Nations and Decolonization: The Role of Afro-Asia,* Nijhoff, 1971; (editor with Hugh Brooks) *Africa and International Organization,* Nijhoff, 1974; *The Organization of African Unity after Ten Years: Comparative Perspectives,* Praeger, 1975; *Egypt, Peace and the Inter-Arab Crisis,* State University of New York at Buffalo, 1979; (editor with I. William Zartman) *The Organization of African Unity after Twenty Years,* Praeger, 1984.

Contributor to *Grolier's Encyclopedia.* Contributor to Middle Eastern and African journals and newspapers published in Egypt, France, Netherlands, Switzerland, United Kingdom, and the United States.

WORK IN PROGRESS: A research project, *International Security in the 1990's.*

SIDELIGHTS: Yassin El-Ayouty writes *CA:* "Having devoted more than forty years to the study of the politics of Africa and the Middle East (both Arab and non-Arab), I have long ago come to the conclusion that international peace, security and development . . . are attainable but only within the context of global human equality of opportunity, dignity, rights and obligations. Only on those bases, can our world, with all its promise and challenges, be gradually evolved into a vast stage for construction, hope and peace."

*   *   *

ELDEFONSO, Edward   1933-

PERSONAL: Born April 20, 1933, in Honolulu, Hawaii; son of Bartold (a laborer) and Cecelia (Jardine) Eldefonso; married Mildred Ann Prastalo, December 1, 1956; children: Jaime Christine, Mitchell Edward. *Education:* San Jose State College (now San Jose State University), B.A., 1959, M.S., 1962,

junior college teaching credential, 1963. *Politics:* "None." *Home:* 5070 Northlawn Dr., San Jose, Calif. 95130. *Office:* 840 Guadalupe Pkwy., San Jose, Calif. 95110.

CAREER: Santa Clara County Juvenile Probation Department, San Jose, Calif., staff member, 1957—, supervisor, 1965—. Teaching instructor at DeAnza College, Cupertino, Calif., and West Valley College, Campbell, Calif., 1963—; lecturer in police science and sociology at several police academies and colleges in California. *Military service:* U.S. Marine Corps Reserve, 1953-57.

WRITINGS: Law Enforcement and the Youthful Offender, Wiley, 1967, 4th edition, 1978; *Youth Problems and Law Enforcement,* Prentice-Hall, 1972; (compiler) *Readings in Criminal Justice,* Glencoe Press, 1973; (with Walter Hartinger) *Corrections: A Component of the Criminal Justice System,* Goodyear Publishing, 1973; (compiler) *Issues in Corrections: A Book of Readings,* Glencoe Press, 1974; (with Hartinger) *Control, Treatment, and Rehabilitation of Juvenile Offenders,* Glencoe Press, 1976.

With Alan R. Coffey: (And Richard C. Grace) *Principles of Law Enforcement,* Wiley, 1968, 3rd edition published as *Principles of Law Enforcement: An Overview of the Justice System,* 1982; *Human Relations: Law Enforcement in a Changing Community,* Prentice-Hall, 1971, 3rd edition, 1982; *Police-Community Relations,* Prentice-Hall, 1971; (and James Sullivan) *Police and Criminal Law,* Goodyear Publishing, 1972; *An Introduction to the Criminal Justice System and Process,* Prentice-Hall, 1974; *Process and Impact of Justice,* Glencoe Press, 1975; *Process and Impact of the Juvenile Justice System,* Glencoe Press, 1976; *Criminal Law: History, Philosophy, and Enforcement,* Harper, 1981.

WORK IN PROGRESS: Probation and Parole, a text.†

*   *   *

ELLIOTT, Lesley   1905-
(Lesley Gordon)

PERSONAL: Born August 5, 1905, in England; daughter of Harry Braine (a small tool salesman) and Mabel Jane (a fashion designer; maiden name, Statham) Gordon; married Frederick Allan Bannister, August 26, 1927 (died, 1970); married Stuart Randall Elliott, 1970 (deceased); children: (first marriage) Rosemary Ann (Mrs. Raymond Few), Hilary Clare (Mrs. Keith Atkinson). *Education:* Educated in East Orange, N.J. and in England. *Home:* "The Mariners," Silfield, Wymondham, Norfolk NR18 9NJ, England.

CAREER: Free-lance writer, 1930—. *Member:* Garden History Society.

WRITINGS—Under name Lesley Gordon: *Sorrowful and Not-So-Sorrowful Tales,* Samuel French, 1937; *The Jenny Lou Books* (juvenile), three volumes, Lutterworth, 1940; *Snips and Snails* (juvenile poems), Lutterworth, 1941; *A Pageant of Dolls* (history), Edmund Ward, 1954; (with Esmee Mascall) *Moppit and Co* (juvenile), Kinheim, Vitgeverij, Heilloo, 1955; *Peepshow into Paradise: A History of Toys,* Harrap, 1958; *Poorman's Nosegay: Flowers from a Cottage Garden,* Collins, 1973; *Green Magic: Flowers, Plants, and Herbs in Lore and Legend,* Viking, 1977; *A Country Herbal,* Mayflower, 1980; (with Jean Lorimer) *A Complete Guide to Drying and Preserving Flowers,* Chartwell, 1982.

Published by Webb & Bower: *Trees,* 1983; *A Year of Flowers,* 1983; *Old Roses,* 1983; *The Ladies' Potpourri of Fashion,* in press; *The Language of Flowers,* in press; *The Mystery and Magic of Trees and Flowers,* in press. Contributor of articles, stories, and poems to magazines since 1930, including American antiques journals.

SIDELIGHTS: Lesley Elliott told *CA:* "My writing career has always played second to my family life. I did, however, try out my story/how-to-make ideas on my own children, so that Easter, summer holiday, and Christmas plays were previewed in our home and appeared in the women's magazines the following year, providing that they had been voted successful by the home critics. Now that the home critics have homes of their own I prefer to concentrate on more demanding writing—in particular, the history and folklore of plants, trees and flowers, and the beauties and eccentricities of women's fashions in the past."

AVOCATIONAL INTERESTS: Travel (France, the Netherlands, Germany, Italy), sculpture, painting (especially flowers), botanical illustration, bookbinding and marbelling, garden history and gardening, collecting old books (especially flower and gardening books).

BIOGRAPHICAL/CRITICAL SOURCES: Los Angeles Times Book Review, December 7, 1980.

*   *   *

ELLIS, Wesley
See WALLMANN, Jeffrey M(iner)

*   *   *

ELLWOOD, Robert S(cott), Jr.   1933-

PERSONAL: Born July 17, 1933, in Normal, Ill.; son of Robert Scott (a teacher) and Knola (Shanks) Ellwood; married Gracia Fay Bouwman (a writer), August 28, 1965. *Education:* University of Colorado, B.A. (magna cum laude), 1954; Berkeley Divinity School, New Haven, Conn., M.Div. (cum laude), 1957; University of Chicago, M.A., 1965, Ph.D., 1967. *Residence:* Pasadena, Calif. *Office:* School of Religion, University of Southern California, Los Angeles, Calif. 90089.

CAREER: Minister in Episcopal church in Central City, Neb., 1957-60; University of Southern California, Los Angeles, assistant professor, 1967-71, associate professor, 1971-75, professor of religion, 1975—, Bishop James W. Bashford Professor of Oriental Studies, 1977—, director of East Asian Studies Center, 1977-81. Lecturer at churches, colleges, and universities. *Military service:* U.S. Navy, chaplain, 1961-62; became lieutenant.

AWARDS, HONORS: Rockefeller Foundation fellowship in religion, 1964-65; Fulbright-Hays fellowship, Japan, 1966-67.

WRITINGS—Published by Prentice-Hall, except as indicated: *Religious and Spiritual Groups in Modern America,* 1973; *One Way: The Jesus Movement and Its Meaning,* 1973; *The Feast of Kingship: Accession Ceremonies in Ancient Japan,* Sophia University Press (Tokyo), 1973; *The Eagle and the Rising Sun: Americans and the New Religions of Japan,* Westminster, 1974; *Many Peoples, Many Faiths,* 1976; *Words of the World's Religions: An Anthology,* 1977; *Introducing Religion: From Inside and Outside,* 1978; *Readings in Religion: From Inside and Outside,* 1978; *Alternative Altars,* University of Chicago Press, 1979.

Mysticism and Religion, 1980; *An Invitation to Japanese Civilization,* Wadsworth, 1980; *Tenrikyo: A Pilgrimage Faith,*

Tenri (Japan), 1982; *Finding the Quiet Mind,* Theosophical Publishing, 1983; *Finding Deep Joy,* Theosophical Publishing, 1984; (with Richard Pilgrim) *Japanese Religion: A Cultural Perspective,* 1985. Contributor to encyclopedias, including *Encyclopaedia Britannica.* Contributor of about twenty articles to academic journals, including *History of Religions, Sewanee Review, Asian Folklore Studies, Journal of Church and State,* and *Anglican Theological Review.*

*   *   *

EMBODEN, William A., Jr.   1935-

PERSONAL: Born February 24, 1935; son of William A. (a priest) and Mildred (an artist; maiden name, Hagquist) Emboden. *Education:* Purdue University, B.S., 1957; Indiana University, M.A., 1960; University of California, Los Angeles, Ph.D., 1965. *Politics:* "Monarchist." *Office:* Department of Biology, California State University, Northridge, Calif. 91330.

CAREER: California State University, Northridge, assistant professor, 1965-70, associate professor, 1970-74, professor of biology, 1974—. Senior curator of botany, Los Angeles Natural History Museum, Los Angeles, Calif., 1967-70. Officer of Harvard University, 1980—.

MEMBER: Sigma Xi.

WRITINGS: Narcotic Plants, Macmillan, 1972; (contributor) Peter T. Furst, editor, *Flesh of the Gods: The Ritual Use of Hallucinogens,* Praeger, 1972; *Sarah Bernhardt,* Crowell-Collier, 1974; *Bizarre Plants,* Macmillan, 1974; *Narcotic Plants of the World,* Macmillan, 1979; (contributor) *American Folk Medicine,* University of California Press, 1980; *Rausch und Realitat,* two volumes, [Cologne], 1981. Contributor to *Terra.*

WORK IN PROGRESS: Three books, *Plants of Shakespeare, Botany of Leonardo da Vinci,* and *The Artist as a Scientist.*

SIDELIGHTS: William A. Emboden, Jr., told *CA:* "I travel and live graciously in a French Normandy chateau situated in the Santa Monica Mountains. During the summer I retire to Paris and Venice where I write."

*   *   *

EMMERSON, Donald K(enneth)   1940-

PERSONAL: Born June 10, 1940, in Tokyo, Japan; son of John Kenneth (a writer and diplomat) and Dorothy (McLaughlin) Emmerson; married Carolyn Holm (a teacher), December 27, 1965; children: Kirsten Holm, Katrina Louise. *Education:* Princeton University, B.A., 1961; Yale University, M.A., 1966, Ph.D., 1972. *Office:* Department of Political Science, University of Wisconsin, 306 North Hall, Madison, Wis. 53706.

CAREER: University of Wisconsin—Madison, instructor, 1970-72, assistant professor, 1972-76, associate professor of political science, 1976—. Visiting fellow at Australian National University, 1975. Has conducted field research in Indonesia, 1967-69, 1974-75.

MEMBER: American Political Science Association.

AWARDS, HONORS: Fulbright-Hays grant and Ford Foundation Southeast Asia fellowship, both 1973-74.

WRITINGS: (Editor and contributor) *Students and Politics in Developing Nations,* Praeger, 1968; (contributor) R. William

Liddle, editor, *Political Participation in Modern Indonesia,* Yale University Press, 1973; (contributor) W. Howard Wriggins and James F. Guyot, editors, *Population, Politics, and the Future of Southern Asia,* Columbia University Press, 1973; *The Bureaucracy in Indonesia,* Center for International Studies, Massachusetts Institute of Technology, 1974; *Indonesia's Elite: Political Culture and Cultural Politics,* Cornell University Press, 1976; *Rethinking Artisanal Fisheries Development: Western Concepts, Asian Experiences,* World Bank, 1980; *Pacific Optimism,* Universities Field Staff International, 1982. Contributor to political science and Asian studies journals.

WORK IN PROGRESS: Research on growth, equality, and technology in poor countries, and on the politics of meaning (space, time, and language).

SIDELIGHTS: Donald K. Emmerson once wrote *CA:* "Growing up in the Foreign Service meant changing countries every two years. So much of my life has been spent overseas and on the move that living in any one place now seems unnatural. My background probably also accounts for my anthropological bent.

"In my pantheon, empathy is a prime god. I enjoy meeting strangers and trying to understand their ways of seeing and doing. I am amazed and grateful that scholar-authors actually get paid for what amounts to intellectual fun. The cup of my luck runneth over."

AVOCATIONAL INTERESTS: California beach-jogging, Balinese sunset-watching, "the company of my family."

BIOGRAPHICAL/CRITICAL SOURCES: Walter Bedell Smith, *My Three Years in Moscow,* Lippincott, 1949; *Foreign Service Journal,* November, 1955, August, 1960.†

* * *

EMMERSON, John K(enneth)   1908-1984

PERSONAL: Born March 17, 1908, in Canon City, Colo.; died of a stroke, March 24, 1984, in Stanford, Calif.; son of John Woods and Margaretta (Hitchcock) Emmerson; married Dorothy McLaughlin, August 18, 1934; children: Dorothy Louise, Donald Kenneth. *Education:* Attended Sorbonne, University of Paris, 1927-28; Colorado College, A.B., 1929; New York University, A.M., 1930; graduate study at Georgetown University, 1932-33. *Home:* 24899 Olive Tree Lane, Los Altos Hills, Calif. 94022. *Office:* Hoover Institution on War, Revolution, and Peace, Stanford University, Stanford, Calif. 94305.

CAREER: University of Nebraska, Nebraska School of Agriculture, Curtis, instructor in history and government, 1930-31; Berlitz School of Languages, Chicago, Ill., assistant director, 1933-35; U.S. Foreign Service, Washington, D.C., Japanese language officer in Tokyo, Japan, 1936-38, vice-consul in Taiwan, 1938-40, third secretary of embassy in Tokyo, 1940-41, foreign service officer in Washington, D.C. and Peru, both 1942, political adviser to General Joseph W. Stilwell, China-Burma-India theater of war, 1943-45, officer in Washington, D.C. and Tokyo, both 1945, assistant chief of Division of Japanese Affairs in the Department of State in Washington, D.C., 1946-47, first secretary of embassy in Moscow, Soviet Union, 1947-49, planning adviser to Bureau of Far Eastern Affairs, 1950-52, counselor and deputy chief of mission at embassy in Karachi, Pakistan, 1952-55, and Beirut, Lebanon, 1955-57, political counselor in Paris, France, 1957, consul general in Lagos, Nigeria, 1958-60, and Salisbury, Rhodesia (now Zimbabwe Rhodesia) and Nyasaland (now Malawi), 1960-

62, minister and deputy chief of mission in Tokyo, 1962-67; Stanford University, Stanford, Calif., diplomat in residence, 1967, senior research fellow at Hoover Institution on War, Revolution, and Peace, 1968-84, lecturer in history, 1973, chairman of U.S.-Japan Relations Program, Northeast Asia-U.S. Forum on International Policy, 1980-84. Research associate of Center for Strategic and International Studies at Georgetown University. Senior adviser to U.S. delegation of United Nations General Assembly, 1956-57; consultant to U.S. State Department, Institute for Defense Analyses, and the Aspen Institute for Humanistic Studies.

MEMBER: Association for Asian Studies, Asiatic Society of Japan (life member), World Affairs Council of Northern California, Japan Society of San Francisco, Phi Beta Kappa.

AWARDS, HONORS: Meritorious service award from U.S. Department of State, 1954; LL.D. from Colorado College, 1968; prize for best book relating to Truman era published during two year period, 1978-79, Harry S Truman Library Institute, 1980, for *The Japanese Thread: A Life in the U.S. Foreign Service.*

WRITINGS: Arms, Yen, and Power: The Japanese Dilemma, Dunellen, 1971; (with Leonard A. Humphreys) *Will Japan Rearm?,* American Enterprise Institute and Hoover Institution, Stanford University, 1973; *The Japanese Thread: A Life in the U.S. Foreign Service,* Holt, 1978. Contributor to *Yearbook on International Communist Affairs.* Contributor to foreign affairs journals and to *Reader's Digest.*

SIDELIGHTS: A 33-year veteran of the Foreign Service, John K. Emmerson was regarded as one of its leading experts on Japan, having served in that country before World War II and returning after the surrender as political adviser to General Douglas MacArthur. He also acted as General Joseph Stilwell's political advisor in the China-Burma-India theater during the war, and he met Mao Tse-tung in Yenan, China in 1944. During the 1960s, he was sent to the U.S. Embassy in Tokyo by John F. Kennedy to serve as minister and deputy chief of mission under Ambassador Edward O. Reischauer. *New York Times Book Review* critic Henry Scott Stokes points out that the merit of Emmerson's book *Arms, Yen, and Power: The Japanese Dilemma* "is that he is very aware of Japanese sensitivities." And *Japanese Thread: A Life in the U.S. Foreign Service* is described by James Thomson in *New York Times Book Review* as "a graceful, vivid and often touching account of the full life lived by the Emmerson family during service in Latin America, the Soviet Union, the Middle East and Africa, as well as East and South Asia—a life constantly near the vortex of contemporary history."

BIOGRAPHICAL/CRITICAL SOURCES: New York Times Book Review, April 9, 1972, March 11, 1979.

OBITUARIES: Washington Post, March 26, 1984; *New York Times,* March 27, 1984; *Chicago Tribune,* March 28, 1984; *Los Angeles Times,* March 28, 1984.†

* * *

ENGDAHL, Sylvia Louise   1933-

PERSONAL: Born November 24, 1933, in Los Angeles, Calif.; daughter of Amandus J. and Mildred Allen (a writer under her maiden name of Butler) Engdahl. *Education:* Attended Pomona College, 1950, Reed College, 1951, and University of Oregon, 1951-52; University of California, Santa Barbara, A.B., 1955; University of Oregon Extension, additional study, 1956-57;

Portland State University, graduate study, 1978-80. *Religion:* Episcopalian. *Home:* 8990 Southwest Camille Tr., Portland, Ore. 97223.

CAREER: Elementary teacher in Portland, Ore., 1955-56; System Development Corp. (computer programming for SAGE Air Defense System), 1957-67, began as programmer, became computer systems specialist, working in Lexington, Mass., Madison, Wis., Tacoma, Wash., and Santa Monica, Calif.; full-time writer, 1968-80; developer and vendor of software for home computers, 1981—.

AWARDS, HONORS: *Enchantress from the Stars* was a 1971 Newbery honor book; Christopher Award, 1973, for *This Star Shall Abide.*

WRITINGS—Novels for young people, except as indicated; all published by Atheneum: *Enchantress from the Stars* (Junior Literary Guild selection), 1970; *Journey between Worlds,* 1970; *The Far Side of Evil,* 1971; *This Star Shall Abide,* 1972; *Beyond the Tomorrow Mountains,* 1973; *The Planet-Girded Suns: Man's View of Other Solar Systems* (nonfiction), 1974; (co-editor) *Universe Ahead: Stories of the Future* (anthology), 1975; (editor) *Anywhere, Anywhen: Stories of Tomorrow* (anthology), 1976; (co-author) *The Subnuclear Zoo: New Discoveries in High Energy Physics* (nonfiction), 1977; *Our World Is Earth* (picture book), 1979; (with Rick Robertson) *Tool for Tomorrow: New Knowledge about Genes* (nonfiction), 1979; *The Doors of the Universe,* 1981.

WORK IN PROGRESS: A book for young people about home computers focused on uses of particular interest to girls; a master's thesis in anthropology on the evolutionary significance of space colonization.

SIDELIGHTS: As a writer, Sylvia Louise Engdahl aims to "bring present-day issues into perspective through speculation about the future as related to the past, with particular emphasis on space exploration, which I believe to be the most significant challenge facing the human race and the only long-range goal that will unite mankind in peace. . . . It is also my belief that today's tendency to equate realism with pessimism is invalid. My science fiction is not intended for fans of that genre; rather, it is directed primarily to young people, who are less interested in the typical space adventure than in the problems that might confront individuals of hypothetical worlds, and deals not so much with technological progress as with the human values I consider important. Unfortunately, this audience is hard to reach since most of my novels are too mature for readers who use children's rooms of libraries, yet are not available in paperback because paperback publishers won't accept science fiction that doesn't appeal to the fan market.

"Being in need of income, and for personal reasons not free to work outside my home, I returned to programming when home computers became common, and this now occupies most of my time. I find the personal computer tremendously exciting and hope to encourage more girls to become involved in it— there seems to be a feeling that computers aren't interesting to girls, just as when I began writing, it was believed science fiction wasn't, and my first novels were considered unusual for having female protagonists. The trouble lies not so much in false premises about women's interests as in false conceptions of both space and computers that lead women themselves to ignore these fields. I hope my future writing will help change such concepts."

BIOGRAPHICAL/CRITICAL SOURCES: Children's Literature Review, Volume II, Gale, 1976.

ENGEL, S(rul) Morris (von)   1931-

PERSONAL: Born March 3, 1931, in Promow, Poland; U.S. citizen; son of Isaac (a rabbi) and Feige-Leah (Pasha) Engel; married Phyllis Chisvin, December 25, 1953; children: Michael, Hartley. *Education:* University of Manitoba, B.A., 1953, M.A., 1955; University of Toronto, Ph.D., 1959. *Office:* School of Philosophy, University of Southern California, Los Angeles, Calif. 90007.

CAREER: University of New Brunswick, Fredericton, assistant professor of philosophy, 1959-61; University of Southern California, Los Angeles, assistant professor, 1962-64, associate professor, 1964-72, professor of philosophy, 1972—.

MEMBER: American Philosophical Association.

AWARDS, HONORS: Canada Council fellow, 1961-62.

WRITINGS: (Translator) S. Ansky, *Dybbuk: Between Two Worlds,* [Winnipeg], 1953, 2nd edition published as *The Dybbuk: Between Two Worlds,* Nash Publishing, 1974; (translator) Rachmil Bryks, *A Cat in the Ghetto,* Bloch Publishing, 1959, 2nd edition published as *Kiddush Hashem,* Behrman, 1977; *The Problem of Tragedy,* Brunswick Press, 1960; *Language and Illumination: Studies in the History of Philosophy,* Nijhoff, 1969; *Wittgenstein's Doctrine of the Tyranny of Language: An Historical and Critical Examination,* Nijhoff, 1971; *With Good Reason: An Introduction to Informal Fallacies,* St. Martin's, 1976, 2nd edition, 1982; *Analyzing Informal Fallacies,* Prentice-Hall, 1980; *The Study of Philosophy,* Holt, 1981; *The Language Trap,* Prentice-Hall, 1984. Author of "The Art of Thinking" television series produced by University of Southern California and broadcast on KNXT-TV, 1973-74. Contributor of more than thirty articles and reviews to journals.

*   *   *

EPSTEIN, Cynthia Fuchs   1933-

PERSONAL: Born November 9, 1933, in New York, N.Y.; daughter of Jesse I. and Birdie (Seider) Fuchs; married Howard Epstein (an editor), July 3, 1954; children: Alexander Maxim. *Education:* Antioch College, B.A., 1955; graduate study, University of Chicago, 1955-56; New School for Social Research, M.A., 1960; Columbia University, Ph.D., 1968. *Home:* 425 Riverside Dr., New York, N.Y. 10025. *Office:* Department of Sociology, Queens College of the City University of New York, Flushing, N.Y. 11367.

CAREER: Researcher for Science Research Associates, New York City, 1956-57, and Save the Children Federation, New York City, 1957; Hadassah, the Women's Zionist Organization of America, New York City, program writer, 1957-60; instructor in sociology at Finch College, New York City, 1961-62, and Barnard College, New York City, 1965; Queens College and Graduate Center of the City University of New York, Flushing, N.Y., 1966—, instructor, 1966-67, assistant professor, beginning 1968, currently professor of sociology. Senior research associate, Columbia University, Bureau of Applied Social Research, 1970-79, and Center for the Social Sciences, 1979-81; resident scholar, Russell Sage Foundation, 1981—.

MEMBER: American Sociological Association, American Association for the Advancement of Science (president), Eastern Sociological Society.

WRITINGS: Woman's Place: Options and Limits in Professional Careers, University of California Press, 1970; (editor with William J. Goode) *The Other Half: Roads to Women's Equality*, Prentice-Hall, 1971; (editor with Rose Laub Coser) *Access to Power: Cross National Studies of Women and Elites*, Allen & Unwin, 1981; *Women in Law*, Basic Books, 1981.

Contributor to *Dissent, Antioch Review, Social Policy*, and to sociology journals and popular magazines.

SIDELIGHTS: Sociologist Cynthia Fuchs Epstein's writings focus on the study of women in the working world. Her first book, *Woman's Place: Options and Limits in Professional Careers*, is, according to *New York Times* critic John Leonard, "sociology with a vengeance (tables, footnotes, clotted prose), but there is more hard data, perception, cross-cultural comparison and historical grasp in this book than in any other tome on the Woman Question that I've ever seen."

Leonard goes on to describe the scope of the book, noting that "Mrs. Epstein looks at American child rearing, role conflict, the professions, women's status in radical movements, the psychological consequences of piercing the Sex Curtain and the ways that other countries cope with the problem."

Once a law student herself, Epstein looks at women in the legal profession in her 1981 book *Women in Law*. Neal Johnston writes in a *New York Times Book Review* article that this volume "is a sociological and historical study of the processes of change in this most central of American professions, quantifying what can be measured and journalistically reporting what cannot. Mrs. Epstein undertakes to describe those women who are attracted to the law and to catalogue their career achievements in every aspect of practice. . . . And she articulates the special (and sometimes terrible) pressures endured by those women who broke the barriers and must now define ways of combining a professional life increasingly free of sexual stereotyping with a personal life still shaped, at least reproductively, by the fact of gender." Epstein, concludes critic Johnston, "tells a success story which the legal world can read with no little pride and which others will read with substantial interest."

BIOGRAPHICAL/CRITICAL SOURCES: New York Times, April 15, 1970; *Saturday Review*, August 29, 1970; *New York Times Book Review*, December 13, 1981.

*   *   *

ESCANDON, Ralph 1928-

PERSONAL: Born May 21, 1928, in Barranquilla, Colombia; son of Antonio J. (a businessman) and Leonor (Hernandez) Escandon; married Lena Hilda Moore (an elementary school teacher), June 6, 1955; children: Willie Rafael. *Education:* Union College, Lincoln, Neb., B.A., 1957; University of Nebraska, M.A., 1959; University of Omaha, additional study, 1966-67; Interamerican University, Saltillo, Mexico, Ph.D., 1968. *Religion:* Seventh-day Adventist. *Home:* 280 Washburn, Angwin, Calif. 94508. *Office:* Department of Modern Languages, Pacific Union College, Angwin, Calif. 94508.

CAREER: University of Nebraska, Lincoln, instructor in Spanish, 1958-60; Creighton University, Omaha, Neb., instructor in Spanish, 1960-62; Cali Junior Academy, Cali, Colombia, principal, 1962-66; University of Omaha (now University of Nebraska at Omaha), assistant professor of Spanish literature, 1966-67; Pacific Union College, Angwin, Calif., associate professor of Latin American literature and history, 1968—, chairman of department of modern languages, 1977-1982.

MEMBER: Phi Sigma Iota.

WRITINGS: Curiosidades matematicas, Editorial Novaro, 1965; *Excentricidades y rarezas*, Editorial Novaro, 1967; *Anecdotas favoritas*, Editorial Novaro, 1970; *Humo y Ceniza* (novel), Editorial Iztaecittuatl, 1972; *Have Fun Being a Christian*, Review and Herald, 1973; *Adelante entusiasta juventud*, Editorial Novaro, 1973; *El origen de muchas cosas*, Editorial Novaro, 1973; *Smoke and Ashes* (novel), Dorrance, 1973; *Curiosidades Biblicas*, Editorial Novaro, 1975.

Sendros de Victoria, Pacific Press Publishing Association, 1977; *Para usted que quierre ser escritor*, Interamerican, 1977; *Intermediate Spanish*, Home Study Institute, 1978; *Proteja a sus hijos*, Pacific Press, 1979; *Vers la victoire*, Pacific Press. 1980; *Ingles para doctores y enfermeras*, Editores Mexicanos Unidos, 1981; *Ingles para secretarias*, Editores Mexicanos Unidos, 1981; *Pensamientos inolvidables*, Diana (Mexico), 1982; *Como llegar a ser vencedor*, Casa Bautista, 1982; *Bilingual Vocabulary for the Medical Profession*, Southwestern, 1982; *Para ti, joven, que quieres triunfar*, Diana, 1983; *Relaciones publicas al alcance de todos*, Editorial Universo, 1983; *Destino sin partida*, Masterbook, 1983; *Como superar los problemas juveniles*, Masterbook, 1983.

Also author of *Como mantener la aromonia en el hogar, Caprichos del idioma, Al borde del abismo*, and *Spanish for Secretaries*. Contributor of articles to periodicals, including *Review and Herald, Jeventud, Spanish for Today, Message, El Vocero*, and *El Gato*.

*   *   *

ESCHHOLZ, Paul A(nderson) 1942-

PERSONAL: Born October 15, 1942, in Hartford, Conn.; son of Paul Arthur (an electrical engineer) and Leone (Anderson) Eschholz; married Eva Lillian Paquin, May 28, 1966; children: William Edward, Sarah Lynn, Ulrich Paul, Karen Louise. *Education:* Wesleyan University, B.A., 1964; University of Vermont, M.A., 1966; University of Minnesota, Ph.D., 1971. *Religion:* Roman Catholic. *Home address:* R.R. 2, Box 2670, Westford, Vt. 05494. *Office:* Department of English, University of Vermont, Burlington, Vt. 05405.

CAREER: University of Vermont, Burlington, instructor in English, 1969-71; Johnson State College, Johnson, Vt., instructor in English, 1971; University of Vermont, assistant professor, 1971-75, associate professor, 1975-78, professor of English, 1978—. Co-founder and publisher with Alfred Rosa of The New England Press, Inc., 1978—.

MEMBER: National Council of Teachers of English, American Dialect Society, Northeast Modern Language Association, New England Association of Teachers of English, Vermont Historical Society, Chittenden County Historical Society, Rowland E. Robinson Memorial Association.

WRITINGS: (Editor with Virginia Clark and Alfred Rosa) *Language: Introductory Readings*, St. Martin's, 1972, 4th edition, 1985; (with Arthur W. Biddle) *Literature of Vermont: A Sampler*, University Press of New England, 1973; (editor with Clark and Rosa) *Language Awareness*, St. Martin's, 1974, 3rd edition, 1982; (editor) *Critics on William Dean Howells*, University of Miami Press, 1975; (contributor) Rowland E. Robinson, editor, *Vermont: A Study of Independence*, Tuttle, 1975; (with Rosa) *Bibliography of Contemporary British and American Fiction, 1950-1970*, Gale, 1977; (editor with Rosa) *Subject and Strategy: A Rhetoric Reader*, St. Martin's, 1978, 2nd edition, 1981; (editor with Rosa) *Models for Writers: Short Essays for Composition,* St. Martin's, 1982.

Contributor to academic journals. Co-editor of *Exercise Exchange: For Teachers of English in High Schools and Colleges,* 1971-80.

WORK IN PROGRESS: The dialect writings of Rowland Evans Robinson, 1833-1900; writing on W. D. Howells and Henry James, and on rhetoric and the writing process.

* * *

ESSLINGER, Pat M.
See CARR, Pat M(oore)

* * *

ETZOLD, Thomas H(erman)   1945-

PERSONAL: Born June 2, 1945, in St. Clair County, Ill.; son of Herman A. (a professor and minister) and Mabel M. (a nurse; maiden name, Traugott) Etzold; married Suzanne E. Burdick, June 12, 1965; children: Klaus C., Ingrid A. *Education:* Indiana University, B.A., 1967, M.A., 1968; Yale University, M.Phil., 1969, Ph.D., 1970. *Office:* United States Arms Control and Disarmament Agency, Washington, D.C. 20451.

CAREER: Yale University, New Haven, Conn., instructor in history, 1970-71; Miami University, Oxford, Ohio, assistant professor of history, 1971-74; Naval War College, Newport, R.I., associate professor, 1974-77, professor of strategy, 1977-84; affiliated with Center for Naval Warfare Studies, 1981-84; Arms Control and Disarmament Agency, Washington, D.C., assistant director, 1984—.

MEMBER: Society for Historians of American Foreign Relations, U.S. Naval Institute, U.S. Strategic Institute, Royal United Services Institute for Defence Studies.

WRITINGS: (With F. G. Chan) *China in the 1920s: Nationalism and Revolution,* F. Watts, 1976; *The Conduct of American Foreign Relations: The Other Side of Diplomacy,* F. Watts, 1977; *Aspects of Sino-American Relations since 1784,* F. Watts, 1978; (with John Lewis Gaddis) *Containment: Documents on American Policy and Strategy, 1945-1950,* Columbia University Press, 1978; *Defense or Delusion: America's Military in the 1980s,* Harper, 1982. Contributor to history and military journals and newspapers.

WORK IN PROGRESS: A book on Henry Kissinger for the series *The American Secretaries of State and Their Diplomacy,* for Littlefield & Rowan.

SIDELIGHTS: Thomas H. Etzold told *CA:* "Francois de Callieres once wrote that, 'A diplomat's speeches should contain more sense than words. That observation is just as useful to writers as to diplomats. The marks of good prose, carefully crafted, are brevity, clarity, and felicity of expression. Without these, great ideas may go unappreciated; with them, even mediocre thoughts can gain at least as much attention as they may deserve.

"As for the literary scene, no matter what the fads of style or the lack of it, or the fads of topics and stances, basic good paragraphing and good topic sentence writing will always carry. Readers are grateful for prose that permits them to grapple with ideas rather than with syntax.

"When writing, I compose in the morning and edit and do library follow-up work in the afternoon and evening. Most people have a time of the day, a portion of it, when they are at their best for a few hours in terms of creativity. A consistent writer needs to figure out what his or her best composition hours are, and, when writing, ruthlessly guard them from trivial interference."

Of Etzold's book, *Defense or Delusion: America's Military in the 1980s,* a *Washington Post Book World* critic says: "The book deals systematically with most major defense issues, and its treatment of these questions is generally balanced and well researched. While much of the military manpower debate is polarized between supporters and foes of the all-volunteer force, Etzold provides us with a valuable discussion of just what manpower problems the draft might and might not solve."

BIOGRAPHICAL/CRITICAL SOURCES: Washington Post Book World, February 7, 1982.

* * *

EWY, Donna   1934-

PERSONAL: Born September 1, 1934, in Denver, Colo.; daughter of Lee K. and Irene Lena (Ginsburg) Hohmann; married Rodger Ewy (a photojournalist), March 1, 1958; children: Marguerite, Suzanne, Rodger, Leon. *Education:* University of Colorado, B.A., 1956; University of Northern Colorado, Ed.D. *Home:* 1315 Northwood, Boulder, Colo. 80302.

CAREER: Teacher in Denver, Colo., Maryland, San Francisco, Calif., and in France, 1958-61. Director, youth programs, Young Women's Christian Association (Y.W.C.A.). *Member:* Colorado Association for Prepared Childbirth.

WRITINGS—All co-authored with husband, Rodger Ewy: *Preparation for Childbirth,* Pruett, 1970, revised edition, New American Library, 1983; *Preparation for Breastfeeding,* Doubleday, 1975, revised edition, 1984; *Guide to a Healthy Pregnancy,* Dutton, 1981; *Guide to Family-Centered Childbirth,* Dutton, 1981; *Guide to Parenting: You and Your Newborn,* Dutton, 1982; *Teenage Pregnancy: Challenges and Choices,* Pruett, 1984; *Death of a Dream: Miscarriage, Stillbirth, and Newborn Loss,* Dutton, 1984.

Other: *Family Passages,* New American Library, 1984. Contributor to photographic journals.

WORK IN PROGRESS: A book on break dancing, with husband R. Ewy; *Walking Tall; Teen Job Almanac.*

SIDELIGHTS: Preparation for Childbirth has been translated into Japanese, German, and Spanish; *Preparation for Breastfeeding* has been translated into Spanish.

* * *

EWY, Rodger   1931-

PERSONAL: Born May 23, 1931, in Denver, Colo.; son of A. W. and M. Jean (Purvis) Ewy; married Donna Hohmann (a photographer and writer), March 1, 1958; children: Marguerite, Suzanne, Rodger, Leon. *Education:* Dartmouth College, B.F.A. (cum laude), 1953. *Home and office:* 1315 Norwood, Boulder, Colo. 80302.

CAREER: Bechtel Corp., San Francisco, Calif., cost engineer, 1956-57; Ewy Photography, free-lance photojournalist in Europe, 1958-61; National Center for Atmospheric Research, Boulder, Colo., photographer, 1963-68; International Business

Machines Corp. (IBM), Boulder, photographer, 1969-74; president, EGA, Inc.; partner, Ewy Associates (metric consultants). Certified metric specialist, U.S. Metric Association. Has produced twenty-eight programs on childbearing and parenting. *Member:* American Association for the Advancement of Science, Colorado Association for Prepared Childbirth.

WRITINGS—All co-authored with wife, Donna Ewy: *Preparation for Childbirth,* Pruett, 1970, revised edition, New American Library, 1983; *Preparation for Breastfeeding,* Doubleday, 1975, revised edition, 1984; *Guide to a Healthy Pregnancy,* Dutton, 1981; *Guide to Family-Centered Childbirth,* Dutton, 1981; *Guide to Parenting: You and Your Newborn,* Dutton, 1982; *Teenage Pregnancy: Challenges and Choices,* Pruett, 1984; *Death of a Dream: Miscarriage, Stillbirth, and Newborn Loss,* Dutton, 1984.

Contributor to photographic journals.

WORK IN PROGRESS: A book on break dancing, with wife D. Ewy.

SIDELIGHTS: Preparation for Childbirth has been translated into Japanese, German, and Spanish; *Preparation for Breastfeeding* has been translated into Spanish.

F

FADER, Shirley Sloan 1931-

PERSONAL: Born February 24, 1931, in Paterson, N.J.; daughter of Samuel Louis (a surgeon) and Miriam (a teacher; maiden name, Marcus) Sloan; married Seymour J. Fader (a professor), June 26, 1951; children: Susan Deborah, Steven Micah Kimhi. *Education:* University of Pennsylvania, B.S., 1952, M.S., 1953. *Home and office:* 377 McKinley Blvd., Paramus, N.J. 07652.

CAREER: Writer. Chairperson, Bergen College Writers' Conference, 1973-76.

MEMBER: American Society of Journalists and Authors (national vice-president, 1976-77; member of national executive council, 1976-79, 1983-86), Authors Guild, Authors League of America, Women's Ink, National Press Club.

WRITINGS: The Princess Who Grew Down (juvenile), Lion Press, 1968; *From Kitchen to Career,* Stein & Day, 1978; *Jobmanship,* Macmillan, 1979; *Successfully Ever After: A Young Woman's Guide to Career Happiness,* McGraw, 1982.

Author of columns "People and You" and "Jobmanship," *Family Weekly,* 1971-81; contributing editor, *Family Weekly,* 1977-81; author of column "How to Get More from Your Job," and contributing editor, *Glamour,* 1978-81; author of columns "Start Here" and "Comment," and contributing editor, *Working Woman,* 1981—; author of column "Women Getting Ahead," *Ladies Home Journal,* 1981—.

Also contributor of several hundred articles to national magazines, including *Mademoiselle, McCall's, Family Circle, Harper's,* and *Cosmopolitan,* and to newspapers, including the *Wall Street Journal* and the *New York Times* Op-Ed page.

WORK IN PROGRESS: Magazine articles.

*   *   *

FAGAN, Brian Murray 1936-

PERSONAL: Born August 1, 1936, in Birmingham, England; naturalized U.S. citizen; son of Brian Walter and Margaret (Moir) Fagan; married Judith Ann Fontana (a registered nurse), December 6, 1969. *Education:* Pembroke College, Cambridge, B.A. (with honors), 1959, M.A., 1962, Ph.D., 1963. *Home:* 170 Hot Springs Rd., Santa Barbara, Calif. 93108. *Office:* Department of Anthropology, University of California, Santa Barbara, Calif. 93106.

CAREER: Livingstone Museum, Livingstone, Northern Rhodesia (now Zambia), keeper of prehistory, 1959-65; British Institute of History and Archaeology in East Africa, Nairobi, Kenya, director of Bantu studies project, 1965-66; University of Illinois at Urbana-Champaign, visiting associate professor of anthropology, 1966-67; University of California, Santa Barbara, associate professor, 1967-68, professor of anthropology, 1969—, director of Center for the Study of Developing Nations, 1969-70, associate dean of research and graduate affairs, 1970-72, associate dean of College of Letters and Science, 1972-73, dean of instructional development, 1973-76.

University of Capetown, lecturer, 1960, visiting professor, 1982; Munro Lecturer, University of Edinburgh, 1967; Richard M. Nixon Visiting Scholar and Lecturer, Whittier College, 1976; lecturer of African history at campuses throughout United States. Zambia Monuments Commission, member, 1960-65, secretary, 1960-62; director of Kalomo/Choma Iron Age project, 1960-63, of Lochinvar research project, 1963-64, and of Bantu studies project in Kenya, Uganda, and Tanzania; conducted archaeological research in Zambia and Northern Nigeria, 1969-70. Has presented papers to numerous conferences in the United States, Africa, England, and Europe. Consultant on innovative instruction, New Mexico State University, 1973; consultant to administrator and head of mission, Evaluation of International Audio-Visual Resource Service, United Nations Fund for Popular Activities, 1976. *Military service:* Royal Navy, 1954-56.

MEMBER: Royal Geographical Society (fellow), Royal Anthropological Institute (fellow), African Studies Association (United States; fellow; chairman of archaeology committee, 1968-69), American Anthropological Association (fellow), Society for American Archaeology, South African Archaeological Society, Prehistoric Society, Current Anthropology (associate), New York Academy of Sciences (fellow), Santa Barbara Yacht Club, Cruising Association (London).

AWARDS, HONORS: Grants from Wenner Gren Foundation, 1967, 1968, and National Science Foundation, 1968-70, 1970-71; Guggenheim fellow, 1972-73; Commonwealth Club Gold Medal for Nonfiction, 1975, for *The Rape of the Nile;* Hanson Cup from Cruising Association, 1975, for a cruise to Scandinavia.

WRITINGS: Southern Africa during the Iron Age, Praeger, 1966, revised edition published as *Southern Africa,* Thames &

Hudson, 1971; (editor) *A Short History of Zambia*, Oxford University Press, 1966, revised edition, 1968; *Iron Age Cultures in Zambia*, Humanities, Volume I: *Kalomo and Kangila*, 1967, Volume II (with S.G.H. Daniels and D. W. Phillipson): *Dambwa, Ingombe Ilede and the Tonga*, 1969.

(Editor) *Introductory Readings in Archaeology*, Little, Brown, 1970; (author of introduction and editorial note) Randall MacIver, *Medieval Rhodesia*, Cass & Co., 1971; (editor) L.S.B. Leakey, *The Stone Age Cultures of Kenya Colony*, Cass & Co., 1971; *In the Beginning: An Introduction to Archaeology*, Little, Brown, 1972, 3rd edition, 1978; *People of the Earth*, Little, Brown, 1974, 2nd edition, 1977; (editor) *Corridors in Time*, Little, Brown, 1974; *The Rape of the Nile*, Scribner, 1975; (with Roland Oliver) *Africa in the Iron Age*, Cambridge University Press, 1975; (editor) *Avenues to Antiquity*, W. H. Freeman, 1976; *Elusive Treasure*, Scribner, 1977; (editor) *Civilization*, W. H. Freeman, 1978; *Archaeology: A Brief Introduction*, Little, Brown, 1978; *Quest for the Past*, Addison-Wesley, 1978; (with Graham Pomeroy) *A Cruising Guide to Santa Barbara Channel*, Capra, 1978; *Return to Babylon*, Little, Brown, 1979.

California Coastal Passages, Capra, 1981; *Cruising Guide to California's Channel Islands*, Western Marine, 1983; *The Aztecs*, W. H. Freeman, 1984; *Clash of Cultures*, W. H. Freeman, 1984; *Bareboating*, International Marine Publishing, 1985.

Contributor: W. W. Bishop and J. D. Clark, editors, *Background to Evolution in Africa*, University of Chicago Press, 1967; Roland Oliver, editor, *The Middle Age of African History*, Oxford University Press, 1968; Leonard M. Thompson, editor, *African Societies in Southern Africa*, Praeger, 1969; Oliver and J. D. Fage, editors, *Papers in African Prehistory*, Cambridge University Press, 1970; J. R. Gray and David Birmingham, editors, *Pre-Colonial African Trade*, Oxford University Press, 1970; P. L. Shinnie, editor, *The African Iron Age*, Oxford University Press, 1971. Also contributor to *UNESCO History of Africa*, Volume II, 1984. Contributor of over one hundred articles and reviews to professional journals and newspapers.

WORK IN PROGRESS: A history of Mesopotamian archaeology.

SIDELIGHTS: Brian Fagan told *CA:* "I became interested in popular writing about archaeology while working in Zambia, where national history had to be created from excavations rather than written records. There I was involved in radio and TV as well as in guidebooks and newspaper writing and scientific articles and monographs. Since coming to the U.S. in 1966, I have been involved in the teaching of large introductory archaeology courses and in much popular lecturing, occupations which led me into textbook writing and then into trade books.

"My trade career began with a chance letter from Scribners about an article I wrote for *Archaeology* on tomb robbers, a letter that led to *The Rape of the Nile* and a whole new vista of writing opportunity. I have continued to write about archaeology for the general public ever since, for the subject is becoming increasingly specialized as it grows. There is a real danger that undisturbed archaeological sites will vanish in North America in the next generation unless the public realizes the immorality of collecting artifacts from Indian sites for personal gain. Such sites are, after all, the archives of American Indian history. I told some of the story of the destruction of American Indian history in my *Elusive Treasure*.

"A lifetime interest has been cruising under sail. We have spent the last three summers sailing in Europe on our 41-foot cutter, *Catticus Rex*, and won the Cruising Association's Hanson Trophy for a cruise to Finland in 1975. I . . . plan to do more writing about sailing in the future.

"I speak French, and [am] deeply involved in the use of media for undergraduate teaching, have an abhorrence for bureaucrats developed when I served as an academic dean, and love cats. Two of them dominate our lives, indeed did everything they could to prevent this paragraph being written by sitting on my pen."

*   *   *

FAIRLEY, M(ichael) C(harles) 1937-

PERSONAL: Born May 13, 1937, in Sittingbourne, Kent, England; son of Charles Frederick and Dorothy (Kay) Fairley; marrried Patricia Cockell, March 30, 1960; children: Jacqueline. *Education:* Studied at Medway and Maidstone Colleges of Art, 1954-62, receiving full technological certificate in printing; Garnett College of Education, London, teacher's certificate, 1966. *Religion:* Church of England. *Office:* Mifair Press and Promotional Services, 10 Torrington Dr., Potters Bar, Hertfordshire EN6 5HR, England.

CAREER: East Kent Gazette, Sittingbourne, England, printer, 1954-63; Thanet School of Art, Margate, England, lecturer in printing, 1964-71; Printing Industry Research Association, Leatherhead, Surrey, England, deputy head of training, 1971-75; Paper and Paper Products Industry Training Board, Star House, Potters Bar, Hertfordshire, England, deputy planning and information manager, 1975-80; Labels & Labelling Publishers, Bickley, Kent, England, founder, director, and editorial consultant, 1977—; WLG Creative Services, London, England, editorial director, 1981-84; Mifair Press and Promotional Services, Hertfordshire, England, managing director, 1984—.

MEMBER: Institute of Printing, National Graphical Association, Institute of Directors.

WRITINGS: Safety, Health, and Welfare in the Printing Industry, Pergamon, 1968; *Materials Handling in the Printing Industry*, Pergamon, 1970; *Print: Technological Change and the Printing Craftsman*, National Graphical Association, 1971; *The Printing Processes-Screen Process*, Printing Industry Research Association, 1972; *The Principles of Moisture Measurement of Paper and Board*, Printing Industry Research Associaton, 1973; *Bar Coding: Where Are We Now?*, Labels & Labelling Publishers, 1983; *Label Printing Processes and Techniques*, Labels & Labelling Publishers, 1984; *Thermal Labelling*, Labels & Labelling Publishers, 1984.

Also author of a wide range of information, careers, and training publications for the Paper and Paper Products Industry Training Board, 1975—; editor of various company newsletters and promotional bulletins, 1980-84. Editor of annual publication, *Directory of Labels and Labelling*. Contributor to *Encyclopedia of Occupational Health and Safety* and *Academic American Encyclopedia;* consultant and feature writer, *Labels and Labelling International*, 1977—; regular contributor to *Print*, 1969-71, and occasional contributor to other periodicals.

SIDELIGHTS: M. C. Fairley once told *CA:* "The main aim of almost all of the books or publications I have written or contributed to has been to explain the nature of industrial problems or technology in a clear, concise and interesting way. This developed from my years as a lecturer in technical education where much of the existing text book or lecture material was too complex for the average reader.''

Fairley recently wrote *CA:* ''[My] philosophy has proved eminently successful and I am now invited to travel all over the world to look at and write about new developments and trends. In the past year alone I have flown over 60,000 miles and written features on developments in countries as diverse as Japan, Australia, Germany, and Italy. Writing in a specialised way has made all of this possible.''

*   *   *

FALK-ROENNE, Arne 1920-

PERSONAL: Born May 12, 1920, in Copenhagen, Denmark; son of Svend and Inge (Andersen) Falk-Roenne; married Katia Bryn, March 7, 1944; children: Adele, Christel, Synnoeve, Arne. *Education:* Attended Frederiksberg Gymnasium, Copenhagen, Denmark; University of Copenhagen, B.A., 1941. *Religion:* Lutheran. *Home:* 64 Rymarksvej, Hellerup, Copenhagen, Denmark.

CAREER: Journalist, beginning 1943, covering much of the world as traveling correspondent for *Allers Familie Journal* (magazine published in Danish, Norwegian, and Swedish).

MEMBER: Danish Writers Association, Danish Journalists Association, Adventurers Club of Denmark.

AWARDS, HONORS: Norwegian-Danish Anker Prize for *Vejen til Betlehem,* 1965.

WRITINGS: Det Bedste for Min Rejsevaluta, [Denmark], 1953; *Eventyrfaerden til Greven af Montechristo's Oe,* [Denmark], 1953; *Eventyrfaerden til Robinson Crusoe's Oe,* Branner & Korch, 1954; *I Udlandet paa Knallert,* [Denmark], 1955; *Se Neapel og Spis Sovs til,* Hirschsprungs Forlag, 1956; *Det var pa Capri,* Hirschsprungs Forlag, 1957; *For Graensen Lukkes,* Hirschsprungs Forlag, 1958; *Hyklere og Myklere pa Mallorca,* Hirschsprungs Forlag, 1958; *Skaebnens Flod,* [Denmark], 1959.

Tafiya, Lohses Forlag, 1960; *Djaevlens Diamanter,* Gyldendals Forlag, 1961; *Tilbage til Tristan,* Lohses Forlag, 1963, translation published as *Back to Tristan,* Allen & Unwin, 1967; *Vejen til Betlehem* (title means ''The Road to Bethlehem''), Lohses Forlag, 1963; *I Morges ved Amazonfloden,* Lohses Forlag, 1964; *Paradis om Bagbord,* Steen Hasselbalchs Forlag, 1965; *Mine venner Kannibalerne,* Steen Hasselbalchs Forlag, 1965; *Vejen Paulus Gik,* Lohses Forlag, 1967; *Sydhavets syv boelger,* Lohses Forlag, 1969; *Doede Indianere sladrer ikke,* Steen Hasselbalchs Forlag, 1969.

I Stanleys fodspor gennem Afrika: 100 aar efter moedet med Livingstone, Lohses Forlag, 1972; (with Farbbildern and Kt.-Skizze) *Wo Salome tanzte,* Stocker, 1973; *Kannibalernes Ny Guinea,* Fremed, 1974; *Dr. Klapperslange: Berentingen orn Bjarne Berboms 32 aar som hvid medicinmand i Sydamerikas urskove,* Fremad, 1975; *Du er Peter: En rejse i apostelens fodspor,* Lohses Forlag, 1976; *Machetebroedre,* Fremad, 1977; *Jorden rundt i 80 dage: 100 aar efter,* Fremad, 1977; *Med Falk-Roenne til Capri-og Napoligolfen,* Lohses Forlag, 1978; *Rejse i faraonernes rige,* Branner & Korch, 1979.

Don Hestedaekken, Delta, 1980; *Paa Biblens stier,* Lohses Forlag, 1982; *Hvor er du, Paradis,* Delta, 1983; *Rom varer hele livet,* Lohses Forlag, 1984. Also author of *Australien, indvandrernes land,* 1983, and television scripts. Contributor of articles to magazines and newspapers.

SIDELIGHTS: Readers of *Allers Familie Journal* (more than a million circulation) have adventured vicariously in such remote spots as Alexander Selkirk's (the real Robinson Crusoe) Island, Masatierra, where Arne Falk-Roenne spent a month in Selkirk's cave. In 1962, Falk-Roenne joined an advance party of Tristaners returning to Tristan de Cunha, where eruption of a dormant volcano the previous year forced evacuation of all the inhabitants to England. He also has visited Pitcairn Island, made four expeditions to remote Amazon tributaries, written about the original German Mennonite sect in Paraguay, searched for descendants of the Incas in Ecuador, and traveled in the New Hebrides, New Guinea, India, Soviet Union, and Africa. Most of Falk-Roenne's books have been published in other Scandinavian countries, and a number in Germany, Netherlands, Czechoslovakia, Austria, Hungary, and the Soviet Union.

*   *   *

FANE, Bron
See FANTHORPE, R(obert) Lionel

*   *   *

FANNING, Robbie 1947-

PERSONAL: Born January 30, 1947, in West Lafayette, Ind.; daughter of J. Edwin (a sociologist) and Roberta (a home economist; maiden name, Edwards) Losey; married Anthony David John Fanning (a writer), 1969; children: Kali Koala. *Education:* Attended Knox College, 1964-66; University of the State of New York Regents External Degree Program, B.S., 1978. *Residence:* Menlo Park, Calif. *Agent:* McIntosh & Otis, 475 Fifth Ave., New York, N.Y. 10017. *Office:* P.O. Box 2634, Menlo Park, Calif. 94026.

CAREER: Lecturer and teacher at short-term workshops on a variety of topics at several locations in United States, beginning 1974; San Jose State University, San Jose, Calif., instructor in writing, 1980—.

MEMBER: International Guild of Craft Journalists, Authors, and Photographers, National Standards Council, Authors League of America, Authors Guild, Embroiderers Guild of America, American Crafts Council, Committee of Small Magazine Editors and Publishers, Center for the History of American Needlework (member of advisory council), California Writers, Peninsula Publishers, Peninsula Stitchery Guild (chairwoman, 1974).

WRITINGS: Decorative Machine Stitchery, Butterick, 1976; (with husband, Tony Fanning) *Here and Now Stitchery* (on ethnic embroidery), Butterick, 1978; (with T. Fanning) *Keep Running,* Simon & Schuster, 1978; *Open Chain's Selected Annotated Bibliography of Self-Publishing,* Fibar Designs, 1978; *Open Chain's Selected Annotated Bibliography of Self-Study in the Needlearts,* Fibar Designs, 1978; *100 Butterflies,* Westminster, 1979; (with T. Fanning) *Get It All Done and Still Be Human,* Chilton, 1980; *The Complete Book of Machine Quilting,* Chilton, 1980. Author of column in *Needle and Thread.* Contributor to national magazines and newspapers, including *Better Homes and Gardens, Good Housekeeping Needlecraft, California Living,* and *Whole Earth Software Catalog.* Editor and publisher of *Open Chain,* 1975-84.

WORK IN PROGRESS: Another juvenile novel; a small business guide; a writing textbook; a book based on her columns.

SIDELIGHTS: Robbie Fanning writes: ''As a writer, I love to communicate clearly and simply my personal enthusiasms, to act as a catalyst between people and ideas, and then to listen and watch the rest of the world. To aspiring writers of any age I offer two words: 'Namaste' (Buddhist for 'I salute the light within you') and 'Persist' (probably more important than talent).''

*   *   *

FANTHORPE, Patricia Alice 1938-

PERSONAL: Born October 2, 1938, in Beetley, England; daughter of Arthur Richard (a lengthman roadworker) and Rosa Margaret (a dressmaker; maiden name, Roberts) Tooke; married Robert Lionel Fanthorpe (a high school headmaster and writer), September 7, 1957; children: Stephanie Dawn Patricia; Fiona Mary Patricia Alcibiadette. *Education:* Attended girls' secondary school in Dereham, England. *Politics:* "Somewhere in the middle." *Religion:* Evangelical Christian. *Home and office:* Rivendell, 48 Claude Rd., Roath, Cardiff CF2 3QA, Wales. *Agent:* Robert Reginald, P.O. Box 2845, San Bernardino, Calif. 92406.

CAREER: Drapery store assistant, 1953-56; in shoe manufacturing, 1956-57; writer, 1957-72; Bailey's Martham, England, horticulturist, 1972-73; International Telephone & Telegraph, Norwich, England, invoice clerk, 1976-79; writer, 1979—.

WRITINGS: (With husband, R. Lionel Fanthorpe) *Spencer's Metric Conversion Tables,* John Spencer, 1970; (with R. L. Fanthorpe) *Spencer's Decimal Payroll Tables,* John Spencer, 1971; (with R. L. Fanthorpe) *Spencer's Metric and Decimal Companion,* John Spencer, 1971; (with R. L. Fanthorpe) *Spencer's Office Guide,* John Spencer, 1971; *Racing Reckoner,* John Spencer, 1972; (with R. L. Fanthorpe) *The Black Lion,* Greystoke Mowbray, 1979; (with R. L. Fanthorpe) *The Holy Grail Revealed,* Newcastle, 1982. Contributor to *Sfear II.*

WORK IN PROGRESS: The Golden Tiger and *Zotala the Priest,* parts two and three of the Derl Wothor trilogy, of which *The Black Lion* was the first volume, both with husband, R. Lionel Fanthorpe.

SIDELIGHTS: Patricia Alice Fanthorpe writes: "I became a writer because Lionel was; if he'd been a plumber I'd have learnt to use a blowlamp instead. Collaboration on our books grew from my typing his manuscripts and discussing science fiction plots when his ideas weren't flowing. We got on to the office guides, decimalisation, and metrication books when the United Kingdom changed currency, weights, and measures in the early seventies. Because the compilation techniques were similar, I then did a racing guide on my own.

"Life with Lionel is tough, unpredictable, exciting, and adventurous. We get the scent of something—like the Rennes-le-Chateau mystery, stop what we're doing, pack a rucksack, catch the first boat to France, and spend the next day climbing the Pyrenees in a rainstorm. We cram thirty hours into the day and ten days into the week.

"After years in the agnostic wilderness, I came back to Christianity when Lionel did, and share his uncompromising evangelical faith, but I don't have his extrovert style—I'd rather share in worship quietly from the back of the church than lead it from the pulpit like he does.

"I think we each have individual talents—in the Biblical sense: Jael had the boldness to kill Sisera; Ruth had the kindness to care for Naomi; Martha had powers of energy and organisation; Mary had a sensitive, intelligent, and contemplative nature. I

believe that God wants us to use our own talents to the full *in our own way*.

"If I have any at all, they lie in the direction of caring for people and animals as individuals. Animals mean a lot to me— I think we've wandered too far from the charge laid on the human race in the first chapter of Genesis: to '*have dominion over*' nature in the sense of *tending and caring for* plant and animal life. That probably makes me a Christian conservationist!''

*   *   *

FANTHORPE, R(obert) Lionel 1935-
(Neil Balfort, Othello Baron, Erle Barton, Lee Barton, Thornton Bell, Noel Bertram, Leo Brett, Bron Fane, Phil Hobel, Mel Jay, Marston Johns, Victor La Salle, Oban Lerteth, Robert Lionel, John E. Muller, Elton T. Neef, Peter O'Flinn, Peter O'Flynn, Lionel Roberts, Rene Rolant, Deutero Spartacus, Robin Tate, Neil Thanet, Trebor Thorpe, Trevor Thorpe, Pel Torro, Olaf Trent, Karl Zeigfreid)

PERSONAL: Born February 9, 1935, in Dereham, England; son of Robert (a shop owner) and Greta Christine (a teacher; maiden name, Garbutt) Fanthorpe; married Patricia Alice Tooke (a writer), September 7, 1957; children: Stephanie Dawn Patricia, Fiona Mary Patricia Alcibiadette. *Education:* Norwich Teachers Training College, certificate, 1963; Open University, B.A., 1974, graduate study, 1980. *Politics:* "Last of Cromwell's Puritan Ironsides; strong on helping the poor and on law and order." *Religion:* "Enthusiastic Evangelical Christian, saved by the Lord Jesus Christ." *Home:* Rivendell, 48 Claude Rd., Roath, Cardiff CF2 3QA, Wales. *Office:* Glyn Derw High School, Penally Road, Ely, Cardiff, Wales.

CAREER: Worked as a machine operator, farm worker, driver, warehouseman, journalist, salesman, storekeeper, and yard foreman during the 1950s; secondary school teacher in Dereham, England, 1958-61 and 1963-67; Gamlingay Village College, Gamlingay, England, tutor, 1967-69; Phoenix Timber Co., Rainham, England, industrial training officer, 1969-72; Hellesdon High School, Hellesdon, England, head of English department, 1972, second master, beginning 1973, deputy head, 1978-79; Glyn Derw High School, Cardiff, Wales, headmaster, 1979—. Former extra-mural tutor for Cambridge University; examiner for Certificate of Secondary Education in English. *Military service:* British Army Cadet Force Officer, 1967-69; became first lieutenant.

MEMBER: British Institute of Management, Mensa, College of Preceptors, Gideons, Judo Club.

AWARDS, HONORS: East of England Judo Championship silver medal, novices' section, Kyu grades, 1977; brown belt, B.J.A., 1978.

WRITINGS—Published by Badger Books, except as indicated: *The Waiting World,* 1958; *Alien from the Stars,* 1959; *Hyperspace,* 1959; *Space-Borne,* 1959; *Fiends,* 1959; *Doomed World,* 1960; *Satellite,* 1960; *Asteroid Man,* 1960; *Out of the Darkness,* 1960; *Hand of Doom,* 1960; *Flame Mass,* 1961; *The Golden Chalice,* 1961; *Space Fury,* 1962, Vega Books, 1963; *Negative Minus,* 1963; *Neuron World,* 1965; *The Triple Man,* 1965; *The Unconfined,* 1966; *The Watching World,* 1966; (with wife, Patricia Alice Fanthorpe) *The Black Lion,* Greystoke

Mobray, 1979; (with P. A. Fanthorpe) *The Holy Grail Revealed*, Newcastle, 1982.

Nonfiction; all published by John Spencer: (With W. H. Farrer) *Spencer's Metric and Decimal Guide*, 1970; (with P. A. Fanthorpe) *Spencer's Metric Conversion Tables*, 1970; (with P. A. Fanthorpe) *Spencer's Office Guide*, 1971; (with P. A. Fanthorpe) *Spencer's Metric and Decimal Companion*, 1971; (with P. A. Fanthorpe) *Spencer's Decimal Payroll Tables*, 1971.

Under pseudonym Erle Barton: *The Planet Seekers*, Vega Books, 1964.

Under pseudonym Lee Barton: *The Unseen*, Badger Books, 1963; *The Shadow Man*, Badger Books, 1966.

Under pseudonym Thornton Bell: *Space Trap*, Badger Books, 1964; *Chaos*, Badger Books, 1964.

Under pseudonym Leo Brett; published by Badger Books: *Exit Humanity*, 1960; *The Microscopic Ones*, 1960; *Faceless Planet*, 1960; *March of the Robots*, 1961; *Mind Force*, 1961; *Black Infinity*, 1961; *Nightmare*, 1962; *Face in the Night*, 1962; *The Immortals*, 1962; *They Never Came Back*, 1962; *The Forbidden*, 1963; *From Realms Beyond*, 1963; *The Alien Ones*, 1963; *Power Sphere*, 1963.

Under pseudonym Bron Fane; published by Badger Books, except as indicated: *Juggernaut*, 1960, published as *Blue Juggernaut*, Arcadia House, 1965; *Last Man on Earth*, 1960; *Rodent Mutation*, 1961; *The Intruders*, 1963; *Somewhere Out There*, 1963; *Softly by Moonlight*, 1963; *Unknown Destiny*, 1964; *Nemesis*, 1964; *Suspension*, 1964; *The Macabre Ones*, 1964; *U.F.O. 517*, 1966.

Under pseudonym Victor La Salle: *Menace from Mercury*, John Spencer, 1954.

Under pseudonym John E. Muller, except as indicated; published by Badger Books, except as indicated: *The Ultimate Man*, 1961; *The Uninvited*, 1961; *Crimson Planet*, 1961; *The Venus Venture*, 1961, published under pseudonym Marston Johns, Arcadia House, 1965; *Forbidden Planet*, 1961; *Return of Zeus*, 1962; *Perilous Galaxy*, 1962; *Uranium 235*, 1962; *The Man Who Conquered Time*, 1962; *Orbit One*, 1962, published under pseudonym Mel Jay, Arcadia House, 1966; *The Eye of Karnak*, 1962; *Micro Infinity*, 1962; *Beyond Time*, 1962, published under pseudonym Marston Johns, Arcadia House, 1966; *Infinity Machine*, 1962; *The Day the World Died*, 1962; *Vengeance of Siva*, 1962; *The X-Machine*, 1962; *Reactor XK9*, 1963; *Special Mission*, 1963; *Dark Continuum*, 1964; *Mark of the Beast*, 1964; *The Negative Ones*, 1965; *The Exorcists*, 1965; *The Man from Beyond*, 1965; *Beyond the Void*, 1965; *Spectre of Darkness*, 1965; *Out of the Night*, 1965; *Phenomena X*, 1966; *Survival Project*, 1966.

Under pseudonym Lionel Roberts, except as indicated; published by Badger Books, except as indicated: *Dawn of the Mutants*, 1959; *Time Echo*, 1959, published under pseudonym Robert Lionel, Arcadia House, 1964; *Cyclops in the Sky*, 1960; *The In-World*, 1960; *The Face of X*, 1960, published under pseudonym Robert Lionel, Arcadia House, 1965; *The Last Valkyrie*, 1961; *The Synthetic Ones*, 1961; *Flame Goddess*, 1961.

Under pseudonym Neil Thanet: *Beyond the Veil*, Badger Books, 1964; *The Man Who Came Back*, Badger Books, 1964.

Under pseudonym Trebor Thorpe: *Five Faces of Fear*, Badger Books, 1960; *Lightning World*, Badger Books, 1960.

Under pseudonym Pel Torro; published by Badger Books, except as indicated: *Frozen Planet*, 1960; *World of the Gods*, 1960; *The Phantom Ones*, 1961; *Legion of the Lost*, 1962; *The Strange Ones*, 1963; *Galaxy 666*, 1963; *Formula 29X*, 1963, published as *Beyond the Barrier of Space*, Tower Books, 1969; *Through the Barrier*, 1963; *The Timeless Ones*, 1963; *The Last Astronaut*, 1963; *The Face of Fear*, 1963; *The Return*, 1964, published as *Exiled in Space*, Arcadia House, 1968; *Space No Barrier*, 1964, published as *Man of Metal*, Lenox Hill, 1970; *Force 97X*, 1965.

Under pseudonym Karl Zeigfreid; published by Badger Books, except as indicated: *Walk Through To-Morrow*, 1962; *Android*, 1962; *Gods of Darkness*, 1962; *Atomic Nemesis*, 1962; *Zero Minus X*, 1962; *Escape to Infinity*, 1963; *Radar Alert*, 1963; *World of Tomorrow*, 1963, published as *World of the Future*, Arcadia House, 1968; *The World That Never Was*, 1963; *Projection Infinity*, 1964; *No Way Back*, 1964; *Barrier 346*, 1965; *The Girl from Tomorrow*, 1965.

Also author of "Supernatural Stories" monographs.

Contributor to periodicals under pseudonyms Neil Balfort, Othello Baron, Erle Barton, Lee Barton, Thornton Bell, Noel Bertram, Leo Brett, Bron Fane, Phil Hobel, Oban Lerteth, Elton T. Neef, Peter O'Flinn, Peter O'Flynn, Lionel Roberts, Rene Rolant, Deutero Spartacus, Robin Tate, Neil Thanet, Trebor Thorpe, Trevor Thorpe, Pel Torro, and Olaf Trent.

WORK IN PROGRESS: Damascus Road, a musical on the life of Saint Paul; *Sonnets from the Scriptures; Fanthorpe's Hammer, or Macabbacus Was Right!*, a collection of controversial Christian essays; *The Golden Tiger* and *Zotala the Priest*, parts two and three of the Derl Wothor trilogy, of which *The Black Lion* was part one, both with wife Patricia Alice Fanthorpe.

SIDELIGHTS: "I started writing when I was sixteen, having read and enjoyed most of the fantasy and science fiction I could get hold of at school," R. Lionel Fanthorpe told *CA*. "This was a mixture of Wells, Verne, Poe, etc., plus the odd paperback by authors whose names didn't register at the time. I have always had a poor memory for authors and titles, but I can recall the plot and characters of a story I've enjoyed for years afterwards. I wrote a parody of John Masefield's 'Sea Fever' beginning—

> I must go back into space again,
> To the lonely space and the stars;
> And all I ask is a rocket ship
> And a job to do on Mars. . . ."

Fanthorpe, who wrote nearly one hundred sixty books from 1957 until 1966, recalled the beginnings of his writing career: "In those days my mother ran a small shorthand and typing school from the front room of our house, and she did all the typing for me. Demand grew over the years. I married Patricia in 1957 and she shared the typing. Demand went on growing. At its peak we were being asked to produce a book a week, or almost a book in a weekend. Communications would arrive from Spencers to the effect that the printer was waiting, could I hurry up. Patricia's sister got called into the typing team. I bought tape recorders and dictated material as fast as I could, despatching reels to the various typists, proofreading the typescripts and sending the manuscripts to Spencers by express mail. They never sent proofs and on some occasions what came out of the printer's end bore only coincidental resemblance to what I'd sent in.

"Spencers almost invariably sent the cover rough to me with a request to write a selection of titles and blurbs that would fit in. When I'd send this, they'd write back saying which ones they'd selected. I wrote the back cover introductions at the same time. Most of these were in-jokes of one sort or another. For example, they produced collections of shorts and insisted that each story appeared under a different pen-name. All my pen-names with the exception of Deutero Spartacus, which is an exercise in exploring the limits of the preposterous, were extractive anagrams based on ROBERT LIONEL FANTHORPE.

"I tried to give my pen-names an international flavour, but it was in the Milligan and Sellers vein. My international authors were music hall caricatures; my Scotsmen said, 'Och aye, the noo,' as a condition of their very existence; my Welshman came out of the infinite, terminated every utterance with, 'Look you, Dai Bach,' and usually worked in coal mines near nonconformist chapels. My French author, Rene Rolant, invariably pronounced *th* as *z* and darkly hinted of his past as a *souteneur* and resistance hero. My all-American boy was Elton T. Neef, known for some obscure reason as the Manhattan Magus, who was a faint shadow of John Wayne mixed with Damon Runyon and Mark Twain. The more blatantly unbelievable it all became, the more stories they bought. Like an impoverished latter-day Sheridan I tried giving characters names that went with their temperaments. He had Mrs. Malaprop and Sir Lucius O'Trigger. I had a gigantic security man with a sloping forehead and a love of fighting. I called him Slam Croberg and featured him in *Android*. It was Kingsley Amis's misfortune to review this for the *Observer* and his delicate artistic soul never fully recovered from the trauma.

"There *are* real characters hidden in some of the stories. It was another form of in-joke. Some I liked and described accordingly. Others I didn't. The reader must guess at those—at least until my mortal remains have gone where no laws of libel can reach. I'm in some of the stories too. The man-I'd-like-to-be is only thinly disguised in "The Attic" by Deutero Spartacus. (I'm the narrator, not the senile villain who gets the chop!) The Bron Fane character Valentine Gregory Stearman is also made in this mould. The nearest real description as opposed to an idealised one is the character of Trader Krells in *The Watching World*."

Addressing himself to the question why an author writes as he does at a particular period in his life, Fanthorpe added: "I am conscious that some experiences have coloured my thinking and led me to emphasize certain characters, lifestyles and philosophies at different stages of my writing. At sixteen and seventeen I was an enthusiastic Christian, a left-wing socialist and an ardent pacifist. In my twenties I was less committed to religion and my political enthusiasm waned. In my thirties I left the church and stopped renewing my subscriptions to the Labour Party. In my forties, I was a vaguely theistic humanist, and sufficient of a Conservative to use my car to convey Conservative voters to the polling station to oblige a friend. I shall be fifty by the time this is printed: I praise and thank God for salvation in Jesus Christ. I'm an enthusiastic evangelical Christian and a member of the Gideons, helping to spread the word of God in hotels, hospitals and schools. I believe that writing should *say* something as well as telling a story: I want all my future writing to say something worthwhile about the Lord Jesus Christ and the new life He offers us.

"My major dislikes are trendy permissiveness and the increasing fads and whims of modern bureaucratic management. I run

my own show, and I'm an old fashioned, autocratic paternalist—the one on whose desk the buck not merely stops but is brought to a crashing, juddering halt. If Moses had worked with a committee the Israelites would still be in Egypt."

*　　*　　*

FASANA, Paul James 1933-

PERSONAL: Born July 20, 1933, in Bingham Canyon, Utah; son of Oreste G. and Mary (Rolando-Calcio) Fasana. *Education:* University of California, Berkeley, B.A., 1959, M.L.S., 1960. *Politics:* Democrat. *Religion:* Roman Catholic. *Home:* 325 West 52nd, Apt. 1G, New York, N.Y. 10019. *Office:* Research Libraries, New York Public Library, 42nd St. and 5th Ave., New York, N.Y. 10018.

CAREER: New York Public Library, New York City, cataloger in Circulation Division, 1960-61; ITEK Laboratories, Lexington, Mass., systems engineer, 1961-63; U.S. Air Force, Cambridge Research Laboratory Library, Bedford, Mass., chief of cataloging, 1963-64; Columbia University Libraries, New York City, assistant coordinator of cataloging, 1964-66, assistant to the director for library automation, 1966-71; Collaborative Library Systems Development, New York City, secretary to planning council, 1968-71; New York Public Library, chief of preparation services, Research Libraries, 1971-79, associate director, Research Libraries, 1980—.

Lecturer in library schools of McGill University, 1966-69, University of Montreal, 1968-69, Rutgers University, 1970-71, Graduate School and University Center of the City University of New York, 1974-76; lecturer or speaker at seminars for American Management Association and information science and library associations. Member of international advisory board, University Microfilms, 1983—.

MEMBER: American Library Association (member of board of directors, Library and Information Technology Division, 1966-67, 1971-73; Resources and Technical Services Division, member of board of directors, 1970-74, president, 1976-77; member of editorial board, Information Technology and Libraries Division, 1978-84), American Society for Information Science (member of council, 1971-74), American National Standards Institute, New York Technical Service Librarians (president, 1971-72), New York Library Club (member of council, 1976-80).

AWARDS, HONORS: Award of merit from New York Technical Services Librarians, 1978; Astor fellowship, 1983-84.

WRITINGS: (Contributor) *Automation and Scientific Communication,* American Documentation Institute, 1963; (editor with L. Denis and contributor) *Proceedings: Colloque sur les implications administratives de l'automatisation dans les bibliotheques,* Montreal University Press, 1968; (editor) *Electronic Data Processing Concepts,* American Society for Information Science, 1968; (editor) *Elements of Information Systems,* American Society for Information Science, 1968; (with others) *A Computer Based System for Reserve Activities in a University Library,* Columbia University Libraries, 1969.

(Editor with Allen Veaner and contributor) *The Collaborative Library Systems Development Project,* M.I.T. Press, 1971; *The Columbia University Libraries Integrated Technical Services System: Acquisition,* U.S. National Science Foundation, 1971; *The Future of the Library Catalog,* Knowledge Industry Publications, 1979; *Closing the Catalog,* Oryx, 1980; (contributor)

Professional Librarians Reader in Library Automation, Knowledge Industry Publications, 1980.

Also author or editor of other reports on automated routines and mechanization for libraries and library orientated organizations. Contributor to numerous library journals. Member of editorial board of *Advanced Technology Library*, 1975—, and *Serials Librarian*, 1976—.

*   *   *

FAULK, Odie B. 1933-

PERSONAL: Born August 26, 1933, in Winnsboro, Tex.; son of Joseph Butler and Leta Verna (Bilbreath) Faulk; married Laura Ella Whalen, August 22, 1959; children: Richard Douglas, Nancy Marie. *Education:* San Angelo College (now Angelo State College), A.A., 1957; Texas Technological College (now Texas Tech University), B.S., 1958, M.A., 1960, Ph.D., 1962. *Politics:* Republican. *Religion:* Presbyterian. *Home:* 216 Kingsbury, Muskogee, Okla. 74403. *Office:* 1047 North York, Muskogee, Okla. 74403.

CAREER: U.S. Marine Corps, 1950-55, left service as staff sergeant; Texas A&M University, College Station, instructor in history, 1962-63; University of Arizona, Tucson, lecturer in history, 1963-65; Arizona Pioneers' Historical Society, Tucson, research historian, 1965-67; Arizona Western College, Yuma, head of social science department, 1967-68; Oklahoma State University, Stillwater, associate professor, 1968-71, professor of history, 1971-77, chairman of history department, 1972-77; Western Heritage Books, Muskogee, Okla., executive editor, 1977—.

MEMBER: American Historical Association, Organization of American Historians, Western History Association, Arizona Pioneers' Historical Society, Texas State Historical Association (fellow), Oklahoma Historical Society.

AWARDS, HONORS: Land of Many Frontiers, North America Divided: The Mexican War, 1846-1848, and *Home of the Brave: A Patriot's Guide to American History* were nominated for Pulitzer Prizes in 1968, 1971, and 1976 respectively; Award of Merit from Texas Civil War Centennial Commission, for *Tom Green: A Fightin' Texan;* Western Heritage Award, Cowboy Hall of Fame, 1972, for *North America Divided: The Mexican War, 1846-1848;* Border Regional Library Association History Award, 1973, for *Tombstone: Myth and Reality.*

WRITINGS: Tom Green: A Fightin' Texan, Texian Press, 1963; (with Ralph Steen) *Government by the People,* Steck, 1964; *The Last Years of Spanish Texas, 1778-1821,* Mouton & Co., 1964.

A Successful Failure, Steck, 1965; (with S. S. McKay) *Texas after Spindletop,* Steck, 1965; (with Sidney Brinckerhoff) *Lancers for the King: A Study of the Frontier Military System of Northern New Spain,* Arizona Historical Foundation, 1965; (editor) *John Robert Baylor: Confederate Governor of Arizona,* Arizona Pioneers' Historical Society, 1966; (editor) *Arizona's State Historical Society,* Arizona Historical Society, 1966; (editor) *John Baptist Salpointe: Soldier of the Cross,* Diocese of Tucson, 1966; (editor) *Prospector, Cowhand, and Sodbuster: Historical Places Associated with the Mining, Ranching, and Farming Frontiers in the Trans-Mississippi West,* National Park Service, 1967; *Too Far North . . . Too Far South: The Controversial Boundary Survey and the Gadsden Purchase,* Westernlore, 1967; (translator and editor) *The Constitution of Occidente: The First Constitution of Arizona, Sonora, and Sinaloa,*

1825-1831, Arizona Pioneers' Historical Society, 1967; *Land of Many Frontiers: A History of the American Southwest,* Oxford University Press, 1968; *The Geronimo Campaign* (Military Book Club selection), Oxford University Press, 1969; (editor) *Derby's Report on Opening the Colorado, 1850-1851,* University of New Mexico, 1969.

Arizona: A Short History, University of Oklahoma, 1970, 2nd edition, 1973; *The Leather Jacket Soldier: Spanish Military Equipment and Institutions of the Late 18th Century,* Socio-Technical Publications, 1971; (with S. V. Connor) *North America Divided: The Mexican War, 1846-1848,* Oxford University Press, 1971; *Tombstone: Myth and Reality,* Oxford University Press, 1972; *This Beats Working for a Living* (Conservative Book Club selection), Arlington House, 1973; *Destiny Road: The Gila Trail and the Opening of the Southwest* (Western Writers of America Book Club selection), Oxford University Press, 1973; (with J. A. Stout) *The Mexican War: Changing Interpretations,* Swallow Press, 1974; *Crimson Desert: Indian Wars of the American Southwest* (Western Writers of America Book Club selection), Oxford University Press, 1974; *Never at a Loss for an Opinion* (Conservative Book Club selection), Arlington House, 1974; (with Stout) *A Short History of the American West,* Harper, 1974.

(With wife, Laura E. Faulk) *The Australian Alternative,* Arlington House, 1975; *The Camel Corps: An Army Experiment,* Oxford University Press, 1976; (with J. A. Carroll) *Home of the Brave: A Patriot's Guide to American History* (Conservative Book Club selection), Arlington House, 1976; *The Modoc People,* Indian Tribal Series, 1976; *Dodge City: The Most Western Town of All,* Oxford University Press, 1977; (with B. M. Jones) *Miracle of the Wilderness: The Continuing American Revolution,* Archer Editions, 1977; (with C. N. Tyson and J. H. Thomas) *The McMan: The Lives of Robert M. McFarlin and James A. Chapman,* University of Oklahoma Press, 1977; (with Welborn Hope and Pendleton Woods) *The Life of a Successful Bank, 1908-1978,* Fidelity Bank (Oklahoma City), 1978; (editor with K. A. Franks and P. F. Lambert) *Early Military Forts and Posts in Oklahoma,* Oklahoma Historical Society, 1978; (with Thomas and Tyson) *The Gentleman: The Life of Joseph A. LaFortune,* Oklahoma Heritage Association, 1979; (editor) *One Man in His Time: The Autobiography of Jack T. Conn,* Oklahoma Heritage Association, 1979; *A Man of Vision: The Life and Career of O. W. Coburn,* Western Heritage Books, 1979.

The Making of a Merchant: R. A. Young and T. G. & Y. Stores, Oklahoma Heritage Association, 1980; *A Specialist in Everything: The Life of Fred S. Watson, M.D.,* Oklahoma Heritage Association, 1981; *A Full Service Banker: The Life of Louis W. Duncan,* Oklahoma Heritage Association, 1981; (with P. Q. Wright) *Coletta: A Sister of Mercy,* Oklahoma Heritage Association, 1981; *Muskogee: City and County,* Five Civilized Tribes Museum (Muskogee, Okla.), 1982; *Dear Everybody: The Life of Henry B. Bass,* Oklahoma Heritage Association, 1982; *Jennys to Jets: The Life of Clarence E. Page,* Oklahoma Heritage Association, 1983; (with B. M. Jones) *Fort Smith: An Illustrated History,* Old Fort Museum (Fort Smith), 1983.

Contributor to professional journals. Assistant editor, *Arizona and the West,* 1963-65.

SIDELIGHTS: Odie B. Faulk, a historian who specializes in the American West, "writes in a dry, matter-of-fact style that suits his objective approach to the fictions and myths we have all stubbornly cherished" about frontier life, according to a critic in the *New York Times Book Review.* Of his book *Land of Many Frontiers: A History of the American Southwest*, N. Scott Momaday writes in the *New York Times Book Review:* "Mr. Faulk . . . has written a concise and responsible study, one in which the disparate elements of this geographic region are brought together in their true proportions. Moreover, there is a fine sense of continuity and organization in the narrative style. Here is a difficult subject treated with precision and insight, confidence and sensitivity."

North America Divided: The Mexican War, 1846-1848 has been translated into Spanish.

BIOGRAPHICAL/CRITICAL SOURCES: New York Times Book Review, February 2, 1969, January 1, 1978.

*   *   *

FAUX, Marian 1945-

PERSONAL: Surname is pronounced "fox"; born July 2, 1945, in Norfolk, Va.; daughter of Donald E. (a businessman) and Lilliam (Walsh) Faux. *Education:* Purdue University, B.A., 1967; graduate study at Roosevelt University. *Office:* 123 West 95th St., New York, N.Y. 10025. *Agent:* Dominick Abel Literary Agency, 498 West End Ave., Apt. 12-C, New York, N.Y. 10024.

CAREER: Robert Snyder Associates, Chicago, Ill., editorial assistant, 1967-68; Douglas Dunhill, Inc., Chicago, editor, 1968-70; Follett Publishing Co., Chicago, senior editor for social science, 1970-74; Henry Regnery Co., Chicago, senior editor, 1973-75; free-lance editor and writer, 1975—. Adjunct professor, Small Business Center, Fashion Institute of Technology.

MEMBER: American Society of Journalists and Authors.

WRITINGS: Drying, Curing, and Smoking Food, Grosset, 1977; (with Marjabelle Stewart) *Executive Etiquette*, St. Martin's, 1979; *The Complete Resume Guide*, Monarch, 1980; *Successful Free-lancing: The Complete Guide to Establishing and Running Any Kind of Free-lance Business*, St. Martin's, 1982; *Clear and Simple Guide to Resume Writing*, Monarch, 1982; *Resumes for Professional Nurses*, Monarch, 1982; *Resumes for Sales and Marketing*, Monarch, 1982; *Childless by Choice: Choosing Childlessness in the Eighties*, Anchor Books, 1984; *Entering the Job Market*, Monarch, 1984.

SIDELIGHTS: In her book *Childless by Choice*, Marian Faux investigates the phenomenon of the childless woman. "Though she often repeats herself, and many of her arguments are familiar, Miss Faux has written a useful book," according to Anatole Broyard in the *New York Times*. "We are inclined to be hypocritical about parenthood, she says, or to rationalize it after the fact. But if women faced their ambivalence before having children, they would probably be better mothers or happier childless wives."

AVOCATIONAL INTERESTS: Reading, collecting American first editions, ballet, theater, travel (Western Europe), Mexico, Virgin Islands.

BIOGRAPHICAL/CRITICAL SOURCES: New York Times, December 24, 1983; *Toronto Globe and Mail*, April 14, 1984.

*   *   *

FERRIS, Tom
   See WALKER, Peter N.

FERSH, Seymour H. 1926-

PERSONAL: Born March 24, 1926, in Poughkeepsie, N.Y.; son of David (a salesman) and Lillian (Hambourg) Fersh; married Harriet Fein, August 31, 1947; children: Donald, Susan, Maryl. *Education:* New York College for Teachers (now State University of New York at Albany), B.A., 1949, M.A., 1950; Yale University, additional study, 1952; Columbia University, additional study, 1953; New York University, Ph.D., 1955. *Home:* Apt. 310, 3060 North Atlantic Ave., Cocoa Beach, Fla. 32931. *Office:* Brevard Community College, Cocoa, Fla. 32922.

CAREER: Social studies teacher in New Paltz, N.Y., 1950-55; New Jersey State College, Montclair, 1955-61, began as assistant professor, became professor of history; The Asia Society, New York, N.Y., education director, 1961-73; Fairleigh Dickinson University, Rutherford, N.J., professor of education, 1973-78; American Association of Community and Junior Colleges, Washington, D.C., director of Office of International Services, 1978-81; Brevard Community College, Cocoa, Fla., coordinator of curriculum development, 1981—. Fulbright professor, India, 1958-59. Assistant director of summer Asian studies program, Rutgers University, New Brunswick, N.J., 1960-66. *Military service:* U.S. Army, 1944-46; became sergeant; received Purple Heart.

MEMBER: Association for Asian Studies, American Historical Association, National Council for the Social Studies.

AWARDS, HONORS: New York State University at Albany distinguished alumni award, 1971.

WRITINGS: The View from the White House: Annual Message to Congress, Public Affairs Press, 1961; *India and South Asia*, Macmillan, 1965, revised edition, 1970; *Learning about Peoples and Cultures*, McDougal, Littell, 1974; *Asia: Teaching about/Learning From*, Teachers College Press, 1978; *The Community College and International Education: A Report of Progress*, Volume I, Brevard Community College, 1981, Volume II, Broward Community College, 1984. Contributor of articles to *Social Education*.

*   *   *

FICKERT, Kurt J(on) 1920-

PERSONAL: Born December 19, 1920, in Pausa, Germany; son of Kurt Alfred (a mechanic) and Martha (Saerchinger) Fickert; married Lynn B. Janda, August 6, 1946; children: Linda (Mrs. Matthew Mosbacher), Jon, Chris. *Education:* Hofstra College (now University), A.B., 1941; New York University, M.A., 1947, Ph.D., 1952. *Politics:* Independent. *Religion:* Lutheran. *Home:* 33 South Kensington Pl., Springfield, Ohio 45504. *Office:* Department of Languages, Wittenberg University, Springfield, Ohio 45501.

CAREER: Hofstra College (now University), Hempstead, N.Y., instructor, 1947-52, assistant professor of German, 1952-53; Florida State University, Tallahassee, instructor in German, 1953-54; Fort Hays Kansas State College, Hays, assistant professor of German and English, 1954-56; Wittenberg University, Springfield, Ohio, assistant professor, 1956-60, associate professor, 1960-67, professor of German, 1967—, chairman, department of languages, 1969-75. *Military service:* U.S. Army Air Forces, 1942-45; served in Pacific theater. *Member:* American Association of Teachers of German, American Association of University Professors, Ohio Poetry Day Association (president, 1971-75), Phi Eta Sigma.

AWARDS, HONORS: Fulbright grant for teachers of German, Germany, 1957; Stephen Vincent Benet Narrative Poem Award, 1968, for "Struggle with Loneliness," from *Poet Lore;* citation for meritorious achievement, Society for German-American Studies, 1973; New England Prize, *Lyric* (magazine), 1976; second prize, Poets and Patrons, 1978; first prize, Yukuhara Haiku Society of Japan, 1978; first prize, Ohio Poetry Society, 1979; second prize, World Order of Narrative Poets, 1980, 1984; National Endowment for the Humanities grant, 1982; Panola Prize, *Lyric,* 1983.

WRITINGS: To Heaven and Back: The New Morality in the Plays of Friedrich Duerrenmatt, University Press of Kentucky, 1972; *Herman Hesse's Quest,* York, 1978; *Kafka's Doubles,* Peter Lang, 1979; *Signs and Portents: Myth in the Work of Wolfgang Borchert,* York, 1980; *Franz Kafka: Life, Work, and Criticism,* York, 1984.

Contributor: *Anthology of German Poetry,* Anchor Books, 1960; *Living in the Present,* Acheron Press, 1982; *Nachrichten aus den Staaten: Deutsche Literatur in den USA,* Olms, 1983. Contributor of articles to *German Quarterly, Monatshefte, Germanic Notes, Contemporary Literature, Explicator,* and *Modern Drama,* of poems to *Lyrica Germanica, German-American Studies, Poet Lore, Bitterroot, Poetry Venture, Speak Out, Lunatic Fringe, Change, Southern Humanities Review,* and *Lyric,* and of a translation of a story from German to *Dimension.*

WORK IN PROGRESS: Neither Right nor Left: The Politics of Individualism in Uwe Johnson's Work.

*   *   *

FIELDING, Temple (Hornaday)   1913-1983

PERSONAL: Born October 8, 1913, in New York, N.Y.; died of a heart attack, May 18, 1983 in Palma, Majorca; son of George T. Fielding II (an executive) and Helen Ross (Hornaday) Fielding; married Nancy Parker (a literary agent and writer), October 17, 1942; children: Dodge Temple. *Education:* Princeton University, B.A. (cum laude), 1939. *Politics:* "Professionally 100 percent a-political." *Religion:* Unitarian Universalist. *Residence:* Palma de Majorca, Spain. *Office:* Fielding Publications, 105 Madison Ave., New York, N.Y. 10016.

CAREER: Professional writer, 1940-83, primarily identified with travel guides to Europe. Wrote for a number of national magazines, 1940-47, doing special correspondence abroad at various times for *Town and Country, Reader's Digest, Saturday Evening Post,* and other magazines; newspaper feature writer for International News Service, *Baltimore Sunday Sun,* and *Christian Science Monitor,* 1940-49; foreign correspondent in Ethiopia for International News Service, 1946; producer of National Broadcasting Co. travel program, "The Fieldings in Europe," 1954; columnist, Hall Syndicate, 1956-57; chairman and president, Fielding Publications, New York, N.Y., 1965-83. *Military service:* U.S. Army, 1940-45; on detached service with Office of Strategic Services for two years, at one point as member of the first American military mission to Tito in Yugoslavia; became major; received Bronze Star and Army Commendation Medal with palm.

MEMBER: American Society of Authors and Journalists (past president), Society of American Travel Writers, Arctic Institute, Overseas Press Club of America (past governor), Temple Fielding's Epicure Club of Europe (founder and former president), Adventurers' Club of New York (past governor), Travelers' Century Club (Los Angeles), Ski Club of Great Britain, Arabian Knights (Cairo), Banshees (New York), Het Jagertje (The Hague), King Christian IV Guild (Denmark), Century Club (New York); honorary member of other clubs and societies in Europe.

AWARDS, HONORS: Flor de Almendro, Commander of Order of Merito Civil, and Knight's Cross of the Order of Isabel la Catolica (all Spain:); Commander of Merito della Repubblica Italiana and gold plaque of merit, Federazione Italiana Pubblici Esercize (both Italy); Gold Cross of Honor (Austria); Knight of the Royal Order of Vasa (Sweden); Knight of the Royal Order of Dannebrog, Knight's Cross of the Order of Haederstegn, and Danish Information Foundation Award (all Denmark); silver medal l'Hospitalite and Officer of the Commanderie de Cotteaux (both France); and other awards from cities in Europe; recipient, Princeton University Medal of Honor and Distinguished Achievement Award, Class of 1939; special citation from President Kennedy, 1963; Red Badge of Courage from U.S. Marine Corps, 1963; Non Sibi, Sed Patriae Award from Marine Corps Reserve Association, 1964.

WRITINGS: New Travel Guide to Europe, Sloane, annually, 1948-49, published as *Fielding's Travel Guide to Europe,* annually, 1950-52, Fielding Publications, annually, 1965-79, published as *Fielding's Europe,* annually, 1979-83; *The Temple Fielding's Selective Shopping Guide to Europe,* Morrow, annually, 1957-65, Fielding Publications, 1965-68, published with wife Nancy Fielding as *Fielding's Selective Shopping Guide to Europe,* 1968-83; (with N. Fielding) *Fielding's Super-Economy Guide to Europe,* published as *Fielding's Super-Economy Europe,* Fielding Publications, 1970-74, published as *Fielding's Low-Cost Europe,* 1974-83. Author of *A Guide to Fort Bragg,* 1942, and contributor to *Deadline Delayed,* 1946.

Also author of various travel pamphlets, including *Quick Currency Guide and Language Tips for Europe, Fielding's World Time Converter, Fielding's World Currency Converter,* and *Fielding's Living Guide Toll-Free Information Service,* 1977. Contributor of columns to *Ladies Home Journal,* 1968-83; also contributor of articles to numerous periodicals, including *Town and Country, Harper's, Life, Coronet, Mademoiselle,* and *Nation's Business.* Contributing editor, *Travel and Leisure,* 1970-83.

SIDELIGHTS: Temple Fielding pioneered the modern travel guide with his *Fielding's Europe,* a guidebook published annually under various names for more than thirty years. Modeled after a humorous orientation booklet that Fielding wrote for arriving army recruits at Fort Bragg during the Second World War, *Fielding's Europe* provides practical advice on such things as where to eat and sleep and what tourist traps to avoid, rather than emphasizing the cultural attractions of Europe.

Fielding's first guide was published in 1948, when many ex-soldiers were returning to Europe with their wives and families. "Rather than dwell on how high the cathedral is or when the entrance was built, Temple thought it more important to tell [travelers] where to get a good meal and a hotel that would treat you right, and which wasn't bombed out," one of his colleagues told the *Washington Post.* Fielding's approach proved to be a popular one and his book, which has sold over three million copies, reigned unchallenged until the 1960s, when the market for budget travel books became highly competitive.

During his lifetime, Fielding, his wife, and several members of their staff would fan out for six months every year, covering twenty-three European countries. Then, from early summer to fall, they incorporated their findings into new editions—rating hotels, restaurants, airlines, motoring conditions, and other categories encountered on a scale which ran from "superb" to "dreadful."

"Our primary obsession wherever we move is to be accepted as Mr. and Mrs. John Smith, routine American tourists," Fielding once told *CA*. "We never voluntarily introduce ourselves. We always insist, as our most basic policy rule, upon paying *all* bills in full. . . . Although we speak from four to six languages (all of them badly), our roles as typical American tourists require that we stick to English when we are in public."

In a *New York Times* interview given the month before his death, Fielding suggested that his major goal had been "easing the path for good-hearted, well-meaning people who didn't know where they were going or what they were going to do when they got there. Europe was a jungle to them so we tried to assuage the hardships, take away the strangeness, make them feel at home. I don't think it's an exaggeration to say that we probably succeeded."

BIOGRAPHICAL/CRITICAL SOURCES: New Yorker, January 6, 1968; *Life*, May 3, 1968; *Time*, June 6, 1969; *Publishers Weekly*, December 8, 1975.

OBITUARIES: New York Times, May 19, 1983; *Washington Post*, May 20, 1983; *Chicago Tribune*, May 20, 1983; *Time*, May 30, 1983; *Newsweek*, May 30, 1983; *Publishers Weekly*, June 3, 1983.†

*   *   *

FINNERTY, Adam Daniel
    See CORSON-FINNERTY, Adam Daniel

*   *   *

FINNERTY, Daniel John
    See CORSON-FINNERTY, Adam Daniel

*   *   *

FITZGIBBON, Russell H(umke)   1902-1979

PERSONAL: Born June 29, 1902, in Columbus, Ind.; died January 8, 1979; son of Thomas Francis and Frances A. (Moore) Fitzgibbon; married Irene Cory, July 6, 1929; children: Alan Lee, Katherine Irene (Mrs. David G. Lilly). *Education:* Hanover College, A.B., 1924; Indiana University, A.M., 1928; University of Wisconsin, Ph.D., 1933. *Religion:* Presbyterian. *Home:* 9729 Pinecrest Dr., Sun City, Ariz. 85351.

CAREER: Hanover College, Hanover, Ind., instructor, 1924-27, assistant professor, 1927-29, associate professor, 1929-32, professor of history and political science, 1932-36; University of California, Los Angeles, assistant professor, 1936-42, associate professor, 1942-48, professor of political science, 1948-64, chairman of department, 1942-43 and 1948-50, director of Center for Latin American Studies, 1959-62, academic assistant to the state-wide university president, 1962-64 and 1967-68; University of California, Santa Barbara, professor of political science, 1964-72. Senior political analyst, Office of Inter-American Affairs, 1944-45; visiting summer professor, Ohio State University, 1952, University of Nebraska, 1954, University of Illinois, 1956, Indiana University, 1960, Georgetown

University, 1963 and 1964, and Arizona State University, 1972-73.

MEMBER: American Political Science Association, Western Political Science Association (member of executive council, 1951-53 and 1957-58; president, 1956-57), Phi Delta Theta (national editor, 1931-36), Pi Sigma Alpha (member of executive council, 1948-50), Pi Gamma Mu, Alpha Phi Gamma.

AWARDS, HONORS: Del Amo Foundation fellowships, 1943-44 and 1959; Doherty Foundation and Social Science Research Council fellowship, 1951; LL.D., Hanover College, 1952; Fulbright research grant, 1958-59; Order of Don Cristobal Colon (Dominican Republic), 1962.

WRITINGS: Cuba and the United States, 1900-1935, G. Banta, 1935; *Visual Outline of Latin American History*, Longmans, Green, 1938; (editor and contributor) *Global Politics*, University of California Press, 1944; (with Flaud C. Wooton) *Latin America, Past and Present*, Heath, 1946; (editor-in-chief) *The Constitutions of the Americas, as of January 1, 1948*, University of Chicago Press, 1948; *Uruguay: Portrait of a Democracy*, Rutgers University Press, 1954.

Latin America: A Panorama of Contemporary Politics, Appleton, 1971, 2nd edition published as *Latin America: Political Culture and Development*, Prentice-Hall, 1981; (editor) Jesus de Galindez, *The Era of Trujillo, Dominican Dictator*, University of Arizona Press, 1973; (editor) *Argentina: A Chronology and Fact Book, 1516-1973*, Oceana, 1974; (editor) *Brazil: A Chronology and Fact Book, 1488-1973*, Oceana, 1974; *Latin American Constitutions: Textual Citations*, Center for Latin American Studies, Arizona State University, 1974.

Contributor of articles to professional journals. Member of international advisory board, *Hispanic American Report*, 1949-62; member of board of editors, *Inter-American Economic Affairs*, 1949-79.†

*   *   *

FLEMING, Susan   1932-

PERSONAL: Born June 12, 1932, in Eliot, Maine; daughter of Maynard F. (a rural mail carrier) and Marjorie (Fernald) Douglas; married Donald Fleming, Jr. (an administrative assistant), April 17, 1965; children: Eric, Gregory. *Education:* Emerson College, A.B. (with high honors), 1953; Harvard University, Ed.M., 1960; Boston University, certificate, 1966. *Home:* 22 Morton St., Needham, Mass. 02194.

CAREER: Teacher at state school in Wrentham, Mass., 1953-54, and at public elementary schools in Ossining, N. Y., 1955-57, Lesington, Mass., 1957-58, and Arlington, Mass., 1958-65; Houghton Mifflin Co., Boston, Mass., editor in elementary reading department, 1966-67; free-lance writer, 1967—. Writing instructor, Lesley College, Cambridge, 1983-84. Reporter for *Needham Reporter*, 1975.

AWARDS, HONORS: The Pig at 37 Pinecrest Drive was selected by Oklahoma Library Association for the Sequoyah Children's Book Awards master list for 1983-84.

WRITINGS—All published by Westminster: *Trapped on the Golden Flyer* (Junior Literary Guild selection), 1978; *The Pig at 37 Pinecrest Drive*, 1981; *Countdown at 37 Pinecrest Drive*, 1982.

Contributor to magazines and newspapers, including *American Baby, Instructor, Christian Home*, and *Boston Herald-American*.

WORK IN PROGRESS: Research in folklore as a basis for another book for children.

SIDELIGHTS: Susan Fleming writes: "I don't know how anyone can get through this world without books. I hide behind them when I need to escape, I lean on them when I need ·inspiration. For many years I enjoyed teaching children to read. Now I enjoy even more the process of writing a book for them. I'll always be a champion of the underdog and children are often underdogs. That's why I like to write about their struggles to gain control over their lives and win recognition."

Trapped on the Golden Flyer has been translated into Japanese.

*   *   *

FLIER, Michael S(tephen)   1941-

PERSONAL: Born April 20, 1941, in Los Angeles, Calif.; son of Albert Alfred (a clockshop owner) and Bonnie Flier. *Education:* University of California, Berkeley, A.B., 1962, M.A., 1964, Ph.D., 1968. *Office:* Department of Slavic Languages and Literatures, 405 Hilgard Ave., University of California, Los Angeles, Calif. 90024.

CAREER: University of California, Los Angeles, assistant professor, 1968-73, associate professor, 1973-79, professor of Slavic languages and literatures, 1979—, chairman of department, 1978-84. Visiting acting assistant professor, University of California, Berkeley, summer, 1968.

MEMBER: Linguistic Society of America, International Linguistic Association, American Association of Teachers of Slavic and East European Languages, Linguistics Association of Great Britain.

AWARDS, HONORS: Inter-University grant for study in Russia, 1966-67; International Research and Exchanges Board fellowship, 1971, for study in Russia and Czechoslovakia, 1978, for research in Russia, Belorussia, and the Ukraine.

WRITINGS: (Editor) *Slavic Forum: Essays in Slavic Linguistics and Literature*, Mouton, 1974; *Aspects of Nominal Determination in Old Church Slavic*, Mouton, 1974; *Say It in Russian*, Dover, 1982; (editor) *American Contributions to the Ninth International Congress of Slavists, Kiev, September, 1983*, Volume I: *Linguistics*, Slavica, 1983; (editor with Henrik Birnbaum) *Medieval Russian Culture*, University of California Press, 1984.

Contributor: Dean S. Worth, editor, *The Slavic Word*, Mouton, 1972; Demetrius J. Koubourlis, editor, *Topics in Slavic Phonology*, Slavica, 1974; L'ubomir Durovic and others, editors, *Studia Linguistica Alexandro Vasilii filio Issatschenko Collegis et Amicis oblata*, De Ridder (Paris), 1977; Richard D. Brecht and Dan E. Davidson, editors, *Soviet-American Russian Language Contributions*, G & G Press, 1978; Birnbaum and others, editors, *American Contributions to the Eighth International Congress of Slavists*, Slavica, 1978.

Kenneth E. Naylor and others, editors, *Slavic Linguistics and Poetics: Studies for Edward Stankiewicz on His Sixtieth Birthday, 17 November, 1980*, Slavica, 1982; Vladimir Markov and Worth, editors, *From Los Angeles to Kiev*, Slavica, 1983. Also contributor to *Phonology in the 1970's*, edited by D. L. Goyvaerts. Contributor of articles and reviews to language journals, including *Russian Linguistics, International Journal of Slavic Linguistics and Poetics, Slavic and East European Journal, Language, Slavic Review, Journal of Linguistics,* and *Russian Review.*

FODOR, Eugene   1905-

PERSONAL: Born October 14, 1905, in Leva, Hungary; came to the United States in 1938, naturalized in 1942; son of Matthew Gyula (a businessman) and Malvine (Kurti) Fodor; married Vlasta Maria Zobel, December 4, 1948; children: Eugene, Jr. *Education:* Attended Sorbonne, University of Paris, 1924-25; University of Grenoble, licencie es economie politique, 1927; graduate study at University of Hamburg. *Home:* Norfolk Rd., Litchfield, Conn. 06759. *Office:* Fodor's Modern Guides, Inc., Box 784, Litchfield, Conn. 06759.

CAREER: Travel correspondent, *Prague Hungarian Journal*, 1930-33; European Travel Guides, London England, travel editor, 1934-38; *Query* (foreign affairs magazine), London, foreign editor, 1937-38; Hyperion Press (publishers of art books), New York, N.Y., editor, 1939-42; Fodor's Modern Guides, Inc., editor and publisher in Paris, France, 1949-64, president in Litchfield, Conn., beginning 1964, chairman of the board in London, beginning 1964. *Military service:* U.S. Army, 1942-47; became captain; received six battle stars and other decorations.

MEMBER: International Federation of Travel Journalists and Writers, International Union of Official Travel Organizations, National Association of Travel Organizations, Society of American Travel Writers, Pacific Area Travel Association, South American Travel Association, Caribbean Travel Association, Caribbean Tourist Association.

AWARDS, HONORS: Grand Prix de Litterature de Tourisme (Paris), 1959; awards from Caribbean Travel Association, 1960, Pacific Area Travel Association, 1960, 1962, National Association of Travel Organizations, 1966, International Travel Book Contest, 1969, British Tourist Authority, 1972, Discover America Travel Organizations, 1975, Travel Hall of Fame, 1978; Vienna Travel Book Exposition honor list, 1963; Silver Medal, Austrian government, 1970; George Washington Prize, American Hungarian Foundation, 1982.

WRITINGS: Editor; published by McKay, except as indicated: *1936 . . . On the Continent*, Aldor, 1936, 2nd edition published as *1937 . . . In Europe*, Houghton, 1937, 3rd edition published as *1938 in Europe*, Houghton, 1938 (published in England as *Aldor's Entertaining Annual*, two volumes, Aldor, 1938).

Britain in 1951, 1951, 3rd edition, 1955; *France in 1951*, 1951, revised edition, 1976; *Italy in 1951*, 1951, revised edition, 1976; *Switzerland in 1951*, 1951, revised edition, 1976; *Benelux: Belgium, the Netherlands, Luxembourg*, 1952, 3rd edition, 1958, published as *Belgium and Luxembourg*, 1959, revised edition, 1976, and *Holland*, 1956, revised edition, 1976; *Scandinavia in 1952*, 1952, revised edition, 1976; *Spain and Portugal in 1952*, 1952, 7th edition, 1966, published (with William Curtis) as *Spain, 1967*, 1967, revised edition published as *Fodor's Spain*, and *Portugal, 1967*, 1967, revised edition published as *Fodor's Portugal*, 1969—; *Woman's Guide to Europe*, 1952, 4th edition, 1956; *Austria, 1953*, 1953, revised edition, 1976; *Germany, 1953*, 1953, revised edition, 1976.

The Men's Guide to Europe, 1955, 2nd edition (with Frederick Rockwell), 1957; *Britain and Ireland, 1956*, 1956, 8th edition, 1967, revised edition (with Robert C. Fisher) published as *Great Britain*, 1968, published as *Fodor's Great Britain*, 1969—, and *Ireland*, 1968, published as *Fodor's Ireland*, 1969—; *Yu-*

goslavia, *1958*, 1958, revised edition, 1976; *Fodor's Jet Age Guide to Europe*, 1959, also published as *Fodor's Guide to Europe*, 1959, 3rd edition, 1967, also published as *Guide to Europe, 1964*, 1964, revised edition, 1976.

Fodor's Guide to the Caribbean, Bahamas, and Bermuda, 1960, revised edition published as *Fodor's Caribbean and the Bahamas*, 1980—; *Greece, 1960*, 1960, revised edition (with Curtis), 1976; *Hawaii, 1961*, 1961, revised edition (with Curtis), 1976; (with Fisher) *Fodor's Guide to Japan and East Asia*, 1962, revised edition, 1974; (with Curtis) *Fodor's Guide to India*, 1963, revised edition, 1976; *The Companion Guide to London*, [London], 1964, [New York], 1965, published as *Fodor's London: A Companion Guide*, McKay, 1975; (with Curtis) *Morocco, 1965-66*, 1965, revised edition, 1976; (with Fisher) *Fodor's Guide to South America, 1966*, 1966, revised edition, 1976; (with Curtis) *Israel, 1967-68*, 1967, revised edition, 1976; (with Curtis) *Turkey, 1969*, 1969, revised edition, 1976; *Fodor's Holland*, 1969—; *Fodor's Ireland*, 1969—; *Fodor's Hawaii*, 1969—.

Czechoslovakia, 1970-71, 1970, revised edition, 1975; *Hungary, 1970-71*, 1970, revised edition, 1976; *Fodor's London*, 1971, revised edition, 1975; Georgina Masson, *Fodor's Rome*, 1971—; Hugh Honour, *Fodor's Venice*, revised edition, 1971; Odile Cail, *Peking*, 1972, revised edition, 1973; (with Majorie Lockett) *Fodor's Mexico*, 1972—; *Europe under 25*, 1972—; *Europe on a Budget*, 1972, revised edition published as *Fodor's Budget Europe*, 1980—; *Fodor's Islamic America: Iran, Afghanistan, Pakistan*, 1973—; (with Curtis) *Islamic Asia*, 1973; (with Curtis) *Fodor's Tunisia*, 1973—; *Paris*, 1974 (published in England as *Fodor's Paris*, Hodder & Stoughton, 1974); *Fodor's Vienna*, 1974; *Fodor's Soviet Union*, 1974—; *Fodor's Far West: California, Oregon, Washington, Idaho, Nevada, Alaska*, 1974—; *Fodor's Germany: West and East*, 1974—.

Fodor's Budget Italy, 1975, revised edition, 1980—; (with Jamake Highwater) *Fodor's Indian America*, 1975; *Fodor's Japan and Korea*, 1975—; *Fodor's Southeast Asia*, 1975—; (with Robert V. Daniels) *Fodor's Europe Talking: A Practical Guide to Nineteen National Languages*, 1975; *Fodor's U.S.A.*, one volume, 1976—; *Fodor's Railways of the World*, 1977; *Fodor's Seaside America*, 1977; *Fodor's Cruises Everywhere*, 1977—; *Fodor's Australia, New Zealand, and the South Pacific*, 1978—; *Fodor's New England*, 1978—; *Fodor's Mid-Atlantic, 1978*, 1978; *Fodor's Rockies and Plains, 1978: Colorado, Idaho, Montana, Nebraska, North Dakota, South Dakota, Utah, Wyoming*, 1978; *Fodor's Only-in-America Vacation Guide*, 1978; *Fodor's Canada*, 1978; *Fodor's Switzerland and Liechtenstein*, 1978; *Fodor's Old South*, 1978; *Fodor's South*, 1979—; *Fodor's Worldwide Adventure Guide: A Handbook of Practical Information for Adventures to Exotic Destinations and Activities outside North America, Covering Africa, Asia, Europe, and South America*, 1979; *Fodor's Sunbelt Leisure Guide*, 1979; *Fodor's Outdoors America*, 1979; *Fodor's People's Republic of China*, 1979—; *Fodor's Budget Travel in America*, 1979; *Fodor's Animal Parks of Africa*, 1979.

Fodor's Alaska, 1980—; *Fodor's Budget Spain*, 1980—; *Fodor's Central America*, 1980—; *Fodor's North Africa*, 1980—; *You Don't Have to Be Rich to Travel Well*, Fodor's Modern Guides, 1981; *Fodor's Budget Japan '81*, Columbus Books, 1981; *Fodor's India and Nepal*, Fodor's Modern Guides, 1981—. Also editor of *Fodor's Bermuda*, *Fodor's Brazil*, *Fodor's Civil War Sites*, *Fodor's California*, *Fodor's Florida*, *Fodor's Egypt*, *Fodor's Iran*, *Fodor's South-West*, *Fodor's Japan and East Asia*, *Fodor's Pennsylvania*, *Fodor's Colorado*, *Fodor's New York: City and State*, *Fodor's Budget France*, *Fodor's Budget Mexico*, *Fodor's Budget Britain*, *Fodor's Budget Caribbean*, and *Fodor's Budget Germany*.

General editor of "Fodor's Shell Travel Guides U.S.A." series, eight volumes, 1966, published as "Fodor's U.S.A.," eight volumes, 1974.

SIDELIGHTS: Eugene Fodor once told *CA* that he "passionately believe[s] that travel is the most effective shortcut to tolerance, understanding and recognition of the others' rights to their own values." Many of his books have been published in French, German, Italian, Spanish, Dutch, Hungarian, and Japanese. In addition to his native Hungarian, Fodor speaks French, German, Italian, Czech, and Slovak.

BIOGRAPHICAL/CRITICAL SOURCES: Times Literary Supplement, October 30, 1981.

*   *   *

FONTENOT, Mary Alice 1910-

PERSONAL: Surname is pronounced *Fon*-te-no; born April 16, 1910, in Eunice, La.; daughter of Elias Valrie and Kate (King) Barras; married Sidney J. Fontenot, September 6, 1925 (died, 1963); married Vincent L. Riehl, Sr., November 14, 1966; children: (first marriage) Edith (Mrs. Burton Ziegler), R. D. (deceased), Julie (Mrs. Michael Landry). *Education:* Attended school in Eunice, La. *Religion:* Roman Catholic. *Home:* 431 Holden Ave., Lafayette, La. 70506. *Office:* Crowley Post-Signal, Crowley, La. 70526.

CAREER: New Era, Eunice, La., reporter, columnist, and women's news writer, 1946-50; *Eunice News*, Eunice, editor, 1950-53; *Daily World*, Opelousas, La., columnist, 1953-57; *Daily Advertiser*, Lafayette, La., women's news reporter, 1958-60; *Rayne Tribune*, Rayne, La., editor, 1960-62; *Daily World*, area editor, 1962-69, columnist, 1969-71; *Crowley Post-Signal*, Crowley, La., columnist and feature writer, 1977—. *Member:* League of American Pen Women, Louisiana Press Women. *Awards, honors:* First prize from National Press Women, 1966; Louisiana Literary Award, Louisiana Library Association, 1976, for *Acadia Parish, La.*, Volume I: *A History to 1900*.

WRITINGS—Published by Claitors: *The Ghost of Bayou Tigre* (juvenile), 1964; (editor) *Quelque Chose Douce* (cookbook), 1964; (editor) *Quelque Chose Piquante* (cookbook), 1966; (with husband, Vincent L. Riehl, Sr.) *The Cat and St. Landry* (biography), 1972; (editor with Mercedes Vidrine) *Beaucoup Bon* (cookbook), 1973; *Acadia Parish, La.*, Volume I: (with Paul B. Freedland) *A History to 1900*, 1976, Volume II: *A History to 1920*, 1979; (with daughter, Julie Landry) *The Louisiana Experience: An Introduction to the Culture of the Bayou State*, 1983. Regular contributor to *Acadiana Profile* magazine.

"Clovis Crawfish" juvenile series; published by Claitors, except as indicated: *Clovis Crawfish and His Friends*, 1962; . . . *and the Big Betail*, 1963; . . . *and the Singing Cigales*, 1964; . . . *and Petit Papillon*, 1966; . . . *and the Spinning Spider*, 1968; . . . *and the Curious Craupaud*, 1970; . . . *and Michelle Mantis*, 1976; . . . *and Etienne Escargot*, Pelican, 1979; . . . *and the Orphan Zo-Zo*, Pelican, 1983.

WORK IN PROGRESS: Early Families of Acadia Parish.

FOTTLER, Myron David 1941-

PERSONAL: Born September 5, 1941, in Boston, Mass.; son of Myron Dustin and Anna (Curley) Fottler; married Carol Ann Szczepaniak (a teacher), August 11, 1972. *Education:* Northeastern University, B.S., 1962; Boston University, M.B.A. (with distinction), 1963; Columbia University, Ph.D., 1970. *Home:* 2509 Shades Crest Rd., Birmingham, Ala. 35216. *Office:* Graduate School of Management, University of Alabama, Birmingham, Ala. 35294.

CAREER: State University of New York at Buffalo, lecturer, 1967-70, assistant professor of industrial relations and of environmental analysis and policy, 1970-75; University of Iowa, Iowa City, associate professor, 1975-76; University of Alabama, University, associate professor, 1976-78, professor of human resources management and health care management, 1978-83; University of Alabama in Birmingham, professor and director of Ph.D. program in administration-health services, 1983—.

MEMBER: Industrial Relations Research Association, Academy of Management (chairperson, Health Care Administration Division, 1984-85).

WRITINGS: Manpower Substitution in the Hospital Industry, Praeger, 1972; *Managing DRGs: A Strategic and Operational Approach,* Aspen Systems Corp., 1985. Contributor of sixty articles to industrial relations, economics, management, and health care journals.

WORK IN PROGRESS: The impact of the new prospective pricing systems on the management of hospitals; employer efforts to contain health care costs; the management of multi-institutional systems in health care.

SIDELIGHTS: Myron D. Fottler told *CA:* "My writings are typically a quantitative and scientifically based attempt to measure the impact of people on the functioning of organizations. I don't believe in a dichotomy between the humanistic and the scientific. Both perspectives are necessary for important research."

* * *

FOX, Levi 1914-

PERSONAL: Born August 28, 1914, in Leicestershire, England; son of John William and Julia (Stinson) Fox; married Jane Richards; children: Roger James, Elizabeth Jane, Patricia Mary. *Education:* Oriel College, Oxford, B.A. (with first class honors), 1936, M.A., 1938; University of Manchester, M.A., 1938. *Home:* 27 Welcombe Rd., Stratford-upon-Avon, England. *Office:* Shakespeare Centre, Stratford-upon-Avon, England.

CAREER: Shakespeare Centre, Stratford-upon-Avon, England, director of Shakespeare Birthplace Trust, 1945—. *Military service:* British Army, 1940-43.

MEMBER: International Shakespeare Association (deputy chairman), Royal Society of Literature (fellow), Royal Historical Society (fellow), Society of Antiquaries of London (fellow).

AWARDS, HONORS: Received doctorate from George Washington University, 1964; New York University medal, 1964; named officer of the Order of the British Empire, 1964; named deputy lieutenant of County of Warwick, 1967.

WRITINGS: The Administration of the Honor of Leicester in the Fourteenth Century, E. Backus, 1940; *The History of Coventry's Textile Industry,* privately printed, 1944; *Leicester Castle* (pamphlet), Leicester Publicity and Development Department, 1944; *Coventry's Heritage: An Introduction to the History of the City,* Coventry Evening Telegraph, 1947, 2nd edition, 1957; (with Percy Russell) *Leicester Forest,* E. Backus, 1948; *Shakespeare's Town, Stratford-upon-Avon: A Pictorial Record with Historical Introduction and Descriptions,* H. & J. Busst, 1949; *Stratford-upon-Avon,* Garland Publishing, 1949.

(Author of introduction and notes) Gerald Gardiner, *Oxford: A Book of Drawings,* Garland Publishing, 1951; *Stratford-upon-Avon: An Appreciation,* Jarrolds, 1952; *The Borough Town of Stratford-upon-Avon,* privately printed, 1953; (editor) *English Historical Scholarship in the Sixteenth and Seventeenth Centuries,* Oxford University Press, 1956; *Stratford-upon-Avon: Official Guide,* privately printed, 1958; *William Shakespeare: A Concise Life* (pamphlet), Jarrolds, 1959; *Shakespeare's Town and Country,* Cotman House, 1959.

Shakespeare's Stratford-upon-Avon: A Souvenir in Colour with Historical Descriptions, J. Salmon, 1962; *Shakespeare's Birthplace: A History and Description,* Jarrolds, 1963; (editor) William Shakespeare, *Sonnets,* Cotman House, 1963; *Stratford-upon-Avon in Colour: A New Pictorial Guide,* Jarrolds, 1963; *The Shakespearian Properties,* Jarrolds, 1964, new edition, 1975; *The Shakespeare Anniversary Book,* Jarrolds, 1964; (editor) *Correspondence of the Reverend Joseph Greene: Parson, Schoolmaster, and Antiquary, 1712-1790,* H.M.S.O., 1965; *Celebrating Shakespeare: A Pictorial Record of the Celebrations Held at Stratford-upon-Avon during 1964 to Mark the Four-Hundredth Anniversary of the Birth of William Shakespeare,* privately printed, 1965; *New Place: Shakespeare's Home* (pamphlet), Jarrolds, 1966; (editor) *A Shakespeare Treasury,* Cotman House, 1966; *A Country Grammar School: A History of Ashby-de-la-Zouch Grammar School through Four Centuries, 1567 to 1967,* Oxford University Press, 1967; (editor) *The Stratford Shakespeare Anthology,* Cotman House, 1968; *The Shakespeare Book,* Jarrolds, 1969, new edition, 1972.

Shakespeare's England, Putnam, 1972; *In Honour of Shakespeare: The History and Collections of the Shakespeare Birthplace Trust,* Jarrolds, 1972; *A Splendid Occasion: The Stratford Jubilee of 1769* (pamphlet), V. Ridler, 1973; *Stratford Past and Present: A Pictorial Record of the Ancient Town of Stratford,* Oxford Illustrated Press, 1975; *Stratford-upon-Avon and the Shakespeare Country,* Jarrolds, 1975; *Shakespeare's Flowers,* Jarrolds, 1978; *Shakespeare's Birds,* Jarrolds, 1978.

The Early History of King Edward VI School, Stratford-upon-Avon, Dugdale Society, 1984. Contributor to Shakespeare studies and history journals.

WORK IN PROGRESS: Research on historical records of Stratford-upon-Avon and Warwickshire.

* * *

FOX, Lucia
See LOCKERT, Lucia (Alicia Ungaro Fox)

* * *

FOX, Michael W(ilson) 1937-

PERSONAL: Born August 13, 1937, in Bolton, England; came to the United States in 1962; son of Geoffrey (a banker) and

Elizabeth (Wilson) Fox; married Bonnie Morrill (marriage ended, August 1, 1964); married Deborah Johnson (a social worker), August 24, 1973; children: (first marriage) Michael Wilson, Jr., Camilla. *Education:* Royal Veterinary College, London, B.Vet.Med., 1962; University of London, Ph.D., 1967, D.Sc., 1976; Alpha School of Massage, Ms.T., 1974. *Office:* Institute for the Study of Animal Problems, 2100 L St. N.W., Washington, D.C. 20037. *Agent:* Eleanor Wood, Blassingame, McCauley & Wood, 225 West 34th St., New York, N.Y. 10122.

CAREER: Psychologist, ethologist, and writer. Jackson Laboratory, Bar Harbor, Me., fellow, 1962-64; State Research Hospital, Galesburg, Ill., medical research associate, 1964-67; Washington University, St. Louis, Mo., assistant professor, 1967-69, associate professor of psychology, 1969-76; Humane Society of the United States, Institute for the Study of Animal Problems, Washington, D.C., director, 1976—. Associate professor at George Washington University. Guest on national television and radio programs. Consultant to zoos, humane societies, and conservation organizations.

MEMBER: British Veterinary Association, British Veterinary Ethology Society (founding member), Royal College of Veterinary Surgeons, Animal Behaviour Society, American Veterinary Medical Association, American Association for the Advancement of Science, American Federation of Television and Radio Artists, Authors Guild, Authors League of America, American Association for Laboratory Animal Care, American Association of Animal Science, American Psychological Association, American Massage and Therapy Association.

AWARDS, HONORS: Christopher Award for Children's Literature, 1973, for *The Wolf; Sundance Coyote* was nominated for Mark Twain Award, 1976; best science book award from National Teacher's Association, 1976, for *Ramu and Chennai: Brothers of the Wild.*

WRITINGS: Canine Behavior, C. C Thomas, 1965; *Canine Pediatrics: Development, Neonatal, and Congenital Diseases,* C. C Thomas, 1966; *Integrative Development of Brain and Behavior in the Dog,* University of Chicago Press, 1971; *Behavior of Wolves, Dogs, and Related Canids,* Harper, 1971; *Understanding Your Dog: Everything You Want to Know about Your Dog but Haven't Been Able to Ask Him,* Coward, 1972; *Understanding Your Cat,* Coward, 1974; *Concepts in Ethology: Animal and Human Behavior,* University of Minnesota Press, 1974; *Between Animal and Man: The Key to the Kingdom,* Coward, 1976; *Understanding Your Pet,* Coward, 1978; *The Dog: Domestication and Behavior,* Garland Publishing, 1978.

The Soul of the Wolf, Little, Brown, 1980; *One Earth, One Mind,* Coward, 1980; *Returning to Eden: Animal Rights and Human Responsibilities,* Viking, 1980; *How to Be Your Pet's Best Friend,* Coward, 1981; *Dr. Michael Fox's Massage Program for Cats and Dogs,* Newmarket, 1981; *Love Is a Happy Cat,* Newmarket, 1982; *The Healing Touch,* Newmarket, 1983; *Farm Animals: Husbandry, Behavior, and Veterinary Practice,* University Park Press, 1983; *The Whistling Hunters: Field Studies of the Asiatic Wild Dog,* State University of New York Press, 1984.

Children's books: *The Wolf,* Coward, 1973; *Vixie: The Story of a Little Fox,* Coward, 1973; *Sundance Coyote,* Coward, 1974; *Ramu and Chennai: Brothers of the Wild,* Coward, 1975; (with Wende Devlin Gates) *What Is Your Cat Saying?,* Cow-

ard, 1977; *Wild Dogs Three,* Coward, 1977; *Whitepaws: A Coyote-Dog,* Coward, 1979.

The Touchlings, Acropolis Books, 1981; *The Way of the Dolphin,* Acropolis Books, 1981; *Lessons from Nature: Fox's Fables,* Acropolis Books, 1982.

Editor: *Abnormal Behavior in Animals,* Saunders, 1968; *Readings in Ethology and Comparative Psychology,* Brooks/Cole, 1973; *The Wild Canids,* Van Nostrand, 1975; (with Richard K. Morris) *On the Fifth Day: Animal Rights and Human Obligations,* Acropolis Press, 1977.

Author of syndicated newspaper column "Ask Your Animal Doctor," 1976—. Contributor to professional journals, including *Behavior, Quarterly Review of Biology,* and *Journal of Mammology.* Editor of *International Journal for Study of Animal Problems;* contributing editor to *McCall's.*

WORK IN PROGRESS: God's Nature and the Animal Soul; Agricultural Nemesis.

SIDELIGHTS: Michael W. Fox told *CA:* "My major motivation behind the adult and children's books I write is to improve the relationship between people and animals and nature; to foster compassion and responsible care through respect and understanding; in essence to encourage *humane stewardship* of all life, upon which the survival and fulfillment of our own species is wholly dependent."

Commenting on Fox's book *The Soul of the Wolf* in a *Time* article, Timothy Foote writes that Fox is a "leader in the growing pack of natural scientists who have lately given wolves a good name. . . . *The Soul of the Wolf* is . . . an illustrated valentine to Fox's four-footed friends, and a moral message for another endangered species, man. . . . By learning about wolves, Fox insists, man can learn about the mysterious intricacies of nature, and thus be encouraged to cease his depredations. In some ways, Fox avers, the world would be a better place to live in if people behaved more like wolves." What comes through in the book, says Foote, is "Fox's overwhelming love of wolves, a sense of communion with them that goes beyond words—something that anyone who has loved a large dog will understand."

BIOGRAPHICAL/CRITICAL SOURCES: New York Times Book Review, July 29, 1973, November 3, 1974, October 26, 1980; *Children's Book World,* November 11, 1973; *Time,* October 6, 1980; *Village Voice,* November 11, 1981.

* * *

FOX-LOCKERT, Lucia
 See LOCKERT, Lucia (Alicia Ungaro Fox)

* * *

FOXX, Jack
 See PRONZINI, Bill

* * *

FRANCOEUR, Robert T(homas) 1931-

PERSONAL: Born October 18, 1931, in Detroit, Mich.; son of George Antoine (a steel consultant) and Julia Ann (Russell) Francoeur; married Anna Kotlarchyk (an accountant), September 24, 1966; children: Nicole Lynn, Danielle Ann. *Education:* Sacred Heart College, B.A., 1953; St. Vincent College, M.A., 1958; University of Detroit, M.S., 1961; University of Delaware, Ph.D., 1966; also attended Fordham University and Johns Hopkins University. *Politics:* Democrat. *Religion:* Roman Catholic. *Home:* 2 Circle Dr., Rockaway, N.J. 07866. *Office:* Department of Biology, Fairleigh Dickinson University, Madison, N.J. 07940.

CAREER: Former Catholic priest; Fairleigh Dickinson University, Department of Biological and Allied Health Sciences, Madison, N.J., instructor, 1965-66, assistant professor, 1966-70, associate professor, 1970-75, professor of human embryology, sexuality, and biomedical ethics, 1975—, former chairman of biological sciences. Visiting professor at twenty-one universities and medical schools; frequent lecturer at colleges, universities, and professional conferences; has appeared on national and local television and radio programs. Has completed documentary programs for Public Broadcasting Authority of New Jersey and Canadian Broadcasting Corp. (CBC). Participant in study of ethical, legal, and social implications of advances in biomedical and behavioral research and technology mandated by the U.S. Congress. Consultant to the United Nations, the American Medical Association, and the New York Bar.

MEMBER: World Future Society, Society for the Scientific Study of Sex, American Association of Sex Educators, Counselors, and Therapists, American College of Sexologists (charter member).

AWARDS, HONORS: Annual award of the Educational Foundation for Human Sexuality, 1978.

WRITINGS: Evolving World, Converging Man, Holt, 1970; *Utopian Motherhood: New Trends in Human Reproduction,* Doubleday, 1970, revised edition, A. S. Barnes, 1972; (author of introduction) Beatrice Bruteau, *Worthy Is the World: The Hindu Philosophy of Sri Aurobindo,* Fairleigh Dickinson University Press, 1971; (contributor) Kenneth Vaux, editor, *To Create a Different Future: Religious Hope and Technological Planning,* Friendship, 1972; (contributor) Seymour Farber and Joseph Alioto, editors, *Teilhard de Chardin: In Quest of the Perfection of Man,* Fairleigh Dickinson University Press, 1972; *Eve's New Rib: Twenty Faces of Sex, Marriage and Family,* Harcourt, 1972; (with wife, Anna K. Francoeur) *Hot and Cool Sex: Cultures in Conflict,* Harcourt, 1974; (editor with A. K. Francoeur) *The Future of Sexual Relations,* Prentice-Hall, 1974.

Becoming a Sexual Person, Wiley, 1982, abridged edition published as *Becoming a Sexual Person: A Brief Edition,* 1984; *Biomedical Ethics: A Guide to Decisions,* Wiley, 1983; (contributor) Eleanor Macklin and Roger Rubin, editors, *Contemporary Familes and Alternative Lifestyles, A Handbook of Research and Theory,* Sage Publications, 1983; (contributor) Lester Kirkendall and Arthur Gravatt, editors, *Marriage and the Family in the Year 2020,* Prometheus, 1984; (contributor) Jose Leyson and others, editors, *Sexual Rehabilitation of the Spinal Cord Injured Patient,* Karger, 1984; (with Martin Evans) *Medical Genetics for Health Professionals,* Wiley, 1985; (contributor) Harvey Gochros and others, editors, *Social Work Practice with the Sexually Oppressed,* Prentice-Hall, 1985.

Contributor of articles to scientific magazines, including *Forum, Journal of Sex Research, Medical Aspects of Human Sexuality, Journal of Allied Health, Journal of Bioethics,* and *Research in Philosophy and Technology.* Special issues editor, *Journal of Sex Research.*

WORK IN PROGRESS: A trade book, co-authored with John Buffum, on the sexual side effects of common medications.

SIDELIGHTS: Robert T. Francoeur told *CA* that his readers have always found it hard to label him or fit him into a comfortable pigeonhole. "I started off in college majoring in philosophy and English," he continued, "and graduated tied for last place in my class because I refused to fit into 'the mold.' Then I shifted gears, pursued Master's degrees in theology and biology. After working for three years as a Catholic priest, my interest in evolution, Teilhard de Chardin, and theology led me into a doctorate in experimental embryology and teaching in a large private secular university. In the past twenty years, I've worn many hats as a 'bioanthropologist,' a theologian, a sexologist, a medical ethicist, a specialist in alternative lifestyles, textbook writer, and expert on the social implications of reproductive technologies. My problem is I'm always looking for the whole picture. Using artificial insemination or embryo transplants to save endangered animal species is interesting in intself, but I'm also interested in the transfer of such technologies to humans and their impact on our values and lifestyles. The challenge of the whole picture leads me into many unusual situations but I really enjoy working and learning with people with different perspectives and professional interests."

BIOGRAPHICAL/CRITICAL SOURCES: Newsweek, November 23, 1970; *Medical World News,* November 27, 1970; *Baltimore Sun,* February 7, 1971.

*   *   *

FRANKLAND, (Anthony) Noble   1922-

PERSONAL: Born July 4, 1922, in Ravenstonedale, England; son of Edward Percy and Maud (Metcalfe-Gibson) Frankland; married Diana Madeline Fovargue Tavernor, February 28, 1944 (died, 1981); married Sarah Katharine Davies, May 7, 1982; children (first marriage): Roger, Linda. *Education:* Trinity College, Oxford, M.A., 1947, D.Phil., 1951. *Home:* Thames House, Eynsham, Oxford, England.

CAREER: Air Ministry, London, England, Air Historical Branch, narrator, 1948-51, Cabinet Office, official military historian, 1951-60; Royal Institute of International Affairs, London, deputy director of studies, 1956-60; Imperial War Museum, London, England, director, 1960-82. Lees Knowles Lecturer at Trinity College, Cambridge, 1963. Member of council of Morley College, 1962-66; trustee of Military Archives Center at King's College, University of London, 1963-82, and Her Majesty's Ship Belfast, 1971-82 (vice-chairman, 1972-82). *Military service:* Royal Air Force, 1941-45, Bomber Command, 1943-45; received Distinguished Flying Cross.

AWARDS, HONORS: Rockefeller Foundation fellowship, 1953; named commander, Order of the British Empire, 1976; named companion, Order of the Bath, 1983.

WRITINGS: (Editor with Vera King) *Documents on International Affairs,* Oxford University Press, Volume I: *1955,* 1958, Volume II: *1956,* 1959, Volume III: *1957,* 1960; *Crown of Tragedy: Nicholas II,* W. Kimber, 1960, published as *Imperial Tragedy: Nicholas II, Last of the Tsars,* Coward, 1961; (with Charles Kingsley Webster) *The Strategic Air Offensive against Germany, 1939-1945,* four volumes, H.M.S.O., 1961; *The Bombing Offensive against Germany: Outlines and Perspectives,* Faber, 1965; *Bomber Offensive: The Devastation of Europe,* Macdonald & Co., 1969; (editor with Christopher Dowling) *Decisive Battles of the Twentieth Century: Land-Sea-Air,* McKay, 1976 (published in England as *Decisive Battles of the Twentieth Century: Land, Sea, Air,* Sidgwick & Jackson, 1976);

Prince Henry: Duke of Gloucester, Weidenfeld & Nicolson, 1980.

Editor with Dowling; "The Politics and Strategy of the Second World War" series; published by University of Delaware Press, 1980: Louis Allen, *Singapore, 1941-1942;* Brian Bond, *France and Belgium, 1939-1940;* Raymond A. Callahan, *Burma, 1942-1945;* Charles Cruickshank, *Greece, 1940-1941;* William Jackson, *Overlord: Normandy, 1944;* Anthony F. Upton, *Finland, 1939-1940;* Geoffrey Warner, *Iraq and Syria, 1941.*

Contributor to *Manual of Air Force Law* and other professional journals.

SIDELIGHTS: "As a dutiful life history of a dutiful English royal prince . . . , this is an admirable book," writes Richard Usborne in the *Times Literary Supplement* of Noble Frankland's *Prince Henry: Duke of Gloucester.* The Duke, according to many reviewers, is an unpromising subject for biography; Usborne and Hugh Montgomery-Massingberd of the London *Times* both mention a day when the entire House of Commons roared with laughter at a facetious suggestion that he be made Commander-in-Chief of the British Army, and Montgomery-Massingberd further describes him as "plodding" and a "royal uncle of little brain." But he praises Frankland's efforts in chronicling the Duke's life: "Dr. Frankland has researched this work most diligently, the facts are presented with exemplary precision and he has certainly earned the CVO [Commander of the Royal Victorian Order] that will presumably come his way as a reward for his efforts. . . . Dr. Frankland sympathetically explains the regimental frustrations [Henry] had to endure for the sake of his princely duties. The Duke's endearing qualities come across nicely in the letters he wrote regularly to [his mother] Queen Mary; a complete edition of these letters might enjoy a success as a sort of *Diary of a Royal Nobody.* There are a few amusing anecdotes to break up the remorseless tedium of the offical record and the hilarious mishaps of the Ethiopian coronation recall Evelyn Waugh."

BIOGRAPHICAL/CRITICAL SOURCES: Times Literary Supplement, April 11, 1980; *Times* (London), April 17, 1980.

*　　*　　*

FRERE, Paul 1917-

PERSONAL: Born January 30, 1917, in Le Havre, France; son of Maurice (an economist) and Germaine (Schimp) Frere; wife's name, Suzanne; children: Marianne, Martine, Nicole. *Education:* University Libre de Bruxelles, Ingenieur Commercial, 1940.

CAREER: Automobile journalist and technical writer. Technical director of automobile branch in Brussels, Belgium, 1947-49, 1951-52; employed with General Motors, Antwerp, Belgium, 1950. Auto race driver for H.W.M., Gordini, Ferrari, Astor Martin, Porsche, 1948-60. Ecole Technique Superieure, Brussels, lecturer, 1950-55.

MEMBER: Internationale Association Journaliste Automobile (vice president), Club Internationale Anciens Pilotes de Grands Prix, Societe Belge des Ingenieurs de l'Automobile (former officer), Association des Journalistes Belges de l'Automobile (president), Societe des Ingenieurs de l'Automobile (Paris), British Racing Drivers' Club.

AWARDS, HONORS: Prix Societe des Ingenieurs de l'Automobile—Charles Faroux, for article, "Revolution in Racing Car Design," 1963.

WRITINGS: La Croisiere Minerva sur la Route des Indes, JaRic, 1954; *Un des vingt au depart,* JaRic, 1956, English translation by Louis Klemantaski published as *On the Starting Grid,* Batsford, 1957; *Je conduis mieux,* Gerard, 1959; *La Course Continue,* JaRic, 1961, English translation by Klemantaski published as *Starting Grid to Checkered Flag,* Batsford, 1962; *Sports Car and Competition Driving,* Bentley, 1963, also published as *Competition Driving,* Batsford, 1963; *Les 800 heures du Mans,* Editions Gamma, 1967; *Bien conduire une voiture sport,* Editions Arts et voyages, 1968.

(With Philippe de Barsy) *Livre d'or du salon de l'automobile, du motocycle et du cycle,* EPE, 1970; *Das Rennen vor dem Rennen: Porsche-Rennwagen zwischen Versuch v. Einsatz,* Motorbuch-Verl, 1971, translation published as *The Racing Porsches: A Technical Triumph,* Arco, 1973; *246 SP-330 P4 Ferraris,* Coburg House, 1972; *Porsche 911 Story,* Arco, 1976, 2nd edition, Aztex, 1981; (translator) Lothar Boschen and Jurgen Barth, *The Porsche Book: A Definitive Illustrated History,* Arco, 1978; *Porsche Racing Cars of the Seventies,* Arco, 1981; *Mercedes-Benz C111: Experimental Cars,* 1981; (with Doug Nye) *Ferrari Daytona,* Arco, 1983.

SIDELIGHTS: Paul Frere's successes in racing include first at Reims in twelve-hour race, 1957 and 1958, first at Le Mans in twenty-four-hour race, 1960, first in South African Grand Prix, 1960.

Porsche 911 Story has been translated into German.†

*　　*　　*

FRIENDLY, Fred W. 1915-

PERSONAL: Surname originally Wachenheimer, but adopted mother's maiden name early in career; born October 30, 1915, in New York, N.Y.; son of Samuel and Therese (Friendly) Wachenheimer; married Dorothy Greene (a magazine researcher; marriage ended); married second wife, Ruth W. Mark (an educator), June, 1968; children: Andrew, Lisa, David, Jon, Michael, Richard. *Education:* Nichols Junior College (now Nichols College), Dudley, Mass. *Residence:* Riverdale, N.Y. *Office:* Graduate School of Journalism, Columbia University, 116th St. and Broadway, New York, N.Y. 10027.

CAREER: Began career in radio in 1938 as writer, producer, and narrator of "Footprints in the Sands of Time," a local series aired in Providence, R.I. (received $8 per broadcast from the sponsor); met Edward R. Murrow in 1948 and collaborated with him on an oral history of the period from 1932 to 1945, which resulted in the best-selling Columbia Records album, "I Can Hear It Now," issued in 1948, and two subsequent albums covering the 1920's and the post-World War II period; became associated with Columbia Broadcasting System in 1951 as joint producer with Murrow of radio network series, "Hear It Now," and eventually, the television series, "See It Now," and "Small World"; executive producer of "CBS Reports," 1959-64, arranging, among other specials, Walter Lippmann's series of conversations on the program.

As president of CBS News, 1964-66, was responsible for the "Town Meeting of the World," "Vietnam Perspective," "National Drivers Test," and other landmark broadcasts; resigned from Columbia Broadcasting System in a celebrated conflict with Network opinions regarding ratings, February, 1966; two months later became Edward R. Murrow Professor of Journalism at Columbia University and adviser on television to the Ford Foundation, New York, N.Y., teaching and directing the

Graduate School's Television Workshop at Columbia. *Military service:* U.S. Army, Information and Education Section, 1941-45; served in the Pacific and Europe; received Legion of Merit, four battle stars, and Soldier's Medal (the last was bestowed for heroism in rescue work following a dock explosion in Bombay, India; Friendly had been discharged from the Army, and was in India for Columbia Broadcasting System at the time).

AWARDS, HONORS: "See It Now" series received thirty-five major awards, garnering in one year (1954) the Overseas Press Club Award, Page One Award of New York Newspaper Guild, National Headliners Club Award, *Saturday Review* Award, *Look* TV Award, and *TV Guide* Gold Medal; "CBS Reports" earned forty major awards, becoming the most decorated series on network television; Friendly personally received ten George Foster Peabody Awards; D.H.L., University of Rhode Island, 1966, and Grinnell University, 1967; annual award for outstanding book dealing with recorded performance, Theatre Library Association, 1977, for *The Good Guys, the Bad Guys and the First Amendment: Freedom of Speech vs. Fairness in Broadcasting.*

WRITINGS: (With Edward R. Murrow) *See It Now*, Simon & Schuster, 1955; *Due to Circumstances beyond Our Control*, Random House, 1967; *The Good Guys, the Bad Guys and the First Amendment: Free Speech vs. Fairness in Broadcasting*, Random House, 1976; *Minnesota Rag: The Dramatic Story of the Landmark Supreme Court Case That Gave New Meaning to Freedom of the Press*, Random House, 1981.

SIDELIGHTS: Long associated with radio and television newscasting, Fred W. Friendly is no stranger to First Amendment rules, regulations, and conflicts. He explores a controversial First Amendment ruling in *Minnesota Rag: The Dramatic Story of the Landmark Supreme Court Case That Gave New Meaning to Freedom of the Press.* The case in question, *Near v. Minnesota*, centers on Jay M. Near, who in the late 1920s published a weekly newspaper, the *Saturday Press*, which "specialized in venemous attacks on Jews," as Aryeh Neier relates in a *Nation* review.

"The *Saturday Press* presented a perfect target for [Minnesota's Public Nuisance Act], which provided that a newspaper could be shut down as a public nuisance if a judge declared it to be 'malicious, scandalous or defamatory,'" continues *Washington Post Book World* critic James F. Simon. "And, indeed, a county judge had no trouble shutting down the *Saturday Press* under the new law." Enter *Chicago Tribune* publisher Robert R. McCormick. Although he recognized that the *Saturday Press* was little more than a bigot's scandal sheet, McCormick sensed a threat to freedom of the press in Minnesota's ruling. So the publisher joined in Near's appeal, and with McCormick's influence and financial backing, the case wound up at the Supreme Court. On June 1, 1931, the justices voted 5 to 4 that "the First Amendment forbids prior restraint of the press such as Minnesota had imposed on [Near's newspaper]," as Neier reports.

Minnesota Rag is "a useful reminder that many great legal precedents protecting the liberty of us all were won by fighting battles on behalf of reprobates," says Neier. Simon notes: "There is never a doubt where Friendly, the passionate advocate of press freedom, stands on the issue in *Near*. His longtime commitment to a free press is conspicuous throughout the book. . . . But in *Minnesota Rag* Friendly eschews sermons in favor of facts. In the process, he destroys a myth that has surrounded the case. As long as *Near v. Minnesota* has been studied, it has been common to assume that the charges leveled

by Near in the *Saturday Press* were false. That assumption is effectively countered by Friendly whose research shows that most of Near's charges of corruption in public office were true. It is this revelation that suggests the singular importance of *Near v. Minnesota* as a constitutional document. The decision stands for the proposition that, with rare exception, our press must be free from government censorship. And the freedom to publish even extends to unscrupulous bigots like Jay M. Near."

BIOGRAPHICAL/CRITICAL SOURCES: America, June 26, 1976; *New Republic*, July 3, 1976; *National Review*, September 17, 1976; *Nation*, June 6, 1981; *New York Times Book Review*, June 7, 1981; *Washington Post Book World*, July 19, 1981.†

*   *   *

FRY, C(harles) George   1936-

PERSONAL: Born August 15, 1936, in Piqua, Ohio; son of Sylvan Jack and Lena Freda Marie (Ehle) Fry; married Brigitte Gertrud Langer, December 28, 1961 (divorced October 2, 1970); married Christel Heischmann, November 24, 1971 (divorced, 1980). *Education:* Capital University, B.A. (with honors), 1958; Ohio State University, M.A., 1961, Ph.D., 1965; Evangelical Lutheran Theological Seminary, B.D. (with honors), 1962, M.Div., 1977; Winebrenner Theological Seminary, D.Min., 1978. *Politics:* Independent. *Home:* 5020 Woodmark, Fort Wayne, Ind. *Office:* Campus Ministry, St. Francis College, Fort Wayne, Ind. 46808.

CAREER: Clergyman of Lutheran Church, vicar in Columbus, Ohio, 1961-62; Wittenberg University, Springfield, Ohio, instructor in history, 1962-63; pastor in Columbus, 1963-66; Capital University, Columbus, instructor, 1963-65, assistant professor, 1966-71, associate professor of religion and history, 1971-75; Concordia Theological Seminary, Fort Wayne, Ind., associate professor of historical theology and director of missions education, 1975-84; St. Francis College, Fort Wayne, protestant chaplain, 1982—.

Visiting professor, Damavand College, 1973-74, Concordia Lutheran Seminary, St. Catharines, Ontario, 1978 and 1982; visiting lecturer, Wittenberg University, 1971, Northern England Institute for Christian Education, University of Durham, 1984; visiting theologian at churches in Columbus, Ohio, 1971-72, National Presbyterian Church of Mexico, 1977 and 1979, conference of the Lutheran churches in Venezuela, 1981, and the Lutheran church in Nigeria, 1983. Member of North American executive committee, Fellowship of Faith for the Muslims, 1970-80; member of North American Conference on Muslim Evangelization, 1977-78; member of Lutheran-Baptist dialogue team, Lutheran Council/United States of America, 1978-81. Member of board, Damavand College, 1976—, Samuel Zwemer Institute, 1977-82, Fort Wayne International Affairs, 1982—, Lutheran Liturgical Renewal, 1983—, Greater Fort Wayne Campus Ministry, 1983—, and Indiana Churches United for Ministry in Higher Education, 1984—.

MEMBER: American Historical Association, American Academy of Religion, Conference on Faith and History, Foundation for Reformation Research (Ohio represenative), Turkish-American Association, United Nations Association for the United States, International Platform Association, American Association of University Professors, Organization of American Historians, Ohio Historical Society, Ohio Academy of History, Phi Alpha Theta, Kappa Alpha Pi. *Awards, honors:* Regional

Council for International Education research grant for study in Turkey, 1969.

WRITINGS: The Supper Guest, Ohio State University Printing, 1971; (with James R. King) *The Middle East: Crossroads of Civilization,* C. E. Merrill, 1973; *The Christian Ministry to Muslims Today,* Fellowship of Faith for Muslims (Toronto), 1977; *A Guide to the Study of the World of Islam,* Fellowship of Faith for Muslims, 1977; (with King) *Islam: A Survey of the Muslim Faith,* Baker Book, 1980, 2nd edition, 1982; (with Duane W. H. Arnold) *The Way, the Truth, and the Life: An Introduction to Lutheran Christianity,* Baker Book, 1982; (with King) *Great Asian Religions,* Baker Book, 1984.

Published by Concordia Theological Seminary Press: *Ten Contemporary Theologians,* 1976; *Islam: An Evangelical Perspective,* 1976; (with Harold H. Zietlow) *Christian Missions: History,* 1976; (with Zietlow) *Christian Missions: Strategy,* 1976; (editor) *European Theology, 1648-1914,* 1976; (editor) *Protestant Theology, 1914-1975,* 1977; (with John M. Drickamer) *Lutheranism in America,* 1979; (with Drickamer) *The Age of Lutheran Orthodoxy, 1530-1648,* 1979; (with Duane W. H. Arnold) *A Lutheran Reader,* 1982; *Raymond Lull: Apostle to the Muslims,* 1983; *Iran and Japan: Two Models of Modernization,* 1983.

Editor: (With Donald E. Bensch, and contributor) *The Middle East in Transition,* Capital University Press, 1970; (with James L. Burke, and contributor) *The Past in Perspective,* MSS Educational Publishing, 1971; (with Burke, and contributor) *The Emergence of the Modern World, 1300-1815,* MSS Educational Publishing, 1971; (with Burke, and contributor) *The Search for a New Europe, 1919-1971,* MSS Educational Publishing, 1971; (with King) *An Anthology of Middle Eastern Literature from the Twentieth Century,* Wittenberg University, 1974.

WORK IN PROGRESS: Protestantism: A Survey; African Religions.

AVOCATIONAL INTERESTS: Hiking, painting, science fiction.

*   *   *

FUCHS, Daniel 1934-

PERSONAL: Born August 12, 1934, in New York, N.Y.; son of Isaac (a manufacturer) and Sadie (Fox) Fuchs; married Cara Skoler, January 25, 1959; children: Margot Lynn, Sabrina. *Education:* Columbia University, A.B., 1955, Ph.D., 1960; Brandeis University, A.M., 1956. *Politics:* Democrat. *Religion:* Jewish. *Home:* 155 Elm St., Tenafly, N.J. 07670. *Office:* Department of English, Speech and World Literatures, College of Staten Island of the City University of New York, 715 Ocean Ter., Staten Island, N.Y. 10301.

CAREER: Rensselaer Polytechnic Institute, Troy, N.Y., instructor in English, 1960-61; University of Michigan, Ann Arbor, instructor in English, 1961-62; University of Chicago, Chicago, Ill., instructor, 1962-64, assistant professor of English, 1964-67; College of Staten Island of the City University of New York, Staten Island, N.Y., assistant professor, 1968-70, associate professor, 1970-82, professor of English, 1983—. Visiting professor, John F. Kennedy Institute of American Studies, Free University of Berlin, 1980-81. Fulbright lecturer in American literature at University of Nantes, 1967-68, and University of Vienna, 1975-76; Yaddo fellow, 1975, 1977.

AWARDS, HONORS: Norman Foerster Prize, for "Ernest Hemingway: Literary Critic," an essay in *American Literature,* 1965; City University of New York faculty research grant, 1972-73, 1979-80.

WRITINGS: The Comic Spirit of Wallace Stevens, Duke University Press, 1963; (contributor) Marston LaFrance, editor, *Patterns of Commitment in American Literature,* University of Toronto Press, 1967; (contributor) Arthur Waldhorn, editor, *Ernest Hemingway,* McGraw, 1972; (contributor) Linda Wagner, editor, *Five Decades of Hemingway Criticism,* Michigan State University Press, 1974.

(Contributor) Duane Macmillan, editor, *The Stoic Strain in American Literature,* University of Toronto Press, 1977; (contributor) *Americana-Austriaca,* Braumuller Verlag, 1979; (contributor) Stanley Trachtenberg, editor, *Critical Essays on Saul Bellow,* G. K. Hall, 1979; (contributor) *Nobel Prize Library,* Helveticus, 1984; *Saul Bellow: Vision and Revision,* Duke University Press, 1984. Contributor to literature journals.

WORK IN PROGRESS: A critical study of Norman Mailer.

SIDELIGHTS: Daniel Fuchs writes *CA:* "I have for some time thought that the primary function of the scholar-critic is to bring learning to bear on contemporary literary issues. I derive this point of view, in part, from having studied (at Columbia University) with Lionel Trilling, F. W. Dupee, Richard Chase and (at Brandeis University) with Irving Howe, and in part, from my own temperament and inclinations."

AVOCATIONAL INTERESTS: Sports, camping, classical music, enology, museums, travel.

*   *   *

FUCHS, Roland J(ohn) 1933-

PERSONAL: Born January 15, 1933, in Yonkers, N. Y.; son of Alois L. and Elizabeth (Weigand) Fuchs; married Gaynell R. McAuliffe (a teacher), June 15, 1957; children: Peter K. Christopher K., Andrew K. *Education:* Columbia University, B.A., 1954, graduate study, 1956-57; Clark University, M.A., 1957, Ph.D., 1959; postdoctoral study at Moscow State University, 1960-61. *Home:* 5136 Maunalani Circle, Honolulu, Hawaii 96816. *Office:* Department of Geography, University of Hawaii at Manoa, 445 Porteus Hall, 2424 Maile Way, Honolulu, Hawaii 96822.

CAREER: University of Hawaii at Manoa, Honolulu, assistant professor, 1958-63, associate professor, 1964-68, professor of geography, 1968—, chairman of department, 1964—, associate dean, College of Arts and Sciences, and director, Asian Studies Language and Area Center, 1965-67. Visiting professor at Clark University, 1963-64, and at National Taiwan University, 1974. Research associate, Ohio State University Research Foundation, summers, 1967, 1968; adjunct research associate, East-West Population Institute, East-West Center, 1980—. Member of National Academy of Sciences and National Research Council committees, boards and delegations; chairman of U. S. national committee for International Geographical Union and National Academy of Sciences, beginning 1973, chairman of International Geographical Union research development committee, 1982—. Consultant to United Nations and to planning studies of Paxton, Mass., 1956, and Sturbridge, Mass., 1957-58.

MEMBER: Association of American Geographers, American Association for the Advancement of Slavic Studies (member of board of directors, 1977—), Population Association of America, American Geographical Society, Pacific Science Association (member of council, 1978—).

AWARDS, HONORS: Award from inter-university committee for travel grants for the Soviet Union, 1960-61; National Science Foundation grants, 1963-65, 1967-69, 1970-71, 1976-78, 1978-79, 1978-80, 1980-82, and 1981-83; Fulbright scholar at Tribhuvan University, 1966-67; National Science Council grant for Republic of China, 1973-74; Rockefeller Foundation grant, 1975; American Council of Learned Societies/Social Science Research Council grant, 1981-82; Honors Award, Association of American Geographers, 1982.

WRITINGS: (Editor with George Demko and contributor) *Geographical Perspectives in the Soviet Union,* Ohio State University Press, 1974; (editor with John Street and contributor) *Geography in Asian Universities: Current Status and Needs,* Oriental Press, 1975; (editor with Demko) *Theoretical Problems in Geography,* Ohio State University Press, 1977; (contributor) H. L. Kostanick, editor, *Population and Migration Trends in Eastern Europe,* Westview, 1977; (editor with Street) *Report: Sino-American Workshop on Land Use Planning,* National Science Council, 1978.

(Co-editor) *Population Distribution Policies in Development Planning,* United Nations, 1981; (contributor with W. T. Chow) G. Hoffman, editor, *The Impact of the Federal System on Regional Development,* University of Texas Press, 1981; (contributor) *National Migration Surveys,* Volume X: *Guidelines for Analysis,* United Nations, 1982; (editor with Demko and contributor) *Geographical Studies on the Soviet Union: Essays in Honor of Chauncy D. Harris,* University of Chicago, Department of Geography, 1984; (contributor) J. I. Clarke, editor, *Geography and Population Approaches and Applications,* Pergamon, 1984. Also contributor to *Allgemeine Stadtgeographie,* edited by P. Schoeller, 1969.

Contributor to *Annals of the Association of American Geographers* and to proceedings of professional organizations, including National Academy of Sciences/National Research Council. Also contributor of numerous articles and reviews to academic journals. Assistant editor of *Economic Geography,* 1963-64; member of editorial advisory committee of *Soviet Geography: Review and Translation,* 1966—.

WORK IN PROGRESS: Research on population growth, modernization, land use change, and environmental degradation.

SIDELIGHTS: Roland J. Fuchs comments: "My major interest is in problems of economic development with particular reference to settlement systems and land use issues in the socialist countries and Asian countries. I have resided in the U.S.S.R., Nepal, and China, and have traveled extensively in Eastern Europe and Southeast Asia. My language competencies include Russian, German, and Chinese (spoken Mandarin)."

G

GALELLA, Ron 1931-

PERSONAL: Born January 10, 1931, in Bronx, N.Y.; son of Vincenzo (a piano and casket maker) and Michelina (a croche beader; maiden name, Marinaccio) Galella; married Betty Burke, April 21, 1979. *Education:* Art Center College of Design, B. Professional Arts, 1957; studied acting and stage direction at Pasadena Playhouse, 1957. *Politics:* Independent. *Religion:* Roman Catholic. *Home and office:* 17 Glover Ave., Yonkers, N.Y. 10704.

CAREER: Ceramic artist with Associated American Artists, 1949-51; free-lance magazine and newspaper photographer, 1955—. Lecturer on photography at various schools and conferences. One man exhibits have been shown at Soho Gallery, Nikon House Gallery, and William M. Lyons Gallery. *Military service:* U.S. Air Force, ground and aerial photographer and camera repairman, 1951-55.

WRITINGS—Self-illustrated with photographs: *Jacqueline,* Sheed & Ward, 1974; *Offguard: A Paparazzo Look at the Beautiful People,* McGraw, 1976.

Photographs have appeared in national magazines, and on covers of *Life, Esquire, People, Newsweek, USA Today, Cosmopolitan, McCall's,* and *Pageant,* and on national television programs.

WORK IN PROGRESS: Shooting Stars, a book of photographs and text.

SIDELIGHTS: Celebrity photographer Ron Galella achieved his own fame—and notoriety—in 1972, when he was involved in a suit and countersuit with Jacqueline Onassis. Galella had followed the former First Lady for months, often at very close range, to obtain some 4000 candid photos of her, which were subsequently published in his book *Jacqueline.* Onassis charged that Galella's methods were an invasion of privacy, and sought a court order to bar him from photographing her again. Galella's opinion, expressed in his *CA* interview: "There's so much hypocrisy involved in this business of celebrities pretending they don't like being photographed and hate the photographers—like Jackie; she's the first to buy the magazines and look at her pictures and collect them." In a letter to *CA,* he emphasized: "Hypocrisy is the greatest evil in this business."

The word *paparazzo* was coined by Italian film director Federico Fellini and means literally "pesky insect." Galella defines it as "a freelance photographer who photographs people offguard and then markets to international publications." Paparazzi sometimes encounter risks other than lawsuits in their work; in pursuit of a good photo, Galella has been assaulted by Richard Burton's chauffeur, has been throttled with his own camera strap by Aristotle Onassis' bodyguards, and has had his jaw broken by Marlon Brando. Trailing celebrities makes it impossible for a paparazzo to lead a normal private life, as Galella explained to Charles Flowers of the *Detroit Free Press:* "Liz Taylor was in town. . . . I said I wish she'd get the hell out of town so I can get back to my life. You can't make a date . . . because Liz Taylor might be going out that night." But all of this inconvenience is, to Galella, preferable to the constraints of working as a staff photographer. He told Flowers that when one asks permission for a photograph, "one of two things will usually happen. They'll either make excuses—'oh, my hair's not done'—or you'll get a trite expression. Expressions on the human face are much more infinite when the person is caught unawares."

Though he has been accused of hounding his subjects, Galella does not see his work as exploitive. He told Flowers: "I'm a romantic. . . . I idolize celebrities in a way. I don't want to make them look bad. I'm trying to portray them as they really are, as real people."

AVOCATIONAL INTERESTS: Ceramic sculpture, drawing.

CA INTERVIEW

CA interviewed Ron Galella by telephone on June 15, 1983, at his home in Yonkers, N.Y.

CA: You're known especially for your photographs of celebrities and the persistence you've shown in getting them. Where did your interest in photography come from?

GALELLA: I was always interested in art in high school, and I got into ceramics after high school—I was still taking art courses in schools here in New York. Then the Korean War came, and I enlisted in the air force to avoid the army and to learn something. I got into photography in the air force for four years; I was lucky. That's where I started my career, actually. Then, under the GI Bill, I went to one of the best schools in the United States, the Art Center College of Design, and graduated in 1968. My work there was in photojournalism.

There was a recession at that time—it was difficult finding work—so I was forced to free-lance. I started my own business, getting published slowly. I offered good pictures; that's the key. Especially in black and white, which I love more than color even to this day. TV oriented the public toward color, and the magazines have gone that way as well. More than fifty percent of the magazines now are in color, so I have to shoot that as well as black and white.

You have to come up with things that the magazines and newspapers don't have, and I did just that with Jackie and her family. I concentrated on getting those pictures, and they put me in business. It was pretty easy to do in one way, because she lived in New York City and I was right here in Yonkers.

I didn't want to work for a magazine. The magazine photographers are usually assigned jobs that are done by appointment; they don't go and stake people out. And though I'd been trained as a life photographer, I found out that it's very difficult to make a living doing free-lance photojournalism stories, although they're very creative and nice to do. My last semester at the Art Center College I did a story on a little girl in nursery school. I spent one day shooting, one day in the dark room, one day mailing photos out—at least three days' work. Finally it sold. The *Daily News* bought it through an agent for $125 for the magazine section. I got half of that—for three days' work. So I found out that celebrity photography was much more lucrative than straight photojournalism stories.

Offering pictures that the press is not getting is the key to success, and it's the whole idea behind paparazzo journalism. Most celebrities give press conferences and interviews to further their careers in film, writing, or whatever. But Jackie wasn't in that category. She shunned the press. There was a void there that I filled by getting those pictures the public hadn't been seeing. And that's what started my paparazzo approach. Paparazzo is a means of getting celebrities in public areas—streets, hotel lobbies, airports, parks—catching them off guard, on the run.

CA: You don't seem to resent being called a paparazzo, as many celebrity photographers do.

GALELLA: Well, a lot of people don't understand the term; that's why I'm trying to make it clear. I don't like to be typed—nobody does—so I resent that part of it, the implication that I'm *only* a paparazzo. A good photographer can do all kinds of work, in all kinds of situations. But paparazzo photography made me famous because of Jackie and all the court battles that evolved from my taking pictures of her. In the second court decision I gave up my right to photograph Jackie and her family.

CA: In addition to your work at the Art Center College, didn't you study acting and directing at the Pasadena Playhouse?

GALELLA: Yes, but that was just a summer session, two months. You see, when I was going to the Art Center College of Design, living in Hollywood, I got very interested in the celebrities. I guess it was more curiosity than actually being a fan; I don't consider myself a fan of the stars, although I've had favorites, of course. But I have an interest in glamour, and naturally in beauty and the magic of photography. So celebrities interested me. I used to crash premiers and take their pictures. And now I make a living taking their pictures.

CA: Are there photographers whose work you formally studied or especially admire?

GALELLA: Oh yes. I think the two foremost photojournalists are Henri Cartier-Bresson and Eugene Smith. Smith passed away a few years ago. Cartier-Bresson shuns publicity. I'm the opposite!

CA: Is there a great deal of competition among celebrity photographers?

GALELLA: Yes, there is, but yet there's a lot of mediocrity. A lot of the new photographers are not trained. I brought my training in life photography to street photography, paparazzo journalism. I was paving new ground and I loved it. Well, with all the publicity from the lawsuits, especially the first court battle in 1972, the word *paparazzo* became known all over America. Everybody with a camera tried to do it.

There was money in it in those days, too, especially at the beginning. In the '60s and early '70s, I would get a thousand dollars a take for photos of Jackie—a thousand for the first sale to a movie magazine or the *National Enquirer*. That was good money then. My best year with Jackie, to give you an idea, was 1970, when I made twenty takes. I made $20,000 from photos of Jackie, and another $20,000 for other photos. (I never photographed just Jackie.) But this also shows that some of the negative publicity was misleading—such as Jackie saying I haunted her like a shadow. The facts show that twenty times were all I got in my best year, 1970.

CA: To get some of your photographs of Jackie, you went to such lengths as wearing assorted disguises, hiding behind coatracks, and even dating her maid. What's the greatest extreme you've ever gone to for a picture?

GALELLA: I had a Greek fisherman take me to Skorpios to take pictures of her there—but none of them were nude pictures; it was another photographer who did that. The coatrack time was one of the most challenging experiences. It was in an intimate Chinese restaurant. Jackie was there with Ari Onassis and Doris Duke and I. M. Pei, the architect. I was invited in by the proprietor after waiting outside. Not knowing, he just said, "Why don't you come in?" He thought Jackie was going to be cooperative. I said, "No, I'll have to sneak these pictures. Just wait; I want to go to my car and get a bag to hide the cameras in, and get the farthest seat from her."

There was a table in the corner behind a coatrack. I had the menu in front of my face and put the cameras under the table in a bag. Not a camera bag, by the way. A paparazzo always tries not to be obvious. The proprietor asked me what I wanted to eat. I said, "The same thing they're eating." When the time came to start taking pictures, I told him to turn the music up so they wouldn't hear the clicks of the camera. I hid behind the coatrack where Jackie's coat was hanging, and shot between the coats. I shot available light, because there was enough flourescent light to do black and white.

The waiters were funny. They knew I was there, and they were trying to pose with Jackie, standing behind her, giving her Oriental drawings, really posing. At the end, I managed to get out without Jackie and her party seeing me, and I photographed her with strobes in color when she left the restaurant.

CA: Most of those photos are in the book Jacqueline, *aren't they?*

GALELLA: Yes. And I did a book after *Jacqueline*. It's called *Offguard;* it was published by McGraw-Hill in 1976.

CA: Since you quit photographing Jacqueline Kennedy Onassis, you've been taking pictures of people like Bo Derek and Brooke Shields. Do you have a new favorite?

GALELLA: When I had to give Jackie up, the question a lot of TV journalists asked me was, "Who's your next subject?" The only one I could think of who would have been of equal importance and interest was Princess Grace and her family. That was my answer then, and I have to say that is my answer now, even though Grace Kelly has passed away.

In 1982, while I was out in Los Angeles (I spend the first four months of every year there with my wife, covering the West Coast), there was a Grace Kelly film festival in Philadelphia, her hometown. I knew about it, but since I had been getting so many photos of her on other occasions, I decided not to go. Well, a reporter from "Entertainment Tonight" interviewed Princess Grace and asked what she thought about being Ron Galella's first subject after Jackie. Her response was, "I'm flattered that Ron would follow me like that, but where is he now? He's slipping!"

CA: Have you found anybody as difficult as Jackie?

GALELLA: Yes, there are people more difficult. There's so much hypocrisy involved in this business of celebrities pretending they don't like being photographed and hate the photographers—like Jackie; she's the first to buy the magazines and look at her pictures and collect them. Brooke Shields's mother has sued a photographer recently—after signing a model release and getting paid for the pictures. She lost, but she almost won. It's unbelievable. She pushed her daughter into the limelight, for profit and publicity, and then went back and tried to get the photographer. She probably had guilt feelings about what she'd done to Brooke.

I have to mention that she's also after me. I've never taken any bad pictures of Brooke. The only deduction I can make is that she's after me because I'm more famous than any other paparazzo, so she'll gain more attention by having me barred from events that Brooke attends. That's what she's been trying to do. She's been successful in a few cases, but not all. Recently Brooke graduated from high school in New Jersey. I and other photographers were there, and we were all bounced out; they had tremendous security, both police and private security. None of us got many pictures. I got about fifteen. I was lucky to get those—it didn't last more than five minutes.

Brooke's mother was difficult with me. She had the police try to get my film. They said they'd arrest me if I didn't surrender it, so I said, "Arrest me." Finally a sympathetic cop took me aside and said, "Get me a roll of film from another camera, one you didn't shoot." So I unwound a blank roll from a black-and-white camera I hadn't used that day and made believe it was the roll I shot.

They were trying to say this was a private event. I said, "A private event? She's a public figure. What are all these press photographers and TV cameras here for? And other photographers like me?" But they didn't demand their film; that's the only difference.

CA: That happens to you a lot, doesn't it?

GALELLA: Yeah. But not always. A lot of people like me. Most of the celebrities do. Even Brooke likes me deep down. Her mother has tried to turn her against me. Many PR people don't like me, though. They try to bar me from events. But most of the stars don't feel that way. Last night, for instance, I followed Farrah Fawcett when she left the theater after a performance. I didn't have an opportunity to photograph her when she came out of the theater, because she was signing autographs; it was impossible to get a good shot with all those people in the way. I figured since she's known me for many years she'd let me take some pictures outside the hotel when she got back there. Well, she knew I was following her and she pulled over. I said, "I just want a few shots of you and I won't bother you." She said, "OK." Then she said, "Wait a minute. I'm a mess." You know, she had just done the show and her hair was still wet. She said, "Why don't we make it another time?" I said, "Fine. You name it." So I have an appointment with her Friday before the theater. Most people are like that. Of course, there are some people like Paul Newman who are nasty to all the press, generally speaking.

CA: And Marlon Brando?

GALELLA: Yes, but Brando is nice to me now. Since the out-of-court settlement for $40,000 for knocking out four of my teeth, he is very nice to me. He shook my hand. And to tell you the truth, he's nice to all the photographers now. I guess he learned his lesson. The $40,000 settlement hurt him, and also his fist sank into my teeth and got infected. He was in the hospital in New York for four days, and he has scars on that hand now.

CA: What was the occasion?

GALELLA: Brando was going to be on Dick Cavett's show when Cavett had the show in New York. This is listed, of course, before the show, and the actual taping was being done at 5:00 in the afternoon for the show being televised that night. So I went to the studio early and browsed around. On the way to Cavett's office I saw a limo driver who told me Brando was coming in by helicopter. There are only three heliports in New York, and I figured the nearest one was the one around 62nd Street, right off the East River. I went there and stalked Brando out.

I was the only photographer there, and the receptionists don't know who's going to be on board any helicopter. By now it was getting close to taping time and I didn't want to miss that, so I started to leave for the studio. Just then a limo driver came into the heliport. The driver knew me, and he told me he was waiting for Brando. So I got Brando coming off the helicopter and getting in the limousine then going to the studio. I followed them to the ABC studio but it was impossible to get a good picture there because of the unbelievable number of press, spectators, and fans. It was just as bad when Brando left the studio after he taped the show, so I figured I'd follow him back to the heliport and get another good take.

I got into my car with a fan who's now a professional photographer, set to follow Brando, who was with Cavett in the limo. But instead of going to the heliport they went to Chinatown. Brando and Cavett got out of the limo, I got out of my car and got about one dozen shots. Cavett knew me, so I'm sure he told Brando who I was sometime during the course of the evening. The two of them stopped and called me over.

Brando said to me, "What do you want that you don't already have?" He was wearing very dark sunglasses so I told him, "I'd like a picture of you without your sunglasses." When Brando said no, I told him that's what editors want to see. Then he slugged me. He caught me off guard, when I wasn't even looking at him. It was a hard blow to the mouth that was such a shock that it sent me four or five feet back into the street. Then I got into my car and drove to Bellevue Hospital. Brando's punch had knocked out four teeth and cracked my lower jawbone. I needed nine stitches in that lip.

CA: The fans and amateur photographers make your job very hard, don't they?

GALELLA: Yeah. The business has changed a lot—mostly for the worse—because of the fans and the mediocre photographers. It's unbelievable. These guys will take some pictures and then run up to the star to get an autograph, and I can't get a good take because they're in the way, blocking. They yell and rave. It's noisy and just terrible. It's hard to get an exclusive now. It's so bad on the West Coast (worse than here in New York) that I've hired two photographers out there to shoot the celebrities at restaurants and other public places, so I'm relieved of part of that. And some of these fans turn semiprofessional and start selling their pictures. That spreads the market out so the buyers can get pictures for almost nothing.

CA: Have you done any teaching, or would you like to?

GALELLA: Yes. For one thing, I've been teaching the two photographers that I hired to work for me. I'm their agent. I have lectured at some schools and conferences. The biggest one was the University of Miami at Coral Gables, Florida. It was the seventeenth annual Wilson Hicks Conference. I prepared a very good slide show for it, showing what paparazzo journalism is about. I've lectured at a photography school in Columbus, Ohio, and one in Boston. I only do it when someone calls and requests an exhibition and a lecture; I mean, I don't have an agent setting up lectures for me. But I do like it.

CA: Do you ever take a vacation from your camera?

GALELLA: That's very difficult! My wife, Betty, had never been to the Bronx Zoo, so last Sunday we went there. I took my camera along just to shoot a few pictures of the animals. They've added a Bengali express monorail that goes through a wild area with animals like deer, peacocks, and bears. It was beautiful. We were kind of late leaving, and when we got on the bus that takes you out of the zoo, guess who was on the same bus? Andy Warhol! He was lost and asked how to get a subway back to the city. I said, "I'll take you to the subway; I have a car in the parking lot." So I got a few pictures of him with the elephant. I printed them up today, in fact. There's a beautiful portrait of him, and it will probably sell.

The point is, you can't leave your camera at home. And you see, it's not work for me; it's pleasure. That's the reason I don't need a vacation. People who don't like their work need a vacation. That's what's wrong with the world: People find no meaning in their work. Of course, some work is bad, like assembly-line work. People who do that kind of work have to have recreation to get by. But I get my kicks from my work. In fact, I've stayed up every night this week until 5:00 or 5:30 in the morning developing pictures. I take the pictures and develop the film the same night so I can get the prints out the next day. It's a tremendous amount of work, and it's only because I love it that I can do it.

It's rare in our modern world that we can do something from beginning to end ourselves. On an assembly line you can't. You have no control. I have *full* control, and I do it in a short time, take the picture one day and have it ready the next day, the finished picture in my hand—a record, something that people will react to, something magic.

BIOGRAPHICAL/CRITICAL SOURCES: Detroit Free Press, September 15, 1974; *Authors in the News,* Volume I, Gale, 1976.

—Interview by Jean W. Ross

*   *   *

GALES, Barbara J.   1940-
(Anne Kristin Carroll)

PERSONAL: Born September 6, 1940, in Houston, Tex.; daughter of Ed C. (a business executive) and Reba (Barnett) Jones; married Ronald E. Wilson, 1958 (divorced, 1962); married Michael R. Denis (a sales manager), April, 1962 (divorced, 1982); married Michael Stephen Gales (an independent investor), December, 1982; children: Ronald E., Michael W. *Education:* Attended University of Houston, Gulf Coast Bible College, and Houston Baptist University. *Politics:* "Conservative Constitutionalist." *Religion:* "Spirit-filled, fundamental, evangelical" Christian. *Home and office:* 3090 Rivermont Pkwy., Alpharetta, Ga. 30201.

CAREER: Writer; marriage counselor at Christian Counseling Center, Atlanta, Ga. Former reservationist for Pan American Airways and Texas International Airways, free-lance model, and administrative assistant.

MEMBER: Freedom Foundation, Campus Crusade for Christ, National Right to Life, Christian Right to Life, Women Who Want to Be Women.

WRITINGS—Under pseudonym Anne Kristin Carroll: (With Darien B. Cooper) *We Became Wives of Happy Husbands,* Victor, 1976; *From the Brink of Divorce: An Evangelical Marriage Counselor Advises How to Save Your Marriage,* Doubleday-Galilee, 1978; *Together Forever,* with workbook, Zondervan, 1982. Also author of cassette tape recordings and workbooks "Marital Dynamics" and "Children: Heartbreak or Happiness."

WORK IN PROGRESS: "A book regarding unusual marriages and marriage partners who, through Christ, were most successful"; a novice's guide to shark fishing.

SIDELIGHTS: Barbara J. Gales told *CA:* "My driving motivation in writing is to share Jesus Christ with others. My vocation, first and foremost, will be to be the best wife possible to the precious and priceless man the Lord gave me as a husband. My avocation, I pray both now and in the future, will be a continuing in-depth study of God's Word, and as important, the daily application of God's truths to my personal life, marriage, and family. Personally, I believe that between the pages of the book called the Holy Bible can be found all the insights and directions for living life to its fullest, of man's heartbreak and problems, and the clear promise of life eternal to all who accept Jesus Christ's substitutionary death at Calvary.

"I believe God's Word is real, alive, and contemporary. I feel it contains clear, vital statements and positions on current issues such as marriage, divorce, politics, the nurturing and discipline of children, sex, homosexuality, government, finances, and life after death.

"I have been most influenced by the following authors and their works: Hal Lindsey (*The Late Great Planet Earth* and *1980s: Countdown to Armegeddon*), Dr. Judson Cornwall (*Let Us Praise* and *Let Us Be Holy*), Paul E. Billheimer (*Destined for the Throne* and *Don't Waste Your Sorrows*), Dan De Haan (*Intercepted for Christ* and *The God You Can Know*), and Dr. Charles Stanley (*Handle with Prayer* and *Is There a Man in the House?*). These books and their authors have helped to shape my Christian direction and to open new doors of thought, worship, praise, and joy."

BIOGRAPHICAL/CRITICAL SOURCES: Atlanta Constitution Journal, September 2, 1978; *Christian Review*, September, 1978.

*   *   *

GALEWITZ, Herb 1928-

PERSONAL: Born July 9, 1928, in Brooklyn, N.Y.; son of Philip and Beckie (Bornstein) Galewitz; married Miriam Nodelman, July 1, 1962; children: Eve, Philip. *Education:* College of the City of New York (now City College of the City University of New York), B.B.A., 1956. *Home:* 612 Grassy Hill Rd., Orange, Ct. 06477. *Office:* 299 Madison Ave., New York, N.Y. 10017.

CAREER: Pocket Books, Inc., New York City, sales administration, 1953-59; Golden Records, New York City, business manager, 1959-65; MGM Records, New York City, artists and repertoire producer, 1965-68; independent record producer and licensing agent, New York City, 1968—. *Military service:* U.S. Army, 1951-53.

AWARDS, HONORS: Nominated for a National Academy of Recording Arts and Sciences "Grammy," 1969, for best record of a musical show in 1968, "You're A Good Man Charlie Brown."

WRITINGS—Editor: The Celebrated Cases of Dick Tracy, Chelsea House, 1971; *Toonerville Trolley*, Scribner, 1972; *Great Comics of the New York News and Chicago Tribune*, Crown, 1972; *Bringing up Father*, Scribner, 1973; *The Gumps*, Scribner, 1974; *Bob and Ray: Write If You Get Work*, Random House, 1975; *Dick Tracy: The Thirties*, Chelsea House, 1978; *Abbie an' Slats*, Ken Pierce, 1983; *Alley Oop*, Ken Pierce, 1984.

*   *   *

GALLAGHER, Richard
See LEVINSON, Leonard

*   *   *

GAMMOND, Peter 1925-

PERSONAL: Born September 30, 1925, in Northwich, Cheshire, England; son of John Thomas (a clerk) and Dorothy (Heald) Gammond; married Elizabeth Ann Hodgson (a teacher), July 31, 1954; children: John Julian, Stephen. *Education:* Attended Wadham College, Oxford, 1943, 1947-50. *Politics:* Socialist. *Religion:* Church of England. *Home and office:* Craven Cottage, Dunboe Pl., Shepperton, Middlesex, England.

CAREER: Decca Record Co., London, England, editor, 1953-60; free-lance writer, 1960—. Composer and broadcaster. *Military service:* British Army, Royal Armoured Corps, 1943-47; became sergeant.

MEMBER: Musicians' Union, Rotary International, Savile Club.

WRITINGS: (Editor and contributor) *The Decca Book of Jazz* (Jazz Book Club selection), Muller, 1958; (editor and contributor) *Duke Ellington: His Life and Music* (Jazz Book Club selection), Roy, 1958.

101 Things, Elek, 1960; (with Peter Clayton) *A Guide to Popular Music*, Phoenix House, 1960, Philosophical Library, 1961; *Terms Used in Music*, Phoenix House, 1960; (with Charles Fox, Alexis Korner, and Alun Morgan) *Jazz on Record*, Hutchinson, 1960, Greenwood Press, 1978; (with James Burnett) *Music on Record: A Critical Guide*, Hutchinson, Volume I, 1962, Volume II, 1962, Volume III, 1963, Volume IV, 1963, Greenwood Press, 1978; (with Clayton) *Know About Jazz*, Blackie & Son, 1963; (with Clayton) *Fourteen Miles on a Clear Night: An Irreverent, Sceptical and Affectionate Book about Jazz Records* (Jazz Book Club selection), P. Owen, 1966; *Bluff Your Way in Music*, Wolfe Publishing, 1966, revised edition, 1984; *The Meaning and Magic of Music*, Hamlyn, 1968, Golden Books, 1970.

Your Own, Your Very Own (music hall scrapbook), Allan, Shepperton, 1971; *One Man's Music*, Wolfe Publishing, 1971; (editor) *Best Music Hall and Variety Songs*, Wolfe Publishing, 1972; *Scott Joplin and the Ragtime Era*, St. Martin's, 1975; (editor) *Music Hall Songbook*, David & Charles, 1975; *Musical Instruments in Colour*, Blandford, 1975, published as *Musical Instruments in Color*, Macmillan, 1976; (contributor) *The Dictionary of Composers*, Book Club Associates, 1977; *The Illustrated Encyclopedia of Recorded Opera*, Salamander, 1979; *The Magic Flute*, Barrie & Jenkins, 1979.

(Editor) *The Music Goes Round and Round*, Quartet Books, 1980; (editor with Raymond Horricks) *Music on Record: Brass Bands*, Stephens, 1980; (editor) *The Good Old Days Songbook*, British Broadcasting Corp. Publications/EMI, 1980; *Offenbach: His Life and Times*, Midas, 1980, Paganiniana, 1981; *An Illustrated Guide to Composers of Opera*, Salamander, 1980; *An Illustrated Guide to Composers of Classical Music*, Salamander, 1980; (editor with Horricks) *Music on Record: The Big Bands*, Stephens, 1981; *Schubert*, Eyre Methuen, 1981; (contributor) *The New Oxford Companion to Music*, Oxford University Press, 1983.

Contributor to "The Great Composers and Their Music" series, for Marshall Cavendish. Also contributor to recording industry journals and newspapers. Editor of *Audio Record Review*, 1966-70; music editor of *Hi-Fi News and Record Review*, 1970-80.

WORK IN PROGRESS: The Bluffer's Guide to British Class; The Bluffer's Guide to Golf; The Bluffer's Guide to Opera; The Oxford Companion to Popular Music; books on Duke Ellington, Jelly Roll Morton, and George Gershwin.

SIDELIGHTS: Peter Gammond writes: "My ambition to be a creative writer was sidetracked, after a period with Decca Record Co., into writing about music and records. It is sometimes frustrating, but at least it is a source of constant commissions. I have always attempted to write about music in understandable terms, and have become increasingly interested in the field of popular music. I am also trying to give more time to writing music, and some fictional work is now under way."

AVOCATIONAL INTERESTS: Tennis, golf, book-collecting.

GARVEY, John 1944-

PERSONAL: Born May 8, 1944, in Decatur, Ill.; son of Hugh Michael (a publisher) and Jane (Driscoll) Garvey; married Regina Carbonell (a musician), June 10, 1967; children: Maria, Hugh Daniel. *Education:* University of Notre Dame, A.B., 1967. *Politics:* "I'm against it." *Religion:* Catholic. *Home:* 1600 Holmes, Springfield, Ill. 62704.

CAREER: Teacher of English, creative writing, and religion in high school in Mishawaka, Ind., 1967-68; Templegate Publishing Co., Springfield, Ill., writer and editor, 1968-71; draft counselor in Springfield, Ill., 1969-73; Sangamon State University, Springfield, publications editor, 1971-73; Templegate Publishing Co., editor, 1973—.

WRITINGS—Published by Thomas More Press, except as indicated: *A Contemporary Meditation on Saints,* 1975; *Saints for Confused Times,* 1976; (editor) *All Our Sons and Daughters: Cults, Their Meaning and the Deprogramming Controversy,* Templegate, 1977; (with Frank Morriss) *Abortion,* 1979; *The Ways We Are Together,* 1983.

Columnist for *Commonweal,* 1975—. Work represented in anthology, *On the Run,* edited by Michael F. McCauley, Thomas More Press, 1974. Contributor of articles to *Critic, Concilium, Katallagete/Be Reconciled, U.S. Catholic,* and *Illinois Times,* and of poems to *Apple* and *Ohio Review.* Editor, *University Today,* 1968-71.

WORK IN PROGRESS: A book, *Hard Questions,* about the problems facing contemporary institutional religion—"the real problems, not the ones the leaders of the churches imagine"; research on the relationship between Christianity and other religions, particularly between Christianity and Judaism and the phenomenon of Christian anti-Semitism.

SIDELIGHTS: John Garvey once wrote *CA:* "I am especially interested in the intersection of religion and great social change, and am lucky to be alive at a time when there is plenty to look at in this area; interesting things may happen when tradition encounters the myths of a new age. (I suspect this interest may have come about as a result of a life-long fascination with mythology, fantasy, and science fiction.) The recent interest on the part of a lot of people in Jung, in the fantasies of Lewis and Tolkien, and in Eastern religion shows that I am not alone— it is all evidence of a search for living symbols, and the need to express, in a new way, realities which are as old as the race. In our time there has been a shift away from a purely intellectual, exteriorized attitude toward dogma to one which emphasizes a personal experience of religious truth, an approach which allows growth and change to reflect the reality of the symbol, while drawing deeper levels of meaning from it.

"When tradition encounters something new it seems awkward—its past is so obvious, like the shell of a tortoise. Traditional religion confronts one set of myths (the most recent ones, perhaps, being a fierce belief in the possibility of personal autonomy, and the belief that one creates one's life in an indifferent universe) with another set, which teaches a kind of mythological ecology: there are true and false things, and choices which align you with or against the universe.

"It is not a case of the new myths being false. They are simply limited. They may take on depth in the encounter with tradition, if tradition can work as a living language, a genuinely informative one. Nor is it a matter of traditional religion being simply true: when it is not living, but has become a smug consolation, tradition can be the most dangerous and limiting myth of all."†

*   *   *

GAULDIE, Enid 1928-

PERSONAL: Born January 29, 1928, in Liverpool, England; daughter of William E. and Annie (Green) Macneilage; married William Sinclair Gauldie (an architect), December 5, 1949; children: Robin, Alison, Becca. *Education:* University of St. Andrews, M.A., 1947, B.Phil., 1967. *Politics:* None. *Religion:* None. *Home and office:* Waterside, Invergowrie by Dundee, Scotland.

CAREER: University of St. Andrews, St. Andrews, Scotland, librarian, 1948; research historian in Dundee, Scotland, 1967-69; writer, 1969—. Visiting lecturer, Duncan of Jordanstone College of Art, Department of Town Planning. Member of board of governors of Duncan of Jordanstone College of Art.

WRITINGS: (With Lenman and Lythe) *Dundee Textile Industry,* Abertay Historical Society, 1969; *Cruel Habitations: A History of Working Class Society,* Allen & Unwin, 1974; *The Scottish Country Miller 1700-1900: A History of Water-Powered Meal Milling in Scotland,* John Donald, 1981; *The Quarries of the Feus* (a history of Invergowrie), Waterside Press, 1981. Also author of short stories and school broadcasts. Contributor to women's magazines.

WORK IN PROGRESS: Research on the Dundee town plan; a work on the Mylnes of Mylnefield; short stories.

SIDELIGHTS: Reviewing Enid Gauldie's *The Scottish Country Miller 1700-1900: A History of Water-Powered Meal Milling in Scotland,* Jim Hunter points out that "the Scottish country miller is, quite literally, a dying breed. It is indicative of Enid Gauldie's approach to her subject that she has talked extensively to the survivors. Mrs. Gauldie, one feels, understands the miller's trade. Her account of milling technology and of millers' work is based on more than a merely academic assessment of the literary and manuscript evidence."

Reviewers commend the author for her practical approach to historical subjects. Hunter, for example, goes on to state in the *Times Literary Supplement* that whereas one recent writer called the one-and-a-half pounds of oatmeal consumed per week per Scot at the turn of this century a sign of decreased meal consumption, Gauldie matter-of-factly reminds readers that it takes only a single ounce to make a bowl of porridge. The critic concludes that the author's work not only sympathetically examines its subject but also "does much to elucidate the effects of the transformation of Scottish rural society in the two centuries following 1700."

AVOCATIONAL INTERESTS: Art, literature, country life, friends.

BIOGRAPHICAL/CRITICAL SOURCES: Times Literary Supplement, August 21, 1981.

*   *   *

GEORGE, Roy E(dwin) 1923-

PERSONAL: Born February 17, 1923, in Liverpool, England; son of Frederick W. (a tugboat captain) and Minnie (Crabtree) George; married Jean Morgan, September 12, 1949; children: Michele, Karen. *Education:* University of London, B.Sc., 1949,

Ph.D., 1967; University of Bristol, M.A., 1956. *Home:* 147 Joffre St., Dartmouth, Nova Scotia, Canada. *Office:* Dalhousie University, Halifax, Nova Scotia, Canada.

CAREER: South Western Gas Board, Bath, England, assistant personnel manager, 1949-56; National Coal Board, Burnley, England, areas staff manager, 1956-60; St. Mary's University, Halifax, Nova Scotia, assistant professor of commerce, 1960-63; Dalhousie University, Halifax, associate professor, 1963-65, professor of commerce, 1965-73, William A. Black Professor of Commerce and professor of economics, 1973—. Consultant to Canadian government agencies, private industry, and trade unions. Member of board of directors, Maritime Chamber of Commerce, 1971-72. *Military service:* Royal Air Force, flight sergeant, 1941-46. *Member:* Canadian Economics Association, Canadian Association of University Teachers (vice-president, 1965-66; treasurer, 1966-67). *Awards, honors:* Canada Council leave fellowship and research grant.

WRITINGS: Technological Redundancy in a Small Isolated Society, Industrial Relations Centre, McGill University, 1969; *Leader and Laggard: Manufacturing Industry in Nova Scotia, Quebec and Ontario,* University of Toronto Press, 1970; *The Life and Times of Industrial Estates Limited,* Institute of Public Affairs, Dalhousie University, 1974; *Targeting High-Growth Industry,* Institute for Research on Public Policy, 1983.

Contributor: R. C. Bellan and W. H. Pope, editors, *The Canadian Economy, Problems and Options,* McGraw/Ryerson, 1981; A. Tupper and G. B. Doern, editors, *Crown Corporations and Public Policy in Canada,* Institute for Research on Public Policy, 1982; Lewis R. Fischer and Eric W. Sagar, editors, *Merchant Shipping and Economic Development,* Memorial University of Newfoundland, 1982.

WORK IN PROGRESS: Research on governmental industrial development policies.

*　　*　　*

GERMANICUS
See DUNNER, Joseph

*　　*　　*

GEYMAN, John P. 1931-

PERSONAL: Born February 9, 1931, in Santa Barbara, Calif.; son of Milton John (a physician) and Betsy (Payne) Geyman; married Emogene Deichler (a teacher), June 9, 1956; children: John Matthew, James Caleb, William Sabin. *Education:* Princeton University, A.B., 1952; University of California, M.D., 1960. *Religion:* Unitarian. *Home:* 2325 92nd Ave. N.E., Bellevue, Wash. 98004. *Office:* School of Medicine, University of Washington, Seattle, Wash. 98195.

CAREER: Private practice of medicine, Mount Shasta, Calif., 1963-69; director of family practice residency program at Community Hospital of Sonoma County, Santa Rosa, Calif., and assistant clinical professor of ambulatory and community medicine at School of Medicine, University of California, San Francisco, 1969-71; University of Utah, College of Medicine, Salt Lake City, associate professor of community and family medicine and chairman, Division of Family Practice, 1971-72; University of California, Davis, School of Medicine, professor of family practice, vice-chairman of Department of Family Practice, and director of family practice residency program, 1972-76; University of Washington, Seattle, professor of fam-

ily medicine and chairman of department, 1977—. Trustee, College of Siskiyous, 1969. *Military service:* U.S. Navy, 1952-55; became lieutenant junior grade.

MEMBER: American Academy of Family Physicians, Society of Teachers of Family Medicine, American Board of Family Practice (fellow).

WRITINGS—All published by Appleton-Century-Crofts: *The Modern Family Doctor and Changing Medical Practice,* 1971; *Family Practice: Foundation of Changing Health Care,* 1980; (editor) *Archives of Family Practice,* Volume I, 1980, Volume II, 1981; *Family Practice: An International Perspective in Developed Countries,* 1983.

Contributor to medical journals. Founding editor, *Journal of Family Practice,* 1974—.

*　　*　　*

GIBSON, Morgan 1929-

PERSONAL: Born June 6, 1929, in Cleveland, Ohio; son of George Miles and Elizabeth (Leeper) Gibson; married Barbara Browne (a university lecturer and poet), August 31, 1950 (divorced, 1972); married Keiko Matsui (a poet and teacher), September 14, 1978; children: (first marriage) Julia, Lucy. *Education:* Oberlin College, B.A., 1950; University of Iowa, M.A., 1952, Ph.D., 1959; Wayne State University, graduate study, 1958-59. *Politics:* "Anarcho-pacifist." *Religion:* Buddhist. *Home address:* P.O. Box 212, Frankfort, Mich. 49635.

CAREER: Shimer College, Mount Carroll, Ill., instructor in English and humanities, 1953-54; Wayne State University, Detroit, Mich., instructor, 1954-59, teaching fellow in history, 1958-59; American International College, Springfield, Mass., assistant professor of English, 1959-61; University of Wisconsin—Milwaukee, 1961-72, began as assistant professor, became associate professor of English; Goddard College, Plainfield, Vt., member of graduate faculty, 1972-75; Osaka University, Toyonaka-shi, Osaka, Japan, visiting professor of language and culture, 1975-79; Michigan State University, Lansing, Mich., lecturer in creative writing, 1979; University of Illinois at Urbana-Champaign, visiting associate professor of comparative literature, 1982-83; Indiana University at Bloomington, associate researcher in comparative literature, 1984—; professor of English, Chukyo University, Nagoya, Japan. Publisher, Great Lakes Books, Milwaukee, Wis., 1956-58. Lecturer on contemporary literature and culture; has read his poetry in Kyoto, Boston, London, San Francisco, Chicago, Detroit, and other cities, and on campuses. Teacher at Afro-American writers' workshop, in freedom schools sponsored by civil rights organizations, and at Free University of Milwaukee.

MEMBER: P.E.N., Academy of American Poets, Poetry Society of America, Buddhist Publishing Society.

AWARDS, HONORS: Gage Prize for Fiction, Oberlin College, 1950; First Prize in fiction, *Mutiny Magazine,* 1961; Uhrig Award for excellent teaching, University of Wisconsin—Milwaukee, 1965; several grants for summer research and writing, University of Wisconsin—Milwaukee, 1966-67.

WRITINGS: (With Barbara Gibson) *Our Bedroom's Underground* (poems), Kenwood Press, 1964; *Mayors of Marble* (poems), Great Lakes Publishing, 1966; (editor) *The Arts of Activism* (anthology), Arts in Society, 1969; *Stones Glow Like Lovers' Eyes* (poems), Morgan Press, 1970; *Kenneth Rexroth* (a critical study), Twayne, 1972; *Dark Summer*, Morgan Press, 1977; *Speaking of Light* (poems), Morgan Press, 1979; (with wife, Keiko Gibson) *Kokoro: Heart Mind*, Kokoro, 1980; *The Great Brook Book* (poetic fictions), Four Zoas Press, 1981; (translator with Hiroski Murakami) *Tantric Poetry of Kukai (Kobo Daishi) Japan's Buddhist Saint*, Mahachula Buddhist University (Bangkok), 1982.

Also author of *Revolutionary Rexroth: Poet of Erotic Wisdom*. Author of two plays, "Strongroom" and "Madame C.I.A.," performed at numerous universities on tour. Poetry, fiction, and essays have appeared in *Choice, Chicago Review, IO, Massachusetts Activist, Prospetti* (Italy), *Poesie Vivante* (Switzerland), and numerous other literary anthologies and periodicals in the United States and England. Author of biweekly column, "Provincial Anarchy," published in *Kaleidoscope* (Milwaukee underground newspaper); former poetry editor, *Arts in Society* (publication of University of Wisconsin Extension).

WORK IN PROGRESS: A book of poems; studies in Buddhist meditation and philosophy.

SIDELIGHTS: Morgan Gibson told *CA:* "Whatever I write and do not throw away—poems, stories, essays—enacts a philosophic quest. What is Truth? Justice? Beauty? How can we be free? Happy? How can we realize life wholly—and death too? These questions cannot be explicitly, finally answered, but they focus consciousness like Zen koans, shocking us awake. 'The Word / leads us from our somnolence to the World.'

"This quest has taken me from Christianity (more than two centuries of Gibsons were protestant preachers), through revolutionary (though always pacifistic) activism for a quarter of a century, to a way of life in Japan (and later even in America) that might be called Buddhist—'Looking into waves within / for the face before I was born.' These waves are often stormy; the face is often blurred. My quest and writings have been best understood and encouraged by the late Kenneth Rexroth and Paul Goodman, and by my wife Keiko Matsui Gibson, whose 'empty Heart-mind smiled / when my way was lost.' Thanks to her, and to countless enlightening beings, I have glimpses of 'the light / of not trying / for light,' when 'I stay in tune with the Great Brook, changes flowing away.'"

Gibson studied world literature and philosophy independently with Kenneth Rexroth and Paul Goodman. He also spent time in Kyoto, Japan, with Buddhist philosopher Masao Abe. For more information on Gibson's work and friendship with Kenneth Rexroth, see the "*CA* Interview" section of Rexroth's entry in this volume.

*   *   *

GIDAL, Nachum
See GIDAL, Tim N(achum)

*   *   *

GIDAL, Sonia (Epstein)   1922-

PERSONAL: Born September 23, 1922, in Berlin, Germany; daughter of Michael and Ellen (Lipschutz) Epstein; married Tim Gidal (a writer and photographer), July 4, 1944 (divorced, 1970); children: Peter. *Education:* Attended high school in Berlin, Germany, and boarding school in Israel. *Home:* Blue Ball, Blue Ball Hill, Totnes, South Devon, England.

CAREER: Press photographer, 1941-45; teacher of arts and crafts in Mount Vernon, N.Y., 1950-52; writer, 1951—.

MEMBER: Society of Authors.

WRITINGS—All juveniles; with Tim Gidal, except as indicated; published by Pantheon, except as indicated: (Sole author) *Meier Shfeya: A Children's Village in Israel*, illustrated with photographs by T. Gidal, Behrman, 1950; *Follow the Reindeer* (Junior Literary Guild selection), 1959; *Sons of the Desert*, 1960; *Henrietta Szold: Mother of Ten Thousand*, Schocken, 1966.

"My Village" series: *My Village in Austria*, 1956; . . . *in India*, 1956; . . . *in Ireland*, 1957; . . . *in Yugoslavia*, 1957; . . . *in Norway*, 1958; . . . *in Israel*, 1959; . . . *in Greece*, 1960; . . . *in Switzerland*, 1961; . . . *in Italy*, 1962; . . . *in Spain*, 1962; . . . *in Denmark*, 1963; . . . *in England*, 1963; . . . *in Germany*, 1964; . . . *in Morocco*, 1964; . . . *in France*, 1965; . . . *in Japan*, 1966; . . . *in Finland*, 1966; . . . *in Brazil*, 1968; . . . *in Korea*, 1968; . . . *in Ghana*, 1969; . . . *in Thailand*, 1970; (sole author) . . . *in Portugal*, 1972; (sole author) . . . *in Hungary*, 1974.

Also author of documentary films "My Friend Chico," 1974, and "The Dancing Turtles," 1974, for children's television. Contributor to filmstrips.

AVOCATIONAL INTERESTS: Skiing and swimming, the theater and modern art.†

*   *   *

GIDAL, Tim N(achum)   1909-
(Nachum Gidal, Nahum Gidalewitsch)

PERSONAL: Original name, Ignaz Gidalewitsch; born May 18, 1909, in Munich, Germany; came to the United States, 1947; naturalized, 1953; son of Abraham (a manufacturer) and Pauline (Eiba) Gidalewitsch; married Sonia Epstein (a writer), July 4, 1944 (divorced, 1970); married Pia Lis, 1980; children: (first marriage) Peter. *Education:* Attended University of Munich, 1928-29, and University of Berlin, 1929-31; University of Basel, Ph.D., 1935. *Home:* 16 Nili St., Jerusalem, Israel. *Agent:* Witkin Gallery, 41 East 57th St., New York, N.Y. 10019. *Office:* Hebrew University of Jerusalem, Mount Scopus, Jerusalem, Israel.

CAREER: Photo-reporter and journalist for *Muenchner Illustrierte Zeitung* and *Woche* in Berlin, Germany, 1929-33, and for British and American magazines in Palestine, 1936-38; *Picture Post*, London, England, principal photo-reporter, 1938-40; free-lance photographer in Jerusalem, Palestine (now Israel), 1940-42, 1945-48, and free-lance writer, 1948-54; New School for Social Research, New York City, lecturer in visual communication, 1955-58; free-lance photographer and writer, 1958-70; Hebrew University of Jerusalem, Jerusalem, Israel, senior lecturer in visual communication, beginning 1971. Photographs have been exhibited in one-man shows at numerous galleries, including Israel Museum, Jerusalem, 1975, Photographers' Gallery, London, 1976, Witkin Gallery, New York City, 1978, Galerie Nagel, Berlin, 1979, and Gundlach Galerie, Hamburg, 1981. Editorial consultant to *Life*, 1953-54. *Military service:* British Eighth Army, reporter and chief photographer for *Parade* in North Africa and the Mediterranean, 1942-43, and with British Fourteenth Army in China, Burma, India, and the Middle East, 1943-44; became captain; received North Africa Star, Burma Star, and Italy Star.

MEMBER: Royal Photographic Society (fellow), Deutsche Gesellschaft fuer Photographie.

AWARDS, HONORS: Kalvin Prize, Israel Museum, 1980.

WRITINGS: (Under name Nachum Gidal; with Bertha Badt-Strauss) *Juedische kinder in Erez Israel,* Brandus, 1936; (illustrator with Robert Capa and Jerry Cooke) Isidor F. Stone, *This Is Israel,* Boni & Gaer, 1948; (illustrator) Sonia Gidal, *Meier Shfeya: A Children's Village in Israel,* Behrman, 1950; (under name Nahum Gidalewitsch) *Bildbericht und Presse: Ein Beitrag zur Geschichte und Organisation der illustrierten Zeitungen,* [Tuebingen], 1956; (with S. Gidal) *Follow the Reindeer* (Junior Literary Guild selection), Pantheon, 1959; (with S. Gidal) *Sons of the Desert,* Pantheon, 1960; (with S. Gidal) *Henrietta Szold: Mother of Ten Thousand,* Schocken, 1966; *Goldweights of the Ashanti: Nachum T. Gidal Collection,* Central Press, 1971; *Deutschland: Beginn des modernen Photojournalismus,* Bucher, 1972, translation by Maureen Oberli-Turner published as *Modern Photojournalism: Origin and Evolution, 1910-1933,* Macmillan, 1973.

"My Village" series; with S. Gidal; published by Pantheon: *My Village in Austria,* 1956; *. . . in India,* 1956; *. . . in Ireland,* 1957; *. . . in Yugoslavia,* 1957; *. . . in Norway,* 1958; *. . . in Israel,* 1959; *. . . in Greece,* 1960; *. . . in Switzerland,* 1961; *. . . in Italy,* 1962; *. . . in Spain,* 1962; *. . . in Denmark,* 1963; *. . . in England,* 1963; *. . . in Germany,* 1964; *. . . in Morocco,* 1964; *. . . in France,* 1965; *. . . in Japan,* 1966; *. . . in Finland,* 1966; *. . . in Brazil,* 1968; *. . . in Korea,* 1968; *. . . in Ghana,* 1969; *. . . in Thailand,* 1970.

Contributor to periodicals, including *Life, Pageant, Friends, Creative Camera, 35mm Photography,* and *Bildjournalist.*

SIDELIGHTS: Collections of photographs by Tim N. Gidal are housed at the Victoria and Albert Musuem in London, the Berlinische Galerie in Berlin, the Photo Museum in Munich, the Israel Museum in Jerusalem, the City Art Museum in Melbourne, the University of Texas at Austin, and the International Museum of Photography at the George Eastman House in Rochester, N.Y.

AVOCATIONAL INTERESTS: Biblical archaelogy, ancient history, theater, travel, nature, music.

BIOGRAPHICAL/CRITICAL SOURCES: Martha E. Ward and D. A. Marquardt, *Authors of Books for Young People,* Scarecrow, 1967; *Creative Camera,* September, 1974; *Camera,* January, 1975; *London Magazine,* December, 1976.†

*　　*　　*

GIDALEWITSCH, Nahum
　See GIDAL, Tim N(achum)

*　　*　　*

GILBERT, Julie Goldsmith
　See DANIEL, Julie Goldsmith

*　　*　　*

GILBERT, Sandra M(ortola)　1936-

PERSONAL: Born December 27, 1936, in New York, N.Y.; daughter of Alexis Joseph (a civil engineer) and Angela (Caruso) Mortola; married Elliot Lewis Gilbert (a professor of English), December 1, 1957; children: Roger, Katherine, Susanna. *Education:* Cornell University, B.A., 1957; New York University, M.A., 1961; Columbia University, Ph.D., 1968. *Office:* Department of English, Princeton University, Princeton, N.J. 08544.

CAREER: Queens College of the City University of New York, Flushing, lecturer in English, 1963-64, 1965-66; Sacramento State College (now California State University, Sacramento), lecturer in English, 1967-68; California State College (now California State University), Hayward, assistant professor of English, 1968-71; St. Mary's College, Moraga, Calif., lecturer in English, 1972; Indiana University at Bloomington, associate professor of English, 1973-75; University of California, Davis, 1975-85, began as associate professor, became professor of English; Princeton University, Princeton, N.J., professor of English, 1985—.

MEMBER: Modern Language Association of America.

WRITINGS: Shakespeare's "Twelfth Night," Thor Publishing, 1964; *Two Novels by E. M. Forster,* Thor Publishing, 1965; *D. H. Lawrence's "Sons and Lovers,"* Thor Publishing, 1965; *The Poetry of W. B. Yeats,* Thor Publishing, 1965; *Two Novels by Virginia Woolf,* Thor Publishing, 1966; *Acts of Attention: The Poems of D. H. Lawrence,* Cornell University Press, 1973; *In the Fourth World: Poems,* University of Alabama Press, 1978; (with Susan Gubar) *The Madwoman in the Attic: The Woman Writer and the Nineteenth-Century Literary Imagination,* Yale University Press, 1979; (editor with Gubar) *Shakespeare's Sisters: Feminist Essays on Women Poets,* Indiana University Press, 1979.

The Summer Kitchen: Poems, Heyeck, 1983; *Emily's Bread: Poems,* Norton, 1984; (editor with Gubar) *The Norton Anthology of Literature by Women,* Norton, 1985. Contributor to anthologies, including *Best Little Magazine Fiction,* 1971, *Bicentennial Poetry Anthology,* 1976, *Contemporary Women Poets,* 1978, and *The Poetry Anthology,* 1978. Contributor of fiction and poetry to *Mademoiselle, Poetry, Epoch, Nation, New Yorker,* and other magazines.

WORK IN PROGRESS: Blood Pressure, a collection of poems; *No Man's Land: The Place of the Woman Writer in the Twentieth Century,* with Susan Gubar.

SIDELIGHTS: In *The Madwoman in the Attic: The Woman Writer and the Nineteenth-Century Literary Imagination,* "Sandra Gilbert and Susan Gubar offer a bold new interpretation of the great 19th-century woman novelists, and in doing so they present the first pervasive case for the existence of a distinctly female imagination," writes Le Anne Schreiber in the *New York Times Book Review.* As Carolyn See notes in the *Los Angeles Times Book Review,* the authors examine how attitudes toward women and woman writers held by men and women alike shaped the literature of Jane Austen, Charlotte and Emily Bronte, Emily Dickinson, George Eliot, and Mary Shelley. According to See, Gilbert and Gubar reveal how these woman novelists used the "essentially destructive myth [that a woman writer was an aberration, 'the Devil Herself']—and their own fears about it—to create their own myths, their own world views."

Rosemary Ashton describes *The Madwoman in the Attic* in the *Times Literary Supplement* as a "purposefully written book essentially without a thesis," whose "authors exhaust the reader with . . . formidable but unconvincing rhetoric." She adds, "It is hard not to suspect that they found just what they were looking for, and equally hard to give acceptance to their 'findings.'" Yet, in a *Washington Post Book World* review, Carolyn G. Heilbrun writes, "At last, feminist criticism, no longer capable of being called a fad, is clearly and coherently mapped out.'' Heilbrun concludes, ''*The Madwoman in the Attic,* by revealing the past, will profoundly alter the present, making it possible, at last, for woman writers to create their own texts.''

BIOGRAPHICAL/CRITICAL SOURCES: Washington Post Book World, November 25, 1979; *New York Times Book Review,* December 9, 1979; *Los Angeles Times Book Review,* March 2, 1980; *Times Literary Supplement,* August 8, 1980.

*   *   *

GILMER, Ann
See ROSS, W(illiam) E(dward) D(aniel)

*   *   *

GLAHE, Fred R(ufus)   1934-

PERSONAL: Born June 30, 1934, in Chicago, Ill.; son of Frederick William (an executive) and Frances (Welch) Glahe; married Nancy S. Behrent, June 24, 1961. *Education:* Purdue University, B.S., 1957, M.S., 1962, Ph.D., 1964. *Religion:* Roman Catholic. *Home:* 3870 Cloverleaf Dr., Boulder, Colo. 80302. *Office:* Department of Economics, Campus Box 256, University of Colorado, Boulder, Colo. 80309.

CAREER: General Motors Corp., Allison Division, Indianapolis, Ind., engineer, 1957-61; Battelle Memorial Institute, Columbus, Ohio, research economist, 1964-65; University of Colorado, Boulder, assistant professor, 1965-68, associate professor, 1968-73, professor of economics, 1973—. *Military service:* U.S. Army, 1958; became second lieutenant. U.S. Army Reserve, 1958-64; became captain.

MEMBER: American Economic Association, Mont Pelerin Society, Philadelphia Society, Omicron Delta Epsilon, Phi Delta Theta.

WRITINGS: Macroeconomics: Theory and Policy, Harcourt, 1973, 3rd edition, 1985; *Implications of Regional Development in the Middle East for U.S. Trade, Capital Flows, and Balance of Payments,* International Research Center for Energy and Economic Development, 1977; *Microeconomics: Theory and Applications,* Harcourt, 1981.

Editor: *Readings in Econometric Theory,* Colorado Associated University Press, 1970; *The Collected Papers of Kenneth E. Boulding,* Volumes I-II: *Economics,* Colorado Associated University Press, 1971-72; *Guide to Graduate Study in Economics and Agricultural Economics in the U.S. and Canada,* American Economic Association, 1975; *Adam Smith and the Wealth of Nations: Bicentennial Essays, 1776-1976,* Colorado Associated University Press, 1978; *The American Family and the State,* Ballinger, 1985.

*   *   *

GLOVACH, Linda   1947-

PERSONAL: Surname is pronounced *Glo*-vack; born June 24, 1947, in Rockville Centre, N.Y.; daughter of John Maurice (a maintenance engineer) and Elvira (Martone) Glovach. *Education:* Attended Farmingdale University, 1965-66, Art Students League of New York, 1966-68, and California Art Center College of Design, 1969. *Politics:* Liberal. *Home and office:* 237 8th Ave. Sea Cliff, Long Island, N.Y.

CAREER: Free-lance artist. Has worked as a secretary and a hostess at Disneyland, Anaheim, Calif. Speaker in grade schools in Brentwood, N.Y., and local Long Island libraries and schools.

MEMBER: Defenders of Wildlife, Society for Animal Rights, Catholic Society for Welfare of Animals, Library Club of Bayshore.

AWARDS, HONORS: Art Students League of New York award for book illustration, 1970.

WRITINGS—Children's books, all self-illustrated; published by Prentice-Hall: *Hey, Wait for Me! I'm Amelia,* 1971; *The Cat and the Collector,* 1972; *The Little Witch's Black Magic Cookbook,* 1972; *The Little Witch's Black Magic Book of Disguises* (Junior Literary Guild selection), 1973; *The Rabbit and the Rainmaker,* 1974; *The Little Witch's Black Magic Book of Games,* 1974; *The Little Witch's Christmas Book,* 1974; *The Little Witch's Halloween Book,* 1975; *The Little Witch's Thanksgiving Book,* 1976; (with Charles Keller) *The Little Witch Presents a Monster: Joke Book,* 1976; *The Little Witch's Book of Yoga,* 1979.

The Little Witch's Birthday Book, 1981; *The Little Witch's Carnival Book,* 1982; *The Little Witch's Spring Holiday Book,* 1983; *The Little Witch's Valentine Book,* 1984. Also author of *The Little Witch's Dinosaur Book.*

WORK IN PROGRESS: Two novels for teenagers, *Laura's Story* and *The Sugar-Coated Kid;* a picture book, *Beebo and His Friends;* another ''Little Witch'' book; research on San Juan Capistrano mission in California, for a picture book for children.

SIDELIGHTS: Linda Glovach has lived a year in Haiti and the Virgin Islands. *Avocational interests:* Biking, running, traveling, gardening, and raising cats and Afghan hounds.

*   *   *

GODFREY, Michael A.   1940-

PERSONAL: Born June 29, 1940, in Washington, D.C.; son of Arthur M. (an entertainer) and Mary (Bourke) Godfrey. *Education:* University of North Carolina, earned B.S. degree. *Religion:* ''Nature.'' *Home:* 108 High St., Carrboro, N.C. 27510.

CAREER: Air-Care, Inc., Rocky Mount, N.C., manager and commercial pilot, 1967; Peat, Marwich, Mitchell & Co., Washington, D.C., financial consultant, 1969-70; University of North Carolina at Chapel Hill, director of systems design, 1970-76; free-lance writer and nature photographer, working in print and video, and video producer, 1976—. *Military service:* U.S. Air Force, 1963-66; served in Asia.

AWARDS, HONORS: CINE Golden Eagle, for film ''A Closer Look.''

WRITINGS: A Closer Look (also see below), Sierra Club Books, 1975; *Winter Birds of the Carolinas and Nearby States,* Blair, 1976; *Sierra Club Naturalists Guide to the Piedmont,* Sierra Club Books, 1980; (and producer) ''The Awards in the Visual Arts'' (television script), Public Broadcasting Systems, 1983.

Also author and director of film ''A Closer Look,'' based on book of the same title.

WORK IN PROGRESS: ''Birds of North America: A Video Guide,'' for video cassette.

SIDELIGHTS: Michael A. Godfrey writes: ''My personal and professional orientation is toward seeing and expressing the life processes which are close at hand, accessible, but easily overlooked.''

AVOCATIONAL INTERESTS: White-water canoeing, rock climbing, running, American literature.

*   *   *

GOERING, Helga
  See WALLMANN, Jeffrey M(iner)

*   *   *

GOLDSTEIN, Jeffrey H(askell)   1942-

PERSONAL: Born August 11, 1942, in Norwalk, Conn.; son of Robert and Sylvia (Schwartz) Goldstein; married Helene Feinberg, August 22, 1973 (divorced). *Education:* University of Connecticut, B.A., 1964; Boston University, M.S., 1966; Ohio State University, Ph.D., 1969. *Religion:* Jewish. *Home:* 419 Iven Ave., Wayne, Pa. 19087. *Office:* Department of Psychology, Temple University, Philadelphia, Pa. 19122.

CAREER: Temple University, Philadelphia, Pa., assistant professor, 1969-72, associate professor, 1972-78, professor of psychology, 1978—. Visiting associate professor at University of Massachusetts, 1973-74. Consultant to National Science Foundation, U.S. Department of Labor, and Canada Council.

MEMBER: International Society for Research on Aggression (fellow), American Psychological Association (fellow), Society of Experimental Social Psychology, Society for the Psychological Study of Social Issues, Authors League of America.

WRITINGS: (Editor with Paul E. McGhee and contributor) *The Psychology of Humor,* Academic Press, 1972; *Aggression and Crimes of Violence,* Oxford University Press, 1975; (contributor) Patricia Golden, editor, *The Research Experience,* F. T. Peacock, 1976; (contributor) Antony J. Chapman and Hugh C. Foot, editors, *It's a Funny Thing, Humor,* Pergamon, 1977; (editor and contributor) *Sports, Games, and Play,* Wiley, 1977; *Social Psychology,* Academic Press, 1978; (editor and contributor) *Sports Violence,* Springer-Verlag, 1983; (with McGhee) *Handbook of Humor Research,* Springer-Verlag, 1983.

Contributor to more than a dozen psychology, sociology, anthropology, and communications journals. Member of editorial board of *Journal of Applied Social Psychology.*

WORK IN PROGRESS: Reporting Science: The Case of Aggression.

SIDELIGHTS: Jeffrey H. Goldstein writes: ''As an experimental social pschologist, I believe my work should deal with important aspects of behavior, such as aggression and positive emotions, and some effort should be made by scientists to communicate their work to the interested public. Therefore I have written, and continue to write, trade books as well as textbooks.''

*   *   *

GOOCH, Stan(ley Alfred)   1932-

PERSONAL: Born June 13, 1932, in London, England; son of Albert Alfred (a clerk) and Annie Emily (Gatty) Zuch; married Ruth Senior, April 1, 1961 (divorced, 1965). *Education:* King's College, London, B.A. (honors), 1955; Birkbeck College, London, B.Sc. (honors), 1963. *Politics:* None. *Religion:* None. *Home and office:* 11 Crossfield Rd., London N.W.3, England.

Agent: David Higham Associates, 5-8 Lower John St., Golden Sq., London WlR 4HA, England.

CAREER: Teacher and head of modern language department at boys' school in London, England, 1958-61; teacher of maladjusted children at special schools in London, 1961-64; senior research psychologist for National Children's Bureau, 1964-68; free-lance writer, 1968—. Lecturer in psychology at Hatfield College of Technology, 1965, and at Brunel University, 1968.

WRITINGS—Published by Wildwood House, except as indicated: *Four Years On,* Humanities, 1966; *Total Man,* Allen Lane, 1972, Holt, 1973; *Personality and Evolution,* 1973; *The Neanderthal Question,* 1977; *The Paranormal,* 1978, John M. Fontana, 1979; *Guardians of the Ancient Wisdom,* 1979, John M. Fontana, 1980.

The Double Helix of the Mind, 1980; *The Secret Life of Humans,* Dent, 1981; *Creatures from Inner Space,* Rider, 1984. Contributor to education and psychology journals.

WORK IN PROGRESS: Generation Five, a novel.

SIDELIGHTS: Stan Gooch writes: ''I became a writer out of a deep dissatisfaction with current (psychological, cultural, religious), accounts of the nature, evolution, and potential of man. Also, although successful in my earlier career, I had never found a job which could satisfy me. I have now been a full-time writer (and writing consultant and journalist) for ten years, and the thought of ever being anything else has never entered my head. My greatest satisfaction has been in seeing my allegedly wild ideas and my name increasingly appearing in books by significant authors (Colin Wilson, Lyall Watson, Arthur Janov, etc.).''

*   *   *

GOODWIN, Craufurd D(avid) W(ycliffe)   1934-

PERSONAL: Born May 23, 1934, in Montreal, Quebec, Canada; son of George and Roma (Stewart) Goodwin; married Nancy Sanders, June 7, 1958. *Education:* McGill University, B.A., 1955; Duke University, Ph.D., 1958. *Home address:* P.O. Box 957, Hillsborough, N.C. 27278. *Office:* Department of Economics, Duke University, Durham, N.C. 27706.

CAREER: Courtauld's Canada Ltd., Montreal, Quebec, economic research assistant, summer, 1955; University of Windsor, Windsor, Ontario, lecturer in economics, 1958-59; Duke University, Durham, N.C., visiting assistant professor of economics and executive secretary of Commonwealth Studies Center, 1959-60; Australian National University, Canberra, honorary research fellow, 1960-61; York University, Toronto, Ontario, assistant professor of economics, 1961-62; Duke University, assistant professor, 1962-63, associate professor, 1963-68, professor of economics, 1968—, assistant to provost, 1962-64, assistant provost, 1964-68, vice-provost for International Studies, 1969-71, director of International Programs, 1969-71. Officer in Charge of European and International Affairs, Ford Foundation, 1971-77. *Member:* American Economic Association, Economic History Association, Canadian Economics Association.

WRITINGS—All published by Duke University Press, except as indicated: *Canadian Economic Thought,* 1961; *Economic Enquiry in Australia,* 1966; (with W. B. Hamilton and Kenneth Robinson) *A Decade of the Commonwealth: 1955-1964,* 1966; (editor with I. B. Holley) *The Transfer of Ideas,* 1968; (editor with R.D.C. Black and A. W. Coat) *The Marginal Revolution in Economics*, 1973; *The Image of Australia*, 1974; (editor and contributor) *Exhortation and Controls: The Search for a Wage-Price Policy, 1945-71*, Brookings Institution, 1975; *Energy Policy in Perspective*, Brookings Institution, 1981; *Absence of Decision*, Institute of International Education, 1983; *Fondness and Frustration*, Institute of International Education, 1984. Editor, *History of Political Economy*.

* * *

GOODWIN, Suzanne
(Suzanne Ebel; Cecily Shelbourne, a pseudonym)

PERSONAL: Born in London, England; daughter of Clement (a director) and Charlotte (a musician; maiden name, Collins) Ebel; married John Goodwin (publicity director for National Theatre), October, 1948; children: Marigold Goodwin Sebastian, James, Timothy. *Education:* Educated at Roman Catholic convent schools in England and Belgium. *Home:* 52-A Digby Mansions, Hammersmith Bridge Rd., London W6 9DF, England. *Agent:* Curtis Brown Ltd., 1 Craven Hill, London W.2, England.

CAREER: Former journalist for *London Times;* Young & Rubicam, New York, N.Y., public relations director in London office, 1950-72; full-time writer, 1972—. *Awards, honors:* Best Romantic Novel of the Year award from the Romantic Novelists Association, 1964, for *Journey from Yesterday.*

*WRITINGS—*Under name Suzanne Goodwin; all novels: *The Winter Spring*, Bodley Head, 1978; *The Winter Sisters*, Bodley Head, 1980; *Emerald*, Magnum Publications, 1980; *Julia's Sister*, Severn House Publishers, 1981; *Floodtide*, Sphere Books, 1983; (with Jill Bennett) *Godfrey, a Special Time Remembered*, Hodder & Stoughton, 1983.

Under name Suzanne Ebel; romantic novels, except as indicated: *Journey from Yesterday*, Collins, 1964; *The Half Enchanted*, Collins, 1965; *The Love Campaign*, Collins, 1966; *A Perfect Stranger*, Collins, 1967; *Name in Lights*, Collins, 1967; *A Most Auspicious Star*, Collins, 1968; *Somersault*, Collins, 1969; *Portrait of Jill*, Collins, 1970; *Dear Kate*, Collins, 1970; *To Seek a Star*, Collins, 1971; *The Family Feeling*, Collins, 1972; *Girl by the Sea*, Collins, 1973; *Guide to the Cotswolds* (nonfiction), Ward, Lock, 1973; *Music in Winter*, Collins, 1974; *A Grove of Olives*, Collins, 1975; *River Voices*, Collins, 1976; *London's Riverside* (nonfiction), Luscombe, 1976; *The Double Rainbow*, Collins, 1977; *A Rose in the Heather*, Collins, 1978.

Under pseudonym Cecily Shelbourne: *Stage of Love*, Putnam, 1977.

Author of "Chords and Dischords" (radio play), aired by British Broadcasting Corp. in 1975. Contributor of stories to magazines.

WORK IN PROGRESS: A novel, set in wartime London and featuring the American Eagle Squadron, entitled *Sisters.*

SIDELIGHTS: Suzanne Goodwin writes: "I have written since I was a teenager. I write regularly every day, sometimes for as long as nine hours. I feel that writing has something strongly in common with painting: it catches the mood, the character, the flavour of life. We own a flat in the south of France, I speak fluent French, and the French influence of art and nature has an effect on my writing, as the English atmosphere does."

BIOGRAPHICAL/CRITICAL SOURCES: Times (London), February 25, 1983.

* * *

GORDON, Donald Ramsay 1929-

PERSONAL: Born September 14, 1929, in Toronto, Ontario, Canada; son of Donald and Maisie Gordon; married December 21, 1953; wife's name Helen Elizabeth (an anesthetist); children: Donald John, Bruce, Keith. *Education:* Queen's University, B.A. (with honors), 1953; University of Toronto, M.A., 1955; London School of Economics and Political Science, graduate study, 1956-63. *Home:* 134 Iroquois Place, Waterloo, Ontario, Canada N2L 2S5.

CAREER: Canadian Press, Toronto, Ontario, writer and filing editor, 1949-55; *Financial Post,* Toronto, assistant editor, 1955-56; affiliated with Clyde Brothers Circus, Oklahoma City, Okla., 1956; European correspondent in London, England for Canadian Broadcasting Corp., 1957-63; University of Calgary, Calgary, Alberta, assistant professor, 1963-65, associate professor of political science, 1965-66; University of Waterloo, Waterloo, Ontario, assistant professor, 1966-67, associate professor of political science, 1967-69, associate professor in Faculty of Arts, part-time, 1969-70; Earthrise, Inc., Ottawa, Ontario, director and project coordinator, 1970; University of Waterloo, associate professor of political science, part-time, 1970-71, associate professor in Arts 100 Project, 1971-72, associate professor of Arts 100 communications, 1972-75; consultant, 1975—; Image Corporation, Waterloo, chief writer, 1981—.

Member, Royal Commission on the Status of Women in Canada, 1967; research consultant to Senate Committee on the Mass Media in Canada, 1969-70, and to Royal Commission on Violence in the Communications Industry, 1976-77. Co-host of "20,000,000 Questions" on CBC Television, 1966-67; presenter of arctic film, "The Edge of Evolution," 1978.

MEMBER: Association of Canadian Radio and Television Artists, University Film Association, Kropotkin Institute (director, 1960—). *Awards, honors:* Ford Foundation communications fellowship, 1954; International Institute of Education travel and research award, 1962-63; Canada Council research award, 1969; Kropotkin Institute Prize, 1981.

WRITINGS: Language, Logic, and the Mass Media, Holt, 1966; (contributor) J. King Gordon, editor, *Canada as a Middle Power*, Canadian Institute of International Affairs, 1966; *The New Literacy*, University of Toronto Press, 1971; *The Rock Candy Bandits* (juvenile), McBain, 1984; *Fineswine*, McBain, 1984. Writer of pamphlets and reports, including "Mass Media and the Rule of Law in Canada," report for Task Force on Government Information, 1969. Contributor to *Canadian Commentator, MacLean's, Toronto Globe and Mail, Times, Spectator, New Statesman, Financial Post,* and other publications, and to television in Canada, the United States, and England.

WORK IN PROGRESS: The 10th Summit, a novel; "The Canadian Communications System," a research paper on mass media policies, systems, and practices in Canada.

SIDELIGHTS: Donald Ramsay Gordon told *CA:* "A relatively uneventful male menopause has allowed me to discover the right stuff in human sexuality, most notably nuzzles and hugs. As a consequence I am abandoning research into alternate philosophies to replace empiricism in favour of joyous swoops into the arms of selected maidens. A small monograph on this subject and its effects on medicare is contemplated. I have also discovered with publication (at last) of a novel that Graham Greene is *absolutely right* in his theory that book editors hate words, especially long ones.''

*   *   *

GORDON, Doreen
  See CHARD, Judy

*   *   *

GORDON, Lesley
  See ELLIOTT, Lesley

*   *   *

GORMLEY, Gerard (Joseph)   1931-

PERSONAL: Born June 15, 1931, in Boston, Mass.; son of James Joseph (an automobile dealer) and Helen L. (Eagan) Gormley; married Patricia M. Cieminski, November, 1953 (divorced, 1971); children: Pamela K., Patrick G., Sean J. *Education:* Northeastern University, A.E.E., 1961. *Politics:* ''Independent.'' *Religion:* ''Independent.'' *Agent:* Boston Literary Agency, P.O. Box 1472, Manchester, Mass. 01944.

CAREER: Ewen Knight Corp., Natick, Mass., publications manager, 1955-61; Impact Advertising, Inc., Boston, Mass., founder and president, 1961-70; Think, Inc., Manchester, Mass., president, 1970—. *Military service:* U.S. Navy, submarine duty, 1951-55.

MEMBER: Authors Guild, Authors League of America, Ocean Research and Education Society, American Management Associations, American Marketing Association.

AWARDS, HONORS: National advertising effectiveness award from United Technical Publishers, 1968.

WRITINGS: The Doll (novel), Pinnacle Books, 1977; *A Dolphin Summer* (fiction based on fact), Taplinger, 1985.

WORK IN PROGRESS: Night of the Fang, a novel of terror and suspense in a small town ravaged by packs of feral dogs; *Swiftly Swim My Brothers, Laughing,* a fictional account of life in a free dolphin tribe; *The Dolphin Chronicles,* a novel about an ocean swimmer who denounces humanity and lives with a tribe of dolphins; *The Woman within the Wall,* the ''haunting tale of a nineteenth-century Irish beauty whose spirit transcends the grave to seek vengeance against a contemporary Anglo-American family for wrongs committed 150 years earlier; *Untitled,* a novel about child/adult sexuality and its impact on a middle-class American family (based largely on fact).''

SIDELIGHTS: Gerard Gormley told *CA:* ''Many writers work only three to four hours daily, but I have difficulty limiting myself to an eight-hour day. For me, writing is more addiction than occupation.

''Although my interests are varied, I'm a thorough researcher, perhaps overly so for a novelist. I'm a plotter, but not a plodder. I usually chapter-block each novel to some degree, but if one of my characters has a better idea, I'm always open to suggestion.

''Upon completion of a novel in 1978, I purposely avoided plotting my next work and embarked on a subconscious binge. For six months, I wrote whatever came spiraling out of my mind—bits of phrasing, scenes, characterizations, snatches of dialogue, childhood memories, etc. My notes filled more than

five hundred pages. Despite glimmers of an underlying theme, I had no idea whether the notes had the makings of a story. Still, I liked much of the material. I grouped the notes into categories, then shelved the material in favor of a more carefully (for me) plotted book. *Untitled* refuses to remain on the shelf for long, though. Off and on over the past six years, I've repeatedly reworked the material, and now have a rough draft of what could be the most important novel I've ever written. Topic: our national worship of youth, the sexual problems it causes, and the hypocrisy surrounding it.''

AVOCATIONAL INTERESTS: ''Reading good books,'' whale watching, ocean swimming, ocean rowing, bicycling, cross-country skiing.

*   *   *

GOTTFRIED, Martin   1933-

PERSONAL: Born October 9, 1933, in New York, N.Y.; son of Isidore (a book dealer) and Rachel (Weitz) Gottfried; married Judith Houchins (marriage ended); married Jane Lahr (an artist), April 15, 1968; children: Maya (daughter). *Education:* Columbia University, B.A., 1955, attended Law School, 1955-57. *Politics:* Independent. *Religion:* None. *Home:* 17 East 96th St., New York, N.Y. 10028. *Agent:* William Morris Agency, 1350 Avenue of the Americas, New York, N.Y. 10019.

CAREER: Village Voice, New York City, music critic, 1960-62; Fairchild Publications, New York City, editor, 1962-63; drama critic for *Women's Wear Daily,* 1963-72; drama critic for *New York Post,* 1973-77, *Saturday Review,* 1977—, and *Cue/New York,* 1978—. Also drama critic for WPAT radio. *Military service:* U.S. Army, Military Intelligence, 1957-59. *Member:* New York Drama Critics Circle, Dramatists Guild.

AWARDS, HONORS: Rockefeller Foundation grant, 1966-67, 1967-68; George Jean Nathan Award for Dramatic Criticism, 1968, for *A Theater Divided.*

WRITINGS: A Theater Divided, Little, Brown, 1968; *Opening Nights,* Putnam, 1969; *Broadway Musicals,* Abrams, 1979; *Jed Harris: The Curse of Genius,* Little, Brown, 1983. Also author of a play, ''The Director,'' 1972. Contributor to national magazines.

WORK IN PROGRESS: Several plays.

SIDELIGHTS: Martin Gottfried has been covering the Broadway beat since 1963 for such periodicals as *Women's Wear Daily, New York Post,* and *Saturday Review.* He is an unabashed fan of the musical in particular; he saw his first, ''Oklahoma!,'' as a young New Yorker and years later, as Gottfried tells *Chicago Tribune* columnist Richard Christiansen, ''I get the same kick in the pants when I hear that overture or listen to the walk-out music. I'm 10 years old again and still getting a bang out of it.''

Gottfried's admiration for what he calls America's ''one major contribution to the theatre'' has resulted in his work *Broadway Musicals.* A lavish, oversized compilation of historical information, criticism, and summary, illustrated with nearly four hundred photographs from every era of the musical, Gottfried's book ''looks like the ultimate coffee table object,'' notes Christiansen, ''but [the author], who says he only wants to write 'book books,' has tried to make his text a lot more than gray wrapping paper for the color photographs.'' Indeed, Gottfried's devotion to musicals does not affect his view of the modern Broadway scene. ''Producers today are becoming merchandisers, which I do not like. They're more concerned about their television commericals for the shows than they are about the shows themselves,'' he states to Christiansen.

"Still, even with these gloomy thoughts," says Christiansen, "Gottfried manages to be enthusiastic about almost any aspect of the Broadway musicals he loves." Says the author: "Writing the book was an education for me, and I guarantee that anyone who reads the chapter on lyric writing will get an education, too. Just think of that great mystery of making the words match the music. . . . And the wonder is that you even have some composers like [Irving] Berlin and Cole Porter and [Stephen] Sondheim who write the words *and* the music. That's absolutely amazing!''

Another of Gottfried's Broadway-related books centers on the life and career of one of the most respected—and hated— producer/directors of the 1920s and 1930s, Jed Harris. According to Jonathan Yardley's *Washington Post* review of the author's *Jed Harris: The Curse of Genius,* Gottfried's subject "pioneered what quickly became the Broadway style, described by his biographer as 'clever, tense, urban, dynamic and, above all, contemporary.'" Associated with such landmark productions as "The Front Page," "The Royal Family," and "Our Town," Harris was known not only for his almost unerring instinct for matching the right talent with the right material, but also for his legendary hot temper and "compulsive meanness," as Yardley puts it.

For instance, Yardley cites Gottfried's anecdotes in *Jed Harris* relating to the producer's marriages: "Harris' first . . . was in 1925, to Anita Greenbaum; as they drove away from the ceremony he said, 'Well you got what you wanted. Doesn't it make you happy?' His second was in 1938, to Louise Platt: 'On the trip back to California, Jed told her how sorry he was that he had married her.' His third was in 1957, to Bebe Allen, who ended it a few months later; the lipstick message she left on the mirror for Harris can't be printed in a family newspaper." Playwright George S. Kaufman, according to the author, so despised Harris that he "said when he died he wanted to be cremated and have his ashes thrown in Jed Harris' face." The book, says Yardley, "is fascinating less as a show-biz biography than as the chronicle of a man who spent virtually his entire adult life bringing gratuitous grief to others and destroying himself in the process." In a *New York Times Book Review* piece on *Jed Harris,* the actor/producer/director John Houseman recalls the subject's "notorious magnetism, which he exploited and abused and which played such a vital part in his theatrical activity." Thus, "I have known actors who had every reason to loathe and despise him but who, years later, spoke with awe and gratitude of his intuitive understanding of their acting problems. . . . I have known others who appeared in the same productions and feel only hatred for him."

Houseman concludes his review by "wishing that more space had been devoted to an investigation of the creative 'genius' who, in his brief and brilliant career, left an indelible mark upon the theater of his time and less to the neurotic eccentricities through which he destroyed himself." Yardley also notes the author's concentration on Harris's stormy personal life, but nonetheless finds the book "oddly compulsive reading. . . . [*Jed Harris* is] filled with one vividly recalled horror story after another; though some may find [the work] to be merely one long sick joke, others will be, as rather against my better judgment I was, hugely amused by it."

BIOGRAPHICAL/CRITICAL SOURCES: Time, November 5, 1967; *Chicago Tribune,* December 4, 1979; Martin Gottfried,

Jed Harris: The Curse of Genius, Little, Brown, 1983; *Washington Post,* December 28, 1983; *New York Times Book Review,* February 5, 1984.†

*   *   *

GOVINDA, Anagarika Brahmacari 1898- (Lama Anagarika Brahmacari Govinda)

PERSONAL: Born May 17, 1898, in Waldheim, Germany; now a citizen of India. *Education:* Studied at University of Freiburg, University of Naples, University of Cagliari, and at Buddhist monasteries in Ceylon. *Home:* 122 Lomita Dr., Mill Valley, Calif. 94941.

CAREER: Helped to organize Buddhist movements in Europe, Ceylon, Burma, and India; former general secretary, International Buddhist University Association; lecturer at Visva-Bharati University, Santiniketan, West Bengal, India, for several years; Patna University, Patna, India, readership lecturer, 1936- 37; became a personal pupil of Tomo Geshe Rimpoche; spent several years in Tibet, eventually joining the bKah-rgyud-pa order; became lama; former acharya (head) of Buddhist order of Arya Maitreya Mandala, with centers in India, Europe, and America.

WRITINGS: Gedanken und Gesichte (title means "Thoughts and Visions"), Pandora (Dresden), 1926; *Rhythmische Aphorismen* (title means "Rhythmic Aphorisms"), Pandora, 1927; *Abhidhammattha-Sangaha* (a compendium of Buddhist philosophy), Benares Verlag (Munich), 1930; *The Psycho-Cosmic Symbolism of the Buddhist Stupa,* [Santiniketan], India, 1935, Dharma, 1976; *Art and Meditation,* Roerich Centre of Art and Culture (Allahabad), 1936; *The Psychological Attitude of Early Buddhist Philosophy and Its Systematic Representation according to Abhidhamma Tradition* (readership lectures at Patna University, 1936-37), Allahabad Law Journal Press, c. 1937, Dutton, 1961; *Some Aspects of Stupa Symbolism,* Allahabad & London (Kitabistan), 1940; (author of introductory essay and commentaries) *The Tibetan Book of the Dead,* Oxford University Press, 1947, revised and enlarged edition, 1965; *Grundlagen tibetischer Mystik, nach den esoterischen Lehren des Grossen Mantra Om Mani Padme Hum,* Rascher (Zurich), 1957, translation published as *Foundations of Tibetan Mysticism, according to the Great Mantra Om Mani Padma Hum,* Dutton, 1959.

Mandala: Meditationgedichte und Betrachtungen, Origo Verlag (Zurich), 1960, 2nd enlarged edition, 1961; (author of Buddhist section) *Die Antwort der Religionen* (title means "The Answer of Religions"), Szczesny Verlag (Munich), 1964; *The Way of the White Clouds: A Buddhist Pilgrim in Tibet,* Hutchinson, 1966, Shambala, 1970; *Creative Meditation and Multidimensional Consciousness,* Quest Books, 1976; *Pictures of India and Tibet,* Irisiana, 1978; *The Inner Structure of the I Ching: The Book of Transformations,* Weatherhill, 1981; *Auf den Wege zur Freiheit* (title means "On the Way to Freedom"), [Munich], 1983. Also author of *The Fundamentals of Buddhism,* published in German, Altmann (Leipzig), 1920. Contributor to other works on Buddhist thought, art, and tradition; contributor to journals in the United States, Europe, and India.

WORK IN PROGRESS: A book, *Paintings and Poetry.*

SIDELIGHTS: Several of Anagarika Govinda's books have been issued in translation in Germany, Japan, France, Spain, Argentina, Sweden, Holland, Italy, and other countries.

GOVINDA, Lama Anagarika Brahmacari
  See GOVINDA, Anagarika Brahmacari

*   *   *

GRAHAM, Carlotta
  See WALLMANN, Jeffrey M(iner)

*   *   *

GRANBY, Milton
  See WALLMANN, Jeffrey M(iner)

*   *   *

GRAY, Martin 1926-

PERSONAL: Born April 27, 1926, in Warsaw, Poland; came to United States in 1947, naturalized citizen, 1952; son of Henry (an industrialist) and Ida (Feld) Gray; married Dina Cult, December 12, 1959 (died October 3, 1970); married Virginia Eraerts, March 6, 1976; children: (first marriage) Nicole, Suzanne, Charles, Richard (all died October 3, 1970); (second marriage) Barbara. *Education:* Educated in Poland. *Home:* Les Barons, 83141 Tanneron, France. *Office:* Dina Gray Foundation, 8 rue de Babylone, 75007 Paris, France.

CAREER: Wholesale antique dealer in New York, N.Y., 1950-60; agriculturalist in Tanneron, France, 1960-70; founder and president of Dina Gray Foundation, Paris, France, 1971—; writer and lecturer, 1971—. Founder of human rights movement ''The Human House.'' *Military service:* Warsaw ghetto fighter, 1939-43; arrested and sentenced to concentration camps, including Treblinka, from which he escaped. Soviet Army, 1944-46; became captain; participated in the battle of Berlin; received numerous decorations, including Order of Alexandre Nevsky, Order of the Fatherland's War, Order of the Red Star, Medal of Berlin, and Medal of Victory.

AWARDS, HONORS: Dag Hammarskjold prize, 1973, for *Au nom de tous les miens.*

WRITINGS: (With Max Gallo) *Au nom de tous les miens* (autobiography), Laffont, 1971, translation by Anthony White published as *For Those I Loved,* Little, Brown, 1972; *Le Livre de la vie: Pour trouver le bonheur, le courage, et l'espoir,* Laffont, 1973, translation published as *A Book of Life: To Find Happiness, Courage, and Hope,* Seabury, 1975; *Les Forces de la vie,* Laffont, 1975, translation published as *The Force of Life,* New American Library, 1978; *Les Pensees de notre vie* (title means ''Thoughts of Our Life''), Laffont, 1977; *La Vie renaitra de la nuit* (title means ''Life Arises Out of Night''), Laffont, 1977.

Le Nouveau Livre (title means ''The New Book''), Laffont, 1980; *J'ecris aux hommes de demain* (title means ''I Write to the Men of Tomorrow''), Laffont, 1983. Writer of a weekly column in *Bonne Soiree* (women's magazine).

SIDELIGHTS: Martin Gray's books express his response to the tragedies which have marred his life. After losing his family in the Warsaw ghetto and the concentration camps of Poland during World War II, he established a new life for himself in the United States and later on his estate in France, seeking happiness through his relationship with his wife and children. When all of them perished in a forest fire in 1970, he refused to submit to despair, deciding instead to establish the Dina Gray Foundation as a memorial to his wife. The foundation's

goal is to fight against natural disasters, fires, and pollution which menace the life of man just as war has in the past.

In an interview with Marci Shatzman of the *Philadelphia Bulletin,* Gray related the origins of his philosophy. ''During the war I knew I had to survive. . . . It was not so much my life that was precious, but life itself. That is what my father told me, and I understood. I remember, before my father was shot, he told me, 'Today we must kill. But remember life. Life is precious and you must give it.' I think this is the secret. . . . I try to live by those words. There is some of the beast and some of the man in all of us,'' he concluded. ''The secret is to remain a man among wolves.''

When asked about coping with personal tragedy, Gray told *CA:* ''I am not a philosopher, a scientist, nor a saint. I am simply a man who has had lots of experiences, and I've learned not from books but from life. I know no recipes. I know no infallible methods. When it comes to such serious questions to such grave problems as courage, hope, and happiness, no miracles. In fact the only, the only true miracle, is Life, and it is in life that one must find the resources that give the means to achieve courage, hope, and happiness. What is important in our life is to know oneself. To learn to utilize the unsuspected forces that are in us and to share them. Herein is the true meaning of man's life. A life reduced to itself is no life. It is an amputation of life.

''Unselfishly we must turn toward others. Not to be an adversary but a friend. It is not always easy but it is the only way finally to be at peace with oneself.

''Life is always to go beyond.''

MEDIA ADAPTATIONS: Martin Gray's autobiography, *For Those I Loved,* was filmed as an eight-hour television series and a theatrical film, starring Michael York.

BIOGRAPHICAL/CRITICAL SOURCES: Martin Gray, *Au nom de tous les miens,* Laffont, 1971; *Philadelphia Bulletin,* February 7, 1974; *Authors in the News,* Volume I, Gale, 1976.

*   *   *

GRAYSON, Richard (A.) 1951-

PERSONAL: Born June 4, 1951, in Brooklyn, N.Y.; son of Daniel (a businessman) and Marilyn (a nutritionist; maiden name, Sarrett) Grayson. *Education:* Brooklyn College of the City University of New York, B.A., 1973, M.F.A., 1976; Richmond College of the City University of New York, M.A., 1975. *Home:* 2732 South University Dr., Davie, Fla. 33328.

CAREER: Fiction Collective, Brooklyn, N.Y., editorial assistant, 1975-77; Long Island University, Brooklyn, lecturer in English, 1975-78; City University of New York, lecturer in English at Kingsborough Community College, Brooklyn, 1978-81, and Brooklyn College, Brooklyn, 1979-81; Broward Community College, Fort Lauderdale, Fla., instructor in English, 1981-83; full-time writer, 1983—.

MEMBER: Authors Guild, Authors League of America, Associated Writing Programs, Mensa, Brooklyn College Alumni Association (member of board of directors, 1973—), Phi Beta Kappa.

AWARDS, HONORS: Ottillie Grebanier Drama Award, Brooklyn College, 1973; scholarships from National Arts Club, 1977, to study at Bread Loaf Writer's Conference, and from Santa Cruz Writing Conference, 1978; fellowships from Virginia Center for the Creative Arts, 1979 and 1981, MacDowell Colony, 1980, Florida Arts Council, 1982, and Millay Colony for the Arts, 1984.

WRITINGS: Disjointed Fictions, X Archives, 1978; *With Hitler in New York and Other Stories*, Taplinger, 1979; *Lincoln's Doctor's Dog and Other Stories*, White Ewe, 1982; *I Brake for Delmore Schwartz*, Zephyr Press, 1983; *Eating at Arby's: The South Florida Stories* (pamphlet), Grinning Idiot Press, 1983.

Contributor of short stories to more than one hundred magazines, including *Epoch, Texas Quarterly, Confrontation, Shenandoah, Carleton Miscellany*, and *Transatlantic Review*.

WORK IN PROGRESS: An Unauthorized Autobiography; a collection of short stories, *Money in Escarola: The West Side Stories;* a novel, *Modern Demographics*.

SIDELIGHTS: Unconventional, imaginative, and possessed of an offbeat sense of humor, Richard Grayson is the author of several collections of short stories that examine life from a perspective many critics find refreshingly different. Originally published in a variety of small magazines, his stories "are full of insanity, nutty therapists, cancerous relatives, broken homes, fiction workshops, youthful theatricals at Catskill bungalow colonies and the morbid wizardry of telephone-answering machines," notes Ivan Gold in the *New York Times Book Review*. Some also feature such unlikely "characters" as the voice of the cold that "assassinated" President William Henry Harrison in 1841 and Sparky, Abraham Lincoln's doctor's puppy, who grows up to become a successful politician and lecturer. (The latter story was inspired by an article Grayson once read that stated most recent best-sellers have dealt with presidents, diseases, or animals—hence, "Lincoln's Doctor's Dog.") As Mark Bernheim observes in *Israel Today*, "Grayson is able to create a full range of masks from behind which the artist peers out to make his criticisms of artificial modern life."

Commenting in *Best Sellers*, Nicholas J. Loprete, Jr., also asserts that Grayson's stories "display a versatility which commands attention. . . . [The author] can parody human excess and human frailty, parent-child relationships, and recreate a 1960's scene with poignancy. . . . He is serious and comic, charming, given to outrageous puns, and a sharp-eyed observer of and participant in Life's absurdities."

In short, declares Lynne Gagnon in the *Ventura County News*, "Richard Grayson gets the prize for making us laugh about the ridiculous insaneness surrounding our lives. But the award is two-fold; he also forces us to examine people and what they do to us. And more importantly what we do to them."

Grayson himself once told *CA:* "Writing has been the primary way I've defined myself; at first it was therapy, but now, I hope, it has become something more. I see the writer's first job as giving the lowdown on himself, and through himself, on humanity. As I reluctantly leave the longest adolescence in history, I find myself—happily—becoming less self-conscious, more patient. I would like to avoid becoming pompous, but I'm afraid statements like these are among the mine fields on the road to absurd self-importance. I have a lot to learn about writing (and other things)."

Even though Grayson is, according to Bernheim and a few other critics, a promising young writer "genuinely poised for flight with a recognizable voice and content his own," he still has had to rely, for the most part, on his other talents—mainly teaching—to earn a living. In mid-1983, when his stint as an English instructor at Fort Lauderdale's Broward Community College came to an end, he found himself in a rather desperate situation: suddenly unemployed and with no prospective teaching posts on the horizon. He then resolved to pursue a new line of work. Declaring himself a Democrat and member of the Committee for Immediate Nuclear War, Grayson announced his intention to run for the presidency of the United States in 1984 as Florida's "favorite grandson." "I figured the presidency pays pretty well, $200,000 a year, and you get to live rent-free," he explained to reporters. "I urge all unemployed people to run."

One of Grayson's first tasks after declaring his candidacy was choosing a running mate. Though at one point he considered actress Meryl Streep for the position, mainly because he liked the sound of the slogan "Streep for Veep," he finally settled on Jane Wyman, star of the television series "Falcon Crest" and ex-wife of President Ronald Reagan. Why Wyman? "She's had experience dumping Reagan so I know . . . she'll be thrilled by the opportunity," Grayson remarked. "Plus we need a woman on the ticket to bridge the gender gap, and since she owns a vineyard on 'Falcon Crest' we should get the wino vote. But poor Maureen Reagan. Who do you think she will vote for—mom or dad?"

The candidate's many proposals included making El Salvador the fifty-first state and replacing the Kissinger Commission with Bianca Jagger and members of the teenage rock group Menudo. Grayson also advocated nuclear war as the solution to many of the country's ills. "In addition to solving problems like boredom, street people, and soap operas," he maintained, "it will get rid of poverty, racism, and environmental contamination. I say it's either now or never."

Grayson even had a plan for those people who voiced the concern that, if elected, he would be barred from serving as president until 1986, when he reaches the minimum legal age of thirty-five. Far from being a disadvantage, the candidate said, his youth could be a definite advantage. "Since a president often causes more problems than he solves, I think having the country in limbo for two years until I'm old enough to serve will be good for it," he explained. "It's the New Deferralism."

BIOGRAPHICAL/CRITICAL SOURCES: Kings Courier, August 7, 1978; *Aspect*, Number 72/73, 1979; *Los Angeles Times*, July 17, 1979; *Ventura County News*, February 4, 1980; *Orlando Sentinel*, April 18, 1982, January 14, 1984; *Best Sellers*, May, 1982; *Israel Today*, May 8, 1983; *Athens Daily News*, July 18, 1983; *New York Times Book Review*, August 14, 1983; *USA Today*, October 15, 1983; *Des Moines Register*, October 21, 1983; *Miami News*, April 13, 1984.

*   *   *

GREEN, Hannah
  See GREENBERG, Joanne (Goldenberg)

*   *   *

GREENBERG, Joanne (Goldenberg)   1932-
  (Hannah Green)

PERSONAL: Born September 24, 1932, in Brooklyn, N.Y.; daughter of Julius Lester and Rosalie (Bernstein) Goldenberg; married Albert Greenberg, September 4, 1955; children: David, Alan. *Education:* American University, B.A. *Religion:* Jewish. *Home:* 29221 Rainbow Hills Rd., Golden, Colo. 80401. *Agents:*

Lois Wallace, Wallace & Sheil Agency, Inc., 177 East 70th St., New York, N.Y.; William Morris Agency, 1350 Ave. of the Americas, New York, N.Y. 10019.

CAREER: Writer. Adjunct professor of anthropology, Colorado School of Mines, 1983—. Medical officer, Lookout Mountain Fire Department; certified emergency medical technician.

MEMBER: Authors Guild, Authors League of America, P.E.N., American Civil Liberties Union, National Association of the Deaf, Colorado Authors' League.

AWARDS, HONORS: Harry and Ethel Daroff Memorial Fiction Award, 1963, and William and Janice Epstein Fiction Award, 1964, both from the National Jewish Welfare Board, both for *The King's Persons;* Marcus L. Kenner Award from the New York Association of the Deaf, 1971; Christopher Book Award, 1971, for *In This Sign;* Frieda Fromm-Reichman Memorial Award from the American Academy of Psychoanalysis, 1971; honorary doctorates from Western Maryland College, 1977, and Gallaudet College, 1979; Rocky Mountain Women's Institute Award, 1983.

WRITINGS—All published by Holt: *The King's Persons* (novel), 1963; (under pseudonym Hannah Green) *I Never Promised You a Rose Garden* (autobiographical novel), 1964; *The Monday Voices* (novel), 1965; *Summering* (short stories), 1966; *In This Sign* (novel), 1968; *Rites of Passage* (short stories), 1971; *Founder's Praise* (novel), 1976; *High Crimes and Misdemeanors* (short stories), 1979; *A Season of Delight* (novel), 1981; *The Far Side of Victory* (novel), 1983. Contributor of articles, reviews, and short stories to numerous periodicals, including *Hudson Review, Virginia Quarterly, Chatelaine,* and *Saturday Review.*

SIDELIGHTS: "Joanne Greenberg is a charming writer who writes about our current social problems without being doctrinaire or propagandistic or stuffy," states J. Mitchell Morse in the *Hudson Review.* As a novelist and short-story writer, Greenberg writes on subjects that are, according to Thomas Lask in the *New York Times,* "astonishingly varied: the farm life of a poor white; the world of the deaf, the family circle of great aunts from the old country, suburban academia and much else. She makes them all tangible." And John Nicholson describes Greenberg in this manner in the London *Times:* "Greenberg is a professional storyteller of the old school, who believes in putting plausible characters into interesting situations and letting them get on with it."

Greenberg's first book, *The King's Persons,* is a historical novel set in twelfth-century England. In it, she examines the resentment that existed between the Jewish moneylenders of York and the local Christian barons. Although this bitterness began over financial matters, it soon developed into general feelings of hatred and religious bigotry that spread to others in the community, resulting in the massacre of many Jewish people.

The King's Persons was highly praised for its attention to historical detail and Greenberg's sensitive portrayal of her characters. "Greenberg's first novel recreates a little known aspect of English history with attention to the nuances of commonplace life usually lost amid the panoply of historical romances that are preoccupied with large and glamorous movements," writes G. E. Grauel in *Best Sellers.* Pamela Marsh remarks in the *Christian Science Monitor* that "the special fascination of this book lies in its background." Marsh continues: "Strangely enough the final, inevitable massacre, appalling though it was,

touches less closely than all the small tragedies and humiliations that happen along the way to people we have grown to care about." And a reviewer for *Time* notes that "with painstaking care, [Greenberg] has woven each of the skeins of medieval life into a vivid tapestry that shows the loutishness and insensitivity of the baronial landholders, the obtuseness of the peasantry, the twisted fervor of churchmen who found virtue in the wholesale slaughter of heretics, and the disturbing contrast between the warmth of Jewish communal life and the demeaning nature of usury."

Greenberg's second—and most popular—novel tackles a completely different subject matter. Written under the pseudonym Hannah Green, *I Never Promised You a Rose Garden* is the story of a young girl's long and difficult battle against schizophrenia. The book is based on Greenberg's own struggle with mental illness and follows the main character, Deborah Blau, as she retreats from reality to her mythical kingdom of Yr, attempts suicide, enters a mental hospital, and undergoes treatment and intensive therapy. R. V. Cassill remarks in the *New York Times Book Review* that Greenberg "has done a marvelous job of dramatizing the internal warfare in a young psychotic. She has anatomized, in full detail, the relationship between a whole, sick human being and the clinical situation—including doctors, other patients and the abstract forces of institutional life." And a reviewer for the *Times Literary Supplement* remarks that in *I Never Promised You a Rose Garden* Greenberg "tries to create the whole world of the mental hospital as the schizophrenic sees it, as the doctor sees it, as the nurses see it, and as the parents, terrified and ignorant, see it from outside. . . . [Greenberg] is excellent when conveying relief and delight at the freedom from lies, and most of all the freedom to call mad mad, crazy crazy. She is excellent too on the inventiveness of the insane."

Due to the sensitive and highly personal nature of the book, Greenberg decided to publish *I Never Promised You a Rose Garden* under a pseudonym. She explains her reason for adopting the Hannah Green name in a *Saturday Review* article written by Rollene W. Saal: "I used the pseudonym when I wrote *Rose Garden* because my children were small. I wanted to protect them. Even so, a schoolmate asked my younger son if he was going to go crazy like his mother. It was like being hit in the face."

Greenberg's third novel, *The Monday Voices,* follows the character of Ralph Oakland, an employee of the Department of Rehabilitation, as he tries to help his handicapped and disadvantaged clients. W. G. Rogers describes *The Monday Voices* in the *New York Times Book Review* as "somber, disheartening, grand and gripping." Rogers goes on to remark: "Few books stick so closely to a theme . . . [Oakland] never lifts his nose from the grindstone, and the reader never does, either. Nor does he want to. The final note is optimistic. . . . There could be no better plea for society's support of the lame, the halt and the blind."

In This Sign, Greenberg's fourth novel, was praised for its sensitive and enlightening description of a deaf couple's trials and tribulations during their nearly fifty years of marriage. A reviewer for the *Times Literary Supplement* writes that *In This Sign* "usually avoids the excesses of sentimentality expected of a novel about the deaf, while technically Joanne Greenberg has managed to find a way of writing conversations between deaf and hearing with inordinate skill, as well as the less usual situations between deaf and deaf."

"Those who protect their heartstrings at all costs from being tugged at by professional writers would do well to avoid Joanne Greenberg's *In This Sign*," comments R. R. Davies in the *New Statesman*. "As a stolid family chronicle it resembles the less vigorous works of Zola in its deliberate, almost deterministic progress. Its skill . . . consists in its coming to terms with the problem of deafness, not merely in its readily imaginable practical implications but in the more fundamental sense of what can and cannot be said with the hands. I was surprised by the tact of the book." And Ruth Nadelhaft states in the *Library Journal* that *In This Sign* is an "unsettling, haunting book. . . . The isolation and the often frenzied rage of the deaf couple are unforgettably vivid. . . . Reading this book is not easy; but it ends with hard-earned laughter and is worth the struggle."

The publication of *Founder's Praise* and *A Season of Delight*, both of which revolve around religious themes, followed *In This Sign*. *Founder's Praise*, for example, explores three generations of an American family and their involvement with the formation of a grass roots religion. J. R. Frakes remarks in the *New York Times Book Review:* "The bulk of [Greenberg's] darkly beautiful and disturbing novel is devoted to the rise and dissolution of [a] new religion. . . . Tough issues [are] dealt with dramatically and persuasively in this gnarled book, which never indulges in cheap mockery or cynical patronizing of the religious impulse."

In *A Season of Delight* the reader is introduced to Grace Dowben, who is trying to cope with her children's rejection of their traditional Jewish background. Norma B. Williamson states in the *National Review* that "Greenberg takes a woman who could fill about half a dozen popular stereotypes and exposes the unique human being beneath. Grace Dowben is a middle-aged Jewish housewife, attempting to deal with the pain and sense of loss engendered by the finality of her children's leaving home. Her son has become a Moonie and her daughter has embraced radical feminism, and both have rejected the traditions that have always been a vital part of Grace's life." And Ellen Sweet explains in *Ms.* that *A Season of Delight* "is about [Dowben's] efforts to come to terms with their choices and with her own feelings. . . . Thanks to Joanne Greenberg's funny/sad, sensitive treatment, we don't have to put up with parody, either."

In *The Far Side of Victory*, Greenberg's more recent novel, young Eric Gordon, after having too much to drink, drives down a snowy Colorado highway and collides with another car. As a result, five passengers in the other car—two men and three children—die; the only survivor, Helen, is the wife of one of the men and the mother of the three children. Gordon receives a sentence of fifteen months probation and proceeds to get his life back in order. Eventually Gordon meets, falls in love with, and marries Helen, the woman who survived the crash he caused. Over the years they have three children. Thirteen years after the original accident another freakish one occurs—this time killing Helen and Gordon's three children. Greenberg's novel has been compared to a Greek tragedy. Remarks Elaine Kendall in the *Los Angeles Times:* "The spare style, the inexorable progress of events and the rigid symmetry of plot all follow accepted classical principles. The characters are obedient to the capricious whims of the gods, the fundamental lesson of the book more dreadful than ordinary mortal can bear." On the other hand, a reviewer for the *Washington Post Book World* believes that "what Greenberg is writing about in her gentle and perceptive book is how hard it is to know the people you love—and how that knowledge, once gained, must be tenderly held."

In addition to the respect critics have for her ability to write sensitive, heart-warming, and intelligent novels, Greenberg has been praised for her skillful short story writing. While reviewers agree that Greenberg successfully handles the technical transition from writing novels to short stories, they note that her topics do not change, for Greenberg still seeks out and explores the problems of the less fortunate. For example, in a *Los Angeles Times Book Review* article concerning *High Crimes and Misdemeanors*, Leah Fritz explains that "in her short stories, Greenberg rails against the unfairness of life and invokes all sorts of unearthly powers—sublime and absurd—to redress it. She despairs of mundane remedies for mundane ills." Fritz goes on to state: "Greenberg's characters use their [brains] to outwit an assortment of evils running the gamut from the perils of city streets to terminal disease, from the disenfranchisement of mental patients to the problems of an amateur cocaine smuggler, from attempted suicide to just plain boredom. . . . Greenberg produced fabrications as layered and light as good strudel." And also writing about *High Crimes and Misdemeanors*, Ellen Carter notes in *Voyager* that this is "an outstanding collection of short stories reminiscent of the late Flannery O'Connor, many concerned with the problems of belief by contemporary man. . . . Beware, these stories will haunt you."

In a review of *Rites of Passage*, Joyce Carol Oates states in *Book World* that "this group of twelve excellent short stories is all the more remarkable for its being not only artistically 'beautiful' but morally and spiritually beautiful as well. . . . In story after story, she sets forth characters populating entirely believable, dense, frightening worlds (or visions of worlds—because her people suffer in their isolation), sometimes establishing contact with another person, sometimes reaching out but failing, sometimes falling back, selfishly, content in failure." And finally, Norma B. Williamson comments in the *National Review* that in all of her writing "Greenberg clearly believes in traditional values, along with such old-fashioned themes as good and evil, but there is humor and compassion in her treatment of both, making her always a joy to read."

MEDIA ADAPTATIONS: I Never Promised You a Rose Garden was filmed by New World Pictures in 1977.

BIOGRAPHICAL/CRITICAL SOURCES: Best Sellers, March 1, 1963, May 1, 1964, July 1, 1965, August 1, 1966, December 1, 1970; *Christian Science Monitor*, March 14, 1963, March 16, 1977; *Time*, March 29, 1963, January 21, 1980, January 19, 1984; *Library Journal*, February 15, 1964, November 15, 1970, October 1, 1976; *New York Times Book Review*, May 3, 1964, July 11, 1965, October 31, 1976, February 3, 1980; *Book Week*, May 3, 1964, July 18, 1965, March 19, 1972; *Saturday Review*, July 18, 1964, September 10, 1966, January 22, 1972; *Times Literary Supplement*, August 13, 1964, November 18, 1965, October 15, 1971, May 19, 1978; *New Statesman*, August 14, 1964, September 3, 1971; *Atlantic*, August, 1965, February 3, 1980; *Hudson Review*, winter, 1966-67.

New Republic, February 13, 1971; *New York Times*, March 18, 1972; *New Yorker*, April 15, 1972; *New York Review of Books*, May 4, 1972; *Top of the News*, April, 1977; *Contemporary Literary Criticism*, Gale, Volume VII, 1977, Volume XXX, 1984; *Washington Post Book World*, March 2, 1980, October 2, 1983; *Los Angeles Times Book Review*, March 16, 1980, October 27, 1983; *National Review*, May 2, 1980, October 15, 1982; *Voyager*, June, 1980; *Ms.*, July, 1981; *Commentary*, May, 1982; *Times* (London), January 19, 1984.

—*Sketch by Margaret Mazurkiewicz*

GREENBERG, Simon 1901-

PERSONAL: Born January 8, 1901, in Russia; came to the United States in 1905, naturalized citizen, 1924; son of Morris (a wine expert) and Bessie (Chaidenko) Greenberg; married Betty Davis, December 13, 1925; children: Moshe, Daniel Asher. *Education:* City College (now of the City University of New York), B.A., 1922; attended American School of Oriental Studies and Hebrew University of Jerusalem, 1924-25; Jewish Theological Seminary, rabbi and M.H.L., 1925; Dropsie College, Ph.D., 1932. *Home:* 420 Riverside Dr., New York, N.Y. 10025. *Office:* Jewish Theological Seminary, 3080 Broadway, New York, N.Y. 10027.

CAREER: Rabbi of Jewish congregation in Philadelphia, Pa., 1925-46; Jewish Theological Seminary, New York, N.Y., lecturer, 1932-40, associate professor, 1940-46, professor of education, 1946-72, professor of homiletics, 1948-72, provost, 1946-52, vice-chancellor and faculty vice-president, 1952; initiator and administrator of Israel Project in Jerusalem, 1972—. Director of University of Judaism, 1948-58, president, 1958-66, chancellor, 1966-72. Executive director of United Synagogue of America, 1950-53.

MEMBER: American Association for Jewish Education, Religious Education Association, Rabbinical Assembly of America (president, 1938-40), Educators Assembly of United Synagogue of America, Conference on Science, Philosophy, and Religion (fellow).

AWARDS, HONORS: D.D. from Jewish Theological Seminary, 1958; Sam Rothberg Award from Hebrew University of Jerusalem, 1977, for contributions to Jewish education in the diaspora; Mordecai M. Kaplan Medal from University of Judaism, 1977.

WRITINGS: Living as a Jew Today, Behrman, 1939; *The Ideals and Values of the Prayer Book,* Jewish Theological Seminary of America, 1940; *The Harishon Textbook Series,* five volumes, United Synagogue of America, 1941; *The First Year in the Hebrew School: A Teacher's Guide,* United Synagogue of America, 1945; *Foundation of a Faith,* Burning Bush Press, 1968.

Words of Poetry, privately printed, 1970; *The Ethical in the Jewish and American Heritage,* Ktav, 1977; *A Jewish Philosophy and Pattern of Life,* Jewish Theological Seminary of America, 1981; *A Guide to Daily Bible Study for the Jewish Community,* Year of the Bible, 1983.

WORK IN PROGRESS: A Jewish Philosophy of Life.

SIDELIGHTS: Simon Greenberg writes: "Since 1972 I have been spending some six months of the year in Jerusalem. I initiated and have been guiding and nurturing the seminary's special Israel Project devoted to building joint educational projects with Israeli institutions for developing more effective methods for transmitting Jewish religio-cultural values while maintaining a policy of freedom of thought and intellectual integrity. We have met with considerable response particularly from a goodly number of intellectuals identified with the non-religious kibbutzim (communal settlements).

"Having taught homiletics at the seminary for more than three decades, I plan to formulate my reflections on the role of the rabbi as Darshan—as interpreter of the written and oral Jewish tradition and its relevancy to the present day life of the individual and community."

GREENE, A(lvin) C(arl) 1923-
(Arthur C. Randolph, Mateman Weaver)

PERSONAL: Born November 4, 1923, in Abilene, Tex.; son of Alvin Carl and Marie (Cole) Greene; married Betty Jo Dozier, May 1, 1950; children: Geoffrey, Mark, Eliot, Meredith Elizabeth. *Education:* Attended Phillips University, 1942, and Kansas State College of Pittsburg (now Pittsburg State University), 1943; Abilene Christian College (now University), B.A., 1948; graduate study at Hardin-Simmons University, 1951, and University of Texas at Austin, 1968-70. *Religion:* Presbyterian. *Home and office:* 4359 Shirley Dr., Dallas, Tex. 75229. *Agent:* Charles Neighbors, 7600 Blanco Rd., San Antonio, Tex. 78216.

CAREER: Abilene Reporter-News, Abilene, Tex., member of staff, 1948-52, amusements editor, 1952-59; *Dallas Times Herald,* Dallas, Tex., book editor and editorial columnist, 1960-68, editor of editorial page, 1963-65; KERA-Television, Dallas, executive producer, 1970-71, news commentator, 1970-77; book reviewer, MacNeil/Lehrer News Hour, 1983—. Special instructor and head of department of journalism, Hardin-Simmons University, 1957, University of Texas at Austin, 1973, and Southern Methodist University, 1976. Owner of book store in Abilene, 1952-57. *Military service:* U.S. Navy and U.S. Marines, 1942-46; served in Pacific theater and China; became pharmacist's mate second class.

MEMBER: PEN International, Writers Guild of America, Texas Institute of Letters (fellow; president, 1969-71). *Awards, honors:* Texas Institute of Letters award, 1963 and 1973; award from National Conference of Christians and Jews, 1964; Dobie-Paisano fellowship, 1968.

WRITINGS: A Personal Country, Knopf, 1969, 3rd edition, 1983; (editor and contributor) *Living Texas: A Gathering of Experiences,* Hendrick-Long Co., 1970; *The Last Captive,* Encino Press, 1972, 2nd edition, 1982; *The Santa Claus Bank Robbery* (nonfiction), Knopf, 1972; (contributor) *Growing Up in Texas,* Encino Press, 1972; *Dallas: The Deciding Years,* Encino Press, 1973, 2nd edition, 1982; *A Christmas Tree,* Encino Press, 1973, miniature edition, Somesuch Press, 1980; *Views in Texas,* Encino Press, 1974.

A Place Called Dallas, Dallas County Heritage Society, 1975; (contributor) Evelyn Oppenheimer and Bill Porterfield, editors, *The Book of Dallas,* Doubleday, 1976; (with Roger Horchow) *Elephants in Your Mailbox,* Times Books, 1980, tape edition, 1983; *The 50 Best Books on Texas,* Pressworks, 1981, 2nd edition, 1982; (contributor) Edward Weems, editor, *A Texas Christmas Miscellany,* Pressworks, 1983; *The Highland Park Woman* (short stories), Shearing Publishing, 1983; *Dallas U.S.A.,* Texas Monthly, 1984; (editor and compiler) *Dobie: Being Frank,* Wind River Press, 1985. Author of column, *Dallas News,* 1983—. Executive editor, *Southwestern Historical Quarterly,* 1968-69.

WORK IN PROGRESS: An encyclopedia, *A Companion to Texas,* for Oxford University Press.

SIDELIGHTS: A. C. Greene tells *CA* that, in order to write, a writer first must feel that "there's something to be said. This, I think, is something a writer faces most often, no matter who he is. Every morning, when a writer wakes up and takes pen and pencil or his yellow pad or typewriter or word processor and sits down to a blank page, he is hit by a wave of disbelief:

Who are you trying to kid? You think you're going to say something that anyone gives a damn about? That's the greatest danger a writer faces, the loss of belief in what he's doing. That's the greatest because you have to keep convincing yourself. It never goes away. You have to think that you're saying something or revealing one little point in life that never has quite been revealed in quite this fashion about quite this type of situation. And then you write.''

BIOGRAPHICAL/CRITICAL SOURCES: New Yorker, March 14, 1970, September 16, 1972; *Saturday Review,* July 1, 1972; *Detroit News,* July 23, 1972; *Dallas Times Herald Sunday Magazine,* October 30, 1977; Patrick Bennett, *Talking with Texas Writers: Twelve Interviews,* Texas A & M University Press, 1980; *Dallas News Dallas Life Magazine,* October 3, 1982; *Post* (Houston), December 26, 1982; *New York Times Book Review,* March 4, 1984; *American Way,* April, 1984.

*   *   *

GREGG, Charles T(hornton)   1927-

PERSONAL: Born July 27, 1927, in Billings, Mont.; son of Charles Thornton (a broker) and Gertrude (Hurst) Gregg; married Elizabeth Whitaker (an operating room nurse), December 20, 1957; children: Paul, Diane, Brian, Elaine. *Education:* Attended Reed College, 1948-50; Oregon State University, B.S., 1952, M.S., 1955, Ph.D., 1959. *Politics:* Liberal. *Religion:* Unitarian Universalist. *Home:* 424 Kiva, Los Alamos, N.M. 87544. *Office:* Los Alamos Scientific Laboratory, MSM881, P.O. Box 1663, Los Alamos, N.M.

CAREER: Oregon State University, Corvallis, instructor in agricultural chemistry, 1955-59; Johns Hopkins University, Baltimore, Md., research fellow in physiological chemistry, 1959-63; University of California, Los Alamos Scientific Laboratory, Los Alamos, N.M., biochemist, 1963—. Visiting professor at Free University of Berlin, 1973-74. *Military service:* U.S. Navy, 1944-46; served in Pacific theater.

MEMBER: American Association for the Advancement of Science (fellow), American Society for Microbiology, Authors Guild, Authors League of America, American Society of Biological Chemists (fellow).

AWARDS, HONORS: U.S. Public Health Service fellowship, 1959-63.

WRITINGS: Plague!, Scribner, 1978, 2nd edition, University of New Mexico Press, 1985; *A Virus of Love and Other Tales of Medical Detection,* Scribner's, 1983. Also author of an unproduced play, ''Patriots/Traitors.''

Contributor: Ronald W. Estabrook and Maynard E. Pullman, editors, *Methods in Enzymology,* Volume X: *Oxidation and Phosphorylation,* Academic Press, 1967; George H. Rothblat and Vincent J. Cristafalo, editors, *Growth, Nutrition, and Metabolism of Cells in Culture,* Volume I, Academic Press, 1972; Diether Neubert and Hans-Jochen Merker, editors, *New Approaches to the Evaluation of Abnormal Embryonic Development,* George Thieme (Stuttgart), 1975; Rudoph Weber, editor, *The Biochemistry of Animal Development,* Volume III: *Molecular Aspects of Animal Development,* Academic Press, 1975.

Contributor to *Proceedings* of the British Pharmacology Society Symposium on Stable Isotopes, 1978, and to *Proceedings* of the Third International Conference on Stable Isotopes; contributor of about forty articles to scientific journals.

SIDELIGHTS: Charles T. Gregg writes: ''I considered myself a writer for a very long time before I had anything published. I wrote short stories, a two-act play, magazine articles and queries, and half of a novel, and I accumulated a stack of rejection slips to attest to my status as a writer.

''I finally concluded that first I had to get a publisher's attention and I could do that best by using my technical background to write on a subject that would be difficult for someone without my training (or the genius of Camus) to handle. It worked— hence the book *Plague!* My next book will also be nonfiction, though not biomedical, since I don't want to be typecast. Then I would like to complete the novel that I turned away from some years ago when I lost control of it. Ideally, I would like to move back and forth between fiction and nonfiction, but it remains to be seen whether or not I can write salable fiction at all.''

Of his book *A Virus of Love and Other Tales of Medical Detection, Los Angeles Times* book reviewer Carolyn See notes: ''Several of the essays here—the ones based on both hard facts and accounts of detection—are interesting reading, particularly on Legionnaires' disease, a recent outbreak of botulism and the first part of a chapter on birth defects, dealing specifically with the marketing of Thalidomide in Europe.''

AVOCATIONAL INTERESTS: Reading, sailing, hiking, playing squash.

BIOGRAPHICAL/CRITICAL SOURCES: Los Angeles Times, March 16, 1983.

*   *   *

GRIFFITHS, Michael C(ompton)   1928-

PERSONAL: Born April 7, 1928, in Cardiff, Wales; son of Charles Idris Ewart and Myfanwy (Jones) Griffiths; married Valerie Kipping (a theological teacher), July 21, 1956; children: John Anderson, Elizabeth Bronwen, Nigel Timothy, Stephen Glyndwr. *Education:* Peterhouse College, Cambridge, B.A., 1952; Ridley Hall, Cambridge, M.A., 1954. *Religion:* Christian. *Home:* ''Wetherby,'' Green Lane, Northwood, Middlesex, HA6 2UV England. *Office:* London Bible College, Green Lane, Northwood, Middlesex, England.

CAREER: Traveling secretary, Inter-Varsity Fellowship, 1954-57; Overseas Missionary Fellowship, missionary in Japan, 1958-68, general director in Singapore, 1969-80; London Bible College, Middlesex, England, principal, 1980—. *Military service:* Royal Army Medical Corps, 1947-49; became corporal.

AWARDS, HONORS: D.D., Wheaton College, 1974.

WRITINGS—Published by Inter-Varsity Press, except as indicated: *Consistent Christianity,* 1960; *Christian Assurance,* 1962; *Take My Life,* 1967; *Give Up Small Ambitions,* 1970; *Three Men Filled with Spirit,* Overseas Missionary Fellowship, 1970; *Take Off Your Shoes,* Overseas Missionary Fellowship, 1971.

Cinderella with Amnesia, 1975; *Changing Asia,* Lion Publishing, 1977; *Cinderella's Betrothal Gifts,* Overseas Missionary Fellowship, 1978; *Shaking the Sleeping Beauty,* 1980; *What on Earth Are You Doing?,* 1983; *The Example of Jesus,* Hodder & Stoughton, 1985. Contributor to journals and newspapers.

WORK IN PROGRESS: Several books.

SIDELIGHTS: Michael C. Griffiths has travelled widely in the Far East, Europe, Australia, New Zealand, South Africa, and

North America. He speaks Japanese fairly well, and knows some German. His books have been translated into German, Chinese, Japanese, Indonesian, Vietnamese, Urdu, French, Portuguese, Dutch, Swedish, Hungarian, and Korean.

AVOCATIONAL INTERESTS: Mountains, fishing, collecting alpine plants.

*   *   *

GROSS, Joel 1951-

PERSONAL: Born March 22, 1951, in New York, N.Y.; son of David Charles (an editor) and Esther (Pearl) Gross; married Linda Sanders, May, 1973. *Education:* Queens College of the City University of New York, B.A. (with high honors in English), 1971; Columbia University, M.A. (with high honors), 1973. *Politics:* Liberal Democrat. *Religion:* Jewish. *Home:* 165 East 66th St., New York, N.Y. 10021.

CAREER: Writer.

WRITINGS—Novels, except as indicated: *Bubble's Shadow,* Crown, 1970; *The Young Man Who Wrote Soap Operas,* Scribner, 1975; *1407 Broadway,* Seaview, 1978; *The Books of Rachel,* Seaview, 1979; *Maura's Dream,* Seaview, 1981; *Home of the Brave,* Seaview, 1982; *This Year in Jerusalem,* Putnam, 1983; *The Lives of Rachel,* American Library, 1984; "Clean Sweep" (play), first produced at the Perry Street Theatre in New York City, February 10, 1984.

*   *   *

GROSS, Theodore L(awrence) 1930-

PERSONAL: Born December 4, 1930, in New York, N.Y.; son of David (a teacher) and Anna Gross; married Selma Bell (a teacher), August 27, 1955; children: Donna, Jonathan. *Education:* University of Maine, B.A., 1952; Columbia University, M.A., 1957, Ph.D., 1960. *Office:* College of Letters and Science, Pennsylvania State University, Capitol Campus, Middletown, Pa. 17057.

CAREER: City College of the City University of New York, New York, N.Y., instructor, 1958-61, assistant professor, 1961-64, associate professor, 1964-68, professor of English, 1968-78, chairman of department, 1970-72, dean of humanities, 1972-78; Pennsylvania State University, Capitol Campus, Middletown, provost and dean, 1979-83, dean of College of Letters and Science, 1983—. Visiting professor at University of Nancy, 1963-64, 1968-69, and Kyoto American Studies summer seminar, 1978.

MEMBER: Modern Language Association of America, National Council of Teachers of English (director of commission on literature), Association of Departments of English (member of executive committee).

WRITINGS: Albion W. Tourgee, Twayne, 1963; *Thomas Nelson Page,* Twayne, 1967; (editor with Norman Kelvin) *An Introduction to Fiction,* Random House, 1967; (editor with James A. Emanuel) *Dark Symphony: Negro Literature in America,* Free Press, 1968; (editor) *Representative Men: Cult Heroes of Our Time,* Free Press, 1970; *Annotated Bibliographies: Hawthorne, Melville,* Free Press, 1971; *The Heroic Ideals in American Literature,* Free Press, 1971; (editor) *A Nation of Nations: Ethnic Literature in America,* Free Press, 1971; (editor) *The Literature of American Jews,* Free Press, 1973; (general editor) *America in Literature,* two volumes, with teachers

manual, Wiley, 1978; *Academic Turmoil: The Reality and Promise of Open Education,* Doubleday, 1981.

Contributor: Seymour L. Gross and John Edward Hardy, editors, *Images of the Negro in American Literature,* University of Chicago Press, 1966; Clayton L. Eichelberger, editor, *American Literary Realism: 1870-1910,* University of Texas Press, 1967; Louis D. Rubin, editor, *Bibliographical Checklist of Southern Literature,* Louisiana State University Press, 1968; C.W.E. Bigsby, editor, *The American Negro Writer,* Everett Edwards, 1969. General editor, "Studies in Language and Literature," Harper, 1975-77. Contributor of articles and reviews to professional journals, including *Phylon, Critique, College English, South Atlantic Quarterly,* and *Yale Review.*

WORK IN PROGRESS: A Partnership in Education.

SIDELIGHTS: In the 1970s, open enrollment to universities, a policy that provided underpriviledged students access to higher education, was a hotly debated issue in the academic world, and Theodore L. Gross found himself embroiled in this controversy. When open enrollment was put into effect at the City College of the City University of New York, where Gross was a dean of humanities, there was tremendous conflict between the demands of traditional coursework and the abilities of students from poor educational backgrounds. Students became frustrated; professors resented having to teach basic skills; traditional subjects gave way to remedial and career-oriented programs. Anger and tensions grew. In 1978 Gross wrote an essay that critically examined the open admissions policy. Publication of the article in *Saturday Review* sparked a furor that eventually forced Gross to resign his position.

In his book *Academic Turmoil: The Reality and Promise of Open Education,* Gross "expands his original, gripping essay and proposes solutions born of that turmoil," writes Jack Curtis in the *Los Angeles Times Book Review.* "Viewing open enrollment as a logical and moral imperative of the democratic credo, Gross' battle lies with the program's implementation. Administrators, instructors, the community and students expected and attempted too much, too fast. . . . To preserve the university's traditional goals, Gross, no romantic, seeks to adjust the humanities to professional needs, to the urban environment."

In the *New York Times Book Review,* Joseph Featherstone describes the book as portraying "a demoralized university in a city unwilling to pay for yesterday's good educational intentions. . . . Making access to higher education more democratic was bound to change the way the liberal arts were taught, Professor Gross says. The question is whether they still matter. Professor Gross thinks they do, and drawing on his City College experience, he has a battery of suggestions. Writing is his prescription for sound learning: he has a series of proposals to put writing at the center of the curriculum. . . . [He is] most interesting on the subject of writing, where he makes good sense. But he is never explicit about how writing is supposed to incorporate all the old values of academic humanism, and he's also unclear about the role of the college in all this. Unless I misread him, Professor Gross seems to be saying that most of the problems lie in secondary education and ever lower grades. . . . This may be true but it ducks the question of what, in fact, colleges have to offer students who show up more or less uneducated. Higher education may be bankrupt as Professor Gross says it is, but it's hard to see what he'd put in its place." Curtis concludes: "Gross' integration of the humanities, career tracks and urban needs challenges educators to reshape and the general public to understand the university's purposes and procedures. As Gross intones, only an open society can ensure the success of open admissions."

BIOGRAPHICAL/CRITICAL SOURCES: New York Times, November 26, 1968, July 22, 1971; *Christian Science Monitor,* December 12, 1968; *Ramparts,* October, 1969; *Books Abroad,* winter, 1970; *New Republic,* December 29, 1973; *Prairie Schooner,* fall, 1974; *New York Times Book Review,* February 3, 1980; *Los Angeles Times Book Review,* March 30, 1980.

*   *   *

GROTH, Alexander J(acob)   1932-

PERSONAL: Surname legally changed, 1953; born March 7, 1932, in Warsaw, Poland; became U.S. citizen, 1953; son of Jacob (an accountant) and Maria (Hazenfus) Goldwasser; married Marilyn Wineburg, December 15, 1961; children: Stevin James, Warren Adrian. *Education:* City College (now City College of the City University of New York), B.A. (magna cum laude), 1954; Columbia University, M.A., 1955, Ph.D., 1960. *Politics:* Independent. *Religion:* Jewish. *Home:* 603 Georgetown Pl., Davis, Calif. 95616. *Office:* Department of Political Science, University of California, Davis, Calif. 95616.

CAREER: City College of the City University of New York, New York, N.Y., instructor in political science, 1960-61; Harpur College (now State University of New York at Binghamton), assistant professor of political science, 1961-62; University of California, Davis, assistant professor, 1962-67, associate professor, 1967-71, professor of political science, 1971—.

MEMBER: American Political Science Association, Western Political Science Association, Far Western Slavic Conference, Phi Beta Kappa.

AWARDS, HONORS: Grant from American Council of Learned Societies and Social Science Research Council, 1965-66.

WRITINGS: Revolution and Elite Access, Institute of Governmental Affairs, University of California, 1966; *Eastern Europe after Czechoslovakia,* Foreign Policy Association, 1969; *Comparative Politics: A Distributive Approach,* Macmillan, 1971; *Major Ideologies: An Interpretative Survey of Democracy, Socialism, and Nationalism,* Wiley, 1971, 2nd edition, Robert E. Krieger, 1983; *People's Poland: Government and Politics,* Chandler & Sharp, 1972.

(Co-author) *Contemporary Politics: Europe,* Winthrop Publishing, 1976; (co-editor) *Comparative Resource Allocation,* Sage, 1984; *Progress and Chaos: Modernization Rediscovery of Religion and Authority,* Robert E. Krieger, 1984. Contributor to political science journals.

WORK IN PROGRESS: Research on public policy aspects of comparative politics.

*   *   *

GRUB, Phillip D.   1932-

PERSONAL: Born August 8, 1932; son of Carl D. and Barbara (Johnson) Grub. *Education:* Eastern Washington State College (now Eastern Washington University), B.A. in economics and B.A. in education (both with highest honors), 1953; George Washington University, M.B.A., 1960, Ph.D., 1964. *Residence:* Arlington, Va. *Office:* School of Government and Business Administration, George Washington University, Washington, D.C. 20052.

CAREER: George Washington University, Washington, D.C., began as assistant professor, 1954, associate professor, 1967-72, professor of business administration, 1972-74, Aryamehr Professor of Multinational Management, 1974—, chairman of department of business administration, 1968-70, special assistant to the president for International Program Development, 1974-79, currently director of International Business Programs. Visiting lecturer in business administration, Eastern Washington State College (now Eastern Washington University), 1960-62; Distinguished Visiting Professor of International Business, Ecole Superiere des Sciences Economiques et Commerciales, Paris, 1970; Distinguished Visiting Professor of International Marketing, Helsinki School of Economics, Finland, 1971; visiting professor of international business administration, Cleveland State University, 1972-73; guest lecturer, Romanian Institute of Management, CEPECA, 1976.

Member of International Relations Committee, American Assembly of Collegiate Schools of Business, 1975-78; chairman of board of governors, African Institute for Economic Development, 1980—. Co-owner and co-manager of 7G Ranch, Medical Lake, Wash., 1962-70; member of board of directors and chairman of executive committee, Diplomat National Bank, 1977-80; associate director, CICCO and Associates, 1978—; member of board of directors, OZMA Corporation, 1979-80. Member of President's Regional Export Expansion Council, 1968—; director, Ohio World Trade-Education Center, 1972-73; member of board of directors and executive secretary, United States-Japan Culture Center, 1979—. Headed first official U.S. seminar team in marketing and management to Eastern Europe for the U.S. Departments of Commerce and State, 1968; led team to Second Asian International Trade Fair in Tehran, Iran, 1969; led delegation of U.S. industrial research and development specialists to the Autumn International Exposition, Bucharest, Romania, 1970; chairman of international conference on "The Role of Multinational Corporations in Economic Development," Alexandria, Egypt, co-sponsored by the Academy of International Business, the U.S. Department of State, and the Government of Egypt, 1977; co-chairman of International Symposium on Technology Transfer, Seoul, Korea, co-sponsored by the Federation of Korean Industries, UNIDO, and the Academy of International Business, 1978; has conducted numerous other seminars and conferences.

International public speaker; gives an average of more than 30 major addresses annually to Kiwanis, Rotary, and Lion's Clubs, labor and industry groups, colleges and universities, and foreign chambers of commerce; has also appeared on television and at press conferences and has given radio interviews concerning international politics and business issues. Management consultant to businesses, governments, and organizations, including Federation of Korean Industries, General Electric Corporation, U.S. Civil Service Commission, Central Bank of Malaysia, U.S. Departments of Commerce and State, and governments of Sweden, Iran, Qatar, and Egypt; member of Ohio Governor's Advisory Committee on World Trade, 1972-73, and International Real Estate Advisory Board, Donaldson, Lufkin and Jennerette, 1981—. *Military service:* U.S. Army, 1954-56; served in Japan as public information specialist, acted as assistant director of the Office of Public Information Headquarters.

MEMBER: Academy of International Business (treasurer, beginning 1969; president, 1975-77; fellow), Association of International Executives, Kiwanis International, Academy of Management, American Economic Association, American Management Association.

AWARDS, HONORS: Citation from U.S. Department of Commerce, 1968; named one of Outstanding Educators of America, 1970; Distinguished Alumnus Award, Eastern Washington State College, 1970; one of three delegates named by President Gerald Ford to represent the U.S. at the Bicentennial Ceremony in Genoa, Italy, 1976; International Founders Award, High-12 International, 1979, for outstanding service to the United States of America.

WRITINGS: (With Karel Holbik) *American-East European Trade: Controversy, Progress, Prospects,* National Press, 1968; (with Norma M. Loeser) *Executive Leadership: The Art of Successfully Managing Resources,* MDI Publications, 1969; (with Mika S. Kaskimies) *International Marketing in Perspective,* Sininen Kirja Oy (Helsinki), 1971; (with Ashok Kapoor), *The Multinational Enterprise in Transition,* Darwin Press, 1972; (with Robert F. Dyer and Charles V. Jackson) *A Handbook for Term Papers, Theses and Dissertations,* George Washington University, 1974; (with Tan Chwee Huat, Kwan Kuen-Chor, and George Rott) *East Asia Dimensions of International Business,* Prentice-Hall, 1982; (with Fariborz Ghadar and Dara Khambata) *Multinational Corporations in Transition,* Volume II, Darwin Press, 1983. Also author of monographs. Contributor of case studies to Harvard University Intercollegiate Case Clearinghouse Series on Multinational Business and Developing Countries. Contributor of numerous articles and reviews to professional journals.

WORK IN PROGRESS: A revision of *Executive Leadership;* a book tentatively entitled *Host Government-Multinational Corporate Conflict: Developing a Code of Conduct for Multinational Corporations.*

SIDELIGHTS: Phillip D. Grub writes that he has conducted research in "more than 80 countries, with major work in Japan, Korea, Malaysia, Indonesia, Iran, Egypt, Kuwait, Saudi Arabia, Yugoslavia, Finland, France, Poland, and the People's Republic of China. [My] specific focus has been varied and included development of an industrial trade zone in Egypt, tourism development, the organization and development of a university in Qatar." Furthermore, he indicates he has conducted a considerable amount of research and consulting "on export development for emerging countries, technology transfer, joint-venture negotiation, and developing information and control systems for multinational corporations. On an international scale, major research emphasis has been on the social responsibility of business, economic and business development in emerging countries, and long-range planning."

Many of Grub's writings have been translated into foreign languages.

* * *

GUGLIOTTA, Bobette   1918-
(Bobette Bibo)

PERSONAL: Surname is pronounced Gu-*lyot*-ta; born November 8, 1918, in Chicago, Ill.; daughter of Irving M. (a music composer) and Aline (Waite) Bibo; married Guy Frank Gugliotta (a naval officer and marine engineer), June 2, 1940; children: Guy Bibo. *Education:* Attended Stanford University, University of Southern California, and University of California, Los Angeles. *Home:* 25351 Moody Rd., Los Altos Hills, Calif. 94022.

CAREER: Foothill International League, Los Altos Hills, Calif., founder and first chairman, 1962-65; Young Women's Christian Association (YWCA), Honolulu, Hawaii, master of ceremonies on beach club radio program, 1965-66; Recording for the Blind, Palo Alto, Calif., reader and auxiliary member, 1969—. Founded University of Hawaii foreign student program, 1965-66.

MEMBER: Authors League of America.

WRITINGS: Nolle Smith: Cowboy, Engineer, Statesman, Dodd, 1971; *Katzimo, Mysterious Mesa,* Dodd, 1974; (contributor under name Bobette Bibo) *Mickey Mouse: Fifty Happy Years,* Crown, 1977; *Pigboat 39: An American Sub Goes to War,* University Press of Kentucky, 1984.

Also contributor of chapter to Houghton Mifflin fifth grade reader, 1980 and 1986 editions. Contributor to *Good Housekeeping, Virginia Quarterly Review, Woman,* and other periodicals and newspapers.

WORK IN PROGRESS: Women of Mexico, biographies of Mexican women from the conquest to the twentieth century, "intended for our growing Hispanic-American population."

SIDELIGHTS: Bobette Gugliotta told *CA:* "I wrote my first story (about Mickey Mouse) at age eleven for Walt Disney. Upon return from three years residence in Ecuador, I ran across a volume entitled *Mickey Mouse: Fifty Happy Years.* My work, "The Story of Mickey Mouse," was reprinted under my maiden name Bobette Bibo. It was a pleasure to know I'd gone on writing and that a ten year publication drought had broken with [my] current book, *Pigboat 39.* But is it worth the stamina and effort when you might be doing other fascinating things with live people? When you're young, you're sure it's worth any amount of toil. As you get older, you begin to wonder. But by then—you're hooked."

BIOGRAPHICAL/CRITICAL SOURCES: Los Altos Town Crier, December 29, 1971; *Palo Alto Times,* January 11, 1972.

* * *

GUY, Rosa (Cuthbert)   1928-

PERSONAL: Born September 1, 1928, in Trinidad; came to United States in 1932; daughter of Henry and Audrey (Gonzales) Cuthbert; married Warner Guy (deceased); children: Warner. *Agent:* Ellen Levine Literary Agency, Inc., 432 Park Ave. S., Suite 1205, New York, N.Y. 10016.

CAREER: Writer.

MEMBER: Harlem Writer's Guild (president).

AWARDS, HONORS: The Disappearance was named to the "Best Books for Young Adults 1979" list, by the Young Adult Services Division of the American Library Association.

WRITINGS—Novels, except as indicated: *Bird at My Window,* Lippincott, 1966; (editor) *Children of Longing* (anthology), Holt, 1971; *The Friends,* Holt, 1973; *Ruby: A Novel,* Viking, 1976; *Edith Jackson,* Viking, 1978; *The Disappearance,* Delacorte, 1979; *Mirror of Her Own,* Delacorte, 1981; (translator and adaptor) Birago Diop, *Mother Crocodile: An Uncle Amadou Tale from Senegal* (story), Delacorte, 1981; *A Measure of Time,* Holt, 1983; *New Guys around the Block,* Delacorte, 1983; *Paris, Pee Wee and Big Dog,* Gollancz, 1984, Delacorte, 1985; *I Heard a Bird Sing,* Delacorte, 1986. Also author of one-act play, "Venetian Blinds," 1954. Contributor to *Cosmopolitan* and *Freedomways.*

WORK IN PROGRESS: A book, *Alexander Hamilton: The Enigma; Benidine,* a novel dealing with a Trinidadian family in New York; research in African languages.

SIDELIGHTS: Rosa Guy often writes about black teenagers, but her themes appeal to readers of all ages. And, although one of Guy's publishers once indicated that her "'literary themes stem from the fact that she is a black and a woman,'" Katherine Paterson indicates in *Washington Post Book World,* "a great strength of Guy's work is her ability to peel back society's labels and reveal beneath them highly individual men and women." Her novel *Edith Jackson* is described by Brian Baumfield in *Times Literary Supplement* as "a vigorous, uncompromising" book, with characters who "live and breathe and are totally credible. The West Indian speech may prove difficult for some, but it is a raw novel of urgency and power, which readers of sixteen and older will find a moving experience." *New York Times Book Review* critic Selma G. Lanes comments that, in reading *New Guys around the Block,* "the reader cannot resist rooting for" the author's main character, "with his intelligence and growing self-awareness, as he negotiates the booby traps of a difficult life." Alice Walker points out in *New York Times Book Review* that, at "the heart of" Guy's novel *The Friends* is "the fight to gain perception of one's own real character; the grim struggle for self-knowledge and the almost killing internal upheaval that brings the necessary growth of compassion and humility *and courage,* so that friendship (of any kind, but especially between those of notable economic and social differences) can exist."

A Measure of Time is a departure from Guy's fiction for youths.

In the opinion of Stuart Schoffman in *Los Angeles Times,* it "is a black *Bildungsroman* in the tradition of Claude McKay, Ralph Ellison and James Baldwin, a sharp and well-written meld of storytelling and sociology. Which is to say it is hardly an Alger tale, or if anything a bitter parody." The heroine of the novel, Dorine, born poor in Alabama, begins working as a maid when she is eight. Molested by her boss, she runs to Cleveland as a teenager with the money she has saved. There, she becomes a prostitute, and later, in Harlem during its 1920's renaissance, she takes up a career as a high-class shoplifter, a profession that sees her through the depression in style but eventually sends her to prison. She is released and regains a modest success as a small businesswoman. Susan Isaacs describes her in *New York Times Book Review* as "a brash and intelligent guide; her observations about people and places are funny, pointed and often moving," although "the other characters in this novel do not come to life. . . . Only Dorine stands on her own—she and the Harlem setting are vividly described, filled with life and a pleasure to read about."

BIOGRAPHICAL/CRITICAL SOURCES: Washington Post, January 9, 1966; *New York Times Book Review,* November 4, 1973, July 2, 1978, December 2, 1979, October 4, 1981, August 28, 1983, October 9, 1983; *Times Literary Supplement,* September 20, 1974, December 14, 1979, July 18, 1980, August 3, 1984; *Washington Post Book World,* November 11, 1979; *Times Educational Supplement,* June 6, 1980; *Los Angeles Times,* August 24, 1983; *Contemporary Literary Criticism,* Volume XXVI, Gale, 1983; *Dictionary of Literary Biography,* Volume XXXIII: *Afro-American Fiction Writers after 1955,* Gale, 1984.

H

HAASE, John 1923-

PERSONAL: Born August 21, 1923, in Frankfurt, Germany; son of Fred W. and Selma (Rosenthal) Haase; married Jean Rosenblatt, 1948; children: Robert, Leslie, Tracy, Peter. *Education:* University of California, Los Angeles, A.A., 1942, B.S., 1944, D.D.S., 1948. *Agent:* Russell & Volkening, 551 Fifth Ave., New York, N.Y. 10176.

CAREER: Private practice, dentistry, Los Angeles, Calif., beginning 1948. *Military service:* U.S. Army, 1941-42.

MEMBER: American Dental Association, American Academy of Oral Roentgenology, Royal Society of Health, Authors League of America, Dramatists Guild, Alpha Omega, Executives Club.

WRITINGS: The Young Who Sin, Avon, 1958; *Road Show,* Simon & Schuster, 1960 (published in England as *The Sherbet Colours,* Heinemann, 1961); *The Fun Couple,* Simon & Schuster, 1961; *Erasmus—with Freckles,* Simon & Schuster, 1963; *Me and the Arch Kook Petulia,* Coward, 1967; *The Noon Balloon to Rangoon,* Simon & Schuster, 1967; *The Nuptials: A Novel,* Simon & Schuster, 1969; *Seasons and Moments,* Simon & Schuster, 1971; *Big Red,* Harper, 1980.

Short story, "Countdown," anthologized in *The Year's Best Science Fiction for 1961.* Contributor to dental journals, *Los Angeles Times, New Yorker,* and other magazines.

MEDIA ADAPTATIONS: Play adapted from *The Fun Couple,* opened in New York, October, 1962; *Me and the Arch Kook Petulia* was filmed as "Petulia," Warner Bros., 1967.

BIOGRAPHICAL/CRITICAL SOURCES: Saturday Evening Post, October 7, 1961; *Punch,* January 31, 1968; *National Observer,* June 17, 1968; *Los Angeles Times,* May 4, 1980.†

*   *   *

HADLEY, Leila 1925-

PERSONAL: Born September 22, 1925, in New York; daughter of Frank Vincent (a sportsman) and Beatrice (Eliott) Burton; married Arthur T. Hadley, March, 1944 (divorced August, 1947); married Yvor H. Smitter, January, 1953 (divorced August, 1969); married William C. Musham, May 29, 1976; children: (first marriage) Arthur T. III; (second marriage) Victoria, Matthew, Caroline. *Education:* Attended University of

Witwatersrand. *Religion:* Presbyterian. *Home and office:* 300 East 75th St., New York, N.Y. 10021. *Agent:* Peter Matson, Literistic Ltd., 32 West 40th St., Suite 5F, New York, N.Y. 10018.

CAREER: Diplomat (magazine), New York City, associate editor, 1965-67; *Saturday Evening Post,* New York City, cartoon editor, 1967, associate women's editor, 1968; *Palm Beach Life,* Palm Beach, Fla., book reviewer and feature writer, 1970-73.

MEMBER: Royal Society for Asian Affairs, Society of American Travel Writers, Society of Women Geographers.

WRITINGS: Give Me the World, Simon & Schuster, 1958; *How to Travel with Children in Europe,* Walker, 1963; (with John Barclay) *Manners for Young People,* Random House, 1966; *Fielding's Guide to Traveling with Children in Europe,* Morrow, 1972, revised edition, 1974, 2nd revised edition published as *Fielding's Europe with Children,* Fielding Travel Books, 1984; *Traveling with Children in the U.S.A.,* Morrow, 1976; *Tibet: 20 Years after the Chinese Takeover,* Imperial Printing Press (Dharamsala), 1979.

Contributor to *Town and Country, Woman's Day, Travel and Camera, Newsday, New York Times,* and *Saturday Evening Post.*

WORK IN PROGRESS: A fictionalized memoir, entitled *Dharamsala,* for Random House; articles.

*   *   *

HAINES, Gail Kay 1943-

PERSONAL: Born March 15, 1943, in Mt. Vernon, Ill.; daughter of Samuel Glen (an atomic plant foreman) and Audrey (Goin) Beekman; married Michael Philip Haines (an oral surgeon), May 8, 1964; children: David Michael, Cindy Lynn. *Education:* Washington University, St. Louis, Mo., A.B., 1965. *Home:* 4145 Lorna Court S.E., Olympia, Wash. 98503.

CAREER: Mallinckrodt Chemical Works, St. Louis, Mo., analytical chemist, 1965-66; writer, 1969—.

WRITINGS—All juvenile: The Elements, F. Watts, 1972; *Fire,* Morrow, 1975; *Explosives,* Morrow, 1976; *Supercold/Superhot,* F. Watts, 1976; *What Makes a Lemon Sour?,* Morrow,

1977; *Brainpower*, F. Watts, 1978; *Natural and Synthetic Poisons*, Morrow, 1979; *Cancer*, F. Watts, 1980; *Baking in a Box, Cooking on a Can*, Morrow, 1981; *Test Tube Mysteries*, Dodd, Mead, 1982.

WORK IN PROGRESS: The Great Nuclear Power Debate, for Dodd, Mead.

SIDELIGHTS: Gail Kay Haines writes: "I have always been fascinated by science, especially reading and writing about it. Chemistry is my favorite, because it is the science I know the most about, but writing books keeps me learning all kinds of things from up-to-minute research to ancient history. I think children want more than just the basic science information they get in school—they want to know what is going on today and what the future holds, and that is what other juvenile nonfiction writers and I try to explore."

* * *

HALDANE-STEVENSON, James Patrick   1910-
(J. P. Stevenson, James Patrick Stevenson; Tomos Radyr, a pseudonym)

PERSONAL: Surname originally Stevenson; born March 17, 1910, in Llandaff, Wales; son of Graham Morton (an engineer) and Jane (Thomson) Stevenson; married Leila Mary Flack, November 5, 1938 (divorced, 1967); married Joan Talbot Smith, August 6, 1983; children: (first marriage) Alan, Keith, Janet. *Education:* St. Catherine's College, Oxford, B.A., 1933, M.A., 1941; University of Lausanne, B.es L., 1934. *Home:* 3 Argyle Sq., Ainslie Ave., Canberra 2601, Australia.

CAREER: Ordained Anglican clergyman, 1935. Westminster Bank, Birmingham, England, clerk, 1927-30; curate of Anglican church in Lambeth, England, 1935-38; British Army, chaplain, 1939-55, served at Dunkirk and Cassino; rector of Anglican church in Wongan Hills, Australia, 1956-59; vicar of North Balwyn, Melbourne, Australia, 1959-80; writer, 1980—. *Member:* Freemen of London, Athenaeum Club (London), Melbourne Club, Naval and Military Club (Melbourne), National Press Club (Canberra).

WRITINGS—Under name J. P. Stevenson, except as indicated: (Editor under name James Patrick Stevenson) *In Our Tongues*, S.P.C.K., 1944; *Religion and Leadership*, Allied Commission (Vienna), 1948; *Crisanzio and Other Poems*, privately printed, 1948; *Beyond the Bridge* (autobiography), Angus & Robertson, 1973; *The Backward Look* (family history), St. Silas' Press, 1976.

Work represented in anthologies, including: *Soldiers Also Asked*, edited by Ronald Selby Wright, Oxford University Press, 1943; *Padre Presents*, edited by Wright, Longmans, Green, 1943; *Poems from Italy*, edited by Siegfried Sassoon, Harrap, 1945; *Songs of Australia*, Bayside Press, 1977.

Contributor to *Australian Encyclopaedia* and *Australian Dictionary of Biography*. Author of articles on Wales under pseudonym Tomos Radyr. Australian correspondent for *Le Monde*, 1969-73. Contributor to *Poetry Review, Poetry Today, Guardian, New Statesman, Spectator*, and to church journals and newspapers.

WORK IN PROGRESS: Monarchy in Crisis.

SIDELIGHTS: James Patrick Haldane-Stevenson told *CA* he sees in the British monarchy "an exemplar of excellence in a shoddy world, a link between forty-seven widely different countries, and a bulwark against continual erosion of constitutional government." *Avocational interests:* Cornish antiquities.

BIOGRAPHICAL/CRITICAL SOURCES: Women's Weekly, December 4, 1963; *Heidelberger*, September 22, 1970; *Yr Enfys*, March-April, 1972; *Times* (London), October 10, 1977; *Bulletin*, July 11, 1978; *Church Scene*, November 29, 1979; *Progress Press* (Melbourne), April 2, 1980.

* * *

HALEY, Gail E(inhart)   1939-

PERSONAL: Born November 4, 1939, in Charlotte, N.C.; daughter of George C. (an advertising manager) and P. Louise (Bell) Einhart; married Joseph A. Haley (a mathematician), August 15, 1959; married second husband, Arnold F. Arnold (a designer, writer, and artist), February 14, 1966; married third husband, David Considine, September 3, 1983; children: (second marriage) Marguerite Madeline, Geoffrey David. *Education:* Attended Richmond Professional Institute, 1957-59, and University of Virginia, 1960-64. *Agent:* Curtis Brown Ltd., 575 Madison Ave., New York, N.Y. 10022. *Office:* Edwin Duncan Hall, Appalachian State University, Boone, N.C. 28608.

CAREER: Manuscript Press, New York, N.Y., vice-president, beginning 1965; Appalachian State University, Boone, N.C., currently writer-in-residence and curator of Gail Hailey Collection of the Culture of Childhood. Artist, illustrator of children's books and educational material, and designer of toys and fashion items; graphics and illustrations exhibited at libraries and museums in southern states and New York. Work included in permanent collections at the University of Minnesota, Jacksonville (Fla.) Children's Museum, University of Southern Mississippi, and Appalachian State University. Toured Great Britain in one-woman multimedia show "Get into a Book."

AWARDS, HONORS: Caldecott Medal, American Library Association, 1971, for *A Story, a Story;* Czechoslovak Children's Film Festival Award for best animated children's film of the year, 1974; Kate Greenaway Medal for illustration, British Library Association, 1976, and Kadai Tosho award (Japan), both for *The Post Office Cat*.

WRITINGS—All self-illustrated: *My Kingdom for a Dragon*, Crozet Print Shop, 1962; *The Wonderful Magical World of Marguerite: With the Entire Cast of Characters Including Rocks, Roses, Mushrooms, Daisies, Violets, Snails, Butterflies, Breezes, and Above All—the Sun*, McGraw, 1964; *Round Stories about Things That Live on Land*, Follett, 1966; *Round Stories about Things That Live in Water*, Follett, 1966; *Round Stories about Things That Grow*, Follett, 1966; *Round Stories about Our World*, Follett, 1966.

A Story, a Story, Atheneum, 1970; *Noah's Ark*, Atheneum, 1973; *Jack Jouett's Ride*, Viking, 1973; *The Abominable Swampman*, Viking, 1975; *The Post Office Cat*, Scribner, 1976; *Go Away, Stay Away!*, Scribner, 1977; *Costumes for Plays and Playing*, Methuen, 1978; *A Story, a Day*, Methuen, 1979; *Gail Haley's Costume Book*, Magnet Books, Volume I: *Dress Up and Have Fun*, 1979, Volume II: *Dress Up and Play*, 1980; *The Green Man*, Scribner, 1980; *Birdsong*, Crown, 1984. Contributor of children's stories to magazines.

Illustrator: *The Skip Rope Book*, Dial, 1962; *One, Two, Buckle My Shoe*, Doubleday, 1964; *The Three Wishes of Hu*, Putnam, 1964; *Koalas*, Prentice-Hall, 1965; *Which Is Which?*, Prentice-

Hall, 1966; *P.S. Happy Anniversary*, World Publishing, 1966; *Peek-A-Boo Book of Puppies and Kittens*, Nelson, 1966; *All Together, One at a Time*, Atheneum, 1971. Also illustrator of syndicated column, "Parents and Children," written by Arnold F. Arnold.

WORK IN PROGRESS: Jack and the Bean Tree, for Crown.

SIDELIGHTS: Gail E. Haley writes: "More than a personal catharsis, my work is an effort designed to stimulate verbal and visual responses and a preparation for literacy. My books are for children. They are also frames of reference for the story reader who needs to dramatize, explain, and discuss the ideas I express, the pictures I draw and the words I use. My object is to involve both adult and child." She also explained that "a child brings his own understanding and experience to the book and is enriched by what the book gives him back. He must supply movement, image, sound and sequence of time. This is a far greater challenge to his brain than sitting passively before a TV set and having these things fed to him without any effort on his part." Haley appeared in a documentary film, "Animating Picture Books."

MEDIA ADAPTATIONS: A Story, a Story was made into a filmstrip, 1972, and an animated film, 1973, both produced by Weston Woods Studios. *Jack Jouett's Ride* was made into a filmstrip, Weston Woods Studios, 1975. An animated film with the same title is planned.

BIOGRAPHICAL/CRITICAL SOURCES: New York Times Book Review, April 12, 1970, November 8, 1970; *Publishers' Weekly*, September 6, 1971; *Charlotte (N.C.) Observer*, July 29, 1973.

*   *   *

HALL, Douglas John   1928-

PERSONAL: Born March 23, 1928, in Ingersoll, Ontario, Canada; son of John D. (a railway worker) and L. Irene (Sandick) Hall; married Rhoda Catherine Palfrey, May 28, 1960; children: Mary Kate, Christopher, Sara, Lucia. *Education:* University of Western Ontario, B.A., 1953; Union Theological Seminary, M.Div., 1956, S.T.M., 1957, Th.D., 1963. *Home:* 5562 Avenue Notre-Dame-de-Grace, Montreal, Quebec, Canada. *Office:* Faculty of Religious Studies, McGill University, 3520 University St., Montreal, Quebec, Canada.

CAREER: Ordained minister of United Church of Canada, 1956; St. Andrew's United Church, Blind River, Ontario, pastor, 1960-62; University of Waterloo, Waterloo, Ontario, principal of St. Paul's United College, 1962-65; St. Andrew's College, Saskatoon, Saskatchewan, McDougald Professor of Systematic Theology, 1965-75; McGill University, Montreal, Quebec, associate professor of Christian theology, 1975—. Guest professor, Universitat Siegen, Siegen, West Germany, 1981; guest lecturer in Canada, the United States, West Germany, and East Germany. Member of theological committee of North American Alliance of Reformed Churches. *Member:* Canadian Theological Society.

WRITINGS: (Editor with Samuel Terrien and others) Paul Scherer, *Love Is a Spendthrift*, Harper, 1960; *Hope Against Hope*, World Student Christian Federation, 1971; *The Reality of the Gospel and the Unreality of the Churches*, Westminster, 1975; *Lighten Our Darkness: Toward an Indigenous Theology of the Cross*, Westminster, 1976; *The Canada Crisis*, Anglican Book Centre, 1981; *Has the Church a Future?*, Westminster, 1981; *The Steward: A Biblical Symbol Come of Age*, Friendship, 1982.

WORK IN PROGRESS: Rethinking Christ: A Theology for the Post-Christian Era; a three volume work, *A North American Contextual Theology; Theology Is an Earth Science; The Christian Mission: Stewarding Life in the Kingdom of Death.*

SIDELIGHTS: Douglas John Hall writes: "My primary concern is that of a Christian theologian who tries to understand the human situation in the light of the 'Gospel of the Cross.' I attempt to work out a theological posture indigenous to the North American experience."

*   *   *

HALL, Elizabeth   1929-

PERSONAL: Born September 17, 1929, in Bakersfield, Calif.; daughter of Edward Earl (an accountant) and Ethel Mae (Butner) Hall. *Education:* Bakersfield College, A.A., 1947; Fresno State College (now California State University, Fresno), B.A., 1964. *Residence:* Waccabuc, N.Y. *Agent:* McIntosh & Otis, Inc., 475 Fifth Ave., New York, N.Y. 10017.

CAREER: Shafter Branch Library, Shafter, Calif., librarian, 1958-66; University of California, Irvine, librarian, 1966-67; *Psychology Today*, Del Mar, Calif., associate editor, 1967-68, assistant managing editor, 1968-72, managing editor, 1972-75, managing editor in New York City, 1975-76; Harcourt Brace Jovanovich, Inc., New York City, editor of *Human Nature* (magazine), 1976-79; writer and behavioral science journalist, 1979—.

MEMBER: American Association for the Advancement of Science, Society for Research in Child Development, Gerontological Society, Authors Guild.

AWARDS, HONORS: National Media Award honorable mention from American Psychological Foundation, 1974, for *Why We Do What We Do*, and 1976, for *From Pigeons to People.*

WRITINGS: Voltaire's Micromegas, Golden Gate, 1967; *Phoebe Snow*, Houghton, 1968; *Stand Up, Lucy!*, Houghton, 1971; *Why We Do What We Do: A Look at Psychology*, Houghton, 1973; *From Pigeons to People: A Look at Behavior Shaping*, Houghton, 1975; (editor) *Developmental Psychology Today*, 2nd edition (Hall was not associated with earlier edition), CRM Books, 1975, 3rd edition (and contributor with Robert E. Schell), 1979, 4th edition, Random House, 1983; *Possible Impossibilities: A Look at Parapsychology*, Houghton, 1977; *Child Psychology Today*, Random House, 1982; (editor) *Psychology Today: An Introduction*, 5th edition (Hall was not associated with earlier editions), Random House, 1982; (with Ray Rosen) *Sexuality*, Random House, 1984; (with Marion Perlmutter) *Adult Development and Aging*, Wiley, 1985.

Films; all with Peter Drucker; all produced by Bureau of National Affairs Films; all 1971: (With John Humble) "The Manager as Entrepreneur"; (with Vermont Royster) "Tomorrow's Customs"; (with Charles De Carlo) "The Future of Technology"; (with De Carlo) "Coping with Technological Change"; (with Jerry Wurf) "Who's Gonna Collect the Garbage?"; (with Robert Hansberger) "Social Needs as Business Opportunities"; (with Hansberger) "Pollution Control—The Hard Decision"; (with Dan Seymour) "The Multinational Corporation"; (with Humble) "The Innovative Organization."

Films; with B. F. Skinner; all produced by CRM Films; all 1972: "A Conversation with B. F. Skinner"; "Token Economy: Behaviorism Applied"; "Business, Behaviorism and the Bottom Line."

HALSEY, Martha T. 1932-

PERSONAL: Born May 5, 1932, in Richmond, Va.; daughter of James D. and Martha (Taliaferro) Halsey. *Education:* Goucher College, A.B., 1954; State University of Iowa, M.A., 1956; Ohio State University, Ph.D., 1964. *Politics:* Democrat. *Religion:* Episcopalian. *Home:* 151 W. Prospect Ave., State College, Pa. 16801. *Office:* Pennsylvania State University, 350 North Burrowes Building, University Park, Pa. 16802.

CAREER: Pennsylvania State University, University Park, assistant professor, 1964-70, associate professor, 1970-79, professor of Spanish, 1979—.

MEMBER: American Association of Teachers of Spanish and Portuguese, Modern Language Association of America, American Association of University Professors, Northeast Modern Language Association.

AWARDS, HONORS: American Philosophical Society grants, 1970 and 1979; grant from the Institute for the Arts and Humanistic Studies, Pennsylvania State University, 1978.

WRITINGS: (Editor with Donald Bleznick) Antonio Buero Vallejo, *Madrugada*, text book edition, Ginn, 1969; *Antonio Buero Vallejo*, Boston Publishing, 1970; (editor) Buero Vallejo, *Hoy es fiesta* [Salamanca, Spain], 1980; (editor) Rodriguez Mendez, *Los inocentes de la Moncloa* [Salamanca, Spain], 1982; (editor) Jose Martin Recuerda, *El enganao* [and] *Caballos desbocaos* [Madrid, Spain], 1983. Contributor of articles and reviews to literary journals including *Hispania, Romanic Review, Romance Notes, Comparative Literature Studies, Contemporary Literature,* and *Revista de Estudios Hispanicos.* Editorial associate, *Modern International Drama, Kentucky Romance Quarterly, Hispanic Review, Estreno, South Atlantic Bulletin,* and *Hispanofila.*

WORK IN PROGRESS: A study of the recent generation of Spanish playwrights, including Carlos Muniz, Antonio Gala, Ricardo Buded, Lauro Olmo, and Martin Recuerda; an anthology of essays on Spain's theater of the 1870s and 1880s.

SIDELIGHTS: Martha T. Halsey writes *CA:* "I believe that studying another language and literature is like looking into the soul of another people. I am most interested in the interrelationship between the theater and Spain's transition from the Franco dictatorship to democracy."

*　　　*　　　*

HALSTOCK, Max
See CAULFIELD, Malachy Francis

*　　　*　　　*

HAMBURGER, Kaete 1896-

PERSONAL: Born September 21, 1896, in Hamburg, Germany (now West Germany); daughter of John (a banker) and Hertha Hamburger. *Education:* Studied philosophy and literature at University of Berlin and University of Munich, 1917-22, received Dr.Phil., 1922. *Home:* Hegelstrasse 51, Stuttgart, West Germany.

CAREER: University of Stuttgart, Stuttgart, West Germany, professor of literature, beginning 1957.

MEMBER: International P.E.N., International Federation of University Women, Goethe-Gesellschaft, Deutsche Schiller-Gesellschaft, Thomas Mann-Gesellschaft, Verdienstkrewz der Bundesrepublik Deutschland, Modern Language Association of America (honorary member).

AWARDS, HONORS: Dr.H.C., Modern Language Association of America.

WRITINGS: (Editor) Betty Heimann, *System und Methode in Hegels Philosophie,* [Leipzig], 1927; *Thomas Mann und die Romantik,* Junker & Duennhaupt, 1932; *Thomas Manns Roman "Joseph und seine Brueder,"* Bermann-Fischer, 1945, 2nd edition published as *Der Humor bei Thomas Mann,* Nymphenburger Verlagshandlung, 1965, 3rd edition published as *Thomas Manns biblisches Werk,* Nymphenburger Verlagshand, 1981; *Schiller: Problemen i hans verk* (in Swedish), Natur & Kultur, 1947.

Leo Tolstoi: Gestalt und Problem, L. Lehnen, 1950, 2nd edition, Vandenhoeck & Ruprecht, 1963; *Die Logik der Dichtung,* Ernst Klett, 1957, 2nd edition, 1968, 3rd edition, Ullstein-Taschenbuch, 1980, translation by Marilynn Rose published as *The Logic of Literature,* Indiana University Press, 1973; *Von Sophokles zu Sartre: Griechische Dramenfiguren antik und modern,* Kohlhammer, 1962, translation by Helen Sebba published as *From Sophocles to Sartre: Figures from Greek Tragedy, Classical and Modern,* Ungar, 1969; (editor) Thomas Mann, *Das Gesetz,* Ullstein, 1964; *Philosophie der Dichter: Novalis, Schiller, Rilke,* Kohlhammer, 1966; (editor and contributor) *Rilke in neuer Sicht,* Kohlhammer, 1971; *Rilke: Eine Einfuehrung,* Ernst Klett, 1976; *Wahrheit undaesthetische Wahrheit,* Klett-Cotta, 1979.

Contributor: H. W. Seiffert and B. Zeller, editors, *Festgabe fuer Eduard Berend,* Hermann Boehlaus Nachfolger, 1959; H. Holtzhauer and Zeller, editors, *Studien zur Goethezeit: Festschrift fuer Lieselotte Blumenthal,* Hermann Boehlaus Nachfolger, 1968; H. Kreuzer, editor, *Gestaltungsgeschichte und Gesellschaftsgeschichte,* J. B. Metzlersche Verlagsbuchhandlung, 1969; B. Hueppauf and D. Sternberger, editors, *Ueber Literatur und Geschichte: Festschrift fuer Gerhard Storz,* Athenaeum, 1973; V. J. Guenther and H. Koopmann, editors, *Untersuchungen zur Literatur als Geschichte: Festschrift fuer Benno V. Wiese,* Erich Schmidt, 1973; H. Ruediger, editor, *Literatur und Dichtung,* Kohlhammer, 1973; U. Schweikert, editor, *Jean Paul,* Wissenschaftliche Buchgesellschaft, 1974.

Koopmann, editor, *Thomas Mann,* Wissenschaftliche Buchgesellschaft, 1975; H. J. Schrimpf, editor, *Gerhart Hauptmann,* Wissenschaftliche Buchgesellschaft, 1976; W. Keller, editor, *Beitraege zur Poetik des Dramas,* Wissenschaftliche Buchgesellschaft, 1976; G. Gillespie and E. Lohner, editors, *Herkommen und Erneuerung: Festschrift fuer Oskar Seidlin,* Max Niemeyer, 1976; *Probleme der Moderne: Festschrift fur W. Sokel,* Max Niemeyer, 1983.

Contributor to *Jahrbuch der deutschen Schillergesellschaft, Handbuch der deutschen Gegenwartsliteratur,* and of more than ninety papers and articles to professional journals, magazines, and newspapers in Germany, England, Sweden, Netherlands, and the United States.

BIOGRAPHICAL/CRITICAL SOURCES: Times Literary Supplement, October 9, 1981.

*　　　*　　　*

HAMILTON-EDWARDS, Gerald (Kenneth Savery) 1906-

PERSONAL: Born July 24, 1906, in Southsea, Hampshire,

England; son of Frederick Charles (a lieutenant general, Royal Marines) and Nona Louisa (Stevens) Edwards. *Education:* Keble College, Oxford, B.A., 1927, M.A., 1932; University of London, Diploma in Librarianship, 1930. *Politics:* Conservative. *Home:* 32 Bowness Ave., Headington, Oxford OX3 0AL, England.

CAREER: Writer. Plymouth Proprietary Library, Plymouth, England, assistant librarian, 1937-39; University of London, Queen Mary College, London, England, assistant librarian, 1945-47; Devon County Library, England, librarian of Pymstock branch, 1947-48, regional librarian for South West Devon, 1948-54; Society of Genealogists, London, secretary, 1955. Part-time teacher in technical and grammar schools. Member of Plymouth City Libraries and Museum Committee, 1932—, and Oxford City Council, 1967-72. Governor of Oxford Polytechnic, 1967-72, and Magdalen College School, 1970-72. *Military service:* British Army, Royal Signals, Territorial Army, 1934-55; on active service, 1939-45; became major; received Territorial Decoration, 1946, and Coronation Medal, 1953.

MEMBER: Library Association (fellow), Royal Overseas League (chairman of Plymouth branch, 1953-54), Society of Genealogists (fellow), Scottish Genealogy Society, English Speaking Union, Society of Authors, Radio Writers Association, Oxfordshire Family History Society (president, 1980—), Oxford Society.

WRITINGS: The Stevens Family of Plymouth, privately printed, 1947; *Twelve Men of Plymouth*, privately printed, 1951; *The Leisured Connoisseur*, privately printed, 1954; (editor) *A Cadet in the Baltic: The Letters of Frederick Edwards, 1855-1857*, privately printed, 1956; (editor) Nona Louisa Edwards, *My Memory Walks beside Me*, privately printed, 1963; *In Search of Ancestry*, M. Joseph, 1966, published as *Tracing Your British Ancestors: A Guide to Genealogical Sources*, Walker & Co., 1967, 3rd edition published as *In Search of British Ancestry*, Genealogical Publishing, 1974, 4th edition, 1983; *In Search of Scottish Ancestry*, Genealogical Publishing, 1972, 2nd edition, Phillimore, 1983; *In Search of Army Ancestry*, Phillimore, 1977; (compiler and author of introduction) *Perthshire Marriage Contracts, 1687-1809*, privately printed, 1978; *Paris in My Youth and Other Poems*, privately printed, 1982.

Also author of short stories and radio scripts for British Broadcasting Corp.; contributor to *Dictionary of National Biography*, and to *Trident, Apollo, Weekly Scotsman, Westcountry Magazine, Times, Times Literary Supplement, Independent*, and other publications.

AVOCATIONAL INTERESTS: Music, art, photography, economics.

*   *   *

HARCOURT, Palma
(John Penn)

PERSONAL: Born in Jersey, Channel Islands; married Jack H. Trotman. *Education:* Attended Jersey Ladies College; earned M.A. from St. Anne's College, Oxford. *Home:* Champ de Rousset, Mont Felard, St. Lawrence, Jersey, Channel Islands. *Agent:* Murray Pollinger, 4 Garrick St., London W.C.2, England.

CAREER: Writer. *Member:* Crime Writers' Association (Britain), Army and Navy Club (London).

*WRITINGS—*Published by Collins, except as indicated: *Climate for Conspiracy*, 1974; *A Fair Exchange*, 1975, McKay,

1976; *Dance for Diplomats*, 1976; *At High Risk*, 1977; *Agents of Influence*, 1978; *A Sleep of Spies*, 1979; *Tomorrow's Treason*, 1980, Scribner, 1981; *The Twisted Tree*, 1982; *Shadows of Doubt*, 1983; *The Distant Stranger*, Beaufort Book Co., 1984. Also contributor of short stories to *Winter's Crimes 14*, Macmillan, 1983, and *John Creasey Anthology*, 1984.

Under pseudonym John Penn, with husband Jack H. Trotman; published by Scribner, except as indicated: *Notice of Death*, Collins, 1982; *An Ad for Murder*, 1983; *Deceitful Death*, Collins, 1983; *Stag-Dinner Death*, 1984; *A Will to Kill*, 1984; *Mortal Term*, 1985.

WORK IN PROGRESS: A Cloud of Doves, for Collins, and *A Matter of Conscience; A Deadly Sickness*, under pseudonym John Penn.

SIDELIGHTS: Some of Palma Harcourt's books have been translated into Danish and Norwegian, and several have been translated into Italian and German.

*   *   *

HARDING, James   1929-

PERSONAL: Born May 30, 1929, in Bath, Somerset, England; married Gillian Russell, January 28, 1956; children: Rupert, Lucy. *Education:* Sorbonne, University of Paris, Diplome de la civilisation francaise, 1948; University of Bristol, B.A. (with honors), 1950; University of London, Ph.D., 1973. *Home:* 100 Ridgemount Gardens, Torrington Place, London WC1E 7AZ, England. *Agent:* Tony Peake, London Management, 235-241 Regent St., London W1A 2JT, England; and Kurt Hellmer, 52 Vanderbilt Ave., New York, N.Y. 10017.

CAREER: Copywriter and advertising executive in advertising agencies and mass-magazine publishing houses, London, England, 1952-64; lecturer, broadcaster, and author in French and English, 1965—. *Military service:* Royal Air Force, 1950-52; served as flying officer. *Member:* Classical Association.

WRITINGS: Saint-Saens and His Circle, Fernhill, 1965; *Sacha Guitry: The Last Boulevardier*, Scribner, 1968; *The Duke of Wellington*, Morgan Grampian, 1968, published as *Wellington*, A. S. Barnes, 1969; (author of introduction) Richard Doddridge Blackmore, *The Maid of Sker*, Anthony Blond, 1968; *Massenet*, Dent, 1970, St. Martin's, 1971; *Boulanger*, Scribner, 1971 (published in England as *General Boulanger*, W. H. Allen, 1971); *Rossini*, Crowell, 1971; *The Ox on the Roof*, St. Martin's, 1972; (editor and author of preface) *Lord Chesterfield's Letters to His Son*, Folio Society, 1973; *Gounod*, Stein & Day, 1973; *Lost Illusions: Paul Leautaud and His World*, Allen & Unwin, 1974, Fairleigh Dickinson University Press, 1975; *Eric Satie*, Praeger, 1975.

Folies de Paris: The Rise and Fall of French Operetta, Chappell, 1978; *Jacques Offenbach*, Riverrun Press, 1980; *Maurice Chevalier: His Life*, Secker & Warburg, 1982; *Jacques Tati, Frame by Frame*, Secker & Warburg, 1984. Contributor to numerous journals, periodicals, reference works and dictionaries.

WORK IN PROGRESS: A biography of James Agate, drama critic and writer, for Eyre-Methuen.

SIDELIGHTS: Reviewing James Harding's biography of the composer Jacques Offenbach, Joseph McLellan writes in the *Washington Post:* "It seems impossible to be bored by James Harding's biography, . . . which reads more like a novel about the composer than a scholarly study. Harding has dug out colorful material from all relevant sources and a few that are only marginally relevant. . . . There are detailed pages on Offenbach eating breakfast, Offenbach directing a rehearsal, a soiree at the Offenbachs'. Even the most minor characters are usually introduced with a short, colorful description and often an anecdote or two that may have little to do with Offenbach. It is a very splendidly readable book and very much in the spirit of the subject.''

AVOCATIONAL INTERESTS: French music, literature, and theatre, and English literature of the 18th, 19th, and 20th centuries; collecting manuscripts of French authors, musicians, and composers.

BIOGRAPHICAL/CRITICAL SOURCES: Washington Post, April 9, 1981; *Los Angeles Times,* April 26, 1981; *Times Literary Supplement,* January 23, 1983.

*   *   *

HARE, F(rederick) Kenneth   1919-

PERSONAL: Born February 5, 1919, in Wylye, Wiltshire, England; became Canadian citizen, 1951; son of Frederick Eli and Irene (Smith) Hare; married Suzanne Alice Bates, 1941 (divorced, 1952); married Helen Neilson Morrill, December 26, 1953; children: (first marriage) Christopher John; (second marriage) Elissa, Robin. *Education:* University of London, B.Sc. (with first class honors), 1939; University of Montreal, Ph.D., 1950. *Home and office:* Trinity College, 6 Hoskin Ave., Toronto, Ontario, Canada M5S 1H8.

CAREER: University of Manchester, Manchester, England, assistant lecturer in geography, 1940-41; McGill University, Montreal, Quebec, assistant professor, 1945-49, associate professor, 1949-52, professor of geography and meteorology, 1952-64, chairman of geography department, 1950-62, dean of Faculty of Arts and Sciences, 1962-64; University of London, London, England, professor of geography and head of department at King's College, 1964-66, master of Birkbeck College, 1966-68, fellow of King's College, 1967—; University of British Columbia, Vancouver, president, 1968-69; University of Toronto, Toronto, Ontario, professor of geography and physics, 1969-76, university professor, 1976—, provost of Trinity College, 1979—, director of Institute for Environmental Studies, 1974-79; Department of the Environment, Canadian Government, Ottawa, Ontario, director-general of research coordination (on leave from University of Toronto), 1972-73.

Visiting scientist, University of Wisconsin, 1969; Lansdowne Visitor, University of Victoria, 1981; distinguished visitor, University of British Columbia, 1982. Chairman of board, Arctic Institute of North America, 1963; member of board of directors of Resources for the Future (U.S.), 1968-80, John Wiley & Sons, 1973—, and Wiley Publishers of Canada, 1973—; *ex officio* member of board of governors, Trinity College School, 1979—. Member of National Research Council (Canada), 1962-64, and Natural Environment Research Council (United Kingdom), 1965-68; co-chairman of National Academy of Sciences/ Royal Society of Canada committee on acid precipitation, 1980-1982. Vice-chairman, Thea and Leon Koerner Foundation, 1968-69. Trustee of Stanstead College, 1956-77, Canadian-Scandinavian Foundation, 1956-60, and Thomas Coram Fields Trust, 1967. Member of Advisory Committee on Natural Resources (United Kingdom), 1965-66, and Canadian Broadcasting Corp. advisory committee on science and technology, 1982—. *Wartime service:* British Air Ministry, meteorologist, 1941-45.

MEMBER: Royal Society of Canada (fellow), Canadian Association of Geographers (president, 1963-64), Royal Meteorological Society (president, 1967-68), Royal Geographical Society, Royal Canadian Geographical Society (fellow), Canadian Geographical Society, Arctic Institute, American Geographical Society (fellow), American Meteorological Society (fellow), Glaciological Society, Geographical Association, Institute of British Geographers, American Association for the Advancement of Science (fellow), Geologists' Association, Canadian Meteorological and Oceanographic Society, Faculty Club of McGill University, Faculty Club of University of Toronto, York Club (Toronto), Athenaeum Club (London).

AWARDS, HONORS: Meritorious Achievement Citation, Association of American Geographers, 1961; President's Prize, Canadian branch of Royal Meteorological Society, 1961, 1962; Patterson Medal, Atmospheric Environment Service (Canada), 1973; Massey Medal, Royal Canadian Geographical Society, 1974; Patron's Medal, Royal Geographical Society, 1977; award for scholarly distinction, Canadian Association of Geographers, 1979; Centenary Medal, Royal Society of Canada, 1982; faculty award, University of Toronto, 1982. LL.D., Queen's University of Kingston, 1964, University of Western Ontario, 1968, and Trent University, 1979; D.Sc., McGill University, 1969, Adelaide University, 1974, and York University, 1978; D.S. Litt., *iure dignitatis,* Thorneloe College of Laurentian University, 1984.

WRITINGS: The Restless Atmosphere, Hutchinson, 1953, 4th edition, Harper, 1966; (with L. Dudley Stamp) *Physical Geography for Canada,* Longmans, Green, 1953; (with Svenn Orvig) *The Arctic Circulation,* Arctic Meteorology Research Group, McGill University, 1958; (with Orvig) *Arctic Meteorology Research Group Publications in Meteorology,* McGill University, 1958; *A Photo-Reconnaissance Survey of Labrador-Ungava,* Department of Mines and Technical Surveys (Ottawa), 1959.

(With R. J. Murgatroyd, B. W. Boville, S. Teweles, and A. Kochanski) *The Circulation in the Stratosphere, Mesosphere and Lower Thermosphere,* World Meteorological Organization, 1965; *On University Freedom in the Canadian Context* (Plaunt lectures at Carleton University), University of Toronto Press, 1967.

(With M. K. Thomas) *Climate Canada,* Wiley, 1974; (editor with R. A. Bryson and contributor) *Climates of North America,* Elsevier Scientific Publishing, 1974; (with H. Schiff) *Atmospheric Exchange Processes and the Ozone Problem,* Institute for Environmental Studies, University of Toronto, 1976; (with A. M. Aikin and J. M. Harrison) *The Management of Canada's Nuclear Wastes,* Department of Energy, Mines and Resources (Ottawa), 1977.

Contributor: *Geography,* Odhams, 1948; L. Dudley Stamp and S. W. Wooldridge, editors, *The London Essays in Geography* (memorial volume to L. R. Jones), Harvard University Press, 1950; Griffith Taylor, editor, *Geography in the Twentieth Century,* Philosophical Library, 1951; *Compendium on Meteorology,* American Meteorological Society, 1951; George W. Hoffman, editor, *A Geography of Europe,* Ronald, 1953, 3rd edition, 1969; R. R. Platt, editor, *Finland and Its Geography,* American Geographical Society, 1955; *Melanges geographiques canadiens offerts a Raoul Blanchard,* University of Laval Press, 1959.

H. A. Estrin and D. M. Goode, editors, *College and University Teaching,* W. C. Brown, 1964; *The Graduate School and Its*

Faculty, Council of Graduate Schools in the United States, 1966; J. T. Spinks and G. O. Arlt, *Development of Graduate Programs in Ontario Universities,* [Toronto], 1966; G. Johnston and W. Roth, editors, *The Church in the Modern World,* Ryerson, 1967; Arnold Court, editor, *Eclectic Climatology,* Association of Pacific Coast Geographers, 1968; H. Steppler, editor, *The Food Resources of Mankind,* Agri-World Press, 1968; John Warkentin, editor, *Canada: A Geographical Interpretation,* Methuen, 1968; *Memorial Volume to Sir Dudley Stamp,* Institute of British Geographers, 1969.

R. E. Beamish, editor, *Dilemmas of Modern Man,* Great West Life Assurance Co., 1974; D. R. Deskins, Jr., G. Kish, J. D. Nystuen, and G. Olsson, editors, *Geographic Humanism, Analysis and Social Action,* Michigan Geographical Publications, University of Michigan, 1977; *Desertification and Its Causes,* Pergamon Press for United Nations Environmental Programme, 1977; L. E. St. Pierre and G. R. Brown, editors, *Future Sources of Organic Raw Materials—CHEMRAWN I,* Pergamon, 1980; Mortimer J. Adler, editor, *The Great Ideas Today: 1982,* Encyclopaedia Britannica, 1982; M. J. Pasqualetti and K. David Pijawka, editors, *Nuclear Power: Assessing and Managing Hazardous Technology,* Westview, 1984.

Author of regional studies and technical reports for Air Ministry (London) and co-author of education studies in Canada. Contributor of more than sixty articles to *Arctic, Weather,* and other scientific journals. Associate editor (in the past or currently), *Geographical Review, Journal of Applied Meteorology, Environmental Research, Geografiska Annaler, Environmental Geology,* and *Journal of Biogeography.*

WORK IN PROGRESS: Research on the future supply and demand of water in Canada; a study on lead pollution in Canada and a study on "the so-called nuclear winter phenomenon" both on behalf of the Royal Society of Canada.

SIDELIGHTS: F. Kenneth Hare told *CA:* "The social applications of science need not be gibberish. They touch on great issues, and should be written as far as possible in the literary tradition. To write anything is hard work. To write well is still harder—and possibly requires the right genes, as well as genius. I don't have either—so I sweat my papers out."

AVOCATIONAL INTERESTS: Singing in choirs, playing the piano, and music generally; gardening, watching the sky and landscape.

*   *   *

HARGREAVES, Mary W(ilma) M(assey)   1914-

PERSONAL: Born March 1, 1914, in Erie, Pa.; daughter of Albert Edward (a factory foreman) and Bess (Childs) Massey; married Herbert Walter Hargreaves (a college professor), August 24, 1940. *Education:* Bucknell University, A.B., 1935; Radcliffe College, M.A., 1936, Ph.D., 1951. *Politics:* Democrat. *Religion:* Methodist. *Home:* 237 Cassidy Ave., Lexington, Ky. 40502. *Office:* Department of History, University of Kentucky, Lexington, Ky. 40506.

CAREER: Harvard University, Business School, Cambridge, Mass., research editor, 1937-39; University of Kentucky, Lexington, associate editor, Clay Papers project, 1952-72, project director, 1972-79, assistant professor, 1964-69, associate professor, 1969-73, professor of history, 1973-84, professor emeritus, 1984—.

MEMBER: American Association of University Women (branch president, 1957-59; member of state board, 1957-69), Amer-

ican Historical Association, Organization of American Historians, Agricultural History Society (member of executive committee, 1969-78, president, 1976), American Association of University Professors, Southern Historical Association, Phi Beta Kappa (chapter secretary, 1964-69; chapter president, 1970-71), Phi Alpha Theta, Sigma Tau Delta.

WRITINGS: Dry Farming in the Northern Great Plains, Harvard University Press, 1957; (editor with James F. Hopkins) *The Papers of Henry Clay,* University Press of Kentucky, Volume I, 1959, Volume II, 1961, Volume III, 1963, Volume IV, 1971, Volume V, 1973, Volume VI, 1981; (contributor) James E. Wright and Sarah Z. Rosenberg, editors, *The Great Plains Experience: Readings in the History of a Region,* University of Mid-America, 1978; (contributor) Brian W. Blouet and Frederick C. Luebke, editors, *The Great Plains: Environment and Culture,* University of Nebraska Press, 1979; (contributor) Mabel E. Deutrich and Virginia C. Purdy, editors, *Clio Was a Woman: Studies in the History of American Women,* Howard University Press, 1980; *The Presidency of John Quincy Adams,* University of Kansas Press, in press.

Contributor of articles to *Agricultural History* and other historical publications.

*   *   *

HARMON, William (Ruth)   1938-

PERSONAL: Born June 10, 1938, in Concord, N.C.; son of William Richard (a textile executive) and Virginia (Pickerel) Harmon; married Lynn Chadwell, December 20, 1965; children: Sally Frances, William Richard Harmon II. *Education:* University of Chicago, A.B., 1958, A.M., 1968; University of North Carolina at Chapel Hill, M.A., 1968; University of Cincinnati, Ph.D., 1970. *Politics:* Democrat. *Religion:* None. *Home:* 108A Stallings Rd., Chapel Hill, N.C. 27514. *Office:* Department of English, University of North Carolina, Chapel Hill, N.C. 27514.

CAREER: U.S. Navy, active duty as officer, 1960-67, reserve service, 1967—, with current rank of lieutenant commander; University of North Carolina at Chapel Hill, instructor, 1970-71, assistant professor, 1971-72, associate professor, 1973-77, professor of English, 1977—, department chairman, 1972-77.

MEMBER: Modern Language Association of America, Academy of American Poets, American Anthropological Association, South Atlantic Modern Language Association.

AWARDS, HONORS:—Military: Navy Commendation Medal with V; Vietnamese Staff Service Honor Medal, first class. Civilian: Fellowships include Rockefeller Foundation humanities fellowship, Ford Foundation fellowship, and Elliston Poetry Fund scholarship; research grants from Kenan Fund.

WRITINGS—Poetry, except as indicated: *Treasury Holiday,* Wesleyan University Press, 1970; *Legion: Civic Choruses,* Wesleyan University Press, 1973; *The Intussuception of Miss Mary America,* Kayak Books, 1976; *Time in Ezra Pound's Work* (criticism), University of North Carolina Press, 1977; (editor) *The Oxford Book of American Light Verse,* Oxford University Press, 1979; *One Long Poem,* Louisiana State University Press, 1982; *Invoices and Bagatelles,* Wesleyan University Press, in press.

Work anthologized in *Quickly Aging Here: Some Poets of the 1970's,* edited by Geof Hewitt, Doubleday, 1969, and in a Pushcart selection. Contributor to journals, including *Antioch*

Review, Carolina Quarterly, Poetry, Kenyon Review, Sewanee Review, Ploughshares, and San Francisco Review.

WORK IN PROGRESS: A volume of poems entitled *To a Friend: Translations;* a book of critical pieces entitled *A Scythian Suite;* a volume of essays on T. S. Eliot.

SIDELIGHTS: William Harmon told *CA:* "I try to avoid subjecting what I do to any very agonizing scrutiny. Poetry is so demanding that, certainly, I would not write it if I did not absolutely as a matter of necessity have to. Teaching, criticism, editing, and other such academic or belletristic pastimes make up a much less ulcerating regimen."

Harmon later wrote: "Addendum ('LXXIV): Jubilate agno: My prose grows less mandarin-florist, I hope, wincing now at 'belletristic . . . regimen' [above]. I seem to attend more to rose-colored bats and punctuation than I used to. Is this senility?"

BIOGRAPHICAL/CRITICAL SOURCES: Antioch Review, fall/winter, 1970-71; *New York Times,* August 9, 1979; *Washington Post Book World,* August 19, 1979.

*   *   *

HARRIS, Alice Kessler   1941-

PERSONAL: Born June 2, 1941, in Leicester, England; daughter of Żoltan and Ilona (Elefant) Kessler; married Jay Evans Harris, August 28, 1960 (divorced, 1974); married Bertram Silverman, January 22, 1982; children: (first marriage) Ilona Kay. *Education:* Goucher College, B.A. (cum laude), 1961; Rutgers University, M.A., 1963, Ph.D., 1968. *Home:* 141 East 88th St., New York, N.Y. 10028. *Office:* Department of History, Hofstra University, Hempstead, N.Y. 11550.

CAREER: Hofstra University, Hempstead, N.Y., assistant professor of history, 1968-73; Sarah Lawrence College, Bronxville, N.Y., professor of history and women's studies, 1974-76, director of Women's Studies Program, 1974-76; Hofstra University, associate professor, 1977-81, professor of history, 1981—, co-director of Center for the Study of Work and Leisure, 1977—. Chairman, Columbia University Seminar on Women in Society, 1983-84; member, Columbia University Seminar in American Civilization.

MEMBER: American Association of University Professors (treasurer of Hofstra University chapter, 1969-71), American Historical Association (member of committee on women historians, 1983-86), Organization of American Historians (member of program committee, 1982), Women in the Historical Profession (member of coordinating committee), American Studies Association, American Civil Liberties Union (member of academic freedom committee, 1971-77), Berkshire Conference of Women Historians (member of program committee, 1982-84).

AWARDS, HONORS: National Endowment for the Humanities fellowship, 1976-77; Radcliffe Institute fellowship, 1977; Philip Taft Prize, 1982, for *Out to Work: A History of Wage-Earning Women in the U.S.*

WRITINGS: (Editor with Blanche Cook and Ronald Radosh) *Past Imperfect: Alternative Essays in American History,* Random House, 1972; (author of introduction) William Ladd, *On the Duty of Females to Promote the Cause of Peace,* Garland, 1972; (author of introduction) George Cone Beckwith, *The Peace Manual; or, War and Its Remedies,* Garland, 1972; (author of introduction) Anzia Yezierska, *Bread Givers,* Bra-

ziller, 1975; (editor) Yezierska, *The Open Cage: Collection,* Persea Books, 1979; *Women Have Always Worked,* McGraw, 1980; *Out to Work: A History of Wage-Earning Women in the U.S.,* Oxford University Press, 1982.

Contributor: *Cooperative History of the United States,* Dushkin, 1974; Richard Edwards and others, editors, *Labor Market Segmentation,* Lexington Books, 1975; Ronald Grele, editor, *Envelopes of Sound,* Precedent Publishing, 1975; Bernice Carroll, editor, *Liberating Women's History,* University of Illinois Press, 1976.

*   *   *

HARRIS, Jessica L.
See MILSTEAD, Jessica L(ee)

*   *   *

HART, Edward L.   1916-

PERSONAL: Born December 28, 1916, in Bloomington, Idaho; son of Alfred A. (a government employee and farmer) and Sarah C. (Patterson) Hart; married Eleanor May Coleman (a musician), December 15, 1944; children: Edward Richard, Paul L., Barbara, Patricia. *Education:* University of Utah, B.S., 1939; University of Michigan, M.A., 1941; Oxford University, D.Phil., 1950. *Politics:* Democrat. *Religion:* Church of Jesus Christ of Latter-day Saints (Mormon). *Home:* 1401 Cherry Lane, Provo, Utah 84601. *Office:* Department of English, A230 JKBA, Brigham Young University, Provo, Utah 84601.

CAREER: University of Utah, Salt Lake City, instructor in English, 1946; University of Washington, Seattle, assistant professor of English, 1949-52; Brigham Young University, Provo, Utah, assistant professor, 1952-55, associate professor, 1955-59, professor of English, 1959—. Visiting professor of English, University of California, Berkeley, 1959-60; visiting professor, Arizona State University, summer, 1968. Member of board, Utah Arts Council, 1977—. *Military service:* U.S. Navy, Japanese language translator and interpreter, 1942-46; became lieutenant.

MEMBER: Modern Language Association of America, American Society for Eighteenth-Century Studies (charter member), Rocky Mountain Modern Language Association (president, 1958), Utah Academy of Sciences, Arts, and Letters, Phi Beta Kappa, Phi Kappa Phi (president of local chapter, 1971-73).

AWARDS, HONORS: Rhodes scholar, Oxford University, 1939; American Council of Learned Societies fellow, 1942; American Philosophical Society grant, 1964; Redd Award in Humanities, Utah Academy, 1976; College of Humanities Distinguished Faculty Award, Brigham Young University, 1977.

WRITINGS: (Editor) John Nichols, *Minor Lives: A Collection of Biographies,* Harvard University Press, 1971; (editor) *Instruction and Delight,* Brigham Young University Press, 1976; *Mormon in Motion* (biography), Windsor Books, 1978; *To Utah* (poems), Brigham Young University Press, 1979; *God's Spies* (lectures on scholarship), College of Humanities, Brigham Young University, 1983. Also author of monograph "More Than Nature Needs," Brigham Young University, 1983. Contributor of articles to journals, including *PMLA, Shakespeare Quarterly, Studies in English Literature, Western Humanities Review,* and *Literature and Psychology;* contributor of poems to journals, including *Beloit Poetry Journal* and *Western Humanities Review.*

HARTMAN, Olov 1906-1982

PERSONAL: Born May 7, 1906, in Stockholm, Sweden; died April 28, 1982; son of Carl August (a Salvation Army officer) and Anna (Karlsson) Hartman; married Ingrid Ohlsson, July 14, 1929; children: Lars, Anna-Britta (Mrs. Sten-Bertil Risberg), Per, Ingrid (Mrs. Per Soederberg), Hans, Sven, Karin. *Education:* University of Uppsala, teol.cand., 1932. *Home:* Kaerrvaegen 19, Sigtuna, Sweden.

CAREER: Church of Sweden, clergyman assigned to pastoral work in different dioceses and parishes, 1932-38; perpetual curate in Naесšjoe, Sweden, 1938-48; Sigtuna Foundation, Sigtuna, Sweden, director, doing pastoral counseling and leading conferences, 1948-70; associate court chaplain, Sweden, beginning 1965.

MEMBER: P.E.N., Sveriges Foerfattarefoerening, Sveriges Dramatikerfoerbund.

AWARDS, HONORS: Gustaf VI Adolf's Minnesmedalj; Nordstjerneorden; D.D. from University of Lund; Wallin Prize, 1972; Prize of the Nine, 1976.

WRITINGS: Opium foer folket, Sveriges kristliga Studentroerelses Bokfoerlag, 1935; *Dopets gaava foerpliktar,* Svenska kyrkans Diakonistyrelses Bokfoerlag, 1939.

Ett heligt arv, Svenska kyrkans Diakonistyrelses Bokfoerlag, 1940; *I tid och otid,* Svenska kyrkans Diakonistyrelses Bokfoerlag, 1941; *Att bedja Guds ord,* C.W.K. Gleerup Bokfoerlag, 1943; *I noed och lust,* Svenska kyrkans Diakonistyrelses Bokfoerlag, 1943; *Att foelja en stjaerna,* Svenska kyrkans Diakonistyrelses Bokfoerlag, 1945; *Stormvarning,* Svenska kyrkans Diakonistyrelses Bokfoerlag, 1948; *Doed med foerhinder* (novel), Norlin, 1948; *Helig maskerad* (novel), Norlin, 1949, translation by Karl A. Olsson published as *Holy Masquerade,* Eerdmans, 1963.

Maenniskor i roett (novel), Norlin, 1950, translation by Eric J. Sharpe published as *Marching Orders,* Eerdmans, 1970; *Natten skulle lysa saasom dagen* (sermons), Svenska kyrkans Diakonistyrelses Bokfoerlag, 1951; *Aer Gud moralisk?* (booklet of radio sermons), Radiotjaenst, 1951; *Medmaenskligt* (essays), Raben & Sjoegren, 1952; *Den heliga staden* (drama), Raben & Sjoegren, 1953; *Saasom i en spegel* (sermons), Svenska kyrkans Diakonistyrelses Bokfoerlag, 1953; *Kunst und Christentum* (booklet of essays), [Hamburg], 1953; *Profet och timmerman* (church drama), Raben & Sjoegren, 1954; *Stenfisken* (short stories), Raben & Sjoegren, 1954; *Borg och bro: En bok om Sigtunastiftelsen,* Svenska kyrkans Diakonistyrelses Bokfoerlag, 1955, translation by Margareta Angstroem published as *The Sigtuna Foundation,* S.C.M. Press, 1955; *Oxens tecken* (sermons), Svenska kyrkans Diakonistyrelses Bokfoerlag, 1955.

Jordiska ting (essays), Raben & Sjoegren, 1956, translation and introduction by Eric J. Sharpe published as *Earthly Things,* Eerdmans, 1968; *Livets krona* (church drama), Raben & Sjoegren, 1956; *Adam och Eva: En Studie i biblisk aektenskapssyn,* Svenska kyrkans Diakonistyrelses Bokfoerlag, 1957; *Den brinnande ugnen* (church drama), Raben & Sjoegren, 1958; *Innanfoer* (novel), Raben & Sjoegren, 1958, translation by Elsa Kruuse published as *The Sudden Sun,* Fortress, 1964; *Oeppna kyrkan* (essays), Svenska kyrkans Diakonistyrelses Bokfoerlag, 1958; *Brusande Vaag* (autobiographical novel; also see below), Raben & Sjoegren, 1959; *Tre kyrkospel,* Raben & Sjoegren,

1959, translation by Brita Stendahl published as *Three Church Dramas,* Fortress, 1966.

Gud i nattens timmar (sermons), Svenska kyrkans Diakonistyrelsens Bokfoerlag, 1960; *Staellet om toernbusken* (essays on Christianity and theology), Raben & Sjoegren, 1961; *Korsfararen* (three-act miracle play), Raben & Sjoegren, 1962; *Marias oro* (church drama), Raben & Sjoegren, 1961, translation by Sharpe published as *Mary's Quest,* Faith Press, 1963; *Ett fritt evangelium* (essays), Svenska kyrkans Diakonistyrelsens Bokfoerlag, 1963; *Dag Hammarskjoeld og hans Gud,* Kristeligt dagblad, 1964; *Vad aer det: En katekes i ord och bild,* Raben & Sjoegren, 1965; *Medan synagogfoerestaandaren vaentar* (sermons), Svenska kyrkans Diakonistyrelsens Bokfoerlag, 1966; *Eld och Kontrapunkt* (two plays), Raben & Sjoegren, 1967; *Den borttraengda himlen* (sermons, 1951-67), Svenska kyrkans Diakonistyrelsens Bokfoerlag, 1967; (compiler) *Bibeln laest i dag* (essays), Raben & Sjoegren, 1967; (compiler) *Att bli gammal* (lectures), Verbum, 1967; *Baeraren* (drama), Raben & Sjoegren, 1968, translation by Brita Stendahl published as *On That Day,* Fortress, 1968; *Jordbaevningen i Lissabon,* Raben & Sjoegren, 1968; *Tiden aer kort,* Verbum, 1969.

Efter oss (drama), Raben & Sjoegren, 1970; *Miljoevesper Maessa och Meditation* (two liturgies), Verbum, 1971; *Vad aer da en maenniska* (sermons), Verbum, 1972; *Tva spel* (two plays), Verbum, 1972; *Trefaldighetsmaessa* (liturgy), Hakan Ohlssons, 1973; *Massa for rattvisan* (liturgy), Hakan Ohlssons, 1973; *En ay Manniskosonens dagar* (meditations), Verbum, 1973; *Den korsfasta skapelsen* (meditations), Verbum, 1973; *Profeten Jesus och hans vaenner* (essays), Verbum, 1975; *Med Gud och hans vaenskap* (liturgy), Nordiska Musikfoerlaget, 1976; *Brusande vag* (first part of memoirs; adaptation of autobiographical novel of same title), Raven & Sjoegren, 1977; *Klartechen,* Raben & Sjoegren, 1977; *Livstecken* (second part of memoirs), Raben & Sjoegren, 1977; *Faardriktning* (third part of memoirs), Raben & Sjoegren, 1979.

Faagelstraeck (fourth part of memoirs), Raben & Sjoegren, 1982; *Landet som inte kan koopas,* Proprius, 1982; *Livstraadet,* Evangeliska Fosterlands stiftelsens forlag, 1982; *Med Gud paa jorden,* Verbum, 1983.

Omnibus volumes: *The Crucified Answer: The Fortress Press Book for Lent and Easter,* translation by Gene L. Lund, Fortress, 1967; *The Birth of God: Readings for Advent, Christmas, and Epiphany,* translation by Lund, Fortress, 1969.

AVOCATIONAL INTERESTS: Fishing, ornithology, music ("with an accent on baroque").

BIOGRAPHICAL/CRITICAL SOURCES: Kai Henmark, *Orden foervandlas till haender Om Olov Hartman som prosaberaettre,* in *En fagel av eld,* Raben & Sjoegren, 1962; *Vaar Loesen,* Number 5-6, 1966 (issue honoring Hartman on his sixtieth birthday); *Earthly Things,* introduction by Eric J. Sharpe, Eerdmans, 1968; *Kirkens Verden,* August, 1971; George Robert Jacks, "Five Dramas of the Swedish Church-Drama Movement Discussed with Reference to Hartman's Theology and Symbolism" (doctoral dissertation), Columbia University, 1972; *Svenska Dagbladet,* December 5, 1972.†

*   *   *

HARWOOD, Gina
    See BATTISCOMBE, E(sther) Georgina (Harwood)

HASSLER, Donald M. (II) 1937-

PERSONAL: Born January 3, 1937, in Akron, Ohio; son of Donald M. (a businessman) and Fran (Parsons) Hassler; married Diana Cain, October 8, 1960 (died September 19, 1976); married Sue Smith, September 13, 1977; children: (first marriage) Donald M. III, David. *Education:* Williams College, B.A., 1959; Columbia University, M.A., 1960, Ph.D., 1967. *Religion:* Presbyterian. *Home:* 1226 Woodhill, Kent, Ohio 44240. *Office:* Department of English, Kent State University, Kent, Ohio 44240.

CAREER: University of Montreal, Montreal, Quebec, instructor in English, 1961-65; Kent State University, Kent, Ohio, assistant professor, 1967-71, associate professor, 1971-77, professor of English, 1977—, director of experimental college, 1973—.

MEMBER: Modern Language Association of America, American Society for Eighteenth-Century Studies, Keats-Shelley Association, American Association of University Professors, Science Fiction Research Association, Ohio Poets Association, Phi Beta Kappa.

AWARDS, HONORS: Woodrow Wilson fellow, 1959.

WRITINGS: The Comedian as the Letter D: Erasmus Darwin's Comic Materialism, Nijhoff, 1973; *On Weighing a Pound of Flesh* (poetry), Defiance College Publications, 1973; *Erasmus Darwin*, Twayne, 1974.

(Contributor) Theodore Besterman, editor, *Studies on Voltaire and the Eighteenth Century*, Voltaire Foundation, 1976; (contributor) Joseph Olander and Martin Greenberg, editors, *Isaac Asimov*, Taplinger, 1977.

Comic Tones in Science Fiction, Greenwood Press, 1982; *Hal Clement*, Starmont House, 1982; *Patterns of the Fantastic*, Starmont House, 1983.

Work appears in annual anthologies of Ohio Poets Association, 1969—. Contributor to *Hiram Poetry Review, Canadian Poetry, Fiddlehead, Descant, Canadian Forum*, and other periodicals.

WORK IN PROGRESS: A collection of poems; a collection of essays on the relation of modern science fiction to the eighteenth century; a book on Isaac Asimov.

*   *   *

HASTINGS, March
See LEVINSON, Leonard

*   *   *

HAUCK, Paul A(nthony) 1924-

PERSONAL: Born September 15, 1924, in Germany; naturalized U.S. citizen in 1949; son of John and Elizabeth (Koenig) Hauck; married Marceleen T. Steenburgen, 1953; children: Kathryn (Mrs. Henry Holladay), Melanie, Stephanie. *Education:* Drew University, B.A., 1948; University of Utah, M.A., 1951, Ph.D., 1953. *Home:* 2365 18th St., Apt. D, Moline, Ill. 61264. *Office:* Suite 302, Safety Building, Rock Island, Ill. 61201.

CAREER: Psychologist in Butte, Mont., 1953-55; State Hospital, East Moline, Ill., chief psychologist, 1955-60; Western Mental Health Center, Marshall, Minn., director, 1960-67; Peoria Mental Health Center, Peoria, Ill., chief psychologist, 1967-68; clinical psychologist in Rock Island, Ill., 1968—. Diplomate, American Board of Professional Psychology, 1961.

MEMBER: American Psychological Association (founder; president, 1959-60).

WRITINGS—All published by Westminster, except as noted: *The Rational Management of Children*, Libra, 1967, 2nd edition, 1972; *Reason in Pastoral Counseling*, 1972; *Overcoming Depression*, 1973; *Overcoming Frustration and Anger*, 1974; *Overcoming Worry and Fear*, 1975; (with Edmund S. Kean) *Marriage and the Memo Method*, 1975; *How to Do What You Want to Do: The Art of Self Discipline*, 1976; *Marriage Is a Loving Business*, 1977; *How to Stand Up for Yourself*, 1979.

Brief Counseling with RET, 1980; *Overcoming Jealousy and Possessiveness*, 1981; *The Three Faces of Love*, 1984. Contributor of weekly column to *Human Scene*.

SIDELIGHTS: Paul A. Hauck's books have been translated into nine foreign languages, including French, Spanish, Danish, and Swedish.

*   *   *

HAWKINS, Robert 1923-

PERSONAL: Born April 6, 1923, in Highmore, S.D.; son of Francis Edwards (a builder) and Lunetta (Bloomenrader) Hawkins. *Education:* Trinity College, Hartford, Conn., B.A., 1945; University of Edinburgh, graduate study, 1947-48. *Politics:* Republican. *Religion:* Episcopalian. *Office:* The Hotchkiss School, Lakeville, Conn. 06039.

CAREER: The Hotchkiss School, Lakeville, Conn., master in English, beginning 1945.

WRITINGS: (Editor with Denise Restout) *Landowska on Music*, Stein & Day, 1964; *Preface to Poetry*, Basic Books, 1965; (editor) Robert Louis Stevenson, *Dr. Jekyll and Mr. Hyde*, Dell, 1966; (editor with John G. Bowen) William Shakespeare, *Macbeth*, Basic Books, 1967; *Printed Matter: An Anthology of Black Moss* (poems), Sun Parlor Advertising Co., 1970; (compiler) *The Kent Family Chronicles Encyclopedia: With Condensations of the John Jakes Novels and Essays about America from 1770 to 1877*, Bantam, 1979; (with Donald Mueting) *Pinball Reference Guide*, Mead Co., 1979; *The Christmas Tree Farm*, Messner, 1981.

WORK IN PROGRESS: Two books in collaboration with Denise Restout, *Biography of Landowska* and *What Is Music?*; editing *Julius Caesar* with John G. Bowen.

SIDELIGHTS: Robert Hawkins is competent in French and Italian. *Avocational Interests:* Ornithology and cooking.†

*   *   *

HAYASHI, Tetsumaro 1929-

PERSONAL: Born March 22, 1929, in Sakaide, Japan; son of Tetsuro (a clergyman) and Shieko (Honjyo) Hayashi; married Skiko Sakuranti, April 14, 1960; children: Richard Hideki. *Education:* Okayama University, B.A., 1953; Wilmington College, Wilmington, Ohio, further study, 1954-55; University of Florida, M.A., 1957; Kent State University, M.A. in L.S., 1959, Ph.D., 1968. *Politics:* Democrat. *Home:* 1405 North Kimberly Lane, Muncie, Ind. 47306. *Office:* Department of English, Ball State University, Muncie, Ind. 47306.

CAREER: Culver-Stockton College, Canton, Mo., assistant professor of English and associate director of library, 1959-63; Kent State University, Kent, Ohio, instructor in English, 1965-68; Ball State University, Muncie, Ind., assistant professor, 1968-72, associate professor, 1972-77, professor of English, 1977—.

MEMBER: International John Steinbeck Society (president, 1983—), Modern Language Association of America, John Steinbeck Society of America (co-founder; director, 1966-77; president, 1977-83), American Library Association, Shakespeare Association of America, Association for Asian Studies, Midwest Modern Language Association.

AWARDS, HONORS: Folger Shakespeare Library senior fellowship, 1972; American Philosophical Society fellowship, 1975, 1981; American Council of Learned Societies fellowship, 1976.

WRITINGS—Published by Scarecrow, except as indicated: *Amerika bunka sobyo* (title means "Sketches of American Culture"), Tarumi Shobo (Tokyo), 1960; *John Steinbeck: A Concise Bibliography, 1930-65*, 1967, updated edition published as *A New Steinbeck Bibliography, 1929-71*, 1973; *Arthur Miller Criticism, 1930-1967*, 1969, 2nd edition published as *An Index to Arthur Miller Criticism*, 1976; *A Textual Study of "A Looking Glass for London and England," by Thomas Lodge and Robert Greene*, Ball State University, 1969.

(Editor) Thomas Lodge and Robert Green, *A Looking Glass for London and England: An Elizabethan Text* (based on Hayashi's doctoral thesis), 1970; *Robert Greene Criticism: A Comprehensive Bibliography*, 1971; (editor with Richard Astro) *Steinbeck: The Man and His Work* (proceedings of Steinbeck Conference), Oregon State University Press, 1971; *Shakespeare's Sonnets: A Record of 20th Century Criticism*, 1972; (editor) *Steinbeck's Literary Dimension*, 1973; *A Textual Study of Robert Greene's Orlando Furioso*, Ball State University Press, 1973; *A Study Guide to Steinbeck: A Handbook to His Major Works*, Volume I, 1974, Volume II, 1979; *A Study Guide to Steinbeck's "The Long Valley,"* Pierian, 1976; (with Kenneth D. Swan) *Steinbeck's Prophetic Vision of America*, Taylor University, 1976; (editor) *John Steinbeck: A Dictionary of His Fictional Characters*, 1976; *The Poetry of Robert Greene*, International Steinbeck Congress, 1976.

(Editor and compiler) *Steinbeck and Hemingway: Dissertation Abstracts and Research Opportunities*, 1980; (editor) *William Faulkner: Research Opportunities and Dissertation Abstracts*, McFarland & Co., 1982; *A New Steinbeck Bibliography, 1971-1981*, 1983; (editor) *Eugene O'Neill: Research Opportunities and Dissertation Abstracts*, McFarland & Co., 1983; *Arthur Miller and Tennessee Williams: Research Opportunities and Dissertation Abstracts*, McFarland & Co., 1983.

Contributor of more than 100 articles to journals in America, Europe, Japan, and India, and twelve short stories to American periodicals. General editor, "Steinbeck Monograph" series. Editor, *Steinbeck Quarterly*, 1968—.

*   *   *

HAYS, David G(lenn)   1928-

PERSONAL: Born November 17, 1928, in Memphis, Tenn.; son of Oliver Glenn (a warehouse manager) and Adele (de Long) Hays; married Marguerite Thompson (a physician and researcher), February 4, 1950 (separated, 1974); children: Dorothy Adele, Warren Stith Thompson, Thomas Glenn. *Education:* Harvard University, B.A., 1951, M.A., 1954, Ph.D.,

1956. *Politics:* Democrat. *Home:* Twin Willows, Wanakah, N.Y. 14075. *Office:* Department of Linguistics, State University of New York at Buffalo, Buffalo, N.Y. 14222.

CAREER: Center for Advanced Study in the Behavioral Sciences, Stanford, Calif., fellow in sociology, 1954-55; RAND Corp., Santa Monica, Calif., social scientist, 1955-68; State University of New York at Buffalo, professor of linguistics, 1968—. Lecturer at University of Southern California, 1956-58, and University of California, Los Angeles, 1950. Visiting scientist in computational linguistics, Euratom Research Center, Ispra, Italy, 1962-63; member of automatic language processing advisory committee, National Academy of Sciences, 1964-66; director of Linguistics Institute, 1971. Member of Mathematical Social Science Board, 1967-71; National Science Foundation, member of social science advisory committee, 1970-72, chairman, 1972.

MEMBER: Association for Computational Linguistics (president, 1964), International Committee on Computational Linguistics (chairman, 1965-69).

AWARDS, HONORS: Bronze Medal, University of Brno, 1971, and University of Pisa, 1973; Chancellor's Award for Excellence in Teaching, 1975.

WRITINGS: Report of a Summer Seminar on Computational Linguistics, RAND Corp., 1964; (editor) *Readings in Automatic Language Processing*, American Elsevier, 1966; (editor) *Introduction to Computational Linguistics*, American Elsevier, 1967; (with Bozena Henisz-Dostert and Marjorie L. Rapp) *Computational Linguistics: Bibliography, 1966*, RAND Corp., 1967; (contributor) *Linguistics: Teaching and Interdisciplinary Relations*, School of Language and Linguistics, Georgetown University, 1974; (contributor) *Theories of Alienation*, Nijhoff, 1976; *Cognitive Structures*, foreword by Raoul Naroll, Human Relations Area Files, 1981.

Also author of several studies published by RAND Corp. Editor of Elsevier's "Mathematical Linguistics and Automatic Language Processing" series. Contributor of about forty-five articles to journals. Editor, *American Journal of Computational Linguistics*, 1974—.

WORK IN PROGRESS: Research on cross-cultural linguistics.†

*   *   *

HEFLIN, Donald
See WALLMANN, Jeffrey M(iner)

*   *   *

HEGGOY, Alf Andrew   1938-

PERSONAL: Born December 15, 1938, in Algiers, Algeria; naturalized U.S. citizen, 1959; son of W. N. (a missionary and author) and Hariet (Berggreen) Heggoy; children: Ingrid, Eric and Brian (twins). *Education:* Randolph-Macon College, B.A., 1959; Duke University, M.A., 1961, Ph.D., 1963. *Politics:* Independent. *Religion:* Methodist. *Home:* 135 Fairlane Dr., Athens, Ga. 30607. *Office:* Department of History, University of Georgia, Athens, Ga. 30601.

CAREER: Researcher in France and North Africa, 1963-65; University of Georgia, Athens, assistant professor, 1965-69, associate professor, 1969-77, professor of history, 1977—. Visiting assistant professor of history, North Carolina Wesleyan College, 1962-63; social science analyst, U.S. Army Research Office, summer, 1963. Volunteer fireman, Danielsville, Ga., 1974-78.

MEMBER: Middle East Studies Association, African Studies Association, American Association of University Professors, French Colonial Historical Society (vice-president, 1974-75; president, 1976-78, 1980-82), Southern Historical Association, Pi Gamma Mu, Phi Alpha Theta.

AWARDS, HONORS: Institute of International Education grant, 1963-64; Army Research Office of Durham grant, 1964-65; selected outstanding honors professor, University of Georgia, 1972, 1974; Joseph H. Parlss Award, 1974, for excellence in the teaching of history.

WRITINGS: The African Policies of Gabriel Hanotaux, University of Georgia Press, 1972; *Insurgency and Counterinsurgency in Algeria,* Indiana University Press, 1972; *Historical Dictionary of Algeria,* Scarecrow, 1981; (editor) *Through Foreign Eyes,* University Press of America, 1982; *The Military in Imperial History: The French Connection,* Garland Publishing, 1984.

Contributor to *Muslim World, African Historical Studies, African Studies Review, International Journal of Middle East Studies,* and other publications. Editor, *Proceedings* of the French Colonial Historical Society, 1975-78.

WORK IN PROGRESS: Oral Sources for North African Studies: Social and Intellectual History of Algeria, completion expected in 1985.

SIDELIGHTS: Alf Heggoy told *CA* that he seeks "to explain North African history and the French colonial experience to American readers—not just to fellow specialists." He is fluent in French and Norwegian, and reads Spanish, Danish, Swedish, German, and Italian.

*   *   *

HEIDBREDER, Margaret Ann
   See EASTMAN, Ann Heidbreder

*   *   *

HEIM, Alice (Winifred)   1913-

PERSONAL: Born April 19, 1913, in London, England; daughter of Felix (a company director) and Lucie (Steinhard) Heim; children: (adopted) Jessica Lucie, Quentin Felix. *Education:* Newnham College, Cambridge, M.A., 1936, Ph.D., 1939. *Home:* 8 Bateman St. Cambridge CB2 1NB, England.

CAREER: Cambridge University, Cambridge, England, instructor and researcher in educational, clinical, experimental, and psychometric psychology, 1939-78. Has given talks on BBC radio; lecturer on animal rights and psychological topics; industrial consultant.

MEMBER: British Psychological Society (fellow), British Association for the Advancement of Science (president, 1978-79), Experimental Psychology Society, Clare Hall (Cambridge; fellow emeritus), Cambridge Scientist Lunch Club (president, 1970-72).

WRITINGS: The Appraisal of Intelligence, Methuen, 1954, N.F.E.R. Publishing Co., 1970; *Intelligence and Personality,* Penguin, 1970; *Psychological Testing,* Oxford University Press, 1974; *Teaching and Learning in Higher Education,* N.F.E.R. Publishing Co., 1976.

Barking Up the Right Tree, Pelham Books, 1980; *Thicker than Water?: Adoption: Its Loyalties, Pitfalls and Joys,* Secker & Warburg, 1983; *Understanding Your Dog's Behavior,* Open Books Publishing, 1984.

Deviser of tests of perceptual reasoning for five- to ten-year-olds, a vocabulary scale for all ages, French versions of a reasoning test and the Brook Reaction Test of interests and personality, and of various tests of intelligence, interests, and personality. Contributor of papers to British, American, and French psychological journals. Member of editorial board, *Occupational Psychology,* 1970-73.

WORK IN PROGRESS: A book on aging, entitled *Where Did I Put My Spectacles?*

SIDELIGHTS: Alice Heim's *Thicker than Water?: Adoption: Its Loyalties, Pitfalls and Joys* is called "an excellent book meriting endless praise" by a *Medical Book News* critic. The work "can be read with gratitude by any actual or would-be parent," according to the *Sunday Telegraph* reviewer.

Heim told *CA,* "Unlike most experimental psychologists, I consider that experience is as important as behavior, that human beings are more interesting than rats—but that the latter deserve humane treatment."

AVOCATIONAL INTERESTS: Travel in Corsica, Turkey, Israel, France, Austria, Yugoslavia, Germany, and the United States; chamber music; theatre and films.

BIOGRAPHICAL/CRITICAL SOURCES: Times Literary Supplement, May 20, 1983; *Sunday Telegraph* (London), June 29, 1983; *Medical Book News,* September, 1983.

*   *   *

HEIMBERG, Marilyn Markham
   See ROSS, Marilyn (Ann) Heimberg

*   *   *

HELD, Jacqueline   1936-

PERSONAL: Born May 27, 1936, in Poitiers, France; daughter of Raymond (a teacher) and Simone (a teacher; maiden name, Gazeau) Bonneau; married Claude Held (a poet and teacher), March 25, 1961; children: Luc, Pascale, Veronique. *Education:* Sorbonne, University of Paris, licence and secondary teaching certificate (C.A.P.E.S.), 1958. *Home:* 257, rue des Tertres, Boigny, 45800 Saint-Jean-de-Braye, France.

CAREER: Taught philosophy and child psychology in Laon, France, 1960-67; teacher of psychology and juvenile literature in Orleans, France, beginning 1967; currently head of juvenile literature program, University of Paris XIII, Villetaneuse, France. Member of board of administration, Centre de Recherche et d'Information sur la Litterature pour la Jeunesse (Research and Information Center for Children's Literature), 1973—; member, Commission de Recherche sur la Litterature de Jeunesse, Ministere du Temps Libre, de la Jeunesse et des Sports. Director with husband, Claude Held, of magazine *Racines.* Has appeared on various radio and television programs. Consultant to Swedish radio and television networks on programs intended for teachers of French.

MEMBER: International Research Society for Children's Literature, Societe Internationale de Recherche sur le Fantastique, l'Irreel, et l'Etrange en Litterature.

AWARDS, HONORS: Television prize of juvenile literature, 1970; Best Book Award from "Loisirs Jeunes" for *Poiravechiche*, 1973, and *Le Navire d'Ika*, 1975; *Le Chat de Simulombula* was named one of fifty best books of the year in Grand Prix de Litterature de Jeunesse competition; Prix Jean Mace and Grand Prix des Treize, both for *La Part du vent*.

WRITINGS—For children, except as indicated: *Patatou, l'hippopotame* (title means "Patatou the Hippopotamus"), Dupuis, 1970; *Le Chat de Simulombula* (title means "The Cat of Simulombula"), Harlin Quist, 1970; *Les Piquants d'Arsinoe* (title means "Arsinoe's Prickles"), Magnard, 1970; *Jil et Jacinthe a la neige*, Editions du Seneve, 1970; *Jil et Jacinthe au jardin*, Editions du Seneve, 1970; *Jil et Jacinthe a la ferme*, Editions du Seneve, 1970; *La Tortue pattue, trapue, ventrue, barbue* (title means "The Fat, Squat, Bearded Tortoise"), Dessain & Tolra, 1971; *Jil et Jacinthe a la mer* (title means "Jil and Jacinthe at the Sea"), Dessain & Tolra, 1972; *Jil et Jacinthe au cirque* (title means "Jil and Jacinthe at the Circus"), Dessain & Tolra, 1972; *Jil et Jacinthe au zoo* (title means "Jil and Jacinthe at the Zoo"), Dessain & Tolra, 1972; *Jil et Jacinthe a la campagne*, Dessain & Tolra, 1972; *Le Pommier des Perloupettes* (title means "The Perloupettes' Apple-Tree"), L'Ecole des Loisirs, 1972; *Le Lion de Bouddha* (title means "The Lion of Buddha"), L'Ecole des Loisirs, 1973; *Arsinoe et Monsieur Printemps* (title means "Arsinoe and Mr. Spring"), Magnard, 1973; *La Part du vent* (title means "This Side of the Wind"), Duculot, 1974; *Le Navire d'Ika* (title means "Ika's Ship"), La Farandole, 1974.

Petipaton, le garcon-poisson, Flammarion, 1975, published as *Fabian, the Fish-Boy*, Addison-Wesley, 1976; *Objet volant non identifie* (title means "Unidentified Flying Object"), La Farandole, 1975; *La Tortue, le hamster, le chat, la lune, et la television* (title means "The Turtle, the Hamster, the Cat, the Moon, and the Television"), La Farandole, 1975; *Mais ou est donc Arsinoe?* (title means "But Where Then Is Arsinoe?"), Magnard, 1976; *Teddy-douce-oreille* (title means "Sweety-Ear Teddy"), Magnard, 1976; *Les Enfants d'Aldebaran* (title means "The Children of Aldebaran"), La Farandole, 1976; *Dikidi et la sagesse: Antifables* (title means "Dikidi and Wisdom: Antifables"), Delarge-Ruy Vidal, 1976; *La Voiture-baobab* (title means "The Baobab-Automobile"), Duculot, 1977; *Le Journal de Manou* (title means "Manou's Diary"), Hatier, 1977; *L'Imaginaire au pouvoir: Les Enfants et la litterature fantastique* (adult nonfiction; title means "For a Rising Power of Imagination: Children and Fantasy Literature"), Editions Ouvrieres, 1977; *Les Inventions de Motimo et Batiba*, Hatier, 1977; *Nouveaux Exploits de Motimo et Batiba*, Hatier, 1978; *Dragons de papier*, L'Ecole des Loisirs, 1978; *Un par un vont les Indiens*, Hatier, 1979; *Petit Guillaume de Sologne*, La Farandole, 1979.

Hans le trop bavard, La Farandole, 1980; *La Voiture sauvage*, Bordas, 1981; *Le Secret de Polichinelle*, Editions G. P., 1982; *Contes de terre et de lune*, L'Ecole des Loisirs, 1983; *Histoires d'ecole*, La Farandole, 1983; *Tania et le drole de bestiau*, Magnard, 1984.

With husband, Claude Held: *Poiravechiche (Les Legumes)* (poems; title means "About Vegetables"), Grasset, 1973; *Hamster rame* (poems; title means "Mr. Hamster Rows"), L'Ecole des Loisirs, 1974; *Lune vole* (poems; title means "The Moon Flies"), L'Ecole des Loisirs, 1976; *Le Chat qui n'etait pas botte* (title means "The Cat That Had No Boots"), Oeuvre Suisse, 1976; *Le Crocodile-aspirateur*, Magnard, 1977; *Les Voyages interplanetaires de Grand'Pere Coloconte*, L'Ecole

des Loisirs, 1978; *Expedition sur la planete Eras*, Bordas, 1978; *Une Giraffe a l'ecole*, La Farandole, 1979; *Vous avez dit bizarre*, Hatier, 1979; *Le Pecheur de soleil*, Dessain & Tolra, 1979; *L'Inconnu des herbes rouges*, Bordas, 1979.

Le Dragon-baryton, Magnard, 1980; *L'Autre de Starros*, Magnard, 1980; *La Fausse Table chinoise*, Editions Universitaires, 1981; *It etait une fois demain* (poetry anthology), La Farandole, 1983; *Seize Histoires pour rire ensemble* (anthology), Magnard, 1983; *Quinze Voyages vers le temps des planetes*, Magnard, 1984.

"Lis-tout poesie" series; with C. Held; all published by Magnard: *Il est une ile*, 1979; *Tatous, matous, caribous*, 1979; *Histoires biscornues*, 1981; *Cache-cache et devinettes*, 1981; *Le Marchand de sable*, 1981; *Le Mouton-nuage*, 1982; *L'Escargot sot*, 1982; *Parole de crocodile*, 1983.

"Lis-tout prose" series; with C. Held; published by Magnard: *Tatiana prend l'autobus*, 1983.

Translator from original English with C. Held; all published by Duculot: Tony Ross, *Hugo et l'homme qui volait les couleurs*, 1977; Ross, *Hugo et la chaussette magique*, 1977; Fay Maschler, *Mounette et Petit J font les courses*, 1978; Maschler, *Mounette et Petit J ont un bebe*, 1978; Maschler, *Mounette et Petit J quittent la ville*, 1978.

Also author, with C. Held, of *Trois Enfants dans les etoiles: 1001 Histoires*, Seghers. Director of "Anthologie-Poche 2001" collection, Magnard. Contributor of chapters on juvenile literature to books and of articles and stories to professional publications and children's magazines. French correspondent, *Rinascita della scuola*.

SIDELIGHTS: Jacqueline Held writes: "Inside the literary field for the young, I feel spontaneously attracted by the poetic and fantastic trends. Writing in the twentieth century for children of the twentieth century, I try to point out the possibilities of strangeness and dream that lie constantly under the most obvious elements of everyday life: the telephone, the car, the fridge, the plane. . . . Such dream is no evasion but, on the contrary, a way of rediscovering the world, a way of taking possession of it."

*   *   *

HELLER, Peter 1920-

PERSONAL: Born January 11, 1920, in Vienna, Austria; naturalized U.S. citizen; son of John (a businessman) and Margarete (Steiner) Heller; married Katrina Ely Burlingham, 1944 (divorced, 1951); married Christiane Menzel, August 20, 1951; children: (first marriage) Anne; (second marriage) Joan Heller Humphreys, Vivian, Stephen, Eve. *Education:* McGill University, Licentiate of Music and B.A., 1944; Columbia University, M.A., 1945, Ph.D., 1951. *Home:* 280 Brompton Rd., Williamsville, N.Y. 14221. *Office:* Department of Modern Languages, Clemens Hall, State University of New York, Buffalo, N.Y. 14260.

CAREER: Columbia University, New York, N.Y., instructor in German, 1948-51; Harvard University, Cambridge, Mass., instructor in German, 1951-54; University of Massachusetts—Amherst, associate professor, 1954-59, professor of German, 1959-61, Commonwealth Professor, 1961-68; State University of New York at Buffalo, professor of German and comparative literature, 1968—, head of German department, 1968-71.

MEMBER: Modern Language Association of America.

AWARDS, HONORS: Fulbright research grants for study in Germany, 1954-56; participated in National Endowment for the Humanities summer seminars for college and secondary school teachers, 1979, 1983, 1984; Guggenheim fellow, 1982.

WRITINGS: (With F. C. Ellert) *German One,* Heath, 1962; (contributor) *Masterpieces of Western Literature,* W. C. Brown, 1966; *Dialectics and Nihilism: Essays on Lessing, Nietzsche, Mann, and Kafka,* University of Massachusetts Press, 1966; (with Edith Ehrlich) *German Fiction and Prose,* Macmillan, 1967.

(With Ehrlich and J. Schaefer) *German Essays and Expository Prose,* Macmillan, 1969; (contributor) *Franz Kafka: His Place in World Literature,* Texas Tech University Press, 1971; (contributor) *Benn-Wirkung Wider Willen,* Athenaeum (Frankfurt), 1971; *Von den Ersten und Letzten Dingen,* De Gruyter (Berlin), 1972; *Prosa in Versen* (poetry), Blaeschke, 1974; *Menschentiere* (poetry), Lyrik und Prosa, 1975; *Probleme der Zivilisation,* Bouvier, 1978; *Emigrantenlitaneien* (poetry), Blaeschke, 1978.

(Editor) *Modern German Studies,* Bouvier, 1978—; *Studies on Nietzsche,* Bouvier, 1980; (editor with Ed Dudley) *American Attitudes toward Foreign Languages and Foreign Cultures,* Bouvier, 1983; (with Guenther Bittner) *Eine Kinderanalyse bei Anna Freud, 1929-1932,* Koenigshausen & Neumann, 1983.

Contributor to *Encyclopaedia Britannica.* Contributor of articles and reviews to *German Life and Letters, Lyrica Germanica, Germanic Review, Massachusetts Review, Modern Language Forum, Malahat Review,* and other publications.

WORK IN PROGRESS: A book of fables; a book on the experience of being a refugee.

* * *

HELLIE, Richard   1937-

PERSONAL: Born May 8, 1937, in Waterloo, Iowa; son of Ole I. (a journalist) and Elizabeth (a teacher; maiden name, Larsen) Hellie; married Jean Laves (a Russian language translator), December 23, 1961; children: Benjamin. *Education:* University of Chicago, A.B., 1958, A.M., 1960, Ph.D., 1965; graduate study at Russian Research Center, Harvard University, 1962-63, and University of Moscow, 1963-64. *Religion:* Atheist. *Home:* 4917 South Greenwood Ave., Chicago, Ill. 60615-1582. *Office:* Department of History, University of Chicago, 1126 East 59th St., Box 78, Chicago, Ill. 60637-1587.

CAREER: Rutgers University, New Brunswick, N.J., assistant professor of Russian history, 1965-66; University of Chicago, Chicago, Ill., assistant professor, 1966-71, associate professor, 1971-80, professor of Russian history, 1980—.

MEMBER: American Historical Association, American Association for the Advancement of Slavic Studies, American Society for Legal History, Historians of Early Modern Europe, Society for Peasant History, Society for Labor History.

AWARDS, HONORS: Ford Foundation fellowship, 1962-65; Quantrell grant, 1969; University of Chicago social science research grants, 1970-84; Herbert Baxter Adams Prize in European history, American Historical Association, 1972, for *Enserfment and Military Change in Muscovy;* Guggenheim fellowship, 1973-74; National Endowment for the Humanities fellowship, 1978-79, grant, 1982-83; Vucinich Prize honorable mention, 1983, for *Slavery in Russia, 1450-1725.*

WRITINGS: (Compiler, editor, and translator) *Muscovite Society: Readings for Introduction to Russian Civilization,* Syllabus Division, University of Chicago, 1967; (contributor) Thomas Riha, editor, *Readings in Russian Civilization,* University of Chicago Press, 2nd edition, 1969; *Enserfment and Military Change in Muscovy,* University of Chicago Press, 1971; (contributor) S. F. Platonov, *Ivan the Terrible,* edited and translated by Joseph L. Wieczynski, Academic International Press, 1974; *Slavery in Russia, 1450-1725,* University of Chicago Press, 1982; (editor and translator) *The Law Code (Ulozhenie) of 1649,* Charles Schlacks, 1984.

Contributor to encyclopedias, including *Encyclopaedia Britannica, Modern Encyclopedia of Russian and Soviet History,* and *Modern Encyclopedia of Russian and Soviet Literatures.* Contributor of articles and reviews to numerous journals, including *Russian History, Historian, American Historical Review, Slavic Review, Journal of Modern History,* and *Russian Review.* Member of editorial board, *Slavic Review,* 1979-81.

WORK IN PROGRESS: Editing "Arcadius Kahan's study of the eighteenth-century economy, for University of Chicago Press; a price series for Russia in the seventeenth century, possibly leading to a general model of the economy as a whole."

SIDELIGHTS: "With the publication of Richard Hellie's important new study [*Enserfment and Military Change in Muscovy*], we have not only an impressive work of synthesis [on the enserfment of the Russian peasantry] but a major contribution to Muscovite history; the author has made the salutary attempt to place the evolution of peasant status in the context of military changes," declares a *Times Literary Supplement* reviewer. Examining the process as both history and sociology, Hellie creates "a work which no serious student of Muscovite Russia can afford to ignore," the critic continues, pointing out that the author's "handling of the complex terminology of the Muscovite social structure and military matters is masterly." In another *Times Literary Supplement* review, I. de Madariaga calls *Enserfment and Military Change in Muscovy* "a work of fundamental importance for the understanding of pre-Petrine Russia in general and serfdom in particular."

Commenting on Hellie's *Slavery in Russia, 1450-1725,* Madariaga states that the "new book is a most welcome addition to the growing number of scholarly studies in English on Muscovite Russia and reveals the same masterly combination of analysis and synthesis" as the author's treatment of enserfment. In both works, Hellie examines documents and laws of the times and presents not only the statistical facts concerning enserfment and slavery but draws sociological conclusions about the image, position, and lives of those who were drawn into serfdom or who sold themselves into slavery. Both *Times Literary Supplement* reviewers commend the author for his thorough presentation of documents—laws, court cases, dowries—as well as his illumination of the human stories that lie behind the factual material.

BIOGRAPHICAL/CRITICAL SOURCES: Times Literary Supplement, March 31, 1972, August 19, 1983.

* * *

HELLYER, Paul (Theodore)   1923-

PERSONAL: Born August 6, 1923, in Waterford, Ontario, Canada; son of Audrey Samuel (a farmer) and Lulla Maude (Anderson) Hellyer; married Ellen Jean Ralph, June 1, 1945; children: Mary Elizabeth, Peter Lawrence, David Ralph. *Ed-*

ucation: Curtiss-Wright Technical Institute of Aerodynamics, diploma in aeronautical engineering, 1941; University of Toronto, B.A., 1949. *Religion:* United Church. *Home:* 506-65 Harbour Sq., Toronto, Ontario, Canada M5J 2L4.

CAREER: Fleet Aircraft Manufacturing Co. Ltd., Fort Erie, Ontario, 1942-44, began as junior draftsman, became group leader in engineering department; House of Commons, Ottawa, Ontario, representative from Davenport riding, 1949-57, and Trinity riding, 1958-74; *Toronto Sun*, Toronto, Ontario, author of syndicated column "Comment—Paul Hellyer," 1974—. Proprietor of Mari-Jane Fashions (Toronto), 1945-56; president of Curran-Hall Ltd., 1951-62, Trepil Realty Ltd., 1951-62, and Hendon Estates Ltd., 1959-62; member of Toronto Board of Trade. Distinguished visitor at York University, 1969-70. Member of Canadian Privy Council and Associate Minister of National Defence, 1957-69, Minister of National Defence, 1963-67, Minister of Transport, 1967-69, minister responsible for housing and urban affairs, 1968-69, acting Prime Minister, 1968-69; founding chairman of Action Canada (populist movement), 1971—; committee chairman and opposition spokesman on industry, trade, and commerce for Progressive Conservative Caucus, 1973. *Military service:* Royal Canadian Air Force, 1944. Canadian Army, Royal Canadian Artillery, 1945-46.

MEMBER: North Atlantic Treaty Organization (NATO) Parliamentary Association, Commonwealth Parliamentary Association, Royal Society for the Encouragement of Arts, Manufactures and Commerce (fellow), Canadian Association for Adult Education, Canadian Authors Association, Ontario Club.

WRITINGS: Agenda: A Plan for Action, Prentice-Hall, 1971; *Exit Inflation*, Nelson, 1981; *Jobs for All: Capitalism on Trial*, Methuen (Scarborough, Ontario), 1984. Contributor to *Queen's Quarterly*.

SIDELIGHTS: Paul Hellyer told *CA:* "My central thesis has been that the division between Left and Right in politics, between East and West in the world, is based on a false premise, i.e., that it is not possible to operate a decentralized private capital system with full employment and stable prices. If the premise is wrong, as I believe, then the whole superstructure of bandaid programs designed to alleviate the symptoms has to be re-examined. While, theoretically, politics is the vehicle for the re-examination, the rigidity of bureaucracies and the reluctance to innovate makes the introduction of new ideas difficult."

AVOCATIONAL INTERESTS: Swimming, waterskiing, skin and scuba diving, stamp collecting.

*   *   *

HENDERSON, Philip (Prichard)   1906-1977

PERSONAL: Born February 17, 1906, in Barnes, Surrey, England; died September 13, 1977; married Millicent Rose, 1938 (divorced, 1947); married Belinda Hamilton (a painter), 1948; children: John Sebastian, Julian Urskwick. *Education:* Attended Bradfield College. *Address:* 25 Christchurch Hill, London NW3, England. *Agent:* A. M. Heath & Co., 40-42 William IV St., London WC2N 4DD, England.

CAREER: Writer. Everyman's Library, London, England, assistant editor, 1929-32; *British Book News*, London, co-editor, 1943-46; British Council, London, editor of feature articles, 1959-63, assistant editor of publications and recorded sound section, 1963-64; Chatto & Windus, London, editor, 1964-66.

Wartime service: National Fire Service, fireman, 1939-43. *Awards, honors:* Arts Council award, 1967.

WRITINGS: (Editor) *Shorter Novels*, Dutton, Volume I: *Elizabethan and Jacobean*, 1929, reprinted, 1949, Volume II: *Jacobean and Restoration*, 1930, reprinted, 1949 (published in England as *Seventeenth Century*, Dent, 1930), Volume III: *Eighteenth Century*, 1930, reprinted, 1954; (editor) Thomas Nash, *The Unfortunate Traveller*, Verona Society, 1930; *First Poems*, Dutton, 1930; (editor) John Skelton, *The Complete Poems*, Dutton, 1931, 4th edition, 1964; *A Wind in the Sand* (poems), Boriswood, 1932; (editor and author of introduction) Edmund Spenser, *The Shepherd's Calendar, and Other Poems*, Dutton, 1932; *Events in the Early Life of Anthony Price* (novel), Boriswood, 1935; (author of additional selections) Thomas Caldwell, *The Golden Book of Modern English Poetry, 1870-1920*, Dent, 1935; *Literature and a Changing Civilization*, John Lane, 1935, reprinted, Norwood, 1978; *The Novel Today: Studies in Contemporary Attitudes*, John Lane, 1936, reprinted, Folcroft, 1973; *And Morning in His Eyes: A Book about Christopher Marlowe*, Boriswood, 1937, reprinted, Haskell, 1972; *The Poet and Society*, Secker & Warburg, 1939, reprinted, Norwood, 1975.

(Editor and author of introduction) George Crabbe, *Poems*, Lawson & Dunn, 1946; (editor and author of introduction) Emily Bronte, *Poems: Selected*, Lawson & Dunn, 1947; (editor) *The Letters of William Morris to His Family and Friends*, Longmans, Green, 1950, reprinted, AMS Press, 1976; (editor and author of introduction) Bronte, *Complete Poems*, Folio Society, 1951; (editor) Bronte, *Wuthering Heights* [and] *Selected Poems*, Dent, 1951; *Christopher Marlowe*, Longmans, Green, 1952, 2nd edition, Barnes & Noble, 1974; *Samuel Butler: The Incarnate Bachelor*, Cohen & West, 1953, Indiana University Press, 1954; *The Life of Laurence Oliphant: Traveller, Diplomat and Mystic*, R. Hale, 1956, reprinted, Arden Library, 1981; *Richard Coeur de Lion: A Biography*, R. Hale, 1958, Norton, 1959, reprinted, Greenwood Press, 1976.

(With Oswald Doughty and H.J.C. Grierson) *Dante Gabriel Rossetti* [and] *William Morris* [and] *Algernon Charles Swinburne* (the first by Doughty, the second by Henderson, the third by Grierson), University of Nebraska Press, 1965; (with J. B. Bamborough, Ian Scott-Kilvert, and Clifford Leech) *Christopher Marlowe* [and] *Ben Jonson* [and] *John Webster* [and] *John Ford* (the first by Henderson, the second by Bamborough, the third by Scott-Kilvert, the fourth by Leech), University of Nebraska Press, 1966; *William Morris: His Life, Work, and Friends*, McGraw, 1967, 2nd edition, 1973; *Swinburne: Portrait of a Poet*, Macmillan, 1974; *Tennyson: Poet and Prophet*, Routledge & Kegan Paul, 1978.

SIDELIGHTS: Philip Henderson's 1974 book *Swinburne: Portrait of a Poet*, says a *New Yorker* critic, is "a literate, thoughtful biography by a scholar who believes that Swinburne was a much better poet than either contemporary or recent taste has recognized." "In Philip Henderson," writes Ian Fletcher in a *Times Literary Supplement* review, "the poet has found something approaching a proper biographer: luminously sane, aware of the comic aspects of the subject's life and genius, but never condescending, never using Swinburne as point of departure for amateur psychologizing, deploying a strong narrative line."

AVOCATIONAL INTERESTS: Music, architecture, English medieval churches, painting, bird life, getting away from cities as often as possible.

BIOGRAPHICAL/CRITICAL SOURCES: New York Times Book Review, January 21, 1968; *New York Review of Books*, May

23, 1968, November 28, 1974; *New Yorker,* September 14, 1968, September 16, 1974; *Times Literary Supplement,* November 21, 1975.†

*   *   *

HENLEY, Wallace (Boynton)   1941-

PERSONAL: Born December 5, 1941, in Birmingham, Ala.; son of Wallace Boynton and Wilfred (Vassar) Henley; married Mary Irene Lambert, September 4, 1961; children: Mary Lauri, Travis Wallace. *Education:* Samford University, B.A., 1964; Southwestern Baptist Theological Seminary, additional study, 1964-65.

CAREER: Ordained Baptist minister, 1962; Central Park Baptist Church, Birmingham, Ala., associate pastor, 1963; Travis Avenue Baptist Church, Fort Worth, Tex., minister of youth education, 1964-66; Antioch Baptist Church, Nuremberg, West Germany, pastor, 1966; Mobile College, Mobile, Ala., director of public relations, 1966-68; *Birmingham News,* Birmingham, religion editor and editorial writer, 1968-70; Cabinet Committee on Education, Washington, D.C., assistant director, 1970-71; staff assistant to the President of the United States, Washington, D.C., 1971-73; Old Spanish Fort Baptist Church, Mobile, pastor, 1973-77; McElwhin Baptist Church, Birmingham, pastor, 1978—. Host of "Know Your News," on Alabama Educational Television Network, 1968-69.

MEMBER: Birmingham Press Club, Sigma Delta Chi.

AWARDS, HONORS: R. S. Reynolds Award from the Presbyterian Church in the United States, 1969, for excellence in religion journalism; Green Eyeshade Award from Atlanta chapter of Sigma Delta Chi, 1970, for writing on the evolution of Birmingham's race relations; award from Alabama Associated Press, 1973, for a study of a changing suburb of Birmingham.

WRITINGS: Enter at Your Own Risk, Revell, 1974; *The White House Mystique,* Revell, 1976; (contributor) Frank Mead, editor, *Tarbell's Teacher's Guide,* Revell, 1976; *Rebirth in Washington: The Christian Impact in the Nation's Capital,* Good News, 1977; *Europe at the Crossroads,* Good News, 1978; *The Roman Solution,* Tyndale, 1984. Contributor to church magazines.

SIDELIGHTS: Religious work has taken Wallace Henley to Central America, Europe, and Asia. He is also one of the people who helped to organize the White House prayer breakfast.

*   *   *

HENSLEY, Joe L.   1926-

PERSONAL: Born March 19, 1926, in Bloomington, Ind.; son of Ralph Ramon and Frances Mae (Wilson) Hensley; married Charlotte R. Bettinger, June 18, 1950; children: Michael Joseph. *Education:* Indiana University, A.B., 1950, LL.B., 1955. *Politics:* Democrat. *Religion:* Presbyterian. *Home:* 2315 Blackmore, Madison, Ind. 47250. *Office:* Fifth Judicial Circuit Courthouse, Madison, Ind. 47250.

CAREER: Admitted to State Bar of Indiana, 1955; Metford & Hensley, Attorneys at Law, Madison, Ind., associate, 1955-71; Ford, Hensley & Todd, Attorneys at Law, Madison, partner, 1971-73; Hensley, Todd, & Castor, Madison, partner, 1973-75; Eightieth Judicial Circuit, Indiana, judge pro-tempore, 1975-76; Fifth Judicial Circuit, Indiana, judge, 1977—. Indiana General Assembly, member of Assembly, 1961-62, prosecuting attorney of Fifth Judicial Indiana Circuit, 1963-

66. *Military service:* U.S. Navy, hospital corpsman, 1944-46, journalist in Korea, 1951-52.

MEMBER: Mystery Writers of America, Science Fiction Writers of America, Indiana State Bar Association, Jefferson County Bar Association.

WRITINGS—Published by Doubleday, except as indicated: *The Color of Hate,* Ace, 1961; *Deliver Us to Evil,* 1971; *Legislative Body,* 1972; *The Poison Summer,* 1974; *Song of Corpus Juris,* 1974; *Rivertown Risk,* 1977; *A Killing in Gold,* 1978; *Minor Murders,* 1980; *Outcasts,* 1981; *Final Doors* (short stories), 1981. Contributor of more than fifty science fiction and suspense stories to magazines.

SIDELIGHTS: Joe L. Hensley, a judge and former attorney in Indiana, is creator of a series of whodunits featuring Don Robak. With a background similar to the author's, lawyer Robak defends the innocent and tries to identify the guilty in Indiana. Hensley "always uses his knowledge [of the state and its judicial system] . . . to enhance his well-woven novels of chicanery and murder," states Alice Cromie in the *Chicago Tribune Book World.*

Hensley told *CA:* "Time is a very difficult thing. I must find mine in odd places. I have no intention, at least now, of stopping being a judge. My stories are at least partially the result of that life. Although they usually take the suspense form, my books are about people who must live in this complicated and devious world all of us try our best to exist within. I find that I can't easily stop writing. So I get up earlier, work harder, and hope to get more done. It isn't fun anymore, but it's something I do. I'm glad I do it and I doubt that anything could make me stop."

BIOGRAPHICAL/CRITICAL SOURCES: Washington Post Book World, February 15, 1981; *New York Times Book Review,* March 1, 1981; *Chicago Tribune Book World,* June 21, 1981.

*   *   *

HERMAND, Jost   1930-

PERSONAL: Born April 11, 1930, in Kassel, Germany (now West Germany); son of Heinz and Annelies (Hucke) Hermand; married Elisabeth Jagenburg, 1956. *Education:* University of Marburg, D.Phil., 1955. *Home:* 845 Terry Pl., Madison, Wis. 53711. *Office:* Department of German, University of Wisconsin, Madison, Wis. 53706.

CAREER: Free-lance writer, 1955-58; University of Wisconsin—Madison, assistant professor, 1958-61, associate professor, 1961-63, professor of German, 1963-67, Vilas Research Professor of German, 1967—. Visiting professor at Harvard University, Free University of Berlin, University of Bremen, University of Marburg, and University of Texas.

AWARDS, HONORS: American Council of Learned Societies fellowship, 1963.

WRITINGS: (With Richard Hamann) *Deutsche Kunst und Kultur,* five volumes, Akademie, 1959-75; *Von Mainz nach Weimar,* Metzler, 1969.

Pop International, Athenaeum (Frankfurt), 1971; *Unbequeme Literatur,* Stiehm, 1971; *Der Schein des schoenen Lebens,* Athenaeum, 1972; *Streitobjekt Heine,* Fischer Atheneum, 1975; *Der fruehe Heine,* Winkler, 1976; *Stile, Ismen, Etiketten,* Athenaeum (Frankfurt), 1978; (with Frank Trommler) *Die Kultur der Weimarer,* Nymphenburger, 1978; *Sieben Arten an Deutschland zu Leiden,* Athenaeum, 1979.

Orte: Irgendwo, Athenaeum, 1981; *Konkretes Hoeren: Zum Inhalt der Instrumental-musik,* Argument, 1981; *Die Kultur der Bundesrepublik,* Volume I, Nymphenburger, 1985; (with James Steakley) *Writings of German Composers,* Continuum, 1985.

*　　*　　*

HERRING, George C., Jr. 1936-

PERSONAL: Born May 23, 1936, in Blacksburg, Va.; son of George C. (a university administrator) and Gordon (Saunders) Herring; married Nancy Walton, March 15, 1958; children: John Walton, Lisa Susanne. *Education:* Roanoke College, B.A., 1957; University of Virginia, M.A., 1962, Ph.D., 1965. *Home:* 175 Muir Lane, Georgetown, Ky. 40324. *Office:* Department of History, University of Kentucky, Lexington, Ky. 40506.

CAREER: Ohio University, Athens, assistant professor of history, 1965-69; University of Kentucky, Lexington, associate professor, 1969-80, professor of history, 1980—, chairman of department, 1973-76. *Military service:* U.S. Navy, 1958-60.

MEMBER: American Historical Association, Society for the History of American Foreign Relations, Organization of American Historians.

WRITINGS: Aid to Russia, 1941-1946, Columbia University Press, 1973; *The Diaries of Edward R. Stettinius,* New Viewpoints, 1975; *America's Longest War: The United States and Vietnam, 1950-1975,* Wiley, 1979; *The Secret Diplomacy of the Vietnam War,* University of Texas, 1983. Editor of *Diplomatic History,* 1982—.

*　　*　　*

HESKETH, Phoebe Rayner 1909-

PERSONAL: Born January 29, 1909, in Preston, Lancashire, England; daughter of Arthur Ernest (a physician and radiologist) and Amy Gertrude (Fielding) Rayner; married Aubrey Hesketh, September 30, 1931; children: Martin, Richard, Catherine. *Education:* Attended Cheltenham Ladies' College. *Religion:* Church of England. *Home:* 10 The Green, Heath Charnock, Chorley PR6 9JH, Lancashire, England.

CAREER: Bolton Evening News, Bolton, England, woman's page editor, 1942-45; poet and free-lance writer for magazines and radio; Arts Council lecturer for schools, colleges and other institutions.

AWARDS, HONORS: Greenwood prize of Poetry Society of London, 1946 and 1963; Royal Society of Literature fellow, 1971—.

WRITINGS—Poetry, except as indicated: *Poems,* Sheratt & Hughes, 1939; *Lean Forward Spring!,* Sidgwick & Jackson, 1948; *No Time for Cowards,* Heinemann, 1950; *Out of the Dark,* selected by Richard Church, Heinemann, 1954; *Between Wheels and Stars,* Heinemann, 1956; *The Buttercup Children,* Hart-Davis, 1958; *Prayer for Sun,* Hart-Davis, 1966; *My Aunt Edith* (biography), P. Davies, 1966.

Rivington: The Story of A Village (prose), P. Davies, 1972; *A Song of Sunlight,* Chatto & Windus, 1974; *Preparing to Leave,* Enitharmon Press, 1977; *The Eighth Day: Selected Poems,* Enitharmon Press, 1980.

Contributor of articles and poems to *Country Life, Times Literary Supplement, Poetry Review, Countryman, Encounter, Observer, Sunday Times,* and other journals. Radio scripts

include "Lift Up Your Hearts," "Woman's Hour," and "Thought for the Day."

BIOGRAPHICAL/CRITICAL SOURCES: Times Literary Supplement, August 21, 1981.

*　　*　　*

HEUER, John (Michael) 1941-

PERSONAL: Surname is pronounced *Hoy*-er; original name J. Michael Kaudy, name legally changed in 1942; born January 21, 1941, in LaCrosse, Wis.; adopted son of Carl Edward (a police chief) and Gertrude (a clerical worker; maiden name, Meitner) Heuer; married Patricia Weinrich, December 5, 1965 (divorced October 2, 1975); married Maryellen McCabe, December 16, 1978; children: (second marriage) Erinnisse Roerich. *Education:* Attended St. Norbert College, 1959-61, and New York University, 1961-62. *Politics:* Liberal. *Religion:* Vedanta-Agni Yoga. *Home:* 315 West 84th St., New York, N.Y. 10024. *Agent:* Robert A. Freedman, Brandt & Brandt Literary Agents, Inc., 1501 Broadway, New York, N.Y. 10036.

CAREER: Bon Marche, Inc., New York City, in sales and customer service, 1966-71; National Starch & Chemical Corp., New York City, in traffic and distribution, 1971-74; H. M. Keiser, Inc., New York City, supply supervisor, 1974-75; freelance writer, 1975-78; Winslow Hotel Corp., New York City, public relations writer, 1978-80; L. S. Wegman Co., New York City, technical editor, 1981-83; M. Joseph Zink & Co., New York City, video/film staff writer, 1983—. Circle Repertory Co., company member, 1972—, resident playwright, 1975—; associated with Circle in the Square Theatre Workshop, Writer's Stage Company Workshop, Mark Epstein Mime Co., and Four Winds Theatre Workshop. Has performed in film and stage productions since 1959, including the original Circle Repertory production of "The Hot l Baltimore." *Member:* Dramatists Guild. *Awards, honors:* Younger audiences program grant from New York State Council on the Arts, 1975.

WRITINGS—Published plays: *Cavern of the Jewels* (two-act juvenile; first produced in New York City at Circle Repertory Co., April 2, 1976), Dramatists Play Service, 1976; *Innocent Thoughts, Harmless Intentions* (first produced in New York City at Circle Repertory Co., December 4, 1974), Dramatists Play Service, 1980.

Unpublished plays: "The Good Shepherd" (one-act), first produced in New York City at Four Winds Studio-in-a-Garden, March 7, 1966; "This Unsettled Earth" (one-act), first produced in New York City at Playwrights' Workshop Club, March 15, 1967; "When Day Becomes Night" (three-act), first produced in New York City at Bastiano's Cellar Studio, October 15, 1967; "Mrs. Tidings' Mason-Dixon Medicine Man" (two-act), first produced in New York City at Circle Repertory Co., June 11, 1973.

Films: "Ivory Colt," Motion Picture Treatment, 1980; "Chinatown Mission," Motion Picture Treatment, 1982.

Also author of industrial films and of plays "Magnificent Ebonyfyre's Midnight Circus," 1977, and "Daughtersmiths," 1979. Author of storyline for television movie "Victoria's Dixie Drummer," 1981, and of scripts for series "Love, Sidney," NBC-TV, 1981-82.

WORK IN PROGRESS: "Rameau LaBesque."

SIDELIGHTS: John Heuer writes: "As a playwright I am particularly interested in working toward the development of a kind of theatre which concerns itself with the human condition in such a manner as to make the casting of performers able to transcend racial, color or ethnic considerations, an expression of theatre that will have itself focus more directly on an actor or actress' ability rather than the surface. I have begun this experiment in 'Cavern' and am continuing it in my current work.''

For his play "Innocent Thoughts, Harmless Intentions," Heuer is "to be commended," according to Ginnine Gocuzza writing in *Villager*, "not only for his complex, well-spun story, but for creating living men and women who make mistakes, who prey upon their victims and are themselves victimized."

Clive Barnes comments on "Innocent Thoughts, Harmless Intentions" in a *New York Post* article, stating that "this is a play of style, compassion and thought. . . . Heuer hits desperately hard in this play. It is a brutal assessment of society . . . and its savage way with a non-conformist. . . . It draws you into its orbit, and makes you part of its feeling." It's the kind of play, concludes Barnes, "that makes you think about the nature of theater. But even more important, it forces you to thrill to its moment."

BIOGRAPHICAL/CRITICAL SOURCES: New York Post, March 7, 1980; *New York Times*, March 8, 1980; *Record*, March 10, 1980; *Villager*, March 13, 1980.

* * *

HIGGINS, Don 1928-

PERSONAL: Born October 8, 1928, in Georgetown, S.C.; son of James Stone (a railroad agent) and Belle (Boone) Higgins; married Margaret Way, September 21, 1957; children: Phoebe, Don, Jr., Liz. *Education:* Attended Hendrix College, 1946-47, and College of William and Mary, 1947-48; Pratt Institute, diploma (with honors), 1951. *Politics:* Independent. *Religion:* Protestant. *Home:* 415 Central Park W., New York, N.Y. 10025. *Office:* SSC&B Advertising, 1 Dag Hammarskjold Plaza, New York, N.Y.

CAREER: Free-lance illustrator in New York City, 1951-64; Young & Rubicam, New York City, television art director, 1964-66; Dancer-Fitzgerald-Sample, New York City, vice-president and executive art director, 1966-70; Grey Advertising, Inc., New York City, vice-president and creative supervisor, 1970-77; Leo Burnett, Inc., Chicago, Ill., vice-president and creative director, 1977-80; SSC&B Advertising, New York City, vice-president and associate creative director, 1980—. *Awards, honors:* Ida C. Haskell traveling scholarship.

WRITINGS—Self-illustrated juveniles, except as indicated: *I Am a Boy*, Golden Press, 1966; *I Am a Girl*, Golden Press, 1966; *Papa's Going to Buy Me a Mocking Bird*, Seabury, 1968; *Catlin* (adult novel), St. Martin's, 1980.

WORK IN PROGRESS: A book, *A Bend in the Pee Dee;* a novel about advertising.

SIDELIGHTS: Don Higgins's adult novel, *Catlin*, features eleven-year-old Chester St. Clair and twelve-year-old Catlin. The young narrators' boy-girl friendship blossoms when Chester and his mother move to a small South Carolina town after Chester's father is committed to an institution for the mentally ill. Through the eyes and actions of the pair—and an assortment of other characters of all ages and backgrounds—the reader learns the romantic scandals, financial dealings, and personalities of the insular community's population. Most of the in-

habitants are, like Chester, St. Clairs. At the head of the expansive clan is Miss Sissy, restaurateur, who employs most of her St. Clair relatives and also acts as surrogate parent or mentor to an assortment of young people. "Don Higgins takes a number of risks—cuteness and confusion, to name two—by making his narrator a child who tells his own story in Pogo-like dialect, but he pulls it off without a hitch," concludes a *New Yorker* critic.

BIOGRAPHICAL/CRITICAL SOURCES: Don Higgins, *Catlin,* St. Martin's, 1980; *New Yorker*, April 21, 1980; *Chicago Tribune*, May 11, 1980; *National Review*, August 8, 1980.

* * *

HILL, Lorna 1902-

PERSONAL: Born February 21, 1902, in Durham, England; daughter of G. H. and Edith (Rutter) Leatham; married V. R. Hill (a clergyman); children: Shirley Victorine (Mrs. E. F. Emley). *Education:* University of Durham, B.A., 1926. *Religion:* Anglican. *Home:* Brockleside, Keswick, Cumberland, England. *Agent:* A. M. Heath & Co. Ltd., 40-42 William IV St., London, WC2N 4DD, England.

CAREER: Author of children's books.

WRITINGS: The Vicarage Children, Evans Brothers, 1961; *More About Mandy*, Evans Brothers, 1963; *The Secret*, Evans Brothers, 1964; *The Vicarage Children in Skye*, Evans Brothers, 1966; *La Sylphide: The Life of Maria Taglioni*, Evans Brothers, 1967; *The Other Miss Perkin*, R. Hale, 1978; *Scent of Rosemary*, R. Hale, 1978, Pinnacle Books, 1980.

"Marjorie" series: *Marjorie & Co.*, Art & Education, 1948, Thomas Nelson, 1956; *Stolen Holiday*, Art & Education, 1948, Thomas Nelson, 1956; *Border Peel*, Art & Education, 1950, Thomas Nelson, 1956; *No Medals for Guy*, Thomas Nelson, 1962.

"Sadler's Wells" series: *A Dream of Sadler's Wells*, Evans Brothers, 1950, Holt, 1955, new edition, Piccolo Books, 1972; *Veronica at the Wells*, Evans Brothers, 1951, new edition, Piccolo Books, 1972, published as *Veronica at Sadler's Wells*, Holt, 1954; *Masquerade at the Wells*, Evans Brothers, 1952, new edition, White Lion, 1976, published as *Masquerade at the Ballet*, Holt, 1957; *No Castanets at the Wells*, Evans Brothers, 1953, new edition, Piccolo Books, 1972, published as *Castanets for Caroline: A Story of Sadler's Wells*, Holt, 1956; *Jane Leaves the Wells*, Evans Brothers, 1953; *Ella at the Wells*, Evans Brothers, 1954; *Return to the Wells*, Evans Brothers, 1955; *Rosanna Joins the Wells*, Evans Brothers, 1956; *Principal Role*, Evans Brothers, 1957; *Swan Feather*, Evans Brothers, 1958; *Dress Rehearsal*, Evans Brothers, 1959; *Back Stage*, Evans Brothers, 1960; *Vicki in Venice*, Evans Brothers, 1962.

"Patience" series, published by Burke Publishing: *They Called Her Patience*, 1951; *It Was All Through Patience*, 1952; *Castle in Northumbria*, 1953; *So Guy Came Too*, 1954; *The Five Shilling Holiday*, 1955.

"Dancing Peel" series, published by Thomas Nelson: *Dancing Peel*, 1954; *Dancer's Luck*, 1955; *The Little Dancer*, 1956; *Dancer in the Wings*, 1958; *Dancer in Danger*, 1960; *Dancer on Holiday*, 1962.

AVOCATIONAL INTERESTS: Scottish dancing, fell walking, swimming, gardening, photography, and music.

HINCHLIFFE, Arnold P.   1930-

PERSONAL: Born December 3, 1930, in Dewsbury, Yorkshire, England. *Education:* University of Manchester, M.A., Ph.D.; Yale University, M.A. *Home:* 19 Craigweil Ave., Didsbury, Manchester, England. *Office:* Department of English, University of Manchester, Manchester, England.

CAREER: University of Manchester, Manchester, England, currently senior lecturer in English literature. *Military service:* British Army, Royal Engineers, 1948-50; became sergeant.

WRITINGS: Private File (poems), Manchester Institute of Contemporary Arts, 1967; *Harold Pinter,* Twayne, 1967; (editor with C. B. Cox) *Casebook on "The Wasteland,"* Macmillan, 1968; *The Absurd: Critical Idiom Number 5,* Methuen, 1969; *British Theatre, 1950-1970,* Basil Blackwell, 1974; *Modern Verse Drama: Critical Idiom Number 32,* Methuen, 1977; (editor) *Drama Criticism: Developments since Ibsen,* Macmillan, 1979; *John Osborne,* G. K. Hall, 1984; (editor) *T. S. Eliot: The Plays—A Casebook,* Macmillan, in press; *Volpone: Text and Performance,* Macmillan, in press.

WORK IN PROGRESS: T. S. Eliot: The Critical Debate, for Macmillan.

*   *   *

HIRO, Dilip

PERSONAL: Born in Sind, Pakistan. *Education:* Virginia Polytechnic Institute and State University, M.S. *Home:* 31 Waldegrave Rd., Ealing, London W5 3HT, England.

CAREER: Writer.

MEMBER: Royal Institute of International Affairs.

AWARDS, HONORS: Award from Chicago Film Festival, 1975, for "A Private Enterprise."

WRITINGS: A Triangular View (novel), Dobson, 1969; *Black British, White British,* Eyre & Spottiswoode, 1971, revised edition, Monthly Review Press, 1973; *To Anchor a Cloud: A Play in Three Acts* (first produced in London, England, at Collegiate Theatre, September 25, 1970), Writers Workshop (Calcutta, India), 1972; *The Untouchables of India,* Minority Rights Group (London), 1975; *Inside India Today,* Routledge & Kegan Paul, 1976, revised edition, Monthly Review Press, 1977; "Apply, Apply, No Reply" (television play; also see below), first broadcast by British Broadcasting Corp. Television, June 12, 1976; "A Matter of Honor" (television play), first broadcast by Granada Television, 1976; "A Clean Break: A Play in One Act" (also see below), first produced in London at Ravi Shankar Hall, November 24, 1977; *Apply, Apply, No Reply* [and] *A Clean Break* (one-act plays), Writers Workshop, 1978.

Interior, Exchange, Exterior (poems), Writers Workshop, 1980; *Inside the Middle East,* McGraw, 1982; *Iran under the Ayatollahs,* Routledge & Kegan Paul, 1984. Also author of a feature film, "A Private Enterprise," 1975.

Author of scripts for television serial "Parosi," 1977-78. Contributor to magazines and newspapers, including *New Society, Wall Street Journal, Nation, International Herald Tribune,* London *Sunday Times,* and *New Statesman.*

WORK IN PROGRESS: A travel book on the Middle East.

BIOGRAPHICAL/CRITICAL SOURCES: New York Times Book Review, January 29, 1978.

*   *   *

HOBEL, Phil
See FANTHORPE, R(obert) Lionel

*   *   *

HODGE, P(aul) W(illiam)   1934-

PERSONAL: Born November 8, 1934, in Seattle, Wash.; son of Paul H. and Frances (Bakeman) Hodge; married Ann Uran, June 14, 1961; children: Gordon, Erik, Sandra. *Education:* Yale University, B.S., 1956; Harvard University, Ph.D., 1960. *Residence:* Seattle, Wash. *Office:* Department of Astronomy, University of Washington, Seattle, Wash. 98195.

CAREER: Harvard University, Cambridge, Mass., lecturer in astronomy, 1960; University of California, Berkeley, assistant professor of astronomy, 1961-65; University of Washington, Seattle, associate professor, 1965-69, professor of astronomy, 1969—, associate dean, 1971-73, 1978-79. Physicist at Smithsonian Astrophysical Observatory, 1956-75. Member of board of directors, Astronomical Society of the Pacific, 1968-74; section chairman, American Association for the Advancement of Science, 1978-79, 1984-85.

MEMBER: International Astronomical Union, American Astronomical Society, American Geophysical Union, Committee on Space Research of International Council of Scientific Unions.

AWARDS, HONORS: Beckwith Prize, 1956; National Science Foundation fellow, 1960-61; Bart J. Bok Prize, 1962.

WRITINGS: (With J. C. Brandt) *Solar System Astrophysics,* McGraw, 1963; *Galaxies and Cosmology,* McGraw, 1965; *The Large Magellanic Cloud,* Smithsonian Press, 1967; *Concepts of the Universe,* McGraw, 1969; *The Revolution in Astronomy,* Holiday House, 1970; (reviser) Harlow Shapley, *Galaxies,* Harvard University Press, 1972; *Astronomy Study Guide,* McGraw, 1973; *Concepts of Contemporary Astronomy,* McGraw, 1974, 2nd edition, 1978; (with F. Wright) *The Small Magellanic Cloud,* University of Washington Press, 1977; *Atlas of the Andromeda Galaxy,* University of Washington Press, 1981; *Interplanetary Dust,* Gordon & Breach, 1981; *Galaxies,* Harvard University Press, 1984; (editor) *The Universe of Galaxies,* Freeman, 1984. Contributor of about three hundred papers to astronomy journals.

*   *   *

HOFFMANN, Peter (Conrad Werner)   1930-

PERSONAL: Born August 13, 1930, in Dresden, Germany (now East Germany); son of Wilhelm (a librarian) and Elfriede Frances (a sculptor; maiden name, Mueller) Hoffmann; married Helga Luise Hobelsberger (a teacher), July 22, 1959; children: Peter Friedrich Georg Wilhelm, Susan Judith Gudula. *Education:* Attended University of Stuttgart, 1953-54, University of Tuebingen, 1954-55, University of Zurich, 1955, and Northwestern University, 1955-56; University of Munich, Ph.D., 1961. *Home:* 4332 Montrose Ave., Montreal, Quebec, Canada H3Y 2A9; and Rosshaustrasse 4, Stuttgart 70, West Germany. *Agent:* Niedieck Linder A. G., Holzgasse 6, CH-8039 Zurich, Switzerland. *Office:* Department of History, McGill University, 855 Sherbrooke St. W., Montreal, Quebec, Canada H3A 2T7.

CAREER: University of Maryland, Heidelberg, Germany, lecturer in history, 1961-65; University of Northern Iowa, Cedar Falls, assistant professor, 1965-68, associate professor of history, 1968-70; McGill University, Montreal, Quebec, professor of history, 1970—. Lecturer at Schiller College, 1964-65. Member, Canadian Committee for the History of the Second World War and American Committee for the History of the Second World War.

MEMBER: Wuerttembergischer Geschichts und Altertumsverein, Deutsche Schillergesellschaft, Sigma Alpha Epsilon.

WRITINGS: *Die diplomatischen Beziehungen zwischen Wuerttemberg und Bayern im Krimkrieg und bis zum Beginn der Italienischen Krise, 1853-1858* (title means "Diplomatic Relations between Wuerttemberg and Bavaria during the Crimean War and to the Beginning of the Italian Crisis, 1853-1858"), W. Kohlhammer Verlag, 1963; *Widerstand, Staatsstreich, Attentat: Der Kampf der Opposition gegen Hitler* (title means "Resistance, Coup d'Etat, Assassination: The Struggle of the Opposition to Hitler"), R. Piper, 1969, 3rd edition, 1977, translation by Richard Barry published as *The History of the German Resistance, 1933-1945*, M.I.T. Press, 1977; *Die Sicherheit des Diktators: Hitlers Leibwachen, Schutzmassnahmen, Residenzen, Hauptquartiere* (title means "The Security of the Dictator: Hitler's Bodyguards, Protective Measures, Residences, Headquarters"), R. Piper, 1975.

Hitler's Personal Security, M.I.T. Press, 1979; *Widerstand gegen Hitler und das Attentat vom 20. Juli 1944* (title means "Resistance to Hitler and the Assassination Attack of 20 July 1944"), R. Piper, 1979, 2nd edition, 1984.

Contributor: Franklin H. Littell and Hubert G. Locke, editors, *The German Church Struggle and the Holocaust*, Wayne State University Press, 1974; Hans Juergen Schultz, editor, *Der zwanzigste Juli: Alternative zu Hitler?* (title means "The Twentieth of July: Alternative to Hitler?"), Kreuz Verlag, 1974; George L. Mosse, editor, *Police Forces in History*, Sage Publications, 1975.

Edgar Denton III, editor, *Limits of Loyalty*, Wilfred Laurier University Press, 1980; Czeslaw Madajczyk, editor, *Inter arma non silent Musae: Wojna i kultura, 1939-1945*, Panstwowy Instytut Wydawniczy, 1982; Militaergeschichtliches Forschungsamt, editor, *Vortraege zur Militaergeschichte 5: Der militaerische Widerstand gegen Hitler und das NS-Regime, 1933-1945* (title means "Lectures on Military History, 5: The Military Resistance to Hitler and to the National-Socialist Regime, 1933-1945"), Verlag E. S. Mittler & Sohn, 1984.

Contributor to German, Italian, Canadian, and American history journals.

WORK IN PROGRESS: Studying the intellectual background of the Stauffenberg brothers and the correspondence of William I of Wuerttemberg.

BIOGRAPHICAL/CRITICAL SOURCES: *Times Literary Supplement*, July 2, 1970; *Newsweek*, April 25, 1977; *Washington Post*, May 15, 1977; *Economist*, May 28, 1977; *New York Times*, June 13, 1977; *New York Review of Books*, September 15, 1977.

*   *   *

HOFFMANN, Stanley (H.)   1928-

PERSONAL: Born November 27, 1928, in Vienna, Austria; came to the United States, 1955, naturalized citizen, 1960; married Inge Schneier. *Education:* Institut d'Etudes Politiques, diploma, 1948; Harvard University, M.A., 1952; University of Paris, LL.D., 1953. *Home:* 91 Washington Ave., Cambridge, Mass. 02140. *Office:* Center for European Studies, Harvard University, Cambridge, Mass.

CAREER: French Political Science Association, Paris, France, assistant, 1952-53; Harvard University, Cambridge, Mass., instructor, 1955-57, assistant professor, 1957-59, associate professor, 1959-63, professor of government, 1963—, Douglas Dillon Professor of the Civilization of France, 1980—, chairman of Center for European Studies.

MEMBER: American Academy of Arts and Sciences, American Political Science Association, American Society of International Law, Council on Foreign Relations, Association Francaise de Science Politique.

AWARDS, HONORS: Carnegie Prize in International Organization, 1955; Prix Alphonse Bentinck, 1982.

WRITINGS: *Organisations internationales et pouvoirs politiques des etats* (title means "International Organizations and Political Powers of States"), A. Colin, 1954; *Le Mouvement Poujade* (title means "The Poujade Movement"), A. Colin, 1956; *Contemporary Theory in International Relations*, Prentice-Hall, 1960; (with Laurence Wylie and others) *In Search of France*, Harvard University Press, 1963; *The State of War*, Praeger, 1965; *Gulliver's Troubles; or, The Setting of American Foreign Policy*, McGraw, 1968; (editor) *Conditions of World Order*, Houghton, 1968; (editor) *The Relevance of International Law*, Schenkman, 1968; *Decline or Renewal?: France Since the 1930's*, Viking, 1974; *Sur la France* (title means "On France"), Editions du Seuil, 1976; *Primacy or World Order*, McGraw, 1978.

(Editor) *The Fifth Republic at Twenty*, State University of New York Press, 1981; *Duties beyond Borders*, Syracuse University Press, 1981; *Dead Ends*, Ballinger, 1982. Contributor to *Foreign Policy, Foreign Affairs, Daedalus,* and *New York Review of Books*.

WORK IN PROGRESS: Studies of the French Fifth Republic and of France, 1934-44.

*   *   *

HOGAN, Michael   1943-

PERSONAL: Born July 14, 1943, in Newport, R.I.; son of Francis Xavier (a businessman) and Anna (Mack) Hogan; married Cynthia Hooper, April 1, 1964 (divorced, 1967); children: Francis Garrison, Melissa Akie. *Education:* Attended Stonehill College, 1961-64; University of Arizona, B.A., 1977, LL.B., 1980. *Home:* 2107 South Winstel, Tucson, Ariz. 85713. *Agent:* Larry Fassler, P.O. Box 26507, Tucson, Ariz. 85726.

CAREER: Poet. Cold Mountain Press, Austin, Tex., associate editor, 1972-76; Cochise College, Douglas, Ariz., writer-in-residence, 1977-78; teacher and poet in artists-in-the-schools program, Tucson, Ariz., and Denver, Colo., 1978-79; consultant on institutional programs to National Endowment for the Arts, 1979-80; consultant to Colorado Humanities Program and Western States Arts Council, 1980-81; legal consultant to Tritex Investments of Arizona, 1981-82; legal advisor to Babanto Investment Corp., 1983—. Editor for Pushcart Press, 1977-78.

MEMBER: Committee of Small Magazine Editors and Publishers.

AWARDS, HONORS: International P.E.N. Award for poetry, 1975; Joseph Fels Award, 1976; Pushcart Prize for poetry from Pushcart Press, 1976; National Endowment for the Arts fellowship, 1976-77; Colorado Humanities Program fellowship, 1978-79; award for excellence in teaching from Colorado P.T.S.A., 1979.

WRITINGS: Letters for My Son, Unicorn Press, 1975; *If You Ever Get There, Think of Me,* Emerald City Press, 1975; *Soon It Will Be Morning,* Cold Mountain Press, 1976; *April, 1976,* Cold Mountain Press, 1976; *Risky Business,* Great Raven Press, 1977; *Rust,* Turkey Press, 1977; (editor) *Do Not Go Gentle,* University of Arizona Press, 1977; (co-editor) *The American Microcosm,* Greenfield Review Press, 1978; *A Lion at a Cocktail Party,* Gallimauphry, 1978; (contributing editor) *The Pushcart Prize: Best of the Small Presses,* Avon/Pushcart, 1978-83.

Annotated Directory of American Correctional Institutions, U.S. Government Printing Office, 1980; *Manual for Writers in Prisons, and Selected Markets,* U.S. Government Printing Office, 1980; *The Broken Face of Summer,* Windriver Books, 1982; (co-editor) *The Light from Another Country,* Greenfield Review Press, 1984. Guest editor, *Greenfield Review,* 1978.

WORK IN PROGRESS: "Currently putting the final touches on a volume of prose and poetry entitled *The Terrace, St. Tropez;* revising and expanding *Living Is No Laughing Matter,* a project begun in 1978 to explore the existential elements of psychic survival in prisons and prison camp environments; working on a book of tales tentatively entitled *Further Adventures of Snake.*"

SIDELIGHTS: Michael Hogan told *CA* that his first book was published while he was in prison. It was well received by critics, he believes, because "it was written in prison and the work *defined the place,* instead of the opposite." Convinced of "the efficacy of writing as a tool to define one's life," Hogan set up writing workshops for ex-offenders under the auspices of the U.S. Department of Labor.

BIOGRAPHICAL/CRITICAL SOURCES: American Poetry Review, January, 1976; *America,* September 11, 1976; *Hudson Review,* spring, 1977.

*　　*　　*

HOGENDORN, Jan S(tafford) 1937-

PERSONAL: Born October 27, 1937, in Lahaina, Hawaii; son of Paul Earl and Helen (Stafford) Hogendorn; married Dianne Hodet (a librarian), September 6, 1960; children: Christiaan Paul. *Education:* Wesleyan University, Middletown, Conn., B.A., 1960; London School of Economics and Political Science, M.Sc., 1962, Ph.D., 1966; additional study at Harvard University, 1962-63. *Politics:* Democrat. *Religion:* Unitarian Universalist. *Home:* R.F.D. 1, North Vassalboro, Me. 04962. *Office:* Department of Economics, Colby College, Mayflower Hill, Waterville, Me. 04901.

CAREER: Boston University, Boston, Mass., instructor in economics, 1963; Colby College, Waterville, Me., assistant professor, 1966-69, associate professor of economics, 1969—, Grossman Professor of Economics, 1976, chairman of department, 1972-80. Ford Foundation professor of development economics, Robert College, Istanbul, Turkey, 1971-72; Fulbright professor of economic history, Ahmadu Bello University, 1975. Associate, Columbia University, 1977—; research associate, University of Birmingham, 1980.

MEMBER: American Economic Association, Royal Economic Society, African Studies Association, Society for Religion in Higher Education (fellow), American Association of University Professors, Phi Beta Kappa.

AWARDS, HONORS: Fulbright fellow in England, 1960-61, and Nigeria, 1975; Danforth fellow, 1965-66; recipient of grants from the Mellon Foundation and the Social Science Research Council.

WRITINGS: Managing the Modern Economy, Winthrop, 1972; *Markets in the Modern Economy,* Winthrop, 1975; *Modern Economics,* Winthrop, 1975; *Nigerian Groundnut Exports,* Oxford University Press, 1978; (with Henry Gemery) *The Uncommon Market: Essays in the Economic History of the Atlantic Slave Trade,* Academic Press, 1979; (with Wilson Brown) *The New International Economics,* Addison-Wesley, 1979; *The Grossman Lectures at Colby College,* Colby College Press, 1984.

WORK IN PROGRESS: The Shell Money of the Slave Trade.

SIDELIGHTS: Jan S. Hogendorn specializes in development economics and international trade. He lived in Africa in 1965.

*　　*　　*

HOGG, Quintin McGarel 1907-
(Lord Hailsham of St. Marylebone)

PERSONAL: Born October 9, 1907, in England; son of Douglas McGarel (first Viscount Hailsham) and Elizabeth (Trimble Brown) Hogg; married Mary Evelyn Martin, April 18, 1944; children: Douglas Martin, Mary Claire, Frances Evelyn, James Richard Martin, Katharine Amelia. *Education:* Christ Church, Oxford, first class honors, moderations, 1928, first class honors, literae humaniores, 1930. *Politics:* Conservative. *Religion:* Church of England. *Home:* The Corner House, 13 Heathview Gardens, Putney Heath, London S.W. 15, England. *Office:* House of Lords, London SW1, England.

CAREER: Succeeded father as second Viscount and Baron Hailsham, 1950. Barrister, Lincoln's Inn, 1932; Queen's Counsel, 1953; bencher of Lincoln's Inn, 1956. Member of Parliament for Oxford City, 1938-50; undersecretary of state for air, in coalition and caretaker government, 1945; First Lord of the Admiralty, 1956-57; Minister of Education, 1957; deputy leader of the House of Lords, 1957-60; Lord Privy Seal, 1959-60; Minister for Science and Technology, 1959-64; chairman of Conservative Party, 1959; Lord President of the Council and leader of the House of Lords, 1960-64; member of Parliament for St. Marylebone, London, 1963-70; Secretary of State for Education and Science, 1964; House of Lords, High Lord Chancellor, 1970-74, 1979—. John Findley Green Foundation Lecturer, 1960; Richard Dimbleby Lecturer, 1976; Hamlyn Lecturer, 1983. Fellow, All Soul's College, Oxford University, 1931-38, 1961—; rector, University of Glasgow, 1959-62; treasurer, Lincoln's Inn, 1975; chancellor, University of Buckingham, 1983—. *Military service:* British Army, Rifle Brigade, 1939-45; served in Africa (wounded), and in Middle East; became major.

MEMBER: Royal Society (fellow), Classical Association (president, 1960-61), Institute of Civil Engineers (honorary), Carlton Club, Alpine Club, Marylebone Cricket Club.

AWARDS, HONORS: D.C.L. from Westminster College, Fulton, Mo., 1960, University of Newcastle, 1964, and Oxford University, 1974; LL.D. from Cambridge University, 1963,

University of Delhi, 1972, St. Andrews University, 1979, and University of Leeds, 1982.

WRITINGS: The Law of Arbitration, Butterworth, 1936; *One Year's Work,* Hurst & Blackett, 1944; *The Law and Employers' Liability,* Stevens & Sons, 1944; *The Times We Live In* (booklet), Signpost, 1944; *Making Peace,* S.C.M. Press, 1945; *The Left Was Never Right,* Faber, 1945; *The Purpose of Parliament,* Blandford, 1946; *The Case for Conservatism,* Penguin, 1947, revised edition published as *The Conservative Case,* 1959; (with W. R. Inge and Walter Elliot) *God, King and Empire,* Hutchinson, 1947; *Parliament: A Reader's Guide,* Cambridge University Press, 1948; (contributor) Tudor Rees and H. V. Usill, editors, *They Stand Apart: A Critical Survey of Homosexuality,* Macmillan, 1955; (with Robert McEwen) *The Law Relating to Monopolies, Restrictive Trade Practices and Resale Price Maintenance,* Butterworth, 1956; *Toryism and Tomorrow* (pamphlet), Conservative Political Centre, 1957; *A New Faith in Ourselves,* Conservative and Unionist Central Office, 1957; *Shaftsbury: A New Assessment,* Shaftsbury Society, 1958.

Interdependence: A Policy for Free Peoples, Conservative Political Centre, 1960; *Vos Exemplaria Graeca,* J. Murray, 1961; (with Winston Churchill) *The Iron Curtain, Fifteen Years After 1960* [and] *The Sinews of Peace* (the former by Hogg, the latter by Churchill), Westminster College, 1961; *The Need for Faith in a Scientific Age,* Glasgow University, 1961; *Science and Government,* University of Southampton, 1961; *National Excellence,* Conservative Political Centre, 1963; *Science and Politics,* Faber, 1963, Encyclopaedia Britannica Press, 1964, reprinted, Greenwood Press, 1983; *The Human Intellect on the Throne of Society,* University of New Brunswick, 1965; *The Brain Drain,* Conservative Political Centre, 1967; *The Devils Own Song, and Other Verses,* Hodder & Stoughton, 1968; *The Door Wherein I Went,* Collins, 1975; *Dilemma of Democracy: Diagnosis and Prescription,* Collins, 1978, revised edition, 1979.

Also author of *Hamlyn Revisited: The British Legal System,* 1983. Editor of *Laws of England,* twenty-four volumes, 4th edition, Butterworth, 1972—.

AVOCATIONAL INTERESTS: Shooting, walking, and other outdoor pursuits.†

* * *

HOLLEY, I(rving) B(rinton), Jr. 1919-

PERSONAL: Born February 8, 1919, in Hartford, Conn.; son of Irving B. (a businessman) and Mary (Sharp) Holley; married Janet Carlson, October 9, 1945; children: Janet Turner (Mrs. Hans H. Wegner), Jean Carlson (Mrs. William F. Schmidt III), Susan Sharp. *Education:* Attended Oxford University, 1937; Amherst College, B.A., 1940; Yale University, M.A., 1942, Ph.D., 1947. *Religion:* Episcopalian. *Home:* 2506 Wrightwood Ave., Durham, N.C. 27705. *Office:* Department of History, Duke University, Durham, N.C. 27706.

CAREER: Industrial College of Armed Forces, member of faculty, 1945-47; Duke University, Durham, N.C., instructor, 1947-50, assistant professor, 1950-54, associate professor, 1954-61, professor of history, 1961—. Visiting professor, U.S. Military Academy, 1974-75, National Defense University, 1978-79; professor emeritus, Air War College, 1981—. Lecturer at Army War College, U.S. Army Command and General Staff College, U.S. Army School of International Studies, Air War College, and Air Command and Staff College. Associate staff

member, Army Research Office, 1963-72. Health Planning Council of Central North Carolina, member, 1964-72, chairman, 1971-72. Trustee, Air Force Historical Foundation, 1973—, and American Military Institute, 1973-76. National Aeronautics and Space Administration, consultant on Project Saturn with University of Alabama, 1967-71, member of advisory committee on history, 1974-81; advisory committee chairman, Air Force Historical Program, 1970-79; member, Department of Defense advisory committee on R.O.T.C. affairs, 1971-73. *Military service:* U.S. Army Air Forces, 1942-47. U.S. Air Force Reserve, 1947-81, retired as major general; received Legion of Merit, 1976, and Distinguished Service Medal, 1981.

MEMBER: American Historical Association, Organization of American Historians, Society for History of Technology (advisory council member, 1967), American Institute of Aeronautics and Astronautics (associate fellow, 1966—), Phi Beta Kappa (Duke University chapter president, 1970-71). *Awards, honors:* Social Science Research Council awards, 1955-56, 1961-62; Smithsonian Institution fellow, 1968-69; civilian service awards from U.S. Army, 1975, and U.S. Air Force, 1979.

WRITINGS: The Evolution of the Liaison Type Airplane, 1917-1944, U.S. Air Force Historical Study, 1946; *The Development of Aircraft Gun Turrets in the Army Air Forces, 1917-1944,* U.S. Air Force Historical Study, 1947; *Ideas and Weapons,* Yale University Press, 1953, 2nd edition, Archon Books, 1971, 3rd edition, U.S. Government Printing Office, 1983; *Buying Aircraft: Air Material Procurement for the Army Air Forces,* U.S. Government Printing Office, 1963; (contributor) M. Kranzberg and C. W. Purcell, Jr., editors, *Technology in Western Civilization,* Oxford University Press, 1967; (editor with C.D.W. Goodwin) *The Transfer of Ideas: Historical Essays,* South Atlantic Press, 1968; *An Enduring Challenge: The Problem of Air Force Doctrine,* U.S. Air Force Academy, 1974; *General John Palmer, Citizen Soldiers and the Army of a Democracy,* Greenwood Press, 1982.

Also author of a research and development policies study, *Rotary-Wing Aircraft in the Army Air Forces,* 1946. Contributor of chapters to proceedings of military history symposium at U.S. Air Force Academy, 1969, and to U.S. Army Command and General Staff College texts. Contributor of reviews to periodicals, including *Journal of Southern History, Air University Review, American Historical Review, Journal of American History, Isis, Technology and Culture, Aerospace Historian, South Atlantic Quarterly,* and *Science.* Member of editorial board, *South Atlantic Quarterly,* 1966—; member of advisory boards, *Aerospace Historian,* 1969—, *Air University Review,* 1977—.

* * *

HOLLISTER, Leo E. 1920-

PERSONAL: Born December 3, 1920, in Cincinnati, Ohio; son of William Burton and Ruth (Appling) Hollister; married Louise P. Palmieri, February 1, 1950 (divorced); children: Stephen, David, Cynthia, Matthew. *Education:* University of Cincinnati, B.S., 1941, M.D., 1943. *Home:* 3237 Benton St., Santa Clara, Calif. 95051. *Office:* Veterans Administration Hospital, 3804 Junipero Serra Blvd., Palo Alto, Calif. 94304.

CAREER: Veterans Administration Hospital, Palo Alto, Calif., chief of Medical Service, 1953-60, associate chief of staff, 1960-70, medical investigator, 1970—. Certified by American Board of Internal Medicine, 1951 and 1974. Member of executive committee of Veterans Administration Cooperative

Studies of Chemotherapy in Psychiatry, 1956-74; chairman of committee on the problems of drug dependence, National Academy of Sciences-National Research Council, beginning 1969; chairman of psychotomimetic agents advisory committee, U.S. Food and Drug Administration-National Institute of Mental Health, 1970-74. *Military service:* U.S. Naval Reserve, active duty, 1945-46, 1950-51; became commander.

MEMBER: American Therapeutic Society (president), American College of Neuropsychopharmacology (former president), Collegium Internationale Neuropsychopharmacologicum (former president), American College of Physicians (president), American Society for Pharmacology and Experimental Therapeutics, American Society of Clinical Pharmacology and Chemotherapy (former president). *Awards, honors:* Meritorious Service Award, U.S. Veterans Administration, 1960; William S. Middleton Award for outstanding achievement in medical research, 1966.

WRITINGS: Chemical Psychoses, LSD and Related Drugs, C. C Thomas, 1968; (editor with Jonathan O. Cole) *Schizophrenia,* Medcom, 1970; *Clinical Use of Psychotherapeutic Drugs,* C. C Thomas, 1973; *Clinical Pharmacology of Psychotherapeutic Drugs,* Churchill Livingstone, 1978, 2nd edition, 1983; (editor with B. Saletu and P. Berner) *Neuro-Psychopharmacology: Proceedings of the 11th Congress of the Collegium Internationale Neuro-Psychopharmacologium, Vienna, July 9-14, 1978,* Pergamon, 1979; *Psychotherapeutic Drugs: An Ultra-Short Practice,* State Mutual Book, 1979. Also author of more than 200 scientific and medical papers; editor of *Yearbook of Drug Therapy,* 1980-82.

WORK IN PROGRESS: A revision of *Clinical Use of Psychotherapeutic Drugs.*

*   *   *

HOLMES, Edward M(orris)   1910-

PERSONAL: Born September 27, 1910, in Montclair, N.J.; son of Edward Huntington and Helen (Sinsabaugh) Holmes; married Jane Marshall Colyer (a librarian), June 27, 1936; children: Caroline (Mrs. Lawrence E. Marsh), Virginia, Constance (Mrs. Daniel McCarthy). *Education:* Dartmouth College, A.B., 1933; University of Maine, M.Ed., 1954; Brown University, M.A., 1956, Ph.D., 1962. *Politics:* Democrat. *Religion:* "Unaffiliated." *Office:* Department of English, E-M Building, University of Maine, Orono, Me. 04473.

CAREER: Has worked as a clerk, salesman, stage carpenter, seaman, business manager of a health cooperative, news reporter, and organizer of fishermen's cooperatives and credit unions; principal of high school in Princeton, Me., 1944-45; head of English department of high school in Ellsworth, Me., 1947-54; Farmington State Teachers College (now University of Maine at Farmington), instructor in English, 1954-55; University of Maine at Orono, instructor, 1956-62, assistant professor, 1962-64, associate professor, 1964-68, professor of English, 1968-74, Lloyd Elliot Professor of English, 1974-77, professor emeritus, 1977—. Visiting professor, Prince of Wales College, Prince Edward Island, 1968-69. Second selectman, Town of Tremont, 1946-47. *Awards, honors:* Emily Clark Balch Prize, 1971, for "Drums Again."

WRITINGS: Faulkner's Twice-Told Tales: His Re-Use of His Material, Mouton, 1966; *Driftwood,* Puckerbrush Press, 1972; *A Part of the Main,* University of Maine Press, 1972; *Mostly Maine,* University of Maine Press, 1977.

Contributor to anthologies: *The Down East Reader,* edited by Nathan Fuller, Lippincott, 1962; *A Handful of Spice,* edited by Richard Sprague, University of Maine Press, 1968; *A Dartmouth Reader,* edited by Francis Brown, Dartmouth Publications, 1969; *Bear, Man, and God,* edited by Utley, Bloom, and Kinney, Random House, 1971; *The Best American Short Stories of 1972,* edited by Martha Foley, Houghton, 1972; *New England Short Stories,* edited by Hillyer and Silitch, Yankee, Inc., 1974; *Over to Home and from Away,* edited by Jim Brunelle, Guy Gannet, 1981; *An Anthology of Maine Literature,* edited by Lecker and Brown, University of Maine Press, 1982. Contributor of about fifty stories and articles to New England journals.

*   *   *

HOMOSAP
See NUTTALL, Jeff

*   *   *

HONAN, Park   1928-

PERSONAL: Born September 17, 1928, in Utica, N.Y.; married, 1952; children: three. *Education:* University of Chicago, M.A., 1951; University of London, Ph.D., 1959. *Office:* School of English, University of Leeds, Leeds LS2 9JT, England.

CAREER: Connecticut College, New London, instructor, 1959-61, assistant professor of English, 1961-62; Brown University, Providence, R.I., assistant professor, 1962-65, associate professor of English, 1965-68; University of Birmingham, Birmingham, England, 1968-84, began as lecturer, became reader of English; University of Leeds, Leeds, England, professor of English and American literature, 1984—. *Member:* Modern Language Association of America. *Awards, honors:* Guggenheim fellowship, 1962-63, and 1973-74.

WRITINGS: Browning's Characters: A Study in Poetic Techniques, Yale University Press, 1961; (co-editor) *Shelley,* Dell, 1962; (author of introduction) *Falkland,* Cassell, 1967; (with William Irvine) *The Book, the Ring, and the Poet: A Biography of Robert Browning,* McGraw, 1974; *Matthew Arnold: A Life,* McGraw, 1981. Contributor to literary journals. British editor, *Novel: A Forum on Fiction,* 1968—.

SIDELIGHTS: "At the beginning of [*Matthew Arnold: A Life,* an] excellent new critical biography, Park Honan nails his colors to the mast: an understanding of Arnold, he writes, 'is more useful to us than an understanding of any other Englishman of the last century,'" as Robert Bernard Martin states in a *Washington Post Book World* review. Honan's study of one of Victorian England's most celebrated poet/critics resulted from ten years of research and in its scope is said to be the most complete biography of Arnold since Lionel Trilling's *Matthew Arnold,* published in 1939.

Arnold, born in 1822 to Rugby School's famous headmaster Thomas Arnold, "turns out to be a character somewhat less delightful than his poetry and criticism," according to Herbert Mitgang in the *New York Times.* Indeed, the Victorian figure was often criticised as a fop or a dandy and was given to overindulgence in food and drink (Arnold died in 1888, his heart attack no doubt fueled by his 238-pound weight). But at the same time, the poet could be a compassionate champion of social reform; as a school inspector, Arnold was committed to improving education throughout England. In his prose writings, particularly his "pieces on education and *Culture and*

Anarchy . . . , [Arnold] exhorted the ascendent middle class, his Philistines, to augment economic power with love of thought and beauty,'' Laurie Stone remarks in *Village Voice,* adding that while ''not always savvy about the uses of dissent and revolution, Arnold was forever the optimist, the smart voice speaking plainly and from the inside out, and his life is beautifully delineated in [Honan's] loving and intelligent biography.''

The author, Stone continues, ''is especially lucid on the modern element in Arnold. The poetry of [Alfred, Lord] Tennyson and [Robert] Browning seems callow beside Arnold's grown-up verse. He was the first to describe how decorum breeds estrangement and self-deception and blocks feelings.'' Jean Strouse of *Newsweek* notes that Honan ''traces the influences of Epictetus, Spinoza and Goethe on Arnold's thought as he follows the rebellious young man from Rugby to Oxford.''

The author makes a bold statement in *Matthew Arnold:* he reveals that the mysterious ''Marguerite'' of Arnold's love poems is Mary Claude, ''a French Protestant exile born in the Freidrichstadt district of Berlin, who summered in the Lake District [where Arnold lived] and became close to the Clough family, Arnold's best friends,'' as Mitgang relates. ''He was 25, she two years older; neither was married when they began a series of heavy-breathing, star-gazing, moonlight walks.'' They arranged a romantic rendezvous in the Alps, but when Arnold arrived he found that Mary had returned to England. ''Professor Honan speculates that [the poet] may have been 'half-relieved' by the unconsummated tryst,'' says Mitgang.

Arnold went on to marry Frances Lucy Wightman. His biographer, states Strouse, ''is at his best telling the moving story of the couple's growing love and understanding of each other as they struggle with poverty, the deaths of three of their six children, Arnold's exhausting travels as an inspector of schools and his complex transformation from poet to social critic. Though Arnold changed hats, his lofty concerns remained the same: he looked directly at the spiritual isolation of modern man and strove incessantly to articulate an adequate response, to find a sense of wholeness in culture . . . to see life steadily and see it whole.'' ''It is not apropos of Arnold the poet that . . . Honan sees and shows most,'' remarks *New York Times Book Review* critic Christopher Ricks. ''He is conventional and laudatory here, and never directly confronts the challenge that Arnold's prose offers to Arnold's poetry—the challenge that wit, irony, energy, surprise, incisive knowledge of life as it is lived must make to a poetry of sensitive enervation, a poetry which even at the time was thought of as a 'melodious whine.' Mr. Honan wants to be able to think equally highly of the poetry and the prose. This sounds splendidly catholic, but it isn't possible, since the strength and rhythmical felicity of the prose constitute a critique—explicit and implicit—of the debility of so much of the poetry. No, where [the author] is himself strong is not in relating Arnold's poetry to Arnold's living but in relating Arnold to his life.''

BIOGRAPHICAL/CRITICAL SOURCES: Park Honan, *Matthew Arnold: A Life,* McGraw, 1981; *New York Times,* July 18, 1981; *New York Times Book Review,* August 9, 1981; *Washington Post Book World,* August 16, 1981; *Times Literary Supplement,* August 28, 1981; *Los Angeles Times Book Review,* September 6, 1981; *Newsweek,* September 7, 1981; *Times* (London), September 10, 1981; *Spectator,* September 12, 1981; *Village Voice,* September 23, 1981; *New York Review of Books,* December 17, 1981.

HONDERICH, Ted 1933-

PERSONAL: Born January 30, 1933, in Baden, Ontario, Canada; son of John William (a pamphleteer and printer) and Rae Laura (a teacher; maiden name Armstrong) Honderich; married Margaret Penman, 1957; married second wife, Pauline Goodwin, 1964; children: Kiaran, John Ruan. *Education:* University of Toronto, B.A., 1959; University of London, Ph.D., 1969. *Politics:* Socialist. *Religion:* None. *Home:* 4 Keats Grove, Hampstead, London N.W. 3, England. *Office:* Department of Philosophy, University College, University of London, Gower St., London W.C. 1, England.

CAREER: Previously lecturer at University of Sussex, Sussex, England; University of London, University College, London, England, 1964—, began as lecturer and reader in department of philosophy, currently professor of philosophy. Visiting professor at Yale University and City University of New York, 1970-71.

WRITINGS: Punishment: The Supposed Justifications, Harcourt, 1969, revised edition, Penguin, 1971; (editor) *Essays on Freedom of Action,* Routledge & Kegan Paul, 1973; (editor) *Social Ends and Political Means,* Routledge & Kegan Paul, 1976; *Three Essays on Political Violence,* Basil Blackwell, 1977; (editor) *Philosophy as It Is,* Penguin, 1979; *Violence for Equality: Inquiries in Practical Philosophy,* Penguin, 1980; (editor) *Morality and Objectivity,* Routledge & Kegan Paul, 1984; *Philosophy through Its Past,* Penguin, 1984. Contributor of articles to books and periodicals. Editor, ''International Library of Philosophy and Scientific Method.,'' ''The Arguments of the Philosophers,'' and ''The Problems of Philosophy.''

WORK IN PROGRESS: A book on determinism.

SIDELIGHTS: Ted Honderich's *Violence for Equality: Inquiries in Political Philosophy* is labelled a ''courageous swim against the current'' of political thought by reviewer Laurie Taylor in the London *Times.* A series of essays, the book examines the targets of violence in Britain and the feasibility of fomenting social change or ''rectify[ing] social imbalances'' through violent acts. The work also considers the moral dilemmas of determining which circumstances justify the use of illegal force to end miseries that remain unchecked by conventional government action.

BIOGRAPHICAL/CRITICAL SOURCES: Times (London), March 1, 1980.

*　　　*　　　*

HONE, Joseph 1937-

PERSONAL: Born February 25, 1937, in London, England; son of Nathaniel and Bridget Hone; married Jacqueline Mary Yeend, March, 1963; children: Lucy, William. *Education:* Attended University of London, 1953-54. *Home:* Manor Cottage, Shutford, near Banbury, Oxfordshire, England. *Agent:* Deborah Rogers, 49 Blenheim Crescent, London W11, England.

CAREER: Writer. English teacher in grammar school in Drogheda, Ireland, 1956; third assistant director to film-makers John Ford (''The Rising of the Moon''), Mark Robson (''The Little Hut''), John Gilling (''Interpol''), Joseph Losey (''The Gypsy and the Gentleman''), and Denys de la Patelleire (''Retour de Manivelle''), 1956-57; Egyptian Ministry of Education, Cairo, teacher of English in Heliopolis and Suez, 1957-58;

Rupert Hart-Davis (publishers), London, England, editorial assistant, 1958-59; Envoy Productions (play producers), Dublin, Ireland, co-founder and co-producer of plays and musicals, 1960-62; British Broadcasting Corp. (BBC)—Radio, London, England, producer in talks and current affairs department, 1963-66; United Nations, Secretariat, New York, N.Y., radio and television officer for Office of Public Information, 1967-68; World Bank, Washington, D.C., producer of radio programs dealing with the bank's various projects in India and Southeast Asia, 1968-69; free-lance broadcaster (mainly for BBC), 1969—.

WRITINGS—Novels, except as indicated: *The Private Sector,* Hamish Hamilton, 1971, Dutton, 1972; *The Sixth Directorate,* Dutton, 1975; *The Dancing Waiters* (travel memoirs), Hamish Hamilton, 1975; *The Paris Trap,* Secker & Warburg, 1977; *The Oxford Gambit,* Random House, 1980; *Gone Tomorrow* (travel book), Secker & Warburg, 1981; *The Valley of the Fox,* Secker & Warburg, 1983. Contributor to screenplay, "King and Country"; author of radio scripts for BBC. Contributor of articles and reviews to magazines and newspapers, including *New Statesman.* Radio and television critic for *Listener.*

WORK IN PROGRESS: Children of the Country, an African travel book, for Morrow.

SIDELIGHTS: "Joseph Hone's 'Sixth Directorate,' which was published in 1975, is one of the best suspense novels of the last 10 years," writes Anatole Broyard in the *New York Times.* The critic substantiates his claim by noting that the work "has elegance, wit, sympathy, irony, surprise, action, a rueful love affair and a melancholy Decline of the West mood. Only the crimes in its pages separate the book from what is known as serious novels." Assessing *The Oxford Gambit* in the *New York Times Book Review,* Peter Andrews agrees that Hone's ficiton "aims a bit higher up the scale of literary distinction [than most suspense or spy novels] and succeeds admirably." With *The Oxford Gambit,* the British author "brings considerable honor to the Graham Greene tradition of writing espionage novels," Andrews concludes.

Commenting on Hone's travel book, *Gone Tomorrow,* Erik de Mauny writes in the *Times Literary Supplement:* "[The author] has the traveller's knack of arriving in a place just as something interesting is happening—on his first evening in Barcelona, they were dancing the *sardana* on the Cathedral steps right in front of his hotel—and a keen eye for local eccentricity." While de Mauny does find "one or two minor irritations and errors" in the work, he calls it an "admirable collection."

Hone's books have appeared in French, Dutch, Swedish, and Spanish editions.

MEDIA ADAPTATIONS: The Sixth Directorate was adapted as a screenplay for Tony Richardson in 1976.

BIOGRAPHICAL/CRITICAL SOURCES: Times Literary Supplement, October 3, 1980, March 12, 1982; *New York Times Book Review,* November 16, 1980; *New York Times,* March 2, 1984.

*   *   *

HOPCRAFT, Arthur   1932-

PERSONAL: Born November 29, 1932, in Essex, England; son of Arthur (a grocer) and Bertha Hopcraft. *Education:* Educated at state schools in England, 1937-49. *Home:* 44 Holmes Rd., Twickenham, Middlesex, England. *Agent:* A. P. Watt & Son, 26-28 Bedford Row, London WCIR 4HL, England.

CAREER: Free-lance writer, playwright, and screenwriter. Reporter in England on local newspapers, 1949-51, and on local and national newspapers, 1953-64, including *Daily Mirror,* 1957-79, and *The Guardian,* 1959-64. *Military service:* British Army, 1951-53.

WRITINGS: Born to Hunger, Houghton, 1968; *The Football Man: People and Passions in Soccer,* Collins, 1968, revised edition, Penguin, 1971; *The Great Apple Raid,* Heinemann, 1970; *Mid-Century Man,* Hamish Hamilton, 1982. Author of screenplay, with Kathleen Tynan, "Agatha," for Warner Bros., 1979.

Also author of television plays for Granada, 1971-76, and British Broadcasting Corporation, 1972-75, including "The Panel," "Katapult," "The Reporters," "Jingle Bells," "Wednesday Love," "The Mosedale Horseshoe," and "Tinker, Tailor, Soldier, Spy." Columnist for *Nova* (magazine), 1968-69; sportswriter for *Observer,* 1964-73; contributor to *Sunday Times Magazine, New Statesman,* and *Observer Magazine,* 1964-80.

WORK IN PROGRESS: Two television series, "Bleak House" and "Ernest Hemingway."

SIDELIGHTS: Arthur Hopcraft writes: "Early in his career Ernest Hemingway wrote a note to himself, instructing that he was to write 'one true sentence.' I believe that he thus defined the business of writing. Also, if I may be forgiven the pun, he delivered himself—and the rest of us—a life sentence."

BIOGRAPHICAL/CRITICAL SOURCES: New York Times, February 9, 1979; *Chicago Tribune,* March 2, 1979; *Times Literary Supplement,* April 16, 1982.

*   *   *

HOPKINS, Jasper (Stephen, Jr.)   1936-

PERSONAL: Born November 8, 1936, in Atlanta, Ga.; son of Jasper Stephen, Sr. (a barber) and Willie Ruth (Sorrow) Hopkins; married Gabriele Voigt, December 13, 1967. *Education:* Wheaton College, Wheaton, Ill., A.B., 1958; Harvard University, A.M., 1959, Ph.D., 1963. *Office:* Department of Philosophy, University of Minnesota, 355 Ford Hall, 224 Church St. S.E., Minneapolis, Minn. 55455.

CAREER: Case Western Reserve University, Cleveland, Ohio, assistant professor, 1963-68; University of Massachusetts—Boston, associate professor, 1969-70; University of Minnesota, Minneapolis, associate professor, 1970-74, professor of philosophy, 1974—. Visiting associate professor, University of Arkansas, spring, 1969; visiting professor of philosophy, University of Graz, 1981-82.

AWARDS, HONORS: Fellowship for research in Munich, 1967-68, and translation fellowship, 1979, both from National Endowment for the Humanities; American Council of Learned Societies fellowship for research in Paris, 1973-74; Guggenheim fellowship for research in Paris, 1980-81; National Humanities Center fellowship, 1983-84.

WRITINGS: (Editor, translator, and author of introduction with Herbert Richardson) St. Anselm of Canterbury, *Truth, Freedom, and Evil: Three Philosophical Dialogues,* Harper, 1967; (translator and author of introduction with Richardson) St. Anselm of Canterbury, *Trinity, Incarnation, and Redemption: Theological Treatises,* Harper, 1970; *A Companion to the Study of St. Anselm,* University of Minnesota Press, 1972; (editor and translator with Richardson) *Anselm of Canterbury,* Edwin

Mellen, Volume I: (editor and translator with Richardson) *Monologion; Proslogion; Debate with Guanilo; A Meditation on Human Redemption*, 1974, Volume II: (editor and translator with Richardson) *Philosophical Fragments; De Grammatico; On Truth; Freedom of Choice; The Fall of the Devil; The Harmony of the Foreknowledge, the Predestination, and the Grace of God with Free Choice*, 1976, Volume III: (editor and translator with Richardson) *Two Letters Concerning Roscelin; The Incarnation of the Word; Why God Became a Man; The Virgin Conception and Original Sin; The Procession of the Holy Spirit; Three Letters on the Sacraments*, 1976, Volume IV: (sole author) *Hermeneutical and Textual Problems in the Complete Treatises of St. Anselm*, 1976.

A Concise Introduction to the Philosophy of Nicholas of Cusa, University of Minnesota Press, 1978, 2nd edition, 1980; *Nicholas of Cusa on God as Not-other: A Translation and an Appraisal of "De Li Non Aliud,"* University of Minnesota Press, 1979, 2nd edition, Banning Press, 1983; *Nicholas of Cusa on Learned Ignorance: A Translation and an Appraisal of "De Docta Ignorantia,"* Banning Press, 1981; *Nicholas of Cusa's Debate with John Wenck: A Translation and an Appraisal of "De Ignota Litteratura" and "Apologia Doctae Ignorantiae,"* Banning Press, 1981, 2nd edition, 1984; *Nicholas of Cusa's Metaphysic of Contraction*, Banning Press, 1983.

WORK IN PROGRESS: Nicholas of Cusa's Dialectical Mysticism: Text, Translation, and Interpretive Study of "De Visione Dei"; third revised edition of *A Concise Introduction to the Philosophy of Nicholas of Cusa*.

*   *   *

HORN, John L(eonard) 1928-

PERSONAL: Born September 7, 1928, in St. Joseph, Mo.; son of John L. (a sailor) and Nellie Rae (Weldon) Horn; married Darlene Dimmitt, November 15, 1950 (divorced, 1954); married Bonnie Colleen Hoskins, July 30, 1955; children: (second marriage) John Leonard, Jr., James Bryan, Julie Lynn, Jennifer Lee. *Education:* University of Denver, B.A., 1956; University of Melbourne, additional study, 1956-57; University of Illinois, A.M., 1961, Ph.D., 1965. *Home:* 196 South Corona, Denver, Colo. 80209. *Office:* Department of Psychology, University of Denver, Denver, Colo. 80210.

CAREER: University of Denver, Denver, Colo., assistant professor, 1961-65, associate professor, 1965-69, professor of psychology, 1969—. Research associate, University of Illinois, summer, 1964; postdoctoral fellow, University of Wisconsin, summer, 1965; visiting lecturer, University of California, Berkeley, 1967; visiting research associate, Institute of Psychiatry, University of London, 1972-73; visiting research scientist, University Hospital, Lund, Sweden, 1982. Trustee, Institute for Research in Moral and Personality Adjustment; member of board of directors, Metropolitan Group Homes. *Military service:* U.S. Army, 1950-52.

MEMBER: American Psychological Association (fellow), American Association for the Advancement of Science (fellow), Psychometric Society, Society of Multivariate Experimental Psychology, Phi Beta Kappa, Sigma Xi, Phi Kappa Phi, Phi Delta Theta, Psi Chi.

AWARDS, HONORS: Fulbright fellowship to Australia, 1956-57; U.S. Office of Education postdoctoral fellowship, 1965; Creative Talents Award, 1965; Fulbright-Hays speaker award,

1973; annual award from Society of Multivariate Experimental Psychology, 1973, for distinguished publications in multivariate psychology.

WRITINGS: (With R. B. Cattell) *The Handbook for the Motivational Analysis Test*, Institute for Personality and Ability Testing, 1962, revised edition, 1964; (with K. W. Wanberg and F. M. Foster) *The Alcohol Use Inventory*, Psych Systems (Baltimore), 1983; (with H. A. Skinner) *Alcohol Dependence Scale (ADS)*, Addiction Research Foundation (Toronto), 1984; (editor) *An Evaluation of the Evolution of a Personality Theory*, Multivariate Behavioral Research, 1984.

Contributor: Cattell, editor, *Handbook of Multivariate Experimental Psychology*, Rand McNally, 1966; L. R. Goulet and P. B. Baltes, editors, *Life-Span Development Psychology*, Academic Press, 1970; A. R. Mahrer, editor, *New Approaches in Personality Classification*, Columbia University Press, 1970; P. D. Knott, editor, *Student Activism*, W. C. Brown, 1971; R. H. Dreger, editor, *Multivariate Personality Research*, Claitor's Book Store, 1972; N. Rosenberg, editor, *Contributions to an Understanding of Alcoholism*, U.S. Government Printing Office, 1973; J. R. Royce, editor, *Multivariate Analysis and Psychological Theory*, Academic Press, 1973.

S. Gerson and A. Raskin, editors, *Genesis and Treatment of Psychologic Disorders in the Elderly*, Raven Press, 1975; Cattell and Dregor, editors, *Handbook of Modern Personality Theory*, Appleton-Century-Crofts, 1977; S. Hooks, P. Kurtz, and M. Todorovich, editors, *The Ethics of Teaching and Scientific Research*, Prometheus Books, 1977; R. T. Osborne, C. E. Noble, and N. Weyl, editors, *Human Variation: The Biopsychology of Age, Race, and Sex*, Academic Press, 1978; P. B. Baltes, editor, *Lifespan Development and Behavior*, Academic Press, 1978; G. A. Marlatt, P. E. Nathan, and T. Loberg, editors, *Alcoholism: New Directions in Behavioral Research and Treatment*, Plenum, 1978.

L. W. Poon, editor, *Aging in the 1980's*, American Psychological Association, 1980; R. Tissot, editor, *Etats deficitaires cerebraux lies a l'age*, George et cie S. A. Librairie De L'Universite, 1980; *Drugs and Methods in C.V.D.*, Pergamon, 1981; B. B. Wolman, editor, *Handbook of Developmental Psychology*, Prentice-Hall, 1982; F.I.M. Craik and S. E. Trehub, editors, *Aging and Cognitive Processes*, Plenum, 1982; R. N. Emde and R. J. Harmon, editors, *Continuities and Discontinuities in Development*, Plenum, 1984; Wolman, editor, *Handbook of Intelligence*, Wiley, 1984.

Also contributor to *Constancy and Change in Human Development*, edited by O. G. Brim and J. Kagan, 1980. Contributor of articles to fifteen books. Contributor to encyclopedias and reference books, including *Encyclopedia of Psychology, International Encyclopedia of Neurology, Psychiatry, Psychoanalysis and Psychology*, and *International Lexicon of Psychology*. Contributor of more than fifty articles to professional journals. Member of editorial board, *Journal of Educational Measurement*, 1968-69, *Multivariate Behavioral Research*, 1968, and *Applied Psychological Measurement*, 1976-81.

SIDELIGHTS: John L. Horn told *CA*: "I did not adjust well in the business society of the [United States]. I was lucky to find the sanctuary known as the university: it provides a protected environment for some kinds of poorly adapted creatures. In this environment I have been able to do some thinking and writing. I am very grateful to the society that provides such sanctuaries.

"My good fortune may indicate a principle: some work that is important for a civilized society (which is not to say that my work is of this kind) is best promoted through non-profit means, as in a university. Here one can take the long view and try things for which there is little chance of success but which, if successful, genuinely improve conditions in this universe. Much science, art and literature can be produced only under such circumstances. All of us should be grateful for a society that provides such sanctuaries."

*   *   *

HOUCK, Carter 1924-

PERSONAL: Born May 2, 1924, in Washington, D.C.; daughter of David Thomas (a farmer) and Eliza (Mason) Greene; married Louis Talmadge Houck, February 3, 1945 (divorced December, 1965); married A. Grant Holt; children: (first marriage) Linda Page, Carl Thomas. *Education:* Attended College of William and Mary, 1941-43, University of Connecticut, 1962-65, and Hunter College of the City University of New York, 1965-68. *Politics:* Independent. *Religion:* Episcopalian. *Home:* 230 Dolphin Cove Quay, Stamford, Conn. 06902.

CAREER: Sewing teacher, Singer Sewing Co., 1943-44; pattern maker, Butterick Co., 1944-45; *Fort Worth Star-Telegram*, Fort Worth, Tex., author of column "Sewing," 1950-51; *Parents' Magazine*, New York City, author of column "Sewing," 1962-72; *Lady's Circle*, New York City, editor of *Needlework*, 1971-78, and *Patchwork*, 1971—. Part-owner of Rag Doll (fabric shop), 1968-74.

MEMBER: New York Embroiderers Guild, Appalachian Mountain Club (vice-chairperson of executive committee).

WRITINGS: (With Joanne Schreiber) *Betty Crocker's Good and Easy Sewing Book for You and Your Family*, Universal Publishing, 1972; *Warm as Wool, Cool as Cotton: Natural Fibers and Fabrics and How to Work with Them*, illustrations by Nancy Parker, Seabury, 1975; *American Quilts and How to Make Them*, photographs by Myron Miller, Scribner, 1975; *The Big Bag Book*, photographs by Miller, Scribner, 1977; (editor) *Patchwork Patterns*, Dutton, 1979; *The Boat Buff's Book of Embroidery*, photographs by Miller, Scribner, 1979.

Nova Scotia Patchwork Patterns: Full-Sized Templates and Instructions for 12 Quilts, Dover, 1981; *101 Folk Art Designs for Counted Cross-Stitch and Other Needlecrafts*, Dover, 1982; (with Cyril Nelson) *The Quilt Engagement Calendar Treasury*, Dutton, 1983; (editor) Carol Wien, *The Great American Log Cabin Quilt Book*, Dutton, 1984. Contributor to magazines, including *Appalachia*, *Trail Walker*, and *Action Vacations*.

WORK IN PROGRESS: Trails for Hiking and Backpacking in New Jersey, for Countryman Press; editing *Make a Gift for Baby*, for Dutton.

SIDELIGHTS: Carter Houck writes: "As a small child growing up on a farm a mile from the highway in the Virginia Piedmont, I had to do a great deal of making my own fun. The Depression struck farming in that area an almost deadly blow when I was five years old, which meant that new cars, movies, coats that weren't hand-me-downs from wealthy city cousins, and a lot of other things I never missed, were unknown to me. What I did have was a horse, a whole menagerie of pets, including occasional wild ones that boarded for a while, and a great deal of delightful neglect. That sort of neglect enabled me to climb trees and swing from the branches, use the tools in my father's workshop, sew on my mother's treadle machine, and some-

times play wild imaginative games with my brother. I still hold conversations with cats, dogs, horses, or any other animals that will hold still for long enough to listen.

"I lived with an assortment of very different relatives, mostly in cities. One uncle had an exquisite townhouse in Washington, D.C., which is now a parking lot. One aunt lived on the Main Line of Philadelphia, complete with swimming pool and tennis court, cottage at the shore, and two bratty children. One aunt was the penurious widow of a minister. She counted the grains of sugar on the cereal, the drops of water in the shower, and all of my sins.

"As life has a habit of doing, all things come full circle, and the little girl who'd used the treadle machine as a rainy-day toy headed straight for design school and the Big City.

"I have never lost the habit of writing down descriptions of things I see, places I go, emotions that I cannot share easily. I carry a camera now when I travel, but I find that words paint a clearer picture for me. I see many things around me in terms of needlework designs, and I want to share these things that are a pleasure to me with anyone who will listen. Teaching small groups isn't enough—I can reach a much larger audience by writing. I do, however, like the contact and feedback of teaching workshops.

"When anyone comes to me and asks about being a writer or designer and about working free-lance, I suggest that being used to being alone and keeping oneself amused are helpful character traits. Being creative alone is only possible if being alone is comfortable and even fun."

*   *   *

HOWARD, C(hester) Jeriel 1939-

PERSONAL: Born March 14, 1939, in Wharton, Tex.; son of Chester (a service manager for B. F. Goodrich) and Alma Howard. *Education:* Union College, Lincoln, Neb., B.A., 1961; Texas Christian University, M.A., 1962; Ph.D., 1967. *Home:* 1400 North State Parkway, Chicago, Ill. 60610. *Office:* Department of English, Northeastern Illinois University, 5500 North St. Louis, Chicago, Ill. 60625.

CAREER: Southwestern Union College, Keene, Tex., instructor in English, 1962-64; Union College, Lincoln, Neb., assistant professor of English, 1964-66; Texas Christian University, Fort Worth, instructor in English, 1966-67; Tarrant County Junior College, Fort Worth, chairman of English department, 1967-69; Bishop College, Dallas, Tex., associate professor of English, 1970-79; Northeastern Illinois University, Chicago, Ill., professor of English, 1979—. Guest instructor, Texas Wesleyan College, 1967; guest professor, East Texas State University, summer, 1968.

MEMBER: National Council of Teachers of English, Conference on College Composition and Communication.

WRITINGS: (With Coramea Thomas) *Contact: A Textbook in Applied Communications*, Prentice-Hall, 1970, 4th edition, 1984; (compiler with Richard F. Tracz) *The Responsible Man: Essays, Short Stories, Poems*, Canfield Press, 1970, 2nd edition published as *The Responsible Person*, 1975; (with Tracz) *Tempo: A Thematic Approach to Sentence-Paragraph Writing*, Canfield Press, 1971; (with Donald Gill) *Desk Copy: Modern Business Communications*, Canfield Press, 1971; *The Age of Anxiety*, Allyn & Bacon, 1972; *Technique*, Canfield Press, 1972, 2nd edition, 1977; *—30—A Journalistic Approach to Freshman Composition*, Goodyear Publishing 1973.

Reprise: A Review of the Basics in Grammar and Composition, Goodyear Publishing, 1975, 2nd edition, Scott, Foresman, 1980; *Writing Effective Paragraphs,* Winthrop Publishers, 1976; *Writing for a Reason,* Scott, Foresman, 1980; (with Tracz) *The Paragraph Book,* Little, Brown, 1982.

WORK IN PROGRESS: The Essential Handbook and Rhetoric, with Tracz; *The Practical Essayist,* with Sheridan Baker.

* * *

HOWKINS, John   1945-

PERSONAL: Born August 3, 1945, in Northampton, England; son of Walter and Lesley (Stops) Howkins. *Education:* Keele University, B.A., 1968; Architectural Association, diploma in town planning, 1972.

CAREER: Free-lance journalist. International Institute of Communications, London, England, editor of *InterMedia* magazine, 1975—; British Academy of Film and Television Arts, London, England, editor of *Vision* magazine, 1977—. Director of Whittet Books; member of executive committee of British Standing Conference on Broadcasting, 1975—.

MEMBER: National Union of Journalists, Critics Circle, Guild of Broadcasting Journalists.

WRITINGS: Understanding Television, Sundial, 1976; (editor) *Vision and Hindsight: The Future of Communications,* International Institute of Communications, 1976; *The Media in China,* Nord Media, 1980; *Mass Communication in China,* Nord Media, 1980, Longman, 1982; *New Technologies, New Policies?,* New York Zoetrope, 1982. Contributor to *Encyclopaedia Britannica* and to periodicals, including *Sunday Times* (London) and *Time Out.*

WORK IN PROGRESS: A book, *TV Is Only the Beginning.*†

* * *

HOWORTH, M. K.
See BLACK, Margaret K(atherine)

* * *

HSU, Kai-yu   1922-1982

PERSONAL: Born July 5, 1922, in China; became U.S. citizen; died January 4, 1982; married Jeanne M. Horbach, 1950; children: Jean-Pierre, Roland. *Education:* National Tsing Hua University, B.A., 1944; University of Oregon, M.A., 1948; Stanford University, Ph.D., 1959. *Office:* Department of Comparative Literature, San Francisco State University, San Francisco, Calif. 94132.

CAREER: Chinese World Daily, San Francisco, Calif., successively reporter, foreign news editor, and associate editor, 1948-52; Stanford Research Institute, Stanford, Calif., assistant analyst, China Project, 1952-53; U.S. Army Language School, Monterey, Calif., instructor in Chinese-Mandarin department, 1953-55; Stanford University, Stanford, Calif., research assistant, China Project, 1955-56, lecturer, then instructor, 1956-59; San Francisco State University, San Francisco, Calif., associate professor, 1959-63, professor of humanities and foreign languages, 1963-82, chairman of department of foreign languages, 1960-65, world literature department, 1968-69, and department of comparative literature, 1974-82, director, Chinese-Mandarin teaching materials development project,

1961-66, foreign language instruction in Spanish, Chinese, and Russian, 1962-65, area studies, 1963-67, and Chinese culture text project, 1966-70. Director, Carnegie Chinese Project, beginning 1962. Chairman, Advisory Committee on Chinese Language Instruction in California Public Schools, 1962-67, Asian Studies Council of California State Colleges, and Pacific Area Intercollegiate Council on Asian Studies, 1967-70. *Military service:* Chinese Army, 1943-47; chief interpreter, Chinese Air Force Detachment in United States, 1945-46; military aide, Chinese Embassy, Washington, D.C., 1946-47.

MEMBER: Association for Asian Studies, Modern Language Association of America, Philological Association of the Pacific Coast, Foreign Language Association of Northern California.

AWARDS, HONORS: American Council of Learned Societies award for travel to Belgium, 1960; National Endowment for the Humanities senior fellowship for travel to the People's Republic of China, 1973.

WRITINGS: (Contributor) *China Handbooks,* Human Relations Area Files, Yale University, 1956; (editor and translator) *Twentieth-Century Chinese Poetry,* Doubleday, 1963; *Chinese: Mandarin,* Levels I, II, III, and IV, Altoan Press, 1965-67; (contributor) Howard L. Boorman, editor, *Biographical Dictionary of Republican China,* Columbia University Press, 1967; *Chou En-lai: China's Gray Eminence,* Doubleday, 1968; *Asian-American Authors,* Houghton, 1972; *Chinese Civilization,* Asian Language Publications, 1972; *From Dragon to Man,* Asian Language Publications, 1972; *The Chinese Literary Scene: A Writer's Visit to the People's Republic,* Random House, 1975; (with Fang-yu Wang) *Ch'i Pai-shih's Paintings,* Art Book Co. (Taipei, Taiwan), 1979; *Wen I-to,* Twayne, 1980; (editor with Ting Wang) *Literature of the People's Republic of China,* Indiana University Press, 1980.

Also author with sons, Jean-Pierre and Roland Hsu, of *Our China Trip,* 1974. Contributor to *Encyclopaedia Britannica, Philosophical Reviews, Show,* and language journals. Editor of Oriental languages section, *MLA Abstracts,* and *MLA-Chinese Conference Newsletter.*†

* * *

HULSE, Stewart H(arding), Jr.   1931-

PERSONAL: Surname rhymes with "pulse"; born August 25, 1931, in Elizabeth, N.J.; son of Stewart Harding and Katharine (Jones) Hulse; married Nancy Huppertz, August 14, 1954; children: Stephen, Jennifer, Melissa. *Education:* Williams College, A.B., 1953; Brown University, Sc.M., 1955, Ph.D., 1957. *Home:* Chapel Ridge Rd., Lutherville, Md. 21093. *Office:* Department of Psychology, Johns Hopkins University, Baltimore, Md. 21218.

CAREER: Johns Hopkins University, Baltimore, Md., instructor, 1957-58, assistant professor, 1958-63, associate professor, 1963-69, professor of psychology, 1969—.

MEMBER: American Psychological Association (fellow), American Association for the Advancement of Science (fellow), Acoustical Society of America, Animal Behavior Society, Pavlovian Society, The Sound Group, Psychonomic Society, Eastern Psychological Association, New York Academy of Sciences, Johns Hopkins Club (secretary, 1971-73, president, 1974-79), Sigma Xi.

AWARDS, HONORS: Research support from National Institute of Mental Health, 1958-59, and National Science Foundation, 1959-77, 1980—.

WRITINGS: (With James Deese) *The Psychology of Learning,* 3rd edition (Hulse was not associated with earlier editions), McGraw, 1967, 5th edition, 1980; (contributor) G. H. Brown, editor, *The Psychology of Learning and Motivation,* Volume VII, Academic Press, 1973; (editor with H. Fowler and W. K. Honig) *Cognitive Processes in Animal Behavior,* Erlbaum, 1978; (contributor with J. Cynx and J. Humpal, and with D. S. Olton and M. L. Shapiro) H. L. Roitblat, T. G. Bever, and H. S. Terrace, editors, *Animal Cognition,* Erlbaum, in press; (contributor with Cynx and Humpal) P. D. Balsam and A. Tomie, editors, *Context and Learning,* Erlbaum, in press; (contributor with Humpal and Cynx) J. Gibbon and L. Allan, editors, *Timing and Time Perception,* New York Academy of Sciences, in press.

Also contributor to *Music Perception.* Contributor to psychology journals. Consulting editor, *Journal of Experimental Psychology,* 1965-74; editor, Journal Supplement Abstract Service, *General Psychology,* 1974-77; associate editor, *Animal Learning and Behavior,* 1976-82.

*   *   *

HUNT, James Gerald 1932-

PERSONAL: Born February 2, 1932, in Denver, Colo.; son of Newell M. and Rosalind G. Hunt; married, 1956; children: three. *Education:* Michigan Technological University, B.S., 1954; University of Illinois, M.A., 1957, Ph.D., 1966. *Office:* College of Business Administration, Texas Tech University, Lubbock, Tex. 79409.

CAREER: General Motors Corp., Pontiac, Mich., project engineer in power development section of Pontiac Motor Division, 1954-56; U.S. Steel Corp., Detroit, Mich., personnel assistant at Michigan Limestone Division, 1957-58; West Virginia Institute of Technology, Montgomery, instructor in business administration, 1958-61; instructor, Millikan University, 1962-63; University of Illinois at Urbana-Champaign, Urbana, instructor in industrial administration, 1963-66, research associate, 1965-66; Southern Illinois University at Carbondale, assistant professor, 1966-69, associate professor, 1969-72, professor of administrative sciences, 1972-81; Texas Tech University, Lubbock, professor, 1981-84, Paul Whitfield Horn Professor of Management, 1984—, area coordinator of management, 1981—. Visiting scholar, University of Aston, 1980. Management development consultant. Manuscript reviewer for Dryden Press and Scott, Foresman, 1973—, and for Richard D. Irwin, Inc., West Publishing, and Science Research Associates, all 1975—.

MEMBER: Academy of Management (vice-president of Midwest Division, 1974-75; president, 1976-77; president, organizational behavior division, 1978-79; member of board of governors, 1978), Southern Management Association, Midwest Business Administration Association.

AWARDS, HONORS: Ford Foundation grant, summer, 1968; National Institute of Mental Health grant, 1970-73; grants from Office of Naval Research and Smithsonian Institution, 1973, 1975, 1977, 1979, and 1981, from Army Research Institute, 1973, 1975, 1977, 1980, and 1983, and from NATO, 1981.

WRITINGS: (Editor with E. A. Fleishman and contributor) *Current Developments in the Study of Leadership,* Southern Illinois University Press, 1973; (editor with Lars L. Larson) *Contingency Approaches to Leadership,* Southern Illinois University Press, 1974; (editor with Larson) *Leadership Frontiers,*

Comparative Administration Research Institute, 1975; (editor with Larson) *Leadership: The Cutting Edge,* Southern Illinois University Press, 1977; (editor with Larson) *Crosscurrents in Leadership,* Southern Illinois University Press, 1979.

(With Richard N. Osborn and Lawrence R. Jauch) *Organization Theory: An Integrated Approach,* Wiley, 1980; (editor with others) *Leadership: Beyond Establishment Views,* Southern Illinois University Press, 1981; (with Osborn and John R. Schermerhorn, Jr.) *Managing Organizational Behavior,* Wiley, 1982, 2nd edition, 1985; (editor with others) *Leaders and Managers: International Perspectives on Managerial Behavior and Leadership Research,* Pergamon, 1984; *Managerial Behavior and Leadership,* Science Research Associates, 1984; (editor with John D. Blair) *Leadership on the Future Battlefield,* Pergamon, 1985.

Contributor: M. S. Wortman and Fred Luthans, editors, *Emerging Concepts in Management,* Macmillan, 1969; Gene Dalton, editor, *Motivation and Control in Organizations,* Irwin-Dorsey, 1970; S. Chilton, editor, *Readings in Educational Administration,* MSS Educational Publishing, 1970; W. K. Graham and Karlene Roberts, editors, *Comparative Studies in Organizational Behavior,* Holt, 1972.

Contributor to proceedings and to professional journals. Guest editor of *Organization and Administrative Sciences,* June, 1975; editor, *Journal of Management,* 1983—. Member of editorial review board of *Journal of Business Research,* 1973—, and *Academy of Management Review,* 1975—; manuscript reviewer for *Business Perspectives,* 1967-73, *Organization and Administrative Sciences, Journal of Applied Social Psychology,* and *Journal of Applied Psychology,* all 1973—.

*   *   *

HUNT, William Dudley, Jr. 1922-

PERSONAL: Born March 23, 1922, in New Orleans, La.; son of William Dudley (a civil engineer) and Ruth (Lee) Hunt; married Julia Wellborn, June 9, 1942 (divorced, 1953); married Gwendolyn Munson, June 19, 1954; children: (first marriage) William Dudley III, Walter W.; (second marriage) Ruth Lee II, Stephen C. M., Gwendolyn M. II, John M. *Education:* Jacksonville State University, B.A., 1949; Tulane University, B.Arch., 1957. *Religion:* Episcopal. *Home address:* Box 228A, Route 4, Gloucester, Va. 23061. *Office address:* Box 670, Gloucester, Va. 23061.

CAREER: Private practice of architecture, 1951-64; *Architectural Record,* New York City, senior editor, 1958-63; American Institute of Architects, Washington, D.C., publisher of *American Institute of Architects Journal,* 1964-72, publishing director, 1970-72; John Wiley & Sons, Inc., New York City, architecture editor, 1972-82. Director, Product Systems for Architects and Engineers, 1970-71. Member, architectural review board, Rye, N.Y., 1963. Consultant to Alcoa and U.S. Steel Co., 1963-68. Consulting editor, Dodge Books, 1958-65, McGraw-Hill Book Co., 1965-72, John Wiley & Sons, Inc., 1982—. *Military service:* U.S. Army Air Forces, pilot and engineering officer, 1942-45; became first lieutenant. U.S. Air Force Reserve, 1945-82; retired as lieutenant colonel.

MEMBER: American Institute of Architects (fellow), Authors Guild, Authors League of America, Tau Sigma Delta.

AWARDS, HONORS: Design award, Dallas Museum of Fine Arts, 1958; merit award, American Society of Landscape Architects, 1980; outstanding academic book award, Authors

League of America, and American Association of the Professions book award, both 1981, both for *Encyclopedia of American Architecture*.

WRITINGS: Contemporary Curtain Wall, Dodge Books, 1958; (editor and contributor) *Hotels, Motels, Restaurants, and Bars*, Dodge Books, 1960; (editor and contributor) *Hospitals, Health Centers and Clinics*, Dodge Books, 1961; (editor and contributor) *Office Buildings*, Dodge Books, 1961; (editor and contributor) *Organizing for Successful Practice*, Dodge Books, 1962; *Comprehensive Architectural Services*, McGraw, 1965; *Creative Cost Control*, McGraw, 1967; *Total Design*, McGraw, 1972.

Encyclopedia of American Architecture, McGraw, 1980; (co-editor) *Architectural Graphic Standards*, Wiley, 1981; (co-editor and contributor) *Architects' Data*, Granada, 1981; *American Architecture: A Field Guide*, Harper, 1984; *The Excitement of Architecture*, Harper, 1985. Contributor of articles to *American Institute of Architects Journal, Architectural Record*, and other professional architectural magazines.

* * *

HUNTER, J(ames) A(lston) H(ope) 1902-

PERSONAL: Born February 12, 1902, in Tigre, Argentina; son of James Hope (an industrialist) and Mamuela Leopoldina (Luna) Hunter. *Education:* Educated at private schools in England, and at Royal Naval Colleges at Osborne and Dartmouth, England. *Address:* c/o Westminster Bank Ltd., 96 Kensington High St., London W.8, England.

CAREER: Royal Navy, 1918-45, midshipman to commander; Control Commission for Germany, chief finance officer for German sea and inland water shipping, 1946-52; writer of syndicated mathematical newspaper feature, "Fun with Figures," with more than 8,000 mathematical teasers published since 1952.

MEMBER: British Mathematical Association, Mathematical Association of America.

WRITINGS: Fun with Figures, Oxford University Press, 1956, revised edition, Dover, 1977; *Figures for Fun*, Phoenix House, 1957; *Figurets: More Fun with Figures*, Oxford University Press, 1958, published as *More Fun with Figures*, Dover, 1966 (published in England as *More Figures for Fun*, Phoenix House, 1959); *Figures Are Fun*, five books and manual for elementary grades four to eight, Copp, 1959; (with Joseph S. Madachy) *Mathematical Diversions*, Van Nostrand, 1963, revised edition, Dover, 1976; *Hunter's Math Brain Teasers*, Bantam, 1965, revised edition published as *Mathematical Brain-Teasers*, Dover, 1976; *Challenging Mathematical Teasers*, Bantam, 1975, revised edition, 1983; *Entertaining Mathematical Teasers*, Bantam, 1975, revised edition, 1983.

Also author of *Some Tough Teasers*, 1979. Author of monthly magazine feature, "Puzzler." Former associate editor, *Recreational Mathematics*.

* * *

HUTCHINSON, G(eorge) Evelyn 1903-

PERSONAL: Born January 30, 1903, in Cambridge, England; came to United States in 1928, naturalized in 1941; son of Arthur (a mineralogist) and Evaline (Shipley) Hutchinson; married July 30, 1933. *Education:* Cambridge University, B.A., 1924, M.A., 1928. *Home:* 269 Canner St., New Haven, Conn.

Office: Department of Biology, Osborn Memorial Laboratories, Yale University, 165 Prospect St., New Haven, Conn. 06511.

CAREER: University of the Witwatersrand, Johannesburg, Transvaal, Republic of South Africa, senior lecturer in zoology, 1926-28; Yale University, New Haven, Conn., instructor in biology, 1928-31, assistant professor, 1931-41, associate professor, 1941-45, professor, 1945, Sterling Professor of Zoology, 1946-71, emeritus professor and senior research biologist, 1971—, fellow of Saybrook College. Biologist for Yale University expedition to northern India in 1932 and other scientific investigations in Italy, England, South Africa, and the United States. Consultant to Bingham Oceanographic Laboratory.

MEMBER: Societas Internationalis Limnologicae (president, 1964-65), National Academy of Sciences, American Philosophical Society, American Society of Zoologists, American Society of Naturalists, Ecological Society of America, Limnology Society of America (vice-president, 1938; president, 1948), British Ecological Society (honorary member), Austrian Academy of Sciences (corresponding member), Linnaean Society of London, Royal Entomological Society of London, Royal Society of London (foreign member), Cambridge Natural History Society.

AWARDS, HONORS: Received honorary degrees from Lawrence College, 1954, Princeton University, 1961, Niagara University, Washington University, 1973, Duke University, 1975, Northwestern University, and Cambridge University; Franklin Medal, 1979; Daniel Girard Elliot Medal, 1984.

WRITINGS—Published by Yale University Press, except as indicated: *The Clear Mirror*, Cambridge University Press, 1937; *The Itinerant Ivory Tower*, 1952; (editor and compiler) *A Preliminary List of the Writings of Rebecca West*, Yale University Library, 1957; *A Treatise on Limnology*, Wiley, Volume I, 1957, Volume II, 1967, Volume III, 1975; *The Enchanted Voyage*, 1963; *The Ecological Theater and the Evolutionary Play*, 1965; *An Introduction to Population Ecology*, 1978; *The Kindly Fruits of the Earth: Recollections of an Embryo Ecologist*, 1979. Author of scientific papers on aquatic insects, limnology, and ecology theory.

WORK IN PROGRESS: Volume IV of *A Treatise on Limnology*.

AVOCATIONAL INTERESTS: Art history, animal iconography, particularly of insects in medieval painting.

* * *

HUTTON, J(oseph) Bernard 1911-?

PERSONAL: Born July 7, 1911, in Bohemia; deceased; son of Frederick William (a businessman) and Margaret (Anton) Hutton; married Ellen Kohl, October 10, 1940 (died, 1950); married Pearl Gold (a company director), December 12, 1950; children: (first marriage) Thomas Edward, Marion Margaret; (second marriage) Harold Frederick. *Education:* University of Berlin, degree in literature.

CAREER: Halo Noviny, Prague, Czechoslovakia, foreign news editor, 1933-34; *Vecherniaya Moskva*, Moscow, U.S.S.R., foreign news editor, 1934-38; Czechoslovak Embassy, London, England, press and cultural attache, 1945-48; free-lance journalist, lecturer, and broadcaster, 1948-57; diplomatic and special correspondent, Thomson Newspapers, 1957-61, and

Topic Journal, 1961-63; free-lance writer, journalist, broadcaster, lecturer, and psychic researcher, beginning 1963. Guest lecturer on economics and politics, University of Moscow, 1936-37.

MEMBER: International Federation of Journalists, Society of Authors, National Union of Journalists, Society for Psychical Research, Paternosters, Monday Club.

AWARDS, HONORS: Honorary degree, University of Moscow, 1936; Military Cross, 1943; Knight of Mark Twain, 1973; Man of Achievement, Cambridge University, 1973.

WRITINGS: Frogman Spy, Obolensky, 1960 (published in England as *Frogman Extraordinary,* Neville Spearman, 1960); *Danger from Moscow,* Neville Spearman, 1960; *School for Spies: The ABC of How Russia's Secret Service Operates,* Neville Spearman, 1961, Coward, 1962; *Stalin, the Miraculous Georgian,* Neville Spearman, 1961; (with Jack Fishman) *The Private Life of Josif Stalin,* W. H. Allen, 1962; *The Traitor Trade,* Obolensky, 1963; *Out of This World,* Psychic Press, 1965, published as *On the Other Side of Reality,* Award Books, 1969; *Healing Hands,* W. H. Allen, 1966, McKay, 1967, 2nd revised edition, W. H. Allen, 1978; *Commander Crabb Is Alive,* Award Books, 1968; (with Liam Nolan) *The Life of*

Smetana: The Pain and the Glory, Harrap, 1968; *Struggle in the Dark: How Russian and Other Iron Curtain Spies Operate* (sequel to *School for Spies*), Harrap, 1969.

The Fake Defector, Howard Baker, 1970; *Hess: The Man and His Mission,* Bruce & Watson, 1970, Macmillan, 1971; *The Great Illusion* (autobiography), Bruce & Watson, 1970; *Women Spies,* W. H. Allen, 1971, published as *Women in Espionage,* Macmillan, 1972; *The Subverters,* Arlington House, 1972 (published in England as *The Subverters of Liberty,* W. H. Allen, 1972); *Lost Freedom,* Bruce & Watson, 1973; *The Healing Power: The Extraordinary Spiritual Healing of Mrs. Leah Doctors and "Dr. Chang," Her Spirit Guide,* Frewin, 1975; *Step into the Unknown: A Study of All Aspects of Parapsychology,* Frewin, 1976; (with others) *Les Guerisseurs psi, guerisseurs de l'impossible: guerisons miraculeuses et guerisons, spontanees, regeneration des organes, les "chirugiens" philippins, influence a distance et imposition des mains, les charlatans, chamans et sorciers, la medecine magique en Chine,* Tchou, 1978.

SIDELIGHTS: J. Bernard Hutton spoke German, Czech, Slovak, and Russian, and understood other languages.

AVOCATIONAL INTERESTS: Classical music, travel.

I

IGLAUER, Edith
   See DALY, Edith Iglauer

* * *

IKO, Momoko 1940-

PERSONAL: Born March 30, 1940, in Wapato, Wash.; daughter of Kyokuo (a farmer and laborer) and Natsuko (Kagawa) Iko. *Education:* University of Illinois, B.A. (with honors), 1961; also attended Instituto Allende and University of Iowa. *Address:* c/o McCloden, P.O. Box 172, Hollywood, Calif. 90028.

CAREER: High school English teacher in Chicago, Ill., 1961-64; Ridgeway Hospital, Chicago, Ill., teacher of emotionally disturbed elementary school children, 1964-65; writer, 1965—; associated with administrative support service agencies in Los Angeles, Calif., 1979—. Head of gerontology project for Japanese American Service Committee, 1975; staff writer for KABC-TV and KNBC-TV, 1976; teacher of adult education courses, Truman College, Chicago City Colleges, 1977; visiting artist, Kearney Street Poets and JAM Workshop, and director, Asian American Theatre Company, San Francisco, fall, 1978; film grant selector, American Film Institute, 1980-81; visiting artist, Basement Workshop, 1981; artist-in-residence, Japanese American Cultural & Community Center and California Arts Council, 1982-83. Consultant to various organizations and agencies.

MEMBER: Writers Guild (East).

AWARDS, HONORS: Playwriting awards from East-West Players, 1970 and 1971; playwriting grant from Rockefeller Foundation, 1976; National Endowment for the Arts grant, 1977; Zellenbach San Francisco Grant, 1978.

WRITINGS—Plays: "Gold Watch" (two-act), first produced in Los Angeles, Calif., at Inner City Cultural Center, spring, 1972; "When We Were Young" (two-act), first produced in Los Angeles by East-West Players, autumn, 1974; "Hollywood Mirrors" (comedy/satire), first produced in San Francisco, Calif., by Asian American Theatre Co., fall, 1978; "Second City Flat," first produced in Los Angeles, 1978; "Flowers and Household Gods," first produced in New York, N.Y., by the Pan Asian Repertory Theater, 1981.

Films; for Japanese-American Service Committee: "Social Services: Seeking a Human Dimension," 1975; "Issei: A Quality for Survival," 1975; "Values and Attitudes I, II, III," 1975; "Whatever Will Be," 1981.

Work anthologized in *Aiiieeee: Anthology of Asian-American Writers,* Howard University Press, 1975; *Counterpoint: Perspectives on Asian America,* University of California Press.

WORK IN PROGRESS: Mama Mountain: Interconnecting Short Stories.

SIDELIGHTS: "In Momoko Iko's moving . . . play, 'Flowers and Household Gods,' . . . we see a Japanese-American family over three generations indelibly influenced by the internment experience during World War II," explains Mel Gussow in the *New York Times.* Set in Chicago in 1968, the play shows how different family members were affected by the experience. Gathered together for the family matriarch's funeral, the relatives dredge up old memories and disturb "old wounds." "Falling into alcoholism and infidelity, [the Kagawas] seem incapable of helping one another," Gussow comments, likening the group to Simon Gray's English family in "Close of Play." Concludes the critic: "The playwright has given her characters a bedrock of specificity. . . . The play is marked by a certitude."

BIOGRAPHICAL/CRITICAL SOURCES: New York Times, April 21, 1981.

* * *

INNES, Brian 1928-
   (Neil Powell)

PERSONAL: Born May 4, 1928, in London, England; son of Stanley George (a civil servant) and Laura (Thornton) Innes; married Felicity Wilson, October 4, 1956 (divorced); children: Simon Alexander. *Education:* King's College, London, B.Sc., 1949; also attended Chelsea School of Art, Central School of Arts and Crafts, and London School of Printing. *Home:* 74 Woodland Rise, London N10, England. *Agent;* Jonathan Clowes Ltd., 22 Prince Albert Rd., London NW7 7ST, England.

CAREER: Benn Brothers Ltd. (publishers), London, England, assistant editor of *Chemical Age,* 1953-55; Maclean-Hunter (Publishers), London, assistant editor of *British Printer,* 1955-

1959, associate editor, 1959-60; Paul Hamlyn Ltd. (publishers), London, art director, 1960-62; Animated Graphic and Publicity Designers, London, director, 1963-65; Immediate Books (book production), London, proprietor, 1965—. Production consultant, Bancroft & Co. Ltd.; design consultant, BPC Publishing Ltd.

MEMBER: Institute of Printing (associate), Society of Authors, Authors' Club, Society of Industrial Artists and Designers, National Union of Journalists, Institute of Journalists.

WRITINGS: The Book of Pirates, Bancroft & Co., 1966; *The Book of Spies: 4000 Years of Cloak and Dagger,* Bancroft & Co., 1967, Grosset, 1969; *The Book of Revolutions,* Bancroft & Co., 1967; *The Book of Outlaws,* Bancroft & Co., 1968.

My Best Book of Flight, Purnell, 1970; *The Saga of the Railways,* Purnell, 1973; *Horoscopes: How to Draw and Interpret Them,* Orbis Books, 1976, Arco, 1978; (editor) *Rococo to Romanticism: Art and Architecture 1700-1850,* Garland Publishing, 1976; *The Tarot: How to Use and Interpret the Cards,* Orbis Books, 1977, Arco, 1978; (editor with Ian Ward) *World of Automobiles: An Illustrated Encyclopedia of the Motor Car,* twenty-two volumes, Purnell, 1977; (under pseudonym Neil Powell) *The Supernatural: Alchemy, the Ancient Science,* Aldus Books, 1977, enlarged edition (with Stuart Holroyd) published as *Mysteries of Magic,* 1979.

(Under pseudonym Neil Powell) *The Book of Change: How to Understand and Use the I Ching,* Orbis Books, 1980; *The Red Baron Lives!,* New English Library, 1981; *The Book of the Havana Cigar,* Beaufort Book Co., 1983. Co-editor, "Facts of Print" series, Vista Books, 1958. Contributor to *Man, Myth, and Magic, American Destiny,* and *On Four Wheels;* also contributor to *Encyclopaedia Britannica,* 1964. Contributor to *Guardian, Scotsman,* and other periodicals.

WORK IN PROGRESS: Man and His Art, for Card Publications; art director of "Cordon Bleu Cookery Course," for BPC; art director of *Pictorial Knowledge,* for International Learning Systems Corp.†

*   *   *

ITZIN, Catherine 1944-

PERSONAL: Born May 29, 1944, in Iowa City, Iowa; daughter of Frank H. (in social work) and Neva (a social worker; maiden name, Smith) Itzin; married R. J. Hawkes, September 3, 1966 (divorced July, 1976); children: Caitlin Sarah, Nicholas Charles. *Education:* University of Iowa, B.A., 1967; University of London, M.Phil., 1970. *Agent:* Deborah Rogers, Deborah Rogers Literary Agency, 49 Blenheim Cres., London W11 2EF, England; and Phil Kelvin, Goodwin Associates, 19 London St., London W2 1HL, England.

CAREER: City Literary Institute, London, England, lecturer in English drama and playwriting, 1971-78; writer. Script editor and producer of radio drama for British Broadcasting Corp., 1973-75. Member of House of Commons Current Arts and Policy Advisory Committee, 1975-76. Trustee Sheltered Housing Assistance for the Disabled, 1976—; manager of Loughborough Infants School, 1976-77; governor of Loughborough Juniors School, 1977-78. Director, Tricycle Theatre, 1977-83.

MEMBER: British Theatre Institute (founder; member of council, 1972—), Theatre Writers Union, Explorations in Feminism Publishing Collective, Vassall Neighborhood Council, Phi Beta Kappa.

AWARDS, HONORS: Second prizes from BBC-TV competition for new writers, 1969, for "I'll Huff and I'll Puff," and Platt Arts Foundation playwriting competition, 1970, for "The Gifts of the Magi."

WRITINGS: Alternative Theatre Handbook, TQ Publications, 1976; *New Playwrights Directory,* TQ Publications, 1977; *Stages in the Revolution: Political Theatre in Britain since 1968,* Methuen, 1980, second edition, 1982; *Splitting Up: Single Parent Liberation,* Virago, 1980; *Tax Law and Child Care: The Case for Reform,* National Council for One Parent Families, 1980; *New Theatre Voices of the Seventies,* Methuen, 1981; *The Directory of Playwrights, Directors and Designers,* John Offord Publications, 1983; *The Good Schools Guide for Parents and Young People,* Methuen, 1985. Also author of *British Alternative Theatre Directory,* published annually, 1979—.

Plays: "Cuckolds" (one-act), first produced in London, England, at Little Theatre, May, 1970; "Infants, Lunatics and Married Women" (one-act radio play), produced on stage in New York, N.Y., by Westbeth Feminist Collective, October 13, 1974; (with Ann Mitchell) "Ever After," produced in London at Tricycle Theatre, 1982; "Let's Murder the Moonshine," produced by BBC Radio 3, October, 1984.

Co-editor, *Theatre Quarterly, Theatrefacts,* and *New Plays,* all 1971-77; drama critic, *Tribune,* 1972-80, *Time Out,* and *Plays and Players.*

WORK IN PROGRESS: Ages of Women: The Double Jeopardy of Ageism and Sexism, for Methuen; a television play about smoking.

SIDELIGHTS: "I am an American exiled in England," Catherine Itzin told *CA.* "In the seventies I combined full-time work as a mother with founding and editing *Theatre Quarterly,* a serious and internationally acclaimed theatre journal, and regularly reviewing plays for *Tribune,* the national weekly newspaper of the Labor Movement, whose literary pages were once edited by George Orwell. My commitment was primarily to the socialist theatre movement in England, which I eventually wrote about in *Stages in the Revolution: Political Theatre in Britain since 1968.*"

Of this work *Times Literary Supplement* critic Irving Wardle remarks: "[The book] is the first comprehensive study [of that era in theatre], and is a remarkable feat of organization. It runs through the decade [1968-78] year by year, each section introduced with a summary of key events before focusing on a particular group of artists; and interweaving chapters on writers and groups with chapters on subsidy, Equity, and the development of such institutions as the Independent Theatre Council and the Theatre Writers' Union, whose muscle the author convincingly demonstrates."

"During the mid and late seventies," continues Itzin, "I gradually came to a feminist conclusion of women's oppression—of *my* oppression. As a worker—the 'double shift,' two jobs, the one as a mother unpaid, the other as a writer low paid. As a mother—doing an immensely valuable job of child-rearing in isolation, and unpaid, with inadequate resources for child care. As a wife—the appropriation in marriage of my sexual and domestic services. My political consciousness-raising really came when I was divorced and living with very young children as a single parent. In an attempt to obtain tax relief on my childcare expenses I challenged the Inland Revenue in a highly-publicized test case [resulting in the book] *Tax Law and Child Care: The Case for Reform..*

"At the end of the seventies I decided that all my future energies would be devoted to writing about women and women's oppression with a view to ending that oppression. I do this for myself and my liberation; for my daughter and for my son, for women and men from an understanding of the damage that is done both to victims of an oppression and also to the oppressors, whose humanity is diminished and life limited by their oppressor role. In the past [few] years I have trained and now teach Revaluation Co-counselling and am now the Area Reference Person for counsellors in South East London. I do a lot of group work and lead workshops on issues of addictions, racism, anti-semitism, and sexism."

BIOGRAPHICAL/CRITICAL SOURCES: Times Literary Supplement, March 20, 1981.

J

JACK, Homer A(lexander) 1916-

PERSONAL: Born May 19, 1916, in Rochester, N.Y.; son of Alexander (an artist) and Cecilia (Davis) Jack; married Esther Rhys Williams, November 23, 1939; married Ingeborg Kind, June 14, 1972; children: (first marriage) Alexander, Lucy. *Education:* Cornell University, B.S., 1936, M.S., 1937, Ph.D., 1940; Meadville Theological School, B.D., 1944. *Politics:* Independent. *Home:* 489 Willow Rd., Winnetka, Ill. 60093. *Office:* Lake Shore Unitarian Universalist Society, 614 Lincoln Ave., Winnetka, Ill. 60093.

CAREER: Unitarian minister in Lawrence, Kan., 1942-43; Chicago Council against Racial and Religious Discrimination, Chicago, Ill., executive director, 1943-48; Unitarian minister in Evanston, Ill., 1948-59; American Committee on Africa, New York City, a founder and associate director, 1959-60; National Committee for a Sane Nuclear Policy, New York City, a founder and executive director, 1960-64; Unitarian Universalist Association of the United States and Canada, Division of Social Responsibility, Boston, Mass., director, 1964-70; World Conference on Religion and Peace, New York City, secretary-general, 1970-83; Lake Shore Unitarian Universalist Society, Winnetka, Ill., minister, 1984—. A founder of congress of Racial Equality (CORE), 1942, and International Confederation for Disarmament and Peace.

AWARDS, HONORS: Thomas H. Wright Award for better race relations, City of Chicago, 1949; D.D., Meadville Theological School, 1971; Niwano Peace Prize, 1984.

WRITINGS: Disarmament Workbook, World Conference on Religion and Peace, 1978; *Disarm—or Die,* World Conference on Religion and Peace, 1983.

Editor: *The Biological Field Stations of the World,* Chronica Botanica, 1945; *The Wit and Wisdom of Gandhi,* Beacon Press, 1951; *To Albert Schweitzer: A Festschrift,* privately printed, 1955; *The Gandhi Reader,* Indiana University Press, 1956; *Religion and Peace,* Bobbs-Merrill, 1966; *World Religions and World Peace,* Beacon Press, 1968, *Religion for Peace,* Gandhi Peace Foundation, 1973; *World Religion/World Peace,* World Conference on Religion and Peace, 1979; *Religion in the Struggle for World Community,* World Conference on Religion and Peace, 1980.

Contributor to *Christian Century, Saturday Review, New York Times Magazine, Bulletin of Atomic Scientists,* and other publications. Editor, *Africa Today,* 1959-60.

SIDELIGHTS: Homer Jack first visited Albert Schweitzer in Africa in 1952, and he was present at Ghana's achievement of independence in 1957. He was an observer at the Asian-African Conference in Bandung, Indonesia, 1955, the All-African People's Conference in Ghana, 1958, and other international conferences. His work in race relations in the United States includes association with Martin Luther King, Jr., beginning in 1956.

*   *   *

JACKSON, James P(ierre) 1925-

PERSONAL: Born December 10, 1925, in Paris, France; son of Kenneth M. and Germaine (Lepaute) Jackson; married Charlene Duncan, August 10, 1957; children: Keith Allen, Glenn Stuart. *Education:* University of Missouri, A.B., 1950, M.A., 1957. *Home address:* Route 2, Box 136A, Marthasville, Mo. 63357.

CAREER: Missouri Department of Conservation, Jefferson City, conservation education consultant, 1951-61; junior high school science teacher in Ladue, Mo., 1961-63; Washington Public High School, Washington, Mo., biology teacher, 1963—, chairman of science department, 1965—. Writer and photographer. Member of advisory council for University of Missouri's School of Forestry, Fisheries, and Wildlife. *Military service:* U.S. Navy, 1944-46; became lieutenant junior grade. *Member:* Conservation Federation of Missouri (member of board of directors), Audubon Society of Missouri (past president).

WRITINGS: The Biography of a Tree (self-illustrated with photographs), Jonathan David, 1978; *Pulse of the Forest,* American Forestry Association, 1980; *Passages of a Stream: A Chronicle of the Meramec,* University of Missouri Press, 1984. Contributor of articles to national wildlife and outdoor periodicals, including *American Forests, National Wildlife, American West,* and *National Parks & Conservation.*

WORK IN PROGRESS: A book on the ecology of the central U.S. high plains region.

SIDELIGHTS: James P. Jackson told *CA:* "As one whose educational training and lifelong interests have been in natural science, I consider myself a specialist. Part of my motivation consistently has been the protection and preservation of our natural heritage. I am a devoted environmentalist. The outlet for such devotion is my writing combined with my photographic efforts. I strive for accuracy and quality in both media.

"*The Biography of a Tree* is a fictionalized story about a long-lived white oak tree, about the effects it had on other life forms of the forest, and about how it was affected by them. My effort was to depict the struggles and successes of the growing, and finally aging tree, in terms of the limitations imposed upon it by nature."

Dennis Drabelle writes in the *Washington Post* of *The Biography of a Tree:* "Nothing is so engrossing as science in the hands of a savvy wordsmith. . . . The writer who can explain complex physical processes with clarity and elan entertains without gimmicks. James Jackson is such an entertainer. . . . In simple but evocative prose, interspersed with dozens of excellent full-page photos, he recounts the [oak] tree's 265 years."

BIOGRAPHICAL/CRITICAL SOURCES: Washington Post, January 16, 1979.

* * *

JACKSON, John N(icholas)   1925-

PERSONAL: Born December 15, 1925, in Nottingham, England; son of Alexander (a teacher and clergyman) and Phyllis E. (Oldfield) Jackson; married Kathleen M. Nussey, May, 1951; children: Andrew, Susan, Paul. *Education:* University of Birmingham, Birmingham, England, B.A., 1949; University of Manchester, Ph.D., 1960. *Religion:* Anglican. *Home:* 80 Marsdale Dr., St. Catharines, Ontario, Canada. *Office:* Department of Geography, Brock University, St. Catharines, Ontario, Canada.

CAREER: Herefordshire County Council, Herefordshire, England, research officer, 1950-53; Hull County Borough, Hull, England, senior planning assistant, 1954-56; University of Manchester, Manchester, England, lecturer in geography, 1956-65; Brock University, St. Catharines, Ontario, professor of applied geography, 1965—, head of department, 1965-70. *Military service:* Royal Navy. *Member:* Royal Town Planning Institute.

WRITINGS: Surveys for Town and Country Planning, Hutchinson University Library, 1963; *Recreational Development and the Lake Erie Shore,* Niagara Region Development Council, 1968; *The Industrial Structure of the Niagara Region,* Brock University, 1971; *The Canadian City: Space, Form, Quality,* McGraw-Ryerson, 1972; (editor with J. Forrester) *Practical Geography,* McGraw-Ryerson, 1972; *Welland and the Welland Canal,* Mika, 1975; *St. Catharines, Ontario: Its Early Years,* Mika, 1976; *A Planning Appraisal of the Welland Urban Community,* Department of Public Works (Ottawa), 1976; *Land Use Planning in the Niagara Region,* Niagara Region Study Review Commission, 1976; (with John Burtniak) *Railways in the Niagara Peninsula,* Mika, 1976; (contributor) Lorne H. Russwurm and Ken B. Beesley, editors, *The Rural-Urban Fringe: Canadian Perspectives,* Department of Geography, Atkinson College, York University, 1981; (with Fred A. Addis) *The Welland Canals: A Comprehensive Guide,* Welland Canals Foundation, 1982.

WORK IN PROGRESS: A study of settlement change across the international border, entitled *The Niagara Frontier: Land-*

scape in Evolution; Urban Characteristics and the Changing Regional Format in the Niagara Peninsula, 1900 to Present; Urban Form, Regional Growth: Quality, Expectations and Reality in Western Europe and North America.

* * *

JACKSON, Mark
See KURZ, Ron

* * *

JAMES, Robert (Vidal) Rhodes
See RHODES JAMES, Robert (Vidal)

* * *

JARCHOW, Merrill E(arl)   1910-

PERSONAL: Surname pronounced "Jarko"; born September 25, 1910, in Stillwater, Minn.; son of Louis D. (a sheriff) and Elsie (Bruntlett) Jarchow; married Doris A. Vrenegor (a dance teacher), March 21, 1943; children: Barbara (Mrs. Keith Slater), Susan (Mrs. William Alrich). *Education:* University of Minnesota, B.A., 1930, M.A., 1933, Ph.D., 1941. *Politics:* Republican. *Religion:* Methodist. *Home:* 203 Oak, Northfield, Minn. 55057. *Office:* Carleton College, Northfield, Minn. 55057.

CAREER: South Dakota State College (now University), Brookings, instructor, 1935-37, assistant professor, 1937-40, associate professor of history, 1940-41; Carleton College, Northfield, Minn., associate professor, 1946-67, historian-in-residence, 1967—, dean of men, 1946-67. Trustee, Shattuck School, Faribault, Minn., 1954-74. *Military service:* U.S. Navy, 1943-46; became lieutenant.

MEMBER: Organization of American Historians, American Historical Association, National Association of Deans and Advisers of Men (member of executive committee, 1948-50), National Association of Student Personnel Administrators, Minnesota Historical Society (member of council, 1954-62), Phi Beta Kappa, Northfield Golf Club (president, 1961).

WRITINGS: (With R. W. Murchie) *Population Trends in Minnesota,* University of Minnesota Press, 1936; (contributor) A. R. Buchanan, editor, *The Navy's Air War,* Harper, 1946; *The Earth Brought Forth,* Minnesota Historical Society, 1949, reprinted, [New York], 1970; (with L. A. Headley) *Carleton: The First Century,* Carleton College, 1966.

Minnesota's Private Liberal Arts Colleges: Their History and Contributions, Minnesota Historical Society, 1973; *Donald J. Cowling,* Carleton College, 1974; *In Search of Fulfillment: Episodes in the Life of D. Blake Stewart,* North Central Publishing, 1974; (with William M. Werber) *Circling the Bases,* [Naples], 1978; *Amherst H. Wilder and His Enduring Legacy to Saint Paul,* [Saint Paul], 1981; *Letters to Alice: Life at Carleton from Strong to Sallmon,* Carleton College, 1982.

WORK IN PROGRESS: A book based on the diary of Winifred Fairbank, 1907-1940.

* * *

JARVIS, Ana C(ortesi)   1936-

PERSONAL: Born September 6, 1936, in Asuncion, Paraguay; came to the United States in 1962, naturalized citizen, 1966; daughter of Santiago (a musician) and Dolores (Bures) Cortesi;

married Bill Jarvis (a systems analyst), February 1, 1963; children: Ronald, Michelle. *Education:* California State College, San Bernardino, B.A., 1968; University of California, Riverside, M.A., 1970, Ph.D., 1973. *Home and office:* 1128 East 26th St., San Bernardino, Calif. 92404.

CAREER: University of California, Riverside, instructor in Spanish, 1968-72; San Bernardino Valley College, San Bernardino, Calif., instructor in Spanish, 1973-75; Riverside City College, Riverside, Calif., instructor in Spanish, 1975—. Interpreter for "Point Four," an American government program in Paraguay.

WRITINGS: Por los senderos de lo hispanico (title means "Along the Hispanic Path"), Wiley, 1967; *Career Education and Foreign Languages,* Houghton, 1975; *Como se dice . . .?* (title means "How Does One Say . . .?"), Heath, 1977, 2nd edition, 1982; (with Raquel Lebredo and Francisco Mena) *Continuemos!: Curso intermedio de espanol,* Heath, 1979; (with Lebredo) *Basic Spanish Grammar* (with workbooks), Heath, 1980, 2nd edition, 1983; (with Lebredo) *Aventuras Literarias,* Heath, 1983; (with Lebredo) *Nuestro Mundo,* Heath, 1983.

WORK IN PROGRESS: A novel in Spanish; a book of poems.

SIDELIGHTS: Ana C. Jarvis comments briefly: "I firmly believe that Americans *need* to study foreign languages and cultures. I will continue to work toward fulfilling my dream: to see the day when *all* Californians are bilingual."†

*   *   *

JAY, Mel
See FANTHORPE, R(obert) Lionel

*   *   *

JEAN, Gabrielle (Lucille) 1924-
(Sister Jean de Milan)

PERSONAL: Born April 8, 1924, in Lowell, Mass.; daughter of Alfred (an electrician) and Claudia (Guillemette) Jean. *Education:* Rivier College, A.B., 1954; Boston College, M.Ed., 1957, Ph.D., 1961. *Home:* 975 Varnum Ave., Lowell, Mass. 01854. *Office:* Saint Luke Institute, 2420 Brooks Dr., Suitland, Md. 20746.

CAREER: Roman Catholic nun of Order of Sisters of Charity, Ottawa, name in religion, Sister Jean de Milan; science and mathematics teacher in Roman Catholic high school for girls, Lowell, Mass., 1954-59; Marillac College, Normandy, Mo., instructor in psychology and education, 1961-62; Rivier College, Nashua, N.H., assistant professor of psychology and education, 1962-64; Rhode Island College, Providence, associate professor of psychology, 1964-71, chairman of department, 1967-69; Roger Williams College, Bristol, R.I., professor of psychology, 1972-74; House of Affirmation, Whitinsville, Mass., staff psychologist, 1974-76; D'Youville Manor Nursing Home, Lowell, Mass., administrator, 1976-81; long-term care specialist for Massachusetts Department of Elder Affairs, 1981; Center for Applied Research in the Apostolate, Washington, D.C., coordinator of health care research, 1981-83; Saint Luke Institute, Suitland, Md., coordinator of health plan, 1983—. Instructor in sociology and psychology, School of Nursing, St. Joseph's Hospital, 1957-61; part-time teacher, University of Rhode Island, 1971-72. Abstractor for American Psychological Association, 1982—.

MEMBER: American Psychological Association, American Association of Homes for the Aging, American College of Health Care Administrators (fellow), American Educational Research Association, American Personnel and Guidance Association, National Vocational Guidance Association, Psychologists Interested in Religious Issues, Association of Massachusetts Homes for the Aging (vice-president, 1977-79; president, 1979-80).

WRITINGS: Future of the Healing Ministry in the Mission of the Church, Center for Applied Research in the Apostolate, 1982; *Survey of the U.S. Bishops on Health,* Center for Applied Research in the Apostolate, 1982. Contributor of articles to religion and psychology journals.

Editor: Bernhard Haering, *Shalom: Peace,* Farrar, Straus, 1967; Haering, *Acting on the Word,* Farrar, Straus, 1968; Haering, *A Theology of Protest,* Farrar, Straus, 1970; Haering, *Hope Is the Remedy,* St. Paul, 1971, Doubleday, 1972; Haering, *Medical Ethics,* Fides, 1973, revised edition, Fides/Claretion, 1975; Haering, *Faith and Morality in a Secular Age,* Doubleday, 1973; *Sin in a Secular Age,* Doubleday, 1974; *Beatitudes—The Social Dimension,* [St. Paul, England], 1976.

*   *   *

JEFFREY, William
See PRONZINI, Bill
and WALLMANN, Jeffrey M(iner)

*   *   *

JENSEN, Peter
See WALLMANN, Jeffrey M(iner)

*   *   *

JENTZ, Gaylord A.   1931-

PERSONAL: Born August 7, 1931, in Beloit, Wis.; son of Merlyn Adair and Delva (Mullen) Jentz; married JoAnn Mary Hornung, August 6, 1955; children: Katherine, Gary, Loretta and Rory (twins). *Education:* University of Wisconsin, B.A., 1953, J.D., 1957, M.B.A., 1958. *Religion:* Congregational. *Home:* 4106 North Hills Dr., Austin, Tex. 78731. *Office:* GSB 4.138, University of Texas, Austin, Tex. 78712.

CAREER: Admitted to Wisconsin Bar, 1957; University of Oklahoma, Norman, 1958-65, began as instructor, became associate professor of business law; University of Texas at Austin, College of Business Administration, associate professor, 1965-68, professor of business law, 1968—, chairman of department of general business, 1968-74, 1980—, Herbert D. Kelleher Professor of Business Law, 1982. University of Wisconsin, 1957-65, began as visiting summer instructor, became visiting professor. *Military service:* U.S. Army, 1953-55.

MEMBER: American Arbitration Association (member of national panel), American Business Law Association (president, 1971-72), Southern Business Law Association (president, 1966-67), Southwestern Social Science Association, Texas Association for College Teachers (president, 1971-72), Wisconsin State Bar Association, Phi Kappa Phi (president, 1983-84).

AWARDS, HONORS: College of Business Administration Foundation Advisory Council Distinguished Contributions Award, 1979; American Business Law Faculty Award of Excellence, 1981; College of Business Administration and Student Council Service Award, 1983; James C. Scarboro Memorial Award from Colorado Graduate School of Banking, 1983.

WRITINGS: Texas Uniform Commercial Code: Practical Aspects on Secured Transactions (monograph), Bureau of Business Research, University of Texas, 1966, revised edition, 1975; (with others) *Business Law: Text and Cases*, 2nd edition, Allyn & Bacon, 1968; (with others) *Business Law: Text and Cases*, Dryden, 1978; (with others) *Business Law: Key Issues and Concepts*, Grid Publishing, 1978; (with others) *West's Business Law: Text and Cases*, 2nd edition (Jentz was not associated with earlier edition), West, 1983; (with others) *West's Business Law: Alternate UCC Comprehensive Edition*, 2nd edition (Jentz was not associated with earlier edition), West, 1983.

Contributor to business and legal journals. Deputy editor, *Social Science Quarterly*, 1966—; *American Business Law Journal*, staff editor of case comments and digest section, 1967-69, editor-in-chief, 1969-74, advisory editor, 1974—.

*   *   *

JOHNS, Marston
See FANTHORPE, R(obert) Lionel

*   *   *

JOHNSTON, Bruce F(oster)   1919-

PERSONAL: Born September 24, 1919, in Lincoln, Neb.; son of Homer K. and Ethel (Hockett) Johnston; married Harriet L. Pollins, March 31, 1944; children: Bruce C., Patricia C. *Education:* Cornell University, B.A., 1941; Stanford University, A.M., 1950, Ph.D., 1953. *Home:* 676 Alvarado Row, Stanford, Calif. 94305. *Office:* Food Research Institute, Stanford University, Stanford, Calif. 94305.

CAREER: U.S. Department of Agriculture, Milwaukee, Wis., field representative for Agricultural Marketing Administration, 1941-42; Supreme Commander of the Allied Powers in Japan, General Headquarters, Tokyo, chief of food branch of Economic and Scientific Section, 1945-48; U.S. Mission to North Atlantic Treaty Organization (NATO) and European Regional Organizations, Paris, France, agricultural economist in Food and Agriculture Division, 1952-54; Stanford University, Stanford, Calif., associate professor of agricultural economics and associate economist at Food Research Institute, 1954-59, professor and economist, 1959—. Member of committee on agricultural economics, Social Science Research Council, 1962-66; member of advisory board, Foreign Area Fellowship Program, 1963-66; member of advisory panel on development problems for Policy Planning Council, U.S. Department of State, 1966-68; chairman and rapporteur, Joint FAO/WHO Expert Committee on Nutrition, 1974-76; co-organizer of the Working Group on Agriculture and Rural Development of the Project on United States-Mexico Relations. Consultant to World Bank, Pakistan Institute of Development Economics, Government of Ghana, and the United Nations. *Military service:* U.S. Army, 1942-46; became captain.

MEMBER: American Economic Association, American Farm Economic Association, African Studies Association (fellow; member of board of directors, 1962-65), Western Economic Association, Western Farm Economic Association, Telluride Association, Phi Beta Kappa, Phi Kappa Phi.

AWARDS, HONORS: Guggenheim fellowship for study of food economies in East Africa, 1962.

WRITINGS: (With Mosaburo Hosoda and Yoshio Kusumi) *Japanese Food Management in World War Two*, Stanford University Press, 1953; *The Staple Food Economies of Western Tropical Africa*, Stanford University Press, 1958.

Agricultural Development and Economic Transformation: Japan, Taiwan, and Denmark, Food Research Institute, Stanford University, 1960; (contributor) M. J. Herskovits and Mitchell Harwitz, editors, *Economic Transition in Africa*, Northwestern University Press, 1964; (editor with Herman M. Southworth) *Agricultural Development and Economic Growth*, Cornell University Press, 1967; (contributor) Erick Thorbecke, editor, *The Role of Agriculture in Economic Development*, National Bureau of Economic Research, 1969; (with Peter Greaves and others) *Manual on Food and Nutrition Policy*, Food and Agricultural Organization (of the United Nations), 1969; (editor with Kazuski Ohkawa and Hiromitsu Kaneda and contributor) *Agriculture and Economic Growth: Japan's Experience*, Tokyo University Press, 1969.

(Contributor) Harrison Brown and Edward Hutchings, Jr., editors, *Are Our Descendants Doomed?: Technological Change and Population Growth*, Viking, 1972; (with Peter Kilby) *Agricultural Strategies, Rural-Urban Interactions, and the Expansion of Income Opportunities*, Organization for Economic Co-operation and Development Centre, 1972; (with Kilby) *Agriculture and Structural Transformation: Economic Strategies in Late-Developing Countries*, Oxford University Press, 1975; (with William C. Clark) *Food, Health, and Population: Policy Analysis and Development Priorities in Low-Income Countries*, International Institute for Applied Systems Analysis, 1979; (with K. R. M. Anthony, W. O. Jones, and V. C. Uchendu) *Agricultural Change in Tropical Africa*, Cornell University Press, 1979; (with Clark) *Redesigning Rural Development: A Strategic Perspective*, Johns Hopkins University Press, 1982.

All published by Institute for Development Studies, University of Nairobi: *Objectives and Scope of a Food and Nutrition Policy*, 1974; *The Agriculture-Industry Continuum*, 1974; (editor with Sidney B. Westley) *Proceedings of a Workshop on Farm Equipment Innovations for Agricultural Development and Rural Industrialization*, 1975; (with Westley and Martin David) *Workshop on a Food and Nutrition Strategy for Kenya*, 1975; (with Anthony J. Meyer) *Nutrition, Health, and Population in Strategies for Rural Development*, 1976.

Contributor to *Journal of Political Economy*, *American Economic Review*, *Food Research Institute Studies*, *Tropical Agriculture*, and *Journal of Economic Literature*.

WORK IN PROGRESS: "Research on agricultural and rural development in Sub-Saharan Africa and in Mexico with particular attention to appropriate technologies for small farmers and to health, nutrition, and population strategies."

*   *   *

JOHNSTONE, Lammy Olcott   1949-

PERSONAL: Born January 23, 1949, in New York, N.Y.; daughter of Edmund Frank (in advertising) and Janet (Olcott) Johnstone; married Walter J. Carlson (a public relations company president), December 3, 1971 (divorced, 1980). *Home:* Silvermine Rd., Silvermine, Norwalk, Conn. 06850. *Office:* Folio Publishing Corp., 125 Elm St., New Canaan, Conn. 06840.

CAREER/WRITINGS: Beverly Hills Times, Beverly Hills, Calif., feature editor, 1964-66; reporter in society department for *New*

York Daily News; Advertising News of New York, New York City, associate editor, 1968-72, managing editor, 1972-77; *Trib,* New York City, senior editor, 1977-78; communications columnist, Gannet Newspapers, 1979-82; Folio Publishing Corp., New Canaan, Conn., marketing director, 1983—.

Notable assignments include an interview with Martin Luther King and coverage of the Watts riots. On-air reporter for "Grandstand," an NBC-TV nationally televised weekly sports/news program. U.S. correspondent for *Campaign* (British business journal); contributor to consumer and business publications and to popular magazines, including *Ladies' Home Journal* and *American Home.*

SIDELIGHTS: Lammy Olcott Johnstone told *CA:* "Regarding my move to the business side of the publishing industry, I feel it is an opportunity more editors/writers should try and take advantage of.

"The old adage of separation of church and state as it applies to the editorial field is no longer applicable in this day and age. We should, rather, work hand-in-hand to preserve the power of print and strengthen its force within the communications media mix. If not, we could well find ourselves not only subservient to our cousins in TV/video but, years down the road, non-existent because of them.

"Of course, one should not give up [one's] writings for the sake of business involvement. To marry the two entities is the most ideal situation. It's a situation both sectors of the industry should strive more diligently for."

*   *   *

JONES, David Pryce
    See PRYCE-JONES, David

*   *   *

JONES, J. Farragut
    See LEVINSON, Leonard

JONES, Penelope   1938-

PERSONAL: Born February 17, 1938, in Rochester, N.Y.; daughter of Gikas (in business) and Metaxia (Jebeles) Critikos; married Graham Starr Jones II (a patent attorney), July 5, 1959; children: Candida Starr, Kimberley Jebeles. *Education:* Smith College, B.A., 1959. *Home:* 8 Jeffrey Lane, Chappaqua, N.Y. 10514.

CAREER: Writer, 1976—. Secretary, 1959-60; Country Day Nursery, Chappaqua, N.Y., teacher, 1977-82; teacher, Bedford Christian School, 1982—. Actress with Southbury Playhouse, summer, 1974; member of Dobbs Ferry Village Players; member of board of directors, past president, and casting director and producer of Chappaqua Drama Group. Volunteer remedial reading teacher at Children's Village, 1963-65; volunteer reader for Chappaqua Library.

MEMBER: Chappaqua Garden Club.

WRITINGS—Juveniles; all published by Bradbury: *I Didn't Want to Be Nice,* 1977; *I'm Not Moving,* 1979; *Holding Together,* 1981; *The Stealing Thing,* 1983.

SIDELIGHTS: Penelope Jones writes: "I feel very strongly about the importance of children learning to love books at the preschool level. In addition to the boundless possibilities for developing the imagination, being read to gives the young child an enormous amount of assurance, understanding, and sheer pleasure, which will have positive effects throughout his life. Having this conviction, I am particularly interested in helping young children to understand that their feelings of hostility, jealousy, and fear are legitimate—everyone has them."

*   *   *

JORDAN, Leonard
    See LEVINSON, Leonard

K

KAHN, Hannah 1911-

PERSONAL: Born June 30, 1911, in New York, N.Y.; daughter of David and Sarah (Seigelbaum) Abrahams; married Frank M. Kahn (deceased); children: Melvin A., Daniel Lyon, Vivian Dale. *Education:* Florida Atlantic University, B.A., 1972; also attended Miami Dade Community College. *Politics:* Liberal Democrat. *Religion:* Jewish. *Home:* 3301 Northeast 5th Ave., Apt. 318, Miami, Fla. 33137.

CAREER: Whitecraft Industries, Miami, Fla., interior decorator, beginning 1937. Guest lecturer at Barry College; poet in residence, College of Du Page; teacher of creative writing at Miami Dade Community College, 1972-73. Has conducted poetry seminars for Southeast Writers Conference and at Armstrong College. Past member of board of directors of Florida Council for Retarded Children.

MEMBER: Academy of American Poets (member of advisory board), Poetry Society of America (southern vice-president), Poetry Society of Virginia, Poetry Society of Georgia, Dade County Association for Retarded Citizens (charter member; past president), Phi Lambda Phi.

AWARDS, HONORS: Winner of more than twenty-five awards for poetry from societies in Virginia, Florida, and Georgia, and from *Lyric* magazine; winner of International Sonnet Competition, Poetry Society of Great Britain and America; winner of annual award, Poetry Society of America.

WRITINGS: Eve's Daughter (poems), Hurricane House, 1963, 5th edition, privately printed, 1981; (editor with Orma Jean Surbey) *Wind Song* (poems), Olivant, 1969; *Time, Wait* (poems), University Presses of Florida, 1983.

Represented in anthologies, including *I Hear My Sisters Saying*, Crowell, and *Poetry: The Essence of Being Human*, McGraw. Contributor of more than four hundred poems to periodicals, including *Harper's, Saturday Review, Commonweal, Saturday Evening Post, American Scholar*, and *New York Times*. Former poetry review editor for *Miami Herald*.

SIDELIGHTS: "A willingness to probe the blackness, to find sweetness where others might not, gives [Hannah Kahn] the poet's edge over the rest of us," according to Georgia Tasker in the *Miami Herald*. "Using herself as a catalyst," continues Tasker, "she both lives her feelings and steps away to describe them. She tempers theatricalities, however, with common sense and a sureness that her aim is true when it comes to expressing certain emotions. It is because you know that her poetry flows from the spring of her own experience that you let her get away with it." Describing Kahn's collection of poems entitled *Eve's Daughter*, Tasker remarks: "Some of them sing with pure sentiment; a few are merely singsong. Yet, there is enough of the woman coming through the book, revealed and vulnerable, that you respect her enormously for her grace and forgive her blunders."

Kahn explained to *CA:* "Ever since I was a child I loved poetry, but it never occurred to me that I might myself someday be a poet. I had little formal education; went to work when I was fifteen. Though born in New York, I lived in a small town from ages twelve to fifteen. I was ill during those years and did not attend high school (which was five miles away). I had acceptances from literary magazines such as *American Scholar* before I continued my education. At the age of fifty I started—one night a week—taking classes at Miami Dade Community College. Twelve years later at age sixty-two I got my degree."

BIOGRAPHICAL/CRITICAL SOURCES: William G. Doster, editor, *The Differing Eye*, Glencoe Press, 1970; Richard P. Janero and D. E. Gearhart, editors, *Human Worth*, Holt, 1972; *Miami Herald*, March 21, 1976; *Authors in the News*, Volume II, Gale, 1976.

*　　*　　*

KAISER, Harvey H. 1936-

PERSONAL: Born July 8, 1936, in New York, N.Y.; son of Jerome (a carpenter) and Rachel T. (a bookkeeper) Kaiser; married Linda Pembroke (a physical therapist), September 20, 1960; children: Sven-Erik, Robert, Christina. *Education:* Rensselaer Polytechnic Institute, B.Arch., 1959; Syracuse University, M.Arch., 1965, Ph.D., 1974. *Home:* 304 Brookford Rd., Syracuse, N.Y. 13224. *Office:* Syracuse University, Syracuse, N.Y. 13210.

CAREER: Architect in Goteborg, Sweden, 1960-61; Sargent, Webster, Crenshaw & Foley, Syracuse, N.Y., associate partner, 1962-72; Syracuse University, Syracuse, associate professor of architecture and vice-president for facilities administration, 1973—. Private architecture practice in Syracuse, 1970-72. President of Urbanistics, Inc.; member of board of directors, Syracuse University Theatre Corporation; member of board of trustees of Everson Museum of Art and of Russell Sage College. Consultant, U.S. Department of Justice and other agencies. *Military service:* U.S. Army Reserve, 1959-67; became captain.

MEMBER: American Institute of Architects, American Planning Association, American Institute of Consulting Planners, American Institute of Certified Planners, Association of University Architects, Association for the Protection of the Adirondacks, National Trust for Historic Preservation, National Association of College and University Business Officers, National Council of Architecture Registration Boards, Association of Physical Plant Administrators of Universities and Colleges.

AWARDS, HONORS: American-Scandinavian fellowship, 1960-61; National Endowment for the Arts fellowship, 1978-79, 1983-84; Academy for Educational Development fellowship, 1980-81.

WRITINGS: The Building of Cities: Development and Conflict, Cornell University Press, 1978; *Mortgaging the Future: The Cost of Deferring Maintenance,* Association of Physical Plant Administrators of Universities and Colleges, 1979; *Managing Facilities More Effectively: New Directions in Higher Education,* Jossey-Bass, 1980; *Facilities Audit Workbook,* Association of Governing Boards of Universities and Colleges, 1982; *Great Camps of the Adirondacks,* Godine, 1982; *Crumbling Academe: Capital Renewal and Replacement in Higher Education,* Association of Governing Boards of Universities and Colleges, 1984. Contributor of articles to periodicals, including *New York Times, House Beautiful, Old House Journal, Historic Preservation,* and *Signature.*

WORK IN PROGRESS: Landmarks in the Landscape, a study of public policy needed to preserve historic architecture in the western U.S. national parks.

SIDELIGHTS: Harvey H. Kaiser told *CA:* "My passion as an architect-social scientist is to encourage public policy for the preservation of historic architecture in rural and urban settings by combining writing and photography. Related to this is publishing guidance for higher education facilities management in stewardship of campus environments."

*   *   *

KAMM, (Jan) Dorinda   1952-

PERSONAL: Born October 17, 1952, in Hempstead, N.Y.; daughter of John Frederick (an accountant) and Janice (Snediker) Kamm. *Education:* Graduated from high school in Franklin Square, New York. *Home:* 82 New Hyde Park Rd., Franklin Sq., New York, N.Y. 11010.

CAREER: Writer.

WRITINGS—Published by Zebra Books, except as indicated: *Cliff's Head* (gothic novel), Lenox Hill, 1972; *Devil's Doorstep* (gothic novel), Lenox Hill, 1973; *The Marly Stones* (murder mystery), 1977; *Drearloch* (romantic suspense novel), 1978; *Shadow Game* (romantic suspense novel), 1979; *Kingsroads Legacy* (suspense novel), 1981.

WORK IN PROGRESS: Editing a mystery, *The Tenth Rook,* for Kensington Publishing.

SIDELIGHTS: Dorinda Kamm told *CA* that, as a young writer, she feels that what she produces in her early years is especially important. She sees it as an encouragement to others her age who want to write yet lack the direction to achieve something.

Kamm feels that many beginning writers think they lack the maturity and education to attempt a writing career. She thinks they should work *now,* "when the desire is greatest and the reward is so much sweeter."

AVOCATIONAL INTERESTS: Reading, collecting poetry, animals, long walks.

*   *   *

KAMRANY, Nake M.   1934-

PERSONAL: Born August 29, 1934, in Kabul, Afghanistan; son of Shair M. and Fia (Farukh) Kamrany; married Barbara Gehlke, December 6, 1957 (divorced September, 1967); married Sajia Walizada, November 12, 1978; children: (first marriage) Shair John, Lilia Joy; (second marriage) Dennis Wali. *Education:* University of California, Los Angeles, B.S., 1959; University of Southern California, M.A. and Ph.D., 1962; University of West Los Angeles, J.D., 1981. *Home:* 201 Ocean Ave., Santa Monica, Calif. 90402. *Office:* Department of Economics, University of Southern California, Los Angeles, Calif. 90089.

CAREER: University of Southern California, Los Angeles, lecturer, 1960-62, assistant professor of economics, 1962-63; Battelle Memorial Institute, Columbus, Ohio, senior economist, 1963-65; University of Southern California, associate professor of economics, 1965-66; System Development Corp., Santa Monica, Calif., senior social scientist, 1965-69; International Bank for Reconstruction and Development (World Bank), Washington, D.C., senior economist, 1969-71; University of Southern California, associate professor, 1971-72, director of economic research and professor of economics, Information Sciences Institute, 1972—, currently director of Program in Productivity and Technology. Visiting professor, University of California, Los Angeles, 1966-68. Consultant to the United Nations and the U.S. Government.

MEMBER: Society for International Development, Association for Asian Studies, American Economic Association, Association for Comparative Economics, Association for Afghanistan Studies.

AWARDS, HONORS: Clune Award of University of Southern California, 1960, 1961, 1962.

WRITINGS: (Contributor) H. R. Hamilton, editor, *Systems Simulation for Regional Analysis,* MIT Press, 1968; *Peaceful Competition in Afghanistan: American and Soviet Models for Economic Aid,* Communication Service Corp., 1969; (with John Elliott) *Technology, Productivity, and Public Policy: A National Needs Analysis,* Center for Policy Alternatives, Massachusetts Institute of Technology, 1975; (editor) *The New Economics of the Less Developed Countries: Changing Perceptions in the North-South Dialogue,* Westview, 1978; *International Economic Reform,* University Press of America, 1977; *The New Economics of the Less Developed Countries,* Westview Press, 1978.

Economic Issues of the Eighties, Johns Hopkins University Press, 1980; *U.S. Options for Energy Independence,* Lexington Books, 1982. Contributor of articles and reviews to journals in his field.

WORK IN PROGRESS: Economic Systems Revisited.

SIDELIGHTS: Nake M. Kamrany told *CA:* "[I] write to express and record my ideas concerning the major issues confronting the individual, the family, the city, the nation, and the international community. This pursuit draws me into a continuous questioning of the role of men and women to achieve a dynamic definition of the quality of life.''

*   *   *

KANET, Roger E(dward) 1936-

PERSONAL: Born September 1, 1936, in Cincinnati, Ohio; son of Robert George (a skilled worker) and Edith Mary (Weaver) Kanet; married Joan Alice Edwards (a registered nurse and hospital administrator), February 16, 1963; children: Suzanne Elise, Laurie Alice. Education: Xavier University, Cincinnati, Ohio, A.B., 1961; Berchmanskolleg, Pullach/Munich, Germany, Ph.B., 1960; Lehigh University, M.A., 1963; Princeton University, A.M., 1965, Ph.D., 1966. Religion: Roman Catholic. Home: 1007 South Victor St., Champaign, Ill. 61821. Office: Department of Political Science, University of Illinois at Urbana-Champaign, Urbana, Ill. 61801.

CAREER: University of Kansas, Lawrence, assistant professor, 1966-69, associate professor of political science, 1969-74, director of undergraduate studies, 1969-70, associate chairman, 1970-71; University of Illinois at Urbana-Champaign, visiting associate professor, 1973-74, associate professor, 1974-78, professor of political science, 1978—, director of graduate studies, 1975-78. Joint senior fellow, Research Institute on Communist Affairs and Russian Institute, Columbia University, 1972-73; associate, Center for Advanced Study, University of Illinois at Urbana-Champaign, 1981-82. Member, University of Illinois at Urbana-Champaign Russian and East European Center, 1974—, Office of Arms Control, Disarmament and International Security, 1978—, African Studies Program, 1982—. Program chairman, First International Slavic Conference, 1974. Kansas State Parents' Association for Hearing-Handicapped Children, co-founder, vice-president, 1969-70, president, 1970-71.

MEMBER: International Studies Association, International Political Science Association, American Political Science Association, American Association for the Advancement of Slavic Studies (chairman of bibliography and documentation committee, 1971-74), Midwest Political Science Association, Midwest Slavic Conference (program chair, 1981), Central Slavic Conference (president, 1966-67; program chair, 1967), Kansas Political Science Association (program chairman, 1970).

AWARDS, HONORS: Grants from American Council of Learned Societies, 1972-73, 1978, NATO Faculty Research Program, 1976, and International Research and Exchanges Board, 1976; campus award for excellence in undergraduate teaching, University of Illinois at Urbana-Champaign, 1981.

WRITINGS: (Editor) The Behavioral Revolution and Communist Studies: Applications of Behaviorally Oriented Political Research on the Soviet Union and Eastern Europe, Free Press, 1971; (with others) The Political and Legal Implications of the Development and Implementation of Remote Sensing Devices, Center for Research, University of Kansas, 1971; (editor with Ivan Volgyes) On the Road to Communism: Essays on Soviet Domestic and Foreign Politics, University Press of Kansas, 1972; (editor) The Soviet Union and the Developing Nations, Johns Hopkins University Press, 1974; (compiler) Soviet and East European Foreign Policies: A Bibliography of English and Russian Language Publications, 1967-71, Clio Press, 1974.

(Editor with Donna Bahry) Soviet Economic and Political Relations with the Developing World, Praeger, 1975; (editor with Maurice D. Simon) Background to Crisis: Policy and Politics in Gierek's Poland, Westview, 1981; (editor) Soviet Foreign Policy in the 1980s, Praeger, 1982; (editor) Soviet Foreign Policy and East-West Relations, Pergamon, 1982; (with Daniel N. Nelson) Government and Politics in Eastern Europe, Westview, 1985.

Contributor: Harry G. Shaffer and Jan S. Prybyla, editors, From Underdevelopment to Affluence: Western, Soviet, and Chinese Views, Appleton, 1968; Prybyla, editor, Communism and Nationalism, Pennsylvania State University, 1969.

Erik Hoffman and Frederic Fleron, Jr., editors, The Soviet Foreign Policy Process, Aldine, 1971; Edward J. Czerwinski and Jaroslaw Piekalkiewicz, editors, The Soviet Invasion of Czechoslovakia: Its Effects on Eastern Europe, Praeger, 1972; Ellen Mickiewicz, editor, Handbook of Soviet Social Science Data, Free Press, 1973; Lenard J. Cohen and Jane P. Shapiro, editors, Communist Systems in Comparative Perspective, Anchor Books, 1974; Charles Gati, editor, The Politics of Modernization in Eastern Europe: Testing the Soviet Model, 1974; Bernard Eissenstat, editor, The Soviet Union: The Seventies and Beyond, Lexington Books, 1975; Gati, editor, The International Politics of Eastern Europe, Praeger, 1976; Francis Heller, editor, The Korean War: A Twenty-five year Perspective, Regents Press of Kansas, 1977; Jae Kyu Park and Melvin Gurtov, editors, Southeast Asia in Transition: Regional and International Politics, Kyung Nam University (Seoul), 1977; Tadao Ishikawa and Park, editors, Tenkanki no Tonan Ajia: Sekai no Ajia Mondai no Ken-i ga katuru Tonon Ajia no Tenbo, Seiko Shobo (Tokyo), 1977; Park, editor, Jeon Hwan Ki ui Dongnam Asia: Ji Yok Chungchi mit Kukje Kwan Kye, Bak Yung Sa (Seoul), 1977; Andrew Gyorgy and James A. Kuhlman, editors, Innovation in Communist Systems, Westview, 1978.

Donald R. Kelley, editor, Soviet Politics in the Brezhnev Era, Praeger, 1980; Stephen F. Cohen, Alexander Rabinowitch, and Robert Sharlet, editors, The Soviet Union Since Stalin, Indiana University Press, 1980; Warren Weinstein and Thomas H. Henriksen, editors, Soviet and Chinese Aid to African Nations, Praeger, 1980; Ronald H. Linden, editor, The Foreign Policies of East Europe: New Approaches, Praeger, 1980; Michael Radu, editor, Eastern Europe and the Third World, Praeger, 1981; W. Raymond Duncan, editor, Soviet Policy in Developing Countries, Robert E. Krieger, 1981; Henriksen, editor, Communist Powers and Sub-Saharan Africa, Hoover Institution, 1981; Robert H. Donaldson, editor, The Soviet Union and the Developing Countries: Successes and Failures, Westview, 1981; Francis Conte and Jean-Louis Martres, editors, L'Union Sovietique dans les Relations Internationales, Economica (Paris), 1982; Bruce E. Arlinghaus, editor, Arms for Africa: Military Assistance and Foreign Policy in the Developing World, Lexington Books, 1982; Georg Brunner and Horst Herlemann, editors, Sicherheitspolitik und Internationale Beziehungen der Sowjetunion, Berlin-Verlag, 1982; John F. Copper and Daniel S. Papp, editors, Communist Nations' Military Assistance, Westview, 1983; Michael J. Sodaro and Sharon L. Wolchik, editors, Foreign and Domestic Policy in Eastern Europe in the 1980s, St. Martin's, 1983.

General editor, publications from the First International Slavic Conference, 1974, Second World Congress for Soviet and East European Studies, 1980. Contributor to encyclopedias. Contributor of more than one hundred fifty articles and reviews to periodicals.

WORK IN PROGRESS: A book-length study of Soviet and East European policy in Africa.

*   *   *

KANTER, Rosabeth Moss 1943-

PERSONAL: Born March 15, 1943, in Cleveland, Ohio; daughter of Nelson Nathan (an attorney) and Helen (a teacher; maiden name, Smolen) Moss; married Stuart A. Kanter, June 15, 1963 (died March 24, 1969); married Barry A. Stein (a management consultant), July 2, 1972. *Education:* Attended University of Chicago, 1962-63; Bryn Mawr College, B.A. (magna cum laude), 1964; University of Michigan, M.A., 1965, Ph.D., 1967; post-doctoral study at Harvard University, 1975-76. *Residence:* Cambridge, Mass. *Office:* Department of Sociology, Yale University, New Haven, Conn. 06520; and Goodmeasure, Inc., P.O. Box 3004, Cambridge, Mass. 02139.

CAREER: University of Michigan, Ann Arbor, instructor in sociology, 1967; Brandeis University, Waltham, Mass., assistant professor of sociology, 1967-73; Harvard University, Cambridge, Mass., associate professor of administration, 1973-74; Brandeis University, associate professor of sociology, 1974-77; Yale University, New Haven, Conn., associate professor, 1977-78, professor of sociology, 1978—, chairman of department, 1982, chairman of University Council on Priorities and Planning, 1982-83; Goodmeasure, Inc. (management consultants), Cambridge, partner, 1977-80, chairman of the board, 1980—.

Visiting professor of organizational psychology and management, Massachusetts Institute of Technology, Sloan School of Management, 1979-80. Visiting scholar at Newberry Library, 1973, Harvard University, 1975—, and Norwegian Research Council on Science and Humanities, September, 1980. Faculty member at Young President's Organization of International University (Hong Kong), 1976; Sigma Chi scholar-in-residence, Miami University (Oxford, Ohio), October, 1978. Blazer Lecturer at University of Kentucky, 1974; Davidson Lecturer at University of New Hampshire, 1975; W. K. Kellogg Foundation Fiftieth Anniversary Lecturer, American Association for Higher Education, April, 1979. Director, American Center for Quality of Work Life, 1978-82, Educational Fund for Individual Rights, 1979-84, and National Organization for Women, Legal Defense and Education Fund, 1979—; trustee, American Leadership Forum, 1981—. Member of planning task force of Cambridge Institute's New City Project, 1969-71; expert witness before Equal Employment Opportunities Commission, 1976-77; consultant to Russell Sage Foundation, Ford Foundation, and U.S. Department of State.

MEMBER: International Association of Applied Social Scientists, American Association for Higher Education, American Sociological Association (member of executive council, 1982-85), American Orthopsychiatric Association, American Legal Studies Association, National Training Laboratories Institute for Applied Behavioral Science (dean, 1973—), Society for the Study of Social Problems, Society for the Psychological Study of Social Issues, Sociologists for Women in Society, Law and Society Association, Eastern Sociological Society (member of executive committee, 1975-78), Committee of 200 (founding member, 1982), Yale Club (New York City and New Haven).

AWARDS, HONORS: U.S. Office of Education grant, 1969-72; National Institute of Mental Health grant, 1973-74; Guggenheim fellowship, 1975-76; I. Peter Gellman Award, Eastern Sociological Society, 1978; C. Wright Mills Award of 1977, 1978, for *Men and Women of the Corporation;* William F. Donner Foundation grant, 1979-80; McKinsey Award, 1979, for article, "Power Failure in Management Circuits," in *Harvard Business Review;* Athena Award, Intercollegiate Association of Women Students, 1980; Professional Woman of the Year award, International Association of Personnel Women, 1981; Woman of the Year award, New England Women Business Owners Association, 1981; award for best article, *Hospital Forum,* 1982; Russell Sage Foundation grant, 1983-84; honorary Master of Arts degree, Yale University, 1978; honorary Doctor of Science degree, Bucknell University, 1980; honorary Doctor of Humane Letters degrees, Westminster College and Babson College, both 1984.

WRITINGS: Commitment and Community: Communes and Utopias in Sociological Perspective, Harvard University Press, 1972; (editor and contributor) *Communes: Creating and Managing the Collective Life,* Harper, 1973; (editor with Marcus Millman, and contributor) *Another Voice: Feminist Perspectives on Social Life and Social Science,* Doubleday, 1975; *Work and Family in the United States: A Critical Review and Research and Policy Agenda,* Russell Sage Foundation, 1976; *Men and Women of the Corporation,* Basic Books, 1977; (editor) *Life in Organizations,* Basic Books, 1979; *A Tale of "O",* Harper, 1980; *The Change Masters: Innovation for Productivity in the American Corporation,* Simon & Schuster, 1983.

Contributor: J. Rabow, J. A. Winter, and M. Chesler, editors, *Vital Problems for American Society,* Random House, 1968; C. G. Bennello and D. Roussopoulos, editors, *The Case for Participatory Democracy,* Richard Grossman, 1971; M. Gordon, editor, *The Nuclear Family in Crisis,* Harper, 1972; Rabow, editor, *Sociology: Students and Society,* Goodyear Publishing, 1972; L. K. Howe, editor, *The Future of the Family,* Simon & Schuster, 1972; A. Effrat, editor, *Perspectives on Political Sociology,* Bobbs-Merrill, 1972; M. P. Effrat, editor, *The Community: Approaches and Applications,* Free Press, 1974.

J. Heiss, editor, *Marriage and Family Interaction,* Rand McNally, 2nd edition (Kanter was not included in 1st edition), 1976; *Schooling and Capitalism,* Routledge & Kegan Paul, 1976; W. R. Burke, editor, *Current Issues and Strategies in Organization Development,* Behavioral Publications, 1976; W. Feigelman, editor, *Sociology Full Circle,* Praeger, 2nd edition (Kanter was not included in 1st edition), 1976; M. Rosenbaum and A. Snadowsky, editors, *The Intensive Group Experience,* Free Press, 1976; A. Sargent, editor, *Beyond Sex Roles,* West Publishing, 1976; M. Blaxall and B. Reagan, editors, *Women and the Workplace: The Implications of Occupational Segregation,* University of Chicago Press, 1976; W. R. Burke, editor, *Current Issues and Strategies in Organization Development,* Behavior Publications, 1976.

P. T. Golembiewski and A. Blumberg, editors, *Sensitivity Training and the Laboratory Approach,* 3rd edition, F. E. Peacock, 1977; G. K. Phelan, editor, *Family Relationships,* Burgess, 1978; P. Worsley, editor, *Modern Sociology: Introductory Readings,* Penguin, 1978; R. A. Farrell and V. L. Swigert, editors, *The Substance of Social Deviance,* Alfred Publishing, 1978; S. Boocock and J. Demos, editors, *Turning Points: Historical and Sociological Essays on the Family,* University of Chicago Press, 1978; D. Nichol and M. Croke, editors, *The United Nations and Decision-Making: The Role of Women,* Volume II, UNITAR, 1978.

R. L. Ellis and M. J. Lopetz, editors, *Essential Sociology*, Scott, Foresman, 1979; A. Westin, editor, *Sourcebook on Individual Rights in the Corporation*, Educational Foundation on Individual Rights, 1979; R. S. Ratner, editor, *Equal Opportunity Policy for Women*, Temple University Press, 1979; R. Alvarez and K. G. Lutterman, editors, *Discrimination in Organizations: Using Social Indicators to Manage Social Change*, Jossey-Bass, 1979; R. A. Webber, editor, *Management Pragmatics*, Irwin, 1979; G. Levinger and O. C. Moles, editors, *Divorce and Separation*, Basic, 1979; J. Case and R. Taylor, editors, *Co-ops, Communes, and Collectives*, Pantheon, 1979.

O. Grusky and G. A. Miller, editors, *The Sociology of Organizations: Basic Studies*, revised edition, Free Press, 1980; A. Etzioni and E. W. Lehman, editors, *Reader in Complex Organizations*, Holt, 1980; S. Graubard, editor, *A New America*, Norton, 1980; A. Westin, editor, *Individual Rights in the Corporation*, Pantheon, 1980; M. A. Morgan, editor, *Managing Organizational Careers*, Van Nostrand, 1980; J. H. Leavitt, L. R. Pondy, and D. M. Boje, *Readings in Managerial Psychology*, 3rd edition, University of Chicago Press, 1980; C. Alderfer and C. Cooper, editors, *Advances in Experiential Social Processes*, Volume II, Wiley, 1980; (author of foreword) Daniel Zwerdling, *Workplace Democracy*, Harper, 1980.

L. Richardson and V. A. Taylor, editors, *Sex and Gender Reader*, Heath, 1981; F. A. Kramer, editor, *Perspectives on Public Bureaucracy*, 3rd edition, Winthrop Publishing, 1981; *The Changing Character of the Public Workforce*, U.S. Office of Personnel Management, 1981; E. Boyer, *Common Learning: A Carnegie Colloquium on General Education*, Carnegie Foundation, 1981; Kahn-Hut and others, editors, *Women and Work: Problems and Perspectives*, Oxford University Press, 1982; J. Rothschild-Whitt and F. Lindenfields, editors, *Workplace Democracy*, Porter Sargent, 1982; F. S. Lane, editor, *Current Issues in Public Administration*, St. Martin's, 1982; P. Stewart and M. Cantor, editors, *Work and Occupations: Autonomy, Power and Control*, Sage, 1982; D. Perlman and C. Cozby, editors, *A Social Problems Perspective on Social Psychology*, Holt, 1982.

E. G. Collins, editor, *Executive Success*, Wiley, 1983; Porter and Allen, editors, *Organizational Influence Processes*, Scott, Foresman, 1983; W. B. Littrell, G. Sjobert, and L. A. Zurcher, editors, *Bureaucracy as a Social Problem*, Jai Press, 1983; Richard G. Hamermesh, editor, *Strategic Management*, Wiley, 1983; Z. Rubin, *Doing unto Others*, Prentice-Hall, 1984; E. Carmen and P. Ricker, editors, *The Gender Gap and Psychotherapy*, Plenum, 1984; P. Osterman, editor, *Internal Labor Markets*, MIT Press, 1984; J. Kimberly and R. Quinn, editors, *New Futures: The Challenge of Transition Management*, Irwin-Dorsey, 1984; W. Powell and P. DiMaggion, editors, *Handbook of Nonprofit Organizations*, Yale University Press, 1985.

Contributor of about fifty articles and reviews to sociology, education, psychology, and psychiatry journals. Member of editorial boards of *Journal of Applied Behavioral Science*, 1970-73, "Rose Monograph Series," American Sociological Association, 1973-76, *American Sociologist*, 1976-78, *Administrative Science Quarterly*, 1979-82, *Human Resource Management*, 1982—, and *Organizational Dynamics*, 1983—. Associate editor, *Sociological Symposium*, 1972-76, *Sociological Inquiry*, 1973-76, and *American Sociological Review*, 1978-81. Consulting editor, *Journal of Voluntary Action Research*, 1972-76, and *American Journal of Sociology*, 1975-77; contributing editor, *Working Papers for a New Society*, 1977-80.

SIDELIGHTS: "All her adult life, [Rosabeth Moss] Kanter, a highly respected management consultant, has studied that traditionally amorphous institution, the corporation, trying to understand it, to explain it, and, ultimately, to make it a better place for everyone," writes Carol Kleiman in the *Chicago Tribune*. Kanter's *The Change Masters: Innovation for Productivity in the American Corporation* is "an effort to discover why some firms succeed in maintaining innovation and growth while others retard individual initiative." Tom Redburn, commenting in the *Los Angeles Times*, goes on to say that the book "provides some of the most revealing glimpses into the day-to-day workings of several successful companies." "To the layman," states Anatole Broyard, "'The Change Masters' explains a great deal and does it very persuasively." The *New York Times* critic adds, "Though Miss Kanter sometimes uses the word innovation as if it were a mantra, it may well be."

Kanter's main point, in both her work as a consultant and her writings, is that most corporate structures impede communication between upper echelon executives and workers. Workers feel cut off from decision making and problem solving. Believing they are powerless, they end up as either "movers," those obviously slated for promotion to positions of increasing power, or "stuck" workers, who continue to perform (often less and less productively) but realize the future holds no more than an automatic raise every twelve months. Management, while wielding power in the eyes of the workers, actually is caught in the middle. Managers are in the position of passing along information and enforcing decisions with which they had little or nothing to do. They appear powerful but usually don't know what the future holds. Kanter told Kleiman that "to her, the ideal corporate state is one in which executives in lofty positions get to know their employes, where they can relax and communicate with them—and where employes can do the same. 'We are all people,' says Kanter, 'people of the organization.'" The author explains: "'I realized very early in college that corporations are among the most powerful entities in society, and if you care about how the world is run, you have to find out about them. My interest has always been in how a complex world is put together.'"

BIOGRAPHICAL/CRITICAL SOURCES: Washington Post Book World, July 3, 1977; *Chicago Tribune*, May 6, 1979; *New York Times*, August 27, 1983; *New York Times Book Review*, October 16, 1983; *Los Angeles Times*, October 20, 1983.

*   *   *

KAPLAN, Fred 1937-

PERSONAL: Born November 4, 1937, in Bronx, N.Y.; son of Isaac (an attorney) and Bessie (Zwirn) Kaplan; married Gloria Taplin (a teacher), May 28, 1959; children: Benjamin, Noah, Julia. *Education:* Brooklyn College (now Brooklyn College of the City University of New York), B.A., 1959; Columbia University, M.A., 1961, Ph.D., 1966. *Home:* 42 Highland Place, Great Neck, N.Y. 11020. *Office:* Department of English, Queens College of the City University of New York, Flushing, N.Y. 11367; and Graduate School and University Center of the City University of New York, 33 West 42nd St., New York, N.Y. 10036.

CAREER: Lawrence University, Appleton, Wis., instructor in English, 1962-64; California State College (now University), Los Angeles, assistant professor of English, 1964-67; City University of New York, Queens College, Flushing, N.Y., associate professor, 1967-71, professor of English, 1971—, Graduate School and University Center, New York, N.Y., professor of English, 1979—. Fulbright professor, University of Copenhagen, 1973-74.

MEMBER: Modern Language Association of America, Dickens Society, Tennyson Society.

AWARDS, HONORS: City University of New York research grant, 1968-69, 1976-78, 1980-85; Guggenheim fellow, 1976-77; National Endowment for the Humanities, fellowship at Huntington Library, 1981-82, grant, 1983; *Thomas Carlyle: A Biography* was a nominee for National Book Critics Circle award, 1983, and a jury-nominated finalist for Pulitzer Prize, 1984.

WRITINGS: Miracles of Rare Device: The Poet's Sense of Self in Nineteenth-Century Poetry, Wayne State University Press, 1972; *The Hidden Springs of Fiction: Dickens and Mesmerism,* Princeton University Press, 1975.

(Editor) *Dickens' Book of Memoranda: A Photographic and Typographic Facsimile of the Notebook Begun in January, 1855,* New York Public Library, 1981; (editor) *John Elliotson on Mesmerism,* Da Capo Press, 1982; *Thomas Carlyle: A Biography,* Cornell University Press, 1983; (general editor) *The Readers' Advisor,* 13th edition, Bowker, 1985; *Sacred Tears: Sentimentality in Dickens, Thackeray and Carlyle,* University of California Press, 1985; (editor) *Carlyle's "The French Revolution,"* annotated edition, University of California Press, 1985.

Contributor to *Studies in English Literature, Nineteenth-Century Fiction, Victorian Newsletter, Journal of the History of Ideas, Dickens Studies Annual,* and *Carlyle Newsletter.* Editor, *Dickens Studies Annual,* 1980-85.

WORK IN PROGRESS: Charles Dickens: A Biography, for Morrow.

SIDELIGHTS: Fred Kaplan's *Thomas Carlyle: A Biography,* "tells the story of Carlyle's life with descriptive skill, conviction and a sure sense of history," comments Donald Thomas in a *New York Times Book Review* article. As John Clive notes in the *Times Literary Supplement,* Kaplan focuses on Carlyle's childhood in Scotland, his strained marriage, and his chronic gastric disorders, but offers little detail of his works. Carlyle's complicated personality has inspired extreme opinions on his life and works, but of Kaplan Clive writes, "He is sympathetic to his subject, but at the same time does not let his judgements depend on any particular bias." Maureen Corrigan observes in a *Village Voice* article that Kaplan's *Thomas Carlyle* "doubtless will be the definitive [Carlyle] biography for decades, displacing the one written by James Anthony Froude in 1884."

BIOGRAPHICAL/CRITICAL SOURCES: Times Literary Supplement, April 2, 1976, June 3, 1983, April 20, 1984; *Sewanee Review,* October, 1977; *Modern Language Review,* April, 1978; *Washington Post Book World,* August 15, 1982; *New York Times Book Review,* January 8, 1984; *New Yorker,* January 16, 1984; *Los Angeles Times Book Review,* January 29, 1984: *Village Voice,* February 21, 1984.

*   *   *

KARKALA, John A.
   See ALPHONSO-KARKALA, John B.

*   *   *

KARKALA, John B. A.
   See ALPHONSO-KARKALA, John B.

KATZ, John Stuart 1938-

PERSONAL: Born June 21, 1938, in Cincinnati, Ohio; son of Maurice G. (a sales representative) and Helen (Klein) Katz; married second wife, Judith T. Milstein (a professor and psychologist), October 1, 1967; children: (second marriage) Jesse. *Education:* Miami University, Oxford, Ohio, B.A., 1960; Columbia University, M.A., 1961; Harvard University, Ed.D., 1967. *Home:* 37 Colin Ave., Toronto, Ontario, Canada. *Office:* Department of Film, Faculty of Fine Arts, York University, Toronto, Ontario, Canada.

CAREER: High school English teacher in Watertown, Mass., 1962-63; Harvard resident supervisor, public schools of Newton, Mass., 1965-67; University of Toronto, Toronto, Ontario, assistant professor of education at Ontario Institute for Studies in Education, 1967-71, director of film-literature study project, 1967-71; York University, Toronto, Ontario, visiting lecturer, 1971, associate professor of film, 1972—, chairman of department, 1974-78. Visiting scholar, University of California, Berkeley, 1976-77, New York University, 1983-84. Member of Canadian selection committee, UNESCO International Centre of Films for Children and Young People. Broadcaster of weekly radio reviews on Canadian Broadcasting Corp. Member of board of directors, John Grierson Film Seminars, 1964-66, Toronto Film Society, 1968-70, Canadian Film Institute, 1975-77, and Young Filmmakers' Exchange. Member, International Seminar on Teaching of English (York, England), 1971. Programmer and director of film festivals, seminars and conferences.

MEMBER: Modern Language Association of America, University Film Association, Society for Cinema Studies, American Educational Theater Association, Phi Delta Kappa.

AWARDS, HONORS: British Council fellowship, 1967.

WRITINGS: (With Joseph Hansen and others) *A Folklore-Mythology Based Curriculum,* Newton School Foundation, 1966; (contributor) *Screen Education in Canadian Schools,* Canadian Education Association, 1969; (contributor) Bruce Rusk, Tim Hardy, and Bill Tooley, editors, *The Student and the System,* Ontario Institute for Studies in Education, 1970; (editor and contributor) *Perspectives on the Study of Film,* Little, Brown, 1971; (contributor) *Challenge and Change in the Teaching of English,* Allyn & Bacon, 1971; (with Curt Oliver and Forbes Aird) *A Curriculum in Film,* Ontario Institute for Studies in Education, 1972; (contributor) *Popular Media and the Teaching of English,* Goodyear Publishing, 1972; (editor and contributor) *Autobiography: Film, Video, Photography,* Art Gallery of Ontario, 1978; (editor with Jay Ruby and Larry Gross) *Image Ethics,* Longman, in press.

Producer and co-director of documentary films; producer of student-made films. Contributor of about twenty-five articles and reviews to journals. Member of editorial board, *Harvard Educational Review,* 1966-67, *Studies in·Visual Communications,* 1981—; editorial consultant, *Journal of Aesthetic Education,* 1972-75.

WORK IN PROGRESS: "Issac Littlefeather," a film.

*   *   *

KEALEY, Edward J(oseph) 1936-

PERSONAL: Born August 1, 1936, in New York, N.Y.; son of John E. and Margaret (Lyon) Kealey. *Education:* Manhattan College, A.B., 1958; Johns Hopkins University, M.A. and

Ph.D., 1962. *Religion:* Roman Catholic. *Home:* 5639 186th St., Fresh Meadows, N.Y. 11365. *Office:* Department of History, College of the Holy Cross, Worcester, Mass. 01610.

CAREER: College of the Holy Cross, Worcester, Mass., 1962—, began as associate professor, member of faculty in Labor Relations Institute, 1965—, professor of history, 1973—, chairman of department, 1980-83. Lecturer at University of Massachusetts Labor Relations Institute, 1969-74, and St. Edmund's House, Cambridge University, 1977-80. Parliamentarian, American Postal Workers of Massachusetts, 1974—.

MEMBER: American Historical Association, Medieval Academy of America, Catholic Historical Association, Society for Values in Higher Education, Conference of British Studies, Haskins Society (councillor and trustee, 1980—), Massachusetts Archaeological Association.

AWARDS, HONORS: Danforth fellow, 1958-62; *Roger of Salisbury, Viceroy of England* was named "one of the best academic books of 1972" by both *America* and *Choice;* National Endowment for the Humanities summer fellow, 1976; American Philosophical Society fellow, 1980; honorable mention in Alpha Sigma Nu national book award competition for *Medieval Medicus: A Social History of Anglo-Norman Medicine.*

WRITINGS: Roger of Salisbury, Viceroy of England, University of California Press, 1972; *Medieval Medicus: A Social History of Anglo-Norman Medicine,* Johns Hopkins University Press, 1981; *Windmill Pioneers in Twelfth-Century England,* University of California Press, 1985. Contributor to encyclopedias. Contributor of over 100 articles and book reviews to periodicals.

WORK IN PROGRESS: Anglo-Norman Studies and *British and New World Archaeology.*

SIDELIGHTS: Edward J. Kealey told *CA* he is "fascinated by the people and events of the twelfth century and by describing their experience with insight and grace. I enjoy documentary research, archaeological excavation, public lecturing, and historical composition. Soon, I also want to try my hand at narrative poetry and creative fiction."

BIOGRAPHICAL/CRITICAL SOURCES: Times Literary Supplement, March 5, 1982.

*   *   *

KEEBLE, John   1944-

PERSONAL: Born November 24, 1944, in Winnipeg, Manitoba, Canada; naturalized U.S. citizen; son of Raymond Charles William and Olivia (Wallace) Keeble; married Claire Sheldon (a violist), September 4, 1964; children: Jonathan Sheldon, Ezekiel Jerome, Carson R. C. *Education:* University of Redlands, B.A. (magna cum laude), 1966; University of Iowa, M.F.A., 1969. *Politics:* "No comment." *Religion:* "No comment." *Address:* R.R. 2, Box 147-2, Medical Lake, Wash. 99022. *Agent:* Georges Borchardt, Georges Borchardt, Inc., 136 East 57th St., New York, N.Y. 10022.

CAREER: Grinnell College, Grinnell, Iowa, member of staff, 1969-72, writer-in-residence, 1971-72; Eastern Washington University, Cheney, Wash., assistant professor, 1973-77, associate professor of English, 1977—, director of creative writing program, 1982-83.

AWARDS, HONORS: Trustee's Medal, Eastern Washington University, 1980; Guggenheim fellowship, 1982-83.

WRITINGS: (Contributor) *Works in Progress, No. 1,* Literary Guild of America, 1970; *Crab Canyon* (novel), Grossman, 1971; (with Ransom Jeffery) *Mine* (novel), Grossman, 1974; (contributor) Theodore Solotaroff, editor, *American Review, No. 25,* Bantam, 1976; *Yellowfish* (novel), Harper & Row, 1981; (contributor) John Witte, editor, *Dialogues with Northwest Writers: Interviews with Nine Writers, Including Tom Robbins, Mary Barnard, and Richard Hugo,* Northwest Review Books, 1982. Also author of play, "Salt," first performed in New York by The Shade Co., 1975.

WORK IN PROGRESS: A novel, *Ghost Versions,* for Harper & Row.

SIDELIGHTS: John Keeble's *Yellowfish* "is a novel of self-discovery disguised as a thriller," writes Rick DeMarinis in the *Chicago Tribune Book World.* "This is not to say that it fails on either level. On the contrary, John Keeble has managed to convince us that the act of self-discovery is a thrilling, dangerous adventure." The story of a smuggler, Wesley Erks, and his attempt to transport four illegal aliens from British Columbia to San Francisco, *Yellowfish* has been praised for its evocative portrait of the landscape and history of the Pacific Northwest. "The smuggler's route from Vancouver to San Francisco," says Jay Tolson in the *Washington Post,* "provides the occasion for an elaborate discourse on the land—the forests and glaciers, the orchard country, the high desert stretching from Washington to Nevada, the great rivers and mountains— as well as its people and history. An amateur historian, Erks possesses a wealth of information, and his musings, whether they concern the folkways and lore of Native Americans, the travel narratives of early explorers and settlers, or the elaborate patterns of human migration, provide a kind of historical analogue to the central action deepening the significance of the journey."

Los Angeles Times critic Ralph B. Sipper finds the combination of landscape and plot in *Yellowfish* unsatisfactory, and feels that what he describes as "a serious attempt to reflect on huge chunks of Pacific Northwest History" detracts from the novel. "What might have been a competent, fully realized thriller," he continues, "caves in under the ponderous weight of its intentions." De Marinis, however, insists that Keeble's use of setting and history is essential to his story. "In the adventure stories that last, the ones we come back to again and again," he argues, "the lure is this: The exterior odyssey is ultimately interior, and the demons we encounter are the ones that live within us, dictating our lives. John Keeble," he concludes, "has gone after this oldest of themes and has come back with the gold."

BIOGRAPHICAL/CRITICAL SOURCES: Time, February 2, 1980; *New York Times Book Review,* February 10, 1980; *Newsweek,* February 11, 1980; *Los Angeles Times,* February 14, 1980; *Chicago Tribune Book World,* February 17, 1980; *Washington Post,* March 24, 1980; *New Yorker,* April 28, 1980.

*   *   *

KEELING, E. B.
See CURL, James Stevens

*   *   *

KELEMAN, Stanley   1931-

PERSONAL: Born November 17, 1931, in Brooklyn, N.Y.; son of Joe and Rose (Cohen) Keleman; married Gail Hughes;

children: Katherine, Leah, Robert. *Education:* Attended Adelphi University, 1950; Chiropractic Institute of New York, D.C., 1954; attended Alfred Adler Institute, 1960-62. *Office:* 2045 Francisco St., Berkeley, Calif. 94709.

CAREER: Somatic psychologist, philosopher, and former bioenergetic trainer in private practice, Berkeley, Calif., 1968—. Lecturer at colleges and associations.

WRITINGS: Sexuality, Self, and Survival, Lodestar, 1970, 2nd edition published as *The Human Ground: Sexuality, Self, and Survival,* Science & Behavior Books, 1975; *Your Body Speaks Its Mind: The Bio-Energetic Way to Greater Emotional and Sexual Satisfaction,* Simon & Schuster, 1975; *Living Your Dying,* Random House, 1976; *Somatic Reality,* Center Press, 1979; *In Defense of Heterosexuality,* Center Press, 1982; *Emotional Anatomy,* Center Press, 1985.

AVOCATIONAL INTERESTS: Metal sculpting, public speaking, swimming.

*   *   *

KENNEDY, William   1928-

PERSONAL: Born January 16, 1928, in Albany, N.Y.; son of William J. (a deputy sheriff) and Mary (a secretary; maiden name, McDonald) Kennedy; married Ana Daisy (Dana) Sosa (a former actress and dancer); children: Dana, Katherine, Brendan. *Education:* Siena College, B.A., 1949. *Home address:* R.D. 3, Box 508, Averill Park, N.Y. 12018. *Agent:* Liz Darhansoff, 1220 Park Ave., New York, N.Y. 10028. *Office:* Department of English, State University of New York at Albany, 1400 Washington Ave., Albany, N.Y. 12222.

CAREER: Post Star, Glen Falls, N.Y., assistant sports editor and columnist, 1949-50; *Times-Union,* Albany, N.Y., reporter, 1952-56; *Puerto Rico World Journal,* San Juan, assistant managing editor and columnist, 1956; Miami *Herald,* Miami, Fla., reporter, 1957; correspondent for Time-Life publications in Puerto Rico, and reporter for Dorvillier (business) newsletter and Knight Newspapers, 1957-59; *Star,* San Juan, Puerto Rico, founding managing editor, 1959-61; full-time fiction writer, 1961-63; *Times-Union,* Albany, special writer, 1963-70, and film critic, 1968-70; book editor of *Look* magazine, 1971; State University of New York at Albany, lecturer, 1974-82, professor of English, 1983—.

Writer's Institute at Albany, founder, 1983, director, 1984—. Visiting professor of English, Cornell University, 1982-83. Cofounder, Cinema 750 film society, Rensselaer, N.Y., 1968-70; organizing moderator for series of forums on the humanities, sponsored by National Endowment for the Humanities, New York State Library, and Albany Public Library. Panelist, New York State Council on the Arts, 1980-83. *Military service:* U.S. Army, 1950-52; served as sports editor and columnist for Army newspapers; became sergeant.

MEMBER: Writers Guild of America, P.E.N.

AWARDS, HONORS: Award for reporting, Puerto Rican Civic Association (Miami, Fla.), 1957; Page One Award, Newspaper Guild, 1965, for reporting; the *Times-Union* won the New York State Publishers Award for Community Service, 1965, on the basis of several of Kennedy's articles on Albany's slums; NAACP award, 1965, for reporting; Writer of the Year Award, Friends of the Albany Public Library, 1975; D.H.L., Russell Sage College, 1980; National Endowment for the Arts fellowship, 1981; MacArthur Foundation fellowship, 1983; *Ironweed* was

named best book of fiction by the National Book Critics Circle, 1983, and one of 1983's thirteen best books by the *New York Times Book Review;* Pulitzer Prize for fiction, 1984, for *Ironweed;* New York State Governor's Arts Award; honored by the citizens of Albany and the State University of New York at Albany with a "William Kennedy's Albany" celebration, September 6-9, 1984.

WRITINGS—Novels, except as indicated: *The Ink Truck,* Dial Press, 1969, reprinted, Viking, 1984; *Legs,* Coward, 1975; (contributor) *Gabriel Garcia Marquez* (criticism), Taurus Ediciones, 1982; *Billy Phelan's Greatest Game,* Viking, 1978; *Ironweed,* Viking, 1983; *O Albany!: An Urban Tapestry* (nonfiction), Viking, 1983. Also co-author, with Francis Ford Coppola, of screenplay "The Cotton Club," 1984; author of screenplay "Legs," for Gene Kirkwood; author of unpublished novel *The Angels and the Sparrows;* author of monographs and brochures for New York State Department of Education, New York State University System, New York Governor's Conference on Libraries, Empire State College, Schenectady Museum, and New York State Library.

Contributor of short fiction to journals, including *San Juan Review, Epoch,* and *Harper's;* contributor of articles, interviews, and reviews to periodicals, including *New York Times Magazine, National Observer, New York Times Book Review, Washington Post Book World, New Republic,* and *Look.*

WORK IN PROGRESS: Quinn's Book, a novel set in Albany from 1849 to 1870, featuring ancestors of the Albany cycle characters; screenplay adaptations of *Billy Phelan's Greatest Game* and *Ironweed.*

SIDELIGHTS: William Kennedy has made Albany, New York, the subject of his three "Albany cycle" novels, *Legs, Billy Phelan's Greatest Game,* and the Pulitzer Prize-winning *Ironweed,* as well as his first novel, *The Ink Truck,* and his recent collection of essays, *O Albany!: An Urban Tapestry.* "Albany is to this gifted writer what the city of Paterson [, New Jersey] was to William Carlos Williams, and like our great laureate of urban plenitude, he wrests from an unlikely source a special kind of lyricism," Joel Conarroe states in *New York Times Book Review.*

O Albany! was written before *Ironweed*'s spectacular reception secured so much long-overdue literary recognition for Kennedy; he had completed the novel, but hadn't yet published it. *Publishers Weekly* reviewer Joseph Barbato maintains that the essays in *O Albany!* now provide readers of Kennedy's novels with a "nonfiction delineation of Kennedy's imaginative source—an upstate city of politicians and hoodlums, of gambling dens and ethnic neighborhoods, which for all its isolation remains, he insists 'as various as the American psyche' and rich in stories and characters." Christopher Lehmann-Haupt agrees in the *New York Times* that "even more absorbing than the detail and the enthusiasm is the raw material of Mr. Kennedy's fiction, present on every page [of the essays]. Even if one doesn't give a damn for Albany, it is always interesting to watch the author's imagination at play in the city and its history, for one is witnessing the first steps in a novelist's creative process." As Kennedy explains in his introduction to *O Albany!,* "I write this book not as a booster of Albany, which I am, nor as an apologist for the city, which I sometimes am, but rather as a person whose imagination has become fused with a single place, and in that place finds all the elements that a man ever needs for the life of the soul."

Legs, Billy Phelan's Greatest Game, and *Ironweed* are all set in the Albany of the 1930's. Margaret Croyden states in *New*

York Times Magazine that the books "are inexorably linked to [Kennedy's] native city, particularly during the Depression years, when Albany was a wide-open city, run by Irish bosses and their corrupt political machine. This sense of place, one of the most important factors in his books, gives Kennedy's work a rich texture, a deep sense of authenticity." *New York Times* writer Susan Chira adds that Albany, "often dismissed by outsiders as provincial and drab, lives in Mr. Kennedy's acclaimed fiction as a raucous town that symbolizes all that was glorious and corrupt, generous and sordid in the America of the 20's and 30's."

For example, *Ironweed*, "which refers to a tough-stemmed member of the sunflower family," according to Lehmann-Haupt, "recounts a few days in the life of an Albany skid-row bum, a former major-league [baseball player] with a talent for running, particularly running away, although his ambition now, at the height of the Depression, has been scaled down to the task of getting through the next 20 minutes or so." Once Phelan ran from Albany after he threw a rock at a scab and killed him during a trolley strike, setting off a riot, but he was later in the habit of leaving the town and his family to play in the leagues every baseball season. Then he accidentally dropped his newborn son—breaking his neck and killing him—while attempting to change the child's diapers; he picked the baby up by the diapers, as he had done with his other two children, and the safety pin broke. So Francis ran from town and abandoned his family for good.

Now Phelan is back in Albany after a twenty-two year hiatus, reports *New York Review of Books* critic Robert Towers, "lurching around the missions and flophouses of the city's South End." He begins a job as a grave-digger, in the words of *Washington Post* reviewer Curt Suplee, "lost in a boozy nimbus of voices and visions." On a cold Halloween night and the following All Saints' Day in 1938, the weekend of Orson Welles's "War of the Worlds" broadcast, Phelan "encounters the ghosts of his friends, relatives, and murder victims, who shout at him on buses, appear in saloons wearing corsages, talk with him from their graves in St. Agnes's cemetery," comments Mark Caldwell in *Village Voice Literary Supplement*. Lehmann-Haupt reports that the plot culminates in "a violent showdown between a gang of marauding American Legionnaires and a handful of derelicts in a hobo jungle."

Discussing *Ironweed* in an interview with Croyden, Kennedy stated that writers he has valued "always drew upon the specifics of their experience, not free-floating value judgements but the specific of Algeria in Camus, for instance, or the war in Hemingway. . . . The specifics in 'Ironweed'—the traction strike, professional baseball, Irish immigrant experiences, a vast Irish cemetery, an Irish neighborhood, the Erie Canal and so forth—are the elements of life in Albany. Some people say that 'Ironweed' might have had any setting, and perhaps this is true. But the values that emerged are peculiar to my own town and to my own time and would not be the same in a smaller city, or a metropolis, or a city that was not Irish, or wasn't large enough to support a skid row."

Kennedy didn't always think of Albany as a rich fictional source. He grew up in Albany, "the only child of a working-class couple from the Irish neighborhood of North Albany," according to a Boston *Globe and Mail* article, and after graduation from college worked at a small daily before spending two years as a sports writer for an Army weekly. After leaving the Army, he worked for the Albany *Times-Union,* but grew restless with the job. One day, he told Suplee, "I got a great

interview with Satchmo [Louis Armstrong]. And the editor threw it away. The guy said, 'What the hell, he's just another band leader.' . . . I knew I had to break out." Kennedy also thought the town provincial, he explained to Suplee: "I really didn't like Albany—I felt it was an old man's town, moribund, no action." He hired on at a paper in Puerto Rico, which soon flopped, and then the Miami *Herald* before working for the San Juan *Star,* where he was the founding managing editor. "I loved it," he told Suplee. "But then the shine wore off. I didn't aspire to any higher job and I knew I wanted to be a writer." So Kennedy cut his hours to devote himself to writing fiction, studying at one point with Saul Bellow, who encouraged him and helped him find an agent. "Bellow talked about character," Kennedy told a *Newsweek* interviewer. "I stewed on that one for years. He would never tell me precisely what that meant. He said, 'Talent goes a certain distance; the rest of the writer's life has to be carried forward by character.' For me, character has come to mean pursuit of the art—refusal to yield to failure."

Kennedy soon also began to learn what *New York Times Book Review* critic Herbert Mitgang calls "an old truth: the greatest fictional riches can live in the characters and neighborhoods of your own home place." When he was first a reporter in Albany, Kennedy explained to Douglas Bauer in *Washington Post Book World,* "I wrote stories on my day off and they were set in Albany and they were lousy. Then I went away, and worked in Miami and in Puerto Rico. In San Juan, I tried the same thing. I wrote stories about Puerto Rico, and I didn't like them, either. Finally, I said, the hell with it, I'm going to write about Albany and it was the first time a place truly engaged me. I think I needed to be in San Juan to sufficiently fictionalize Albany as a place. I started a novel, and every day I amazed myself at how much I knew about the people I was writing about. I had a concern for them. There was a substance to them that made some sense." As Kennedy told Chira, "I felt I had probably outgrown Albany, the way you outgrow childhood. But I hadn't. When I was writing about Puerto Rico, it was o.k., but then I began to write about Albany, and it seemed to come far more easily, with a richness that was absent in the other work. It proved to me I really didn't need to go off to these exotic places. I felt like I didn't have to go anywhere else. It was really a young writer's education in discovering his own turf."

Kennedy first returned to Albany when his father became ill. *O Albany!* is based in part upon a series of articles Kennedy wrote about city neighborhoods for the *Times-Union* in the mid-1960's, a few years after he returned for good. He concentrated on his fiction, however, supporting himself with free-lance writing and reviewing, as well as part-time journalism and teaching. Kennedy published *The Ink Truck* back then, a novel about an Albany newspaper strike featuring a main character described by *Time* reviewer R. Z. Sheppard, upon the book's reprinting in 1984, as "a columnist named Bailey, a highly sexed free spirit with a loud checkered sports jacket, a long green scarf and a chip on his shoulder as big as the state capitol." "It is my hope," Kennedy told *Library Journal* in 1969, that *The Ink Truck* "will stand as an analgesic inspiration to all weird men of good will and rotten luck everywhere." The novel, Sheppard relates, culminates in "a poignant conclusion, yet it does not show Kennedy at his full spellbinding power. Much of the book is inspired blarney, fun to read and probably fun to write."

When it was originally published, *The Ink Truck* was generally ignored but, as Kennedy indicates in *O Albany!,* he began to view his hometown as "an inexaustible context for the stories I planned to write, as abundant in mythic qualities as it was in political ambition, remarkably consequential greed and genuine fear of the Lord. I saw it as being as various as the American psyche itself, of which it was truly a crucible: It was always a melting pot for immigrants as was New York or Boston, and it epitomizes today the transfer of power from the Dutch, to the English to the ethnic coalitions." In Caldwell's words, Albany's "been run by the Dutch, the English, and the Irish, inhabited by trappers, Indians, soldiers, burghers, farmers, canal-workers, and bureaucrats. It's known every form of government from virtual fiefdom under the Dutch patroons to an old-fashioned and still surviving ward-heeling Democratic machine."

This political landscape figures prominently in Kennedy's novels. For example, in a *Time* review of *Ironweed*, Paul Gray points out that Francis Phelan "would not be [back] in Albany at all if the local Democratic machine were not offering deadbeats $5 for every time they register as voters. Francis does so 21 times before he gets caught and the politicians renege. He now owes his lawyer, who once worked for Legs Diamond, $50 for getting him off on a technicality." Kennedy wrote in *O Albany!* that "it was a common Albany syndrome for children to grow up obsessed with being a Democrat. Your identity was fixed by both religion and politics, but from the political hierarchy came the way of life: the job, the perpetuation of the job, the dole when there was no job, the loan when there was no dole, the security of the neighborhood, the new street-light, the new sidewalk, the right to run your bar after hours or to open a cardgame on the sneak. These things came to you not by right of citizenship. Republicans had no such rights. They came to you because you gave allegiance to Dan O'Connell and his party."

Kennedy's knowledge of Albany's political machinery is firsthand. A Boston *Globe and Mail* reporter indicates that "his father sold pies, cut hair, worked in a foundry, wrote illegal numbers, ran political errands for the Democratic ward heelers, and was rewarded by the Machine by being made a deputy sheriff." And, as Croyden explains, William Sr., "often took his son with him to political clubs and gambling joints where young Bill Kennedy, with his eye and ear for detail and for the tone and temper of Irish-Americans, listened and watched and remembered." Kennedy, writes Doris Grumbach in *Saturday Review*, "knows every bar, hotel, store, bowling alley, pool hall, and whorehouse that every opened in North Albany. He knows where the Irish had their picnics and parties—and what went on at them; where their churches were; where they bet on horses, played the numbers, and gathered for poker. He can re-create with absolute accuracy the city conversations at the Albany *Times-Union*," where the hero of *Billy Phelan's Greatest Game*, Martin Daugherty, works.

Kennedy tends to rely upon his own background and imagination for fictive details and has little use for extensive research. For his novel *Legs*, he said to Mitgang, "I spent a lot of time researching the gangster era, but it's the last time I ever intend to research a novel. It's a self-propelling thing to sit in a library and go down so many false trails. Too much research can overburden the imagination." *Legs*, according to Suplee, "which Kennedy wrote eight times," is a "fictional biography" of Jack 'Legs' Diamond, the "vicious" Irish-American gangster-bootlegger "who in 1931 was finally shot to death in his underwear" at an Albany rooming house. Kennedy's novel chronicles "Legs' attempts to smuggle heroin, his buying of politicians, judges and cops," and his woman-

izing, relates W. T. Lhamon in *New Republic*. A bully and a torturer who frequently betrayed associates, Diamond made many enemies. Several attempts were made on his life, and, to many people, he seemed unkillable.

Though vicious, Diamond was also a glamorous figure. *Listener* critic Tony Aspler indicates that F. Scott Fitzgerald met the gangster on a transatlantic crossing in 1926, and in the words of *Times Literary Supplement* writer Philip French, Diamond "may have been the model" for Fitzgerald's character Jay Gatsby. Legs Diamond, points out Suplee, "evolved into a national obsession, a godsend for copy-short newsmen, a mesmerizing topic in tavern or tearoom. Yet profoundly evil." Croyden writes that "Diamond's legal maneuvering and social doings were in the Albany papers every day," according to Kennedy, who told her that "we were also frequently aswarm with out-of-town newsmen, particularly the New York tabloid crowd, which claimed Jack as its own and regularly gave him pages of space in order to deplore his depredations. A serious effort at deploring Jack was as good for circulation as a kinky Hollywood sex murder."

Kennedy's novel about the gangster is narrated by Diamond's friend and lawyer, Marcus Gorman, the same character who also briefly defends Francis Phelan in *Ironweed*. Gorman is described by Peter S. Prescott in *Newsweek* as a man fascinated "by Jack's 'luminosity,' by this man who 'was alive in a way I was not.'" While writing the novel, Kennedy told Suplee, he tried to analyze Diamond's appeal: "So why do we like him? *That's* the thing. I kept saying to myself, 'Why am I writing about this son of a bitch?'" Suplee notes that "among the book's many answers is Diamond's odd integrity: 'It is one thing to be corrupt. It is another to behave in a psychologically responsible way toward your own evil.' Legs becomes a litmus, huge and hugely awful, at whom folk could gape 'with curiosity, ambivalent benevolence, and a sense of mystery at the meaning of their own response.'" Also, Kennedy said to Croyden, "Legs is another version of the American dream—that you can grow up and shoot your way to fame and fortune. On the other hand, the people that live this kind of life are human beings like you or me. People did love Legs Diamond."

Kennedy's second novel in the Albany cycle, *Billy Phelan's Greatest Game*, explores a similar milieu. An *Atlantic* reviewer indicates that the book is set in "the joints of Albany's Broadway, where his incidental characters, seedy and doomed, endlessly gamble, drink, and whore in pools of artificial light." *Time* critic Paul Gray calls it a "fictional and vivid demimonde of conniving politicians, ward heelers, petty gamblers, and barflies, all caught up in a bizarre kidnapping and extortion plot." Of *Billy Phelan's Greatest Game*, Prescott writes, "the year is 1938, the time is almost always after dark, and the characters . . . are constantly reminded of times further past, of the floods and strikes, the scandals and murders of a quarter century before." The plot of the novel is related by reporter Martin Daugherty. Through his eyes, writes Suplee, "we watch Billy—a pool shark, bowling ace and saloon-wise hustler with a pitilessly rigid code of ethics—prowl among Albany's nighttown denizens. But when kidnappers abduct the sole child of an omnipotent clan (patterned on the family of the late Dan O'Connell, of Albany's Democratic machine), Billy is pushed to turn informer, and faces competing claims of conscience."

Billy Phelan's Greatest Game received a smattering of mildly favorable critical attention, as did *Legs*, but didn't sell particularly well; all three of the author's earlier novels sold only a few thousand copies. The first one hundred pages of *Ironweed*, the story of Billy Phelan's father who left the family when Billy was nine, were originally accepted by Viking, but the book later lost the marketing backing it needed in the house. In 1979, Kennedy agreed it would be best to submit the novel elsewhere. It was rejected twelve more times, and the author was disillusioned—past fifty and in debt—when Saul Bellow wrote Viking, admonishing them for slighting Kennedy's talent and asking them to reconsider their decision not to publish *Ironweed*. Viking heeded Bellow's letter, in which the Nobel Prize-winner referred to Kennedy's "Albany novels," calling them "a distinguished group of books," Kennedy writes *CA*. Kennedy's editor at the house fell upon the idea of reissuing *Billy Phelan's Greatest Game* and *Legs*, then out of print, for simultaneous publication with *Ironweed*, and he made the occasion a publishing event, Kennedy indicates to *CA*, "by focusing on" Kennedy's "long-standing plan to write a 'cycle' of novels." "The three books modify and fortify each other," writes French. "Certain characters recur in the books, most notably the McCall family of political fixers and the lawyer Marcus Gorman." For example, he points out, journalist Martin Daugherty's "playwright father, in his day the peer of Eugene O'Neill, wrote a play about the 1901 [transit] strike called *The Car Barn* that was inspired by Francis Phelan." Through these books, French points out, we also "become familiar with" Albany's landmarks, "like the plush Kenmore Hotel and the public park that boasts statues of both Robert Burns and Moses."

By itself, *Ironweed* did not appear to be a good publishing risk. Perhaps even less commercial than Kennedy's previous novels, the book represents a departure for the author as he adopts new literary structures and devices. Towers writes that, in *Ironweed*, Kennedy "largely abandons the rather breezy, quasi-journalistic narrative voice of his previous fiction and resorts to a more poetically charged, often surrealistic use of language as he re-creates the experiences and mental states of an alcoholic bum." "Throughout the novel," maintains Towers, "Kennedy plays with the contrast between sordid event and exalted illusion, between remembered past and threadbare present." In the opinion of Webster Schott in *Washington Post Book World*, "what William Kennedy has in mind is to tell two stories at once in *Ironweed*. One is the gloriously checkered history of Francis Phelan as young lover of the neighbor lady in silk, star of baseball diamonds in Toronto and Dayton, wrathful killer of at least three men, and joyous victim of sin forever on the run. The other is of a newer Francis Phelan emerging during the crucial present of the novel—three days during which Francis moves from shoveling graves to picking rags. . . .''

And the subject matter is relentlessly downbeat. *Ironweed* portrays "the world of the down-and-outer, the man who drifts by the windows of boarding houses and diners with a slouch hat and a brain whose most vivid images are 20 years old," writes *Detroit News* critic James F. Veseley. In Croyden's words, "drawn against a background of flophouses, bars and soup kitchens, Kennedy's winos are dirty, diseased and depressed, searching for food, baths, beds and warmth in their agonizing quest for survival; men in extremis—outsiders, outlaws—they struggle against a cold and rejecting world. Their hands bitten by dogs, their shoes gone, their feet swollen, their underwear in shreds, yet they fight on until, exhausted, they succumb. But not Francis Phelan."

Despite the book's hopeful resolution, publishers thought *Ironweed* unmarketable and, until Bellow intervened, attempted to convince Kennedy to rewrite it. As Kennedy told a Boston *Globe and Mail* reporter, "They said, 'Too many bums in the book, Bill. Cut a few of 'em out.' They also objected that the book was overwritten, they didn't understand what I was doing in terms of language, they felt that no bum would ever talk like Francis does, or think like he does, that they thought of him only as a bum. They didn't understand that what I was striving for was to talk about the central eloquence of every human being. We all have this unutterable eloquence, and the closest you can get to it is to make it utterable at some point, in some way that separates it from the conscious level of life."

Furthermore, he told Croyden, "I'm interested in the human being concealed within a bum's or a gangster's life. When you take a character into his most extreme condition, you get extreme explanations, and you begin to discover what lurks in the far corners of the soul. I really do believe that that's the way a writer finds things out. I love the surrealistic, the mystical elements of life. There is so much mysteriousness going on in everybody's life." He remarked in the Boston *Globe and Mail* interview: "Legs was an extreme character. Billy Phelan carried himself into the realms of being an outlaw. And, of course, Francis. Francis is an outlaw all his life. He's a man who has fierce loyalties and fierce angers and a kind of enduring principle at the centre of his being. And those extremes seem to me to be where you're coming in touch with the deepest elements of your being. When you're strung out, then you find out who you are and who you are not, what you will do and what you will not do." As Prescott points out, "Like the plant that gives [*Ironweed*] its name, Francis is tougher than the others. He may be at war with himself, yet he's searching for his own kind of grace, which has something to do with what was once unspoiled in his and other people's lives." And Francis does come to grips with his guilt and move on. Kennedy told Suplee, "That's the kind of characters I've been writing about. The refusal to yield to what appears to be fate. If you don't die and you don't quit, then there's a chance."

ADAPTATIONS: Film rights to *Ironweed* and *Legs* have been sold to Gene Kirkwood; film rights to *Billy Phelan's Greatest Game* have been sold to Richard Sylbert and Jerry Wexler.

BIOGRAPHICAL/CRITICAL SOURCES: Library Journal, October 1, 1969; *Washington Post,* October 5, 1969, May 18, 1975, December 28, 1983; *Best Sellers,* October 15, 1969, August, 1975; *Observer,* October 20, 1969; *Legs,* Coward, 1975; *New Republic,* May 24, 1975, February 14, 1983; *Newsweek,* June 23, 1975, May 8, 1978, January 31, 1983, February 6, 1984; *Contemporary Literary Criticism,* Gale, Volume VI, 1976, Volume XXVIII, 1984; *Listener,* May 6, 1976; *Book World,* April 23, 1978; *Saturday Review,* April 29, 1978; *Atlantic,* June, 1978; *Commonweal,* October 13, 1978, September 9, 1983; *Los Angeles Times Book Review,* December 26, 1982, September 23, 1984; William Kennedy, *O Albany!: An Urban Tapestry,* Viking, 1983; *New York Times,* January 10, 1983, September 17, 1983, December 23, 1983, September 22, 1984; *Washington Post Book World,* January 16, 1983, January 29, 1984, October 14, 1984; *New York Times Book Review,* January 23, 1983, November 13, 1983, January 1, 1984, September 30, 1984; *Chicago Tribune,* January 23, 1983; *Time,* January 24, 1983, October 1, 1984; *Detroit News,* January 30, 1983, February 26, 1984; *Village Voice Literary Supplement,* February, 1983, October, 1984; *New Yorker,* February 7, 1983; *New York Review of Books,* March 31, 1983; *Hudson Review,* summer, 1983; *Publishers Weekly,* December 9, 1983; *America,* May 19, 1984; *New York Times Magazine,* August 26, 1984; *Globe and Mail* (Boston), September 1, 1984; *Times Literary Supplement,* October 5, 1984.

—*Sketch by Candace Cloutier*

KESSELMAN, Mark J.

PERSONAL: Son of Paul Kesselman; married Amrita Basy (an assistant professor). *Education:* Cornell University, B.A., 1959; University of Chicago, M.A., 1961, Ph.D., 1965. *Office:* Columbia University, 420 West 118th St., New York, N.Y. 10027.

CAREER: Columbia University, New York, N.Y., assistant professor, 1964-69, associate professor, 1969-73, professor of political science, 1973—. *Member:* Phi Beta Kappa. *Awards, honors:* Guggenheim fellowship, 1968-69; Rockefeller Foundation Humanities Fellowship, 1980-81.

WRITINGS: The Ambiguous Consensus, Knopf, 1967; *The Politics of Power,* Harcourt, 1975, revised edition, 1979; (contributor) Philip Cerney and Martin Schain, editors, *French Politics and Public Policy,* St. Martin's, 1980; (contributor) William Andrews and Stanley Hoffman, editors, *The Fifth Republic at Twenty,* State University of New York Press, 1980; (editor) *The French Workers' Movement: Economic Crisis and Political Change,* Allen & Unwin, 1984. Also contributor to other books. Contributor to political science and sociology journals in America and abroad.

*   *   *

KEZYS, Algimantas   1928-

PERSONAL: Born October 28, 1928, in Vistytis, Lithuania; came to the United States in 1950, naturalized citizen, 1956; son of George (a government employee) and Eugenija (Kolytaite) Kezys. *Education:* Loyola University, Chicago, Ill., M.A., 1956. *Office:* Galerija Art Gallery, 226 West Superior St., Chicago, Ill. 60610; and (studio) 3502 North Paulina St., Chicago, Ill. 60657.

CAREER: Entered Society of Jesus (Jesuits), 1950, ordained Roman Catholic priest, 1961; editor in Chicago, Ill., 1964-67; founder of Lithuanian Photo Library in Chicago, 1966, president, 1966—; founder and director of Lithuanian Library Press, Chicago, 1976—. Director of Lithuanian Youth Center in Chicago, 1974-77. Photographer; first one-man show, 1963; exhibitions held at Art Institute of Chicago, 1965, and at other institutions in the United States and abroad.

WRITINGS: Sventoji auka (with own photographs; title means "The Holy Sacrifice"), Jesuit Fathers of Della Strada, 1965; (photographer) Bruno Markaitis, *Photographs: Algimantas Kezys,* Loyola University Press, 1966; (photographer) William M. Barbieri, *Sidewalk: Reflections and Images,* Maryknoll Publications, 1969.

(Editor and photographer) Francis Thompson, *I Fled Him, Down the Nights and Down the Days,* Loyola University Press, 1970; *Form and Content* (photographs), M. Morkunas, 1972; (editor and photographer) *A Lithuanian Cemetery: St. Casimir Cemetery in Chicago, Ill.,* Lithuanian Photo Library, 1976; (photographer) Tom Collins, *The Search for Jimmy Carter,* Word Books, 1976; *Posters: Algimantas Kezys,* Volumes I-IV, Loyola University Press, 1978-79.

(Photographer) George Lane, *Chicago Churches and Synagogues,* Loyola University Press, 1981; *Chicago-Kezys: Sixty-Four Photographs of Chicago,* Loyola University Press, 1983. Also author of *Portfolio '66,* 1966. Contributor of photographs to *Famous Photographers Annual* and to various magazines, including *Camera.*

WORK IN PROGRESS: A Peek through the Wall; A Walk through the Parks of U.S.A.

SIDELIGHTS: In the introduction to *Form and Content,* Algimantas Kezys writes: "I believe the camera is a mechanical tool for communication between individuals. The process of photographic communication begins with the photographer's inner self. It continues through the mechanics of photography, which act as transmitters of his thoughts, feelings, and vision to another individual.

"I have discovered that my pre-visualization powers are completely dormant, and that my post-visualization dexterity is nonexistent. I can't be either an art director who tells photographers or himself what to shoot, nor a lab technician who produces marvels even from the most ordinary negative material. From my own observation of myself I know that my 'moment of glory' is the moment of seeing and discovering. For me this is the crucial point at which pictures are made or unmade."

BIOGRAPHICAL/CRITICAL SOURCES: Algimantas Kezys, *Form and Content,* M. Morkunas, 1972.

*   *   *

KHAN, Zillur Rahman   1938-

PERSONAL: Born November 21, 1938, in Hoogly, West Bengal (now part of India); son of Abdur Rahman (an educator) and Khadija Khatun (Choudhury) Khan; married Margaret Carol Noe, April 3, 1966; children: Tamiz, Kabir, Mary. *Education:* Dacca University, B.A. (with honors), 1957, M.A., 1958, LL.B., 1959; Claremont Graduate School, M.A., 1965, Ph.D., 1967. *Office:* Department of Political Science, University of Wisconsin, Oshkosh, Wis. 54901.

CAREER: Dacca College, Dacca, East Pakistan (now Bangladesh), lecturer in political science, 1960-63; cantonment executive officer and magistrate of Jessore, East Pakistan, 1963-64; Sonoma State College (now California State College), Sonoma, Calif., assistant professor of anthropology, 1966-67; Dacca University, Dacca, associate professor of political science, 1969-71; University of Wisconsin—Oshkosh, assistant professor, 1967-69, 1971-72, associate professor, 1973-80, faculty senator, 1979—, professor of political science, 1981—, coordinator of Asian studies, 1984—. Bangladesh Foundation of the United States, director, 1973-81, currently president of board of trustees. Distinguished guest speaker at University of Manitoba, 1984.

MEMBER: American Political Science Association, American Society of Public Administration, Association of Muslim Social Scientists (chairman of political science group).

AWARDS, HONORS: Fulbright fellowship, 1964-65; Asian Studies Award, 1965-66; Danforth Foundation award, 1966-67; National Science Foundation grant, 1967.

WRITINGS: (With A.T.R. Rahman) *Autonomy and Constitution Making: The Case for Bangladesh,* Green Book House, 1973; *Leadership in the Least Developed Nation: Bangladesh,* Foreign and Comparative Studies Program, Syracuse University, 1983 (published in Bangladesh as *From Martial Law to Martial Law: Leadership Crisis in Bangladesh,* University Press Ltd., 1984); (with S. A. Khan) *On Constitution and Constitutional Issues,* University Press Ltd., 1983; (with S. A. Khan) *Constitution and Constitutional Issues: Comparative Studies, Analyses and Prospects,* University Press Ltd., 1984; *Nettriter Ubhashankot* (title means "Leadership's Dilemmas"), University Press Ltd., 1984.

Contributor to political science and Asian studies journals, including *Western Political Quarterly, Indian Journal of Political Science, Canadian Review of Sociology and Anthropology, Pacific Affairs, Asian Survey,* and *Third World Review.* Member, editorial board, International Documentation Center, 1972—.

WORK IN PROGRESS: A Political History of Bangladesh; Bureaucracy in Bangladesh; Ziaur Rahman: A Political Biography; Administrative Decentralization.

*   *   *

KING, Edith W(eiss)   1930-

PERSONAL: Born July 16, 1930, in Detroit, Mich.; daughter of Otto A. and Fay (Eskay) Weiss; married Marvin M. King (chief product engineer and manager, Products Division of Samsonite Corp.), December 22, 1951; children: Melissa, Matthew. *Education:* University of Michigan, B.A., 1951; Wayne State University, M.A., 1961, Ed.D., 1966. *Politics:* Democrat. *Religion:* Jewish. *Home:* 3734 South Niagara Way, Denver, Colo. 80237. *Office:* School of Education, University of Denver, Denver, Colo. 80208.

CAREER: Teacher at elementary schools in Michigan, 1951-64; director of cooperative nursery school in Oak Park, Mich., 1959-60; University of Denver, School of Education, Denver, Colo., 1966—, began as associate professor, currently professor of educational sociology. Guest lecturer, Centre for Multicultural Education, University of London, and School of Education, University of Birmingham, both England, 1981. Co-organizer for international conference in Sociology of Education, UNESCO Headquarters, Paris, 1980 and 1984. Director of numerous workshops and faculty member of several projects on multiethnic and multicultural education. Reader for the U.S. Department of Education. Consultant to numerous public school systems in the United States, including Wichita, Kans., Lawrence, Mass., Denver and other school districts in Colorado, and Catholic Archdiocese in Chicago, Ill.; consultant to numerous education agencies in Britain, including BBC Schools Programs, Schools Council, Centre for Multicultural Education, West Midlands Child Guidance Centre, and University of London; consultant to American and British publishers, including University of Illinois Press, Allyn & Bacon, Holt, Rinehart & Winston, Coronet Films and Filmstrips, SRA Associates, Chicago, and Spoken Arts, New Rochelle; consultant to Ethnic Heritage Studies Project at the Social Science Consortium, Boulder, Colo., 1974-75.

MEMBER: International Sociological Association, American Sociological Association, American Educational Studies Association, Sociologists for Women in Society, Western Social Science Association, Sociology of Education Association (England), Phi Beta Kappa, Phi Delta Kappa.

WRITINGS: (With August Kerber) *The Sociology of Early Childhood Education,* American Book Co., 1968; *The World: Context for Teaching in the Elementary School,* W. C. Brown, 1971; *Educating Young Children: Sociological Interpretations,* W. C. Brown, 1973; (with P. Bohannon, I. Morrisset, and W. W. Stevens, Jr.) *The Intercultural Dimension in International/Intercultural Education, Grades K-14* (monograph), Social Science Education Consortium, 1973; (with Joseph Stevens, Jr.) *Administering Early Childhood Education Programs,* Little, Brown, 1976; (with R. P. Cuzzort) *Humanity and Modern Social Thought,* 2nd edition (King was not associated with earlier edition), Dryden, 1976; *Teaching Ethnic Awareness:*

Methods and Materials for the Elementary School, Scott, Foresman, 1980; (with R. P. Cuzzort) *Twentieth Century Social Thought,* Holt, 1980. Also author of "Discovering the World!," filmstrip, records, and teacher's guide on world awareness for young children, Spoken Arts, 1971. Contributor of numerous articles, readings, and reviews to education journals in the United States and England. Consultant to journals, including *Social Education, Contemporary Sociology, Journal of Multicultural Education,* and *Social Science Teacher.*

SIDELIGHTS: The Sociology of Early Childhood Education has been translated into Danish.

*   *   *

KING, James Cecil   1924-

PERSONAL: Born September 14, 1924, in Uniontown, Pa.; son of Joseph Herbert and Eliza Ann (Kelley) King; divorced; children: Christopher Hanbury, Sheila Anne. *Education:* George Washington University, B.A., 1949, M.A., 1950, Ph.D., 1954. *Home:* 9296 Bailey Lane, Fairfax, Va. 22031. *Office:* Academic Center T508E, George Washington University, Washington, D.C. 20052.

CAREER: St. Albans School for Boys, Washington, D.C., teacher of French, German, and Latin, 1952-55; George Washington University, Washington, D.C., assistant professor, 1955-60, associate professor, 1960-65, professor of German and Sanskrit, 1965—. *Military service:* U.S. Army, 1943-46.

MEMBER: American Association of Teachers of German, Linguistic Society of America, Modern Language Association of America, Mediaeval Academy of America, American Association of University Professors, Phi Beta Kappa.

AWARDS, HONORS: German Academic Exchange service grant for research in Europe, 1963.

WRITINGS—Editor: Arnold Littmann, *Peter hat Pech!,* Holt, 1961; (with F. A. Raven and W. K. Legner) *Germanic Studies in Honor of Edward Henry Sehrt,* University of Miami Press, 1968; *Notker der Deutsche, Boethius' Bearbeitung der "Categoriae" des Aristoteles,* Max Niemeyer, 1972; *Boethius' Bearbeitung von Aristoteles' Schrift "De interpretatione",* Max Niemeyer, 1975; *Martianus Capella, "De nuptiis Philologiae et Mercurii",* Max Niemeyer, 1979.

WORK IN PROGRESS: Notker latinus zum Martianus Capella and *Die kleineren Schriften Notkers des Deutschen.*

*   *   *

KING, Norman A.
See TRALINS, S(andor) Robert

*   *   *

KING-HELE, Desmond (George)   1927-

PERSONAL: Surname is pronounced King-Heeley; born November 3, 1927, in Seaford, England; son of Sydney George (in government service) and Bessie (Sayer) King-Hele; married Marie Therese Newman, August 31, 1954; children: Carole, Sonia. *Education:* Trinity College, Cambridge, B.A. (first class honors), 1948, M.A., 1952. *Home:* 3 Tor Rd., Farnham, Surrey, England. *Office:* Royal Aircraft Establishment, Farnborough, Hampshire, England.

CAREER: Royal Aircraft Establishment, Farnborough, England, member of scientific research staff, 1948—, research concentrated on space, 1955—, deputy chief scientific officer, space department, 1968—. Bakerian Lecturer, Royal Society, 1974; Halley Lecturer, Oxford University, 1974. *Member:* Royal Society (London; fellow), Royal Astronomical Society (fellow), Institute of Mathematics and Its Application (fellow), International Academy of Astronautics. *Awards, honors:* Bronze Medal of the Royal Aeronautical Society, 1959, for work on the theory of satellite orbits; Eddington Gold Medal of Royal Astronomical Society, 1971; Charles Chree Medal and Prize of Institute of Physics, 1971.

WRITINGS: Shelley, the Man and the Poet, Yoseloff, 1960 (published in England as *Shelley, His Thought and Work,* Macmillan, 1960), 3rd edition, Macmillan, 1984; *Satellites and Scientific Research,* Routledge & Kegan Paul, 1960, 2nd revised edition, Dover, 1962; *Erasmus Darwin,* Macmillan, 1963, Scribner, 1964; *Theory of Satellite Orbits in an Atmosphere,* Butterworth & Co., 1964; (editor) *Space Research V,* North-Holland Publishing, 1965; *Observing Earth Satellites,* Macmillan, 1966, revised edition, 1983; (editor and author of linking commentary) *The Essential Writings of Erasmus Darwin,* MacGibbon & Kee, 1968, Hillary, 1969; *The End of the Twentieth Century?,* St. Martin's, 1970; *Poems and Trixies,* Mitre Press, 1972; *Doctor of Revolution: The Life and Genius of Erasmus Darwin,* Faber, 1977; (editor) *The Letters of Erasmus Darwin,* Cambridge University Press, 1981; *The RAE Table of Earth Satellites,* Facts on File, 1981, 2nd edition, 1983; *Animal Spirits* (poems), 1983.

Published technical reports for Royal Aircraft Establishment include *Average Rotational Speed of the Upper Atmosphere from Changes in Satellite Orbits,* 1970, and *The Shape of the Earth,* 1970. Contributor of more than 200 scientific and literary papers to *Nature, Keats-Shelley Memorial Bulletin, Proceedings of Royal Society, Planetary and Space Science,* and other journals.

WORK IN PROGRESS: A study of the influence of Erasmus Darwin on the Romantic poets.

SIDELIGHTS: Desmond King-Hele told *CA* that his first book "was begun in the 1950s because I thought that previous books on Shelley failed to bring out his keenly analytical and scientific mind. Today, things are quite different: Shelley is well appreciated and, when revising my book for its third edition, I found that I had to review 85 new books about Shelley published between 1971 and 1982.

"From Shelley," writes King-Hele, "I was led to Erasmus Darwin, the 18th-century physician, who achieved more in a wider variety of subjects than anyone since, as a scientist, an inventor, a poet and a doctor. He has proved endlessly fascinating." In keeping with his enthusiasm, the author has made Darwin the subject of two biographical studies and edited collections of his writings and letters. Reviewing *Doctor of Revolution: The Life and Genius of Erasmus Darwin* in the *Spectator,* Elisabeth Whipp states: "How inspiriting, today, to read of a man who took the whole of human knowledge for his province, unlimited by the constraints of conventional attitudes, or the necessity for reviewing an entire literature on a subject before he felt able to propound upon it. All speculations were grist to his mill, and all problems were assumed to be ultimately soluble."

King-Hele credits Darwin with being ahead of his time and anticipating later developments in areas such as botany, physics, and psychology. Writing in the *Times Literary Supplement,* David Porter outlines the breadth of Darwin's achievements as described by King-Hele: "In countless fields—meteorology, photosynthesis, rocket motors, sewage farms, steam turbines, and submarines, to name a few—Darwin foreshadowed scientific hypotheses indicated a century or more later, and anticipated futuristic technology." As Redmond O'Hanlon points out in a *Times Literary Supplement* review of *The Letters of Erasmus Darwin,* the physician was also "the founding father of modern evolutionary thought; his theory pre-dates Lamarck's, and is in any case less Lamarckian than that of his grandson Charles Darwin." Redmond believes "Darwin's range of interests certainly seem to have inspired his editor towards feats of similar virtuosity. [He] has succeeded," he continues, "in his two biographies and now in this magnificent (and first) edition of the letters, in dragging . . . Darwin's large and various planet, highly supportive of all kinds of life, back into full view."

Aside from his writings on Darwin and Shelley, King-Hele has authored a number of technical works on satellites. Describing his motivation for writing, he states: "I have a bad memory, and a prime incentive for writing books is to record my ideas and findings on a subject before I forget them. That also means including notes and references—how else can I remember where I found the information? I rarely write articles (apart from scientific papers) because they are often mangled by editors, so that (a) I am ashamed at what appears, (b) it does not say what I want to say, and (c) I do not have the incentive to bring the writing to the standard I like. I enjoy writing poems and constantly strive for perfection of style—in vain, of course. But the striving is beneficial and provides an excellent target, carried over to the other books, which are usually revised many times before reaching their final form."

AVOCATIONAL INTERESTS: Tennis, walking in the countryside, enjoying natural beauties.

BIOGRAPHICAL/CRITICAL SOURCES: Times Literary Supplement, December 24, 1971, December 30, 1977, March 19, 1982; *Spectator,* December 3, 1977.

*　　*　　*

KINGHORN, Kenneth Cain   1930-

PERSONAL: Born June 23, 1930, in Albany, Okla.; son of Kenneth (a businessman) and Eloise (Rye) Kinghorn; married Hilda Hartzler, June 4, 1955; children: Kathleen, Kenneth, Kevin, Kent. *Education:* Ball State University, B.S., 1952; Asbury Theological Seminary, B.D., 1962; Emory University, Ph.D., 1965. *Home:* 1083 The Lane, Lexington, Ky. 40504. *Office:* Office of the Dean, Asbury Theological Seminary, Wilmore, Ky. 40390.

CAREER: Ordained United Methodist minister, 1965; Asbury Theological Seminary, Wilmore, Ky., associate professor, 1965-70, professor of history of theology, 1970-82, dean, 1982—.

WRITINGS: Contemporary Issues in Historical Perspective, Word Inc., 1970; *Dynamic Discipleship,* Revell, 1973; *Fresh Wind of the Spirit,* Abingdon, 1975; *Gifts of the Spirit,* Abingdon, 1976; *Christ Can Make You Fully Human,* Abingdon, 1979; *Discovering Your Spiritual Gifts,* Zondervan, 1984. Contributor of articles to periodicals.

*　　*　　*

KINKADE, Richard P(aisley)   1939-

PERSONAL: Born January 7, 1939, in Los Angeles, Calif.;

son of Joseph Marion (a physician) and Elizabeth (Paisley) Kinkade; married Raquel Liebes, June 2, 1962 (divorced, 1977); children: Kathleen, Richard, Jr., Scott Philip. *Education:* Yale University, B.A., 1960, Ph.D., 1965. *Home:* 1200 Paseo Pavon, Tucson, Ariz. 85718. *Office:* College of Arts and Sciences, Faculty of Humanities, University of Arizona, Tucson, Ariz. 85721.

CAREER: University of Arizona, Tucson, assistant professor, 1965-69, associate professor of Romance languages, 1969-71; Emory University, Atlanta, Ga., professor of Romance languages, 1971-77, chairperson of department, 1971-74, director of graduate studies in Spanish, 1971-75, chairperson of Committee on Foreign Languages and Classics, 1976-77; University of Connecticut, Storrs, professor of Romance languages and head of department of Romance and classical languages, 1977-82; University of Arizona, Tucson, dean of faculty of humanities and professor of Spanish and Portuguese, 1982—.

MEMBER: International Association of Hispanists, Modern Language Association of America (member of Bibliography and Research Committee, 1972-75; chairperson of Spanish Section, 1974, 1977; member of executive committee, 1974-78; divisional delegate to national delegate assembly, 1976-78), American Association of Teachers of Spanish and Portuguese, Medieval Academy of America, Academy of American Research Historians on Medieval Spain, South Atlantic Modern Language Association (chairperson of Medieval Section, 1973; member of executive committee, 1973-76).

AWARDS, HONORS: American Council of Learned Societies travel grant, 1974; National Endowment for the Humanities research grant, 1978-79.

WRITINGS: Los "Lucidarios" espanoles (critical edition), Editorial Gredos (Madrid), 1968; (contributor) Staubach, Guerrero, and Bonilla, *Espanol: Lengua activa 2,* Ginn, 1970; (contributor) *Estudios literarios de hispanistas norteamericanos dedicados a Helmut Hatzfeld,* HISPAM (Barcelona), 1974; (with John E. Keller) *Iconography in Medieval Spanish Literature,* University Press of Kentucky, 1984.

Also author of *Homenaj a Agapito Rey,* Indiana University Press. Also contributor to *Actas del primer congreso internacional sobre el arcipreste de Hita,* 1973, and *Actas del congreso internacional de hispanistas,* 1978. Contributor to professional journals. Member of editorial board, *Kentucky Romance Quarterly, Vortice, Revista de Estudios Hispanicos,* and *Scripta Humanistica.*

WORK IN PROGRESS: An edition of *La vida de San Amaro: La leyenda de San Brandan en la Espana medieval,* with Dana A. Nelson; an edition of *La semeianca de mundo,* with James F. Burke, for University Press of Kentucky; a text and anthology of medieval Spanish literature with Keller.

SIDELIGHTS: Richard P. Kinkade has traveled extensively in Mexico and Central America and has lived in Spain.

*   *   *

KINNARD, Douglas 1921-

PERSONAL: Born September 13, 1921, in Morristown, N.J.; son of Frederick Henry (a businessman) and Mary (Toomey) Kinnard; married Wade Tyree (an English professor), July 6, 1951; children: Frederick Douglas. *Education:* U.S. Military Academy, B.S., 1944; Princeton University, M.S., 1948, M.A., 1972, Ph.D., 1973. *Home:* 7349 Eldorado Ct., McLain, Va.

22102. *Office:* U.S. Army Center of Military History, 20 Massachusetts Ave. N.W., Washington, D.C. 20314.

CAREER: U.S. Army, officer, 1944-70, retiring as brigadier general; University of Vermont, Burlington, 1973-83, began as associate professor, became professor of political science, professor emeritus, 1984—, director of area and international studies, 1977-79; U.S. Army Center of Military History, Washington, D.C., chief of military history, 1983—. Served as special assistant to supreme commander Allied headquarters, Paris, 1961-64; commander of 24th Infantry Division artillery, Germany, 1964-65; chief of operations analysis of U.S. Military Assistance Command, Vietnam, 1966-67; chief of staff, II Field Force, Vietnam, 1969-70. Consultant on national security affairs. *Member:* International Institute for Strategic Studies, International Studies Association, American Political Science Association, Northeast Political Science Association, Association of Graduates of U.S. Military Academy, Princeton Graduate Alumni Association, Nassau Club, Army and Navy Club, Princeton Club. *Awards, honors*—Military: Distinguished Service Medal, Distinguished Flying Cross, and numerous others.

WRITINGS: President Eisenhower and Strategy Management, University Press of Kentucky, 1977; *The War Managers,* University Press of New England, 1977; *The Secretary of Defense,* University Press of Kentucky, 1980. Contributor of articles to *Journal of Politics, Polity, Journal of Political and Military Sociology, Naval War College Review, Public Opinion Quarterly,* and *Midwest Review of Public Administration.*

WORK IN PROGRESS: Maxwell Taylor and the American Military Tradition; The Second Indochina War; articles on foreign and defense policy matters.

*   *   *

KINNEY, Arthur F(rederick) 1933-

PERSONAL: Born September 5, 1933, in Cortland, N.Y.; son of Arthur Frederick, Sr. and Gladys Elorsie (Mudge) Kinney. *Education:* Syracuse University, B.A. (magna cum laude), 1955; Columbia University, M.S., 1956; University of Michigan, Ph.D., 1963. *Residence:* 25 Hunter Hill Dr., Amherst, Mass. 01002. *Agent:* McIntosh & Otis, Inc., 475 Fifth Ave., New York, N.Y. 10017. *Office:* Department of English, University of Massachusetts, Amherst, Mass. 01002.

CAREER: Yale University, New Haven, Conn., instructor in English, 1963-66; University of Massachusetts—Amherst, assistant professor, 1966-68, associate professor, 1968-74, professor of English, 1974—, director, bachelor's degree program in individual studies. Affiliate associate professor of English, Clark University, Worcester, Mass., 1971-83. Visiting professor, Oxford University, 1978, University of Liverpool, 1984, Sir Thomas Browne Institute, University of Leiden, 1984. *Military service:* U.S. Army, chaplain, 1966-68.

MEMBER: Modern Language Association of America (chairman of Conference of Editors of Learned Journals, 1971-73, 1981-83), National Council of Teachers of English, Shakespeare Society of America, Milton Society, Malone Society, Renaissance English Text Society (vice-president, 1983-84; president, 1984-86), College English Association, American Studies Association, Renaissance Society of America, Northeast Modern Language Association (executive secretary, 1971-73), New England College English Association (member of board of directors, 1971-73), Michigan Academy of Arts and Letters, Phi Beta Kappa, Phi Kappa Phi, Rho Delta Phi.

AWARDS, HONORS: Jules M. and Avery Hopwood Major Award for Writing, 1961; Breadloaf scholar, 1962; Morse fellow, Yale, 1964, 1965, 1966; senior fellow, Huntington Library, 1972, 1983; senior fellow, Folger Shakespeare Library, 1973; senior fellow, National Endowment for the Humanities, 1977, 1982-83; Fulbright-Hays fellow, New College, Oxford, 1978; university research fellow, University of Massachusetts—Amherst, 1983-84.

WRITINGS: Bear, Man, and God: Seven Approaches to Faulkner's "The Bear," Random House, 1964, revised edition, 1971; *Symposium,* Houghton, 1968; *On Seven Shakespearean Tragedies,* Scarab Press, 1968; *Symposium on Love,* Houghton, 1969; *On Seven Shakespearean Comedies,* Scarab Press, 1969.

(Author of critical and textual notes) H. R., *Mythomystes (1623),* Scolar Press, 1972; *Rogues, Vagabonds, and Sturdy Beggars,* Imprint Society, 1973; *Titled Elizabethans: A Directory of Elizabethan State and Church Officers and Knights with Peers of England, Scotland, and Ireland, 1558-1603,* Shoe String, 1973; *Elizabethan Backgrounds,* Shoe String, 1974; *Dorothy Parker,* Twayne, 1978.

Critical Essays on William Faulkner: The Compson Family, G. K. Hall, 1982; (contributor) James J. Murphy, editor, *Renaissance Eloquence: The Theory and Practice of Renaissance Rhetoric,* University of California Press, 1983; *Nicholas Hilliard's "Art of Limning,"* Northeastern University Press, 1983; *The Sartoris Family,* G. K. Hall, 1984; *Resources of Being: Flannery O'Connor's Library,* University of Georgia Press, 1984; *CELJ Handbook for Journal Editors and Contributors,* Modern Language Association of America, 1984; (contributor) *William Faulkner: Ten Years of Criticism,* University Press of Mississippi, 1984.

Also author of *Markets of Bawdrie: The Dramatic Criticism of Stephen Gosson,* 1975, and of *Faulkner's Narrative Poetics: Style as Vision,* 1978. Editor, Twayne "English Authors" series, and *English Literary Renaissance;* supervisor of "English Literary Renaissance Monographs." Contributor of short stories and essays to periodicals, including *Virginia Quarterly Review, Southern Review,* and *Massachusetts Review.*

WORK IN PROGRESS: Seasons of Discovery: John Skelton, the Priest as Poet; Re-viewing Shakespeare; Philip Sydney: The Death and the Legend.

SIDELIGHTS: Arthur F. Kinney told *CA:* "My writing career began when I adapted the Book of Ruth for a Sunday school Easter play; I was eleven at the time, and the production of that play, to local acclaim anyway, insured my career as a writer. Later teenage journalism gave way to fiction and that to criticism. Now I try to interpret the people, events, and literature of the Elizabethan period—Shakespeare and his age—to those who want some fresh critical interpretations which begin in the background of the age. Writing helps me to think, for writing, I find, not only clarifies one's thought, but fixes it, as if in photographer's acid, in semi-permanent form. Not only the ideas, then, but the expression become vital—since the way you say things defines what it is you are saying—and I find that writing, even more than research and judgement, leads me to new ideas I had not been fully conscious of before sitting down at the typewriter."

*   *   *

KIRK, Philip
    See LEVINSON, Leonard

KITSON CLARK, George Sydney Roberts   1900-1975

PERSONAL: Born June 14, 1900, in Leeds, England; died December 8, 1975; son of Edwin (engineer and lieutenant colonel in the British Territorial Army) and Georgina (Bidder) Kitson Clark. *Education:* Trinity College, Cambridge, B.A., 1921, Litt.D., 1954. *Religion:* Church of England. *Home and office:* Trinity College, Cambridge University, Cambridge CB2 1TQ, England.

CAREER: Cambridge University, Cambridge, England, fellow in history at Trinity College, 1922-75, lecturer in history at Trinity College, 1928-54, and tutor, 1933-45, university lecturer in history, 1929-54, praelector, 1953-75, reader in constitutional history, 1954-67, Birkbeck lecturer, 1967, chairman of Faculty Board of History, 1956-58. Visiting lecturer at University of Pennsylvania, 1953-54; Ford's lecturer at Oxford University, 1960; Maurice lecturer at King's College, University of London, 1960; George Scott fellow at University of Melbourne, 1965; also lecturer in United States, Canada, Switzerland, India, Australia, New Zealand, and Ireland. Founder of Cambridge University Educational Film Council, 1947; first chairman of British University Film Council, 1948-51.

MEMBER: Royal Commonwealth Society (fellow; chairman of Cambridgeshire branch, 1956-66), Royal Institute of International Affairs, Royal Historical Society (fellow), American Academy of Arts and Sciences (foreign honorary member), Athenaeum Club (London).

AWARDS, HONORS: D.Litt., University of Durham, 1960, University of East Anglia, 1970, University of Glasgow, 1971, University of Leeds, 1973.

WRITINGS: Peel and the Conservative Party, G. Bell, 1929, 2nd edition, Cass & Co., 1964; *Sir Robert Peel,* Duckworth, 1936; *The English Inheritance,* S.C.M. Press, 1950; *Elizabeth by the Grace of God* (William Ainslie Memorial Lecture), St. Martins-in-the-Field, 1953; (contributor) J. H. Plumb, editor, *Studies in Social History,* Longmans, Green, 1955; *The Kingdom of Free Men,* Macmillan, 1957.

The Making of Victorian England, Harvard University Press, 1962; (author of introduction) R. T. Shannon, *Gladstone and the Bulgarian Agitation, 1876,* Thomas Nelson, 1963; *The Critical Historian,* Basic Books, 1967; *An Expanding Society: Britain, 1830-1900,* Cambridge University Press, 1967; *Guide for Research Students Working on Historical Subjects,* Cambridge University Press, 1968, 2nd edition, 1969; *Churchmen and the Condition of England, 1832-1885,* Methuen, 1973; (editor) George Malcolm Young, *Victorian England: Portrait of an Age,* Oxford University Press, 1977.

Author of two guides for research students in history, first published by Cambridge University Press, 1958 and 1963, and a booklet on the art of lecturing, published by Heffer & Sons, Cambridge; also author, with Derek Fraser, of a phonotape, "Peel," for BFA Educational Media, 1972. Contributor of articles and reviews to *Economic History Review, Transactions of Royal Historical Society, Journal of Modern History* (Chicago), *University Review* (Ireland), and other journals.

SIDELIGHTS: Cambridge historian George Sydney Roberts Kitson Clark based his book *The Critical Historian* on a lecture he delivered in 1962. The book, according to Allan Nevins in a *Book World* review, "emphasizes and expands the thesis that one of the most important uses of historical education might well be the training of students in the application of the best methods of historical scholarship. . . . Taken as a whole, this book is both a fresh and an incisive treatment, not alone of the best tools for ascertaining truth in history but of the profitable ways in which these tools can be applied to the vast mass of fact and theory in our study of the present-day world."

"Dr. Kitson Clark," wrote a *Times Literary Supplement* reviewer, "has written a thought-provoking [and] valuable . . . book. . . . His object [in *The Critical Historian*] is to warn us against the many traps, sophistications, negligences and downright dishonesties of which the reader of history should be aware." The reviewer also noted that "for anyone who is disposed to take historians on trust this book will provide a valuable antidote."

BIOGRAPHICAL/CRITICAL SOURCES: Robert Robson, editor, *Ideas and Institutions of Victorian Britain: Essays in Honour of G. Kitson Clark*, G. Bell, 1967; *Times Literary Supplement*, November 2, 1967; *Book World*, May 5, 1968.†

*   *   *

KLEIN, Alexander 1918-

PERSONAL: Born November 12, 1918, in Hungary; son of Anton and Rose (Judovitch) Klein; married, 1976. *Education:* City College of New York (now City College of the City University of New York), B.A., 1939. *Home:* 75 Bank St., New York, N.Y. 10014.

CAREER: Free-lance film writer and producer, with Henry Steele Commager, 1945—. Writer, United Jewish Appeal, 1940-41; Caravel Films, New York City, writer and producer of combat-training, documentary, and special films for the U.S. Air Force and U.S. Navy, 1941-45; vice-president in charge of television, J. D. Tarcher Advertising Agency, 1950-53; City College of New York (now City College of the City University of New York), teacher of creative writing, 1950-52; Fordham University, New York City, adjunct professor, 1970-75; director of public relations, CARE, 1972—. Founder, with Norman Thomas, of Arden House convocations on foreign policy, 1957; special counsel to Senator Abraham Ribicoff, 1962, 1968, and 1972; consultant to Theatre of Ideas, 1967-75, and to the National Coalition for a Responsible Congress, 1970.

AWARDS, HONORS: Special citation for U.S. Navy film series, "Fighter Direction: Defense of Fleet against Air Attacks," 1944; Golden Reel Award, 1957, for film on Boys Clubs of America; *Variety* award, 1958, for television film; Israeli Government prize, 1975, for film "Shalom, Baby."

WRITINGS: Armies for Peace, Antioch University Press, 1950; (contributor) William G. Leary and James S. Smith, editors, *Think before You Write*, Harcourt, 1951; (contributor) *Expanding Horizons*, Odyssey Press, 1953; *Courage Is the Key*, Twayne, 1953; *The Empire City*, Rinehart, 1955; *Grand Deception*, Lippincott, 1955; *The Counterfeit Traitor*, Holt, 1958; (contributor) H. Ribalow, editor, *These Your Children*, Barnes, 1958; *The Double Dealers*, Lippincott, 1959.

(Contributor) *Psychology of Mental Health*, Ronald, 1960; *The Fabulous Rogues*, Ballantine, 1960; *The Magnificent Scoundrels*, Ballantine, 1961; *Rebels, Rogues, Rascals*, Ballantine, 1962; (contributor) *Treasury of American Jewish Stories*, Yoseloff, 1962; *That Pellet Woman*, Stein & Day, 1965.

(Editor) *Natural Enemies: Youth and the Conflict of the Generations*, Lippincott, 1970; (editor) *Dissent, Power, and Confrontation*, McGraw, 1972.

Also author of over 200 film scripts, including "Shalom, Baby," 1975, "Daisyfresh," 1977, and "The Savage." Work appears in anthologies, including *Best American Short Stories*. Contributor to *New Republic, Saturday Review*, and other magazines.

MEDIA ADAPTATIONS: The Counterfeit Traitor was filmed by Paramount in 1962; *Grand Deception* has been optioned by Screen Gems for a television series; "The Savage" has been optioned by Metro-Goldwyn-Mayer.

BIOGRAPHICAL/CRITICAL SOURCES: New Republic, February 28, 1970; *Christian Science Monitor*, March 14, 1970; *National Review*, April 7, 1970; *New York Times*, February 24, 1972.

*   *   *

KOHAK, Erazim V. 1933-

PERSONAL: Born May 21, 1933, in Prague, Czechoslovakia; son of Miloslav (a journalist) and Zdislava (Prochazkova) Kohak; married Frances MacPherson, 1955 (divorced, 1976); married Sheree Dukes, 1981; children: (first marriage) Mary Zdislava, Susan Bozena, Katherine MacPherson. *Education:* Colgate University, B.A., 1954; Yale University, M.A., 1957, Ph.D., 1958. *Religion:* Episcopalian. *Address:* R.F.D. 2, Box 15B-Sharon, Jaffrey, N.H. 03452. *Office:* Department of Philosophy, Boston University, 232 Bay State Rd., Boston, Mass. 02215.

CAREER: Gustavus Adolphus College, St. Peter, Minn., assistant professor of philosophy, 1958-60; Boston University, Boston, Mass., assistant professor, 1960-66, associate professor, 1966-71, professor of philosophy, 1971—, chairman of department, 1982-84. Visiting professor of philosophy, Bowling Green State University, 1971.

MEMBER: American Philosophical Association, Society for Phenomenology and Existential Philosophy, Czechoslovak Society for Arts and Sciences, Husserl Circle, Personalistic Discussion Group (chair), Phi Beta Kappa.

WRITINGS: (Translator and author of introduction) Paul Ricoeur, *Freedom and Nature*, Northwestern University Press, 1966; (editor and translator) Thomas G. Masaryk, *Masaryk on Marx*, Bucknell University Press, 1972; (with Heda Kovaly) *The Victors and the Vanquished*, Horizon Press, 1972; (with Kovaly) *Na vlastni kuzi*, Sixty-eight Publishers (Toronto), 1972; *Narod v nas*, Sixty-eight Publishers, 1978; *Idea and Experience*, University of Chicago Press, 1978; *The Embers and the Stars*, University of Chicago Press, 1984; *Certorani s Misou*, St. Michael Press, 1984. Regular contributor to *Dissent, Commonweal*, and *Harper's*. Member of editorial board, *Dissent* and *Philosophical Forum*.

WORK IN PROGRESS: Three Czech Thinkers: Masaryk, Radl, Patocka; a continuing series of philosophic/literary broadcasts for Radio Free Europe Czechoslovak Service.

SIDELIGHTS: Erazim V. Kohak told *CA:* "In a technological age, philosophy, too, tends to become a *techne*, the province of a technician. My aim as a writer is to return it to people. I write of the moral sense of nature to win a place for persons in an increasingly mechanized world, and of the world beyond the powerlines and paved roads, to rediscover nature as the dwelling place of moral subjects, not just a source of raw materials."

*   *   *

KOHL, Herbert   1937-

PERSONAL: Born August 22, 1937, in Bronx, New York; son of Samuel (a building contractor) and Marion Kohl; married Judith Murdock (a teacher and weaver), 1963; children: Antonia, Erica, Joshua. *Education:* Harvard University, A.B. (magna cum laude), 1958; graduate study, University College, Oxford, 1958-59; Teachers College, Columbia University, M.A., 1962, additional graduate study, 1965-66. *Home:* 40561 Eureka Hill Rd., Point Arena, Calif. 95468. *Agent:* Robert Lescher, Lescher & Lescher, Ltd., 155 East 71st St., New York, N.Y. 10021.

CAREER: Elementary school teacher in New York City, 1962-66; Horace Mann-Lincoln Institute, New York City, research associate, 1966-67; Teachers and Writers Collaborative, New York City, director, 1966-67; University of California, Berkeley, visiting associate professor of English education, 1967-68; Other Ways (public alternative high school), Berkeley, Calif., teacher and director, 1968-71; Berkeley Unified School District, Berkeley, consultant on public alternative schools, 1971-72; Center for Open Learning and Teaching, Berkeley, co-director, 1972-77; Coastal Ridge Research and Educational Center, Point Arena, Calif., director, 1978—.

Educational consultant to University of Minneapolis, Des Moines Community Corporation, University of California, San Mateo County Schools, Stockton Unified School District, and other public and private institutions, 1967-73. Member of board, Atari Institute. *Member:* Authors Guild, PEN American Center (member of executive board; coordinator of PEN American Center West), Phi Beta Kappa. *Awards, honors:* Henry fellowship, 1958-59; Woodrow Wilson fellowship, 1959-60; National Endowment for the Arts award for nonfiction article, 1968; National Book Award for Children's Literature, 1977, for *View from the Oak.*

WRITINGS: The Age of Complexity, Mentor, 1965; *The Language and Education of the Deaf,* Center for Urban Education, 1966; *36 Children,* New American Library, 1967; *Teaching the Unteachable,* New York Review of Books, 1967; *The Open Classroom: A Practical Guide to a New Way of Teaching,* Vintage, 1969; *Fables: A Curriculum Unit,* Teachers and Writers Collaborative, 1969.

A University for Our Time, Other Ways, 1970; (editor with Victor Hernandez Cruz) *Stuff: A Collection of Poems, Visions, and Imaginative Happenings from Young Writers in Schools—Open and Closed,* World Publishing, 1970; (author of introduction) Sata Repo, editor, *This Book Is about Schools,* Pantheon, 1970; *Golden Boy as Anthony Cool: A Photo Essay on Names and Graffiti,* Dial, 1972; (editor) *An Anthology of Fables,* Houghton, Volume I, 1972, Volume II, 1973; *Reading: How to—A People's Guide to Alternative Ways of Teaching and Testing Reading,* Dutton, 1973; (editor) *Stories of Sport and Society,* Houghton, 1973; *Games, Math and Writing in the Open Classroom,* Random House, 1973; *Half the House,* Dutton, 1974.

On Teaching, Schocken, 1976; (with wife, Judith Kohl) *View from the Oak* (juvenile), Scribner, 1977; *Growing with Your Children,* Little, Brown, 1978.

A Book of Puzzlements, Schocken, 1981; *Basic Skills: A Plan for Your Children, a Program for All Children,* Little, Brown, 1982; *Atari Games and Recreations,* Reston, 1982; *Insight: Reflections on Reading,* Addison-Wesley, 1982; *Conscience and Human Rights,* Amnesty International, 1983; (with J. Kohl) *Pack, Band, and Colony,* Farrar, Strauss, 1983; *Atari PILOT Games and Recreation for Learning,* Reston, 1983; (with daughter, Erica Kohl) *Whatever Became of Emmett Gold?,* Little, Brown, 1983.

Author of column, "Insight," in *Teacher,* 1968-80. Contributor of articles and reviews to *New York Review of Books, New York Times, Learning Magazine, Times Educational Supplement, Harvard Educational Review, This Magazine Is about Schools, Cultural Affairs, New School Education Journal,* and other publications. Member of editorial board, *People's Yellow Pages* and *Learning Magazine;* member of advisory board, *Interaction.*

SIDELIGHTS: Herbert Kohl is one of the most persistent voices in the call for the reevaluation and reformation of the American educational system. His concept of an "open classroom" has particularly influenced educators and has inspired many alternative educational experiments. In *The Open Classroom: A Practical Guide to a New Way of Teaching,* Kohl explains his theories and the techniques he uses in an open classroom. The goal of such teaching is to help students to make worthwhile educational choices and to find themselves.

In *36 Children,* Kohl details how the use of open classroom techniques was successful in his own teaching in a ghetto elementary school. Nat Hentoff, writing in the *New Yorker,* explains that in this book, "Kohl shows how a sixth-grade class of wary Negro children in East Harlem learned to trust him as a teacher and trust themselves and thereby beat the system. Temporarily. After their one year with Kohl, most of them, too, were mutilated, but they demonstrated in that one year what they could have become—poor as they were, black as they were, and without a head start. In this book, they are trenchant proof that their defeat is the fault not of themselves or their families but of the system."

A *New York Times Book Review* writer describes Kohl's success in the classroom as a "time of intense creative collaboration. . . . Following the children's needs, he let his students sit where they wished, take 10-minute talk periods between subjects, dance once a week in class, and visit his apartment regularly." Amid what would seem like pandemonium by conventional classroom standards of decorum, the reviewer goes on to note that "they began to write, and this sometimes heartbreaking book is as much by the children as by the author. Starting with simple descriptions of their surroundings, some progressed to the perceptive stories, fables and poems that comprise about half the text." Some readers and reviewers have suggested that Kohl included so much of the children's work in *36 Children* as a final act of educational encouragement.

In his own writing about *36 Children,* Kohl says that he was "able to take children who had experienced failure and self-hatred in school and enable them to flower emotionally and intellectually. This involved my throwing out the standard curriculum, reworking the schedule of the day, and most of all, listening and learning from my students and building a curriculum that used the strengths in their lives."

Reading: How to—A People's Guide to Alternative Ways of Teaching and Testing Reading explores the question of illiteracy, suggesting methods that teachers and parents can use to teach reading more effectively. Kohl sees illiteracy as a failure not of the child but of the educational system. "Kohl," writes Barbara Breasted in the *Christian Science Monitor,* "has never met a child who didn't want to learn to read. But this . . . educational reformer has met many adults who make children afraid they can't learn to read. It is the spirit in which reading is taught that needs to be changed."

Examining the assumptions of modern education, Kohl suggests in *Basic Skills: A Plan for Your Child, a Program for All Children* that schools have not concentrated on certain fundamentals which all children should learn. Education's first goal, Kohl writes, is to "develop informed, thoughtful and sensitive citizens." This can be done, he writes, by teaching students six basic skills: "The ability to use language well and thoughtfully, . . . the ability to think through problems and experiment with solutions, . . . the ability to understand scientific and technical ideas and use tools, . . . the ability to use imagination and to participate in and appreciate personal and group expression, . . . the ability to understand how people function in groups, . . . [and] learning how to learn throughout life and to contribute to the nurturance of others." As David G. Savage writes in the *Los Angeles Times Book Review,* Kohl "still is laboring away, trying to reform and redefine public education."

BIOGRAPHICAL/CRITICAL SOURCES: New Republic, December 23, 1967, November 21, 1970; *New Yorker,* March 16, 1968; *Carleton Miscellany,* winter, 1969; *Washington Post Book World,* April 12, 1970, July 11, 1982; *Times Literary Supplement,* December 18, 1970; *Saturday Review,* May 27, 1972; *New York Review of Books,* May 3, 1973; *Christian Science Monitor,* May 23, 1973; *New York Times,* July 9, 1973; *American Libraries,* March, 1975; *Los Angeles Times Book Review,* February 11, 1979, May 2, 1982; *Instructor,* April, 1982.

*   *   *

KOPPITZ, Elizabeth M(unsterberg)   1919-1983

PERSONAL: Born February 9, 1919, in Berlin, Germany; came to United States in 1939; died October 5, 1983, in New York, N.Y. of cancer; daughter of Oskar and Helen F. (Rice) Munsterberg; married Werner Koppitz (a research psychologist), June 14, 1955. *Education:* George Peabody College for Teachers of Vanderbilt University, B.A., 1951; Ohio State University, M.A., 1952, Ph.D., 1955. *Home address:* R.F.D. 1, Box 200, Mount Kisco, N.Y. *Office:* Board of Cooperative Educational Services, Yorktown Heights, N.Y.

CAREER: East Boston Social Center Council, Boston, Mass., arts and crafts instructor, 1942-45; Fisk University Social Center, Nashville, Tenn., head resident, 1945-50; Juvenile Diagnostic Center, Columbus, Ohio, psychologist, 1955; Children's Mental Health Center, Columbus, psychologist, 1956-58; Endicott (N.Y.) public schools, psychologist, 1959; Board of Cooperative Educational Services, Yorktown Heights, N.Y., school psychologist, beginning 1961.

MEMBER: American Psychological Association, National Association of School Psychologists, Westchester Association of School Psychologists.

*WRITINGS—*Published by Grune, except as indicated: *The Bender Gestalt Test with Human Figure Drawing Test* (manual), Ohio Department of Education, 1962; *The Bender Gestalt Test for Young Children,* Volume I, 1964, Volume II: *Research and Application 1963-1973,* 1975; *Psychological Evaluation of Children's Human Figure Drawings,* 1968; *Children with Learning Disabilities: A Five Year Follow-Up Study,* 1971; *The Visual Aural Digital Span Test,* 1977. Contributor to psychology periodicals.

WORK IN PROGRESS: Translation of books into German, Japanese, and Spanish; research on diagnostic tests for middle school children.

AVOCATIONAL INTERESTS: Gardening, art, stamp-collecting, and travel.

OBITUARIES: New York Times, October 12, 1983.

*   *   *

KORNHAUSER, David H(enry)   1918-

PERSONAL: Born March 17, 1918, in Philadelphia, Pa.; son of David Emmanuel (an artist) and Mary Elizabeth (Parker) Kornhauser; married Kyoko Nakamura, February 12, 1948 (died April, 1963); married Michiko Usui, July 20, 1965; children: (second marriage) David Hajime. *Education:* Bucknell University, B.A., 1941; University of Michigan, M.A., 1951, Ph.D., 1956. *Home:* 5089 Maunalani Cir., Honolulu, Hawaii 96816. *Office:* Department of Geography, Room 415, 2424 Maile Way, University of Hawaii, Honolulu, Hawaii 96822.

CAREER: Member of Supreme Commander of Allied Powers headquarters, Osaka, Japan, and Tokyo, Japan, 1946-50; Pennsylvania State University, State College, assistant professor of geography, 1955-56; State University of New York College at New Paltz, associate professor of geography, 1956-63; University of Hawaii, Honolulu, professor of geography and Asian studies, 1963—. *Military service:* U.S. Army, 1943-47; became second lieutenant.

MEMBER: Association of American Geographers, Association of Japanese Geographers, Association for Asian Studies, Pacific Science Association.

AWARDS, HONORS: Fulbright fellow, Tokyo Kyoiku University, Japan, 1959-60, and University of Hawaii, 1964-65; Japan Society for Promotion of Science grant, summer, 1972; Ministry of Education of Japan teaching grant, Mie University, 1977-78; University of Hawaii Foundation/Japanese government grant, 1984-85.

WRITINGS: Urban Japan: Its Foundations and Growth, Longman, 1976; *Japan: Geographical Background to Urban-Industrial Development,* Longman, 1982; (translator with wife, Michiko Kornhauser) Iozawa Tomoya, *Trekking in the Himalayas,* Yama-Kei (Tokyo), 1983; *Studies of Japan in Western Languages of Special Interest to Geographers,* Kokon-Shoin (Tokyo), 1984. Contributor of articles to academic journals.

WORK IN PROGRESS: Research on growth and development of Japanese cities.

AVOCATIONAL INTERESTS: Music, photography.

*   *   *

KOVEL, Joel S.   1936-

PERSONAL: Born August 27, 1936, in Brooklyn, N.Y.; son of Louis and Rose (Farber) Kovel; married Virginia Ryan, April 13, 1962; children: Jonathan, Erin, Molly. *Education:*

Yale University, B.S. (summa cum laude), 1957; Columbia University, M.D., 1961. *Home:* 165 West 91st St., New York, N.Y. 10024. *Office:* Albert Einstein College of Medicine, Yeshiva University, New York, N.Y. 10033.

CAREER: Bronx Municipal Hospital Center, Bronx, N.Y., intern in medical service, 1961-62; assistant resident, later resident in psychiatry at Albert Einstein College of Medicine, Yeshiva University, New York, N.Y., and Bronx Municipal Hospital Center, 1962-64, chief resident in psychiatry at both institutions, 1964-65; Yeshiva University, Albert Einstein College of Medicine, instructor, 1967-69, assistant professor, 1969-74, associate professor, 1974-79, professor of psychiatry, 1979—. Psychoanalyst and psychiatrist in private practice; visiting professor of anthropology at New School for Social Research, 1980—. *Awards, honors:* Nomination for National Book Award in philosophy and religion, 1970, for *White Racism: A Psychohistory.*

WRITINGS: White Racism: A Psychohistory, Pantheon, 1970, reprinted, Columbia University Press, 1984; (contributor) Jean Strouse, editor, *Women in Analysis: Dialogues on Psychoanalytic Views of Femininity,* Grossman, 1974; *A Complete Guide to Therapy: From Psychoanalysis to Behavior Modification,* Pantheon, 1976; *The Age of Desire: Case Histories of a Radical Psychoanalyst,* Pantheon, 1981; *Against the State of Nuclear War,* Pan Books, 1983. Contributor of articles and reviews to *Telos, Social Research, Social Policy, New York Times Book Review,* and *Psychoanalytic Review.* Editorial associate, *Telos.*

SIDELIGHTS: "Psychoanalysts of the world, unite; put Joel [S.] Kovel back on the couch before he has you up against the wall," writes Harvey Mindess in the *Los Angeles Times.* In *The Age of Desire: Case Histories of a Radical Psychoanalyst,* Kovel criticizes his profession, labeling the majority of its practitioners "certifiably out-and-out hacks." "When we feel so rotten that we can't function," explains John Leonard in the *New York Times,* "psychoanalysis purports to be a form of help. It isn't, according to Joel Kovel, . . . nor is any other adjunct of the 'mental health' industry in the Western world. Why not? Because, says Dr. Kovel, 'bourgeois psychology' is in business to abet capitalism. . . . The object of most therapies is not to make us feel worthy, but to get us back to work."

Kovel describes himself as a Marxist psychoanalyst, "and in a sense *The Age of Desire* is a book-length attempt to define that unlikely hybrid," notes Walter Kendrick in *Nation.* In the end, concludes Kendrick, "Kovel acknowledges that there can be no such thing as Marxist psychotherapy, but he maintains that there can be a therapy compatible with Marxism—'a transcendent therapy, one predicated on the movement toward universality.'"

Kovel supports his argument with partially fictionalized case histories, and Seymour Kleinberg writes in the *Village Voice* that when Kovel is discussing "the people he has known so intimately, the book is alive." Kendrick similarly believes the histories "read like tales of real life: Curtis the investment banker, Sarah the spoiled Jewish princess, and Hector the Puerto Rican 'vigilante' are firmly placed in the contexts of race, family, and work, so that we seem to know them—though, as Kovel admits, it's impossible even after years of analysis for an analyst to 'know' his patient."

The fictitiousness, however, bothers some reviewers. While admitting there may be professional reasons for it, Leonard claims "it injures me in my credulity and Dr. Kovel seems to

enjoy it too much." Kleinberg, moreover, suggests that Kovel fictionalizes because "he wants his evidence to conform to his theories, so that one case can symbolize 'the family under capitalism,' and another can invite him to dwell for a bit on the economic and psychological history of women. . . . When he begins to theorize, the prose shifts, in a matter of sentences, into the oracular, thickening, bogging the reader down under the weight of the labor to be profound."

Benjamin DeMott admits in *Psychology Today* that Kovel's glib generalizations and heavy use of jargon weaken *The Age of Desire,* but he maintains that each case history "lights up the interdependencies that [Kovel] claims his profession as a whole neglects—the linkups between the state of individual psyches and the terms of individual participation in history and the public world." Calling the book "as strong and flexible an argument on the side of the party of hope as I've heard in years from within a working professional elite," DeMott concludes that *The Age of Desire* "begins as a probe of the ills of a single sector of American professional life but emerges, before it's done, as a powerful address to a central problem of our time—how to preserve and nourish moral ambition in an immoral society. . . . Refusing to wrestle with [this difficult book] would be an act of self-impoverishment."

BIOGRAPHICAL/CRITICAL SOURCES: New York Times, June 24, 1976, January 14, 1982; *New York Times Book Review,* July 18, 1976; *New Leader,* October 25, 1976; *Times Literary Supplement,* July 15, 1977; Joel S. Kovel, *The Age of Desire: Case Histories of a Radical Psychoanalyst,* Pantheon, 1981; *Psychology Today,* January, 1982; *Village Voice,* January 20-26, 1982; *Nation,* January 30, 1982; *Los Angeles Times,* March 19, 1982.

* * *

KREEFT, Peter 1937-

PERSONAL: Surname is pronounced Krayft; born March 16, 1937, in Paterson, N.J.; son of John (an engineer) and Lucy (Comtobad) Kreeft; married Maria Massi, August 18, 1962; children: John, Jennifer, Katherine, Elizabeth. *Education:* Calvin College, A.B., 1959; graduate study at Yale University, 1959-60; Fordham University, M.A., 1961, Ph.D., 1965. *Religion:* Roman Catholic. *Home:* 44 Davis Ave., West Newton, Mass. 02165. *Office:* Department of Philosophy, Boston College, Chestnut Hill, Mass. 02167.

CAREER: Villanova University, Villanova, Pa., instructor in philosophy, 1961-65; Boston College, Chestnut Hill, Mass., assistant professor, 1965-69, associate professor of philosophy, 1969—.

AWARDS, HONORS: Woodrow Wilson fellowship, 1959-60; Danforth fellowship, 1966-67; *Love Is Stronger than Death* was nominated for the American Book Award in the religion/ inspirational category, 1980.

WRITINGS: C. S. Lewis, Eerdmans, 1969; *The Five Faces of Death,* Harper, 1978; *Love Is Stronger than Death,* Harper, 1979; *Heaven, the Heart's Deepest Longing,* Harper, 1980; *Everything You Ever Wanted to Know about Heaven . . . but Never Dreamed of Asking,* Harper, 1982; *Between Heaven and Hell,* Inter-Varsity Press, 1982; *The Unaborted Socrates,* Inter-Varsity Press, 1983; *The Best Things in Life,* Inter-Varsity Press, 1984; *Yes or No?,* Servant Publications, 1984; (with Richard Purtill and Michael MacDonald) *Philosophical Questions,* Prentice-Hall, 1984.

WORK IN PROGRESS: An introduction to St. Thomas Aquinas; a philosophical commentary on Job.

SIDELIGHTS: Peter Kreeft writes that his main interests are philosophy in literature, philosophy of religion, East-West dialogue, mysticism, and existentialism.

*   *   *

KREJCI, Jaroslav 1916-

PERSONAL: Surname rhymes with "Strachey"; born February 13, 1916, in Czechoslovakia; son of Jaroslav (a civil servant) and Zdenka (Dudova) Krejci; married Anna Cerna (a principal lecturer at Preston Polytechnic), May 11, 1940. *Education:* Charles University, Prague, Dr. Jur., 1945. *Office:* Lonsdale College, University of Lancaster, Lancaster, England.

CAREER: State Planning Office, Prague, Czechoslovakia, secretary to chairman, 1945-48, head of department of national income, 1948-50; State Bank, Prague, research worker, 1950-53; Czechoslovak Academy of Sciences, Prague, research worker, 1968; University of Lancaster, Lancaster, England, lecturer in comparative social and cultural analysis, 1970-76, professor in School of European Studies, 1976-83, professor emeritus, 1983—. External associate professor, Graduate School of Political and Social Sciences, Prague, 1948-50, and Technological University, Prague, 1950-52; member of advisory body for economic analysis for Deputy Prime Minister, Prague, 1968.

MEMBER: International P.E.N., National Association of Soviet and East European Studies, University Association for Contemporary European Studies, Council for European Studies, Czechoslovak Society of Arts and Sciences.

AWARDS, HONORS: Received award for participation in Czech resistance movement during World War II.

WRITINGS: Duchodove rozvrstveni (title means "Income Distribution"), [Prague], 1947; *Uvod do planovaneho hospodarstvi* (title means "Introduction into the Planned Economy"), [Prague], 1949; *Volkseinkommensvergleich: Osterreich CSSR* (title means "National Income Comparison: Austria-Czechoslovakia"), Verlag des Osterreichischen Gewerkschaftsbundes (Vienna), 1969.

Social Change and Stratification in Postwar Czechoslovakia, Columbia University Press, 1972; *Social Structure in Divided Germany,* St. Martin's, 1976; (editor) *Sozialdemokratie und Systemwandel,* Dietz, 1978; (with V. Velimsky) *Ethnic and Political Nations in Europe,* St. Martin's, 1981; *National Income and Outlay in Czechoslovakia, Poland and Yugoslavia,* St. Martin's, 1982; *Great Revolutions Compared,* St. Martin's, 1983.

Contributor: M. S. Archer and L. S. Giner, editors, *Ethnic Problems in Contemporary Europe,* Routledge & Kegan Paul, 1978; P. H. Merkl and Ninian Smart, editors, *Religion and Politics in the Modern World,* New York University Press, 1983; L. Matejka and B. Stolz, editors, *Cross Currents,* Michigan Slavic Publications, 1983.

Contributor to *Review of Income and Wealth, Soviet Studies, Sociological Analysis, Journal of Religious History, Revue d'Etudes Comparatives Est-Ouest, Jahrbuch der Wirtschaft Osteuropas, Religion, History of European Ideas,* and *Promeny.*

WORK IN PROGRESS: Civilization and Social Structure.

SIDELIGHTS: Jaroslav Krejci spent the years from 1954-60 in a labor camp in Czechoslovakia.

*   *   *

KREVOLIN, Nathan 1927-

PERSONAL: Born November 21, 1927, in New Haven, Conn.; son of Abraham and Rebecca (Rich) Krevolin; married Lois Ann Silverman, July 3, 1955; children: Clay, Adam. *Education:* Quinnipiac College, A.S., 1948; Central Connecticut State College (now University), B.S., 1950; Southern Connecticut State College (now University), M.A., 1952; University of Connecticut, professional diploma, 1956, Ph.D., 1960. *Home:* 40 Osage Rd., West Hartford, Conn. 06117. *Office:* Maria Sanford Hall, Central Connecticut State University, New Britain, Conn. 06050.

CAREER: University of Connecticut, Storrs, instructor in business education, 1950-51; secondary school business education teacher in New Haven, Conn., 1951-55, and West Hartford, Conn., 1955-66; Central Connecticut State College (now University), New Britain, associate professor, 1966-73, professor of business education, 1973—. Lecturer in business education for radio and television stations, including "Voice of America," 1967-68. *Military service:* U.S. Army, 1946-47.

MEMBER: National Education Association, National Business Education Association, American Association of University Professors, Eastern Business Education Association, Connecticut Education Association, Connecticut Business Education Association, Kappa Delta Pi, Phi Delta Kappa, Delta Pi Epsilon, Farmington Club.

WRITINGS: Art Typing, Pitman, 1962; (with Louis C. Nanassy) *Junior High Timed Writings,* Pitman, 1963, revised edition published as *Timed Writings for Teenagers,* 1968; (with Alan C. Lloyd) *You Learn to Type!,* with twenty record albums, McGraw, 1966.

(With Nanassy and John E. Whitcraft) *Personal Typing,* with teacher's manual and key, Pitman, 1970; *The Gregg Office Job Training Program: Typist,* with training manual, resource materials, and teacher's manual, McGraw, 1972.

Communication Systems and Procedures for the Modern Office, Prentice-Hall, 1983; *Filing and Records Management,* Prentice-Hall, 1985; (with Whitcraft and Nanassy) *Keyboarding for Personal and Professional Use,* Reston, 1985.

Contributor to textbooks, magazines, handbooks, and yearbooks. Contributor of articles to education journals, including *Journal of Secondary Education, Education Digest, Business Education World, Journal of Business Education, Typewriting News,* and *Balance Sheet.*

AVOCATIONAL INTERESTS: Art, music, tennis, golf, swimming, and travel.

*   *   *

KROCHMAL, Arnold 1919-

PERSONAL: Born January 30, 1919, in New York; son of Morris (an embroiderer) and Leah (Weissman) Krochmal; married Connie Brite (a writer), November 30, 1970; children: Stephen Glen, Maurice Manfred, Walter Lyle. *Education:* Attended New York University, 1937; North Carolina State College, B.S., 1942; Cornell University, M.S., Ph.D. *Religion:* Jewish. *Home:* 119 Bell Rd., Asheville, N.C. 28805.

CAREER: Instructor in horticulture, New Mexico Agriculture Experiment Station, 1947-49; Fulbright professor in Greece, 1952-53; chief research advisor of Wyoming Team, in Kabul, Afghanistan, 1957-59; Panamerican Agricultural School, El Zamorano, Honduras, head of department of horticulture, 1960-61; U.S. Department of Agriculture, assistant officer in charge and research botanist in Virgin Islands, 1961-66, Forest Service, principal economic botanist and project leader for timber-related crops in Berea, Ky., 1961-66, principal economic botanist in Asheville, N.C., 1971-82, affiliated with Institute of Tropical Forestry, Rio Piedras, P.R., 1982-83.

Economic geographer, College of the Virgin Islands, 1964-66; summer visiting professor at Wisconsin State University, 1966; fall visiting professor at Berea College, 1967; guest of Jardin Botanico Uribe, Medellin, Columbia, 1974; senior research fellow at Agricultural University of Wageningen, Holland, 1976-77; guest lecturer, Academy of the U.S.S.R. Main Botanical Garden, 1980; chairperson of Structure of Tropical Rain Forests Working Party, International Union of Forest Research Organizations, 1980—; chairman of Division of Natural Sciences, World University, Hato Rey, P.R., 1982-83; adjunct professor at North Carolina State University, University of North Carolina, and Atlanta University. Consultant to Agency for International Development, Volunteers for International Technical Assistance, International Executive Corps, and the governments of Surinam, Jamaica, Montserrat, Thailand, Dominican Republic, and British Virgin Islands. *Military service:* U.S. Army, 1942-46.

WRITINGS: Horticultura Practica, Panamerican Agricultural School, 1960; (with Russ Walters and Richard Doughty) *Guide to Medicinal Plants of Appalachia,* Forest Service, U.S. Department of Agriculture, 1971; *Indigenous Nuts of the United States,* Forest Service, U.S. Department of Agriculture, 1983. Editor, *Caribbean Agriculture and Science* and *Ceiba.*

With wife, Connie Krochmal: *Guide to Medicinal Plants of the United States,* Quadrangle, 1973; *The Complete Illustrated Book of Dyes from Natural Sources,* Doubleday, 1974; *Indoor Gardening: Green Thumb Guide,* Drake, 1974; *Making It: The Encyclopedia of How to Do It for Less,* Drake, 1975; *Caribbean Cooking,* Quadrangle, 1975; *A Naturalist's Guide to Cooking with Wild Plants,* Quadrangle, 1975. Also author, with C. Krochmal, of *Gardening in the Carolinas,* Doubleday, and of garden column in San Juan *Star.*

WORK IN PROGRESS: Pamphlets on aging, acid rain, cults, and world hunger; three books, *Alternate Healings, Alternate Energy Sources* and *Mental Retardation.*

SIDELIGHTS: Arnold Krochmal told *CA* that his family has a motto: "Words as a bridge, not a wall." Much of the work done by Krochmal and his wife, Connie, has been inspired by that motto and has been "devoted to translating scientific botanical information for the lay person, using understandable words, not scientific jargon," which Krochmal "tried passionately to escape during a thirty-four-year career as a professor and government scientist."

The Krochmals come from dissimilar backgrounds—he is the son of immigrant parents and was raised in the Bronx, while she grew up on a mountain farm in Appalachian Kentucky—but the two writers "share the deep concern that science and research do more than serve as a source of esoteric papers in rarely-read scholarly journals. We feel that citizen and taxpayer has a right to know what is going on in the world of science, and we have and will continue to try to close the gap. We like

to think of ourselves as the Saint Jeromes of the botanical and horticultural community, translating the current dogmas into understandable English. And sometimes the results have been as Saint Jerome knew them—harassment by the 'priesthood' whose monopoly of knowledge is threatened!

"We have been influenced by the writings of two great Cornell professors, Liberty Hyde Bailey and Walter Conrad Muenscher. They mastered the skill and talent of communicating with a broad audience without losing their knowledge or diluting it. For young writers in this area of popularized science writing, we urge a period of apprenticeship. We have worked with a number of young people who were assigned to us in the U.S. Forest Service, helping them learn how to produce readable and correct items.

"We work as a team," Krochmal said of himself and his wife. "We discuss the outline of what we are doing, then move the work back and forth between us. We do an outline first, then fill it in. We use lots of photos and drawings, and knowing where these can be borrowed or commissioned is [a basic skill].

"One of the things we have learned is that we must write what publishers will publish. Great ideas, wonderful concepts, are of little value if no one will publish them. We have also learned to try to work with the editors as best we can. Some are easy to deal with. Others, in the federal government, can be tyrannical and arbitrary. . . . We have the completed manuscripts of three plant books done while working for the U.S. Forest Service as part of job requirements. Not one will be published by them, for one reason or another."

MEDIA ADAPTATIONS: Some of the Krochmal's books were the basis for a U.S. Forest Service slide show entitled "A Forest Is Also Nuts, Berries, and Leaves."

*   *   *

KULSKI, Julian (Eugeniusz) 1929-

PERSONAL: Born March 3, 1929, in Warsaw, Poland; came to United States, 1948, naturalized citizen, 1950; son of Julian Spitoslav (in public administration) and Eugenia Helena (Solecka) Kulski; married Isabel Gagian (an editor), September 3, 1959; children: Helena, Julian. *Education:* Attended Oxford School of Architecture, 1947-48; Yale University, B.Arch., 1953, M.Arch., 1973; Warsaw Institute of Technology, Ph.D., 1966. *Home and office:* Varzara, Orlean, Va. 22128.

CAREER: University of Notre Dame, Notre Dame, Ind., professor of architecture and city planning, 1960-65; George Washington University, Washington, D.C., professor of city planning, 1965-67; Howard University, Washington, D.C., professor of city planning, 1967—. Consultant to U.S. Agency for International Development, World Bank, and municipal and industrial agencies. Chairman of continuing education committee, Association of Collegiate Schools of Architecture, 1964-66.

MEMBER: American Institute of Architects, American Institute of Planners, American Society for Public Administration, American Association of University Professors, American Society of Planning Officials, National Association of Housing and Redevelopment Officials.

WRITINGS: Land of Urban Promise: Continuing the Great Tradition, University of Notre Dame Press, 1967; *Stefan Starzynski w mojej pamieci,* Instytut Literacki, 1968; *Przemiany w Ukladach Urbanistycznych Miast Amerykanskich* (title means

"Evolution of American Urban Systems"), Panstwowe Wydawnictwo Naukowe (Warsaw), 1970; *Architecture in a Revolutionary Era*, Aurora, 1971; *Dying, We Live: The Personal Chronicle of A Young Freedom Fighter in Warsaw (1939-1945)*, Holt, 1979. Contributor to professional journals.

SIDELIGHTS: In *Dying, We Live: The Personal Chronicle of a Young Freedom Fighter in Warsaw (1939-1945)*, Julian Kulski recounts his experiences as a boy partisan in Poland during World War II. Though Kulski himself was not Jewish, his father was a Resistance sympathizer whose efforts to fight the German invaders set an example for the boy. When the fighting escalated, Kulski, whose father was then mayor of Warsaw, was sent to live with his scoutmaster, Ludwik Berger. Berger became the district leader of the youth resistance forces in his area of the city and trained Kulski to be a courier. As a child, Kulski was able to penetrate areas of the city that were inaccessible to adults, and he survived several attacks on the Jewish ghetto where he stationed himself to help the resistance effort later in the war. Written in diary form, with maps and photos of old Warsaw, the book tells "a touching story," according to the *Los Angeles Times,* "one which shows a side of the Polish resistance not often reported." In 1984, Kulski translated the book into Polish.

BIOGRAPHICAL/CRITICAL SOURCES: Washington Post, January 16, 1980; *Los Angeles Times,* May 30, 1980.

*   *   *

KURLAND, Gerald 1942-

PERSONAL: Born July 24, 1942, in Brooklyn, N.Y.; son of Carl (a pharmacist) and Sophia (Spar) Kurland. *Education:* Long Island University, B.A., 1963; Brooklyn College of the City University of New York, M.A., 1964; City University of New York, Ph.D., 1968. *Politics:* Generally conservative. *Religion:* None. *Office:* 6990 Southwest 30th St., Miramar, Fla. 33023.

CAREER: Brooklyn College of the City University of New York, Brooklyn, N.Y., lecturer in history, 1966-75; free-lance writer and editor, mainly of textbooks and adult and juvenile historical works.

MEMBER: American Historical Association, Organization of American Historians, New York State Historical Association, New York Historical Society.

WRITINGS—Published by Simon & Schuster, except as indicated: *Seth Low: The Reformer in an Urban and Industrial Age*, Twayne, 1971; *Western Civilization to 1500 A.D.*, 1971; *Western Civilization from 1500 A.D.*, 1971; *American History to Reconstruction*, 1971; (editor) *Misjudgment or Defense of Freedom: The United States in Vietnam*, 1975; (editor) *The Failure of Diplomacy: The Origins of the Cold War*, 1975; (contributor) John A. Garraty, editor, *Dictionary of American Biography: Supplement Five, 1951-1955*, Scribner, 1977; (contributor) *Dictionary of American Biography: Supplement Six*, Scribner, 1980.

Juvenile books; all published by Story House: *Warren Harding*, 1971; *Thomas Dewey*, 1971; *Walt Disney*, 1971; *Nikita S. Khrushchev*, 1971; *Fidel Castro*, 1972; *George Wallace*, 1972; *Spiro Agnew,* 1972; *Fiorello La Guardia*, 1972; *Alexander Hamilton*, 1972; *Benjamin Franklin*, 1972; *John D. Rockefeller*, 1972; *Samuel Gompers*, 1972; *Mao Tse Tung*, 1972; *Richard Daley*, 1972; *Clarence Darrow*, 1972; *Lyndon B. Johnson,*

1972; *Henry Ford*, 1972; *James R. Hoffa*, 1972; *Lucretia Mott,* 1972; *Thomas Edison*, 1972.

Andrew Carnegie, 1973; *John L. Lewis*, 1973; *Walter Reuther*, 1973; *The Arab-Israeli Conflict*, 1973; *The Cold War, 1945-1963*, 1973; *The Conflict in Vietnam*, 1973; *The Growth of Presidential Power*, 1973; *The Political Machine: What It Is, How It Works*, 1973; *The Supreme Court under Warren*, 1973; *The United States: Policeman of the World?*, 1973; *The Assassination of John F. Kennedy*, 1973; *The Assassination of Robert F. Kennedy*, 1973; *The Convention and the Crisis: Chicago, 1968*, 1973; *The Creation of Bangla Desh*, 1973; *The Cuban Missile Crisis*, 1973; *The Hiroshima Atomic Bomb Blast*, 1973; *The My Lai Massacre*, 1973; *The Suez Crisis, 1956*, 1973; *The Bay of Pigs Invasion*, 1974; *The Czechoslovakian Crisis of 1968*, 1974; *The Hungarian Rebellion of 1956*, 1974; *The Korean War*, 1974; *The Gulf of Tonkin Incident*, 1975; *Lindberg Flies the Atlantic*, 1975; *The Common Market*, 1980; *Communism and the Red Scare*, 1980.

General editor, *Outstanding Personalities of the American Revolution*, six volumes, Story House, 1973, and *Controversial Issues in United States History*, five volumes, Simon & Schuster, 1975. Contributor to *New York Historical Society Quarterly*, *New Jersey History*, *New York History*, *The Historian*, *America*, *History and Life*, and other journals.

*   *   *

KURZ, Ron 1940-
(Mark Jackson)

PERSONAL: Born November 27, 1940, in Baltimore, Md.; son of Gordon L. (an aircraft mechanic) and Dorothy (Driver) Kurz; married Darlene M. Sweet, January 16, 1965 (divorced, 1975); married Shelley Nelkens, June 4, 1981; children: (second marriage) Scott, Daniel. *Education:* Attended Baltimore Community College. *Politics:* Liberal Independent. *Religion:* None. *Home address:* P.O. Box 164, Antrim, N.H. 03440. *Agent:* Bob Eisenbach, Eisenbach-Greene Inc., 760 North La Cienega Blvd., Los Angeles, Calif. 90069.

CAREER: Maryland Department of Corrections, Baltimore, Md., and Jessup, Md., correctional officer, 1963-69; free-lance writer, 1975—. *Military service:* U.S. Army, 1958-61; served in Germany; became sergeant.

MEMBER: Writers Guild of America (East).

WRITINGS: Lethal Gas (novel), M. Evans, 1974; *Black Rococo* (novel), M. Evans, 1976. Contributor to newspapers, including *Baltimore Sun* and *Boston Herald-American.*

Screenplays: "King Frat," Mad Makers, Inc., 1979; (co-author) "Eyes of a Stranger," Warner Bros., 1981; "Friday the 13th, Part II," Paramount, 1981; (co-author) "Off the Wall," Hot Dogs, Inc., 1983. Also author of earlier screenplays under pseudonym Mark Jackson.

WORK IN PROGRESS: A novel; television movies for CBS-TV.

*   *   *

KURZMAN, Dan 1927-

PERSONAL: Born March 27, 1927, in San Francisco, Calif.; son of Joseph (a businessman) and Lillian (a writer; maiden name, Halperin) Kurzman; married Florence Knopf (an editor), February 27, 1977. *Education:* University of California, Berkeley, B.A., 1946; Sorbonne, University of Paris, certificate, 1947. *Address:* c/o H. Knopf, 187 Boulevard, Apt. 36-B, Passaic, N.J. 02055. *Agent:* William Morris Agency, 1350 Avenue of the Americas, New York, N.Y. 10019.

CAREER: Writer. International News Service, Paris, France, correspondent, 1946-48; Marshall Plan Information Division, Paris, feature writer, 1949; National Broadcasting Co. (NBC), New York City, Middle East correspondent, 1950-53; Mc-Graw-Hill World News Service, New York City, Tokyo bureau chief, 1954-60; *Washington Post,* Washington, D.C., foreign correspondent, 1962-68.

MEMBER: Overseas Press Club, P.E.N., National Press Club, Tokyo Foreign Correspondents Club, Overseas Writers Club, State Department Correspondents Club, Authors League of America.

AWARDS, HONORS: Overseas Press Club award for best book on foreign affairs (named the Cornelius Ryan Award in 1978), 1963, for *Subversion of the Innocents,* and 1980, for *Miracle of November: Madrid's Epic Stand, 1936;* Front Page Award, 1964; George Polk Award for international reporting, 1965, from Long Island University; National Jewish Book Award for biography, Jewish Book Council of the Jewish Welfare Board, 1984, for *Ben-Gurion: Prophet of Fire.*

WRITINGS: Kishi and Japan: The Search for the Sun, Obolensky, 1960; *Subversion of the Innocents,* Random House, 1963; *Santo Domingo: Revolt of the Damned,* Putnam, 1965; *Genesis 1948: The First Arab-Israeli War,* World Publications, 1970; *The Race for Rome,* Doubleday, 1975; *The Bravest Battle: The 28 Days of the Warsaw Ghetto Uprising,* Putnam, 1976; *Miracle of November: Madrid's Epic Stand, 1936,* Putnam, 1980; *Ben-Gurion: Prophet of Fire,* Simon & Schuster, 1983. Contributor to several periodicals, including *Washington Star* and Independent News Alliance.

WORK IN PROGRESS: Day of the Bomb, a book on the atomic bombing of Hiroshima, for McGraw-Hill.

SIDELIGHTS: A former foreign correspondent in Europe, the Middle East, and Asia, Dan Kurzman has become a practitioner of a form of history writing closely related to journalism. This "new history," as it is often described, is a synthesis of scholarly research, investigative reporting, and a form of creative writing, which, as Kurzman told *CA* is creative "not in the fictional sense, but in the sense of creating images with facts." Thus, more factually detailed than historical fiction and more dramatic than traditional histories, Kurzman's books appeal to a wide range of readers. Quoted in a *Times Literary Supplement* article, Kurzman explains, "Using the techniques of the novelist and the biographer, I have tried to bring history alive."

As John S. Carroll notes in the *Saturday Review,* Kurzman uses the tools of various trades to compose a picture of history that captures the complexity of the original events. From the historian, he borrows a concern for the events, their chronology and significance. He engages in extensive research of his subject, drawing information from official documents, books, magazines, and newspapers to provide the backdrop for his story.

Acting as a journalist, Kurzman focuses his picture by emphasizing the people involved and their individual experiences. He interviews thousands of participants from major contributors to minor players and makes use of diaries, memoirs, and letters to supplement and substantiate the interviews. Then, to clarify complicated or conflicting information, Kurzman cross-examines key witnesses.

Finally, Kurzman introduces elements of the novel to enhance his picture, exploiting the natural tension of the events to build drama, intertwining the experiences of several individuals to simulate characterization, and finally, adding dialogue quoted from first-hand writings and interviews. Larry Collins, in a *New York Times Book Review* article, writes that Kurzman's technique creates a "whole that conveys the feel, color and emotion of the event as well as its historical significance."

Kurzman's early books—accounts of Japanese prime minister Nobusuke Kishi, Soviet influence in Africa and Asia, and the mid-nineteen-sixties revolt in Santo Domingo—drew some favorable reviews, but *Genesis 1948: The First Arab-Israeli War* was his first work to receive wide attention. Phil Freshman in a *Los Angeles Times Book Review* article calls *Genesis 1948* "the best book I've read on the first Arab-Israeli war." Some reviewers find factual errors in Kurzman's account; others, however, commend his objectivity in handling an issue as volatile as the struggle to reestablish a Jewish state in Palestine. Roderick MacLeish writes in the *Washington Post,* "[Kurzman] declines to reduce Israelis and Arabs to the stereotypes of invincible heroes at war with sleazy rat finks."

In *Miracle of November: Madrid's Epic Stand, 1936,* Kurzman recreates Franco's seige of Madrid during the Spanish Civil War. Writes Robert Kirsch in the *Los Angeles Times,* "This is no romanticized or whitewashed version of events, no facile portrayal of propaganda heroes." In a *New York Review of Books* article, Bernard Knox faults Kurzman's incomplete notation of sources, which he feels makes the book "of no use to the historian." Knox also writes that Kurzman's image of this conflict "fails to give the reader a sense of the unique atmosphere of Madrid in November." On the other hand, *New York Times* writer Richard F. Shepard feels that "Mr. Kurzman has chronicled this epic with the attention and detail and the sense of the human spirit that it requires."

Ben-Gurion: Prophet of Fire, Dan Kurzman's biography of David Ben-Gurion, is the story of Israel's founding father and first prime minister. Phil Freshman points out that Kurzman's research has uncovered new information about Ben-Gurion, especially concerning his private life. In assessing the biography, however, Freshman contends that Kurzman "seems to excuse some of [Ben-Gurion's] formidable faults." Yet, Alden Whitman writes in the *Chicago Tribune Book World* that Kurzman's "reportorial biography is at once coherent and informative. From it, Ben-Gurion emerges as a titan of our times."

MEDIA ADAPTATIONS: Otto Preminger acquired the rights to *Genesis 1948: The First Arab-Israeli War* in 1970; CBS-TV is preparing a television adaptation of *Day of the Bomb.*

BIOGRAPHICAL/CRITICAL SOURCES: Saturday Review, November 27, 1965, June 27, 1970; *Washington Post,* September 3, 1970; *Christian Science Monitor,* December 4, 1970, November 9, 1983; *New York Times Book Review,* December 13, 1970, February 23, 1975, November 28, 1976; February 24, 1980, December 25, 1983; *Times Literary Supplement,* October 13, 1972; *New York Times,* March 7, 1975, November 26, 1976, April 7, 1980; *Los Angeles Times,* February 20, 1980; *Washington Post Book World,* March 2, 1980, January 8, 1984; *New York Review of Books,* November 6, 1980; *Los Angeles Times Book Review,* November 20, 1983; *Detroit News,* December 10, 1983; *Chicago Tribune Book World,* March 4, 1984.

L

LABIN, Suzanne (Devoyon) 1913-

PERSONAL: Born May 6, 1913, in Paris, France; daughter of Louis Leon (a metal worker) and Marie-Eugenie (Leplatre) Devoyon; married Edouard Labin (an electronic engineer), April 4, 1935. *Education:* Ecole des hautes etudes internationales et de journalisme, Diplomee, 1935; Sorbonne, University of Paris, Licenciee es sciences, 1936. *Religion:* Roman Catholic. *Home and office:* 3 rue Thiers, Paris 16, France.

CAREER: Journalist, author, and lecturer. Founder and president of International Conference on Political Warfare, with headquarters in Paris, 1960—. Has launched campaigns in support of the Hungarian Revolution, in support of the Tibetan uprising against the Chinese invasion, in support of the South Vietnamese and their U.S. allies, and against the policy of the West in Katanga. Lecturer (in French, English, and Spanish) in most countries of Asia, Africa, Latin America, and North America; member of the Asian Speakers Bureau (United States) and of the Church League of America Speakers Bureau; producer of film, "Freedom Is at Stake in Berlin," for French television, 1962.

MEMBER: World Anti-Communist League (chairman of French chapter), League of Freedom (president), Societe des gens de lettres, European Freedom Council (president of Committee for Information), Federacion Argentina Entidades Democraticas Anti-Communistas (honorary member), Association for the Study of the Problems of Public Opinion (honorary member of the board).

AWARDS, HONORS: Freedom Prize for *Les Entretiens de Saint-Germain—Liberte aux Liberticides?;* Golden Cross of European merit; Golden Cross of cultural and philanthropic merit; Freedom Award of the Assembly of Captive Nations: Freedom Award of the Freedom Foundation of Valley Forge; Henry Malherbe Prize, Association des Ecrivains Combattants, 1980; Officer of Bernardo O'Higgins Order (Chile), 1982.

WRITINGS: Staline le terrible: Panorama de la Russie sovietique, Editions Self, 1948, translation by Edward Fitzgerald published as *Stalin's Russia,* Gollancz, 1950.

Le Drame de la democratie, Horay, 1954, translation by Otto E. Albrecht published as *The Secret of Democracy,* Vanguard, 1955; *La Conspiration communiste, l'Hydre totalitaire: Comment la museler,* Spartacus, 1957; *Les Entretiens de Saint-*

Germain: Liberte aux liberticides?, Spartacus, 1957; *La Condition humaine en Chine communiste,* La Table Ronde, 1959, translation by Edward Fitzgerald published as *The Anthill: The Human Condition in Communist China,* Stevens & Sons, 1960, Praeger, 1961; *The Technique of Soviet Propaganda* (pamphlet; originally written in French as a report for the tenth anniversary of the North Atlantic Treaty Organization), [London], 1959, expanded version prepared for U.S. Senate published as *The Techniques of Soviet Propaganda,* U.S. Government Printing Office, 1960, revised publication, 1965, also published as *The Unrelenting War: A Study of the Strategy and Techniques of Communist Propaganda and Infiltration,* American-Asian Educational Exchange, 1960.

Il Est moins cinq: Propagande et infiltration sovietiques (further expansion of her report on Soviet propaganda), Berger-Levrault, 1960; (editor) *Vie ou mort de monde libre* (principal speeches at International Conference on Political Warfare, 1960), La Table Ronde, 1961; *Competition U.S.S.R.—U.S.A.: Economique, militaire, culturelle,* La Table Ronde, 1962; *Counter Attack: A Plan to Win the Political Warfare of the Soviets,* American-Asian Educational Exchange, 1963; *Reconnaissance Chine communiste, Ambassades pour subversions,* Editions de la Ligue de la Liberte, 1963, translation published, with an introduction by Senator Thomas J. Dodd, as *Embassies of Subversion,* American Afro-Asian Education Exchange, 1965; *Le Tiers monde entre l'est et l'ouest: Vivre en dollars, voter en roubles,* La Table Ronde, 1964, translation published as *Red Foxes in the Chicken Coop,* Crestwood, 1966; *Vietnam: An Eye-witness Account,* Crestwood, 1964, updated and enlarged edition published as *Sellout in Vietnam?,* Crestwood, 1966.

(Contributor) *Trouble Abroad,* Crestwood, 1965; *La Liberte se joue a Saigon,* Editions de la Ligue de la Liberte, 1965; *Les Colonialistes chinois en Afrique,* Editions de la Ligue de la Liberte, 1965; *DeGaulle ou la France enchainee,* Editions de la Ligue de la Liberte, 1965; *Menaces chinoises sur l'Asie,* La Table Ronde, 1966; *50 Annees de communisme,* Berger-Levrault, 1967, translation published as *Promise and Reality: 50 Years of Soviet "Achievements,"* John Graham, 1967; *Goliath and David: Justice pour la Chine libre,* Editions de la Ligue de la Liberte, 1967; *Le Petit livre rouge: Arme de guerre,* La Table Ronde, 1969.

Hippies, drogues et sexe, La Table Ronde, 1970, translation published as *Hippies, Drugs and Promiscuity,* Arlington House, 1970; *Le Monde des drogues,* France Empire, 1975; *La Violence Politique,* France Empire, 1977.

Chili: Le Crime de Resister, Nouvelles Editions Debresse, 1980, translation published as *Chile: The Crime of Resistance,* Foreign Affairs Publishing Co., Ltd., 1982; *Israel: Le Crime de Vivre,* Nouvelles Editions Debresse, 1981; *Socialisme: La Demagogie du Changement,* Nouvelle Editions Debresse, 1983. Contributor of articles to magazines and newspapers in many countries.

SIDELIGHTS: Many of Suzanne Labin's books have been translated into English and other languages.

AVOCATIONAL INTERESTS: Collecting unusual sculpture, riding horseback, swimming, skiing.

BIOGRAPHICAL/CRITICAL SOURCES: American Legion Magazine, December, 1962.

* * *

LAIR, Jess K. 1926-

PERSONAL: Born October 11, 1926, in Bricelyn, Minn.; son of Merle T. and Bertha (Eggen) Lair; married Jacqueline Carey (a writer), July 7, 1949; children: Janet, Barbara (Mrs. Richard Robinson), Jess, Jr., Joseph, Michael. *Education:* University of Minnesota, B.A., 1948, M.A., 1964, Ph.D., 1965. *Home address:* P.O. Box 249, Bozeman, Mont. 59715.

CAREER: Bruce B. Brewer Advertising Agency, Kansas City, Mo., and Minneapolis, Minn., assistant editor and copywriter, 1951-56; Leo Burnett Advertising Agency, Chicago, Ill., copywriter, 1956-57; owner of a marketing consultant company, Minneapolis, 1957-62; University of Minnesota, Minneapolis, assistant professor, 1963-66, associate professor of writing and speech, 1966-67; Montana State University, Bozeman, associate professor of writing, 1967-69, associate professor of educational psychology, beginning 1968. *Military service:* U.S. Army Air Forces, 1944-45.

MEMBER: American Psychological Association.

WRITINGS—All published by Doubleday: *I Ain't Much Baby, But I'm All I Got,* 1972; *Hey God, What Should I Do Now?,* 1974; *I Ain't Well but I Sure Am Better,* 1975; *Ain't I a Wonder and Ain't You a Wonder, Too!,* 1977; *Sex, If I Didn't Laugh, I'd Cry,* 1979; *I Don't Know Where I'm Going but I Sure Ain't Lost,* 1982; *How to Have a Perfect Marriage with Your Present Mate,* 1984.

* * *

LALLY, Michael 1942-

PERSONAL: Born May 25, 1942, in Orange, N.J.; son of James A. and Irene (Dempsey) Lally; married Carol Lee Fisher, August 8, 1964 (divorced, 1978); married Penelope Dale Milford, February 14, 1982 (separated, 1984); children: (first marriage) Caitlin Maeve, Miles Aaron. *Education:* University of Iowa, B.A., 1968, M.F.A., 1969. *Home:* 1335 26th St., Santa Monica, Calif. 90404.

CAREER: Trinity College, Washington, D.C., instructor, 1969-74; Franklin Library, New York, N.Y., editor, 1976-78. Poet, actor, and musician. Member of board of directors of Print Center, 1972-77, and Washington Film Classroom, 1972; founder and president of Some of Us Press, 1972-75; founder and

publisher, O Press, 1975-79; founder and director of Mass Transit Poetry Project, 1972-76. *Military service:* U.S. Air Force, 1962-66.

MEMBER: National Book Critics Circle, P.E.N., Screen Actors Guild. *Awards, honors:* Discovery Award from New York Poetry Center, 1972; National Endowment for the Humanities fellow, 1974, 1981; award from New York Poets Foundation, 1974.

WRITINGS—Poetry: *What Withers,* Doones Press, 1970; *The Lines Are Drawn,* Asphalt Press, 1970; *Stupid Rabbits,* Morgan Press, 1971; *MCMLXVI Poem,* Nomad Press, 1971; *The South Orange Sonnets,* Some of Us Press, 1972; *Late Sleepers,* Pellet Press, 1973; *My Life,* Wyrd Press, 1975; *Rocky Dies Yellow,* Blue Wind Press, 1975; *Dues,* Stonewall Press, 1975; *Sex/The Swing Era,* Lucy & Ethel Press, 1975; *Mentally, He's a Sick Man,* Salt Lick Press, 1975; *Oomaloom,* Dry Imager, 1975; *Charisma,* O Press, 1976; (editor) *None of the Above,* Crossing Press, 1976; *Catch My Breath* (prose and poems), Salt Lick Press, 1978; *In the Mood,* Titanic Books, 1978; *Just Let Me Do It,* Vehicle Editions, 1978; *White Life,* Jordan Davies, 1980; *Attitude,* Hanging Loose Press, 1982; *Hollywood Magic,* Little Caesar Press, 1982.

Contributor to more than two hundred magazines. Editor of periodicals, including *Iowa Defender, Daily Iowan, Campus Underground,* and *Washington Review of the Arts;* reviewer for *Washington Post,* 1975-80, and *Village Voice,* 1978-80.

WORK IN PROGRESS: A novel; a volume of selected poems; a two-act play; a screenplay.

SIDELIGHTS: Michael Lally comments: "I started out as a musician (piano and bass), mostly jazz, so music, especially American music, has been a great source of inspiration for my work and the generating force behind my ideas on structure and movement, both in poetry and prose."

BIOGRAPHICAL/CRITICAL SOURCES: Sun and Moon Quarterly, spring, 1976; Toby Thompson, *The Sixties Report,* Rawson Wade Publishers, 1979; *The Language Book,* Southern Illinois University Press, 1984.

* * *

LAMONT-BROWN, Raymond 1939-

PERSONAL: Some biographical and bibliographical sources index under name Brown; born September 20, 1939, in Leeds, England; son of James (a civil engineer) and Margaret Isabella (Johnston) Lamont-Brown; married Jean Elizabeth Adamson, April 14, 1973 (died December 11, 1979). *Education:* Attended British Institute of Technology, 1958-59, and School of Oriental and African Studies, 1959-60; Nihon Daigaku, Tokyo, M.A., 1961; Institute of Engineering Technology, M.A., 1963; also attended Bradford Technical College. *Religion:* Anglican. *Home:* 3 Crawford House, 132 North St., St. Andrews, Fife KY16 9AF, Scotland.

CAREER: Yorkshire Electricity Board, Bradford, England, staff member in commercial and accounting departments, 1963-65; free-lance writer, 1965—. Adult education lecturer at University of St. Andrews, 1978—; extra-mural lecturer at University of Dundee, 1982—. Founder of Japan Research Projects, 1965. Editor of M. B. Publications, Ltd., 1967-69.

MEMBER: Royal Geographical Society, Royal Asiatic Society, Japan Society, Society of Authors in Scotland (honorary secretary), Royal Society of Antiquaries of Scotland.

WRITINGS: History of St. Mark's Church, Dewsbury, 1865-1965, Birkdale Books, 1965; *A Book of Epitaphs*, Taplinger, 1967; *Doncaster Rural District Official Guide*, Directory Publications, 1967; *Clarinda: The Intimate Story of Robert Burns and Agnes MacLehose*, M. B. Publications, 1968; *Sir Walter Scott's Letters on Demonology and Witchcraft*, Citadel, 1968; *Robert Burns's Commonplace Book*, S. R. Publishers, 1969.

A Book of Superstitions, Taplinger, 1970; *A Book of Proverbs*, Taplinger, 1970; *A Book of Witchcraft*, Taplinger, 1971; *General Trade in Berwick-on-Tweed, 1894*, Bell, 1972; *Charles Kirkpatrick Sharpe's Historical Account of the Belief of Witchcraft in Scotland*, S. R. Publishers, 1972; *Phantoms of the Sea*, Taplinger, 1972; *Robert Burns's Tour of the Borders*, Boydell Press, 1972; *Phantoms, Legends, Customs, and Superstitions of the Sea*, Taplinger, 1972; *The Magic Oracles of Japan*, Fowler, 1972; *Robert Burns's Tour of the Highlands and Stirlingshire*, Boydell Press, 1973; *A New Book of Epitaphs*, Frank Graham, 1973; *A Casebook of Military Mystery*, Drake, 1974; *Phantoms of the Theatre*, Thomas Nelson, 1977; *Epitaphs Hunting*, Thornhill Press, 1977; *Scottish Epitaphs*, Thornhill Press, 1977; *Growing Up with the Highland Clans*, Wayland, 1978.

Walks for Motorists: Lothian and the Southeast Borders, Warne, 1980; *East Anglian Epitaphs*, Acorn, 1980; *My Fun Book of Scotland*, Holmes McDougall, 1981; *Mary Queen of Scots*, Spurbooks, 1982; *Mysteries and Legends*, Spurbooks, 1982; *Drives around Edinburgh*, Macdonald, 1983; *Drives around Glasgow*, Macdonald, 1983; *Visitor's Guide to St. Andrews*, Alvie, 1983; *Mothers-in-Law*, Alvie, 1983.

With Peter Adamson: *Victorian and Edwardian Fife from Old Photographs*, Ramsey Head Press, 1980; *The Victorian and Edwardian Borderland from Rare Photographs*, Alvie, 1980; *Victorian and Edwardian Dundee and Broughty Ferry*, Alvie, 1981; *Fife, 1910-50*, Alvie, 1982; *St. Andrews: City of Change*, Alvie, 1984.

Contributor of about two hundred fifty articles to magazines all over the world. Managing editor, *Writers' Monthly*, 1984—.

WORK IN PROGRESS: General dictionaries and reference books on literature and history; researching a photographic history of Scotland from Victorian times.

SIDELIGHTS: Raymond Lamont-Brown writes: "I strive, through the written word, to bring a greater understanding of the motivation of the 'Oriental mind' to the West. I have travelled widely in the Far East, and promoted English literature in the Orient. To this may be added a wish to promote the writing of humour and the dissemination of the culture of Scotland."

Lamont-Brown's work has been translated into French, German, Spanish, Japanese, and Hebrew.

*　　*　　*

LANGER, William L(eonard)　1896-1977

PERSONAL: Born March 16, 1896, in Boston, Mass.; died December 26, 1977, in Boston; son of Rudolph E. (a florist) and Johanna (Rockenbach) Langer; married Susanne Knauth (a philosopher), September 3, 1921 (divorced August, 1942); married Rowena Allen Morse Nelson, April 9, 1943; children: (first marriage) Leonard Charles Rudolph, Bertrand Walter; stepchildren: four. *Education:* Harvard University, A.B., 1915, A.M., 1920, Ph.D., 1923; additional study at University of

Vienna, 1921-22. *Home:* 1 Berkeley St., Cambridge, Mass. 02138. *Office:* Department of History, Harvard University, Cambridge, Mass. 02138.

CAREER: Worcester Academy, Worcester, Mass.; teacher of modern languages, 1915-17; Clark University, Worcester, assistant professor, 1923-25, associate professor of history, 1925-27; Harvard University, Cambridge, Mass., assistant professor, 1927-31, associate professor, 1931-36, Archibald Cary Coolidge Professor of History, 1936-64, professor emeritus, 1964-77, director of Russian Research Center, 1954-59, and of Center for Middle East Studies, 1954-56. Lecturer at University of Chicago, summer, 1926; visiting professor, Columbia University, 1931; Harvard lecturer, Yale University, 1933; professor, Fletcher School of Law and Diplomacy, 1933-34, 1936-41.

U.S. Government, Washington, D.C., member of board of analysts, Office of the Coordinator of Information, 1941-42, chief of research and analysis branch, Office of Strategic Services, 1942-45, director of Office of Intelligence Research, Department of State, 1945-46, special assistant to Secretary of State, 1946, assistant director for national estimates, Central Intelligence Agency, 1950-52, member of President's Foreign Intelligence Advisory Board, 1961-69. Trustee, Carnegie Endowment for International Peace; member of advisory board, National War College, 1946-51; president, Harvard Pierian Foundation, 1969-73. Editorial adviser to Houghton Mifflin Co., Harper & Row Publishers, Inc., and American Heritage Publishing Co. *Military service:* U.S. Army, First Gas Regiment, 1917-19; served in France; participated in St.-Mihiel and Argonne Forest engagements; became master engineer junior grade.

MEMBER: American Historical Association (president, 1957), American Philosophical Society, American Academy of Arts and Sciences, Organization of American Historians, Council on Foreign Relations, Massachusetts Historical Society, Phi Beta Kappa, Harvard Club (New York).

AWARDS, HONORS: LL.D. from Harvard University, 1945, and Mills College, 1960; Medal of Merit for wartime service with Office of Strategic Services, 1946; Bancroft Prize (shared with S. Everett Gleason), Columbia University, 1955, for *The Undeclared War, 1940-1941*; D.Phil. from University of Hamburg, 1955; L.H.D. from Yale University, 1956; Center for Advanced Study in the Behavioral Sciences fellow, 1959-60; Litt.D. from Alma College, 1961; Golden Plate Award, American Academy of Achievement, 1966.

WRITINGS: (With Robert B. MacMullin) *With "E" of the First Gas*, Holton, 1919, published as *Gas and Flame in World War I*, Knopf, 1965; *The Franco-Russian Alliance, 1890-1894*, Harvard University Press, 1929, reprinted, Octagon, 1967; *European Alliances and Alignments, 1871-1890*, Knopf, 1931, 2nd edition with supplementary bibliographies, 1950, reprinted, Greenwood Press, 1977; *The Diplomacy of Imperialism, 1890-1902* (sequel to *European Alliances and Alignments, 1871-1890*), Knopf, 1935, 2nd edition with supplementary bibliographies, 1951.

Our Vichy Gamble, Knopf, 1947, reprinted, Shoe String, 1965; (with S. Everett Gleason) *The Challenge to Isolation, 1937-1940*, Harper, 1952, published in two volumes as *The Challenge to Isolation: The World Crisis of 1937-1940 and American Foreign Policy*, 1964; (with Gleason) *The Undeclared War, 1940-1941*, Harper, for Council on Foreign Relations, 1953; (contributor) Arthur P. Dudden, *Woodrow Wilson and* the World of Today, University of Pennsylvania Press, 1957; (contributor) *Goals for Americans*, Prentice-Hall, 1960; *Conyers Read, 1881-1959: Scholar, Teacher, Public Servant*, [Fairfax, Calif.], 1963; (contributor) Evelyn M. Acomb and Marvin L. Brown, editors, *French Society and Culture since the Old Regime*, Holt, 1966; *Political and Social Upheaval, 1832-1852*, Harper, 1969, abridged edition (chapters 10-14) published as *The Revolutions of 1848*, 1971; *Explorations in Crisis: Papers on International History*, edited by Carl E. Schorske and Elizabeth Schorske, Harvard University Press, 1969.

The New Illustrated Encyclopedia of World History, two volumes, Abrams, 1975; *Up from the Ranks: The Autobiography of William L. Langer*, privately printed, 1975, published as *In and Out of the Ivory Tower: The Autobiography of William L. Langer*, Neale Watson, 1977.

Editor: (With Hamilton Fish Armstrong) *"Foreign Affairs" Bibliography: A Selected and Annotated List of Books on International Relations, 1919-1932*, Harper, 1933, published as *"Foreign Affairs" Bibliography, 1919-1932*, Russell, 1960; (and compiler with the assistance of others) *An Encyclopedia of World History: Ancient, Medieval, and Modern, Chronologically Arranged* (revised and modernized version of Karl J. Ploetz's *Epitome of Ancient, Medieval, and Modern History*), Houghton, 1940, revised edition published as *An Encyclopedia of World History: Ancient, Medieval, and Modern, Chronologically Arranged*, 1948, 5th edition, 1972.

Western Civilization, Volume I: *Paleolithic Man to the Emergence of European Powers*, Volume II: *The Struggle for Empire to Europe in the Modern World*, Harper, 1968, 2nd edition published as *Western Civilization*, Volume I: *Prehistory to the Peace of Utrecht*, Volume II: *The Expansion of Empire to Europe in the Modern World*, 1975; *Perspectives in Western Civilization: Essays from "Horizon,"* two volumes, American Heritage Publishing Co., 1972.

"The Rise of Modern Europe" series; published by Harper, except as indicated: Crane Brinton, *A Decade of Revolution, 1789-1799*, 1934, reprinted, Greenwood Press, 1983; Geoffrey Brum, *Europe and the French Imperium, 1789-1814*, 1938, reprinted, Greenwood Press, 1983; Carlton J. Hayes, *A Generation of Materialism, 1871-1900*, 1941, reprinted, Greenwood Press, 1983; Leo Gershoy, *From Despotism to Revolution, 1763-1789*, 1944, reprinted, Greenwood Press, 1983; Penfield Roberts, *The Quest for Security, 1715-1740*, 1947, reprinted, Greenwood Press, 1983; John B. Wolf, *The Emergence of the Great Powers*, 1951, reprinted, Greenwood Press, 1983; Carl J. Friedrich, *The Age of the Baroque, 1610-1660*, 1952, reprinted, Greenwood Press, 1983; Myron P. Gilmore, *The World of Humanism, 1453-1517*, 1952, reprinted, Greenwood Press, 1983; Oron J. Hale, *Great Illusion, 1900-1914*, 1971; Frederick B. Artz, *Reaction and Revolution: 1814-1832*, 1977.

Also author of booklets (mainly reprints from journals), including *A Critique of Imperialism*, 1935, *The Next Assignment*, 1958, *Farewell to Empire*, 1962, *Red Rag and Gallic Bull: The French Decision for War, 1870*, 1962, and *Europe's Initial Population Explosion*, 1963. Contributor of numerous articles to periodicals. Member of editorial board of *Journal of Modern History*, 1929-33, *American Historical Review*, 1936-39, and *Foreign Affairs*, beginning 1955; member of editorial advisory board, *Historical Abstracts*, beginning 1955.

WORK IN PROGRESS: Studies of the European population in the time of Thomas Malthus.

SIDELIGHTS: "William L. Langer was without doubt the most thoroughgoing of modern diplomatic historians, and the outstanding Harvard figure in this field for over thirty years," declared W. N. Medlicott in the *Times Literary Supplement*. Langer distinguished himself as one of the first to examine the intricate system of alliances that contributed to the outbreak of World War I, and his books on the subject are considered classics. A U.S. government official with the Office of Strategic Services (OSS), the Central Intelligence Agency (CIA), and the State Department during and after the Second World War, he also produced authoritative studies of the diplomacy behind American involvement in World War II.

Langer established his reputation with *The Franco-Russian Alliance, 1890-1894*, the first of three books on the political polarization of Europe before World War I. Praising the book in *American Historical Review*, B. E. Schmitt singled out "the skill with which [Langer] makes the reader see the situation as it presented itself at any given moment to a particular government rather than as it appears to the historian who knows what is going to happen." Alexander Baltzly echoed this assessment in *Current History*, claiming there is "no study of late nineteenth century diplomacy that envisages more clearly the complicated milieu in which Bismarck and Caprivi, Freycinet and Ribot, Thiers, Salisbury, Rosebery and Crispi groped their way. Professor Langer approaches his problem as much from the German, the British and Italian angle as from the French or Russian."

In *European Alliances and Alignments, 1871-1890*, Langer traced the diplomatic maneuvering of the period dominated by German Chancellor Otto von Bismarck. "The book is a masterpiece," wrote A. H. Lybyer in the *American Political Science Review*. "Bismarck stands forth throughout as the chief actor in the fateful drama, and the keen discussions of his remarkably successful policies are as vivid and original as anything in the book." Charles Seymour, moreover, considered the work to be "of the first historical importance." Seymour noted in *Current History* that Langer was "the first historian writing in English to utilize [newly published French and German diplomatic documents] for an intensive study of the Bismarckian period; there is no one better versed in the great variety of sources that have been published."

Diplomacy of Imperialism, 1890-1902, the sequel to *European Alliances and Alignments, 1871-1890*, examines the developments in Africa, Asia, and the Near East as they related to events in Europe. Called "one of the finest products of American historical scholarship" by William MacDonald in the *New York Times*, the book greatly enhanced Langer's already significant reputation. E. L. Woodward, for example, wrote in *Spectator*: "It is safe to say that there are not more than half a dozen scholars in the two continents who could have written so good an account of European diplomacy from the fall of Bismarck to the conclusion of the Anglo-Japanese alliance." F. L. Schuman similarly concluded in *Nation* that no scholar "has examined the records of diplomacy with more painstaking care or with sounder critical judgment [than Langer]. No writer has unraveled more brilliantly the peculiar complexities of the period, or presented more lucidly the tangled themes of the cacophonous symphony of power, prestige, and profits, of empire, war, and catastrophe."

With the 1935 publication of *Diplomacy of Imperialism, 1890-1902* and his subsequent appointment as the first Archibald Cary Coolidge Professor of History at Harvard University, Langer ironically "would have liked to [have said] farewell to diplomatic history,'' Medlicott reported. "He was becoming a public figure and a celebrated teacher, with a rigorous seminar technique.'' But Langer's expertise in diplomatic affairs led him into government service when World War II broke out. During the war he was an analyst for the Office of the Coordinator of Information and chief of the research and analysis branch of the OSS. After the war he helped organize the CIA and, despite his return to Harvard, continued to serve the government in various advisory and administrative positions. "All this pointed inexorably to his return, rather against his inclinations apparently, to diplomatic history as the official historian of America's wartime foreign policy,'' noted Medlicott.

At the personal invitation of Secretary of State Cordell Hull, Langer wrote in 1944 *Our Vichy Gamble,* a history of American relations with the pro-Nazi Vichy regime in France from 1940 to 1943. Published in 1947, the book, according to Percy Winner in the *New Republic,* "gives a factual account, readable, entertaining, exciting, frequently depressing, of how and why Washington chose and clung obstinately to Petain, Darlan and the Vichy fascists instead of to de Gaulle and those Frenchmen for whom freedom meant emancipation from fascism as well as from the Germans.''

Langer based his account not only on secret files of the State Department, the OSS, and the army, but also the letters of Hull, President Roosevelt, and Ambassador Leahy. The unrestricted access enjoyed by Langer "prompted the historian Charles A. Beard to voice alarm over what he regarded as 'special favors' enjoyed by some historians,'' Morris Kaplan reported in the *New York Times.* But a much bigger stir was caused by critics who saw *Our Vichy Gamble* as an official defense of Roosevelt's and Hull's unpopular policy. *Time* magazine, whose reviewer hailed the book as being "of the first importance in its field, even for those who do not share [Langer's] outspoken conclusions,'' publicized the controversy by printing Langer's picture with the caption, "Expediency First.''

Nevertheless, *Our Vichy Gamble* was widely recognized as a work of impeccable scholarship. Leo Gershoy expressed the opinion of many reviewers when he said in the *New York Herald Tribune Book Review,* "Whether one agrees or not with his thesis, it is incontestable that Mr. Langer has made a monumental historical contribution.'' R. C. Snyder, moreover, insisted in the *American Political Science Review* that in spite of "an unobtrusive air of defensiveness, [*Our Vichy Gamble*] is not an official apology. For the most part, Langer lets the facts unfold whatever logic there was in the government's policy.''

Langer's last two works in diplomatic history were *The Challenge to Isolation, 1937-1940* and *The Undeclared War, 1940-1941,* both written with S. Everett Gleason. Commissioned by the Council on Foreign Relations to help Americans understand the historical forces underlying the war and America's subsequent emergence as a superpower, the books were acclaimed as landmark studies in the field. In *Saturday Review* Adolph A. Berle called *The Challenge to Isolation, 1937-1940* "the standard, authoritative American work,'' and the *New York Times* reviewer S. F. Bemis considered *The Undeclared War, 1940-1941* to be "the most important and scholarly work in diplomatic history . . . since the epoch-marking contributions . . . on the origins of World War I.''

In addition to diplomatic studies, Langer produced other notable books. He edited *An Encyclopaedia of World History,* which according to Sherwin Smith in the *New York Times Book Review* "has been an invaluable desk-top reference for years.''

His autobiography, *In and Out of the Ivory Tower,* "should be compulsory reading for future teachers of modern international history,'' Medlicott maintained. "But,'' the critic added, "it leaves unsolved the problem, which many of [Langer's] writings raise, of whether any reasonable finality of judgment is possible in such studies. . . . His final verdict was pessimistic in the extreme: 'The writing of contemporary history is like the work of Sisyphus. The constant flow of new materials makes it almost impossible to arrive at any conclusion.'''

AVOCATIONAL INTERESTS: Music (played viola in an amateur quartet).

BIOGRAPHICAL/CRITICAL SOURCES: Current History, March, 1930, November, 1931; *American Historical Review,* April, 1930, October, 1936, July, 1954, June, 1970, October, 1978, February, 1979; *Times Literary Supplement,* May 1, 1930, August 11, 1932, April 18, 1952, January 29, 1954, November 10, 1978; *New York Times,* October 18, 1931, June 7, 1936, April 6, 1947, January 20, 1952, September 6, 1953, December 27, 1977; *Nation,* October 21, 1931, November 20, 1935; *New Republic,* October 21, 1931, November 13, 1935, April 14, 1977; *American Political Science Review,* February, 1932, June, 1936, August, 1947; *Saturday Review of Literature,* August 20, 1932, February 22, 1936, May 3, 1947; *Christian Science Monitor,* October 30, 1935, April 7, 1947; *Spectator,* April 10, 1936, January 15, 1954; *New York Herald Tribune Weekly Book Review,* April 13, 1947; *Time,* April 14, 1947; *Political Science Quarterly,* December, 1947, September, 1952.

Saturday Review, January 19, 1952, September 26, 1953; *New York Herald Tribune Book Review,* November 1, 1953; *Commonweal,* December 11, 1953; *New York Times Book Review,* March 28, 1965, December 7, 1975; William L. Langer, *In and Out of the Ivory Tower: The Autobiography of William L. Langer,* Neale Watson, 1977; *Foreign Affairs,* April, 1978.

OBITUARIES: New York Times, December 27, 1977; *Washington Post,* December 28, 1977.†

—*Sketch by James G. Lesniak*

*   *   *

La REYNIERE
   See COURTINE, Robert

*   *   *

La SALLE, Victor
   See FANTHORPE, R(obert) Lionel

*   *   *

LAURANCE, Alfred D.
   See TRALINS, S(andor) Robert

*   *   *

LAZARUS, Arnold A(llan)   1932-

PERSONAL: Born January 27, 1932, in Johannesburg, South Africa; son of Benjamin and Rachel (Mosselson) Lazarus; married Daphne Ann Kessel, June 10, 1956; children; Linda Sue, Clifford Neil. *Education:* University of the Witwatersrand, B.A. (honors), 1956, M.A., 1957, Ph.D., 1960. *Politics:* Semi-Liberal. *Religion:* Agnostic. *Home:* 56 Herrontown Cir., Princeton, N.J. 08540. *Agent:* Rhoda Weyr, 322 Central Park

W., New York, N.Y. 10025. *Office:* Graduate School of Applied and Professional Psychology, Rutgers University, P.O. Box 819, Piscataway, N.J. 08854.

CAREER: Private psychotherapy practice, Johannesburg, South Africa, 1959-63; Stanford University, Stanford, Calif., visiting assistant professor of psychology, 1963-64; Behavior Therapy Institute, Sausalito, Calif., director, 1966-67; Temple University Medical School, Philadelphia, Pa., professor of psychology, 1967-70; Yale University, New Haven, Conn., director of clinical training, 1970-72; private psychotherapy practice, Princeton, N.J., 1972—; Rutgers University, New Brunswick, N.J. and Piscataway, N.J., professor of psychology and chairman of department, 1972-74, professor, Graduate School of Applied and Professional Psychology, 1974—; Multimodal Therapy Institute, Kingston, N.J., founder and director, 1976—. Diplomate in clinical psychology awarded by American Board of Professional Psychology, 1972, and by International Academy of Professional Counseling and Psychotherapy, 1982. Vice-president of Transvaal Workers Association, Johannesburg, South Africa, 1960.

MEMBER: American Psychological Association (fellow), American Orthopsychiatric Association (fellow), American Academy of Psychotherapists, Association for Advancement of Behavior Therapy (president, 1968), New Jersey Psychological Association.

AWARDS, HONORS: American Board of Professional Psychology distinguished service award, 1982; named distinguished practitioner, National Academy of Practice in Psychology.

WRITINGS: (With Joseph Wolpe) *Behavior Therapy Techniques,* Pergamon, 1966; *Behavior Therapy and Beyond,* McGraw, 1971; (editor with Richard Rubin, Herbert Fensterheim, and Cyril Franks) *Advances in Behavior Therapy,* Academic Press, 1971; *Clinical Behavior Therapy,* Brunner, 1972; (with Allen Fay) *I Can if I Want To,* Morrow, 1975; *Multimodal Behavior Therapy,* Springer Publishing, 1976; *In the Mind's Eye,* Rawson Associates, 1978; *The Practice of Multimodal Therapy,* McGraw, 1981; *Casebook of Multimodal Therapy,* Guilford, 1985.

Contributor of over one hundred papers, articles, and chapters to books and periodicals. Member of editorial panel, *Behavior Research and Therapy,* 1963, *Behavior Therapy,* 1970, *Psychotherapy: Theory, Research, and Practice,* 1970, *Journal of Individual Psychology,* 1976, *Cognitive Therapy and Research,* 1977, *Comprehensive Psychotherapy,* 1979, *Psychotherapy in Private Practice,* 1982, and *Journal of Psychotherapy and the Family,* 1984.

WORK IN PROGRESS: A book demystifying hypnosis; *Marital Myths: Two Dozen Mistaken Beliefs That Can Ruin a Marriage (or Make a Bad One Worse) and What Can Be Done about It.*

SIDELIGHTS: Arnold A. Lazarus told *CA:* "As a professional psychologist in academe and in clinical practice, I used to denigrate psychologists and psychiatrists who wrote 'popular' books, especially those of the 'self-help' variety. Gradually, I have come to change my mind. A picture may be worth a thousand words, and a good self-help book can be worth dozens of psychotherapy sessions. Thus, in 1975 I wrote *I Can if I Want To* with my friend and colleague, Dr. Allen Fay. I am continuing to write clinical textbooks and scientific papers for professional journals, but I am now a firm believer in trying to reach laypeople about useful methods and techniques, rather

than only writing for other psychologists. My book *In the Mind's Eye* tells the layperson how to use mental imagery for personal enrichment."

Lazarus has founded Multimodal Therapy Institutes in New York, New Jersey, Virginia, Pennsylvania, and Ohio.

AVOCATIONAL INTERESTS: Cultivation of deep and special friendships, music, theatre, good food, tennis, country walks.

*   *   *

LEAVENWORTH, Carol 1940-

PERSONAL: Born December 5, 1940, in Oak Park, Ill.; daughter of Frank Gates and Audrey (a designer; maiden name, Melum) Leavenworth; married Vernon Vobejda (divorced, 1975); married Carroll Gaylord Hendricks (a psychologist), April 1, 1978 (marriage annulled); children: (first marriage) Susan Marie, Steven Edward. *Education:* University of Minnesota, B.A., 1965; University of Wisconsin, M.S., 1974. *Residence:* Colorado Springs, Colo. *Office:* 224 East Willamette, Suite 3, Colorado Springs, Colo. 80903.

CAREER: Certified psychotherapist. Virginia Neal Blue Center (social service agency), Colorado Springs, Colo., director, 1974-75; Integral Therapy Associates, Colorado Springs, psychotherapist, 1975-80; Colorado College, Colorado Springs, director of career center, 1976-83; in private practice of psychotherapy, 1983—.

MEMBER: American Association of Counseling and Development, American Psychological Association, Colorado Association of Counseling and Development, Colorado Mental Health Counselors Association, Phi Beta Kappa.

WRITINGS: (With Gay Hendricks) *How to Love Every Minute of Your Life,* Prentice-Hall, 1978; (with Hendricks) *Cool and Creamy: The Ice Cream and Frozen Yogurt Book,* Prentice-Hall, 1979; *Love and Commitment,* Prentice-Hall, 1981; *Family Living,* Prentice-Hall, 1982, 2nd edition, 1984.

WORK IN PROGRESS: Research on issues related to masculinity and femininity.

SIDELIGHTS: Carol Leavenworth comments on her development as a writer: "Three years before the publication of *How to Love Every Minute of Your Life,* Gay Hendricks asked me to work with him on a book for the lay audience about personal growth and problem solving. I didn't have much confidence in myself as a writer, but I agreed because I knew we had something fresh and helpful to say on the subject. I was excited by the challenge of sharing our ideas in writing. I wasn't surprised that starting the book was easier than finishing it. At the time I found working against a deadline to be the strongest motivator in completing the work I had begun. In the process I learned that writing for others about growth and problem solving enhances my own growth as a person and as a psychotherapist. Right now the thing I like most about writing is that it helps me organize my thoughts while looking at ordinary problems in new ways. It keeps me excited about what I am doing."

*   *   *

LEBOWITZ, Fran(ces Ann) 1951(?)-

PERSONAL: Born in Morristown, N.J.; daughter of Harold and Ruth Lebowitz (furniture store proprietors). *Residence:* New York, N.Y.

CAREER: Writer. Previously worked at a number of "colorful and picturesque" jobs in New York City, including bulk mailing, taxi driving, apartment cleaning, poetry reading, and selling advertising for *Changes* magazine.

WRITINGS—Humorous essays: *Metropolitan Life,* Dutton, 1978; *Social Studies,* Random House, 1981. Former author of columns, "I Cover the Waterfront," in *Interview,* and "The Lebowitz Report," in *Mademoiselle,* 1977-79. Contributor of book and film reviews to *Changes* magazine.

WORK IN PROGRESS: A novel.

SIDELIGHTS: "Fran Lebowitz is not only the funniest woman in America," Edmund White writes in the *Washington Post Book World,* "she is also the guardian of the proprieties. Like all satirists she is a moralist, and like most moralists she is conservative. She is for the eternal verities of sleep, civilized conversation and cigarette smoking. The list of what she is against is somewhat longer."

As author of two bestselling books, *Metropolitan Life* and *Social Studies,* and a monthly column published in Andy Warhol's *Interview* magazine, Lebowitz has become recognized as a talented author of satirical essays on the trendy aspects of urban life. Descriptions of Lebowitz have run the gamut from "daring" by *New York Times* reviewer Anatole Broyard, and "right on the mark" by Jean Strouse in *Newsweek,* to "an unlikely and perhaps alarming combination of Mary Hartman and Mary McCarthy" by John Leonard in the *New York Times.* She has also been compared to various other humorists, notably Erma Bombeck, Dorothy Parker, and Oscar Wilde.

"[Lebowitz] disapproves of virtually everything, particularly fads, trends, and the relaxation of social and personal restraints in general," remarks Vic Sussman in the *Washington Post Book World.* Scot Haller comments in the *Saturday Review:* "Chronicling the baroque customs and bizarre behavior of the American species near the end of the 20th century, Lebowitz sounds like Dorothy Parker in Gomorrah, or Emily Post in hysterics. From cafe society to the coffee-klatsch crowd, no social set or disorder escapes her infectious wrath." And finally, Paul Rudnick observes in *New Times* that "Lebowitz's pose is neither establishment lackey nor avant-garde artiste; she has followed the Noel Coward tradition of an intensely civilized, titillating frivolity. Her work is marvelously entertaining and intentionally superficial; any subversiveness is masked by a declaration of triviality. She can insult anyone she likes, as long as the offense is smothered in charm and wit. It is a remarkably difficult tightrope to navigate."

Lebowitz's first book, *Metropolitan Life,* was generally greeted with overwhelmingly favorable reviews and soon became a bestseller. Richard Locke, for example, describes *Metropolitan Life* as a "remarkable collection of satirical pieces." Continues the critic in his *New York Times Book Review* article: "Though she is young in years, her book *Metropolitan Life* exhibits an exceptional ferocity and tone of camp authority that deserve attention. She may lack the mimetic range and dramatic flair of her distinguished elders—she tends toward the firm didactic statement or a desperate Basic English sneer—but she epitomizes the 70's New York know-it-all fashion-magazine/artistic world, and I confess I'm head over heels at her feet." And A. J. Anderson writes in *Library Journal* of *Metropolitan Life:* "Unpredictable variety is the keynote of [Lebowitz's] musings; she discourses on everything from the pros and cons of children to digital clocks and pocket calculators, always projecting a light-hearted and sometimes nonsensical view of things."

One reviewer who does not agree with those who praise *Metropolitan Life* is Madora McKenzie. In a *Christian Science Monitor* review, McKenzie writes: "Apparently Miss Lebowitz wrote these pieces while sucking on lemon drops, because sour grapes crop up so often. . . . All her imagination and energies are devoted to exposing and ridiculing indignities and indemnities of life; she cannot seem to come up with any palatable alternatives." However, Jill Robinson remarks in the *New York Times Book Review* that *Metropolitan Life* "introduces an important humorist in the classic tradition. The satire is principled, the taste impeccable—there is character here as well as personality. . . . Astringent, meticulous with language, Miss Lebowitz is a sort of Edwin Newman for the chic urban-decay set."

In general, Lebowitz's second book, *Social Studies,* was greeted with the same degree of enthusiasm as *Metropolitan Life.* Hall, again writing in *Saturday Review,* declares that "for the most part, *Social Studies* is a textbook example of astute, acerbic social comedy. . . . The quick-witted, quick-tempered Lebowitz may be the funniest chronic complainer on the scene." And Anatole Broyard comments in the *New York Times* that one of Lebowitz's most entertaining qualities is that "she never gets used to anything. She experiences customs and situations as if they were all done on purpose to her. And the funniest thing of all is that she's right."

Reviewing *Social Studies* for the *Los Angeles Times Book Review,* Elaine Kendall maintains that "most of the time [Lebowitz is] both original and brave, taking on subjects everyone would like to laugh at but few people dare—highly charged topics that arouse emotional response, some of it furious." Finally, Peter Grier states in the *Christian Science Monitor* that in *Social Studies* Lebowitz "makes W. C. Fields look like St. Francis of Assisi. . . . Not everyone may think Fran Lebowitz is funny. . . . *Social Studies* might offend you. Then again, as Lebowitz says, 'Being offended is the natural consequence of leaving one's home.'"

In her *Los Angeles Times Book Review* article on *Social Studies,* Kendall speculates on why Lebowitz's form of satire is so successful while that of other writers fails. Kendall writes: "Other satirists bite; Lebowitz nibbles. They're corrosive while she's just tart." Even so, writes Glenn Collins in the *New York Times Book Review,* "Lebowitz's wit will not be appreciated by all of the people all of the time. . . . Fran Lebowitz is not exactly brimming over with human compassion. Hers is not an Up-With-People view of personing." While this may be the case, Kendall states that "the humorist who worries excessively about hurt feelings soon runs out of material and winds up doing trite monographs on smog, the only target with no organization dedicated to its defense. If you want to be funny for more than a week or so, you have to be willing to take chances and risk unpopularity."

Concludes Sussman in the *Washington Post Book World:* "Those unfamiliar with Lebowitz might think her a moralist, an elitist, a snob. She is all those. But she is an equal-opportunity snob, venting her disdain regardless of one's race, disability, sexual persuasion, or for that matter, species. Lebowitz is unashamedly Lebowitz, thank goodness, a funny, urbane, intelligent one-woman bulwark against cultural ticky-tack, creeping mellowness, and the excesses of what Mencken dubbed 'boobus Americanus.'"

CA INTERVIEW

CA interviewed Fran Lebowitz by telephone May 25, 1983, at her home in New York City.

CA: You've spoken many times about the sheer difficulty of writing, the lengths that you'll go to to avoid doing it, and the horror of deadlines. Has the success of your books made writing easier for you in any way?

LEBOWITZ: No, not at all. It has made my *life* easier, but not writing. Actually writing has become harder and harder for me. I think that's because I have become more critical.

CA: You began writing very young, producing a Nancy Drew-type novel in elementary school and a volume of poems in your teens. Coming from what you've described as "a family where literary tradition runs largely toward the picture postcard," how did you become interested in writing?

LEBOWITZ: I'm quite sure it was from reading, from being addicted to reading. I was so under the spell of reading. I still am. I read much more than I write—about twelve million times more. I think as soon as I realized that people wrote books and not God, as I imagined when I was very young, I wanted to be one of those people. This probably came out of my desire to be Godlike—there is something very Godlike about writing, you know. It's a kind of holy egomania.

CA: Is reading a great deal still one of the ways you avoid writing?

LEBOWITZ: It's the way I avoid everything. I think reading is actually better than real life. People often accuse me of using it as an escape; well, I think it's an escape to a much better life. I would say I read most of the day. If I didn't need money I'd read all the time.

CA: Who are your favorite writers?

LEBOWITZ: I have so many favorite writers that I'm always loath to start mentioning them because I'm afraid of leaving someone out. Do you mean dead or alive?

CA: It doesn't matter—either.

LEBOWITZ: Well, it matters to me. I prefer dead writers, of course, because you tend not to meet them at parties. Actually I am much more of a fan of writing than of writers. Of humorists, or people who write comedy, my favorite is Oscar Wilde. I would say that he should be everyone's favorite. If I were a dictator, I would make it mandatory that Oscar Wilde be everyone's favorite. I like Evelyn Waugh. Of the lighter comic writers I like Nancy Mitford very much and I like Angela Thirkell quite a bit. She's even lighter than Nancy Mitford. I don't think there are any comic American writers to compare to the English, and I am not an Anglophile; in fact I'm an Anglo*phobe*. There have just never been any real great American comic novelists, with the exception of Twain. We don't really have a class system, which is so valuable to the comic writer. (I'm attempting to rectify the situation by writing a novel. But the only way I'm able to contemplate such a task is by forcing the American public to acknowledge that we of course *do* have a class system.) I like Twain. Thurber I love; he makes me laugh. I like Dorothy Parker. I always hate to say I like Dorothy Parker, but I *do* like Dorothy Parker.

CA: Yes, people are always comparing the two of you.

LEBOWITZ: The only reason that they do is because I'm a girl. I'm very flattered to be compared to Dorothy Parker—I

think she's quite a remarkable writer—but it's really such an inaccurate comparison. She never wrote anything in the form that I write in.

Of living comic writers, I like Terry Southern. He doesn't work anymore, but I wish he did. I thought he was great. Fortunately, there aren't a great many living American comic prose writers! Of living writers who aren't primarily comic writers, my favorite is James Purdy. I would say he is far and away my favorite American writer. And Steven Millhauser is a writer I admire very much.

CA: Yes. He hasn't had enough attention.

LEBOWITZ: I know, and it's criminal. His first novel, *Edwin Mullhouse*, I think is actually the best novel ever written about childhood. It's one of my favorite books. Cynthia Ozick is one of my favorite writers. Philip Roth is a wonderful writer. Ann Arensberg, who wrote just one book, *Sister Wolf*. I like W. M. Spackman quite a bit. You know, I'm such a promiscuous reader, there really are dozens of writers that I like. Of dead writers I like Cheever, and John O'Hara, as unfashionable as that might be. I think he is one of the most underrated American writers ever. And, of course, Nabokov.

CA: Do you ever go back and reread your own writing after you've got it off your hands? I suppose you had to in putting Metropolitan Life *together.*

LEBOWITZ: Both books were written as books. Although some of the pieces from *Metropolitan Life* were in the *Mademoiselle* column before the book came out, they were written for the book. I just published them as I went along because I needed the money. That's the only kind of recycling I've participated in: getting paid for one piece of work as many times as possible. I do reread my work all the time, because I do a lot of readings for colleges. And almost every time I sit down to write, I reread old writings because I can't imagine how I ever did it. That's the main reason I reread—looking for hints as to how I managed to do it.

CA: Your very funny writing seems to grow out of genuine irritation. Has that been with you since you were a little kid?

LEBOWITZ: I've always been enraged. People ask me, "Is this true?"—a question which has always astonished me. How could I make it up? First of all, only since *Metropolitan Life* would it have occurred to anyone that irritation as a pose could be lucrative. My entire life I have been punished for it. In fact, even though I've been successful, I'm still being punished for it. People may in fact admire my attitude, but they certainly don't approve of it. So it doesn't lead to a very smooth life.

Not only have I always been in a state of rage, but I genuinely don't understand why everyone isn't. I don't think of it as being unusual; I think it's the only logical response to life. I think of my writing as an organized and rarified form of a tantrum. It's the only thing that keeps me from being a murderer. There is a very thin line that divides the comic writer from the mass murderer, and, you know, I really have that impulse all the time. So I guess writing or making wisecracks and jokes is a way of not ending up in prison.

People have always told me I'm going to have a heart attack because I get angry and blow up. Every time you get on the subway in New York, it stops between stations for no reason. You sit there for twenty minutes. No one ever tells you why, and everyone just sits there. But I don't. I walk to the front of the train and start screaming at the conductor. Of course it doesn't get any results. People ask me what I hope to achieve from my writing. I never for a second imagined that I was going to change anyone's mind. And I also never for a second imagined that any complaint I would ever make either in writing or in talking would have any effect. Which further enrages me. The last writer who managed to move people to action was Thomas Paine, and the time of the pamphleteer is gone. I think of myself as a kind of pamphleteer, though the likelihood of affecting people by writing in a country where people are basically illiterate is not very great.

CA: Some of the more wonderfully outrageous bits of your advice have to do with children, as in these pointers from Social Studies: *"Never allow your child to call you by your first name. He hasn't known you long enough. . . . Don't bother discussing sex with small children. They rarely have anything to add. . . . Ask your child what he wants for dinner only if he's buying." But a real sympathy for children comes through. Is it from your own difficulties growing up?*

LEBOWITZ: It has to do basically with the fact that I'm quite childlike. I'm always on the child's side. It's both things. I really feel that adults don't get it, and what they don't get is that children are not short adults. Children have a completely different consciousness, so they are approached in the wrong way, especially in modern life. I hear people say, "We're getting a divorce, but the kids understand." Of course they don't understand. It's just a way of assuaging their own guilt for not taking care of their children. I identify with powerlessness. To be in this constant state of rage is to acknowledge what it is like to be a child and constantly have no power. Of course, no one really has any power, you see. But adults have this idea that they have it, because they have it over children. And people always misunderstand my writing about children because they think I'm like W. C. Fields and don't like children. But it's not true. I really prefer them to adults.

CA: School was hardly your favorite place as a youngster. What kind of feelings do you have when you do readings or give commencement addresses at colleges?

LEBOWITZ: I like to talk in front of an audience, because I'm a ham. What I don't like is being at a school. It doesn't make any difference if I'm speaking or if I'm in the school because the second I walk onto school property I feel that someone is going to come over and tell me to go to the gym. I don't like it any better being in the company of the college president than being in the company of other students. When you give the commencement address, you have to have dinner at the president's house and all that kind of stuff. I still feel like the kid even if I'm sitting between the president of the board of trustees and the president of the college; I feel like they're going to suspend me any second. I really don't like anything at all about being in an academic environment except the talking. I like having that audience; it's a response that you don't get from writing.

CA: The great success of Metropolitan Life *was a surprise to its publisher, who thought that it would be of interest primarily to New Yorkers. Why do you think its very sophisticated humor appealed to so many other people as well? Were you as surprised as the publisher?*

LEBOWITZ: First of all, I never thought it was a New York book, as the publisher did. I never *thought* about it, to tell you the truth. I never thought in terms of demographics and I still don't. The idea of the audience is really a television idea, and I resent it in book publishing. The writer should never think of the audience, and publishers should not do so either—they do a great disservice to writing in general to think that way. I never expected the success I had with *Metropolitan Life*. I did expect to *have* success in my life; I just didn't expect it in my first book. I was used to beating my head against a wall for quite some time, so I was very surprised. The book was a *New York Times* success; in fact, it was a John Leonard success. What surprised me was the power of the *New York Times*. I never had any idea before of how powerful it was—not in influencing people, but in influencing other media. It brought the book to the attention of a lot of people by means of the media.

I think that humor is not a matter of demographics. Humor is a matter of sensibility. You can never know who's going to share your own sensibility. You can't know it by age, you can't know it by how rich someone is, you can't know it by where someone lives in the country, you can't know it by anything. Each person's comic sensibility is an individual thing. You can make a guess. This is why TV writing is so terrible: they have to guess what people are going to think is funny. I had no college audience until I was in paperback, and what does that prove? That proves that college students can't afford a book that costs ten dollars. That's *all* it proves. My college audience has increased greatly because I regularly do "Late Night with David Letterman," which is a very popular program among college students. That's given me probably a thousand times bigger college audience than I ever had from my writing.

I would say that basically I have an urban audience, but on the other hand I did lecture dates this year in Shreveport, Louisiana, and San Angelo, Texas—quite small towns—and I got some people. At every little place there's someone who thinks my writing is funny. Quite a lot of people *don't* like it, but you can't tell by saying, "New York humor"—that's what I mean. I don't think I have a genuine mass audience. I'll never have a Michener-size audience. But I certainly always thought I had a bigger audience than the publisher thought I did, and I think that's true of a number of writers who get pounded into some category.

CA: Why do you think publishers do it?

LEBOWITZ: They do it for economic reasons. They do it because they're trying to guess first, and you can't publish like that. If I were a publisher, anything good would be published, because I think a thing that is very good will have enough audience to pay for itself, even if it's a small audience. I think that's part of the duty of publishers. If they want to be in the shoe business, then they should go in the shoe business—and many of them should.

CA: Have you enjoyed the promotion tours?

LEBOWITZ: I love being on TV. It makes me feel more American. And, of course, I like talking about myself, so I like doing interviews. What I hate is traveling. I hate it. I hate it! It's everything I hate, because right away I'm delivering myself knowingly into the hands of incompetent airlines and hotel managers, and I hate having so little ability to affect my own circumstances. That drives me nuts. I'm a very bad traveler.

I mean, I complain. I've had real fights in airplanes, where they say they're going to call the police. And I don't take well to them sitting on the ground for four hours. I'm not one of the complacent ones. I loathe having to eat horrible food and stuff like that. But I like doing the appearances. If I didn't like it, I wouldn't do it. Writers who complain about doing it are lying, because you don't have to. Of course your choice in not doing it is to sell fewer books.

CA: Are you still resisting movie offers for your books?

LEBOWITZ: Yes. I don't want to get involved with it. I receive offers from every major movie studio and also pretty much every major Broadway producer. I think there are two reasons for that. One is that there's really a very small number of funny writers, and the other one is that I say no, which just makes me more attractive. It's now at a point where it has nothing to do with reality.

My saying no is not a moral stance. I do not think it is selling out or immoral to sell your books to the movies. *I* don't do it because I think I am too immature. I could never deal with what happens to you when you get involved with that machine. I *know* what happens; I *see* it happen. And I have really not very much sympathy for writers who come back from Hollywood and say, "You'll never believe how they treat writers out there." Because you know at the outset.

A movie is a cooperative situation. I am not interested in collaborating. I am not interested in relinquishing one iota of control over my work. And there is no way that you can work in the movies without doing that. Every writer that I know who sells books to movies says I'm crazy—you sell the book and you forget about it. I think that's great, but I can't. I am consciously unable to. I keep thinking, well, I'll grow up. A producer called me the other day who has been trying to buy *Metropolitan Life* for five years. I said I still wasn't interested, and he said, "I thought you might have grown up by now," and I said, "Well, I haven't." I have a certain amount of financial difficulty and I hope that I *will* grow up and be able to do that, but at the present time I cannot.

When I write something, that is *the thing*, not raw material for some moronic director and six actors who can't speak English to fool around with. I could never be in a situation where I would have to listen to the literary opinion of an actor. It is out of the question. I have some friends who are playwrights, and I have a friend who is rehearsing a play. She is going nuts. I said to her, "Do you want to know how you direct a play? You go on the stage with a gun and you read it aloud to the actors and you say, 'Just like that.' Then when they do it wrong you shoot them in the leg." So you can see I wouldn't get along very well in the theater.

CA: Is there anything about being recognized now that you don't like?

LEBOWITZ: No. There's nothing I don't like about it. People lie when they say there are things they don't like about it. To become well-known is a separate effort from being just a writer. Writers who genuinely don't want to be celebrities are not. And it is just another big lie people tell people. For instance, Philip Roth does not want to be a celebrity and he's not. Other writers (I won't mention who) go and complain on TV about being celebrities. Well, they don't have to go on. I respect either choice, but you have to admit what you are doing. I really enjoy it. I mean, yeah, sometimes you're walking down the street, you're in a horrible mood, someone comes and talks to you, but so what? That's hardly the worst thing that ever happened to you. The problems with obscurity were greater for me than the problems with fame. I think that a writer has a really perfect amount of fame—enough to get a good table in a restaurant, but not so much that people bother you while you're eating. And it's such a pleasure to have people come up to me on the street and say they enjoy my writing.

CA: How do you deal with mail?

LEBOWITZ: I answer no mail, including mail from relatives, because to answer mail means you have to write. If I am going to go through the effort of writing, then I might as well write on my book. To me it's the same effort. The other day I had to leave a note for the cleaning lady. I was sitting at the table with this pencil and someone came in and said, "What are you doing?" I said, "I have to leave a note for Marina." She said, "You're sitting there for an hour, agonizing over leaving a note for Marina?" The cleaning lady, by the way, is not American and does not speak English well enough to make judgments on my writing. I phone a lot. If someone I know writes me a letter, I call. Other mail I don't answer at all. I am happy to get favorable mail, but I don't answer it. And I am not organized enough to have a secretary.

The hate mail, of course, I wouldn't answer anyway. There's a certain amount of mail from people saying they don't like my books, or what I said on TV—that's normal hate mail. But I would say that the bulk of it is hysterical anti-Semitic mail. This is common to anyone who is recognizably Jewish who goes on television. That is the worst mail I get, and that is frequent. I also get quite a lot of mail from prisoners. This is not from being Jewish. This is from being a girl. Every girl I know who's on TV gets mail from prisoners; people in jail, I've discovered, watch TV all day long. I don't, of course, answer mail from prisoners either, which I wouldn't do even if I answered my other mail, because prisoners get out. I don't believe in being provocative.

CA: Do you want to talk about the novel in progress?

LEBOWITZ: I can't, really. It's not that I don't want to talk about it for any reason other than the fact that, first of all, I'm not far enough along in it. And all my writing always comes out of the writing rather than out of a plan, which makes it difficult to talk about in advance. I could talk about it in a very *sketchy* way. I hate to use the term "working title" because it's kind of a lie at the moment, but the title is *Exterior Signs of Wealth*, a loose translation of a French conspicuous-consumption tax. The reason they have this tax—which is not a modern tax, but quite old—is because even the French were compelled to notice that the French were liars, and the only way to get enough tax revenue was to tax not only reported income but also any display of wealth. I actually was tickled to discover this, because I felt that if anyone deserved such a tax, it was the French. The book, by the way, is not about French people basically, although there are a few French characters. And I just thought it was a funny title. I was lately thinking of changing the title of the book to *Art*, but then I thought, first of all, that's asking for it. And second, I was thinking if it didn't come out the way I wanted it to I would have to change the title to *Craft*.

CA: Very good! What's it about?

LEBOWITZ: It's about rich people who want to be artists and artists who want to be rich people. In other words, it is about a kind of class in society that exists not only in New York but everywhere. It is possible—and not only possible, but it is my life—that no matter what city I go to, I go to the same party. I literally mean the same people—the exact same people, not the same *kind* of people. I've been to the same party in London, Paris, Rome, Milan, Venice; every place I go, I go to the same party. And the people who make up this party are basically these two types of people. I chose these people to write about not only because I am familiar with them (because I am not familiar with a great number of different kinds of people), but because they offer the most comic possibility. Rich people with longings in directions that might be termed pretentious are the most ripe for comic writing because they have the most ridiculous mannerisms.

People ask me why I don't write about the middle class; isn't that funny? It's been done quite a bit, and it's *not* really that funny. Rich people can afford to be funnier than anyone. There's a general idea, not just an American idea, that there's a nobility about the poor. Well, the nobility that exists in the poor is that they cannot afford to behave in a monstrous way. I believe firmly that in almost any given era (there are exceptions, you know) there are approximately ten people alive in the world who have any genuine character. With the exception of those people, if you gave almost anyone, say, twenty-million dollars, he would fairly soon start acting like a monster, because he would be allowed to. Most people act in a nicer way not because they're nicer, but because they have to. This is what the book is about, and it should be done when I'm about ninety-seven.

BIOGRAPHICAL/CRITICAL SOURCES: Christian Science Monitor, March 15, 1978; *New York Times Book Review,* March 26, 1978, April 23, 1978, July 15, 1979, August 23, 1981, February 28, 1982; *New York Times,* March 31, 1978, September 2, 1981; *Library Journal,* April 1, 1978, August, 1981; *Newsweek,* April 10, 1978, September 14, 1981; *Saturday Review,* April 15, 1978, August, 1981; *Washington Post Book World,* April 30, 1978, June 5, 1978, August 30, 1981; *Ms.,* May, 1978; *Harper,* May, 1978; *Time,* May 29, 1978; *Crawdaddy,* June, 1978; *New Times,* July 10, 1978; *Bookviews,* September, 1978; *People,* September 4, 1978; *Contemporary Literary Criticism,* Volume XI, Gale, 1979; *Esquire,* August, 1981; *Los Angeles Times Book Review,* August 30, 1981; *New York,* September 14, 1981; *New Statesman,* February 19, 1982.†

—Sketch by Margaret Mazurkiewicz

—Interview by Jean W. Ross

*   *   *

LEFFERTS, George   1921-

PERSONAL: Born June 18, 1921, in Paterson, N.J.; son of Morris (an entrepreneur) and Elinor (a pianist; maiden name, Jacobs) Lefferts; married Elizabeth Ruth Schaul, December 29, 1942 (divorced, 1970); married Hilary Sares, July 4, 1982; children: (first marriage) Lauren Ruth, Barbara Ellen; (second marriage) Katherine Sares. *Education:* Drew University, B.A. (engineering), 1940; University of Michigan, B.A. (English), 1942. *Home:* Robbins Rest, Fire Island, N.Y. 11782. *Agent:* International Creative Management, 40 West 57th St., New York, N.Y. 10019.

CAREER: National Broadcasting Co. (NBC), New York, N.Y., executive producer, director, and writer, 1947-57; U.S. Department of State, Washington, D.C., producer and writer of films, 1958-61; Bing Crosby Productions, Los Angeles, Calif., executive producer and writer of "Breaking Point" television series, 1962-64; executive producer, American Broadcasting Co. (ABC), 1966-67; president of George Lefferts Associates, Inc., 1968—. Executive producer, "Hallmark Hall of Fame" television series, 1969-70, Smithsonian Institution Television, 1975-76, David Wolper Productions, 1976-78, and Time-Life Films, 1980-83; producer of specials for NBC, 1971-72; producer and writer for NBC Movie of the Week, 1977-78, and of feature films, industrial films, and films for the American Cancer Society and American Heart Association. Sculpture exhibited at Sculpture Gallery, New York, N.Y., 1960. Consultant to Children's Television Workshop, 1981, and Proctor & Gamble Productions, 1984; senior consultant to ABC Program Division, 1981—. *Military service:* U.S. Army, 1942-45.

MEMBER: National Academy of Television Arts and Sciences, Academy of Motion Picture Arts and Sciences, Dramatists Guild, Authors League of America, Writers Guild of America, Christopher Morley Knothole Association, South Bay Cruising Club, Glen Goin Club.

AWARDS, HONORS: Award from Ohio State University, 1955, for "NBC Theatre"; George Foster Peabody Award, 1956, for "Biographies in Sound," 1970, and 1975, for "Benjamin Franklin" mini-series; National Media Award, 1961; Golden Globe Award, 1961, for "Specials for Women," and 1965; Emmy Award, 1962, for "Specials for Women," 1970, for production of "Teacher, Teacher," and 1979, for "Benjamin Franklin" mini-series; Fame Award, 1962; Plaudit Award from Producers Guild, 1963, for "Breaking Point" series, 1968, and 1969; Foreign Press Award, 1963; First Prize, San Francisco Film Festival, 1970; Golden Eagle Certificate, Council on International Nontheatrical Events, Inc. (CINE), 1974, for "Moonflights and Medicine"; New England Journalism Award, 1984, for column in *Litchfield County Times;* Albert Lasker Award for outstanding medical film, for "What Price Health?"

WRITINGS: Special for Women (eight plays originally broadcast on television), introduction by Margaret Mead, Avon, 1962; "The Teenager" (filmscript), American-International, 1965; "Mean Dog Blues" (filmscript), American-International, 1978.

Author of plays, "Nantucket Legend," "The Boat," and "Hey Everybody," first produced in 1970; author and producer of filmscripts, "The Living End," 1959, "The Stake," 1960, and "The Harness," 1972; author of numerous television scripts for programs, including "Kraft Theatre," "Studio One," "Armstrong Theatre," "NBC Theatre," "Alcoa Theatre," and "Chrysler Theatre"; author of twenty-nine television special reports, including "Bravo Picasso," National Broadcasting Co. (NBC), 1969, "Pain," 1971, "What Price Health?," and "Dr. Barnard's Heart Transplant." Also author of syndicated columns; contributor to *Esquire* and other magazines.

*   *   *

LEHMANN, Johannes   1929-

PERSONAL: Born September 7, 1929, in Madras, India; son of Arno (a professor) and Gertrud (Harstall) Lehmann; married Ruth Lindenberg, 1956; children: Christine, Maria. *Education:* Studied at University of Halle-Saale, University of Edinburgh, and Free University of Berlin; University of Berlin, Ph.D. *Home:* 8 Degerlocherstrasse, Stuttgart, Germany. *Office:* Sueddeutscher Rundfunk, Stuttgart, Germany.

CAREER: Lutheran World Federation, Geneva, Switzerland, news editor, 1955-60; German Press Agency, Hamburg, Germany, news editor, 1960-63; Sueddeutscher Rundfunk (Radio Stuttgart), Stuttgart, Germany, head of literature department, 1963—.

MEMBER: Deutscher Schrifstellerverband (writer's association).

WRITINGS: (Editor) *Christliche Erziehung heute* (title means "Christian Education Today"), Ehrenwirth, 1964; (editor) *Ist der Glaube krank? Glaubwuerdigkeit und Unglaubwuerdigkeit der Glaeubigen* (title means "Is the Faith Ill?"), Quell, 1966; (editor) *In allen Zungen: Geistliche Reden durch 15 Jahrhunderte* (title means "In All Tongues: Spiritual Speeches in Fifteen Centuries"), Ehrenwirth, 1966; (translator with Norbert Brieger and Barbara Beuys) *Gute Nachricht fuer Sie* (title means "Good News for You"), Bibelanstalt, 1967; (editor) *Motive des Glaubens: Eine Ideengeschichte des Christentums in 18 Gestalten* (title means "Motives of Faith"), Furche, 1968; *Mao, Marx und Jesus: Ein Vergleich in Zitaten* (title means "Mao, Marx and Jesus: A Comparison in Quotes"), Jugenddienstverlag, 1969.

Jesus-Report: Protokoll einer Verfaelschung, Econ Verlag, 1970, translation by Michael Heron published as *Rabbi J.,* Stein & Day, 1971; *Die Jesus GMBH* (title means "The Jesus Ltd."), Econ Verlag, 1972; *Die Hethiter: Volk der tausend Gotter,* Bertelsmann Verlag, 1975, translation by Maxwell Brownjohn published as *The Hittites: People of a Thousand Gods,* Viking, 1977; *Die Kreuzfahrer* (title means "The Crusaders"), Bertelsmann Verlag, 1976; *Die Staufer: Glanz und Elend eines deutschen Kaisergeschlechts* (title means "Staufer: Glory and Downfall of a German Kaiser-house"), Bertelsmann Verlag, 1978.

Budda: Leben, Lehre, Wirkung (title means "Buddha: Life, Teaching, History") Bertelsmann Verlag, 1980; *Moses: Der Mann aus Aegypten* (title means "Moses: The Man from Egypt"), Hoffmann & Campe, 1983; *Das Geheimnis des Rabbi J.* (title means "The Secret of Rabbi J."), Rasch & Roehring, 1985. Writer of radio plays and features. Contributor to journals.

WORK IN PROGRESS: Short stories; research on early Christianity and mythology in the Near East.

SIDELIGHTS: In addition to German, Johannes Lehmann is competent in Greek, Latin, Hebrew, English, and French. He has traveled in the United States, Near East, and throughout Europe. His *Jesus Report* has been published in Sweden, Denmark, Netherlands, France, and England, and in a paperback edition in Germany.

*   *   *

LEISER, Erwin (Moritz)   1923-

PERSONAL: Born May 16, 1923, in Berlin, Germany; immigrated to Sweden, 1939; son of Hermann (a lawyer) and Emmy (Abrahamsohn) Leiser; married Vera Wagner (a journalist), October 2, 1960; children: Marion, Sandra. *Education:* University of Lund, B.A., 1946. *Home:* 44 Zurichbergstrasse, CH 8028 Zurich, Switzerland.

CAREER: Journalist, beginning 1945; *Morgon-Tidningen,* Stockholm, Sweden, cultural editor, 1950-58; feature writer, Swedish Broadcasting and Television, beginning 1953; director and producer of documentary films in Sweden, 1959-62, and in Switzerland, 1962—. Films include "Mein Kampf," 1960, "Murder through Signature," 1961, "Choose Life," 1963, "Germany Awake," 1968, "NPD," 1969, "The World Is Not for Children," 1972, "From Bebel to Brandt," 1974, "Because They Are Women," 1975, "Women of the Third World," 1975, "The Prime of Their Life," 1978, "The World That Disappeared," 1978, "The Passions of Isaac Bashevis Singer," 1981, and "Life after Survival," 1982.

MEMBER: Swedish P.E.N., Overseas Press Club.

AWARDS, HONORS: Awards at San Francisco, Berlin, Moscow, and Melbourne film festivals; Film Award of city of Zurich; awards for art films at Asolo, Italy, and Montreal, Quebec.

WRITINGS: (Contributor) *Bertolt Brecht,* Det Norske Studentersamfunds Kulturatvalg, 1958; *"Mein Kampf": Documenti su Hitler e il Terzio Reich* (book of the film), Feltrinelli, 1961, translation published as *A Pictorial History of Nazi Germany,* Penguin, 1962; (editor) *Flykt och foervandling* (Swedish translations of Nelly Sachs' poems with original German text of some of the poems), Fib's, 1961; *Waehle das Leben* (book of the film, "Choose Life"), Hans Deutsch, 1963; *Om dokumentaerfilm,* Norstedt, 1967; *Deutschland Erwache! Propaganda im Film des Dritten Reiches,* Rowohlt, 1968, translation published as *Nazi Cinema,* Macmillan, 1975; *Samtal i Berlin,* Norstedt, 1969; *Gud har ingen vaxel,* Norstedt, 1977; *Leben nach dem Ueberleben,* Althemaeum, 1982.

Also author of *Doe foer Hitler,* 1968, and of film portraits "Hans Richter," 1973, "Fernando Botero," 1976, "Edward Kienholz," 1977, "Willem de Kooning," 1979, "Raphael Soyer," 1981, and "Berenice Abbott," 1982. Editor of *International Theatre Yearbook,* 1957-60. Contributor to *Expressen* (Stockholm), *Weltwoche* (Zurich), and other Swedish and Swiss magazines and newspapers.

AVOCATIONAL INTERESTS: Collecting art and records (especially jazz).

BIOGRAPHICAL/CRITICAL SOURCES: Jay Leyda, *Films Beget Films,* Allen & Unwin, 1964; *Variety,* October 22, 1969.

*   *   *

LERTETH, Oban
See FANTHORPE, R(obert) Lionel

*   *   *

LESLY, Philip   1918-

PERSONAL: Born May 29, 1918, in Chicago, Ill.; married Ruth Edwards, October 17, 1940 (divorced December 3, 1971); married Virginia Barnes, May 11, 1984; children: (first marriage) Craig. *Education:* Northwestern University, B.A. (with honors), 1940. *Home:* 155 Harbor Dr., Chicago, Ill. 60601. *Office:* Philip Lesly Co., 130 East Randolph St., Chicago, Ill. 60601.

CAREER: Philip Lesly Co. (public relations counsel), Chicago, Ill., owner, 1949—. Director of National Safety Council, 1967-70. *Military service:* U.S. Navy, 1944.

MEMBER: International Public Relations Association, Public Relations Society of America, Phi Beta Kappa, Mid-America Club.

AWARDS, HONORS: Public Relations Society of America, Silver Anvil Awards, 1946, 1963, 1965, Gold Anvil Award, 1979; voted leading active practitioner, *PR Reporter* international poll, 1978.

WRITINGS: Public Relations: Principles and Procedures, Irwin, 1945; *Public Relations in Action,* Ziff-Davis, 1947; *Public Relations Handbook,* Prentice-Hall, 1950, 3rd edition, 1967; *Everything AND the Kitchen Sink,* Farrar, Straus, 1955; *Lesly's Public Relations Handbook,* Prentice-Hall, 1971, 3rd edition, 1983; *The People Factor,* Dow Jones-Irwin, 1974; *How We Discommunicate,* AMACOM, 1979; *Overcoming Opposition,* Prentice-Hall, 1984.

Also author of bimonthly, *Managing the Human Climate.* Contributor to business and public relations journals. Member of editorial advisory board of *International Public Relations Review, Public Relations Quarterly, Public Relations Review, PR Reporter,* and *Video Monitor.*

SIDELIGHTS: Philip Lesly writes: "I believe only concentration on excellence can bring about the high standards needed to improve any human activity or society. We must encourage the excellent. I concentrate on gaining satisfaction from what is achieved for my clients, my staff, my readers, my family, my friends.

"The writer, even more than other people, must focus on what he or she can uniquely offer, not following what others have done, or what has been proved popular. The way to be recognized for one's special abilities, ideas, and contributions is to focus on what others have not done and cannot do as well. This is especially important if the writer is dealing with an area of expertness aside from writing, such as a professional who is conveying his knowledge and judgment.

"I sold my first writing at the age of eight (to a children's page of a newspaper) because I had a good deal of time to myself, and I was allowed to use an old typewriter. Ever since, blank paper has been a lure to me, calling out to be filled with new thoughts and challenging ideas. I've built my career around communication, with my books and other writing (other than work for clients) being projections of what I've learned and the insights I've gained.

"My influences on national affairs and ways of life have been through invisible works (on behalf of clients), as well as visible (under my name)."

*   *   *

LESSER, R(oger) H(arold) 1928-
(Hakji Damor)

PERSONAL: Born May 31, 1928, in London, England; son of Harold (an accountant) and Esther (a teacher; maiden name, Rogers) Lesser. *Education:* Attended St. Xavier's College (Calcutta, India), 1945-49, and St. Edmund's College (England), 1949-55. *Home and office:* The Cathedral, Ajmer, Rajasthan, India 305001.

CAREER: Ordained Roman Catholic priest, 1955; taught English, history, general science, and social studies in mission school in Udaipur, India, 1955-57; did missionary work among the Bhil tribals in South Rajasthan, India; Cathedral, Ajmer,

Rajasthan, India, assistant parish priest, 1968—. Diocesan director of catechetics, liturgy, and evangelization, 1969—; liason man for mass communications media, 1969—; vigilance member for diocese, 1969—; diocesan chaplain for youth, 1970—; diocesan promoter of the biblical apostolate, 1971—; correspondent for the diocese, 1971—; regional director of natural family planning, 1977—. Has done broadcasting for All India Radio External Services and BBC Hindi Services. Preacher and lecturer. *Member:* International Biographical Association, Writer's Workshop (Calcutta), Sarv Dharam Maitri Sangh (founder and president), Christian Unity Meeting (Ajmer; founder).

WRITINGS: What a Wonderful World!, St. Paul Publications (India), 1958; *The Growing Youth,* St. Paul Publications, 1959.

Tales That Tell, St. Paul Publications, 1960; *More Tales That Tell,* St. Paul Publications, 1961; *I Wonder,* St. Paul Publications, 1961; *Into the World,* St. Paul Publications, 1962; *A Short Cut to Happiness,* St. Paul Publications, 1962; *My G-O-O-D Book,* St. Paul Publications, 1963; *An A-B-C of Goodness,* St. Paul Publications, 1963; *Indian Adventures,* privately printed, 1963; *Kindly Light,* three volumes, St. Paul Publications, 1964; (under pseudonym Hakji Damor) *Hak ni vat* (in Bhili; title means "Way of Happiness"), privately printed, 1966, 2nd revised edition (with Andrew Buria, John Sunni, George D'Souza, and Joseph Pathalil), 1968; *The Bible: My Book,* privately printed, 1969, 2nd revised edition published as *The Bible: Our Book,* Theological Publications (India), 1975.

My Place in the Family of the Trinity, privately printed, 1970; *The Church Indeed Is His Body,* St. Paul Publications, 1970; *Great Love Stories,* privately printed, 1971; *Things Worth Having,* privately printed, 1971, 2nd edition, St. Paul Publications, 1975; *Indian Mosaic,* Writers Workshop (Calcutta), 1972; *Preach the Gospel,* Pontifical Mission Aid Societies (Bangalore, India), 1972; *Peace Is Possible,* Commission for Justice and Peace (Delhi, India), 1973; *Words with God: The Psalms,* privately printed, 1973, revised edition, St. Paul Publications, 1974; *The Family Prayer-Book,* St. Anselm's Press, 1975, revised edition, 1983; (editor) *Development of Personality: A Course of Morals for Non-Christian College Students,* three volumes, All India Association of Christian Higher Education, 1976-78; *The Holy Spirit and Charismatic Renewal,* Theological Publications (India), 1978; *So You Want to Get Married,* St. Paul Publications, 1978; *Helping Young People to Know God Better,* St. Paul Publications, 1979.

The Cross on the Barren Hills, privately printed, 1980; *Twenty-Two Ways of the Cross,* Melaka-Johor Cathetical Services, 1980, revised edition, Asian Trading Corporation, 1983; *lesser lights,* Asian Trading Corporation, 1982; *Take Your Child to God,* St. Paul Publications, 1982; *Parish Councils,* Asian Trading Corporation, 1983; *A Prayer,* St. Paul Publications, 1984.

In Hindi: *Missa Pravesh* (title means "Introduction to the Mass"), privately printed, 1967; (with Baburav Joshi) *Manzil sab ki ek: Rah alag alag* (title means "All Aim at the Same Goal: Only the Ways Then Differ"), privately printed, 1971; *Muktidan* (play; title means "Gift of Salvation"), privately printed, 1976; *Krist Me Navi-Karan* (title means "Renewal in Christ"), privately printed, 1980.

Author of eight pamphlets for Amruthavani Enquiry Centre Secunderabad. Contributor of over six hundred articles, book reviews, and stories to *Catholic World, Catholic Herald, Times of India, Thought,* and other periodicals.

WORK IN PROGRESS: A History of the Roman Catholic Church in Rajasthan; The Good Cathechist; Forced Landing, a novel; "Spiritual Corners," a collection of spiritual essays for *The New Leader,* Madras.

SIDELIGHTS: R. H. Lesser writes: "I was the first English diocesan priest to be ordained in England by an Indian bishop for the Indian mission. My first job was teaching in a school in Udaipur. Then I was posted to work among the Bhil tribals in South Rajasthan where I was asked to start a new mission and train catechists. After fourteen enjoyable years among the tribals, I was posted to my present position. I enjoy and appreciate almost everything, especially Eastern and Western classical music and dancing. I have travelled over most of India, Sri Lanka, Malaysia, Holland, Italy, and England giving retreats and seminars, and am about to give a course on the philosophy of St. Thomas Aquinas in the local government college.

"The longer I live in India, even though I have travelled much in the most beautiful countries in the world, the more I am confirmed in the opinion that India is the best country in the world. I explicated this in a piece I wrote called 'Why India Is My Favourite Country.' With all its faults and flaws, with all the many successive confusions into which it seems to stumble, this vast sub-continent has so much to offer and such great potential.

"I suppose all my writing and work in India springs from my belief, and firm conviction, that Jesus is the ultimate goal and complete satisfaction of the religious strivings of these wonderful people. I do not mean the Jesus as he has most often been represented (or rather misrepresented) by Christians and Christian churches in India. Jesus, I supect, is still an unknown Christ to most of us Christians and, as Raymond Pannikar brilliantly expounded, is very definitely *already* a part of the Hindu religious search."

*   *   *

LEVEN, Charles L(ouis) 1928-

PERSONAL: Born May 2, 1928, in Chicago, Ill.; son of Elie H. (an insurance salesman) and Ruth (Reinach) Leven; married Judith Danoff, September 10, 1950 (divorced, 1968); married Dorothy Wish, December 31, 1970; children: (first marriage) Ronald L., Robert M., Carol E.; (second marriage) Philip W., Alice S. *Education:* Attended Illinois Institute of Technology, 1945, 1946-47, and University of Illinois, 1947-48; Northwestern University, B.S. (with honors), 1950, M.A., 1957, Ph.D., 1958. *Home:* 7042 Delmar, St. Louis, Mo. 63130. *Office:* Department of Economics, Washington University, St. Louis, Mo. 63130.

CAREER: Federal Reserve Bank of Chicago, Chicago, Ill., research assistant, 1949-51, economist, 1951-56; Iowa State University of Science and Technology, Ames, assistant professor of economics, 1957-59; University of Pennsylvania, Philadelphia, assistant professor of economics and regional science, 1959-62; University of Pittsburgh, Pittsburgh, Pa., associate professor of economics, 1962-65, associate director of Center for Regional Economics Studies, 1963-65; Washington University, St. Louis, Mo., professor of economics, 1965—, chairman of faculty of urban and regional science, 1965-69, director of Institute for Urban and Regional Studies, 1965—, chairman of economics department, 1975-80, chairman of urban studies, 1982—.

Visiting professor, University of California, Los Angeles, 1961; special lecturer, Brookings Institution, 1966-76. Member of regional economics advisory committee, U.S. Department of Commerce, 1963; member of advisory committee on small area data. U.S. Bureau of Census, 1965-70; member of research advisory group, Regional Economic Development Insitute, 1965-68; chairman of economic advisory committee, St. Louis Regional Industrial Development Corp., 1969-74. Consultant to industry and to public and private groups, including Army Corps of Engineers, 1967—, Planning and Development Cooperative International, 1970, Puerto Rico Planning Board, 1970, Municipality of Anchorage, 1977, University of Reading, United Kingdom, 1983—, and European Economic Community, 1983—. *Military service:* U.S. Navy, 1945-46.

MEMBER: American Economic Association, Regional Science Association (president, 1963-64), Southern Economic Association, Western Regional Science Association (councillor, 1969-72; president, 1973-74), Mid-Continent Regional Science Association.

AWARDS, HONORS: Social Science Research Council grant, 1960; Committee on Urban Economics grants, 1965, 1966; National Science Foundation grants, 1968, 1975.

WRITINGS: Theory and Method of Income and Product Accounts for Metropolitan Area: Including the Elgin-Dundee Area as a Case Study, Center for Regional Economic Studies, University of Pittsburgh, 1963; *Development Benefits of Water Resource Investments,* Institute for Water Resources, U.S. Army Corps of Engineers, 1969.

(With John Legler and Perry Shapiro) *An Analytical Framework for Regional Development Policy,* M.I.T. Press, 1970; (editor with M. Perlman and B. Chinitz) *Spatial, Regional, and Population Economics: Essays in Honor of Edgar M. Hoover,* Gordon & Breach, 1972; (with J. Little, H. Nourse, and R. Read) *Neighborhood Change: Lessons in the Dynamics of Urban Decay,* Praeger, 1976; (editor) *The Mature Metropolis,* Heath, 1978; *Regional Dynamics of Socioeconomic Change,* Funnpublishers, 1979.

Internal Dynamics of the City, Oxford University Press, 1982; *Human Settlement and Regional Development,* Settlement Department of the Jewish Agency, 1984.

Contributor: Werner Hochwald, editor, *Design of Regional Accounts,* Johns Hopkins Press, 1961; *Economic Study of the Pittsburgh Region,* Volume III: *Region with a Future,* University of Pittsburgh Press, 1963; John Friedmann and William Alonso, editors, *Regional Development and Planning,* M.I.T. Press, 1964; Werner Hirsch, editor, *Studies in Regional Accounts,* Johns Hopkins Press, 1964; Paul Davidson and Eugene Smolensky, editors, *Aggregate Demand and Supply Analysis,* Harper, 1964; Earl Heady, editor, *Research and Education for Regional and Area Development,* Iowa State University Press, 1965; *Lectures on Water Management,* Johns Hopkins University Press, 1965; *Urban Development Models,* Highway Research Board, National Academy of Science, 1968; Lionel Needleman, editor, *Regional Economics,* Penguin, 1968; R. P. Misra, editor, *Regional Planning,* University of Mysore (India), 1969.

Information Systems for Regional Development, Lund Studies in Geography, 1971; *Urban and Social Economics in Market and Planned Economies,* Praeger, 1974; *Regional Sociology and Regional Planning,* Mouton, 1977; *Internal Migrations: A Comparative Perspective,* Academic Press, 1977. Contributor of about twenty articles to scholarly journals.

WORK IN PROGRESS: Economic Impact of Urban Land Use Controls; Metropolitan Change and Development.

SIDELIGHTS: Charles L. Leven told *CA:* "Most of what I have to write is fairly technical. At the same time, I try to make what I have to say as clear as possible to non-professionals since I believe that academic scholarship . . . [has] something of importance to contribute to practical problems of today. It should be conceded that professional economists . . . are probably much better at asking than [at] answering questions, but perhaps taking the question in the right way may be more of a practical contribution than is commonly supposed."

*　　*　　*

LEVINE, Norman 1924-

PERSONAL: Born October 22, 1924, in Ottawa, Ontario, Canada; son of Moses Mordecai and Annie (Gurevich) Levine; married Margaret Payne, January 2, 1952 (died August 15, 1978); married Anne Sarginson, August 10, 1983; children: (first marriage) Cassie, Kate, Rachel. *Education:* McGill University, B.A. (with honors), 1948, M.A., 1949. *Home:* 45 Bedford Rd., St. Ives, Cornwall, England; and 103 Summerhill Ave., Toronto, Ontario, Canada. *Agent:* Dr. Ruth Liepman, Maienburgweg 23, Zurich, Switzerland.

CAREER: Writer. Head of English department, Barnstaple Boys Grammar School, 1953-54; first resident writer, University of New Brunswick, 1965-66. *Military service:* Royal Canadian Air Force, 1942-45; became flying officer.

AWARDS, HONORS: Canada Council fellowship, 1959; Canada Council arts award, 1969 and 1971.

WRITINGS: Myssium (poetry), Ryerson Press, 1948; *The Tightrope Walker* (poetry), Totem Press, 1950; *The Angled Road* (novel), Werner Laurie, 1952; *Canada Made Me* (travel), Putnam, 1958, reprinted, Deneau, 1979; *One Way Ticket* (stories), Secker & Warburg, 1961; (editor) *Canadian Winter's Tales,* Macmillan, 1968; *From a Seaside Town* (novel), Macmillan, 1970; *I Don't Want to Know Anyone Too Well* (stories), Macmillan, 1971; *Selected Stories,* Oberon Press, 1975; *I Walk by the Harbour* (poetry), Fiddlehead Poetry Books, 1976; *In Lower Town,* Commoners, 1977; *Thin Ice* (stories), Deneau, 1979; *Why Do You Live So Far Away?* (stories), Deneau, 1984; *Champagne Barn* (stories), Penguin, 1984.

Contributor of teleplays to the Canadian Broadcasting Co., and the British Broadcasting Co. Contributor of short stories to *Encounter, Vogue, Harper's Bazaar, Sunday Times Magazine, Daily Telegraph Magazine, Saturday Night,* and other periodicals.

WORK IN PROGRESS: Short stories; a novel.

SIDELIGHTS: Norman Levine was the subject of three television films, "Norman Levine Lived Here," made by the Canadian Broadcasting Co. in 1970, "Norman Levine's St. Ives," made by the British Broadcasting Co., 1972, and a film made by TV Ontario, 1980. Some of Levine's work has been translated into German.

BIOGRAPHICAL/CRITICAL SOURCES: Times (London), July 19, 1970; *Times Literary Supplement,* August 28, 1970, March 14, 1980; *Montreal Star,* September 26, 1970.

LEVINSON, Leonard 1935-
(Nicholas Brady, Lee Chang, Glen Chase, Richard Hale Curtis, Gordon Davis, Nelson De Mille, Richard Gallagher, March Hastings, J. Farragut Jones, Leonard Jordan, Philip Kirk, John Mackie, Robert Novak, Philip Rawls, Bruno Rossi, Jonathan Scofield, Jonathan Trask, Cynthia Wilkerson)

PERSONAL: Born in 1935, in New Bedford, Mass.; married twice (first marriage ended by divorce, second by death); children: (first marriage) Deborah. *Education:* Michigan State University, B.A., 1961. *Home:* 347 West 55th St., New York, N.Y. 10019. *Agent:* Barbara Lowenstein & Associates, Inc., Suite 714, 250 West 57th St., New York, N.Y. 10107.

CAREER: Writer, 1971—. Has also worked as a public relations representative, social worker, bartender, cab driver, and waiter. *Military service:* U.S. Army, 1954-57.

MEMBER: National Writers Union, Writers Guild of America (East).

WRITINGS—Under pseudonym Nicholas Brady: *Shark Fighter* (adventure novel), Belmont-Tower, 1975; *Inside Job* (crime novel), Belmont-Tower, 1978.

Under pseudonym Lee Chang: *The Year of the Boar* (crime novel), Manor Publishing, 1975.

Under pseudonym Glen Chase: *Where the Action Is* (crime novel), Leisure Books, 1977.

Under pseudonym Richard Hale Curtis: *Every Man an Eagle,* Dell, 1982.

Under pseudonym Gordon Davis: *Death Train,* Zebra Books, 1980; *Hell Harbor,* Zebra Books, 1980; *Bloody Bush,* Zebra Books, 1980; *The Goering Treasure,* Zebra Books, 1980; *The Liberation of Paris,* Bantam, 1981; *Doom River,* Bantam, 1981; *Slaughter City,* Bantam, 1981; *Bullet Bridge,* Bantam, 1981; *Bloody Bastogne,* Bantam, 1981; *The Battle of the Bulge,* Bantam, 1981.

Under pseudonym Nelson De Mille: *The Terrorists* (crime novel), Leisure Books, 1974.

Under pseudonym Richard Gallagher: *Doom Platoon* (war novel), Belmont-Tower, 1978.

Under pseudonym March Hastings: *Private Sessions* (romantic comedy), Midwood Books, 1974.

Under pseudonym J. Farragut Jones: *Forty Fathoms Down,* Dell, 1981; *Tracking the Wolf Pack,* Dell, 1981.

Under pseudonym Leonard Jordan: *Operation Perfidia* (spy thriller), Warner Books, 1975; *The Bar Studs,* Fawcett, 1976; *Hype!* (novel), Fawcett, 1977; *Cabby,* Belmont-Tower, 1980; *The Last Buffoon,* Belmont-Tower, 1980; *Without Mercy,* Zebra Books, 1981.

Under pseudonym Philip Kirk; all published by Leisure Books: *The Hydra Conspiracy,* 1979; *Smart Bombs,* 1979; *The Slayboys,* 1979; *Chinese Roulette,* 1979; *Love Me to Death,* 1980; *Killer Satellites,* 1980.

Under pseudonym John Mackie; all published by Jove: *Hit the Beach,* 1983; *Death Squad,* 1983; *River of Blood,* 1983; *Meat Grinder Hill,* 1984; *Down and Dirty,* 1984; *Green Hell,* 1984; *Too Mean to Die,* 1984.

Under pseudonym Robert Novak: *The Thrill Killers* (crime novel), Belmont-Tower, 1974.

Under pseudonym Philip Rawls: *Streets of Blood* (crime novel), Manor Publishing, 1975.

Under pseudonym Bruno Rossi; all crime novels published by Leisure Books: *The Worst Way to Die,* 1974; *Night of the Assassins,* 1974; *Headcrusher,* 1974.

Under pseudonym Jonathan Scofield: *Bayonets in No-Man's Land,* Dell, 1982.

Under pseudonym Jonathan Trask: *The Camp,* Belmont-Tower, 1977.

Under pseudonym Cynthia Wilkerson: *Sweeter than Candy,* Belmont-Tower, 1978; *The Fast Life,* Belmont-Tower, 1979.

*　　*　　*

LEVITIN, Sonia (Wolff) 1934-
(Sonia Wolff)

PERSONAL: Born August 18, 1934, in Berlin, Germany; brought to United States in 1938; daughter of Max (a manufacturer) and Helene (Goldstein) Wolff; married Lloyd Levitin (a business executive), December 27, 1953; children: Daniel Joseph, Shari Diane. *Education:* Attended University of California, Berkeley, 1952-54; University of Pennsylvania, B.S., 1956; San Francisco State College (now University), graduate study, 1957-60. *Home:* 1341 Via Gabriel, Palos Verdes Estates, Calif. 90274. *Agent:* Toni Mendez, Inc., 140 East 56th St., New York, N.Y. 10022.

CAREER: Writer and lecturer. Elementary teacher in Mill Valley, Calif., 1956-57; adult education teacher in Daly City, Calif., 1962-64; Acalanes Adult Center, Lafayette, Calif., teacher, 1965-72; teacher of creative writing, Palos Verdes Peninsula, Calif., 1973-76. Founder of STEP (adult education corporation) in Palos Verdes Peninsula, Calif.

MEMBER: Authors League of America, Authors Guild, P.E.N., Society of Children's Book Writers, California Writer's Guild, Moraga Historical Society (founder and former president).

AWARDS, HONORS: Journey to America received the Charles and Bertie G. Schwartz Award for Juvenile Fiction from the Jewish Book Council of America, 1971, and American Library Association Notable Book honors; *Roanoke: A Novel of the Lost Colony* was nominated for Dorothy Canfield Fisher Award, Georgia Children's Book Award, and Mark Twain Award; *Who Owns the Moon?* received American Library Association Notable Book honors; *The Mark of Conte* received Southern California Council on Literature for Children and Young People award for fiction, 1976, and was nominated for California Young Reader Medal award in the junior high category, 1982; *The No-Return Trail* received Golden Spur Award from Western Writers of America, 1978, and Lewis Carroll Shelf Award; Southern California Council on Literature for Children and Young People award for a distinguished contribution to the field of children's literature, 1981.

WRITINGS—Juveniles, except as indicated: *Journey to America* (Junior Literary Guild Selection), Atheneum, 1970; *Rita the Weekend Rat,* Atheneum, 1971; *Who Owns the Moon?,* Parnassus, 1973; *Roanoke: A Novel of the Lost Colony,* Atheneum, 1973; *Jason and the Money Tree,* Harcourt, 1974; *A Single Speckled Egg,* Parnassus, 1975; *The Mark of Conte,* Atheneum, 1976; *Beyond Another Door,* Atheneum, 1977; *The No-Return Trail* (Junior Literary Guild Selection), Harcourt, 1978; *Reigning Cats and Dogs* (adult), Atheneum, 1978; *A*

Sound to Remember (Jewish Book Club selection), Harcourt, 1979.

Nobody Stole the Pie, Harcourt, 1980; (under name Sonia Wolff) *What They Did to Miss Lily* (adult), Harper, 1981; *The Fisherman and the Bird,* Houghton, 1982; *All the Cats in the World,* Harcourt, 1982; *The Year of Sweet Senior Insanity,* Atheneum, 1982; *Smile Like a Plastic Daisy,* Atheneum, 1983. Feature columnist for Sun Newspapers, Contra Costa, Calif., and *Jewish Observer of the East Bay,* Oakland, Calif. Contributor to periodicals, including *Smithsonian, Parent's Magazine, The Writer, Woman's World,* and *San Francisco Magazine.*

WORK IN PROGRESS: An adult novel, *Incident at Loring Groves.*

SIDELIGHTS: Based upon the author's childhood experiences, Sonia Levitin's *Journey to America* is the story of a Jewish family's escape from Nazi Germany. In a review in the *School Library Journal,* Terry M. Cole describes Levitin's first book as "a very moving though never mauldin story with good characterization and a fast pace." Commenting on the author's realistic portrayal of people and events, Zena Sutherland writes in the *Bulletin of the Center for Children's Books* that *Journey to America* is "well-written and perceptive in describing the tensions and reactions of people in a situation of stress." Concludes Elizabeth Minot Graves in *Commonweal,* "[This is] one of the best books of the year, indeed any year."

Levitin's other books feature characters who confront the harsh environment of the unexplored New World as well as such complex contemporary issues as wealth, ESP, and feminism. Levitin told *CA:* "In each book I try to do something quite different from the previous work. Themes and characters might repeat themselves, but I believe that my growth as a writer and as a person depends on accepting new challenges, deepening my experience and my efforts."

BIOGRAPHICAL/CRITICAL SOURCES: School Library Journal, May, 1970; *Commonweal,* May 22, 1970; *New York Times Book Review,* May 24, 1970, November 28, 1976; *Bulletin of the Center for Children's Books,* February, 1971; *Writer,* August, 1972; *Contemporary Literary Criticism,* Volume XVII, Gale, 1981; *Wilson Library Bulletin,* May, 1984.

*　　*　　*

LEVY, Fred D(avid), Jr. 1937-

PERSONAL: Born October 10, 1937, in Chicago, Ill.; son of Fred David and Anne (Adler) Levy; married Judy Reinach, June 12, 1960; children: Sally Ann, Patricia Louise, Sharon Lea. *Education:* Purdue University, B.S., 1959; Yale University, M.A., 1960, Ph.D., 1966. *Home:* 10318 Folk St., Silver Spring, Md. 20902.

CAREER: Syracuse University, Syracuse, N.Y., instructor, 1964-65, assistant professor, 1965-72, associate professor of economics, beginning 1972; U.S. Agency for International Development (USAID), Rio de Janerio, Brazil, economic adviser, 1967-69; consultant to U.S. Agency for International Development, 1969-72, and U.S. Treasury Department, 1972-75; senior economist, World Bank, 1975—. Has presented papers on Latin American debt problems and the economy of Brazil.

MEMBER: American Economic Association, Latin American Studies Association, Society for International Development.

WRITINGS: Economic Planning in Venezuela, Praeger, 1968; *Documentos para o Planejamento da Economia Brasileira,*

Interamerican University Foundation, 1971; (with Sidney C. Sufrin) *Basic Economics: Analysis of Contemporary Problems and Politics,* with workbook and instructor's manual, Harper, 1973; *Chile: An Economy in Transition,* World Bank, 1980; *A Review of Brazilian Agricultural Policies,* World Bank, 1982.

Contributor to *Collier's Encyclopedia;* contributor of articles on economic planning and foreign technical assistance to journals in his field.

WORK IN PROGRESS: World Bank economic studies regarding Brazil, Argentina, Uruguay, and Paraguay.

*   *   *

LI, Tze-chung 1927-

PERSONAL: Born February 17, 1927, in Kiangsu, China; son of Ken-hsiang (a lawyer) and Yu-hsien (Chang) Li; married In-lan Wang (a librarian), October 21, 1961; children: Lily, Rose. *Education:* Soochow University, LL.B., 1948; Southern Methodist University, M.C.L., 1957; Harvard University, LL.M., 1958; Columbia University, M.S., 1965; New School for Social Research, Ph.D., 1963. *Home:* 1104 Greenfield, Oak Park, Ill. 60302. *Office:* Graduate School of Library and Information Science, Rosary College, River Forest, Ill. 60305.

CAREER: Ministry of Justice, Taiwan, China, district judge, 1949-51; Ministry of Defence, Taiwan, section head, 1951-56; Atlantic Fiscal Corp., New York, N.Y., vice-president, 1960-64; Illinois State University, Normal, assistant professor of library science and assistant librarian, 1965-66; Rosary College, River Forest, Ill., associate professor, 1966-74, professor of library science, 1974-82, dean, 1982—. Visiting professor, National Taiwan University, and Soochow University, 1969; director, National Central Library (Taiwan), 1970-72; chairman, Graduate Institute of Library Science (Taiwan), 1971-72; member of board of directors, Center for American Studies (Taiwan), 1971. President, Chinese-American Educational Foundation, 1969-70.

MEMBER: International Association of Orientalist Librarians (area representative, 1971-76), American Library Association, National Librarians Association, Chinese-American Librarians Association (president, 1974-76; executive director, 1976-79), American Association for Chinese Studies, Association of Asian Studies, Organization of Chinese Americans, Chinese Library Association (convenor, 1971-72), Association for Library and Information Science Education.

AWARDS, HONORS: Chinese Government citations, 1963, 1972; Rosary College, Elsie O. and Philip D. Sang award for excellence in teaching, 1971, and outstanding educator, 1982; distinguished service award, Phi Tau Phi Scholastic Honor Society, 1982.

WRITINGS: Lu-hai-k'ung-chun hsing-fa kai-lun (title means "A Treatise on Military Criminal Law") Far East, 1955; *A List of Doctoral Dissertations by Chinese Students in the United States: 1961-1964,* Chinese American Educational Foundation, 1969; *Mei-kuo tushu-kuan yeh-wu* (title means "American Librarianship"), Far East, 1972; (with wife, In-lan Wang) *Chung-wen ts'an-k'ao yung-shu* (title means "A Guide to Chinese Reference Books"), Cheng-chung, 1972; (with Roy Chang) *A Directory of Chinese-American Librarians,* CHCUS, 1977.

Social Science Reference Sources, Greenwood Press, 1980; *Mah Jong: The Rules for Playing the Chinese Game,* CHCUS, 1982; *An Introduction to Online Searching,* Greenwood Press,

1985. Also author of *A Guide to Basic DIALOG Searching,* 1981.

Contributor to law and library journals. Executive editor, *Journal of Library and Information Science,* 1975-79; chairman of editorial board, *International Journal of Reviews in Library and Information Science,* 1984—.

*   *   *

LIHANI, John 1927-

PERSONAL: Surname is pronounced Le-*hon*-ey; born March 24, 1927, in Hnusta, Czechoslovakia; son of John (a molder) and Susanna (Jablonska) Lihani; married Emily G. Kolesar (a librarian), September 9, 1950; children: J. Brian, Robert P., David L. *Education:* Western Reserve University (now Case Western Reserve University), B.S. (magna cum laude), 1948; Ohio State University, M.A., 1950; Tulane University, further study, 1950-51; University of Texas, Ph.D., 1954; postdoctoral study at Yale University and University of Madrid. *Religion:* Lutheran. *Office:* Department of Spanish, University of Kentucky, Lexington, Ky. 40506.

CAREER: University of Texas at Austin, instructor in Spanish, 1953-54; Yale University, New Haven, Conn., instructor, 1954-58, assistant professor of Spanish, 1958-62; University of Pittsburgh, Pittsburgh, Pa., associate professor of Spanish, 1962-69; University of Kentucky, Lexington, professor of Spanish, 1969—. Member of board of directors, National Confederation of American Ethnic Groups, 1969-71.

MEMBER: Modern Language Association of America, American Association of Teachers of Spanish and Portuguese, Linguistic Society of America, Comparative Romance Linguistics Group, American Association of University Professors, Phi Beta Kappa.

AWARDS, HONORS: Morse fellow, 1960-61; Fulbright professor in Colombia, 1965-66; International Research and Exchanges award, 1974; American Philosophical Society award, 1977; American Council of Learned Societies grants, 1980, 1984.

WRITINGS: (Editor) Lucas Fernandez, *Farsas y eglogas,* Las Americas, 1969; *El lenguaje de Lucas Fernandez,* Instituto Caro y Cuervo, 1973; *Lucas Fernandez,* Twayne, 1973; *Bartolome de Torres Naharro,* Twayne, 1979; (editor) *El Poema de Fernan Gonzalez,* Clasicos Ebro, 1984; (compiler) *Manuscript Documents from Spain Dating from the 12th through the 18th Centuries,* University of Kentucky Library Associates, 1984.

Contributor of articles to language and Romance studies journals. Member of editorial board, *Kentucky Romance Quarterly;* associate editor, *Bulletin of the Comediantes;* founding editor, *La Coronica.*

WORK IN PROGRESS: Research on Spanish linguistics, Spanish medieval and renaissance literature, comparative Romance linguistics, global trends in linguistics, and Indo-European languages.

SIDELIGHTS: John Lihani speaks Spanish, Slovak, French, Italian, Portuguese, Russian, Polish, Czech, Serbo-Croatian, German, and has studied Latin, Sanskrit, Greek, Mandarin Chinese, and Roumanian. He has traveled extensively in Europe and North and South America.

*   *   *

LIONEL, Robert
See FANTHORPE, R(obert) Lionel

LITTLEJOHN, David 1937-

PERSONAL: Born May 8, 1937, in San Francisco, Calif.; son of George T. and Josephine (Cullen) Littlejohn; married Sheila Hageman, June 10, 1963; children: Victoria, Gregory David. *Education:* University of California, Berkeley, B.A., 1959; Harvard University, M.A., 1961, Ph.D., 1963. *Home:* 719 Coventry Rd., Kensington, Calif. 94707. *Office:* School of Journalism, University of California, Berkeley, Calif. 94720.

CAREER: University of California, Berkeley, assistant professor of English and journalism, 1963-70, associate professor, 1970-76, professor of journalism, 1976—, associate dean, 1974-78. Critic for KQED, San Francisco, 1965-75, and Public Broadcasting Service, 1971-72; Fulbright professor in France, 1966-67. Consultant to Aspen program on communications and society, 1973-75.

AWARDS, HONORS: American Council of Learned Societies fellow in England and France, 1972-73; National Endowment for the Humanities grant, 1976; National Endowment for the Arts grant, 1984.

WRITINGS: (Editor) *Dr. Johnson: His Life in Letters,* Prentice-Hall, 1965; *Black on White: A Critical Survey of Writing by American Negroes,* Grossman, 1966; *Interruptions* (essays), Viking, 1969; (editor) *Gide: A Collection of Critical Essays,* Prentice-Hall, 1970; (editor) *The Andre Gide Reader,* Knopf, 1971; *Dr. Johnson and Noah Webster: Two Men and Their Dictionaries,* Book Club of California, 1972.

Three California Families, privately printed, 1976; *The Man Who Killed Mick Jagger* (fiction), Little, Brown, 1977; *Going to California* (fiction), Coward, McCann & Geohegan, 1982; *Architect: The Life and Work of Charles W. Moore,* Holt, 1984. Author of approximately two hundred television scripts for Public Broadcasting Service programs. Contributor of over 120 articles and book reviews to journals.

WORK IN PROGRESS: The Last Days of Sir Anthony Craven, a novel; *I Made Them All Up,* a book of stories; *Words about Buildings,* a book on architectural criticism; *An Exotic and Irrational Entertainment,* essays on opera.

SIDELIGHTS: In his novel *Going to California,* David Littlejohn intertwines past and present, paralleling two different journeys across America. For a forty-year-old man and his young bride, the trip home to California from Boston proves as demanding as a similar trip made by the man's great-great-grandmother during the California gold rush. Carolyn See writes in the *Los Angeles Times,* "Littlejohn is a wonder in this *tour de force.* His research—both of the highways of today and the trails of 100 years ago—is perfectly authentic." In the *Times Literary Supplement,* Stephen Fender adds, "*Going to California* offers us a store of close observations . . . of the absurd, often tawdry and sometimes touching human contacts along the road."

In *Architect: The Life and Work of Charles W. Moore,* Littlejohn offers a critical examination of the Post-Modernist architect and the structures for which he is responsible. Paul H. Gleye in the *Los Angeles Times Book Review* calls the book "a 368-page chat, always admiring but nevertheless critical of [its] subject." Gleye concludes, "The author's observations must at times have been uncomfortable for his subject, but in the end, this stance lends humanity to both the author and the architect, as well as to the creative process of architecture."

BIOGRAPHICAL/CRITICAL SOURCES: Los Angeles Times, January 29, 1981; *Times Literary Supplement,* May 15, 1981; *Los Angeles Times Book Review,* July 1, 1984.

*   *   *

LOCK, Dennis (Laurence) 1929-

PERSONAL: Born September 15, 1929, in London, England; son of Douglas Leonard and Marjorie (Rouledge) Lock; married Gladys Nancie Shilling, July 11, 1953. *Education:* Acton Technical College, Higher National Certificate in applied physics, 1955. *Politics:* Conservative. *Religion:* Church of England. *Home:* 29 Burston Dr., Park St., St. Albans, Hertfordshire AL2 2HR, England. *Office:* Seltrust Engineering Ltd., 57/61 Clerkenwell Rd., London EC1M 5SP, England.

CAREER: General Electric Co., Wembley and Stanmore, England, physicist, 1945-48 and 1950-62; Honeywell Controls Ltd., Hemel Hempstead, England, contracts control manager, 1963-68; Herbert-Ingersoll Ltd., Daventry, England, manager of engineering administrative services, 1968-71; Seltrust Engineering Ltd., London, England, office services manager, 1971—. Consultant. *Military service:* Royal Air Force, 1948-50.

MEMBER: British Institute of Management, Institute of Industrial Managers, Institute of Management Services (fellow), Physical Society (fellow), Writers Guild of Great Britain.

WRITINGS—All published by Gower Press, except as indicated: *Project Management,* Canner, 1968, revised edition, 1984; (editor) *Directors' Guide to Management Techniques,* 1970, revised edition, 1972; *Industrial Scheduling Techniques,* 1971; (editor) *Engineers' Handbook of Management Techniques,* 1973; (editor) *Financial Management of Production,* 1975; *Factory Administration Handbook,* 1976; (with others) *Robotics in Practice,* Kogan Page, 1980; (editor) *Gower Handbook of Management,* 1983.

AVOCATIONAL INTERESTS: Music, opera, mountain walking.

*   *   *

LOCKERBIE, D(onald) Bruce 1935-

PERSONAL: Born August 25, 1935, in Capreol, Ontario, Canada; son of Ernest Arthur (a minister) and Jeanette (Honeyman) Lockerbie; married Lory Quayle (a teacher), December 15, 1956; children: Donald Bruce, Jr., Kevin John, Ellyn Beth. *Education:* New York University, A.B., 1956, M.A., 1963. *Politics:* Independent. *Religion:* Episcopalian. *Home:* 7 Peggy Ln., Stony Brook, N.Y. 11790. *Office:* Stony Brook School, Stony Brook, N.Y. 11790.

CAREER: Affiliated with Wheaton College, Wheaton, Ill., 1956-57; Stony Brook School, Stony Brook, N.Y., chairman of Fine Arts department, 1957—. Visiting professor of English, Wheaton College; Staley Foundation lecturer at several colleges. *Member:* National Council of Teachers of English (member of Commission on English Curriculum), Cum Laude Society, New York Athletic Club.

WRITINGS: Billy Sunday, Word Books, 1965; (with Thomas C. Pollock) *The Macmillan English Series,* two volumes, Macmillan, 1969; *Patriarchs and Prophets,* Holt, 1969; *Major American Authors,* Holt, 1970; (with Lincoln Westdal) *Success in Writing,* Addison-Wesley, 1970; *Purposeful Writing,* Addison-Wesley, 1972; *The Way They Should Go,* Oxford University Press, 1972; *The Liberating Word: Art and the Mystery of the Gospel*, Eerdmans, 1974; *Education of Missionaries' Children: The Neglected Dimension of World Mission*, William Carey Library, 1975; *The Cosmic Center*, Eerdmans, 1977; *The Apostles' Creed: Do You Really Believe It?*, Victor, 1977; *A Man under Orders: Lt. General William K. Harrison, Jr.*, Harper, 1978.

Who Educates Your Child?, Doubleday, 1980; *The Timeless Moment: Creativity and the Christian Faith*, Crossway, 1980; *Asking Questions*, Mott Media, 1980; *Fatherlove: Learning to Give the Best You've Got*, Doubleday, 1981; *In Peril on the Sea*, Doubleday, 1984; (editor) Frank E. Gaebelein, *Whatsoever Things: Essays in Christian Aesthetics*, Multnomah, 1985. Contributor of articles to religion and literature journals.

WORK IN PROGRESS: Thinking Like a Christian; The Abdication of Belief; Wisdom and Knowledge: A History and Anthology of Christian Schooling.

BIOGRAPHICAL/CRITICAL SOURCES: Review for Religious, May, 1973; *Christian Century*, January 15, 1975, February 1, 1978.

*   *   *

LOCKERT, Lucia (Alicia Ungaro Fox)   1928-
(Lucia Ungaro de Fox, Lucia Fox, Lucia Fox-Lockert)

PERSONAL: Born March 29, 1928, in Lima, Peru; daughter of Fabricio (an engineer) and Enriqueta (Zevallos) Ungaro; married Hugh Fox, June 9, 1956 (divorced, 1970); married Clinton Lockert (a professor and librarian), June 24, 1972; children: three. *Education:* Universidad Nacional de San Marcos, M.A., 1955; University of Illinois, Ph.D., 1960. *Home:* 1049 Cressenwood Rd., East Lansing, Mich. 48823. *Office:* Department of Romance Languages, Michigan State University, East Lansing, Mich. 48824.

CAREER: University of Sonora, Sonora, Mexico, lecturer, 1961-62; instructor in high schools in Inglewood, Calif., 1962-64; Centro Venezolano-Americano, Caracas, Venezuela, lecturer, 1964-66; San Fernando Valley State College, Los Angeles, Calif., professor, 1966-68; Michigan State University, East Lansing, Mich., assistant professor of romance languages, 1968—. *Member:* American Association of Teachers of Spanish and Portuguese, Institute of International Studies, Latin American Studies Association, Modern Language Association of America.

WRITINGS—Under name Lucia Fox, except as indicated: (Under name Lucia Ungaro de Fox) *Imagenes de Caracas* (poetry), Garcia Hnos (Caracas), 1965; (under name Lucia Ungaro de Fox) *Ensayos hispano-americanos*, M. A. Garcia, 1966; *Redes*, Ediciones Carabela, 1968; *Aceleracion Multiple*, Dead Weight, 1969; *El rostro de la patria en la literatura peruana*, Ediciones Continente, 1970; *La odisae del pajaro*, Empresas Editoras, 1972; *Monstruos aeros y submarinos* (poetry), Superspace, 1974; (under name Lucia Fox-Lockert) *Women Novelists in Spain and Spanish America*, Scarecrow, 1979; *El perfil desnudo* (plays), Ediciones Salesiana, 1980. Contributor to periodicals, including *El rostro de la patria*, *La Tapada*, and *Mosaics*.

WORK IN PROGRESS: Tales of an Indian Princess; studies of the role of higher education, women as motif in Peruvian poetry, and Mexican history and social institutions.

AVOCATIONAL INTERESTS: Working, mainly with women, in Chicano and bilingual groups.

*   *   *

LOCKLIN, Gerald (Ivan)   1941-

PERSONAL: Born February 17, 1941, in Rochester, N.Y.; son of Ivan Ward and Esther (Kindelen) Locklin; married Mary Alice Keefe; married second wife, Maureen McNicholas; married third wife, Barbara Curry; children: (first marriage) James, Heidi, Rebecca; (second marriage) Blake, John; (third marriage) Vanessa, Zachary. *Education:* St. John Fisher College, B.A., 1961; University of Arizona, M.A., 1963, Ph.D., 1964. *Office:* Department of English, California State University, Long Beach, Calif. 90801.

CAREER: California State College at Los Angeles (now California State University, Los Angeles), instructor in English, 1964-65; California State University, Long Beach, 1965—, began as associate professor, currently professor of English.

MEMBER: Phi Beta Kappa.

WRITINGS: Sunset Beach, Hors Commerce Press, 1967; *The Toad Poems,* Runcible Spoon Press, 1970, new edition, Venice Poetry Company, 1975; *Poop, and Other Poems,* Mag Press, 1973; *Toad's Europe,* Venice Poetry Co., 1973; *Locked In,* True Gripp Press, 1973; *Son of Poop,* Maelstrom Press, 1974; (with Koertge and Stetler) *Tarzan and Shane Meet the Toad,* Russ Haas Press, 1975; *The Chase: A Novel,* Duck Down Press, 1976; *The Criminal Mentality,* Red Hill Press, 1976; *The Four-Day Work Week and Other Stories,* Russ Haas Press, 1977; *Pronouncing Borges,* Wormwood Review Press, 1977; *A Weekend in Canada,* Rumba Train Press, 1979; *The Cure,* Applezaba Press, 1979; *Two Summer Sequences,* Maelstrom Press, 1979.

Stanford's Farm, Rumba Train Press, 1980; *Last of Toad,* Venice Poetry Co., 1980; *Two for the Seesaw and One for the Road,* Northwoods Press, 1980; *Poop: Gedichte und stories,* Maro Verlag (West Germany), 1980; *Scenes from a Second Adolescence,* Applezaba Press, 1981; *A Clear and Present Danger to Society,* Four Zoas Night House Press, 1981; *By Land, Sea, and Air,* Maelstrom Press, 1982; *Why Turn a Perfectly Good Toad into a Prince?,* Mt. Alverno Press, 1983; *Fear and Paternity in the Pauma Valley,* Planet Detroit Press, 1984; (with Ray Zepeda) *The Ensenada Poems,* Truly Fine Press, 1984.

Author of *The Case of the Missing Blue Volkswagen,* Applezaba Press, *Frisco Epic,* Russ Haas Press, *Toad's Sabbatical,* Venice Poetry Co., *The Phantom of the Johnny Carson Show,* Illuminati Press, and *The Death of Jean-Paul Sartre and Other Poems,* Ghost Pony Press. Also author of play "The Dentist." Contributor of numerous reviews to *Los Angeles Times* and *Long Beach Independent Press-Telegram,* and of articles to *Coast;* contributor of poems and stories to literary magazines, including *Wormwood Review* and *Transpacific.*

WORK IN PROGRESS: Poems, stories, novels, plays, and literary criticism.

BIOGRAPHICAL/CRITICAL SOURCES: Los Angeles Times Book Review, October 31, 1982.

LOEWEN, James W. 1942-
(James Lyons)

PERSONAL: Born February 6, 1942, in Decatur, Ill.; son of David Frank (a physician) and Winifred (a librarian; maiden name, Gore) Loewen; married Judith Murphy (a teacher), September 16, 1978; children: (previous marriage) Bruce Nicholas, Lucy Catherine. *Education:* Attended Mississippi State University, 1963; Carleton College, B.A. (cum laude), 1964; Harvard University, M.A., 1967, Ph.D., 1968. *Politics:* Independent. *Religion:* Unitarian Universalist. *Home:* 46 Central Ave., South Burlington, Vt. 05401. *Office:* Department of Sociology, University of Vermont, Burlington, Vt. 05401.

CAREER: Tougaloo College, Tougaloo, Miss., assistant professor, 1968-70, associate professor of sociology, 1970-75, chairman of department of sociology and anthropology, 1969-73, chairman of Division of Social Science, 1972-74; University of Vermont, Burlington, associate professor, 1975-83, professor of sociology, 1984—. Director of research, Center for National Policy Review, Washington, D.C., beginning 1978. Has served as an expert witness in numerous civil rights cases for Department of Justice and Lawyers Committee for Civil Rights, beginning 1969; has lectured and presented papers to various professional organizations. Text reviewer for Holt, Rinehart & Winston, Harper & Row, Praeger Publishers, and American Association for State and Local History.

MEMBER: American Sociological Association, Southern Sociological Society, Mississippi Historical Society. *Awards, honors:* Distinguished Teacher Award, Tougaloo College, 1970-71, 1972-73; National Science Foundation postdoctoral fellowship, 1975; Lillian Smith Award for southern nonfiction, 1975, for *Mississippi: Conflict and Change*.

WRITINGS: The Mississippi Chinese: Between Black and White, Harvard University Press, 1971; (with Charles Sallis and others) *Mississippi: Conflict and Change*, Pantheon, 1974, revised edition, 1980; *Social Science in the Courtroom*, Heath, 1983. Also author of booklet *Sociology at Vermont (How, Maybe Even Why, to Major in It)*, 1977, resource packet *If Your State History Is Dull and Boring, Here's How to Fix It*, 1977, and script for documentary film "The Spirit of Kake Walk," 1978. Contributor to national journals and professional publications, sometimes under pseudonym James Lyons. Editor, *Clearinghouse for Civil Rights Research*.

WORK IN PROGRESS: Visitation in Divorce, a "how to" book and review of social science literature for parents without custody; several articles for professional journals.

SIDELIGHTS: James W. Loewen told *CA:* "One of my most vivid memories is of a freshman social science seminar at predominantly black Tougaloo College one morning in the early 1970s. Afro-American history was the subject of the semester, and I needed to find out what my students already knew about it. 'What was Reconstruction?' I asked. 'What images come to your mind about that era?' The class consensus, with but one exception, went like this: Reconstruction was the time when blacks took over the governing of several Southern states, including Mississippi, but they were too soon out of slavery, so they messed up, and the whites had to take back control of the state governments themselves.

"So many misconceptions of fact mar that statement that it's hard to know where to start rebutting it. But the crucial question is: why would a group of black Americans believe a myth about the past that connoted such tragic incapability about their own people? (And whites who believe this myth conclude erroneously that it is only right that blacks be governed by whites, unless the colored races can be helped along toward citizenship via the elixir of education.)

"Their answers were programmed, of course, programmed by their prior 'education.' *Any* history book that celebrates, rather than examines, our heritage has the by-product, intended or not, of alienating all those in the 'out group,' those who have not become affluent, and denies them a tool for understanding their own group's lack of success. Seems as though, incredible as it sounds, the old cliche is correct: the truth will make you free. It's this truth that social science, including history, is hopefully about, and that I've tried to capture in my own writing. 'Performance,' as a previous writer on the South observed, 'is another matter.'"

MEDIA ADAPTATIONS: The Mississippi Chinese: Between Black and White was adapted into a motion picture and produced under the title "Mississippi Triangle" by Third World Newsreel, 1984.

*   *   *

LONEY, Glenn (Meredith) 1928-

PERSONAL: Born December 24, 1928, in Sacramento, Calif.; son of David Merton (a farmer) and Marion (Busher) Loney. *Education:* University of California, Berkeley, A.B., 1950; University of Wisconsin—Madison, M.A., 1951; Stanford University, Ph.D., 1954. *Home:* 3 East 71st St., New York, N.Y. 10021. *Office:* Department of Theatre, Brooklyn College of the City University of New York, Bedford Ave. & Ave. H., Brooklyn, N.Y. 11210.

CAREER: San Francisco State College (now University), San Francisco, Calif., instructor in language arts, 1955-56; Nevada Southern University (now University of Nevada, Las Vegas), instructor in English and theatre, 1955-56; University of Maryland Overseas, professor of English and speech, 1956-59; Hofstra University, Hempstead, N.Y., instructor in theatre, 1959-61; Adelphi University, Garden City, N.Y., instructor in theatre, 1959-61; Brooklyn College of the City University of New York, Brooklyn, N.Y., assistant professor, 1961-67, associate professor, 1967-70, professor of theatre, 1970—; Graduate School and University Center of the City University of New York, New York, N.Y., professor of theatre, 1970—. Member of ad hoc committees, Save the Forum and Save the Library of Performing Arts. *Military service:* U.S. Army, 1953-55.

MEMBER: International Theatre Institute, International Federation of Theatre Research, American Theatre Critics Association, New Drama Forum, American Society for Theatre Research, American Theatre Association, Speech Communication Association, United States Institute for Theatre Technology, American-Scandinavian Foundation (fellow), Drama Desk, Outer Circle of Drama Critics (secretary), Art Deco Society of New York, Phi Beta Kappa, Alpha Mu Gamma.

WRITINGS: Briefing and Conference Techniques, McGraw, 1959; (editor) John Gassner, *Dramatic Soundings*, Crown, 1968; (with Robert Corrigan) *Tragedy*, Houghton, 1971; (with Corrigan) *Comedy*, Houghton, 1971; (with Corrigan) *The Forms of Drama*, Houghton, 1972; (contributor) *Theatre Crafts Book of Costume*, Rodale, 1973; (contributor) *Theatre Crafts Book of Make-Up, Masks, and Wigs*, Rodale, 1974; (editor) *Peter Brook's RSC Production of Midsummer Night's Dream*, Dramatic Publishers, 1974; (editor) *Frank Dunlop/Young Vic Production of Scapino*, Dramatic Publishers, 1975; (with Pat

MacKay) *The Shakespeare Complex*, Drama Book Specialists, 1975; *Your Future in the Performing Arts*, Richards Rosen, 1980; *"The House of Mirth": The Play of the Novel*, Associated University Presses, 1981; *Twentieth-Century Theatre*, two volumes, Facts on File, 1983; *California Gold Rush Plays*, Performing Arts Press, 1983; *Musical Theatre in America*, Greenwood Press, 1984; *Unsung Genius*, F. Watts, 1984.

Theatre critic, *Educational Theatre Journal*, 1965-71, *New York Daily Column*, and *After Dark*. Contributor to periodicals, including *Christian Science Monitor, New York Herald Tribune, New York Times, Life, Reporter, Saturday Evening Post,* and *Smithsonian.* Contributing editor, *Dance, Dramatics, Opera News, Theatre Today, Theatre Crafts,* and other publications; editor, *Art Deco News.*

*　　*　　*

LORD HAILSHAM of ST. MARYLEBONE
See HOGG, Quintin McGarel

*　　*　　*

LOSONCY, Lawrence J.　1941-

PERSONAL: Surname is accented on second syllable; born September 12, 1941, in Detroit, Mich.; son of Joseph Michael (a businessman) and Rose (Laus) Losoncy; married Mary Jan Sibley (a teacher and researcher), August 16, 1965; children: David Lawrence, John Michael, Kristen Mary. *Education:* Sacred Heart Seminary College, B.A., 1963; also attended St. John's Seminary, 1963-65; University of Detroit, M.A., 1968; Wayne State University, Ph.D., 1971. *Politics:* Democrat. *Religion:* Roman Catholic. *Home:* 1701 West Virgin Ave., Tulsa, Okla. 74127. *Office:* Hope Associates, Suite 16, 5550 South Lewis, Tulsa, Okla. 74105.

CAREER: School music teacher and church organist in Lincoln Park, Mich., 1965-68; University of Detroit, Detroit, Mich., instructor in philosophy, 1968; high school religion teacher in Southgate, Mich., 1968-69; Wayne State University, Detroit, instructor in philosophy of education, 1969; Hi-Time Publisher, Elm Grove, Wis., editor, 1969; U.S. Catholic Conference, Washington, D.C., director of Adult Education Division and project director for national study, "The Church's Expanding Role in Adult Education," 1970-72; became professional marriage and family counselor; Oral Roberts University, Tulsa, Okla., associate professor, 1979-82; currently marriage and family therapist with own firm, Hope Associates, in Tulsa. Former national consultant, U.S. Catholic Conference; religious education consultant, Diocese of Trenton, and Immaculate Conception Parish, both in New Jersey, 1972-76.

WRITINGS: Common Sense Vision: A Philosophy of Religious Education, privately printed, 1968; *For Parents: Teaching Religion at Home,* privately printed, 1969; (with wife, Mary Jan Losoncy) *Love,* Ave Maria Press, 1970; (with M. J. Losoncy) *Sex and the Adolescent,* Ave Maria Press, 1971; *The ABC's of Adult Education,* Volume I, U.S. Catholic Conference, 1971; *Land of Promise,* Dimension, 1972; *Religious Education and the Life Cycle,* Catechetical Communications, 1977; *When Your Child Needs a Hug,* Abbey Press, 1978; *Heart Attacks: The Answer Book,* Revell, 1983.

Currently author of column, "Less Than Perfect," *Eastern Oklahoma Catholic.* Editor of bi-monthly "Focus '72," monthly "Financial Aid," and monthly "Footprints."

WORK IN PROGRESS: Good Grieving: Blessed Are They Who Mourn.

SIDELIGHTS: Lawrence Losoncy told *CA:* "I have found working and writing in the service of other people to be a source of unending satisfaction. Our challenge today in literature and in life is to uphold the dignity and individual rights of each person in the face of technology and bureaucracy. Literature has always been such a force for humanizing ourselves."

*　　*　　*

LOTZ, James Robert　1929-
(Jim Lotz)

PERSONAL: Born January 12, 1929, in Liverpool, England; son of John Bowyer (a railway worker) and Mary (Hutcheon) Lotz; married Pat Wicks (a free-lance editor and librarian), December 12, 1959; children: Annette Mary, Fiona Suzanne. *Education:* University of Manchester, B.A. (with honors), 1952; McGill University, M.Sc., 1957; University of British Columbia, additional study, 1964-65 ("ejected from institution"). *Religion:* Christian. *Home address:* Box 3393, Halifax South P.O., Halifax, Nova Scotia, Canada B3J 3J1.

CAREER: Spent some time in Africa as trader after leaving England, and served with the special constabulary in the Kano riots in Nigeria, 1953; later wrote advertising copy in Ottawa, Ontario; Canadian Government, Department of Indian Affairs and Northern Development, Ottawa, Ontario, community planning officer, then research officer, 1960-66; Canadian Research Centre for Anthropology, Ottawa, associate director, 1966-71; St. Francis Xavier University, Coady International Institute, Antigonish, Nova Scotia, assistant professor of community development, 1971-73; freelance writer, teacher, research worker, and consultant, 1973—. *Military service:* Royal Air Force, radio technician, 1947-49. *Member:* Writer's Union of Canada. *Awards, honors:* Queen's Commendation for brave conduct in Kano riots.

*WRITINGS—*Under name Jim Lotz: *Northern Realities: Exploitation of the Canadian North,* Follett, 1971; (editor with wife, Pat Lotz, and contributor) *Pilot, Not Commander: Essays in Memory of Diamond Jenness,* Canadian Research Centre for Anthropology, St. Paul University, 1971; (co-author) *Cape Breton Island,* David & Charles, 1974; *Understanding Canada: Regional and Community Development in a New Nation,* NC Press, 1977; *Death in Dawson,* PaperJacks, 1978; *Murder on the Mackenzie,* PaperJacks, 1979; *Killing in Kluane,* PaperJacks, 1980; *Sixth of December,* PaperJacks, 1981; *History of Canada,* Bison Books, 1984; *The Mounties,* Bison Books, 1984. Contributor of about five hundred articles, technical papers, and reviews to Canadian, American, British, Italian, and German journals.

WORK IN PROGRESS: A history of the Canadian Pacific Railway, for Bison Books; co-writing a book on children's vision; *The Lichen Factor,* a work on the search for symbiosis in social action.

SIDELIGHTS: James Robert Lotz has written a series of successful "northerns"—a Canadian equivalent of the American "western"—which tell of adventures in the Yukon Territory. The popularity of such titles as *Murder on the Mackenzie* and *Killing in Kluane* in Canada "proves my theory that there's an unfilled niche in Canadian writing out there," the author tells Alan Abrams in a *Windsor Star* article.

Lotz goes on to describe himself as "repulsed" by the graphic violence and sex rampant in American novels. "We need something sort of gentle and more—quote—Canadian," he says to Abrams. "There's a lot of fascination with the Canadian existence. You'd be amazed at the misconceptions of Canada and Canadians that people have abroad. . . . I want to reach those readers outside of Canada [by] writing clean-cut adventure stories, which may be an area in which Canadian writing can go in the future."

BIOGRAPHICAL/CRITICAL SOURCES: Windsor Star, February 21, 1981.

* * *

LOTZ, Jim
   See LOTZ, James Robert

* * *

LUCAS, John   1937-

PERSONAL: Born June 26, 1937, in Devon, England; married Pauline van Meeteren; children: Ben, Emma. *Education:* University of Reading, B.A., 1959, Ph.D., 1965. *Politics:* Socialist. *Religion:* None. *Home:* 19 Devonshire Ave. Beeston, Nottinghamshire, England. *Office:* Department of English, University of Loughborough, Leicestershire LE11 3TU, England.

CAREER: University of Reading, Reading, England, lecturer in English, 1961-64; University of Nottingham, Nottingham, England, lecturer, 1964, senior lecturer, 1971-75, reader in English, 1975-77; University of Loughborough, Leicestershire, England, professor of English and drama, 1977—. Visiting professor at Universities of Maryland and Indiana, 1967-68; Lord Byron Professor of English Literature, University of Athens, 1984-85.

WRITINGS: (With John Goode and David Howard) *Tradition and Tolerance in Nineteenth Century Fiction,* Barnes & Noble, 1966; (editor and author of introduction and notes) *A Selection from George Crabbe,* Longmans, Green, 1967.

The Melancholy Man: A Study of Dickens's Novels, Barnes & Noble, 1970; (editor and author of introduction) *Literature and Politics in the Nineteenth Century* (essays), Barnes & Noble, 1971; *About Nottingham,* Byron Press, 1971; *A Brief Bestiary* (poems), Pecten Press, 1972; *Chinese Sequence* (poems), Sceptre Press, 1972; *Arnold Bennett: A Study of His Fiction,* Methuen, 1975; *Egillssaga: The Poems,* Dent, 1975; (editor) W. H. Mallock, *The New Republic,* Leicester University Press, 1975; *The Literature of Change,* Barnes & Noble, 1977; *The 1930's: A Challenge to Orthodoxy,* Harvester Press, 1978.

(Editor with Ian Fletcher) *Poems of G. S. Fraser,* Leicester University Press, 1981; *Romantic to Modern Literature: Essays and Ideas of Culture, 1750-1900,* Harvester, 1982; *The Days of the Week: A Poem Sequence,* Dodman Press, 1983.

WORK IN PROGRESS: A volume of poems; a book about cricket; a study of modern poetry.

SIDELIGHTS: "The time may soon be coming when a book of literary essays will seem the appurtenance of a vanished cult, like volumes of Victorian sermons," writes Graham Hough in his *Times Literary Supplement* review of John Lucas's *Romantic to Modern Literature: Essays and Ideas of Culture, 1750-1900.* "Hence perhaps the slightly defiant air with which [the author] introduces his collection. But discussion of literature falls naturally into the essay form; and for two hundred years or more, up to and including the present, most readable literary criticism has employed this vehicle rather than the treatise or the monograph—the essay, discrete, free-standing, suggestive rather than exhaustive, with a limited subject and designed to be consumed as a single sitting."

Lucas's various pieces, continues Hough, "range from Wordsworth to Forster, and they do not suffer from the essay's habitual defect—that of being a mere exhibition of opinion. They have a ballast of history; and it is to history, character and society that [the author's] study of literature naturally leads. He has no particular axe to grind, but he has a point of view. We could call it roughly the Orwellian point of view. He assumes, extravagant though it may seem, that novels and poems were written by human beings, and should be judged by their bearing on human affairs; and the nature of literarity concerns him not at all."

AVOCATIONAL INTERESTS: Jazz, sports, beer.

BIOGRAPHICAL/CRITICAL SOURCES: Times Literary Supplement, October 2, 1981, March 4, 1983.

* * *

LUKE, Mary M.   1919-

PERSONAL: Born March 24, 1919, in Pittsfield, Mass.; daughter of John Frisbie and Hazel (Fish) Munger; married David L. Luke (divorced January, 1965); children: Melinda Carey. *Education:* Attended Berkshire Business College, 1939. *Politics:* Republican. *Religion:* Episcopalian. *Agent:* Claire Smith, c/o Harold Ober Associates, 40 East 49th St., New York, N.Y. 10017.

CAREER: Writer and historian. Worked for advertising, oil, and tool firms in New York, N.Y., and then for a documentary film company during World War II; RKO Pictures, Hollywood, Calif., secretary to treasurer of the company, 1943-44; Hunt Stromberg Productions, Hollywood, employee in story and publicity departments, 1944.

MEMBER: Ridgefield Library and Historical Association (former treasurer), Silver Spring Country Club.

WRITINGS—All published by Coward: *Catherine, the Queen,* 1967; *A Crown for Elizabeth,* 1970; *Gloriana: The Years of Elizabeth,* 1973; *The Nonsuch Lure,* 1976; *The Ivy Crown: A Biographical Novel of Queen Katherine Paar,* Doubleday, 1984.†

* * *

LUNDSGAARDE, Henry P(eder)   1938-

PERSONAL: Born December 22, 1938, in Copenhagen, Denmark; came to the United States in 1955, naturalized citizen, 1961; married Anette Rothenborg, 1967; children: Peter, Thorsten, Allan and Erik (twins). *Education:* University of California, Santa Barbara, B.A. (with honors), 1961; University of Wisconsin—Madison, M.S., 1963, Ph.D., 1966; postdoctoral study at Harvard University, 1969-70. *Home:* 1815 Meadowlark Lane, Lawrence, Kan. 66044. *Office:* Department of Anthropology, University of Kansas, Lawrence, Kan. 66045.

CAREER: University of Oregon, Eugene, adjunct research assistant in anthropology, 1964-65; University of California, Santa Barbara, assistant professor of anthropology, 1965-69; University of Houston, Houston, Tex., associate professor of anthropology and chairman of department, 1970-72; University of Kansas, Lawrence, professor of anthropology, 1972—, chairman of department, 1972-76. Research associate at University of Vermont, 1976-78. Conducted field research in California, Alaska, Idaho, the Gilbert Islands, Texas, Denmark, and Vermont. Guest lecturer.

MEMBER: American Anthropological Association (fellow), American Society for Criminology, Association for Social Anthropology in Oceania (fellow), Current Anthropology (associate), Society for Medical Anthropology, Association for Political and Legal Anthropology, South Pacific Social Science Association, Tungavalu Society (Gilbert Islands; honorary member).

AWARDS, HONORS: Woodrow Wilson fellowship, 1964-65; National Institute of Mental Health grant, summer, 1966; American Council of Learned Societies fellowship, 1969-70; National Endowment for the Humanities fellowship, summer, 1972; National Center for Health Services Research grant, 1976-78; National Science Foundation grant, 1982-83; Wenner-Gren Foundation for Anthropological Research grant, 1982-83.

WRITINGS: Cultural Adaptation in the Southern Gilbert Islands, Department of Anthropology, University of Oregon, 1966; *Social Changes in the Southern Gilbert Islands, 1938-1964,* Department of Anthropology, University of Oregon, 1967; (contributor) Vern Carroll, editor, *Adoption in Eastern Oceania,* University Press of Hawaii, 1970; (contributor) T. G. Harding and B. J. Wallace, editors, *Cultures of the Pacific: Selected Readings,* Free Press, 1970; *Legal and Behavioral Perspectives on Privacy,* Sigma Information, Inc., 1972; (editor) *Land Tenure in Oceania* (monograph), University Press of Hawaii, 1974.

(Contributor) Niel Gunson, editor, *The Changing Pacific: Essays in Honour of H. E. Maude,* Oxford University Press, 1977; *Murder in Space City: A Cultural Analysis of Houston Homicide Patterns,* Oxford University Press, 1977; (contributor) A. Mamak and G. McCall, editors, *Paradise Postponed: Essays on Social Research and Development in the South Pacific,* Pergamon, 1978; (with P. J. Fisher and D. J. Steele) *A Report of the Ethnographic Study of the Problem-Oriented Medical Information System,* National Center for Health Services Research, 1978; (contributor) Rose, editor, *Lethal Aspects of Urban Violence,* Lexington Books, 1979; (with Fisher and Steele) *Human Problems in Computerized Medicine,* University of Kansas Publications in Anthropology, 1981. Also contributor to *Encyclopedia of Southern Culture.* Contributor of articles and reviews to professional journals.

WORK IN PROGRESS: A book on the Kiribati culture of the Gilbert Islands.

SIDELIGHTS: Reviewing Henry P. Lundsgaarde's *Murder in Space City: A Cultural Analysis of Houston Homicide Patterns,* Larry McMurtry notes that the book "brilliantly reveals not merely that homicide is easy to get away with in Texas, but *why* it is easy to get away with, where its supports are in the culture, and its sanction in the legal system." McMurtry explains in the *New York Times Book Review* that the author believes murder can be linked to cultural patterns "which sustain and possibly even promote violence." In disclosing the hidden elements of these patterns, Lundsgaarde's book is a "provocative, I might say definitive, study," concludes the critic.

BIOGRAPHICAL/CRITICAL SOURCES: New York Times Book Review, February 6, 1977.

LUSSU, Joyce (Salvadori)　1912-
(Joyce Salvadori)

PERSONAL: Born May 8, 1912, in Florence, Italy; daughter of Guglielmo and Giacinta (Galletti) Salvadori; married Emilio Lussu (an Italian senator and writer), June 19, 1944; children: Giovanni. *Education:* University of Heidelberg, student, 1931-32; University of Lisboa, Diplome of Portuguese Literature, 1940; Sorbonne, University of Paris, Licence es Lettres, 1941. *Home:* San Tommaso, Fermo (Ascoli Piceno), Italy.

CAREER: Writer; translator of poetry. *Wartime service:* Captain in the Italian Liberation Corps, 1943-45, received Silver Medal.

MEMBER: Writers Trade Union.

WRITINGS: (Under name Joyce Salvadori) *Liriche,* Ricciardi, 1939; *Fronti e frontiere; Collana della liberazione,* Edizioni U, 1945, 2nd edition, Laterza, 1967, translation by William Clowes published as *Freedom Has No Frontier,* M. Joseph, 1969; (editor) *Donne come te: Inchieste di Luciano della mea,* Edizioni Avanti, 1957; *Poesie d'amore di Nazim Hikmet,* Mondadori, 1965; *Tradurre poesia* (includes poetry translated from various languages), Mondadori, 1967.

Le Inglesi in Italia, Lerici, 1970; *Padre, Padrone, Padreterno,* Mazzotta, 1976; *L'acqua del 2000,* Mazzotta, 1976; *L'uomo che voleva nascere donna,* Mazzotta, 1978; *Che cos'e un marito,* Mazzotta, 1979; *Storia del Fermano,* Il Lavoro Editoriale, 1980; *Il Libro Perogno su donne streghe e sibille,* Il Lavoro Editoriale, 1981; *Donne guerra e societa,* Il Lavoro Editoriale, 1982; *Sherlock nella Marche,* Il Lavoro Editoriale, 1983.

Has translated the work of poets from Portugal, Guinea, Angola, Mozambique, Turkey, Kurdistan, Albania, and Vietnam.

SIDELIGHTS: Joyce Lussu has traveled widely in Africa, the Middle East, China, Cuba, and in every European country, searching out poets not yet known, with a constant interest for the problems of peace, women's liberation, struggles against colonialism, ecology.

*　　*　　*

LUSTBADER, Eric Van　1946-

PERSONAL: Born December 24, 1946, in New York, N.Y.; son of Melvin Harry (a state social security bureau director) and Ruth (Aaronson) Lustbader; married; wife's name Victoria. *Education:* Columbia University, B.A., 1968. *Agent:* Henry Morrison, Inc., 58 West 10th St., New York, N.Y. 10011.

CAREER: Free-lance writer, 1973—. CIS-TRANS Productions (music producers), New York City, owner, 1963-67; elementary school teacher in New York City, 1968-70; *Cash Box* (music trade journal), New York City, associate editor, 1970-72; Elektra Records, New York City, director of international artists and repertory and assistant to the president, 1972-73; Dick James Music, New York City, director of publicity and creative services, 1974-75; Sweet Dream Productions, New York City, owner, 1975-76; NBC-TV, New York City, writer and field producer of news film on Elton John, 1976; CBS Records, New York City, designer of publicity and album covers and manager of media services, 1976-78.

MEMBER: Smithsonian Institution, Metropolitan Museum of Art, Museum of Modern Art, South Street Seaport Museum.

WRITINGS—Novels: *The Ninja*, M. Evans, 1980; *Sirens*, M. Evans, 1981; *Black Heart*, M. Evans, 1982; *The Miko* (sequel to *The Ninja*), Villard Books, 1984. Contributor to popular music magazines, including *Crawdaddy, Good Times*, and *Rock*.

"The Sunset Warrior" cycle; all published by Doubleday: *The Sunset Warrior*, 1977; *Shallows of Night*, 1978; *Dai-San*, 1978; *Beneath an Opal Moon*, 1980.

SIDELIGHTS: Eric Van Lustbader has translated his interest in Oriental culture into source material for his writing. Thus, when he chose the heroic fantasy genre for his first novels, he introduced an Oriental flavor to the classic sword and sorcery tale. Lustbader's "Sunset Warrior" cycle, which includes *The Sunset Warrior, Shallows of Night, Dai-San*, and *Beneath an Opal Moon*, chronicles the adventures of the Bladesman Ronin in a future world rich in Eastern tradition. To this backdrop, the author adds the fast-paced action associated with martial arts, giving a new look to the fantasy-adventure.

After *Beneath an Opal Moon*, Lustbader turned to the murder and suspense thriller. His bestseller *The Ninja* unfolds in a modern historical setting, but Oriental tradition and martial arts remain the underlying framework. Two men, once fellow students of the martial arts in postwar Japan, meet again in modern New York as adversaries. One, a hired assassin or "ninja," stalks a wealthy businessman. The other, an Anglo-Oriental, becomes involved through his relationship with the businessman's daughter. In a *Los Angeles Times Book Review* article, Don G. Campbell writes that at times the fast pace of *The Ninja* can leave the reader confused, but he praises Lustbader's "robust, flamboyant style" and his ability to create "a mood that something terrible is just about to happen."

Black Heart has many of the elements found in *The Ninja*, but to this novel Lustbader adds espionage and political intrigue. A Cambodian refugee, torn by the effects of war, becomes the tool of a powerful American industrialist bent on influencing presidential politics. A former intelligence agent involved in planning the bombing of Cambodia during the Vietnam War is drawn into the intrigue when his friend, the governor of New York, becomes a victim of the plot. In the *New York Times Book Review*, Jack Sullivan criticizes the violent scenes in *Black Heart*. Campbell, however, points out the author's virtuosity in handling such scenes. He writes, "Violent death is an instrument [Lustbader] plays like a fine violin, and few can match him in capturing the creepy mood of inevitability that precedes it."

AVOCATIONAL INTERESTS: Japanese and Mayan history, history of prewar Shanghai, music, ballet.

CA INTERVIEW

CA interviewed Eric Van Lustbader by telephone on April 2, 1984, at his home in New York City.

CA: Before you became a writer, you worked in various capacities in the music business. How did that begin, and how did you go from music to writing?

LUSTBADER: I honestly did not go from music to writing; I have been writing all my life. I became interested in music through the Beatles. When I was in junior high school I started producing a rock 'n' roll band and did that for a number of years, all the way through college. Then I went to work as a writer and associate editor for *Cash Box*, a trade paper like *Billboard*. I created a column called "Insight and Sound,"

which had been there before but just as a publicity column for items like who was playing where, and when. I turned it into an interview column centering on new acts.

Through that I went to work for the president of Elektra Records, Jac Holzman; I was his personal assistant and looked for new acts. But the company had been bought by Warner Communications and Jac was in the process of getting out, so I only worked there for about nine months. I was out of work for a while, but I continued writing free-lance for a number of publications such as *Crawdaddy, Good Times*, and *Rock*. Next I went to work for Elton John's publishing company in this country and became the director of publicity and creative services for them. I left to produce and manage a band for my own company and that lasted about six months—the band split up as we were getting a record contract.

While I was out of work this time I started writing my first book, *The Sunset Warrior*, and then joined CBS Records. I was there for about two and a half years before I left, and by then I had written two more books. The pressures of writing and holding down a job in a business that was not nine to five were really getting to me, so I had to make a decision whether I wanted to write full-time or stay in the music business.

The music business was no longer much fun to be in. Everything was being run by large corporations, by conglomerates, by statistics, by people in button-down collars. It still wasn't the world's easiest decision. I knew in my heart what I wanted to do, but I was making a lot of money in music and it was very secure; at that point, writing was not. I'd written three books that had made a nice amount of money, but not enough for me to live on. But I decided I wanted to write full-time.

CA: Then things moved pretty fast for you, didn't they?

LUSTBADER: Yes. I left CBS in May, 1978, and over that summer I wrote the first draft of *Beneath an Opal Moon*, the fourth book in my fantasy series. My hardcover publisher, Doubleday, had called me up and begged me to do another one, because the other three were doing well. I asked for and got quite a bit of money up front, and I used that to live on while I wrote the first draft of *The Ninja*, which I started right after the first draft of *Beneath an Opal Moon* without taking a break. Then I went back and did the final draft of *Beneath an Opal Moon*.

My agent, Henry Morrison, had no idea that I was writing another book, let alone a book out of the fantasy genre. I just plopped it in his lap one day, I think in October, and really sort of stunned him. The first sale of *The Ninja* was made to Granada Publishing in England. Henry has a good relationship with Mark Barty-King, the editorial director of Granada, and Mark happened to be in this country right after Henry got the book; he called Henry up and said, "Do you have anything big for me?" Henry said, "Do I have a book for *you*." Mark took the book on the plane with him back to London. By the time he got to Heathrow Airport he had read two hundred pages. He called Henry from the airport and said he wanted it. He made Henry an offer and Henry said no. When Henry was relating this to me, I got sort of hysterical and said, "What do you mean, 'no'?" Henry said, "If Mark likes the book now, he's going to go wild over it when he finishes it."

Well, I had to figure Henry knew what he was doing, and sure enough, Mark called a few days later. He'd finished the book and he wanted it. Henry gave him a figure; I was stunned. About a week later Henry played a tape Mark had left on his answering machine. It said he was going to give us the money.

This was before anyone had bought it in America. In fact, it went through about ten publishers before we settled on Evans. I had some misgivings about them because they were so small and had never had a bestseller in fiction. But they really wanted to get on the map, and they convinced us. Interestingly enough, a number of larger companies turned us down because their subsidiary rights people felt the book was so unusual that they would have trouble selling it in paperback.

CA: Herb Katz, your editor on The Ninja, *was quoted in the* New York Times Book Review *as saying he had "never met anyone so totally self-assured about his work." Was it the experience with Granada that gave you such confidence?*

LUSTBADER: No. I must say that I'm my own worst critic—I'm usually very hard on my own work—and I just felt from the beginning that *The Ninja* was good.

CA: Why did you try fantasy first? Was it a genre you had particularly enjoyed reading?

LUSTBADER: Yes. I had loved fantasy almost from the time I learned to read. I was a big fan of Michael Moorcock and Robert Silverberg and people like that. The first thought about writing that came into my mind was to do an heroic fantasy, but while I was doing that I was dealing with an Oriental setting—though it was a future setting, obviously. That's the way my thoughts went from the very beginning.

CA: Where did your interest in the Orient come from?

LUSTBADER: It has to do with a feeling inside myself that the most important thing in life is honor. I started getting interested in the Orient through art, through Japanese woodblock prints. I became fascinated with them and began to read about them, about the artists, about the milieu they came from, about the history of Japan. The more I read, the more I realized I really knew about it without having to read it. I don't want this to sound mystical—it's pretty unexplainable—but it's obvious to me that I can write about the Orient without having seen it. I've never been to Japan. We were supposed to go last year, but I canceled at the last minute because I don't want to go until I've finished writing about it. I have a certain feeling about it, and there are a lot of negative aspects of Japanese society that I don't want to confront. I know about them, I write about them, but I don't want to see them until I'm finished with it. I *have* been to Hong Kong; we did some research for *Black Heart* there.

CA: Yes. You do a great deal of research for your books, don't you?

LUSTBADER: A tremendous amount. I did many personal interviews with Japanese people for *The Ninja,* and with Cambodian refugees for *Black Heart.* To me one of the greatest joys of writing is doing this kind of personal research, meeting people and staying friends with them. I have a lot of friends now whom I've met through the course of my work. One of my best friends is a Cambodian refugee. A lot of the Cambodian character in *Black Heart* is based on his story.

It's funny, I didn't really know anything about Cambodia until I saw an advertisement on television for CARE that had to do with Cambodian refugees. Then I wondered what it would be like to be a child in a country where there had been nothing but war. I didn't know much about it politically or any other

way until I began to meet Cambodian people. Then everything started to fit together. The reason *Black Heart* has a political skew to it is that that was how my research developed. Everything that relates back to Cambodia has a political cast to it, whereas most of my research on Japan has a cultural cast.

CA: How do you feel about the criticism of violence in your work?

LUSTBADER: I'm pretty neutral about it. My books do have violence in them, but frankly, I've read much more violence in many other writers' work. The one who comes to mind first is Stephen King. There's a lot of blood and spewing of guts and real horrible stuff in his books that it would never enter my mind to put into mine. I'm appalled by the violence that surrounds us in modern-day life, and writing about this sort of gets out my anger about it. All my heroes are very violent characters, but they're violent despite themselves; that's the interesting thing. They have violence thrust upon them and they have to do something about it. They have to defend themselves in a certain way. Tracy Richter in *Black Heart,* for instance, is a killer, but he's appalled that he's so good at doing that. It makes him literally crazy that he's like that. I frankly feel that the people who say my books are too violent don't understand what I'm writing about.

CA: How do you feel about sometimes being called an "entertainment" writer?

LUSTBADER: I'm interested in entertaining people, but that's not why I write; I write to inform people. All my books have quite a lot in them that people can learn from, from an historical point of view, from a sociological point of view. I'm always writing with that in mind. But my object is to have as many people as possible read my books. I don't believe it makes any sense at all to write for ten people. Most of what commonly goes for "literature," in the *New York Times* sense, is to my way to thinking pretentious, very difficult to read, and not very enjoyable. I think people are most apt to learn things when they are enjoying themselves; if they can enjoy my story and along the way find themselves remembering facts about history and politics and sociology, then all the better.

I do believe that there are pure "entertainment" writers. James Michener is *not* a pure entertainment writer, or James Clavell, but Judith Krantz is. Sidney Sheldon is. There's nothing to be learned from anything they write. With Michener and Clavell and myself, there are things to be learned about other cultures and other times that the normal person on the street might never know about otherwise.

But I don't like categories, and it amazes me how people feel more secure when they can put labels on things. That's annoying, whether you're labeled an escapist writer or a "serious" writer. I think of myself as a serious writer: I'm very serious about my work; I'm very serious about what I'm trying to say. In *The Miko,* the sequel to *The Ninja,* there are murders and sex, but the underlying structure is all about how and why Japan made a great economic leap forward in the '50s and '60s and '70s. It's also a book about women's rights, the evolution of women in Japan. But there will be a lot of people who can't see anything beyond the fact that, in the opening scene, two people die.

I'm not talking about readers, because I have a tremendous number of readers. I'm talking about critics. I was once a critic, and I know what it's like, but it really annoys me; and I must say that among all the critics, the people at the *New York Times* annoy me most. It's not personal—they do it to everybody they don't feel is writing serious fiction, and anyone who sells more than 500,000 copies, in their opinion, is not writing serious fiction.

When I was a critic, I strove to be very professional about things. I was always amazed at how unprofessional critics could be, how they allow personal feelings to absolutely color everything they write about. I think that's often what happens at the *Times*. With *Sirens,* the reviewer admitted in the review that he read about fifty pages, no more. If I were the editor, I just wouldn't run a review where the reviewer admitted that.

CA: What kind of writing schedule do you keep?

LUSTBADER: I work from somewhere between 6 and 7 in the morning until 11 or 12. I don't keep hours; I write between eight and eleven pages a day. Usually I work six days a week, but I'm not an automaton. There are days when I'm just thinking about the book or working on scenes and I don't do any writing at all. There are some days when I'm not even thinking about the book—I have to get away and just let things percolate in the back of my mind. But when things are going well, I'm generally doing eight to eleven pages a day, six days a week.

We've started working on a word processor. It's fabulous. I don't do the first draft on it; I type that out and my wife Victoria (who's a really fantastic editor and the first editor on all my work) puts the daily work onto the machine. Then when I'm finished with the first draft, I'll go back and get a printout and start to make revisions. From then on I work pretty much on the machine. The only problem is that I can't work steadily at it for many hours a day because the radiation from it bothers me. I get headaches and my eyes start to hurt. But with *The Miko,* which is the first book we used the word processor on, I would say that it saved us, at a minimum, three months' work. It paid for itself just on that book.

CA: Things seem to be going very well for you.

LUSTBADER: Yes. The paperback of *Black Heart* is coming out next month here. Fawcett is advancing 1.4 million copies. It has already been released abroad. I just spoke to my publisher in England, and it's the number one paperback there. Before this book I was the number two bestselling author in South Africa. They advanced 100,000 copies of the paperback of *Black Heart* there, which is the equivalent of about 5 million here in America. They sold out that number; I just got a Telex from the publisher in South Africa saying the book sold 10,000 the first week at the largest retail chain there. That breaks all the records.

That's one of the interesting things about my career, and very gratifying. I'm a bestseller in a tremendous number of countries—in addition to South Africa and England, there's France, Italy, Germany, Holland, New Zealand, Australia, and Japan.

CA: Are there movies in the works?

LUSTBADER: Richard Zanuck and David Brown, the people who did "Jaws" and "Patton," bought *The Ninja* before it was released in hardcover, in 1980. They've been through two directors and four screenwriters and they've just about given up. The rights will revert back to me in a couple of months, and it looks like I'm going to be working on a screenplay myself with a screenwriter. I'm *not* a screenwriter, and I told my agent that if I became involved in this, I didn't want to do it on my own—I wanted to have a seasoned screenwriter to work with. So we're working out the deal for that, and there are producers who have come to us and expressed interest in the project. We may do the thing independently.

CA: What part does music play in your life now?

LUSTBADER: A tremendous part. I write with music on—always rock music; it gets my adrenalin going. If I were to put anything else on, it would put me to sleep. I'm used to working with music. *Cash Box* was a weekly magazine, and there were always deadlines. I worked best right up against deadline with music playing. I'm an album junkie, always haunting record stores for new acts.

CA: You said just after the publication of The Ninja *that you didn't expect success to change your life much. Has it brought some changes?*

LUSTBADER: I think the worst thing that happened was a lot of my friends no longer were my friends, which really confused me. People I'd known for years and years were all of a sudden acting hostile. It didn't occur to me until much later that they were very jealous. But you can't avoid those things, and I was able to weed out the people who were genuinely happy for me from the people who couldn't deal with the fact that I had become successful.

The thing that's changed my life most—the best thing that's happened—is meeting my wife and falling in love with her and getting married. But success has changed my life some. We rent a house out in Southampton, and we're about to build a house. We can go away to Hong Kong or anywhere and go first class if we want to. I can stop in at Tiffany's and buy my wife something if I want to. But I don't very often do those things.

I didn't go crazy when I got a lot of money. I think a lot of it had to do with two things. My father brought me up very well. Even though we were well off, I always had less money than any of my friends had; he gave me a smaller allowance. I complained, of course, but he did the right thing. I never had enough money to buy everything I wanted in a given week. That was good because I had to learn to set priorities. The first time I wanted something expensive—it was a Nikon camera—I went out and worked for it. I never asked my parents for it.

The other thing was, working in the music business, I was the first American writer to discover Elton John and write about him. We became very good friends. I went on tour with him when no one knew him, when some people knew him, when a lot of people knew him. And I saw how having a great deal of money and fame changed him. I think that helped me quite a bit when the same kind of thing happened to me.

BIOGRAPHICAL/CRITICAL SOURCES: Los Angeles Times Book Review, June 22, 1980, April 10, 1983; *New York Times Book Review,* June 7, 1981, April 10, 1983, September 23, 1984; *Publishers Weekly,* August 17, 1984.

—*Interview by Jean W. Ross*

* * *

LYONS, James
See LOEWEN, James W.

M

MACCOBY, Michael 1933-

PERSONAL: Surname is pronounced *Mack*-oby; born March 5, 1933, in Mount Vernon, N.Y.; son of Max (a rabbi) and Dora (Steinberg) Maccoby; married Sandylee Weille (a portrait painter), December 19, 1959; children: Anne Alexandra, Maria Jzette, Nora Harriet, Max Francis. *Education:* Harvard University, B.A., 1954, Ph.D., 1960; studied at New College, Oxford, 1954-55, University of Chicago, 1955-56, and Mexican Institute of Psychoanalysis, 1960-64. *Home:* 4825 Linnaean Ave. N.W., Washington, D.C. 20008.

CAREER: University of Chicago, Chicago, Ill., instructor in social science, 1955-56; Harvard University, Cambridge, Mass., secretary of committee on educational policy, 1956-60; research fellow, U.S. Public Health Service, 1960-63; psychotherapist in private practice in Mexico City, Mexico, and Washington, D.C., 1962—; member of faculty, Washington School of Psychiatry, 1974—. Visiting and resident fellow, Institute for Policy Studies, Washington, D.C., 1969-77. Visiting professor of social psychology, Universidad Nacional Autonoma de Mexico, Mexico City, 1960-61; lecturer in psychology, University of California, Santa Cruz, 1967-68; fellow, Center for Advanced Study in the Behavioral Sciences, Stanford, Calif., 1968-69. Member of board of directors, Centro Intercultural de Documentacion, Cuernavaca, Mexico, 1966-69; research associate for program on technology and society, Harvard University, 1970-73, and program on science, technology, and public policy, 1974—, director of program on technology, public policy, and human development, 1978—; consultant to American Telephone and Telegraph, and the Communications Workers of America, 1980—, and to Swedish Council on Management and Working Life, 1981—.

MEMBER: American Psychological Association, American Anthropological Association, International Council for the Quality of Working Life, Phi Beta Kappa.

AWARDS, HONORS: Woodrow Wilson fellowship, Oxford University, 1954-55.

WRITINGS: (Author of introduction) Barbara O'Brien, *Operators and Things: The Inner Life of a Schizophrenic,* Arlington Press, 1959; (with Erich Fromm) *Social Character in a Mexican Village,* Prentice-Hall, 1970; (author of introduction) David C. H. Sheppard and Neal Q. Herrick, *Where Have All the Robots Gone?,* Macmillan, 1972.

(Author of introduction) Herrick, *The Quality of Work and Its Outcomes,* Academy for Contemporary Problems, 1975; *The Gamesman: The New Corporate Leaders,* Simon & Schuster, 1976; *The Lender: A New Face for American Management,* Simon & Schuster, 1981; *Management in Government and Technoservice Industries,* Simon & Schuster, 1985.

Contributor: J. Roosevelt, editor, *The Liberal Papers,* Doubleday, 1961; J. M. Potter and others, editors, *Peasant Society: A Reader,* Little, Brown, 1967; Jerome S. Bruner and others, editors, *Studies in Cognitive Growth,* Wiley, 1967; Ralph Stavins, editor, *Television Today: The End of Communication and the Death of Community,* Institute for Policy Studies, 1969; J. H. Skolnick and others, editors, *Crisis in American Institutions,* Little, Brown, 1970; David C. McClelland and others, editors, *The Drinking Man,* Free Press, 1972.

Phillip Brenner, Robert Borosage, and Bethany Weidner, editors, *Exploring Contradictions: Papers from the Congressional Staff Seminars on Political Economy,* McKay, 1974; R. Fairfield, editor, *Humanizing the Workplace,* Prometheus Books, 1974; B. Lenkerd and P. C. Reining, editors, *Village Viability in Contemporary Society,* Westview Press, 1980; E. W. Colgazier, Jr. and S. B. Lundsteldt, editors, *Managing Innovation,* Pergamon, 1982. Also contributor to many psychiatry and social science journals in United States and Mexico.

WORK IN PROGRESS: Research project on technology, work, and character.

SIDELIGHTS: Michael Maccoby earned some critical attention with his 1976 study *The Gamesman: The New Corporate Leaders,* in which the author defined the executive of the 1970s as "cool, pragmatic, flexible, fascinated by challenges and above all eager to win, and willing to be manipulative for that purpose," according to Bernard A. Weisberger in a *Washington Post* review. The gamesman, continues Weisberger, "was a creation of the adventurous business climate of the '60s, and took his place alongside other managerial types—the craftsman, the jungle fighter, the company man—who emerged at earlier stages of economic development."

In the 1980s, with its different social and economic conditions, the gamesman has been replaced by the subjects of Maccoby's next book, *The Leader: A New Face for American Management.* The leaders of business and industry in this decade, as Weisberger notes in his review, evolved from a social ethic "more individualistic and resistant to authority than it once was; what's more, the men and women of the workplace are less willing to commit themselves totally to their jobs. . . . To bring out the best in such people—which, for Maccoby, is the true function and art of leadership—tomorrow's managers will have to be flexible, humane, involved and caring; 'less charismatic and narcissistic than past leaders,' . . . and recognizing that it is 'logical and necessary . . . to share the functions of leadership.'"

BIOGRAPHICAL/CRITICAL SOURCES: Michael Maccoby, *The Leader: A New Face for American Management,* Simon & Schuster, 1981; *Detroit News,* December 20, 1981; *Washington Post,* December 28, 1981.

*   *   *

MacISAAC, David 1935-

PERSONAL: Born June 22, 1935, in Boston, Mass.; son of John L. (a marketing clerk) and Mary (a credit manager; maiden name, Mullen) MacIsaac; married Charlotte Wade, July 19, 1959; children: Donna Marie, Paul, Pamela, Patrick. *Education:* Trinity College, Hartford, Conn., A.B., 1957; Yale University, A.M., 1958; Duke University, Ph.D., 1970. *Politics:* "Eccentric." *Home and office:* 3411 Royal Carriage Dr., Montgomery, Ala. 36116.

CAREER: U.S. Air Force, career officer, 1958-81, retired as lieutenant colonel; freelance writer and consultant, 1981-82; Air University, Air Power Research Institute, Maxwell Air Force Base, Ala., senior research fellow and visiting professor, 1982-84; freelance writer and consultant, 1984—. Personnel officer with Strategic Air Command in Texas, 1959-61, and at Torrejon Air Base in Spain, 1961-64; Air Force Academy, instructor, 1964-66, assistant professor, 1968-70, associate professor, 1971-76, professor of history, 1976-78; member of Air Force advisory group in Vietnam, 1971; visiting professor at U.S. Naval War College, 1975-76; chief of history of warfare studies at Air War College, 1979-81. Fellow of Woodrow Wilson International Center for Scholars, Smithsonian Institution, 1978-79.

MEMBER: American Military Institute, Air Force Association, United States Naval Institute, American Committee on the History of the Second World War, Inter-University Seminar on the Armed Forces and Society, Phi Beta Kappa.

AWARDS, HONORS—Military: Bronze Star. Civilian: Woodrow Wilson fellow, Yale University, 1958.

WRITINGS: (Editor) *The Military and Society: Proceedings of the Fifth Military History Symposium,* U.S. Government Printing Office, 1975; *Strategic Bombing in World War II: The Story of the U.S. Strategic Bombing Survey,* Garland Publishing, 1976; (editor and author of introductions) *The U.S. Strategic Bombing Survey,* ten volumes, Garland Publishing, 1976; *The Air Force in an Age of Strategic Paradox, 1945-1984,* Air University Press, 1985.

Contributor: M. D. Wright and Lawrence Paszek, editors, *Soldiers and Statesmen: Proceedings of the Fourth Military History Symposium,* U.S. Government Printing Office, 1973; David H. White, editor, *Proceedings of the Citadel Conference on War and Diplomacy,* Citadel, 1976; A. F. Hurley and R. C. Ehrhart, editors, *Air Power and Warfare: Proceedings of the Eighth Military History Symposium,* U.S. Government Printing Office, 1979; James Titus, editor, *War and the Home Front in the Twentieth Century,* U.S. Government Printing Office,

1984; Peter Paret, editor, *Makers of Modern Strategy: New Edition,* Princeton University Press, 1985.

Consultant, *Bombers over Japan,* by Keith Wheeler, Time-Life, 1982. Contributor to *Dictionary of American History;* contributor of more than fifty articles and reviews to history and military journals.

SIDELIGHTS: "My writing thus far has been pretty straightforward stuff, history and all that, relating almost exclusively to military affairs," David MacIsaac told *CA.* "For the past five years it has centered increasingly on questions of nuclear weapons policy, indeed a dismal field of speculation. I'm about ready to start looking for a topic from the eighteenth century or so—before aircraft, before nukes, before security-classified documents, and before copying machines. Much of what I have written about of late so nearly fulfills the requirements for fiction that I might even give that a try."

*   *   *

MACKIE, John
See LEVINSON, Leonard

*   *   *

MACLEAN, Fitzroy (Hew) 1911-

PERSONAL: Born March 11, 1911, in Cairo, Egypt; son of Charles Wilberforce (a British Army officer) and Gladys (Royle) Maclean; married Veronica Fraser (daughter of 16th Baron of Lovat), January 12, 1946; children: Charles, James. *Education:* Cambridge University, M.A. (with first class honors), 1932. *Politics:* Conservative. *Religion:* Church of Scotland. *Home:* Strachur House, Strachur, Argyllshire, Scotland.

CAREER: Diplomatic Service, third secretary, 1933, transferred to Paris, 1934, transferred to Moscow, 1937, second secretary, 1938, transferred to Foreign Office, 1939; resigned from Diplomatic Service and enlisted as private in Cameron Highlanders, 1941, became second lieutenant, joined First Special Air Service Regiment and became captain, 1942, lieutenant-colonel and brigadier, 1943, commander of British Military Mission to Yugoslav Partisans, 1943-45, head of Special Refugee Commission, Germany, Austria, and Italy, 1947; member of Parliament, Lancaster Division, 1941-59, Bute and North Ayrshire, 1959-74; War Office, parliamentary under-secretary of state and financial secretary, 1954-57. Lee Knowles Lecturer at Cambridge University, 1953. Member of United Kingdom delegation to North Atlantic Assembly, 1962-74; member, Council of Europe, 1972-74.

MEMBER: Cable Television Association (president), Great Britain—U.S.S.R. Association (past president), British Yugoslav Society (president).

AWARDS, HONORS—Military: Croix de Guerre (France), 1943; Commander, Order of the British Empire, 1944; Order of Kutusov (U.S.S.R.), 1944; Partisan Star 1st Class, 1945; Yugoslav Order of Merit, 1969; Yugoslav Order of the Flag, 1981. Civilian: Created Baronet of Strachur and Glensmain, 1957; LL.D., Glasgow University, 1969; D.Litt., Acadia University, 1970; LL.D., Dalhousie University.

WRITINGS: Eastern Approaches (Book Society choice in England), J. Cape, 1949, published as *Escape to Adventure,* Little, Brown, 1950, special edition with new introduction by Charles W. Thayer, Time, 1964, reprinted, Atheneum, 1984; *The Heretic: The Life and Times of Josip Broz-Tito,* Harper,

1957, published as *Tito, the Man Who Defied Hitler and Stalin*, Ballantine, 1957 (published in England as *Disputed Barricade: The Life and Times of Josip Broz-Tito, Marshal of Jugoslavia*, J. Cape, 1957); *A Person from England, and Other Travelers to Turkestan*, Harper, 1958; *Back to Bokhara*, Harper, 1959.

(Author of introduction) *Yugoslavia*, photographs by Toni Schneiders and others, Thames & Hudson, 1969; *A Concise History of Scotland*, Viking, 1970; *The Battle of the Neretva*, Panther Books, 1970; *To the Back of Beyond*, Little, Brown, 1975; *To Caucasus: The End of All the Earth*, Little, Brown, 1976; *Take Nine Steps*, Atheneum, 1978; *Holy Russia*, Atheneum, 1979; *Tito: A Pictorial Biography*, McGraw, 1980.

WORK IN PROGRESS: An anthology of West Highland tales; a life of Bonny Prince Charlie.

SIDELIGHTS: Fitzroy Maclean has traveled widely in the Balkans, the Caucasus, Near East, Middle East, Central Asia, Mongolia, and in European Russia.

BIOGRAPHICAL/CRITICAL SOURCES: New Yorker, May 30, 1970; *New York Times*, October 21, 1980.

* * *

Mac NAMARA, Donal E(oin) J(oseph) 1916-

PERSONAL: Born August 13, 1916, in New York, N.Y.; son of Daniel Patrick and Rita (Chambers) Mac Namara; married Margaret Scott (a lawyer), June, 1953; children: Brian Scott. *Education:* Columbia University, B.Sc., 1939; New York University, M.P.A., 1946; Air Command and Staff College, U.S. Air Force, diploma, 1948. *Politics:* "Independent Liberal." *Religion:* Roman Catholic. *Home:* 206 Christie Hghts., Leonia, N.J. 07605. *Office:* 444 West 56th St., New York, N.Y. 10019.

CAREER: Rutgers University, New Brunswick, N.J., instructor in political science, 1948-49; University of Southern California, Los Angeles, assistant professor of police administration, 1949-50; New York Institute of Criminology, New York City, assistant dean, 1950-55, dean, 1955-65; City University of New York, New York City, professor of criminology at John Jay College of Criminal Justice, 1965—, and at Bernard M. Baruch College, 1966—. Managing partner, Flath, Weston & MacNamara Associates, 1958-69; vice-president, Character Underwriters, Inc. Visiting lecturer at University of Louisville, 1950—, and State University of New York, 1950-56; visiting professor at Florida State University, 1959, and University of Utah, 1961, 1962. Chairman of law enforcement institutes and lecturer in Graduate School of Public Administration, New York University, 1950-57; coordinator of police science program, Brooklyn College of the City University of New York, 1957-63; senior instructor, Center for Correctional Training, 1963-65. Assistant director of Delinquency Control Institute, 1949-50; director of Traffic Management Survey Fund, Inc., 1958-68, and Crime Show Consultants; executive vice-president of Bronx Real Estate Board. Consultant to New York Housing Authority, 1955, New Jersey Law Enforcement Council, 1957-59, Commonwealth of Puerto Rico, 1960, and Probation and Parole Officers Association. *Military service:* U.S. Army, Military Police and Intelligence, 1942-46; became major.

MEMBER: International Association of Chiefs of Police, Societe Internationale de Criminologie, Association Internationale de Droit Penal, American Association for the Advancement of Science (fellow), American Society of Criminology (fellow; secretary, 1949-51; vice-president, 1953-55, 1958-60; presi-

dent, 1961), Association for the Psychiatric Treatment of Offenders, Institute of Social and Behavioral Science, Academy of Criminalistics (fellow; president, 1959-63), American League to Abolish Capital Punishment (president), American Sociological Association (fellow), National Council on Crime and Delinquency, American Correctional Association. *Awards, honors:* Herbert A. Bloch Award, American Society of Criminology, 1967.

WRITINGS: The Moorestown, New Jersey, Police Survey, Donal E. J. MacNamara & Associates, 1965; *Law Enforcement in Bergen County, New Jersey*, [New York], 1967; *Problems of Sex Behavior*, Crowell, 1969; *Perspectives on Correction*, Crowell, 1971; (editor with Edward Sagarin) *Corrections: Problems of Punishment and Rehabilitation*, Praeger, 1973; (editor with Marc Riedel) *Police: Perspectives, Problems, Prospects*, Praeger, 1974; *Criminal Justice*, Dushkin, 1976; (with Sagarin) *Sex, Crime, and the Law*, Free Press, 1977; (with Lloyd McCorkle) *Crime, Criminals, and Corrections*, John Jay Press, 1982; (with Philip J. Stead) *New Dimensions in Transnational Crime*, John Jay Press, 1982; *Deviants: Victims or Victimizers?*, Sage, 1983. Editor-in-chief, *Criminology: An Interdisciplinary Journal*, 1976—; editor, *Journal of Corrective Psychiatry;* member of editorial boards, *Abstracts of Criminology and Penology* and *Abstracts of Police and Forensic Science*.

WORK IN PROGRESS: Crime and Delinquency in the U.S.S.R.; Social Pathology among the Irish Tinkers.

SIDELIGHTS: Donal E.J. Mac Namara told *CA:* "I am a liberal, somewhat eclectic behavioral scientist with a strong bias against the punitive-repressive approach to those unable or unwilling to live by society's laws. I favor decriminalizing the penal code, eliminating criminal sanctions against consensual and/or victimless crimes (e.g., gambling, narcotics use, alcoholism, most sex offenses), humanizing our penal institutions, and adopting a much more tolerant and permissive attitude toward the eccentricities, idiosyncrasies, and even the peccadillos of our fellow men."

* * *

MAHONEY, John Leo 1928-

PERSONAL: Born February 4, 1928, in Somerville, Mass.; son of John Leo (a printer) and Margaret (Daly) Mahoney; married Ann Marie Dowd (a dental hygienist), September 1, 1956; children: John, Patricia, William. *Education:* Boston College, A.B., 1950, A.M., 1952; Harvard University, Ph.D., 1957. *Politics:* Democrat. *Religion:* Roman Catholic. *Home:* 8 Sutherland Rd., Lexington, Mass. 02173. *Office:* Department of English, Boston College, Chestnut Hill, Mass. 02167.

CAREER: Boston College, Chestnut Hill, Mass., instructor, 1955-58, assistant professor, 1958-61, associate professor, 1961-65, professor of English, 1966—, chairman of department, 1962-67, 1969-70. Visiting professor, Harvard University, summers, 1963, 1965, 1969, 1971, 1980, 1983. Trustee, St. John's Seminary, 1980—, and Katherine Gibbs School, 1983—. *Military service:* U.S. Army, 1946-47.

MEMBER: Modern Language Association of America, American Society of Eighteenth-Century Studies, American Association of University Professors, Wordsworth-Coleridge Association, New England Modern Language Association. *Awards, honors:* Boston College-Mellon Foundation grant, 1981-82.

WRITINGS: (Editor) *William Duff's Essay on Original Genius,* Scholars' Facsimiles & Reprints, 1963; (editor) *Dryden's Critical Essays,* Bobbs-Merrill, 1965; (editor) *The English Romantics: Major Poetry and Critical Theory,* Heath, 1978; *The Enlightenment and English Literature,* Heath, 1981; *The Logic of Passion: The Literary Criticism of William Hazlitt,* Fordham University Press, 1981; (contributor) James Engell, editor, *Harvard English Studies: The Age of Johnson,* Harvard University Press, 1984. Also author of *The Whole Internal Universe: Imitation and the New Defense of Poetry in British Criticism, 1660-1830.* Contributor to journals in his field.

WORK IN PROGRESS: The Persistence of Tragedy: Episodes in the History of Drama; William Wordsworth: A Literary Life.

* * *

MAITLAND, Margaret
See WALLMANN, Jeffrey M(iner)

* * *

MALLEN, Bruce E. 1937-

PERSONAL: Born September 4, 1937, in Montreal, Quebec, Canada; son of Mitchell (a retailer) and Mary (Epstein) Mallen; married Marcia Abramson (a registered nurse), December 12, 1965; children: Howard, Jay, Reesa. *Education:* Sir George Williams University (now Concordia University), B.Comm. and B.A., 1958; Columbia University, M.Sc., 1959; University of Michigan, M.B.A., 1960; New York University, Ph.D., 1963.

CAREER: P. S. Ross & Partners (management consultants), Montreal, Quebec, senior marketing consultant, 1962-64; Bruce Mallen & Associates Inc. (marketing consultants), Montreal, president, 1964—; Concordia University, Sir George Williams Campus, Montreal, lecturer, 1964-65, associate professor, 1965-67, professor of marketing and chairman of department, 1967-71, chairman of graduate studies in business, beginning 1968, acting dean, faculty of commerce and administration, 1970-71.

Visiting professor of marketing, Universite Laval, Quebec, 1968-70; visiting scholar, Graduate School of Management, University of California, Los Angeles, 1978-79; part-time lecturer, McGill University. Speaker and researcher on Ford Foundation-sponsored world tour, 1968; World Bank economic development assignment in Togo, Africa, summer, 1969. Consultant to Consulate General of Japan in Montreal and Canadian Council of Resource Ministers.

MEMBER: American Marketing Association (president, Montreal chapter, 1969-70; international director, 1970-71), Association of Industrial Advertisers (former president), Industrial Marketers (former president), American Economic Association, Montreal Economic Association, Advertising and Sales Executive Club of Montreal (director), Sales and Marketing Executives of Montreal (former director).

WRITINGS: (With M. Kelly) *The Role of Sales Management in Modern Marketing,* Canadian Manufacturers Association, 1963; (editor with I. A. Litvak) *Marketing: Canada,* McGraw, 1964, 2nd edition, 1968; (editor) *The Marketing Channel: A Conceptual Viewpoint,* Wiley, 1967; (editor with Litvak) *Annotated Bibliography on Marketing in Canada,* American Marketing Association, 1967; (with R. Rotenberg) *The Costs and Benefits of Evening Shopping to the Canadian Economy,* National Retailers' Institute, 1969.

Marketing in the Canadian Environment, Prentice-Hall (Scarborough, Ontario), 1973; *A Preliminary Paper on the Levels, Causes and Effects of Economic Concentration in the Canadian Retail Food Trade: A Study of Supermarket Power,* Food Prices Review Board (Ottawa), 1976; *Principles of Marketing Channel Management: Interorganizational Distribution Design and Relations,* Lexington Books, 1977; (with V. H. Kirpalani and R. Savitt) *Principles of Marketing in Canada,* Prentice-Hall (Scarborough, Ontario), 1980.

Contributor: B. Israelsson and C. Roos, editors, *Marketing Guide: Canada,* General Export Association of Sweden, 1970; V. P. Buell, editor, *Handbook of Modern Marketing,* McGraw, 1970; D. Leighton and D. Thompson, editors, *Canadian Marketing: Problems and Prospects,* Wiley, 1973; *Modern Marketing,* Random House, 1975. Contributor to marketing and management journals.

Former editor, *Canadian Marketer* (journal of Federation of Canadian Marketing); member of editorial board, *Journal of Marketing* (American Marketing Association), and *International Journal of Physical Distribution* (United Kingdom).

SIDELIGHTS: Bruce E. Mallen told *CA* that he is a "capitalist at heart," with ownership and control interest in various companies. He is competent in French. *Avocational interests:* Reading philosophy and history, skiing, handball.†

* * *

MALONE, Michael (Christopher) 1942-

PERSONAL: Born November, 1942, in North Carolina; son of Thomas Patrick (a psychiatrist) and Faylene (Jones) Malone; married Maureen Quilligan (a professor of English), May 17, 1975; children: Margaret Elizabeth. *Education:* Attended Syracuse University; earned B.A. and M.A. from University of North Carolina; further graduate study at Harvard University. *Politics:* Democrat. *Religion:* Episcopalian. *Home:* 32 Commerce St., Clinton, Conn. 06413. *Agent:* Peter Matson, 264 Fifth Ave., New York, N.Y. 10001.

CAREER: Writer. Instructor at various colleges.

MEMBER: Authors Guild, Authors League of America, Dramatists Guild, National Book Critics Circle.

WRITINGS—Novels, except as indicated: *Painting the Roses Red,* Random House, 1975; *The Delectable Mountains,* Random House, 1977; *Psychetypes* (nonfiction), Dutton, 1977; *Heroes of Eros: Male Sexuality in the Movies* (nonfiction), Dutton, 1979; *Dingley Falls,* Harcourt, 1980; *Uncivil Seasons,* Delacorte, 1983. Contributor of articles and reviews to magazines, including *Viva, Nation, Human Behavior, Harper's, Playboy, Mademoiselle,* and *New York Times Book Review.*

WORK IN PROGRESS: Handling Sin, a novel.

SIDELIGHTS: A town "inhabited by more homey, colorful characters than all of Winesburg, Ohio, Raintree County and Batavia, N.Y., put together," is how the setting of Michael Malone's novel *Dingley Falls* is described by *New York Times Book Review* critic Alan Cheuse. "There are scores of [characters]," continues Cheuse, "all neatly listed in a cast sheet preceding the first chapter—and they stroll, stalk, hitchhike, jog, or drive police cars, motorcycles, bicycles, jalopies, sports cars or fire engines along the town's simple streets and bordering highways. Each is convinced that life in Dingley Falls, U.S.A., is neither comic nor tragic but merely life."

Calling *Dingly Falls* "a wonderful novel, impressive in every way, and constantly absorbing and entertaining," Susan Fromberg Schaeffer goes on to note in the *Chicago Tribune Book World* that the book "takes its structure from a metaphor Malone uses early in the [novel]: that of the spider and his web. Just as each person is at the center of his own web, so each web is entangled in larger webs, and the plot of 'Dingley Falls' is to uncover the two largest webs in which the townspeople are entangled. First they are entangled in the web of the government, which has built a secret Army base on the outskirts of town (the base's personnel test out their poisons on Dingleyan guinea pigs), and lastly, they are entangled in God's web. So beautifully is this novel rendered, scene by scene, character by character, sentence by sentence, that the end of the journey is much less important than the journey itself—as indeed it should be. Everything in this book sparkles and rings true."

While *Washington Post* reviewer Pat McNees doesn't agree that every word in *Dingley Falls* rings true—the critic labels the book "schizophrenic in tone and concept"—McNees ultimately finds that this "imperfect novel [is] so full of energy and gems of characterization, so successful at creating a sense of place and people, that you forgive it its excesses and awkwardness, are sorry when it's finished, and look forward to the author's next book. There's talent there, and life. One senses Malone will grow."

BIOGRAPHICAL/CRITICAL SOURCES: New York Times Book Review, May 11, 1980, November 13, 1983; *Washington Post,* May 26, 1980; *Chicago Tribune Book World,* June 15, 1980, November 28, 1983; *Los Angeles Times Book Review,* August 10, 1980; *Nation,* August 30, 1980.

*　　　*　　　*

MALY, Eugene H.   1920-1981

PERSONAL: Born September 6, 1920, in Cincinnati, Ohio; died, 1981; son of Robert John and Florence (Bill) Maly. *Education:* Athenaeum of Ohio, A.B., 1941, graduate study, 1941-43; additional study at University of Cincinnati, 1944-45, and Hebrew Union College, Cincinnati, 1945-46; Angelicum University, Rome, S.T.D., 1948; Pontifical Biblical Institute, Rome, S.S.D., 1959.

CAREER: Roman Catholic priest. Athenaeum of Ohio, Mount St. Mary's of the West, Norwood, instructor, 1950-55, assistant professor, 1955-59, associate professor, 1959-60, professor of Sacred Scripture, beginning 1960. Lecturer at institutions, workshops, and institutes.

MEMBER: Catholic Biblical Association of America (president, 1962-63), Society of Biblical Literature, National Association of Professors of Hebrew.

WRITINGS: The Epistles of Saints James, Jude, Peter, Liturgical Press, 1960; *The Book of Wisdom* (commentary), Paulist Press, 1962; *The World of David and Solomon,* Prentice-Hall, 1966; *Prophets of Salvation,* Herder & Herder, 1967; (contributor) R. E. Brown and others, editors, *The Jerome Biblical Commentary,* Prentice-Hall, 1968; *The First Book of Samuel* [and] *The Second Book of Samuel,* Liturgical Press, 1970; *Sin: Biblical Perspectives,* Pflaum/Standard, 1973; (editor) *Good News Bible: The Bible in Today's English Version* (Catholic study edition), Sadlier, 1979; *Romans,* Michael Glazier, 1979; *The Word Alive: Commentaries and Reflections on the Scripture Readings for all Sundays, Solemnities of the Lord,*

Holy Days, and Major Feasts for the Three-Year Cycle, Alba House, 1982. Contributor to religious and theological journals. Chairman of editorial board, *The Bible Today,* beginning 1962.

SIDELIGHTS: Eugene H. Maly speaks French, German, Italian, Spanish, Latin, Greek, and Hebrew.†

*　　　*　　　*

MANCHEL, Frank   1935-

PERSONAL: Born July 22, 1935, in Detroit, Mich.; son of Lee and Olga (Fluhr) Manchel; married Sheila Wachtel, 1958; children: Steven Lloyd, Gary Howard. *Education:* Ohio State University, A.B., 1957; Hunter College (now Hunter College of the City University of New York), M.A., 1960; Columbia University, Ed.D., 1966. *Home:* 5 Cranwell Ave., South Burlington, Vt. 05401. *Office:* Office of the Dean, College of Arts and Sciences, University of Vermont, Burlington, Vt. 05401.

CAREER: High school instructor in English, New Rochelle, N.Y., 1958-64; Southern Connecticut State College, New Haven, assistant professor of English, 1964-67; University of Vermont, Burlington, associate professor of English and speech, 1967-71, professor of communication and theater, 1971-77, associate dean of College of Arts and Sciences, 1977—, director of La Mancha Project in Composition (cooperative program with Vermont high schools, exploring techniques in improving writing skills). Visiting professor, University of Bridgeport, summer, 1967. Member of George Peabody Board, 1983—. Chairman of the Governor's Committee on Children and Youth, 1973. *Military service:* U.S. Army, Medical Corps, 1957. U.S. Army Reserve, 1957-63.

MEMBER: National Council of Teachers of English, American Federation of Film Societies (chairman of executive board), Society for Cinema Studies (member of executive committee), American Film Institute, British Film Institute.

AWARDS, HONORS: Simmonds Foundation grant for research in England, 1970; *Terrors of the Screen* was nominated for a National Book Award; *Cameras West* was chosen as an "Ambassador Book" by the English Speaking Union.

WRITINGS: Movies and How They Are Made (juvenile), Prentice-Hall, 1968; *When Pictures Began to Move* (juvenile), illustrations by James Caraway, Prentice-Hall, 1968; *When Movies Began to Speak* (juvenile), Prentice-Hall, 1969; *Terrors of the Screen* (Junior Literary Guild selection), Prentice-Hall, 1970; (contributor) Sheila Schwartz, editor, *Readings in the Humanities,* Macmillan, 1970; *Cameras West* (Junior Literary Guild selection), Prentice-Hall, 1972; *Film Study: A Resource Guide,* Fairleigh Dickinson University Press, 1973.

Published by F. Watts: *Yesterday's Clowns: The Rise of Film Comedy,* 1973; *The Talking Clowns,* 1976; *An Album of Great Science Fiction Films,* 1976, revised edition, 1982; *Women on the Hollywood Screen,* 1977; *Gangsters on the Screen,* 1978; *The Box-Office Clowns: Bob Hope, Jerry Lewis, Mel Brooks, Woody Allen,* 1979; *Great Sports Movies,* 1980; *An Album of Modern Horror Films,* 1983. Contributor of articles and reviews to film and other professional journals.

SIDELIGHTS: Frank Manchel maintains that "the demand for comedy of all kinds seems to be a permanent fixture of society. When life goes sour, people want to laugh. It is not unusual, therefore, that the most popular figures in film history have been great jesters. . . . The comedian's art is based on the difference between what is and what is possible. . . . Their aim, which has been the aim of all great comedy since the beginning of time, is to criticize the world in the belief that things can be better.''

Movies and How They Are Made has been translated into Portuguese.

BIOGRAPHICAL/CRITICAL SOURCES: Variety, January 15, 1969, October 22, 1969; *Saturday Review,* August 16, 1969.

* * *

MANNING, Peter K(irby) 1940-

PERSONAL: Born September 27, 1940, in Salem, Ore.; son of Kenneth G. and Esther A. (Gibbard) Manning; married Victoria Shaughnessy, September 3, 1961 (divorced, 1981); children: three. *Education:* Willamette University, B.A., 1961; Duke University, M.A., 1963, Ph.D., 1966. *Home:* Northwind Farms, East Lansing, Mich. 48823. *Office:* Department of Sociology, 201 Berkey Hall, Michigan State University, East Lansing, Mich. 48824-1111; and Center for Socio-Legal Studies, Wolfson College, Oxford University, Oxford OX2 6UD, England.

CAREER: Duke University, Durham, N.C., instructor, 1964-65; University of Missouri—Columbia, assistant professor, 1965-66; Michigan State University, East Lansing, assistant professor, 1966-70, associate professor of sociology, 1970-74, professor of sociology and psychiatry, 1974—; Oxford University, Wolfson College, Oxford, England, senior principal scientific officer, Center for Socio-Legal Studies, 1984-86. Visiting research fellow, Goldsmith's College, University of London, 1972-73; visiting fellow, Law Enforcement Assistance Administration, National Institute of Law Enforcement and Criminal Justice, 1974-75, and Balliol College, Oxford, 1982-83; visiting professor, Portland State University, 1976, Purdue University, 1977, State University of New York at Albany, 1982, and Massachusetts Institute of Technology, 1982. Has participated in, and presented papers at, professional meetings. Consultant to several agencies, including Police Executive Research Forum, KOBA Associates, and U.S. Department of Justice.

MEMBER: International Sociological Association, Society for the Study of Social Problems (chairman of social problems theory section, 1971—; member of program committee, 1978), National Deviancy Conference, American Sociological Association, Society for the Study of Social Problems, Society for the Study of Symbolic Interaction, Association of Humanist Sociology, British Sociological Association, British Society of Criminology, Royal Anthropological Institute (fellow), Western Society of Criminology, Midwest Sociological Society, North Central Sociological Association, Ohio Valley Sociological Society (section head of Medical Sociology, 1967; program chairman, 1970), Pi Gamma Mu.

AWARDS, HONORS: Research grants from Michigan State University, National Science Foundation, U.S. Department of Justice, and All University Research Institution; alumni citation, Willamette University, 1981.

WRITINGS: (Editor with Marcello Truzzi) *Youth and Sociology,* Prentice-Hall, 1972; (editor with Robert B. Smith and contributor) *Social Science Methods: An Introduction,* Free Press, 1972; (editor) *Youth: Divergent Perspectives,* Wiley, 1973; (with Martine Zucker) *The Sociology of Mental Health and Illness,* Bobbs-Merrill, 1976; *Police Work: The Social Organization of Policing,* MIT Press, 1977; (editor with John

Van Maanen) *Policing: A View from the Streets,* Goodyear Publishing, 1978; (with Lawrence John Redlinger and Jay R. Williams) *Police Narcotics Control: Patterns and Strategies,* United States Government Printing Office, 1979; *The Narcs' Game: Organizational and Informational Limits on Drug Law Enforcement,* MIT Press, 1980; (editor with Smith) *Handbook of Social Science Methods,* Volume II: *Qualitative Methods,* Ballinger, 1982.

Contributor: Jack D. Douglas, editor, *Understanding Everyday Life,* Aldine, 1970; Russell Kleis, editor, *Social Relevance in Continuing Education,* Continuing Education Service, Michigan State University, 1970; Douglas, editor, *Crime and Justice in American Society,* Bobbs-Merrill, 1971; James Henslin, editor, *Studies in the Sociology of Sex,* Appleton, 1971, 2nd edition, Schocken, 1978; Ralph Blankenship, editor, *Colleagues in Organizations: The Social Construction of Professional Work,* Wiley, 1971; Henslin, editor, *Down to Earth Sociology,* Free Press, 1972; (with Horacio Fabrega, Jr.) Douglas and Robert A. Scott, editors, *Theoretical Perspectives on Deviance,* Basic Books, 1972; Douglas, editor, *Research on Deviance,* Random House, 1972; Douglas, editor, *Introductory Sociology,* Free Press, 1972; (with C. Richard Fletcher, Larry T. Reynolds, and James O. Smith) Paul Roman and Harrison Trice, editors, *Current Perspectives in Psychiatric Sociology,* Science House, 1972.

(With Fabrega) George Psathas, editor, *Phenomenological Sociology,* Wiley, 1973; Richard Quinney, editor, *Criminal Justice in America: A Critical Understanding,* Little, Brown, 1974; Isadore Silver, editor, *The Crime Control Establishment,* Prentice-Hall, 1974; R. J. Havighurst, editor, *Youth,* National Society for the Study of Education, 1975.

Anthony L. Guenther, editor, *Criminal Behavior and Social Systems,* Rand McNally, 1976; Niederhoffer and Blumberg, editors, *The Ambivalent Force,* Dryden, 1976; (with L. J. Redlinger) P. E. Rock, editor, *Drugs and Politics,* Transaction Books, 1977; Douglas and Johnson, editors, *Official Deviance,* Lippincott, 1977; Sagarin, editor, *Fundamentals of Sociology,* Holt, 1977; Larry K. Gaines and Truett Ricks, editors, *Managing the Police Organization: A Book of Readings,* West Publishing, 1978; Sagarin, editor, *Sociology: The Basic Concepts,* Holt, 1978; Arnold Trebach, editor, *Drugs, Crime and Politics,* Prager, 1978.

Simon Holdaway, editor, *British Police,* Edward Arnold, 1979, Sage, 1980; Carl Klockars, editor, *Deviance and Its Relation to the Ethics of Social Research,* Volume III: *Annual Reviews of Studies of Deviance,* Sage, 1979; Jason Ditton, editor, *The View from Goffman,* Macmillan, 1980; R.V.G. Clarge and J. M. Hough, editors, *The Effectiveness of Policing,* Gower, 1980; *Five Year Outlook for Science and Technology in the United States,* National Science Foundation, 1980; J. Lowinson and P. Ruiz, editors, *Substance Abuse in the United States: Clinical Problems and Perspectives,* Williams & Wilkins, 1981.

Rita Donelan, editor, *The Maintenance of Order in Society,* Minister of Supply and Services (Ottawa, Canada), 1982; Ida Harper Simpson and Richard L. Simpson, editors, *Research in the Sociology of Work,* Volume II, JAI Press, 1983; C. D. Phillips and G. P. Whitaker, editors, *Evaluating Performance of Criminal Justice Agencies,* Sage, 1983; Norm Denzin, editor, *Studies in Symbolic Interaction,* JAI Press, 1984; Louis A. Radelet, editor, *The Criminal Justice System,* Macmillan, 1985.

Also contributor to Keith Hawkins and John Thomas, editors, *Regulatory Policy-Making,* in press, Rob Baldwin and Paul

Fenn, editors, *Regulation in Britain*, Oxford University Press, in press, Andrew Rutherford, editor, *Criminal Justice in the Eighties*, Martin Robertson, in press, and Thomas J. Cottle and Robert Weiss, editors, *The Narrative Voice*, Basic Books, in press. Contributor to a number of proceedings. Contributor of articles and reviews to periodicals, including *Sociology and Social Research, Sociological Quarterly, Youth and Sociology, Mental Health Digest, Urban Life and Culture*, and *British Journal of Criminology*.

Editor, *Urban Life*, 1977-83; associate editor, *American Sociological Review*, 1975-78, and *Deviant Behavior: An Interdisciplinary Journal*, 1978—; advisory editor, *American Journal of Sociology*, 1981-84, and *Howard Journal of Criminal Justice*, 1983—; editorial consultant, *Criminal Justice and Behavior: An International Journal*, 1983—; member of editorial review board, *Sociological Quarterly*, 1968-73.

WORK IN PROGRESS: The Social Organization of Narcotics Law Enforcement: A Comparative Analysis; Signifying Calls; (with Keith Hawkins) *Decision-Making;* (with H. Fabrega) a chapter in *Social Science and Medicine;* other books and articles.

*   *   *

MARCUM, John A(rthur) 1927-

PERSONAL: Born August 21, 1927, in San Jose, Calif.; son of Arthur I. (a draftsman) and Dorothy (Curtner) Marcum; married Gwendolyn Groomes, October 17, 1964; children: Andrea, Edmund, Arthur. *Education:* Stanford University, B.A., 1949, Ph.D., 1955; Columbia University, M.A., 1951; Institute of Political Science, University of Paris, postdoctoral study, 1952-54. *Politics:* Democrat. *Religion:* Protestant. *Home:* 2214 Ocean St. Ext., Santa Cruz, Calif. *Office:* Office of the Academic Vice Chancellor, University of California, Santa Cruz, Calif. 95064.

CAREER: Colgate University, Hamilton, N.Y., instructor, 1956-57, assistant professor of political science, 1957-61; Lincoln University, Lincoln University, Pa., professor of political science and director of African Program, 1961-68, director of African Language and Area Center, 1965-68; University of California, Santa Cruz, Merrill College, visiting professor, 1969-70; University of Denver, Center on International Relations, Denver, Colo., visiting professor, 1970-72; University of California, Santa Cruz, Merrill College, professor of politics and provost, 1972-78, academic vice chancellor, 1978—.

Visiting lecturer at Wharton School of Finance and Commerce, University of Pennsylvania, 1962-63, and East African Program, Syracuse University, summers, 1965, 1966; U.S. Department of State, lecturer on Africa, 1961-63, member of advisory council on African affairs, 1963-68; lecturer for Peace Corps training projects, 1964-65. Member of board of directors, African Student Service, 1962-66; member of national council, South African Education Program, 1980—, and Council for the International Exchange of Scholars, 1983—; member of board of trustees, World Affairs Council of Northern California, 1978—; member of management committee, U.S.-South Africa Leader Exchange Program, 1979—; member of advisory committee on investment to southern Africa, Executive Council of Episcopal Church, 1968; also member of numerous other committees. Consultant, Ford Foundation, 1974, and Rockefeller Foundation, 1978-79. *Military service:* U.S. Naval Reserve, 1945-46.

MEMBER: African Studies Association (vice-president, 1973-74; president, 1974-75), American Political Science Association, American Civil Liberties Union, Phi Beta Kappa.

AWARDS, HONORS: Fulbright scholar in France, 1952-54; Ford Foundation international relations fellowship in Africa, 1958-59, research grant, 1976; Fulbright-Hays grant for research in Africa, 1966-67; African studies award, Pacific Coast Africanist Association, 1982; L.L.D., Temple University, 1982.

WRITINGS: The Challenge of Africa, New Leader, 1960; *The Angolan Revolution*, MIT Press, Volume I: *The Anatomy of an Explosion, 1950-1962*, 1969, Volume II: *Exile Politics and Guerilla Warfare, 1962-1976*, 1978; *The Politics of Indifference: Portugal and Africa, a Case Study in American Foreign Policy*, Eastern African Studies, Syracuse University, 1972; *Education, Race and Social Change in South Africa*, University of California Press, 1982.

Contributor: *Pan-Africanism Reconsidered*, University of California Press, 1962; William Lewis, editor, *New Forces in Africa*, Public Affairs Press, 1962; (with Allard Lowenstein) Davis and Baker, editors, *Southern Africa in Transition*, Praeger, 1966; *Lectures: Institute on Africa*, Board of Education (Philadelphia, Pa.), 1969; G. Daniels, editor, *Southern Africa: A Time for Change*, Friendship Press, 1969; G. W. Shepherd, editor, *Race and American Foreign Policy*, Basic Books, 1970; R. Dale and C. Potholm, editors, *Southern Africa in Perspective*, Free Press, 1972; Helen Kitchen, editor, *Africa from Mystery to Maze*, Heath & Co., 1976; Gwendolen Carter and Patrick O'Meara, editors, *Southern Africa in Crisis*, Indiana University Press, 1977, revised edition published as *Southern Africa: The Continuing Crisis*, 1979.

Contributor of written testimony on hearings before the subcommittee on African affairs of the committee on foreign relations, United States Senate, 1975-76; also contributor to *Encyclopedia of World Biography*, McGraw, 1973, and *World Book Encyclopedia*, Field Educational Publications, 1976. Contributor of articles to periodicals, including *Africa Report, Colgate Alumni News, Journal of Human Relations, Freedom and Union*, and *New Leader*. Member of editorial board, *Journal of African Studies;* executive editor, *Africa Today*, 1970-72.

*   *   *

MARCUS, Edward 1918-

PERSONAL: Born April 29, 1918, in Brooklyn, N.Y.; son of Herman and Rose (Marayna) Marcus; married Mildred Rendl (an economist), 1956. *Education:* Harvard University, B.S., 1939, M.B.A., 1941; King's College, Cambridge, graduate study, 1946-47; Princeton University, Ph.D., 1950. *Religion:* None. *Home address:* P.O. Box 814, New Canaan, Conn. 06840. *Office:* Department of Economics, Graduate School and University Center, City University of New York, 33 West 42nd St., New York, N.Y. 10036.

CAREER: Federal Reserve Board, Washington, D.C., economist in division of international finance, 1950-52; City University of New York, Brooklyn College, Brooklyn, N.Y., beginning 1952, began as assistant professor, professor of economics, beginning 1962, chairman of department, 1966-79, Graduate School and University Center, New York, N.Y., began as professor of economics, currently professor emeritus. Visiting professor at New York University, 1960-61, and at Maxwell Center, Syracuse, N.Y., 1961. Consultant to Ira Haupt

& Co., 1955-58, National Academy of Sciences, 1959, and U.N. Conference on Trade and Development, 1966. *Military service:* U.S. Army, 1941-42. U.S. Coast Guard Reserve, active duty, 1942-46; became commander.

MEMBER: American Economic Association, American Finance Association, African Studies Association, Society for International Development, American Association of University Professors, Canadian Economic Association, Economic Society of South Africa, Canadian Political Science Association, Royal Economic Society, Metropolitan Economics Association (New York; president, 1966-67), Phi Beta Kappa.

AWARDS, HONORS: Merrill Foundation grant, 1953.

WRITINGS: Canada and the International Business Cycle, 1927-1938, Bookman Associates, 1954; (with wife, Mildred Rendl Marcus) *Investment and Development Possibilities in Tropical Africa,* Bookman Associates, 1960, reprinted, Arno, 1977; (with M. R. Marcus) *International Trade and Finance,* Pitman, 1965; (with M. R. Marcus) *Monetary and Banking Theory,* Pitman, 1965; (contributor with M. R. Marcus) *Management Sciences in the Emerging Countries,* Pergamon, 1965; (with M. R. Marcus) *Economic Progress and the Developing World,* Scott, Foresman, 1971; (with M. R. Marcus) *Economics,* Kendall/Hunt, 1978; (editor with Nathan Schmukler) *Inflation through the Ages: Economic, Social, Psychological and Historical Aspects,* Brooklyn College Press, 1981. Contributor to professional journals.

SIDELIGHTS: Edward Marcus is competent in French, Swedish, and German.

* * *

MARGENAU, Henry 1901-

PERSONAL: Born April 30, 1901, in Bielefeld, Germany; naturalized U.S. citizen; son of Frederick and Karoline (Wagemann) Margenau; married Louise Margarethe Noe, May 28, 1932; children: Rolf Carl, Annemarie Louise, Henry F., Jr. *Education:* Midland Lutheran College, A.B., 1924; University of Nebraska, M.Sc., 1926; Yale University, Ph.D., 1929. *Home:* 173 Westwood Rd., New Haven, Conn. 06525. *Office:* 44 S.P.L., Yale University, New Haven, Conn. 06520.

CAREER: University of Nebraska, Lincoln, instructor in physics, 1926-27; Yale University, New Haven, Conn., assistant professor, 1931-40, associate professor, 1940-45, professor of physics, 1945-47, professor of physics and natural philosophy, 1947-49, Eugene Higgins Professor of Physics and Natural Philosophy, 1949—. Distinguished visiting professor, University of Pennsylvania, 1959; visiting professor at University of Heidelberg, University of Fribourg, University of Tokyo, University of California, University of Washington, Seattle, Whitman College, Haverford College, and Carleton College. Member of Institute for Advanced Study, 1939-40; member of radiation weapons committee, Institute for Defense Analysis. Member of World Council of Churches Committee on Atomic War, 1954-56. Consultant to Lockheed Aviation Co., RAND Corp., U.S. Air Force, and U.S. Navy.

MEMBER: International Academy of Philosophy of Science (vice-president, 1975-80), American Academy of Arts and Sciences, Philosophy of Science Association (president, 1950-60).

AWARDS, HONORS: L.H.D., Carleton College, 1954; Michigan State University Centennial Award, 1955; D.Sc., University of Nebraska, 1957, Hartwick College, 1964, Stonehill

College, 1981; LL.D., Dalhousie University, 1960, Rhode Island College, 1962; D.Pub.Serv., Midland College, 1965; De Vane Medal, 1971; Wilbur Cross Medal, 1981.

WRITINGS: (With R. D. Lindsay) *Foundations of Physics,* Wiley, 1936, Ox Bow, 1981; (with G. M. Murphy) *Mathematics of Physics and Chemistry,* Van Nostrand, Volume I, 1943, 2nd edition, 1956, Volume II, 1964; *Nature of Physical Reality,* McGraw, 1950; *Open Vistas,* Yale University Press, 1963; *Ethics and Science,* Van Nostrand, 1966; *Scientific Indeterminism and Human Freedom,* Archabby Press, 1968; *Theory of Intermolecular Forces,* Pergamon, 1969; (editor) *Integrative Principles of Modern Thought,* Gordon & Breach, 1972; *Physics and Philosophy: Selected Essays,* Reidel, 1978; (with L. LeShan) *Einstein's Space and Van Gogh's Sky,* Macmillan, 1982; *The Miracle of Existence,* Ox Bow, 1983. Consulting editor, Time-Life Science Series. Contributor of about two hundred research articles to journals.

WORK IN PROGRESS: Philosophy of Quantum Mechanics.

* * *

MARSDEN, Peter (Richard Valentine) 1940-

PERSONAL: Born April 29, 1940, in London, England; son of Sidney L.V. and Emily Sylvia (Lynde) Marsden; married Frances Elizabeth McKerrell; children: (previous marriage) Paul Stephen Valentine, Mark Richard Valentine; Katie-May McKerrell (stepdaughter). *Education:* Attended Kilburn Polytechnic, 1957. *Politics:* Liberal. *Religion:* Church of England. *Home:* 21 Meadow Lane, Lindfield, Sussex RH16 2RJ, England. *Office:* Museum of London, London Wall, London EC2Y 5HN, England.

CAREER: Museum of London, London, England, archaeologist, 1959—. Director and secretary, Nautical Museums Trust (creators of Shipwreck Heritage Centre), Hastings, East Sussex, England. *Member:* Society of Antiquaries (fellow), Institute of Field Archaeologists, Society for Nautical Archaeology (member of committee), Society for Nautical Research, Committee for Nautical Archaeology (member of committee).

WRITINGS: The Wreck of the Amsterdam, Hutchinson, 1974, Stein & Day, 1975; *Roman London,* Thames & Hudson, 1980; *The Marsden Family of Paythorne and Nelson, 1666-1981,* privately printed, 1981. Contributor to magazines and newspapers.

WORK IN PROGRESS: A revised edition of *The Wreck of the Amsterdam;* a book, *Saxon and Medieval London,* for Thames & Hudson.

SIDELIGHTS: Reviewing Peter Marsden's *Roman London,* Philip Howard notes that the author "stands back from his excavations to give a broad historical reconstruction of Roman London for the general reader, with 160 photographs, plans, and drawings." Writing in the London *Times,* Howard concludes that "Peter Marsden's piecing together of the ancient jig-saw is punctilious and persuasive." Marsden told *CA* that his interest in old ships and archaeology, exploration, and discovery is motivated by "extreme curiosity and the challenge of the unknown. Also," he adds, "writing books while commuting forty miles by train each day is a worthwhile use of the journey time."

AVOCATIONAL INTERESTS: Planetary geology ("including Earth") and family history.

BIOGRAPHICAL/CRITICAL SOURCES: Times (London), December 11, 1980.

*   *   *

MARSHALL, Hermine H(alprin)   1935-

PERSONAL: Born April 21, 1935, in Newark, N.J.; daughter of Hyman H. (a businessman) and Anita (Ackerman) Halprin; married Sumner Marshall (a physician), August, 1956; children: Randolph, Gregory, Bradley. *Education:* Wellesley College, B.A., 1957; Bank Street College of Education, M.S., 1959; Syracuse University, graduate study, 1959-61; University of California, Berkeley, Ph.D., 1967. *Home:* 27 Norwood Ave., Kensington, Calif. 94707. *Office:* Department of Education, University of California, Berkeley, Calif. 94720.

CAREER: Worked as a kindergarten teacher in New York, 1958-60; California State College (now University), Hayward, assistant professor of education, 1967-68; University of California, Berkeley Education Extension, instructor in education, 1965-75; University of California, Berkeley, lecturer in education, 1969-77, assistant research educator, 1973-77; California State College, Sonoma (now Sonoma State University), lecturer, 1977-78; University of California, Berkeley, assistant research psychologist, 1979-83, associate research psychologist, 1983-84. Visiting lecturer at San Francisco State College (now University), 1967, 1984.

MEMBER: American Psychological Association, American Educational Research Association, National Association for the Education of Young Children, Society for Research in Child Development, Phi Beta Kappa, Pi Lambda Theta, Phi Delta Kappa.

WRITINGS: (Contributor) E. D. Evans, editor, *Children: Readings in Behavior and Development*, Holt, 1968; *Positive Discipline and Classroom Interaction: A Part of the Teaching-Learning Process*, C. C Thomas, 1972; *Dimensional Occurrence Scale: Manual*, School of Education, University of California, 1976; *Manual for Revised Reciprocal Category System*, School of Education, University of California, 1976; *Task Involvement Scan*, School of Education, University of California, 1976; (co-author) *Teacher-Initiated Statements and Questions*, School of Education, University of California, 1980; *Classroom Dimensions Observation System*, Department of Psychology, University of California, 1982.

Also author of *Self-Evaluation of Openness*. Contributor to professional journals, including *Child Development*, *Journal of Educational Psychology*, *Early Childhood Education*, *Young Children*, *Journal of Classroom Interaction*, and *Review of Educational Research*.

*   *   *

MARSZALEK, John F(rancis, Jr.)   1939-

PERSONAL: Surname is pronounced *Mars*-ah-lack; born July 5, 1939, in Buffalo, N.Y.; son of John F. (a grocer) and Regina (Sierakowski) Marszalek; married Jeanne A. Kozmer, October 16, 1965; children: John F. III, Christopher H., James S. *Education:* Canisius College, A.B., 1961; University of Notre Dame, A.M., 1963, Ph.D., 1968. *Religion:* Roman Catholic. *Home:* 108 Grand Ridge, Starkville, Miss. 39759. *Office:* Department of History, Mississippi State University, Mississippi State, Miss. 39762.

CAREER: Canisius College, Buffalo, N.Y., instructor, 1967-68; Gannon University, Erie, Pa., assistant professor, 1968-

72, associate professor of history, 1972-73; Mississippi State University, Mississippi State, associate professor, 1973-80, professor of history, 1980—. *Military service:* U.S. Army, 1965-67; became captain.

MEMBER: American Historical Association, Organization of American Historians, Mississippi Historical Society.

AWARDS, HONORS: National Endowment for the Humanities Summer Award for Younger Humanists, 1971, travel grant, 1984; American Council of Learned Societies grant, 1973-74; travel grant, Cushwa Center for the Study of American Catholicism, University of Notre Dame.

WRITINGS: Court Martial: A Black Man in America, Scribner, 1972; (with Sadye Wier) *A Black Businessman in White Mississippi, 1886-1974*, University Press of Mississippi, 1977; (editor) *The Diary of Miss Emma Holmes, 1861-1866*, Louisiana State University Press, 1979; *Sherman's Other War: The General and the Civil War Press*, Memphis State University Press, 1981.

Contributor to *Dictionary of American Biography*, *Dictionary of American Negro Biography*, and *Encyclopedia of the South*. Contributor of articles and reviews to journals, including *Civil War Times Illustrated*, *Georgia Historical Quarterly*, *American Heritage*, *American Historical Review*, *Civil War History*, and *Journal of American History*.

WORK IN PROGRESS: With Douglas Conner, *Bringing Hope: The Autobiography of a Black Physician*, for University Press of Mississippi; a biography of General William T. Sherman; articles on nineteenth-century blacks and on Civil War topics.

SIDELIGHTS: John F. Marszalek told *CA:* "I am a teacher and writer of American history. I aim to produce accurate, objective accounts of the American past with emphasis on the human side of history. In my writings, I try to tell the stories of individuals, some well known, others not, whose lives were not only significant in themselves, but who also illuminated the ages in which they lived."

*   *   *

MARTIN, Geoffrey John   1934-

PERSONAL: Born March 9, 1934, in London, England; son of Charles Walter (an education officer) and Elizabeth K. (Doughty) Martin; married Norma Jean Bechtel, January, 1965; children: Thaddius Stuart, Amanda Gale. *Education:* London School of Economics and Political Science, B.Sc., 1956; Kings College, London, P.G.C.E., 1957; University of Florida, M.A., 1958. *Home:* 189 Banks Rd., Easton, Conn. 06612. *Office:* Department of Geography, Southern Connecticut State University, New Haven, Conn. 06515.

CAREER: Eastern Michigan University, Ypsilanti, assistant professor of geography, 1959-65; Wisconsin State University, Platteville (now University of Wisconsin—Platteville), assistant professor of geography, 1965-66; Southern Connecticut State University, New Haven, professor of geography, 1966—, chairperson of department, 1976-79.

MEMBER: Association of American Geographers (chairperson of committee on association history and archives; councillor, 1980-83).

AWARDS, HONORS: National Council for Geographic Education grant, 1968, for *Mark Jefferson: Geographer;* American Council of Learned Societies grant-in-aid for *Ellsworth Hun-*

tington: His Life and Thought; American Philosophical Society grant for *The Life and Thought of Isaiah Bowman;* National Geographic Society grant, 1982; Association of American Geographers award, 1983; National Science Foundation grant, 1984.

WRITINGS: Mark Jefferson: Geographer, Eastern Michigan University Press, 1968; *Ellsworth Huntington: His Life and Thought,* Archon Books, 1973; (with P. E. James) *The History of the Association of American Geographers,* Association of American Geographers, 1979; *The Life and Thought of Isaiah Bowman,* Shoe String Press, 1980; (with James) *All Possible Worlds: A History of Geographical Ideas,* Wiley, 1981. Contributor of articles to various journals.

WORK IN PROGRESS: A History of Geography in North America.

AVOCATIONAL INTERESTS: International chess playing.

* * *

MARTIN, William C. 1937-

PERSONAL: Born December 31, 1937, in San Antonio, Tex.; son of Lowell Curtis (in agribusiness) and Joe Bailey (Brite) Martin; married Patricia Summerlin, December 31, 1957; children: Rex William, Jeffrey Summerlin, Elisabeth Dale. *Education:* Abilene Christian College, B.A., 1958, M.A., 1960; Harvard Divinity School, B.D., 1963; Harvard University, Ph.D., 1969. *Politics:* Democrat. *Religion:* Protestant. *Home:* 2148 Addison, Houston, Tex. 77001. *Agent:* Gerard F. McCauley, P.O. Box AE, Katonah, N.Y. 10536. *Office:* Department of Sociology, Rice University, Houston, Tex. 77251.

CAREER: Traveling salesman for Southwestern Co., summers, 1956-61; high school instructor and chaplain in Wellesley, Mass., 1965-68; Rice University, Houston, Tex., instructor, 1968-69, assistant professor, 1969-73, associate professor, 1973-79, professor of sociology, 1979—, chairman of department, 1983—, Master of Sid W. Richardson College, 1976-81; writer. Member of numerous professional committees; president, board of directors, Fellowship for Racial and Economic Equality, 1970-71, and House of Carpenters, Inc. (non-profit housing corporation. Has spoken and presented papers at professional meetings.) Consultant, American Sociological Association Teaching Project.

MEMBER: American Sociological Association, Society for the Scientific Study of Religion, Religious Research Association, Popular Culture Association, Texas Institute of Letters.

AWARDS, HONORS: George R. Brown Award for Superior Teaching, Rice University, 1974, 1976, 1977; George R. Brown Award for Excellency in Teaching, Rice University, 1975, 1982; J. Frank Dobie/Paisano Fellowship, Texas Institute of Letters, 1980; National Headliner Award, 1982, for contributions to *Texas Monthly* magazine.

WRITINGS: The Layman's Bible Encyclopedia, Southwestern Co., 1964; *These Were God's People: A Layman's Bible History,* Southwestern Co., 1966; *Christians in Conflict,* Center for the Scientific Study of Religion, 1972; (author of text) Geoff Winningham, *Going Texan,* Kelsey, 1972.

Contributor: *The Minister's Taped Digest,* Word, 1970; Eric Artzt and Renatus Hartog, editors, *Violence: Causes and Solutions,* Dell, 1970; H. Prakash Sethi, editor, *Business Corporations and the Black Man,* Chandler, 1970; Bill C. Malone and Judith McCulloh, *Stars of Country Music: From Uncle*

Dave Macon to Johnny Rodriguez, University of Illinois Press, 1972; George H. Lewis, editor, *Side-Saddle on the Golden Calf: Social Structure and Popular Culture in America,* Goodyear, 1972; James M. Salem, editor, *A New Generation of Essays,* W. C. Brown, 1972; Andrew M. Greely, editor, *Unsecular Man,* Schocken, 1972; Bernard J. McGarney and Virginia Lee Owen, editors, *Economics: A Synergetic Approach,* Dryden, 1973; John A Perry, editor, *The Social Web,* Canfield Press, 1973; James Burl Hogin and Robert E. Yarber, editors, *Phase Blue,* revised edition, Science Research Associates, 1974; Joseph R. Trimmer, editor, *American Oblique,* Houghton, 1975.

Dean S. Dorn, Robert M. Kloss, and Ron E. Roberts, editors, *Sociology with a Human Face,* C. V. Mosby, 1976; Reed Geertsen and Richard A. Sundeen, editors, *Eighty-One Techniques for Teaching Sociological Concepts,* American Sociological Association, 1979; Louis C. Reichman and Barry J. Wishart, editors, *Modern Sociological Issues,* Macmillan, 1979; *Readings in Rhetoric,* fourth edition, Macmillan, 1979; David Birch and Frederic Rissover, editors, *Mass Media and the Popular Arts,* McGraw, 1980; Glen Gavligio and David Raye, editors, *Society as It Is,* second edition, Macmillan, 1980; David E. Harrell, Jr., editor, *Varieties of Southern Evangelicalism,* Mercer University Press, 1981; Lawrence Hlad, editor, *Reader in Sociology,* Ginn, 1982.

Contributor to *Dictionary of Southern Religion;* contributor of articles and reviews to periodicals, including *Atlantic, Harper's, Esquire,* and *Texas Monthly.*

WORK IN PROGRESS: The Electric Preacher: Radio and Television Evangelism in America, for Atlantic/Little-Brown.

* * *

MARX, Gary T. 1938-

PERSONAL: Born October 1, 1938, in Hanford, Calif.; son of Donald and Ruth Marx; married Phyllis A. Rakita. *Education:* University of California, Los Angeles, B.A., 1960; University of California, Berkeley, M.A., 1962, Ph.D., 1966. *Office:* Department of Urban Studies and Planning, Massachusetts Institute of Technology, 77 Massachusetts Ave., Cambridge, Mass. 02139.

CAREER: Traveled around the world, preparing for the study of comparative race and ethnic relations, 1963-64; University of California, Berkeley, research associate, Survey Research Center, 1965-67, lecturer in sociology, 1966-67; Harvard University, Cambridge, Mass., assistant professor of social relations, 1967-69, lecturer, 1969-73, research associate, Harvard-Massachusetts Institute of Technology Joint Center for Urban Studies, 1967-73; Massachusetts Institute of Technology, Cambridge, associate professor, 1973—. Visiting associate professor or lecturer, Boston College, spring, 1973, fall, 1974, University of California, Santa Barbara, summer, 1974, Wellesley College, fall, 1975, Boston University, spring, 1976, University of California, San Diego, 1977-78; State University of New York at Albany, 1980-81. Has presented papers at professional meetings. Consultant to National Advisory Commission on Civil Disorder, 1967, Urban Institute, 1970—, and Police Foundation, 1971—.

MEMBER: American Sociological Association (member of executive council, 1973-76), American Political Science Association, Society for the Study of Social Problems, Society for the Psychological Study of Social Issues, Eastern Sociological Society.

AWARDS, HONORS: Guggenheim fellow in England and France, 1970-71; also recipient of research grants, 1970-72, 1973-75.

WRITINGS: The Social Basis of the Support of a Depression Era Extremist: Father Coughlin, Survey Research Center, University of California, Berkeley, 1962; *Protest and Prejudice,* Harper, 1967, edition with postscript, Torchbooks, 1969; (editor with others) *Confrontation: Psychology and the Problems of Today,* Scott, Foresman, 1970; (editor) *Radical Conflict: Tension and Change in American Society,* Little, Brown, 1971; (with others) *Inquiries in Sociology,* Allyn & Bacon, 1972; (editor) *Muckraking Sociology: Research as Social Criticism,* Transaction Books, 1972; (reviser with N. Goodman) *Society Today,* 4th edition, Random House, 1982; (editor with Goodman) *Sociology: Classic and Popular Approaches,* Random House, 1980.

Contributor: A. Mier and E. Rudwick, editors, *Readings in Negro Life and History,* Atheneum, 1967; C. E. Lincoln, editor, *Is Anybody Listening to Black America?,* Seabury, 1968; M. Minnis and W. Cartwright, editors, *Sociological Perspectives: Readings in Deviant Behavior and Social Problems,* W. C. Brown, 1968; T. Moran and R. Roth, editors, *Law and Order: A Panacea?,* Proceedings of the Fifth Annual Police Seminar of Northeastern University, 1968; C. Bonjean and N. Glenn, editors, *Blacks in America: An Anthology,* Chandler Publishing, 1969; P. Washburn and C. Larson, editors, *Power, Participation and Ideology,* McKay, 1969.

M. Goldschmid, editor, *The Negro American and White Racism,* Holt, 1970; C. Anderson, editor, *Sociological Essays and Research: Introductory Readings,* Dorsey, 1970; J. F. Szwed, editor, *Black Americans: A Second Look,* Basic Books, 1970; P. Rose, editor, *Study of Society,* Random House, 1970; H. Nelsen and others, editors, *The Black Church in America,* Basic Books, 1971; G. Gavligio and D. Raye, editors, *Society as It Is,* Macmillan, 1971; D. Boesel and P. Rossi, editors, *Cities under Siege,* Basic Books, 1971.

D. A. Wilkinson, editor, *Black Revolt: Strategies of Protest,* McCuchan Publishing, 1972; G. Thielbar and S. Feldman, editors, *Issues in Social Inequality,* Little, Brown, 1972; E. Greer, editor, *Black Political Power: A Reader,* Allyn & Bacon, 1972; M. Wolfgang and J. Short, editors, *Collective Violence,* Aldine, 1972; S. Guterman, editor, *The Personality Patterns of Black Americans,* Glendessary, 1972; Guterman, editor, *Black Psyche,* Glendessary, 1972; C. Glock, editor, *Religion in Sociological Perspective,* Wadsworth, 1973; S. McNall, editor, *The Sociological Perspective,* Little, Brown, 1973; B. Franklin and F. Kohout, editors, *Social Psychology and Everyday Life,* McKay, 1973; S. Wasby, editor, *American Government and Politics,* Scribner, 1973.

B. Beit-Hallahmi, editor, *Research in Religious Behaviour,* Brooks/Cole, 1974; W. Newman, editor, *The Social Meanings of Religion,* Rand McNally, 1974; *Privacy in a Free Society,* Roscoe Pound American Trial Lawyers' Association, 1974; C. Reasons, editor, *Criminology: A Radical Perspective,* Goodyear, 1974; R. Evans, editor, *Social Movements,* Rand McNally, 1974; J. Rosenbaum and C. Sederberg, editors, *Vigilantism,* University of Pennsylvania, 1975; E. Viano, editor, *Criminal Justice Research,* Heath, 1976; (with M. Useem) J. Rothman, editor, *Issues in Race and Ethnic Relations,* Peacock, 1977; J. Douglas, editor, *Official Deviance,* Lippincott, 1977.

D. Larsen, editor, *Performance Measures and Analytical Tools,* Heath, 1978; J. McCarthy and M. Zald, editors, *The Dynamics*

of Social Movements, Winthrop, 1979; H. Blalock, editor, *Social Theory and Research: A Critical Appraisal,* Free Press, 1981; M. Jackson and J. Wood, editors, *Social Movements,* Brooks/Cole, 1982; P. Manning and R. Smith, editors, *An Introduction to Social Research,* Ballinger, 1982; J. Johnson and L. Savitz, editors, *Legal Processes and Corrections,* Wiley, 1982; S. Kadish, editor, *Encyclopedia of Crime and Justice,* Macmillan, 1983; C. Klockars, editor, *Police Issues,* McGraw-Hill, 1983.

Also contributor to W. Hefferman and T. Stroup, editors, *Police Ethics: Hard Choices in Law Enforcement,* John Jay, in press; J. Kitsuse and J. Schneider, editors, *Studies in the Sociology of Social Problems,* Albex, in press; D. Kelly, *Deviant Behavior: Readings in the Sociology of Deviance,* St. Martin's, in press. Contributor to *World Book Encyclopedia* and *Encyclopaedia Britannica.* Contributor of articles to numerous periodicals, including *Nation, Phylon, New Republic, Contemporary Sociology, Yale Law Journal, New York Times,* and *Los Angeles Times.*

Associate editor, *Social Problems,* 1969-75, and *American Sociological Review,* 1972-75; advisory editor, *Politics and Society,* 1970-73; member of editorial board, *Annual Review of Sociology,* 1978-84, and *Journal of Conflict Resolution,* 1984—.

WORK IN PROGRESS: A Necessary Evil: The Problems and Possibilities of Undercover Police Work, for Twentieth Century Fund; *Ironies of Social Control,* for University of California Press; *Collective Behavior and Collective Behavior Process,* for Prentice-Hall.

*   *   *

MASSIE, Robert K(inloch) 1929-

PERSONAL: Born January 5, 1929, in Lexington, Ky.; son of Robert K. and Mary (Kimball) Massie; married Suzanne Rohrbach (a writer), December 18, 1954; children: Robert, Susanna, Elizabeth. *Education:* Yale University, B.A., 1950; Oxford University, B.A., 1952. *Home:* 60 West Clinton Ave., Irvington, N.Y. 10533.

CAREER: Collier's, New York City, reporter, 1955-56; *Newsweek,* New York City, writer and correspondent, 1956-62; *USA-1,* New York City, writer, 1962; *Saturday Evening Post,* New York City, writer, 1962-65; free-lance writer, 1965—; Princeton University, Princeton, N.J., Ferris Professor of Journalism, 1977; Tulane University, New Orleans, La., Mellon Professor of Humanities, 1981. *Military service:* U.S. Naval Reserves, 1952-55; became lieutenant, junior grade.

MEMBER: Authors Guild, Authors League of America, P.E.N.

AWARDS, HONORS: Christopher Award, 1976, for *Journey;* American Book Award nomination in biography, American Library Association notable book citation, and Pulitzer Prize in biography, all 1981, for *Peter the Great: His Life and World.*

WRITINGS: Nicholas and Alexandra (biography), Atheneum, 1967; (with wife, Suzanne Massie) *Journey,* Knopf, 1975; *Peter the Great: His Life and World* (biography), Knopf, 1980; (author of introduction) *The Romanov Family Album,* Vendome, 1982.

WORK IN PROGRESS: A book on the arms race between England and Germany before World War I.

SIDELIGHTS: Robert K. Massie's research into Russian history stems from a very personal source. It was his son's hemophilia, a hereditary, incurable blood disease, and Massie's investigation of it, that led him to study Alexis, the male heir of the last ruling family of Russia, Czar Nicholas II and Empress Alexandra Romanov. Alexis was also afflicted with hemophilia, a fact that contributed to the 1917 downfall of the royal family, thus affecting the Russian Revolution. Massie's research led to the best-selling biography *Nicholas and Alexandra,* a book highly praised by such critics as S. J. Laut who, writing in *Best Sellers,* described the work as "intimate history at its magnificent best." Remarks Robert Payne in the *New York Times Book Review:* "Massie's canvas is the whole of Russia, the Czar and Czarina merely the focal points. . . . What emerges is a study in depth of the reign of Nicholas, and for perhaps the first time we meet the actors in the drama face to face in their proper setting."

The profits from the book and the successful film adapted from it provided Massie with the time and funds to help his son, Robert, cope with life as a hemophiliac. In 1975 Massie and his wife, Suzanne, chronicled young Bobby's courage in facing his condition, and their own involvement in the boy's life, in the book *Journey.* "The chapters written by Robert tend to deal with technical details," notes Peter Stoler in a *Time* article. "Suzanne concentrates on her personal anguish and the years of caring for Bobby. If she sometimes seems to overwrite, the book proves how thoroughly she has earned the right to do so. Her descriptions of the emotional and physiological effects of hemophilia on exhausted parents, as well as children, are heartrending. Its portrait of Bobby Massie's enduring courage and the decency and devotion of those who helped him makes *Journey* a remarkable human document."

"The substance of the book shifts from the mastery of pain to the mastery of life, and it is done in part by a turning outward in contrast to the Romanovs' [of *Nicholas and Alexandra*] secretiveness and withdrawal," comments *New York Times Book Review* critic Elizabeth Hegeman of *Journey.* She continues: "The authors skillfully weave into their story important information about hemophilia in order to dispel harmful misinformation. They are determined to try to change those American institutions that fail to support the chronically ill."

Indeed, *Journey* contains a harsh indictment of America's "pitifully inadequate health plans, the workings of hospitals and the politics of the Red Cross which, charge the Massies, places the welfare of drug companies above that of hemophilia victims," according to *Newsweek* reviewer Margo Jefferson. Hegeman says that the authors describe "the grotesque folly of trying to raise enough money for the hemophilia society through charity balls and premieres and the inadequacy of the 'patchwork' uncoordinated charities and agencies set up to help special need groups." Massie "points to the subsidized medical care of Army dependents and wasteful Blue Cross policies which insist on in-patient care for reimbursement."

However, notes Hegeman, Robert Massie's "restrained yet passionate condemnation should not be mistaken for a self-serving plea for more money for hemophiliacs. It is the statement of a father who feels guilty over using so much of the precious blood derivative *even though he pays for it,* because he has carefully thought out his connection to society and he knows that something is deeply wrong with our social policy if blood is treated as a commodity to be exchanged for money." "Bobby Massie is more fortunate than most hemophiliacs," summarizes Stoler. "His parents were not wealthy, but they were determined. . . . The result of their efforts—and courage—is obvious." Young Massie was a student at Princeton

University at the time of *Journey's* publication and, despite his condition, he "served as an aide to Scoop Jackson, learned to fly, [swam] more than 1,500 yards a day in college, working out regularly with the swimming team," Stoler remarks. "*Journey* makes hauntingly clear that Bobby's spirit is intact. In a postscript the boy rejects the suggestion, sometimes made to him, that his ordeal has been a blessing in disguise. But he writes, 'If [in] having vanquished braces, bleeding, pain, self-consciousness, boredom, and depression, I have not added in any way to my appreciation of this life that has been given me, then that indeed would be a misfortune to be pitied.'"

Having completed his most personal work, Massie turned back to the rich vein of Russian history with *Peter the Great: His Life and World.* The architect of modern Russia, Peter the Great was an imposing 17th-century figure; obsessed with learning all he could about Western ways, the ruler "sent Russian youths abroad to study arts and crafts unknown in the Russia of his day: shipbuilding in particular. But first he went himself and worked in Dutch and English shipyards as a laborer to learn the shipwright's trade. He set up medical schools and learned to perform surgical operations himself. . . . He even carried about with him a set of dentist's instruments which he was always ready to use on his friends, to their understandable alarm. He organized urban fire services—and whenever possible took personal charge of the operations. And he would show visitors his horny hands and point out the obvious moral," as Kyril Fitzlyon relates in the *New York Times Book Review.*

The czar's obsessive characteristics often resulted in the torture of those he saw as standing in the way of progress—among them his son, Alexis. But in the author's view, "Peter was not a sadist," recalls *Newsweek's* Walter Clemons. "Of his earlier presence at the torture of members of a Streltsy [palace guard] revolt, Massie observes: 'To us this seems brutal and degrading; to Peter it seemed necessary. . . . Peter never hesitated to be a participant in the enterprises he commanded, whether on the battlefield, on shipboard, or in the torture chamber. . . . He would not sit back and wait for someone to bring back the news that his command had been obeyed.'"

A London *Times* critic feels that the author's admiration for his subject colors his view of the facts, and remarks that "the urge to show Peter in the best light must spring partly from the relief of writing about a monarch who could, and did, do everything for himself, after devoting so many years to Peter's descendants who, between them, barely seemed able to tie up a ribbon or fasten a stud." And John Leonard, in the *New York Times,* criticizes Massie for the fact that "there is, in [*Peter the Great*], no thesis. . . . Peter's spotty education, his voracious curiosity, his epileptic convulsions, his talent with his hands, his ignorance of literature, his humor and his terror—all are merely reported and forgiven, like the weather."

Clemons is also aware that the author's biography "may draw adverse comment because [Massie] suspends conclusive judgment. He is bewitched by Peter. [But] what he offers is the story, detailed and urgently readable, of a very complicated man." Massie "has by no means written a conventional academic study, to place its subject in accurate scholarly perspective," Condren comments. "Yet his book could serve as a model for what scholarly writing ought to be. He has preeminently brought Peter to life for us. Whether describing his enchantment with youthful war games and shipbuilding or following him through military campaigns in the Balkans and against Sweden, Massie relentlessly pursues the man behind the monarch. His account captivates and enraptures." And to

Fitzlyon, the book's "only serious drawback in the eyes of some readers may be its enormous length [the work runs more than nine hundred pages]. This could have been slightly modified by abridging digressions on the politics and history of countries other than Russia. Nevertheless, it is an enthralling book, beautifully edited, with a first-rate index and excellent illustrations. . . . It would be surprising if it did not become the standard biography of Peter the Great in English for many years to come, as fascinating as any novel and more so than most."

MEDIA ADAPTATIONS: Nicholas and Alexandra was adapted into a film of the same title, and was released by Columbia Pictures in 1971; an adaptation of *Peter the Great* is scheduled by NBC-TV as a ten-hour miniseries.

CA INTERVIEW

CA interviewed Robert K. Massie by telephone on March 7, 1984, at his home in Irvington, New York.

CA: You have lived in the North all of your professional life. Did you consider moving back to the South after you got out of the navy, since your background is Southern?

MASSIE: My father and grandfather were both from Virginia. They had gone to Kentucky because my grandfather was an Episcopal minister and he went to a church there. After I left Oxford, I went into the navy for five years. When I got out, I was twenty-six and married, and my wife was about to have our first child. I was interested in writing. I did actually go back to Nashville, to the *Nashville Tennesseean*, where I was offered a job; but the pay was very low, even by comparison with the junior officer's salary I had been getting in the navy. I didn't see how we could manage it.

I came up to New York looking for a job—in fact, I had about fifty-five interviews, as I recall—and finally got something in a branch of journalism, working for *Collier's*. I was there when it collapsed. Then I went to *Newsweek* and was there for five years. I did book reviews, then wrote foreign news and was the United Nations correspondent. Then I went to the *Saturday Evening Post*, where I was a contract writer; I wrote eight articles a year—political profiles and that kind of thing. While I was still there, I began working on *Nicholas and Alexandra*.

CA: In Journey *(1975), you and your wife wrote about your son's hemophilia. With the difficulty and worry involved in coping with that, was it hard for you to write?*

MASSIE: Bobby was born the first summer I was working, and we didn't discover he had hemophilia until the following winter, just about a week after I began at *Newsweek*. It wasn't easy, but it was harder for my wife; she was also a journalist, and she had to stay home. Life was very iffy. We didn't have much money and medical care was expensive. Yes, there were a lot of problems.

CA: Your son graduated from Princeton and then from Yale Divinity School. Where is he now?

MASSIE: He's now married and is one of several ministers at Grace Church in New York City. He will probably be going back to get a Ph.D. in ethics.

CA: Have conditions improved for hemophiliacs in the years since Journey *was published?*

MASSIE: There's been very little change medically, no real advance in treatment. They still use the fraction that came out in 1968. Most hemophiliacs treat themselves once they reach a certain age. This gives them a great deal more mobility and gives their life a different dimension. As far as money is concerned, the patchwork quilt we have in America for caring for people hasn't become any more logical. But there is the Medicaid program at the bottom, which helps people who couldn't even begin to afford help. The people who are still exposed are those in the middle, the people who aren't on welfare or in a very low income group. There are various state programs that help somewhat.

CA: Journey must have helped to educate a lot of people.

MASSIE: I believe it has. Certainly the Red Cross's first reaction to the book was hostile. I heard there was talk of a lawsuit. I was shown an advisory that went around when the book came out, advising all the local Red Cross chapters to pay special attention if the Massies should come to town hawking their book. But only two or three years later I was invited to be a speaker at the Red Cross national convention. We made our peace. A few of the senior administrative staff were still angry, but I said in my speech, "The reason we're upset is that you collect the best blood in the country, and that's fine. But you could do better."

CA: Prices for blood fractions were very high, weren't they?

MASSIE: They were; they still are. The problem with this whole thing is the overall high price of medical care, which makes everybody back off and say, we can't do any better. Modern technology has produced these two-million- and four-million-dollar machines that every hospital thinks it has to have. I'm very concerned about this. I no longer believe that we can just reorganize medical care by having the federal government do it all. We must achieve better distribution of medical services, and we must also put some kind of cap on medical expenses. Perhaps we can't afford optimum care for everybody for every disease. This poses an enormous problem in ethics as well as in economics.

CA: According to what you said in the preface to Nicholas and Alexandra, *you wrote that book because of your son. Did you have an interest in Russian history before that?*

MASSIE: No, not at all. I knew what I suppose everybody knows about Rasputin, the stereotype, but I had no real interest whatever in the history of Russia.

CA: You had just looked into history to find cases similar to your son's?

MASSIE: Yes. When something unusual happens in your life, you are curious to see what has happened before. We were busy trying to find out how to deal with this disease, talking to a lot of other families, to doctors and social workers and people like that about hemophilia in mid-twentieth-century America. But I knew a bit of the story of the Tsarevich Alexis and I was curious to find out how his family had dealt with it, what was all this business about hypnotism and so forth. So I started doing a lot of reading at the New York Public Library.

There was no thought of a book; I was just curious to know what had happened. I read whatever I could find and I began to notice a discrepancy. The general narrative historians swept pretty quickly by this whole business of the boy's illness with a sentence or two. I found that it was much more complicated than that. The links that even I could find, with very little background in the field, between the illness and what was happening politically were very much in evidence and were important.

But I sat on it. Bobby was born in 1956, and I didn't start the book until '64. What happened actually was that I had done a couple of articles on the state of Mississippi in 1962. Then James Meredith was introduced into the University of Mississippi's law school by five hundred U.S. Marshals and the 82nd Airborne Division. I was down there covering that and had proposed a book on it. I was all set to begin writing when my publisher found out that Walter Lord, who was a very well-known writer, was also doing it. So my publisher, I suppose wisely, said he didn't want to publish an unknown Mr. Massie on the same subject that the well-known Mr. Lord was writing about, and asked me if there was anything else I'd like to do. I said tentatively that I would like someday to tackle the whole question of hemophilia in the Russian imperial family and its connection with what happened politically. They encouraged me to write a proposal, which I did. They asked me how long I thought it would take; I said a year, perhaps. So they gave me a tiny handful of money and I started. And of course a year later I was still working at the *Post* and trying to dovetail the two lives. The more I learned, the more excited I got.

CA: Did you consider learning Russian while you were doing research for the book?

MASSIE: Yes, but the splendid thing—the gratuitous thing—at that point was finding out that Nicholas and Alexandra, who wrote to each other practically every day when they were apart, wrote to each other in English. Alexandra was German, but her mother died when she was very little and she spent a lot of time in England. Most of the Anglo-German royal family spoke both languages. So Alexandra's English was that of an Englishwoman, and of course Russian wasn't very easy for her. Nicholas had been trained in German, French, and English as well as Russian. Alexandra did learn Russian as she went along. But their correspondence is in English, which made it much easier for me.

Also, most of the government documents have been translated, and most of the memorabilia that I used was from the memoirs of people who got away and published books either in French or English right after the Revolution. On top of that, I had somebody translate Russian material for me. But then I went to Russia with my wife, and I began to learn how to speak railway-station Russian and to read it in a simple way.

CA: Did you do much of the actual research in Russia?

MASSIE: Not for *Nicholas and Alexandra*, no. This was back in the '60s. Nicholas was then—and still is—very much a political rather than a historical figure. The story is still loaded with counterrevolutionary tones. For example, when we went to see the palace at Yalta in 1967, we weren't actually able to get in; it was a sanitarium. Why are you so interested, people asked. We said it was because that was where President Roosevelt and Mr. Churchill and Mr. Stalin met. Now the palace is open and the connection with the family is acknowledged. They have made some progress in admitting their history.

CA: I understand you weren't altogether happy with the film. What were your objections?

MASSIE: I felt it could have been better. Of course it could have been much worse. But there was a lack of Russianness about it. It was filmed in Spain, and I thought that showed. The "Russians" standing around all had long, thin faces and soulful black eyes rather than high cheekbones. The script was very wooden. My feeling was that they tried to do too much. They tried to cover not only the story of the family in three hours, but the whole of the Revolution. Scenes were cut, and I thought it was jerky and spiritless.

Then I had problems with the producer, Sam Spiegel, because he said that I was going to be very much involved, but as soon as I signed the contract it was goodbye. I saw the script only two years later, when the actress who played the empress—who was horrified to hear that I hadn't seen it—showed it to me. It was filled with errors. I sat down and wrote Mr. Spiegel a letter saying that the errors having to do with hemophilia were really unacceptable. Here's a film taken from a book that makes a major point about the importance of hemophilia in the relationship between the boy and Rasputin and the empress, and between the empress and her husband, and on Rasputin's effect on policy.

There's no scene in the film in which Rasputin is with the boy. There *was* a scene, but medically speaking, it was all wrong: the child is bleeding and Rasputin comes in and performs a miracle; the boy straightens his bleeding arm and gets up and plays the balalaika. This is absurd. So they just cut it and didn't bother to reshoot it. I learned something about the movie business—how much money is wasted on perks. A producer puts himself on an expense account for three and a half years and drives around in Rolls Royces. But they can't reshoot an important scene.

And we had a major fight, which you may have read about in *Journey*, about the premiers. At the time I was very worked up about it; I don't know if I'd do the same thing now. But here was a film based on a factual story that revolved around a disease, and the premieres were given to medical charities that had nothing to do with that disease, simply because people involved with hemophilia weren't social enough.

CA: Did Peter the Great *grow out of the interest you developed during the writing of* Nicholas and Alexandra?

MASSIE: Yes. As I said earlier, I really didn't know much about Russian history in the beginning. While I was working on *Nicholas and Alexandra,* I was giving myself a course and reading as much as I could. I was fascinated by Peter. There were glimpses of his character, stories and legends about him, but I couldn't find any biography which really captured him. After thinking about it for a while, I thought I could try one.

CA: You spent some time in Russia working on Peter the Great. *What was it like working there?*

MASSIE: I went quite often—I guess now I've been twelve or thirteen times. Of course Peter was a subject the Russians were enthusiastic about. I applied for and received official and scholarly and other help and toured around meeting various people. I remember walking the Poltava battlefield with a wonderful young student. It wasn't like doing research in the West, because Russia is a different country. I had no problem. And I was surprised, because, even though *Nicholas and Alexandra* was well known by then from tourists bringing it in and its having been passed around hand-to-hand and copied, nevertheless I still encountered no problems.

CA: Do you think there's a good market for biography now in this country?

MASSIE: Excellent. I taught a course at Tulane in 1981, and I'm ninety-nine percent sure I'm going to be doing a version of that this fall at Yale. Students in high school and college don't have much to do with biography, because history professors don't have time to stop and examine the life of any single person. They're trying to cover a lot of ground quickly, so they stick to narrative texts. In literature courses, professors would rather have students read the novels or poems than a life of the writer. But once students graduate, if they continue to read serious nonfiction, it's often in the form of biography, because biography is a splendid mixture of the excitement, the adventure, the challenge of a single life. We're all interested in how people meet the specific challenges they face, and also the context of the life.

CA: Speaking of context, one of the interesting things you did in Peter the Great *was branch off into the lives of such people as Louis XIV and Charles XII, which certainly helped bring Peter's time to life.*

MASSIE: I had to write the kind of book that I like to read, and people have reacted favorably to that. I am happy to have that kind of material on any period, but I thought it was particularly relevant in this book because most people don't have any idea how Russian history relates to anybody else's history before the Revolution, or who was a contemporary of whom. Since a great determining factor of Peter's life was his interest in the West, and his visits to the West galvanized him into doing what he did in Russia, I thought it was essential to bring in these other historical figures. And there was the wonderful comparison—I made it implicit rather than explicit—between Louis XIV and Peter the Great. Not many people realize that they were contemporaries.

In fact, I actually did fifteen or twenty pages on the American colonies at the time of Peter. Harvard was already established, for example. What life was like in Boston, New York, Philadelphia. But even before I got it to my editor, I knew I had a problem of length. I thought, Well, I can justify London, Paris, and Amsterdam, but Boston had very little to do with Peter's life! So those pages are in a folder somewhere, without a home.

CA: In addition to the course at Tulane, you taught a course in nonfiction at Princeton and were obviously successful, judging by the fact that some of your students there are making a living by writing. What's your secret?

MASSIE: They were already very good. I think all I did was encourage them, and also point out some of the pitfalls. The course has a grand title—which I didn't give it—The Literature of Fact. It's usually taught by John McPhee, who is a Princeton institution, but John was off doing his book on Alaska that spring.

Probably because of John's reputation, there were a lot of applications, maybe sixty, and you could take sixteen. These were people submitting work they had already done. I wasn't very democratic. I didn't choose people who needed help the most; I chose those who were already the best. These people

had skills and motivation, and I brought in people from the world of journalism and publishing to give them some guideposts and, as I said, a combination of encouragement and *dis*couragement—it's not fair to get people cranked up and then have them break their hearts for four or five years.

I enjoyed it very much. I plan to incorporate into this biography course at Yale a good deal of writing, and I hope to work it out so that I can spend time with the students going over their work. This is what I would like to have had. It's hard—it takes an enormous amount of time. But it's very valuable. And it's fun for me.

CA: Would you like to comment on the book you're working on now?

MASSIE: It's about the coming of the First World War, specifically in terms of the arms race between England and Germany. It covers 1897 to 1914. It's about the dynasties—Edward VII and the Kaiser—and the problems the Kaiser and the Germans had in feeling inferior to England, and their foolish mistake in challenging British sea power, thus bringing Britain into the alliance structure on the opposite side. It's not, however, as my daughter said, going to be just about boats; it's mostly about people, and the relationship between Germany and England. I'm trying now to rope it in, so to speak. I've done a great deal of reading. I haven't done any writing yet, because I'm trying to reduce it to something manageable.

BIOGRAPHICAL/CRITICAL SOURCES: Time, August 18, 1967; May 19, 1975, November 10, 1980; *New York Times Book Review,* August 20, 1967, May 11, 1975, November 2, 1980, November 16, 1980; *Newsweek,* August 28, 1967, May 26, 1975, October 20, 1980; *Best Sellers,* September 1, 1967; *Publishers Weekly,* September 18, 1967; Robert and Suzanne Massie, *Journey,* Knopf, 1975; *Times Literary Supplement,* March 19, 1967, April 24, 1981; R. Massie, *Peter the Great: His Life and World,* Knopf, 1980; *Saturday Review,* October, 1980; *New York Times,* October 7, 1980; *Atlantic,* November, 1980; *Chicago Tribune Book World,* November 9, 1980; *Washington Post Book World,* November 23, 1980; *New Yorker,* November 24, 1980; *Los Angeles Times Book Review,* November 30, 1980; *Commentary,* December, 1980; *New Republic,* December 27, 1980; *Times* (London), February 5, 1981; *New York Review of Books,* March 19, 1981.

—*Sketch by Susan Salter*

—*Interview by Walter W. Ross*

*   *   *

MATARAZZO, James M. 1941-

PERSONAL: Born January 4, 1941, in Stoneham, Mass.; son of Angelo Michael (a candy-maker) and Anna (Finamore) Matarazzo; married Alice Marie Keohane, September 3, 1966; children: James M., Jr., Susan Eileen. *Education:* Boston College, B.S., 1963, M.A., 1972; Simmons College, M.S., 1965; University of Pittsburgh, Ph.D., 1978. *Home:* 146 Cottage Park Rd., Winthrop, Mass. 02152. *Office:* Graduate School of Library and Information Science, Simmons College, 300 The Fenway, Boston, Mass. 02115.

CAREER: Massachusetts Institute of Technology, Cambridge, assistant science librarian, 1965-67, documents librarian, 1967-68, serials librarian, documents librarian, and head of technical reports, 1968-69; Simmons College, Graduate School of Library and Information Science, Boston, Mass., lecturer, 1968, instructor, 1969-70, assistant professor, 1971-73, associate professor, 1973-80, professor of library science, 1980—, acting assistant director, 1974-75, assistant dean, 1975-79, associate dean, 1979—. Library consultant to corporations, including New England Electric System, Conoco Chemicals Co., Cahnens Publishing Co., and John Hancock Mutual Life Insurance Co. *Member:* Special Libraries Association (president, Boston chapter, 1979-81, member of executive board, 1983-85), American Library Association (member of committee on accreditation, 1979-82, member of council, 1979-87, member of committee on program evaluation and support, 1982-86).

WRITINGS: Library Problems in Science and Technology, Bowker, 1971; (editor with James M. Kyed) *Scientific, Technical, and Engineering Societies: Publications in Print, 1974-75,* Bowker, 1974; (editor) *The Serials Librarian: Acquisitions Case Studies,* Faxon, 1975; (editor with Kyed) *Scientific, Medical, and Engineering Societies: Publications in Print, 1976-77,* Bowker, 1977; (contributor with James G. Williams and Ian I. Mitroff) Allen Kent and Thomas J. Galvin, editors, *Library Resource Sharing,* Dekker, 1977; (contributor with Galvin) E. J. Josey, editor, *The Information Society: Issues and Answers,* Oryx Press, 1978; (contributor with Williams and Evalyn Clough) Kent and Galvin, editors, *The On-Line Revolution in Libraries,* Dekker, 1978; (editor with Kyed) *Scientific, Engineering and Medical Societies: Publications in Print, 1979-80,* Bowker, 1979; (contributor) *Library Education and Resistance to Technology,* U.S. Office of Education, 1980; *Closing the Corporate Library: Case Studies in the Decision-Making Process,* Special Libraries Association, 1981; (editor with Kyed) *Scientific, Engineering and Medical Societies: Publications in Print, 1980-81,* Bowker, 1981. Contributor of articles and reviews to library journals.

WORK IN PROGRESS: Research on corporate libraries and the reasons for their excellence, for Special Libraries Association.

* * *

MATTILL, A(ndrew) J(acob), Jr. 1924-

PERSONAL: Born August 2, 1924, in St. Joseph, Mo.; son of Andrew Jacob (an accountant), and Ruth Florence (Hanne) Mattill; married Mary Elizabeth Bedford, March 31, 1960. *Education:* University of Chicago, B.A. (with honors), 1949; Evangelical Theological Seminary, Naperville, Ill., B.D., 1952; Vanderbilt University, Ph.D., 1959. *Home address:* Route 2, Box 49, Gordo, Ala. 35466-9516.

CAREER: Armour & Co., South St. Joseph, Mo., assistant to paymaster, 1943-45; ordained to ministry of Evangelical United Brethren Church, 1952, transferred ordination and membership to Churches of God in North America, 1966, dropped ordination and membership, 1977, ordained to ministry of Unitarian Universalist Fellowship, Tuscaloosa, Ala., 1979; pastor of Evangelical United Brethren Church, Vassar, Kan., 1952-54; Berry College, Mount Berry, Ga., 1958-62, began as assistant professor, became associate professor of Bible; Livingstone College, Salisbury, N.C., professor of Bible, 1962-65; Winebrenner Theological Seminary, Findlay, Ohio, Bucher Professor of New Testament and registrar, 1965-75; private scholar, engaged in New Testament research on a farm near Gordo, Ala., 1975—.

Part-time minister, Liberty Universalist Church, Louisville, Miss., 1977—, and Unitarian Universalist Fellowship, Tuscaloosa, 1979-84. Substitute letter carrier, U.S. Postal Service,

Gordo, 1979—. *Military service:* U.S. Army, 1945-47; served in France; became sergeant. *Member:* Society of Biblical Literature. *Awards, honors:* Scholarship through New York University for postdoctoral work in Israel, 1959; American Association of Theological Schools grant for sabbatical year in Germany, 1972-73.

WRITINGS: The Wets Are All Wet (booklet), Christian Action League, 1965; (with wife, Mary Elizabeth Mattill) *A Classified Bibliography of Literature on the Acts of the Apostles,* E. J. Brill, 1966; (translator; Paul Feine and Johannes Behm, revisers) W. G. Kuemmel, *Introduction to the New Testament,* 14th revised edition, Abingdon, 1966; *The Church in a Revolutionary World* (booklet), Central Publishing House of the Churches of God in North America, 1968; (contributor) W. W. Gasque and R. P. Martin, editors, *Apostolic History and the Gospel,* Paternoster, 1970; *A Religious Odyssey* (booklet), Scott Recording Laboratory, 1977; (contributor) C. H. Talbert, editor, *Perspectives on Luke-Acts,* Association of Baptist Professors of Religion, 1978; *Luke and the Last Things,* Western North Carolina Press, 1979; *A Christ for These Days,* Church of the Larger Fellowship, 1979; (translator) Albert Schweitzer, *The Problem of the Lord's Supper,* Mercer University Press, 1982; *Jesus and the Last Things,* Flatwoods Free Press, 1983. Author of weekly column, "World of Religion," *Pickens County Advertiser,* 1982-83. Contributor of articles and reviews to religious journals.

WORK IN PROGRESS: Ingersoll Attacks the Bible; A New Faith for a New Age; The Seven Mighty Blows, a book on science and religion.

SIDELIGHTS: A. J. Mattill told *CA* that his current works are "free-thought studies [that] seek to show the inadequacy of traditional religions and set forth the basic elements of a rational religion."

* * *

MAY, William E(ugene) 1928-

PERSONAL: Born May 27, 1928, in St. Louis, Mo.; son of Robert William (an oil company executive) and Katherine (Armstrong) May; married Patricia Ann Keck, October 4, 1958; children: Michael, Mary Patricia, Thomas, Timothy, Patrick, Susan, Kathleen. *Education:* Catholic University of America, B.A., 1950, M.A., 1951; Marquette University, Ph.D., 1968. *Politics:* "Independent, with more democratic than republican leanings." *Religion:* Roman Catholic. *Home:* 4412 Saul Rd., Kensington, Md. 20895. *Office:* Department of Theology, Catholic University of America, Washington, D.C. 20064.

CAREER: Newman Press, Westminster, Md., associate editor, 1954-55; Bruce Publishing Co., Milwaukee, Wis., associate editor, 1955-66, trade book editor-in-chief, 1966-68; Corpus Instrumentorum, Inc., Washington, D.C., editor-in-chief of Corpus Books, 1969-70; Catholic University of America, Washington, D.C., assistant professor of religion, 1971-74, associate professor of moral theology, 1974—.

MEMBER: American Philosophical Association, American Catholic Philosophical Association, Society for Christian Ethics, College Theology Society (chairman of Chicago region, 1968), Fellowship of Catholic Scholars.

AWARDS, HONORS: College Theology Society award, 1971, for best work published by a member, for *Christ in Contemporary Thought;* Cardinal Wright Award for contributions to Catholic thought, Fellowship of Catholic Scholars, 1980; Thomas

Linaire Award, National Federation of Catholic Physicians Guilds, 1983.

WRITINGS—Published by Franciscan Herald, except as indicated: *Christ in Contemporary Thought*, Pflaum, 1970; (editor) Jopseh Fletcher and Thomas Wassmer, *Hello, Lovers!*, Corpus Publications, 1970; *Becoming Human: An Invitation to Christian Ethics*, Pflaum, 1975; *The Meaning and Nature of Chastity*, 1976; *Human Existence, Medicine, and Ethics*, 1977; *Sex, Love, and Procreation*, 1977; *The Unity of the Moral and Spiritual Life*, 1978; *Sex, Marriage, and Chastity*, 1981; (editor) *Principles of Catholic Moral Life*, 1981; *Sex and the Sanctity of Human Life*, Christendom Publications, 1984. Contributor to periodicals, including *American Journal of Jurisprudence, Homilectic and Pastoral Review, Communio*, and *Linacre Quarterly*.

WORK IN PROGRESS: Studies in Natural Law.

*   *   *

McCAIG, Donald   1940-
(Snee McCaig; Steven Ashley, a pseudonym)

PERSONAL: Born 1940, in Butte, Mont.; married; wife's name, Anne (a breeder of Rambouillet sheep). *Education:* Montana State University, B.A.; attended various graduate schools. *Residence:* Williamsville, Va. *Agent:* Knox Burger Associates Ltd., 39½ Washington Sq. S., New York, N.Y. 10012.

CAREER: Writer. Teacher of philosophy at Wayne State University, Detroit, Mich., and University of Waterloo, Waterloo, Ontario, in the mid-1960s; copywriter and copychief for advertising agencies in Detroit and New York, N.Y., including Gilbert Advertising and Young & Rubicam; producer of "Murray the K's" rock-and-roll radio show, American Broadcasting Co. (ABC-Radio); sheep and hay crop farmer in Highland County, Va. Organizer and first chief of a volunteer fire department in Highland County.

MEMBER: P.E.N., United States Border Collie Club, Virginia Border Collie Association (president).

WRITINGS—Novels, except as indicated: (Under pseudonym Steven Ashley) *Caleb, Who Is Hotter than a Two-Dollar Pistol*, McKay, 1975; (under name Snee McCaig) *Last Poems* (poetry), Alternative Press, 1975; (under pseudonym Steven Ashley) *Stalking Blind*, Dial, 1976; *The Butte Polka*, Rawson, Wade, 1980; *Nop's Trials* (Book-of-the-Month Club alternate selection), Crown, 1984. Also author of numerous novels under undisclosed pseudonyms. Contributor to periodicals, including *Harper's, Atlantic*, and *Blair and Ketchum's Country Journal*.

WORK IN PROGRESS: A book on training Border Collies, with sheepdog trainer Jack Knox.

SIDELIGHTS: With "a face the color of beefsteak, hands like knots on a tree, and blond-turning-gray sideburns that [remind] you of honeysuckle patches clamoring to be cut back," Donald McCaig looks more like a backwoods farmer than a New York City adman-turned-novelist, according to Isaac Rehert in the *Baltimore Sun*. McCaig has, in fact, abandoned a "fast lane" advertising career to farm and write on his 18th-century homestead in mountainous western Virginia. There, he and his wife Anne raise Rambouillet sheep and harvest alfalfa for hay. McCaig also has cultivated a literary crop of three suspense novels, a book of poetry, an unspecified number of genre works under pseudonyms, and a novel about a man and his farm dog that Roy E. Perry, writing in the *Nashville Banner*, claims "has all the earmarks of a classic."

McCaig's suspense novels—*Caleb, Who Is Hotter than a Two-Dollar Pistol, Stalking Blind*, and *The Butte Polka*—unfold largely in rural communities quite different from the cement jungles usually associated with crime fiction. Reviewers consistently note the author's ability to portray rural places and populations without lapsing into generalities or caricature. McCaig "knows his country people, and successfully manages to give the feeling of the rugged individualists who live a little apart from urban civilization," says Newgate Callendar, who calls *Stalking Blind* "curiously absorbing and sensitive" in the *New York Times Book Review*. Norma B. Hawes, assessing *The Butte Polka* in *National Review*, likewise commends the novelist's "raw vitality and gritty realism" in an "essentially grim tale set in a grim climate." Critics attribute a large part of McCaig's achievement to his spare, bare-bones prose. "The language throughout [*The Butte Polka*] is raw," notes Susan M. Wilcox in *Library Journal*. A *New Yorker* critic adds that McCaig's protagonist "tells the story in short, tough sentences that convey precisely how his anger and his grief are barely restrained by stoicism," and concludes that *Butte* is "a powerful performance."

Despite such critical approval, it wasn't until publication of the dog story, *Nop's Trials*, that McCaig's writings brought him tangible fame and fortune. In fact when *Caleb*, McCaig's first suspense novel, sold a few thousand copies, the author bragged to a fellow farmer, "Last year we made about as much money writing as we lost on the sheep," and the neighbor replied, "I had the same kind of year, but I didn't do no writing," as James Conaway reports in the *Washington Post*. Conaway labels McCaig's sudden success "one of the most dramatic reversals of fortune in recent publishing history, making McCaig the richest subsistence farmer in Highland County." McCaig accounts for the book's success by telling John F. Baker of *Publishers Weekly* that "*Nop* was an easy book to write, a natural, and because no one else is doing anything like it, it fell right into a vacant spot with a clunk."

While a *People* writer characterizes *Nop's Trials* as "a kind of *Lassie* meets *Watership Down*," combining an old-fashioned dog story with the anthropomorphism associated with Richard Adams's work, most critics agree that McCaig has brought his canine and human characters up-to-date, creating an animal story that deals with more complex personalities and issues than those usually embraced by the genre. Notes Edmund Fuller of the *Wall Street Journal*: "The dog story is a genre in itself, from writers as varied as Jack London and Albert Payson Terhune, to be judged by other than purely literary standards. The popular and admired James Herriot calls 'Nop's Trials' a masterly work of its kind. Time will test that, but at the least it is very good in its class, and deserves the success it is likely to have." Many other reviewers approach the story cautiously, remembering the "talking animal" stories read in their youth, and discover that this dog story is, in many ways, different. "They expected, perhaps, a mawkish story and were pleasantly surprised," believes Connie Lauerman, writing in the *Chicago Tribune*. Dannye Romine agrees in his *Charlotte Observer* review that the book is more than he expected, calling *Nop* "a man-loves-dog, man-loses-dog, man-gets-dog-back novel that's surprisingly irresistible."

The novel's plot, although more complex than Romine's summary suggests, does center on the kidnapping, subsequent tribulations, and eleventh-hour rescue of a working Border Collie named Nop. Not yet in his prime, the sheepdog has exhibited exceptional promise in stockdog trials as well as at home on Louis Burkholder's farm. A jealous competitor, drowning his sorrows in a local dive after losing to Nop and Burkholder, lets it be known that he'd pay handsomely for the assurance that the young Border Collie would not beat his dogs in future sheepdog trials. Two redneck crooks take him at his word and, when the opportunity presents itself, steal the basically trusting dog. Nop's gentle yet stoic nature is tested as he passes through the hands of a rodeo roustabout, a bag lady, animal shelter employees, and an assortment of villains. The dog's heroism, unlike that of Lassie or Rin Tin Tin, stems from his drive and talent for survival. He performs no spectacular acts of bravery, such as saving children from burning buildings. Instead, he adapts to the sometimes horrible situations he finds himself in, looks for the good in the humans he encounters, and is prepared, always, to do that for which his breed was bred—to work for man.

Critics praise McCaig's characterizations, both human and canine. "What Donald McCaig has done so well here is to intertwine Nop's story with that of his master, Louis Burkholder, a stock farmer in the Blue Ridge country of Virginia," Bruce Cook states in the *Detroit News*. Although Louis has family and farm troubles to contend with, he is obsessed with finding his dog. "Burkholder is struggling to accept his new son-in-law, his wife is trying to keep peace in the family, and his pregnant daughter wants her father and new husband to like one another," explains Mary Ann Grossman in the *St. Paul Dispatch*. Pitting Burkholder's loyalty to his dog against his love and responsibilities toward his family gives the novel an added dimension, as several reviewers note. While Fuller finds it initially difficult to accept the split in Louis's characterization, he admits that it enriches the book in the end. Cook continues: "[Burkholder's] are ordinary problems, but very real human problems, and [the author] handles them in a realistic, respectful way that says he knows something about the devious indirections of the human psyche. All his characters ring true, and they come from a broad spectrum of society—from millionaires to shopping bag ladies." In addition to the villians and the family members, McCaig presents a city police detective, an assortment of sheepdog trainers and handlers (many of whom are real or based on real people), and even an autistic child for whom tears represent a breakthrough in acknowledging and communicating with the world around him. McCaig tells Lauerman that it is "a sweet story, but not a sentimental story. . . . And the people are like most people. They've got a son-in-law who hasn't got a way of making a living. They've got a marriage that was pretty exciting for a time, and now it's kind of flat."

Discussing the dogs in the book, Fuller notes that "the central problem of all animal stories is the inescapable element of anthropomorphism. In the psychology of his dogs, as seen in the thoughts attributed to them, Mr. McCaig is convincing." The author tells Conaway that he "wanted to have [the dogs] talk in the book, because they do talk. But it's hard to make a language out of shrugs and eye movements. These are very ritualistic, formal dogs. If they spoke, they might use something like Mandarin Chinese, or Elizabethan English." So McCaig set the canine speech apart from that of humans by giving his dogs a very proper-sounding vocabulary filled with "thees" and "thous." "One reason his canine speeches work is simply that McCaig has put dogs' non-verbal, usually ritual and entirely natural communication with each other and other animals into words," writes Beaufort Cranford in the *Detroit News*. "It's easy, for example, to imagine one dog greeting another by bragging about himself, as they often do here, because dogs obviously do that." Robert W. Smith summarizes

in the Cleveland *Plain Dealer:* "Seldom does an animal book for adults come along that makes one want to shout. This is one. . . . [It] will remind readers of such classics as Walter de la Mare's *The Three Royal Monkeys* and Richard Jefferies' *Bevis*. Though it lacks their artistry, McCaig has given it something they didn't have. 'All the thoughts of a turtle,' wrote [Ralph Waldo] Emerson, 'are turtle.' McCaig's dogs think, act, and talk dog—not human. McCaig is also better able to show the interaction of animal and man." Talking to the author about the authenticity of his dog characters, Baker notes that "one of the unforgettable canine characters in the book is called the Stink Dog, who is badly injured defending [her] master against a rampaging cow but survives to take part in another sheepdog trial. 'A true story,' McCaig insists. 'You know, if you're going to toy with people's hearts, you've got to have your facts straight.'"

McCaig investigated the facts behind dog stealing, animal control, and the use of former pets for laboratory experimentation before relating the grim realities in *Nop*. His descriptions of kennel and lab conditions are based, Cranford reports, on newspaper accounts. When Nop's trials become so degrading that he finds himself en route to a small laboratory facility, packed into a foul van with assorted other dogs, the canine hero states very simply McCaig's philosophical view on the respective responsibilities of dog and man. McCaig tells a *Charlotte Observer* critic that "we need to enter into a contract with a dog when we own it. We ask that the dog give up his freedom and be loyal to us. In return, says McCaig, the dog asks of us that we keep him 'in our eyes.' This means literally seeing the dog,' says McCaig." In the novel, the philosophy is stated from Nop's point of view. "If it strikes you as ridiculous that a dog would wax . . . philosophical—or that he would address his fellow dogs in what sounds like the speech of old-time Quakers . . .—then you have a measure of what Donald McCaig has pulled off in this irresistibly compelling story," Christopher Lehmann-Haupt contends in the *New York Times*. "In context, [his] heightened effects work admirably, so effectively are they counterweighted by the gritty details of life in a rural Virginia neighborhood where the big event of the spring is the barbecue given by the fire department's ladies auxiliary on opening day of the trout season." Fuller concludes: "It is impossible not to love the gallant Nop through all his pain and humiliation. . . . I came to the end of Nop's story with a warm glow of satisfaction. Unless you just don't like dogs I think you will find the same rewards—and you won't soon forget Border Collies."

McCaig admits that Nop is based, at least in part, on his own Border Collie, Pip. Bought to help herd the McCaigs' sheep, Pip introduced the author to the world of stock dog training and handling. McCaig, as he relates to Conaway, became obsessed with training and understanding the dog. "I had a real, live E.T.—an alien mind, but definitely a mind" to interact with, the novelist says. "It's an odd thing to say," McCaig adds in his interview with Lauerman, "but training a dog is an intellectual exercise. You have to read another species' mind. You have to know what the dog is thinking or you can't train him. You sit there and watch the dog and you can see it—it sounds like I'm talking mysticism to you and I'm not."

"Border Collies predate the British Kennel Club," he tells Conaway. "They've been bred consistently for 100 years, they're the last working dogs in the world, with some minor exceptions. Bench shows [dog shows] have ruined the other breeds, like the hunting dogs. Border Collies are peasant dogs, and that's protected them." The author explains in *Blair and Ket-*

chum's Country Journal: "A good stock dog can replace three men loading hogs, will fetch your milk cows morning and evening, can pluck goats out of the thicket and sort sheep. Stock dogs improve your poor fences, substitute for good handling facilities, and stabilize your blood pressure when your deaf neighbor's forty cows have busted through the watergate and are standing in your newly planted alfalfa, chowing down. . . . If you do your part of the job, likely your dog will do his. Working a good dog can be lovely: a real connection with an alien mind. One December evening you'll go out to bring in the bred ewes, and it'll be driving snow, and those hummocks way at the far end of the pasture might be sheep and might not too, and the light will be failing. Quietly, you send your dog into the dusk where its knowledge and heart will bring your sheep safely home. That's why stock dogs have one-syllable names: Ben, Nell, Pip, Lass, Cap, Hope. You can cry their names into the teeth of the wind."

Devoted to the Border Collie breed, McCaig worries that his portrayal of Nop's finer qualities will encourage readers to buy Border Collies as pets. "If this [book] has persuaded you to buy a Border Collie for a pet, I'd like to offer a caution," McCaig writes in a note to readers at the back of *Nop's Trials.* "Border Collies are very bright, quick and more than a little weird. They are not suitable for most city apartments. Their working instincts are strong and their self-esteem comes from working well. A bored, mishandled Border Collie can get into awful trouble." Although a member of the United States Border Collie Club and president of the Virginia Border Collie Association, McCaig also emphasizes that he's still a novice where sheepdog training and handling are concerned. When Baker asks the author how his colleagues and mentors feel "about the possibility of a bestselling book on their passionate avocation," McCaig states simply: "They don't have a problem. I write a better book than they do. But they train a better dog than I do."

MEDIA ADAPTATIONS: Film rights to *Nop's Trials* have been sold to producer Martin Bregman.

BIOGRAPHICAL/CRITICAL SOURCES: New York Times Book Review, January 16, 1977; *Library Journal,* March 1, 1980; *Publishers Weekly,* June 13, 1980, April 6, 1984; *National Review,* September 5, 1980; *New Yorker,* October 13, 1980; *Atlantic,* February, 1981; *Sports Illustrated,* April 27, 1981; *Washington Post,* March 26, 1984; *Nashville Banner,* March 31, 1984; *Book and Author Magazine,* March/April, 1984; *Sun* (Baltimore), April 8, 1984; *Detroit News,* April 8, 1984, May 2, 1984; *New York Times,* April 12, 1984; *Wall Street Journal,* April 17, 1984; *Charlotte Observer,* April 23, 1984; *St. Paul Dispatch,* May 1, 1984; *Plain Dealer* (Cleveland), May 13, 1984; *Chicago Tribune,* May 15, 1984; *Los Angeles Times Book Review,* June 3, 1984; *People,* June 4, 1984.†

—*Sketch by Nancy Hebb*

*   *   *

McCAIG, Snee
See McCAIG, Donald

*   *   *

McCALL, Robert B(ooth)   1940-

PERSONAL: Born June 21, 1940, in Milwaukee, Wis.; son of John I. (a metallurgist) and Blanche (Booth) McCall; married

Rozanne Allison (a remedial reading specialist), June 13, 1962; children: Darin, Stacey. *Education:* DePauw University, A.B., 1962; University of Illinois, M.A., 1964, Ph.D., 1965. *Office:* Boys Town Center, Boys Town, Neb. 68010.

CAREER: University of North Carolina at Chapel Hill, assistant professor of psychology, 1966-68; Antioch College, Yellow Springs, Ohio, associate professor of psychology, 1968-77; Fels Research Institute, Yellow Springs, senior scientist and chairman of department of psychology, 1968-71, chief of section on perceptual cognitive development, 1971-77; Boys Town, Boys Town, Neb., senior scientist and science writer, 1977—.

MEMBER: American Association for the Advancement of Science, American Psychological Association (fellow), Society for Research in Child Development, Phi Beta Kappa.

AWARDS, HONORS: National Science Foundation post-doctoral fellow, Harvard University, 1965-66.

WRITINGS: (Author of student guide and programmed units with Lane K. Conn, Jr.) Jerome Kagan and Ernest Havemann, *Psychology: An Introduction,* Harcourt, 1968, 2nd edition (with Havemann) published as *Study Guide with Programmed Units to Accompany Kagan and Havemann's "Psychology: An Introduction,"* 1972, 3rd edition published as *Study Guide with Programmed Units and Learning Objectives to Accompany Kagan and Havemann's "Psychology: An Introduction,"* 1976, 5th edition (with Havemann and J. Segal), 1984; *Fundamental Statistics for Psychology,* Harcourt, 1970, 3rd edition, 1980; (with Kagan) *Change and Continuity in Infancy,* Wiley, 1971; *Intelligence and Heredity,* Learning Systems Co., 1975; *Infants: The New Knowledge,* Harvard University Press, 1979.

Contributor: P. Mussen, editor, *Manual of Child Psychology,* Wiley, 1970, 4th edition, 1983; Dwain N. Walcher and Donald L. Peters, editors, *Early Childhood: The Development of Self-regulatory Mechanisms,* Academic Press, 1971; M. Lewis, editor, *Origins of Intelligence,* Plenum, 1976, 2nd edition, 1983; I. C. Uzgiris and F. Weizmann, editors, *The Structuring of Experience,* Plenum, 1977; J. D. Osofsky, editor, *Handbook of Infant Development,* Wiley, 1979; M. H. Bornstein and W. Kessen, editors, *Psychological Development from Infancy,* Erlbaum, 1979. Contributor and member of editorial board, *Monographs of the Society of Research in Child Development.* Contributing editor, monthly columnist, and feature writer, *Parents,* 1980—. Contributor of articles and reviews to *Journal of Experimental Child Psychology, Child Development, Developmental Psychology, Science, American Psychologist, Journal of Comparative and Physiological Psychology* and other publications. Member of editorial board, *Child Development Journal, Journal of Experimental Child Psychology, Intelligence, Developmental Psychology, Infant Behavior and Development,* and *Journal of Applied Developmental Psychology.*

*   *   *

McCANTS, Olga   1901-
(Sister Dorothea Olga McCants)

PERSONAL: Born November 10, 1901, in Magnolia, Miss.; daughter of Robert Sidney (an architect and contractor) and Daisy (Coney) McCants. *Education:* St. Vincent College, teacher's life certificate, 1923; Our Lady of the Lake College (now University), A.B., 1929; Loyola University, New Orleans, La., M.A., 1934; Catholic University of America, M.A.,

1941; also attended George Peabody College for Teachers, Louisiana State University, Laval University, and University of Wisconsin—Madison. *Home:* 1000 Fairview, Shreveport, La. 71104. *Office:* Daughters of the Cross Convent, 1000 Fairview, Shreveport, La. 71104.

CAREER: Roman Catholic nun of Daughters of the Cross, 1920—; name in religion, Sister Dorothea Olga McCants; St. Vincent Academy and College, Shreveport, La., faculty member in education, 1921-41, principal, 1941-43; principal of Presentation High School, Marksville, La., 1943-47; teacher in Roman Catholic high school in Monroe, La., 1947-63; Marillac College for Young Sisters, St. Louis, Mo., faculty member in education and Latin, 1964-66; Daughters of the Cross Convent, Shreveport, La., archivist, 1970—.

MEMBER: National League of American Pen Women, Louisiana Historical Society, Louisiana Outdoor Drama Association, North Louisiana Historical Association, Historic Preservation (Shreveport). *Awards, honors:* Medallion Award from Louisiana Library Association, 1970, for *They Came to Louisiana.*

*WRITINGS—*Under name Sister Dorothea Olga McCants: (Editor and translator) *They Came to Louisiana* (collection of French historical letters), Louisiana University Press, 1970, 2nd edition with pictorial supplement, Daughters of the Cross Publications, 1983; (translator) Rodolphe Desdunes, *Our People and Our History,* Louisiana State University Press, 1973; *With Valor They Serve,* Claitors, 1975; (translator from French) G. F. de Beauvais, *The Establishment and Growth of the Daughters of the Cross,* Daughters of the Cross Publications, 1975; *Chalkdust and Pencil Shavings,* Daughters of the Cross, 1981.

Also author of religious pamphlets. Contributor to *Catholic Youth Encyclopedia* and *Dictionary of Religious Institutes.* Contributor of over thirty articles and reviews to religious periodicals. Contributing editor of *Vexilla Regis,* 1949-54.

BIOGRAPHICAL/CRITICAL SOURCES: New Orleans States, February 19, 1970, February 20, 1970.

*   *   *

McCANTS, Sister Dorothea Olga
See McCANTS, Olga

*   *   *

McCLELLAND, Doug 1934-

PERSONAL: Born July 16, 1934, in Plainfield, N.J.; son of William Vincent and Elna (Whitlock) McClelland. *Education:* Attended Newark, N.J. public schools. *Home:* 704 Madison Ave., Bradley Beach, N.J. 07720.

CAREER: Office boy for *Newark Star-Ledger,* Newark, N.J., during late 1940s; *Newark Evening News,* Newark, arts editor, 1953-56; *Record World Magazine,* New York, N.Y., editor, 1961-72. Lecturer on motion pictures.

WRITINGS: The Unkindest Cuts, A. S. Barnes, 1972; (contributor) *The Real Stars,* Curtis Publishing, 1973; *Susan Hayward: The Divine Bitch,* Pinnacle, 1973; *Down the Yellow Brick Road,* Pyramid Publications, 1976; *The Golden Age of "B" Movies,* Charterhouse, 1978; (contributor) *Hollywood Kids,* Popular Library, 1978; *Hollywood on Ronald Reagan,* Faber & Faber, 1983; *Hollywood on Hollywood,* Faber & Faber, 1985.

Contributor to *Encyclopedia Year Book, 1969.* Contributor of articles to *After Dark, Films and Filming, Films in Review, Filmograph, Screen Facts,* and *The Many Worlds of Music.* Author of jacket notes for record albums.

SIDELIGHTS: Doug McClelland's *Hollywood on Ronald Reagan* presents more than 300 quotations from people who knew Reagan during his movie-making days. The book "provides intriguing and valuable portraits, but those wishing more will remain dissatisfied" because the author's questions do not probe deeply enough, writes Lary May in the *Los Angeles Times Book Review.* May concludes, "This portrait provides valuable clues, but few answers to the identity of the real Ronald Reagan."

BIOGRAPHICAL/CRITICAL SOURCES: Los Angeles Times Book Review, October 16, 1983.

*   *   *

McCORMICK, (George) Donald (King) 1911-
(Richard Deacon)

PERSONAL: Born December 9, 1911, in Rhyl, Wales; son of Thomas Burnside (a journalist) and Lillie Louise (King) McCormick; married Rosalind Deirdre Buchanan Scott, 1934 (divorced); married Sylvia Doreen Cade, 1947 (deceased); married Eileen Dee Challinor James, 1963; children: Anthony Stuart McCormick. *Education:* Attended Oswestry School. *Politics:* Non-party. *Home:* 8 Barry Court, 36 Southend Rd., Beckenham, Kent, BR3 2AD England.

CAREER: Has worked at a variety of jobs on numerous provincial and British national newspapers, 1931-39; *Gibraltar Chronicle,* Gibraltar, Spain, editor, 1946; Kemsley Newspapers, London, England, foreign correspondent in Northwest Africa, 1946-49, Commonwealth correspondent, 1949-55; *Sunday Times,* London, foreign manager, 1963-73; writer. *Military service:* Royal Navy, 1941-46.

WRITINGS: The Talkative Muse, Lincoln Williams, 1934; *Islands for Sale,* Garnett, 1949; *Mr. France,* Jarrolds, 1955; *The Wicked City: An Algerian Adventure,* Jarrolds, 1956; *The Hell-Fire Club: The Story of the Amorous Knights of Wycombe,* Jarrolds, 1958; *The Mystery of Lord Kitchener's Death,* Putnam, 1959; *The Identity of Jack the Ripper,* Jarrolds, 1959, revised edition, John Long, 1970.

The Incredible Mr. Kavanagh, Putnam, 1960, Devin-Adair, 1962; *The Wicked Village,* Jarrolds, 1960; *The Temple of Love,* Jarrolds, 1962, Citadel, 1965; *Blood on the Sea: The Terrible Story of the Yawl "Migonette,"* Muller, 1962; *The Mask of Merlin: A Critical Study of David Lloyd George,* Macdonald & Co., 1963, published in America as *The Mask of Merlin: A Critical Biography of David Lloyd George,* Holt, 1964; *The Unseen Killer: A Study of Suicide, Its History, Causes and Cures,* Muller, 1964; *Peddler of Death: The Life and Times of Sir Basil Zaharoff,* Holt, 1965 (published in England as *Pedlar of Death: The Life of Sir Basil Zaharoff,* Macdonald & Co., 1965); *The Red Barn Mystery: Some New Evidence on an Old Murder,* John Long, 1967, A. S. Barnes, 1968; *Murder by Witchcraft: A Study of Lower Quinton and Hagley Wood Murders,* John Long, 1968.

Murder by Perfection: Maundy Gregory, the Man behind Two Unsolved Murders, John Long, 1970; *One Man's Wars: The Story of Charles Sweeney, Soldier of Fortune,* Arthur Barker, 1972; *How to Buy an Island,* David & Charles, 1973; *The*

Master Book of Spies (young-adult book), Watts, 1974; *Islands of England & Wales: A Guide to 138 English & Welsh Islands,* Osprey, 1974; *Islands of Scotland: A Guide to 247 Scottish Islands,* Osprey, 1974; *Islands of Ireland: A Guide to 110 Irish Islands,* Osprey, 1974; *The Master Book of Escapades* (young-adult book), Watts, 1975; *Taken for a Ride: The History of Cons & Conmen,* Harwood-Smart, 1976; *Who's Who in Spy Fiction,* Taplinger, 1977; *Approaching 1984,* David & Charles, 1980; *Love in Code,* Methuen, 1980.

Under pseudonym Richard Deacon; nonfiction, except as indicated; published by Muller, except as indicated: *The Private Life of Mr. Gladstone,* 1966; *Madoc and the Discovery of America,* 1967, Braziller, 1968; *John Dee,* 1968; *A History of the British Secret Service,* 1969, Taplinger, 1970; *A History of the Russian Secret Service,* Taplinger, 1972; *The Chinese Secret Service,* 1974 (published in England as *A History of the Chinese Secret Service,* 1974); *William Caxton: The First English Editor,* 1976; *Matthew Hopkins: Witchfinder-General,* 1976; *The Book of Fate: Its Origins and Uses,* 1976; *The Israeli Secret Service,* Hamish Hamilton, 1977, Taplinger, 1978; *The British Connection,* Hamish Hamilton, 1977; *Spy!,* B.B.C. Publications, 1979; *Escape,* B.B.C. Publications, 1980; *A History of the Japanese Secret Service,* 1982, published in America as *Kempei Tai: A History of the Japanese Secret Service,* Beaufort, 1983; *With My Little Eye,* 1982; *Ziba: A Do-It-Yourself Romance* (novel), 1983.

SIDELIGHTS: Donald McCormick told *CA:* "I have—on the principle that it helps to save one from getting stale—switched from one type of nonfiction to another in my books. My first book, *The Talkative Muse,* was a youthfully pretentious dialogue between two friends in the form of essays on a wide range of subjects. A passion for islands has led me to write *Islands for Sale, How to Buy an Island,* and three books on the islands surrounding England, Wales, Scotland and Ireland, large and small. I have also become fascinated in studying the histories of the secret services of the world. I was prompted to tackle the British Secret Service first as a result of doing a biography of John Dee, astrologer to Queen Elizabeth I, who was also a secret agent. Then I found that down the ages there were frequent links between the British and Russian secret services. Not just the notorious Philby link, but that of the quadruple agent, Sidney Reilly, and the fact that Catherine the Great stayed up late at night to decipher messages for the British Ambassador. I then switched to the Chinese secret service largely as a challenge because everybody said it was an impossible subject. I found they had a text book on espionage way back in the fourth century B.C. Finally, I got down to the subject of the Israeli secret service because it seemed to me to be the youngest, smallest and yet most efficient in the whole world and very much part and parcel of the gallant little nation's fight for survival—perhaps a lesson for all of us.

"In the end espionage becomes something of an inescapable obsession. One escapes from it for a time to do another type of book and then, out of one's network of contacts all over the world, a new slant on it presents itself. Lo and behold, there is another book! What fascinated me most about working on *Who's Who in Spy Fiction* was the constantly recurring links between fact and fiction. . . . This is so much more marked in modern times when almost every intelligence service studies the spy fiction of its rivals just in case somebody let leak a little truth. So often the spy fiction books reveal more fact than the spymasters get from their agents! This has been markedly the case with some fiction concerning the CIA."

McCOY, Malachy
   See CAULFIELD, Malachy Francis

*   *   *

McEWAN, Ian (Russell)   1948-

PERSONAL: Born June 21, 1948, in Aldershot, England; son of David (a soldier) and Rose (Moore) McEwan. *Education:* University of Sussex, B.A. (with honors), 1970; University of East Anglia, M.A., 1971.

CAREER: Writer.

AWARDS, HONORS: Somerset Maugham Award, 1976, for *First Love, Last Rites;* Booker Prize finalist, 1981, for *The Comfort of Strangers; Evening Standard* Award for best screenplay, 1983, for "The Ploughman's Lunch."

WRITINGS: First Love, Last Rites (short stories), Random House, 1975; *The Cement Garden* (novel), Simon & Schuster, 1978; *In Between the Sheets* (short stories), Simon & Schuster, 1978; *The Imitation Game* (teleplays; contains "Jack Flea's Celebration," "Solid Geometry," and "The Imitation Game"), J. Cape, 1981; *The Comfort of Strangers* (novel), Simon & Schuster, 1981; *Or Shall We Die: An Oratorio* (first produced at Royal Festival Hall, February, 1983; produced at Carnegie Hall, 1985), J. Cape, 1982; "The Ploughman's Lunch" (film), Greenpoint Films, 1982.

Author of radio play, "Conversations with a Cupboardman," produced by British Broadcasting Corp., 1975. Contributor to *Radio Times* and to literary journals in Europe and the United States, including *Transatlantic Review, American Review, New American Review, Tri-Quarterly,* and *New Review.*

WORK IN PROGRESS: A novel.

SIDELIGHTS: Ian McEwan began writing seriously just before enrolling at the University of East Anglia. That school's faculty included Angus Wilson, a major novelist of the generation preceding McEwan's, to whom the younger writer has been compared. A collection of McEwan's stories, written as his master's thesis, became his first published work, *First Love, Last Rites.* Writing in the *New York Review of Books,* Robert Towers praises the collection as "possibly the most brilliantly perverse and sinister batch of short stories to come out of England since Angus Wilson's *The Wrong Set.*" Towers describes McEwan's England as a "flat, rubble-strewn wasteland, populated by freaks and monsters, most of them articulate enough to tell their own stories with mesmerizing narrative power and an unfaltering instinct for the perfect sickening detail." The "freaks" include an incestuous brother and sister, a man who lives in a cupboard, a child-slayer, and a man who keeps the penis of a nineteenth-century criminal preserved in a jar. "Such writing would be merely sensational if it were not, like Kafka's, so pointed, so accurate, so incapable indeed of being appalled," writes John Fletcher in *Dictionary of Literary Biography.* "In contemporary writing one has to turn to French literature to encounter a similar contrast between the elegance of the language and the disturbing quality of the material; in writing in English McEwan is wholly unique. No one else combines in quite the same way exactness of notation with a comedy so black that many readers may fail to see the funny side at all."

Reviewing *First Love, Last Rites* in *Encounter,* Jonathan Raban declares that the book "oozes with talent as wayward, original and firm in vision as anything since [Jean] Rhys's early novels.'' He attributes the author's success in handling his somewhat distasteful plots to the fact that McEwan's writing takes "nothing for granted, it is surprised by nothing and observant of everything . . . at its frequent best, it has a musical purity matched to music's deep indifference to the merely moral.'' Of the young author's debut, Raban concludes: "*First Love, Last Rites* is one of those rare books which strike out on a new direction in current English fiction. The most important question is what will McEwan do next? His abilities as a stylist and a storyteller are profuse, and these stories are only the first harvest.''

McEwan's next venture, a novel entitled *The Cement Garden,* has been likened to William Golding's *Lord of the Flies.* It is the story of four children's regression into a feral state, possessing the "suspense and chilling impact'' of Golding's book, "but without the philosophy lessons,'' notes William McPherson in *Washington Post Book World.* The four children, Julie, Jack, Sue, and Tom, have been raised in a Victorian house that stands alone among the abandoned ruins of modern pre-fabricated houses. The children's father dies at the moment that Jack, the fifteen-year-old narrator, experiences his first orgasm. When their mother dies a short time later, Jack convinces his siblings that they must bury her secretly rather than be separated and put into foster homes. They carry out his plan, encasing the body in a trunk of wet cement and hiding it in the basement. Julie and Jack then unsuccessfully attempt to assume the parental roles. They lapse into filth and apathy; their youngest brother regresses to an infantile state; flies infest the house as food rots in the kitchen. Eventually the cement in the trunk cracks, filling the house with the scent of the mother's decaying body. In time, Julie's boyfriend, Derek, discovers the corpse; then he stumbles upon Jack and Julie, engaged in incest. The book ends with the orphans' closed world shattered as Derek summons the police to the scene.

Robert Towers describes *The Cement Garden* as "a shocking book, morbid, full of repellent imagery—and irresistably readable, . . . the work of a writer in full control of his materials. As in the short stories, the effect achieved by McEwan's quiet, precise, and sensuous touch is that of magic realism—a transfiguration of the ordinary that has a far stronger retinal and visceral impact than the flabby surrealism of so many 'experimental' novels. The setting and events reinforce one another symbolically, but the symbolism never seems contrived or obtrusive.'' Fletcher also praises McEwan's style; however, he expresses reservations about this type of subject matter. "The novel would be rather silly if its tone were not so obsessive and sustained, and if the sharpness of detail and observation were not so intense,'' he states. "It is difficult to see how McEwan can develop much further this line in grotesque horror and black comedy, with a strong admixture of eroticism and perversion.''

Anne Tyler, in the *New York Times Book Review,* states: "Ian McEwan is a skillful writer, absolutely in control of his material.'' But she goes on to question the validity of such a bleak tale: "What makes the book difficult is that these children are not—we trust—real people at all. They are so consistently unpleasant, unlikable and bitter that we can't believe in them . . . and we certainly can't identify with them. Jack's eyes, through which we're viewing this story, have an uncanny ability to settle upon the one distasteful detail in every scene, and to dwell on it. . . . It seems weak-stomached to criticize a novel on these grounds, but if what we read makes us avert our gaze entirely, isn't the purpose defeated? Jack, we're being told, has been so damaged and crippled that there's no hope

for him. But if it's a foregone conclusion that there's no hope whatsoever, we tend to lose hope in the book as well.''

Other critics consider McEwan's ability to gain reader sympathy for these children to be one of the major strengths of his novel. Paul Gray writes in *Time* magazine: "Jack, 15, [is] unattractive in a manner that only adolescent males can fully achieve. . . . Without any redeeming charm, he is nonetheless capable of evoking sympathy. . . . Seen from the inside, the characters are simply beleaguered children trying to cope and, ultimately, failing. Outsiders find their degeneration criminal; the book shows the inadequacy of such a judgement.'' John Leonard, in the *New York Times,* finds, "The odd thing is that the reader comes to root for [the children] . . . and against Derek, the moneyed snooker player who would invade their dream with his rationality and the authority of his disgust.'' Leonard calls the novel "remarkable because it takes materials so familiar from recent literature as to amount to a kind of dross of modernism—the psychopathology of family life, sinister shifts in sex roles, infantile regression, libidinal politics, tribal mores—and transmutes them into something dark and glowing. . . . Just about everything of craft that can be done right is done right in *The Cement Garden,* from the cement at the beginning to the sledgehammer at the end. . . . Disquieting, I suppose, is the word for this novel, as well as 'accomplished' and 'astonishing.' Mr. McEwan sneaks up and stabs us in the heart.''

McEwan's collection of short stories *In Between the Sheets* has also attracted a great deal of critical attention. Some reviewers praise the less sensational nature of this book, citing in particular "Psychopolis,'' "Two Fragments: March 199-,'' and the title story as examples of a new restraint on McEwan's part. However, *In Between the Sheets* does include stories about teenage lesbians, a romantic ape who laments the end of his affair with a woman writer, and a man who eats ground glass, washes it down with juice, and hurls himself under a train. "McEwan is experimenting more,'' writes V. S. Pritchett in the *New York Review of Books.* In this critic's view, the collection demonstrates McEwan's versatility and contains what he terms "two encouraging breaks with 'mean' writing. [These two stories] enlarge his scene.'' "Two Fragments: March 199-'' takes its theme and style from George Orwell's *Nineteen-eighty-four.* It describes a London that has been half-destroyed by a war or revolution; its inhabitants have been reduced to a life of scavenging. Pritchett feels that McEwan treats the theme of a future society well, with a "far greater sense of physical and emotional dissolution'' than Orwell, and Terence Winch of *Washington Post Book World* says that McEwan's prose, "like Orwell's, is as clear as a windowpane.'' He calls McEwan "a gifted story-teller and possibly the best British writer to appear in a decade or more.''

In contrast to his earlier works, McEwan's next novel, *The Comfort of Strangers,* features two well-groomed, respectable adults. Colin and Mary are on holiday in Venice when they are drawn into a web of horror that climaxes in sadomasochistic murder. Though continuing to praise McEwan's gifts as a storyteller—calling him "a black magician''—John Leonard finds the book's plot contrived and unbelievable. His review concludes: "This novel, by a writer of enormous talent, is definitely diseased.'' Stephen Koch, too, faults the plot while praising McEwan's craftsmanship. "McEwan proceeds through most of this sickly tale with subtlety and promise,'' Koch writes in the *Washington Post Book World.* "The difficulty is that all this skill is directed toward a climax which, even though it is duly horrific, is sapped by a certain thinness and plain banality at its core. After an impressive wind-up, the sado-masochistic fantasy animating *The Comfort of Strangers* is revealed as . . . a sado-masochistic fantasy. And not much more. . . . Yet *The Comfort of Strangers* has real interest as a novel. . . . In all his recent fiction, McEwan seems to be reaching toward some new imaginative accommodation to the sexual questions of innocence and adulthood, role and need that have defined, with such special intensity, his generation. . . . I honor him for his effort.''

''As the best young writer on this island,'' writes Andrew Sinclair in the London *Times,* ''McEwan's evocation of feeling and place and his analyses of mood and relationship remain haunting and compelling. Yet his obsession with the thin skin between life and death, his concentration on menace and perversion, narrow his vision. His plots are cautionary tales with compulsory deadly endings. . . . His promise has been in walking on brittle ice; his achievement will be in his treading on solid ground.'' Fletcher concludes: ''One hopes that [McEwan] is not cultivating a contemporary form of Gothic to the point of self-indulgence. If he is not—if, in other words, he can develop and deepen an already formidable talent—then he is likely to become one of the greatest British writers of his generation.''

BIOGRAPHICAL/CRITICAL SOURCES: Encounter, June, 1975, January, 1979; *London Magazine,* August/September, 1975, February, 1979; *Virginia Quarterly Review,* autumn, 1975; *Times Literary Supplement,* January 20, 1978, September 29, 1978, October 9, 1981; *New Review,* autumn, 1978; *Washington Post Book World,* October 29, 1978, August 5, 1979, June 28, 1981; *Time,* November 17, 1978; *New York Times,* November 21, 1978, August 14, 1979, June 15, 1981; *New York Times Book Review,* November 26, 1978, August 26, 1979, July 5, 1981; *Chicago Tribune Book World,* November 26, 1978, September 30, 1979, July 19, 1981; *New York Review of Books,* March 8, 1979, January 24, 1980; *Listener,* April 12, 1979; *Contemporary Literary Criticism,* Volume XIII, Gale, 1980; *Times* (London), February 16, 1981, October 8, 1981; *Dictionary of Literary Biography,* Volume XIV: *British Novelists since 1960,* Gale, 1983; *Monthly Film Bulletin,* June, 1983.

—*Sketch by Joan E. Marecki*

* * *

McGANN, Jerome J(ohn) 1937-

PERSONAL: Born July 22, 1937, in New York, N.Y.; son of John Joseph (a printer) and Marie V. (Lecouffe) McGann; married Anne P. Lanni (a teacher), August 20, 1960; children: Geoffrey, Christopher, Jennifer. *Education:* Le Moyne College, B.S., 1959; Syracuse University, M.A., 1962; Yale University, Ph.D., 1966. *Home:* 1221 Arden Rd., Pasadena, Calif. 91106. *Office:* Department of Humanities, California Institute of Technology, Pasadena, Calif. 91125.

CAREER: University of Chicago, Chicago, Ill., assistant professor, 1966-69, associate professor, 1969-72, professor of English, 1972-76; Johns Hopkins University, Baltimore, Md., professor of English, 1976-81; California Institute of Technology, Pasadena, Doris and Henry Dreyfus Professor of Humanities, 1981—.

MEMBER: Modern Language Association of America.

AWARDS, HONORS: Fulbright fellow, 1965; Fels fellow, 1965; American Philosophical Society fellow, 1967; Guggenheim

fellow, 1970-71 and 1975-76; Melville Cane Award, 1973, for *Swinburne;* National Endowment for the Humanities fellow, 1974-76.

WRITINGS: Fiery Dust: Bryon's Poetic Development, University of Chicago Press, 1968; (editor) Edward Bulwer-Lytton, *Pelham,* University of Nebraska Press, 1972; *Swinburne: An Experiment in Criticism,* University of Chicago Press, 1972; *Don Juan in Context,* University of Chicago Press, 1976; (editor) *Lord Byron: The Complete Poetical Works,* Volumes I-III, Oxford University Press, 1980-81; *The Romantic Ideology,* University of Chicago Press, 1983; *A Critique of Modern Textual Criticism,* University of Chicago Press, 1983; *The Beauty of Inflections,* Oxford University Press, 1985.

Plays: (Adapter) George Gordon Byron, ''Cain,'' produced in Chicago, Ill., 1968; (adapter) William Blake, ''Marriage of Heaven and Hell,'' produced in Chicago, 1970.

Poetry: *Air Heart Sermons,* Pas de loup Press, 1975; (with Janet Kauffman) *Writing Home,* Coldwater Press, 1977; (with James Kahn) *Nerves in Patterns,* X Press, 1979.

WORK IN PROGRESS: Lord Byron: Poetry and Prose, for Oxford University Press.

SIDELIGHTS: Since 1970, Jerome J. McGann has spent countless hours and traveled numerous miles in search of material for a comprehensive critical edition of the works of British Romantic poet Lord Byron. The first such collection to appear since the turn of the century, *Lord Byron: The Complete Poetical Works* will, upon completion, contain nearly fifty never-before-published poems in addition to some 350 more familiar titles. Thanks to McGann's diligence, even a substantial number of these will undergo some significant changes; the author uncovered many old manuscripts and printer's proofs that have led to textual revisions in some cases. Described by *New York Times* writer Richard Eder as ''not merely a Byron scholar but a Byron enthusiast,'' McGann has made the establishment of an accurate record of the poet's work his primary goal.

Accompanying the poems are McGann's observations on the text itself and his comments on the historical context. Unlike the generation of critics who preceded him, McGann believes strongly that important insights can be gained by examining not just the internal structure of a poem, but the external influences on the poet as well—especially, perhaps, in Byron's case. ''You can't read him without being involved in his connections,'' the scholar explained to Eder. ''His interest was not words but what they stand for, as in Auden: a window to reality. He can't write the equivalent of a well-wrought urn; each of his poems is deeply involved in its times.'' In short, concludes Eder, ''studying texts and editions, for [McGann], is not an object in itself but a way or reaching some of the most essential values in literature.''

BIOGRAPHICAL/CRITICAL SOURCES: New York Times, March 27, 1980; *Village Voice Literary Supplement,* November, 1983.

* * *

McINNIS, Noel F. 1936-

PERSONAL: Born October 29, 1936, in Freeport, Ill.; son of Frederick (a musician) and Carol (Thompson) McInnis; married June Knudsen, December 21, 1958 (divorced, 1975); married Rita Pearce, April 15, 1979; children: (first marriage) Holly, Scott. *Education:* Kendall College, A.A., 1956; Northwestern

University, B.S., 1958, M.A., 1962. *Home:* 3128 Cofer Rd., Falls Church, Va. 22042.

CAREER: Kendall College, Evanston, Ill., director of admissions, 1959-60, chairman of social science department, 1965-67, director of educational advancement, 1965-70; Center for Curriculum Design (non-profit educational foundation), Evanston, director, 1970-74; free-lance writer and educational consultant, 1974-78; Ernest Holmes College, Los Angeles, Calif., member of faculty, 1978—; *Brain Mind Bulletin,* Los Angeles, managing editor, 1980-83. *Military service:* U.S. Army Reserve, 1960-66.

WRITINGS: (Editor with others) Robert Theobald, *An Alternative Future for America* (speeches and essays), Swallow Press, 1968, revised and enlarged edition published as *An Alternative Future for America Two,* 1970; (editor with Richard L. Heiss) *Can Man Care for the Earth?,* Abingdon, 1971; *You Are an Environment: Teaching/Learning Environmental Values,* Center for Curriculum Design, 1972, 2nd edition, Museum and Science Center, 1977; (editor with others) *Somewhere Else: A Living/Learning Catalog,* Swallow Press, 1973.

(Editor with Don Albrecht) *What Makes Education Environmental,* Data Courier, 1975; (co-author) *The Whole Earth Happens as You Do: The Balance of Lifekind,* Environments for Learning, 1975; *How One-derful to Be,* Supper-Money Press, 1977; *Everywhere I Go, There I Am,* Supper-Money Press, 1977; *New World Directory,* International Co-Operation Council, 1978; (editor with wife, Rita McInnis) *Happy Birth Day Planet Earth,* Foundation for Co-Creation, 1984.

WORK IN PROGRESS: The Book of Co-Creation and *The Power of Commitment.*

*   *   *

McKENNA, A. Daniel
See CORSON-FINNERTY, Adam Daniel

*   *   *

McKENNA, George   1937-

PERSONAL: Born March 2, 1937, in Chicago, Ill.; son of Robert Emmet (a steel mill worker) and Helen (Norton) McKenna; married Sylvia Iafolla, August 29, 1964; children: Laura, Maria, Christopher. *Education:* Attended University of Illinois at Chicago Circle, 1955-57, University of Chicago, 1957-59, University of Massachusetts, 1959-60, and Fordham University, 1961-66. *Home:* 162 Newcomb Rd., Tenafly, N.J. 07670. *Office:* City College of the City University of New York, New York, N.Y. 10031.

CAREER: Associated with City College of the City University of New York, New York, N.Y.

WRITINGS: (Editor and contributor) *American Populism,* Putnam, 1974; *American Politics: Ideals and Realities,* McGraw, 1976; (editor with Stanley Feingold) *Taking Sides on Controversial Social Issues,* Dushkin, 1978, 3rd edition (with Kurt Finsterbusch), 1984.

Media Voices, Dushkin, 1982; *A Guide to the Constitution: That Delicate Balance,* Random House, 1984; (editor with Feingold) *Taking Sides on Controversial Political Issues,* 4th edition (McKenna was not associated with earlier editions), Dushkin, 1985.

WORK IN PROGRESS: Research on the U.S. Constitution.

SIDELIGHTS: George McKenna writes: "My motivation flows in some measure from fear of having to return advances."

*   *   *

McLEOD, Wallace (Edmond)   1931-

PERSONAL: Born May 30, 1931, in Toronto, Ontario, Canada; son of Angus Edmond (a printing pressman) and Mary A. E. (Shier) McLeod; married Elizabeth M. Staples (a teacher), July 24, 1957; children: Betsy, John, James, Angus. *Education:* University of Toronto, B.A., 1953; Harvard University, A.M., 1954, Ph.D., 1966; also studied at American School of Classical Studies, Athens, Greece, 1957-59. *Politics:* Conservative. *Religion:* Presbyterian. *Home:* 399 St. Clements Ave., Toronto, Ontario, Canada M5N 1M2. *Office:* Victoria College, University of Toronto, Toronto, Ontario, Canada M5S 1K7.

CAREER: Trinity College, Hartford, Conn., instructor in classical languages, 1955-56; University of British Columbia, Vancouver, instructor in classics, 1959-61; University of Western Ontario, London, lecturer in classics, 1961-62; University of Toronto, Victoria College, Toronto, Ontario, assistant professor, 1962-66, associate professor, 1966-74, professor of classics, 1974—, associate chairman, 1975-78, acting chairman of undergraduate classics department, 1978-79. *Member:* Classical Association of Canada, American Philological Association, Society of Archer-Antiquaries, Ancient Free and Accepted Masons. *Awards, honors:* Canada Council fellowship, 1970-71.

WRITINGS: Composite Bows from the Tomb of Tut'ankhamun, Oxford University Press, 1970; (editor and contributor) *Beyond the Pillars: More Light on Freemasonry,* Grand Lodge of Canada, 1973; (editor and contributor) *Meeting the Challenge: The Lodge Officer at Work,* Grand Lodge of Canada, 1976; (editor and author of introduction) *The Sufferings of John Coustos: A Facsimile Reprint of the First English Edition, Published at London in 1746,* Masonic Book Club, 1979; (editor and contributor) *Whence Come We?: Freemasonry in Ontario, 1764-1980,* Grand Lodge of Canada, 1980; *Self Bows and Other Archery Tackle from the Tomb of Tut'ankhamun,* Griffith Institute, 1982. Contributor of articles and reviews to professional journals. *Phoenix,* associate editor, 1965-70, acting editor, 1973.

WORK IN PROGRESS: Inscribed Pottery from the Middle Bronze Age at Lerna; Crusaders' Castles of the Argolid.

SIDELIGHTS: Wallace McLeod participated in archaeological excavations at Lerna, Greece, and Gordion, Turkey, in 1958.

*   *   *

McMANNERS, John   1916-

PERSONAL: Born December 25, 1916, in Durham, England; son of Joseph (a clergyman of the Church of England) and Ann (Marshal) McManners; married Sarah Carruthers Errington, December 27, 1952; children: Hugh, Helen, Peter, Ann. *Education:* Oxford University, B.A. (first class honors), 1938, M.A., 1946; University of Durham, Diploma in Theology, 1947. *Home:* 71 Cunliffe Close, Oxford, England. *Office:* All Souls College, Oxford University, Oxford OX1 1DP, England.

CAREER: Clergyman, Church of England, 1947—; Oxford University, St. Edmund Hall, Oxford, England, fellow and chaplain, 1948-56; University of Sydney, Sydney, New South Wales, Australia, professor of history, 1960-68; University of

Leicester, Leicester, England, professor of history, 1968-72; Oxford University, Regius Professor of Ecclesiastical History, 1973—. Senior visiting fellow, All Souls College, Oxford University, 1967-68; visiting professor of British Academy, Institut Catholique, Paris, 1972; director d'etudes associe, Pratique des Hautes Etudes, Section IV, Paris, 1980-81. Trustee, National Portrait Gallery, London, 1971—. *Military service:* British Army, 1939-45; became major; decorated Officer, Order of King George I of the Hellenes.

MEMBER: Australian Academy of the Humanities (fellow), British Academy (fellow), Ecclesiastical History Society (president, 1977-78).

AWARDS, HONORS: Wolfson Literary Prize, 1982, for *Death and the Enlightenment: Changing Attitudes to Death among Christians and Unbelievers in Eighteenth-Century France.*

WRITINGS: (Editor with John M. Wallace-Hadrill) *France: Government and Society,* Methuen, 1957, 2nd edition, 1970; *French Ecclesiastical Society under the Ancient Regime: A Study of Angers in the Eighteenth Century,* Manchester University Press, 1960; (with R. M. Crawford) *The Future of the Humanities in the Australian Universities* (booklet), Melbourne University Press, for Australian Humanities Research Council, 1965; *Lectures on European History, 1789-1914: Men, Machines, and Freedom,* Basil Blackwell, 1966, Barnes & Noble, 1967, reprinted as *European History, 1789-1914: Men, Machines, and Freedom,* Harper, 1969; *The Social Contract and Rousseau's Revolt against Society* (lecture), Leicester University Press, 1968; *The French Revolution and the Church,* S.P.C.K., for Church Historical Society, 1969, Harper, 1970.

Church and State in France, S.P.C.K., for Church Historical Society, 1972; (contributor) D. Baker, editor, *Church, Society, and Politics,* Basil Blackwell, 1975; (contributor) Baker, editor, *Religious Motivations: Biographical and Sociological Problems for the Church Historian,* Basil Blackwell, 1978; *Death and the Enlightenment: Changing Attitudes to Death among Christians and Unbelievers in Eighteenth-Century France,* Oxford University Press, 1981.

Contributor to *New Cambridge Modern History,* Volumes VI and VIII.

WORK IN PROGRESS: Further studies on French ecclesiastical life in the eighteenth century.

SIDELIGHTS: In *Death and the Enlightenment: Changing Attitudes to Death among Christians and Unbelievers in Eighteenth-Century France,* John McManners examines the evolution of French attitudes towards death, religion, and a belief in the afterlife. He finds that immense societal changes were brought about in France by a dramatic rise in population and an increased average life expectancy during the eighteenth century. These changes resulted in French society becoming more secularized. Traditional religious beliefs were widely questioned and some once-religious activities, like burial, were no longer exclusively handled by the church. "McManners writes beautifully and at times movingly," Owen Chadwick states in the *Times Literary Supplement.* He concludes that "this is that rare combination: a learned and scholarly book with not a page in it that is arid."

BIOGRAPHICAL/CRITICAL SOURCES: Times Literary Supplement, May 14, 1982.

McNALLY, Raymond T.   1931-

PERSONAL: Born May 15, 1931, in Cleveland, Ohio; son of Michael Joseph and Marie (Kinkoff) McNally. *Education:* Attended University of Paris, 1951-52; Fordham University, A.B. (highest honors), 1953; Free University of Berlin, Ph.D., 1956; University of Leningrad, postdoctoral studies, 1961. *Politics:* Democrat. *Office:* Carney Hall 201, Boston College, Chestnut Hill, Mass. 02167.

CAREER: John Carroll University, Cleveland, Ohio, instructor in history, 1956-58; Boston College, Chestnut Hill, Mass., assistant professor, 1958-61, associate professor, 1962-69, professor of history, 1970—, director of Slavic and East European Center, 1964-74. Fulbright faculty research appointment to Romania, 1969-70, and to the Soviet Union, 1980-81.

MEMBER: American Association of Slavic Studies, American Historical Society.

AWARDS, HONORS: American Exchange Scholar to the U.S.S.R., 1961; American Philosophical Society research grant, 1961; American Council of Learned Societies and Social Science Research Council grant, 1965.

WRITINGS: The Major Works of Peter Chaadayev, University of Notre Dame Press, 1969; *Chaadayev and His Friends: An Intellectual History of Peter Chaadayev and His Russian Contemporaries,* Diplomatic Press, 1971; (with Radu Florescu) *In Search of Dracula: A True History of Dracula and Vampire Legends,* New York Graphic Society, 1972; (with Florescu) *Dracula: A Biography of Vlad the Impaler, 1431-1476,* Hawthorne, 1973; (compiler) *A Clutch of Vampires: These Being among the Best from History and Literature,* New York Graphic Society, 1974; (editor with Florescu) *The Essential "Dracula": A Completely Illustrated and Annotated Edition of Bram Stoker's Classic Novel,* Mayflower, 1979; *Dracula Was a Woman: In Search of the Blood Countess of Transylvania,* McGraw, 1983.

Contributor of articles to *Forschungen zur Osteuropaischen Geschichte, Slavic and East European Review, Russian Review, Slavic Review,* and *Journal of the History of Ideas.*

SIDELIGHTS: An authority on the vampire in folklore and fiction, Raymond T. McNally has written several studies about the sources for the vampire myth. His *In Search of Dracula: A True History of Dracula and Vampire Legends* surveys the host of vampire legends to be found in Europe and documents some of the actual crimes which gave rise to the legends. In *Dracula: A Biography of Vlad the Impaler, 1431-1476* and *Dracula Was a Woman: In Search of the Blood Countess of Transylvania,* McNally takes a close look at the lives of two historical figures who inspired Bram Stoker's novel *Dracula.*

Both *In Search of Dracula* and *Dracula: A Biography* detail the life of the historic Dracula, a 15th-century Romanian prince named Vlad the Impaler. A cruel and sadistic ruler, Vlad was nonetheless a hero among his people for his battles against the invading Turks. He was instrumental in stopping the Turks from conquering Eastern Europe. His atrocities, however, earned him a fearsome reputation. He was called the Impaler because he enjoyed impaling Turkish prisoners on sharpened wooden posts and displaying them in his courtyard. While hundreds of unfortunate victims writhed in agony, Vlad would set up a table outside and eat his dinner. His treatment of his own people was equally cruel and bloody. He once invited a number of his enemies to a banquet, then locked them in the banquet hall and set it on fire. Because of such activities, Vlad became a terrible character in local folktales. It was through such folktales that Bram Stoker learned of the cruel and sadistic prince. When Stoker wrote his novel *Dracula,* he modeled his vampire count on the real-life Vlad the Impaler.

Another historical source for *Dracula* was the Hungarian countess Elizabeth Bathory. Known as the "Blood Countess," Bathory was responsible for torturing and killing several hundred young girls and bathing in their blood. The countess believed the blood would preserve her youth. Details about the murders were suppressed by the Hungarian nobility for over one hundred years. In *Dracula Was a Woman,* McNally sorts the grisly facts about the countess from the many legends surrounding her. "Never before has [Bathory] been treated so thoroughly and factually in English," writes Joseph McClellan in the *Washington Post Book World.* "McNally tells his horror tale with a fair degree of scholarly objectivity." P. A. Duhamel states in the *Boston Herald* that *Dracula Was a Woman* is "an account impressive in its grim details and astonishing in its revelations of the power of a cruel aristocrat."

Speaking of his work, McNally told *CA:* "I believe that behind almost every fairy tale and behind almost any story which gets repeated often enough across the centuries there is some hidden historical reality. I have journeyed throughout the modern world in search of such cases."

BIOGRAPHICAL/CRITICAL SOURCES: Atlantic, November, 1972; *New York Times Book Review,* January 14, 1973; *Time,* January 15, 1973; *Saturday Review,* February, 1973; *Commonweal,* March 2, 1973; *Choice,* April, 1973; *Harper's,* April, 1973; *Los Angeles Times Book Review,* August 31, 1980; *Library Journal,* March 15, 1983; *Boston Herald,* April 24, 1983; *Los Angeles Times,* May 10, 1983; *Washington Post Book World,* May 28, 1983; *Globe,* August 9, 1983.

*   *   *

MECH, Dave
  See MECH, L(ucyan) David

*   *   *

MECH, L(ucyan) David   1937-
  (Dave Mech)

PERSONAL: Surname rhymes with "peach"; born January 18, 1937, in Auburn, N.Y.; son of Lucyan Frank (a foreman laborer in a chemical plant) and Margaret C. (Nade) Mech; married Betty Ann Smith, August 30, 1958; children: Sharon E., Stephen D., Nicholas E., Christopher A. *Education:* Cornell University, B.S., 1958, Purdue University, Ph.D., 1962; University of Minnesota, postdoctoral study, 1962-63. *Politics:* Independent. *Home:* 1315 66th Ave. N.E., Minneapolis, Minn. 55432. *Office:* U.S. Fish and Wildlife Service, North Central Forest Equipment Station, Folwell Ave., St. Paul, Minn. 55108.

CAREER: University of Minnesota, Museum of Natural History, Minneapolis, research associate, 1963-66; Macalester College, St. Paul, Minn., assistant professor of biology and research associate, 1966-69; U.S. Fish and Wildlife Service, North Central Forest Experiment Station, St. Paul, wildlife research biologist, 1969—.

Lecturer on wolf ecology and research and on animal-tracking, Serengeti Research Institute in Tanzania, 1970, and over 200

other institutions. Has appeared on network television in the National Broadcasting Co. specials, "The Wolf Men" and "Our Endangered Wildlife," and on the "Dick Cavett Show."

MEMBER: Ecological Society of America, American Society of Mammalogists, Wildlife Society, Minnesota Zoological Society (member of board of directors).

AWARDS, HONORS: National Institutes of Health fellowship, 1963-64; Special Achievement Award of U.S. Bureau of Sport Fisheries and Wildlife, 1970; Special Achievement Award from U.S. Fish and Wildlife Service, 1970; Terrestial Wildlife Publication Award from Wildlife Society, 1972, and Best Wildlife Book award from Symposium on Threatened and Endangered Wildlife, 1974, both for *The Wolf: The Ecology and Behavior of an Endangered Species;* Civil Servant of the Year award from U.S. Fish and Wildlife Service, 1973; award for distinguished service in science education and research, Minnesota Academy of Science, 1981; special achievement award, U.S. Fish and Wildlife Service, 1981.

WRITINGS: (With M. E. Nelson) *Deer Social Organization and Wolf Predation in Northeastern Minnesota,* Wildlife Monographs, 1961; *The Wolves of Isle Royale,* U.S. Government Printing Office, 1966; *The Wolf: The Ecology and Behavior of an Endangered Species,* Natural History Press, 1970; (editor with L. D. Frenzel, Jr., and contributor) *Ecological Studies of the Timber Wolf in Northeastern Minnesota,* North Central Forest Experiment Station (St. Paul), 1971; (with D. G. Schneider and J. R. Tester) *Movements of Female Raccoons and Their Young as Determined by Radio-Tracking,* Animal Behavior Monographs, 1971; (with S. H. Fritts) *Dynamics, Movements, and Wolf Predation in Northwestern Minnesota,* Wildlife Monographs, 1981; *Handbook of Animal Radio-Tracking,* University of Minnesota Press, 1983.

Contributor of over 100 articles and reviews, some under name Dave Mech, to scientific publications, and about seventy articles to popular periodicals and newspapers, including *Reader's Digest, Naturalist, Sports Afield, Outdoor Life, Animal Kingdom,* and *National Geographic.*

WORK IN PROGRESS: Further ecological and behavioral research on timber wolves in northern Minnesota.

SIDELIGHTS: L. David Mech told *CA:* "Although I thoroughly enjoy writing, it happens to form only a small part of my regular career, which is wildlife research. The research itself takes me into the field to work with many interesting wilderness animals, and I must say that I enjoy that more. Nevertheless, there is something very intellectually satisfying, when all the field work is done, the data collected, the results analyzed, and the conclusions drawn, to integrate them all and be able to relive the entire grand experience and try to convey what was learned to an audience. I could easily enjoy an entire lifetime devoted to field work, and another devoted entirely to writing; wedding the two interests gives me the best of both."

AVOCATIONAL INTERESTS: Wildlife photography, music.

BIOGRAPHICAL/CRITICAL SOURCES: New York Times Book Review, June 14, 1970, May 17, 1981.

*   *   *

MEEHAN, Eugene J(ohn)   1923-

PERSONAL: Born September 16, 1923, in Peckville, Pa.; son of James (an accountant) and Anna (Harvilchuck) Meehan; married Ruth J. Patterson, 1946 (divorced, 1949); married Alice Elizabeth McCuskey, September 26, 1949; children: (first marriage) Kathleen Ann, Eileen. *Education:* Attended University of Kentucky, 1946; Ohio State University, B.A., 1950, M.A., 1951; London School of Economics, Ph.D., 1954, postdoctoral study, 1954-57. *Home:* 125 Frontenac Forest, Frontenac, Mo. 63131. *Office:* Department of Political Science, University of Missouri, St. Louis, Mo. 63131.

CAREER: U.S. Department of the Air Force, assistant chief of education and libraries in London, England, 1953-57; U.S. Armed Forces Institute, Madison, Wis., educational adviser, 1957-58; Rutgers University, New Brunswick, N.J., lecturer, 1958-60, assistant professor of political science, 1960-65; Brandeis University, Waltham, Mass., associate professor of political science, 1965-68; University of Illinois at Urbana-Champaign, professor of political science, 1969-70; University of Missouri—St. Louis, professor of political science, 1970—. Fellow, Netherlands Institute for Advanced Study, 1980-81. Consultant to Inter-American Foundation, 1973—, University of Costa Rica, 1978—, and U.S. Agency for International Development (USAID). *Military service:* U.S. Army Air Forces, 1942-45; became captain; received Distinguished Flying Cross.

WRITINGS: Introductory Social Studies, U.S. Government Printing Office, 1957; *Introductory Physical Science,* U.S. Government Printing Office, 1959; *The British Left Wing and Foreign Policy: A Study of the Influence of Ideology,* Rutgers University Press, 1960; (with Paul A. Samuelson and Robert Bierstedt) *Modern Social Science,* McGraw, 1964; *The Theory and Method of Political Analysis,* Dorsey, 1965; (with John P. Roche and Murray S. Stedman, Jr.) *The Dynamics of Modern Government,* McGraw, 1966; *Contemporary Political Thought: A Critical Study,* Dorsey, 1967; *Explanation in Social Science: A System Paradigm,* Dorsey, 1968; *Value Judgment and Social Science: Structures and Processes,* Dorsey, 1969.

Foundations of Political Analysis: Empirical and Normative, Dorsey, 1971; (contributor) Wolfram F. Hanreider, editor, *Comparative Foreign Policy,* McKay, 1972; (contributor) George Graham, editor, *The Post-Behavioral Era,* McKay, 1972; *Public Housing Policy: Convention Versus Reality,* Center for Urban Policy Research, Rutgers University, 1975; (contributor) Stuart S. Nagel, editor, *Policy Studies and the Social Sciences,* Lexington Books, 1975; (contributor) Frank P. Scioli, Jr. and Thomas J. Cook, editors, *Methodologies for Analyzing Public Policies,* Lexington Books, 1975; *The Distribution of Public Assistance and Benefits in the St. Louis Metropolitan Area, 1970-1977,* Metropolitan Data Center (St. Louis), 1975; *Introduccion al Pensamiento Critico* (translation of the original English manuscript; title means "Introduction to Critical Thought"), Editorial Trillas, 1975.

(Contributor) Donald Phares, editor, *A Decent Home and Environment,* Ballinger, 1977; *El Pensamiento Critico: Una Introduccion* (translation of the original English manuscript; title means "Critical Thought: An Introduction"), two volumes, University of Costa Rica, 1979; *In Partnership with People: The Inter-American Foundation, 1969-1978,* U.S. Government Printing Office, 1979; *The Quality of Federal Policymaking: Programmed Disaster in Public Housing,* University of Missouri Press, 1979; *Reasoned Argument in Social Science: Linking Research to Policy,* Greenwood Press, 1981; *Economics and Policymaking: The Tragic Illusion,* Greenwood Press, 1982; (contributor) Donald Rosenthal, editor, *Urban Revitalization,* Sage Publications, 1982.

Also author of manuscript *Education for Critical Thought,* which was published in Spanish translation, University of Costa

Rica, 1981; also contributor to *Wisconsin Seminar on Natural Resources Policy in Relation to Economic Development,* Volume I, 1980, *Progress in Rural Extension and Community Development,* edited by Jones and Rolls, Wiley, *Symposium on Creativity in Science Teaching,* edited by R. Zeledon, National Council for Scientific and Technological Research, Costa Rica, and *The Economic Revitalization of America,* edited by Terry Buss, Kennikat. Contributor to political science journals, including *Journal of the Inter-American Foundation, Urban Affairs Quarterly,* and *Journal of Housing.* Member of editorial board, *Journal of Politics.*

WORK IN PROGRESS: Two books, *The Normative Dimension of Human Action* and *Reasoning and Argument in Law and in Scientific Inquiry.*

SIDELIGHTS: Eugene J. Meehan wrote *CA:* "The central concerns in all of my work for the past 25 years have been (1) development of a conception of knowledge (empirical *and* normative) that can serve as a guide to justifiable and corrigible action and (2) development of training materials, at all levels from kindergarten through graduate school, that will maximize the likelihood that the individual student will learn how to learn from experience, and both know that learning has occurred and be able to improve on the knowledge acquired."

*　　*　　*

MEIER, Matt S(ebastian) 1917-

PERSONAL: Born June 4, 1917, in Covington, Ky.; son of Matthias John (a barber) and Mary (Berberich) Meier; married Bettie C. Beckman (a secretary), September 21, 1946; children: Gary Peter, Guy Patrick, G. Paul, G. Philip, Pepe. *Education:* University of Miami, Coral Gables, Fla., A.B. (magna cum laude), 1948; University of the Americas, Mexico City, Mexico, M.A. (magna cum laude), 1949; University of California, Berkeley, Ph.D., 1954. *Politics:* Democrat. *Religion:* Roman Catholic. *Home:* 603 Glen Alto Dr., Los Altos, Calif. 94022. *Office:* Department of History, University of Santa Clara, Santa Clara, Calif. 95053.

CAREER: High school teacher in Oroville, Calif., 1954-55; Bakersfield College, Bakersfield, Calif., instructor in Latin American history, 1955-63; University of Santa Clara, Santa Clara, Calif., 1963—, began as assistant professor, currently Patrick A. Donohue, S. J. Professor of the College of Arts and Sciences, chairman of department of history, 1968-71, 1976—. Fulbright professor in Argentina, 1958-59. *Military service:* U.S. Army, Signal Corps, 1943-46; became technical sergeant.

MEMBER: American Historical Association, American Association of University Professors (local president, 1962-63, 1970-71), Pacific Coast Council on Latin American Studies (president, 1964-65).

WRITINGS: (Contributor) Ellwyn R. Stoddard, editor, *Borderlands Sourcebook,* University of Oklahoma Press, 1983; (compiler) *Bibliography of Mexican American History,* Greenwood Press, 1984.

With Feliciano Rivera: *The Chicanos: A History of Mexican Americans,* Hill & Wang, 1972; *A Bibliography for Chicano History,* R. & E. Research Associates, 1972; (editors) *Readings on La Raza: The Twentieth Century,* Hill & Wang, 1973; *Dictionary of Mexican American History,* Greenwood Press, 1981.

WORK IN PROGRESS: Dictionary of Mexican American Biography, for Greenwood Press.

SIDELIGHTS: "I believe very strongly," Matt S. Meier told *CA,* "in the importance of a maximum number of Americans, both Anglo and Chicano, expanding their understanding of the historical reasons for the current position of Mexican Americans, social, political, and economic. Only with knowledge and deeper understanding can progress come."

The *New Republic* reviewer calls *The Chicanos: A History of Mexican Americans* "especially good; it is not long or pretentious, nor is it especially polemical. Rather the authors in a quiet but determined way want to educate their readers, presumably the Anglos. . . . It would be nice if a few Texas Rangers, so exclusively Anglo, so powerful and sure of themselves, so willing to use force to keep 'them' in line, were to read what Meier and Rivera have to say, and even nicer if senators like John Tower or Barry Goldwater, or Peter Dominick, who represent so many Chicanos, also dipped into these pages. But those strong and and influential senators have limited time, and have long ago learned whose voices to heed, the voices of the owners of factory-farms rather than of men and women who without exaggeration can simply be called subjects."

BIOGRAPHICAL/CRITICAL SOURCES: New Republic, August 19, 1972; *New York Review of Books,* August 31, 1972; *Congressional Record,* October 25, 1972; *California Historical Quarterly,* summer, 1973.

*   *   *

MELLINKOFF, Ruth   1924-

PERSONAL: Born December 18, 1924, in Marshall, Minn.; daughter of N. Ben and Dorothy (Aaron) Weiner; married David Mellinkoff (a professor of law), July 10, 1949; children: Daniel. *Education:* University of Minnesota, B.A., 1947; University of California, Berkeley, M.A., 1963; University of California, Los Angeles, Ph.D., 1967, postdoctoral study, 1970-74. *Home:* 744 Holmby Ave., Los Angeles, Calif. 90024. *Office:* Center for Medieval and Renaissance Studies, University of California, Los Angeles, Calif. 90024.

CAREER: University of California, Los Angeles, research associate, 1974—. Member of board of governors, University of Judaism.

MEMBER: Medieval Academy of America (councillor, 1983-86).

WRITINGS: Something Special Cookbook, Ritchie, 1959, revised edition, 1971; *The Uncommon Cookbook,* Ritchie, 1968; *The Horned Moses in Medieval Art and Thought,* University of California Press, 1970; *The Just Delicious Cook Book,* Ritchie, 1974; *The Easy, Easier, Easiest Cookbook,* Warner Paperbacks, 1980; *The Mark of Cain,* University of California Press, 1981; *The Invisible Cook,* Pangloss Press, 1984. Contributor to *Journal of Jewish Art, Anglo-Saxon England,* and *Speculum.*

WORK IN PROGRESS: Images of Infamy: The Dishonored, Disreputable, and Despised in the Art and Thought of the Late Middle Ages and Renaissance.

BIOGRAPHICAL/CRITICAL SOURCES: Times Literary Supplement, August 21, 1981.

*   *   *

MEMMI, Albert   1920-

PERSONAL: Born December 15, 1920, in Tunis, Tunisia; son of Francois (an artisan) and Marguerite (Sarfati) Memmi; married Germaine Dubach; children: Daniel, Dominique, Nicolas. *Education:* University of Algiers, licence en philosophie, 1943; Sorbonne, University of Paris, Dr. es lettres, 1970. *Home:* 5 rue St. Merri, 75004 Paris, France. *Office:* University of Paris, 92 Nanterre, France.

CAREER: High school teacher of philosophy in Tunis, Tunisia, 1953-56; Center of Educational Research, Tunis, director, 1953-57; National Center of Scientific Research, Paris, France, researcher, 1958-60; University of Paris, Sorbonne, Ecole pratique des hautes etudes, assistant professor, 1959-66, professor of social psychology, 1966-70; University of Paris, Nanterre, France, professor of sociology, 1970—. School of Higher Studies in Social Sciences, conference director, 1958, director of department of social sciences, 1975-78; Walker Ames Professor, University of Seattle, 1972.

MEMBER: Societe des Gens de Lettres, P.E.N. Club (France; vice-president), Academie des Sciences d'Outremer.

AWARDS, HONORS: Commander of Ordre de Nichan Iftikhar (Tunisia); Chevalier de la Legion d'Honneur; Officier of Tunisian Republique; Officier des Arts et des Lettres; Officier des Palmes Academiques; Prix Carthage (Tunis), 1953; Prix Feneon (Paris), 1954; Prix Simba (Rome).

WRITINGS—In English: *La Statue du sel* (novel), introduction by Albert Camus, Correa, 1953, translation by Edouard Roditi published as *Pillar of Salt,* Criterion, 1955, reprinted, O'Hara, 1975; *Agar* (novel), Correa, 1955, translation by Brian Rhys published as *Strangers,* 1958, Orion Press, 1960; *Portrait du colonise precede du portrait du colinisateur,* introduction by Jean-Paul Sartre, Buchet/Chastel, 1957, translation by Howard Greenfield published as *The Colonizer and the Colonized,* Orion Press, 1965, reprinted, Beacon Press, 1984.

Portrait d'un Juif, Gallimard, 1962, translation by Elisabeth Abbott published as *Portrait of a Jew,* Orion Press, 1962; *La Liberation d'un Juif,* Gallimard, 1962, translation by Judy Hyun published as *The Liberation of a Jew,* Orion Press, 1966; *L'Homme domine,* Gallimard, 1968, new edition, Payot, 1973, translation published as *Dominated Man: Notes Towards a Portrait* (collection of essays), Orion Press, 1968; *Le Scorpion ou la confession imaginaire* (novel), Gallimard, 1969, translation by Eleanor Levieux published as *The Scorpion or the Imaginary Confession,* Grossman, 1971, 2nd edition, J. Philip O'Hara, 1975.

Juifs et Arabes, Gallimard, 1974, translation by Levieux published as *Jews and Arabs,* J. Philip O'Hara, 1975; *La dependance: esquisse pour un portrait du dependant,* Gallimard, 1979, translation published as *Dependence,* Beacon Press, 1983.

Other works: *La Poesie algerienne de 1830 a nos jours: approches socio-historiques,* Mouton, 1963; (editor) *Anthologie des ecrivains maghrebins d'expression francaise,* two volumes, Presence africaine, 1964, revised and updated edition, 1965; (with Paul Hassan Maucorps) *Les Francais et le racisme,* Payot, 1965; *Ecole pratique des hautes etudes,* Mouton, 1965.

Albert Memmi: un entretien avec Robert Davies suivi d'itineraire de l'experience vecue a la theorie de la domination, Reedition Quebec, 1975; *La Terre interieure entretiens avec Victor Malka,* Gallimard, 1976; *Le Desert: ou, La vie et les aventures de Jubair Ouali El-Mammi* (novel), Gallimard, 1977; *La Racisme,* Gallimard, 1982.

Work represented in textbooks and in numerous anthologies.

SIDELIGHTS: The English translations of Albert Memmi's works have been well-received in the United States. In his autobiographical novels *Pillar of Salt* and *Strangers*, Memmi, who grew up in a traditional Jewish household in Tunisia, colorfully describes life in North Africa. "But these novels are far more than exotic Durrellian travel guides," a *New York Times* critic writes, "for Memmi, like a Tunisian Balzac graced with Hemingway's radical simplicity and sadness, gave us this world through the voice of a quiet, well-behaved, quite charmingly sad but earnest young man who was slowly disintegrating before our eyes." These novels "today remain two of the best works to appear in Europe after the war," the critic concludes, comparing them to Albert Camus's *The Stranger* and *The Plague.*

Man's alienation from himself and from others is a major theme in Memmi's novel *The Scorpion.* In the story, the protagonist, Emile Memmi, expresses the self-doubts that Memmi sees as a part of the human condition. Although the *New York Times* critic does not consider *The Scorpion* to be completely successful as a novel, he does comment that "the audacious form and technique of the book are totally unprecedented in Memmi: a richly interwoven net of autobiography, diary, commentary, aphorism, parable, *faux memoire* and novel-within-the-novel. . . ."

In *Portrait du colonise, Portrait d'un Juif,* and some of his other books, Memmi explores the theories of colonization and the rule and the exploitation of minorities, concluding that once the exploited gain their freedom, they become like those who ruled them. He details the Jews' complicity in this schema in *The Liberation of a Jew,* as *Nation* contributor David Joravsky explains: "The Enlightenment and the democratic revolutions have undermined the belief of Jews that they are chosen to hold a spiritual fortress against gentile assault until the true Messiah comes. The overwhelming majority of Jews leave the besieged life as soon as the gentiles offer a way out. They prefer peace in their own time, on almost any terms the gentiles offer. Memmi calls this 'self-rejection.' He doesn't bother with superficial things like beards, clothes or diet. He goes straight to such fundamentals as name, language, characteristic ideas and national allegiance. In all these essentials Jews come close to complete 'self-rejection,' but hold back at the very end, indulging in curiously ambiguous or whimsical acts of 'self-acceptance'—like changing the name from Silverstein to Silvers, or arguing that Jewishness is an advantage because it is a burden."

Translations of Memmi's books have been published in Israel, Italy, Germany, England, Spain, Argentina, Yugoslavia, Japan, and other countries.

BIOGRAPHICAL/CRITICAL SOURCES: Nation, May 22, 1967; *Research in African Literatures,* Volume I, number 1, 1970; *New York Times,* May 22, 1971; *Best Sellers,* July 1, 1971; *Los Angeles Times,* August 17, 1984.

*   *   *

MEYER, Ben F. 1927-

PERSONAL: Born November 5, 1927, in Chicago, Ill.; son of Ben F. (a banker) and Mary (Connor) Meyer; married Denise Oppliger, March 27, 1969. *Education:* University of Santa Clara, S.T.M., 1958; Biblical Institute, Rome, Italy, S.S.L., 1961; Gregorian University, Rome, Italy, S.T.D. (summa cum laude), 1965. *Politics:* Democrat. *Religion:* Roman Catholic. *Home:* 2160 Lakeshore Rd., Apt. 1008, Burlington, Ontario,

Canada. *Office:* Department of Religious Studies, McMaster University, Hamilton, Ontario, Canada.

CAREER: Graduate Theological Union, Berkeley, Calif., assistant professor of religion, 1965-68; McMaster University, Hamilton, Ontario, associate professor, 1969-74, professor of religious studies, 1974—.

MEMBER: Society of Biblical Literature, Catholic Biblical Association, Studiorum Novi Testamenti Societas.

AWARDS, HONORS: Fulbright fellow, Germany, 1964-65; Canada Council fellowship in Greece and Switzerland, 1976-77, 1983-84.

WRITINGS: The Man for Others, Bruce, 1970; *The Church in Three Tenses,* Doubleday, 1971; *The Aims of Jesus,* S.C.M. Press, 1979; *Early Christian Self-Definition,* Center for Hermeneutical Studies (Berkeley), 1980; (editor with E. P. Sanders) *Jewish and Christian Self-Definition: Self-Definition in the Greco-Roman World,* Fortress, 1983.

Also author of television documentary, "Christianity," Ontario Educational Authority, 1973.

WORK IN PROGRESS: A New Mankind.

SIDELIGHTS: Ben F. Meyer has traveled throughout the Near East, Europe, and South America, and has a secondary residence in Switzerland.

*   *   *

MEYERS, Joan Simpson 1927-

PERSONAL: Born September 20, 1927, in Boulder, Colo.; daughter of George Gaylord (a paleontologist and professor) and Lydia (Pedroja) Simpson; married Alfred Meyers, 1952 (divorced); children: Trina Anne, Peter Alexander. *Education:* University of Michigan, B.A., 1951. *Office:* Harcourt Brace Jovanovich, Inc., 757 Third Ave., New York, N.Y. 10017.

CAREER: Partisan Review, New York City, staff member, 1960; Basic Books, Inc., New York City, editor, 1961-63; Columbia Broadcasting System-Columbia Records, New York City, literary editor, 1964-66; Harcourt Brace Jovanovich, Inc., New York City, editor, 1966—.

WRITINGS: Poetry and a Libretto, A. Swallow, 1965; (with George Whitaker) *Dinosaur Hunt,* Harcourt, 1965; (editor) *John Fitzgerald Kennedy: As We Remember Him,* Atheneum, 1965; *Buying and Selling a Home in Today's Market: Your Guide for the 1980s,* Dell, 1983.

WORK IN PROGRESS: A novel; poetry; nonfiction.†

*   *   *

MICHAEL, Wolfgang F(riedrich) 1909-

PERSONAL: Born February 23, 1909, in Freiburg, Germany; naturalized U.S. citizen; son of Wolfgang W. (a university professor) and Else (Wehrenpfennig) Michael; married Hadassah Posey, December, 1937 (divorced, 1948); married Marian Pendergrass (a journalism teacher), 1952; children: (first marriage) Hadassah H., Michael Hiscott, Dorothea F., Felton P. *Education:* Attended University of Freiburg, University of Berlin, and University of Marburg; University of Munich, Ph.D., 1934. *Home:* 405 West 37th St., Austin, Tex. 78705. *Office:* Department of German, University of Texas, Austin, Tex. 78712.

CAREER: Bryn Mawr College, Bryn Mawr, Pa., instructor in German, 1939; Chestnut Hill College, Philadelphia, Pa., assistant professor of German, 1939-47; University of Texas at Austin, assistant professor, 1946-51, associate professor, 1951-61, professor of German, 1961—.

MEMBER: Internationale Vereinigung der Germanisten, Modern Language Association of America, American Association of Teachers of German, Mediaeval Academy of America.

WRITINGS: Die Anfaenge des Theaters zu Freiburg in Breisgau, Joseph Waibal, 1934; *Die geistlichen Prozessionsspiele in Deutschland,* Johns Hopkins Press, 1947; *Fruehformen der deutschen Buehne,* Gesellschaft fuer Theatergeschichte, 1963.

Das deutsche Drama des Mittelalter, Walter De Gruyter, 1971; (editor) Thomas Brunner, *Tobias,* Peter Lang, 1978; (editor with Hubert Heinan) Brunner, *Von der Heirat Isaacs,* Peter Lang, 1983; (editor with Barbara Koenneker) Johan Narhamer, *Historia Jobs,* Peter Lang, 1983; *Das deutsche Drama der Reformationszeit,* Peter Lang, 1984. Contributor to language journals.

WORK IN PROGRESS: Critical Bibliography of German Medieval Drama.

*   *   *

MICHAELS, Philip
See van RJNDT, Philippe

*   *   *

MICHAELSON, L(ouis) W.   1917-

PERSONAL: Born March 27, 1917, in Denver, Colo.; son of Max and Helen (Weiner) Michaelson; married wife, Anne; children: Marcy, David. *Education:* University of Denver, B.A., 1954, Ph.D., 1969; University of Iowa, M.A., 1956. *Home:* 1406 Lakeshore Dr., Fort Collins, Colo. 80521. *Office:* Department of English, Colorado State University, Fort Collins, Colo. 80521.

CAREER: Colorado State University, Fort Collins, assistant professor of creative writing, 1958—, tennis coach, 1969-72. *Member:* Phi Beta Kappa. *Awards, honors:* Prizes for short fiction, Galileo Press, 1983, and Colorado Council of Arts and Humanities, 1984.

WRITINGS—Poetry, except as indicated: *New Shoes on an Old Man,* Pierian, 1968; *Songs of My Divided Self,* Southwest Press, 1969; *Everyone Revisited,* Prairie Gate Press, 1974; *On My Being Dead and Other Stories* (short-story collection), Galileo Press, 1983. Contributor of stories and poems to periodicals, including *Esquire, Saturday Evening Post, Saturday Review,* and *New York Times.*

WORK IN PROGRESS: A novella, *Summer Work.*

SIDELIGHTS: L. W. Michaelson wrote *CA:* "My new book *On My Being Dead and Other Stories,* in a sense, refutes Barbara Tuchman's *A Distant Mirror,* in which she contends the fourteenth century was the worst. Actually my stories bring out nerve gas, wars, atom bombs, mental illness, divorce, etc., etc., and contend our own twentieth century is Numero Uno for any contest on the world's worst century—the 1300s has bubonic plague, but we had Hitler and two atom explosions killing thousands."

AVOCATIONAL INTERESTS: Travel in Mexico.

MIDDLEBROOK, (Norman) Martin   1932-

PERSONAL: Born January 24, 1932, in Boston, England; married Mary Sylvester, September 7, 1954; children: Jane, Anne, Catherine. *Education:* Attended schools in England. *Politics:* Independent. *Religion:* Roman Catholic. *Home and office:* 48 Linden Way, Boston, Lincolnshire, England. *Agent:* A. P. Watt & Son, 26-28 Bedford Row, London, England.

CAREER: Poultry farmer in Boston, England, 1956-81. *Military service:* British Army, 1950-52.

WRITINGS: The First Day on the Somme, Allen Lane, 1971, Norton, 1972; *The Nuremberg Raid,* Allen Lane, 1973, Morrow, 1974; *Convoy,* Allen Lane, 1976, Morrow, 1977; (contributor) Edward Marshal and Michael Carver, editors, *The War Lords,* Weidenfeld & Nicolson, 1976; (with Patrick Mahoney) *Battleship,* Allen Lane, 1977, Scribner, 1979; *The Kaiser's Battle,* Allen Lane, 1978; (editor) *Private Bruckshaw's Diaries,* Scolar Press, 1979; *The Battle of Hamburg,* Allen Lane, 1980; *The Peenemunde Raid,* Bobbs-Merrill, 1982; *The Schweinfurt-Regensburg Mission,* Scribner, 1983.

WORK IN PROGRESS: The Bomber Command War Diaries; Operation Corporate: The Falklands War.

SIDELIGHTS: Martin Middlebrook told *CA:* "In my opinion there is no such thing as a 'last word' in history, and anyone who thinks he/she has written a 'definitive' book is a fool." *Avocational interests:* Golf, skiing, local government, travel, giving guided tours of the Western Front battlefields.

BIOGRAPHICAL/CRITICAL SOURCES: Times Literary Supplement, December 26, 1980.

*   *   *

MIHAILOVICH, Vasa D.   1926-

PERSONAL: Born August 12, 1926, in Prokuplje, Yugoslavia; son of Dragutin V. (a postmaster) and Vidosava (Petkovic) Mihailovich; married Branka Jancetovic, 1957; children: Draggan Paul, Zoran Mark. *Education:* Wayne State University, B.A., 1956, M.A., 1957; University of California, Berkeley, Ph.D., 1966. *Politics:* Democrat. *Religion:* Serbian Orthodox. *Home:* 821 Emory Dr., Chapel Hill, N.C. 27514. *Office:* Department of Slavic Languages, University of North Carolina, Chapel Hill, N.C. 27514.

CAREER: University of North Carolina at Chapel Hill, instructor, 1961-63, assistant professor, 1963-68, associate professor, 1968-75, professor of Slavic languages, 1975—.

MEMBER: Modern Language Association of America, American Association of Teachers of Slavic and East European Languages (vice-president, 1969-71), American Association for the Advancement of Slavic Studies, Southern Conference on Slavic Studies.

WRITINGS: (Editor) *Modern Slavic Literatures,* Ungar, Volume I, 1972, Volume II, 1976; (editor) *Introduction to Yugoslav Literature,* Twayne, 1973; (editor) *Yugoslav Literature in English: A Bibliography of Translations and Criticisms, 1821-1975,* Slavica, 1976; (editor) *White Stones and Fir Trees: An Anthology of Contemporary Slavic Literature,* Fairleigh Dickinson University Press, 1977; (editor) *Contemporary Yugoslav Poetry,* University of Iowa Press, 1977; *Stari i novi vilajet* (prose poems), Kosovo, 1977.

Bdenja (prose poems), Kosovo, 1980; *Emigranti i druge price* (short stories), Srpska misao, 1980; *Krugovi na vodi* (prose poems), Yugoslavica, 1982; (editor) *Landmarks in Serbian Culture and History*, Serb National Federation, 1983; (editor) *A Comprehensive Bibliography of Yugoslav Literature in English, 1593-1980*, Slavica, 1984.

Guest editor of Yugoslav and Russian issues of *Literary Review*, 1968, 1970. Contributor of articles to *World Literature Today, Books Abroad, Saturday Review, Slavic and East European Journal, Slavic Review*, and *Encyclopedia Americana*.

WORK IN PROGRESS: Serbian Poetry from the Beginnings to the Present, an anthology; translating Njegos's *Gorski vijenac* into English.

*   *   *

MIKHAIL, E(dward) H(alim)   1928-

PERSONAL: Born June 29, 1928, in Cairo, Egypt; emigrated to Canada in 1966; son of Halim and Mathilda (Phares) Mikhail; married Isabelle Bichai, July 22, 1954; children: May, Carmen. *Education:* Cairo University, B.A. (with honors), 1947, B.Ed., 1949; Trinity College, Dublin, D.E.S., 1959; University of Sheffield, Ph.D., 1966. *Politics:* Conservative. *Religion:* Christian. *Home:* 6 Crestwood Blvd. W., Lethbridge, Alberta, Canada. *Office:* Department of English, University of Lethbridge, Lethbridge, Alberta, Canada.

CAREER: Cairo University, Cairo, Egypt, 1949-66, began as lecturer, became assistant professor; University of Lethbridge, Lethbridge, Alberta, associate professor, 1966-72, professor of English, 1972—. *Member:* International Association for the Study of Anglo-Irish Literature, Canadian Association for Irish Studies, Modern Language Association of America, Association of Canadian University Teachers of English, British Drama League, American Committee for Irish Studies. *Awards, honors:* Six Canada Council research grants, 1967-74.

WRITINGS: Social and Cultural Setting of the 1890's, Garnstone Press (London), 1969; *John Galsworthy the Dramatist: A Bibliography of Criticism*, Whitston Publishing, 1971; *Sean O'Casey: A Bibliography of Criticism*, University of Washington Press, 1972; *Comedy and Tragedy: A Bibliography of Critical Studies*, Whitston Publishing, 1972; *A Bibliography of Modern Irish Drama, 1899-1970*, University of Washington Press, 1972; *Dissertations on Anglo-Irish Drama*, Rowman & Littlefield, 1973; (editor with John O'Riordan) *The Sting and the Twinkle: Conversations with Sean O'Casey*, Barnes & Noble, 1974; *J. M. Synge: A Bibliography of Criticism*, Rowman & Littlefield, 1975.

Contemporary British Drama, 1950-1976: An Annotated Critical Bibliography, Rowman & Littlefield, 1976; *J. M. Synge: Interviews and Recollections*, Barnes & Noble, 1977; *W. B. Yeats: Interviews and Recollections*, two volumes, Barnes & Noble, 1977; *English Drama, 1900-1950: A Guide to Information Sources*, Gale, 1977; *Lady Gregory: Interviews and Recollections*, Rowman & Littlefield, 1977; *Oscar Wilde: An Annotated Bibliography of Criticism*, Rowman & Littlefield, 1978; *A Research Guide to Modern Irish Dramatists*, Whitston Publishing, 1979; *Oscar Wilde: Interviews and Recollections*, two volumes, Barnes & Noble, 1979; *The Art of Brendan Behan*, Barnes & Noble, 1979; *Brendan Behan: An Annotated Bibliography of Criticism*, Barnes & Noble, 1979; *An Annotated Bibliography of Modern Anglo-Irish Drama*, Whitston Publishing, 1981; *Lady Gregory: An Annotated Bibliography*

of Criticism, Whitston Publishing, 1982; *Brendan Behan: Interviews and Recollections*, two volumes, Barnes & Noble, 1982.

WORK IN PROGRESS: Sean O'Casey: A Reference Guide; The Letters of Brendan Behan; The Abbey Theatre: Interviews and Recollections.

BIOGRAPHICAL/CRITICAL SOURCES: Times Literary Supplement, April 18, 1980, April 22, 1983.

*   *   *

MILES, Keith
     See TRALINS, S(andor) Robert

*   *   *

MILLER, Conrad
     See STRUNG, Norman

*   *   *

MILLER, George (Eric)   1943-

PERSONAL: Born January 19, 1943, in Buffalo, N.Y.; son of Ralph L. and Lois (Wolfe) Miller; married Dorothy Ryan (a writer and researcher), September 5, 1964 (divorced August 23, 1979); married Rachel McClain (an editor and technical writer), November 8, 1979; children: Lisa, Jon, Craig, Valerie. *Education:* Pennsylvania State University, B.A., 1964, M.A., 1966; University of Connecticut, Ph.D., 1969. *Home:* 13 Turnbridge Rd., Newark, Del. 19713.

CAREER: University of Delaware, Newark, assistant professor, 1969-74, associate professor, 1974-81, professor of English, 1981—. *Member:* Modern Language Association of America. *Awards, honors:* Folger Shakespeare Library fellow, 1973.

WRITINGS: (With Dorothy Miller) *Picture Postcards in the United States, 1893-1918*, C. N. Potter, 1976; (with Thomas Gravell) *A Catalogue of American Watermarks, 1690-1835*, Garland Publishing, 1979; *A Pennsylvania Album*, Pennsylvania State University Press, 1979; (with Gravell) *A Catalogue of Foreign Watermarks Found on Paper Used in America, 1700-1835*, Garland Publishing, 1983; *Edward Hyde, Earl of Clarendon*, Twayne, 1983. Contributor to literature journals and popular magazines. Editor of *Teaching Writing*.

WORK IN PROGRESS: An introductory composition textbook; editing an anthology of essays for college use.

*   *   *

MILLER, Tom   1947-

PERSONAL: Born August 11, 1947, in Washington, D.C.; son of Morris (a judge) and Sara (an artist; maiden name, Levy) Miller. *Education:* Attended College of Wooster, 1965-68. *Politics:* "Yes." *Religion:* None. *Agent:* Theron Raines, Raines & Raines, 71 Park Ave., New York, N.Y. 10016. *Office address:* P.O. Box 50842, Tucson, Ariz. 85703.

CAREER: Writer. Visiting lecturer in creative writing, University of Arizona, 1980; participant in Artists-in-Education Program, Arizona Commission on the Arts, 1983—. Participated in Reporters and Editors Workshop on the Caribbean, Miami, 1983. *Awards, honors:* National Endowment for the Arts fellow, 1978.

WRITINGS: The Assassination Please Almanac, Regnery, 1977; *On the Border: Portraits of America's Southwestern Frontier*, Harper, 1981. Also author of documentary television programs. Contributor to *New York Times, Rolling Stone, Nation, Esquire*, and other publications.

WORK IN PROGRESS: Arizona: The Land and the People; books about travels in South America.

SIDELIGHTS: Tom Miller's *On the Border: Portraits of America's Southwestern Frontier* is "concerned less with the political issues it raises than with ordinary people's lives," according to Tamar Jacoby in the *New York Times Book Review*. Based on a four-month tour of America's southwest, the book provides a look at the often-illegal activities to be found along the Mexican-American border. Miller writes of smugglers, cockfight promoters, disk jockeys who broadcast from Mexico, and a host of others. "Miller," writes Jacoby, "has drawn a lively sketch of this unruly, unpredictable place."

BIOGRAPHICAL/CRITICAL SOURCES: New York Times Book Review, July 12, 1981; *New York Review of Books*, October 22, 1981.

*   *   *

MILNE, Lorus J.

PERSONAL: Born in Toronto, Ontario, Canada; son of Charles S. (a businessman) and Edna S. (Johnson) Milne; married Margery Greene (a writer, lecturer, and teacher). *Education:* University of Toronto, B.A. (honors), 1933; Harvard University, M.A., 1934, Ph.D., 1936. *Politics:* Republican. *Home:* 1 Garden Lane, Durham, N.H. 03824. *Office:* Spaulding Life Sciences Building, University of New Hampshire, Durham, N.H. 03824.

CAREER: Associate professor and professor at universities and colleges in Texas, New York, Virginia, Pennsylvania, and Vermont; University of New Hampshire, Durham, professor of zoology, 1948—. Visiting professor of environmental technology, Florida International University, 1974. Consultant-writer for American Institute of Biological Sciences; consultant-leader under UNESCO to New Zealand Department of Education; exchangee to South Africa under United States-South Africa Leader Exchange Program. Jointly appointed with wife as "Keepers of the Swans," 1968—, by town of Durham, N.H. *Member:* American Association for the Advancement of Science, Animal Behavior Society, American Society of Zoologists, Woods Hole Marine Biological Laboratory Corporation, Sigma Xi, Explorers Club.

WRITINGS: Machine Shop Methods, Prentice-Hall, 1950.

All with wife, Margery Milne: *A Multitude of Living Things*, Dodd, 1947; *The Biotic World and Man*, Prentice-Hall, 1952, 3rd edition, 1965; *The Mating Instinct*, Little, Brown, 1954; *The World of Night*, Harper, 1956, reprinted, 1981; *Paths across the Earth*, Harper, 1958; *Animal Life*, Prentice-Hall, 1959; *Plant Life*, Prentice-Hall, 1959.

(And with Ralph Buchsbaum and Mildred Buchsbaum) *The Lower Animals: Living Invertebrates of the World*, Doubleday, 1960; *The Balance of Nature*, Knopf, 1960; (and with the editors of *Life*) *The Mountains*, Time-Life Books, 1962; *The Senses of Animals and Men*, Atheneum, 1962; *The Valley: Meadow, Grove, and Stream*, Harper, 1963; *Water and Life*, Atheneum, 1964; *Living Plants of the World*, Random House, 1967, 2nd edition, 1975; *Patterns of Survival*, Prentice-Hall,

1967; *The Ages of Life: A New Look at the Effects of Time on Mankind and Other Living Things*, Harcourt, 1968; *North American Birds*, Prentice-Hall, 1969.

The Nature of Life: Earth, Plants, Animals, Man, and Their Effect on Each Other, Crown, 1970; *The Cougar Doesn't Live Here Any More: Does the World Still Have Room for Wildlife?*, Prentice-Hall, 1971; *The Arena of Life: The Dynamics of Ecology*, Doubleday, 1972; *Invertebrates of North America*, Doubleday, 1972; *The Animal in Man*, McGraw-Hill, 1972; (with Franklin Russell) *The Secret Life of Animals*, Dutton, 1975; *A World Alive*, New Hampshire Publishing, 1977; *Ecology Out of Joint: New Environments and Why They Happen*, Scribner, 1977; *The Audubon Society Field Guide to North American Insects and Spiders*, Knopf, 1980; *Gadabouts and Stick-at-Homes: Wild Animals and Their Habitats*, Scribner, 1980; *A Time to Be Born: An Almanac of Animal Courtship and Parenting*, Sierra Books, 1982; *The Audubon Society Book of Insects*, Abrams, 1983. Also author of *Insect Worlds: A Guide for Man in Making the Most of the Environment*, 1980, with others, of *The Audubon Society Encyclopedia of Animal Life*, 1982, *Concise Book of Living Invertebrates*, and *Laboratory Manual in General Biology*.

Books for young people; all with Margery Milne: *Famous Naturalists*, Dodd, 1952; *Because of a Tree*, Atheneum, 1963; *The Crab That Crawled Out of the Past*, Atheneum, 1965; *Gift from the Sky*, Atheneum, 1967; *The Phoenix Forest*, Atheneum, 1968; *The Nature of Animals*, Lippincott, 1969; *When the Tide Goes Far Out*, Atheneum, 1970; *The Nature of Plants*, Lippincott, 1971; *The How and Why of Growing*, Atheneum, 1972; *Because of a Flower*, Atheneum, 1975; *Dreams of a Perfect Earth*, Atheneum, 1982; *Nature's Clean-up Crew: The Burying Beetles*, Dodd, 1982; *Nature's Great Carbon Cycle*, Atheneum, 1983; *The Mystery of the Bog Forest*, Dodd, 1984.

Contributor to *Encyclopaedia Britannica, Time, National Geographic*, and other publications. Associate editor, *Fauna*.

SIDELIGHTS: About seventeen of Lorus Milne's books have been issued in foreign editions.

BIOGRAPHICAL/CRITICAL SOURCES: Books and Bookmen, December 4, 1967; *Book World*, January 14, 1968; *New York Times Book Review*, June 30, 1968; *Children's Book World*, November 3, 1968; *Best Sellers*, June 1, 1969; *New Yorker*, December 20, 1969; *Washington Post Book World*, July 11, 1982; *Chicago Tribune Book World*, December 5, 1982; *Los Angeles Times Book Review*, February 6, 1983.

*   *   *

MILNE, Margery

PERSONAL: Born in New York, N.Y.; daughter of S. Harrison (a businessman) and Beatrice (Gutman) Greene; married Lorus J. Milne (a professor of zoology, writer, and lecturer). *Education:* Hunter College (now Hunter College of the City University of New York), B.A., 1933; Columbia University, M.A., 1934; Radcliffe College, M.A., 1936, Ph.D., 1939. *Politics:* Republican. *Home:* 1 Garden Lane, Durham, N.H. 03824.

CAREER: Instructor, assistant professor, or lecturer at colleges and universities in Maine, Virginia, Pennsylvania, Massachusetts, Vermont, and New Hampshire. Consultant-writer for American Institute of Biological Sciences; consultant, Department of Education, Wellington, New Zealand. Jointly appointed with husband as "Keepers of the Swans," 1968—, by town of Durham, N.H. *Member:* Conservation Foundation,

Nature Conservancy, Society of Women Geographers, Phi Beta Kappa, Phi Sigma, Sigma Xi.

WRITINGS—All with husband, Lorus J. Milne: *A Multitude of Living Things*, Dodd, 1947; *The Biotic World and Man*, Prentice-Hall, 1952, 3rd edition, 1965; *The Mating Instinct*, Little, Brown, 1954; *The World of Night*, Harper, 1956, reprinted, 1981; *Paths across the Earth*, Harper, 1958; *Animal Life*, Prentice-Hall, 1959; *Plant Life*, Prentice-Hall, 1959.

(And with Ralph Buchsbaum and Mildred Buchsbaum) *The Lower Animals: Living Invertebrates of the World*, Doubleday, 1960; *The Balance of Nature*, Knopf, 1960; (and with the editors of *Life*) *The Mountains*, Time-Life Books, 1962; *The Senses of Animals and Men*, Atheneum, 1962; *The Valley: Meadow, Grove, and Stream*, Harper, 1963; *Water and Life*, Atheneum, 1964; *Living Plants of the World*, Random House, 1967, 2nd edition, 1975; *Patterns of Survival*, Prentice-Hall, 1967; *The Ages of Life: A New Look at the Effects of Time on Mankind and Other Living Things*, Harcourt, 1968; *North American Birds*, Prentice-Hall, 1969.

The Nature of Life: Earth, Plants, Animals, Man, and Their Effect on Each Other, Crown, 1970; *The Cougar Doesn't Live Here Any More: Does the World Still Have Room for Wildlife?*, Prentice-Hall, 1971; *The Arena of Life: The Dynamics of Ecology*, Doubleday, 1972; *Invertebrates of North America*, Doubleday, 1972; *The Animal in Man*, McGraw, 1972; (and with Franklin Russell) *The Secret Life of Animals*, Dutton, 1975; *A World Alive*, New Hampshire Publishing, 1977; *Ecology Out of Joint: New Environments and Why They Happen*, Scribner, 1977; *The Audubon Society Field Guide to North American Insects and Spiders*, Knopf, 1980; *Gadabouts and Stick-at-Homes: Wild Animals and Their Habitats*, Scribner, 1980; *A Time to Be Born: An Almanac of Animal Courtship and Parenting*, Sierra Books, 1982; *The Audubon Society Book of Insects*, Abrams, 1983. Also author of *Insect Worlds: A Guide for Man in Making the Most of the Environment*, 1980, with others, of *The Audubon Society Encyclopedia of Animal Life*, 1982, *Concise Book of Living Invertebrates*, and *Laboratory Manual in General Biology*.

Books for young people; all with Lorus J. Milne: *Famous Naturalists*, Dodd, 1952; *Because of a Tree*, Atheneum, 1963; *The Crab That Crawled Out of the Past*, Atheneum, 1965; *Gift from the Sky*, Atheneum, 1967; *The Phoenix Forest*, Atheneum, 1968; *The Nature of Animals*, Lippincott, 1969; *When the Tide Goes Far Out*, Atheneum, 1970; *The Nature of Plants*, Lippincott, 1971; *The How and Why of Growing*, Atheneum, 1972; *Because of a Flower*, Atheneum, 1975; *Dreams of a Perfect Earth*, Atheneum, 1982; *Nature's Clean-up Crew: The Burying Beetles*, Dodd, 1982; *Nature's Great Carbon Cycle*, Atheneum, 1983; *The Mystery of the Bog Forest*, Dodd, 1984.

Contributor of natural history articles to *Audubon Magazine*, *American Scholar*, *Natural History Magazine*, *New York Times Magazine*, *Scientific America*, and other periodicals, and of research reports to biology journals.

BIOGRAPHICAL/CRITICAL SOURCES: Books and Bookmen, December, 1967; *Book World*, January 14, 1968; *New York Times Book Review*, June 30, 1968; *Children's Book World*, November 3, 1968; *New Yorker*, December 20, 1969; *Washington Post Book World*, July 11, 1982; *Chicago Tribune Book World*, December 5, 1982; *Los Angeles Times Book Review*, February 6, 1983.

MILSTEAD, Jessica L(ee) 1939-
(Jessica L. Harris)

PERSONAL: Born June 4, 1939, in Bryans Road, Md.; daughter of Jesse Woodrow and Margret (Downs) Milstead; married Robert Harris (a plastics engineer), June 4, 1960 (divorced). *Education:* Eastern Nazarene College, A.B., 1960; Columbia University, M.S., 1965, D.L.S., 1969. *Home:* 251 Great Hill Rd., Ridgefield, Conn. 06877. *Office:* NewsBank, Inc., 58 Pine St., New Canaan, Conn. 06840.

CAREER: High school library assistant in Shorewood, Wis., 1960-61; Midwest Translation Bureau, Milwaukee, Wis., editor and translator, 1961-62; Bethel (Conn.) Public Library, library assistant, 1963-64; Rothines Associates, New York City, research associate, 1965-69; Columbia University, New York City, assistant professor of library service, 1969-72; Queens College of the City University of New York, Flushing, N.Y., assistant professor of library science, 1972-74; St. John's University, Jamaica, N.Y., associate professor of library and information science, 1974-79; Research Publications, Inc., Woodbridge, Conn., manager of indexing department, 1979-82; NewsBank, Inc., New Canaan, Conn., vice-president and editorial director, 1982—.

MEMBER: American Library Association, American Society of Indexers (secretary, 1968-69), Society of Indexers (London), Association for Computing Machinery, American Society for Information Science, Special Libraries Association, New York Library Club, Beta Phi Mu, Phi Delta Lambda.

WRITINGS—Under name Jessica L. Harris, except as indicated: (With Theodore C. Hines) *Computer Filing of Index, Bibliographic, and Catalog Entries*, Bro-Dart Foundation, 1966; *Subject Analysis: Computer Implications of Rigorous Definition*, Scarecrow, 1970; (contributor) Hilda Feinberg, editor, *Indexing Specialized Formats*, Scarecrow, 1983; (under name Jessica L. Milstead) *Subject Access Systems*, Academic Press, 1984.

Contributor of articles and reviews to professional journals. *Annual Review of Information Science and Technology*, index and bibliographic editor, 1974-75, compiler of cumulative index for volumes 1-10, 1976.

*   *   *

MINER, Matthew
See WALLMANN, Jeffrey M(iner)

*   *   *

MITCHELL, Don(ald Earl) 1947-

PERSONAL: Born October 15, 1947, in Chicago, Ill.; son of Wayne Treleven (an electrical engineer) and Elizabeth (Bowker) Mitchell; married Cheryl Warfield, November 29, 1969; children: Ethan, Anais. *Education:* Swarthmore College, A.B., 1969. *Politics:* Democrat. *Religion:* Protestant. *Home:* R.D. 2, Vergennes, Vt. 05491. *Agent:* Blanche C. Gregory, Inc., 2 Tudor City Pl., New York, N.Y. 10017.

CAREER: American Baptist Board of Education and Publication, Valley Forge, Pa., staff member, 1971; The New School, Wayne, Pa., high school teacher, 1972; writer, and sheep breeder at Treleven Farm in Vermont, 1973—.

WRITINGS: Thumb Tripping (also see below), Little, Brown, 1970; *Four-Stroke,* Little, Brown, 1973; *The Souls of Lambs,* Houghton, 1979; *Moving UpCountry,* Yankee, Inc., 1984. Also author of *Heretical Passions;* author of "Thumb Tripping," Avco Embassy Pictures Corp., 1969-70. Work anthologized in *Best Short Stories of 1971,* Houghton. Columnist, *Boston Magazine,* 1979—. Contributor to *Harper's, Atlantic, Esquire, Shenandoah, Viva, Country Journal,* and *Yankee.*

WORK IN PROGRESS: Meat, a detective novel.

SIDELIGHTS: Don Mitchell told *CA:* "I still like to think of myself as a novelist, but for the past several years my novelistic efforts have been sandbagged by real life: becoming a parent, learning the skills of an amateur architect/builder, and struggling to profitably manage a jewel of a farm in Vermont. If it weren't for having to produce a monthly magazine column, I'd have little at this point to underpin my identity as a writer at all. But I know I will return to the novel, and I can buy off my sense of discipline—and guilt—by reminding myself how important it is that novelists live life fully and well. When I go back to the problems of writing fiction, I expect it will be with fresh energies and fresh capital. And fresh eyes."

BIOGRAPHICAL/CRITICAL SOURCES: New York Times Book Review, August 2, 1970; *Best Sellers,* August 15, 1970; *Wall Street Journal,* April 23, 1979.

* * *

MITCHELL, Margaretta K. 1935-

PERSONAL: Born May 27, 1935, in Brooklyn, N.Y.; daughter of Conrad William (a realtor) and Margaretta (Rice) Kuhlthau; married Frederick C. Mitchell (a publisher), May 23, 1959; children: Margaretta Anne, Catharine Francesca, Julia Warren. *Education:* Smith College, B.A. (magna cum laude), 1957; graduate study, Boston Museum School, 1958-59, and Escuela de Bellas Artes, Madrid, 1959-60. *Religion:* Episcopalian. *Home:* 280 Hillcrest Rd., Berkeley, Calif. 94705.

CAREER: Photographer. Work has been exhibited at numerous galleries and museums, including International Center of Photography, New York City, San Francisco Museum of Modern Art, and Focus Gallery, San Francisco. Has taught at several schools and workshops; assistant at Ansel Adams Workshop, 1973.

MEMBER: American Society of Magazine Photographers, Society for Photographic Education, Institute for Historical Study, San Francisco Women Artists, Phi Beta Kappa.

AWARDS, HONORS: National Endowment for the Arts grant, 1978-79; California Council for the Humanities grant, 1980; L. J. and Mary C. Skaggs Foundation grants, 1981; California Council for the Arts grant, 1981-82.

WRITINGS: Gift of Place, Scrimshaw Press, 1969; (with Dorothea Lange) *To a Cabin,* Grossman, 1973; (author of introduction) Imogen Cunningham, *After Ninety,* University of Washington Press, 1977; *Recollections: Ten Women of Photography,* Viking, 1979; (contributor) *Contemporary Photographers,* St. Martin's, 1982; (author of introduction) Cynthia MacAdams, *Rising Goddess,* Morgan & Morgan, 1982.

Also author of slide/film presentation, "Dance for Life," 1978, and of booklet, "The American Family," 1980. Contributor of articles and photographs to magazines and journals, including *Darkroom, Camera Arts, Popular Photography, 35mm Photography, Invitation to Photography,* and *Ramparts.*

WORK IN PROGRESS: Isadora Duncan and Her California Dance Tradition.

SIDELIGHTS: Margaretta Mitchell told *CA:* "As a photographer, I specialize in portraiture. I also am now striving to work for designers and writers in the corporate world for my living. At the same time I am producing photogravures for my own delight. As a writer I write about photographers and photography."

BIOGRAPHICAL/CRITICAL SOURCES: New York Times Book Review, November 25, 1979; *Washington Post Book World,* December 2, 1979.

* * *

MITCHELL, W.J.T. 1942-

PERSONAL: Born March 24, 1942, in Anaheim, Calif.; son of Thomas Miles (a miner) and Leona (an accountant; maiden name, Gaertner) Mitchell; married Janice Misurell (a composer), August 11, 1968; children: Carmen, Gabriel. *Education:* Michigan State University, B.A., 1964; Johns Hopkins University, M.A., and Ph.D. *Politics:* "Left-Liberal." *Religion:* Agnostic. *Home:* 1331 East 50th St., Chicago, Ill. 60615. *Office:* Department of English, University of Chicago, Chicago, Ill. 60637.

CAREER: Ohio State University, Columbus, assistant professor, 1968-73, associate professor of English, 1973-77; University of Chicago, Chicago, Ill., associate professor of English, 1977-80, professor of English and art and design, 1980—, visiting professor, School of Criticism and Theory, 1983.

MEMBER: P.E.N., Conference of Editors of Learned Journals, Academy of Literary Studies, Modern Language Association of America, American Society for Eighteenth Century Studies.

AWARDS, HONORS: American Philosophical Society fellow, 1970; National Endowment for the Humanities fellow, 1977-78; Guggenheim fellow, 1980-81.

WRITINGS: Blake's Composite Art, Princeton University Press, 1978; (editor) *The Language of Images,* University of Chicago Press, 1980; *On Narrative,* University of Chicago Press, 1981; *The Politics of Interpretation,* University of Chicago Press, 1983. Work represented in anthologies.

Contributor of articles and reviews to language and eighteenth-century studies journals. Co-editor of *Critical Inquiry.*

WORK IN PROGRESS: Iconology: Image, Text, Ideology, on the interaction of verbal and pictorial structures in the arts, and the values they embody.

SIDELIGHTS: W.J.T. Mitchell comments: "The central commitment of my professional life is the theory and practice of criticism, conceived as a method of rigorous intellectual inquiry applicable to all subjects of human concern. I am especially interested in expanding our comprehension of the cognitive nature of artistic works, and overcoming the isolated 'aestheticism' which opposes the arts to practical and scientific matters. I have [also] come to feel that the issues of power and value are equally important (along with the cognitive) in our grasp of the arts."

* * *

MOFFETT, Judith 1942-

PERSONAL: Born August 30, 1942, in Louisville, Ky.; daughter of James S. (a commercial artist) and Margaret (a secretary; maiden name, Cowherd) Moffett; married Edward B. Irving, Jr., March 17, 1983. *Education:* Hanover College, A.B. (cum laude), 1964; Colorado State University, M.A., 1966; University of Wisconsin—Madison, further graduate study, 1966-67; University of Pennsylvania, M.A., 1970, Ph.D., 1971. *Home:* 608 Meadowvale Lane, Media, Pa. 19063. *Office:* Department of English, University of Pennsylvania, Philadelphia, Pa. 19104.

CAREER: University of Lund, Lund, Sweden, Fulbright lecturer in American studies, 1967-68; Pennsylvania State University, Behrend College, Erie, assistant professor of English, 1971-75; writer, 1975—; University of Iowa, Iowa City, teacher of writing, 1977-78; University of Pennsylvania, Philadelphia, assistant professor of English, 1978—. *Awards, honors:* Eunice Tietjens Memorial Prize from *Poetry*, 1973, for two poems; grants from Pennsylvania State Institute for the Arts and Humanistic Studies, 1973, American Philosophical Association, 1973, Nathhorsts Foundation, 1973, Swedish Institute, 1973 and 1976, and Ingram Merrill Foundation, 1976 and 1980; Fulbright travel grant, 1973-74; Borestone Mountain Poetry Award, 1975, for "Cecropia Terzine"; Levinson Prize from *Poetry*, 1976; University of Pennsylvania faculty research grant, 1979 and 1983; translation prize from Swedish Academy, 1982, for translation of *Gentleman, Single, Refined and Selected Poems, 1937-1959* by Hjalmar Gullberg; National Endowment for the Humanities translation grant, 1983, for an anthology of nineteenth-century Swedish poetry; National Endowment for the Arts creative writing fellowship, 1984.

WRITINGS: Keeping Time (poems), Louisiana State University Press, 1976; (translator from the Swedish) Hjalmar Gullberg, *Gentleman, Single, Refined and Selected Poems, 1937-1959*, Louisiana State University Press, 1979; *James Merrill: An Introduction to the Poetry*, Columbia University Press, 1984; *Whinny Moor Crossing* (poems), Princeton University Press, 1984.

WORK IN PROGRESS: Translations, introduction, and notes for an anthology of nineteenth-century Swedish poetry containing selections from the work of seven poets; "learning to write science fiction."

*   *   *

MOMADAY, N(avarre) Scott   1934-

PERSONAL: Surname is pronounced *Ma*-ma-day; born February 27, 1934, in Lawton, Okla.; son of Alfred Morris (a painter and teacher of art) and Mayme Natachee (a teacher and writer; maiden name, Scott) Momaday; married first wife, Gaye Mangold, September 5, 1959; married Regina Heitzer, July 21, 1978; children: (first marriage) Cael, Jill, Brit (all daughters). *Education:* University of New Mexico, A.B., 1958; Stanford University, M.A., 1960, Ph.D., 1963. *Home:* 1041 West Roller Coaster Rd., Tucson, Ariz. 85704. *Office:* Department of English, University of Arizona, Tucson, Ariz. 85721.

CAREER: University of California, Santa Barbara, assistant professor, 1963-65, associate professor of English, 1968-69; University of California, Berkeley, associate professor of English and comparative literature, 1969-73; Stanford University, Stanford, Calif., professor of English, 1973-82; University of Arizona, Tucson, professor of English, 1982—. Artist; has exhibited his drawings and paintings in galleries. Trustee, Museum of American Indian, Heye Foundation, New York City,

1978—. Consultant, National Endowment for the Humanities, National Endowment for the Arts, 1970—.

MEMBER: Modern Language Association of America, American Studies Association, Gourd Dance Society of the Kiowa Tribe.

AWARDS, HONORS: Academy of American Poets prize, 1962, for poem "The Bear"; Guggenheim fellowship, 1966-67; Pulitzer Prize for fiction, 1969, for *House Made of Dawn;* National Institute of Arts and Letters grant, 1970; shared Western Heritage Award with David Muench, 1974, for nonfiction book *Colorado, Summer/Fall/Winter/Spring;* Premio Letterario Internazionale Mondello, Italy, 1979.

WRITINGS: (Editor) *The Complete Poems of Frederick Goddard Tuckerman*, Oxford University Press, 1965; *The Journey of Tai-me* (retold Kiowa Indian folktales), with original etchings by Bruce S. McCurdy, limited edition, University of California, Santa Barbara, 1967, enlarged edition published as *The Way to Rainy Mountain*, illustrated by his father, Alfred Momaday, University of New Mexico Press, 1969; *House Made of Dawn* (novel), Harper, 1968, limited edition, Franklin Library, 1977; *Colorado, Summer/Fall/Winter/Spring*, illustrated with photographs by David Muench, Rand McNally, 1973; *Angle of Geese and Other Poems*, David Godine, 1974; *The Gourd Dancer* (poems), illustrated by the author, Harper, 1976; *The Names: A Memoir*, Harper, 1976.

Also author of film script of Frank Water's novel, *The Man Who Killed the Deer*. Contributor of articles and poems to periodicals; a frequent reviewer on Indian subjects for *New York Times Book Review*.

WORK IN PROGRESS: A study of American poetry in the middle period, *The Furrow and the Glow: Science and Literature in America, 1836-1866* (tentative title), for Oxford University Press; a novel; a book on storytelling, for Oxford University Press.

SIDELIGHTS: N. Scott Momaday's poetry and prose reflect his Kiowa Indian heritage in structure and theme, as well as in subject matter. "When I was growing up on the reservations of the Southwest," he told Joseph Bruchac in *American Poetry Review*, "I saw people who were deeply involved in their traditional life, in the memories of their blood. They had, as far as I could see, a certain strength and beauty that I find missing in the modern world at large. I like to celebrate that involvement in my writing." Roger Dickinson-Brown indicates in the *Southern Review* that Momaday has long "maintained a quiet reputation in American Indian affairs and among distinguished *literati*" for his brilliance and range, "his fusion of alien cultures, and his extraordinary experiments in different literary forms." Momaday believes that his poetry, in particular, grows from and sustains the Indian oral tradition, he commented to Bruchac. And his Pulitzer Prize-winning novel *House Made of Dawn* is described by Baine Kerr in *Southwest Review* as an attempt to "transliterate Indian culture, myth, and sensibility into an alien art form without loss." *The Way to Rainy Mountain* melds myth, history, and personal recollection into a narrative about the Kiowa tribe, while Momaday's *The Names: A Memoir* explores the author's heritage in autobiographical form.

The Names is composed of tribal tales, boyhood memories, and genealogy, reports *New York Times Book Review* critic Wallace Stegner. Momaday's quest for his roots, writes Edward Abbey in *Harper's*, "takes him back to the hills of Kentucky and north to the high plains of Wyoming, and from there, in memory and imagination, back to the Bering Straits.'' Stegner describes it as ''an Indian book, but not a book about wrongs done to Indians. It is a search and a celebration, a book of identities and sources. Momaday is the son of parents who successfully bridged the gulf between Indian and white ways, but remain Indian,'' he explains. ''In boyhood Momaday made the same choice, and in making it gave himself the task of discovering and in some degree inventing the tradition and history in which he finds his most profound sense of himself.'' *New York Review of Books* critic Diane Johnson agrees that ''Momaday does not appear to feel, or does not discuss, any conflict of the Kiowa and white traditions; he is their product, an artist, heir of the experiences of his ancestors and conscious of the benignity of their influence.''

Momaday is only half Kiowa. His mother, Mayme Natachee Scott, is descended from early American pioneers, although her middle name is taken from a Cherokee great-grandmother. Momaday's memoir also includes anecdotes of such Anglo-American ancestors as his grandfather, Theodore Scott, a Kentucky sheriff. His mother, however, preferred to identify in her imagination with her Indian heritage, adopting the name Little Moon when she was younger and dressing Indian style. She attended Haskell Institute, an Indian school in Kansas, where she met several members of the Kiowa tribe; eventually she married Momaday's father, also a Kiowa. The author grew up in New Mexico, where his mother, a teacher and writer, and his father, an artist and art teacher, found work among the Jemez Indians in the state's high canyon and mountain country, but he was originally raised among the Kiowas on a family farm in Oklahoma. Although Momaday covers his Anglo-American heritage in the memoir, he prefers, like his mother, ''to imagine himself *all* Indian, and to 'imagine himself' back into the life, the emotions, the spirit of his Kiowa forebears,'' comments Abbey. He uses English, his mother's language, according to Abbey, to tell ''his story in the manner of his father's people, moving freely back and forth in time and space, interweaving legend, myth, and history.''

Momaday doesn't actually speak Kiowa, but, in his work, he reveals the language as not only a reflection of the physical environment, but also a means of shaping it. The title of *The Names*, reports Richard Nicholls in *Best Sellers*, refers to all ''the names given by Scott Momaday's people, the Kiowa Indians, to the objects, forms, and features of their land, the southwestern plains, and to its animals and birds.'' When he was less than a year old, Momaday was given the name Tsoaitalee or ''Rock-tree-Boy'' by a paternal relative, after the 1,200-foot volcanic butte in Wyoming, which is sacred to the Kiowas and is known to Anglo-Americans as Devil's Tower. ''For the Kiowas it was a place of high significance,'' points out Abbey. ''To be named after that mysterious and mythic rock was, for the boy, a high honor and a compelling one. For among the Indians a name was never merely an identifying tag but something much more important, a kind of emblem and ideal, the determing source of a man or woman's character and course of life.''

The Indian perception of man's relationship to the earth is a central concern in Momaday's writing; he told Bruchac: ''I believe that the Indian has an understanding of the physical world and of the earth as a spiritual entity that is his, very much his own. The non-Indian can benefit a good deal by having that perception revealed to him.'' And, he explained, his own particular ''growing up'' within the Indian culture was a ''fortunate'' upbringing. ''On the basis of my experience, trusting my own perceptions, I don't see any validity in the separation of man and landscape. Oh, I know that the notion of alienation is very widespread, in a sense very popular. But I think it's an unfortunate point of view and a false one, where the relationship between man and the earth is concerned. Certainly it is one of the great afflictions of our time, this conviction of alienation, separation, isolation. And it is certainly an affliction in the Indian world. But there it has the least chance of taking hold, I believe, for there it is opposed by very strong forces. The whole world view of the Indian is predicated upon the principle of harmony in the universe. You can't tinker much with that; it has the look of an absolute.''

This view does not preclude conflict, however. Momaday's theme in his poem ''Rainy Mountain Cemetery,'' Dickinson-Brown points out, ''is as old as our civilization: the tension, the gorgeous hostility between the human and the wild—a tension always finally relaxed in death.'' And, ultimately, even the violent, discontinuous sequence of events in *House Made of Dawn* conveys what Vernon E. Lattin calls in an *American Literature* review ''a new romanticism, with a reverence for the land, a transcendent optimism, and a sense of mythic wholeness.'' Momaday's ''reverence for the land,'' according to Lattin, is comparable ''to the pastoral vision found in most mainstream American literature,'' but with ''essential differences.'' Dickinson-Brown argues that Momaday's use of landscape in *House Made of Dawn* ''is peculiar to him and to his Indian culture. It is a landscape and a way of living nowhere else available.'' In Kerr's words, here, Momaday ''may in fact be seeking to make the modern Anglo novel a vehicle for a sacred text.''

House Made of Dawn tells ''the old story of the problem of mixing Indians and Anglos,'' reports *New York Times Book Review* critic Marshall Sprague. ''But there is a quality of revelation here as the author presents the heart-breaking effort of his hero to live in two worlds.'' In the novel's fractured narrative, the main character, Abel, returns to the prehistoric landscape and culture surrounding his reservation pueblo after his tour of duty in the Army during World War II. Back home, he kills an albino. He serves a prison term and is parolled, unrepentant, to a Los Angeles relocation center. Once in the city, he attempts to adjust to his factory job, like his even-tempered roommate, Ben, a modern Indian, who narrates parts of the novel. During his free time, Abel drinks and attends adulterated religious and peyote-eating ceremonies. He can't cope with his job; and, ''because of his contempt,'' Sprague indicates that he's brutally beaten by a Los Angeles policeman, but returns again to the reservation ''in time to carry on tradition for his dying grandfather,'' Francisco. The novel culminates in Abel's running in the ancient ritual dawn race against evil and death.

According to Kerr, the book is ''a creation myth—rife with fabulous imagery, ending with Abel's rebirth in the old ways at the old man's death—but an ironic one, suffused with violence and telling a story of culture loss.'' The grandfather, he maintains, ''heroic, crippled, resonant with the old ways, impotent in the new—acts as a lodestone to the novel's conflicting energies. His incantatory dying delirium in Spanish fixes Momaday's symbolic compass . . . , and around his dying the book shapes its proportions.'' Francisco is ''the alembic that transmutes the novel's confusions,'' he comments. ''His retrospection marks off the book's boundaries, points of reference, and focal themes: the great organic calendar of the black mesa—the house of the sun (which locates the title)—as a central Rosetta stone integrating the ceremonies rendered in Part One, and the source place by which Abel and [his brother] could 'reckon where they were, where all things were, in time.'"

Momaday meets with difficulties in his attempt to convey Indian sensibility in novelistic form, Kerr relates. The fractured narrative is open to criticism, in Kerr's opinion, and the "plot of *House Made of Dawn* actually seems propelled by withheld information, that besetting literary error," he writes. Of the novel's structure, Dickinson-Brown writes that the sequence of events "is without fixed order. The parts can be rearranged, no doubt with change of effect, but not always with recognizable difference. The fragments thus presented *are* the subject. The result is a successful depiction but not an understanding of what is depicted: a reflection, not a novel in the comprehensive sense of the word." Kerr also objects to the author's overuse of "quiet, weak constructions" in the opening paragraph and indicates that "repetition, polysyndeton, and *there* as subject continue to deaden the narrative's force well into the book." *Commonweal* reviewer William James Smith agrees that "Mr. Momaday observes and renders accurately, but the material seems to have sunken slightly beneath the surface of the beautiful prose." Lattin maintains, however, that the novel should also be regarded as "a return to the sacred art of storytelling and myth-making that is part of Indian oral tradition," as well as an attempt "to push the secular mode of modern fiction into the sacred mode, a faith and recognition in the power of the word." And a *Times Literary Supplement* critic points out Momaday's "considerable descriptive power," citing "a section in which Tosamah [a Los Angeles medicine man/priest] rehearses the ancient trampled history of the Kiowas in trance-like visionary prose that has moments of splendour."

John "Big Bluff" Tosamah, Kerr argues, "in his two magnificent 'sermons,' is really an incarnation of the author, Momaday's mouthpiece, giving us what we've been denied: interpretation of Indian consciousness, expatiation on themes." According to Lattin, he is "a more complex religious figure" than his thoroughly Christian counterpart, Father Olguin, the Mexican priest who works on the reservation. "In the first sermon, 'The Gospel According to St. John,' Tosamah perceives the Book of John as an overwrought creation myth, applies the lightning bolt concept of the Word to the Kiowa myth of Tai-me, and apotheosizes the Indian gift of the human need for a felt awe of creation," Kerr relates. Tosamah, he indicates, "is an intriguing, well-crafted interlocutor, but also a slightly caricatured self-portrait—like Momaday a Kiowa, a man of words, an interpreter of Indian sensibility."

Tosamah's sermon on Kiowa tribal history appears in a slightly altered form in Momaday's *The Way to Rainy Mountain,* and in a review of that book, *Southern Review* critic Kenneth Fields points out that Momaday's writing exemplifies a "paradox about language which is often expressed in American Indian literature." Momaday himself has written that "by means of words can a man deal with the world on equal terms. And the word is sacred," comments Fields. "On the other hand . . . the Indians took for their subject matter those elusive perceptions that resist formulation, never entirely apprehensible, but just beyond the ends of the nerves." In a similar vein, Dickinson-Brown maintains that Momaday's poem "Angle of Geese" "presents, better than any other work I know . . . perhaps the most important subject of our age: the tragic conflict between what we have felt in wilderness and what our language means." What Momaday must articulate in *The Way to Rainy Mountain,* Fields argues, is "racial memory," or "the ghostly heritage of [his] Kiowa ancestors," and "what it means to feel himself

a Kiowa in the modern American culture that displaced his ancestors."

Described by Fields as "far and away [Momaday's] best book," *The Way to Rainy Mountain* relates the story of the Kiowas' journey 300 years ago from the Yellowstone down onto the plains, where they acquired horses, and, in the words of John R. Milton in *Saturday Review,* "they became a lordly society of sun priests, fighters, hunters, and thieves, maintaining this position for 100 years, to the mid-nineteenth century," when they were all but destroyed by the U.S. Cavalry in Oklahoma. And when the sacred buffalo began to disappear, Fields indicates, "the Kiowas lost the sustaining illumination of the sun god," since, as Momaday explains, the buffalo was viewed as "the animal representation of the sun, the essential and sacrificial victim of the Sun Dance." "Momaday's own grandmother, who had actually been present at the last and abortive Kiowa Sun Dance in 1887, is for him the last of the Kiowas," relates Fields.

Here, Momaday uses form to help him convey a reality that has largely been lost. His text is made up of twenty-four numbered sections grouped into three parts, The Setting Out, The Going On, and The Closing In. These parts are in turn divided into three different passages, each of which is set in a different style type face. The first passage in each part is composed of Kiowa myths and legends, the second is made up of historical accounts of the tribe, and the third passage is a personal autobiographical rendering of Momaday's rediscovery of his Kiowa homeland and roots. "In form," points out Fields, "it resembles those ancient texts with subsequent commentaries which, taken altogether, present strange complexes of intelligence; not only the author's, but with it that of the man in whose mind the author was able to live again."

By the end of the last part, however, writes Nicholas, the three passages begin to blend with one another, and "the mythic passages are no longer mythic in the traditional sense, that is Momaday is creating myth out of his memories of his ancestors rather than passing on already established and socially sanctioned tales. Nor are the historical passages strictly historical, presumably objective, accounts of the Kiowas and their culture. Instead they are carefully selected and imaginatively rendered memories of his family. And, finally, the personal passages have become prose poems containing symbols which link them thematically to the other two, suggesting that all three journies are products of the imagination, that all have become interfused in a single memory and reflect a single idea."

Dickinson-Brown considers the book's shape a well-controlled "associational structure," distinctively adapted to the author's purpose. The form, according to Fields, forces Momaday "to relate the subjective to the more objective historical sensibility. The writing of the book itself, one feels, enables him to gain both freedom and possession. It is therefore a work of discovery as well as renunciation, of finding but also of letting go." Thus Momaday can view his heritage objectively and in a positive light. Momaday explained to Bruchac: "The Indian has the advantage of a very rich spiritual experience. As much can be said, certainly, of some non-Indian writers. But the non-Indian writers of today are culturally deprived, I think, in the sense that they don't have the same sense of heritage that the Indian has. I'm told this time and time again by my students, who say, 'Oh, I wish I knew more about my grandparents; I wish I knew more about my ancestors and where they came from and what they did.' I've come to believe them. It seems to me that the Indian writer ought to make use of that advantage. One of his subjects ought certainly to be his cultural investment in the world. It is a unique and complete experience, and it is a great subject in itself.''

CA INTERVIEW

CA interviewed N. Scott Momaday by telephone on December 16, 1983, at his home in Tucson, Arizona.

CA: When you won the 1969 Pulitzer Prize in fiction for House Made of Dawn, *were you as surprised as the newspaper accounts reported you to be?*

MOMADAY: At least as surprised; I couldn't have been more surprised.

CA: Instead of using the resulting attention for personal gain, you have made it a means of promoting your Indian cultural heritage, beginning perhaps with your course in American Indian literature at the University of California at Berkeley, which was said to be the first in the country. Is American Indian literature being taught widely now?

MOMADAY: I think so. I have no idea how many departments of native American studies there are in the country now, but there are a good many and some of them, I'm sure, are quite distinguished.

CA: In the acknowledgments to The Way to Rainy Mountain *(1969), you thanked the ''kinsmen who willingly recounted . . . the tribal history and literature'' to you. Were there many people who told you the Kiowa legends, besides your father, your grandmother Aho, and her friend Ko-sahn?*

MOMADAY: There were quite a few. Most of the stories, at least the core stories, I had from my father. Then when I set out to make the collection for *The Way to Rainy Mountain,* I talked to a number of people in Oklahoma, mostly older people who were themselves in close touch with the oral tradition of the tribe; I would say maybe six or eight such people.

CA: Did they realize that you would be putting the stories into book form, that they would be written down?

MOMADAY: I think some did, yes. I'm sure I mentioned my intention to several of them. They were quite receptive and I ran into no objections.

CA: In your very unusual autobiography, The Names *(1976), you told about your ancestors on both sides, which included some Kentucky history and French and English forebears on your mother's side. Had the ancestry already been traced, or did you do most of it yourself?*

MOMADAY: It had been sketchily traced through the family. My mother and her sister, both very much interested in family history, had looked into some of those matters. But when I was writing *The Names* I discovered that I could get only so far with it. Beyond that, there simply were no records whatever.

CA: The photographs in that book were marvelous. Did they already belong to the family?

MOMADAY: Yes. They were in my mother's possession, a kind of a family album. They were enormously helpful, of course, in patching that family history together.

CA: How did the Indian name Mammedaty become the family surname?

MOMADAY: Mammedaty was my paternal grandfather's name—at that time, people had but one name. That was the name that was given to him as a child, and that was the only name that he had. But during his lifetime the missionaries came in, and the Indians adopted the Christian tradition of the surname and the Christian name. And so my grandfather was given the name John, and he became known as John Mammedaty then, and Mammedaty simply became the surname of his family. It was passed down. Some of my relatives in Oklahoma still use that spelling, but my father abbreviated it to Momaday.

CA: You've taught your children the Indian stories and traditions as your parents and grandparents taught them to you. One of your daughters said she wanted to be a painter (like you and your father, Al Momaday) and a writer (like you and your mother). Is she moving in that direction?

MOMADAY: Yes. I think she's more interested in painting than in writing at the moment, but she is very much interested in both, and that pleases me, of course.

CA: Do you find time now for painting as well as writing?

MOMADAY: Yes, I do. I find that I can do both things. I go through long periods of time in which I'm doing one and not the other, but I do both. I'm having an exhibit in January, so I'm having to put together some drawings and paintings for that, and I'm also under contract to finish a novel. So I'm fairly busy with both things.

CA: Where is the exhibit going to be?

MOMADAY: It's going to be in Scottsdale, Arizona, at a gallery where my father exhibited frequently, called the Ohl Gallery.

CA: In your poetry as well as your prose you celebrate the earth and man's tie to it. You've said that ''the American Indian has a unique investment in the American landscape.'' Are you actively involved in ecological causes?

MOMADAY: I wouldn't say actively. I'm very much interested of course in things that are being done to conserve resources, but I'm not a joiner so I don't belong to organizations; I'm not active in that way. What I do is try to indicate my feelings about the land in my writing.

CA: You were writing in college as an undergraduate. Did you start writing seriously much before that?

MOMADAY: No. I think I had wanted to be a writer, as so many young people do, but I didn't know what that meant until I was an undergraduate. Then I started writing poems and kept up the writing of poetry pretty much through graduate school. Then I turned to prose.

CA: You don't seem to have gone through the tribulations that many writers endure to get their work published. Your doctoral dissertation became your first published book, The Complete Poems of Frederick Goddard Tuckerman *(1965). What happened after that, with* House Made of Dawn?

MOMADAY: Well, I had started writing *House Made of Dawn* when I left Stanford in 1963 as a graduate student. When I graduated I went to Santa Barbara, which was my first teaching post, and there I started writing *House Made of Dawn*. I had a letter one day from Frances McCullough, who had been the editor of the literary magazine at Stanford, called *Sequoia*. She had published some of my poems there when I was a student and she was a student (she was an undergraduate student at that time), and when we both left Stanford, she went to New York and entered a publishing house—I've forgotten which one. But anyway, she moved over to Harper & Row after a time, and she wrote to me and asked me if I had a sufficient number of poems for a book that I might be willing to submit. I didn't have enough and I told her that, but I said, "I happen to be working on a novel. Why don't I send you some of that?" So I sent her what I had; it must have been, oh, two chapters, say. Harper & Row accepted the novel, and that's how it all happened. It was all quite a fluke, really. I was very fortunate, and believe me, it's not lost upon me. I'm grateful.

CA: How were you attracted to nineteenth-century American literature, and to Frederick Tuckerman in particular?

MOMADAY: When I got to Stanford I didn't really know much about American literature. In fact, when I went there it was as a fellow in creative writing, and I did not intend to take an advanced degree at first. I thought, well, I'll go, and this is a good opportunity to write, since they're paying my way for a year. But when I got to Stanford, Yvor Winters, who became my close friend and advisor, talked me into staying on through graduate school. I think it was he who really got me interested in Tuckerman. I didn't know Tuckerman when I went to Stanford, but Winters had taught some of Tuckerman's poems in one of his courses. I got particularly interested in that period, I think, mainly because of my deep admiration of the poems of Emily Dickinson. But then when I was thinking about a dissertation I boiled it down to a couple of choices, and Tuckerman turned out to be the most feasible—I had discovered that his manuscripts were collected in one place and it would not be difficult to work with them. So I selected Tuckerman on that basis.

CA: Do you feel that there is a kinship between nineteenth-century American literature and the Indian folklore and mythology that you've done so much work in?

MOMADAY: Yes, to some extent, because a lot of nineteenth-century writers were discovering the indigenous America and they became painters, especially interested in wilderness landscapes. And a lot of the poets were writing about Indians. I think there is some affinity.

CA: Is more Indian folklore being written down now?

MOMADAY: I think so. What was written down formerly was done mostly by anthropologists and ethnographers. There is a good body of that material in such publications as the Smithsonian bulletins. But I think now there is an interest across a wider range. A lot of people who are not necessarily scientists are becoming interested in Indian folklore—writers, for example, who see some possibility of incorporating that particular level of mythology into their own writing. That interest is very healthy, I think.

CA: In The White Man's Indian *(1978), Robert F. Berkhofer, Jr., wrote, "Native Americans were and are real, but the* Indian *was a White invention and still remains largely a White image, if not stereotype." In the past few years of awakening*

pride among Indians and other ethnic groups, has the stereotype begun to break down?

MOMADAY: I think it has. I think the stereotype is still there, and indeed it may not be necessarily a bad thing that we do have this invention of the Indian by the white man because it does function, sometimes, in a creative way in artistic expression. I'm thinking of such things as the Wild West show and the great tradition of Western films, which were not authentic but were nonetheless viable as art forms. That stereotype persists, as I say; but at the same time, apart from it, we have another view of the Indian and a much more viable one. The Indian himself has given us that view. I think he's concerned to do that at this time, and we will know more about who and what he really is as time goes on. There's been a big explosion in that way, beginning perhaps with Dee Brown's *Bury My Heart at Wounded Knee*. Since the publication of that book in 1970, there have been a lot of books that have given us a different and much more accurate view of the Indian world.

CA: You have indeed cited Bury My Heart at Wounded Knee *as a turning point in the recognition of the "fundamental diversity and individuality" of American Indians. Do you think the tribes can retain their individuality and still function well in a larger culture? Is there a kind of a delicate balance that has to be maintained?*

MOMADAY: That's a very difficult question, and I really don't know the answer to it. I have the impression that it is possible for one to retain tribal identity and at the same time function in the non-Indian world, but that's about all I can say about it. The question is, what does it mean to retain a tribal identity? I believe an Indian is someone who thinks of himself as an Indian, which is a pretty broad kind of a definition. But I know that my kinsmen, for example, the Kiowas, as dispersed as they are now, do feel that they are Kiowas and have ways of celebrating that identity. They always return to Oklahoma, for example, for ceremonial occasions and really keep that heritage alive within themselves. I think it must be possible to keep on in that way—and may be more possible now than it was a generation ago.

CA: What about fiction with an Indian focus? Is there much of a body of good fiction?

MOMADAY: Not much, but a growing body. There are some people around who are gifted writers of fiction. I'm thinking of James Welch and Leslie Silko and Simon Ortiz—more poets than writers of fiction, by the way, which I find interesting and also reasonable because I think poetry is closer to Indian oral tradition than is fiction. But we're going to see many more Indian novelists in the future.

CA: Considering the upcoming art exhibit, it may be a bad time to ask you what kind of a writing schedule you keep. Under normal conditions, do you write on a steady schedule?

MOMADAY: Yes. I try to build up to a fairly rigid schedule. Writing, I find, goes on in the mind for a long time before you really put anything down on paper. And I've just begun, really, to make that transition. Last summer I made a good beginning on the novel; I've set down, oh, ten or fifteen thousand words. When I'm really writing I do it in the morning. I find that I can write about six hours and that's all. But I try to do it every day and get an early start when I think my energies are at their very best.

CA: Are you teaching at all now?

MOMADAY: I just finished the spring term and I'm on leave now until September. It's badly needed time.

CA: Beyond the novel, what's in the future?

MOMADAY: I want to keep painting and writing. And I want to write a book on storytelling eventually. I haven't really begun that, but I have thought about it a good deal and I've signed a contract with Oxford for it, though I don't have a deadline yet. I'm interested in the origin of storytelling and the function of the storyteller and what his relationship is to his listener. There is an awful lot to be learned about that. I will, of course, focus on American Indian storytelling, but I also want to be able to make references to other ancient forms of storytelling. That's something in the future, and it may be the next thing I turn to after the novel.

BIOGRAPHICAL/CRITICAL SOURCES: New York Times Book Review, June 9, 1968, June 16, 1974, March 6, 1977; *Best Sellers,* June 15, 1968, April, 1977; *Nation,* August 5, 1968; *Commonweal,* September 20, 1968; *Listener,* May 15, 1969; *New York Times,* May 16, 1969, June 3, 1970; *New Yorker,* May 17, 1969; *Times Literary Supplement,* May 22, 1969; *Spectator,* May 23, 1969; *Observer,* May 25, 1969; *Saturday Review,* June 21, 1969; *Southwest Review,* summer, 1969, spring, 1978; *Washington Post,* November 21, 1969; N. Scott Momaday, *The Way to Rainy Mountain,* University of New Mexico Press, 1969.

Southern Review, winter, 1970, January, 1978, April, 1978; *Indians of Today,* edited by Marion E. Gridley, I.C.F.P., 1971; Marion E. Gridley, *Contemporary American Indian Leaders,* Dodd, 1972; *Contemporary Literary Criticism,* Gale, Volume II, 1974, Volume XIX, 1981; *South Dakota Review,* winter, 1975-76; N. Scott Momaday, *The Names: A Memoir,* Harper, 1976; *Atlantic,* January, 1977; *New York Review of Books,* February 3, 1977; *Harper's,* February, 1977; *Sewanee Review,* summer, 1977; *World Literature Today,* summer, 1977; *American Indian Quarterly,* May, 1978; *American Literature,* January, 1979; *American Poetry Review,* July/August, 1984.

—*Sketch by Candace Cloutier*

—*Interview by Jean W. Ross*

*   *   *

MONTES, Antonio Llano   1924-

PERSONAL: Born January 17, 1924, in Havana, Cuba; came to United States in 1962; son of Manuel (a businessman) and Blandina Montes; married Aurora Bellido; married Silvia Casado, August 10, 1957 (divorced); married Anita Llano, July 15, 1966 (divorced February, 1978); children: Mary, Alina, Tony, John, Danny. *Education:* University of Havana, B.A., 1948, J.D., 1952. *Religion:* Roman Catholic. *Home:* 4275 Northwest South Tamiami Channel Dr., Z-304, Miami, Fla. 33126. *Agent:* Cadena Capriles, Plaza Panteon, Caracas, Venezuela. *Office address:* P.O. Box 431, Shenandoah St., Miami, Fla. 33145.

CAREER: Carteles, Havana, Cuba, columnist, 1950-58; *Diario de la Marina,* Havana, travel editor, 1956-58; *Diari El Nacional,* Havana, columnist, 1956-58; Channel 4 Television, Havana, reporter and commentator, 1957-60; *Ultimas Noticias,* Caracas, Venezuela, journalist, 1960-63; *Elite,* Caracas, travel editor, 1960-65; *Carteles,* Santo Domingo, Dominican Re-

public, editor and publisher, 1963-65; *La Nacion,* Santo Domingo, news editor, 1963-65; *Yates y Pesca,* Miami, Fla., editor and publisher, 1965-68; *El Mundo,* Caracas, columnist, 1970—; *Directorio Industrial U.S.A.,* Miami, editor and publisher, 1973-75; currently news editor, commercial representative, and director of U.S. Office of Cadena de Publicaciones Capriles. Notable assignments include the Costa Rican War, 1950, the Santo Domingo Revolution, 1965, and the civil wars in El Salvador, 1979-80, and Angola, 1981. Member of board of directors, Aquapol Corp.

WRITINGS: (Editor) *Libro Blanco Fuerzas Armadas Dominicanas,* C.A. (Santo Domingo), 1964; *Santo Domingo: Barricadas de Odios,* Editores Mexicanos Unidos, 1966; *Manson, Dios o Diablo?,* Lithoformas Editores, 1973; *La Dinastia,* Lithoformas Editores, in press. Also author of "Tras la Noticia" column, *Carteles,* 1950-58, and "Observando" column, *Diaria El Nacional,* 1956-58.

WORK IN PROGRESS: A sequel to *La Dinastia,* entitled *Miserias y Grandezas de un Exilio,* the story of the first five years of Cuban exile in Miami, Venezuela, and other parts of the world.

SIDELIGHTS: Antonio Llano Montes was a reporter in Cuba during the Costa Rican War. He told *CA:* "In this war the revolutionary forces took me prisoner, and General Anastasio Somoza Sr. liberated me. In the revolution in Santo Domingo (1965), I was principle adviser of General Elias Wessin. I have been personal friends with the following presidents: Romulo Betancourt of Venezuela, Dumarsse Estime of Haiti, Jose Figueres of Costa Rica, Carlos Andres Perez of Venezuela, Miguel Idigoras of Guatemala, Licenciado Raphael Bonelly of the Domican Republic, and Donald Reid Cabral of the Domican Republic."

"One of my special interests," Montes added, "was to study the Maya civilization, therefore I made trips to Yucatan, Campeche, Tabasco, Quintana Roo and Honduras throughout the years 1953-56. I have also made many trips to Europe, North Africa, South America, Central America, the Caribbean, and the Middle East."

*   *   *

MOONEY, Christopher F(rancis)   1925-

PERSONAL: Born February 23, 1925, in Bayonne, N.J.; son of Christopher and Frances (Behan) Mooney. *Education:* Loyola University, A.B., 1950, M.A., 1954; Woodstock College, S.T.L., 1958; Institut Catholique, Paris, S.T.D., 1964; University of Pennsylvania, J.D., 1978. *Home:* 200 Barlow Rd., Fairfield, Conn. 06430.

CAREER: Roman Catholic priest of the Society of Jesus (Jesuits); Canisius College, Buffalo, N.Y., professor of theology, 1959-61; St. Peter's College, Jersey City, N.J., professor of theology, 1959-61; Fordham University, New York City, professor of theology, 1964-69, chairman of department, 1965-69; Woodstock College, New York City, president of the college, 1969-74; Yale University, Law School, New Haven, Conn., graduate fellow, 1974-75; St. Joseph's College, Philadelphia, Pa., visiting professor, 1975-76; University of Pennsylvania, Law School, Philadelphia, assistant dean, 1978-80; Fairfield University, Fairfield, Conn., academic vice-president, 1980—.

MEMBER: American Bar Association, National Association of College and University Attorneys, Catholic Biblical Association, Catholic Theological Society of America, Society for the Scientific Study of Religion, Religious Education Association, American Academy of Religion.

AWARDS, HONORS: Best scholarly article of the year award, Catholic Press Association, 1964, for "Anxiety in Teilhard de Chardin"; National Catholic Book Award, 1966, for *Teilhard de Chardin and the Mystery of Christ.*

WRITINGS: Teilhard de Chardin and the Mystery of Christ, Harper, 1966; (editor and author of introduction) *The Presence and Absence of God,* Fordham University Press, 1969; (editor and author of introduction) *Prayer: The Problem of Dialogue with God,* Paulist Press, 1969; *The Making of Man,* Paulist Press, 1971; *Man without Tears,* Harper, 1975; *Religion and the American Dream,* Westminster, 1977; *Inequality and the American Conscience,* Paulist Press, 1982.

Contributor of articles to *Theological Studies, Harvard Theological Review, Downside Review, Scripture, Religious Education, Social Research, Continuum,* and other journals. Member of editorial board, *Concilium,* 1970—.

WORK IN PROGRESS: Study of the interface between the disciplines of religion and law and between religious and legal values.

*   *   *

MOORE, John Norton   1937-

PERSONAL: Born June 12, 1937, in New York, N.Y.; son of William Thomas (a nuclear engineer) and Lorena (Norton) Moore; married Barbara Schneider (an engineer), December 12, 1981. *Education:* Drew University, A.B., 1959; Duke University, LL.B. (with distinction), 1962; University of Illinois, LL.M., 1965. *Home:* 824 Flordon Dr., Charlottesville, Va. 22901. *Office:* School of Law, University of Virginia, Charlottesville, Va. 22901.

CAREER: Attorney; admitted to Bars of Florida, 1962, Illinois, 1963, Virginia, 1969, District of Columbia, 1974, and U.S. Supreme Court, 1973; University of Florida, Gainesville, assistant professor of law, 1963-65; University of Virginia, Charlottesville, associate professor, 1965-68, professor of international law, 1968-76, Walter L. Brown Professor of Law, 1976—, director of Center for Oceans Law and Policy and Center for Law and National Security. Counselor on international law, U.S. Department of State, 1972-73. Chairman, U.S. National Security Council Task Force on the Law of the Sea; U.S. ambassador to Third United Nations Conference on the Law of the Sea, 1973-76. Member of Council on Foreign Relations; member of U.S. delegation to United Nations, 1972-75; member of State Department Advisory Panel on International Law. Berkeley International Legal Studies Program fellow, 1963; National Institute of Health fellow, Yale Law School, 1965-66. Consultant in international law to Naval War College, National War College, and Judge Advocate General's School of the Army, and to the President's Intelligence Oversight Board, 1982—.

MEMBER: International Law Association, American Society of International Law, American Bar Association (chairman, Committee on Law and National Security), Phi Beta Kappa, Cosmos Club, Order of the Coif.

AWARDS, HONORS: Sesquicentennial fellow of Center for Advanced Studies at the University of Virginia, 1971-72; fellow, Woodrow Wilson International Center for Scholars, 1976;

alumni achievement award in the arts, Drew University, 1976; Phi Beta Kappa Award, for *Law and the Indo-China War;* Hardy Cross Dillard Memorial Award in International Law, 1984.

WRITINGS: Law and the Indo-China War, Princeton University Press, 1972; (editor) *The Arab-Israeli Conflict,* three volumes, Princeton University Press, 1972, revised edition, 1977; (editor) *Law and Civil War in the Modern World,* Johns Hopkins University Press, 1975; (with others) *Deep Seabed Mining in the Law of the Sea Negotiation: Toward a Balanced Development System,* Michie Co., 1978; (editor with Richard B. Lillich) *Readings in International Law from the Naval War College Review, 1947-1977,* Naval War College Press, 1980; (with Filho Pires) *Ocean Law,* two volumes, Federal Publications, in press. Also author of *Law and the Grenada Mission,* 1984.

Author of numerous articles on oceans policy, national security, and congressional-executive relations in foreign policy. Member of editorial board, *American Journal of International Law,* 1972, and *Marine Technology Society Journal,* 1976—.

WORK IN PROGRESS: Materials on law and national security.

*   *   *

MOORE, Regina
See DUNNE, Mary Collins

*   *   *

MOORSOM, Sasha   1931-

PERSONAL: Born January 25, 1931, in Hampshire, England; daughter of Raisley and Ann (Thomson) Moorsom; married Michael Young (a sociologist and writer), 1961; children: Sophie, Toby. *Education:* Girton College, Cambridge, B.A. (first class honors), 1953. *Politics:* Labour. *Religion:* "Free-thinker." *Home:* 67 Gibson Sq., London N.1., England.

CAREER: British Broadcasting Corp., London, England, features producer, 1953-61; *Where* (education journal), Cambridge, England, editor, 1962-64; free-lance journalist, 1964-68; Inner London Education Authority, London, teacher, 1968-71; writer, 1971—. *Awards, honors:* Prizes from Author's Club and *Yorkshire Post,* both 1977, for *Lavender Burning.*

WRITINGS: (Translator) *Perrault's Fairy Tales,* Doubleday, 1972; *Lavender Burning* (novel), Coward, 1976 (published in England as *A Lavender Trip,* Bodley Head, 1976); *In the Shadow of the Paradise Tree* (novel), Routledge & Kegan Paul, 1983.

Work anthologized in *Dartington Anthology.* Author of column, "Information," *Listener,* 1965-68. Contributor of poems to magazines, including *New Statesman* and *Observer.*

SIDELIGHTS: Sasha Moorsom's novel *In the Shadow of the Paradise Tree* concerns Jessica Miles, an Englishwoman who moves to Africa to teach media studies at a university. She finds herself "at the center of political disturbance in an imaginary military regime," writes Marion Glastonbury in *New Statesman.* Jessica also "finds her feminism severely tested," Christopher Hope maintains in the *Times Literary Supplement,* "by Moslem polygamy and female circumcision." "The story of a liberated woman in an illiberal land, *In the Shadow of the Paradise Tree* has its moments," Hope concludes. "Sasha Moorsom can be vividly and grimly funny."

BIOGRAPHICAL/CRITICAL SOURCES: Listener, June 3, 1976; *New Statesman,* June 4, 1976, April 22, 1983; *Observer,* June

6, 1976; *Times Literary Supplement,* June 11, 1976, June 3, 1983; *New York Times Book Review,* December 26, 1976.

* * *

MORGAN, Dan 1925-

PERSONAL: Born December 24, 1925, in Holbeach, Lincolnshire, England; son of Cecil (a tailor) and Lilian Kate (Morley) Morgan; married 1949, wife's name Jean (divorced); married, wife's name Georgina Evelyn; children: Glenn Dan. *Education:* Educated in Spalding, Lincolnshire, England. *Home and office:* 1 Chapel Lane, Spalding, Lincolnshire PE11 1BP, England. *Agent:* Laurence Pollinger Ltd., 18 Maddox St., London W1R 0EU, England; and Robert P. Mills, Ltd., 156 East 52nd St., New York, N.Y. 10022.

CAREER: Has worked as a musician; Dan Morgan (a menswear retail business), Spalding, Lincolnshire, England, managing director, 1958—. *Military service:* British Army, Medical Corps, 1947-48.

MEMBER: Science Fiction Writers of America, Society of Authors.

WRITINGS: Playing the Guitar, Bantam, 1967; *Spanish Guitar,* Corgi Books, 1982; *Beginning Windsurfing,* Corgi Books, 1982; (with Nick Penny) *You Can Play the Guitar,* Carousel (London), 1983.

Science fiction: *The New Minds,* Avon, 1969; *The Several Minds,* Avon, 1969; *Mind Trap,* Avon, 1970; (with John Kippax) *A Thunder of Stars,* Ballantine, 1970; (with Kippax) *Seed of Stars,* Ballantine, 1972; *The High Destiny,* Berkley Publishing, 1973; (with Kippax) *The Neutral Stars,* Ballantine, 1973; *Inside,* Berkley Publishing, 1974; *The Country of the Mind,* Corgi Books, 1975; *The Concrete Horizon,* Millington Books, 1976.

Contributor to anthologies, including *New Writings in SF.* Contributor to science fiction magazines in Great Britain and the United States.

WORK IN PROGRESS: A revised edition of *Playing the Guitar;* a book on computer systems; a television play; a monthly column for *Menswear* magazine.

SIDELIGHTS: Dan Morgan told *CA:* "Despite a continuing business commitment, I'm pleased to report that I have managed to ease myself back into writing. Science fiction is being rather neglected, although its influence is clearly apparent in the play I am working on. I used to think that fiction of one kind or another was the only 'real' writing, but I found my recent excursions into instructional books very rewarding both financially and intellectually. Although I have never really thought of myself as a teacher, I have discovered that there is something very satisfying in finding out about a subject and then devising a technique for passing that experience on to others." Morgan's *Playing the Guitar* has sold over 300,000 copies.

* * *

MORRIS, (Murrell) Edward 1935-

PERSONAL: Born September 21, 1935, in Elkview, W.Va.; son of Charles Sennet (a laborer) and Mary Elizabeth (a laborer; maiden name, Pauley) Morris; married Norma Chapman (a photographer), February 6, 1960; children: Erin, Christopher (deceased), Jason, Rachel. *Education:* Morris Harvey College,

B.A., 1958; Ohio University, M.S., 1959. *Politics:* Socialist. *Religion:* None. *Home:* 1710 Clough St., Bowling Green, Ohio 43402. *Office: Billboard,* 14 Music Cir. E., Nashville, Tenn. 37203.

CAREER: Findlay College, Findlay, Ohio, instructor in English, 1960-63; Alice Lloyd College, Pippa Passes, Ky., assistant professor of English, 1965-66; Edinboro State College, Edinboro, Pa., assistant professor of English, 1967-70; Brookside Children's Home, Charleston, W.Va., childcare worker, 1971-72; Appalachia Educational Laboratory, Charleston, W.Va., staff writer and editor, 1972-74; free-lance writer, 1974-76; *Writer's Digest,* Cincinnati, Ohio, assistant editor, 1976-78; free-lance writer, 1978-81; *Billboard,* Nashville, Tenn., writer and editor, 1981—.

WRITINGS: (With Freida Gregory) *TV: The Family School,* Avatar Press, 1976; (with wife, Norma Morris) *Free and Low-Cost Publicity for Your Musical Act,* Media Modes, 1978.

Poems anthologized in *Poems from Bowling Green,* edited by Frederick Eckman, Winesburg Editions, 1967, and *Poems from the Hills, 1970,* edited by William Plumley, Morris Harvey College Press, 1970. Also author of publicity releases for CBS/Epic Records, RCA Records, and Warner Brothers Records. Contributor to numerous magazines, including *TV Guide, Writer's Digest, Mechanix Illustrated, Mother Earth News, Advertising Age, Bluegrass Unlimited, Country Music,* and *International Musician.*

WORK IN PROGRESS: Studying country and bluegrass music.

SIDELIGHTS: Edward Morris writes: "Writing is appealing to me because it allows me to earn a living without going out-of-doors. As much as I enjoy good writing (doing it or reading it) I have almost no faith in its ability to change people's lives. And I have identical qualms about teaching. Had I been a religious man, I would have tried to sell my soul to write like Peter DeVries or S. J. Perelman."

* * *

MORRISEY, George L(ewis) 1926-

PERSONAL: Born December 6, 1926, in Brooklyn, N.Y.; son of George Sims and Elizabeth (Pounds) Morrisey; married Carol Beverley Putnam (a corporate secretary), August 21, 1948; children: Lynn Carol Morrisey Rosiska, Steven Lewis. *Education:* Springfield College, B.S., 1951, M.Ed., 1952. *Home:* 8022 San Dimas Circle, Buena Park, Calif. 90620. *Office address:* MOR Associates, P.O. Box 5879, Buena Park, Calif. 90622.

CAREER: Young Men's Christian Association, professional director of organizations in El Paso, Tex., 1952-56, and Los Angeles, Calif., 1956-61; First Western Bank and Trust, Los Angeles, administrative assistant, 1961-62; Rockwell International, Downey, Calif., management development specialist, 1962-68; McDonnell Douglas Corp., Long Beach, Calif., manager of management training, 1968-70; Postal Service Management Institute, Los Angeles, manager of West Coast Center, 1970-72; MOR Associates (management consultants), Buena Park, Calif., founder and president, 1972—. Young Men's Christian Association, North Orange County, member of board of directors, 1964-82, chairman, 1976. *Military service:* U.S. Army, 1945-47.

MEMBER: International Management by Objective Institute (member of board of directors, 1976—), American Society for

Training and Development, National Speakers Association (member of board of directors, 1982—). *Awards, honors:* Publication award from American Society for Training and Development, 1972-73.

WRITINGS—Published by Addison-Wesley, except as indicated: *Effective Business and Technical Presentations: Managing Your Presentations by Objectives and Results,* 1968, 2nd edition, 1975; *Management by Objectives and Results for Business and Industry,* 1970, 2nd edition, 1977; *Appraisal and Development through Objectives and Results,* 1972; *Performance Appraisal Instruction Kit,* 1972; (with Paul A. Jordan) *Effective Presentations Instruction Kit,* 1975; *Management by Objectives and Results in the Public Sector,* 1976; *Getting Your Act Together: Goal Setting for Fun, Health and Profit,* Wiley, 1980; *Performance Appraisals in the Public Sector,* 1983; *Performance Appraisals in Business and Industry,* 1983.

Author of numerous audio cassette programs, including "Management by Objectives and Results Overview," Addison-Wesley, 1972, "Women and MORe: Winning Techniques for Goal Setting," MOR Associates, 1977, and "Getting Your Act Together: Goal Setting for Fun, Health and Profit," MOR Associates, 1983; also author of videos, "Management by Objectives and Results," Addison-Wesley, 1975, and "How to Get Organized: MBO for Individuals," MOR Associates, 1979, and a film, "Getting Your Act Together: Goal Setting for Fun, Health and Profit," Salenger Educational Media, 1980. Contributor of more than twenty articles to professional journals.

WORK IN PROGRESS: Performance Appraisals in the Public Sector; Peformance Appraisals in Business and Industry.

SIDELIGHTS: George L. Morrisey told *CA:* "All [my] publications, teaching and consulting efforts are directed at helping individuals and organizations, in both the public and private sectors, achieve worthwhile results. They are oriented to providing specific tools, techniques and processes in a 'how to' approach. The 'Management by Objective and Results' (MOR) process, which is at the heart of all [my] publications, is a systematic, practical approach to management that recognizes that *people,* not pieces of paper, get the job done."

*   *   *

MORRISON, Kristin (Diane) 1934-

PERSONAL: Born April 22, 1934, in Los Angeles, Calif.; daughter of Robert Wood and Mary-Louise (Allec) Morrison. *Education:* Immaculate Heart College, B.A., 1957; St. Louis University, M.A., 1960; Harvard University, Ph.D., 1966. *Home:* 358 Arborway, Boston, Mass. 02130. *Office:* Department of English, Boston College, Chestnut Hill, Mass. 02167.

CAREER: Immaculate Heart College, Los Angeles, Calif., instructor in English, 1960-61; South Carolina State College, Orangeburg, professor of English, 1966-67; New York University, Washington Square College of Arts and Sciences, New York, N.Y., assistant professor of English, 1967-69; Boston College, Chestnut Hill, Mass., 1969—, began as associate professor, currently professor of English. Member of selection committee for Kent fellowships, Danforth Foundation, 1969—.

MEMBER: American Association of University Professors, Women's Equity Action League.

AWARDS, HONORS: Woodrow Wilson fellow, 1958; Kent fellow, 1964.

WRITINGS: (With Michael Anderson, Jacques Guicharnaud, and Jack D. Zipes) *Crowell's Handbook of Contemporary Drama,* Crowell, 1971; *In Black and White,* Free Press, 1972.

(Contributor) Morris Beja, S. E. Gontarski, and Pierre Astier, editors, *Samuel Beckett: Humanistic Perspectives,* Ohio State University Press, 1983; *Canters and Chronicles: The Use of Narrative in the Plays of Samuel Beckett and Harold Pinter,* University of Chicago Press, 1983; (contributor) Francois Pitavy, editor, *William Faulkner's "Light in August,"* Garland Publishing, 1983; (contributor) Clifford Davidson, C. J. Gianakaris, and John H. Stroup, editors, *Drama in the Twentieth Century: Comparative and Critical Essays,* AMS Press, 1984. Contributor to scholarly journals.

*   *   *

MORSE, Peter 1935-

PERSONAL: Born October 29, 1935, in Chicago, Ill.; son of John Boit (an artist) and Margaret (McLennan) Morse; children: Daniel. *Education:* Yale University, B.A., 1957. *Home:* 1717 Mott-Smith, Honolulu, Hawaii 96822.

CAREER: Assistant to U.S. Congressman Charles M. Teague, 1957-60; businessman in Santa Barbara, Calif., 1960-65; Smithsonian Institution, Washington, D.C., associate curator of graphic arts, 1965-67; Honolulu Academy of Arts, Honolulu, Hawaii, research associate, 1967—. Consultant for the Charlot Collection, University of Hawaii, 1981-83. *Member:* American Society of Composers, Authors and Publishers, Appraisers Association of America.

WRITINGS: John Sloan's Prints: A Catalogue Raisonne of the Etchings, Lithographs and Posters, Yale University Press, 1969; *Jean Charlot's Prints,* University Press of Hawaii, 1976; *Popular Art: The Example of Jean Charlot,* Capra, 1978; *Jean Charlot's Prints: Supplement,* University of Hawaii Press, 1983; *Antoni Waterloo's Prints,* Abaris, in press. Composer of film score for "House Made of Dawn." Contributor of articles on prints and Hawaiian history to magazines. Member of editorial board, Tamarind Institute.

WORK IN PROGRESS: Hokusai's Prints, with Roger S. Keyes, completion expected in 1988; *The Lahainaluna Engravings.*

AVOCATIONAL INTERESTS: Inventor.

*   *   *

MOSKOW, Michael H. 1938-

PERSONAL: Born January 7, 1938, in Paterson, N.J.; son of Jacob and Sylvia (Edelstein) Moskow; married Constance Bain, December 18, 1966; children: Robert, Eliot, Lisa. *Education:* Lafayette College, A.B., 1959; University of Pennsylvania, M.A., 1962, Ph.D., 1965. *Home:* 400 Sheridan Rd., Winnetka, Ill. 60093.

CAREER: High school teacher of English and history in Paterson, N.J., 1960-61; Drexel Institute of Technology (now Drexel University), Philadelphia, Pa., instructor in economics, 1963-64; Lafayette College, Easton, Pa., instructor in economics, 1964-65; Drexel Institute of Technology, assistant professor of management, 1965-67; Temple University, Philadelphia, Pa., associate professor of economics, and director of Bureau of Economic and Business Research, 1967-69; U.S. President's Council of Economic Advisers, Washington, D.C., senior staff economist, 1969-71; U.S. Department of Labor, Washington, D.C., executive director of construction industry collective bargaining commission, 1970-72, deputy under-secretary, 1971-72, assistant secretary for policy, evaluation, and research, 1972-73; U.S. Department of Housing and Urban Development, Washington, D.C., assistant secretary for policy development and research, 1973-75; director, Council on Wage and Price Stability, 1975-76; U.S. Department of Labor, undersecretary of labor, 1976-77; vice-president of corporate development and planning, Esmark, Inc., 1977-80; executive vice-president, Estronics (division of Esmark, Inc.), 1980-82; president and chief executive officer, Velsicol Chemical Corp., 1982—.

Consultant to Associated Council for the Arts, Rockefeller Brothers Fund, and other public and private agencies. *Military service:* U.S. Army, 1959-60; became first lieutenant.

MEMBER: American Arbitration Association (member of national panel of arbitrators), American Economics Association, Industrial Relations Research Association.

WRITINGS: Teachers and Unions, University of Pennsylvania Press, 1966; (with Myron Lieberman) *Collective Negotiations for Teachers,* Rand McNally, 1966; (editor with Stanley Elam) *Employment Relations in Higher Education,* Phi Delta Kappa, 1966; (editor with Elam and Lieberman) *Readings on Collective Negotiations in Public Education,* Rand McNally, 1967; *Labor Relations in the Performing Arts: An Introductory Survey,* Associated Council for the Arts, 1969.

(With J. Joseph Lowenberg and Edward C. Koziara) *Collective Bargaining in Public Employment,* Random House, 1970; (editor with Lowenberg) *Collective Bargaining in Government,* Prentice-Hall, 1972; *Strategic Planning in Business and Government,* Committee for Economic Development (New York, N.Y.), 1978. Contributor of more than twenty articles to professional journals.

* * *

MOUNTBATTEN, Richard
  See WALLMANN, Jeffrey M(iner)

* * *

MUELLER, John E(rnest) 1937-

PERSONAL: Born June 21, 1937, in St. Paul, Minn.; son of Ernst A. (a manufacturer) and Elsie (Schleh) Mueller; married Judith A. Reader, September 6, 1960; children: Karl, Karen, Susan. *Education:* University of Chicago, A.B., 1960; University of California, Los Angeles, M.A., 1963, Ph.D., 1965. *Politics:* Democrat. *Home:* 246 Roslyn St., Rochester, N.Y. 14619. *Office:* Department of Political Science, University of Rochester, Rochester, N.Y. 14627.

CAREER: University of Rochester, Rochester, N.Y., assistant professor, 1965-69, associate professor, 1969-72, professor of political science, 1972—, professor of film studies, 1984—, director of dance archive, 1973—. *Awards, honors:* National Science Foundation grant, 1968-70; National Endowment for the Humanities grant, 1972-73; de la Torre Bueno Prize for most distinguished book-length manuscript on dance, 1973, for *Astaire Dancing: The Musical Films.*

WRITINGS: (Editor) *Approaches to Measurement in International Relations,* Appleton, 1969; *War, Presidents and Public Opinion,* Wiley, 1973; *Films on Ballet and Modern Dance,* American Dance Guild, 1974; (contributor) Ellen P. Stern, editor, *The Limits of Military Interventions,* Sage Publications,

1977; *Dance Film Directory,* Princeton Books, 1979; (contributor) Harrison E. Salisbury, editor, *Vietnam Reconsidered,* Harper, 1984; (contributor) Peter Braestrup, editor, *Vietnam as History,* University Press of America, 1984; *Astaire Dancing: The Musical Films,* Knopf, in press. Author of "Film," column in *Dance,* 1974—. Contributor of articles to political science, film, and dance journals.

WORK IN PROGRESS: Research on Vietnam policy; research on dance films, choreography, and the ballets of George Balanchine.

* * *

MULLER, Gilbert H(enry) 1941-

PERSONAL: Born November 8, 1941, in Brooklyn, N.Y.; son of Henry G. and Mildred (Tweed) Muller; married Laleh Mostafavi, June 25, 1964; children: Parisa, Darius. *Education:* University of Kentucky, B.A., 1963; Stanford University, M.A., 1966, Ph.D., 1967. *Home:* 21 Monfort Rd., Port Washington, N.Y. 11050. *Office:* LaGuardia Community College of the City University of New York, 31-10 Thomson Ave., Long Island City, N.Y. 11100.

CAREER: Pahlavi University, Shiraz, Iran, assistant professor of English and American literature, 1967-71; LaGuardia Community College of the City University of New York, Long Island City, N.Y., 1971—, began as assistant professor, currently professor of English and American literature.

MEMBER: Modern Language Association of America, American Studies Association, American Federation of Teachers, Professional Staff Congress, College English Association, New York State Teachers Association.

AWARDS, HONORS: Woodrow Wilson fellowship, 1963; Parks Award, 1972, for *Nightmares and Visions: Flannery O'Connor and the Catholic Grotesque;* National Endowment for the Humanities fellowship, 1973, 1979; University Research Awards, 1974, 1981; Fulbright fellowship, 1978; Mellon fellowship, 1982.

WRITINGS: Nightmares and Visions: Flannery O'Connor and the Catholic Grotesque, University of Georgia Press, 1972; *Comparison and Contrast,* Harper, 1974; *The Basic English Handbook,* Harper, 1978; (with Harvey S. Wiener) *The Short Prose Reader,* McGraw, 1979, 3rd edition, 1985; *The McGraw-Hill Reader,* McGraw, 1982; *John A. Williams,* Twayne, 1984; *The McGraw-Hill Introduction to Literature,* McGraw, 1985; *The American College Handbook,* Harper, 1985.

Contributor to *Nation, New Republic, Georgia Review, Studies in Short Fiction,* and to *New York Times.*

WORK IN PROGRESS: A book on William Faulkner's short fiction; a study of Chester Himes.

* * *

MULLER, John E.
  See FANTHORPE, R(obert) Lionel

* * *

MYRES, Sandra Lynn 1933-

PERSONAL: Born May 17, 1933, in Columbus, Ohio; daughter of George Y. (a physician) and Lucille (Stockdale) Swickard; married Charles E. Myres (a chemist), July 2, 1953 (divorced,

1973). *Education:* Attended Rice University, 1950-51; Texas Technological College (now Texas Tech University), B.A., 1957, M.A., 1960; Texas Christian University, Ph.D., 1967. *Home:* 2019 Terlingua, No. 148, Arlington, Tex. 76010. *Office:* Department of History, University of Texas, Arlington, Tex. 76019.

CAREER: Schreiner Institute (now College), Kerrville, Tex., instructor in history, 1960-61; University of Texas at Arlington, assistant professor, 1967-71, associate professor, 1971-82, professor of history, 1982—. Executive director, Texas Committee for the Humanities and Public Policy, 1973-75.

MEMBER: Organization of American Historians, American Association for State and Local History, Western History Association, Westerners International (president, 1984), Society of Southwest Archivists, Society for Historical Archaeology, Texas State Historical Association, Fort Worth Westerners. *Awards, honors:* National Endowment for the Humanities research fellowship, 1979; Huntington-Hayes fellowship, 1980; Fulbright research fellowship, 1982.

WRITINGS: S. D. Myres: Saddlemaker, privately printed, 1961; (editor) *Force without Fanfare,* Texas Christian University Press, 1968; *The Ranch in Spanish Texas: 1690-1800,* Texas Western Press, 1969; (editor with Harold M. Hollingsworth) *Essays on the American West,* University of Texas Press, 1969.

One Man, One Vote: Gerrymandering vs. Reapportionment, Steck, 1970; (with Edward Overman) *Urban Texas Today,* Institute for Urban Affairs, University of Texas at Arlington, 1971; (contributor) *Indian Tribes of Texas,* Texian Press, 1971; (editor with Margaret F. Morris) *Essays on U.S. Foreign Relations,* University of Texas Press, 1974; (contributor) *Broken Treaties and Forked Tongues,* Caxton, 1976; (editor) *Cavalry Wife: The Diary of Eveline M. Alexander, 1866-1867,* Texas A&M University Press, 1977; (contributor) *The American Military on the Frontier,* Office of Air Force History and the United States Air Force Academy, 1978.

Ho for California!: Women's Overland Diaries from the Huntington Library, Huntington Library, 1980; *The Native Americans in Texas,* American Press, 1981; (author of introduction) Sophie Poe, *Buckboard Days,* University of New Mexico Press, 1981; (author of introduction) Frances Roe, *Army Letters from an Officer's Wife,* University of Nebraska Press, 1981; *Westering Women and the Frontier Experience,* University of New Mexico Press, 1982; (contributor) Michael Malone, editor, *Historians and the American West,* University of Nebraska Press, 1983; (author of introduction) Teresa Viele, *"Following the Dream,"* University of Nebraska Press, 1984.

Contributor to *McGraw-Hill Encyclopedia of World Biography* and *Readers Encyclopedia of the American West;* contributor to history journals.

WORK IN PROGRESS: Plainswomen: Settlers on the Frontier, a book on women on the Great Plains, with Glenda Riley; *Victoria's Daughters,* a comparative study of frontier women in Australia, New Zealand, Canada, and the American West.

SIDELIGHTS: Sandra Lynn Myres told *CA:* "As both teacher and author, I believe one activity enhances the other. I find my research adds to my classroom activities and enables me to bring new material to the attention of my students, and frequently my students contribute new ideas or directions for research. For me, writing is an avocation which melds with my teaching career."

N

NAGEL, Stuart S(amuel)   1934-

PERSONAL: Born August 29, 1934, in Chicago, Ill.; son of Leo I. (a store owner) and Florence (Pritikin) Nagel; married Joyce Golub, September 1, 1957; children: Brenda Ellen, Robert Franklin. *Education:* Attended University of Chicago, 1955; Northwestern University, B.S., 1957, J.D., 1958, Ph.D., 1961. *Politics:* Democratic Party. *Religion:* Jewish. *Home:* 1720 Park Haven, Champaign, Ill. 61820. *Office:* Department of Political Science, University of Illinois at Urbana-Champaign, Urbana, Ill. 61801.

CAREER: Pennsylvania State University, University Park, instructor in political science, 1960-61; University of Arizona, Tucson, assistant professor of political science, 1961-62; University of Illinois at Urbana-Champaign, assistant professor, 1962-64, associate professor, 1965-67, professor of political science, 1968—, member of University Research Board, 1962—.

Visiting fellow, National Institute of Law Enforcement and Criminal Justice, U.S. Department of Justice, 1974-75. Occasional part-time general legal practice, 1958—; assistant counsel, U.S. Senate Subcommittee on Administrative Practice, Washington, D.C., 1966; trial attorney, National Labor Relations Board, Chicago, Ill., 1966; attorney and director, Office of Economic Opportunity Legal Services Agency, Champaign, Ill., 1966-70. Consultant to government agencies, commercial research firms, and university research bureaus.

MEMBER: International Association for Philosophy of Law and Social Philosophy, Policy Studies Organization (secretary-treasurer), Law and Society Association, American Bar Association, American Political Science Association, International Academy of Forensic Psychology (member of board of governors, 1971—), Midwest Political Science Association.

AWARDS, HONORS: Research grants from Illinois Center for Education in Politics, 1963, American Council of Learned Societies, 1964-65, Center for Advanced Study in the Behavioral Sciences, Palo Alto, Calif., 1964-65, East-West Center of Hawaii, 1965, National Science Foundation, 1970-73, and Ford Foundation, 1975-79; Russell Sage research fellow, Yale Law School, 1970-71.

WRITINGS: (Editor) *Evaluation Charts on Delay in Administrative Proceedings,* U.S. Government Printing Office, 1966; (editor) *Questionnaire Survey on Delay in Administrative Pro-*ceedings, U.S. Government Printing Office, 1966; *The Legal Process from a Behavioral Perspective,* Dorsey, 1969; (editor) *Law and Social Change,* Sage Publications, 1970; (editor) *New Trends in Law and Politics Research,* Law & Society Association, 1971; (editor) *The Rights of the Accused in Law and Action,* Sage Publications, 1972; (editor) *Law and Social Change,* Sage Publications, 1973; *Comparing Elected and Appointed Judicial Systems,* Sage Publications, 1973; *Minimizing Costs and Maximizing Benefits in Providing Legal Services to the Poor,* Sage Publications, 1973; *Policy Studies Directory,* Policy Studies Organization, 1973, revised edition, 1976; (editor) *Environmental Politics,* Praeger, 1974.

(Editor) *Policy Studies and the Social Sciences,* Heath, 1975; (editor) *Policy Studies in America and Elsewhere,* Heath, 1975; *Improving the Legal Process,* Heath, 1975; (editor) *Political Science Utilization Directory,* Policy Studies Organization, 1975; *Operations Research Methods,* Sage Publications, 1976; *The Applications of Mixed Strategies: Civil Rights and Other Multi-Activity Policies,* Sage Publications, 1976; (editor) *Modeling the Criminal Justice System,* Sage Publications, 1977; *Legal Policy Analysis,* Heath, 1977; *Legal Process Modeling,* Sage Publications, 1977; (editor) *Policy Studies Review Annual,* Sage Publications, 1977; (editor) *Policy Studies Grants Directory,* Policy Studies Organization, 1977; *Too Much or Too Little Policy: The Example of Pretrial Release,* Sage Publications, 1977; *Decision Theory and the Legal Process,* Heath, 1978; *Policy Analysis: In Social Science Research,* Sage Publications, 1978; (editor) *Policy Research Centers Directory,* Policy Studies Organization, 1978; (editor) *Policy Studies Personnel Directory,* Policy Studies Organization, 1979.

(Editor) *Improving Policy Analysis,* Sage Publications, 1980; (editor) *Policy Publishers and Associations Directory,* Policy Studies Organization, 1980; *The Policy Studies Handbook,* Lexington Books, 1980; *Policy Evaluation: Making Optimum Decisions,* Praeger, 1982; (editor) *Encyclopedia of Policy Studies,* Dekker, 1983; (editor) *The Political Science of Criminal Justice,* C. C Thomas, 1983; (editor) *Basic Literature in Policy Studies: A Comprehensive Bibliography,* JAI Press, 1984; *Contemporary Public Policy Analysis,* University of Alabama Press, 1984; (editor) *Cross-National Policy Studies Directory,* Policy Studies Organization, 1984; *Equity as a Policy Goal,* Bowling Green State University, 1984; (editor) *Productivity and Public Policy,* Sage Publications, 1984; *Public Policy: Goals, Means, and Methods*, St. Martin's, 1984; (editor) *Public Policy Studies: A Multi-Volume Treatise*, JAI Press, 1984; *Law, Policy, and Evaluation*, Kennikat, 1984.

Contributor: Glendon Austin Schubert, editor, *Judicial Decision-Making*, Free Press, 1963; Schubert, editor, *Judicial Behavior: A Reader in Theory and Research*, Rand McNally, 1964; *Should Law Enforcement Agencies in the U.S. Be Given Greater Freedom in the Investigation and Prosecution of Crime?*, U.S. Government Printing Office, 1965; Simon Dinitz and Walter C. Reckless, editors, *Critical Issues in the Study of Crime*, Little, Brown, 1968; Raymond W. Mack and Kimball Young, editors, *Principles of Sociology*, 4th edition, Van Nostrand, 1968; Frederick Wirt and Willis Hawley, editors, *New Dimensions of Freedom in America*, Chandler Publishing, 1969; Theodore L. Becker, editor, *The Impact of Supreme Court Decisions: Empirical Studies*, Oxford University Press, 1969; Richard Quinney, *Crime and Justice in Society*, Little, Brown, 1969.

Robert I. Mendelsohn and James R. Klonoski, *The Politics of Local Justice*, Little, Brown, 1970; Abraham S. Blumberg, editor, *Law and Order: The Scales of Justice*, Aldine, 1970; *Political and Legal Obligation: Nomos XII*, Atherton, 1970; Norman Johnston and others, editors, *Sociology of Punishment and Correction*, 2nd edition, Wiley, 1970; Irving L. Horwitz and Mary S. Strong, *Sociological Realities*, Harper, 1971; Thomas R. Dye, *The Measurement of Policy Impact*, Florida State University Press, 1971; Becker and Vernon Murray, editors, *Government Lawlessness in America*, Oxford University Press, 1971.

Fred W. Grupp, Jr. and Marvin Maurer, editors, *Political Behavior in the United States*, Appleton, 1972; Gresham M. Sykes and others, editors, *Law and Social Science Research*, University of Denver Law School, 1972; Gary T. Marx, editor, *Muckraking Sociology: Research as Social Criticism*, Dutton, 1972; Joseph R. Fiszman and Gene S. Poschman, editors, *The American Political Arena*, Little, Brown, 1972; Robert Weissberg and Mark Nadel, editors, *Democracy and the American Political System*, Wiley, 1972; Becker and Malcolm Feeley, editors, *The Impact of Supreme Court Decisions*, Oxford University Press, 1973; Walter D. Burnham, editor, *Politics/America*, Van Nostrand, 1973; Abraham S. Blumberg, editor, *Law and Order: The Scales of Justice*, Dutton, 1973; L. Papayanopoulous, editor, *Democratic Representation and Apportionment*, New York Academy of Sciences, 1973; Matthew Holden and Dennis Dresang, editors, *What Government Does*, Sage Publications, 1974.

Horowitz and Charles Nanry, editors, *Sociological Realities II*, Harper, 1975; Tom Cook and Frank Scioli, editors, *Methodologies for Analyzing Public Policies*, Lexington Books, 1975; Lester Milbrath, editor, *Environmental Policy*, Sage Publications, 1975; Dorothy James, editor, *Analyzing Poverty Policy*, Heath, 1975; Gordon Tullock, editor, *Frontiers of Economics*, University Publications, 1975; Charles Jones and Robert Thomas, editors, *Public Policy-Making in a Federal System*, Sage Publications, 1976.

G. Dorsey and G. Doyle, editors, *Freedom and Equality*, Oceana, 1977; John Gardiner, editor, *Public Law and Public Policy*, Praeger, 1977; Rita Simon, editor, *Research in Law and Sociology*, Jai Press, 1977; William Starbuck, editor, *Handbook of Organizational Design*, Elsevier, 1977; *Nationalizing Government: Public Policies in America*, Sage Publications, 1978; *Law and Ecological Change*, William S. Hein, 1978; *The Policy Cycle*, Sage Publications, 1978; *The Criminology of De-*

viant Women, Houghton, 1978; *Perspectives on the Costs and Benefits of Applied Social Research*, Abt Associates, 1979; *Courts, Judges, and Politics: An Introduction to the Judicial Process*, Random House, 1979; *Urban Policymaking*, Sage Publications, 1979; *Policy Studies and Public Choice*, Sage Publications, 1979.

Lawyer's Ethics: Contemporary Dilemmas, Transaction Books, 1980; *The Practice of Policy Evaluation*, St. Martin's, 1980; *Criminal Justice System: Materials on the Administration and Reform of the Criminal Law*, Little, Brown, 1980; *Teaching Public Policy*, Florida State University, 1980; *The Sociology of Law*, Free Press, 1980; *Why Policies Succeed or Fail*, Sage Publications, 1980; *Fiscal Stress and Public Policy*, Sage Publications, 1980; *Public Policy and Policy Analysis: Political Science Reading Lists and Course Outlines*, Eno River Press, 1981; *Frontiers of Applied Political Science*, ASU Political Research and Evaluation Program, 1981; *The Trial Process*, Plenum, 1981; *Handbook of Political Behavior*, Plenum, 1981; *American Politics: Political Science Reading Lists and Course Outlines*, Eno River Press, 1981; *Handbook of Organizational Design*, Oxford University Press, 1981; *Public Policy Analysis*, Prentice-Hall, 1981; *Psychology of the Courtroom*, Academic Press, 1981; *Teaching Public Administration*, University of Missouri Public Administration, 1981; *Evaluation and Criminal Justice Policy*, Sage Publications, 1981; *Optimizing and Evaluating Public Policy*, Lexington Books, 1981.

Supreme Court Activism and Restraint, Columbia University Press, 1982; *Values, Ethics, and the Practice of Policy Analysis*, Lexington Books, 1982; *Operations Research Applications*, Sangamon State University, 1983; *Criminal Justice in South Africa: Selected Aspects of Discretion*, Juta (Cape Town), 1983; *Handbook on Public Organizations Management*, Dekker, 1983; *Scarce Natural Resources: The Role of Public Policymaking*, Sage Publications, 1983; *The Impact of Social Psychology on Procedural Justice*, C. C Thomas, 1984; *Making and Managing Policy: Formulation, Analysis Evaluation*, Dekker, 1984; *Social Sciences and Public Policy*, Kennikat, 1984; *The Private Exercise of Public Functions*, Kennikat, 1984.

Contributor of articles to over fifty journals, including *Policy Studies Journal, American Behavioral Scientist, Public Opinion Quarterly,* and *American Bar Association Journal.* Editor, *Policy Studies Journal;* member of editorial board, *Law and Society Review*, 1966—; member of editorial advisory board, *Sage Criminal Justice System Annuals*, 1971—; member of editorial board, *Journal of Politics*, 1972—.

WORK IN PROGRESS: Controversial Issues in Public Decision-Science; "the continuation of my work in public policy analysis with particular emphasis on applications to the legal system and also attempts to make decision-science more understandable to the general public."

SIDELIGHTS: Stuart Nagel told *CA:* "There is a need for social scientists to show more interest in applying their knowledge and skills to important policy problems. There is also a need for policy-makers and policy-appliers to become more aware of the relevant knowledge and skills that social scientists have developed. I have tried to stimulate closer relations between social science and public policy by such relevant activities as writing articles, authoring books, editing journals, and founding associations. Those activities will hopefully result in promoting more applications of social science to important public policy problems."

NARANG, Gopi Chand 1931-

PERSONAL: Born January 1, 1931, in Dukki, Baluchistan, India; son of Dharam Chand (a civil servant) and Tekan (Bai) Narang; married Tara Rani (a teacher; divorced, 1972); married second wife, Manorma (a teacher); children: Arun, Tarun. *Education:* Panjab University, B.A. (with honors in Persian), 1950; University of Delhi, M.A. (with honors in Urdu), 1954, Ph.D., 1958, Diploma in Linguistics, 1961. *Home:* D 252 Sarvodaya Enclave, New Delhi-17, India. *Office:* Department of Urdu, Jamia Millia University, New Delhi-25 India.

CAREER: University of Delhi, Delhi, India, 1957-74, began as lecturer, associate professor of Urdu language and literature, 1961-74; Jamia Millia University, New Delhi, India, professor of Urdu and chairman of department, 1974—. Visiting professor in department of Indian studies, University of Wisconsin, 1963-65, 1968-70. Regular broadcaster on All India Radio and Delhi Television; member of board of directors, Jamia Publishing House; member of executive board and convener of Urdu advisory board, Sahitya Academi; chairman of Urdu committee, National Council of Educational Research and Training (India); convener, Bharatiya Inanpith Literary Award committee. Member of Indian Government delegation to 27th Orientalist International Congress, University of Michigan, 1967.

MEMBER: Urdu Association of India (member of executive committee), American Oriental Society, Linguistic Society of America, Modern Language Association of America, Association for Asian Studies, Linguistic Society of India, Royal Asiatic Society of London (fellow), All India P.E.N.

AWARDS, HONORS: Ghalib Prize of Indian Government for best scholarly work of 1962, for *Urdu Masnawiyan;* Commonwealth fellowship, 1963; U.P. Urdu Academy Prize, 1972, for *Karbal Katha ka Lisaniyati Mutaliya;* Mir Award for total literary services, 1976; President of Pakistan's Gold Medal, 1978, for distinguished scholarly work on the poet Igbal; national award from National Council of Educational Research and Training, 1980; Association for Asian Studies award, 1982, for services to Urdu language and literature; award from Aligarh Alumni Association, Washington, D.C., 1982, for Urdu scholarship; Ghalib Memorial Award, 1983; special award from Bihar Urdu Academy, 1983; Sahitya Kala Parishad Award, 1984.

WRITINGS: (Editor) *Miraj ul-Ashiqeen,* Azad Kitab Ghar, 1957; *Teaching Urdu as a Foreign Language,* Azad Kitab Ghar, 1960, 2nd edition, 1963; *Urdu Masnawiyan,* Maktaba Jamia, 1962; *Karkhandari Dialect of Delhi Urdu,* Munshi Ram Manohar Lal, 1963; (editor) *Adabi Tahreerin,* Sab Ras Kitab Ghar, 1964; *Readings in Literary Urdu Prose,* University of Wisconsin Press, 1968; (editor) *Manshurat,* Anjuman taraqqi-e-Urdu, 1968.

(Co-author) *Karbal Katha ka Lisaniyati Mutaliya,* Maktaba Shahrah, 1970; (editor) *Aemughan-e-Malik,* Maktaba Jamia, 1973; (editor) *Imla Namah,* Urdu Development Board, 1974; *Puranon ki Kahaniyan,* National Book Trust (India), 1976; (editor) *Igbal Jamia ke Musannifin ki Nazar men,* Maktaba Jamia, 1978; (co-author) *Wazahati Kitabiyat,* Urdu Promotion Bureau, 1979.

(Editor and translator) *Indian Poetry Today,* Volume IV: *Modern Urdu Poetry,* Indian Council for Cultural Relations, 1980; (editor) *Urdu Afsanah: Riwayat aur Masail,* Educational Publishers, 1981; *Anis Shanasi,* Educational Publishers, 1981; *Sa-*

far Ashna, Educational Publishers, 1982; *Igbal Ka Fann,* Educational Publishers, 1983; *Usloobiyat-e-Mir,* Educational Publishers, 1984.

WORK IN PROGRESS: An anthology of Urdu short stories in English translation; *Lisani Nikat; Tangeedi Izharat; Ilmi Magalat.*

*   *   *

NASH, N. Richard 1913-
(N. Richard Nusbaum)

PERSONAL: Original name, Nathan Richard Nusbaum; born June 7, 1913, in Philadelphia, Pa.; son of Shael Leonard (a bookbinder) and Jennie (Singer) Nusbaum; married Helena Taylor, 1935 (divorced, 1954); married Janice Rule, March, 1956 (divorced, 1956); married Katherine Copeland, November, 1956; children: (first marriage) one son; (third marriage) two daughters. *Education:* University of Pennsylvania, B.S., 1934. *Agent:* Joan Scott, Writers & Artists Agency, 162 West 56th St., New York, N.Y. 10019.

CAREER: Playwright, screenwriter, television writer, and novelist. Producer of musical "Wildcat," with Michael Kidd, first produced on Broadway at Alvin Theatre, December 16, 1960. Instructor in philosophy and drama at numerous colleges and universities, including Bryn Mawr College and Princeton University. *Wartime service:* Office of War Information, World War II.

MEMBER: Authors League of America, Writers Guild of America, Academy of Motion Picture Arts and Sciences, Dramatists Guild.

AWARDS, HONORS: Maxwell Anderson Verse Drama Award, 1940, for "Parting at Imsdorf"; International Drama Award (Cannes, France) and Prague Award, both 1954, both for "See the Jaguar"; Karl Gosse Award, 1957, for "The Rainmaker"; Archer Award, 1960, for "Handful of Fire"; also recipient of Orbeal Award, Cannes Theatre Laurel, and Europa Prize for Literature.

WRITINGS—Plays: (Under name N. Richard Nusbaum) *So Wonderful! (In White)* (one-act), Samuel French, 1937; (under name N. Richard Nusbaum) *Incognito* (three-act), Samuel French, 1941; (under name N. Richard Nusbaum) *Parting at Imsdorf* (one-act), Samuel French, 1941; (under name N. Richard Nusbaum) *Sky Road: A Comedy of the Airways* (three-act), Row, Peterson & Co., 1941; *Second Best Bed* (first produced on Broadway at Ethel Barrymore Theatre, June 3, 1946), Samuel French; *The Young and Fair* (first produced in New York City at Fulton Theatre, November 22, 1948), Dramatists Play Service; *See the Jaguar* (three-act; first produced on Broadway at Court Theatre, December 3, 1952), Dramatists Play Service, 1953.

The Rainmaker (three-act; first produced on Broadway at Court Theatre, October 28, 1954), Random House, 1955, musical adaptation published and produced as *110 in the Shade* (first produced on Broadway at Broadhurst Theatre, October 24, 1963), Tams-Witmark; *Girls of Summer* (three-act; first produced on Broadway at Longacre Theatre, November 19, 1956), Samuel French, 1957; *Handful of Fire* (three-act; first produced on Broadway at Martin Beck Theatre, October 1, 1958), Samuel French, 1959; *Wildcat* (musical adaptation first produced on Broadway at Alvin Theatre, December 16, 1960), Tams-Witmark; *The Happy Time* (two-act musical adaptation; first produced on Broadway at Broadway Theatre, January 18, 1968), Dramatic Publishing Co., 1969; *Echoes* (two-act; first produced in New York City at Bijou Theatre, February 26, 1973), Samuel French, 1973; *Sarava* (musical based on "Dona Flor and Her Two Husbands," by Jorge Amado; first produced in New York City at Mark Hellinger Theater, 1979), Mitch Leigh. Also author of *Rouge Atomic*, Dramatists Play Service.

Books: *Cry Macho*, Delacorte, 1975; *East Wind, Rain*, Atheneum, 1977; *The Last Magic*, Atheneum, 1978; *Aphrodite's Cave*, Doubleday, 1980; *Radiance*, Doubleday, 1983. Also author of two books on philosophy, *The Athenian Spirit* and *The Wounds of Sparta*.

Screenplays: "Nora Prentiss," Warner Bros., 1946; (author of adaptation with Arthur Sheekman) "Welcome Stranger," Paramount, 1946; (with Harry Clork) "The Sainted Sisters" (adapted from the short story, "The Sainted Sisters of Sandy Creek," by Elisa Bialk), Paramount, 1948; (with Sheekman) "Dear Wife" (sequel to the play, "Dear Ruth," by Norman Krasna), Paramount, 1950; "The Vicious Years," Film Classics, 1950; (with Harvey S. Haislip) "The Flying Missile," Columbia, 1951; (with Gertrude Berg) "Molly" (adapted from the radio serial, "The Goldbergs," by Berg), Paramount, 1951; "Maru Maru," Warner Bros., 1952; (with John D. Klorer) "Top of the World," United Artists, 1955; "The Rainmaker" (based on the author's play of the same title), Paramount, 1956; "Porgy and Bess" (adapted from the folk opera by George Gershwin), Columbia, 1959.

Teleplays: "House in Athens," National Broadcasting Co. (NBC); "The Rainmaker" (based on the author's play of the same title), NBC; "The Brownstone," NBC; "The Happy Rest," NBC; "The Young and Fair" (based on the author's play of the same title), NBC; "The Arena," NBC; "Welcome Home," American Broadcasting Co. (ABC); "The Joker," ABC. Also contributor of teleplays to "Philco Playhouse," "General Electric Theater," "U.S. Steel Hour," "Television Playhouse," and "Theater Guild of the Air."

WORK IN PROGRESS: A novel, telling the story of Jesus Christ from the points of view of Mary Magdalene and Judas.

SIDELIGHTS: Perhaps known best for his immensely popular "The Rainmaker," in recent years N. Richard Nash has concentrated on novel writing. His seriousness about this genre is exemplified by his diligence: he spent seven years researching and writing *East Wind, Rain*.

In "The Rainmaker," a "con man" brings rain to a drought-stricken land while awakening the potential for love in a spinster. Understandably, Nash's first novel, *Cry Macho*, brought a comparison to the famous romantic comedy. Arthur Ramirez writes in *Southwest Review:* "In . . . *Cry Macho*, Nash returns to a dusty setting and spiritually and emotionally drained characters. In both works the characters are colorful, the backdrop is picturesque, the action and narrative focus outrageously larger than life, and the message ultimately positive and reassuring. But the touch of artistry in connecting various threads is absent, nor is there a hypnotic presence in *Cry Macho* equal to the intriguing rainmaker-conman." But, Ramirez continues, "psychoanalysis and Women's Lib . . . cause Nash to move away from his portrait of a spinster in distress . . . to a more modern union of strength and kindness, giving and taking."

Nash drew upon both experience and thorough research in creating his best-selling Pearl Harbor novel, *East Wind, Rain*. "I first got interested in the Japanese," he told Arnold W. Ehrlich in *Publishers Weekly*, "when I served with OWI [Of-

fice of War Information] on the West Coast in World War II. Then after the war I went to Hawaii, and what do you think I became? A bum. Literally, I looked and behaved like a wreck. And you you know what stopped me from being a bum?. . . Sheer terror. I lived a hand-to-mouth existence. I actually lived in the wilderness—the Big Island of Hawaii. The experience obviously stuck even though I went back to Hawaii nine times to do research on the book." In addition, Nash says he "made a thorough and complete pest of myself at the Naval library at Pearl Harbor. . . . I must have interviewed at least 100 Navy people, starting with ex-admirals on down to sailors who served at the base before the Japanese attack and who have retired in Hawaii."

Writing in the *New York Times Book Review*, Joe David Bellamy terms the novel a combination of "a love story with a saga of revenge with the mysteries of espionage in an exotic locale at a historic moment." In addition to this setting, "Nash . . . shows he has a fairly impressive grasp of both [character and plot] and the initiative to put them to work on a mixture of sure fire recipes for clearing out bookstore windows." Bellamy states, "It is undoubtedly a rarity to find a novel of entertainment that is this well written."

While enjoying the praise surrounding *East Wind, Rain*, Nash found that critics have made some disturbing distinctions in their treatment of the book. "What annoys me," he told Ehrlich, "is how critics treat a book like [*East Wind, Rain*]. First they call it popular entertainment—that's OK with me—then they say, 'Isn't it amazing that the book is so beautifully written.' I think critics who make a distinction between popular entertainment and good writing are helping to popularize bad fiction."

Nash crossed half the globe to treat a new subject in *The Last Magic*. *Kirkus Reviews* describes the plot: "The pope is dying, radical terrorists are attacking Catholic clergy (an excessively gory crucifixion of a cardinal), and liberal Father Michael Farris, a favorite of the pope, is eager to do whatever he can to hold the Church together." The plot thickens with the aid of "much heavy-breathing revelations of dull secrets," but is plagued by "a strange absence of action or momentum."

James Walt, meanwhile, is convinced that Nash is a "suspense novelist" and, in a *New Republic* review, explains the author's focus on violence: "Today's violence plays into his hands and lends an air of truth to episodes in his novels that a quieter age would have dismissed as lunatic or diabolic. In *The Last Magic*," Walt expands, "Nash lets up on the sensationalism—a trifle. His theme, all the same, betokens the ambitious writer: the ability of Catholicism to survive. . . . It is a flawed but powerful book. Nash makes his point about universal violence too well; but ideas underlie his melodrama, and his lowest and loftiest characters illustrate his mastery of dialogue."

AVOCATIONAL INTERESTS: Making furniture.

CA INTERVIEW

CA interviewed N. Richard Nash by telephone on March 15, 1984, at his home in New York City.

CA: You've distinguished yourself as a playwright, screenwriter, television writer, and novelist. How did a young man who grew up fighting on the streets of South Philadelphia become interested in literature and writing?

NASH: It was pure escape, I guess. I was a Depression child, and you have to run away from all that. I'm still running away; I'm a dreadful romantic, and the kind of writing I do makes up worlds that don't exist and probably never could.

CA: Did you start reading early?

NASH: Oh yes. I was an avid reader. I read when I was four, and by the time I got to high school, I had run through two or three libraries.

CA: Were there some especially strong motivators or influences along the way?

NASH: I think two things, Shakespeare and the Bible. The odd thing about the Bible is that I do not come from a religious family and I myself am not religious. The Bible hit me as one of the great pieces of literature of all time. I suppose religion scorns that kind of approach to something that is meant to be a matter of great spirit. To me it *was* a matter of great spirit, except that it was the literary spirit. Also Mark Twain, Hawthorne, Dickens, Thackeray—except for Mark Twain and Hawthorne, the English writers were more an influence than the American ones.

CA: Before you became a playwright, you had written two books of philosophy, The Athenian Spirit *and* The Wounds of Sparta. *How did you go from philosophy to writing plays?*

NASH: I did one of the philosophy books while I was still in college, and the second one was done right after college. I majored in both philosophy and literature, and I thought I was going to be a teacher of philosophy. But I very soon decided that that was going a little bit too far afield from the world, so I contented myself with just writing those two books, both of them very slim volumes. They're both long out of print now. As a matter of fact, the only people I know who have any copies are two of my sisters!

While I was still in college I began teaching at a small junior college in Bryn Mawr and at Bryn Mawr College. I started out teaching philosophy, but as something on the side, totally extracurricular, I was directing plays. At Bryn Mawr College in those days, the women were always playing men's parts. I hated that. So I wrote a one-act play for women, it was performed at Bryn Mawr, and the Philadelphia *Evening Bulletin* reviewed it and said marvelous things about it. I thought, My goodness, should I be doing this? Then I wrote a second play, a full-length play. The authorities at Bryn Mawr College would not allow it to be produced because there were about a half-dozen four-letter words in it. In those days you didn't dare. So I thought, if they won't do it here, I'll see if I can't do it elsewhere; and it was done on Broadway. Actually it was my second play on Broadway, but that wasn't the chronology of its writing; it was the first full-length play I wrote.

CA: "The Rainmaker," probably the best-known of your plays, was first produced on Broadway in October, 1954, and later produced in a musical version, as a movie, and on television. Do you have a favorite production of "The Rainmaker?"

NASH: You know, it's been odd. They've all been *kind* of favorites. I thought Geraldine Page, who played it on the stage, was wonderful. Then Inga Swenson, who played it in the musical, was wonderful. The only person whose casting I resented was Katie Hepburn. Before she was cast in it, Hal Wallis, who

was doing the picture, came to me and said, "Do you have any suggestions?" I gave him a list of people I thought should play the film. He read the list and said it was very interesting, but what did I think of Hepburn? I said, *"She's* not on my list. She's too old for the part; she comes from the wrong part of the country; her speech is wrong. She's not at all right for it." Wallis said, "I think you're absolutely right, but unfortunately she has the part." And she was marvelous! All of the things I said I still think are accurate, but she has such radiance, she irradiated the part.

CA: The play still seems to be very popular. Is it done a lot?

NASH: It's a strange thing that has been happening to it. They tell me at Samuel French that the average life of a Broadway play, if it has been a hit, is five to seven years. Here's a play that's now thirty years old, and every year the royalties on it increase.

About 1979 or 1980 I heard about a survey that was done with a large sampling of college students. They were asked, among other things, what plays they thought would be most likely to endure. Well, I guessed it so wrong, and I've been in the theater all my life. Number one was "Our Town." Number two was Eugene O'Neill's "Desire Under the Elms." I'm amazed that the students knew it so well. I think "Desire Under the Elms" is in fact O'Neill's best play, but I wouldn't have thought they'd be sophisticated enough to know that. Number three was "The Rainmaker." And who was the only playwright who had two plays on the list? I would have thought O'Neill, but it was Tennessee Williams, with "A Streetcar Named Desire" and "The Glass Menagerie." It was a surprising list, and I was rather flattered to be on it.

CA: Did you act in any of your plays?

NASH: I was the world's worst actor. When I was in college, I thought I was going to be an actor, but I was dreadful! You've never seen such an intellectual actor—I *thought* every line. I was slow on the uptake of every cue. I was in maybe a half-dozen plays, and directors used to tear their hair when they couldn't get at mine.

CA: Some of your screenplays were adaptations—for example, "Molly," from the radio serial "The Goldbergs," "The Rainmaker" from your own play, and "Porgy and Bess" from the Gershwin folk opera.

NASH: "Porgy and Bess" I'm rather proud of; that was a good job, I thought. But I've done some terrible ones.

CA: Do you find adaptations harder to do in some ways than original screenplays?

NASH: Actually they're considerably easier, except that when you're doing adaptations, generally you're doing them for films, and I hate working in Hollywood. I think Hollywood is literally the most corrupt city in the world; I mean that very seriously. When you think of corruption, you think in terms of money and power. But Hollywood has a much deeper corruption. It corrupts the mind. So if you're going to be writing for pictures, it's a terrible place to be. This is not a cop-out; most of the things I do badly I blame on myself. But a lot of things I've done in pictures were because Hollywood is that kind of a city to work in. I've done bad things in theater, and there they're more or less exclusively the playwright's fault because what goes on the stage is entirely up to the playwright. He can say no—the Dramatists Guild protects him in that way. But in pictures, the writer has no say whatsoever about what goes up there on the screen.

CA: You were writing for TV in that time that's called in retrospect the Golden Age of Television. Any comments you'd like to make on being involved in that period of television, or the differences between then and now?

NASH: It was sheer joy. We all had a most marvelous time. We sparked one another. It was a feisty group; there was Paddy Chayefsky, Gore Vidal, myself, Robert Alan Aurthur, Horton Foote. We used to fight with one another and help one another. We were interested and alive and, most important in those days, we had a producer by the name of Fred Coe who thought that the writer was next to God. What we wanted to get on the camera we got on the camera. It's totally different now. Television is the stepbrother of motion pictures, and the same values pertain. In fact, in television I think the values are on an even lower scale.

If you watch old television now, you notice something interesting. All of the scenes were right up close; you never saw a distance shot, a long shot. This meant you had a chance to talk about people, intimately. Now when you see a television show, it's just like a B movie. The automobile is much more important than the human spirit. That made for a great difference in the kind of human qualities that you were allowed to dramatize.

CA: I think the closest thing we see now to those old shows are the "Masterpiece Theatre" productions.

NASH: Exactly. Even their camera work is the way we used to do it. For example, in "Brideshead Revisited," you would get a few long shots used as establishing shots, just a few, and then everything else was played right on the faces of the people.

CA: With Cry Macho, *published in 1975, you became a novelist. What was it like making the change to writing novels?*

NASH: That was an odd experience. *Cry Macho* was originally a motion picture script. It was sent around to all the studios and unanimously rejected. I thought, that doesn't seem like such objectionable material; I wonder what would happen if I turned it into a novel? So in about two weeks I turned it into a novel and sold it. And immediately after it came out, it got sold to films!

I had the same experience with "The Rainmaker." That did the rounds for about a year and a half with no takers. Then when it opened on Broadway, every major studio bid for it, and it brought the highest price that had then been established.

CA: You are known for doing a lot of research for your novels. Is that an especially enjoyable part of the process for you?

NASH: I love it. I'm doing a new book right now that's the story of Jesus told from the points of view of Mary Magdalene and Judas. My research on that goes back twenty-eight years.

CA: Was it a book in your mind twenty-eight years ago?

NASH: No, I was going to do it as a play, but I never found the language of it. Finally I realized that the language of Jesus should be for the most part offstage, and that's why it was

difficult to write as a play; it takes an awful lot of gall to put dialogue in the mouth of Jesus Christ.

CA: After the publication of East Wind, Rain *you criticized reviewers for calling your book "popular entertainment" and then expressing surprise that it was also well written, as if one precluded the other. Do you think reviewers are as guilty of that now?*

NASH: Well, more or less all my life as a novelist, which has been pretty short, I've been getting these surprise reviews. Reviewers seem to be a bit shocked that anybody who writes a popular book should be able to parse a sentence. It's a shame, because if you go back in the history of literature, you realize that some of our greatest writers have written popular books—Dickens, Thackeray, Fielding, Smollett, Mark Twain; you can make a long list. Unfortunately, reviewers write about popular novels as being one kind and—I don't know what you'd call the others—"modern" novels as being another kind. That sort of thinking is exactly what has killed poetry in the last fifty years. At one time poetry was read by every literate person. Now very few people read it, and I lay that charge to the critics who have made poetry a kind of "special" art. That's too bad.

CA: There does seem to be a trend back to the good story, though, in what critics would call literature.

NASH: Yes, I think that's true. I'm delighted that with *Radiance* I've been getting predominantly excellent reviews on both the story and the writing. I'm very grateful for that. I agree that the trend right now is not to make that bifurcation. I know in the theater the age of the unstructured play is passing. Some of the most successful plays in recent years have been plays that told a story well. I think what it boils down to is a recognition on the part of critics that accidentalism should not necessarily be rewarded. It actually takes some skill to write a fine play or a well-structured novel.

CA: Do you think of yourself as a novelist now, or is that too confining?

NASH: I think of myself as a novelist *right* now, because I'm working on a novel. But next week I'm going to be working on a play, and then I'll think of myself as a playwright! I have a new play that I'm just finishing. Really I'm doing the novel and the play more or less simultaneously.

CA: In addition to all the writing, you've somehow found time to teach philosophy and drama. Do you enjoy teaching?

NASH: I'm the easiest catch as a teacher; a dollar a year and I'll do it. I love teaching. I think, as a matter of fact, that it's the thing I do best in the world. I do that better than write, or direct, or anything else. Really I'm a very good teacher, and you notice I haven't said I'm a good writer!

CA: How do you find time?

NASH: I don't anymore teach on a full-year basis; what I do is a series of lectures here and a series there. I'm going to be doing a series at Southern Methodist University this coming summer and a series up at Yale in 1985.

CA: Are the lectures to be on drama?

NASH: The ones at Southern Methodist are going to be on the relationships of the various writing arts: drama, the novel, the screenplay, the musical, even poetry for a minute or so.

CA: What's in the future in writing? Is there anything you'd like to do that you haven't tried yet?

NASH: There *is* a narrative poem. I started a narrative poem four or five years ago; I wrote forty-four pages and threw it away. Then I started it again and wrote about eight pages and threw it away. One of these days I'll find a way of telling that particular story..

BIOGRAPHICAL/CRITICAL SOURCES: New York Times Book Review, July 13, 1975, March 6, 1977; *Southwest Review,* autumn, 1976; *Kirkus Reviews,* December 1, 1976, July 15, 1978; *New York Times,* February 11, 1977, February 12, 1979; *Observer,* March 19, 1977; *Saturday Review,* March 19, 1977; *Publishers Weekly,* June 6, 1977; *Virginia Quarterly,* autumn, 1977; *New Republic,* September 30, 1978; *West Coast Review of Books,* November, 1978; *New Yorker,* November 6, 1978.†

—*Interview by Jean W. Ross*

*   *   *

NEEF, Elton T.
  See FANTHORPE, R(obert) Lionel

*   *   *

NELKIN, Dorothy   1933-

PERSONAL: Born July 30, 1933, in Boston, Mass.; daughter of Henry and Helen (Fine) Wolfers; married Mark Nelkin (a physicist and professor at Cornell University), August 31, 1952; children: Lisa, Laurie. *Education:* Cornell University, B.A., 1954. *Office:* Science, Technology, and Society Program, Department of Sociology, Cornell University, Ithaca, N.Y. 14850.

CAREER: Cornell University, Ithaca, N.Y., director of migrant labor project, 1966-69, senior research associate in science, technology, and society program, 1969—, member of graduate faculty in public policy, 1971—.

AWARDS, HONORS: Guggenheim fellowship, 1983.

WRITINGS: On the Season: Aspects of the Migrant Labor System, New York State School of Industrial and Labor Relations Press, 1970; (with William H. Friedland) *Migrant: Farm Workers in America's Northwest,* Holt, 1971; *Nuclear Power and Its Critics: The Cayuga Lake Controversy,* Cornell University Press, 1971; *The Politics of Housing Innovation: The Fate of the Civilian Industrial Technology Program,* Cornell University Press, 1971; *The University and Military Research: Moral Politics at M.I.T.,* Cornell University Press, 1972; *Methadone Maintenance: A Technological Fix,* Braziller, 1973.

Science Textbook Controversies, MIT Press, 1977; *Technological Decisions and Democracy,* Sage Publications, 1977; *The Atom Besieged,* MIT Press, 1982; *The Creation Controversy: Science or Scripture in the Schools,* Norton, 1982; *Workers at Risk,* University of Chicago Press, 1984.

AVOCATIONAL INTERESTS: Playing cello, tennis.

BIOGRAPHICAL/CRITICAL SOURCES: Los Angeles Times Book Review, December 26, 1982; *Washington Post Book World,* December 26, 1982.

NELLI, Humbert S(teven)   1930-

PERSONAL: Born January 12, 1930, in Chicago, Ill.; son of Humbert Orazio (a professor of insurance) and Florence (Purcelli) Nelli; married Elizabeth Thomson, December 28, 1961; children: Steven, Christopher, William. *Education:* University of Georgia, B.C.S., 1951; Columbia University, M.A., 1956; University of Chicago, Ph.D., 1965. *Home:* 127 Westgate Dr., Lexington, Ky. 40504. *Office:* Department of History, University of Kentucky, Lexington, Ky. 40506.

CAREER: Karlsfeld Ordnance Depot, Munich, Germany, civilian chief of management branch, 1953-55; Fordham University, Bronx, N.Y., assistant professor of history, 1965-67; University of Kentucky, Lexington, 1967—, began as assistant professor, currently professor of history. *Military service:* U.S. Army, 1951-53.

MEMBER: American Historical Association, Organization of American Historians, American Italian Historical Society (member of executive board), American Academy of Political and Social Sciences, Urban History Group, Immigration History Group, Phi Alpha Theta.

AWARDS, HONORS: American Association for State and Local History award, 1966; University of Kentucky research award, 1972; National Endowment for the Humanities, research grant, 1972-73, youth grant, 1978-79; Hallam Book Award, 1977; Southern Regional Education Board research grant, 1981-82; Anisfield-Wolf Award in Race Relations, 1983.

WRITINGS: The Italians in Chicago, 1880-1930: A Study in Ethnic Mobility, Oxford University Press, 1970; (contributor) Raymond Mohl and Neil Betten, editors, *Urban America in Historical Perspective,* Weybright, 1970; (contributor) Kenneth Jackson and Stanley Schultz, editors, *Cities in American History,* Knopf, 1972; (contributor) Mohl and James Richardson, editors, *The Urban Experience: Themes in American History,* Wadsworth, 1972; (contributor) Francesco Cordasco, editor, *Studies in Italian-American Social History: Essays in Honor of Leonard Covello,* Rowman & Littlefield, 1975; *The Business of Crime: Italians and Syndicate Crime in the United States,* Oxford University Press, 1976; (editor) *The United States and Italy: The First Two Hundred Years,* American Italian Historical Association, 1977.

From Immigrants to Ethnics: The Italian Americans, Oxford University Press, 1983; *The Winning Tradition: University of Kentucky Basketball,* University Press of Kentucky, 1984; (contributor) Roger D. Bridges and Rodney O. Davis, *Illinois: Its History and Legacy,* River City, 1984. Contributor to history journals, and to *Mercurio, American Journal of Sociology* and *Chicago Tribune.*

WORK IN PROGRESS: A book examining the Italian experience in the United States.

BIOGRAPHICAL/CRITICAL SOURCES: Los Angeles Times Book Review, April 3, 1983; *New York Times Book Review,* April 24, 1983.

*   *   *

NEVITT, H(enry) J(ohn) Barrington   1908-

PERSONAL: Born June 1, 1908, in St. Catharines, Ontario, Canada; son of Robert Barrington (a clergyman) and Selma L. (Melville) Nevitt; married Constance Elsie Johnson, June 28,

1941; children: Richard Barrington, Amy Becker. *Education:* University of Toronto, B.A.Sc., 1934; McGill University, M.Eng., 1945; also attended University of Santander in Spain, 1933, and University of Western Ontario, 1960. *Religion:* Christian. *Home:* 2 Clarendon Ave., Apt. 207, Toronto, Ontario, Canada M4V 1H9.

CAREER: Worked in radio telegraph stations, 1920-30; bush pilot, Ontario Provincial Air Service, 1930-31; Zavod Elektropribor, Leningrad, Soviet Union, research and development engineer, 1932-33; Northern Electric Co., Montreal, Quebec, manufacturing engineer, 1934-39; Canadian Pacific Telegraph and Defence Communications, Montreal, systems engineer, 1939-44; Sir George Williams College, Montreal, lecturer in history and philosophy of science, 1943; RCA Corp., executive engineer in Montreal and New York City, 1944-47; L. M. Ericsson Telephone Co., Stockholm, Sweden, consultant on projects in Europe and the Americas, 1947-60; Royal Commission for Government Organization, Ottawa, Ontario, consultant, 1960-63; Ontario Development Corp., Toronto, Ontario, manager, 1963-64, director of innovations and management training, 1964-76. Honorary director, Institut fuer Informationsentwicklung, Vienna, Austria; honorary correspondent, United Nations Center for Industrial Development and UNESCO. Visiting professor at universities in Europe and the Americas.

MEMBER: Institute of Electrical and Electronic Engineers (fellow), Institution of Electrical Engineers (United Kingdom; fellow), American Association for the Advancement of Science (fellow), Engineering Institute of Canada (fellow), Society for General Systems Research, American Management Association (consulting member), Discoveries International (Tokyo and Rome), Association of Professional Engineers of the Province of Ontario. *Awards, honors:* LL.D., Concordia University, 1984.

WRITINGS: (With Marshall McLuhan) *Take Today: The Executive as Dropout,* Harcourt, 1972; *ABC of Prophecy: Understanding the Environment,* Canadian Futures Publications, 1980; *The Communication Ecology: Re-Presentation Versus Replica,* Butterworths (Toronto), 1982.

Contributor: Don Toppin, editor, *This Cybernetic Age,* Human Development Corp., 1969; Tony H. Bonaparte and John E. Flaherty, editors, *Peter Drucker: Contributions to Business Enterprise,* New York University Press, 1970; Stanley Winkler, editor, *Computer Communications: Impacts and Implications,* Institute of Electrical and Electronic Engineers, 1972; Jacques Roger, editor, *Seminari Interdisciplinari di Venezia: La Teoria dell'Informazione,* Il Mulino (Bologna), 1974; Anthony Debons and William J. Cameron, editors, *Perspectives in Information Science,* Noordhoff (Leyden), 1975; George Singer and Glen Williams, editors, *Industrial Design and Aesthetics,* School of Industrial Design, Carleton University, 1978; Singer, editor, *Industrial Design and the Common Object,* School of Industrial Design, Carleton University, 1979; Vello Hubel, editor, *Design Trialogue at Trent,* Ontario College of Art, 1980; George Lasker, editor, *Applied Systems and Cybernetics,* Pergamon, 1980; Debons, editor, *Information Science in Action: Systems Design,* Martinus Nijhoff (The Hague), 1981.

Contributor to proceedings and to *Technology and Culture, Canadian Journal of Communication, Explorations,* and other publications.

WORK IN PROGRESS: "Continuing research, in collaboration with mavericks, academics, business, and cultural institutions, on the physical, psychic, and social effects of man's techno-

logical extensions, past and present, by process pattern recognition; also research on circumventing economic crises."

SIDELIGHTS: H. J. Barrington Nevitt told *CA:* "I am particularly interested in sharpening perception of intercultural barriers to communication, stimulating the processes of invention, and anticipating the effects of innovation by using all our wits and senses. I am now involved in exploring the conflicts and complementarities of art and science, East and West, in order to organize current ignorance for continuing dialogue to transform breakdowns into breakthroughs." Nevitt has a working knowledge of French, German, Spanish, Portuguese, Italian, Swedish, and Russian, obtained, along with a smattering of other languages, through work and residence abroad.

* * *

NEWTON, Suzanne 1936-

PERSONAL: Born October 8, 1936, in Bunnlevel, N.C.; daughter of Hannis T. and Billie (O'Quinn) Latham; married Carl R. Newton (a civil servant), June 9, 1957; children: Michele, Erin, Heather, Craig. *Education:* Duke University, A.B., 1957. *Home:* 841-A Barringer Dr., Raleigh, N.C. 27606.

CAREER: Writer. Writer-in-residence at Meridith College, 1984-85.

MEMBER: North Carolina Writer's Conference, Authors Guild, Authors League of America.

AWARDS, HONORS: American Association of University Women (North Carolina chapter) award for juvenile literature, 1971, for *Purro and the Prattleberries,* 1974, for *Care of Arnold's Corners,* 1977, for *What Are You Up To, William Thomas?,* 1978, for *Reubella and the Old Focus Home,* and 1981, for *M. V. Sexton Speaking; I Will Call It Georgie's Blues* was named an American Library Association notable book and best book for young adults, and *New York Times* and *New York Times Book Review* best book of the year, all 1983.

WRITINGS—All juveniles; published by Westminster, except as indicated: *Purro and the Prattleberries,* 1971; *Care of Arnold's Corners* (Junior Literary Guild selection), 1974; *What Are You Up To, William Thomas?* (Junior Literary Guild selection), 1977; *Reubella and the Old Focus Home,* 1978; *M. V. Sexton Speaking,* (Junior Literary Guild selection), Viking, 1981; *I Will Call It Georgie's Blues,* Viking, 1983; *An End To Perfect,* Viking, 1984.

Contributor of short stories, poems, and articles to *Home Life, Parents' Magazine, Human Voice Quarterly, Southern Poetry Review,* and *Long View Journal.*

WORK IN PROGRESS: A sequel to *An End To Perfect.*

SIDELIGHTS: Suzanne Newton told *CA:* "Writing is a part of me, but so is the business of enabling people to 'become.' I am involved in the Poetry-in-the-Schools project in North Carolina, in which poets and writers go into public school classrooms for a week at a time to help young people find the poetry that is inside them. It has been an exciting experience to see children find freedom in word creations of their own.

"As for my own writing, . . . I have a tendency to create 'heroic' characters—that is, people who risk, who dare against great odds, who are more visionary than anyone in their circumstances has a right to be, who stand up against the opposition and say all the smart things—although their knees knock—that I used to lie in bed at night and wish I had said. . . .

An interesting thing has happened, though. The characters have become my models. As a result of creating them, I have come out of my shy, fearful self and have begun to risk and dare along with them! What I hope is that perhaps they may have that same effect upon some of my young readers.''

* * *

NICHOLS, Nina (Marianna) da Vinci 1932-
(Cornelia Tree)

PERSONAL: Born December 21, 1932, in New York, N.Y.; daughter of Giovanina da Vinci; divorced; children: Peter. *Education:* Attended Hunter College of the City University of New York and Columbia University; New York University, Ph.D., 1971. *Home:* 305 West 13th St., New York, N.Y. 10014; and 495 Three Mile Harbor, East Hampton, N.Y. *Agent:* Ellen Levine Literary Agency, 370 Lexington Ave., New York, N.Y. *Office:* Department of English, Rutgers University, New Brunswick, N.J. 08903.

CAREER: Writer. Rutgers University, New Brunswick, N.J., instructor, 1970-71, assistant professor, 1971-77, associate professor of English, 1977—. Has also worked as a psychotherapist and in advertising agencies. Lecturer on the theater and on women's writings. *Member:* Modern Language Association of America, Women's Institute, PEN, Poets and Writers.

WRITINGS: (Editor with J. Benjamin) *Celtic Bull*, University of Tulsa, 1968; *Man, Myth, Monument*, Morrow, 1975; (under pseudonym Cornelia Tree) *Child of the Night*, Bantam, 1983; (contributor) *The Female Gothic*, Eden Press Women's Publications (Montreal), 1983. Also ghostwriter of material. Contributor to literary journals and popular magazines, including *Ariel, Denver Quarterly,* and *New Republic.*

WORK IN PROGRESS: Romantic Paradigm: Portraits of a Heroine; a novel; a series of stories to be read aloud.

SIDELIGHTS: Nina da Vinci Nichols told *CA:* "I've been writing something on and off all my life. Sometimes it finds a shape—a poem, an essay, a story; often enough it remains a fragment that waits on later, fuller, expression. For me, writing is an act of discovery and therefore achingly slow. What comes readily, a turn of phrase, a seemingly fresh image, too often restates the already familiar which need not have been stated at all. Many words peel away without loss before I reach a genuine one. Perhaps we all talk too much on this, our 'information age.'''

* * *

NIGRO, Felix A(nthony) 1914-

PERSONAL: Born August 8, 1914, in Brooklyn, N.Y.; married Edna Helen Nelson, July 28, 1938; children: Lloyd G., Kirsten F. *Education:* University of Wisconsin, B.A., 1935, M.A., 1936, Ph.D., 1948. *Home:* 199 West View Dr., Athens, Ga. 30602. *Office:* Department of Political Science, University of Georgia, 203A Baldwin Hall, Athens, Ga. 30601.

CAREER: Public Administration Service, Chicago, Ill., member of staff, 1937-38; Social Science Research Council, Committee on Public Administration, Washington, D.C., researcher, 1938-39; National Resources Planning Board, Washington, D.C., administrative analyst, 1939-40; National Youth Administration, Washington, D.C., chief of classification, 1940-42; Office of Emergency Management, Wash-

ington, D.C., senior classification officer, 1942-43; War Shipping Administration, Washington, D.C., administrative analyst, 1943-44; National Housing Agency, Washington, D.C., assistant personnel officer, 1944-45; United Nations Relief and Rehabilitation Administration, Washington, D.C., management analyst, 1945-46; Griffenhagen & Associates (management consultants), Chicago, staff member, 1946-47; University of Texas, Main University (now University of Texas at Austin), assistant professor of political science, 1948-49; University of Puerto Rico, Rio Piedras, visiting professor of public administration, 1949-51; Florida State University, Tallahassee, associate professor of public administration, 1951-52; Institute of Inter-American Affairs, Montevideo, Uruguay, and El Salvador, public administration field consultant, 1952-54; J. L. Jacobs & Co. (management consultants), Chicago, senior associate, 1954; University of Puerto Rico, associate professor of public administration, 1954-56; United Nations Advanced School of Public Administration, San Jose, Costa Rica, lecturer in personnel administration, 1956-57; Southern Illinois University at Carbondale, professor of government, 1957-61; San Diego State College (now University), San Diego, Calif., professor of political science, 1961-65; University of Delaware, Newark, Charles P. Messick Professor of Public Administration, 1965-69; University of Georgia, Athens, professor of political science, 1969—.

Lecturer, United Nations International Training Center (El Salvador), 1951, Pan-American Sanitary Bureau on Water Finance and Administration regional conference (Mexico), 1960, and Public Administration Center (Guatemala), 1961; lecturer in personnel administration, School of Public Administration (Spain), 1975; visiting professor, University of Southern California, spring, 1960, summers, 1966-68, San Jose State College (now University), summer, 1961, University of Delaware, summer, 1963, University of Wisconsin, summer, 1964, and North Carolina State University, 1969; Simon fellow, University of Manchester, fall, 1972. Member of New Castle County (Delaware) Personnel Board, 1967-69; member of City of Newark (Delaware) Board of Ethics, 1967-69. Arbitrator, Federal Mediation and Conciliation Service; arbitrator and factfinder, Florida Public Employment Relations Commission. Consultant to Venezuelan Ministry of Health, 1952, and Ministry of Finance, 1958, and to Uruguayan Ministry of Health, 1952-53.

MEMBER: International Personnel Management Association, National Academy of Public Administration, American Society for Public Administration, American Arbitration Association, American Association of University Professors, National Labor Panel, Phi Beta Kappa, Phi Kappa Phi, Phi Eta Sigma.

WRITINGS: University Training for the Public Service (pamphlet), Civil Service Assembly, 1938; *Recruitment of Firemen* (pamphlet), Public Administration Service, 1940; (editor) *Public Administration: Readings and Documents,* Rinehart, 1951; *Conferencias sobre gerencia administrativa,* Government of El Salvador, 1951; *Conferencias sobre administracion de personal,* Government of El Salvador, 1953; *El concepto moderno de administracion de personal* (pamphlet), Government of Guatemala, 1956; *Administracion de personal,* United Nations Advanced School of Public Administration (Central America), 1957; *Public Personnel Administration,* Holt, 1959; *Modern Public Administration,* Harper, 1965, 6th edition (with son, Lloyd G. Nigro), 1984; *Management-Employee Relations in the Public Service,* Public Personnel Administration, 1969; (with L. G. Nigro) *The New Public Personnel Administration,*

F. E. Peacock, 1976, 2nd edition, 1981; (editor with L. G. Nigro) *Readings in Public Administration*, Harper, 1983.

Contributor: *Panorama general del servicio civil*, Ministry of Labor, Government of Honduras, 1956; *Seminario de servicio civil*, Ministerio de Trabajo y Bienestar Social (Guatemala), 1957; *Rethinking the Philosophy of Employee Relations in the Public Service*, International Personnel Management Association, 1968; *Labor Management Policies for State and Local Governments*, U.S. Government Printing Office, 1969; *Managing Government's Labor Relations*, Manpower Press, 1973; (with L. G. Nigro) Charles H. Levine, editor, *Managing Human Resources: A Challenge to Urban Governments*, Volume XIII, Sage Publications, 1977. Contributor of about sixty-five articles in Spanish and English to professional journals.

WORK IN PROGRESS: With Lloyd G. Nigro, a seventh edition of *Modern Public Administration* and a third edition of *The New Public Personnel Administration*.

*   *   *

NIVEN, Larry
See NIVEN, Laurence Van Cott

*   *   *

NIVEN, Laurence Van Cott   1938-
(Larry Niven)

PERSONAL: Born April 30, 1938, in Los Angeles, Calif.; son of Waldemar Van Cott (a lawyer) and Lucy (Doheny) Niven; married Marilyn Joyce Wisowaty, September 6, 1969. *Education:* Attended California Institute of Technology, 1956-58; Washburn University of Topeka, A.B., 1962; University of California, Los Angeles, graduate study, 1962-63. *Home and office:* 3961 Vanalden, Tarzana, Calif. 91356.

CAREER: Writer. *Member:* Science Fiction Writers of America. *Awards, honors:* Hugo Award, World Science Fiction Convention, 1967, for story "Neutron Star," 1971, for novel *Ringworld*, 1972, for story "Inconstant Moon," 1975, for story "The Hole Man," and 1976, for novelette "The Borderland of Sol"; Nebula Award, Science Fiction Writers of America, 1970, for *Ringworld;* Ditmar Award, 1972, for *Ringworld;* E. E. Smith Memorial Award, 1978; LL.D., Washburn University of Topeka, 1984.

WRITINGS—All under name Larry Niven; novels: *World of Ptavvs*, Ballantine, 1966; *A Gift from Earth*, Ballantine, 1968; *Ringworld*, Ballantine, 1970; (with David Gerrold) *The Flying Sorcerers*, Ballantine, 1971; *Protector*, Ballantine, 1973; (with Jerry Pournelle) *The Mote in God's Eye*, Simon & Schuster, 1974; (with Pournelle) *Inferno*, Pocket Books, 1976; *A World Out of Time*, Holt, 1976; (with Pournelle) *Lucifer's Hammer*, Playboy Press, 1977; *The Magic Goes Away*, Ace Books, 1978; *The Ringworld Engineers*, Holt, 1980; *The Patchwork Girl*, Ace Books, 1980; (with Pournelle) *Oath of Fealty*, Simon & Schuster, 1981; (with Steven Barnes) *Dream Park*, Ace Books, 1981; (with Barnes) *The Descent of Anansi*, Pinnacle Books, 1982; *The Integral Trees*, Ballantine, 1984; (with Pournelle) *Footfall*, Ballantine, 1985.

Story collections; published by Ballantine, except as indicated: *Neutron Star*, 1968; *The Shape of Space*, 1969; *All the Myriad Ways*, 1971; *The Flight of the Horse*, 1973; *Inconstant Moon*, Gollancz, 1973; *A Hole in Space*, 1974; *Tales of Known Space*, 1975; *The Long ARM of Gil Hamilton*, 1976; *Convergent Series*, 1979.

Editor: *The Magic May Return*, Ace Books, 1981; *More Magic*, Berkley Publishing, 1984.

Contributor: Harlan Ellison, editor, *Dangerous Visions: 33 Original Stories*, Doubleday, 1967; Reginald Bretnor, editor, *The Craft of Science Fiction*, Harper, 1976.

Work appears in anthologies. Contributor of short stories to *Magazine of Fantasy and Science Fiction, Galaxy, Playboy*, and other magazines.

WORK IN PROGRESS: Limits, Niven's Laws, and *The Time of the Warlock*, all story collections.

SIDELIGHTS: Larry Niven's science fiction novels are speculations about the technologies of the future. Niven's speculations closely follow current trends in scientific research to their logical conclusions, while his visions of the future are usually optimistic. According to Raymond J. Wilson III, writing in the *Dictionary of Literary Biography*, "much of Larry Niven's fiction reveals a love affair with technology. Niven's protechnology heroes take the positive position that the problems raised by technology can be solved and are, in any case, a small price to pay for the benefits of technological advance." Niven's heavy emphasis on science in his science fiction is acknowledged by the author himself. Speaking to Jeffrey Elliot in *Science Fiction Review*, Niven explains: "I wait for the scientists' [research] results and then write stories about them. . . . I try to make my stories as technically accurate as possible." This devotion has paid off. Gerald Jonas states in the *New York Times Book Review* that "there is a certain type of science fiction story that is completely incomprehensible to the non-SF reader. Devotees know it as the 'hard science' story. . . . Devotees recognize Larry Niven as one of the masters of this rather specialized subgenre."

In *Ringworld* and *The Ringworld Engineers*, Niven extrapolates from current scientific speculation about creating artificial planets to imagine Ringworld, an artificial planet shaped like a giant hoop. It is a million miles wide, has a diameter of 190 million miles, and is built in orbit around a sun. Along its outer edge is a range of thousand-mile-high mountains to keep the atmosphere from spinning off as the planet rotates. The top surface of Ringworld—an area three million times larger than the surface of the Earth—has been terraformed to sustain life, while the underside is made of an incredibly strong material. Between Ringworld and the sun are a series of orbiting screens which serve to block sunlight at regular intervals to simulate night and day. The planet is, Bud Foote writes in the *Detroit News*, the "greatest of fictional artifacts."

Ringworld is based on speculations first made by prominent physicist Freeman Dyson. Dyson foresees a time when humanity will acquire the necessary technology to convert the gaseous planets of our solar system into heavier elements and use this material to construct a string of artificial planets in Earth's orbit. This project would provide mankind with more room for its expanding population. While strictly adhering to scientific possibility, Niven's *Ringworld* takes Dyson's idea a step further, envisioning a single huge planet rather than many smaller ones. As Niven states in *Ringworld Engineers*, Dyson "has no trouble believing in Ringworld."

By the time the stories of *Ringworld* and *Ringworld Engineers* take place, the builders of the planet are long dead, and Ringworld is populated by the barbarian descendants of the builders, who no longer understand the advanced technology which created their world. Because of the immense space available on the planet, an area impossible for any human to explore in a lifetime, there are a wide variety of races and cultures which have evolved on Ringworld. In both books, this immense diversity is lavishly presented. In *Ringworld,* a human expedition crash lands on the planet and is forced to journey across its width to safety, encountering many different peoples along the way. In *Ringworld Engineers,* some stabilizer rockets which keep Ringworld in proper orbit have been removed by a culture using them to power their spaceships. An Earthling and an alien set out to find the repair center of Ringworld so they can make the repairs needed to get the planet back in orbit again. Their search takes them through a host of cultures. Speaking of *Ringworld Engineers,* Galen Strawson of the *Times Literary Supplement* states that "the book is alive with detail. There is *rishathra,* sex between species; there are silver-haired vampires with supercharged pheromones; there are shadow farms and flying cities, quantities of different social forms and incompatible social *mores.* Faults of contruction cease to matter in the steady stream of invention. This is in part a guidebook to (a minute fragment of) the Ringworld."

Niven had not originally intended to write a sequel to *Ringworld,* but the amount of interest science-fiction readers showed in the award-winning novel, and certain technical questions they raised, eventually convinced Niven to write *Ringworld Engineers.* Besides explaining a few engineering details about the planet's construction, *Ringworld Engineers* also includes new ideas suggested by Niven's readers. As Strawson explains, Niven wrote the book "partly to answer questions and partly to incorporate details not of his own imagining." Because of this, Strawson sees a problem in the novel's structure. "The incidents [in *Ringworld Engineers*] often seem set up to provide frames for the imparting of information about Ringworld's construction; so that although they are individually well conceived and executed, and jointly testify to Niven's remarkable powers of imagination, they fail to develop smoothly into one another." James Blish, writing in the *Magazine of Fantasy and Science Fiction,* finds fault with *Ringworld.* "The backdrop is a staggering invention," Blish believes, "but what is happening in the foreground is mostly conventional to the point of pettiness." Despite some criticism, the Ringworld books have proven to be enormously popular. Foote expresses the hope of many readers that "Niven does still more Ringworld books; it's a big world, and there is a lot of material there."

BIOGRAPHICAL/CRITICAL SOURCES: Magazine of Fantasy and Science Fiction, September, 1971; *New York Times Book Review,* January 12, 1975, October 26, 1975, October 17, 1976, November 13, 1977; *New Republic,* October 30, 1976; *Contemporary Literary Criticism,* Volume VIII, Gale, 1978; *Analog,* March, 1978, February, 1979; *Science Fiction Review,* July, 1978; *Future,* #3, 1978; Larry Niven, *The Ringworld Engineers,* Holt, 1980; *Detroit News,* April 20, 1980; *Times Literary Supplement,* November 7, 1980; *Dictionary of Literary Biography,* Volume VIII: *Twentieth-Century American Science-Fiction Writers,* two volumes, Gale, 1981; *Los Angeles Times Book Review,* April 19, 1981, November 8, 1981, November 21, 1982; *Washington Post Book World,* December 27, 1981, February 26, 1984; Charles Platt, *Dream Makers, Volume II: The Uncommon Men and Women Who Write Science Fiction,* Berkley Publishing, 1983.

—*Sketch by Thomas Wiloch*

*   *   *

NORRIS, Leslie 1921-

PERSONAL: Born May 21, 1921, in Merthyr Tydfil, Gla-

morganshire, Wales; son of George William (an engineer) and Janie (Jones) Norris; married Catharine Mary Morgan (a teacher), July 31, 1948. *Education:* Attended Training College, Coventry, England, 1947-49, University of Southampton Institute of Education, 1955-58. *Politics:* Liberal. *Home:* Plas Nant, Northfields Lane, Aldingbourne, Chichester, Sussex, England.

CAREER: Assistant teacher in Yeovil, Somerset, England, 1949-52; deputy head teacher in Bath, Somerset, 1952-55; head teacher in Chichester, Sussex, England, 1955-58; Training College, Bognor Regis, Sussex, lecturer in English, beginning 1958. Resident poet, Eton College, 1977. Visiting poet, University of Washington, 1973, 1980, 1981, and Brigham Young University, 1983-84. Lecturer, Institutes of Education at University of Southampton and University of Reading. *Military service:* Royal Air Force, 1940-42; invalided out.

AWARDS, HONORS: Welsh Arts Council Award, 1967, 1968, 1978, and 1980; Arts Council Award, 1969; Alice Hunt Bartlett Prize of Poetry Society, 1970, for *Ransoms;* Cholmondeley Poetry Award, 1978; David Higham Prize for fiction, 1978; Katherine Mansfield Triennial Short Story Award, 1981.

WRITINGS—Poetry, except as indicated: *The Tongue of Beauty,* Favil Press, 1943; *Poems,* Falcon Press, 1946; *The Ballad of Billy Rose,* Northern House, 1964; *Finding Gold,* Chatto & Windus, 1967; *The Loud Winter,* Triskel Press, 1967; *Curlew,* Armstrong, 1969.

(Editor) *Vernon Watkins, 1906-1967* (nonfiction), Faber, 1970; *Ransoms,* Chatto & Windus, 1970; *His Lost Autumn,* Sceptre Press, 1972; *Glyn Jones* (nonfiction), University of Wales Press, 1973; *Mountains, Polecats, Pheasants and Other Elegies,* Chatto & Windus, 1973; *Stone and Fern,* Southern Arts Association, 1973.

Sliding and Other Stories (short stories), Scribner, 1976; *At the Publishers',* Priapus Press, 1976; *Ravenna Bridge,* Sceptre Press, 1977; *Islands off Maine,* Tidal Press, 1977; *Merlin and the Snake's Egg,* Viking, 1978; (editor) *Tributes to Andrew Young,* Tidal Press, 1978.

Water Voices, Chatto & Windus, 1980; *Walking the White Fields: Poems 1967-1980,* Atlantic-Little, Brown, 1980.

Also author of short radio plays for school programs of British Broadcasting Corp., and featured, with Dannie Abse, on sound recording "Poems," Argo, 1974. Contributor of poems to poetry magazines, some of them reprinted in anthologies; also contributor to *New Yorker, Atlantic,* and other periodicals.

WORK IN PROGRESS: Verse translations from medieval Welsh.

SIDELIGHTS: Some of Leslie Norris's poetry, as published in the collection *Walking the White Fields: Poems 1967-1980,* represents work of "extraordinarily refreshing clarity whose magic lies not in symbolist indirection, nor solely in its lovely musicality, but . . . in the absolute realism of its vision," according to Peter Clothier in a *Los Angeles Times Book Review* article. The poet once told *CA* that he works "slowly and with great pain, [producing] about six poems a year."

BIOGRAPHICAL/CRITICAL SOURCES: Punch, April 5, 1967; *Times Literary Supplement,* April 23, 1970, July 25, 1980; *Los Angeles Times Book Review,* November 2, 1980.

*   *   *

NOVAK, Robert
See LEVINSON, Leonard

NUNEZ, Ana Rosa 1926-

PERSONAL: Born July 11, 1926, in Havana, Cuba; came to the United States in 1965, naturalized citizen, 1971; daughter of Jorge Manuel (an architect and professor) and Carmen G. (Burgos) Nunez. *Education:* Academia Baldor, Bachiller en Letras, 1945; Instituto de Segunda Ensenanza, Bachiller en Letras, 1945; attended University of Michigan, 1953; University of Havana, Doctora en Filosofia y Letras, 1954, Bibliotecaria, 1955. *Religion:* Roman Catholic. *Home:* 2130 Southwest 14th Ter., Apt. 4, Miami, Fla. 33145. *Office:* Otto G. Richter Library, University of Miami, Coral Gables, Fla. 33124.

CAREER: Colegio Cima, Havana, Cuba, professor of English as a second language, 1947-49; College of Wooster, Wooster, Ohio, assistant professor in department of Spanish, 1949-50; Tribunal de Cuentas de la Republica de Cuba, Havana, head librarian, 1950-61; University of Miami, Otto G. Richter Library, Coral Gables, Fla., 1966—, assistant professor, 1969-72, associate professor, 1972-80, professor, 1980—, assistant reference librarian, 1969-72, reference librarian, 1972—. Elementary school teacher in Havana, Cuba, 1950-52; assistant professor in summer school, University of Havana, 1950-52; librarian for Academia de Ciencias Genealogicas, 1956-59. Cruzada Educativa Cubana, executive assessor, 1968—, lecturer, 1973; judge for literary competitions; has given poetry readings and lectures. Cultural consultant to Patronato Teatro Las Mascaras y de Forum; counselor, Federation of Cuban Students, University of Miami.

MEMBER: Circulo de Cultura Panamerica, Artistic and Cultural Society of the Americas (president, 1974-76), Instituto de Cultura Hispanica (honorary librarian; member of executive council, 1973—), Colegio Nacional de Doctores en Ciencias y Filosofia y Letras, Colegio Nacional de Bibliotecarios Universitarios (founder; vice-president of executive committee, 1957-59), Asociacion Bibliografica Jose Toribio Medina (Colombia), Sociedad Cubana de Filosofia, Seminar of Latin American Acquisition Materials, Florida Library Association, Dade County Library Association, Sociedad de Escritores, Pintores, y Artistas (Miami; honorary member), Cuban Women's Club (Miami), Sigma Delta Pi (honorary member), Phi Alpha Theta.

AWARDS, HONORS: Scholarship from New York Institute of International Education, 1949; Medalla Juan Enrique Dunant from Spanish Red Cross, 1958; third prize in poetry from Circulo de Escritores y Poetas Iberoamericanos de Nueva York, 1966, for unpublished version of *Sol de un solo dia;* Diploma de Reconocimiento from International Young Men's Christian Association (YMCA), 1970; Diploma de Honor Juan J. Remos from Cruzada Educativa Cubana, 1971; Lincoln-Marti Prize from U.S. Department of Health, Education and Welfare, 1972; Gran Orden del Merito Ciudadano en reconocimiento de destacada labor a la Comunidad from Liceo Cubano, 1973; Order of St. Helene (Greece); Premio Jose de la Luz y Caballero from Cruz Educativa Cubana, 1981.

WRITINGS: La vida bibliografica de don Antonio Bachiller y Morales (title means "Bibliographic Life of don Antonio Bachiller y Morales"), Libraria Marti, 1955; *Un dia en el verso 59* (poems; title means "One Day in Verse 59"), Atabex, 1959; (translator with Ana Maris Brul and Margot Gomez Calvo) *Fernando Broada: Sintesis de su obra artistica,* [Havana], 1959; *Gabriela Mistral: Amor que hirio* (poems; title means "Gabriela Mistral: Love That Hurt"), Atabex, 1961; *Las siete lunas de enero* (poems; title means "The Seven Moons of

January"), Cuadernos del Hombre Libre, 1967; *La Florida en Juan Ramon Jiminez* (title means "Florida in Juan Ramon Jimenez"), Ediciones Universal, 1968; *Loores a la palma real* (title means "Praises to the Royal Palm"), Ediciones Universal, 1968, 2nd edition, Ediciones Continentales, 1976; *Bando* (poems; title means "Edict"), Armando Cordova, 1969.

(Editor and contributor) *Poesia en exodo: El exilio cubano en su poesia, 1959-1969* (anthology; title means "Poetry in Exodus: The Cuban Exile in Poetry"), Ediciones Universal, 1970; *Requiem para una isla* (poems; title means "Requiem for an Island"), Ediciones Universal, 1970; (contributor) *Nuestro Gustavo Adolfo Becquer, 1870-1970* (title means "Our Gustavo Adolpho Becquer"), Ediciones Universal, 1970; *Viaje al cazabe* (title means "Journey to Cazabe"), Ediciones Universal, 1970; *Del paredon al siglo* (poems; title means "From the Shooting Wall to the Century"), Ediciones Universal, 1971; *Escamas del Caribe: Haikus de Cuba* (title means "Scales from the Caribbean: Haikus of Cuba"), Ediciones Universal, 1971; (contributor) *Mijares,* Ediciones Universal, 1971; (contributor) *Res,* [Miami], 1973; *Los oficialeros* (title means "Humble Workers"), Ediciones Universal, 1973.

Algunas fuentes para el servicio de referencia en materia legal cubana (title means "Some Reference Sources on Cuban Legal Material"), Ediciones Universal, 1975; (with Florinda Alzaga) *Ensayo de diccionario del pensamiento vivo de La Avellaneda* (title means "Dictionary of the Living Thoughts of La Avellaneda"), Ediciones Universal, 1975; (editor with Alzaga) *Antologia de la poesia religiosa de La Avellaneda* (title means "Anthology of the Religious Poetry of La Avellaneda"), Ediciones Universal, 1975; *Sol de un solo dia* (poems), Atabex, 1975; (contributor) *Atlas Poetica,* Ediciones Continentales, 1976; (translator) Mildred Merrick, *Exhibition of Rare Cuban Books/ Exhibicion de libros raros cubanos: Catalogue,* [Coral Gables], 1979.

Author of prologue; all published by Ediciones Universal: Humberto J. Pena, *Ya no habra mas domingos* (title means "No More Sundays Left"), 1971; Jose Sanchez Boudy, *Cuentos a luna llena* (title means "Short Stories at Full Moon"), 1971; Ricardo Pau-Llosa, *Veinticinco poemas,* 1973; Esparanza Rubido, *Mas alla del azul,* 1975; Donald A. Randolph, *Tu, papel y yo,* 1975; Dolores F. Rovirosa, *Antonio J. Valdes: Historiador cubano,* 1980. Also author of prologue to Raoul Garcia Iglesias's *Mediodia.*

Work represented in anthologies, including: *Antologia de poesia espanola, 1965-1966* (title means "Anthology of Spanish Poetry"), edited by L. Jiminez Martos, Aguilar, 1967; *Verde yerba,* [Barcelona], 1967; *Un catauro de folklore cubano* (title means "A Basket of Cuban Folklore"), edited by Antonio Carbajo, Language Research Press, 1968; *Poesia en mesa redonda: Antologia latinoamericana, 1948-1968* (title means "Poetry in Round Table: Anthology of Latin American Poetry, 1948-1968"), edited by Antonio de Undurraga, Ediciones de la Revista Caballo de Guego, 1969; *Cinco poetisas cubanas, 1935-1969: Mercedes Garcia Tuduri, Pura del Prado, Teresa Maria Rojas, Rita Geada, Ana Rosa Nunez* (title means "Five Cuban Poetesses, 1935-1969: Mercedes Gardia Tuduri, Pura del Prado, Teresa Maria Rojas, Rita Geada, Ana Rosa Nunez"), Ediciones Universal, 1970; *Poesia negra del Caribe y otras areas: Black Poetry of the Americas—A Bilingual Anthology,* edited by Hortensia Ruiz del Vizo, Ediciones Universal, 1972; *La ultima poesia cubana: Antologia de poesia cubana contemporanea,* edited by Orlando Rodriguez Sardinas, Hispanova, 1973; *Cinquenta poetas modernos: Antologia de la poesia moderna de America Latina y Espana*, edited by Pedro V. Roig, [Miami], 1973; *Antologia de cuento y poesia cubano americana*, Bilingual Press, 1983.

Also author of *Aspectos de una vida entre libros* and *Tierra del mar;* editor, with Jose E. Fernandez, of *Manach y las artes plasticas cubanas;* translator of Pierre Seghers's *Piranese: Poema.*

Co-editor of "Las horas blancas" in *El Habenero,* 1974—. Contributor of poems and articles to numerous newspapers and magazines in the United States, Europe, Cuba, and other Latin American countries.

WORK IN PROGRESS: Editing, with Jose E. Fernandez, *Antologia de literature infantil* (title means "Anthology of Children's Literature"); an anthology of Nunez's poems from 1957 to 1976, entitled *Sin sol pero con sal* (title means "Without Sun, Yet with Salt"); *Andres y otros cuentos* (title means "Andrew and Other Stories"); a book of poems, *Mis dos voces* (title means "My Two Voices").

SIDELIGHTS: Ana Rosa Nunez writes: "I know that I am alone with my poetry, and I also know that I have broken the original silence with my poems. But as long as each one of them can have a life of its own I am rewarded, deep in my silent world. In a poem I have put a great effort in letting silence win. Poetry does not begin with the poet who writes the poem. It really begins with the person who reads it. I believe in the order of the chaos established in the soul when the abyss is not yet forgotten. I believe in Bruegel as the master of surrealism, as the man who gave the inner man his place in a world built to fit hope and tomorrows. I do not trust fame, best-sellers, or book jackets. I believe and trust in the isolation of a sincere creator who wishes to give an order to the resemblance of the light that inherits everyday's light. I believe in Liberty and I stand for everything that could restore Human Dignity."

*   *   *

NUSBAUM, N. Richard
  See NASH, N. Richard

*   *   *

NUTTALL, Jeff   1933-
  (Peter Church, Homosap)

PERSONAL: Born July 8, 1933, in Clitheroe, Lancashire, England; son of Kenneth (a teacher) and Hilda (Addison) Nuttall; married Jane Louch, July, 1954; children: Sara, Daniel, Toby, Timmy Willy. *Education:* Graduated from Herford School of Art, 1951, and Bath Academy of Art, 1953. *Politics:* Anarchist. *Religion:* "Dionysian." *Home:* 392 Halifax Rd., Todmorden, Lancashire, England. *Office:* Liverpool Polytechnic, Liverpool, England L39 RH.

CAREER: Teacher in secondary modern schools in England, 1956-68; Bradford College of Art, Bradford, England, lecturer in fundamental studies department, 1968-70; Leeds College of Art, Leeds, England, lecturer in fine arts, 1970-81; Liverpool Polytechnic, Liverpool, England, head of fine art, 1981—. Has worked as a writer, painter, cartoonist, jazz band trumpeter and pianist; edited a mimeographed literary journal, *My Own Mag.* Participant in various political campaigns, especially in the British Campaign for Nuclear Disarmament. *Military service:* Royal Army Education Corps.

*WRITINGS—*Poetry: (With Keith Musgrove) *The Limbless Virtuoso,* Writers Forum, 1963; *Songs Sacred and Secular,* privately printed, 1964; *Pieces of Poetry,* Coptic Press, 1965; *Poems I Want to Forget,* Turret, 1965; *Isabel,* Turret, 1967; *Journals,* Unicorn Bookshop, 1968; (with Alan Jackson and William Wantling) *Penguin Modern Poets 12,* Penguin (Harmondsworth), 1968; *Love Poems,* Unicorn Bookshop, 1969; *Poems, 1963-69,* Fulcrum Press, 1970; *Selected Poems,* Horizon Press, 1970; *Objects,* Trigram, 1976; *Sun Barber,* Poet and Peasant, 1976; *What Happened to Jackson,* Aloes, 1978; *The Patriarchs: An Early Summer Landscape,* Aloes, 1978; *Grape Notes/Apple Music,* Rivelin, 1979.

Prose: *Come Back, Sweet Prince* (novelette), Writers Forum, 1966; *The Case of Isabel and the Bleeding Foetus* (fiction), Beach Books Text and Documents, 1967; *Mr. Watkins Got Drunk and Had to Be Carried Home* (fiction), Writers Forum, 1968; *Oscar Christ and the Immaculate Conception* (fiction), Writers Forum, 1968; *Bomb Culture* (social criticism), MacGibbon & Kee, 1968, Delacorte, 1969; *Pig* (fiction), Fulcrum Press, 1969.

(Editor) *25: Writing from Leeds Pyrotechnic,* Art and Design Press, 1971; *The Fox's Lair,* Aloes, 1974; *The House Party* (fiction), Basilike, 1975; *Man, Not Man,* Unicorn, 1975; *The Anatomy of My Father's Corpse,* Basilike, 1975; *Fatty Feedemall's Secret Self,* Jack Press, 1975; *Snipe's Spinster,* Calder & Boyars, 1975.

(With Rodick Carmichael) *Common Factors, Vulgar Factions,* Routledge & Kegan Paul, 1977; *King Twist: A Portrait of Frank Randle* (biography), Routledge & Kegan Paul, 1978; *The Gold Hole* (novel), Quartet, 1978; *Performance Art: Memoirs and Scripts,* two volumes, J. Calder, 1979; *Muscle,* Rivelin, 1982.

Plays: "Barrow's Boys," first produced in Bradford, Yorkshire, 1972; "Kosher," first produced in Bradford, Yorkshire, 1972.

Scriptwriter for The People Show, an underground theatre group which has appeared throughout the United Kingdom. Contributor of poetry and prose, sometimes under pseudonyms, to various underground newspapers and magazines.

SIDELIGHTS: In *Bomb Culture,* Jeff Nuttall divides society into two groups: those born before the atomic bomb who believe there is a future, and those born since the bomb who believe there is no future. A reviewer for *Newsweek* regards *Bomb Culture* as a "guidebook" to the underground, one in which "war, violence, brutality and destructive imagination are the central energies Nuttall locates in his inventory of postwar theater, music, painting, poetry and popular culture." Lewis Bates of *Punch,* on the other hand, believes the book is too esoteric for the "common reader," calling it "an invaluable record of recent frenzies from the inside." "To Nuttall and the children of the Bomb," writes George Thayer of the *Washington Post,* "the past is irrelevant and the future nonexistent: The world is so impossible to them that the only reality is now—instant gratification and wisdom through the use of drugs, withdrawal into anarchy and mysticism." Thayer faults Nuttall for his too subjective listing of Allen Ginsberg, William Burroughs, R. D. Laing, Tim Leary, Criton Tomazos, Alexander Trocchi and the Beatles as "the major artistic impulses of the new culture"; he states rather that these have been major influences on Nuttall himself. Writing in the *Times Literary Supplement,* Michael Neve states that *Bomb Culture,* "a study of the underground movement of the mid to late 1960s, is the only English work that actually seemed to be part of the world that it spoke of.''

Nuttall has perhaps been most closely associated with William Burroughs. According to a 1967 *Life* article by Barry Farrell, Nuttall's *My Own Mag* was an important vehicle for beginning underground writers and ''the principal mouthpiece for William Burroughs.'' Nuttall was instrumental in publishing Burroughs' letters and experiments in ''cut-up writing'' in the early underground days. Nuttall told Farrell in 1966: '''Burroughs, all of us—we're decaying men, for God's sake. We're all decaying, clearly. Playing around with drugs, playing around with every possible sexual deviation. . . . But the curious, impressive thing is that so many artists are able to go through these things as intelligent men—not as totally unprincipled sensual men. If you go through these things to some purpose, it can be even noble. It's as if, with your own rot, you refuel and invigorate—you fertilize this very scorched earth for those yet to come.'''

BIOGRAPHICAL/CRITICAL SOURCES: Life, February 17, 1967; *Punch*, November 27, 1968; *New Statesman*, November 29, 1968, March 19, 1971; *Books and Bookmen*, February, 1969; *London Magazine*, February, 1969, November, 1969; *Times Literary Supplement*, April 24, 1969, April 14, 1978, November 24, 1978, February 15, 1980; *Spectator*, July 26, 1969, May 3, 1975; *Newsweek*, August 4, 1969; *Washington Post*, August 22, 1969; *Saturday Review*, August 23, 1969; *Poetry*, February, 1971, May, 1972; *Observer*, December 10, 1978.

O

OATES, Wallace Eugene 1937-

PERSONAL: Born March 21, 1937, in Los Angeles, Calif.; son of Eugene A. (a business executive) and Irene (Young) Oates; married Mary Irby (a college teacher), September 6, 1959; married Grace Mary Garry (a writer), January 13, 1979; children: (first marriage) Catherine, Christopher, Mary Nora. *Education:* Stanford University, M.A., 1959, Ph.D., 1965. *Home:* 4606 Clemson Rd., College Park, Md. 20740. *Office:* Department of Economics, University of Maryland, College Park, Md. 20742.

CAREER: San Diego State College (now University), San Diego, Calif., part-time instructor in economics, 1961-62; San Jose State College (now University), San Jose, Calif., part-time instructor in economics, 1962-65; Princeton University, Princeton, N.J., assistant professor, 1965-71, associate professor, 1971-74, professor of economics, 1974-79; University of Maryland, College Park, professor of economics, 1979—. *Military service:* U.S. Navy, 1959-62; became lieutenant junior grade.

MEMBER: American Economic Association, National Tax Association, Royal Economic Society, Public Choice Society.

AWARDS, HONORS: John Simon Guggenheim fellow, 1974-75; senior Fulbright-Hays research scholar, 1974-75.

WRITINGS: Fiscal Federalism, Harcourt, 1972; *Introduction to Econometrics,* Harper, 1974, revised edition, 1981; *The Theory of Environmental Policy,* Prentice-Hall, 1975; *Fiscal Zoning and Land Use Controls,* Lexington Books, 1975; *Financing the New Federalism,* Johns Hopkins University Press, 1975.

The Political Economy of Fiscal Federalism, Lexington Books, 1977; *Essays in Labor Market Analysis,* Wiley, 1977; *Economics, Environmental Policy, and the Quality of Life,* Prentice-Hall, 1979.

Contributor of articles to periodicals, including *American Economic Review, Quarterly Journal of Economics,* and *Journal of Political Economy.*

WORK IN PROGRESS: A study of the use of economic incentives for protection of the environment (supported by the National Science Foundation); studies in state and local government finance.

O'FLINN, Peter
See FANTHORPE, R(obert) Lionel

*   *   *

O'FLYNN, Peter
See FANTHORPE, R(obert) Lionel

*   *   *

O'GRADY, Desmond (James Bernard) 1935-

PERSONAL: Born August 27, 1935, in Limerick, Ireland; son of Leonard Joseph and Elizabeth Anne (Bourke) O'Grady; married Olga Nora Jwaideh, 1957 (divorced); children: (first marriage) Deirdre Anne Maria; (with Florence Tamburro) Leonard John Jules. *Education:* Attended National University of Ireland, 1954-56; Harvard University, M.A., 1964, Ph.D., 1982. *Residence:* Ballynagarde, Ballyneety, Limerick, Ireland.

CAREER: Poet; translator. Former English teacher in Paris, France and Rome, Italy, at Harvard University, Cambridge, Mass., and at Roxbury Latin School, West Roxbury, Mass.; Overseas School, Rome, senior English master, beginning 1965; American University of Cairo, Cairo, Egypt, distinguished visiting professor, 1971, visiting poet-in-residence, 1975-76. Has given poetry readings throughout the United States, Europe, and North Africa. Irish Representative to Congress of the Community of European Writers, Florence, 1962, and Congress of European Literary Editors and Publishers, Belgrade, 1968. *Member:* Community of European Writers.

*WRITINGS—*Poetry: *Chords and Orchestrations,* Echo Press (Limerick, Ireland), 1956; (with others) *New Work by Five Poets,* [Rome], 1957; (with others) *A Reading of New Poems,* [Rome], 1958; (with others) *Poems,* [Rome], 1959; *Reilley,* Phoenix Press (London), 1961; *Professor Kelleher and the Charles River,* Carthage Press, 1964; *The Dark Edge of Europe,* MacGibbon & Kee, 1967; *Separanzioni* (poems in English with Italian translations opposite), Editizioni Raporti Europi, 1968; *The Dying Gaul,* MacGibbon & Kee, 1968; *Hellas,* New Writers' Press (Dublin), 1971; *Separations,* Goldsmith Press (Dublin), 1973; *Stations,* illustrations by Margo Veillon, American University in Cairo Press, 1976; *His Skaldcrane's*

Nest, Gallery Press (Dublin), 1979; *The Headgear of the Tribe,* Gallery Press, 1979; *The Wandering Celt,* Gallery Press, 1983. Also author of *Sing Me Creation.*

Translator of poetry: *Off Licence,* Dolmen, 1968; *The Gododdin,* illustrations by Margo Veillon, Dolmen, 1976; *A Limerick Rake,* Gallery Press, 1978; *Grecian Glances,* Inkling Press, 1981; *Trawling the Tradition,* Gallery Press, 1983. Translator of works from Irish, Scottish, Welsh, French, Italian, Spanish, Greek, German, Turkish, Armenian, Persian, Arabic, Russian, Swedish, Czech, and Slavic.

Contributor to many anthologies including *The Norton Anthology of Modern Poetry, The New Irish Poetry, The Castle Poets, The Patrick Kavanagh Anthology,* and *Soundings 72.* Contributor of poetry, reviews, stories, essays, and travelogues to periodicals, including *Transatlantic Review, Botteghe Oscure, Atlantic, Poetry Ireland, Irish Times,* and *Arena.*

WORK IN PROGRESS: The Unauthorized Version, collected translations; *Shards,* lyric fragments; *The Mass,* a free translation and adaptation of the Roman Latin Mass; *Inheritance,* imaginative autobiographical prose.

SIDELIGHTS: Desmond O'Grady told *CA:* "I began writing poems in boarding school in Ireland. At that time I first practiced the styles of Milton and the English and French romantics, later the English and American moderns. The writers who influenced me most in style and technique then were Hopkins, Joyce, Pound and Patrick Kavanagh. I wrote mostly about what concerns young people: nature, love, change or process, death, as I experienced them growing up in the west of Ireland. Through Joyce's influence the architecture of groups or collections of poems became very important to me so that I saw and wrote in interrelated sequences. *Reilley* was the first elaborate, if strongly influenced, sequence.

"When I left Ireland in the fifties to live on the Continent and in America, themes of social criticism, love, separation, loss, exile, concerned me. At that time, too, a reaction to the way of life in Ireland combined with what most young poets ambitiously aspire to—writing the long poem in the shadow of *The Waste Land*—became a preoccupation. My attempt in *The Scattering* was not successful. *The Dying Gaul* was a later and more satisfying attempt.

"Because I have travelled a lot in North Africa, Asia, Europe and America, and read in the literature of these places, I began to translate into English some of the poetry of these languages as a way to begin a day's work, or to keep my writing hand moving when not writing poems of my own, or to get closer to the methods of composition of poets who interested me. The thing was to get from under the shadow of Yeats. Again, because I had a serious interest in Celtic literature and culture, I developed a Celtic rather than a Greco-Roman attitude to form for my collections of poems. Making my *The Gododdin* from Welsh into English affected me greatly in this, and Anglo-Saxon poetic devices solved many problems. And because so many of my friends have been painters, sculptors and ballad singers, I developed more of an artist's method of working, of *making,* so that even my translations may hardly be called that but rather my version of their originals as a painter or sculptor would use, or a singer sing, the work of another—ancient or modern—to render his own version of his own style.

"For me, therefore, my poem is a made artifact as detached from me as a painting, sculpture or vase would be from its maker—no matter how intense the autobiographical element may be. There are exceptions, where the poem sings itself.

But these are rare indeed. I write poems to attempt to order the general chaos of my experience and through that order hopefully understand my life and motives better and also in the hope that I give readers an expression and understanding of our common daily experience. There is a structure of intercyclical and expanding circles that make the whole of my work cohere for me so that I see my total production to date, in verse and verse translation together, as ultimately one book. . . . My prose I intend as a backdrop to my verse. The poems are epiphanic moments in the general narrative of my life.

"My attitude to routine and artistic discipline was formed by a Cistercian monk, Dom. Eugene Boylan, and my attitude to language was formed mostly by Ezra Pound. Every word must work in the line and every line bend its unique tension. My way of seeing things owes much to archeology and anthropology—particularly in collections like *The Dying Gaul* and *Sing Me Creation* where the poems, like ruins on an archeological site, may read naturally enough to the eye but where much else may be found under the surface with a little careful digging. I also like to echo or refer back to old poems in the new ones, like artists might in their work, or put in faces, places, things that I have been involved with. I believe in the daily effort and in ceaseless revision. Tinkering.

"Looking at the poems and translations I have done in the past twenty years, I see them thematically and not chronologically, and as a single work that will expand spherically as I continue to write. I began with subject matter and in a language drawn from the place and people of my origins in the west of Ireland. I proceeded through various journeyings that constitute a single journey and recorded the experiences of separation from the places, people and paraphernalia encountered in that journey.

"Today I find myself confronted with my own *wyrd* in the sequence of poems called *The Wandering Celt.* It is the *persona* of Reilley, the wandering Celt, the dying Gaul who journeys. He records the experience of his wanderings in an attempt to connect what he left with what he found. . . . You might say mine is a poetry of quest."

BIOGRAPHICAL/CRITICAL SOURCES: New Statesman, September 15, 1967; *Punch,* December 25, 1968.

*   *   *

OLDER, Julia 1941-

PERSONAL: Born May 25, 1941, in Chicago, Ill.; daughter of David Drake and Martha Louise (Dalrymple) Older. *Education:* University of Michigan, B.A., 1963; Conservatorio Arrigo Boito, diploma, 1966; Instituto San Miguel de Allende, M.F.A., 1969. *Home and office address:* P.O. Box 174, Hancock, N.H. 03449. *Agent:* Martha Millard, 357 West 19th St., New York, N.Y. 10011.

CAREER: Writer and musician. Institute for Cross-Cultural Research, Washington, D.C., librarian, 1967-68; teacher of English at a preschool in Celaya, Mexico, 1968-69; G. P. Putnam's Sons, New York, N.Y., assistant to children's book editor, 1969-70; receptionist, 1971; Orchestra de Sao Paulo, Sao Paulo, Brazil, flutist, 1972-73. *Awards, honors:* Avery Hopwood Prize from University of Michigan, 1963, for "The Green Bench and Other Poems"; Yaddo residency, 1972, 1983; MacDowell Colony residency, 1973; Mary Roberts Rinehart grant, 1974; Ossabaw residency, 1978.

WRITINGS: (Illustrator) *The Wood Stove and Fireplace Book,* Stackpole, 1976; *Appalachian Odyssey: 2000 Miles on the Appalachian Trail from Georgia to Maine,* Stephen Greene Press, 1977; *Soup and Bread,* Stephen Greene Press, 1978; *New Hampshire Dining Guide,* Phoenix Press, 1979; *Cooking without Fuel: The Forgotten Art of Fireless Cooking,* Yankee Books, 1982; *Oonts and Others* (poems), Unicorn Press, 1982; *Endometriosis: A Woman's Guide to a Common but Often Undetected Disease,* Scribner, 1984.

Co-author of review column "Dining in New Hampshire" in *New Hampshire Times,* 1976-78. Contributor to anthologies. Contributor of short stories, articles, book reviews, and poems to journals, including *Amicus Journal, Christian Science Monitor,* and *New Letters.*

WORK IN PROGRESS: Celia, a biographical novel based on the New Hampshire poet Celia Thaxter; *The Girl with the Cloak,* a collection of short stories; *Hermaphrodite in America,* a book-length poem; *The Original Child,* an oratorio libretto; a song cycle of poems set to music for piano and voice; *A Little Wild,* a chapbook of animal-related poems with four original woodblock prints; *Echoes from the Cave,* a collection of poems; *Umbanda,* a personal account of spiritual beliefs and the history of this urban Brazilian-African cult.

SIDELIGHTS: Julia Older told *CA:* "I've turned off the television for good and highly recommend the benefits of peace and constructive concentration that follow such a decision.

"Music and poetry have combined in exciting new forms— the continuous poem orchestrated for several voices, working on more levels than the 'what I had for breakfast' outlook. Today it seems that poets want to be safe, hang onto academia and hang out at workshops. I've noticed not much growth happens that way. Juilliard turns out scrambling competitive musicians and [University of] Iowa turns out scrambling competitive poets made and manufactured in competitive America. They have signed all the right forms and done the right things. But few of them have any historical perspective, or respect the traditions that allow us to approach the edges of creation without fear. As a musician I want to hear and play New Music. As a poet I want to write and live unsafe poems."

*   *   *

ORGEL, Stephen (Kitay) 1933-

PERSONAL: Born April 11, 1933, in New York, N.Y.; son of Samuel Z. (a physician) and Esther (an attorney; maiden name, Kitay) Orgel. *Education:* Columbia University, B.A., 1954; Harvard University, Ph.D., 1959. *Office:* Department of English, Johns Hopkins University, Baltimore, Md. 21218.

CAREER: Harvard University, Cambridge, Mass., instructor in English, 1959-60; University of California, Berkeley, assistant professor, 1960-66, associate professor, 1966-72, professor of English, 1972-75; Johns Hopkins University, Baltimore, Md., professor of English, 1975-81, Sir William Osler Professor, 1981—.

MEMBER: Modern Language Association of America, Renaissance Society of America, American Society for Theatre Research, Shakespeare Association.

AWARDS, HONORS: Woodrow Wilson fellowship, 1954-55; American Council of Learned Societies fellowship, 1967-68, 1973-74; National Endowment for the Humanities senior fellow, 1982-83.

WRITINGS: The Jonsonian Masque, Harvard University Press, 1965, reprinted, Columbia University Press, 1981; (editor) Ben Jonson, *The Complete Masques,* Yale University Press, 1969; (editor) *Christopher Marlowe: Complete Poems and Translations,* Penguin, 1971; (with Roy Strong) *Inigo Jones: The Theatre of the Stuart Court,* two volumes, University of California Press, 1973; (with John Harris) *The King's Arcadia,* Arts Council of Great Britain, 1973.

The Illusion of Power: Political Theater in the English Renaissance, University of California Press, 1975; (editor) D. J. Gordon, The Renaissance Imagination: Essays and Lectures, University of California Press, 1976; (editor) *Cebes in England,* Garland Publishing, 1980; (with Guy Lytle) *Patronage in the Renaissance,* Princeton University Press, 1981.

General editor of "The Renaissance and the Gods" series, Garland Publishing, 1976. Also general editor of four other series. Editor-in-chief, *ELH* (journal of English literary history).

WORK IN PROGRESS: Imagining Shakespeare; editing an edition of *The Tempest* for Oxford University Press.

*   *   *

ORNATI, Oscar A(braham) 1922-

PERSONAL: Born July 11, 1922, in Trieste, Italy; came to United States in 1939; naturalized U.S. citizen, 1943; son of Julius (a businessman) and Anna (Klar) Ornati; married Winifred Benes, 1946 (died October, 1980); children: Lee, Susan, Molly. *Education:* Hobart College, B.A., 1949; Harvard University, M.A., 1950, Ph.D., 1955. *Politics:* Democrat. *Religion:* Jewish. *Home:* 100 Bleecker St., Apt. 5A, New York, N.Y. 10012. *Office:* Department of Management, Graduate School of Business, New York University, 100 Trinity, New York, N.Y. 10003.

CAREER: Cornell University, New York State School of Industrial and Labor Relations, Ithaca, N.Y., assistant professor of economics, 1952-57; New School for Social Research, New York City, associate professor, 1957-61, professor of economics, 1961-66; New York University, New York City, professor of economics and manpower management, 1966—. Visiting professor in Italy in Trieste, 1955-56, Milan, 1982, and Venice, 1984. Principal, Arthur Young & Co., 1973-78. Chief of economic development, Office of Economic Opportunities (OEO), 1965-66. Vice-president, Humanic Designs Corp., Manhasset, N.Y., 1969-73, and Meredith Assocs., Westport, Conn., 1973-83. Appointed to New York State Task Force on Poverty; director, National Committee on American Foreign Policy; director, Council on Municipal Performance. Arbitrator in public and private labor disputes; member of Federal Mediation Conciliation Service and National Mediation Board. Consultant to numerous government agencies and various corporations. *Military service:* U.S. Army, interpreter for Allied Military Government in Italy, 1943-46.

MEMBER: National Academy of Arbitrators, American Economic Association, Industrial Research Association. *Awards, honors:* Order of the British Empire.

WRITINGS: Jobs and Workers in India, Cornell University Press, 1955; *Poverty amid Affluence,* Twentieth Century Fund, 1965; *Transportation Needs of the Poor,* Praeger, 1971; (with Katzell, Yankelovich, Fein, and Nash) *Work, Productivity and Job Satisfaction: An Evaluation of Policy-Related Research,* Psychological Corp., 1975; *Staffing and Budgeting the Per-*

sonnel Function, American Management Association, 1981; *Employees Benefit Handbook,* Warren, Gorham & Lamont, 1982-84. Also author of *E.E.O.: Avoiding Compliance Headaches,* and *How to Eliminate Discriminatory Practices: A Guide to EEO Compliance.* Contributor of numerous articles to journals in his field.

SIDELIGHTS: Oscar A. Ornati told *CA:* "When I first went to work I cared only to be a good teacher. I began to write because research had to be reported out and I needed that for both my career and to have something new and exciting to tell my students. There followed a number of years with a small stream of reasonably dull professional articles. Now my thrust is to make the regularities of the world of the social sciences clear to the nonspecialist; I would like the general public to be as excited as I am about manpower planning, collective bargaining, etc. I find current writing in economics, business, social problems abysmal. What is important is too often buried in jargon, while most of what is well written is either wrong or trivial."

*   *   *

O'SHEA, Sean
   See TRALINS, S(andor) Robert

*   *   *

O'TOOLE, Rex
   See TRALINS, S(andor) Robert

*   *   *

OWEN, Philip
   See PHILIPS, Judson (Pentecost)

*   *   *

OWENS, Virginia Stem   1941-
   (Eugenia Adams)

PERSONAL: Born March 4, 1941, in Houston, Tex.; daughter of Clarence Lamar (in U.S. Air Force) and Esther (a secretary; maiden name, Adams) Stem; married David Clinton Owens (a clergyman), December 26, 1959; children: Alyssa Claire, Amy Laury. *Education:* North Texas State University, B.A., 1965; University of Kansas, M.A., 1969; Iliff School of Theology, M.A.R., 1975. *Politics:* None. *Religion:* United Presbyterian. *Residence:* Huntsville, Tex. 77340. *Agent:* Sandra Hintz, 2879 North Grant Blvd., Milwaukee, Wisc. 53210.

CAREER: Northeast Missouri State University, Kirksville, instructor in English, 1969-70; writer, 1970—. Also worked as beekeeper, houseparent for mentally retarded boys, researcher, and library cataloger.

WRITINGS: (Under pseudonym Eugenia Adams) *Assault on Eden,* Eerdmans, 1978; *The Total Image,* Eerdmans, 1980; *A Taste of Creation,* Judson, 1980; *And the Trees Clap Their Hands,* Eerdmans, 1983; *A Feast of Families,* Zondervan, 1983; *Wind River Winter,* Zondervan, 1985. Contributor to periodicals, including *Theology Today, Christian Century, One World,* and *Mother Earth News.*

WORK IN PROGRESS: Language as a spiritual enterprise; life in Texas at the turn of the century.

SIDELIGHTS: Virginia Stem Owens writes: "I've never wanted to do anything but write—except for reading. Unfortunately, I never had anything to write about until my nebulous and somewhat insubstantial life coalesced in the cosmic drama of Christ. I was at one time involved in radical politics, the women's movement, ecology activism, etc. Now I have no causes, although I retain my horror of our technological society. At this point I have no desire to influence either society or individuals. I'm only interested in how the story turns out.

"I have an east Texas background rich in the oral tradition of story-telling. Thanks to affluence and television, that will not survive my generation. *Sic transit gloria.* My family is very important to me, almost mythologically so. We are like secret refugees from some unarticulated homeland."

P

PAGE, Joseph A(nthony) 1934-

PERSONAL: Born April 13, 1934, in Boston, Mass.; son of Joseph E. (an attorney) and Eleanor M. (a teacher; maiden name, Santosuosso) Page; married Martha Gil-Montero. Education: Harvard University, A.B., 1955, LL.B., 1958, LL.M., 1964. Agent: Carl Brandt, Brandt & Brandt Literary Agents, Inc., 1501 Broadway, New York, N.Y. 10036. Office: Law Center, Georgetown University, 600 New Jersey Ave. N.W., Washington, D.C. 20001.

CAREER: National Association of Claimants Counsel of America, Watertown, Mass., assistant editor-in-chief of NACCA Law Journal, 1960-63; University of Denver, Denver, Colo., assistant professor of law, 1964-68; Georgetown University, Washington, D.C., associate professor, 1968-73, professor of law, 1973—. Member of bars of Massachusetts and District of Columbia. Consumer advocate; has worked with a number of Ralph Nader's groups in the area of consumer safety. Military service: U.S. Coast Guard Reserve, 1958-67; became lieutenant.

WRITINGS: The Revolution That Never Was: Northeast Brazil, 1955-1964, Grossman, 1972; (with Mary Win O'Brien) Bitter Wages: The Nader Report on Disease and Injury on the Job, Grossman, 1973; The Law of Premises Liability, Anderson, 1976; Peron: A Biography, Random House, 1983. Contributor of articles and reviews to law journals, popular magazines, and newspapers, including New Republic, Nation, Atlantic, New York Times Magazine, and Progressive.

SIDELIGHTS: Joseph A. Page's Peron: A Biography is the story of Argentine political strongman Juan Domingo Peron, who first rose to power in 1943 and who is believed by many political observers to exert a great deal of influence on that country's government even today, many years after his death in 1974. For more than forty years Argentines have been sharply divided into Peronist and anti-Peronist camps. Explains Mario Del Carril in the Washington Post Book World: "When . . . Peron became the dominant political figure in Argentina, . . . his followers made social justice their flag, while his opponents insisted on preserving civic freedoms and institutional autonomies." Today, "social justice" is espoused by the influential Justicialist Party, a Peronist coalition, while "civic freedom" is advocated by the anti-Peronist Radical Civic Union. Most other political factions in Argentina are aligned along these same lines, and, as Del Carril points out, when Argentines go to the polls, "whether they admit it or not," they still vote as either Peronists or anti-Peronists.

Alberto Manguel, writing in the Toronto Globe and Mail, states, "For those unfamiliar with the character of Peron and Argentina, [Peron: A Biography] provides a comprehensive picture of the man and his era; for those who knew him and lived through his three presidencies, Page's book has the vividness of a nightmare." Manguel, whose father was a diplomat in Peron's regime, believes that "not only has the author managed to capture the personality of the man and sense of what Argentina is (a task at which V. S. Naipaul failed dismally in The Return of Eva Peron), but he has also managed to put his finger on the paradox of the archetypal dictator: a seemingly unremarkable man who suddenly becomes the symbol of his country and his times."

Del Carril expresses the opinion that "Joseph A. Page's extensively documented political biography of Peron is a valiant, though I believe unsuccessful, attempt to come to terms with this most controversial, confusing and brilliant of Argentina's military/politicians. Page . . . has labored under two handicaps: many facts about Peron's life are not yet available and Page himself is not professionally equipped to go into depth about the history and culture of Argentina." On the other hand, Jonathan Kandell maintains in the New York Times Book Review that "Mr. Page's account of Peron's career and the people who surrounded him fills huge gaps in our understanding of one of South America's master politicians and the movement he created" and calls Peron: A Biography "a clearly written, definitive study, the first biography that traces the legendary caudillo [leader] from birth to power to exile and back to power and death. This is a considerable feat of historical writing because the passions aroused by Peron in his nation are so great." Concludes Malcolm Boyd in a Los Angeles Times Book Review article, "This is a handsomely researched biography, surprising in its revelations, written with commendable style."

Peron: A Biography was translated into Spanish by Page's wife, Martha Gil-Montero, and was published in two volumes in 1984. The work was a best-seller in Argentina.

BIOGRAPHICAL/CRITICAL SOURCES: New York Times Book Review, September 4, 1983; Washington Post Book World,

September 4, 1983; *Los Angeles Times Book Review,* October 16, 1983; *Toronto Globe and Mail,* March 17, 1984.

* * *

PALLISTER, Janis L(ouise)   1926-

PERSONAL: Born January 12, 1926, in Rochester, Minn.; daughter of George L. (an engineer) and Edith (Reed) Pallister. *Education:* University of Minnesota, B.A. (cum laude), 1946, M.A., 1948, Ph.D., 1964; also attended University of Wisconsin, 1950-52; Sorbonne, University of Paris, Certificat, 1959. *Politics:* Independent. *Religion:* Roman Catholic. *Home:* 211 State St., Bowling Green, Ohio 43402. *Office:* Department of Romance Languages, Bowling Green State University, Bowling Green, Ohio 43402.

CAREER: Black Hills Teachers College (now Black Hills State College), Spearfish, S.D., instructor in French, Spanish, and English, 1948-50; translator, Minnesota Mining and Manufacturing, 1953-54; Colby College, Waterville, Me., instructor in French, 1959-61; Bowling Green State University, Bowling Green, Ohio, instructor, 1961-65, assistant professor, 1965-68, associate professor, 1968-71, professor of French, 1971-78, university professor, 1979—.

MEMBER: American Association of Teachers of French, Modern Language Association of America, American Literary Translators Association, African Studies Association, African Literature Association, American Council on the Teaching of Foreign Languages, Modern Humanities Research Association, American Association of University Professors, Renaissance Society of America, Paul Claudel Society of America, Mediaeval Academy of America, Lambda Alpha Psi, Pi Delta Phi, Phi Sigma Iota, Sigma Delta Pi, Phi Kappa Phi.

AWARDS, HONORS: Greater University fellowship, 1959; Tozer Foundation fellowship, 1969; Columbia University Translation Center award, 1978; National Endowment for the Humanities grant, 1980; North East Modern Language Association grant for Canadian studies, 1983; Canadian government research grant, 1984.

WRITINGS: The World View of Beroalde de Verville, Vrin, 1971; *Mon Autre Lyre,* J. & C. Transcripts, 1971; *The Planting,* New Voices, 1972; *The Green Balloon* (poems), Northwoods Press, 1976; *Confrontations,* Westburg Associates, 1977; *Esanzo,* Naaman, 1977; *The Bruised Reed,* Naaman, 1978; (with Ramona Conmier) *Waiting for Death: The Philosophical Significance of "En attendant Godot,"* University of Alabama Press, 1979.

(With Michael Giordano) *Bibliographic Notes on Beroalde de Verville's "Le Moyen de Parvenir,"* PSCFL, Bibliotheque 17, 1981; (translator from the French) Ambroise Pare, *On Monsters and Marvels,* University of Chicago Press, 1982; *Sursum Corda* (poems), Gergon Press, 1982; *At the Eighth Station* (poems), Gergon Press, 1984.

Contributor of more than eighty poems in English, Spanish, and French, and about thirty articles and reviews to professional and literary journals, including *Poetry Review, Poet and Critic, Beyond Baroque, L'Esprit Createur, French Review,* and *Romance Notes.*

SIDELIGHTS: Janis L. Pallister speaks French and Spanish, and reads German, Italian, Old French, Old Provencal, Portuguese, and Latin.

PARISH, David   1932-

PERSONAL: Born October 3, 1932, in Niagara Falls, N.Y.; son of Wheaton H. and Alma (Kurkowski) Parish; married Ava H. Hughart, November 23, 1963; children: David Andrew. *Education:* Buffalo State Teachers College, B.S., 1954, M.S., 1961; University of Buffalo (now State University of New York at Buffalo), Ed.M., 1958; State University of New York College at Geneseo, M.L.S., 1967, graduate study, 1974—. *Religion:* Methodist. *Home:* 5 Crossett Rd., Geneseo, N.Y. 14454. *Office:* Milne Library, State University of New York College at Geneseo, Geneseo, N.Y. 14454.

CAREER: Reading teacher in elementary public schools in Niagara Falls, N.Y., 1957-66; State University of New York College at Geneseo, academic librarian, 1967—, head of government publication section. Co-chairman of State Government Document Planning Committee, 1973-75; member of Geneseo Campus United Ministry Council. *Military service:* U.S. Army, 1955-56.

MEMBER: American Library Association, National Education Association, New York State Library Association (past president of government document committee), State University Professionals, State University of New York Library Association, Livingston County Historical Society (member of board of directors), Phi Delta Kappa, Masons, Rotary. *Awards, honors:* Geneseo Foundation grant, 1973, 1981; New York State Library Association grants, 1978, 1981; State University of New York College at Geneseo faculty grant, 1981.

WRITINGS: (With Sally Wynkoop) *Directory of Government Agencies,* Libraries Unlimited, 1969; *Milne Library State Classification Scheme* (pamphlet), Milne Library, State University of New York College at Geneseo, 1969; *State Government Reference Publications: An Annotated Bibliography,* Libraries Unlimited, 1974, 2nd edition, 1981; *Bibliography of U.S. and State Government Bibliographies* (monograph), State University of New York College at Geneseo, 1975; *The Church in the Valley: History of the Geneseo United Methodist Church,* privately printed, 1975; (editor with Ivan L. Kaldor and Stephen Torok, and contributor) *Proceedings of the First Annual Government Document Workshop,* School of Library and Information Science, State University of New York College at Geneseo, 1976; (coauthor and editor) *History of the Livingston County Mutual Insurance Company* (monograph), privately printed, 1977; *Changes in American Society, 1960-1978, as Reflected in Official Government Publications,* Scarecrow, 1981; *Bibliography of State Government Bibliographies, 1970-1980,* Libraries Unlimited, 1983; *Changes in American Economics and Science, 1950-1980, as Reflected in Official Government Publications,* Scarecrow, 1984.

Author of a column on popular state publications for *Government Publications Review,* 1976—. Contributor of reviews and articles to numerous local and professional journals, including *Communicator* and *Government Document Review.* Editor of *DttP—New York State* (government document taskforce newsletter), 1973—, and *Trestle-Board,* 1976—; co-editor of *Livingstone,* 1973—.

WORK IN PROGRESS: Bibliography of State Bibliographies, 1970-1983; History of Geneseo Methodist Church, 1975-1983.

* * *

PARSIFAL
See CURL, James Stevens

PEACE, Richard 1938-

PERSONAL: Born July 6, 1938, in Detroit, Mich.; son of Claude Vernon (a stationary engineer) and Helen (Brinkman) Peace; married Judy Jean Boppell, September 13, 1963; children: Elizabeth Jean, Jennifer Joan, Stephen Richard, Jonathan Charles. *Education:* Yale University, B.E., 1960; Fuller Theological Seminary, B.D., 1964; University of Natal, Ph.D. candidate. *Home:* 479 Bay Rd., South Hamilton, Mass. 01982.

CAREER: African Enterprises, Inc. (missionary organization), Pasadena, Calif., and Pietermaritzburg, South Africa, director of special projects, working in the field of city evangelism in Africa, 1964-71; Clear Light Productions (multimedia production house), Newton, Mass., director of publications, 1971-73; Education Development Center (curriculum development house), Newton, assistant to manager of media services, 1974-77; Gordon-Conwell Theological Seminary, Hamilton, Mass., associate professor of evangelism and media, 1977—. Ordained minister of United Church of Christ. *Member:* Sigma Xi, Tau Beta Pi.

WRITINGS: Learning to Love God, Zondervan, 1968; *Learning to Love Ourselves,* Zondervan, 1968; *Learning to Love People,* Zondervan, 1968; *Witness,* three volumes, Zondervan, 1971; *A Leader's Guide to Witness,* Zondervan, 1971; *Pilgrimage: A Workbook of Christian Growth,* Action House Publishers, 1976; (consulting editor) *Hearing and Doing: Discipleship and Mission in Today's Cultures,* P.I.M., 1979; *Giving Away Your Faith and Keeping It Too,* David Cook, 1979; *A Church's Guide to Evangelism,* E.A.N.E., 1982; (contributor) *Search the Scriptures,* Serendipity, 1983; *Small Group Evangelism,* Inter-Varsity Press, 1984.

Author of taped lectures for witness course; also author of film scripts, including "Freedom '66" and "Chris Begins Again," and animation scripts for the national PBS-TV series, "Infinity Factory." Contributor to religious journals.

WORK IN PROGRESS: A Bible study series, for Serendipity.

*   *   *

PEARSALL, Ronald 1927-

PERSONAL: Surname is pronounced *Peer*-sall; born October 20, 1927, in Birmingham, England; son of Joseph (an engineer) and Elsie Caroline (Rawlins) Pearsall. *Education:* Studied art, 1950-52, and attended Birmingham College of Art, 1952-54. *Politics:* Conservative. *Religion:* Church of England. *Home:* Thornecroft, Landscove, Ashburton, Devon TQ13 7LX, England.

CAREER: Writer. Traveled about England, 1954-61, working variously as bank clerk, cinema manager, wine waiter, dance hall musician, private detective, composer, and at other short-term jobs in twenty cities. Lecturer in Sweden for British Council, 1964. *Military service:* British Army, Royal Corps of Signals, 1945-48.

MEMBER: Society for Psychical Research, London Library.

WRITINGS: Scarlet Mask (spy thriller), Lloyd Cole, 1941; *Is That My Hook in Your Ear?,* Stanley Paul, 1966; *Worm in the Bud,* Macmillan, 1969, published as *The Worm in the Bud: The World of Victorian Sexuality,* Penguin, 1983; *The Table Rappers,* St. Martin's, 1972; *Victorian Sheet Music Covers,*

Gale, 1972; *Victorian Popular Music,* Gale, 1972; *Collecting Mechanical Antiques,* Arco, 1973; *Edwardian Life and Leisure,* St. Martin's, 1973; *Collecting and Restoring Scientific Instruments,* Arco, 1974; (with Graham Webb) *Inside the Antique Trade,* Reid & Son, 1974; *Edwardian Popular Music,* Fairleigh Dickinson University Press, 1975; *Night's Black Angels: The Forms and Faces of Victorian Cruelty,* McKay, 1975.

Popular Music of the Twenties, Rowman & Littlefield, 1976; *Public Purity, Private Shame: Victorian Sexual Hypocrisy Exposed,* Weidenfeld & Nicholson, 1976; *The Alchemists,* Weidenfeld & Nicholson, 1976; *Conan Doyle: A Biographical Solution,* St. Martin's, 1977; *Tides of War,* M. Joseph, 1978; *The Iron Sleep,* M. Joseph, 1979; *Tell Me, Pretty Maiden: The Victorian and Edwardian Nude,* Webb & Bower, 1981; *Practical Painting,* Winchmore Publishing, 1984.

Contributor to *Punch, Quarterly Review, Motoring, Homes and Gardens, Field History Today, Books & Bookmen, Ideal Home, Music Review,* and other periodicals in Britain, United States, Canada, and Australia.

SIDELIGHTS: Scarlet Mask, a paperback, was published when Ronald Pearsall was fourteen ("the firm decamped without paying me any royalties"). Pearsall told *CA* that he is "looking for an adventurous publisher to commission an encyclopedia of spiritualism of 250,000 words."

BIOGRAPHICAL/CRITICAL SOURCES: Home and Gardens, August, 1964.

*   *   *

PEARSON, Susan 1946-

PERSONAL: Born December 21, 1946, in Boston, Mass.; daughter of Allen M. and Chloris (Horsman) Pearson. *Education:* St. Olaf College, B.A., 1968. *Home:* 4545 Aldrich Ave. S., Minneapolis, Minn. 55409.

CAREER: Volunteers in Service to America (VISTA), Columbia, S.C., volunteer worker, 1968-69; Quaker Oats Co., Minneapolis, Minn., sales representative, 1969-71; Viking Press, New York City, assistant, 1971-72; Dial Press, New York City, editor, 1972-78; Carolrhoda Books, Minneapolis, editor-in-chief, 1978-84; writer.

AWARDS, HONORS: Izzie was named *New York Times* outstanding book of the year and Child Study Association children's book of the year, 1975.

WRITINGS—For children; published by Dial, except as indicated: *Izzie,* 1975; *Monnie Hates Lydia,* 1975; *That's Enough for One Day, J.P.!,* 1977; *Monday I Was an Alligator,* Lippincott, 1979; *Molly Moves Out,* 1979; *Karin's Christmas Walk,* 1980; *Saturday I Ran Away,* Lippincott, 1981.

WORK IN PROGRESS: Picture books and juvenile novels.

*   *   *

PEDEN, Margaret Sayers 1927-

PERSONAL: Surname is pronounced *Pea*-den; born May 10, 1927, in West Plains, Mo.; daughter of Harvey Monroe (a horseman) and Eleanor Green (James) Sayers; married Robert Norwine, August, 1949 (divorced, 1961); married William Harwood Peden (a professor and writer), September 18, 1965; children: (first marriage) Kerry (Mrs. James Dunning), Kyle Robert; (second marriage) Eliza (Mrs. Carl Mitchell), Sally

Monroe (stepdaughters). *Education:* University of Missouri—Columbia, A.B., 1948, M.A., 1963, Ph.D., 1966. *Politics:* Independent. *Religion:* Protestant. *Home:* 408 Thilly Ave., Columbia, Mo. 65201. *Office:* 11 Arts and Science, University of Missouri—Columbia, Columbia, Mo. 65201.

CAREER: University of Missouri—Columbia, assistant professor, 1966-70, associate professor, 1970-75, professor of Spanish, 1975—, Catherine Paine Middlebush Professor of Romance Languages, 1979—, chairperson of department of Romance languages, 1975-77.

MEMBER: P.E.N., American Association of Teachers of Spanish and Portuguese, American Literary Translators' Association, Missouri Modern Language Association, Phi Sigma Iota, Sigma Delta Pi.

AWARDS, HONORS: Byler Distinguished Professor Award, 1977, and distinguished faculty award, 1981, both from University of Missouri—Columbia; American Association of University Women fellow, 1978-79; National Endowment for the Arts fellow, 1981; Rockefeller scholar in Bellagio, Italy, 1983.

WRITINGS: Emilio Carballido, Twayne, 1980; (editor) *The Latin American Short Story: A Critical History,* Twayne, 1983.

Translator: Emilio Carballido, *The Norther,* University of Texas Press, 1968; Carballido, *The Golden Thread and Other Plays,* University of Texas Press, 1970; Egon Wolff, *Paper Flowers* (play), University of Missouri Press, 1971; (with Lysander Kemp) Octavio Paz, *The Siren and the Seashell* (critical essays), University of Texas Press, 1976; Horacio Quiroga, *The Decapitated Chicken and Other Stories,* University of Texas Press, 1976; Carlos Fuentes, *Terra Nostra,* Farrar, Straus, 1976; Faustino Gonzalez Aller, *Nina Huanca,* Viking, 1977; Fuentes, *The Hydra Head,* Farrar, Straus, 1978.

Fuentes, *Burnt Water* (short stories), Farrar, Straus, 1980; Sor Juana Ines de la Cruz, *Woman of Genius: The Intellectual Autobiography of Sor Juana Ines de la Cruz,* Lime Rock Press, 1982; Fuentes, *Distant Relations,* Farrar, Straus, 1982; Pablo Neruda, *Passions and Impressions,* Farrar, Straus, 1983. Also translator of *El canto del coqui,* by Catryna Ten Eyck Seymour.

Contributor of articles to linguistics and literature journals. Member of numerous editorial boards.

WORK IN PROGRESS: Translating Octavio Paz's *Sor Juana Ines de la Cruz; or, the Pitfalls of Faith,* for Harvard University Press, Carlos Fuentes' *The Old Gringo,* for Farrar, Straus, *Selected Poems of Sor Juana Ines de la Cruz,* and Pablo Neruda's *Elemental Odes.*

*　　*　　*

PENN, John
    See HARCOURT, Palma

*　　*　　*

PENTECOST, Hugh
    See PHILIPS, Judson (Pentecost)

*　　*　　*

PERKIN, Harold (James) 1926-

PERSONAL: Born November 11, 1926, in Stoke-on-Trent, England; son of Robert James (a building worker) and Hilda

(Dillon) Perkin; married Joan Griffiths, 1948; children: Deborah, Julian. *Education:* Jesus College, Cambridge, B.A. (first class honors with distinction), 1948, M.A., 1952. *Home:* 1-0 Grove End House, Grove End Rd., London NW8 9HR, England. *Office:* Department of History, Northwestern University, Evanston, Ill. 60201.

CAREER: University of Manchester, Manchester, England, assistant lecturer in extramural education, 1950-51, lecturer in social history, 1951-65; University of Lancaster, Lancaster, England, senior lecturer, 1965-67, professor of social history, 1967-84, founding director of Centre for Social History, 1976-84; William Marsh Rice University, Houston, Tex., Mellon Distinguished Professor of the Humanities, 1984; Northwestern University, Evanston, Ill., professor of history, 1984—. Davis fellow, Princeton University, 1979-80; fellow, National Humanities Center, North Carolina, 1982-83. *Military service:* Royal Air Force, education officer, 1948-50.

MEMBER: Royal Historical Society (fellow), Social History Society (founding chairman), Association of University Teachers (past president), Economic History Society, Labour History Society, History of Education Society, Cumberland and Westmorland Antiquarian and Archaeological Society.

WRITINGS: The Origins of Modern English Society, 1780-1880, Routledge & Kegan Paul, 1969; *New Universities in the United Kingdom,* Organization for Economic Co-operation and Development, 1969; *Key Profession: The History of the Association of University Teachers,* Routledge & Kegan Paul, 1969; *The Age of the Railway,* Panther Books, 1970; *History: An Introduction for the Intending Student,* Routledge & Kegan Paul, 1970; *The Age of the Automobile,* Quartet Books, 1976; *The Structured Crowd: Essays in English Social History,* Harvester Press, 1981. Editor of "Studies in Social History," Routledge & Kegan Paul, 1957—. Contributor of more than forty articles to periodicals.

WORK IN PROGRESS: An interpretation of the development of English society since 1880, with special reference to professionalization.

SIDELIGHTS: Harold Perkin told *CA* that "as the first professor of social history in Britain," he has always encouraged research and teaching in that field as widely as possible. "My first aim," he writes, "is to understand what is happening to modern industrial and post-industrial society throughout the world." According to Stephen Koss in the *Times Literary Supplement,* "twenty-five years and eleven stimulating exercises separate the opening and closing essays in [Perkin's] impressive collection" *The Structured Crowd: Essays in English Social History.* Koss indicates that Perkin "began in 1953 by asking rather beseechingly, 'What is Social History?'; he concludes in 1977 with a comprehensive institutional and bibliographical survey which effectively answers the question." "As assembled here," states Koss, "Perkin's own writings and addresses throughout the intervening period testify to a steady process of development, both methodological and territorial." Paul Barker reports in the London *Times* that most of the essays "have been published before, in various more-or-less obscure journals. And some, it has to be said are academic in the Dryasdust sense. But when Professor Perkin moves away from the grand generalities of 'What is social history?,' and starts to have fun with the details, it's like the sun coming out at Blackpool."

In conclusion, Koss maintains that "difficult questions are Harold Perkin's stock-in-trade, and he does not shy away from the complexities they involve. Occasionally as when he states the 'false antithesis' between nineteenth-century collectivism and individualism, the difficulty of the question is somewhat exaggerated to make a pedagogical point. More typically, as when he investigates the interplay between 'Land Reform and Class Conflict in Victorian Britain,' the result is brilliant."

BIOGRAPHICAL/CRITICAL SOURCES: Times Literary Supplement, April 17, 1969, September 18, 1969, March 26, 1971, April 17, 1981; *Times* (London), March 12, 1981.

* * *

PERKINS, Edward A., Jr. 1928-

PERSONAL: Born September 23, 1928, in Portland, Ore.; son of Edward A. and Blanche (Burkland) Perkins; married Marilyn (Loyce) Apted (a secretary), January 28, 1955; children: Michael Edward, Jeffrey Craig, Robert Harold, Deana May. *Education:* University of Washington, Seattle, B.A., 1953; Stanford University, M.A., 1956; Oregon State University, Ed.D., 1963. *Home:* 135 Rollingwood Dr., Athens, Ga. 30605. *Office:* Department of Business Education, University of Georgia, Athens, Ga. 30602.

CAREER: High school teacher in Seattle, Wash., 1953-56, and in Burlingame, Calif., 1956-58; Oregon State University, Corvallis, instructor, 1958-61; Washington State University, Pullman, assistant professor, 1961-64, associate professor, 1964-69, professor of office administration and business education, 1969-81, director, Office Occupations Research and Development Project, 1965-68, chairman of department of office administration, 1972-78, acting chairman of department of management and administrative systems, 1978-80; University of Georgia, Athens, head of department of business education, 1981—. Visiting summer professor, Utah State University, 1962, 1965. *Military service:* U.S. Air Force, 1946-49; became sergeant. U.S. Air Force Reserve, 1953—; currently captain.

MEMBER: American Business Communications Association, Academy of Management, National Business Education Association, Western Business Education Association (executive board; historian, 1966-67), Washington State Business Education Association (president, 1966), Eastern Washington Business Education Association (president, 1965-66), Southern Business Education Association, Delta Pi Epsilon, Phi Delta Kappa, Kappa Delta Pi.

WRITINGS: (With C. E. Reigel) *Executive Typewriting,* Gregg, 1966, 2nd edition, 1980; (with Reigel and T. Lockwood) *Practice for Professional Typing,* Gregg, 1968; *Vocational Business Education,* Washington State Coordinating Council for Occupational Education, 1974.

Also author of *Typing for the Air Force* and "Mimeograph Textbook Curriculum" series, both 1971, and "Fluid Instruction" series and *Reprographics in Business Education,* both 1972. Contributor to business education journals.

AVOCATIONAL INTERESTS: Sports, youth development programs.

* * *

PERRY, Roger 1933-

PERSONAL: Born August 4, 1933, in Enfield, England; son of Gerald Alfred Amos and Frances Mary (Everett) Perry; married Shirley Pettifer, December 18, 1974. *Education:* Christ's

College, Cambridge, B.A., 1957, M.A., 1961. *Home:* The Chestnuts, Orford, Suffolk IP12 2NT, England.

CAREER: British Broadcasting Corp., Bristol, England, field research assistant in natural history unit, 1958-62; UNESCO, Department for the Advancement of Science, Charles Darwin Research Station, Galapagos Islands, Ecuador, director, 1964-70; British Ministry of Overseas Development, Christmas Island, Gilbert Islands, wildlife adviser, 1977-79; writer. Conducted field studies in the northern Andes, 1957-58, 1971, 1972, the Amazon, 1962-63, and Patagonia, 1973, 1974, 1975. *Military service:* British Army, Airborne Division, 1952-54. *Member:* Royal Geographical Society (fellow), Ecuadorian Institute of Natural Sciences (honorary member).

*WRITINGS—*All for young people: *The Galapagos Islands,* Dodd, 1972; *Patagonia: Windswept Land of the South,* Dodd, 1974; *Wonders of Llamas,* Dodd, 1977; *Wonders of Water Lilies,* Dodd, 1982; (editor) *Key Environment: Galapagos,* Pergamon, 1984. Contributor to magazines, including *Country Life, Illustrated London News, Wildlife,* and *Pacific Discovery.*

AVOCATIONAL INTERESTS: Mountain travel.

* * *

PESSEN, Edward 1920-

PERSONAL: Born December 31, 1920, in New York, N.Y.; son of Abraham and Anna (Flashberg) Pessen; married Adele Barlin, November 25, 1940; children: Beth (Mrs. Michael Shub), Abigail (Mrs. Richard Wolf), Dinah (Mrs. Abraham Attman), Jonathan, Andrew. *Education:* Columbia University, B.A., 1947, M.A., 1948, Ph.D., 1954. *Home:* 853 East 18th St., Brooklyn, N.Y. 11230. *Office:* Department of History, Bernard M. Baruch College of the City University of New York, 17 Lexington Ave., New York, N.Y. 10010; and Graduate Center of the City University of New York, 33 West 42nd St., New York, N.Y. 10036.

CAREER: College of the City of New York (now City College of the City University of New York), New York City, lecturer in history, 1948-54; Fisk University, Nashville, Tenn., associate professor of history, 1954-56; Staten Island Community College (now Staten Island Community College of the City University of New York), Staten Island, N.Y., professor of history and head of department of social and humanistic studies, 1956-70; Graduate Center of the City University of New York, New York City, professor, 1968-72, distinguished university professor of history, 1972—; Bernard M. Baruch College of the City University of New York, New York City, professor, 1970-72, distinguished university professor of history, 1972—. *Military service:* U.S. Army, Infantry, 1944-45; received Purple Heart and Bronze Star. *Member:* American Historical Association, Organization of American Historians, Society for Historians of the Early American Republic (president-elect, 1984-85), Southern Historical Association.

AWARDS, HONORS: First prize, State University of New York competition for essays on the improvement of teaching, 1959; first prize, Daughters of the Founders and Patriots of America essay competition, 1966; Pulitzer Prize nomination, 1968, for *Most Uncommon Jacksonians;* National Book Award nomination, 1974, for *Riches, Class, and Power before the Civil War;* Guggenheim fellow, 1977-78; Rockefeller fellow, 1978; Kerr Prize, New York State Historical Association, 1978.

WRITINGS: Most Uncommon Jacksonians: The Radical Leaders of the Early Labor Movement, State University of New

York Press, 1967; *Jacksonian America: Society, Personality, and Politics,* Dorsey, 1969, revised edition, 1978; (editor and contributor) *New Perspectives on Jacksonian Parties and Politics,* Allyn & Bacon, 1969; *Riches, Class, and Power before the Civil War,* Heath, 1973; (editor and contributor) *Three Centuries of Social Mobility in America,* Heath, 1974; (editor) *Jacksonian Panorama,* Bobbs-Merrill, 1976; (editor and contributor) *The Many-Faceted Jacksonian Era,* Greenwood Press, 1977; *The Log Cabin Myth: The Social Backgrounds of the Presidents,* Yale University Press, 1984.

Contributor: James Bugg, Jr., editor, *Jacksonian Democracy: Myth or Reality?,* Holt, 1964; J. Godechot, editor, *La Presse Ouvrier, 1819-1850,* Centre National de la Recherche Scientifique (Paris), 1966; Charles Rehmus and Doris McLaughlin, editors, *Labor and American Politics,* University of Michigan Press, 1966; Howard Quint, Dean Albertson, and Milton Cantor, editors, *Main Problems in American History,* Dorsey, 1968, revised edition, 1978.

Frank Otto Gatell, editor, *Essays in Jacksonian America,* Holt, 1970; J. R. Johnson, J. A. Hall, and C. D. Farquhar, editors, *Selected Readings in American History,* San Jacinto College Press, 1970; Herbert J. Bass, editor, *The State of American History,* Quadrangle, 1970; Michael McGiffert, editor, *American Social Thought before the Civil War,* Addison-Wesley, 1972; Armin Rappaport and Richard Traina, editors, *Source Problems in American History,* Macmillan, 1972; Ari Hoogenboom and Olive Hoogenboom, editors, *An Interdisciplinary Approach to American History,* Prentice-Hall, 1973; Harry Sievers, editor, *Six Presidents from the Empire State,* Sleepy Hollow Restorations, 1974; John Garraty and J. Sternstein, editors, *Encyclopaedia of American Biography,* Harper, 1974; Herbert G. Gutman, editor, *Readings in American Social History,* Prentice-Hall, 1974; J. H. Cary and J. Weinberg, editors, *The Social Fabric: American Life from 1607 to the Civil War,* Little, Brown, 1975; R. L. Garner and P. E. Stebbins, editors, *Individualism and Community: A Thematic Approach to the History of the United States,* Pennsylvania State University Press, 1975.

A. F. Davis and H. D. Woodman, editors, *Conflict and Consensus in Early American History,* Heath, 1976; J. S. Ezell and others, editors, *Readings in American History,* Houghton, 1976; P. Stewart and J. L. Bugg, editors, *Jacksonian Democracy,* Dryden, 1976; Philip C. Dolce and George H. Shaw, editors, *Power and the Presidency,* Scribner, 1976; Richard B. Morris, editor, *Bicentennial History of the American Worker,* U.S. Department of Labor, 1976; C. E. Starnes and J. H. Turner, editors, *Inequality: Privilege and Poverty in America,* Goodyear Publishing, 1976; R. E. Beringer, editor, *Historical Analysis: Contemporary Approaches to Clio's Craft,* Wiley, 1978; I. Yellowitz, editor, *Essays in the History of New York City,* Kennikat, 1978; A. Eisenstadt, A. Hoogenboom, and H. L. Trefousse, editors, *Before Watergate: Problems of Corruption in American Society,* Brooklyn College Press/Columbia University Press, 1978.

W. D. Rubinstein, editor, *Wealth and the Wealthy in the Modern World,* Helm, 1980; J. Frese and J. Judd, editors, *An Emerging Independent Economy,* Sleepy Hollow Press, 1980; Gerald N. Grob and George Billias, editors, *Interpretations of American History,* Free Press, 1982; Henry Graff, editor, *The Presidents: A Reference History,* Scribner, 1984.

Contributor to *Encyclopaedia Britannica* and *Encyclopedia of American History;* also contributor to periodicals, including *Political Science Quarterly, New York History, Pennsylvania History, The Nation, South Atlantic Quarterly,* and *New York Times.*

WORK IN PROGRESS: American Society in the Early Nineteenth Century, for Heath; *Social Mobility in American History,* for Yale University Press; *America's Cold War Foreign Policy and Its Disastrous Consequences* and *The Golden Age of American Popular Songs, 1920-1945,* both for University of Illinois Press.

SIDELIGHTS: Edward Pessen writes: "As a child I dreamed of becoming a history professor and the GI Bill—my reward for being shot at by the Germans in World War II—gave me the opportunity to make my dream come true. When I became a historian, I had no idea that I could write books that anyone might be interested in. Involved as teacher, department chairman, co-founder of a new college, father, jazz singer, and golfer, I did not publish my first book until I was 46.

"To my delight and amazement, people thought well of my first book, *Most Uncommon Jacksonians: The Radical Leaders of the Early Labor Movement.* In writing my next book, *Jacksonian America: Society, Personality, and Politics,* an iconoclastic synthesis of the period 1825-1850, I discovered that I loved to write and that I was brimming over with things to say. Discovering that some of the most pervasive and influential ideas about American history are based on very slim evidence, I get special pleasure from performing thorough and original research that enables me to puncture or demolish myths. *Riches, Class, and Power before the Civil War* challenges Alexis de Tocqueville's egalitarian portrait of pre-Civil War America, and *The Log Cabin Myth* [: *The Social Background of the Presidents*] refutes the notion that most of the presidents were born to humble or modest circumstances.

"Perhaps because I hope to break with my 'typecasting' as a Jacksonian era specialist, the two books I am now working on concern the twentieth century. The first, a scathing critique of our post-World War II foreign policy, was motivated by my dismay at the appalling consequences of this policy, its ideological extremism, its departure from our pragmatic tradition, and the absence of searching criticism it has received. The second, which began as a study of the social origins of the great popular songwriters (to test the accuracy of the 'myth' that most of them were born on the Lower East side of New York City to Russian Jewish immigrant parents), has evolved into a labor of love on the songs I have sung for more than fifty years, an essay in which I hope to do justice to the charming poetry in the best of Larry Hart, Ira Gershwin, Cole Porter, Irving Berlin, Dorothy Fields, Gus Kahn, Oscar Hammerstein II, and the several dozen other lyricists and composers who created the great songs of the 1920s and 1930s.

"In recent years I have come to regard history as more art than science. Perhaps on reflection the two categories are not as irreconcilable as we sometimes assume they are. Good art requires vast knowledge. Good science best reveals itself in luminous prose and is perhaps no less subjective than is art. In any case, my ideal is to write a history that combines the qualities of the two. My tactics are to try to write good sentences—clear, varied, carriers of important and perhaps interesting intellectual freight. My strategy is to put these sentences at the disposal of what I trust are searching questions about the past. My professional ideology is to follow the evidence along the perverse paths it often takes and to question the past not only about what happened but also about what did not happen and why."

BIOGRAPHICAL/CRITICAL SOURCES: New York Times, June 20, 1968.

*   *   *

PHILIPS, Judson (Pentecost) 1903-
(Philip Owen, Hugh Pentecost)

PERSONAL: Born in 1903, in Northfield, Mass.; son of Arthur (an opera singer) and Frederikco (an actress; maiden name, Pentecost) Philips; married Norma Burton (an actress), 1951; children: David, Caroline, John, Daniel. *Education:* Columbia University, B.A., 1925. *Home:* Emmons Lane, Canaan, Conn. 06018. *Agent:* Brandt & Brandt, 101 Park Ave., New York, N.Y. 10017. *Office:* 1501 Broadway, New York, N.Y. 10036.

CAREER: Writer. *New York Tribune,* New York, N.Y., high school sports reporter, beginning 1926; *Harlem Valley Times,* Amenia, N.Y., co-owner and editor, 1949-56; *Lakeville Journal,* Lakeville, Conn., political columnist and book reviewer, beginning 1951; Sharon Playhouse, Sharon, Conn., founder and director, 1951-72; WTOR-Radio, Torrington, Conn., talk-show host, 1970-76.

MEMBER: Mystery Writers of America (founding member and past president).

AWARDS, HONORS: First prize in Dodd, Mead's mystery competition, 1939, for *Cancelled in Red;* Mystery Writers of America Grand Master Award, 1973.

WRITINGS—Published by Dodd, except as indicated: (With Robert W. Wood, Jr.) *Hold 'Em Girls! The Intelligent Woman's Guide to Men and Football,* Putnam, 1936; (with Thomas M. Johnson) *Red War,* Doubleday, 1936; *The Death Syndicate,* I. Washburn (New York), 1938; *Death Delivers a Postcard,* I. Washburn, 1939; *Murder in Marble; a Detective Story,* 1940; *Odds on the Hot Seat,* 1941; *The Fourteenth Trump,* 1942; *Killer on the Catwalk,* 1959.

Whisper Town, 1960; *Murder Clear, Track Fast,* 1961; *A Dead Ending,* 1962; *The Dead Can't Love,* 1963; *The Laughter Trap,* 1964; *The Black Glass City: A Peter Styles Mystery,* 1965; *The Twisted People: A Peter Styles Mystery,* 1965; *The Wings of Madness: A Peter Styles Mystery Novel,* 1966; *Thursday's Folly: A Peter Styles Mystery Novel,* 1967; *Hot Summer Killing: A Peter Styles Mystery Novel,* 1968.

Nightmare at Dawn: A Peter Styles Mystery Novel, 1970; *Escape a Killer,* 1971; *The Vanishing Senator,* 1972; *The Larkspur Conspiracy,* 1973; *The Power Killers,* 1974; *Walk a Crooked Mile,* 1975; *Five Roads to Death,* 1977; *A Murder Arranged: A Peter Styles Murder Mystery,* 1978; *Why Murder?: A Peter Styles Murder Mystery,* 1979.

Death Is a Dirty Trick, 1980; *Target for Tragedy: A Peter Styles Mystery Novel,* 1982.

Under pseudonym Philip Owen: *Mystery at a Country Inn,* Berkshire Traveller Press, 1979.

Under pseudonym Hugh Pentecost: *Cancelled in Red,* 1939; *The 24th Horse,* 1940; *I'll Sing at Your Funeral,* 1942; *The Brass Chills,* 1943; *Cat and Mouse,* Royce (New York), 1945; *The Dead Man's Tale,* Royce, 1945; *Secret Corridors* (short stories), Century House, 1945; *Death Wears a Copper Necktie and Other Stories* (short stories), Edwards (London), 1946; *Memory of Murder: Four Novelettes,* Ziff-Davis, 1947; *Where the Snow Was Red,* 1949; *Shadow of Madness,* 1950; *Chinese Nightmare,* Dell, 1951; *Lieutenant Pascal's Tastes in Homi-cides,* 1954; *The Assassins,* 1955; *The Obituary Club,* 1958; *The Lonely Target,* 1959.

The Kingdom of Death, 1960; *Choice of Violence,* 1961; *The Deadly Friend,* 1961; *The Cannibal Who Overate,* 1962; (editor) *Cream of the Crime: The 15th Mystery Writers of America Anthology,* Holt, 1962; *The Tarnished Angel,* 1963; *The Shape of Fear,* T. V. Boardman, 1963, Dodd, 1964; *Only the Rich Die Young,* 1964; *Sniper,* 1965; *Hide Her From Every Eye: A John Jericho Mystery Novel,* 1966; *The Creeping Hours: A John Jericho Mystery Novel,* 1966; *The Evil That Men Do,* 1966; *The Golden Trap,* 1967; *Dead Woman of the Year: A John Jericho Mystery Novel,* 1967; *The Gilded Nightmare: A Pierre Chambrun Mystery Novel,* 1968; *Girl Watcher's Funeral: A Pierre Chambrun Mystery Novel,* 1969; *The Girl With Six Fingers: A John Jericho Mystery Novel,* 1969.

Around Dark Corners: A Collection of Mystery Stories, 1970; *A Plague of Violence,* 1970; *The Deadly Joke,* 1971; *Don't Drop Dead Tomorrow,* 1971; *Birthday, Deathday,* 1972; (contributor with Robert Hayden and Lawson Carter) *How I Write,* Harcourt, 1972; *The Champagne Killer,* 1972; *Walking Dead Man,* 1973; *The Beautiful Dead,* 1973; *Bargain With Death,* 1974; *The Judas Freak,* 1974; *Time of Terror,* 1975; *Honeymoon with Death,* 1975; *Backlash,* 1976; *Die after Dark,* 1976; *Five Roads to Death,* 1977; *The Day the Children Vanished,* Hale (London), 1977; *The Steel Palace,* 1977; *Murder as Usual,* 1977; *The Fourteen Dilemma,* 1977; *Deadly Trap,* 1978; *Death After Breakfast,* 1978; *Random Killer,* 1979; *The Homicidal Horse,* 1979.

Beware Young Lovers, 1980; *Death Mask,* 1980; *Murder in Luxury,* 1981; *Sow Death, Reap Death: A Julian Quist Mystery Novel,* 1981; *Murder as the Curtain Rises,* 1981; *Past, Present, and Murder: A Julian Quist Mystery Novel,* 1982; *With Intent to Kill: A Pierre Chambrun Mystery Novel,* 1982; *The Copycat Killers,* 1983; *Murder in High Places: A Pierre Chambrun Mystery Novel,* 1983; *Murder out of Wedlock,* 1983; *Remember to Kill Me,* 1984; *The Price of Silence,* 1984.

Plays: "Lonely Boys," first produced in Sharon, Conn. at Sharon Playhouse, 1954; "The Lame Duck Party," first produced at Sharon Playhouse, 1977.

Author of filmscripts, including "General Crack," produced by Warner Bros., 1930. Also author of television scripts, including "Studio One," "The Ray Milland Show," "The U.S. Steel Hour," "Hallmark Hall of Fame," and "Robert Montgomery Presents"; contributor of scripts to the television series, "The Web." Author of radio scripts in the 1940s, including "Suspense," "Father Brown," and "The Whisper Men." Contributor of stories to periodicals, including *Saturday Evening Post, Liberty, Collier's, American, Ellery Queen's Mystery Magazine,* and *Cosmopolitan.*

SIDELIGHTS: Judson Philips, better known to mystery fans as Hugh Pentecost, is one of America's most prolific authors of detective fiction. In his fifty-year career he has produced more than a hundred novels and countless short stories, making him an acknowledged "old pro" of whodunit fiction. As Newgate Callendar reports in the *New York Times Book Review,* Philips's "name is a guarantee of smooth writing, an ingenious story-line, and convincing characterization." Seargeant Cuff adds in *Saturday Review* that the author's work is marked by "complications of the sort only a top pro could handle with clarity and at a brisk pace."

Among Philips's most popular works are the series featuring characters Peter Styles, John Jericho, Pierre Chambrun, and

Julian Quist. Styles, the one investigator Philips writes of under his own name, is a one-legged magazine columnist presented as a crusader for justice and the American way of life. The journalist-turned-detective has battled a small-town fascistic army, confronted a gang of young psychopaths, and fought a terrorist group operating amid an atmosphere of racial tension. The Jericho novels, like the Styles books, "peer over and again at the prejudices and violence of our society" notes a *New York Times Book Review* critic. Jericho is a talented artist, and this position allows the author to sketch views of the seamier side of the artistic community and its wealthy supporters. Chambrun, the managing director of Manhattan's Hotel Beaumont, may be Philips's best-known investigator. Although confined to the posh hostelry, Chambrun sees an assortment of characters—including numerous celebrities—come and go, bringing with them the complications of crime that allow him to do his sleuthing. Callendar calls Julian Quist "a wish-fulfillment of our times . . . tall, lean, handsome." Head of a public relations firm, the decisive Quist usually moves through the world of entertainers or the super rich. Often accompanied by an assortment of beautiful women, "Quist may be all slick invention, but he's fun to have around," concludes Haskel Frankel in *Saturday Review*.

Critics generally cite Philips's fast pacing, straightforward yet forceful language, and his feel for timely subjects as reasons for his popularity. "He is never at a loss for a new twist of plot or character," notes a writer for *West Coast Review of Books*. "One can depend on all of his novels to have the power to hold the attention of the reader to the very last page of the book." While, occasionally, reviewers fault the author for producing too many mysteries with too much in common, most appreciate what a *Los Angeles Times Book Review* critic calls "vintage Pentecost—tough, taut, immaculately plotted." Concludes Cuff: "Judson Philips . . . is as pro as they come."

CA INTERVIEW

CA interviewed Judson Philips (Hugh Pentecost) by telephone October 24, 1983, at his home in Canaan, Connecticut.

CA: Your first novel was published in 1935, and you've done more than a hundred since, in addition to short stories, plays, movies, and radio and television scripts. There has to be more of an explanation for this output than hard work, though surely that's made it possible. Have you enjoyed it enormously?

PHILIPS: Well, I've never done anything else. I sold my first short story when I was a junior in college in 1923; that's sixty years ago. I set out in life wanting to be an actor. My mother was an actress; my father was an opera singer. I got a job when I was eighteen years old in a silent movie with a star named Elaine Hammerstein, who I suppose was the grandniece of Oscar Hammerstein. There weren't very many parts for eighteen-year-old kids, and while this was a good one and it all went very well, I never could get any jobs again. I finally wrote a script that had a part for an eighteen-year-old boy; I sold the script but I didn't get the part! So I became a writer.

CA: You've said that you work four to five hours a day, before lunch—and no more unless you're not happy with what you've done on a particular day. How did you discipline yourself to work so steadily?

PHILIPS: I have to eat, for one thing. And I'll tell you, I have been a sports nut ever since I was a small boy, and until a few years ago, I liked to play golf. If I were going to indulge myself in outdoor pleasures and activities, I had to have a regular working schedule. Also, experience told me that I was at my best, I had more energy, getting started early and working in the morning. I must say that I'm not a great rewriter. If something goes real haywire and I've gotten off-line in the story, I don't sit down and redo scenes very often. I edit, of course, but usually what comes first is the best.

CA: Mysteries have intricate plots; they're like puzzles with many pieces that have to fit together precisely. How much of a plot do you know before you start writing?

PHILIPS: I would say eighty percent. Sometimes the characters in a story will take your arm and twist you in another direction finally. One of the things that happened to me along the way is that I used to do a lot of novelettes for *American*. It was a monthly magazine published by Crowell-Collier, which also did *Collier's*. At one stage of my life those two magazines were the basis of my income, and they both folded within six months of each other. (I don't think that had anything to do with me; I like to think not.)

Anyway, they would assign me to special backgrounds of one kind or another, varying all the way from a chemical factory in New Jersey to the harbor pilots in New York. I would go out with absolutely no idea where a story might lie in a particular field. This taught me something, and I got good at it. People would write in and say, "That's the Boundbrook factory in New Jersey," because I was so accurate in my facts. So special backgrounds became a specialty of mine and stories came out of those backgrounds. In effect, I would be looking for something that couldn't happen anywhere else. You only have a certain number of possibilities if you're doing a puzzle story, and the reader is bound to guess right once in a while. You try to be as honest as you can and not come up with the butler, you know. You're playing a two-handed game: You're trying to be on the level and you're trying to be deceitful.

CA: Do you still enjoy going out and finding out about a new field altogether?

PHILIPS: Physically now it's not as much fun as it used to be. I am eighty years old now and I like to be anchored where I am right this minute, right in front of my typewriter. Travel isn't that much fun anymore; I'm more comfortable at home. So a lot of the research that I do now may come out of special reading of some kind. But I did enjoy the research. Now I am embarked on a story with a kind of rural background. Part of it takes place at a county fair, and I did this fall go up and spend some time in the neighboring town of Great Barrington, Massachusetts, where they have a fair. That gave me some information I didn't have before I went. But I'm not going to fly to Tibet!

CA: Do mysteries become more or less popular with social and economic changes?

PHILIPS: I think mysteries are a little bit less popular now than they used to be, but the reason is the price—I can remember when a hardcover book sold for two dollars. Now it sells for ten. The hardcover book is selling less and less in the bookstore and more exclusively to libraries. On the other hand, foreign sales, while they don't amount to too much in money, are very popular: Italy, Spain, and England and Germany particularly. I get published in all kinds of places, and the translations sell in considerable quantity. They're not a get-rich-quick thing for the writer but, nonetheless, you don't sneeze them off because there are a lot of them.

CA: Do you get a lot of mail from other countries as well as here?

PHILIPS: I wouldn't say I get a lot. Mail is peculiar. As time has gone by (I don't know whether this is because I now look like the Lincoln Memorial or what), I get more letters than I used to. I don't think I'm any better, you understand, but I seem to get 'em. But I've also noticed in the last couple of years or so that an awful lot of people seem to be making collections of mysteries—I guess on the assumption that they're going to disappear; I don't know.

CA: Do you have a favorite character among the ones you've created who've gone on through a series of novels?

PHILIPS: I suppose the most popular one from the public's point of view has been the hotel manager Pierre Chambrun. He's the least popular with me—I mean I enjoy working with him less than with some others—because he's limited to the hotel. I can't get him out on the streets, you know. At one time I was very fond of a character named Jericho who was an artist, a painter, traveled all over the world, crusaded against violence. But he didn't do well in books and I keep him alive now by writing an occasional short story about him for *Ellery Queen's Mystery Magazine.* Then, early on, there was a Dr. John Smith. He was a psychiatrist (I was being analyzed at the time). I think the striking thing about him was that he was one of the few people who could register at a hotel with the name John Smith and they would know it was really his name! A very neutral little gray man. But this was kind of fun because I was dealing more with psychological clues rather than material clues. And I was very hot on it at the time that I did it because I was lying on my back, once a day, five days a week. Anyway, it was one way to get even with my analyst.

CA: Let's talk a bit about some of the writing you've done besides the novels.

PHILIPS: I had a piece of advice when I first got into the field from another writer, George Harmon Coxe, who had a character that was very popular for years called Flashgun Casey, a newspaper photographer. I was talking with George on the phone the other day, and when he said goodbye, he said, "Goodbye, kid." I'm eighty; he's eighty-two! Very early on in the game George told me, "You should work in all the mediums you get a chance to work in because things are going to change over the years." And he was so right. I started out in the pulps and went on to the so-called slicks. I worked in radio; radio disappeared. I work in television; I did some film work. In other words, I got involved with most of the mediums that were available for moneymaking. Finally, so many people got in the act in some of these public mediums like films and television, there were so many fingers in the pie, that I got sick of it.

CA: How do you think that other writing affected your fiction?

PHILIPS: My stuff is fairly heavily larded with dialogue. It may be that writing for radio and later for television and films helped to produce a kind of style which was action in words. But I hadn't thought of it in particular; each one has its own special quality. When I'm writing an ordinary fiction piece, I tell myself that what I'm doing is describing a movie, and I try to tell it that way. I'm not an internal writer; I don't go very deeply into the insides of people except as they reveal them themselves.

I've done some books that are first-person stories, but usually the first-person storyteller is not the hero; he's somebody who's observing the hero. If you're stuck with an "I" character you can't go anywhere that he doesn't go. You're limited by his personal action. I learned that I would entrap myself if I did this, so when I use the first-person storyteller, he is not the key figure. For example, in the hotel stories it's the public-relations man there who describes what goes on, but it's Chambrun, the manager, who is really the detective. Well, the master, Conan Doyle, did this.

CA: And Sherlock Holmes was an early hero of yours, you've said. Do you read a lot of mysteries?

PHILIPS: I read almost no mysteries for the simple reason that it's so easy to copy. Now, I'd like to imitate Hemingway, or Dashiell Hammett, perhaps, but I'd like to stop there; I don't want to imitate everybody else, good as they may be. And I'm an instinctive mimic.

CA: You went to Hollywood in 1929 and, as you've said, grew very disillusioned with it because of all the fingers in the pie. Who were some of the people you worked with?

PHILIPS: One of the people that I worked with primarily, and went out there to do a film for, was John Barrymore. It was a film called "General Crack." I'm not sure that it wasn't his first talkie. And in that cast was Lowell Sherman, who was a famous Broadway actor. Barrymore and Lowell Sherman didn't get along very well. Sherman was of course playing the villain and Barrymore was playing the hero. It was a costume piece and Sherman played the king, which meant wearing a lot of ermine furs and such stuff, and Barrymore would keep him waiting on the set, under the lights, until he was wringing wet with sweat.

There was a scene in which Barrymore was supposed to leap through a window with drawn sword, and as usual he kept Sherman waiting and waiting under the lights, sweating. Then he leaped through the window, brandishing his sword, stopped dead in his tracks and said, "Somebody's left a nail in that window; it's torn my tights." So they had to stop while the wardrobe mistress fixed his tights. He repeated this and it happened again that his tights were torn. What we didn't know at this point was that there was a little boy in the office who wanted to go to the horse races. Barrymore had said, "Just stick around, I'll get to take you." So, he jumps through the window the third time and the third time he announced that his tights were split, took them off in front of everybody, tore them into a thousand pieces, and headed for the race track.

My father was an opera singer and became a voice teacher. In the early days that I recall, a great many stage actors came to him for voice problems. There was of course no amplification in those days; you had to be heard at the top of the second balcony. A lot of good actors came to my father: Barrymore was one of them, Roland Young, Ozgood Perkins, Frank Morgan, a whole lot of people of that period. I got to know them all personally, and Barrymore got me the job to go out to Hollywood because he was sure there was nobody literate enough there to write dialogue for him, so I went out and wrote the dialogue for him in "General Crack."

CA: You had done some sports reporting in high school for the New York Tribune, *and in 1949 you bought an interest in the weekly* Harlem Valley Times. *Did you have any idea of becoming more a newspaperman than a novelist at that time?*

PHILIPS: Oh, no. The *Harlem Valley Times* was and is a little weekly newspaper in a small town; it covers two or three towns in the area. I guess every writer at some point wants to own a newspaper. My grandfather bought a newspaper once in Darien, Connecticut, when I was about ten or twelve years old, so maybe it was a tradition in the family. My real second interest in life has always been theater and performing arts. And I did, in 1951, found the Sharon [Connecticut] Playhouse, an Equity summer theater that is still going. When I bought that, I sold out my interest in the *Harlem Valley Times*. I had bought the *Harlem Valley Times* with a friend and he stayed on in the business. But when I was trying to put on a show every week during the summer, it just got to be too much.

CA: You wrote some plays specifically for the Sharon Playhouse, didn't you?

PHILIPS: I did two plays for them. Neither of them did very well anywhere else. The first play had been a television special on CBS. What had originally been a short story became a television special and then I made a play out of it, *Lonely Boy* [produced, 1954]. It had probably gotten a little worked over, you know. Then I did *The Lame Duck Party* [produced, 1977].

CA: You did many radio and television plays.

PHILIPS: Yes. One year I did eighteen scripts for a show called "The Web," which was a Goodson-Todman production. One of the absurdities about that was that if you got clearance, the advertiser didn't have to approve the script; the producer could just say go. I got clearance, so when they were having trouble with scripts Frank Heller, the producer, would just say to me, "We're going to need one this week." And I would do it and nobody would have to look at it—until we were being sponsored by Kent cigarettes and we got a directive from the front office saying that no villains could smoke long cigarettes. Can you believe it?

The process was that the cast would read the script and then they would begin rehearsing. In this particular script, a murder had taken place on a train. The conductor is standing there and the villain is dying on the floor. Somebody says, "We better get him a doctor," and the lady detective says, "Let him die. It'll save the state a lot of money." That was the last line in the film. The advertising executive who was there for the reading said he felt that was a little strong. So Frank said, "Go ahead. Why don't we go through it again; you'll have another line for us, Jud, won't you?" I said, "Sure." So we got there finally and he said, "What is the other line?" I said, "Well, give the son of a bitch a short cigarette!" I lost my clearance.

CA: You've pretty much avoided the kind of glamorous image that we impose on our writers in this country. Has it been hard to do, especially in view of your long career?

PHILIPS: No, I don't think so. I think probably if I thought this was the way to sell books in any noticeable quantity, I might have tried it. But I'm not very tall, and when I was a young man, I was kind of overweight. I was married quite a few times. I was married first for two years and then for four years and then for six years and then for thirteen years and now for thirty-two years, and it reminds me of the Italian tenor singing in Milan. He sings the aria from "Pagliacci," and when it's all over they give him huge applause: "Encore, encore!" He sings it over again, and more applause and the "Encore, encore!" Then he comes down to the footlights and says, "I'm sorry, I have to go on with the opera," and some guy up in the balcony shouts down at him, "You'll sing it until you get it right!" I guess that's what I did with my love life; I finally got it right.

CA: Do you hear from many beginning writers trying to get published?

PHILIPS: Not a great many. I was one of the founders of the Mystery Writers of America, and when I was its third president (as Hugh Pentecost) and was so active with them, I used to get a lot of inquiries. Now, not so much; but I wouldn't know what to tell anybody now anyway. The whole picture's changed. You have to realize that there was a time—I'm talking now about the 1940s and 1950s—when we had the *Saturday Evening Post* and *Collier's* and *Liberty,* and you could see eight or ten short stories a week in each one, plus serials. That was the short-story market. Both the *Post* and *Collier's* published serials and paid well. *American,* which was a monthly, published a mystery novelette once a month. There were all kinds of markets. People in those days were constantly asking how you could break into the magazines because that's where the money was. Well, there really aren't any magazines anymore except for women's and how-to's. There's so little fiction. The only short stories I do anymore I do out of affection and regard for Fred Dannay, who was half of Ellery Queen, though he has now died. It was the only market for the mystery that really was consistent, so I still do about three or four a year for them.

CA: Off and on there's been talk of an autobiographical novel that you were working on. Is it still in the works? Is an actual autobiography a possibility?

PHILIPS: At one time I was talking about doing a book—in this last marriage, when I got it right. I have a son from that marriage who is now twenty-six years old and I just had a visit from a son from my first marriage who is fifty-eight years old. That's the absurdity of my life. I talked about writing a book which would be autobiographical because I have children and grandchildren scattered all over the place. But I never really did that. I did a novel; I finished it about three years ago, but it never quite happened. I should do something about it. Carl Brandt, my agent, was very pleased with the first two-thirds of it but then he thought it didn't work after that. I knew it wasn't for Dodd Mead, my mystery publishers, before they even saw it. It's sitting in the drawer that I'm facing now with guilt. No, it was not autobiographical—it was not a story about Judson Philips or Hugh Pentecost—but it was full of autobiography, if you know what I mean.

CA: Is there anything you haven't done that you'd like to try?

PHILIPS: Well, I'd like to play centerfield for the Yankees. I've got a black Labrador dog here that can catch a fly ball that I throw over the top of a tree. No, I've never really wanted to make a living any other way, except in the very beginning I did want to be an actor. Obviously this stuck with me because I went on to become a theatrical impresario and I did some acting. I once had a production here of "Death of a Salesman." The actor who was to play Willie Loman fell in the bathtub the night before we went into rehearsal, so I took over and played the part. There was a writer here named Clyde Brion

Davis, a novelist who had won a Pulitzer Prize, and he wrote me a letter that went something like this: "I have always admired you as a top writer of suspense fiction; I have thought you had great courage to keep the Sharon Playhouse going, but when I heard that you were going to play Willie Loman in *Death of a Salesman,* I went to the theater with some trepidation." He said, "I went, I saw, you conquered, and I have one question for you: 'How are you on the pipe organ?'" Acting was really what I wanted to do, but I would never have made it as successfully as I made it being a writer. I'm better offstage.

BIOGRAPHICAL/CRITICAL SOURCES: Times Literary Supplement, December 2, 1965, February 23, 1967, January 25, 1968, April 24, 1969, June 11, 1970, November 6, 1970, February 26, 1971, May 26, 1972, August 17, 1973, September 6, 1974, July 9, 1976; *New York Times Book Review,* August 6, 1967, February 23, 1969, March 30, 1969, June 8, 1969, September 21, 1969, April 5, 1970, January 24, 1971, June 20, 1971, October 3, 1971, January 16, 1972, May 28, 1972, August 20, 1972, November 5, 1972, June 10, 1973, June 17, 1973, November 18, 1973, December 9, 1973, March 10, 1974, June 16, 1974, October 20, 1974, January 19, 1975, August 3, 1975, June 12, 1977, January 22, 1978, July 2, 1978; *Books and Bookmen,* February, 1968, September, 1973; *Punch,* March 5, 1969, September 3, 1979; *Observer,* August 24, 1969, October 18, 1970, January 24, 1971, May 14, 1972, July 1, 1973, July 14, 1974, April 11, 1976, March 18, 1979.

Saturday Review, March 28, 1970, August 1, 1970, December 26, 1970, September 25, 1971, December 25, 1971, September 9, 1972, November 25, 1972; *New Yorker,* January 8, 1972, September 20, 1976; *Book World,* December 17, 1972, June 17, 1973; *Hartford Courant,* June 30, 1974; *Authors in the News,* Volume I, Gale, 1976; *New York Times,* May 4, 1978; *Chicago Tribune Book World,* March 28, 1982, August 15, 1982, December 19, 1982, May 22, 1983, January 29, 1984.†

—*Interview by Jean W. Ross*

*   *   *

PHILLIPS, Jill (Meta) 1952-

PERSONAL: Born October 22, 1952, in Detroit, Mich.; daughter of Leyson Kirk (a writer and editor) and Leona A. (a writer and researcher; maiden name, Rasmussen) Phillips. *Education:* Attended high school in Covina, Calif. *Politics:* Conservative Republican ("avidly Anti-Communist"). *Religion:* "Existentialist Christian." *Home:* 851 North Garsden Ave., Covina, Calif. 91724. *Office:* P.O. Box 4213, Covina, Calif. 91723; or P.O. Box 260, Glendora, Calif. 91740.

CAREER: Book Builders, Charter Oak, Calif., ghost writer, literary critic, and counselor, 1968-74; writer, 1974—.

MEMBER: Young Americans for Freedom.

WRITINGS—Published by Gordon Press, except as indicated: (Editor with mother, Leona Rasmussen Phillips, and contributor) *A Directory of American Film Scholars,* 1975; *The Good Morning Cookbook,* Pelican, 1976; *George Bernard Shaw,* Volume I: *A Review of the Literature—An Annotated Bibliography,* 1976; (author of introduction) L. R. Phillips, *D. W. Griffith: Titan of the Film Art—A Critical Study,* 1976; *T. E. Lawrence: Portrait of the Artist as Hero—Controversy and Caricature in the Biographies of "Lawrence of Arabia,"* 1977; (with L. R. Phillips) *The Occult: Hauntings, Witchcraft, Dreams, and All Other Avenues of Paranormal Phenomena,* 1977; *D. H.*

Lawrence: A Review of the Biographies and Literary Criticism, 1978; (with L. R. Phillips) *Film Appreciation: An Outline and Study Guide for Colleges and Universities,* 1978; *The Archaeology of the Collective East: An Annotated Bibliography,* 1979; *Annus Mirabilis: Europe in the Dark and Middle Centuries,* 1979.

The Darkling Plain: The Great War in History, Biography, Diary, Poetry, Literature, and Film, 1981; *The Sterile Promontory: The Second World War in History, Biography, Diary, Poetry, Literature, and Film,* 1982; (contributor) *The Book of Lists #3,* Morrow, 1983; (with L. R. Phillips) *The Dark Frame: Occult Cinema,* 1984.

Contributor of articles, poems, and reviews to *New Guard* and *San Gabriel Valley Tribune.*

WORK IN PROGRESS—All for Gordon Press: *The Films of Montgomery Clift; Music and the Cinema; George Bernard Shaw,* Volume II: *A Review of the Dramas,* Volume III: *A Review of the Films and Filmed Plays; The Black Death and Peasants Revolt; The Liberated Mind: Conservatives, Communists, and Women in Twentieth-Century Society; The Trinity of Evil: Hitler, Himmler, and Heydrich; The Art of David Lean; The Operas of Gian-Carlo Menotti; Geoffrey Plantagenet; Isabel of Hainault; The Apple Cookbook; The Holiday Cookbook; The Wet Priest,* a novel; *Sarah,* a novel; *Everywhere, Christmas,* a novel; books on medieval society and history.

SIDELIGHTS: Jill Phillips told *CA:* "'Art' is personal, intractable. It is important, however, for the artist to serve more than art. Everyone has a personal responsibility to use his/her talent to awaken others. History is the key: we *could* learn from it if we would only study and acknowledge it. Too many people live only in the now. We should see life as a fixed cosmic experience which extends through all time. Yesterday, today, tomorrow are indivisible, and the past is a long shadow which will not be dispelled."

AVOCATIONAL INTERESTS: Politics, music, movies, books; collecting perfumes, tea, and cats.

*   *   *

PHILLIPS, Leona Rasmussen 1925-

PERSONAL: Born November 11, 1925, in Powellsville, Ohio; daughter of Niels (a Lutheran clergyman) and Clara (Potratz) Rasmussen; married Leyson Kirk Phillips (a writer and editor), November 6, 1948; children: Jill, Glen, Sally, Donna, Dorothy. *Education:* Attended University of Michigan. *Politics:* Conservative Republican. *Religion:* Lutheran. *Home:* 851 North Garsden Ave., Covina, Calif. 91724. *Office:* P.O. Box 4213, Covina, Calif. 91723.

CAREER: Has worked as stenographer and switchboard operator; *Tracks,* Cleveland, Ohio, correspondent, 1943-47; writer, 1950—.

WRITINGS—Published by Gordon Press, except as indicated: *You Can Write,* Book Builders, 1966; (editor with daughter, Jill Phillips, and contributor) *A Directory of American Film Scholars,* 1975; *D. W. Griffith: Titan of the Film Art—A Critical Study,* 1976; *Colonial Days and the Revolutionary War: An Annotated Bibliography,* 1976; *Adolf Hitler and the Third Reich: An Annotated Bibliography,* 1977; (with J. Phillips) *The Occult: Hauntings, Witchcraft, Dreams, and All Other Avenues of Paranormal Phenomena,* 1977; *Chinese History: A Bibliography,* 1978; *Christmas: An Annotated Bibliography,* 1978;

Edgar Allan Poe: An Annotated Bibliography, 1978; *Silent Cinema: An Annotated Critical Bibliography*, 1978; (with J. Phillips) *Film Appreciation: An Outline and Study Guide for Colleges and Universities*, 1978; *Twixt Wind and Water*, Ashley Books, 1983.

SIDELIGHTS: Leona Phillips writes: "In the fifties I began writing in the field of fiction and since then have written twenty-seven full-length novels; the subject backgrounds involve: biographical, historical, political, religious, romance, sports, occult, musical, cinema, and every-day life. I have published no fiction, but some day they will all be in print. I have written hundreds of poems (the rhyming kind), lyrics to some of my fictional books and about fifteen plays and screenplays. There is one important truth a writer must realize. Anytime the written word reaches out, it influences. The farther it reaches, the greater the influence. It is necessary that the writer be factual without being pedantic, and that he write with sincerity without undue bias. Nevertheless, I feel that if it is acceptable for other writers to inflict their un-Christian and un-American beliefs and ideas on me and my children, then I am at liberty to try and convince them with my own Christian and patriotic ideas. We can only hope that the day never dawns when moral ideas are considered harmful."†

* * *

PHILLIPS, Paul 1938-

PERSONAL: Born November 3, 1938, in Hong Kong; Canadian citizen; son of Richard G. (an accountant) and Mary D. (a teacher; maiden name, Ricketts) Phillips; married Donna C. Speers (a public relations consultant), September 13, 1958; children: Erin, Nicole. *Education:* Attended Victoria College (now University of Victoria), 1956-58; University of Saskatchewan, B.A. (with distinction), 1962, M.A., 1963; London School of Economics and Political Science, Ph.D., 1967. *Home address:* R.R. 2, Dugald, Manitoba, Canada R0E 0K0. *Office:* University College, University of Manitoba, Winnipeg, Manitoba, Canada.

CAREER: University of Victoria, Victoria, British Columbia, instructor in economics, 1965-66; British Columbia Federation of Labor, Victoria, research director, 1966-68; Simon Fraser University, Burnaby, British Columbia, visiting assistant professor of economics, 1968-69; University of Manitoba, Winnipeg, assistant professor, 1969-75, associate professor, 1975-79, professor of economics, 1979—. Manitoba Economic Development Advisory Board, member, 1972-79, research director, 1974-75; chairman of Milk Control Board of Manitoba, 1975-80; member of Dairy Board of Manitoba, 1975—; commissioner of People's Food Commission, Manitoba, 1979-80; member of board of Community Unemployed Help Centre. Winnipeg Folk Festival, member of board of directors, 1976, chief stage coordinator. Manuscript and grant applicant reader for various publishers, journals, and organizations. Dairy industry consultant to Manitoba Department of Agriculture labour arbitrator. *Military service:* Royal Canadian Air Force Reserve, pilot, 1956-61; became flying officer.

MEMBER: Canadian Association of University Teachers, Social Science Federation of Canada (member of aid to publications committee), Manitoba Opera Association (vice-president and chairman of production committee), Springfield Polo Club (captain).

WRITINGS: No Power Greater: A Century of Labour in British Columbia, Boag Foundation, 1967; (with J. Seldon) *Macro Economic Theory and the Canadian Economy*, Heath, 1972, 2nd edition, 1983; (with Seldon) *Micro Economic Theory and the Canadian Economy*, Heath, 1973, 2nd edition, 1983; (editor) *Incentives, Location, and Regional Development*, Economic Development Advisory Board, 1975; (editor and contributor) *Manpower Issues in Manitoba*, Economic Development Advisory Board, 1975; *The Mining Frontier in B.C., 1880-1920*, National Museum of Canada, 1975; *Regional Disparities*, Lorimer, 1978, revised edition, 1982; (editor and author of introduction) H. C. Pentland, *Labour and Capital in Canada: 1640-1860*, Lorimer, 1981; (with daughter, Erin Phillips) *Women and Work*, Lorimer, 1983.

Contributor: J. Saywell, editor, *Canadian Annual Review*, University of Toronto Press, 1966-68; G. Shelton, editor, *British Columbia and Confederation*, University of Victoria Press, 1967; Henry C. Klassen and A. W. Rasporich, editors, *Prairie Perspectives II*, Holt, 1973; M. Gunderson, editor, *Collective Bargaining in the Essential and Public Service Sectors*, University of Toronto Press, 1975; A. R. McCormack and I. MacPherson, editors, *Cities in the West*, National Museums of Canada, 1975; W. Gagne, editor, *Nationalism, Technology, and the Future of Canada*, Macmillan, 1976; Klassen, editor, *The Canadian West*, Compoint Publishing, 1977; D. J. Bercuson, editor, *Canada and the Burden of Unity*, Macmillan, 1977; A. Artbise, editor, *Town and City: Aspects of Western Canadian Urban Development*, Canadian Plains Research Centre, 1980; (with Stephen Watson) Michael S. Cross and Gregory S. Kealy, editors, *Readings in Canadian Social History*, Volume V, McClelland & Stewart, 1984. Contributor to *New Canadian Encyclopaedia* and to academic journals.

WORK IN PROGRESS: "Unequal Exchange, Surplus Value, and the Commercial-Industrial Question," in *Festschrift for Irene Spry*, edited by Duncan Cameron; "The Underground Economy: The B.C. Mining Frontier, 1850-1920," in *British Columbia Social History*, edited by Rennie Warburton; a study of Canadian economic history; a study of the development of the labour process in Canada in the period of industrialization.

SIDELIGHTS: Paul Phillips writes: "I think it was John Kenneth Galbraith who decided, after the lack of attention to his first book on war-time price controls, that he would write for the general public rather than for academe. While I still write for a professional audience, my main interest is in communicating with the general reader interested in contemporary economy. Unless the issues of current economic policy are understood by the electorate, the future of democracy will wither in the hands of economic technicians."

* * *

PLAIN, Belva 1919-

PERSONAL: Born October 9, 1919, in New York, N.Y.; daughter of Oscar and Eleanor Offenberg; married Irving Plain (a physician), June 14, 1941 (died December, 1982); children: three. *Education:* Graduated from Barnard College. *Residence:* South Orange, N.J. *Agent:* Dorothy Olding, Harold Ober Associates, Inc., 40 East 49th St., New York, N.Y. 10017.

CAREER: Writer.

*WRITINGS—*All novels; all published by Delacorte: *Evergreen* (Literary Guild selection), 1978; *Random Winds*, 1980; *Eden Burning*, 1982; *Crescent City*, 1984. Contributor of several dozen short stories to periodicals, including *McCall's, Good Housekeeping, Redbook,* and *Cosmopolitan.*

WORK IN PROGRESS: A novel, "a family story, not ethnic, that takes place in England and New York."

SIDELIGHTS: Belva Plain told *CA* that "the seed" for her best-selling family saga, *Evergreen,* "was planted when my own nice suburban middle-class children first thought of asking who their forebears were. But it was not until my children began presenting me with grandchildren that their questions merged in my mind with the whole mystique of the past and finally took shape in this, my first novel.

"I had always been curious about my own grandmother, who came here from Europe alone at the age of sixteen. Such courage! I think of her still saying a final goodbye and sailing toward an unknown world so long ago. She never saw her people again.

"Of course, all that is a common American adventure: the loneliness, the struggles and failures—and sometimes, the rise to shining affluence. In such ways *Evergreen* is everybody's story whether he be of Irish, Italian, Polish, or any other stock. Yet there is a special Jewish aspect to the book, too. I was and am weary of reading the same old story, told by Jewish writers, of the same old stereotypes: the possessive mothers, the worn-out fathers and all the rest of the neurotic, rebellious, unhappy, self-hating tribe. I admit that I wanted to write a *different* novel about Jews, and a truer one."

All of Plain's books have been published abroad in eleven languages.

MEDIA ADAPTATIONS: Evergreen was produced as a miniseries by the National Broadcasting Co. in 1985.

BIOGRAPHICAL/CRITICAL SOURCES: New York Times Book Review, July 30, 1978, August 22, 1982.

*   *   *

POOL, Ithiel de Sola   1917-1984

PERSONAL: Born October 26, 1917, in New York, N.Y.; died March 11, 1984, in Cambridge, Mass., of cancer; son of David de Sola (a rabbi) and Tamar (Hirshenson) Pool; married Jean Mackenzie (a psychologist), March 5, 1956; children: Jonathan, Jeremy, Adam. *Education:* University of Chicago, B.A., 1938, M.A., 1939, Ph.D., 1951. *Politics:* Democrat. *Religion:* Jewish. *Home:* 105 Irving St., Cambridge, Mass. 02138. *Office:* Center for International Studies, Massachusetts Institute of Technology, Cambridge, Mass. 02139.

CAREER: Hobart and William Smith Colleges, Geneva, N.Y., assistant professor, 1942-48, associate professor of political science, 1948-49, chairman of Division of Social Science, 1942-49; Stanford University, Stanford, Calif., research associate at Hoover Institution on War, Revolution, and Peace, 1949-53; Massachusetts Institute of Technology, Cambridge, associate professor, 1953-59, professor, 1959-84, became Ruth and Arthur Sloan Professor of Political Science, chairman of department, 1959-61, 1965-69. Visiting lecturer, Yale University, 1953-54; visiting professor, Keio University, Tokyo, 1976. Member of scientific advisory board of U.S. Air Force, 1961-63, Defense Science Board, 1968-70, and Surgeon General's Committee on Television and Children's Behavior, 1970-71. Consultant to RAND Corp., 1951-84.

MEMBER: American Political Science Association, American Association for Public Opinion Research, American Sociological Association, Council on Foreign Relations, American Academy of Arts and Sciences (fellow), Churchill College,

Cambridge University (fellow), Cosmos Club (Washington, D.C.).

AWARDS, HONORS: Center for Advanced Study in the Behavioral Sciences fellowship, 1957-58; Woodrow Wilson Award of American Political Science Association, 1964, for *American Business and Public Policy.*

WRITINGS: (With Nathan Leites) *Communist Propaganda in Reaction to Frustration,* Library of Congress, Experimental Division for the Study of Wartime Communications, Document No. 27, 1942.

(With others) *Symbols of Internationalism,* Stanford University Press, 1951; *The Comparative Study of Symbols,* Stanford University Press, 1952; (with Robert North) *Kuomintang and Chinese Communist Elites,* Stanford University Press, 1952; (with others) *The "Prestige Papers,"* Stanford University Press, 1952; (with others) *Symbols of Democracy,* Stanford University Press, 1952, reprinted, Greenwood Press, 1981; (with others) *Satellite Generals: A Study of Military Elites in the Soviet Sphere,* Stanford University Press, 1955, reprinted, Greenwood Press, 1975; (editor) *Studies in Political Communication,* Princeton University, 1958; *Indian Images of America,* Center for International Studies, Massachusetts Institute of Technology, 1958; (editor) *Trends in Content Analysis,* University of Illinois Press, 1959.

(Editor with Raymond Bauer) *American Businessmen and International Trade Code Book and Data from a Study on Attitudes and Communications,* Free Press of Glencoe, 1960; *Communication and Values in Relation to War and Peace,* Institute for International Order, 1961; *Science and Public Policy,* MIT Press, 1961; (with Barbara Adler) *The Out-of-Classroom Audience of WGBH: A Study of Motivation in Viewing,* Center for International Studies, Massachusetts Institute of Technology, 1963; (with Wilbur Schramm and Jack Lyle) *The People Look at Educational Television: A Report of Nine Representative ETV Stations,* Stanford University Press, 1963; (with Bauer and Lewis Anthony Dexter) *American Business and Public Policy,* Atherton Press, 1963, 2nd edition, 1972; (with Robert P. Abelson and Samuel Popkin) *Candidates, Issues and Strategies: A Computer Simulation of the 1960 Presidential Election,* MIT Press, 1964, revised edition, 1965; (editor) *Contemporary Political Science,* McGraw, 1967; (editor) *The Prestige Press: A Comparative Study of Political Symbols,* MIT Press, 1969.

(With Herbert E. Alexander) *Politics in a Wired Nation,* Educational Resources Information Center, 1971; (with Philip J. Stone and Alexander Szalai) *Communications, Computers, and Automation for Development,* UNITAR, 1971; (co-editor) *Handbook of Communication,* Rand McNally, 1973; (editor) *Talking Back: Citizen Feedback and Cable Technology,* MIT Press, 1973; (with others) *Inventory of Survey Questions about the Interests of the American Public,* Center for International Studies, Massachusetts Institute of Technology, 1974; *The Social Impact of the Telephone,* MIT Press, 1977.

Forecasting the Telephone, Ablex Publishing, 1982; *Technologies of Freedom,* Belknap Press, 1983. Also compiler of *Reprints of Publications on Vietnam, 1966-1970,* 1971.

Contributor: Bert Hoselitz, editor, *Industrialization and Society,* UNESCO, 1963; Wilbur Schramm, editor, *The Science of Human Communication,* Basic Books, 1963; Lucian W. Pye, editor, *Communications and Political Development,* Princeton University Press, 1963; *Refocusing Government Communications Policy: A Report of the Proceedings of Four Washington*

Staff Seminars on Communications Policy, Aspen Institute for Humanistic Studies, 1976.

WORK IN PROGRESS: Research on the social effects of communication systems.

OBITUARIES: New York Times, March 13, 1984; *Washington Post,* March 13, 1984.†

*   *   *

POWELL, Neil
    See INNES, Brian

*   *   *

POWERS, Robert M(aynard)   1942-

PERSONAL: Born November 9, 1942, in Lexington, Ky.; son of Ralph D. and Eddie M. (Vaughn) Powers; married Patricia L. Burgdorf, September 1, 1961 (divorced, 1970); children: Michelle M. *Education:* University of Edinburgh, certificate, 1968; University of Arizona, B.A., 1969. *Agent:* Maggie Noach Agency, London, England. *Office address:* P.O. Box 12158, Denver, Colo. 80212.

CAREER: Writer, 1970—. *Member:* Authors Guild, Authors League of America, Aviation/Space Writers Association, Royal Astronomical Society of Canada, Royal Astronomical Society (London; fellow), Webb Society (London). *Awards, honors:* Richard Grand Foundation grant for legal and educational research, 1968; Aviation Space Writers Association national award for best book, 1979, 1980, and 1981; *Library Journal* award for best book, 1980.

WRITINGS: Viking Mission to Mars, Martin-Marietta, 1975; *Planetary Encounters,* Stackpole, 1978; *Turquoise,* Stackpole, 1978; *Shuttle: The World's First Spaceplane,* Stackpole, 1979; *The Coattails of God: The Ultimate Space Flight—the Trip to the Stars,* Warner Books, 1982; *Mars,* Houghton, 1984.

WORK IN PROGRESS: Das Projekt, a novel.

SIDELIGHTS: Robert M. Powers writes: "I had the misfortune, at the age of five, to be given a college astronomy textbook to find an answer to what should have been an innocent childish question. Somewhere in the mid-sixties, while working at a job I detested, I saw via television a Ranger vehicle impact on the Moon. I quit my job and began writing about space."

AVOCATIONAL INTERESTS: Racing antique cars, jumping horses ("both of which get in the way of writing").

*   *   *

PRABHUPADA, A.C. Bhaktivedanta   1896-1977
    (A. C. Bhaktivedanta Swami, A.C. Bhaktivedanta
    Swami Prabhupada)

PERSONAL: Born September 1, 1896, in Calcutta, India; died November 14, 1977, in Vridaban, India. *Education:* University of Calcutta, B.A., 1920. *Religion:* "Krishna Consciousness" (Vaisnava). *Address:* c/o Bhaktivedanta Book Trust, 3764 Watseka Ave., Los Angeles, Calif. 90034.

CAREER: Leader of Hare Krishna movement in the United States. Former manager of a chemical company, then proprietor of drug and chemical concern, became swami and minister of philosophy, religion, and theology; International Society for Krishna Consciousness in the United States, New York City,

founder, 1965, and acharya (teacher), later established 108 temples in major cities around the world. Founder of Vedic farm community in West Virginia, 1968; introduced Vedic system of primary and secondary education to United States in 1972, schools now in Dallas, Tex., Los Angeles, Calif., Port Royal, Pa. and Vrndavana, India. Co-founder of Bhaktivedanta Book Trust, 1972.

WRITINGS—Published by Iskcon Press, except as indicated: *Two Essays, Krsna: The Reservoir of Pleasure and Who Is Crazy?,* 1967; *Teachings of Lord Caitanya: A Treatise on Factual Spiritual Life,* 1968; *Krsna, The Supreme Personality of Godhead: A Summary Study of Srila Vyasadeva's Srimad-Bhagavatam, Tenth Canto,* 1970; *Transcendental Teachings of Prahlad Maharaj,* 1970; *Krsna Consciousness: The Topmost Yoga System,* 1970; *Easy Journey to Other Planets by Practice of Supreme Yoga,* 1970; *The Perfection of Yoga,* 1972, revised edition, Collier, 1973; *Prahlad: A Story for Children from the Ancient Vedas of India,* edited by Mohanananda das Adhikari, Iskcon Children's Press, 1973.

Published by Bhaktivedanta Book Trust: *Beyond Birth and Death,* 1972; *On the Way to Krsna,* 1973; *Raja-vidya: The King of Knowledge,* 1973; *Elevation to Krsna Consciousness,* 1973; *Teachings of Lord Caitanya: The Golden Avatara,* 1974; (translator with Acyutananda Svami and Jayasacinandana dasa Adhikari) *Songs of the Vaisnava Acaryas,* 1974; *Krsna Consciousness, the Matchless Gift,* 1974; *Perfect Questions, Perfect Answers: Conversations between His Divine Grace A.C. Bhaktivedanta Swami Prabhupada and Bob Cohen, a Peace Corps Worker in India,* 1977; *The Science of Self Realization,* 1977; *Teachings of Lord Kapiladeva: The Son of Devahuti,* 1977; *Teachings of Queen Kunti,* 1978; *Life Comes from Life: Morning Walks with A.C. Bhaktivedanta Swami Prabhupada and Swarupa Damodara Singh,* 1979; *The Path of Perfection: Yoga for the Modern Age,* 1979; *Search for Liberation,* 1981; *Sri Namamrta: The Holy Nectar of the Holy Name,* 1982. Also author of *Coming Back: The Science of Reincarnation.*

Translator and author of commentary: *Bhagavad-Gita As It Is,* Macmillan, abridged edition, 1968, complete edition, Collier, 1972; *Sri Isopanisad: The Knowledge That Brings One Nearer to the Supreme Personality of Godhead, Krsna,* Iskcon Press, 1969; *Nectar of Devotion: A Summary Study of Srila Rupa Gosvami's "Bhakti-nasamrta-sindhu,"* Iskcon Press, 1970, published as *Nectar Of Devotion: The Complete Science of Bhakti Yoga,* Bhaktivedanta Book Trust, 1970; *Srimad Bhagavatam, First Canto,* three volumes, *Second Canto,* two volumes, *Third Canto,* four volumes, *Fourth Canto,* four volumes, *Fifth Canto,* two volumes, *Sixth Canto,* three volumes, *Seventh Canto,* three volumes, *Eighth Canto,* three volumes, *Ninth Canto,* three volumes, *Tenth Canto,* three volumes, Bhaktivedanta Book Trust, 1972-80; *Sri Caitanya Caritamrta of Krsnadasa Kaviraja Gosvami,* seventeen volumes, Bhaktivedanta Book Trust, 1973-77; *The Nectar of Instruction: An Authorized English Presentation of Srila Rupa Gosvami's "Sri Upadesamrta,"* Bhaktivedanta Book Trust, 1975. Also author of shorter publications.

Editor of *Back to Godhead* magazine, 1974-77.

SIDELIGHTS: A.C. Bhaktivedanta Prabhupada brought the Hare Krishna movement to the United States in 1965, arriving in New York with only a pair of cymbals and $50 in rupees to found the International Society for Krishna Consciousness and spread the teachings of Lord Krishna, a deity in Hindu mythology. A former Calcutta chemist and Sanscrit scholar, the Swami was married and the father of three children, but he renounced his family when instructed by his spiritual teacher to carry his message to the West. Prabhupada's arrival in America coincided with an era in which young people were beginning to rebel against traditional western society and experiment with drugs, so his asceticism was appealing to many. He started out by sitting on an East Village sidewalk and reciting the now-familiar Hare Krishna chant, and soon was conducting religious classes in New York City, preaching about the ancient Vedic scriptures which formed the basis of Hinduism. Prabhupada was regarded by his followers as one in a long line of Hindu-inspired teachers that can be traced back 5,000 years. According to a *New York Times* obituary, central to the Swami's teachings is the "belief that the souls of outsiders will be elevated by hearing the name Krishna." Prabhupada went on to establish 108 temples in major cities around the world.

OBITUARIES: New York Times, November 16, 1977.†

* * *

PRABHUPADA, A. C. Bhaktivedanta Swami
See PRABHUPADA, A. C. Bhaktivedanta

* * *

PREISS, Byron (Cary)

PERSONAL: Born in New York, N.Y.; son of Edmund (an attorney) and Pearl (a corporate officer) Preiss. *Education:* University of Pennsylvania, B.A. (with honors), 1973; Stanford University, M.A., 1974. *Religion:* Jewish. *Agent:* Sterling Lord, Sterling Lord Agency, Inc., 660 Madison Ave., New York, N.Y. 10021. *Office:* 128 East 56th St., New York, N.Y. 10022.

CAREER: National Periodical Publications, Inc., New York City, director of EDUgraphics program, 1970; Children's Television Workshop, New York City, editor and writer for "Electric Company," 1972-73; elementary school teacher in Philadelphia, Pa., 1973; American Broadcasting Co. (ABC-Television), San Francisco, Calif., head writer, 1974; writer and director of own films, 1974-76; Harcourt Brace Jovanovich, Inc., New York City, independent editor, 1976-77; writer and lecturer. Proprietor of Byron Preiss Visual Publications, Inc., New York City. *Member:* Sigma Alpha Mu, Friar's Club.

WRITINGS: The Electric Company Joke Book (juvenile), Western Publishing, 1973; *The Silent "E's" from Outer Space* (juvenile), Western Publishing, 1973; (with Ralph Reese) *One Year Affair* (adult), Workman Publishing, 1976; *Fiction Illustrated* (adult), four volumes, Pyramid Publications, 1976; *Starfawn* (science fiction), Pyramid Publications, 1976; *Son of Sherlock Holmes* (mystery), Pyramid Publications, 1977; (with Michael Reaves) *Dragonworld,* Bantam, 1979, revised edition, 1983; *The Beach Boys,* Ballantine, 1979, revised edition published as *The Beach Boys: The Authorized Biography,* St. Martin's, 1983; *The First Crazy Word Book: Verbs* (juvenile), F. Watts, 1982; (with William Stout) *The Little Blue Brontosaurus,* illustrations by Don Morgan and Stout, Caedmon, 1983; (with Michael Sorkin) *Not the Webster's Dictionary,* Wallaby Books, 1983; *The Bat Family,* illustrations by Kenneth Smith, Caedmon, 1984. Author of screenplays, "Five on the Feiffer Side" and "Hunger."

Editor: (And contributor) *Weird Heroes,* Pyramid Publications, Volume I, 1974, Volume II, 1975, Volume III: (with Ron Goulart) *Quest of the Gypsy,* 1976, Volume IV: *Nightshade,* 1976, Volume V: *Phoenix,* 1977, Volume VI, 1977; *Schlomo*

Raven (adult), Pyramid Publications, 1976; (and adaptor) *The Authorized Illustrated Book of Roger Zelazny,* illustrations by Gray Morrow, Baronet, 1978, published as *The Illustrated Roger Zelazny,* Ace Books, 1979; *The Dinosaurs,* Bantam, 1981; Samuel R. Delany, *Distant Stars,* Bantam, 1981; *The Art of Leo and Diane Dillon* (monograph), introduction by Harlan Ellison, Ballantine, 1981; Sean Kelly and Ted Mann, *The Secret,* illustrations by Overton Loyd, John Jude Palencar, and John Pierard, Bantam, 1982; *The Words of Gandhi,* introduction by Richard Attenborough, Newmarket, 1982; *The Time Machine,* two volumes, Bantam, 1984.

WORK IN PROGRESS: The Planets, for Bantam.

SIDELIGHTS: Byron Preiss writes that he has "spent much time working with children in a schoolroom environment, developing solutions to learning problems using visual materials; this resulted in more sophisticated and extensive work with the Children's Television Workshop and National Periodicals and the emergence of a new reading technology involving the use of the graphic story medium to support traditional learning activities."

BIOGRAPHICAL/CRITICAL SOURCES: New York Times Book Review, March, 1974; *Mediascene,* summer, 1976; *Tales of Texas,* winter, 1976; *Los Angeles Times,* January 2, 1977; *Ellery Queen Mystery Magazine,* February, 1977.

* * *

PRESCOTT, Peter S(herwin) 1935-

PERSONAL: Born July 15, 1935, in New York, N.Y.; son of Orville (a writer and critic) and Lilias (Ward-Smith) Prescott; married Anne Lake (a professor of English), June 22, 1957; children: David Sherwin, Antonia Courthope. *Education:* Harvard University, A.B. (magna cum laude), 1957; Sorbonne, University of Paris, additional study, 1957-58. *Politics:* Democrat. *Home and office:* 81 Benedict Hill Rd., New Canaan, Conn. 06840. *Agent:* Sterling Lord Agency, 660 Madison Ave., New York, N.Y. 10021.

CAREER: E. P. Dutton & Co., New York City, senior editor, 1958-67; *Women's Wear Daily,* New York City, literary editor, 1964-68; *Look,* New York City, book review editor, 1968-71; *Newsweek,* New York City, general editor and book critic, 1971—, senior writer, 1978—. Instructor, Publishers' School for Writers, 1964-65; lecturer, U.S. State Department, 1978; associate, Graduate School of Journalism, Columbia University, 1979—. Constable of town of New Canaan, 1969-73. *Military service:* U.S. Army Reserve, 1958-64.

MEMBER: International P.E.N. (member of executive board, American Center, 1974-76), Authors Guild (member of council, 1971—; foundation vice-president, beginning 1972, currently president), Authors League of America (member of council, 1973-76), Century Association, Coffee House, Country Club of New Canaan, Phi Beta Kappa.

AWARDS, HONORS: Guggenheim fellow, 1977; George Polk Award for criticism, 1978; First Prize, Robert F. Kennedy Book Awards, 1981, for *The Child Savers: Juvenile Justice Observed.*

WRITINGS: A World of Our Own: Notes on Life and Learning in a Boys' Preparatory School, Coward, 1970; *Soundings: Encounters with Contemporary Books,* Coward, 1972; *A Darkening Green: Notes from the Silent Generation,* Coward, 1974; *The Child Savers: Juvenile Justice Observed,* Knopf, 1981.

WORK IN PROGRESS: Never in Doubt: Encounters with Contemporary Books (sequel to *Soundings: Encounters with Contemporary Books*); "a book on writing with style."

SIDELIGHTS: A selection of reviews originally written for *Look, Newsweek,* and other periodicals, Peter S. Prescott's *Soundings: Encounters with Contemporary Books* examines a cross section of the books published in the mid 1960s and early 1970s, including works by Saul Bellow, Michael Crichton, Aleksandr Solzhenitsyn, Joyce Carol Oates, Kate Millett, and E. B. White. *Soundings* also illuminates the role of the book reviewer, which, as Prescott writes in the book's preface, is not to "present the infallible truth about books," but rather to "offer a reader . . . a certain perspective, a certain tone of discourse." In a *New York Times Book Review* article, George Stade writes that at times Prescott lapses "into the style of the blurb," but for the most part, Stade finds, "the prose of these reviews is lucid, succinct, and graceful." Calling the reviews "good-humored," "shrewd," "practical," and "ripe with common sense," he concludes, "[Prescott] is unfailingly humane, lively, and considerate of his reader."

In the *Child Savers: Juvenile Justice Observed*, Prescott reports on New York City's Family Court, an institution whose proceedings are not usually open to journalists. The author observed numerous court cases and interviewed judges, lawyers, caseworkers, the children, and their families to reveal what Franklin E. Zimring in the *New York Times Book Review* calls the "chronic frustration" of the system. Michiko Kakutani writes in the *New York Times,* "Mr. Prescott succeeds in giving the reader an understanding of the complexities—and some of the emotional costs—of New York City's juvenile justice system." And Alan Brinkley, summing up *The Child Savers* in an *Atlantic* review, calls it "a study that is intelligent and eloquent, and that expresses both outrage and compassion."

CA INTERVIEW

CA interviewed Peter S. Prescott by telephone on August 8, 1984, at his home in New Canaan, Conn.

CA: In the introduction to Soundings *(1972), a collection of your critical writing, you described yourself as "a clear case of arrested development: The only boy in the fourth grade who actually likes writing book reports finds, in adult life, that writing book reports is still what he wants to do." Knowing something of your literary antecedents, I'm sure that concern for books was nurtured and supported from early on.*

PRESCOTT: That's quite true; my father was a critic.

CA: Did working in publishing (at E. P. Dutton, 1958-1967) before you became a full-time reviewer give you some perspective you might not have had otherwise?

PRESCOTT: I think it did, because after all, I had been a professional reader of books, if I can use that phrase, since I got out of college. I think I said in that same introduction that it was simply a question of turning my attention from an audience consisting of perhaps half a dozen people, at the same firm that I had worked for, to the outside world to increase that audience. I enjoyed the act of writing the reports that I had to write on all the books and manuscripts that crossed my desk.

CA: Many books are published; relatively few are reviewed. How does the selection process work? How many bad books are you likely to read for every good book?

PRESCOTT: I try not to read all of any book that I don't actually review—I don't have the time—so I spend a good part of each day simply screening books. I say a good part—between an hour and two hours a day, even on vacation. The books pour into my house. They also pour into the office. I rarely go to the office; I try to stay away from it as much as possible, because I can't get any real work done there. I stay at home, I look at these books, I sift them through my hands. I have at least three stages of decision-making. The first is when I tear open the packages. I can tell at once that a book on advanced sailboat design, or a book on diets for the last six months of pregnancy, is not a book that is going to command our attention at *Newsweek*. You don't even have to open the book; you just know from the start that that is not a book for you.

Then there is another group of books—also small—that you are absolutely sure are going to command your attention, unless for some reason they are squeezed out by other such books that are even *more* demanding of attention. For instance, I opened the mail today and two books fell out: one is an oral history of the black soldier in Vietnam; the other, a book by Antonia Fraser on the lot of women in the seventeenth century. Both of those are of commanding interest, it seems to me—to me personally, because I'm interested in the subjects, and the books look as if they were extremely well done. So the odds are very high that we will review those two books.

In between the advanced sailboat design and the Antonia Fraser come the great hoard of other books. With these books it's impossible to tell at once if they are suitable for review. You have to put them aside for when you can spend more time on them. These constitute almost all fiction except the fiction by the big-name authors. We know, for instance, that we will automatically review the new book by Saul Bellow or Philip Roth or Norman Mailer. But the hard part comes in trying to find the good novel by someone you've never heard of, or the best of all the nonfiction books that might be interesting, though you haven't had time to determine the author's qualifications or his past record yet. So I would say that almost half the books that cross my desk, so to speak, are books that will require a further look. I spend a great deal of my time trying to *find* the time to give these books the attention they deserve. And of course we can't do it entirely efficiently; we do find that we just miss things. We do have to spend roughly half, and probably more, of our time on the books that we know we are going to review.

CA: Have you made any discoveries that you are especially proud of among new authors?

PRESCOTT: Oh, sure I have, but if the question is put that way it's extremely difficult to answer. For one thing, I don't think any critic should take any great pride in saying that he has made a discovery. It's the editor whose job is on the line, the editor who is required to show a profit on his balance sheet at the end of the year, the editor who has to take a certain number of commercial books in which he can't really take pride except for the huge sums that they may earn. And also, for his own integrity and pride, he has to take a risk on young people of whom no one has ever heard, yet in whose work he believes. So it is they who make these discoveries. If they are good editors, or if they work for a good firm that communicates well with the critics, then they can make some part of their enthusiasm known to us. If we're alert, we won't let the best of these unknown books pass by. But sometimes the book publishers don't make that enthusiasm known to us efficiently.

CA: Is there ever pressure from publishers or agents to review specific books?

PRESCOTT: I think I can say I've never heard from an agent, ever—except my own, and that's for my own work. No, agents know that would be futile. So do publishers. Sometimes an editor will write an individual letter. They don't call, really. I've always discouraged that, because I just don't have time to field phone calls. I think agents and publishers know, on the whole, that any attempt to apply pressure to a critic would be counterproductive. I can recall once a publisher trying very hard to get me to pay attention to a book that she said had made a great difference in her life. I knew this person, I liked her, I was even fond of her. I expressed my doubts about the book, but she said, "Oh, no, no, you haven't tried it." So I tried it, and since I had invested my time in it and the author was famous, I decided that I would review it. It was a terrible book! I made sarcastic fun of it. I think publishers realize that it just isn't the thing to do. They can send the book, they can send the publicity material with it, but individual contact with book critics should usually be avoided, I think.

CA: If book reviewing still ranks, as you said some years ago, "somewhere between cleaning chimneys and calling people up to ask what television program they are watching," what are the rewards?

PRESCOTT: The rewards are several, one of which is that I'm able to make a pretty decent living at it. I don't have to take a shower after I work. I can work at home, I can work pretty much at my own pace, I answer to people far less than almost anyone else ever does. I am involved in the communication of ideas, and those ideas are—despite the fact that so many of the books are very bad—the most important that our human society has to offer, because books are still the repository, the means of communication, of ideas that are worth something next week, or the week after that. Most of what is worth saying in our society finds its way into book form. So in a sense I'm being paid to continue my education in public. More important, the critic mediates between the artist and his audience. He introduces, explains. encourages and objects. John Simon has said that without criticism, the artist today has no serious response. I believe that.

CA: Do you read the work of other reviewers much?

PRESCOTT: I try to keep abreast of it, which means I look to see what they are doing. If the book they are talking about interests me, or if it's a critic who interests me, yes, I do read it. Of course it's a part of my job to know what's being done in the daily and Sunday *Times* and what's being done in *Time* magazine and half a dozen other publications. But I rarely read reviews all the way through, unless there's a strong reason to do it, because for the most part I already know about those books and have had to make up my own mind about them before those reviews appear.

CA: Are you still teaching the seminar "Reviewing the Arts"?

PRESCOTT: Yes, and I'm teaching a second seminar called "Writing with Style."

CA: What can be taught about reviewing? What do you stress?

PRESCOTT: I've never been convinced that anybody can teach anybody to write—*well,* at least. But I am convinced that people can learn to write well if they have the capacity to fix their eye on a text in a way that is unlike that which the ordinary critic uses, and can also learn to read very critically, analytically, so that they can ask themselves, what is the writer doing with this paragraph, what is he doing with this sentence, why is he making this transition here, why is he using the first person, how does he introduce irony, and where does he come to the main subject. If you can learn to decipher a text, in the sense of trying to figure out what the writer of that text had in mind as he was doing it, then you can learn how it's done. Of course there's still the great bridge: now that you know how it's done, can you do it yourself?

I try to teach primarily problems of style, which involve trying to get the student to develop a tone of voice that has some authority, because that is what all journalists who write the kind of stuff I teach have to have. The writing I teach is what appears in the back of newspapers and the back of magazines—anyplace where opinion is allowed, a first person is also allowed. This is advocacy journalism, where you're trying to persuade your readers that this is worthwhile or that isn't or please think like me in this regard. So I talk about the establishment of an authority on the part of the journalist, establishing a tone of voice and a personal tone which is not simply what I call "the naked I," but is a persona, a first person manufactured for the occasion itself.

CA: How do you feel about the bestseller lists?

PRESCOTT: Depressed, always. The books on them are uniformly rotten; it's hard to find anything of substance. If you were to look at last Sunday's *Times* bestseller list, you'd see in fifteenth place Saul Bellow's new book, *Him with His Foot in His Mouth and Other Stories,* which is probably the best work of fiction that has come out this year, but there it is in fifteenth place. The average book of good quality doesn't ever see the bestseller list.

CA: What about awards? Are there too many?

PRESCOTT: I don't think there are too many; I've won a few, so I'm glad to have awards around! Any way you can encourage a writer is good. It's such a dismal life and so few writers can make a living doing it. You may have heard of a survey that shows that the average writer in this country makes under $5000 a year. There are so few means of encouragement, I think any award is good.

CA: In A World of Our Own *(1970), you wrote about your alma mater, Choate, during the troubled school year of 1967-1968, when traditional concepts of authority were rapidly falling by the way. Do you think the prep schools still have a legitimate and important role in our society?*

PRESCOTT: I do indeed—which isn't to say that there aren't some bad schools or some snobbish schools or schools that have the opportunity to be more imaginative and firm in their instruction than they in fact are. I'm sure that that is still true. But the schools were always, even in those dim days that I wrote about, exciting places to be when you consider the alternative, the public high school, which is rarely a very exciting place to be. And insofar as these schools serve as areas where experimentation can be made, areas where students can be required to work harder or stretch their imaginations more than they would in the public high school, I'm all for them. I think, too, that they have by and large improved since I wrote that book. I was fortunate—in terms of my book, at least—that I chose to observe those schools, by accident, at a time when they were really tottering on the brink of extinction. But they have somehow pulled themselves together again, and society has changed to a certain extent too. They did try to find themselves again, and they did that largely by turning away from being single-sex schools and becoming coed schools. I think a great deal of their renewed life and vigor has to do with that. These schools now seem to have much more of a sense of the real world about them than they had in the late 1960s.

CA: You wrote in that book, "The Age of the Great Headmaster is over." Has that reversed itself to any extent?

PRESCOTT: No, I don't think so. The great headmasters existed because of a certain combination of beliefs. Those beliefs are gone; we're not going to see their like again, ever. They simply are extinct, worn out. The idea that in my book I call Christian Humanism, for instance, is not alive and well in our society today. That isn't to say that there will not appear someday, in some prep school, some titanic individual who might in some ways serve the same purpose that these headmasters did. But I expect he or she would not be the same kind of person, because to be a great headmaster in the same sense that I intended the phrase meant a continuity of interests, a shared system of belief and outlook that existed for at least four centuries. Now, if you were going to have a really dynamic leader, he or she would have a completely different vocabulary and a very different perspective.

CA: The bit of history in A World of Our Own, *your account of the Christian Humanist legacy of the great fifteenth-century teacher Vittorino and how his tradition was carried through until recent time, was most interesting.*

PRESCOTT: Thank you. I always feel you have to put some history in. I put some history in *The Child Savers* as well. But you should save it for chapter two, because you want to make sure you've caught the reader's attention before you hit him with all that stuff!

CA: In The Child Savers *(1981) you dealt with the juvenile justice system in New York City and the opposite kind of young people from those in* A World of Our Own—*"the outcasts, the inarticulate, the violent," as you called them, whose lives are affected by that system. The book was shocking, both in the problems it related about the judicial system and in its revelation of the horrors that are commonplace for so many young people. Were the research and writing emotionally difficult?*

PRESCOTT: Writing is always emotionally difficult. The research was not as difficult for me as it was for the extraordinarily able and very decent young people whom I was looking at closely, the lawyers. They were involved in a professional way—their careers, and to an extent their lives, depended on what happened to these kids—and they could not step away from their jobs as I did every day. I was a journalist, and I was a commuter to the courts. At the end of each day I would come back to my exurban home and I could put it out of my mind for a while. But these young people could not do that. They had a commitment to it that I didn't have. And it was certainly emotionally damaging to them, there's no question about it. For me it was just endlessly fascinating, because I

didn't have that emotional commitment to what was going on. Writers, I think, have a sliver of ice in their hearts.

CA: Have you had a lot of response to the book?

PRESCOTT: Oh yes. It seems to have been read by everybody in the system, which is a good thing, and I'm told that I offended the family court judges. That's all right with me; I guess they loom up as the villains of the book. They have the responsibility for what happens to these kids, and they don't exercise it properly. They have the key to the resources that might help these children, and they don't use those properly either. So if they were offended, that's all right. Everybody else seems to have liked the book, except for a few prosecutors, so I'm pleased. But I don't think it's going to change the system. As I said in the introduction to the book, the problems are just too ingrown. No one really sees a way out of it, and certainly one book isn't going to make a great deal of difference, though it could make some.

CA: In the acknowledgments to your books you have given such heartfelt credit to your wife, Anne Lake Prescott, that I wondered if you would like to elaborate on her help in your work.

PRESCOTT: My wife is a professor of English at Barnard College. She probably works harder than I do; she has to go into the city more often than I do, and she's a scholar as well as a teacher so she's constantly working late into the night on articles and reviews and books of her own. That she takes the time to defend me from the outside world when that's necessary, or that she takes the time to pore over very carefully what I write and point out that this phrase isn't quite right or that phrase is downright ungrammatical, or simply to tell me that the experimental thing that I've tried to do and am a little nervous about is OK, that it works—this is immensely helpful. Not only that, but, to be very blunt, I've had maybe fifteen editors in my life, and she has a better sense of words than any of them. So Anne has always been my chief editor. She knows what the language is and how it should work in a way that other editors that I've had simply don't.

CA: Is there something in the works that you can talk about?

PRESCOTT: There's always something in the works—in this case, two books. One is a collection of reviews, a sequel to *Soundings* and a book very much like it, called *Never in Doubt.* It has the same subtitle as *Soundings, Encounters with Contemporary Books.* That is just about ready to go. Beyond that there will be a book on writing with style, based on my experiences and my theories that I've developed in the two seminars I've taught, a combination of exemplary texts and my own advice aimed at the journalist and the would-be journalist. I think that will give the book its particular flavor. There has been no such book specifically on examples of journalistic style from, say, Shaw's reviews up to the present.

CA: So there's no fiction incubating?

PRESCOTT: No. I've been tempted to write fiction, but I've always managed to suppress the urge.

CA: Are there any other comments you'd like to make on your work?

PRESCOTT: Well, I suppose if there's anything interesting in my particular career as a writer it's that I'm trying to divide my time—not equally, by any means—between discussions of literary matters and discussions of social matters. For me, that's an interesting balance. Every week I have to be there in the back pages of *Newsweek,* and always in the same context. It seems to me that if you're going to stay alive and alert and fresh, so to speak, it's of the utmost importance that you spend some of your time, indeed a large measure of your time, doing something else on the outside; otherwise you become a hack. That is the great peril of journalists, that they become hacks very quickly. They begin to turn stuff out in a machine-like way. I've now been writing criticism for over twenty years, and I'm very alert that the problem exists; it lurks like some kind of monster in a child's dream outside the window at night. You musn't let it in; you must not succumb to the temptation to do things in a mechanical way. The way I handle this is to do a different kind of writing, to do something else. I write books; I do a small amount of humor writing. That puts me in a different gear and helps me come back to the reviewing with a fresh approach. I also do a fair amount of *pro bono* work. I'm on the board of the Authors Guild and president of the Authors Guild Foundation. That takes my mind off my own problems and gives me a chance to talk to other writers and see what the problems of writers around the country are.

The humor is important. I think you can see in looking at *A World of Our Own,* in *A Darkening Green,* even in *The Child Savers.* To a certain extent in the reviews I write there is occasionally a humorous note. I think it's the only way to maintain your sanity. You cannot write about these very serious subjects—or even those subjects that are not so serious—without humor, or you run the risk of losing your audience's attention. And besides, I have the eye of the satirist anyway, the eye of the ironist, because I go into situations in which people are taking themselves tremendously seriously and it is pretty funny to watch, even though the most horrible things are unfolding in front of you. Even when people's lives are being ruined in front of you, as they were in *The Child Savers,* the process by which this happens has its own macabre humor, and I don't want to lose sight of that.

BIOGRAPHICAL/CRITICAL SOURCES: New York Times Book Review, October 11, 1970, August 16, 1972, May 5, 1974. June 14, 1981; *New York Times,* October 14, 1970. September 9, 1981: *Washington Post,* October 16, 1970; *Newsweek,* October 26, 1970, April 29, 1974; *Saturday Review/World,* May 4, 1974; *New Yorker,* May 6, 1974; *Atlantic,* June 1981; *Washington Post Book World,* June 14, 1981.

—*Interview by Jean W. Ross*

*   *   *

PRINCE, Carl E.   1934-

PERSONAL: Born December 8, 1934, in Newark, N.J.; son of Phillip G. and Anne (Silver) Prince; children: Elizabeth, Jonathan. *Education:* Rutgers University, B.A. (with honors), 1956, M.A., 1958, Ph.D., 1963. *Politics:* Democrat. *Religion:* Jewish. *Home:* 35 Korwell Circle, West Orange, N.J. 07052. *Office:* Department of History, New York University, 19 University Pl., New York, N.Y. 10003.

CAREER: Fairleigh Dickinson University, Madison, N.J., instructor in history, 1960-63; Seton Hall University, South Orange, N.J., assistant professor, 1963-66, associate professor of history, 1966-68; New York University, New York, N.Y., associate professor, 1968-75, professor of history, 1975—, acting chairman of department, Washington Square College,

1971-72, 1978—. Visiting assistant professor of history at Rutgers University, 1962-66; associate, Columbia University Seminar in Early American History. Member of advisory historical committee, New Jersey Tercentenary Commission, 1963-64; chairman, Linden (N.J.) chapter of Independent Voters for Johnson, 1964, and West Orange (N.J.) Citizens against the Vietnam War, 1965-70; coordinator, Essex County (N.J.) Citizens for McCarthy, 1968; advisor to Democratic Party delegation to New Jersey Constitutional Convention, 1968; member, West Orange Bicentennial Committee, 1976. Member of executive board, New Jersey Catholic Historical Records Commission and United Negro College Fund Archives; trustee, Bet Yeled Hebrew Folk School.

MEMBER: American Historical Association, Organization of American Historians, Institute of Early American History and Culture (associate), American Association for State and Local History, American Association of University Professors, Society for Historians of Early American Republic (member of executive board; president, 1983-84), New Jersey Historical Society (fellow).

AWARDS, HONORS: Frank Weil Institute fellow, 1965; postdoctoral fellow at Hebrew Union College, 1966; National Endowment for the Humanities younger scholar fellow, 1968-69; Fulbright scholar in Israel, 1972-73.

WRITINGS: Middlebrook: American Eagle's Nest, Somerset Press, 1958; *New Jersey's Jeffersonian Republicans: The Genesis of an Early Party Machine, 1789-1817,* University of North Carolina Press, 1967; *The Federalists and the Origins of the Civil Service,* New York University Press, 1977; (editor) *The Papers of William Livingston,* Volume I: *June 11, 1774-June 30, 1777,* Volume II: *July 1, 1777-December, 1778,* New Jersey Historical Commission, 1979. Contributor to regional history journals.

WORK IN PROGRESS: Editing additional volumes of the papers of William Livingston, for the New Jersey Historical Commission.

*   *   *

PRINGLE, Laurence P.   1935-
(Sean Edmund)

PERSONAL: Born November 26, 1935, in Rochester, N.Y.; son of Laurence Erin (a realtor) and Marleah (Rosehill) Pringle; married Judith Malanowicz (a librarian), June 23, 1962 (divorced, 1970); married Alison Newhouse (a free-lance editor), July 14, 1971 (marriage ended); married Susan Klein (a teacher), March 13, 1984; children: (first marriage) Heidi Elizabeth, Jeffrey Laurence, Sean Edmund. *Education:* Cornell University, B.S., 1958; University of Massachusetts, M.S., 1960; Syracuse University, graduate study, 1960-62. *Residence:* West Nyack, N.Y.

CAREER: Free-lance writer, editor, and photographer. High school science teacher in Lima, N.Y., 1961-62; American Museum of Natural History, *Nature and Science* (children's magazine), New York, N.Y., associate editor, 1963-65, senior editor, 1965-67, executive editor, 1967-70. Faculty member, New School for Social Research, 1976-78.

AWARDS, HONORS: Three of Laurence Pringle's books were named "Notable Books" by the American Library Association: *Listen to the Crows,* 1976, *Death Is Natural,* 1977, and *Wild Foods: A Beginner's Guide to Identifying, Harvesting, and Cooking Safe and Tasty Plants from the Outdoors,* 1978; Special Conservation Award, National Wildlife Federation, 1978; Eva L. Gordon Award, American Nature Society, 1983.

WRITINGS—Children's books, except as indicated: *Dinosaurs and Their World,* Harcourt, 1968; *The Only Earth We Have,* Macmillan, 1969; (editor) *Discovering the Outdoors: A Nature and Science Guide to Investigating Life in Fields, Forests, and Ponds,* Natural History Press, 1969.

(Editor) *Discovering Nature Indoors: A Nature and Science Guide to Investigations with Small Animals,* Natural History Press, 1970; *From Field to Forest,* World Publishing, 1970; *In a Beaver Valley: How Beavers Change the Land,* World Publishing, 1970; *One Earth, Many People: The Challenge of Human Population Growth,* Macmillan, 1971; *Ecology: Science of Survival,* Macmillan, 1971; *Cockroaches: Here, There and Everywhere,* Crowell, 1971; *This Is a River: Exploring an Ecosystem,* Macmillan, 1971; *From Pond to Prairie: The Changing World of a Pond and Its Life,* Macmillan, 1972; *Pests and People,* Macmillan, 1972; *Wild River* (adult book; self-illustrated), Lippincott, 1972; *Estuaries: Where Rivers Meet the Sea,* Macmillan, 1973; *Into the Woods: Exploring the Forest Ecosystem,* Macmillan, 1973; *Follow a Fisher,* Crowell, 1973; *Twist, Wiggle, and Squirm: A Book about Earthworms,* Crowell, 1973; *Recycling Resources,* Macmillan, 1974.

Energy: Power for People, Macmillan, 1975; *City and Suburb: Exploring an Ecosystem,* Macmillan, 1975; *Chains, Webs, and Pyramids: The Flow of Energy in Nature,* Crowell, 1975; *Water Plants,* Crowell, 1975; *The Minnow Family: Chubs, Dace, Minnows, and Shiners,* Morrow, 1976; *Listen to the Crows,* Crowell, 1976; *Our Hungry Earth: The World Food Crisis,* Macmillan, 1976; *Death Is Natural,* Four Winds, 1977; *The Hidden World: Life under a Rock,* Macmillan, 1977; *The Controversial Coyote: Predation, Politics, and Ecology,* Harcourt, 1977; *The Gentle Desert: Exploring an Ecosystem,* Macmillan, 1977; *Animals and Their Niches: How Species Share Resources,* Morrow, 1977; *The Economic Growth Debate: Are There Limits to Growth?* F. Watts, 1978; *Dinosaurs and People: Fossils, Facts, and Fantasies,* Harcourt, 1978; *Wild Foods: A Beginner's Guide to Identifying, Harvesting, and Cooking Safe and Tasty Plants from the Outdoors,* Four Winds Press, 1978; *Nuclear Power: From Physics to Politics,* Macmillan, 1979; *Natural Fire: Its Ecology in Forests,* Morrow, 1979.

Lives at Stake: The Science and Politics of Environmental Health, Macmillan, 1980; *What Shall We Do with the Land?: Choices for America,* Crowell, 1981; *Frost Hollows and Other Microclimates,* Morrow, 1981; (contributor) Betsy Hearne and Marilyn Kaye, editors, *Celebrating Children's Books: Essays on Children's Literature in Honor of Zena Sutherland,* Lothrop, 1981; (contributor) *Beyond Fact: Nonfiction for Children and Young People,* American Library Association, 1982; *Vampire Bats,* Morrow, 1982; *Water: The Next Great Resource Battle,* Macmillan, 1982; *Radiation: Waves and Particles, Benefits and Risks,* Ridley Enslow, 1983; *Wolfman: Exploring the World of Wolves,* Scribner, 1983; *Feral: Tame Animals Gone Wild,* Macmillan, 1983; *The Earth Is Flat, and Other Great Mistakes,* Morrow, 1983; *Being a Plant,* Crowell, 1983.

Contributor to *Audubon, Ranger Rick's Nature Magazine, Highlights for Children,* and *Smithsonian,* sometimes under the pseudonym Sean Edmund.

SIDELIGHTS: In an essay titled "Science Done Here" in *Celebrating Children's Books: Essays on Children's Literature in Honor of Zena Sutherland,* wildlife biologist and children's author Laurence P. Pringle writes about his views on the current state of science in our culture. "The nineteenth-century philosopher Soren Kierkegaard," says Pringle, "told of a man who saw a sign in a shop window: 'Philosophy Done Here.' He rushed into the shop to buy some, only to be told that the sign itself was for sale.

"The subject here is science books, and Kierkegaard's story can easily be adapted to the late twentieth century: change the words to 'Science Done Here' and put them on a T-shirt. . . .

"To do science is to acknowledge that the world is a complex place but that the complexity can be explored and understood, and that there is order and unity in its diversity. At its core, science is a hopeful activity. Psychiatrist Karen Horney believed that young children are naturally joyful, unafraid, warm, and spontaneous. To this I think we can add curious and hopeful. Since science at its best stands for hope, curiosity, truthfulness, and the joy of discovery, you might suppose that children would clamor for more science in their lives. This is not the case.

"Science teaching is scarce in elementary and middle schools, and many science programs reinforce the notion that doing science means memorizing facts, jargon, and numbers that seem irrelevant to everyday life. . . .

"We live in an age when decisions involving science and technology can have enormous effects on everyone. Scientific knowledge—or a lack of it—plays a vital part in food-growing, health, and energy matters, for example. Decisions about such matters affect the quality of our lives, and perhaps the lives of many generations to come. . . .

"The doing of science depends on such special human qualities as curiosity, passion, creativity, and veracity. Partly because of these characteristics, science has been called the greatest hope of the human race. Children's books have a vital role to play. They can make science and the universe more accessible to young people. They can stand for and appeal to the finest characteristics and highest aspirations of the human species."

BIOGRAPHICAL/CRITICAL SOURCES: New York Times Book Review, November 9, 1969, May 24, 1970, December 10, 1978; *Scientific American,* December, 1975; *Washington Post Book World,* November 13, 1977; *Times Literary Supplement,* March 28, 1980; Betsy Hearne and Marilyn Kaye, editors, *Celebrating Children's Books: Essays on Children's Literature in Honor of Zena Sutherland,* Lothrop, 1981; *Children's Literature Review,* Volume IV, Gale, 1984.

*   *   *

PRONZINI, Bill 1943-
(Jack Foxx, Alex Saxon; William Jeffrey, a joint pseudonym)

PERSONAL: Born April 13, 1943, in Petaluma, Calif.; son of Joseph (a farm worker) and Helene (Guder) Pronzini; married Laura Patricia Adolphson, May 15, 1965 (divorced, 1967); married Brunhilde Schier, July 28, 1972. *Politics:* Liberal Democrat. *Home address:* P.O. Box 27368, San Francisco, Calif. 94127. *Agent:* Clyde Taylor, Curtis Brown Ltd., 575 Madison Ave., New York, N.Y. 10022.

CAREER: Petaluma Argus-Courier, Petaluma, Calif., reporter, 1957-60; writer, 1969—.

MEMBER: Authors League of America, Authors Guild, Mystery Writers of America (member of board of directors), Science Fiction Writers of America, Western Writers of America, Writers Guild of America West.

WRITINGS: (Under pseudonym Alex Saxon) *A Run in Diamonds*, Pocket Books, 1973; (editor) *Midnight Specials: An Anthology for Train Buffs and Suspense Afficionados*, Bobbs-Merrill, 1977; (with Barry N. Malzberg) *Night Screams*, Playboy Press, 1979; (editor with Malzberg) *The End of Summer*, Ace Books, 1979.

(Editor with Malzberg) *Bug-Eyed Monsters*, Harcourt, 1980; *A Killing in Xanadu*, Waves Press, 1980; *Gun in Cheek: A Study of "Alternative" Crime Fiction*, Coward, McMann & Geoghegan, 1982; *The Gallows Land*, Walker & Co., 1983; (with John Lutz) *The Eye*, Mysterious Press, 1984; (editor with Martin H. Greenberg) *The Lawmen*, Fawcett, 1984; (with Marcia Muller) *Child's Ploy*, MacMillan, 1984; (with Muller) *Witches' Brew*, MacMillan, 1984.

All published by Random House: *The Stalker*, 1971; *Panic!*, 1972; (editor) *The Edgar Winners: Thirty-third Annual Anthology of the Mystery Writers of America*, 1980.

All published by Putnam: *Snowbound*, 1974; (with Malzberg) *The Running of Beasts*, 1976; *Games*, 1976; (with Malzberg) *Acts of Mercy*, 1977.

All published by St. Martin's: (Editor with Malzberg) *Shared Tomorrows: Science Fiction Is Collaboration*, 1979; (with Malzberg) *Prose Bowl*, 1980.

All published by Doubleday: (Editor with Joe Gores) *Tricks or Treats*, 1976; (editor with Malzberg) *Dark Sins, Dark Dreams: Crime in Science Fiction*, 1978; (with Jack Anderson) *The Cambodia File*, 1981; (editor with Greenberg) *Reel West*, 1984; *Starvation Camp*, 1984.

All published by Arbor House: *Werewolf!*, 1979; (editor) *Voodoo!: A Chrestomathy of Necromancy*, 1980; (editor) *Mummy!: A Chrestomathy of Crypt-ology*, 1980; (editor) *The Arbor House Necropolis*, 1981; (editor with Greenberg and Malzberg) *The Arbor House Treasury of Horror and the Supernatural*, introduction by Stephen King, 1981; (editor with Greenberg and Malzberg) *The Arbor House Treasury of Mystery and Suspense*, introduction by John D. MacDonald, 1981; (editor) *Creature!: A Chrestomathy of "Monstery,"* 1981; *Masques*, 1981; (editor) *Specter!: A Chrestomathy of "Spookery,"* 1982; (editor) *The Arbor House Treasury of Great Western Stories*, 1982; (editor) *The Arbor House Treasury of Detective and Mystery Stories from the Great Pulps*, 1983.

All published by Morrow: (With Muller) *The Web She Weaves*, 1983; (editor with Greenberg) *The Western Hall of Fame: An Anthology of Classic Western Stories Selected by the Western Writers of America*, 1984; (co-editor) *The Mystery Hall of Fame: An Anthology of Classic Mystery and Suspense Stories, Selected by the Mystery Writers of America*, 1984.

"Nameless Detective" mysteries; published by St. Martin's, except as indicated: *The Snatch*, Random House, 1971; *The Vanished*, Random House, 1973; *Undercurrent*, Random House, 1973; *Blowback*, Random House, 1977; (with Collin Wilcox) *Twospot*, Putnam, 1978; *Labyrinth*, 1980; *Hoodwink*, 1981; *Scattershot*, 1982; *Bindlestiff*, 1983; *Casefile: The Best of the "Nameless Detective" Stories*, 1983; *Nightshades*, 1984; *Quicksilver*, 1984; (with Muller) *Double*, 1984; *Bones*, 1985.

Under pseudonym Jack Foxx; all published by Bobbs-Merrill: *The Jade Figurine*, 1972; *Dead Run: A Novel of Suspense*, 1975; *Freebooty: A Novel of Suspense*, 1976; *Wildfire*, 1978.

With Jeffrey M. Wallmann, under joint pseudonym William Jeffrey: *Duel at Gold Buttes*, Leisure Books, 1982; *Border Fever*, Leisure Books, 1983; *Day of the Moon*, R. Hale, 1983.

Contributor to anthologies; also contributor of over two hundred short stories and articles to magazines, including *Argosy, Ellery Queen's Mystery Magazine*, and *Magazine of Fantasy and Science Fiction*.

SIDELIGHTS: "Pronzini . . . is a master of suspense who here has turned confusing political history into taut adventure." Thus Jeff Gillenkirk describes Bill Pronzini's part in *The Cambodia File*, a novel written in collaboration with columnist Jack Anderson. Drawn from Anderson's reports of American involvement in Cambodia during the Vietnam War, Pronzini creates a dramatic story set during the U.S. withdrawal from Cambodia and the revolution that followed. Gillenkirk credits Pronzini for "movingly portraying the human consequences of the Nixon/Kissinger Cambodian 'incursion.'"

Pronzini's books have been translated into sixteen languages and published in more than thirty countries.

MEDIA ADAPTATIONS: Several of Pronzini's books have been optioned for films, including *The Jade Figurine, Snowbound* (Columbia Pictures), *Panic!* (Hal Wallis Productions), *Games* (Sara Films), and *Night Screams* (Soge Films).

AVOCATIONAL INTERESTS: Sports, old movies and radio shows, book collecting.

BIOGRAPHICAL/CRITICAL SOURCES: New York Times Book Review, March 2, 1980; *Washington Post Book World*, January 18, 1981, April 18, 1982; *Los Angeles Times*, March 12, 1981; *Village Voice Literary Supplement*, February, 1984; *Globe and Mail*, April 7, 1984.

*   *   *

PRUDDEN, Bonnie 1914-

PERSONAL: Born January 29, 1914, in New York, N.Y.; daughter of Harry J. (a newspaper representative) and Nell (Russell) Prudden; children: Joan Hirschland Meijer, Susan Hirschland Sussman. *Education:* Attended Columbia University Extension, Grand Central School of Art, and Weidman-Humphrey School of Dance. *Home address:* Prospect Hill, Stockbridge, Mass. 01262. *Agent:* Willis Wing, Falls Village, Conn. 06031. *Office:* Bonnie Prudden, Inc., Stockbridge, Mass. 01262.

CAREER: Physical fitness expert. Director of ski patrols and Red Cross disaster units, New York, N.Y., and Westchester, N.Y., 1939-49; founder and director of Institute for Physical Fitness, White Plains, N.Y., beginning 1950, and Stockbridge, Mass., beginning 1960; founder and director of Bonnie Prudden School for Physical Fitness and Myotherapy, Stockbridge, beginning 1979. Made regular appearances on "Home Show" and "Today Show" television programs for three years; has appeared as a guest on numerous major television and radio programs; former host of "The Bonnie Prudden Show," syndicated television series. Has conducted fitness workshops since 1955.

AWARDS, HONORS: Safety Award from Eastern Amateur Ski Association; Service to Youth Award from Young Men's Christian Association (Y.M.C.A.); M.H. from Springfield College; honorable mention from American Medical Association for work in hypokinetic disease; annual grants from *Reader's Digest* since 1967.

WRITINGS: Basic Exercise No. 1, Institute for Physical Fitness, 1956; *Is Your Child Really Fit?,* Harper, 1956; *Improve Your Body* (manual), Equitable Life, 1959; *Bonnie Prudden's Fitness Book: A Picture Guide with Exercises and Reducing Plans,* Ronald, 1959; *Executive Fitness* (manual), Equitable Life, 1960; *How to Keep Slender and Fit after Thirty,* Geis, 1961, revised edition, 1969; *Fitness for You* (talking book for the blind), Library of Congress, 1964; *How to Keep Your Child Fit from Birth to Six,* Harper, 1964; *Teenage Fitness,* Harper, 1965, revised edition, Dial, 1983; *Quick Rx for Fitness,* Grosset, 1965; *Bowling and Fitness* (manual), American Machine & Foundry, 1967; *Fit for Life* (manual), Girls Clubs of America, 1967.

Fitness from Six to Twelve, Harper, 1972, revised edition, Dial, 1983; *Your Baby Can Swim,* Reader's Digest Press, 1974, published as *Teach Your Baby to Swim,* Dial, 1983; *How to Keep Your Family Fit and Healthy,* Reader's Digest Press, 1975; *Exer-Sex,* Bantam, 1978; *Pain Erasure the Bonnie Prudden Way,* M. Evans, 1980; *Bonnie Prudden's Guide to Pain-Free Living,* Dial, 1984; *The After-Fifty Crowd* (tentative title), Ballantine, 1985.

Audio-visual materials: "Peter and the Koos" (film), Institute for Physical Fitness, 1967; "Keep Fit . . . Be Happy" (film strips with manuals), Pathescope Educational Films, 1971; "Alive and Feeling Great" (film), Girls Clubs of America, 1974; "Your Baby Can Swim" (film), Institute for Physical Fitness, 1974; "Living Pain Free" (video cassette), 1984. Author of record albums "Keep Fit . . . Be Happy," Volume I, 1960, Volume II, 1961, "Fit to Ski," 1962, "Fitness for Baby and You," 1962, "Executive Fitness," 1963, "Fitness for Teens," 1963.

Also author of *Muscular Fitness and Orthopedic Disability,* 1953, *We're Physical Mollycoddlers,* 1956, and *Hypokinetic Disease,* 1956. Columnist for *Sports Illustrated* for three years. Contributor of articles to technical journals and popular periodicals, including *New York Journal of Medicine* and *Journal of American Association for Health, Physical Education, and Recreation.*

SIDELIGHTS: Bonnie Prudden was invited to conduct a presentation on physical fitness for President Dwight D. Eisenhower, following which the president established his Council on Youth Fitness. This was later to become the President's Council on Physical Fitness under John F. Kennedy. "This in turn," writes Prudden, "led to the current interest in fitness."

Prudden told *CA:* "I got into the 'fitness business' by accident. I noticed my children were not getting what I would consider physical education in school, so I started my own physical fitness classes, which later grew first to a school and then to an international institute. Using six tests devised by Dr. Hans Kraus and Dr. Sonya Weber, I tested thousands of children all over the world. American children proved to be the weakest in the world." It was Prudden's report on these findings that attracted the attention of President Eisenhower and led him to establish the Council on Youth Fitness. Continues the author, "At the time the report was made, there was not one current book on physical fitness other than those found in schools, which were of no value to the public.

"I wrote my first book, *Basic Exercise No. 1,* so that my students and teachers, and other teachers further removed, would have some information on exercise. The second book, *Is Your Child Really Fit?,* contained information on the state of fitness, what was causing our problems—and what to do about it at

home where the trouble starts. *How to Keep Your Child Fit from Birth to Six, Fitness from Six to Twelve,* and *Teenage Fitness* were written to bring further information into the home, since the schools continued to provide nothing of value. *How to Keep Slender and Fit after Thirty* was written to provide the awakening women with a safe and useful program that would help them become fit and slender and *do them no harm.* Their burgeoning interest led to the records 'Keep Fit . . . Be Happy,' 'Fitness for Baby and You,' and the book *Exer-sex.* As interest slowly grew, athletes began to understand the value of pre-season training, . . . so the record 'Fit to Ski' was cut. This was followed by 'Executive Fitness,' so that men, too, would have something *safe* as well as successful to follow, something other than jogging, which had already begun to take its toll. Long before Title IX promised girls equal time in P.E. [physical education] with boys (a promise unfulfilled to this day), I put out the record 'Fitness for Teens.'

"One very important motivator, as far as my later writings are concerned, is pain. Seriously injured as a young skier, I went the usual route taken by people with back pain. In my search, I found two doctors who helped, Dr. Hans Kraus, with whom I wrote several medical papers, and Dr. Janet Travell, the White House physician during the Kennedy Administration. They used injections into an entity called a trigger point to alleviate muscle pain. I worked with doctors for forty years, providing pre- and post-operation exercises as well as special exercises for conditions such as MS [multiple sclerosis], and even pre-season training for Olympic skiers.

"In 1976 I discovered that there was a way to provide the same pain relief, using the same as well as many more trigger points, but without injection. This became known as myotherapy, and I wrote *Pain Erasure the Bonnie Prudden Way* to bring it to the people. By this time the whole nation had fallen into the hands of incompetent providers of 'fitness,' and the need for help for damaged muscles had soared. In addition, the fitness level of children had dropped even further due to TV, the school bus, and a continued lack of exercise. We have been eminently successful with myotherapy and now have a two-year school for people interested in learning the art of non-invasive pain relief that also lasts. The new book *Bonnie Prudden's Guide to Pain-Free Living* [deals with] all our latest discoveries, especially 'Quick Fix,' or how to get rid of a backache, headache, knee pain, bursitis, etc., temporarily but at once.

"The after-fifty crowd has interested me since 1979, when the government took a hand in the fitness programs designed for those over sixty. Too little, too late, and all wrong. Then, when Mt. Sinai Hospital approached me to write the first in their series of books designed to help older Americans, I was delighted. *Anything* would be better than what was out there, and I felt there were many reasons why my work would be very much better indeed. For one thing, I was seventy and, therefore, one of the crowd. I was still an athlete able to conduct fitness workshops five hours a day for a week at a time—for young people. I had had two total hip repacements (that old ski injury finally caught up), but no one would know unless I told them. And, best of all, I hated what those working with older people said we were.

"If I were to give advice to aspiring writers, I would say, live it first, and *then* write about it. Have something of importance to say, and then, for heaven's sake, say it simply. If, by some chance (and I don't believe it's chance at all) you have a bad time in life, figure you had something to learn, and learn it.

Later, it will be grist for your mill, probably indirectly. I'm sure I've been influenced by other writers. I read all the time and everybody. I started to write when I was very small, I really can't say who [my early influences were.] I can say what, however: They were always direct, and they always had something of value to give.

"I am saddened by the current literary scene. I deal with many young people in my school for physical fitness and myotherapy. We always ask what enrolling students read during the year prior to entering the school. Although many already hold degrees from so-called 'good' colleges and universities, they don't read, they can't write, and they find spelling harder than a foreign language, of which most are Greek to them. This is not the fault of the student; it begins at home when children are read to—or not read to. Some day, when I am very old, I shall take up golf and write for the children of parents who care about them."

* * *

PRYCE-JONES, David   1936-

PERSONAL: Indexed in some sources under Jones; born February 15, 1936, in Vienna, Austria; son of Alan (a writer) and Therese (Fould-Springer) Pryce-Jones; married Clarissa Caccia, July 29, 1959; children: Jessica, Candida, Adam. *Education:* Magdalen College, Oxford, B.A., 1959, M.A., 1963. *Address:* c/o A. D. Peters, 10 Buckingham St., London W.C. 2, England. *Agent:* Wallace & Sheil Agency, Inc., 177 East 70th St., New York, N.Y. 10021.

CAREER: Writer. Teacher at writers workshop, University of Iowa, 1964-65, California State College, Hayward (now California State University, Hayward), 1968 and 1970, and University of California, Berkeley, 1972. *Military service:* British Infantry, 1954-56.

WRITINGS—Novels: *Owls and Satyrs,* Longmans, Green, 1960; *The Sands of Summer,* Holt, 1963; *Quondam,* Holt, 1965; *The Stranger's View,* Weidenfeld & Nicolson, 1967, Holt, 1968; *Running Away,* Weidenfeld & Nicolson, 1971; *The England Commune,* Quartet, 1975; *Shirley's Guild,* Weidenfeld & Nicolson, 1979.

Nonfiction: *Graham Greene* (critical study), Oliver & Boyd, 1963; (contributor) M. Sissons and P. French, editors, *The Age of Austerity,* Hodder & Stoughton, 1963; *Next Generation: Travels in Israel,* Weidenfeld & Nicolson, 1964, Holt, 1965; *The Hungarian Revolution* (history), Benn, 1969, Horizon Press, 1970; *The Face of Defeat* (history), Holt, 1972; (editor) *Evelyn Waugh and His World* (essays), Little, Brown, 1973; *Unity Mitford: A Quest* (biography), Weidenfeld & Nicolson, 1976, published as *Unity Mitford: An Enquiry into Her Life and the Frivolity of Evil,* Dial, 1977; *Vienna,* Time-Life, 1978; *Paris in the Third Reich: A History of the German Occupation, 1940-1944,* Holt, 1981; *Cyril Connolly: Journal and Memoir,* Collins, 1983, Ticknor & Fields, 1984.

Translator: G. Prassinos, *The Traveller* (novel), Harvill Press, 1962; M. Rheims, *Art on the Market,* Athenaeum, 1962; Pierre Marsay, *Leaving Standing Still* (novel), Quartet Books, 1977.

Literary editor, *Time and Tide,* 1960-61; drama critic, *Spectator,* 1963-64.

WORK IN PROGRESS: A novel.

SIDELIGHTS: In 1976, just before the appearance of his first work of biography, David Pryce-Jones found himself embroiled in a bitter controversy. Disturbed by a portrait they believed was unfair, the biographee's family at first tried to suppress publication of the book, then (when that tactic failed) set out to discredit it. As Hyam Maccoby recalled in *Commentary,* "All hell broke loose. The English press from the intellectual *Times Literary Supplement* to the popular dailies was filled with recriminations for weeks." The unlikely cause of all this commotion was Unity Mitford, the almost-forgotten member of a well-known family that has made, in the words of Lynn Darling of the *Washington Post,* "one of the more stunning contributions to the lore of English upper-class eccentricity."

One of six sisters, including writers Jessica and Nancy Mitford, Unity Mitford was only nineteen when she traveled to Germany and attended a rally at which Adolf Hitler spoke. It was a case of instant hero-worship, the beginning of "a strange sexless love affair," as Maccoby described it. The tall, blond, Nordic-looking Unity contrived a way to meet her idol in a Munich cafe, and the two soon became friends. From 1935 to 1939, the young Englishwoman was a highly visible member of Hitler's inner circle. She enthusiastically embraced fascism and anti-Semitism and entertained the possibility of one day presiding as empress over a joint German-British Aryan empire. So devoted was she to both her homeland and her adoptive country that she could not bear the thought of a conflict between the two. Consequently, on September 3, 1939, the day Germany and Great Britain issued a mutual declaration of war, twenty-five-year-old Unity Mitford went to a Munich park and shot herself in the head—but without the desired result. After a long convalescence in Germany, the permanently brain-damaged young woman was quietly sent back (via neutral Switzerland) to her family in England, where she lingered on in a kind of half-life until 1948, when the bullet in her head suddenly shifted and killed her.

In the early stages of researching his book on the life of Unity Mitford, Pryce-Jones approached her friends and acquaintances and the surviving members of her family and requested their assistance and cooperation. According to *New York Times Book Review* critic Stephen Koss, the author "received varying degrees of encouragement." Explained Koss: "Nancy graciously welcomed him to her home at Versailles, where she was soon to die, and regaled him with anecdotes, most of which he subsequently 'discovered were set pieces.' Diana, Lady Mosley [wife of Sir Oswald Mosley, founder and head of the British Fascists Union], granted him an interview in her Paris flat, shared recollections and suggested contacts. Jessica . . . was particularly cooperative. Of the surviving members of the family, only Deborah, now Duchess of Devonshire, declined to assist." For the most part, friends of the family were also very willing to talk candidly and at great length about their memories of Unity.

On the eve of the biography's publication, however, the Mitford sisters (especially Diana and Deborah) had second thoughts about the project. In an attempt to suppress and discredit the book, the Mitfords filed a lawsuit. "They declared that the biography was unauthorized, inaccurate, and unfair," reported Noel Annan in the *New York Review of Books.* "They denounced Mr. Pryce-Jones for going around and passing himself off as persona grata with the family, when in fact he was not, and on those grounds inveigling many of Unity's acquaintances to give him information which he then twisted to suit his thesis. When his informants complained and asked to be shown the proofs of what they were alleged to have said, Mr. Pryce-Jones then—so the indictment read—either forgot to send proofs or left in offending passages which he had agreed to delete. His book was tendentious, unimaginative, and insensitive to the tragedy which befell Unity Mitford's parents, and toward the delusion which afflicted and finally destroyed the girl herself.'' The disagreement eventually led to a televised confrontation between Pryce-Jones and Mosley, the Mitford's representative.

After the objections of the Mitford sisters became public, some of the family friends who had talked with Pryce-Jones protested that they had been misrepresented and misquoted. A team of reporters from the London *Sunday Times* investigated this charge (the most serious leveled against the author) and concluded, as Maccoby stated, ''that Pryce-Jones's interviews, as published, were in accordance with the notes he made at the time of the interviews, that he had submitted the written-up interviews to all his interviewees for criticism or comment, and had incorporated any objections in the final version; and that the present retractions of some of the interviewees were made on vague or questionable grounds.''

By this time, the controversy had grown to include not only the principals, but also some of the book reviewers charged with evaluating *Unity Mitford.* (Diana Mosley, Unity's sister, was among those who reviewed the biography; her article appeared in *Books and Bookmen.*) In what Annan termed ''the most dazzling piece of invective'' to appear anywhere, Lord Lambton, commenting in the *Spectator,* first denied there was any need for a full-length study of what he believed was best described as ''an impressionable girl's adoration of the Fuehrer,'' then proceeded to criticize the author's writing ability, insult his father (writer Alan Pryce-Jones), and attack Lord Weidenfeld (of the publishing company Weidenfeld & Nicolson) for defending ''such a shoddy, inaccurate, dull, little book.''

In sharp contrast to this emotional reaction (and others like it) were the more measured observations of those critics who devoted their reviews almost entirely to the issues raised by the biography and the furor surrounding its publication. Most of the debate centered around not only the question raised by Lord Lambton—namely, whether Unity's life warranted such a thorough examination—but also what conclusions could be drawn from her actions and the actions of those who tried so diligently to see to it that the biography was never published.

The Mitfords, for example, argued that Unity had been nothing more than a stage-struck young girl and that Pryce-Jones's treatment of the whole tragic affair had caused them unnecessary pain. Pamela Hansford Johnson more or less concurred with the Mitfords' evaluation of Unity, writing in the *Listener* that the young woman ''was neither strange nor devious, nor, to my mind, interesting. From her early years and debutante days, she appears to have been maladjusted. . . . This entire history of an obsessed girl is less a tragedy than a profound irritant; and the book does nothing to dispel that feeling. . . . [Her life was one of] childish, stony-hearted naughtiness, and little more.''

Commenting in the *New Republic,* Peter Stansky noted that ''Pryce-Jones seems to wish to depict Unity as some sort of rebel, which is to endow her with a kind of historical significance she doesn't deserve: the 'mirror image' of the young men and women on the left in the 1930s. I'm afraid the explanation is simpler and more awful, that she took the anti-Semitism of her family to its extreme, and failed to allow for the paradoxes of English character which frequently combined total beastliness of expression with decency of action.''

Annan agreed that Unity was basically ''an insignificant bit part player in [a] particular act of history'' but dismissed the notion that she had been wronged by her biographer. ''Since the days when they were young,'' observed the reviewer, ''the Mitford sisters have been news; and those who live by the sword of publicity have to accept that if they fall from grace, whether or not deservedly, they will perish by the sword. . . . If you go on the stage, your family cannot object if the critics judge you to have put on a bad act.'' In fact, declared Annan, ''Pryce-Jones can hardly be said to have written the book which the subject deserved''—that is, a book containing a more thorough analysis of Unity's socioeconomic class with its ''aristocratic notion of politics'' that tended to excuse rather than condemn her association with the Nazis.

Koss also found it impossible to sympathize with those who felt Pryce-Jones had been unfair. After pointing out that the author's research ''unearthed materials that his patrons would have preferred to leave in obscurity,'' the critic went on to state: ''It is a measure of [the family's] naivete, indeed their arrogance, to have assumed that a 'fair' portrait of Unity would be an uncritical one. . . . Denied access to Unity's diaries, . . . Pryce-Jones was forced to rely on printed sources. . . . With commendable enterprise, he also traced people who knew Unity.'' Though Koss acknowledged that ''the transcript-like structure of the narrative . . . makes for a good deal of repetition and defies the canons of chronology,'' and that ''some of the author's gibes at the British class system are . . . crude and gratuitous,'' he nevertheless concluded: ''Despite these intrinsic problems—paradoxically even because of them—the cumulative effect is riveting. Admittedly, a vacuum persists at the core of the book. But, as demonstrated conclusively by those who were her acquaintances, and especially by those who remain her apologists, that vacuum was Unity Mitford herself.''

Other critics were not so quick to assign Unity such a minor role in history. In his *New Statesman* review, for instance, David Caute maintained that ''it would be a great mistake to conclude that [Unity] was too insignificant a figure to merit a full-scale biography.'' Caute then proceeded to suggest that her true importance lay in what Stansky, Annan, and Koss only hinted at—the extent to which she reflected the prevailing attitudes of the English upper class. ''Pryce-Jones has borrowed some of the novelist's traditional ammunition and recreated the life-style of an entire class by close attention to detail which may seem deceptively trivial,'' explained the reviewer. ''This class is still with us. It is this class which . . . launched a concerted campaign to suppress the book.''

Maccoby was also convinced that deeply-entrenched prejudices had a major impact on the way Pryce-Jones's biography was received in certain circles. ''The clue that disposes one to think that Unity is after all a figure of some significance is the defensive, almost hysterical, tone of those who took the line that she was not,'' wrote the critic in his review of *Unity Mitford.* ''This seemed to indicate that the exposure of Unity had touched a raw nerve. If Pryce-Jones's book was so trivial, why did they get so upset? The conclusion presented itself that Unity was in some way representative of the English upper class. Her anti-Semitism, though bizarre in its manner of expression, was a faithful image of upper-class anti-Semitism, even though its faithfulness was that of a caricature, which by exaggeration brings out the essential features. . . . Too much of the evidence provided by [the author] shows that Unity Mitford was not quite so freakish and unrepresentative as she has been made out to be.''

In short, concluded Maccoby, "it is these people Mr. Pryce-Jones is telling us about in his excellent study, in which he approaches his subject in the spirit of a dedicated field-working anthropologist. His book is not just about Unity Mitford. It is about the class to which she belonged, and that is why it aroused such passions."

BIOGRAPHICAL/CRITICAL SOURCES: Books and Bookmen, November, 1976, September, 1979; *Listener,* November 11, 1976; *New Statesman,* November 12, 1976, July 20, 1979; *Economist,* November 13, 1976; *Spectator,* November 13, 1976, September 1, 1979, November 21, 1981; *Times Literary Supplement,* November 26, 1976, November 6, 1981, July 8, 1983; *Encounter,* February, 1977; *New York Times Book Review,* May 8, 1977, September 27, 1981; *Washington Post Book World,* May 8, 1977, March 25, 1984; *New York Review of Books,* May 12, 1977; *Newsweek,* May 30, 1977; *Saturday Review,* June 25, 1977; *Commentary,* July, 1977, January, 1982; *New Republic,* August 20, 1977; *National Review,* September 16, 1977; *Washington Post,* May 14, 1979, June 6, 1979; *New Yorker,* January 15, 1982; *Progressive,* June, 1982; *Times* (London), July 14, 1983; *New York Times,* March 24, 1984; *Los Angeles Times Book Review,* July 8, 1984.

—*Sketch by Deborah A. Straub*

R

RACHLEFF, Owen S(pencer) 1934-

PERSONAL: Surname is pronounced *Rack*-leff; born July 16, 1934, in New York, N.Y.; son of Harold Kirman (a banker) and Theresa (Friedman) Rachleff. *Education:* Columbia University, B.F.A., 1956; University of London, M.A., 1958. *Home:* 135 East 71st St., New York, N.Y. 10021.

CAREER: Writer. Harry N. Abrams, Inc. (publisher), New York City, house writer and editor, 1963-67; American Heritage Publishing Co., New York City, staff writer and editor, 1967-68; teacher at New School for Social Research, beginning 1968; New York University, New York City, assistant professor of humanities, 1968-74; Hofstra University, adjunct assistant professor, 1972-78.

Professional actor, 1975—, appearing in Off-Broadway productions, including "Catsplay," 1978, "The Lesson," 1978, "Arms and the Man," 1980, "Waltz of the Toreadors," 1980, "Escoffier: King of Chefs," 1981, 1982, 1983, 1984, "A New Way to Pay Old Debts," 1983; appeared in films "The Dain Curse," 1977, "A Question of Honor," 1981, and on television in series "The Bloodhound Gang," Public Brodcasting Service, and soap opera "All My Children," American Broadcasting Companies, Inc., 1980.

MEMBER: Actors Equity Association, Screen Actors Guild, American Federation Television and Radio Artists, Dramatists Guild, Authors League.

AWARDS, HONORS: MacDowell Colony fellowship, 1965; A.B.A. White House Selection, 1970.

WRITINGS: Rembrandt's Life of Christ, Abradale Press, 1966; *Young Israel: A History of the Modern Nation,* Lion Press, 1968; *Great Bible Stories and Master Paintings: A Complete Narration of the Old and New Testaments,* Abrams, 1968; *An Illustrated Treasury of Bible Stories,* Abradale Press, 1970; *The Occult Conceit: A New Look at Astrology, Witchcraft and Sorcery,* Cowles Book Co., 1971; *The Magic of Love,* C. R. Gibson, 1972; *Sky Diamonds: The New Astrology,* illustrations by Robert Rappaport, Hawthorn, 1973; *The Secrets of Superstitions: How They Help and How They Hurt,* Doubleday, 1976; *Exploring the Bible,* Abbeville Press, 1980; *Eric's Image* (novel), Tower Books, 1982; *The Occult in Art,* Alpine, 1984. Film and theatre critic, *Midstream* magazine, 1972-77.

Plays: "Cain," produced in St. Petersburg, Florida, 1965; "Javelin," produced Off-Broadway, 1966; "From the Classifieds," produced Off-Broadway, 1970; "Uncle Money," produced Off-Broadway, 1980; *Escoffier: King of Chefs* (first produced at St. Clement's Theatre in New York City, 1981), Broadway Play Publishng Co., 1983; (adaptor) "Tosca 1943," based on the play "La Tosca," by Victorien Sardou, produced Off-Broadway, 1984.

WORK IN PROGRESS: A book, *The Theatre in Art,* for Alpine Fine Arts; "The Fabulous Fontaine," a musical play.

* * *

RACHLIN, Nahid

PERSONAL: Born in Abadan, Iran; came to the United States in 1962, naturalized citizen, 1969; daughter of Manoochehr (a lawyer) and Mohtaram Bozorgmehri; married Howard Rachlin (a professor of psychology); children: Leila. *Education:* Lindenwood College, B.A. *Home:* 501 East 87th St., New York, N.Y. 10028. *Agent:* Harriet Wasserman, 230 East 48th St., New York, N.Y. 10017.

CAREER: Writer. Research assistant, Children's Hospital, Boston, Mass., 1968-69; adjunct assistant professor of creative writing, Continuing Education Division, New York University, 1979—.

AWARDS, HONORS: Bennett Cerf Award from Columbia University, 1974, for short story, "Ruins"; Doubleday-Columbia fellowship for creative writing, 1974-75; Wallace Stegner fellowship, 1975-76; National Endowment for the Arts fiction grant, 1979; P.E.N. syndicated fiction project prize, 1983.

WRITINGS: Foreigner (novel), Norton, 1978; *Married to a Stranger,* Dutton, 1983. Contributor of stories to popular magazines and literary journals, including *Redbook, Shenandoah, Four Quarters, Confrontation,* and *Aratat.*

WORK IN PROGRESS: A novel, tentatively entitled *Dump-View Acres.*

SIDELIGHTS: Nahid Rachlin comments: "I have always written fiction rather than nonfiction because I feel that only fiction can convey the complexity of character and situation that I see around me. I think that the purpose of fiction in society is to provide models for alternate courses of life—not so much as a guide for action but as a vehicle for understanding people. *Foreigner,* my first published novel, for instance, seems autobiographical because of many parallels in the protagonist's life and my own life (a young woman coming to the U.S., marrying an American and then returning home for a visit).

"The same with my second novel, *Married to a Stranger,* which is about a young woman in Iran, yearning to break through the rigid traditions around her." According to Barbara Thompson in the *New York Times Book Review,* "Rachlin captures the range of forces that were brought to bear on personal relationships in the changing political and social setting of the last years of Shah Mohammed Reza Pahlevi's reign. She shows us not only the tranquil inner courtyards with sweets and gossip exchanged by the fishpond, the flower bedecked bridal chamber, but also the political, social and religious factions contending for primacy in the streets outside." Carolyn See describes it as "a woman's novel in a very particular sense," in the *Los Angeles Times.* "The reader has the feeling that these are the facts, ma'am; perhaps the real facts of one ordinary relationship, matter-of-factly described against the larger background of a country ripped by war and revolution. But it's the single human beings who are important here; that is, perhaps, what makes it a woman's novel."

BIOGRAPHICAL/CRITICAL SOURCES: Los Angeles Times, September 16, 1983; *New York Times Book Review,* October 2, 1983.

* * *

RADYR, Tomos
    See HALDANE-STEVENSON, James Patrick

* * *

RAMKE, Bin   1947-

PERSONAL: Born February 19, 1947, in Port Neches, Tex.; son of Lloyd Binford (an engineer) and Melba (Guidry) Ramke; married Linda Keating (a textiles artist), May 31, 1967. *Education:* Louisiana State University, B.A., 1970; University of New Orleans, M.A., 1971; Ohio University, Ph.D., 1975. *Politics:* "Only among close friends." *Religion:* "Poetry." *Home:* 2020 South Monroe, Denver, Colo. 80210. *Office:* Department of English, University of Denver, Denver, Colo. 80208.

CAREER: Columbus College, Columbus, Ga., assistant professor of English, beginning 1975; currently associate professor of English, University of Denver, Denver, Colo.

MEMBER: Modern Language Association of America, P.E.N., Associated Writing Programs.

AWARDS, HONORS: Yale Younger Poets Award from Yale University Press, 1977, for *The Difference between Night and Day.*

WRITINGS: Any Brass Ring (poetry chapbook), Ohio Review, 1977; *The Difference between Night and Day* (poems), Yale University Press, 1978; *White Monkeys* (poems), University of Georgia Press, 1984. Assistant editor of *Ohio Review,* 1973-75.

WORK IN PROGRESS: The Cats of Balthus.

SIDELIGHTS: "In *The Difference between Night and Day,* Bin Ramke shows an unusual maturity in both vision and technique," says Peter Stitt in the *Georgia Review.* A critic for the *New York Times Book Review,* however, feels that "Ramke's

poems embody many of the strengths and failings brought to mind by the phrase 'younger poet': he has a rich imagination, and he often overspends it wastefully." Stitt perceives the matter differently, insisting "his manipulation of images and figures of speech gives his poems a striking density of texture and complexity of theme." In addition, Stitt believes Ramke's "command of the formal elements of verse is truly impressive—his strong supple rhythms reflect the movement our poets have recently made away from, up from, the plain style." He concludes: "Bin Ramke is a poet of very large talent."

Describing the course of his writings, Ramke told *CA:* "My early interest and training was in mathematics and physics. Curiously, my movement away from those disciplines ten years ago paralleled the major movements *within* them during the same time—toward cosmology, toward the large unanswerable, the first and last questions: toward a concern for a *logos.* I still admire accuracy, discipline, precision, and seek those qualities in my own work. And yet *The Difference between Night and Day* is a book about where to stand, not in order to move the world, but to be moved by it. I still stand, if not by, at least in the vicinity of [this] book, but have moved more, in my third book, into *personae,* more interesting, more outrageous, versions of myself. And since the death of my father, my work has become a quarrel with him, an *apologia.*"

BIOGRAPHICAL/CRITICAL SOURCES: Times Literary Supplement, October 20, 1978; *New York Times Book Review,* November 12, 1978; *Georgia Review,* fall, 1978.

* * *

RAMSEY, (Arthur) Michael   1904-

PERSONAL: Born November 14, 1904, in England; son of Arthur Stanley (a mathematics don at Cambridge University) and Agnes (Wilson) Ramsey; married Joan Alice Hamilton, April 8, 1942. *Education:* Cambridge University, B.A., 1927, M.A., 1930, B.D., 1950; also attended Cuddesdon Theological College. *Home:* 16 South Bailey, Durham England.

CAREER: Ordained deacon in Church of England, 1928, and priest, 1929; Church of St. Nicholas, Liverpool, England, curate, 1928-30; subwarden, Lincoln Theological College, 1930-36; Boston Parish Church, Lincolnshire, England, lecturer, 1936-38; St. Benedict's Church, Cambridge, England, vicar, 1938-40; University of Durham, Durham, England, Van Mildert Professor of Divinity, 1940-50; Cambridge University, Cambridge, Regius Professor of Divinity and fellow of Magdalene College, 1950-52; bishop of Durham, 1952-56; archbishop of York, 1956-61; archbishop of Canterbury, 1961-74. Examining chaplain to bishop of Chester, 1932-39. Select preacher to Cambridge University, 1934, 1940, 1948; canon, Durham Cathedral, 1940-50; select preacher to Oxford University, 1945-46; canon of Caistor and prebendary, Lincoln Cathedral, 1951-52; Hulsean Preacher, Cambridge University, 1969-70. Trustee of British Museum, 1963-69. *Member:* World Council of Churches (president, 1961-68), Cambridge Union (president, 1926).

AWARDS, HONORS: Doctorate in divinity from University of Durham, 1951, University of Edinburgh, University of Leeds, University of Hull, and Cambridge University, all 1957, Victoria University of Manchester, 1961, and University of London, 1962; honorary fellow of Magdalene College, Cambridge University, 1952—, Merton College, Oxford University, 1974—, and Keble College, Oxford University, 1975—; D.Cl. from Oxford University, 1960, and University of Kent, 1966; honorary master of the bench, Inner Temple, 1962; D.Litt. from University of Keele, 1967.

WRITINGS: The Gospel and the Catholic Church, Longmans, Green, 1936; *The Resurrection of Christ,* Presbyterian Board of Christian Education, 1946; *The Glory of God and the Transfiguration of Christ,* Longmans, Green, 1949; *F. D. Maurice and the Conflicts of Modern Theology,* Cambridge University Press, 1951; *Durham Essays and Addresses,* S.P.C.K., 1956.

An Era of Anglican Theology, Scribner, 1960; *Oratory and Literature,* English Association, 1960; *Introducing the Christian Faith,* S.C.M.P., 1961; *Unity, Truth, and Holiness,* Fellowship of St. Alban and St. Serbius, 1961; *The Narratives of the Passion,* Mowbray, 1962; *Christianity and the Supernatural,* Althone, 1963; *Image Old and New: On the Problem of Finding New Ways to State Old Truths,* Forward Movement, 1963; *Canterbury Essays and Addresses,* Seabury, 1964; *Beyond Religion?,* S.P.C.K., 1964; *Christ Crucified, for the World,* Mowbray, 1964; *Sacred and Secular: A Study in the Other Worldly and This Worldly Aspects of Christianity,* Longmans, Green, 1965; *The Meaning of Prayer,* Morehouse, 1965; *Problems of Christian Belief,* BBC Publications, 1966; *God, Christ, and the World: A Study in Contemporary Theology,* Morehouse, 1969.

(With Leon-Joseph Cardinal Suenens) *The Future of the Christian Church,* Morehouse, 1970; *The Christian Priest Today,* S.P.C.K., 1972; (with Robert E. Terwillizer and A. M. Allchin) *The Charismatic Christ,* Morehouse, 1973; *Canterbury Pilgrim,* S.P.C.K., 1974; (with others) *Come Holy Spirit,* Morehouse, 1976; *Holy Spirit,* S.P.C.K., 1977; *Jesus and the Living Past,* Oxford University Press, 1980; *Be Still and Know,* Collins, 1982.

SIDELIGHTS: When Michael Ramsey succeeded to the episcopacy of York in 1956, many feared that his Anglo-Catholicism would prove a threat to Christian reunion, according to a *Newsweek* writer. But he retired as Archbishop of Canterbury, eighteen years later, "to a chorus of nearly unqualified praise—including comparisons with such giants of English ecclesiastical history as Saint Anselm and Thomas a Becket." The *Newsweek* writer continues: "In a fitting farewell to Ramsey's episcopacy, the House of Commons . . . approved a reform that he has been advocating since becoming Primate—the granting of ecclesiastical affairs to the Church of England. The church's historic ties with the state will remain. The Queen is still its Supreme Governor and the Prime Minister will continue to appoint its bishops. But Church officials may now reform doctrine and liturgy without approval from . . . Parliament."

One of Ramsey's dreams was to see Anglican reconciliation with Roman Catholicism. He helped further that cause in 1966 when he became the first Archbishop of Canterbury to officially visit Rome, exchanging a "kiss of peace" with Pope Paul VI.

In his writings, Ramsey has been less conciliatory. For example, in "The Menace of Fundamentalism," an article published in 1956, Ramsey attacks fundamentalism as heretical, singling out American evangelist Billy Graham as a preacher of the "grossest doctrines." Most of Ramsey's full-length works, however, have been either studies of the New Testament or broad expositions of Christian doctrine. Of his own perception of God, Ramsey says, "I enjoy Him. I think about Him, tell Him of my worries."

BIOGRAPHICAL/CRITICAL SOURCES: J. B. Simpson, *The Hundredth Archbishop of Canterbury,* Harper, 1960; *Newsweek,* December 16, 1974.

RANDALL, Diane
    See ROSS, W(illiam) E(dward) D(aniel)

*   *   *

RANDOLPH, Arthur C.
    See GREENE, A(lvin) C(arl)

*   *   *

RANDOLPH, Ellen
    See ROSS, W(illiam) E(dward) D(aniel)

*   *   *

RAWLS, Philip
    See LEVINSON, Leonard

*   *   *

REICH, Bernard   1941-

PERSONAL: Born December 5, 1941, in Brooklyn, N.Y.; son of Moe and Rosalyn (Hartglass) Reich; married Madelyn Sue Ingber, June 16, 1963; children: Barry, Norman, Michael, Jennifer. *Education:* City College of the City University of New York, B.A. (cum laude), 1961; University of Virginia, M.A., 1963, Ph.D., 1964. *Religion:* Jewish. *Home:* 13800 Turnmore Rd., Wheaton, Md. 20906. *Office:* Department of Political Science, George Washington University, Washington, D.C. 20052.

CAREER: George Washington University, Washington, D.C., assistant professor, 1964-67, 1968-70, associate professor, 1970-76, professor of political science and international affairs, 1976—, head of department of political science, 1976-82.

Visiting assistant professor at University of Virginia, spring, 1969; visiting professor at Baltimore Hebrew College, 1975-78. Member of adjunct faculty at U.S. Defense Intelligence School, 1975—; professorial lecturer at Johns Hopkins University, 1978-80; chairperson of Middle East studies at Foreign Service Institute, U.S. Department of State, 1979—; adjunct professor at Defense Institute of Security Assistance Management, 1983—; lecturer at National War College, Foreign Service Institute, U.S. Military Academy, U.S. Naval Academy, Inter-American Defense College, and foreign colleges and universities. Visiting research associate at Tel Aviv University, 1971-72. Participant in international seminars; testified before U.S. Congress; member of advisory council, International Security Studies Program, Woodrow Wilson International Center for Scholars, 1982—; senior advisor, Frost and Sullivan Country Consultation Service, 1983—; consultant to U.S. Department of State and Research Analysis Corp.

MEMBER: International Institute for Strategic Studies, Middle East Institute, Middle East Studies Association (fellow), Phi Beta Kappa, Delta Phi Epsilon (honorary member).

AWARDS, HONORS: Fulbright grant for study in Egypt, summer, 1965; National Science Foundation fellowship for study in Israel, 1971-72; American specialist grant, U.S. Department of State, 1978; American participant grant, U.S. International Communication Agency, 1978-79, 1980, 1981, 1982, 1983, and 1984; special travel grant, International Research and Exchanges Board, 1984.

WRITINGS: Crisis in the Middle East, 1967: Implications for U.S. Policy, Research Analysis Corp., 1968, revised edition published as *Background of the June War,* 1968; (co-author) *A Strategic Appraisal of the Middle East: Eastern Arab States and Israel,* Research Analysis Corp., 1968, revised edition published as *Israel and the Eastern Arab States: A Strategic Source Book,* 1968; *The Cyprus Problem,* Research Analysis Corp., 1969.

(Co-author) *The Persian Gulf: Implications for U.S. Security Policy,* Research Analysis Corp., 1970, revised edition published as *Persian Gulf,* 1971; *The United States and the Northern Tier: Some Problems of Security and Defense Policy in Turkey and Iran,* Research Analysis Corp., 1971; *Israel in Paperback* (bibliography), Middle East Studies Association, 1971; *Israel and the Occupied Territories,* U.S. Department of State, 1974; (with Arnon Gutfeld) *Arzot Habrit Vehasechsuch Yisraeli-Aravi* (title means "The United States and the Israeli-Arab Conflict"), Maarachot (Tel Aviv), 1977; *Quest for Peace: United States-Israel Relations and the Arab-Israeli Conflict,* Transaction Books, 1977.

(Editor with David Long, author of introduction, and contributor) *Government and Politics of the Middle East and North Africa,* Westview, 1980; *United States Middle East Policy in the Carter and Reagan Administrations,* Graduate School of International Studies, University of Miami, 1984; *The United States and Israel: Influence in the Special Relationship,* Praeger, 1984; *Israel: A Political Profile,* Westview, 1984. Also author of technical reports.

Contributor: Tareq Ismael, editor, *Governments and Politics of the Contemporary Middle East,* Dorsey, 1970; Howard R. Penniman, editor, *Israel at the Polls: The Knesset Elections of 1977,* American Enterprise Institute for Public Policy Research, 1979; Robert O. Freedman, editor, *World Politics and the Arab-Israeli Conflict,* Pergamon, 1979.

Economic Consequences of the Revolution in Iran, Joint Economic Committee, U.S. Congress, 1980; *The Political Economy of the Middle East: 1973-1978,* Joint Economic Committee, U.S. Congress, 1980; *The Middle East and the United States: Perceptions and Policies,* Transaction Books, 1980; Edward A. Kolodziej and Robert E. Harkavy, editors, *Security Policies of Developing Countries,* Lexington Book, 1982; Richard Dean Burns, editor, *Guide to American Foreign Relations since 1700,* American Bibliographical Center-Clio Press, 1983; George E. Delury, editor, *World Encyclopedia of Political Systems and Parties,* two volumes, Facts on File, 1983; G. R. Berridge and A. Jennings, editors, *The United Nations, Power Politics and Diplomacy,* Macmillan (London), 1984; Paul Marantz and Janice Gross Stein, editors, *Peacemaking in the Middle East: Problems and Prospects,* Croom Helm, 1984; Penniman and Daniel Elazar, editors, *Israel at the Polls, 1981,* Indiana University Press, 1984.

Contributor to *Yearbook on International Communist Affairs, Concise Encyclopedia of the Middle East,* and *Collier's Year Book;* also contributor of numerous articles to political science and international affairs journals.

Editor, "Nations of the Contemporary Middle East" series, Westview. Member of board of advisory editors of *Middle East Journal,* 1977—. Consulting editor of *New Middle East,* 1971-73.

WORK IN PROGRESS: Articles and chapters for several books on United States-Middle East policy and on Israeli politics.

SIDELIGHTS: Bernard Reich has toured the Middle East and North Africa as a guest of the governments of Saudia Arabia, Egypt, and Morocco, and the Soviet Union as a guest of the U.S.S.R. Academy of Sciences.

Reich's writing has been translated into Hebrew.

*   *   *

REID, Sue Titus   1939-

PERSONAL: Born November 13, 1939, in Bryan, Tex.; daughter of Andrew Jackson, Jr. and Lorraine (Wylie) Titus. *Education:* Texas Woman's University, B.S. (with honors), 1960; University of Missouri, M.A., 1962; University of Iowa, J.D., 1972. *Office:* College of Law, University of Tulsa, 3120 East Fourth Pl., Tulsa, Okla. 74104.

CAREER: Cornell College, Mount Vernon, Iowa, instructor, 1963-65, assistant professor, 1965-69, associate professor of sociology, 1969-72, acting chairman of department, 1969-72; admitted to Iowa State Bar, 1972; Coe College, Cedar Rapids, Iowa, associate professor of sociology and chairman of department, 1972-74; University of Washington, School of Law, Seattle, associate professor, 1974-78; University of Tulsa, College of Law, Tulsa, Okla., professor of law, 1978—. Visiting summer professor, University of Nebraska, 1970; visiting distinguished professor of law and sociology, University of Tulsa, 1977-78; visiting professor, University of San Diego School of Law, 1981-82; George Beto Professor of Criminal Justice, Sam Houston State University, 1984-85. Executive associate, American Sociological Association, 1976-77.

MEMBER: American Sociological Association, American Society of Criminology, American Bar Association, Midwest Sociological Society (member, board of directors, 1970-72), Iowa Bar Association.

WRITINGS: Crime and Criminology, Dryden, 1976, 4th edition, 1985; (editor with David L. Lyon) *Population Crisis: An Interdisciplinary Perspective,* Scott, Foresman, 1976; *The Correctional System: An Introduction,* Holt, 1981; (contributor with Lorna Keltner) *Encyclopedia of Crime and Justice,* Macmillan, 1984; (with Keltner) *Criminal Justice,* Holt, 1985.

*   *   *

REIMAN, Donald H(enry)   1934-

PERSONAL: Born May 17, 1934, in Erie, Pa.; son of Henry Ward (a teacher) and Mildred A. (a teacher; maiden name, Pearce) Reiman; married Mary Warner (a rare book restorer and conservator), September 21, 1958 (divorced); married Helene Dworzan (a writer and teacher), October 3, 1975; children: (first marriage) Laurel Elizabeth. *Education:* College of Wooster, B.A., 1956; University of Illinois, M.A., 1957, Ph.D., 1960. *Politics:* Democrat. *Religion:* Presbyterian. *Home:* 6495 Broadway, Bronx, N.Y. 10471. *Office:* Carl H. Pforzheimer Library, Room 815, 41 East 42nd St., New York, N.Y. 10017.

CAREER: Duke University, Durham, N.C., instructor, 1960-62, assistant professor of English, 1962-64; University of Wisconsin—Milwaukee, associate professor of English, 1964-65; Carl H. Pforzheimer Library, New York, N.Y., editor of *Shelley and his Circle,* 1965—. Adjunct professor of English, City University of New York, 1967-68; adjunct professor of English and senior research associate, Columbia University, 1969-74; visiting professor of English, St. Johns University, 1974-75; and University of Washington, 1981.

MEMBER: Modern Humanities Research Association, Modern Language Association of America, Keats-Shelley Association of America (treasurer, 1973—), Charles Lamb Society, Byron Society, Wordsworth-Coleridge Association, Society for Textual Scholarship, Association for Documentary Evidence, Bibliographical Society of America, English Institute, American Association of University Professors, Common Cause, Phi Beta Kappa, Phi Kappa Phi.

AWARDS, HONORS: American Council of Learned Societies grant, 1961-62, study fellow, 1963-64; associate fellow, Center for Advanced Study, Wesleyan University, 1963-64; National Endowment for the Humanities summer stipend, 1978; Litt.D., College of Wooster, 1981.

WRITINGS: Shelley's "Triumph of Life": A Critical Study, University of Illinois Press, 1965; *Percy Bysshe Shelley,* Twayne, 1968; (editor) *Shelley and his Circle,* Harvard University Press, Volumes V-VI, 1973, Volumes VII-VIII, 1984; (editor) *The Romantics Reviewed,* nine volumes, Garland Publishing, 1972; (with Doucet Devin Fischer) *Byron on the Continent,* New York Public Library, 1974; (editor) *The Romantic Context: Poetry,* 128 volumes, Garland Publishing, 1976-79; (with Sharon B. Powers) *Shelley's Poetry and Prose,* Norton, 1977; *English Romantic Poetry, 1800-1835,* Gale, 1979; (editor) *The Manuscripts of the Younger Romantics,* Volumes I-XI, Garland Publishing, 1984; (editor) *The Bodleian Shelley Manuscripts: A Facsimile Edition, with Full Transcriptions and Scholarly Apparatus,* Volume I, Garland Publishing, 1984.

Contributor: Frank Jordan, editor, *The English Romantic Poets: A Review of Research and Criticism,* 3rd revised edition (Reiman was not associated with earlier editions), Modern Language Association of America, 1972; John D. Baird, editor, *Editing Texts of the Romantic Period,* Hakkert (Toronto), 1972; M. H. Abrams, editor, *Norton Anthology of English Literature,* Norton, 1974; (and editor with others) *The Evidence of the Imagination,* New York University Press, 1978.

Also contributor to *The Reader's Encyclopedia of English Literature, New Catholic Encyclopedia,* and *Encyclopedia Americana.* Contributor of over eighty articles and reviews on English and American literature to scholarly journals. Member of editorial board, *Keats-Shelley Journal,* 1968-73, *PMLA,* 1969-70; member of advisory board, *Milton and the Romantics,* 1975-80, *Studies in Romanticism,* 1977—, *Romanticism Past and Present,* 1980—.

WORK IN PROGRESS: Intervals of Inspiration: Skepticism and the Psychology of Romanticism, essays on most of the major English Romantics; essays on the poetry of A. R. Ammons and on other contemporary American poets; an essay on the interrelations of real and fictional fathers and daughters during the English Romantic period; a series of responses to lectures by major literary theorists under the general title *Romanticism and Contemporary Criticism;* a book under the working title *The Sociology of Romantic Poetry,* based in part on *The Romantic Context: Poetry;* Volumes IX-XII of *Shelley and His Circle.*

SIDELIGHTS: Donald H. Reiman told *CA:* "Beginning my scholarly career with a dissertation on one poem by Shelley, I have worked outward by employing the same techniques to literary works in other areas. I try to be eclectic in my approach, giving attention to textual problems, historical and biographical background, philosophical presuppositions underlying the work of art, and aesthetic problems of formal integrity, symbolism, and prosody. I hope ultimately to publish studies of major

British and American poets from Chaucer and Shakespeare through the post-Modernists."

*   *   *

RENAN, Sheldon (Jackson) 1941-

PERSONAL: Born June 29, 1941, in Portland, Ore.; son of George Donald (owner of a food distributing firm) and Louise (Esterly) Renan; married Barbara Stross (an educational consultant), March 14, 1966 (divorced); children: George, Ingrid, Lisa. *Education:* Yale University, B.A., 1963. *Home:* 1528 Franklin St., Santa Monica, Calif. 90404.

CAREER: Advertising copywriter in New York, San Francisco, and Tokyo, 1964-68; University of California Art Museum, Berkeley, director of film programs, 1968-70, director of Pacific Film Archive, 1971-74; became producer for Public Broadcasting Service; film and television producer and director, Renan Group, 1975—. Member of junior council, Museum of Modern Art, New York, N.Y., 1965-66.

WRITINGS: An Introduction to the American Underground Film, Dutton, 1967 (published in England as *The Underground Film: An Introduction to Its Development in America,* Studio Vista, 1969); *I Am Joe's Eye* (also see below), Reader's Digest, 1983; *Treasure* (also see below), Warner Books, 1984.

Screenplays; self-produced and directed; distributed by Pyramid, except as indicated: "Basic Film Terms," 1970; "Basic Television Terms: A Video Dictionary," 1976; "The Electronic Rainbow: An Introduction to Television," 1977; "Burn Emergency," 1977; "Eye Emergency," 1978; "I Am Joe's Eye," 1983; (with J. David Wyles) "Treasure," distributed by Vestron, 1984.

Television series; self-produced for Public Television Service, 1975: (With Edwin O. Reischauer and Donald Richie) "The Japanese Film"; "The International Animation Festival."

Also author of film scripts for commercial shorts and film criticism. Contributor of short stories to literary magazines, and articles to periodicals, including *Film Culture, Art Voices,* and *San Francisco Magazine.*

SIDELIGHTS: Sheldon Renan has lived in Japan for a total of twelve months over a six year period.

BIOGRAPHICAL/CRITICAL SOURCES: Observer Review, July 7, 1968.

*   *   *

RENAULT, Rick
See WALLMANN, Jeffrey M(iner)

*   *   *

RESKIND, John
See WALLMANN, Jeffrey M(iner)

*   *   *

REXROTH, Kenneth 1905-1982

PERSONAL: Born December 22, 1905, in South Bend, Ind.; moved to Chicago, Ill., at the age of twelve; died June 6, 1982, in Montecito, Calif., of a heart ailment; son of Charles Marion (a wholesale druggist) and Delia (Reed) Rexroth; married Andre Deutcher, 1927 (died, 1940); married Marie Kass, 1940 (divorced, 1948); married Marthe Larsen, 1949 (divorced, 1961); married Carol Tinker (a poet), 1974; children: (by third marriage) Mary, Katharine. *Education:* Attended the Chicago Art Institute and the Art Students League, New York, N.Y.; largely self-educated. *Politics:* None.

CAREER: Poet, translator, playwright, essayist, and painter. Worked as mucker, harvest hand, packer, fruit picker, forest patrolman, factory hand, and attendant in a mental institution. Held one-man art shows in Los Angeles, Santa Monica, New York, Chicago, Paris, and San Francisco. *The Nation,* San Francisco correspondent, beginning 1953. Co-founder of the San Francisco Poetry Center; columnist for the *San Francisco Examiner.* Taught at various universities, including San Francisco State University, University of California, Santa Barbara, and University of Wisconsin—Milwaukee. Lectured and gave poetry readings throughout the world. *Military service:* Conscientious objector.

MEMBER: National Institute of Arts and Letters.

AWARDS, HONORS: California Literature Silver Medal Award for poetry, 1941, for *In What Hour,* 1945, for *The Phoenix and the Tortoise,* and 1980, for *The Morning Star;* Guggenheim fellowship in poetry, 1948 and 1949; Eunice Teitjens Award, 1957; Shelley Memorial Award, 1958; Amy Lowell fellowship, 1958; Longview Award; Chapelbrook Award; National Institute of Arts and Letters grant, 1964; Rockefeller grant, 1967; Akademische Austausdienfp, 1967; Academy of American Poets' Copernicus Award, 1975.

WRITINGS: (Contributor) Louis Zukofsky, *Objectivists Anthology,* Humphries, 1932; *In What Hour* (poetry), Macmillan, 1940; *The Phoenix and the Tortoise* (poetry), New Directions, 1944; *The Art of Wordly Wisdom* (poetry), Decker Press, 1949.

The Signature of All Things: Poems, Songs, Elegies, Translations, and Epigrams, New Directions, 1950; *Beyond the Mountains* (verse plays; produced in New York at Cherry Lane Theatre, December 30, 1951), New Directions, 1951, reprinted, 1974; *The Dragon and the Unicorn* (poetry; originally published in part in *New Directions Annual,* 1950-51), New Directions, 1952; *Thou Shalt Not Kill* (poetry), Good Press, c. 1955; *In Defense of the Earth* (poetry), New Directions, 1956.

The Homestead Called Damascus (poem; first published in *Quarterly Review of Literature,* 1957), New Directions, 1963; *Natural Numbers: New and Selected Poems,* New Directions, 1963; (contributor) William Arrowsmith and Roger Shattuck, editors, *The Craft and Context of Translation,* Doubleday, 1964; *An Autobiographical Novel,* Doubleday, 1966; *The Collected Shorter Poems of Kenneth Rexroth,* New Directions, 1967; (contributor) *Penguin Modern Poets 9,* Penguin, 1967; *The Heart's Garden, the Garden's Heart* (poems and calligraphic designs), Pym-Randall Press, 1967; *Collected Longer Poems of Kenneth Rexroth,* New Directions, 1968; *The Spark in the Tender of Knowing* (poetry), Pym-Randall, 1968.

Sky Sea Birds Tree Earth House Beasts Flowers, Unicorn Press, 1971; *American Poetry: In the Twentieth Century* (essays), Herder, 1971; *The Rexroth Reader,* edited and with a foreword by Eric Mottram, Cape, 1972; *New Poems,* New Directions, 1974; *The Silver Swan: Poems Written in Kyoto, 1974-75* (also see below), Copper Canyon Press, 1976; *On Flower Wreath Hill* (poem; also see below), Blackfish Press, 1976; *The Morning Star* (includes *The Silver Swan, On Flower Wreath Hill,* and *The Love Songs of Marichiko*), New Directions, 1979;

Saucy Limericks and Christmas Cheer, Bradford-Morrow, 1980; *Selected Poems,* New Directions, 1984.

Essays: *Bird in the Bush: Obvious Essays,* New Directions, 1959; *Assays,* New Directions, 1962; *Classics Revisited,* Quadrangle Books, 1968; *The Alternative Society: Essays from the Other World,* Herder, 1970; *With Eye and Ear,* Herder, 1970; *The Elastic Retort: Essays in Literature and Ideas,* Seabury, 1973; *Communalism: From Its Origin to the Twentieth Century,* Seabury, 1974.

Editor: (And author of introduction) D. H. Lawrence, *Selected Poems,* New Directions, 1948; *New British Poets: An Anthology,* New Directions, 1949; *Fourteen Poems of O. V. de Lubicz-Milosz,* Peregrine Press, 1952; (and translator) *One Hundred Poems from the Japanese,* New Directions, 1955.

(And translator with Ling O. Chung) *The Orchid Boat: Women Poets of China,* Herder, 1972; Czeslav Milosz, *The Selected Poems of Czeslav Milosz,* Seabury, 1973; David Meltzer, *Tens: Selected Poems, 1961-71,* McGraw, 1973; (and author of introduction) Jessica Tarahata Hagedorn and others, *Four Young Women: Poems,* McGraw, 1973; (and translator) *One Hundred More Poems from the Japanese,* New Directions, 1974; *The Buddhist Writings of Lafcadio Hearn,* Ross-Erikson, 1977; (and translator with Ikuko Atsumi) *The Burning Heart: The Women Poets of Japan,* Seabury, 1977; (and author of introduction and translator with Atsumi) Kazuko Shiraishi, *Seasons of Sacred Lust—Selected Poems,* New Directions, 1978.

Translator: *One Hundred Poems from the French,* Jargon, 1955, reprinted, Pym-Randall, 1970; *One Hundred Poems from the Chinese,* New Directions, 1956; *Thirty Spanish Poems of Love and Exile,* City Lights, 1956, reprinted, Kraus Reprint, 1973; (and author of introduction) *Poems from the Greek Anthology,* University of Michigan Press, 1962; Pierre Reverdy, *Selected Poems,* New Directions, 1969; *Love and the Turning Year: 100 More Chinese Poems,* New Directions, 1970; (with Chung) *Li Ch'ing Chao: The Complete Poems,* New Directions, 1979.

Also author of shorter works of poetry, including broadsides and "Lament for Dylan Thomas," c. 1955, and "As the Full Moon Rises," published by Old Marble Press; author of autobiographical work *Excerpts from a Short Life,* 1981. Contributor of poetry, translations, essays, and criticism to numerous popular and academic periodicals.

SIDELIGHTS: In a reminiscence written for the *Los Angeles Times Book Review,* Kenneth Rexroth's friend and former student Thomas Sanchez portrayed the author as a "longtime iconoclast, onetime radical, Roman Catholic, Communist fellow traveler, jazz scholar, I.W.W. anarchist, translator, philosopher, playwright, librettist, orientalist, critical essayist, radio personality, newspaper columnist, painter, poet and longtime Buddhist." While Rexroth played all these roles, he is best recognized for his contributions to modern American poetry. The length and breadth of his career resulted in a body of work that not only chronicles his personal search for visionary transcendence but also reflects the artistic, cultural, and political vicissitudes of more than half a century. Commented John Unterecker in a 1967 *New York Times Book Review:* "Reading through all of Kenneth Rexroth's shorter poems is a little like immersing oneself in the literary history of the last forty years; for Rexroth experimented with almost all of the poetic techniques of the time, dealt, at least in passing, with all of its favorite themes."

A prolific painter and poet by age seventeen, Rexroth traveled through a succession of avant-garde and modernist artistic movements, gaining a reputation as a radical by associating with labor groups and anarchist political communities. He experimented amid Chicago's "second renaissance" in the early 1920s, explored modernist techniques derived from the European-born "revolution of the word," played an integral part in the anarchist-pacifist politics and poetic mysticism that pervaded San Francisco's Bay Area in the 1940s, and affiliated himself with the "Beat Generation" in the mid-1950s. Intellectually as well as artistically eclectic, Rexroth scorned institutionalized education and criticism, calling American academics "corn belt Metaphysicals and country gentlemen," as M. L. Rosenthal noted in *The Modern Poets*. After quitting school in his early teens, the poet pursued a curriculum of self-education that included not only literature from diverse cultures and times but encompassed science, philosophy, theology, anthropology, Oriental thought and culture, and half a dozen languages. William R. McKaye of the *Washington Post* emphasized: "In an era in which American colleges crank out graduates who seemingly have never read anything, Rexroth . . . [appeared] well on the way to having read everything. And 'everything' is not just the standard European classics in translation: it is the Latins and Greeks in the original; it is the Japanese and Chinese; it is poetry of all kinds; finally, as a sort of spicy sauce over all, it is such . . . curiosities as the literature of alchemy, the writings of 18th and 19th century Anglican divines and the 'Religio Medici' of Sir Thomas Browne."

Critics have classified and discussed Rexroth as a member of one or another of the century's literary movements—Objectivist, Cubist, Imagist, West Coast, or Beat, for example—because of his diversity, outspoken individualism, and far-ranging interests. He has been labeled a nature poet, an erotic poet, and a polemicist. Rexroth scholar Morgan Gibson believes such categorizing obscures the achievement and import of the author's work as a whole. In his critical study *Kenneth Rexroth*, Gibson pointed out that the poems—spanning sixty years—illustrate a constant struggle "against despair in a world gone mad, a world in which collectives of strangers, equipped with runaway technology, push each other toward extinction." Rexroth's search for a way to transcend what he saw as decaying traditions in a decadent society led to "oceanic, ecstatic illuminations of the oneness of all beings," which affirmed his "sense of mission as philosophical artist and poet." Writing in *Dictionary of Literary Biography Yearbook: 1982*, Gibson explained that this direction appeared early and gave a sustained focus to the poet's career. "I was astonished by [Rexroth's] vision of the creative process of the universe, extending from the molten core of the earth through eons of evolution revealed by the geologic ladder of fossils, culminating in the union of lovers lying under the turning stars, and all passionately realized in lyric poetry," stated Gibson, recalling his reaction to Rexroth's first major work, *The Homestead Called Damascus*.

Reportedly written in 1922 when Rexroth was seventeen, *The Homestead Called Damascus* did not appear in its entirety until it was published in a 1957 *Quarterly Review of Literature*, according to Brown Miller and Ann Charters in *Dictionary of Literary Biography*. Consisting of four sections, the "musically eloquent" long poem traces two brothers' search for liberation from "the bourgeois-Christian-Classical tradition in a state of decadence," Gibson explained. While the protagonists' attempts to escape merely lead from "innocence into the experience of despair," the poem represents Rexroth's initial explorations of the individual, nature, and love as possible ways to transcend the evils of past and present human condi-

tions. Sharing some of the characteristics of Symbolist poetry, in which integral ideas are presented through a variety of emotive images rather than intellectual exposition, *Homestead* illustrates one facet of Rexroth's early, informed interest in the modernist techniques developed during the twentieth century's first decades.

Active as a painter as well as a poet throughout his life, Rexroth also experimented in the Cubist mode during the 1920s and 1930s. Applied initially to art and then to literature, Cubism took the elements of experience, or images, and broke them into fragments of their original form. The pieces then were recombined to created new compositions. The poet's "most ambitious experiment in literary Cubism," believed Gibson, was the long poem "Prolegomenon to a Theodicy." Published in Louis Zukofsky's *Objectivists Anthology* in 1932, but not widely reviewed until it was included in *The Art of Worldly Wisdom* (1949), "Prolegomenon" "represents Rexroth's tortured struggle for a faith that transcends the vision of *Homestead*. . . . As a way out of despair, he seems to be moving in the direction of [T. S.] Eliot, towards self-sacrificial acceptance of traditional Christian mysteries," Gibson noted. Intensely interested in the contemplative side of Christian faith—to the point of almost becoming a Catholic postulant in his early twenties—Rexroth nonetheless found no viable, optimistic resolution in the mysteries of the faith. "Prolegomenon," as Gibson emphasized in his book, contains far more Christian imagery than any of the poet's subsequent works.

"Prolegomenon" and the shorter experimental poems included in *The Art of Worldly Wisdom* (1949) met with little critical acclaim from reviewers, possibly because the prevailing styles had been explored by established and aspiring poets alike during the preceding decades. Commenting on what he considered to be the book's dated techniques, Dudley Fitts pointed out in *Saturday Review of Literature* that "the more freakish poems—Mr. Rexroth would reject the epithet—heavily influenced by Gertrude Stein and the surrealists, are in the familiar (and today how archaic in tone!) manner to which most of us who were experimenting in the late [1920s] did obeisance." David Daiches added in *New York Herald Tribune Weekly Book Review*: "They are exhausting poems to read; we feel that at any moment we will be able to seize the poem as a whole and wrest its inner core of meaning from it; but that moment never comes, and the perceptions, images and propositions disintegrate on all sides, leaving us aware of having experienced something but not sure what it was. It seems that the poetic energy here is greater than the control, and that a centrifugal tendency is working to pull the parts of the poem off in different directions." However, Gibson considered Rexroth's experiments in Cubism important to the poet's development. They provided a showcase for both humor and philosophy and, more significantly, served "as a means of discovering new rhythmic possibilities in American speech."

Rexroth's poems of the 1930s, largely collected in his first published book *In What Hour* (1940), show additional modernist experimentation but, for the most part, move toward either introspection or direct statement. The author reacted strongly to the political and economic upheaval of his times, favoring polemical poems on topics such as the Spanish Revolution and the electrocution of American radicals Nicola Sacco and Bartolomeo Vanzetti. (Immigrants, Sacco and Vanzetti were accused of robbery and murder and executed in 1927 despite worldwide protests that they were innocent victims of persecution.) Set beside such topic-pieces, Rexroth's "introspective harmonies," reflecting those in *Homestead* according to Gibson, illustrated the poet's shift "from the horror of modern history . . . toward the mysterious processes of nature." In the poem "Toward an Organic Philosophy," which Steven Stepanchev called "Rexroth's best poem of the 1930s" in *New Leader,* the poet contemplated mountains and stars, developing his view of "the chain of dependence which runs through creation." "The relationship of stone, ice and stars is systematic and enduring," concluded Rexroth. Against this backdrop of constancy, he believed, the individual must love, accept moral responsibility, and search for transcendence within the perpetual decline and renewal of the universe. Gibson observed: "To find transcendence in the natural process of creation out of destruction is a chilling 'solution' to the problem of value, but it offered Rexroth a firmer foundation than the Christian apocalyptics we find in his *Prolegomenon.* In . . . 'Toward an Organic Philosophy' there is a more positive sense of transcendence through natural communion."

George Woodcock, writing in *New Leader,* felt that "the pattern of the most attractive kind of Rexroth poem" was established in "Toward an Organic Philosophy" and similar pieces. Defining the design, Woodcock noted that "the writer visits a scene that has special meaning for him, a particular beauty and links with memory; in describing the present and evoking the past, he comes in the end to the thought which the whole poem has been hunting, securely trapped in a mesh of imagery." While Ruth Lechlitner also praised *In What Hour,* commenting in *Books* that it contained "much finely reasoned, eloquent and mature work," other reviewers found the volume's diversity too great to create a coherent whole. "Mr. Rexroth has been confused by attendance on multiple demands," Rolfe Humphries claimed in *New Republic.* "At his best, he is a simple-minded man, with a liking for outdoors . . . and a decent reverence for nature and the stars. Of these he writes well; his observation is direct and immediate." Yet, continued Humphries, "Mr. Rexroth's other aspect, the erudite indoor ponderer over many and difficult texts, is less deserving of encouragement." While maintaining that the poet demonstrated "a flair for phrase," John Ritchie similarly was troubled by the work's unevenness. "A great deal of the time [Rexroth] is esoteric. At other times he seems to wilfully twist his lines into angular forms. One comes to the conclusion that Mr. Rexroth is not a poet whose work gives much indication of necessity," the critic summarized in the *Christian Science Monitor.*

Published in 1944, *The Phoenix and the Tortoise* earned greater critical approbation. Called "much more coherent in style and theme than his first book" by Gibson, the volume focused less on experimentation and politics and, instead, initiated a study of "the 'integral person' who, through love, discovers his responsibility for all in a world of war, cold war, and nuclear terror." The true achievement of *The Phoenix and the Tortoise* and Rexroth's next book, *The Signature of All Things,* was the emergence of "poems that affirm more convincingly than ever the transcendent power of personal love," Gibson stated. At the time, reviewers commented favorably on the change in Rexroth's style since he first appeared as an Objectivist-Cubist in the 1920s and 1930s. Wrote Vivienne Koch in *Weekly Book Review,* "Quietly, but with a solid sense of direction that is rare, Kenneth Rexroth . . . has arrived at a poetic maturity that is marked at once by passion and by control." A *Canadian Forum* critic believed the book's mystical love lyrics shared a loose affinity with the work of D. H. Lawrence (whose selected poems Rexroth would edit in 1948) and added: "The writing, in spite of occasional Eliot and Lawrence cadences, is admi-

rably clear and intelligent. . . . [Rexroth] is seldom obscure and even more seldom without something interesting to say, and his poetry makes, on its surface level, thoroughly enjoyable reading." While Leo Kennedy, in *Book Week,* said the 39-year-old author wrote "smoothly and cleanly and is certainly a young poet to watch sharply," the *Canadian Forum* reviewer concluded, like Koch, that Rexroth had found his personal, mature voice. The work's "competence and assurance," wrote the critic, "suggest that he has already found a style which he will not be likely to transcend in [the] future; but all that that means is that [this] volume shows achievement rather than promise."

James Laughlin, founder of the New Directions Publishing Corporation which published and kept in print most of Rexroth's books, agreed that the poet found his mature style in *The Phoenix and the Tortoise* and *The Signature of All Things* (1950). "When he hit his true vein, a poetry of nature mixed with contemplation and philosophy, it was magnificent," Laughlin claimed in a tribute written for *Dictionary of Literary Biography Yearbook: 1982.* "Read 'The Signature of All Things,'" he urged. "It, how shall I put it, pulls everything in human life together. It is all there, all the things we cherish, all our aspirations, and over it all a kind of Buddhist calm." Reviewing *The Signature of All Things* in the *New York Times,* Richard Eberhart outlined both Rexroth's intent and his accomplishment: "Mr. Rexroth's purpose is to make a particular kind of poem which will be classical in its restraint, but without severity; personal, revealing, and confessional, without being sentimental; and it must, according to his bent, eschew symbolism and any kind of ambiguous imagery for a narrative or statement strength based on noun and verb, but not weakened by adjectives."

Critics consistently noted the increasing directness of Rexroth's language and the accessibility of his images. A contributor to *U.S. Quarterly Booklist* observed that "there is much less explicit philosophizing [in *The Signature of All Things*] than in *The Phoenix and the Tortoise.*" Echoing such praise, T. H. Ferril focused on the work's clean structure in a *San Francisco Chronicle* review. "There is fastidious architecture here and, in summary, the poems strike me as having been written by a gifted man with a fine ear, a fun-loving and overcast poet inclined toward sentimentality." However, the intimate tone, despite Eberhart's claim, was called overly personal by several critics. Convinced the book made readers feel cut off from the poet's subjects, Howard Griffin, for example, wrote in *Saturday Review of Literature:* "All the poems remain very personal, often even addressed to individuals. Except for such outstanding achievements as the title poem . . . the contents show little urgency of expression or compelling drive." Selden Rodman added in *New York Herald Tribune Book Review,* "If [Rexroth] would ignore momentarily the pursuing Furies and his own imagined shrinkings under their lash, he could write about the larger world with as much humanity as Frost and as much compassion as Blake."

In another long poem, *The Dragon and the Unicorn,* Rexroth addressed "the larger world" by chronicling his postwar tour through Europe. The work "is Rexroth's major effort to work out a philosophy of love and community," Gibson explained. Here, the poet-narrator is presented as a transcendent individual in whom "the sophisticated traveler, the dialectical philosopher, the anarchist polemicist, and the lover and visionary unite." While Gibson admitted that "the poem suffers from the predominance of abstract thought over direct visionary experience," he felt that "nevertheless, Rexroth communicates as a man of comprehensive wisdom and deep affection.'' Dudley Fitts agreed that the work was less engaging than previous volumes, writing in *New Republic,* ''This account of Rexroth's travels operates on many levels of which the surface one—narrative, anecdote, description—though the most entertaining, is the least ponderable.'' His main criticism, however, was ''from the point of view of technic: too much of it—whole pages of it—is flat, uncadenced prose.'' Other reviewers concurred, including W. T. Scott. ''Objection will be made, I'm sure, that much of *The Dragon and the Unicorn* is not poetry. This is true,'' he wrote in *New York Herald Tribune Book Review.* ''It contains, nevertheless, a great deal of bright observation and a cranky hard-headedness of intelligence.''

Those who praised the work emphasized the author's clear projection of his narrative personality. Writing in *Nation,* Humphries pointed out that the poem contained ''a lot of fun . . . possibly a bit too much minstrelsy about tarts with hearts of gold, but a philosophical anarchist,'' he added, ''same as anybody else, is entitled to his conventions.'' Eberhart described the work as ''poetic art and cultural history, with personal evaluation of a fascinating kind, managed with freshness of insight and always some new excitement.'' He maintained that the work was ''all of a piece. The reader is invited to a grand tour of the whole sensibility of the author. Nobody should miss a fabulous voyage.''

The form Rexroth adopted in his mature work, which he called ''natural numbers,'' was unrhymed and syllabic rather than metrically regular. Generally varying from seven to nine syllables per line, the structure allowed him to emphasize the ''natural cadences of speech,'' which Gibson pointed out had been important to the poet from the days of his earliest Cubist experiments. Looking back to the 1950s, Karl Malkoff remarked in a 1970 *Southern Review:* ''Rexroth . . . never stopped experimenting with rhythms, which not surprisingly are crucial to the success of his poems. Here his work is most vulnerable; here his successes, when they come, are most striking. When . . . Rexroth hit upon the seven syllable line as a temporary resolution, he was accused of writing prose broken up into lines. . . . Actually, on rereading, Rexroth's ear proves reasonably reliable.'' When he published his first collection of selected work in 1963, the poet entitled it *Natural Numbers: New and Selected Poems,* thus reaffirming the importance of an element critics had dismissed earlier as ineffective or unimportant.

Rexroth's tetralogy of verse plays in ''natural numbers,'' *Beyond the Mountains* (1951), proves not only his devotion to the natural patterns of speech but indicates his knowledge of classical Greek and Oriental literature. Gibson claimed in his study that the author's ''poetic, philosophical, and visionary powers [reached] their epitome'' in the four dramas ''Phaedra,'' ''Iphigenia at Aulis,'' ''Hermaios,'' and ''Berenike.'' While the characters were based in Greek tragedy, Rexroth's style reflected Japanese *Noh* drama. As Gibson related, an ''important quality of *Noh* found in Rexroth's plays is *yugen,* a term derived from Zen Buddhism and defined by Arthur Waley as 'what lies beneath the surface'; the subtle, as opposed to the obvious; the hint, as opposed to the statement.'' Although several commentators felt *Beyond the Mountains* suffered from obscurity or was more complex than necessary—including R. W. Flint who wrote in *Poetry* that the ''plotting has been just a shade too ambitious for [Rexroth's] poetic gift''—the renowned poet William Carlos Williams applauded both the work's language and form. ''Rexroth is one of the leading craftsmen of the day,'' proclaimed Williams in the *New York Times.*

''There is in him no compromise with the decayed line of past experience. His work is cleanly straightforward. The reek of polluted Shakespeare just isn't in it, or him. I don't know any Greek, but I can imagine that a Greek, if he knew our language as we ought to but don't, would like the athletic freshness of the words.''

A common concern for poetry as straightforward, spoken language was only one of the links between Rexroth and the Beat Generation. Quoting Jack Kerouac's definition found in *Random House Dictionary,* Charters defined the term Beat Generation as '''members of the generation that came of age after World War II who, supposedly as a result of disillusionment stemming from the Cold War, [espoused] mystical detachment and relaxation of social and sexual tension.' Emerging at a time of great postwar change, the Beat Generation was more than a literary movement, but at its heart was its literature.'' Charters and Miller explained how Rexroth came to be connected with the movement: ''By the mid-1950s many of the poets who were to become famous as Beat writers—Lawrence Ferlinghetti, Allen Ginsberg, Jack Kerouac, Michael McClure, Gary Snyder, Philip Whalen—had moved to San Francisco, attracted by the climate of radical poetry and politics, and they were soon part of Rexroth's circle. . . . Considering the diverse aspects of Rexroth's interests in avant-garde art, radical politics, and Eastern philosophy, one can understand why he seemed the perfect mentor for the Beats.''

Rexroth occupied a central position in the Bay Area's literary community at the time. Characterized as ''anarchopacifist in politics, mystical-personalist in religions, and experimental in esthetic theory and practice'' by Gibson, the community revolved around the Pacifica Foundation, with its public arts radio station, and the Poetry Center at San Francisco State College, both of which Rexroth helped establish. As a contributor to *Nation,* the *San Francisco Chronicle,* and the *New York Times,* he also wielded a certain critical power across the country. Rexroth used these forums to champion the younger poets' work in articles like his February, 1957, *Nation* review entitled ''San Francisco's Mature Bohemians.'' Most instrumental in linking Rexroth with the Beats, however, may have been the frequent poetry readings—often to jazz accompaniment—that Rexroth attended or helped organize from 1955 to 1957.

Rexroth considered the readings essential to foment ''poetry as voice, not as printing,'' as he told readers in his *American Poetry: In the Twentieth Century* (1971). ''The climacteric was not the publication of a book, it was the famous Six Gallery reading, the culmination of twenty years of the oral presentation of poetry in San Francisco.'' In 1955, the year of the Six Gallery reading that featured Rexroth as master of ceremonies and the first presentation of Ginsberg's controversial long poem *Howl,* ''Kenneth Patchen, Lawrence Ferlinghetti, and myself,'' related Rexroth, ''were doing poetry to jazz all over the country. It didn't really matter if the *Hudson Review* printed us or not. . . .'' Supporting the Beats morally with reviews and with his presence at their events, including his series of readings at the Cellar jazz club, Rexroth earned the title ''Godfather of the Beats.'' ''Kenneth Rexroth seemed to appear everywhere at their side like the shade of Virgil guiding Dante through the underworld,'' Alfred Kazin wrote in *Contemporaries.* ''Rexroth . . . suddenly became a public figure.''

While Rexroth enjoyed recognition before his association with the Beats, his public visibility did increase as the Beat Generation flourished from 1955 to 1958. Undoubtedly influencing the Beats more than they influenced him, the poet nonetheless was considered part of the school he instructed by many conservative or academic critics. As such, he often was dismissed or opposed as being part of a nonconformist craze. Some reviewers looked beyond the image to assess the poet's work itself, however. "Rexroth's *In Defense of the Earth* [1956] showed him the strongest of West Coast anarchist poets because he is a good deal more than a West Coast anarchist poet," emphasized Rosenthal. "He is a man of wide cultivation and, when not too busy shocking the bourgeois reader (who would like nothing better), a genuine poet." Added Gibson: "Rexroth's book of the Beat period, *In Defense of the Earth*, . . . is no period piece. . . . These poems of love and protest, of meditation and remembrance, stand out as some of his most deeply felt poems."

In Defense of the Earth included an elegy for Dylan Thomas, "Thou Shalt Not Kill," which has been considered one of the poet's most explicitly "Beat" works. A catalogue of his generation's defeated artists, the poem shares stylistic affinity with Ginsberg's *Howl,* as critics noted, but it also illustrates the author's knowledge of classical and traditional elegiac forms. Reviewers generally overlooked the work's traditional elements. "'Thou Shalt Not Kill' has a magnificently passionate and bitter beginning whose power carries over to, and is taken up by, the later *ubi sunt* stanzas which call the roll of the modern poets who have died, sickened, given up, been imprisoned, or gone mad," Rosenthal commented. "Yet the poem as a whole is sacrificed to the self-indulgent pleasure of the poet in love with his own voice." Other critics agreed that the poem, although less impassioned and stricter in form than *Howl,* sacrificed competence or art to unbridled ranting. The work's range of feeling—tenderness and bewilderment leading to prophetic rage and accusation—led Gibson, however, to proclaim "Thou Shalt Not Kill" to be Rexroth's "best protest poem." Considering the poem's message and Rexroth's concern as a morally responsible individual, Gibson added: "Rexroth seems to be saying that anyone who thrives, or even survives, in an anti-personal culture has climbed on the 'mountain of death.' The successful have helped create . . . a culture that destroys the young and talented, if not in war then in the acquisitive society at home. . . . As a successful poet, does [he] take any of the guilt? Certainly his assumption of total moral liability . . . would lead to the insight that much of his rage and indignation are explosions from his own involvement in the very culture that he denounces."

Despite the vehement support Rexroth expressed for the birth of the Beat Generation, he became disillusioned when he saw the movement's more prominent members become "hipsters." He noted in his 1959 critical collection, *Bird in the Bush: Obvious Essays:* "The Beat Generation may once have been human beings—today they are simply comical bogies conjured up by the Luce publications. . . . Success, alas, as it almost always does, led to the worst kind of emotional suicide. Those to whom that kind of success was a temptation have become the trained monkeys, the clowning helots of the Enemy. They came to us late, from the slums of Greenwich Village, and they departed early, for the salons of millionairesses." Gibson concluded that Rexroth's change of sentiment was motivated by the Beats' corruption of their "basic values soon after . . . the famous Six Gallery reading. . . ." Brown and Charters, however, state that the poet "seemed to have become jealous of [the Beats'] success and widespread attention from the national press. He had fought for many years for his own recognition as a poet," they pointed out, "and as [the Beats']

popularity increased, his growing hostility toward [them] was expressed in a series of articles over the next several years. He said that he broke with [them] because of what he regarded as their lack of artistic discipline, but his harshly critical reviews of important experimental books . . . alienated him from the writers whom he had helped." In fact, Rexroth remained supportive of certain aspects of some Beat writers' works while condemning the movement as a whole. Several critics now note this point, attributing both Rexroth's animosities and his preferences to an individual integrity not influenced by blind allegiance—or enmity—to any literary collective.

Rexroth's collections of essays illuminate this fiercely independent intellect. As a critic, he was "erudite as Aristotle but colloquial as Socrates, dialectical as Marx but as funny as Mark Twain" and often "full of surprises," according to Gibson. His subjects ranged from the ordinary to the highly specialized. Reviewing *Assays* (1962) in the *New York Times Book Review,* Milton Crane noted: "Mr. Rexroth is nowhere more attractive and successful than in his efforts to naturalize and interpret the exotic—witness the opening essay on 'Sung Culture' or the deeply sympathetic discussions of 'The Holy Kabbalah,' 'American Indian Songs,' or 'Science and Civilization in China.'" However, Crane continued, Rexroth's tone tended "easily to become shrill—and, at worst, absurd." A *Booklist* critic likewise praised the author's "cleverness and perspicacity" while fearing that these qualities "frequently degenerate into mere flippancy."

Rexroth's appraisals of contemporary works and ways often opposed current academic criticism, which may account for the mixed reviews his critical collections elicited. His work, Kenneth Paul pointed out in *Washington Post,* was "not the arid criticism of a publish-or-perish academician." It was, rather, "the thoughtful offering of a citizen bibliophile, a highly skilled, enthusiastic amateur." "Mr. Rexroth," added Emile Capouya, "conceives it to be his function not only to give information but to make judgments." The critic went on in his *Saturday Review* article on *Assays* to say, "Often, in the cases in which the unspecialized reader can form an opinion, Mr. Rexroth's views seem at once illuminating and idiosyncratic— but this is another word for original, and is what one expects of an extraordinary mind." Generally, reviewers concurred, Rexroth's comments disclosed the complicated pathways of his intellect and personality. Woodcock found this illumination one of the most fascinating aspects of Rexroth's treatise on the American underground, *The Alternative Society* (1970). "*The Alternative Society* is interesting primarily for the character it projects, that argumentative, opinionated personality which is indeed part of Rexroth. . . . These pieces may not be criticism," Woodcock summarized in *New Leader,* "[for the] picture presented is highly personal and impressionistic, jeweled with the fragments of knowledge an accomplished polymath loves to display. It is perhaps the intuitive grasp of connections and analogies that is most important . . . and the flashes of wisdom that repeatedly illuminate his running comments on the contemporary scene."

Rexroth's position as a central yet independent figure in American literature was strengthened not only by his political and critical opinions and his association with the Beats but by a personal account of his youth entitled *An Autobiographical Novel.* According to Dean Stewart, writing in the *Los Angeles Times Book Review,* the 1966 work "did most to enhance [Rexroth's] image as a living historical personality; his essays in book form and spreading reputation as a keen social critic and insightful philosopher also helped." Yet, while his role as the "outsider's insider" in the literary world became widely acknowledged, serious attention to his own poetry seemed to receive secondary consideration. Commented Stewart: "For a poet who has constantly said he'only writes prose for money,' Rexroth rivals H. L. Mencken as a terse and cogent critic. But like Mencken, the largely forgotten lexicographer, little-read essayist and much remembered personality, Rexroth may share a similar descending fame from poet to translator to essayist to personality."

Illustrative of critics' approach to *An Autobiographical Novel* was George Woodcock's review focusing on the poet's. personality rather than on how the artist's experiences influenced his work: "[This book] is Rexroth as he looks and talks, the essence of his talent as a raconteur and the total image he presents to others. . . . [His] memories are full of content, and they have been played over by a mind that has probed into a multitude of the ideas which world literature and the thought of the past have made available to twentieth-century man. Rexroth is an autodidact, member of a dying kind, and, like many men who have avoided an excess of formal education, he is able to make his own original and often brilliant syntheses of happenings, impressions and theories." A *Newsweek* reviewer pointed out, also, that the autobiography's forceful presentation of Rexroth's character might account for critics' comments. "The trouble," the reviewer wrote, "is that though [Rexroth] may be telling the notarized and certified truth, the reader can scarcely bring himself to believe more than every other word of it. The fault throughout lies in the tone. . . . [He] seems, sadly, unable to see himself in human perspective—the man of august years looking back bemusedly upon the bumptious boy he was. But it is exactly this failure of perspective that is both Rexroth's strength and weakness."

Gibson emphasized that in order to appreciate the importance of what Rexroth presents in *An Autobiographical Novel* the reader must understand Rexroth's world view as it evolves through all his works. Integral to the development of the poet's vision were his translation of foreign verse (both contemporary and ancient) and his study of Oriental thought. Rexroth felt an artistic kinship with the Greeks and Romans of classical times and with Japanese and Chinese writers. As Peter Clothier pointed out in a *Los Angeles Times* review of Rexroth's last Japanese translations: "The sharpness of focus and the directly experiential quality of . . . [oriental] poets are close to Rexroth's own aesthetic. . . . Rexroth has long championed this directness and simplicity of diction in poetry, a clarity of image and emotion clearly compatible with the Japanese aesthetic." Although, as Gibson commented, literary critics have yet to explore the relationships between Rexroth's translations and his own poetry, it has been generally recognized that his later poems are characterized by a serenity and quiet intensity that reflects Oriental art and philosophy.

The Heart's Garden, the Garden's Heart (1968), *New Poems* (1974), and *The Morning Star* (1979)—Rexroth's major poetry collections published after his autobiography—illustrate both his involvement with Oriental culture and his final resolutions of philosophical and technical concerns. Rexroth was, stated Victor Howes in the *Christian Science Monitor,* looking "for a sort of day-to-day mysticism." It was "a poetry of direct statement and simple clear ideas," the critic continued. "A poetry free of superfluous rhetoric. One might call it a poetry of moments." Agreed Richard Eberhart in *Nation,* "Rexroth . . . settled down to the universal validity of stating simple and deep truths in a natural way." "Though he [had] always been a visionary, he spent more than three decades searching for a philosophical rationale for his experience, for history, and for nature. In the 1960s he seems to have abandoned that kind of quest in favor of pure visionary experience," Gibson summarized. "[*The Heart's Garden, the Garden's Heart*], an extended Buddhist-Taoist meditation written in Japan, shows the depths of his resignation and enlightenment."

Written as Rexroth celebrated his sixtieth birthday, *The Heart's Garden, the Garden's Heart* did not "aim at giving answers to final questions that have none," explained Luis Ellicott Yglesias in the *New Boston Review.* "Instead it is a meditation on a handful of central images that have been treasured for centuries because they have the virtue of clarifying experience to the points of making it possible to relinquish life with the facility of a ripe apple dropping from its branch." Woodcock, who recognized in Rexroth's earlier works a dialogue between the poet's "conceptualizing mind" and his "experiencing sensibility," felt the two were reconciled in the volume. Out of the fusion "there appears a unique contemplative intensity," the critic stated in *New Leader.* "What has been forged is a supercharged imagism in which every physical object, every scene, every picture the poet creates, is loaded with burdens of meaning that cannot otherwise be expressed." This reconciliation of the immediate and the enduring continued in *New Poems,* which Herbert Leibowitz said were composed "of a flash or revelatory image and silent metamorphoses." Describing what he saw as Rexroth's achievement, Leibowitz continued in the *New York Times Book Review:* "Syntax is cleared of the clutter of subordinate clauses, that contingent grammar of a mind hesitating, debating with itself, raging against death and old age. The dynamics of his poems are marked *piano*—even storms are luminous rather than noisy." The quietness, as well as a vital eroticism, carried over to Rexroth's volume of verse *The Morning Star.* Containing three previously published collections, including the sequence that Rexroth pretended was translated from the Japanese ("The Love Songs of Marichiko"), the book offers a "directness and clarity" not usually associated with Western art, according to David Kirby in the *Times Literary Supplement.* "How different this is from the Rexroth of *The Phoenix and the Tortoise* (1944), who sounds like Lawrence and Pound and Whitman, or the one who wrote ['Thou Shalt Not Kill''] in *In Defense of the Earth.* . . . Now he appears to belong, or to want to belong, at least as much as a publishing writer can, to the Buddhist bodhisattvas [or other Eastern religious]."

"Revolutionary and conservative, worldly and spiritual, Asian and western ideas from traditions that my seem irreconcilable were uniquely harmonized in Rexroth's world view as expressed [throughout] his philosophical poetry and essays," Gibson wrote in his study *Kenneth Rexroth.* Just how—and why—the poet accomplished this synthesis has yet, the scholar told *CA,* to be explicated. Concluded Douglas Dunn in *Listener:* "Insufficient credit has been granted to Rexroth's identity as an old-fashioned, honest-to-God man of letters of downright independence of mind. . . . His temper [was] too independent, too scholarly, for cut-and-dried allegiances. He [turned] his back on Eliot and Pound. He [had] the irritating habit—for the mediocre, that is, the literary side-takers—of liking some but not all of certain poets or movements. Like all good examples in modern poetry, he has been seen as a figure instead of as a creator; as a representative rather than as a participant. That he is all four of these persons at once comes as a sweet discovery from a reading of his work instead of from side-glances at other people's estimates of his reputation."

CA INTERVIEW

Morgan Gibson, a professor and writer, studied world literature and philosophy with Kenneth Rexroth and Paul Goodman from 1976 to 1978. He also studied Buddhism with Masao Abe in Kyoto, Japan. Author of the critical studies *Kenneth Rexroth* (Twayne, 1972) and *Revolutionary Rexroth: Poet of Erotic Wisdom,* Gibson has taught literature and creative writing at numerous universities, including Wayne State University, American International College, the University of Wisconsin—Milwaukee, Goddard College, Indiana University, and Osaka University (Japan). He travels throughout the United States and Japan to lecture and give readings of his original poetry. Details of his career, writings, and additional biographical information may be found in Gibson's *Contemporary Authors* entry in this volume.

In November, 1982, Gibson talked with *CA* about his late friend, Kenneth Rexroth.

CA: When did you first meet Kenneth Rexroth?

GIBSON: I met him in the early '60s, when he came to the University of Wisconsin at Milwaukee, where I was teaching then. He was poet in residence for the summer of 1964 and came back later on several occasions. We became friends from that first meeting. We had corresponded a little bit before that; I'd sent him poems and he had read some of them over KPFA on his poetry program in San Francisco. After the first meeting we saw each other every couple of years. I'd try to meet him when he came to the Midwest to give readings, and I went out to California several times to talk with him there. When he visited Japan in the mid 1970s, he and his wife Carol Tinker stayed with me for several weeks. We toured Japan for poetry readings.

CA: Did he influence or strengthen the direction of your work in any way?

GIBSON: I think so, largely by giving me confidence, helping me realize that poetry can be derived from direct speech rather than from artificial stylistic tricks. In the last ten years or so, I've been very much interested in the Japanese and Buddhist qualities in Rexroth's poetry, and particularly the poetry of Kūkai, or Kōbō Daishi, a great Buddhist leader in Japan over a thousand years ago. I embarked on a translation of Kūkai with a Japanese poet largely because of Kenneth's encouragement.

CA: From early on, Rexroth seemed to have a certain disrespect for conventional classroom learning.

GIBSON: He never completed high school. He did audit courses at the University of Chicago when he was in his teens, and also at the Art Institute, where he studied painting. But he had no interest in sitting through a four-year degree program.

CA: Did any of that attitude show up later in his own teaching?

GIBSON: I sat in on a number of his classes at the University of Wisconsin at Milwaukee and one at the University of California at Santa Barbara also—and found that his teaching methods ranged from a very close interpretation of the classics to a much more freewheeling presentation of recent work. His reading of classic poetry particularly—either in English or in Chinese, Japanese, or other languages—was accompanied by very close commentary. On the other hand, he wouldn't discuss

more recent poetry—especially twentieth-century poetry—with that kind of detailed attention. His judgments of contemporary poetry tended to be much more spontaneous and general, in both his conversation and his writing, and sometimes they seemed extreme; but they were always based on his own precise knowledge.

CA: Did he form many close friendships among his students?

GIBSON: Yes, he did. He encouraged student writers a good deal. In fact, at the University of California at Santa Barbara he taught a course for people who were writing songs. I visited that class. Some of his students have gone on to do quite remarkable work. John Solt may be one of the most impressive; he's now a graduate student working on his doctorate in the Harvard Japanese program. Several others are writers, artists, and so forth.

CA: Was Rexroth's own writing influenced at all by commentary and criticism from other poets?

GIBSON: Not much when I knew him, though that might not have been the case earlier. He was a very close friend of Yvor Winters and many other poets. It's possible that in the 1920s and 1930s, maybe 1940s, he paid more attention to their criticism—maybe from William Carlos Williams, for example. But when I knew him it wasn't so, because there were no living American poets whom he felt he could learn much from. After Williams died, he felt there wasn't that much criticism he needed to respect or pay attention to.

CA: Where did his great interest in languages come from?

GIBSON: He traveled to Europe with his parents when he was quite young, and I think his knowledge of French, at least, goes back to those early trips. When he moved to the West Coast he had Chinese and Japanese friends who helped him learn those languages. He always made a point of working very closely with an informant in Chinese and Japanese when he did translations. He did know the languages—he studied them all his life—and based his translations on direct reading of the original, but he would always try to work closely with a Chinese or Japanese poet or scholar.

Of course he was working in an international climate of excitement concerning new developments in all of the arts. We've moved so far away from that feeling that it's hard for us to recover it, but certainly during the 1920s and 1930s, and even to some extent a few years after World War II, there was a tremendously optimistic enthusiasm about all of the arts as media for changing the consciousness of the entire world and bringing in an entirely new way of life. In that spirit it was easier to learn languages, and Rexroth always felt propelled to search out the new literature in all languages wherever he moved around the world.

CA: I remember reading that he was interested in "The Revolution of the Word" as it was exemplified in the writing of Gertrude Stein and other experimental writers in Paris in the 1920s and 1930s, yet he didn't like Paris much and chose not to stay there.

GIBSON: That was interesting to me too. One of the anarchists—Alexander Berkman—actually advised him to come back to America and base his writing on his American experience. He remarked that if Rexroth stayed in Paris, he might become just another expatriate artist instead of doing something original out of the American experience. William Carlos Williams, who had similar feelings, may also have influenced Rexroth in that direction.

CA: Did he continue to paint throughout his life?

GIBSON: Yes, he did, though I don't know how late in his life he kept it up as a regular discipline. The Santa Barbara Museum of Art had a retrospective show of his work just a few months before he died and issued a catalog that indicates something of the tremendous scope of his work over the years. He was respected as a painter even before he began getting his poetry published. At that time his painting was Cubist. He did keep it up, and I think it interacted with his poetry pretty continuously too.

CA: Do you expect a growth or renewal of interest in Rexroth's work?

GIBSON: There's been a burst of interest recently among scholars. I welcome that, because while many, many poets all over the world admire his work, few scholarly critics have done serious pieces about it. Some have reviewed it, and over the years there have been a number of short essays, but mine is the only book by a single author about his work. Recently, though, in both Japan and the United States there's been a new interest in treating his work. *For Rexroth,* a festschrift edited by Geoffrey Gardner, came out in 1980. The University of Maine started a new journal, *sagetrieb,* which had a special issue on Rexroth. And I'm working on a new book. In Japan recently there have been two special issues of journals devoted to Rexroth's work.

CA: The poet Louis Simpson wrote in 1967: "It wasn't easy for Kenneth Rexroth to write poems. Rexroth has been excluded from the front ranks of fame, not by the Establishment . . . but by his own temperament." Do you agree?

GIBSON: That's something I'm very curious about and don't have complete answers to—why Rexroth has been neglected by many people who you would think might take a serious interest in his work. I have some intuitions as to what happened. I think, first of all, Rexroth's mind was far more complex and philosophical than the minds of most literary people in the United States. His long philosophical poems are quite difficult because they're based upon Oriental traditions as well as European: Christian, Buddhist, and other traditions. His sense of history is phenomenal. His sense of literature all over the world is far more sophisticated and widespread than the knowledge of most American critics. I think that might have caused some fear, on the part of many critics, which led them to neglect him.

He also entered into many civil wars with writers and critics and groups of literary people. He never cared for the New York literary establishment. (Though of course that didn't include New Directions, which isn't really part of the establishment anyway. James Laughlin has always gone his own way, sometimes in the face of disapproval by other literary people in New York. Laughlin has courageously sponsored new literature for many decades.) Rexroth alienated certain critics on that score, and they tended to reject him out of hand as a "West Coast nature poet."

In addition, he had no use for the New Criticism and the kind of formalist criticism that grew up from the '40s on. And there

was of course a dispute between him and the Beat Generation from the late '50s on. He had originally encouraged some of the Beat writers, but he later criticized the movement for its commercialism and corruption. There's probably been a mutual problem between Rexroth and other literary people. He was quite outspoken. He never compromised his judgment of anybody, and by being that way, he might have scared off people who were in some ways interested in his work.

CA: In championing the Beats' cause early and then later becoming disillusioned with them, he may have lost credence with both anti-Beat and pro-Beat factions.

GIBSON: Yes. In fact, I've been rather disappointed that some of the obituaries and journalistic comments since his death have linked him primarily with the Beats. Many have called him the grandfather of the Beats, and that title put him into a rage ever since the early 1950s. His reputation has been linked with the Beats in a way that is quite superficial. Many people don't understand, first of all, that he was of an older generation, and second, that his own viewpoint and his own poetry were developed in quite an independent way from the Beats'. He didn't depend on them; they depended on him. Third, his evaluation of each poet was extremely independent. He judged particular poems of particular poets at certain times in their careers. When Ginsberg became a celebrity and depended more on his image in the press than on the quality of his poetry, Rexroth started criticizing that. I think it's unfortunate that Rexroth's tremendous accomplishments and the great range of his writing have so often been linked in the public mind with the Beat Generation.

CA: Off and on throughout his life Rexroth was involved in various manifestations of the counterculture. Did he take part personally in the activism of the 1960s?

GIBSON: I know he did some traveling to take part in readings against the Vietnam War, but I can't give a detailed answer about his participation on the West Coast. By the '60s Kenneth had become somewhat suspicious, if not cynical, where political activity was concerned. He regarded himself still as an anarchist, an independent critic of American foreign policy and militarism. As part of his independence, maybe he didn't want to jump into the activism as much as other poets like Robert Bly did. It puzzled me at the time. I was very active in antiwar readings, mostly with Bly, and when I wrote to Kenneth about this I would be surprised by his sarcastic responses. He was totally opposed to the war, and he always encouraged draft resistance and criticism of the war. But he was cautious of movements by then, because he had gone through so many movements in the '20s and '30s, and some of them had betrayed their original ideals. He was not so much a movement person by then as an independent visionary and prophet.

CA: Had he thought of doing another autobiography?

GIBSON: I understand that there are other sections of his autobiography that have not been published. *Excerpts from a Life,* a fairly short book published in 1981, might be called a second volume of his autobiography, though it's by no means comparable to *An Autobiographical Novel.* There are other sections. I'm not sure what plans there are for bringing them out, but I know Rexroth was working on bringing his autobiography at least into the 1950s and maybe even beyond that.

CA: In your 1972 critical volume, Kenneth Rexroth, *you discussed his amazing objectivity in writing about the events of his early life. "By objectivity," you explained, "I do not mean that he is always right or even accurate. . . . I mean that he has that rare ability to look at his own life with the kind of amused interest and detached curiosity that we expect of historians more than from poets. . . ."*

GIBSON: That came out of the objectivism of the literary movement he had been associated with in the '20s and early '30s, and it came out of his whole attitude toward poetry. He was one of the very few poets, I think, to insist that poetry be written from a clear and even rational mind. That is, he saw no contradiction between being rational and being prophetic, being passionate, in his poetry. His early cubist poems assisted him in that discipline of keeping his own mind very clear and steady, and looking at his own life in that objective way.

CA: What does your new book, Revolutionary Rexroth: Poet of Erotic Wisdom, *cover?*

GIBSON: It goes considerably beyond my earlier book, because Rexroth wrote many books in the last ten years of his life, after my book came out in 1972. Much of his work was directly influenced by his experience in Japan; he visited Japan five times and lived there for at least a year one of those times. The writing of the last twelve years or so of his life was even more richly influenced by Asian culture than his earlier work had been. My new book attempts to take into account that last ten or twelve years of his work, but also covers his entire body of work from a new point of view. I'm interested in approaching the work philosophically and seeing the depth and range of his world view.

CA: Is anyone writing his biography?

GIBSON: I don't have plans to do a detailed biography, but I know of several people who would be qualified and would be interested in doing it, and I think that might be the next project someone would want to undertake. His papers are collected at the University of California at Los Angeles and the University of Southern California, so it would be possible for a biographical scholar to do quite a bit on his life. However, it's going to be extremely difficult for anyone to examine the range of his life, to track down everything he did. It would have to be researched internationally, and of course many of Rexroth's contemporaries are dead now, so it's becoming increasingly difficult and increasingly sad trying to reconstruct his career.

The area I find so interesting is his religious synthesis of Buddhism and Christianity. Many reviewers have omitted that. So many critics who have looked at one book at a time have failed to realize that he had a consistent spiritual outlook from the '20s on. He has often been thought of as a kind of agnostic rebel, which is simply not true. That satirical and rebellious side of his character was very pronounced, of course, but it should be understood in the context of his contemplative vision, Christian and Buddhist. His funeral was Catholic, in fact.

BIOGRAPHICAL/CRITICAL SOURCES—Books: Horace Gregory and Marya Zaturensk, *A History of American Poetry, 1900-1940,* Harcourt, 1946; Mary McCarthy, *The Groves of Academe,* Harcourt, 1952; Babette Deutsch, *Poetry in Our Time,* Columbia University Press, 1956; Wolfgang Bernard Fleishman, editor, *Encyclopaedia of World Literature,* Volume III, Ungar, 1957; John C. Thirlwall, editor, *The Selected Letters of William Carlos Williams,* McDowell/Obolensky, 1957;

Jack Kerouac, *The Dharma Bums,* Signet Books, 1958; Kenneth Rexroth, *Bird in the Bush: Obvious Essays,* New Directions, 1959; Lawrence Lipton, *The Holy Barbarians,* Messner, 1959.

M. L. Rosenthal, *The Modern Poets: A Critical Introduction,* Oxford University Press, 1960; Joseph Warren Beach, *Obsessive Images,* University of Minnesota Press, 1960; Daniel Aaron, *Writers on the Left: Episodes in American Literary Communism,* Harcourt, 1961; Thomas Parkinson, *A Casebook on the Beat,* Crowell, 1961; Rexroth, *Assays,* New Directions, 1962; John Ciardi, *In Fact,* Rutgers University Press, 1962; Alfred Kazin, *Contemporaries,* Little, Brown, 1962; Rexroth, *An Autobiographical Novel,* Doubleday, 1966; James Hartzell and Richard Zumwinkle, *Kenneth Rexroth: A Checklist of His Published Writings,* Friends of the University of California Library (Los Angeles), 1967.

Ruby Cohn, *Dialogue in American Drama,* Indiana University Press, 1971; David Meltzer, *The San Francisco Poets,* Ballantine, 1971; Rexroth, *American Poetry: In the Twentieth Century,* Herder, 1971; Morgan Gibson, *Kenneth Rexroth,* Twayne, 1972; *Contemporary Literary Criticism,* Gale, Volume I, 1973, Volume II, 1974, Volume VI, 1976, Volume XI, 1976, Volume XXII, 1982; Geoffrey Gardner, editor, *For Rexroth,* Ark, 1980; *Dictionary of Literary Biography,* Volume XVI: *The Beats: Literary Bohemians in Postwar America,* 1983; *Dictionary of Literary Biography Yearbook: 1982,* Gale, 1982.

Periodicals: *New Republic,* August 12, 1940, August 8, 1949, February 9, 1953, February 18, 1957, September 16, 1957; *Christian Science Monitor,* August 31, 1940, July 11, 1967, January 9, 1969, September 14, 1970, February 6, 1980; *Christian Century,* September 4, 1940, July 1, 1970, May 19, 1971; *Boston Transcript,* October 7, 1940; *Poetry,* November, 1940, June, 1950, May, 1956, June, 1957, July, 1963, December, 1967, April, 1969; *Living Age,* November, 1940; *Books,* December 22, 1940; *Canadian Forum,* December, 1944; *Book Week,* December 24, 1944; *New Yorker,* December 30, 1944, March 26, 1949, May 20, 1950, February 4, 1956, May 3, 1958.

Weekly Book Review, January 14, 1945; *New York Times,* December 19, 1948, August 6, 1950, January 28, 1951, February 15, 1953, January 1, 1956, November 22, 1964, July 23, 1967, August 17, 1968, July 10, 1970; *Kirkus Reviews,* February 1, 1949, April 1, 1970, May 15, 1971, November 1, 1972, February 1, 1973, September 1, 1974, November 1, 1974, November 1, 1979; *Nation,* February 12, 1949, June 10, 1950, September 28, 1957, June 6, 1966, March 18, 1968, April 22, 1968, March 24, 1969, December 31, 1973; *Booklist,* March 1, 1949, April 1, 1969, November 1, 1973, February 1, 1975, February 15, 1975, October 15, 1976, July 1, 1978, October 1, 1979; *San Francisco Chronicle,* May 29, 1949, March 12, 1950, January 29, 1956, February 10, 1957; *Saturday Review of Literature,* June 4, 1949, September 17, 1949, May 20, 1950; *New York Herald Tribune* [*Weekly*] *Book Review,* June 12, 1949, October 2, 1949, May 7, 1950, February 19, 1956; *Library Journal,* June 15, 1949, July, 1970, August, 1971, July, 1972, September 15, 1972, December 15, 1972, October 15, 1974, January 15, 1975, September 1, 1976, September 15, 1977, October 15, 1979, November 15, 1979.

U.S. Quarterly Booklist, June, 1950; *Saturday Review,* June 16, 1956, November 9, 1957, February 12, 1966, March 15, 1969; *Quarterly Review of Literature,* Volume IX, number 2, 1957; *Life,* September 9, 1957; *Evergreen Review,* Volume I, number 4, 1957; *Commentary,* December, 1957; *Time,* December 2, 1957, February 25, 1966; *Comparative Literature,* Volume X, 1958; *Reporter,* April 3, 1958, March 3, 1960, May 19, 1966; *New York Herald Tribune,* May 7, 1950, February 1, 1953; *Spectator,* March 13, 1959; *Studies,* summer, 1959.

Hudson Review, spring, 1960, summer, 1967, summer, 1968, autumn, 1968, summer, 1971, autumn, 1974; *Minnesota Review,* spring, 1962, fall, 1962; *New Leader,* April 24, 1967, February 17, 1969, October 27, 1969, September 21, 1970; *New York Times Book Review,* July 23, 1967, November 16, 1969, February 15, 1970, October 4, 1970, March 23, 1975, November 23, 1980; *Harper's,* August, 1967; *Carleton Miscellany,* fall, 1967; *Kaleidoscope* (Milwaukee), December 8-21, 1967; *Sydney Southerly* (Sydney, Australia), Volume XXVIII, 1968; *Washington Post,* August 29, 1968, February 11, 1971; *National Observer,* December 9, 1968; *Los Angeles Free Press,* January 10, 1969; *Publishers Weekly,* September 1, 1969, April 13, 1970, September 28, 1970, January 1, 1973, October 8, 1979; *Choice,* November, 1969, October, 1971, October, 1972, January, 1974, April, 1974, March, 1975, June, 1975, May, 1977, March, 1978, July/August, 1978.

Southern Review, spring, 1970; *Book Review,* March, 1971; *Times Literary Supplement,* April 30, 1971, June 16, 1972, March 25, 1977, May 30, 1980; *Journal of Library History,* May 17, 1971; *Best Sellers,* August 1, 1971, February, 1980; *Antioch Review,* number 3, 1971; *Prairie Schooner,* winter, 1971-72; *American Literature,* March, 1972; *Virginia Quarterly Review,* summer, 1973, spring, 1975; *America,* August 4, 1973, December 20, 1975; *Journal of Asian Studies,* November, 1973, May, 1978; *Washington Post Book World,* January 6, 1974, June 29, 1975, March 12, 1978; *London Magazine,* April/May, 1974; *Commonweal,* December 6, 1974.

Progressive, June, 1975; *Psychology Today,* July, 1975; *American Association of Political and Social Science Annals,* September, 1975; *Ohio Review,* winter, 1976; *New Statesman,* January 2, 1976; *Kliatt Paperback Book Guide,* winter, 1977, spring, 1978; *Listener,* June 16, 1977; *Library Review,* autumn, 1977; *New Boston Review,* Volume III, number 3, December, 1977; *World Literature Today,* winter, 1978, spring, 1978, autumn, 1978, winter, 1981; *Los Angeles Times,* October 3, 1978, February 5, 1980; *American Poetry Review,* November, 1978; *Los Angeles Times Book Review,* August 3, 1980, June 20, 1982; *Parnassus,* spring, 1981; *Kyoto Review,* Vol. XV, fall, 1982; *sagetrieb,* Vol. II, no. 3, winter, 1983.

OBITUARIES: New York Times, June 8, 1982; *Los Angeles Times,* June 8, 1982; *Washington Post,* June 9, 1982; *Detroit Free Press,* June 9, 1982; *Times* (London), June 12, 1982; *Newsweek,* June 21, 1982; *Publishers Weekly,* June 25, 1982; *AB Bookman's Weekly,* September 6, 1982.

[Sketch reviewed by Morgan Gibson]

—*Sketch by Nancy Hebb*

—*Interview by Jean W. Ross*

*   *   *

RHEA, Nicholas
   See WALKER, Peter N.

*   *   *

RHODES, Albert   1916-1977

PERSONAL: Born May 10, 1916, in Sheffield, Yorkshire,

England; died March 1, 1977; son of Ernest (a blacksmith and farrier) and Annie (Cartwright) Rhodes; married Eileen Evelyn Collins, July 29, 1939; children: Peter, Jennifer. *Education:* Attended Chesterfield Technical College, 1930-34. *Politics:* Liberal. *Religion:* Church of England. *Address:* c/o Eileen E. Rhodes-Bennett, 2 Southcliffe Rd., Friars Cliff, Christchurch, Dorset, England.

CAREER: Novelist and managing director of Rhodes Engineering Ltd. Committee member of Writers' Summer School. *Military service:* British Army, 1939-45; became sergeant.

MEMBER: Writers' Guild of Great Britain, Writers' Action Group, Independent Writers' Club.

WRITINGS—Novels; all published by Dobson: *Butter on Sunday,* 1964; *A Summer of Yesterday,* 1967; *Calico Bloomers,* 1968; *Shout into the Wind,* 1975. Also author of radio and stage plays.

WORK IN PROGRESS: Derbyshire Lead Mining; television scripts.

SIDELIGHTS: Albert Rhodes was forty-eight when his first book was published; he once described himself as a compulsive writer, getting up at six o'clock to write for an hour daily before going to his business. *Butter on Sunday* was adapted for a trilogy of one-hour plays aired by British Broadcasting Corp.†

*   *   *

RHODES JAMES, Robert (Vidal)   1933-

PERSONAL: Indexed in some sources under James; born April 10, 1933, in Murree, India; son of William Rhodes (a lieutenant colonel, Indian Army) and Violet (Swinhoe) James; married Angela Margaret Robertson, August 18, 1956; children: Lucy Victoria Margaret, Emma Jenneffee, Charlotte Elizabeth, Katherine Alexandra Stirling. *Education:* Worcester College, Oxford, M.A., 1955. *Religion:* Church of England. *Home:* The Stone House, Gransden, Sandy, Bedfordshire, England. *Agent:* Anthony Sheil Associates, 2-3 Morwell St., London WC1B 3AR, England. *Office:* House of Commons, London SW1A 0AA, England.

CAREER: Historian and biographer. House of Commons, London, England, assistant clerk, 1955-61, senior clerk, 1961-64; Oxford University, All Souls College, Oxford, England, fellow, 1965-68, and 1979-82; Stanford University, Stanford, Calif., Kratter Professor of European History, 1968; University of Sussex, Institute for Study of International Organisation, Sussex, England, director, 1969-73, professorial fellow, 1973; Executive Office of the Secretary General of the United Nations, New York, N.Y., principal officer, 1973-76; House of Commons, London, Conservative member of Parliament for Cambridge, 1976—, parliamentary private secretary to Foreign and Commonwealth Office, 1979—.

Founder member, Study of Parliament Group, 1964; United Kingdom participant, United Nations Subcommittee on Prevention of Discrimination and Protection of Minorities, 1972-73. Lecturer on military history at Royal Military Academy, Sandhurst, 1965, Imperial Staff College, 1966, and Royal United Service Institute, 1966. Consultant to United Nations Conference of Human Environment, 1971-72.

MEMBER: United Nations Association, Royal Society of Literature (fellow), Royal Historical Society (fellow), Committee on Atlantic Studies, Travellers Club, Century Association.

AWARDS, HONORS: John Llewellyn Rhys Memorial Prize, 1962, for *An Introduction to the House of Commons;* Heinemann Award, Royal Society of Literature, 1964, for *Rosebery: A Biography of Archibald Philip, Fifth Earl of Rosebery;* North Atlantic Treaty Organization, fellowship, 1965-66, professorship, 1967.

WRITINGS: Lord Randolph Churchill: Winston Churchill's Father, Weidenfeld & Nicolson, 1959, A. S. Barnes, 1960; *An Introduction to the House of Commons,* Collins, 1961; *Rosebery: A Biography of Archibald Philip, Fifth Earl of Rosebery,* Weidenfeld & Nicolson, 1963, Macmillan, 1964; *Gallipoli,* Macmillan, 1965; *Standardization and Production of Military Equipment in NATO,* Institute for Strategic Studies, 1967; (with A.J.P. Taylor, J. H. Plumb, Basil Lidell Hart, and Anthony Storr) *Churchill Revised: A Critical Assessment,* Dial, 1969.

(Compiler) *The United Nations,* Jackdaw Publications, 1970; *Churchill: A Study in Failure, 1900-1939,* Weidenfeld & Nicolson, 1970; *Britain's Role in the United Nations,* United Nations Association, 1971; *The Constitutional Year Book, 1885-1939,* Harvester Press, 1971; *Staffing the United Nations Secretariat,* Institute for the Study of International Organisation, University of Sussex, 1971; *Ambitions and Realities: British Politics, 1964-1970,* Harper, 1972; *The Policy Debate,* Interbook, 1975; *The British Revolution: British Politics, 1880-1939,* Hamish Hamilton, Volume I: *From Gladstone to Asquith, 1880-1914,* 1975, Volume II: *From Asquith to Chamberlain, 1914-1939,* 1976, 2nd edition published in one volume, Knopf, 1976; *Victor Cazalet: A Portrait,* Hamish Hamilton, 1976; *Albert, Prince Consort,* Hamish Hamilton, 1983.

Editor: Henry Channon, *"Chips": The Diaries of Sir Henry Channon,* Weidenfeld & Nicolson, 1967; J.C.C. Davidson, *Memoirs of a Conservative: J.C.C. Davidson's Memoirs and Papers, 1910-1937,* Weidenfeld & Nicolson, 1969; *The Czechoslovak Crisis, 1968,* Weidenfeld & Nicolson, 1969; *Winston S. Churchill: His Complete Speeches, 1897-1963,* eight volumes, Bowker, 1974, abridged edition published as *Churchill Speaks: Winston S. Churchill in Peace and War,* Chelsea House, 1980, 2nd edition, 1982.

Contributor: Anthony Moncrieff, editor, *Suez Ten Years After,* B.B.C. Publications, 1967; *Essays From Divers Hands,* Oxford University Press, 1967; *Churchill: Four Faces and the Man,* Penguin, 1969; *International Administration,* Oxford University Press, 1971; Hugh Seton-Watson, editor, *Tomorrows in Europe,* University of South Carolina Press, 1973; *The Prime Ministers,* Volume II, Allen & Unwin, 1975. Contributor to periodicals, including *History Today, Spectator, New Statesman, Observer,* and *Daily Telegraph.*

WORK IN PROGRESS: Sir Anthony Eden.

SIDELIGHTS: In a *Times Literary Supplement* review of Robert Rhodes James's *The British Revolution: British Politics, 1880-1939,* Paul Johnson describes Rhodes James as "an unusual phenomenon in British historiography—he is a professional historian who declines to belong, except for brief periods, to the academic world. The first decade of his career he spent as a Clerk of the House of Commons, occupying an unrivalled coin of vantage on British politics." Furthermore, Johnson points out, Rhodes James is experienced as a member of Parliament and has served as a principal officer of the United Nations Secretary General. "The strength of [the author's] book is his profound understanding of Parliament," claims Johnson, "and particularly the House of Commons, of the way

in which it functions, the manner in which it controls (or fails to control) governments and, above all, the unconscious subtlety with which it shapes the personalities and determines the effectiveness of our leaders."

A *Times Literary Supplement* critic describes Rhodes James's approach to *Ambitions and Realities,* an earlier account of British politics from 1964, when Harold Wilson restored the Labour Party to office, until 1970, when the Conservative Party again took control of the government: Rhodes James, the reviewer indicates, "is an accomplished contemporary historian and biographer who wants to vindicate an older method of interpreting and analysing politics, in which literary style and human and political insight are at least as important as the priestly laying-on of slide-rules."

Of Rhodes James's book *Albert, Prince Consort,* a critic in the London *Times* comments that Prince Albert's "life is a wonderful subject for a biography and Rhodes James weaves sympathetically and with skill the rich tapestry of his activities. He also destroys a number of myths that have clouded some historians' vision of the Prince Consort." A.J.P. Taylor, reviewing the book in the *Observer Review,* indicates that Rhodes James presents "Albert's private life as well as his public one. There is a full account of his marriage with Queen Victoria, treating both the deep happiness of the married pair and also the difficulties raised by the Queen's temperament and the Prince's anomalous position in the political world." Excluded from official business while Lord Melbourne was prime minister, the prince only began to exercise real political authority and act as Victoria's advisor while Prime Minister Robert Peel was in power. Albert supported the arts and became independently involved in town planning efforts, building projects, and social reforms. Rhodes James writes *CA* that Albert was "an architect and designer in his own right," active in "the natural sciences and industrial design, and the true founder of modern universities in Britain." Although he later suffered personal and political defeats and became disillusioned and disappointed, Prince Albert, Taylor concludes, "was a man of great character and of noble achievement. In Robert Rhodes James's book he receives a worthy tribute. Indeed this is one of the finest biographies I have ever read."

AVOCATIONAL INTERESTS: Sailing, cricket, the theatre, literature.

BIOGRAPHICAL/CRITICAL SOURCES: Times Literary Supplement, July 24, 1969, May 21, 1970, December 11, 1970, June 9, 1972, May 28, 1976, July 8, 1977; *New York Review of Books,* July 23, 1970; *Times* (London), November 24, 1983; *Observer Review,* December 4, 1983.

*   *   *

RICE, Donald L. 1938-

PERSONAL: Born August 5, 1938, in East Greenwich, R.I.; son of Walter Lewis and Edna (Tunnicliff) Rice; married Dorothy Bundy, May 20, 1961; children: Aaron Lewis. *Education:* Attended Urbana College, 1960-62, Skidmore College, 1976-77. *Politics:* Democrat. *Home:* 1109 West Vine St., Mt. Vernon, Ohio 43050.

CAREER: Worked for various newspapers in Ohio, Wisconsin, Rhode Island, Massachusetts, 1957-66; Cooper-Bessemer (engine manufacturer), Mt. Vernon, Ohio, technical editor, 1966-72; Photo Documents Corp., Mt. Vernon, production manager, 1972-73; free-lance advertising, 1973—.

AWARDS, HONORS: Ohio Arts Council playwriting prize, 1974, for "The Situation on Earth."

WRITINGS—Published by Van Nostrand, except as indicated: *The Agitator: A Schism Anthology*, American Library Association, 1972; *Publish Your Own Magazine*, McKay, 1978; *Animals: A Picture Sourcebook*, 1979; *Birds: A Picture Sourcebook*, 1980; *Fishes, Reptiles and Amphibians: A Picture Sourcebook*, 1981; (editor) *The Friendly Stars*, 1982.

Also author of plays "The Situation on Earth," 1974, and "Software," produced in 1979. Contributor of satires, short stories, poetry, and plays to periodicals, including *Apalachee Quarterly, Nexus, Starwind, Unicorn, Green Egg*, and *Vile*. Founder and editor of *Schism: A Journal of Divergent American Opinions*, 1969-75.

WORK IN PROGRESS: "Uncounted books, plays, short stories, etc."

SIDELIGHTS: Donald L. Rice told *CA:* "I find myself achieving a life-long goal: Curmudgeonry. In my case this has taken the form of rejecting most of contemporary fiction (including my own). Why waste precious spare time reading current bestsellers or, worse yet, poorly written, badly edited (usually autobiographical) small press novels? Nearly every book in both categories will disappear with hardly a bibliographic trace—and for good reasons. So why waste time reading them when there are novels of Thomas Hardy's yet to be read, or Jane Austen's, or Turgenev's or, for that matter, James Hilton's? Fortunately, in thinking this way, I belong to a tiny minority."

*   *   *

RICKMAN, H(ans) P(eter)   1918-

PERSONAL: Born November 11, 1918, in Prague, Czechoslovakia; son of Ernst (a lawyer) and Grete (Wollin) Weisskopf; adopted by stepfather, 1929; married Muriel Edith Taylor, May 5, 1947 (died May 28, 1981). *Education:* Educated in Czechoslovakia, 1924-38 (with one year at a university); University of London, B.A. (with honors), 1941, M.A., 1948; New College, Oxford, D.Phil., 1943. *Home:* 12 Fitzroy Ct., 57 Shepherds Hill, London N.6., England. *Office:* Department of Social Sciences and Humanities, City University, London, England.

CAREER: University of Hull, Hull, England, staff tutor in philosophy and psychology, 1949-61; City University (formerly Northampton College of Advanced Technology), London, England, senior lecturer, 1961-67, reader, 1967-82, visiting professor in philosophy, 1982—. Life governor, Imperial Cancer Research Fund. *Military service:* British Army, intelligence and education posts, 1944-47. *Member:* Aristotelian Society, Royal Institute of Philosophy, Oxford Union, Association of University Teachers.

WRITINGS: Meaning in History: Dilthey's Thought on History and Society, Allen & Unwin, 1961, published as *Pattern and Meaning in History*, Harper, 1962; *Preface to Philosophy*, Schenkman, 1964, published as *The Use of Philosophy*, Routledge & Kegan Paul, 1973; *Living with Technology*, Zenith, 1966; *Understanding and the Human Studies*, Heinemann, 1967; (editor) Wilhelm Dilthey, *Selected Writings*, Cambridge University Press, 1976; *Wilhelm Dilthey: Pioneer of the Human Studies*, University of California, 1979; *The Adventure of Reason: The Uses of Philosophy in Sociology*, Greenwood Press, 1983. Contributor to *Encyclopedia of Philosophy*, 1967, *Symposium Volume on VICO*, 1969, 1981, and *The Hero in Transition*, 1983. Also contributor of more than thirty articles to

Fortnightly, Hibbert Journal, German Life and Letters, British Journal of Sociology, and other journals.

WORK IN PROGRESS: Six articles; a short book on change.

SIDELIGHTS: H. P. Rickman told *CA:* "One of the major concerns of my research and writing is how philosophy can help the social sciences to become more relevant and rigorous without aping the physical sciences."

*   *   *

RIKKI
See DUCORNET, Erica

*   *   *

ROBARD, Jackson
See WALLMANN, Jeffrey M(iner)

*   *   *

ROBERTS, Dan
See ROSS, W(illiam) E(dward) D(aniel)

*   *   *

ROBERTS, David
See COX, John Roberts

*   *   *

ROBERTS, Grant
See WALLMANN, Jeffrey M(iner)

*   *   *

ROBERTS, Lionel
See FANTHORPE, R(obert) Lionel

*   *   *

ROBERTS, Robert C(ampbell)   1942-

PERSONAL: Born January 28, 1942, in Wichita, Kan.; son of Arthur Verne (a lawyer) and Elisabeth (Euwer) Roberts; married Elizabeth Vanderkooy (a teacher), December 18, 1976. *Education:* Wichita State University, B.A., 1965, M.A., 1970; Yale University, B.D., 1970, Ph.D., 1973; attended Oxford University, 1970-71. *Religion:* Christian. *Home:* 1013 Willow St., Wheaton, Ill. 60187. *Office:* Department of Philosophy, Wheaton College, Wheaton, Ill. 60187.

CAREER: Western Kentucky University, Bowling Green, assistant professor of philosophy, 1973-84; Wheaton College, Wheaton, Ill., professor of philosophy and psychological studies, 1984—.

WRITINGS: Rudolf Bultmann's Theology, Eerdmans, 1976; *Spirituality and Human Emotion*, Eerdmans, 1983; *The Strengths of a Christian*, Westminster, 1984; (contributor) Robert Perkins, editor, *Soren Kierkegaard's Two Ages: A Commentary*, Mercer University Press, 1984. Contributor to theology journals.

WORK IN PROGRESS: A book on Kierkegaard; a philosophical account of moral psychology.

ROBINS, Lee N(elken) 1922-

PERSONAL: Born August 29, 1922, in New Orleans, La.; daughter of Abraham and Leona (Reiman) Nelken; married Eli Robins (a physician), February 22, 1946; children: Paul, James, Thomas, Nicholas. *Education:* Radcliffe College, B.A., 1942, M.A., 1943, Ph.D., 1951. *Home:* 1 Forest Ridge, Clayton, Mo. 63105. *Office:* Washington University Medical School, 4940 Audubon, St. Louis, Mo. 63110.

CAREER: Washington University, Medical School, St. Louis, Mo., research assistant in department of psychiatry and neurology, 1954-58, research instructor, 1958-59, research assistant professor, 1959-62, research associate professor, 1962-66, research professor of sociology, 1966-68, professor of sociology in psychiatry, 1968—. Member of task panel, President's Commission on Mental Health. Member of National Advisory Council on Drug Abuse, and of World Health Organization's expert advisory panel on mental health.

MEMBER: International Sociological Association, International Epidemiological Association, American Sociological Association (fellow), Society for the Study of Social Problems, American Public Health Association, Society for Life History Research in Psychopathology, American Psychopathological Association, Society for Epidemiological Research, Institute of Medicine, American Association for Psychiatry, Midwest Sociological Society.

AWARDS, HONORS: Research grants from National Institute of Mental Health, National Institute on Drug Abuse, and National Institute on Alcohol Abuse and Alcoholism; Research Scientist Award, United States Public Health Service, 1970—; Pacesetter Research Award, National Institute on Drug Abuse, 1978; Paul Hoch Award, American Psychopathology Association, 1978; Graduate Society medal, Radcliffe College, 1979; Rema Lapousse Award, American Public Health Association, 1979.

WRITINGS: (With Noah Weinstein and Lester Glick) *1959 Survey of Current Practices and Procedures of Missouri Juvenile Courts,* privately printed, c. 1959; *Deviant Children Grown Up,* Williams & Wilkins, 1966; (editor with David N. Nurco and Lloyd D. Johnston) *Conducting Follow-Up Research on Drug Treatment Programs,* National Institute on Drug Abuse, 1977; (editor with Paula J. Clayton and John K. Wing) *The Social Consequences of Psychiatric Illness,* Brunner, 1980. Also author of two monographs, *A Follow-Up of Vietnam Drug Users,* 1973, and *The Vietnam Drug User Returns,* 1974, both for Special Action Office.

*   *   *

ROBINSON, Robert (Reginald) 1922-

PERSONAL: Born March 10, 1922, in Orillia, Ontario, Canada; son of William Reginald (an insurance agent) and Alberta May (Ball) Robinson; married Marian Cecile Sabine (a freelance writer), April 9, 1949; children: Paul, Derek, Trevor, Andrea. *Education:* Attended University of Toronto, 1942-45, and Yale University, summer, 1954. *Religion:* Christian. *Home:* 5 Shouldice Ct., Willowdale, Ontario, Canada M2L 2S3. *Office:* RRR Communications, Inc., 55 Adelaide St., East Toronto, Ontario, Canada MSC 1K6.

CAREER: Maclean-Hunter Publishing Co. Ltd., Toronto, Ontario, writer and editor, 1946-51; Health League of Canada,

Toronto, public relations director and magazine editor, 1951-53; Addiction Research Foundation, Toronto, director of education, 1953-57; A. V. Roe Canada Ltd., Toronto, coordinator of public relations for a group of companies, 1957-59; Addiction Research Foundation, director of education, 1959-70 (producer of films "Margin for Safety," 1960, "Hospitality," 1960, "It's Best to Know," 1961, "Understanding Alcohol," 1964, "The Curious Habits of Man," 1968, "The Argument," 1969, "US," 1970, "Hotel Dieu," 1970, "Two Festivals," 1971); RRR Communications, Inc., Toronto, president, 1972—. Technical adviser and consultant for about a dozen films on social problems.

WRITINGS: How about a Drink, illustrated by son, Derek Robinson, Westminster, 1973; *Scrap Arrow* (novel), General Publishing, 1975; *On the Rocks* (juvenile), Scholastic Publications, 1979; *La Colere et l'Espoir* (juvenile), Editions Heritage, 1981; *Hume,* Highway Book Shop, 1981. Editor, *SIDS,* 1974. Managing editor, *Journal of Otolaryngology.*

*   *   *

RODRIGUEZ-ALCALA, Hugo (Rosendo) 1917-

PERSONAL: Born November 25, 1917, in Asuncion, Paraguay; U.S. citizen; children: Hugo Luis Ramiro Antonio, Marina Renee, Kimberly, Christopher Jose. *Education:* University of Asuncion, J.D., 1943; Washington State University, M.A., 1950; University of Wisconsin, Ph.D., 1963. *Religion:* Roman Catholic. *Home:* Mariscal Lopez 775, Asuncion, Paraguay.

CAREER: Secretary to supreme court justice in Paraguay, 1943-47; Rutgers University, New Brunswick, N.J., assistant professor, 1956-58; University of Washington, Seattle, 1958-63, began as associate professor, became professor; University of California, Riverside, professor of Spanish, beginning 1963, currently professor emeritus, chairman of department, 1965-67. *Military service:* Paraguayan Army, 1934-35. *Member:* International Association of Hispanists, Institute of Latin-American Literature, Modern Language Association of America, Paraguayan Academy of the Language. *Awards, honors:* First prize, Paraguayan Ministry of Education, for *Horas liricas,* 1939.

WRITINGS: La danza de la muerte, [Asuncion], 1937; *Estampas de la guerra,* Editorial Zampiropolos, 1939; *Horas liricas* (poems), Imprenta Nacional, 1939.

Francisco Romera: Vida y obra, Columbia University Press, 1951; (with Everett W. Hesse) *Cinco yanquis en Espana,* Ronald, 1955; (contributor) *La cultura y la literatura iberoamericana,* Ediciones de Andrea, 1957; *Korn, Romero, Guiraldes, Unamuno, Ortega,* Ediciones de Andrea, 1958; *Mision y pensamiento de Francisco Romero,* National University of Mexico Press, 1959.

Abril que cruza el mundo (poetry), Editorial Estaciones, 1960; *Ensayos de norte a sur,* University of Washington Press, 1960; (contributor) *Homenaje a Alejandro Korn (1860-1960),* Universidad Nacional de la Plata, 1960; (with William Wilson) *Por tierras de sol y de espanol,* Ronald, 1963; (with Sally Rodriguez-Alcala) *Un pais hispanico visto por dentro,* Prentice-Hall, 1965; *El arte de Juan Rulfo,* Instituto Nacional de Bellas Artes, 1965; (editor with S. Rodriguez-Alcala) *Cuentos neuvos del sur,* Prentice-Hall, 1967; *Literatura paraquaya,* Centro Editor de America Latina, 1968.

Historia de la literatura paraguaya, Ediciones de Andrea, 1970; *Palabras de los dias: Poemas,* Facultad de Humanidades y

Educacion, Universidad del Zulia, 1972; *Narrativa hispa-noamericana*, Editorial Gredos, 1973; *El canto del aljibe*, Universidad Nacional Autonoma de Mexico, 1973; (editor and author of foreword) *Nine Essays on Romulo Gallegos*, Latin American Studies Program, University of California, 1979; *Literatura de la Ilustracion*, Editorial La Muralla, 1979.

Literatura de la Independencia, Editorial La Muralla, 1980; *El porton invisible*, Editorial Alcandara, 1983; *Relatos de norte y sur*, Editorial Napa, 1983.

Contributor of about one hundred articles, translations, short stories, poems, and reviews to yearbooks, journals, and newspapers in North and South America, Mexico, and Europe; articles include a series of twenty-two about Brazil published in *El Pais*, 1940.

* * *

ROGERS, H(ugh) C(uthbert) Basset 1905-

PERSONAL: Born June 11, 1905, in Wylam-on-Tyne, England; son of Hugh Stuart (a brigadier general) and Kathleen Mary (Ridley) Rogers; married Eileen Elizabeth Clare Condon, July 10, 1928; children: Sheila Mary (Mrs. J. A. Bird), Hugh Stephen. *Education:* Attended Royal Military College, 1923-24. *Politics:* Conservative. *Religion:* Roman Catholic. *Home:* 209 Reading Rd., Wokingham, Berkshire RG11 16J, England. *Agent:* A. M. Heath, 40-42 William IV St., London WC2N 4DD, England.

CAREER: British Army, career officer, 1924-55, retired as colonel; writer, 1955—; British Foreign Office, London, England, member of staff, 1956-70. Campaigned in Northwest frontier of India, 1929-30; assigned to 2nd Corps Signals in France and Belgium, 1939-40; commander of 2nd Corps Signal Regiment, 1942; deputy chief signal officer in South Eastern Command, 1943; chief signal officer in Persia and South Iraq, 1944; commander of 3rd General Headquarters Signal Regiment in Egypt, 1945-46; chief signal officer of Northern Ireland, 1949-52; member of staff, Organisation and Training Division, Supreme Headquarters, Allied Powers Europe, 1952-55. *Member:* Society for Army Historical Research, Navy Records Society, Naval Review Society, Irish Military History Society, Army and Navy Club. *Awards, honors:* Officer of the Order of the British Empire, 1940.

WRITINGS: The Pageant of Heraldry, Seeley Service, 1955; *Mounted Troops of the British Army*, Seeley Service, 1959, 2nd edition, 1967; *Weapons of the British Soldier*, Seeley Service, 1960; *Turnpike to Iron Road*, Seeley Service, 1961; *Troopships and Their History*, Seeley Service, 1963; *Tanks in Battle*, Seeley Service, 1965; *Battles and Generals of the Civil Wars, 1642-1651*, Seeley Service, 1968.

The Last Steam Locomotive Engineer, R. A. Riddles, Allen & Unwin, 1970; *Artillery through the Ages*, Seeley Service, 1971, published as *A History of Artillery*, Citadel, 1975; *Chapelon: Genius of French Steam*, Ian Allan, 1972; *Confederates and Federals at War*, Ian Allan, 1973; *Napoleon's Army*, Ian Allan, 1974; *G. J. Churchward: A Locomotive Biography*, Allen & Unwin, 1975; *The British Army of the Eighteenth Century*, Allen & Unwin, 1977; *Thompson and Peppercorn: Locomotive Engineers*, Ian Allan, 1979; *The British Army Today and Tomorrow*, Ian Allan, 1979; *Transition from Steam*, Ian Allan, 1980; *Bulleid Pacifics at Work*, Ian Allan, 1980; *Riddles and the "9Fs,"* Ian Allan, 1982; *Napoleon's Army*, Hippocrene, 1982; *Steam from Waterloo*, David & Charles, in press. Also author of *Wellington's Army*, Ian Allan.

WORK IN PROGRESS: Military Logistics in the Twentieth Century; British Express Locomotives and Their Engineers.

SIDELIGHTS: H. C. Basset Rogers writes: "My predominant interest is in military and naval history, with a secondary interest in railways and their history. I spent three years at Supreme Headquarters Allied Powers Europe on the staff of Generals Eisenhower and Gruenther, and I hold that North Atlantic Treaty Organization defence in general and British and American defence in particular are of primary importance in the world today. I do not believe anything else is vital, because without adequate defence none of the values we cherish can survive."

* * *

ROHRLICH, George F(riedrich) 1914-

PERSONAL: Born January 6, 1914, in Vienna, Austria; came to United States in 1938; naturalized citizen; son of Egon (an attorney) and Rosa (Tenzer) Rohrlich; married Laura Ticho (a research economist), February 3, 1946; children: Susannah T., David E., Daniel M. *Education:* University of Vienna, Dr. Jur., 1937; Consular Academy of Vienna, diplomate, 1938; Harvard University, Ph.D., 1943. *Politics:* Democrat. *Religion:* Jewish. *Home:* 7913 Jenkintown Rd., Cheltenham, Pa. 19012. *Office:* School of Business Administration, Temple University, Philadelphia, Pa. 19122.

CAREER: Sweet Briar College, Sweet Briar, Va., instructor in economics and government, 1942-45; U.S. Office of Strategic Services, Washington, D.C., consultant and senior analyst, 1944-45; U.S. Department of State, Washington, D.C., senior economic analyst, 1945-47; Supreme Commander for Allied Powers, Social Security Division, Public Health and Welfare Section, Tokyo, Japan, chief of economic analysis branch, 1947-50; U.S. Social Security Administration, Bureau of Old Age and Survivors Insurance, Baltimore, Md., chief of disability research branch, 1950-53; U.S. Department of Labor, Bureau of Employment Security, Unemployment Insurance Service, Washington, D.C., chief of Division of Actuarial and Financial Services, 1953-59, chief of Division of Program and Legislation, 1957-58; International Labour Office, Social Security Division, Geneva, Switzerland, senior staff member, 1959-64; University of Chicago, Chicago, Ill., visiting professor of social policy and economics, 1964-67; Temple University, Philadelphia, Pa., professor of economics and social policy, 1967-81, professor emeritus, 1981—, director of Institute for Social Economics and Policy Research, 1968-81.

Research associate, National Planning Association, 1950-52. Senior staff member, President's Commission on Veterans' Pensions, 1955-56. Guest professor, University of Trieste, Institute for Comparative Labor Law and Social Security, 1966; senior lecturer in social policy, Columbia University, 1968-69; Fulbright research scholar, Victoria University, Wellington, New Zealand, 1980; guest lecturer, Pennsylvania State University, 1983; guest lecturer in Brasilia and other Brazilian cities, 1984. U.S. observer, First International Conference of Social Security Actuaries and Statisticians (Brussels), 1956; general reporter, Sixth International Congress on Labor Law and Social Legislation (Stockholm), 1966; member, World Health Organization-International Labour Office Joint Committee of Experts on Personal Health Care and Social Security, 1970; external collaborator, Puerto Rican Commission on Universal Health Insurance, 1973-74; director of research, Commission on an Integral Social Security System (Puerto Rico), 1975-76. Technical adviser, National Commission on Railroad

Retirement, 1971-72; member of board of directors, Regional Health and Welfare Council of Greater Philadelphia, 1968-70. Consultant to National Commission on State Workmen's Compensation Laws, 1972; expert consultant on socio-economic policies and programs, National Planning Department of the Government of Colombia, 1974; consultant at an international conference on accident prevention and compensation, Geneva, Switzerland, 1979.

MEMBER: International Society for Labor Law and Social Security, American Association for the Advancement of Science, Association for Social Economics (member of executive council, 1975-76; first vice-president, 1978, president, 1978-79), Association for Evolutionary Economics, American Economic Association, Industrial Relations Research Association (charter member), American Risk and Insurance Association, American Association of University Professors (member of executive committee, Temple University Chapter, 1974-75), Eastern Economic Association.

AWARDS, HONORS: Harvard refugee scholar, 1939-41; Brookings Institute fellow, 1942; Ford Foundation fellow, 1966; cited as distinguished member of the Association for Social Economics, *Review of Social Economy,* 1983; Volume X of *International Review of Social Economics* was dedicated to Rohrlich.

WRITINGS: (With Louis Hartz, Charles M. Hardin, and William S. McCauley) *Civil-Military Relations: Bibliographical Notes on Administrative Problems of Civilian Mobilization,* Public Administration Service, 1940; *Funds and Accounts in the Federal Government,* Graduate School of Public Administration, Harvard University, 1944; (with Margaret T. Mettert) *Japanese Social Insurance Systems,* Supreme Commander for the Allied Powers, 1951; (with Robert M. Ball and Robert J. Myers) *Pensions in the United States,* U.S. Government Printing Office, 1952; *Veterans' Non-Service-Connected Pensions,* U.S. Government Printing Office, 1956; (editor) *Report on the Asian Regional Training Course in Social Security Administration,* International Labour Office, 1961; *Benefits in the Case of Industrial Accidents and Occupational Diseases,* four volumes, International Labour Office, 1962-64; *Report to the Government of Tanganyika on an Exploratory Social Security Survey with a View to Establishing a National Provident Fund,* International Labour Office/TAP/Tanganyika, 1963.

(Co-author) *Personal Health Care and Social Security,* World Health Organization, 1971; *Social Economics—Concepts and Perspectives* (monograph), Academic Publishers, 1974; (editor) *Environmental Management: Economic and Social Dimensions,* Ballinger, 1976. Contributor to *Encyclopedia of Social Work,* National Association of Social Workers, Volume II, 16th edition, 1971, 17th edition, 1977.

Contributor: Lyman Bryson, editor, *Conflicts of Power in Modern Culture,* Harper, 1947; *Basic Papers on Social Work,* Japan Social Work Association, 1949; Bryson and others, editors, *Perspectives on a Troubled Decade,* Harper, 1950; Bryson and others, editors, *Freedom and Authority in Our Times,* Harper, 1953; *Essays in Honor of Makoto Suetka,* Seibundo, 1965; Sar A. Levitan and others, editors, *Towards Freedom from Want,* Harper, 1968; George R. Iden, editor, *Federal Programs for the Development of Human Resources,* U.S. Government Printing Office, 1968; E. M. Kassalow, editor, *The Role of Social Security in Economic Development,* U.S. Government Printing Office, 1968.

(And editor) *Social Economics for the 1970s: Programs for Social Security, Health and Manpower,* Dunellen, 1970; Jo-

seph W. Eaton, editor, *Migration and Social Welfare,* National Association of Social Workers, 1971; Michael S. March, editor, *Staff Papers Supporting the Report to the President and the Congress by the Commission on Railroad Retirement,* Volume III: *The Relationship of the Railroad Retirement System to Old-Age, Disability, and Survivors' Insurance within the National Social Security Framework,* U.S. Government Printing Office, 1972; C. Arthur Williams, Jr., editor, *Compendium on Workmen's Compensation,* U.S. Government Printing Office, 1973; *Collected Papers,* Volume II, Polish Academy of Sciences, 1973; *Apendices del Informe de la Comision Sobre Seguro de Alud Universal,* Commission on Universal Health Insurance (Puerto Rico), 1974. Contributor of about thirty-five articles to professional journals.

WORK IN PROGRESS: Toward an Economic Rationale in Support of Collective Liability Concepts.

SIDELIGHTS: George F. Rohrlich told *CA:* "I am interested in reconnecting the field of economics to the broader social setting in which it operates—and which, in its turn, is part and parcel of our environment or habitat. Obviously, this suggests a holistic perspective. John Maurice Clark (1884-1963)—in my view the most perceptive among American economists—has had the greatest and most lingering impact upon my thinking. His challenge to the economics profession, posed more than half a century ago, was to formulate the 'one consistent set of laws' which governs *both* 'free exchange' *and* 'social reform.' It is this challenge which informs and motivates my own quest for what he called 'an economics of responsibility' in lieu of the 'economics of irresponsible conflict.'"

*   *   *

ROLANT, Rene
    See FANTHORPE, R(obert) Lionel

*   *   *

ROMERO, Patricia W.
    See CURTIN, Patricia (W.) Romero

*   *   *

RONSON, Mark
    See ALEXANDER, Marc

*   *   *

ROSENBAUM, Peter S.   1940-

PERSONAL: Born March 26, 1940; son of LeRoy S. and Phoebe (Weiss) Rosenbaum; married Joan Grossman, July 15, 1962. *Education:* Wesleyan University, Middletown, Conn., B.A., 1962; Massachusetts Institute of Technology, Ph.D., 1965.

CAREER: International Business Machines Corp., Research Division, Yorktown Heights, N.Y., manager of language learning group, 1965-69; Columbia University, Teachers College, New York, N.Y., associate professor of linguistics and education, 1969—.

MEMBER: International Reading Association, Linguistic Society of America, Association for Computing Machinery, National Council of Teachers of English (member of committee on research, 1970—), Association for Machine Translation and Computational Linguistics, American Educational Research Association, Linguistic Circle of New York, Phi Beta Kappa, Phi Delta Kappa.

AWARDS, HONORS: Woodrow Wilson fellowship.

WRITINGS: The Grammar of English Predicate Complement Constructions, M.I.T. Press, 1967; (with Roderick A. Jacobs) Grammar, Volumes I-IV, Ginn, 1967-69; (with others) "Ginn Language and Composition Series," Ginn, 1968; (with Jacobs) English Transformational Grammar, Blaisdell, 1968; (compiler with Jacobs) Readings in English Transformational Grammar, Ginn, 1970; (with Jacobs) Transformations, Style, and Meaning, Xerox College Publishing, 1971; Peer-Mediated Instruction, Teachers College Press, 1973; Spelling: A PMI System, Holt, 1973. Also author, with Jacobs, of An Introduction to Transformational Grammar, Ginn. Writer of articles and scientific reports.†

* * *

ROSENBLOOM, Noah H. 1915-

PERSONAL: Born September 29, 1915, in Radom, Poland; son of Michael and Sarah Leah (Weingelb) Rosenbloom; married Pearl Cohen, May 16, 1946; children: Leah Marion, Michaelle Nathanyah. Education: Yeshiva University, B.R.E. and Rabbi, 1942, D.H.L., 1948; Columbia University, M.A., 1945; New York University, Ph.D., 1958. Home: 1066 East 85th St., Brooklyn, N.Y. 11236. Office: Stern College, Yeshiva University, 253 Lexington Ave., New York, N.Y. 10016.

CAREER: Rabbi in Steubenville, Ohio, 1942-43, Philadelphia, Pa., 1944-48, and Brooklyn, N.Y., 1949—; Hunter College (now Hunter College of the City University of New York), New York City, instructor in Hebrew literature, 1949-54; Yeshiva University, New York City, professor of Hebraic philosophy and literature, 1954—.

MEMBER: Rabbinical Council of America.

WRITINGS: Luzzatto's Ethico: Psychological Interpretation of Judaism, Yeshiva University Press, 1965; Tradition in an Age of Reform, Jewish Publication Society, 1976; The Threnodist and Threnody of the Holocaust, Kibbutz of Ghetto Fighters (Israel), 1980; (translator) I. Katzehelson, The Song of the Murdered Jewish People, [Israel], 1980; The Exodus Epic of the Enlightenment and Exegesis, Mass Publishing House (Jerusalem), 1983.

Contributor to Jewish philosophy and theology journals. Member of editorial board, Tradition.

* * *

ROSENFIELD, John M(ax) 1924-

PERSONAL: Born October 9, 1924, in Dallas, Tex.; son of John M. and Clarie (Burger) Rosenfield; married Ella Ruth Hopper, 1948; children: Sarah Ann, Paul Thomas. Education: Attended University of Texas, 1941-43; University of California, Berkeley, B.A., 1945; Southern Methodist University, B.F.A., 1947; University of Iowa, M.F.A., 1949; Harvard University, Ph.D., 1959. Home: 75 Coolidge Rd., Arlington, Mass. 02174. Office: Harvard University Art Museums, Cambridge, Mass. 02138.

CAREER: University of Iowa, Iowa City, instructor in history of art, 1949-50, 1952-54; University of California, Los Angeles, assistant professor of history of art, 1957-60; Harvard University, Cambridge, Mass., research fellow, 1960-65, associate professor of fine arts, 1965-68, professor of history of art, 1968—, Abby Aldrich Rockefeller Professor of Oriental Art, 1974—, acting director of art museums, 1982—, chairman

of department of fine arts, 1971-76. Lecturer at University of Maryland, 1960-62, and Northeastern University, 1964-67; trustee, Museum of Fine Arts, Boston, 1975-77. Military service: U.S. Army, 1943-46, 1950-51; served in Southeast Asia during World War II; became technical sergeant.

MEMBER: American Academy of Arts and Sciences, College Art Association, Association for Asian Studies, Association for Oriental Studies.

AWARDS, HONORS: American Council of Learned Societies grant for research in Japan, 1962-64; Harvard University traveling fellowship in Asia and Middle East, 1967.

WRITINGS: The Dynastic Arts of the Kushans, University of California Press, 1966; (translator) S. Noma, Arts of Japan, Ancient and Medieval, Kodansha (Tokyo), 1966; Japanese Arts of the Heian Period, Asia Society (New York), 1967; (editor with Shujiro Shimada) Traditions of Japanese Art: Selections from the Kimiko and John Powers Collection, Fogg Art Museum, Harvard University, 1970; (editor with Fumiko E. and Edwin A. Cranston) The Courtly Tradition in Japanese Art and Literature: Selections from Hofer and Hyde, Fogg Art Museum, Harvard University, 1973.

(Editor) Song of the Brush: Japanese Paintings from the Sanso Collection, Seattle Art Museum, 1979; (with Elizabeth Ten Grotenhuis) Journey of the Three Jewels: Japanese Buddhist Paintings from Western Collections, Asia Society, 1979; The Japanese Courier: Painting, Calligraphy, and Poetry from the Fogg Art Museum, the Phillip Hofer Collection, Santa Barbara Museum of Art, 1980. Editor, Archives of Asian Art, 1973-84, and Japanese Arts Library, 1977—.

WORK IN PROGRESS: The history of Asian art, Japanese calligraphy.

* * *

ROSENTHAL, Donald B. 1937-

PERSONAL: Born July 14, 1937, in Brooklyn, N.Y. Education: Brooklyn College (now Brooklyn College of the City University of New York), B.A. (summa cum laude), 1958; University of Chicago, M.A., 1960, Ph.D., 1964. Office: State University of New York at Buffalo, Amherst Campus, Buffalo, N.Y. 14260.

CAREER: State University of New York at Buffalo, assistant professor, 1964-68, associate professor, 1968-72, professor of political science, 1972—.

MEMBER: American Political Science Association, Policy Studies Organization, American Society for Public Administration.

AWARDS, HONORS: American Institute of Indian Studies fellow, 1963-64; postdoctoral fellowship from University of Chicago Committee on Southern Asia, 1966-67; joint grant from American Institute of Indian Studies and Social Science Research Council-American Council of Learned Societies for research in India, 1970; National Association of Schools of Public Affairs and Administration fellow, 1977-78; senior fellow, Rockefeller Institute of Government, Albany, N.Y., 1983.

WRITINGS: (With Robert L. Crain and Elihu Katz) The Politics of Community Conflict, Bobbs-Merrill, 1969; The Limited Elite, University of Chicago Press, 1971; (editor) The City in Indian Politics, Thomson Press (India), 1976; The Expansive Elite, University of California Press, 1977; Sticking-Points and Ploys *in Federal-Local Relations,* Center for the Study of Federalism, 1979; (editor) *Urban Revitalization,* Sage Publications, 1980.

Contributor: James Q. Wilson, editor, *City Politics and Public Policy,* Wiley, 1968; Terry N. Clark, editor, *Community Structure and Decision-Making,* Chandler Publishing, 1968; Rajni Kothari, editor, *Caste in Indian Politics,* Orient Longmans, 1970; David A. Caputo and Richard L. Cole, editors, *Revenue Sharing,* Lexington Books, 1976; Barry Bozeman and Jeffrey Strausman, editors, *New Directions in Public Administration,* Books/Cole, 1984; Robert Eyestone, editor, *Policy Studies,* Jai Press, 1984.

Contributor of articles and reviews to social science journals.

WORK IN PROGRESS: A study of the design and implementation of a federal program (the Section 8 Neighborhood Strategy Area program) to promote neighborhood revitalization.

*   *   *

ROSS, Clarissa
    See ROSS, W(illiam) E(dward) D(aniel)

*   *   *

ROSS, Dan
    See ROSS, W(illiam) E(dward) D(aniel)

*   *   *

ROSS, Dana
    See ROSS, W(illiam) E(dward) D(aniel)

*   *   *

ROSS, Marilyn
    See ROSS, W(illiam) E(dward) D(aniel)

*   *   *

ROSS, Marilyn (Ann) Heimberg   1939-
    (Marilyn Markham Heimberg)

PERSONAL: Born November 3, 1939, in San Diego, Calif.; daughter of Glenn J. (a businessman) and Dorothy (a real estate broker; maiden name, Scudder) Markham; married T. M. Ross (an advertising executive), May 25, 1977; children: Scott, Steve, Kevin, Laurie. *Education:* Attended San Diego State University. *Religion:* Church of Religious Science. *Home:* 5644 La Jolla Blvd., La Jolla, Calif. 92037.

CAREER: Manager of a woman's ready-to-wear business, 1959-69; San Diego-South Bay Trade Schools, San Diego, Calif., director of marketing, 1969-74; marketing consultant, advertising copywriter, and writer, 1974-80; co-founder of About Books, Inc. (nationwide writing and publishing consulting service), 1980—. President, Communication Creativity, La Jolla, Calif., beginning 1978; co-founder and director, Copy Concepts, La Jolla, beginning 1978. Instructor, San Diego Community College District, 1975-77. Member of board of directors of Research Electronics Co. *Member:* Authors League of America, Authors Guild.

AWARDS, HONORS: First place in nonfiction from Southern Division of California Press Women, 1977, for "Business Bites Back at Internal Crime," 1978, for *Creative Loafing: Shoestring Guide to New Leisure Fun,* and 1979, for *Encyclopedia*

of Self-Publishing: How to Successfully Write, Publish, Promote and Sell Your Own Work.

WRITINGS: (Under name Marilyn Markham Heimberg) *Discover Your Roots: A New, Easy Guide for Tracing Your Family Tree,* Communication Creativity, 1977; (under name Marilyn Markham Heimberg) *Finding Your Roots: How to Trace Your Ancestors and Record Your Family Tree,* Dell, 1978; *Creative Loafing: A Shoestring Guide to New Leisure Fun,* Communication Creativity, 1978; (with husband, T. M. Ross) *The Encyclopedia of Self-Publishing: How to Successfully Write, Publish, Promote and Sell Your Own Work,* Communication Creativity, 1979, 2nd edition, 1980. Also author of *The Force of Us,* 1980. Ghost writer and editor. Contributor to over fifteen magazines, including *Essence, National Enquirer, Coronet, Catholic Digest,* and *Westways.* Editor of *People in Motion* (company newsletter), 1971-74.

WORK IN PROGRESS: The Encyclopedia of Self-Publishing, a revised and expanded edition, for Writer's Digest.

SIDELIGHTS: Marilyn Heimberg Ross writes: "To me, communication is a vital facet of life. It is the catalyst that helps us understand ourselves and others better. I hope to use the written and spoken word to enlighten and entertain on a broad scope. It is important to me that others be encouraged to enjoy the abundance in life that I have discovered. Towards this goal, I lecture and consult on various aspects of writing and publishing, and find great personal satisfaction in assisting promising writers."

AVOCATIONAL INTERESTS: Ranching.

*   *   *

ROSS, W(illiam) E(dward) D(aniel)   1912-
    (Dan Ross; Leslie Ames, Rose Dana, Ruth Dorset, Ann Gilmer, Diane Randall, Ellen Randolph, Dan Roberts, Clarissa Ross, Dana Ross, Marilyn Ross, Jane Rossiter, Tex Steel, Rose Williams, pseudonyms)

PERSONAL: Born November 16, 1912, in Saint John, New Brunswick, Canada; son of William Edward (a military man) and Laura Frances (an actress; maiden name, Brooks) Ross; married Charlotte Edith MacCormack (died, 1958); married Marilyn Ann Clark (an editor), July 2, 1960. *Education:* Attended Provincetown Theatre School, New York, N.Y., 1934; further study at University of Chicago, University of Oklahoma, Columbia University, and University of Michigan. *Politics:* None. *Religion:* Anglican. *Home:* 80 Horton Rd., East Riverside, Saint John, New Brunswick, Canada E2H IP8. *Agent:* Martha Millard, 357 West 19th St., New York, N.Y. 10011.

CAREER: Worked as traveling actor and actor manager with own company, 1930-48; film distributor for own company, for Paramount, and for Monogram Films, 1948-57; writer, 1957—. Member of panel of judges for Gibson National Literary Award, given yearly for best first novel in Canada. *Wartime service:* Served with British Entertainment Services during World War II.

MEMBER: Canadian Authors Association (former president), Playwrights Canada, Mystery Writers of America, Authors Guild, Authors League of America, Western Writers of America, Society of Authors (United Kingdom), Christian Press, Riverside Country Club, Lotus Club, Union Club of Boston, Union Club of Saint John.

AWARDS, HONORS: Dominion Drama Festival Prize for Play-wrighting, 1934; Queen Elizabeth Silver Jubilee Medal, 1978, for contributions to popular fiction.

WRITINGS: Alice in Love, Popular Library, 1965; *Fog Island,* Paperback Library, 1965, published under pseudonym Marilyn Ross, Popular Library, 1977; *Journey to Love,* Bouregy, 1967; *Love Must Not Waver,* R. Hale, 1967; *Winslow's Daughter,* Bouregy, 1967; *Our Share of Love,* R. Hale, 1967; *Let Your Heart Answer,* Bouregy, 1968; *Christopher's Mansion,* Bouregy, 1969; *Luxury Liner Nurse,* R. Hale, 1969; *The Need to Love,* Avalon, 1969.

Sable in the Rain, Lenox Hill, 1970; *The Web of Love,* R. Hale, 1970; *An Act of Love,* Bouregy, 1970; *Magic Valley,* R. Hale, 1970; *This Man I Love,* R. Hale, 1970; *The Whispering Gallery,* Lenox Hill, 1970, published under name Dan Ross, Manor, 1977; *Beauty Doctor's Nurse,* Lenox Hill, 1971; *The Yesteryear Phantom,* Lenox Hill, 1971; *King of Romance,* R. Hale, 1971; *The Room without a Key,* Lenox Hill, 1971; *Music Room,* Dell, 1971; *Wind over the Citadel,* Lenox Hill, 1971; *Rothhaven,* Avalon, 1972; *The House on Mount Vernon Street,* Lenox Hill, 1972; *Mansion on the Moors,* Dell, 1974.

Nightmare Abbey, Berkeley, 1975; *One Louisburg Square,* Belmont-Tower, 1975; *Witch of Goblin's Acres,* Belmont-Tower, 1975; *Dark Is My Shadow,* Manor, 1976; *Summer's End,* Fawcett World, 1976; *House on Lime Street,* Bouregy, 1976; *Pattern of Love,* Bouregy, 1977; *Shadows over Garden,* Belmont-Tower, 1978; *Return to Barton,* Avalon, 1978.

Published by Arcadia House: *The Ghost of Oaklands,* 1967; *The Third Spectre,* 1967, published under name Dan Ross, Macfadden-Baitell, 1969; *Dark Villa of Capri,* 1968; *The Twilight Web,* 1968; *Behind Locked Shutters,* 1968, published under name Dan Ross, Manor, 1975; *Dark of the Moon,* 1968; *Queen's Stairway,* 1978; *The Dark Lane,* 1979; *Magic of Love,* 1980; *Phantom of Edgewater Hall,* 1980; *Nurse Ann's Secret,* 1980; *Onstage for Love,* 1981; *Nurse Grace's Dilemma,* 1982; *This Uncertain Love,* 1982; *Flight to Romance,* 1983; *The Ghostly Jewels,* 1983; *Rehearsal for Love,* 1984; *A Love Discovered,* 1984; *Nurse Janice's Dream,* 1984.

Under name Dan Ross: *The Castle on the Cliff,* Bouregy, 1967; *Nurse in Love,* Avalon, 1972; *Murder Game* (play), Playwrights Press, 1982; *Moscow Maze,* Dorchester, 1983; *This Frightened Lady* (play), Marginal, 1984.

Under pseudonym Leslie Ames: *Bride of Donnybrook,* Arcadia House, 1966; *The Hungry Sea,* Arcadia House, 1967; *The Hidden Chappel,* Arcadia House, 1967; *The Hill of Ashes,* Arcadia House, 1968; *King's Castle,* Lenox Hill, 1970.

Under pseudonym Rose Dana: *Citadel of Love,* Arcadia House, 1965; *Down East Nurse,* Arcadia House, 1967; *Nurse in Jeopardy,* Arcadia House, 1967; *Labrador Nurse,* Arcadia House, 1968; *Network Nurse,* Arcadia House, 1968; *Whitebridge Nurse,* Arcadia House; *Department Store Nurse,* Lenox Hill, 1970.

Under pseudonym Ruth Dorset: *Front Office Nurse,* Arcadia House, 1966; *Hotel Nurse,* Arcadia House, 1967; *Nurse in Waiting,* Arcadia House, 1967.

Under pseudonym Ann Gilmer: *The Fog and the Stars,* Avalon, 1963; *Winds of Change,* Bouregy, 1965; *Private Nurse,* Bouregy, 1969; *Nurse on Emergency,* Bouregy, 1970; *Skyscraper Nurse,* Bouregy, 1976; *Nurse at Breakwater Hotel,* Arcadia, 1982.

Under pseudonym Diane Randall: *Dragon Lover,* Jove, 1981.

Under pseudonym Ellen Randolph: *Personal Secretary,* Avalon, 1963; *The Castle on the Hill,* Avalon, 1964; *Nurse Martha's Wish,* Arcadia, 1983.

Under pseudonym Dan Roberts: *The Wells Fargo Brand,* Arcadia House, 1964; *The Cheyenne Kid,* Arcadia House, 1965; *Durez City Bonanza,* Arcadia House, 1965; *Outlaw's Gold,* Arcadia House, 1965; *Stage to Link City,* Arcadia House, 1966; *Wyoming Range War,* Arcadia House, 1966; *Yuma Brand,* Arcadia House, 1967; *The Dawn Riders,* Arcadia House, 1968.

Under pseudonym Clarissa Ross: *Mistress of Ravenswood,* Arcadia House, 1966; *The Secret of Mallet Castle,* Arcadia House, 1966; *Fogbound,* Arcadia House, 1967, published under name Dan Ross, Manor, 1976; *Let Your Heart Answer,* Valentine, 1968; *Secret of the Pale Lover,* Magnum, 1969; *Beware the Kindly Stranger,* Lancer, 1970; *Gemini in Darkness,* Magnum, 1970; *Glimpse into Terror,* Magnum, 1971; *The Spectral Mist,* Magnum, 1972; *Phantom of Glencourt,* Magnum, 1972; *Whispers in the Night,* Bantam, 1972; *China Shadow,* Avon, 1974; *Drafthaven,* Avon, 1974; *Ghost of Dark Harbor,* Avon, 1974; *A Hearse for Dark Harbor,* Avon, 1974.

Dark Harbor Hunting, Avon, 1975; *Evil of Dark Harbor,* Avon, 1975; *Terror at Dark Harbor,* Avon, 1975; *Durrell Towers,* Pyramid, 1976; *Jade Princess,* Pyramid, 1977; *Moscow Mists,* Avon, 1977; *A Scandalous Affair,* Belmont-Tower, 1978; *Kashmiri Passions,* Warner Brothers, 1978; *Istanbul Nights,* Jove, 1978; *Flame of Love,* Belmont-Tower, 1978; *Wine of Passion,* Belmont-Tower, 1978; *Casablanca Intrigue,* Warner Brothers, 1979; *So Perilous My Love,* Leisure Press, 1979, *Eternal Desire,* Jove, 1979.

Fan the Wanton Flame, Pocket Books, 1980; *Only Make Believe,* Leisure Press, 1980; *Masquerade,* Pocket Books, 1980; *Venetian Affair,* Jove, 1980; *Beloved Scoundrel,* Belmont-Tower, 1980; *Fortune's Mistress,* Popular Library, 1981; *Satan Whispers,* Leisure Press, 1981; *Summer of the Shaman,* Warner Brothers, 1982; *The Dancing Years,* Pinnacle, 1982.

Under pseudonym Dana Ross; published by Paperback Library: *Demon of Darkness,* 1975; *Lodge Sinister,* 1975; *This Shrouded Night,* 1975; *The Raven and the Phantom,* 1976.

Under pseudonym Marilyn Ross; published by Warner, except as indicated: *Phantom of Fog Island,* 1971; *The Long Night of Fear,* 1972; *Mistress of Moorwood Manor,* 1972; *Night of the Phantom,* 1972; *The Sinister Garden,* 1972; *Witch of Bralhaven,* 1972; *Behind the Purple Veil,* 1973; *Face in the Shadows,* 1973; *House of Ghosts,* 1973; *Don't Look Behind You,* 1973; *Marta,* 1973; *Step into Terror,* 1973; *The Amethyst Tears,* Ballantine, 1974; *The Vampire Contessa,* Pinnacle, 1974; *Witches Cove,* 1974; *Cameron Castle,* 1975; *The Ghost and the Garnet: Birthstone No. One,* Ballantine, 1975; *Satan's Island,* 1975; *Shadow over Emerald Castle,* Ballantine, 1975; *Brides of Saturn,* Berkeley, 1976; *Temple of Darkness,* Ballantine, 1976; *The Twice Dead,* Fawcett, 1978.

Published by Paperback Library: *The Locked Corridor,* 1965; *Beware My Love!,* 1965; *Dark Shadows,* 1968; *The Foe of Barnabas Collins,* 1969; *Barnabas, Quentin and Dr. Jekyll's Son,* 1971; *Dark Stars over Seacrest,* 1972; *Phantom of the Swamp,* 1972.

Published by Popular Library: *A Garden of Ghosts,* 1974; *Loch Sinister,* 1974; *Dark Towers of Fog Island,* 1975; *Fog Island Secret,* 1975; *Ghost Ship of Fog Island,* 1975; *Phantom of the Thirteenth Floor,* 1975; *Ravenhurst,* 1975; *The Widow of Westwood,* 1976; *The Curse of Black Charlie,* 1976; *Haiti Circle,*

1976; *Phantom Wedding,* 1976; *Shadow over Denby,* 1976; *Stewards of Stormhaven: Cellars of the Dead,* 1976; *Waiting in the Shadows,* 1976; *Cauldron of Evil,* 1977; *Death's Dark Music,* 1977; *Mask of Evil,* 1977; *Phantom of the Snow,* 1977; *This Evil Village,* 1977; *Delta Flame,* 1978; *Rothby,* 1978; *Horror of Fog Island,* 1978; *Beloved Adversary,* 1981; *Forbidden Flame,* 1982.

Under pseudonym Jane Rossiter; published by Avalon: *Backstage Nurse,* 1963; *Love Is Forever,* 1963; *Summer Star,* 1964.

Under pseudonym Rose Williams; published by Arcadia House, except as indicated: *Five Nurses,* 1964; *Nurse in Doubt,* 1965; *Nurse Diane,* 1966; *Nurse in Spain,* R. Hale, 1967; *Nurse in Nassau,* 1967; *Airport Nurse,* 1968.

Also writes under pseudonym Tex Steel. Contributor of short stories to *Saint Mystery Magazine, Mike Shayne Mystery Magazine,* and other periodicals.

WORK IN PROGRESS: Several novels, including *Denver's Lady, Stormy Crossing, Summer Returns,* and a novel version of the author's play *Murder Game.*

SIDELIGHTS: While he has produced dozens of popular gothic thrillers, nurse romances, and western adventures, W. E. D. Ross stresses the literary value in his works. "I honestly don't consider myself a hack," he tells David Dee in a *Chicago Tribune Book World* interview. "A hack is motivated entirely by money, and I'm not. I'm making money. I do well. But every word I write is sincere.

"Some of the academics," Ross continues, "have a jaundiced view of my writing. I don't mind that. I'm dealing in another area of writing. I'm an entertainer. I'm here to give my readers a good read." The author concludes to Dee: "I can't imagine ever not writing. When I get letters from fans, some of whom have been reading my books for years now, I get a special joy. People can call me a hack or anything they like, but I enjoy what I'm doing and the readers enjoy what they're reading. That's what matters really, isn't it?"

Ross's novels have been published in several foreign languages. The author's papers have been collected by Boston University.

BIOGRAPHICAL/CRITICAL SOURCES: Chicago Tribune Book World, October 16, 1983.

*   *   *

ROSSI, Bruno
See LEVINSON, Leonard

*   *   *

ROSSI, Ernest Lawrence   1933-

PERSONAL: Born March 26, 1933, in Bridgeport, Conn.; son of Angelo (a carpenter) and Mary (De Libro) Rossi; married Sheila Peabbles (a clinical psychologist), August 10, 1962 (divorced, 1977); children: Lisa, April. *Education:* University of Connecticut, B.S., 1954; Washington State University, M.S., 1957; Temple University, Ph.D., 1961. *Office:* 11980 San Vincente Blvd., Los Angeles, Calif. 90049.

CAREER: Clinical psychologist in private practice, Los Angeles, Calif., 1962—; Analytical Psychology Clinic, Los Angeles, member of staff and clinic committee, 1969—; University of California, Los Angeles, member of extension faculty,

1972—. C. G. Jung Institute of Los Angeles, member of executive board, 1975, training analyst, 1976; member of board of directors, Centro per lo Studio della Personalita, Naples, Italy. Workshop leader and trainer in teaching seminars, American Society of Clinical Hypnosis, Ericksonian Hypnotherapy Congresses, 1974—. Volunteer consultant, Westminister Neighborhood Association, Watts, Calif.

MEMBER: International Association of Analytical Psychology (Jungian Psychology), American Psychological Association, American Society of Clinical and Experimental Hypnosis.

AWARDS, HONORS: U.S. Public Health fellow, 1961-62, 1962-64.

WRITINGS—Published by Irvington, except as indicated: *Dreams and the Growth of Personality: Expanding Awareness in Psychotherapy,* Pergamon, 1972; (with Milton H. Erickson) *Hypnotic Realities: The Induction of Clinical Hypnosis and Forms of Indirect Suggestion,* Irvington, 1976; *Hypnotherapy: An Exploratory Casebook,* 1979; (editor) *The Collected Papers of Milton H. Erickson, M.D. in Hypnosis,* four volumes, 1980; *Experiencing Hypnosis: Therapeutic Approaches to Altered States,* 1981; (editor) *Healing in Hypnosis: The Seminars, Workshops, and Lectures of Milton H. Erickson,* Volume I, 1983. Contributor of articles and reviews to more than ten psychology journals and magazines. Member of editorial board, *American Journal of Clinical Hypnosis,* 1977—, *Psychological Perspectives,* 1980, and *Ericksonian Monographs,* 1983.

WORK IN PROGRESS: Ultradian Health and Healing: Biological Rhythms in Everyday Life.

SIDELIGHTS: Ernest Lawrence Rossi wrote *CA:* "All my writing is an effort to explain something to myself. My first book, *Dreams and the Growth of Personality,* was written while in post-doctoral training. . . . The director of my program did not want me to present some unusually interesting material [about] a patient whom I [considered] a psychological genius. The director felt [that] I was too inexperienced and would make a fool of myself before the august body of psychoanalysts. . . . I wrote it all up in the form of a book that some people now feel is [a] valid extension of classical psychoanalytic theory. My second book, *Hypnotic Realities,* was my effort to understand the teachings of another genius, Milton H. Erickson. My third book, *Hypnotherapy: An Exploratory Casebook,* is yet another effort to understand and extend current developments in the process of psychotherapy. I write because I can clearly see how my mind is inferior to others'; the writing is the scaffolding I throw up in order to reach what I feel I should know."

*   *   *

ROSSITER, Jane
See ROSS, W(illiam) E(dward) D(aniel)

*   *   *

ROTH, Alexander
See DUNNER, Joseph

*   *   *

ROTH, Robert Howard   1933-

PERSONAL: Born January 15, 1933, in Newark, N.J.; son of Max and Marion (Gurkewitz) Roth; married Estelle Goldstein, June 16, 1957; children: Lisa, Neil. *Education:* Juilliard School of Music, B.S., 1953; Columbia University, M.A., 1956, Ed.D., 1960. *Home:* 111 Gallinson Dr., Murray Hill, N.J. 07974. *Office:* Madison Medical Center, 28 Walnut St., Madison, N.J. 07940.

CAREER: Kean College of New Jersey, Union, instructor, 1960-63, assistant professor, 1963-65, associate professor, 1965-68, professor of psychology, 1968—; Madison Medical Center, Madison, N.J., private practice in clinical psychology, 1969—.

MEMBER: American Psychological Association, American Orthopsychiatric Association (fellow), American Group Psychotherapy Association, American Personnel and Guidance Association, American Association for the Advancement of Science, National Council on Family Relations, National Institute for the Psychotherapies, Sigmund Freud Society of America, Eastern Psychological Association, New Jersey Psychological Association, New Jersey Academy of Science, New York Academy of Sciences.

WRITINGS—Editor: *Abnormal Psychology: Disorders of Behavior and Experience*, Selected Academic Readings, 1968; *Psychology of Personality*, Selected Academic Readings, 1968; *The Parameters of Personality*, MSS Educational Publishing, 1970; *Studies in Psychopathology*, MSS Educational Publishing, 1970; *Studies in Abnormal Psychology*, Xerox College Publishing, 1972; *Theoretical and Applied Studies in Personality*, Xerox College Publishing, 1972; *Psychological Studies in Personality*, Xerox College Publishing, 1978; *Abnormal Psychology in Perspective*, Xerox College Publishing, 1978.

Editor; published by Ginn: *Disorders of Behavior and Experience*, 1979, 2nd edition, 1981; *Personality in Perspective*, 1980, 2nd edition, 1982; *Contemporary Studies in Psychopathy*, 1983.

*   *   *

ROTHCHILD, Donald (Sylvester)   1928-

PERSONAL: Born August 11, 1928, in New York, N.Y.; son of Sylvester E. (a businessman) and Alice (Levy) Rothchild; married Edith Lee White (a psychiatric social worker), 1953; children: Derek, Maynard. *Education:* Kenyon College, B.A. (with high honors), 1949; University of California, Berkeley, M.A., 1954; Johns Hopkins University, Ph.D., 1958. *Politics:* Democrat. *Office:* Department of Political Science, University of California, Davis, Calif. 95616.

CAREER: Colby College, Waterville, Me., instructor, 1957-59, assistant professor, 1959-62, associate professor of political science, 1962-65; University of California, Davis, associate professor, 1965-69, professor of political science, 1969—. Fulbright lecturer, Makerere University, 1962-64; senior lecturer, University of Nairobi, 1966-67; Ford Foundation visiting professor, University of Zambia, 1970-71; director, Ghana Study Center, University of Ghana, 1975-77. *Military service:* U.S. Army, 1960-62.

MEMBER: African Studies Association, American Political Science Association, International Studies Association, International Political Science Association, Western Political Science Association, Phi Beta Kappa.

AWARDS, HONORS: Fellow, Hebrew University of Jerusalem, 1980.

WRITINGS: Toward Unity in Africa, Public Affairs Press, 1960; (contributor) Gwendolen M. Carter, editor, *Politics in Africa: Seven Cases*, Harcourt, 1966; (contributor) Carter, editor, *Na-*

tional Unity and Regionalism in Eight African States, Cornell University Press, 1966; (editor) *Politics of Integration: An East African Documentary*, East African Publishing House, 1968; (editor with C. J. Gertzel and Maure Goldschmidt) *Government and Politics in Kenya*, East African Publishing House, 1969, International Publications Service, 1972.

Racial Bargaining in Independent Kenya: A Study of Minorities and Decolonization, Oxford University Press, for Institute of Race Relations, 1973; (co-author) *Scarcity, Choice, and Public Policy in Middle Africa*, University of California Press, 1978; (co-editor) *Eagle Entangled*, Longman, 1979.

(Co-editor) *State Versus Ethnic Claims*, Westview, 1983; (co-editor) *Eagle Defiant*, Little, Brown, 1983. Contributor to *Harper's* and to political science and African studies journals.

WORK IN PROGRESS: Ethnicity and Public Policy.

*   *   *

ROTHWELL, Kenneth J(ames)   1925-

PERSONAL: Born October 13, 1925, in Perth, Australia; son of Horace P. and Violet (Hoddinott) Rothwell; married Alida Eidner, October 17, 1952; children: Kylie, Karin, Andrew Carlson. *Education:* University of Western Australia, B.A., 1949, M.A., 1954; University of Stockholm, graduate study, 1952; Harvard University, Ph.D., 1960. *Home address:* Box 124, Durham, N.H. 03824. *Office:* Department of Economics, University of New Hampshire, Durham, N.H. 03824.

CAREER: Reserve Bank of Australia, economic assistant, 1946-55; Harvard University, Cambridge, Mass., research associate, 1955-57; Bucknell University, Lewisburg, Pa., assistant professor of economics, 1957-60; Dartmouth College, Hanover, N.H., assistant professor, 1961-63; University of New Hampshire, Durham, associate professor, 1963-67, professor of economics, 1967—, dean of School of Business and Economics, 1966-67.

Visiting professor, University of Western Australia, 1965, Institute of Social Studies, The Hague, 1971, and University of Stockholm, 1971-72; coordinator of international programs, New England Center, 1967—. Associate director, Indonesian Cultural foundation, 1970; director of agricultural research, Agency for International Development (Korea), 1971—; affiliated with United Nations Missions to Indonesia, Ethiopia, and Iran, 1974-75. Consultant to Pan American Union, Academy for Interscience Methodology, and United Nations Center for Development, Planning, Programs, and Policy. *Military service:* Royal Australian Air Force, 1943-45; became flight lieutenant.

MEMBER: American Economic Association, Society for International Development, Latin American Studies Association, Association for Asian Studies.

AWARDS, HONORS: Ford faculty fellowship from Massachusetts Institute of Technology, 1961.

WRITINGS: (With M. O. Clement and R. D. Pfister) *Theoretical Issues in International Economics*, Houghton, 1967; *New England Professional Schools and World Affairs; With a Directory of Professional Schools and International Education in New England*, New England Center for Continuing Education, 1968; (editor) *Administration and Management in Developing Countries*, New England Center for Continuing Education, 1970; *New England-Japan Commercial and Educational Exchanges*, New England Center for Continuing Education,

1972; *Administrative Issues of Developing Economies,* Heath, 1972; *The Scope of Management and Administration Problems in Development,* Institute of Social Studies, 1973; (editor) *New England-Japan Trade and Exchange Potentials: A Conference Report,* New England Center for Continuing Education, 1973; (editor with Bernard K. Gordon) *The New Political Economy of the Pacific,* Ballinger, 1975.

Also author of *The Planning and the Realisation of Economic Development,* Institut Ilmu Pemerintahan, Biro Research dan Publikaski, 1969, and editor of *Higher Education and Accelerated Change,* New England Center for Continuing Education, 1971. Contributor to professional journals and magazines.

WORK IN PROGRESS: Research on inflation theory and development economics, and comparative fiscal policy.

*   *   *

ROWE, A(lbert) W(ard) 1915-

PERSONAL: Born July 1, 1915, in St. Ives, Cornwall, England; son of Anthony (a harbor master) and Margaret (Ninnes) Rowe; married Joan Whipp, January 24, 1945; children: Gillian, Janet, Isabel. *Education:* University of London, B.A. (with honors in English), M.Phil., L.R.A.M., Teachers Certificate, and Diploma in Education. *Home:* 57A Pearson Park, Hull, Yorkshire, England.

CAREER: Former lecturer at a training college and headmaster at David Lister Comprehensive School, Hull, Yorkshire, England; radio and television broadcaster. *Military service:* Royal Air Force, 1939-45.

WRITINGS: (With Gareth Walters) *Harmonica and Recorder Teacher's Manual,* with pupils' primary and secondary books, Hohner, 1958; *The Education of the Average Child,* Harrap, 1959; (with Walters) "Worcester" series (graded part pieces for harmonica and recorder), two books, Hohner, 1959.

The New Hohner Melodica Tutor, Hohner, 1961; "English through Experience" series, five books (Books I-IV with Peter Emmens), Blond Educational, 1963-67, revised edition, 1975; *Desk Book of Plain English,* Basil Blackwell, 1965, revised edition, 1979; (contributor) Brian Jackson, editor, *English Versus Examinations,* Chatto & Windus, 1965; (editor) *People Like Us: Short Stories for Secondary Schools,* Faber, 1965; (editor) "Active Anthologies" series, five books, Blond Educational, 1967-69; *Language for Living,* Basil Blackwell, 1967.

The School as a Guidance Community, Pearson Press, 1971; (with Jim Roberts) *Making the Present: A Social and Economic History of Britain, 1918-72,* Hutchinson, 1975; (translator) Frederico Garcia Lorca, *Poems* (translations from the first nineteen poems from *Poema del cante hondo*), Aquila-Phaeton Press, 1975; *English Teaching and Its Contribution to Secondary Education,* Hart-Davis, 1975; *English for Living,* four volumes, Macmillan, 1975-76; *Language Matters,* Wheaton, 1977; *Pollen Girl,* Macmillan, 1977; *St. Ives Boy's Summer: Poems,* Aquila, 1977; *Language Links,* Wheaton, 1978; *The Sword of Fate,* Hutchinson, 1978.

Positive English, four volumes, Macmillan, 1980; *Language Skills,* Wheaton, 1981; *Enjoying Poetry,* Macmillan, 1982. Author of booklets and pamphlets, some for use in primary schools. Contributor of articles and reviews to professional journals.

WORK IN PROGRESS: Two books, *Changing a School* and *Educating Ordinary Children;* a two-book anthology of prose

and verse for primary schools; research into attitudes of secondary school pupils towards school and life.

AVOCATIONAL INTERESTS: Sports (especially rugby football), travel in Europe and America, reading (especially poetry and novels), music, playing clarinet and harmonica.†

*   *   *

RUARK, Gibbons 1941-

PERSONAL: Born December 10, 1941, in Raleigh, N.C.; son of Henry Gibbons (a minister) and Sarah (Jenkins) Ruark; married Kay Stinson, October 5, 1963; children: Jennifer Kay, Emily Westbrook. *Education:* University of North Carolina at Chapel Hill, A.B., 1963; University of Massachusetts, M.A., 1965. *Office:* Department of English, University of Delaware, Newark, Del. 19711.

CAREER: University of North Carolina at Greensboro, instructor in English, 1965-68; University of Delaware, Newark, assistant professor, 1968-73, associate professor, 1973-83, professor of English, 1983—.

AWARDS, HONORS: National Arts Council awards for poetry, 1968, and 1971, for *A Program for Survival;* National Endowment for the Arts fellowship, 1979.

WRITINGS: (Editor with Robert Watson) *The Greensboro Reader,* University of North Carolina Press, 1968; *A Program for Survival* (poems), University Press of Virginia, 1971; *Reeds* (poems), Texas Tech Press, 1978; *Keeping Company* (poems), Johns Hopkins University Press, 1983.

Contributor: *American Literary Anthology #1,* Farrar, Strauss, 1968; Lionel Stevenson and others, editors, *Best Poems of 1968,* Pacific Books, 1969; X. J. Kennedy, editor, *Messages,* Little, Brown, 1973; Stevenson and others, editors, *Best Poems of 1974,* Pacific Books, 1975; Kennedy, editor, *Introduction to Poetry,* Little, Brown, 1982; Kennedy, editor, *Introduction to Literature,* Little, Brown, 1983; *1984 Anthology of Modern Poetry,* Monitor Book, 1984; Dave Smith and David Bottoms, editors, *The Morrow Anthology of Younger American Poets,* Morrow, 1984.

WORK IN PROGRESS: Poems.

SIDELIGHTS: Gibbons Ruark is described by James Whitehead in *Saturday Review* as "quiet, reflective; in fact nostalgia is his vision, particularly in memories of his dead father. . . . Ruark accepts and loves the family that raised him, and he accepts and loves the family he is raising in turn. Affirming family and friends, he makes marvelous poetry in the process."

The poems in *A Program for Survival* are, according to Michael Hefferan's review in *Midwest Quarterly,* "of a high and difficult sort, not easily achieved and less easily contrived. These poems took a long time: nothing here was slapped down unrevised, nothing here depends for its effects on cryptic, half-digested talk to obfuscate some basic vacancy. . . . There is an emotional authenticity about all these poems that makes them almost overpowering with a kind of uncanny, unrelenting force. They stay in the mind because they have been, many of them, driven there so deeply they will not pry loose."

A tape recording of Ruark's poems has been placed in the archives of the Library of Congress.

BIOGRAPHICAL/CRITICAL SOURCES: Midwest Quarterly, Volume XII, 1971; *Virginia Quarterly Review,* autumn, 1971;

Saturday Review, December 18, 1971; *Contemporary Literary Criticism*, Volume III, Gale, 1975.

*　　*　　*

RULON, Philip Reed 1934-

PERSONAL: Born February 20, 1934, in Delaware, Iowa; son of Wayne M. and R. Hannah Rulon; married Annette K. Rulon, January 2, 1976; children: Philip Scott, Douglas Matthew; adopted children: Yvonne Winkler Thompson, William Payne Thompson, Ann Marie Thompson. *Education:* Washburn University, B.A., 1963; Kansas State Teachers' College (now Emporia State University), M.A., 1965; Oklahoma State University, Ed.D., 1967; University of Texas, postdoctoral study, 1974. *Politics:* Democrat. *Religion:* Episcopalian. *Home:* Saddlerock Ranch, R.R. 2, Rock Ridge Dr., Sedona, Ariz. 86336. *Office:* Department of History, Northern Arizona University, Flagstaff, Ariz. 86002.

CAREER: Oklahoma State University, Stillwater, instructor in history, 1964-67; Northern Arizona University, Flagstaff, 1967—, began as assistant professor of history, currently director of Research Center for Excellence in Education. Summer lecturer at Oklahoma State University, 1965, at Kansas State Teachers' College (now Emporia State University), 1967, 1969. Consultant to Arizona Council on the Humanities and Public Policy. Member of committee on history in the classroom, National Advisory Board. *Military service:* U.S. Army, 1957-59.

MEMBER: American Historical Association, History of Education Society, Society for History Education, National Council for the Social Sciences, Oklahoma Academy of Science, Phi Kappa Phi, Phi Alpha Theta. *Awards, honors:* Recipient of eleven research grants from Northern Arizona University, and of grants from Lyndon Baines Johnson Foundation, American Historical Association, and U.S. Office of Education.

WRITINGS: Oklahoma State University: A History, Oklahoma State University Press, 1975; *Compassionate Samaritan: The Life of Lyndon Baines Johnson*, Nelson-Hall, 1981; *Letters from the Hill Country: The Correspondence of Rebekah and Lyndon Baines Johnson*, Thorp Springs Press, 1983; (with William H. Lyon) *Speaking Out: An Oral History of the American Past*, two volumes, Burgess, 1981. Contributor to education and history journals. Member of editorial board, *Historian*, 1974-79.

WORK IN PROGRESS: Navajo Traders.

*　　*　　*

RUNKLE, Gerald 1924-

PERSONAL: Born January 5, 1924, in Akron, Ohio; son of Frank I. (a businessman) and Alberta (Abbett) Runkle; married Audrey Colchin, June 24, 1947; children: Randall, Elizabeth, Sarah. *Education:* Oberlin College, A.B., 1948; Yale University, M.A., 1950, Ph.D., 1951. *Politics:* Democrat. *Home:* 445 Buena Vista, Edwardsville, Ill. 62025. *Office:* Department of Philosophy, Southern Illinois University, Edwardsville, Ill. 62026.

CAREER: University of Georgia, Atlanta Division (now Georgia State University), assistant professor, 1951-55, associate professor of philosophy, 1955; Doane College, Crete, Neb., associate professor of philosophy, 1955-59; Southern Illinois University, Edwardsville, associate professor, 1959-64, pro-

fessor of philosophy, 1964—, chairman of department, 1959-64, dean, School of Humanities, 1964-73. *Military service:* U.S. Army Air Forces, 1942-46; became lieutenant. *Member:* American Association of University Professors, American Society for Political and Legal Philosophy, American Philosophical Association.

WRITINGS: A History of Western Political Theory, Ronald, 1968; *Anarchism: Old and New*, Dell, 1972; *Good Thinking*, Holt, 1978, 2nd edition, 1981; *Ethics: An Examination of Contemporary Moral Problems*, Holt, 1982; *Theory and Practice*, Holt, 1984.

Contributor of articles to *Atlanta Economic Review, Theology Today, Ethics, Journal of Politics, Comparative Studies in Society and History, Darshana International*, and *Journal of the History of Philosophy*.

*　　*　　*

RUTHERFORD, Ward 1927-

PERSONAL: Born October 27, 1927, in Richmond, England; son of Edward Thomas (a marine engineer) and Lydia (a journalist; maiden name, Jones) Rutherford; married Marilyn Aikens Cowes (a teacher), August 5, 1955; children: Sarah Julia, Luke Edward, Martin Richard. *Education:* Educated in the United Kingdom. *Politics:* Radical. *Religion:* Anglican. *Home:* 76 Stanford Ave., Brighton, Sussex BN1 6FE, England. *Agent:* Douglas Rae, 28 Charing Cross Rd., London W1, England.

CAREER: Channel Television, Jersey, United Kingdom, head of news, 1962-65; British Broadcasting Corp. (BBC), London, reporter, 1965-67; writer. Member, Teilhard Centre for the Future of Man.

MEMBER: Writers Guild, Crime Writers Association, Society of Sussex Authors.

WRITINGS: The Gallows Set, Bles, 1969; *Kasserine: Baptism of Fire*, Ballantine, 1970; *Great Big Laughing Hannah*, Bles, 1971; *The Fall of the Philippines*, Ballantine, 1971; *The Untimely Silence: The Story of the Jersey Sex Attacks*, Hamish Hamilton, 1972; *Genocide: The Nazi Persecution of the Jews*, Ballantine, 1973.

The Russian Army in World War I, Cremonesi, 1975, published as *The Ally: The Russian Army in World War I*, 1977; *Jersey*, David & Charles, 1976; *Hitler's Propaganda Machine*, Bison Books, 1978; *The Druids and Their Heritage*, Cremonesi, 1978, published as *The Druids*, Aquarian, 1983; *Blitzkrieg 1940*, Bison Books, 1979; *Rommel*, Hamlyn, 1981.

Plays: "Fingers," first performed in Worthing, England, at the Connaught Theatre, November 24, 1976.

SIDELIGHTS: Ward Rutherford told *CA:* "As a writer my motivation has always been the belief that modern, western man feels himself to be lost. I believe that this arises from the lack of those central certainties he once obtained from religious belief. His criteria for behavior have thus become negative ones, i.e. why shouldn't I do this or that—rather than positive ones. I realize that it is impossible to expect humanity to return to the old religious ideas with their very rigid structures and that many ethical and moral ideas have been irreversibly changed (sexual morality, for instance, by the advent of the contraceptive pill). On the other hand, I am utterly convinced that humanity needs to find for itself some central, extrinsic point of reference and that, indeed, the need is realized, if only on a sort of subconscious level. My own hints on achieving this arise from the writings of Pierre Teilhard de Chardin. What is basic to this, it seems to me, is his notion that man is deeply enmeshed in his evolutionary process, which with the development of the reflective mind is now become conscious. It is from this that modern man must derive his ideas about himself and about his attitudes to his fellow man, whether or not this includes the notion of a personal or any other kind of God. As I am not a propagandist writer I have never sought to canvas these views through my work, but rather to use them as a matrix out of which my books and their ideas arise.''

Reviewing *The Druids and Their Heritage,* John Leonard writes in the *New York Times:* ''Ward Rutherford, an English novelist and historian, aspires to define what Druids were and weren't. . . . He hasn't much evidence to go on . . . but he conjectures promiscuously in graceful prose. . . . Mr. Rutherford is good-humored. . . . And he is absorbing when he occupies himself with comparisons between the Brahmins and the Druids, the Magi and the Druids, and the Assyrians and the Druids.'' Rutherford's book, Leonard concludes, ''is superbly packaged and nicely written and insists that attention be paid.''

BIOGRAPHICAL/CRITICAL SOURCES: New York Times, March 15, 1979.

* * *

RYCHLAK, Joseph F(rank) 1928-

PERSONAL: Surname is pronounced *Rish*-lock; born December 17, 1928, in Cudahy, Wis.; son of Joseph Walter and Helen (Bieniek) Rychlak; married Lenora Smith, June 16, 1956; children: Ronald, Stephanie. *Education:* University of Wisconsin, B.S., 1953; Ohio State University, M.A., 1954, Ph.D., 1957. *Home:* 916 Michigan Ave., Apartment 2, Evanston, Ill. 60202. *Office:* Department of Psychology, Loyola University of Chicago, 6525 North Sheridan Rd., Chicago, Ill. 60626.

CAREER: Florida State University, Tallahassee, assistant professor of psychology, 1957-58; Washington State University, Pullman, assistant professor of psychology and director of Human Relations Center, 1958-61; St. Louis University, St. Louis, Mo., associate professor, 1961-65; professor of psychology, 1965-69; Purdue University, Lafayette, Ind., professor of psychology, 1969-83; Loyola University of Chicago, Chicago, Ill., Maude C. Clarke Professor of Humanistic Psychology, 1983—. Research consultant for management progress study, American Telephone & Telegraph Corp., 1957-82. *Military service:* U.S. Army Air Forces, 1946-47; U.S. Air Force, 1947-49; became sergeant. *Member:* American Psychological Association (fellow), Society for Projective Techniques (fellow), Phi Beta Kappa. *Awards, honors:* Honored for ''outstanding contribution to human understanding and welfare'' by the International Association for Social Psychiatry, 1971.

WRITINGS: A Philosophy of Science for Personality Theory, Houghton, 1968, 2nd edition, Robert E. Krieger, 1981; *Introduction to Personality and Psychotherapy,* Houghton, 1973, 2nd edition, 1981; (editor) *Dialectic: Humanistic Rationale for Behavior and Development,* Karger, 1976; *The Psychology of Rigorous Humanism,* Wiley-Interscience, 1977; *Discovering Free Will and Personal Responsibility,* Oxford University Press, 1979; *Personality and Life Style of Young Male Managers: A Logical Learning Theory Analysis,* Academic Press, 1982.

RYDEN, Hope

PERSONAL: Born in St. Paul, Minn.; daughter of Ernest E. (a minister) and Agnes (Johnson) Ryden. *Education:* Attended Augustana College, Rock Island, Ill.; University of Iowa, B.A. *Home:* 345 East 81st St., New York, N.Y. 10028. *Agent:* N. S. Bienstock, 850 7th Ave., New York, N.Y. 10019.

CAREER: Free-lance documentary film producer and writer. Drew Associates (affiliate of Time-Life Broadcast), New York City, film producer, 1960-64; Hope Ryden Productions, New York City, film producer, writer, and director, 1965; American Broadcasting Corp., New York City, feature producer for ABC-TV evening news, 1966-68. Free-lance still photographer. Member of board of directors, Defenders of Wildlife, 1977—, Society for Protective Animal Legislation, 1983—, and American Society for Protection of Animals, 1984—.

AWARDS, HONORS: ''Oppie'' award for best book in Americana category, 1970, and *Library Journal* citation as one of 100 best sci-tech titles, 1970, for *America's Last Wild Horses;* Screen Writers Guild nomination for best film documentary, 1970, for ''Missing in Randolph''; New York Public Library citations for *God's Dog* and *America's Last Wild Horses;* Cine Golden Eagle award for ''The Wellsprings''; Emmy Award, Clarion Award, and Society of the Silurians Award, all for ''Angel Dust: Teenage Emergency''; Library of Congress Award, Notable Book award, Outstanding Science Book for Children award, Notable Book in Field of Social Studies award, and ''Children's Choice'' award, all 1978, for *The Little Deer of the Florida Keys;* Humanitarian of the Year Award, American Horse Protection Association, 1979; Joseph Wood Krutch Award, Humane Society of the United States, 1981; Outstanding Achievement Award, Augustana College Alumni Association, 1981; Outstanding Science Book for Children award, 1983, for *Bobcat.*

WRITINGS: America's Last Wild Horses, Dutton, 1970; *The Wild Colt,* Coward, 1972; *Mustangs: A Return to the Wild,* Viking, 1972; *God's Dog,* Coward, 1975; *The Wild Pups,* Putnam, 1975; *The Little Deer of the Florida Keys,* Putnam, 1978; *Bobcat Year,* Viking, 1981; *Bobcat,* Putnam, 1983; *American Bald Eagle,* Putnam, 1985.

Documentary films: ''Susan Starr,'' produced by Drew Associates/Time-Life Films, 1962; ''Jane,'' produced by Drew Associates/Time-Life Films, 1963; ''Mission to Malaya,'' produced by Drew Associates/ABC-TV Network News, 1964; ''Operation Gwamba,'' produced by Hope Ryden Productions and CBS-TV, 1965; ''To Love A Child,'' produced by ABC-TV News, 1969; ''Missing in Randolph,'' produced by ABC-TV News, 1970; ''Strangers in Their Own Land: The Chicanos,'' produced by ABC-TV News, 1971; ''The Wellsprings,'' produced by PBS-TV, 1976; ''Beginning Again at Fifty,'' produced by CBS-TV, 1977; ''The Forties: A Crossroad,'' produced by CBS-TV, 1977; ''Angel Dust: Teenage Emergency,'' produced by CBS-TV, 1978.

Contributor of articles to *Look, Children's Day, National Geographic, Reader's Digest, National Parks,* and *Conservation Magazine;* contributor of photographs to *National Geographic, Time, New York Times, Reader's Digest, Children's Day,* and other periodicals.

SIDELIGHTS: Hope Ryden told *CA:* ''I feel very little attention has been paid to North American wildlife. Most people are more concerned with animals on other continents whose fate is beyond our control. Our own animals are exploited by commercial interests or removed if they have little or no commercial value and stand in the way of fuller exploitation of some other facet of nature. Though many people are enlightened regarding the balance of nature, the concept is not practised in wildlife management. I wish to make this understood.''

*   *   *

RZHEVSKY, Leonid   1905-

PERSONAL: Born August 21, 1905, in Moscow, Russia (now U.S.S.R.); naturalized U.S. citizen, 1970; son of Denis and Elisabeth (de Roberty la Cerda) Surazhevsky; married Agnes Shishkov (a teacher at Columbia University), August 18, 1943. *Education:* Attended Moscow Second University, 1927-30; Lenin Pedagogical Institute, Ph.D., 1941. *Religion:* Russian Orthodox. *Home:* 1 Washington Square Village, Apt. 15-S, New York, N.Y. 10012.

CAREER: Pedagogical Institute, Moscow, U.S.S.R. (also Tula and Orechovo), associate professor of Russian language and literature, 1938-41; University of Lund, Lund, Sweden, university lektor, 1953-63; University of Oklahoma, Norman, professor of Russian literature, 1963-64; New York University, New York City, professor of Slavic literature, 1964-74, professor emeritus, 1974—. Professor of Russian literature, Norwich University Russian School, summers, 1968—. *Military service:* Russian Army, 1941; became lieutenant.

MEMBER: Modern Language Association of America, International P.E.N.

AWARDS, HONORS: L.H.D., Norwich University, 1981.

WRITINGS: Between Two Stars (novel), Chekhov Publishing, 1953; *To This Who Showed Us Light* (novel), Possev Verlag, 1960; *Two on the Stone* (short stories), [Munich], 1960; *Through the Straits* (short stories), [Munich], 1966.

The Language of Creative Writing, New York University Press, 1970; *Three Themes on Dostoevsky,* [Frankfort on the Main], 1972; *Tvorets i podvig* (title means ''Creator and Heroic Deed''), [Frankfort on the Main], 1972, translation by Sonja Miller published as *Solzhenitsyn: Creator and Heroic Deed,* University of Alabama Press, 1978; *Two Strokes of Time* (novel), Possev Verlag, 1976; *Dina* (novel), N.R.S., 1979; *The Sunflower in Revolt* (novel), Hermitage, 1981; *The Falling Stars* (collection of novellas), Hermitage, 1984.

S

SACHS, Albert Louis 1935-
(Albie Sachs)

PERSONAL: Born January 30, 1935, in Johannesburg, South Africa; son of E. S. (a trade unionist) and Ray (Ginsburg) Sachs. *Education:* University of Cape Town, B.A., 1953, LL.B., 1956; University of Sussex, Ph.D., 1972. *Politics:* Anti-apartheid. *Agent:* Tessa Sayle, 11 Jubilee Pl., Chelsea, London SW3 3TE, England. *Office:* Department of Law, Universidade Eduardo Mondlane, C.P. 257, Maputo, Mozambique.

CAREER: Attorney in Cape Town, South Africa, 1957-66; arrested for anti-apartheid activities, October, 1963, and held without charge in solitary confinement for six months; went into exile in England, 1966; senior lecturer in law, University of Southampton, Highfield, England; Universidade Eduardo Mondlane, Maputo, Mozambique, professor of law, 1977—. Part-time writer and legal adviser for a radical weekly journal, 1956-63; speaker on South African political and legal subjects. *Awards, honors:* Anisfield-Wolf Award, 1973, for *Justice in South Africa.*

WRITINGS—All under name Albie Sachs: *The Jail Diary of Albie Sachs,* Harvill, 1966, McGraw, 1967, published as *Jail Diary,* Sphere Books, 1969; *Stephanie on Trial,* Harvill, 1968; *South Africa: The Violence of Apartheid,* Christian Action Publications, 1969, 2nd edition, 1970; *Justice in South Africa,* University of California Press, 1973; (with Joan Hoff Wilson) *Sexism and the Law,* Free Press, 1979; (with Indres Naidoo) *Island in Chains,* Penguin, 1982, published as *Robben Island,* Random House, 1983, published as *Robben Island: Ten Years as a Political Prisoner in South Africa's Most Notorious Penitentiary,* Vintage, 1983.

MEDIA ADAPTATIONS: The Jail Diary of Albie Sachs was adapted for the stage in 1978 by David Edgar; this adaptation was subsequently performed as a teleplay by BBC-TV in 1980.

BIOGRAPHICAL/CRITICAL SOURCES: Albie Sachs, *The Jail Diary of Albie Sachs,* Harvill, 1966, McGraw, 1967; *Atlantic,* April, 1967; *New Yorker,* July 1, 1967; *Statesman,* October 11, 1968; *Punch,* October 30, 1968.

*   *   *

SACHS, Albie
See SACHS, Albert Louis

SACHS, Murray 1924-

PERSONAL: Born April 10, 1924, in Toronto, Ontario, Canada; son of Thomas (a tailor) and Sarah (Roth) Sachs; married Miriam Blank, September 14, 1961; children: Deborah Ruth, Aaron Jacob. *Education:* University of Toronto, B.A., 1946; Columbia University, M.A., 1947, Ph.D., 1952. *Politics:* Independent. *Religion:* Jewish. *Home:* 280 Highland Ave., West Newton, Mass. 02165. *Office:* Department of Romance and Comparative Literature, Brandeis University, Waltham, Mass. 02254.

CAREER: University of California, Berkeley, instructor in French, 1948-50; University of Detroit, Detroit, Mich., lecturer in French, 1951-52; Williams College, Williamstown, Mass., assistant professor of French, 1954-60; Brandeis University, Waltham, Mass., professor of French, 1960—.

MEMBER: Modern Humanities Resaerch Association (England), American Council on Teaching of Foreign Languages, Modern Language Association of America, Asosciation of Teachers of French, Association of Departments of Foreign Languages (president, 1985), Phi Beta Kappa (honorary member).

AWARDS, HONORS: Palmes Academiques by government of France, 1971.

WRITINGS: (Editor with E. M. Grant and R. B. Grant) *French Stories, Plays and Poetry,* Oxford University Press, 1959; *The Career of Alphonse Daudet,* Harvard University Press, 1965; *The French Short Story in the Nineteenth Century,* Oxford University Press, 1969.

Anatole France: The Short Stories, Edward Arnold, 1974; (contributor) Michael Issacharoff, editor, *Langages de Flaubert,* Lettres Modernes, 1976; (contributor) Walton Beacham, editor, *Critical Survey of Short Fiction,* Salem Press, 1981; (contributor) Paula Gilbert Lewis, editor, *Traditionalism, Nationalism and Feminism: Women Writers of Quebec,* Greenwood Press, 1984.

Contributor of articles to various professional journals. Member of editorial advisory board, *Nineteenth-Century French Studies,* 1973—.

WORK IN PROGRESS: A study of the art of Gustave Flaubert; a study of the emergence of the short story as a new literary genre, in Europe and in America.

SIDELIGHTS: Murray Sachs told *CA:* "As a humanist and student of literature, [I have] a cultivated knowledge of literature in five languages (English, French, German, Spanish and Yiddish) and [have] studied some literary works in five other languages (Greek, Hebrew, Italian, Latin and Portuguese). [I] hope to have a reading knowledge of Russian soon."

*   *   *

SACK, John 1930-

PERSONAL: Born March 24, 1930, in New York, N.Y.; son of John Jacob (a clerk) and Tracy Rose (Levy) Sack. *Education:* Harvard University, A.B., 1951; Columbia University, graduate study, 1963-64. *Home:* 2005 La Brea Ter., Los Angeles, Calif. 90046. *Agent:* Lois Wallace, Wallace & Sheil Agency, Inc., 177 East 70th St., New York, N.Y. 10021.

CAREER: Writer and journalist. United Press, correspondent in Peru, 1950, Japan and Korea, 1953-54, and Albany, N.Y., 1954-55; Columbia Broadcasting System, CBS News, documentary writer and producer in New York City and Paris, France, 1961-66; *Esquire,* New York City, correspondent in Vietnam, 1966-67, contributing editor, 1967-78; *Playboy,* Chicago, Ill., contributing editor in Los Angeles, 1978—; KCBS-TV, Los Angeles, newswriter and producer, 1982-84. *Military service:* U.S. Army, 1951-53; served in Korea; war correspondent, *Pacific Stars and Stripes,* 1952-55.

MEMBER: Writers Guild of America, Screen Actors Guild, American Federation of Television and Radio Artists.

WRITINGS: The Butcher, Rinehart, 1952 (published in England as *The Ascent of Yerupaja,* Jenkins, 1954); *From Here to Shimbashi,* Harper, 1955; *Report from Practically Nowhere,* Harper, 1959; *M,* New American Library, 1967, reprinted, Avon, 1985; *Lieutenant Calley,* Viking, 1971 (published in England as *Body Count,* Hutchinson, 1971); *The Man-Eating Machine,* Farrar, Straus, 1973; *Fingerprint,* Random House, 1983. Author of television documentaries. Contributor to magazines, including *Harper's, Atlantic Monthly, Holiday, Town and Country, Playboy, Eros,* and *New Yorker.*

WORK IN PROGRESS: "Searching in the People's Republic of the Congo for the last living dinosaurs," and writing about them for the Associated Press, CBS News, *Playboy,* and Random House.

SIDELIGHTS: John Sack told *CA* that his "best or best-known book" is "*M,* which was excerpted in 1966 as the cover story in *Esquire,* the longest article in *Esquire*'s history." *M* is the story of "M" Company of the 1st Advanced Infantry Training Brigade. "John Sack followed the company from the inanity of a training inspection at Fort Dix to the senseless killing of a seven-year-old girl in Viet Nam," writes Stewart Kampel in the *New York Times.* "He has produced a gripping, honest account, compassionate and rich, colorful and blackly comic, but with that concerned objectivity that makes for great reportage." Writing in *Book Week,* Dan Wakefield praises *M* as "one of the finest, most perceptive books of reportage in recent years. One must go back to Orwell for appropriate comparisons of journalistic excellence." And Robert Kirsch's *Los Angeles Times* review names *M* as "the whole story, one of the most compelling ever told about men in war. This is the way it is."

Sack's *Lieutenant Calley* is the story of the My Lai massacre in Viet Nam. In a letter to *CA,* the author notes that it is his "most infamous book . . . in the course of writing which the federal government arrested and indicted me but never prosecuted me."

A more recent book, *Fingerprint,* has been compared by reviewers to Laurence Sterne's *Tristam Shandy.* Like that classic, writes Michiko Kakutani in the *New York Times, Fingerprint* "begins with the events leading up to the author's conception and birth, and it similarly boasts a narrative positively crammed with digressions and asides." Kakutani continues: "Gifted with an eye for physical detail and a canny ear for dialogue, Mr. Sack is at his best when he sticks closely to the facts of his own life. . . . It is when he attempts to pontificate on the larger evils of society that he becomes trite and moralistic." Reviewing *Fingerprint* in the *Washington Post Book World,* Joseph McLellan criticizes Sack's "polemic, which is . . . a diatribe against what he calls 'efficiency'. . . . In a sense, his complaints resemble what one of his beard follicles might have to say about his efficient habit of shaving. Still, he does write well and there is a germ of truth in what he has to say. . . . In an age when we are teaching computers to become more and more 'user-friendly,' we may hope to see better days ahead—speeded, perhaps, by amorphous howls such as 'Fingerprint.'"

"Sack has hung about since the '50's, participating in the kinks and enthusiasms of the succeeding times while writing about them critically but on the whole amiably," notes Richard Eder in the *Los Angeles Times Book Review.* "He is a sunny man, or a sunny writer, at least: 'Fingerprint,' though a concentrated denunciation of what he sees as the central fallacy of our civilization, draws its originality not so much from the fierceness or cogency of the denunciation as from its exuberance."

Sack's *Lieutenant Calley* has been translated into German, Spanish, French, Portuguese, Italian, and Finnish.

BIOGRAPHICAL/CRITICAL SOURCES: New York Times, March 7, 1967, January 31, 1983; *Los Angeles Times,* March 8, 1967; *Book Week,* March 12, 1967; *Christian Science Monitor,* April 6, 1967; *New York Times Book Review,* May 14, 1967; *Nation,* October 23, 1967; *Los Angeles Times Book Review,* January 2, 1983; *Washington Post Book World,* March 5, 1983.

*   *   *

SAGAR, Keith (Milsom) 1934-

PERSONAL: Born June 14, 1934, in Bradford, Yorkshire, England; son of Harry Heald and Emily (Milsom) Sagar; married Melissa Partridge, 1981. *Education:* King's College, Cambridge, B.A., 1955, M.A., 1957; University of Leeds, Ph.D., 1962. *Politics:* "Ecology." *Religion:* "Ecology." *Home:* 11 Leys Close, Wiswell, Nr. Blackburn, Lancashire, England.

CAREER: University of Leeds, Extra-Mural Department, Leeds, England, administrative assistant, 1957-59; Workers' Educational Association, tutor-organizer, Northeast Derbyshire, England, 1959-63; University of Manchester, Extra-Mural Department, Manchester, England, staff tutor, 1963-74, senior staff tutor in literature, 1974—. *Military service:* British Army, National Service, 1956.

MEMBER: D. H. Lawrence Society (honorary vice-president).

WRITINGS: The Art of D. H. Lawrence, Cambridge University Press, 1966; (contributor) *Criticism in Action,* Longmans, Green,

1969; *Hamlet* (criticism), Basil Blackwell, 1969; *Ted Hughes,* Longman, 1972, revised edition, Profile Books, 1982; *The Art of Ted Hughes,* Cambridge University Press, 1975, revised edition, 1978.

(Contributor) *The Art of Emily Bronte,* Vision Press, 1976; *Emily Bronte: Wuthering Heights,* British Council, 1975; (coauthor) *The Love of Tropical Fish,* Octopus, 1975; *D. H. Lawrence: A Calendar of His Works,* Manchester University Press, 1979; *The Life of D. H. Lawrence,* Eyre Methuen, 1980; *The Reef and Other Poems,* Ilkley Literature Festival, 1980; (contributor) *D. H. Lawrence: The Man Who Lived,* Southern Illinois University Press, 1980; (with Stephen Tabor) *Ted Hughes: A Bibliography,* Mansell, 1983; *D. H. Lawrence: Life into Art,* Penguin, 1985. Contributor to *D. H. Lawrence Review, Sunday Times* (London), *Guardian, Twentieth Century,* and other periodicals.

Editor: D. H. Lawrence, *The Mortal Coil and Other Stories,* Penguin, 1971; D. H. Lawrence, *The Princess and Other Stories,* Penguin, 1971; *Selected Poems of D. H. Lawrence,* Penguin, 1972; (and contributor) *The World Encyclopedia of Tropical Fish,* Octopus, 1978; *D. H. Lawrence: Sons and Lovers,* Penguin, 1981; (and contributor) *A D. H. Lawrence Handbook,* Manchester University Press, 1982; (and contributor) *D. H. Lawrence and New Mexico,* Peregrine Smith, 1982; (with wife, Melissa Partridge) *D. H. Lawrence: The Complete Short Novels,* Penguin, 1982; (and contributor) *The Achievement of Ted Hughes,* Manchester University Press, 1982; *The Letters of D. H. Lawrence,* Volume VII, Cambridge University Press, 1985.

WORK IN PROGRESS: "A vast long-term project provisionally titled *Worshippers of Nature.*"

SIDELIGHTS: Keith Sagar has travelled extensively in the United States, Italy, and places associated with D. H. Lawrence. He told *CA:* "I am depressed by the failure of contemporary criticism to take literature seriously, to relate it to the desperate needs of the contemporary world, and to evince any belief in the creative imagination. Most critics seem to be interested in playing games with literature, and cutting the great writers down to their own size. The only question which matters now is whether we can survive—survive the threat of nuclear war in the short term, and the destruction of nature by other means in the long. All other concerns are relatively trivial. Great imaginative literature is central. It can help to release our creativity, to clarify our awareness of the real and the sacred. It can bring to ecology the psychological and spiritual dimensions which transform it from a merely prudential science into the only adequate religion for our time."

Reviewing Sagar's *The Life of D. H. Lawrence* in the *New York Times,* James Atlas states that "Mr. Sagar writes in a sort of shorthand, as if his readers already knew the story, and makes no effort to explain himself." Other reviewers welcome the book's style, which V. S. Pritchett calls "album-like." Harry Marten praises the heavily-illustrated volume in *Washington Post Book World* as "informative, rewarding in its brevity and pleasing in its clarity." Pritchett in the *New York Review of Books* notes that the "biographical album has the merit of bringing out all the facets of [D. H. Lawrence] and letting them stand." And a *New York Times Book Review* critic states: "For Keith Sagar's lavishly illustrated biography of D. H. Lawrence I have nothing but admiration. . . . [Sagar's] skill . . . results in a biography satisfying in every way: readable, informative, authoritative and set in an attractive format. This is altogether a lovely book."

AVOCATIONAL INTERESTS: The theatre, photography, keeping marine tropical fishes, tennis, squash, and gardening.

BIOGRAPHICAL/CRITICAL SOURCES: New York Review of Books, May 20, 1980; *Washington Post Book World,* June 1, 1980; *New York Times,* June 10, 1980; *New York Times Book Review,* June 29, 1980.

*   *   *

St. GEORGE, Judith   1931-

PERSONAL: Born February 26, 1931, in Westfield, N.J.; daughter of John H. (a lawyer) and Edna P. Alexander; married David St. George (an Episcopal minister), June 5, 1954; children: Peter, James, Philip, Sarah. *Education:* Smith College, B.A., 1952. *Religion:* Episcopalian. *Home:* 290 Roseland Ave., Essex Fells, N.J. 07021.

CAREER: Suburban Frontiers (relocating service), Basking Ridge, N.J., president, 1968-71; writer, 1970—. Teacher, 1979-81. Commissioner on the Brooklyn Bridge Centennial Commission, 1981-83; delegate to White House Conference on Libraries and Information Services.

MEMBER: Authors Guild, Society of Children's Book Writers, Authors League of America, Jean Fritz Workshop.

AWARDS, HONORS: By George, Bloomers! was named among the best books for spring, 1976, by *Saturday Review; The Halloween Pumpkin Smasher* was awarded a special Edgar, Mystery Writers of America, 1978; *Haunted* was named among best mysteries of the year, *New York Times Book Review,* 1980; *The Brooklyn Bridge: They Said It Couldn't Be Built* was cited with several honors, including American Book Award nomination, American Library Association notable book citation, and Jefferson Cup Honor Book Award, all 1982.

WRITINGS—For young people; published by Putnam, except as indicated: *Turncoat Winter, Rebel Spring,* Chilton, 1970; *The Girl with Spunk,* 1975; *By George, Bloomers!,* Coward, 1976; *The Chinese Puzzle of Shag Island,* 1976; *The Shad Are Running,* 1977; *Shadow of the Shaman,* 1977; *The Halloween Pumpkin Smasher,* 1978; *The Halo Wind,* 1978; *Mystery at St. Martin's,* 1979.

The Amazing Voyage of the New Orleans (Junior Literary Guild selection), 1980; *Haunted,* 1980; *Call Me Margo,* 1981; *Mysterious Girl in the Garden,* 1981; *The Brooklyn Bridge: They Said It Couldn't Be Built* (Junior Literary Guild selection), 1982; *Do You See What I See?,* 1982; *In the Shadow of the Bear* (Junior Literary Guild selection), 1983.

SIDELIGHTS: Judith St. George told *CA:* "As a child I loved reading above all else and remember receiving twenty-two books one Christmas. In grammar school I used to write crazy plays, which my friends and I produced. Looking back, I realize my teachers must have had the patience of Job. In college I took every creative writing course available to me. History and mysteries are my two loves. I guess mysteries have to come first, since I find it hard to plot a story without some element of mystery woven into it. On the other hand, historical nonfiction gives me the opportunity to delve into our past and meet fascinating people, as well as do research, which I find as irresistible as eating peanuts."

New York Times Book Review critic Richard Shepard has praise for one of St. George's nonfictions, *The Brooklyn Bridge: They Said It Couldn't Be Built.* The author, says Shepard, "has a knack for narration, so even though you may know a fair amount about the bridge . . . you get caught up in this tale of grit, intelligence and imagination, for it is in the good old Horatio Alger tradition. While she never loses sight of the main characters, she explains with exemplary clarity the engineering problems involved in the building. . . . [St. George] also refers to, but does not become bogged down in, the politics of building the bridge.''

BIOGRAPHICAL/CRITICAL SOURCES: New York Times Book Review, July 13, 1980, January 25, 1981, April 25, 1982.

*   *   *

St. GERMAIN, Gregory
See WALLMANN, Jeffrey M(iner)

*   *   *

SALINGER, Pierre (Emil George) 1925-

PERSONAL: Born June 14, 1925, in San Francisco, Calif.; son of Herbert Edgar (a mining engineer) and Jehanne (Bietry) Salinger; married second wife, Nancy Brook Joy, June 28, 1957 (divorced); married Nicole Gillmann, June 18, 1965; children: (first marriage) Marc (deceased), Suzanne, Stephen; (third marriage) Gregory. *Education:* University of San Francisco, B.S., 1947. *Politics:* Democrat. *Agent:* Sterling Lord Agency, 660 Madison Ave., New York, N.Y., 10021. *Home:* 248 Rue de Rivoli, 75001 Paris, France.

CAREER: San Francisco Chronicle, San Francisco, Calif., began as reporter, became night city editor, 1946-55; *Collier's* (magazine), New York City, West Coast editor and contributing editor, 1955-56; *House and Home* (magazine), New York City, assistant news editor, 1956-57; U.S. Senate Labor Rackets Committee, Washington, D.C., investigator, 1957-59; press secretary to Senator John F. Kennedy, 1959-60, to President Kennedy, 1961-63, and to President Lyndon B. Johnson, 1963-64; U.S. senator from California (appointed to fill vacancy), 1964; Continental Airlines, Los Angeles, Calif., vice-president for international affairs, 1965-68, also vice-president, deputy to the chairman of the board, and a director of subsidiary, Continental Air Services, Inc.; National General Corp. (theaters), Beverly Hills, Calif., vice-president, then consultant, 1965—; president, Fox Overseas Theatres, 1965—; Gramco Development Corporation, Los Angeles, Calif., president, 1968—; *L'Express,* Paris, France, roving editor, 1973-79; ABC News, chief of Paris bureau, 1979-83, chief foreign correspondent, 1983—.

Senior vice-president, AMPROP, Inc., 1969; department chairman, Gramco Ltd., 1970-71. Press officer, Stevenson for President campaign, California, 1952 and 1956, and Richard Graves for Governor of California campaign, 1954. Member of board of directors, National General Productions and California Museum of Science and Industry; trustee, Robert F. Kennedy Memorial Foundation; chairman of board of trustees, American College in Paris. Guest lecturer in journalism, Mills College, 1950-55. *Military service:* U.S. Naval Reserve, active duty, 1943-46; became lieutenant junior grade.

MEMBER: National Health Club (Washington, D.C.).

AWARDS, HONORS: Navy and Marine Corps Medal, 1945; Edward V. McQuade Memorial Award, 1953; George Polk Award, 1982, for documentary, ''America Held Hostage: The Secret Negotiations''; Legion of Honor medal.

WRITINGS: (Editor with Sander Vanocur) *A Tribute to John F. Kennedy,* Encyclopaedia Britannica, 1964; *With Kennedy,* Doubleday, 1966; (editor with Edwin Guthman, Frank Mankiewicz, and John Seigenthaler) *An Honorable Profession: A Tribute to Robert F. Kennedy,* Doubleday, 1968.

On Instructions of My Government (novel), Doubleday, 1971; *Je suis un americain,* Stock, 1975; *La France et le nouveau monde,* Robert Laffont, 1976; *Venezuelan Notebooks,* Saix Boral (Spain), 1979.

America Held Hostage: The Secret Negotiations (also see below), Doubleday, 1981; (with Michael Rice, Johnathan Carr, Henri Pierre, and Jan Reifenberg) *Reporting U.S.-European Relations,* Pergamon, 1982; (with Leonard Gross) *The Dossier,* Doubleday, 1984.

Also author of documentary, ''America Held Hostage: The Secret Negotiations, for ABC News, 1982.

SIDELIGHTS: ABC News chief foreign correspondent and former press secretary to President Kennedy, Pierre Salinger makes use of his many years of travelling and living abroad when he writes. With access to many high-placed contacts throughout the world, Salinger is able to write with authenticity and inside knowledge of the workings of government and society, according to some critics.

Reviewer James Fallows, for example, comments on the book *America Held Hostage: The Secret Negotiations* in a *New York Times Book Review* article. Salinger's international contacts, says Fallows, ''have given him the material for fast-paced, adventure-story reading. He reprints the secret letters and memorandums through which the United States and Iran tried to agree on a 'scenario' in which an international tribunal would hear complaints against the shah (and America) while the hostages were set free. . . . He recounts one instance after another in which agreement seemed imminent—only to slip away, because of misunderstanding or suspicion or simple human error.''

''There are some stunning moments'' in Salinger's account of the hostage crisis, says Bill Stout, writing in the *Los Angeles Times Book Review,* ''such as the foreign policy breakfast of October 19, 1979, when Mondale, Vance, Brzezinski, et al., were unanimous in urging the admission of the shah. Only Jimmy Carter was reluctant. He went along, Salinger says, but with a final comment: 'What are you guys going to recommend that we do when they take our embassy and hold our people hostage?' ''

America Held Hostage: The Secret Negotiations, according to Marvin Zonis writing in a *Chicago Tribune Book World* review, ''adds new details'' to our knowledge of the incident ''as it presents a riveting account of duplicity and decency acted out over four continents for 14 months by scores of characters straight from central casting: a U.S. President rejected by voters; a deposed shah who had become, in the words of his longtime ally, Henry Kissinger, some kind of 'Flying Dutchman' seeking a home; revolutionaries of all descriptions . . . ; ayatollahs and priests . . . ; diplomats. . . . And, of course, all those Iranians.''

The Dossier, the 1984 novel Salinger co-authored with Leonard Gross, displays more of Salinger's talent for authenticity, according to David Evanier's article in the *New York Times Book Review.* ''An air of knowledgeability about government, broadcasting and international intrigue pervades this deft thriller,'' says Evanier. *The Dossier* ''is an intelligently written, suspenseful, tightly structured insider's view of international double-dealing that rarely stumbles into the implausible.''

Similarly, Anne Chamberlin comments on *The Dossier*'s attention to detail in a *Washington Post Book World* review. ''The twenty-eight cliffhanging chapters sweep you from the Oval Office of the White House to the innermost warrens of the CIA, to a country dacha outside Moscow and the best hotels and restaurants on three continents in dazzling succession, described with the knowing eye of a party who has been there in real life.''

AVOCATIONAL INTERESTS: Golf, cooking, music.

BIOGRAPHICAL/CRITICAL SOURCES: New Republic, November 29, 1980; *Los Angeles Times Book Review,* November 29, 1981, August 12, 1984; *Chicago Tribune Book World,* December 6, 1981; *New York Times Book Review,* December 13, 1981, August 19, 1984; *Washington Post Book World,* December 13, 1981, July 30, 1984; *Times Literary Supplement,* July 30, 1982; *New York Times,* July 21, 1984.

*   *   *

SALVADORI, Joyce
See LUSSU, Joyce (Salvadori)

*   *   *

SAMPSON, Edward E. 1934-

PERSONAL: Born December 4, 1934, in Chicago, Ill.; son of Theodore R. and Beatrice Sampson; married Marya Marthas, March 17, 1972. *Education:* University of California, Los Angeles, B.A., 1956; University of Michigan, Ph.D., 1960. *Politics:* ''Variable.'' *Religion:* ''Personal.'' *Office:* Wright Institute, Berkeley, Calif. 94704.

CAREER: University of California, Berkeley, assistant professor, 1960-66, associate professor of psychology, 1966-70; Brunel University, Uxbridge, England, lecturer, 1970-71; Clark University, Worcester, Mass., visiting professor, 1971-72, professor of sociology and adjunct professor of psychology, 1972-82, former chairman of sociology department; Wright Institute, Berkeley, Calif., dean of the graduate school, 1982—.

WRITINGS: Approaches, Contexts, and Problems of Social Psychology, Prentice-Hall, 1964; *Student Activism and Protest,* Jossey-Bass, 1970; *Social Psychology and Contemporary Society,* Wiley, 1971, 2nd edition, 1976; *Ego at the Threshold,* Delta, 1975; (with wife, Marya Marthas) *Group Process for the Health Professions,* Wiley, 1977, 2nd edition, 1981; *Introducing Social Psychology,* New Viewpoints, 1980; *Justice and The Critique of Pure Psychology,* Plenum, 1983.

WORK IN PROGRESS: Not in Control: A Different Place for Humanity in the World.

*   *   *

SAMUELS, Warren J. 1933-

PERSONAL: Born September 14, 1933, in New York, N.Y.; son of Emanuel Abraham (a contractor) and Lillian (Glazer) Samuels; married Sylvia Joan Strake; children: Kathy Joan, Susan Jill. *Education:* University of Miami, Coral Gables, Fla., B.B.A., 1954; University of Wisconsin, M.S., 1955, Ph.D., 1957. *Home:* 4397 Cherrywood Dr., Okemos, Mich. 48864. *Office:* Department of Economics, Michigan State University, East Lansing, Mich. 48824.

CAREER: Assistant professor of economics at University of Missouri—Columbia, 1957-58, and Georgia State College (now University), Atlanta, 1958-59; University of Miami, Coral Gables, Fla., assistant professor, 1959-62, associate professor of economics, 1962-68; Michigan State University, East Lansing, professor of economics, 1968—, director of graduate programs and placement officer, department of economics, 1969-73. Member of subcommittee on energy, Michigan Economic Council, 1976. Participant in professional conferences; guest lecturer at numerous universities, including University of North Carolina, Grand Valley State College, University of Notre Dame, and University of Glasgow. Has given expert testimony before the U.S. Senate and several state government agencies. Consultant in public finance and public utilities fields.

MEMBER: International Institute of Public Finance, Royal Economic Society, American Economic Association, National Tax Association (member of Public Utilities Taxation Committee, 1971-73, 1976-78, 1979-82), American Association of University Professors, American Legal Studies Association, Association for Evolutionary Economics (member of Veblen-Commons Award committee, 1969; chairman of nominating committee, 1971), Association for Comparative Economic Studies, Public Choice Society, Association for Social Economics, Economic History Association, Law and Society Association (member of board of trustees, 1976-79; member of publications committee, 1978—), Policy Studies Organization (member of council, 1976-78), History of Economics Society (member of executive committee, 1972-73; vice-president, 1977, president-elect, 1980-81; president, 1981-82), Transportation and Public Utilities Group, Association for the Study of Grants Economy, Midwest Economics Association, Southern Economic Association, Economic Society of Michigan (president-elect, 1971-72; president, 1972-73).

WRITINGS: The Classical Theory of Economic Policy, Collins & World, 1966; *Pareto on Policy,* Elsevier-North Holland, 1974; (with A. Allan Schmid) *Law and Economics: An Institutional Perspective,* Nijhoff, 1981.

Editor: (With Harry M. Trebing) *A Critique of Administrative Regulation of Public Utilities,* Institute of Public Utilities, Michigan State University, 1972; *The Chicago School of Political Economy,* Division of Research, Graduate School of Business Administration, Michigan State University, 1976; *The Economy as a System of Power,* two volumes, Transaction Books, 1979; *The Methodology of Economic Thought,* Transaction Books, 1980; (with Larry L. Wade) *Taxing and Spending Policy,* Lexington Books, 1980; (with Henry W. Spiegel) *Contemporary Economic Thought,* Jai Press, in press.

Contributor: *Wisconsin Blue Book,* State of Wisconsin, 1956; *Promotion at What Cost?,* Social Planning Division, Detroit City Plan Commission, 1972; F. Wunderlich and W. L. Gibson, Jr., editors, *Perspectives of Property,* Institute for Research on Land and Water Resources, Pennsylvania State University, 1972; Trebing, editor, *Essays on Public Utility Pricing and Regulation,* Institute of Public Utilities, Michigan State University, 1972; Milton Russell, editor, *Perspectives in Public Regulation,* Southern Illinois University Press, 1973; *New Challenges to Public Utility Management,* Institute of Public Utilities, Michigan State University, 1974; Gordon Tullock, editor, *Further Explorations in the Theory of Anarchy,* University Publications (Blacksburg), 1974.

Market Appraisals of Public Utilities for Advalorem Tax Purposes, Center for Management Development, Wichita State University and National Tax Association, 1975; Stuart S. Nagel, editor, *Policy Studies and the Social Sciences*, Lexington Books, 1975; Trebing, editor, *New Dimensions in Public Utility Pricing*, Division of Research, Graduate School of Business Administration, Michigan State University, 1976; Sidney Weintraub, editor, *Modern Economic Thought*, University of Pennsylvania Press, 1977; James M. Buchanan and Richard E. Wagner, *Fiscal Responsibility in Constitutional Democracy*, Nijhoff, 1978; *Workshop Proceedings: Capital Investment Decisions*, Electric Power Research Institute, 1978; Trebing, editor, *Assessing New Pricing Concepts in Public Utilities*, Division of Research, Graduate School of Business Administration, Michigan State University, 1978; Trebing, editor, *Challenges for Public Utility Regulation in the 1980s*, Division of Research, Graduate School of Business Administration, Michigan State University, 1981.

Also author of introduction to Friedrich von Wieser, *The Law of Power;* contributor to *Value Judgements and Income Distribution*, edited by Anderson and Solo. Editor of "Recent Economic Thought" series, Nijhoff. Also contributor to *Encyclopedia of Economics and Business* and *Encyclopedia of Policy Studies*. Contributor of articles and reviews to numerous professional journals, including *Journal of Economic Issues, Wall Street Review of Books, Southern Economic Journal, Journal of Economic History, American Economic Review*, and *Journal of Law and Economics*. Member of editorial board, *Southern Economic Journal*, 1967-68, *History of Political Economy*, 1969—, *Social Science*, 1977—, *Journal of Post-Keynesian Economics*, 1977—, *Policy Studies Journal*, 1979—, and *Interdisciplinary Economics*, 1981—; editor, *Journal of Economic Issues*, 1971-81.

WORK IN PROGRESS: Research on the theory of property rights, institutional economics; aspects of history of economic thought.

SIDELIGHTS: Warren J. Samuels told *CA:* "My principal interests, from the beginning of my graduate work to the present day, have centered on the interrelationships between nominally legal-political and economic processes and on the history of economic thought with regard to economic policy. The two have reinforced each other and are really twin sides of an overarching concern with the making of economically relevant decisions, some by economic actors, some by political actors, and some through our modes of discourse."

*   *   *

SANDERS, James A(lvin)   1927-

PERSONAL: Born November 28, 1927, in Memphis, Tenn.; son of Robert Erastus (a railroad engineer) and Sue (Black) Sanders; married Dora Geil Cargille (a dance instructor and musician), June 30, 1951; children: Robin David. *Education:* Vanderbilt University, B.A. (magna cum laude), 1948, B.D. (with honors), 1951; Theologie Protestante de Paris, theological study, 1950-51; Hebrew Union College, Ph.D., 1955. *Home:* 99 Claremont Ave., New York, N.Y. 10027.

CAREER: Ordained Presbyterian minister, Cincinnati, Ohio, 1955. Vanderbilt University, Nashville, Tenn., instructor in French, 1948-49; Colgate Rochester Divinity School, Rochester, N.Y., assistant professor, 1954-57, associate professor, 1957-60, professor of Old Testament, 1960-65; Union Theological Seminary, New York, N.Y., professor of Old Testament, 1965-68, Auburn Professor of Biblical Studies, 1968-77; currently Elizabeth Hay Bechtel Professor, Claremont Graduate School.

Visiting professor, Rochester Center for Theological Studies, 1970, and Princeton Theological Seminary, 1972, 1974, and 1976. Lecturer at several universities. American Schools of Oriental Research, Jerusalem, Jordan, annual professor, 1961-62, associate trustee, 1963-66, member of committee on Dead Sea Scrolls, 1963—. *Member:* Society of Biblical Literature (associate-in-council, 1963-66; president, 1977-78), American Academy of Religion, American Schools of Oriental Research Alumni Association (president, 1964), Phi Beta Kappa. *Awards, honors:* Fulbright grant, 1950-51; Rockefeller Foundation fellow, 1953-54; Guggenheim fellowship, 1961-62, 1972-73; Litt.D., Acadia University, 1973; S.T.D., University of Glasgow, 1975; Lilly Foundation grant, 1981.

WRITINGS: Suffering as Divine Discipline, Colgate Rochester Divinity School Press, 1955; *The Old Testament in the Cross*, Harper, 1961; *The Psalms Scroll of Qumran Cave 11*, Clarendon Press, 1965; *The Dead Sea Psalms Scroll*, Cornell University Press, 1967; (editor) *Near Eastern Archaeology in the Twentieth Century*, Doubleday, 1970; *Torah and Canon*, Fortress, 1972; *God Has a Story, Too: Sermons in Context*, Fortress, 1979.

Also author of "Luke: The Theological Historican," a series of videotapes for United Methodist Communications, 1981. Contributor to *The Interpreter's Dictionary of the Bible, Harper's Dictionary of Biblical Biography, Encyclopedia Americana*, and *American People's Encyclopedia*. Contributor to theological and other learned journals in the United States, England, France, Israel, and Germany. Member of editorial board, *Journal of Biblical Literature*, 1970-76, *Journal for the Study of Judaism*, 1970—, and *Interpretation*, 1973-78.

*   *   *

SANDOZ, (George) Ellis (Jr.)   1931-

PERSONAL: Born February 10, 1931, in New Orleans, La.; son of George Ellis (a dentist) and Ruby (Odom) Sandoz; married Therese Alverne Hubley, May 31, 1957; children: George Ellis III, Lisa Claire Alverne, Erica Christine, Jonathan David. *Education:* Attended University of North Carolina, 1950; Louisiana State University, B.A., 1951, M.A., 1953; graduate study at Georgetown University, 1952-53, and University of Heidelberg, 1956-58; University of Munich, Dr.oec.publ. (magna cum laude), 1965. *Politics:* Democrat. *Religion:* Baptist. *Home:* 2843 Valcour Ave., Baton Rouge, La. 70820. *Office:* Department of Political Science, Louisiana State University, Baton Rouge, La. 70803.

CAREER: Louisiana Polytechnic Institute, Ruston, instructor, 1959-60, assistant professor, 1960-66, associate professor, 1966-67, professor of political science, 1967-68, director of Center for International Studies, 1966-68; East Texas State University, Commerce, professor of political science and head of department, 1968-78; Louisiana State University, Baton Rouge, professor of political science, 1978—, chairman of department, 1980-81. Fulbright scholar in Germany, 1964-65; visiting summer scholar, Hoover Institution on War, Revolution, and Peace, 1970 and 1973. Member of council, Southwest Alliance for Latin America, 1966-68 and 1973. Member of National Council on the Humanities, 1982-1988. Speaker at professional conferences. Consultant, National Endowment for the Humanities fellowship program, 1977-80. *Military service:* U.S. Marine Corps, 1953-56; became first lieutenant.

MEMBER: American Political Science Association (member of council, 1978-79), American Society for Political and Legal

Philosophy, Conference for the Study of Political Thought, Southwestern Political Science Association (member of executive council, 1970-71; vice-president, 1972-73; president, 1974-75), Southern Political Science Association (member of executive council, 1982-85), Phi Delta Kappa, Sigma Nu, Tau Kappa Alpha, Pi Sigma Alpha.

AWARDS, HONORS: Germanistic Society of America fellow, 1964-65; H. B. Earhart fellow, 1964-65; Fulbright Achievement Award, 1965; National Endowment for the Humanities research grant, 1976-78.

WRITINGS: Political Apocalypse: A Study of Dostoevsky's Grand Inquisitor, Louisiana State University Press, 1971; (contributor) George J. Graham, Jr. and George W. Carey, editors, *The Post Behavioral Era: Perspectives on Political Science,* McKay, 1972; *Conceived in Liberty: American Individual Rights Today,* Duxbury, 1978; (editor with Cecil V. Crabb, Jr.) *A Tide of Discontent: The 1980 Elections and Their Meaning,* Congressional Quarterly, 1981; *The Voegelinian Revolution: A Biographical Introduction,* Louisiana State University, 1981; (editor, and author of introduction) *Eric Voeglin's Thought: A Critical Appraisal,* Duke University Press, 1982; (contributor) Francis Canavan, editor, *The Ethical Dimension of Political Life: Essays in Honor of John H. Hallowell,* Duke University Press, 1983; (contributor) *American Values Projected Abroad,* University of Virginia, 1984.

Author of weekly column, "Southerner Abroad," for *Shreveport Journal,* 1956-58. Contributor of about twenty articles to political affairs journals. Member of board of editors, *Political Science Reviewer,* 1970—, *Modern Age,* 1971—; *Journal of Politics,* 1975—, *Interpretation,* 1980—, and *This World,* 1981—.

WORK IN PROGRESS: A Government of Laws: Essays on the American Founding.

*   *   *

SANGSTER, Jimmy   1927-

PERSONAL: Born December 2, 1927, in North Wales; son of Dudley (in real estate) and Ruth (Bowlden) Sangster; married Monica Hustler (an artist), August 26, 1950; married Sandra Schwartz (an interior designer); children: Mark James. *Education:* Educated in Wales; left school at fifteen to start work in the film industry. *Politics:* "Middle." *Agent:* Ashley Famous Artists, 45 New Bond St., London W.1, England. *Office:* 1 Carlton Tower Pl., Sloane St., London S.W.1, England; and 1590 Lindacrest Dr., Beverly Hills, Calif. 90210.

CAREER: Free-lance assistant film director, 1948-50; free-lance film production manager, 1950-55; free-lance writer and film producer, 1957—. Script consultant, Columbia Broadcasting System (CBS), 1972, and D'Antonia Weitz, 1975. *Military service:* Royal Air Force, 1945-48.

MEMBER: Screen Writers Guild of Great Britain (member of council, 1963-64), Association of Cine and Allied Technicians (London), Directors Guild of America, Writers Guild of America (West).

WRITINGS—Novels: (With Barre Lyndon) *The Man Who Could Cheat Death,* Avon, 1959; *Private I,* Norton, 1967; *Foreign Exchange,* Norton, 1968; *Touchfeather,* Norton, 1968; *Touchfeather Too,* Norton, 1970; *Your Friendly Neighborhood Death Pedlar,* Dodd, 1971.

Screenplays: "The Legacy," Universal Pictures, 1979; (author of story with Mary Rodgers) "The Devil and Max Devlin," Walt Disney Productions, 1981. Also author of "Deadlier than the Male," Universal Pictures, "Maniac," Columbia Pictures, "Scream of Fear," Columbia Pictures, "The Nanny," Twentieth Century-Fox, "The Anniversary," Twentieth Century-Fox, "Fear in the Night," Hammer Films, "The Criminal," and "The Mummy"; also author of three Frankenstein films, three Dracula films, and about thirty other screenplays.

Television scripts: "Motive for Murder" (six-part serial); "The Assassins" (six-part serial); "The Big Deal" (ninety-minute live play); "I Can Destroy the Sun" (ninety-minute live play); "A Taste of Evil." Also author of a number of other television scripts.†

*   *   *

SATTERFIELD, Archie   1933-

PERSONAL: Born June 18, 1933, in Howards Ridge, Mo.; son of Homer and Lucile (Howard) Satterfield. *Education:* Attended St. Louis University, 1956-57, and University of Missouri, 1957-59; University of Washington, B.A., 1963. *Home address:* P.O. Box 405, Edmonds, Wash. 98020.

CAREER: Seaside Signal, Seaside, Ore., reporter, 1963-64; *Longview Daily News,* Longview, Wash., reporter, 1964-66; *Seattle Times,* Seattle, Wash., reporter and assistant magazine editor, 1966-72; *Seattle Post-Intelligencer,* Seattle, Wash., book review editor, 1972-79; editor, *Northwest Edition* (magazine). *Military service:* U.S. Navy, 1952-56; became petty officer third class.

MEMBER: American Society of Journalists and Authors, Authors Guild, Authors League of America, Society of American Travel Writers, Pacific Northwest Writers Conference (vice-president, 1972-73), Seattle Free-Lances (president, 1974-75).

AWARDS, HONORS: State of Washington Governor's Writers Day Award, 1970.

WRITINGS: Moods of the Columbia, Superior, 1968; (with L. Jarman) *Alaska Bush Pilots in the Float Country,* Superior, 1969.

(Editor) *Oregon Coast,* Charles H. Belding, 1972; (with Ray Atkeson) *Washington II,* Charles H. Belding, 1973; (with others) *California: Its Coast and Desert,* Charles H. Belding, 1973; *Chilkoot Pass: Then and Now,* Alaska Northwest Publishing, 1973, 3rd edition published as *Chilkoot Pass: The Most Famous Trail in the North,* 1980; (with R. Atkeson) *Oregon II,* Charles H. Belding, 1974; *The Yukon River Trail Guide,* Stackpole, 1975; (with Merle E. Dowd) *The Seattle Guidebook,* Writing Works, 1975, 5th edition, 1981.

After the Gold Rush, Lippincott, 1976; *The Lewis and Clark Trail,* Stackpole, 1978; *Adventures in Washington,* Writing Works, 1978; *Elton Bennett: His Life and Art,* Writing Works, 1979; *Exploring the Yukon River,* Mountaineers, 1979.

Backroads of Washington, Rand McNally, 1981; *The Alaska Airlines Story,* Alaska Northwest Publishing, 1982; *The Home Front,* Playboy Press, 1982; *Pacific Sea and Shore,* Writing Works, 1982.

With Eddie Bauer; all published by Addison-Wesley; all 1983: *The Eddie Bauer Guide to Family Camping; The Eddie Bauer Guide to Cross-Country Skiing; The Eddie Bauer Guide to Backpacking.*

BIOGRAPHICAL/CRITICAL SOURCES: *Publishers Weekly*, December 4, 1981; *New York Times Book Review*, February 21, 1982; *Chicago Tribune*, April 3, 1983.

* * *

SATTLER, Helen Roney 1921-

PERSONAL: Born March 2, 1921, in Newton, Iowa; daughter of Louie Earl (a farmer) and Hazel (Cure) Roney; married Robert E. Sattler (a chemical engineer), September 30, 1950; children: Richard, Kathryn. *Education:* Southwest Missouri State College (now University), B.S., 1946; Famous Artist's School, Certificate in Commercial Art, 1960. *Politics:* Democrat. *Religion:* Christian. *Residence:* Bartlesville, Okla. 74003.

CAREER: Elementary teacher in Aldrich, Mo., 1941-42, Norwood, Mo., 1942-45, and Marshfield, Mo., 1945-48; Kansas City Public Library, Kansas City, Mo., children's librarian, 1948-49; Standard Oil of New Jersey, elementary teacher at company school on Aruba (Dutch island off Venezuelan coast), 1949-50.

MEMBER: Authors League of America, Authors Guild, Society of Children's Book Writers, Oklahoma Writers Federation, Bartlesville Writer's Association (chairman, 1967-68 and 1981-82).

AWARDS, HONORS: American Library Association Book of Interest, 1973, for *Recipes for Art and Craft Materials;* Oklahoma Cherubim Award and outstanding science trade book for children citation, both 1978, for *Nature's Weather Forecasters;* Children's Choice Award, 1982, for *No Place for a Goat.*

All 1981, for *Dinosaurs of North America:* Golden Kite nonfiction honor book; American Library Association notable children's book; *Boston Globe/Horn Book* nonfiction honor book; chosen as outstanding science trade book for children, National Science Teachers Association; among the books of the year chosen by Library of Congress; Children's Reviewer's choice.

WRITINGS: Kitchen Carton Crafts, Lothrop, 1970; *A Beginning to Read Book of Puzzles*, Denison, 1971; *Holiday Gifts, Favors and Decorations*, Lothrop, 1971; *The Eggless Cookbook*, A. S. Barnes, 1972; *Sockcraft*, Lothrop, 1972; *Jewelry from Junk*, Lothrop, 1973; *Recipes for Art and Craft Materials*, Lothrop, 1973; *Jar and Bottle Craft*, Lothrop, 1974; *Train Whistles*, Lothrop, 1977; *Bible Puzzle Collection*, Baker Book, 1977; *Bible Puzzle Pack*, Baker Book, 1977; *Nature's Weather Forecasters*, Dutton, 1978; *Dollars from Dandelions*, Lothrop, 1979; *Bible Puzzles for Teens*, Concordia, 1979.

Brain Busters, Scholastic Book Services, 1980; *Dinosaurs of North America*, Lothrop, 1981; *No Place for a Goat*, Dutton, 1981; *The Smallest Witch*, Dutton, 1981; *Charley le Mulet*, Harlequin, 1981, translation published as *Morgan the Mule*, Ideals Publishing, 1982; *Noses Are Special*, Abingdon, 1982; *The Illustrated Dinosaur Dictionary*, Lothrop, 1983; *Fish Facts and Bird Brains*, Dutton, 1984; *Baby Dinosaurs*, Lothrop, 1984; *Sharks: The SuperFish*, Lothrop, 1985. Contributor of puzzles, how-to articles, stories, and verse to more than forty magazines, including *Child Life, Junior Discoveries, Jack and Jill, Boys' Life, Cricket*, and *Highlights for Children.*

WORK IN PROGRESS: Pterosaurs: The Flying Reptiles, and *Whales*, both for Lothrop.

SIDELIGHTS: Helen Roney Sattler told *CA:* "I love books and I love children, a perfect combination for either writing or teaching. When I retired from teaching to raise my family,

I turned to writing as a natural second career. Many years of experience working with children as a teacher, mother, and Scout leader led to my creating crafts and puzzles, first for magazine publication, then in books. I believe that puzzles stimulate their minds and that most children can be taught to work with their hands and be creative if shown a few basic designs to get them started. A toy or gift made by themselves is more valuable than an expensive one bought in a store. Creative work need not be expensive. This is what I try to show in my craft books. As my own children matured and left home, it became the role of my grandchildren to inspire my books. I wrote *Train Whistles* for my grandson who could never find enough train books in the library. Then when he was four, he asked me to write him a book about dinosaurs that 'didn't have any mistakes in it.' This resulted in *Dinosaurs of North America.*

"When I began research for this book, I knew very little about dinosaurs. I soon realized the need for a book like *The Illustrated Dinosaur Dictionary*. A book that would define all of those words that I could not find in a regular dictionary. A book that would give the pronunciation of each dinosaur and one that would distinguish between dinosaurs and non-dinosaurian Mesozoic animals. So I wrote one.

"I know that all children, like my grandson, want the facts in their books to be accurate, so I take great pains to research my books carefully. The research for *The Illustrated Dinosaur Dictionary* spanned five years. I read more than one hundred fifty references and visited excavations. I also talked to and corresponded with paleontologists all over North America. My fascination with these creatures has never waned and I never tire of reading about them. I am delighted when I learn something new.

"While researching the book on sharks, I interviewed shark experts and visited a dozen aquariums both in the United States and in Canada. My research on whales [involved] a whale watch trip to Baja California where I played with the grey whales.

"Writing nonfiction for children is almost as much fun as reading [it]. I strive to write books that will capture the interest of all children, especially the reluctant readers."

Dinosaurs of North America is praised by Georgess McHargue in the *New York Times Book Review* as "meticulous," "complete," and "elaborate." "[Sattler's] prose is superbly understandable, with never a hint of condescension. . . . It is not, all in all, an easy book, but a rewarding one, nevertheless." Of *The Illustrated Dinosaur Dictionary*, McHargue writes: "Its elegant artwork is as attractive as it is informative. . . . This present volume is likely to become the premier reference work on the subject."

Sattler has visited most of the fifty states, Canada, Mexico, Haiti, Cuba, and Aruba.

AVOCATIONAL INTERESTS: Painting, drawing, cooking, crafts, puzzle solving, and travel.

BIOGRAPHICAL/CRITICAL SOURCES: *New York Times Book Review*, November 15, 1981, November 13, 1983.

* * *

SAVARIN
See COURTINE, Robert

SAVITZ, Harriet May   1933-

PERSONAL: Born May 19, 1933, in Newark, N.J.; daughter of Samuel and Susan (Trulick) Blatstein; married Ephraim Savitz (a pharmacist); children: Beth, Steven. *Education:* Attended evening classes at Upsala College, one year, and Rutgers University, one year. *Religion:* Jewish. *Home address:* P.O. Box 181, Plymouth Meeting, Pa. 19462. *Agent:* Curtis Brown Ltd., 575 Madison Ave., New York, N.Y. 10022.

CAREER: Writer. Teacher of writing, Philadelphia Writer's Conference; guest lecturer in English literature, University of Pennsylvania. Holds workshops in novel writing; helped organize workshop at Philadelphia's Free Library for the Blind to sensitize the media to the needs of the disabled.

MEMBER: National League of American Pen Women, National Wheelchair Athletic Association, Disabled in Action, VEEP (Very Exciting Education Program), Pennsylvania Wheelchair Athletic Association, Children's Reading Roundtable (Philadelphia; co-founder; member of steering committee, 1966—), Philadelphia Book Sellers Association.

AWARDS, HONORS: Nomination for the Dorothy Canfield Fisher Memorial Children's Book Award, 1971, for *Fly, Wheels, Fly!*; Outstanding Author Award, Pennsylvania School Library Association, 1981; *Run, Don't Walk* was nominated for the California Young Reader Medal in the high school category, 1983-84; received recognition for *Wheelchair Champions,* in celebration of International Year of Disabled Persons.

WRITINGS—Published by John Day: (With M. Caporale Shecktor) *The Moon Is Mine* (short stories for children), 1968; (with Shecktor) *Peter and Other Stories* (juvenile), 1969; *Fly, Wheels, Fly!* (juvenile novel), 1970; *On the Move* (juvenile novel), 1973; *The Lionhearted,* 1975; *Wheelchair Champions—A History of Wheelchair Sports,* 1978.

Published by New American Library, except as indicated: *Run, Don't Walk* (juvenile novel), F. Watts, 1979; *Wait Until Tomorrow* (juvenile novel), 1981; *If You Can't Be the Sun, Be a Star,* 1982; *Come Back, Mr. Magic,* 1983; *Summer's End,* 1984; *The Sweat and the Gold* (research project on the history of regional wheelchair sports competitions in the United States), VEEP, 1984.

Also author of works for Science Research Associates reading program and Lyons & Carnahan readers. Contributor of short stories to collections, including *Short Story Scene.* Contributor to *Encyclopaedia Britannica.* Contributor to magazines and newspapers, including Philadelphia *Inquirer,* Denver *Post, Scholastic, Boys' Life, Children's Friend,* and *Ranger Rick.*

WORK IN PROGRESS: The Wheelchair Express, a book about a quadriplegic who made an 110-mile journey in an electric wheelchair to protest the lack of public transportation accessible to the disabled in his state.

SIDELIGHTS: Harriet May Savitz writes *CA:* "I find the books walk into my life. My father had a laryngectomy. A young boy at the shore wants to commit suicide. The two join together for *Wait Until Tomorrow.*

"A gifted young man I know becomes injured in a hit and run and is left in a coma. An artist friend travels about the world seeking adventure. They come together in *Come Back, Mr. Magic.*

"I belong to a neighborhood watch program and am stunned by the crimes against the elderly. I speak at schools where there is no dress code. The two come together in *If You Can't Be the Sun, Be a Star.*

"I walk down the boardwalk and talk to a fellow stroller. He tells me he is a second generation survivor. I ask, 'What is that?' There is a devastating flood in a mountain town nearby. Someone gives me the news clippings. I move the flood to the shore and include the second generation survivor of the Holocaust and we have *Summer's End.*

"For five years I research *The Sweat and the Gold,* bringing the real people into the story. All the disabled who have inspired me in fiction take their places in this nonfiction book.

"Sometimes I just stand somewhere, sit somewhere, walk somewhere and I feel it. The book. It's around me and if I look carefully, listen intently, and let myself feel its presence, the book introduces itself. 'How do you do,' I say. 'Let's get on with it,' it answers. From that moment on, there is no other world."

Savitz based her book *Fly, Wheels, Fly!* on factual material drawn from her association with a group of paraplegics in the Norristown, Pa., area who have formed an organization known as the Central Penn Wheelers. Member of the organization play basketball and compete in other sports—all from their wheelchairs.

MEDIA ADAPTATIONS: Run, Don't Walk was adapted and produced as an American Broadcasting Company afterschool special by Henry Winkler's production company.

*   *   *

SAXON, Alex
See PRONZINI, Bill

*   *   *

SAXON, Bill
See WALLMANN, Jeffrey M(iner)

*   *   *

SCANZONI, Letha Dawson   1935-

PERSONAL: Born October 9, 1935, in Pittsburgh, Pa.; daughter of James Jackson (a businessman) and Hilda (Koch) Dawson; married John H. Scanzoni (a professor of sociology), July 7, 1956 (divorced, November 2, 1983); children: Stephen, David. *Education:* Attended Eastman School of Music, 1952-54, and Moody Bible Institute, 1954-56; Indiana University, A.B. (with high distinction), 1972. *Politics:* Democrat. *Religion:* Presbyterian. *Home and office:* 4512 Grendel Rd., Greensboro, N.C. 27410.

CAREER: Village Missions, Lookingglass, Ore., rural church, music, and youth worker, 1958-61; writer, 1962—. Speaker at universities and conferences.

MEMBER: Evangelical Women's Caucus (member of executive council, 1978-82), SIECUS Associates, National Organization for Women, National Council on Family Relations, Phi Beta Kappa.

WRITINGS: Youth Looks at Love, Revell, 1964; *Why Am I Here? Where Am I Going?,* Revell, 1966; *Sex and the Single Eye,* Zondervan, 1968, published as *Why Wait?,* Baker Book,

1975; *Sex Is a Parent Affair: Sex Education for the Christian Home*, Regal Books, 1973, revised edition, Bantam, 1982; (with Nancy Hardesty) *All We're Meant to Be: A Biblical Approach to Women's Liberation*, Word Books, 1974; (with John H. Scanzoni) *Men, Women, and Change: A Sociology of Marriage and Family*, McGraw, 1976, revised edition, 1981; (with Virginia Ramey Mollenkott) *Is the Homosexual My Neighbor?: Another Christian View*, Harper, 1978; *Sexuality*, Westminster, 1984.

Contributor: Gary Collins, editor, *The Secrets of Our Sexuality*, Word Books, 1976; Harold Twiss, editor, *Homosexuality and the Christian Faith: A Symposium*, Judson, 1978; *Family Factbook*, Marquis, 1978; Perry Catham, editor, *Christian Social Ethics*, Baker Book, 1979; Lina Mainiero, editor, *American Women Writers*, Ungar, Volume I, 1979, Volume III, 1981; John M. Holland, editor, *Religion and Sexuality*, Association of Sexologists, 1981; Janet Kalven and Mary I. Buckley, editors, *Women's Spirit Bonding*, Pilgrim Press, 1984.

Contributor to *Christian Century, Faith at Work, Daughters of Sarah, SIECUS Report*, and other periodicals. Contributing editor, *Radix;* former editorial associate, *Other Side.*

WORK IN PROGRESS: Contributing to *Women and Religion in America.*

SIDELIGHTS: Letha Scanzoni told *CA:* "As a Christian and a feminist, I am interested in writing about religion and social issues—particularly with regard to changes in male-female roles and relationships. I also do quite a bit of travel and speaking on these subjects. Other areas of interest in my writing and speaking are biblical interpretation, marriage and family, domestic violence, friendship, sex ethics, and sex education. Sociology is of equal interest and is an area in which I try to keep current and plan to do further writing."

AVOCATIONAL INTERESTS: Movies, theater, music (trombonist), pet Persian cat, aerobic excercise.

*   *   *

SCARPITTI, Frank R(oland)   1936-

PERSONAL: Born November 12, 1936, in Butler, Pa.; married Ellen Canfield, September 5, 1959; children: Susan, Jeffrey. *Education:* Fenn College (now Cleveland State University), B.A., 1958; Ohio State University, M.A., 1959, Ph.D., 1962. *Home:* 104 Radcliffe Dr., Newark, Del. 19711. *Office:* Department of Sociology, University of Delaware, Newark, Del. 19711.

CAREER: University of Louisville, Louisville, Ky., instructor in sociology, 1961-62; University of Kentucky, Lexington, instructor in sociology, 1962-63; Rutgers University, New Brunswick, N.J., assistant professor of sociology, 1963-67; University of Delaware, Newark, associate professor, 1967-69, professor of sociology 1969—, chairman of department, 1969-80. Member of juvenile delinquency task force, Governor's Commission on Crime and Administration of Justice; member of study committee, Delaware Law Enforcement Planning Agency; member of board of directors, Delaware Citizens' Crime Commission, 1968-75, and Commission of Criminology and Criminal Justice Education and Standards, 1977-81.

MEMBER: American Sociological Association, Society for the Study of Social Problems, American Society of Criminology (vice-president, 1977-79; president, 1980-81), American Association of University Professors (vice-president of University

of Delaware chapter, 1971-72), Eastern Sociological Society, Alpha Kappa Delta, Phi Kappa Phi, Omicron Delta Kappa.

AWARDS, HONORS: Research fellowship from U.S. Public Health Service, 1960-61; Hofheimer Prize for Research from American Psychiatric Association, 1967; Danforth Foundation associate, 1968.

WRITINGS: (Contributor) Marvin Wolfgang, Leonard Savitz, and Norman Johnston, editors, *The Sociology of Crime and Delinquency*, Wiley, 1962; (contributor) Ruth Cavan, editor, *A Reader in Juvenile Delinquency*, Lippincott, 1964; (contributor) Walter C. Reckless and C. L. Newman, editors, *Interdisciplinary Problems in Criminology*, College of Commerce Publication Service, Ohio State University, 1965.

(Contributor) D. A. Mereness, editor, *Readings in Psychiatric Nursing*, W. C. Brown, 1966; (contributor) Joseph Zubin and Paul Hoch, editors, *The Psychopathology of Schizophrenia*, Grune, 1966; (with Simon Dinitz and Benjamin Pasamanick) *Schizophrenics in the Community: An Experimental Study in the Prevention of Hospitalization*, Appleton, 1967; (with Harry Gold) *Combatting Social Problems: Techniques of Intervention*, Holt, 1967; (contributor) Paul S. Graubard, editor, *Children against Schools*, Follett, 1969; (contributor) Simon Dinitz, Alfred Clarke, and Russell Dynes, editors, *Deviance: Studies in the Process in Stigmatization and Societal Reaction*, Oxford University Press, 1969.

(With John H. McGrath) *Youth and Drugs*, Scott, Foresman, 1970; (contributor) S. H. Frey, editor, *Adolescent Behavior in School*, Rand McNally, 1970; (contributor) Norman Johnston, Leonard Savitz, and Marvin Wolfgang, editors, *Sociology of Punishment and Correction*, 2nd edition (Scarpitti was not associated with earlier edition), Wiley, 1970; (contributor) Peter Garabedian and D. C. Gibbons, editors, *Becoming Delinquent*, Aldine, 1970; (with Richard M. Stephenson) *Group Interaction as Therapy*, Greenwood Press, 1973; *Social Problems*, Holt, 1974, 3rd edition, 1980; (with Paul T. McFarlane) *Deviance: Action, Reaction, Interaction*, Addison-Wesley, 1975.

Drugs and the Youthful User, Sage Publications, 1980; *Women, Crime, and Justice*, Oxford University Press, 1980; (with Alan Block) *Poisoning for Profit*, Morrow, 1985.

Contributor of about twenty-five articles to professional journals, including *Journal of the American Medical Association, Elementary School Journal, Archives of General Psychiatry, Social Forces, Federal Probation, Crime and Delinquency*, and *Journal of Rehabilitation.*

*   *   *

SCHLACHTER, Gail Ann   1943-

PERSONAL: Born April 7, 1943, in Detroit, Mich.; daughter of Lewis E. (an attorney) and Helen (Blitz) Goldstein; married Alfred S. Schlachter, June 18, 1964 (divorced, 1973); children: Sandra Elyse, Eric Brian. *Education:* Attended Santa Monica City College, 1960-62; University of California, Berkeley, B.A., 1964; University of Wisconsin—Madison, M.A. (history and education), 1966, M.A. (library science), 1967; University of Minnesota, Ph.D., 1971; University of Southern California, M.P.A., 1979. *Home:* 240 Las Alturas, Santa Barbara, Calif. 93103. *Office address:* ABC-Clio Information Services, 2040 A.P.S., Box 4397, Santa Barbara, Calif. 93103.

CAREER: University of Wisconsin—Madison, director of Industrial Relations Reference Center and Social Science Graduate Reference Center, 1967-68; University of Minnesota, Minneapolis, lecturer in library science, 1969-70; University of Southern California, Los Angeles, assistant professor of library science, 1971-74; California State University Library, Long Beach, head of department of social sciences, 1974-76; University of California, Davis, assistant university librarian, 1976-81; American Bibliographical Center, ABC-Clio Information Services, Santa Barbara, Calif., director, 1981-82, vice-president for publications, 1982-83, vice-president and general manager, 1983—.

MEMBER: American Library Association, Association of American Library Schools, National Librarians Association, Library Associates, Special Libraries Association, Committee of Small Magazine Editors and Publishers, American Association of University Professors, California Library Association (chapter president, 1977-78, chairman of professional standards committee), Western Independent Publishers, Beta Phi Mu, Alpha Gamma Sigma, Alpha Mu Gamma.

AWARDS, HONORS: Ford Foundation Area fellowship, 1965; Higher Education Act fellowship, 1968-70.

WRITINGS: Library Science Dissertations, 1925-1972: An Annotated Bibliography, Libraries Unlimited, 1974; *Directory of Internships, Work Experience Programs, and On-the-Job Training Opportunities,* Ready Reference Press, 1976; *Minorities and Women: A Guide to Reference Literature in the Social Sciences,* Reference Service Press, 1977; *Directory of Financial Aids for Women,* Reference Service Press, 1978.

The Service Imperative for Libraries: Essays in Honor of Margaret E. Monroe, Libraries Unlimited, 1982; *Library Science Dissertations, 1973-1981,* Libraries Unlimited, 1983; *Directory of Financial Aids for Minorities, 1984/85,* American Bibliographical Center-Clio Press, 1983; *Directory of Financial Aids for the Disabled, 1985/86,* American Bibliographical Center-Clio Press, 1984.

Editor of "Facsimile Reprint Series," California State University. Editor of *Critique: Journal of Southern California Public Policy,* 1976, and of *CARL Newsletter;* book review editor of *Reference Quarterly,* 1978—.

*   *   *

SCHLENDER, William E(lmer) 1920-

PERSONAL: Born October 28, 1920, in Sawyer, Mich.; son of Gust A. and Marie (Zindler) Schlender; married Lela Ruth Pullen, June 9, 1956 (died June 23, 1983). *Education:* Valparaiso University, A.B., 1941; University of Denver, M.B.A., 1947; Ohio State University, Ph.D., 1955. *Religion:* Lutheran. *Home address:* P.O. Box 96, Sawyer, Mich. 49125.

CAREER: U.S. Rubber Co., Mishawaka, Ind., industrial relations assistant, 1941-43, 1946; Bowling Green State University, Bowling Green, Ohio, assistant professor, 1947-50, associate professor of business administration, 1950-53; Ohio State University, Columbus, assistant professor, 1954-57, associate professor, 1957-61, professor of business organization, 1961-65, assistant dean of College of Commerce and Administration, 1959-62, associate dean, 1962-63; University of Texas at Austin, professor of management, 1965-68, department chairman, 1966-68; Cleveland State University, Cleveland, Ohio, dean of College of Business Administration, 1968-75, professor of management, 1975-76; Valparaiso University, Valparaiso, Ind., International Lutheran Laymen's League Professor of Business Ethics, 1976-79, Richard E. Meier Professor

of Management, 1983—. Visiting professor, University of Denver, 1949, Columbia University, 1957-58, and University of Texas at Arlington, 1981-82. Consultant in business. *Military service:* U.S. Army, 1943-45; became staff sergeant; received Bronze Star.

MEMBER: International Council of Small Business, Academy of Management (fellow), American Management Association, Industrial Relations Research Association, Ohio Commodores, Rotary Club, Sigma Iota Epsilon, Phi Kappa Phi, Tau Kappa Epsilon, Beta Gamma Sigma, Alpha Kappa Psi.

WRITINGS: (With Michael James Jucius) *Elements of Managerial Action,* Irwin, 1960, 3rd edition, 1973; (editor with William G. Scott and Alan C. Filley) *Management in Perspective: Selected Readings,* Houghton, 1965; (editor) *Executive Leadership in a Dynamic Society,* Ohio State University College of Commerce and Administration, 1965; (contributor) Donald G. Jones, editor, *Business, Religion, and Ethics,* Oelgeschlager, Gunn & Hain, 1982. Also editor of *Management in a Dynamic Society,* 1965. Contributor to *Encyclopaedia Britannica Yearbook* and to professional journals.

WORK IN PROGRESS: Research on organizational structure of various business institutions and business ethics.

SIDELIGHTS: William Schlender has speaking and reading knowledge of German, reading knowledge of French.

*   *   *

SCHNESSEL, S. Michael 1947-

PERSONAL: Born April 7, 1947, in Hof, West Germany; came to the United States, 1950, naturalized citizen, 1956; son of Samuel and Gertrude Bertha (Arndt) Schnessel. *Education:* Baltimore Junior College, A.A., 1966; Syracuse University, B.A.J., 1968. *Politics:* "To the left, within reason." *Religion:* "Never touch the stuff." *Residence:* Princeton, N.J. *Office address:* P.O. Box 2057, Princeton, N.J. 08540.

CAREER: Robert Rusting Associates (public relations firm), New York City, account executive, 1969-74; New Jersey State Council on the Arts, Trenton, public relations director, 1974-75; *Trentonian,* Trenton, art and theater critic, 1975-81; American Broadcasting Companies, Inc. (ABC-TV), New York City, full-time writer, 1981—. President of Exhumation (gallery for antique posters). Active in community theater, as performer and executive.

AWARDS, HONORS: New Play Award, Southeastern Theatre Conference, and first prize, Jane Gilmore Playwriting Competition, Omaha Community Playhouse, both 1979, for "Visiting Hours"; second prize, John Gassner Memorial Playwriting Awards, New England Theatre Conference, 1980, for "Cassie's Miracle"; honorable mention, Virginia Weisbrod Playwriting Award, Little Theatre of Alexandria, 1980, for "A Widow in the Midnight Sun"; finalist, Forest Roberts Playwriting Awards, Northern Michigan University, 1980, for "The Serpent Smiles"; New Jersey State Council on the Arts playwriting fellowship, 1980.

WRITINGS: A Collector's Guide to Louis Icart, Exhumation, 1973; *Icart,* C. N. Potter, 1976; *Jesse Willcox Smith,* Crowell, 1977; *The Etchings of Louis Icart,* Schiffer, 1982.

Plays: "Visiting Hours," first produced at Omaha Community Playhouse, 1979; "A Widow in the Midnight Sun," first produced at Little Theatre of Alexandria, 1980; "The Serpent Smiles," first produced at Princeton Community Theatre, 1980;

"Galatea's Hands" (staged reading), first production in Trenton, New Jersey, at Mill Hill Playhouse, 1980; "The Day Mr. Donald Disappeared" (staged reading), first production at Princeton Community Theatre, 1980. Also author of staged reading "Cassie's Miracle," first produced in Cambridge, Mass., at The People's Theatre, and of "The Unitron Monster," "Seance," and "My Name is Miranda."

Contributor to journals on antiques and art, and to popular magazines and newspapers, including *Good Housekeeping* and *TV Guide.*

WORK IN PROGRESS: Three plays, "Miki's Day 'N Nite," a comedy, "Crane," a drama, and "Seance," a musical based on the author's play of the same title; four screenplays, "The Thirteenth Floor," "Mr. K Comes to Ergo," "Sky Devil," and "The Renegade and the Prodigy."

*   *   *

SCHOFIELD, Michael 1919-
(Gordon Westwood)

PERSONAL: Born June 24, 1919, in Leeds, England; son of Snowden and Ella (Dawson) Schofield. *Education:* Cambridge University, M.A., 1940. *Home and office:* 28 Lyndhurst Gardens, London NW3 5NW, England.

CAREER: British Social Biology Council, London, England, research director, 1959-62; Central Council for Health Education, London, research director, 1963-65; self-employed researcher and writer, 1973-82. Former member of executive committee, National Council for Civil Liberties; former member of Government Advisory Committee on Drug Dependence and the Wootton Committee. Vice-president of Campaign for Homosexual Equality. *Military service:* Royal Air Force, 1940-45.

WRITINGS: Sexual Behavior of Young People, Longmans, Green, 1965; *Sociological Aspects of Homosexuality,* Longmans, Green, 1965; *Social Research,* Heinemann, 1969; (author of introduction) *The Release Report,* Sphere, 1969; *The Strange Case of Pot,* Penguin, 1971; (author of introduction) *Boy, Girl, Man, Woman,* Calder & Boyars, 1972; *The Sexual Behavior of Young Adults,* Allen Lane, 1973; *Promiscuity,* Gollancz, 1976; *Report of the Committee on the Operation of the Sexual Containment Act,* Davis-Poynter, 1978; (contributor) *Human Sexuality,* Cambridge University Press, 1979.

Under pseudonym Gordon Westwood: *Society and the Homosexual,* Gollancz, 1952; *A Minority: A Report on the Life of the Male Homosexual in Great Britain,* Longmans, Green, 1960.

SIDELIGHTS: Michael Schofield has spent many years supporting various law reform groups. A member of the executive committee of the National Council for Civil Liberties for nine years, he was active in the campaign against censorship and appeared as an expert witness for the defense in several obscenity trials. Schofield was also on the Government Advisory Committee on Drug Dependence and the Wootton Committee, which produced a controversial report on cannabis, suggesting that the law was far too severe. He also campaigned for the Abortion Law Reform Society and for the provision of free contraceptives by the National Health Service.

Schofield, who retired in 1982, told *CA:* "Nearly all my work was motivated by the belief that people would act sensibly if only they could be provided with the necessary information. I now believe, particularly since the Falklands episode, that this belief is false. Most people prefer propaganda to truth and base their decisions on emotion, not fact."

Of Schofield's book, *Sexual Behavior of Young People,* John Gray writes in *Books and Bookmen:* "Schofield presents, in what is sociologically and statistically an almost blameless manner, the results of interviews with 1,870 teenagers in seven different areas of England. . . . Those who have hopes of finding yet another scarifying expose of teenage immorality will be disappointed by this book. The facts are presented dispassionately, and are far less 'shocking' than the exposes would have us believe."

BIOGRAPHICAL/CRITICAL SOURCES: Books and Bookmen, February, 1969.

*   *   *

SCHOLES, Robert (Edward) 1929-

PERSONAL: Surname is pronounced *Skolz;* born May 19, 1929, in Brooklyn, N.Y.; son of Herbert J. (a businessman) and Leila (Imello) Scholes; married Joan Grace Carer (a secretary), January 6, 1951 (died, 1971); married Jo Ann S. Putnam, January 30, 1972; children: (first marriage) Christine, Peter. *Education:* Yale University, A.B., 1950; Cornell University, M.A., 1956, Ph.D., 1959. *Politics:* Ex-Democrat. *Religion:* Ex-Catholic. *Office:* Brown University, Providence, R.I. 02912.

CAREER: University of Virginia, Charlottesville, 1959-63, began as instructor, became assistant professor of English; University of Wisconsin—Madison, visiting fellow at Humanities Institute, 1963-64; State University of Iowa, Iowa City, associate professor, 1964-66, professor of English, 1966-70; Brown University, Providence, R.I., professor of English and comparative literature, 1970—. *Military service:* U.S. Naval Reserve, 1951-55; became lieutenant.

MEMBER: Modern Language Association of America, Semiotic Society of America, National Council of Teachers of English, College English Association.

WRITINGS: The Cornell Joyce Collection: A Catalogue, Cornell University Press, 1961; (editor) *Approaches to the Novel: Materials for a Poetics,* Chandler Publishing, 1961, revised edition, 1966; (editor) *Learners and Discerners: A Newer Criticism* (discussions of modern literature by Harry Levin and others), University Press of Virginia, 1964; (editor with Richard M. Kain) *The Workshop of Daedalus: James Joyce and the Raw Materials for "A Portrait of the Artist as a Young Man",* Northwestern University Press, 1965; (with Robert L. Kellogg) *The Nature of Narrative,* Oxford University Press, 1966; (editor with Richard Eelman) James Joyce, *Dubliners,* Viking, 1966; *The Fabulators,* Oxford University Press, 1967; *Elements of Fiction,* Oxford University Press, 1968; (editor with A. Walton Litz) James Joyce, *Dubliners* (Viking critical edition), Viking, 1969; *Elements of Poetry,* Oxford University Press, 1969; (with Carl H. Klaus) *Elements of the Essay,* Oxford University Press, 1969; (editor) *Poetic Theory/Poetic Practice,* Midwest Modern Language Association, 1969.

(Editor) *The Philosopher-Critic,* University of Tulsa, 1970; (editor) *Some Modern Writers: Essays and Fiction by Conrad, Dinesen, Lawrence, Orwell, Faulkner, and Ellison,* Oxford University Press, 1971; (with Klaus) *Elements of Drama,* Oxford University Press, 1971; *Elements of Writing,* Oxford University Press, 1972; *Structuralism in Literature,* Yale University Press, 1974; *Structural Fabulation,* University of Notre

Dame Press, 1975; (with Eric S. Rabkin) *Science Fiction: History, Science, Vision,* Oxford University Press, 1977; *Fabulation and Metafiction,* University of Illinois Press, 1979.

(With Nancy R. Comley) *The Practice of Writing,* St. Martin's, 1981; *Elements of Fiction: An Anthology,* Oxford University Press, 1981; *Semiotics and Interpretation,* Yale University Press, 1982; *Bridges to Fantasy,* Southern Illinois University Press, 1982; (editor with others) *Elements of Literature Three: Fiction, Poetry, Drama,* Oxford University Press, 1982; *Elements of Literature Five: Fiction, Poetry, Drama, Essay, Film,* Oxford University Press, 1982. Contributor of numerous articles and book reviews to learned journals, literary magazines, and weekly reviews.

SIDELIGHTS: In the introduction to *The Nature of Narrative,* Robert Scholes and Robert L. Kellogg write that they are attacking "our veneration of the novel as a literary form." Dorrit Cohn of Indiana University notes in *Comparative Literature* that the book "aims to re-educate us to a more liberal view of the narrative genre by studying the diversity of its forms from the Homeric epic to the post-novel. . . . The authors' vast erudition is impressive; so are the apparent ease with which they range over the literature of twenty-five centuries and the considerable yield of their comparative readings of specific texts."

Commenting in *South Atlantic Quarterly,* Morris Beja calls *The Fabulators* "a valuable book . . . a sort of gloss on the study" previously written in collaboration with Kellogg. Centrally concerned with the relation between fiction and reality, Scholes evaluates Lawrence Durrell, John Hawkes, Terry Southern, Iris Murdoch, Kurt Vonnegut, and John Barth in terms of their "fabulation," by which he means a "more verbal . . . more fictional . . . less realistic and more artistic kind of narrative" than the traditional novel. "Clearly, Mr. Scholes is writing about an important development in contemporary fiction," declares a critic for the *New York Times Book Review,* "but his case for these writers is weakened by his excessive enthusiasms." In an article on "the pretentious nonsense passing for profundity" published today, *Motive* reviewer James P. Degnan faults Scholes for feeling "compelled to pretend that he is 1) providing us with some kind of special 'literary equipment' . . . ; and 2) that *The Fabulators* documents the death of 'realism' and demonstrates that the 'fabulators,' e.g. Durrell, Hawkes, Southern and the bunch, have replaced the 'realists.'"

Reviewing *Fabulation and Metafiction* in the *New York Times Book Review,* Mark Shechner defines "'fabulation' (or 'metafiction,' 'surfiction' or 'post-modernism')" as "writing that seeks to circumvent the human image in art in order to pursue those recondite truths that a vulgar realism cannot grasp. The distinguishing features of 'fabulation' are an indulgence in fantasy, a cherishing of artifice, linguistic self-consciousness, a delight in form, and a Berkeleyan rejection of the world as unknowable, except as a creation of language, fiction and myth, which are seen as *the* basic realities. Its heroes are [James] Joyce, [Jorge Luis] Borges, [Samuel] Beckett, [Vladimir] Nabokov, Barth, Vonnegut, Hawkes, Robert Coover, William S. Burroughs and William H. Gass," the critic concludes. Shechner finds that "two-thirds" of *Fabulation and Metafiction* is a repeat of material in *The Fabulators,* but nonetheless comments that Scholes's inclusion of authors not considered part of the usual list of "fabulators," such as John Fowles, Durrell, Murdoch, and Bernard Malamud, makes the work "a touch more lively."

Scholes writes that in *Structural Fabulation* he is "asserting that the most appropriate kind of fiction that can be written in the present and the immediate future is fiction that takes place in future time." The author's argument "is an old one, already implicit in [H. G.] Wells, and it constitutes science fiction's favorite alibi," according to Michael Wood in the *New York Review of Books;* specifically, that "the genre prepares us for drastic change, helps us to meet our sudden tomorrows." Moreover, Scholes contends that science fiction "should be considered the dominant literary form of our age, uniting as it does the delights of romantic narrative with reminders of the universe in which we 'know' we live," Stephen Clark adds in the *Times Literary Supplement.*

With Eric S. Rabkin, Scholes presents a general overview of the science fiction (SF) genre in *Science Fiction: History, Science, Vision.* According to Brian Aldiss, writing in the *Times Literary Supplement,* "the blandness of the book . . . points to its having been designed for the proliferating courses in SF in American universities." Although he finds the work unexciting because "the authors are so nice to all concerned . . . [and because] it is sad to find oneself balking at so many statements; when not actually wrong, they represent safe non-judgments," Aldiss praises the book's summary of [Walter M.] Miller's *Canticle for Leibowitz* as "penetrating and thoughtful, reminding one of the merits of Professor Scholes's previous work on structural fabulation."

BIOGRAPHICAL/CRITICAL SOURCES: Robert Scholes and Robert L. Kellogg, *The Nature of Narrative,* Oxford University Press, 1966; Scholes, *The Fabulators,* Oxford University Press, 1967; *Kenyon Review,* January, 1967; *New York Times Book Review,* October 29, 1967, October 7, 1979; *Western Humanities Review,* winter, 1968; *Motive,* March, 1968; *Virginia Quarterly Review,* spring, 1968; *Hudson Review,* summer, 1968; *South Atlantic Quarterly,* summer, 1968; *Canadian Forum,* December, 1968; *Comparative Literature,* spring, 1969; *Times Literary Supplement,* August 2, 1974, February 20, 1976, November 18, 1977, October 15, 1982; Scholes, *Structural Fabulation,* University of Notre Dame Press, 1975; *New York Review of Books,* October 2, 1975.†

*   *   *

SCHROEDER, Albert H(enry) 1914-

PERSONAL: Born March 23, 1914, in Brooklyn, N.Y.; son of Henry W. (an importer) and Ida (LeHovey) Schroeder; married Ella Krienke, January 27, 1945; children: Stephen H., Christine A. (Mrs. Thomas Hueston), Scott G. *Education:* University of Arizona, B.A., 1938, M.A., 1941. *Politics:* Independent. *Religion:* Lutheran. *Home:* 1108 Barcelona Lane, Santa Fe, N.M. 87501.

CAREER: Foreman at archaeological site in Arizona, 1938-39; U.S. National Museum, assistant archaeologist in Mexico, 1940-41; U.S. National Park Service, ranger-naturalist, 1941, 1946, archaeologist in Santa Fe, N.M., 1951-54, Globe, Ariz., 1954-57, and Santa Fe, 1957-67, interpretive specialist, Santa Fe, 1967-73, chief of Division of Interpretation, 1973-76. Expert witness in Indian Land Claims Hearings, 1953-65, 1967-77; chairman of New Mexico Cultural Properties Review Committee, 1969-80. Member of board of managers, School of American Research, 1965-71. *Military service:* U.S. Army, 1942-46; became technical sergeant.

MEMBER: Archaeological Society of New Mexico (president, 1965-71), Historical Society of New Mexico (president, 1979-83), Westerners Corral of Santa Fe (sheriff, 1968).

AWARDS, HONORS: Meritorious Service Award, U.S. Department of Interior, 1956; Distinguished Service Award, U.S. Department of Interior, 1976; L.L.D., New Mexico State University, 1980; recipient of festschrift, *Collected Papers in Honor of Albert Henry Schroeder,* Archaeological Society of New Mexico, 1984.

WRITINGS: Archaeology of Zion National Park (monograph), Department of Anthropology, University of Utah, 1956; *The Archaeological Excavations at Willow Beach, Arizona, 1950* (monograph), Department of Anthropology, University of Utah, 1961; (editor and translator with Daniel S. Matson) Gaspar Castano de Sosa, *A Colony on the Move Journal: 1590-1591,* School of American Research, 1965; *The Hohokam, Sinagua, and the Hakataya* (monograph), Imperial Valley College Museum Society, 1975; (editor) *Southwestern Ceramics: A Comparative Review,* Arizona Archaelogical Society, 1982; (assembler) *The Pratt Cave Studies,* El Paso Archaeological Society, 1983.

Editor; published by Archaeological Society of New Mexico: *Collected Papers in Honor of Lyndon Lane Hargrave,* 1968; *Collected Papers in Honor of Marjorie Ferguson Lambert,* 1976; *Collected Papers in Honor of Bertha Pauline Dutton,* 1979; *Collected Papers in Honor of Helen Greene Blumenschein,* 1980; *Collected Papers in Honor of Erik Kellerman Reed,* 1981.

Also contributor to *Handbook of the North American Indian,* Volume XIV. Contributor of more than one hundred seventy archaeological and historical articles and reviews to journals and other publications. Editor, *La Gaceta* and *Brand Book,* Westerners Corral of Santa Fe, 1970—; member of editorial advisory committee for Southwest section, *Handbook of the North American Indian,* 1971-82.

*   *   *

SCHULLER, Robert (Harold) 1926-

PERSONAL: Born September 16, 1926, in Alton, Iowa; son of Anthony (a farmer) and Jennie (Beltman) Schuller; married Arvella DeHaan, June 15, 1950; children: Sheila, Robert, Jeanne Anne, Carol, Gretchen. *Education:* Hope College, B.A., 1947; Western Theological Seminary, B.D., 1950. *Office:* 12141 Lewis St., Garden Grove, Calif. 92640.

CAREER: Minister, Reformed Church in America. Ivanhoe Reformed Church, Chicago, Ill., pastor, 1950-55; Garden Grove Community Church, Garden Grove, Calif., founder, pastor, 1955—; Hour of Power TV Ministry, Garden Grove, founder and president, 1970—. Founder, Robert H. Schuller Center for Possibility Thinkers, 1976. President of Robert Schuller Institute for Successful Church Leadership; president of Robert Schuller Televangelism Assoc., Inc. President of board of directors, Christian Counseling Service; member of board of directors, Religion in American Life, 1975—. Member of board of education, Reformed Church in America. *Member:* Religious Guild Architects, Phi Kappa Delta, Rotary Club.

AWARDS, HONORS: Washington Honor Medal of Freedoms Foundation, 1962, principle award of Freedoms Foundation, 1974; distinguished alumnus award, Hope College, 1970; LL.D., Azusa Pacific College, 1970, Pepperdine University, 1976, and Barrington College, 1977; D.D., Hope College, 1973; named headliner of the year, Orange County, Calif., and clergyman of the year, Religious Heritage of America, both 1977.

WRITINGS: God's Way to the Good Life, Eerdmans, 1963; *Your Future Is Your Friend: An Inspirational Pilgrimage through the Twenty-Third Psalm,* Eerdmans, 1964; *Move Ahead with Possibility Thinking,* with an introduction by Norman Vincent Peale, Doubleday, 1967; *Self-Love: The Dynamic Force of Success,* with an introduction by Peale, Hawthorne, 1969; *Power Ideas for a Happy Family,* Revell, 1972; *You Can become the Person You Want to Be,* Hawthorn, 1973; *The Greatest Possibility Thinker That Ever Lived,* Revell, 1973; *Your Church Has Real Possibilities,* Regal, 1974; *Love or Loneliness, You Decide,* Hour of Power, 1974.

Positive Prayers for Power-Filled Living, Hawthorn, 1976; *Keep on Believing,* Hour of Power, 1976; *Reach Out for New Life,* Hawthorn, 1977; *Peace of Mind through Possibility Thinking,* Doubleday, 1977; *It's Possible,* Revell, 1978; *Turning Your Stress into Strength,* Harvest House, 1978; *Daily Power Thoughts,* Harvest House, 1978; (with wife, Arvella Schuller) *The Courage of Carol: Pearls from Tears,* Doubleday, 1978; *Discover Your Possibilities,* Ballantine, 1979; (with A. Schuller) *The Peak to Peek Principle,* Doubleday, 1980; *Living Positively One Day at a Time,* Revell, 1981; *Self-Esteem: The New Reformation,* Word, 1982; *Tough Times Never Last but Tough People Do!,* Thomas Nelson, 1983; *Tough-Minded Faith for Tenderhearted People,* Thomas Nelson, 1984.

"Discover" series, published by Harvest House, 1978: *Discover Courage to Face Your Future; . . . Freedom; . . . Health and Happiness; . . . How Life Can Be Beautiful; . . . How to Bloom Where You Are Planted; . . . How to Get Your Priorities Straight; . . . How to Turn Activity into Energy; . . . Self-Love; . . . the Miracles in Your Life; . . . the Power for Overcoming Defeat; . . . Your Opportunities; . . . Your Self-Confidence.* Author of column syndicated to seventy-five newspapers.

SIDELIGHTS: In 1955, a twenty-eight-year-old Reformed minister from the Midwest arrived in California with five hundred dollars and a simple credo: "Find a need and fill it, find a hurt and heal it." *Time* magazine describes how Robert Schuller then realized "the hurt . . . was greatest among agnostic transients flooding the West. The need was a drive-in church to serve this mobile culture. So [he] rented a drive-in theatre near Disneyland." Schuller promoted his new Garden Grove Community Church with the slogan "Come as you are in the family car," and fifty people drove up to hear his first Easter service, which he delivered from atop a refreshment stand.

Some thirty years later, Schuller's flock has multiplied into the thousands who attend services at the controversial Crystal Cathedral in Orange County, Calif., and the millions who follow the minister's "Hour of Power" television shows. Schuller's is one of the most amazing success stories to come from the field of video evangelism. He was among the first to buy television time in the so-called "ghetto hours" of Sunday morning—and saw his "Hour of Power" become a ratings hit in such large markets as New York City. In a 1979 *Saturday Review* article, John Mariani placed Schuller's weekly air-time budget at $70,000, "although many stations take 'Hour of Power' free of charge and punch it into their FCC-mandated 'public interest' slots," the writer adds. "[Schuller] has taken criticism for using show-biz techniques on his broadcasts, [but] there is much less razzle-dazzle on [the program] than on most of the evangelical broadcasts."

Schuller's style, influenced by that of his friend Norman Vincent Peale, is decidedly more low-keyed than that of his many video peers. He is "by far the most palatable of TV preachers,"

Mariani states. "His brand of Christian optimism works especially well in middle-class markets like southern California, and his advisers have sometimes kept his ["Hour of Power"] off stations in the more conservative, fundamentalist enclaves of the South." Schuller's broadcasts draw more than ten million dollars annually in donations.

The minister's "brand of religion is appealing enough," suggests Janet Chase-Marshall in an *US* article. "He never dwells on such dark fundamentalist issues as damnation and retribution. Instead, he talks of the theology of self-esteem and the power of possible thinking (not to be confused with [Peale's] power of positive thinking . . .). Schuller's favorite themes are the dignity of the human spirit, the importance of unconditional love, open communication and the search for self-knowledge. His basic philosophy is self-acceptance; he believes his job is to build people up and make them feel good about themselves."

Schuller has applied his power of possibility theory not only to his congregation but to himself: using televised appeals on the "Hour of Power," the minister was able to raise upwards of eighteen million dollars to construct the Crystal Cathedral on his Garden Grove estate. Designed by noted architect Philip Johnson, the cathedral, dedicated in 1980, is a "four-pointed, knife-edged star, whose walls contain 10,661 different panels of glass, each one of which seems to reflect the surrounding fountains and grounds in a different way," according to a *Newsweek* article. "The building is huge, longer than a football field, more than 120 feet high," and, as some have pointed out, larger than the Notre Dame Cathedral in Paris. The structure seats three thousand and is "one of the most spectacular religious edifices in the world," as *Newsweek* concludes.

The popular church became the center of controversy in 1983, when the California State Board of Equalization ruled that the Crystal Cathedral must forfeit its tax-exempt status and Schuller must pay more than $600,000 in property tax to the state. *Humanist* writer Donald W. Foster reports that "what jiggled the tax men is that Schuller has been so grandly successful as a church fundraiser, fetching, for example, $500 and more for his Possibility Thinker ballpoint pens and his plaster-of-Paris Isiah eagles." According to an interview the minister had with Charles Trueheart in *Publishers Weekly*, the Board also objected to the fact that "admission was being charged to such secular activities as musical concerts and weight reduction classes." But Schuller "contends that his church's fundraising practices are no different from those of any other religious group," Foster says. "As a 'possibility thinker,' he has simply operated on a larger scale."

The financial entanglement served as an ironic touch to the career of a renowned evangelist who has gone out of his way to avoid controversy. While other religious figures such as Jerry Falwell have taken political stands, Schuller, "with the acumen of a politician, . . . sees little point in taking positions if they serve to alienate and divide," notes Trueheart. As a mainline minister Schuller is opposed to "evangelists' penchant for labeling politicians who disagree with them 'godless,'" as Seth Cagin explains in another *US* feature. Schuller tells him, "Their attacks are doing responsible religion untold damage."

While he is the author of many inspirational books, often drawn from his sermons, Schuller is also the subject of two unauthorized biographies, *Robert Schuller: The Inside Story*, by Michael and Donna Nason, and *Mountains into Goldmines: Robert Schuller and the Gospel of Success*, by Dennis Voskuil. "One of [the minister's] weaknesses, as reported by both Vos-

kuil and by the Nasons in their [books], is his occasional deep sensitivity to criticism," offers Trueheart in the *Publishers Weekly* interview. Schuller responds in the article: "I'm not sensitive to criticism if criticism is honest and fair *and* if it's noncontroversial. . . . [Even controversial criticism is acceptable] *if* a person is given equal time, before the same audience. I was raised this way. Sensitive to criticism? I think it's a strong sense of social justice in the treatment of a human being."

"I would like to be remembered as an encourager," Schuller tells Megan Rosenfeld of the *Washington Post*. "I was asked to come to Flint, Michigan, a depressed city, and *I* was the man they could agree on," the minister relates to Trueheart. "The labor unions liked what I was espousing, the capital managers liked it, the blacks liked it, the Jews liked it, the Catholics liked it, the Protestants liked it. Gosh! I went back to my hotel room that night, and I said, 'You've answered my prayers, Lord. I am a repairer of bridges.'"

BIOGRAPHICAL/CRITICAL SOURCES: Saturday Review, February 3, 1979; *US,* February 6, 1979, September 1, 1981; *Time,* February 24, 1979; *People,* September 29, 1980; *Newsweek,* October 6, 1980; Michael and Donna Nason, *Robert Schuller: The Inside Story,* Word, 1983; Dennis Voskuil, *Mountains into Goldmines: Robert Schuller and the Gospel of Success,* Eerdmans, 1983; *Publishers Weekly,* March 4, 1983; *Washington Post,* August 17, 1983; *Christian Century,* November 23, 1983; *Humanist,* January/February, 1984.

—*Sketch by Susan Salter*

*   *   *

SCHULTZ, Harry D.

PERSONAL: Born September 11; son of Harry J. (owner of a drug store chain) and Theresa (Stachowiak) Schultz; married Gladys Irene Roosevelt, 1947 (divorced, 1952); married Dawn Courtman (an economist), August 24, 1963 (divorced, 1971). *Education:* Attended Los Angeles City College, 1941-43. *Politics:* Republican. *Religion:* Protestant. *Home address:* P.O. Box 5414, Amsterdam, Netherlands. *Office address:* P.O. Box 141, Clarens-Montreux, 1815, Switzerland.

CAREER: Owner and publisher, at various times, of thirteen newspapers in Palm Springs, North Hollywood, Lake Arrowhead, San Bernardino, and other California locations, 1946-57; stockbroker, 1959-60; stock market trader in Europe, 1960-64; publisher of monthly "International Harry Schultz Letter," 1964—, currently with offices in England, Canada, the Netherlands, Bermuda, and Switzerland. Financial adviser; organizer of international monetary seminars in New York and Los Angeles, 1967, London, 1968, Montreal, 1971, and Bermuda, 1973. Candidate for California State Assembly, 1948. *Military service:* U.S. Army Air Forces, 1943-46. *Member:* International Investment Letters Association (president, 1973—), National Press Club (Washington, D.C.), San Bernardino County Newspaper Publishers Association (president, 1956-57).

AWARDS, HONORS: Nominated for Pulitzer Prize in editorial writing, 1964, for editorial campaign conducted by *Palm Springs Limelight News;* Liberty Award, Congress of Freedom, 1969; named Knight of the Holy Cross, Rome, 1973; named Man of the Year by World Gold Association, 1980, and Benelux Libertarian Society, 1982; Freedom Fighter Extraordinaire award, Coalition for Peace through Security, 1982.

WRITINGS: Bear Markets—How to Survive and Make Money in Them, Prentice-Hall, 1964; (with Samson Coslow) *A Trea-*

sury of Wall Street Wisdom, Investors' Press, 1966; *Handbook for Understanding Swiss Banks,* Public Press, 1967; *The International Monetary Muddle,* La Jolla Rancho Press, 1969; (co-author) *The Dollar Devaluation: Mechanics and Timing,* Financial & Economic Research Corp., 1971; *What the Prudent Investor Should Know about Switzerland and Foreign Money Havens,* Arlington House, 1971; *Panics and Crashes: How You Can Make Money Out of Them,* Arlington House, 1972, revised edition, 1980; *You and Gold,* Financial & Economic Research Corp., 1973; *Inflation and Inflation Hedges,* Financial & Economic Research Corp., revised edition, 1974; *Financial Tactics and Terms for the Sophisticated International Investor,* Harper, 1974; (with James E. Sinclair) *How the Experts Buy and Sell Gold Bullion, Stocks and Coins,* Arlington House, 1975; *Schultz's Bear Market Strategy,* Dow Jones-Irwin, 1981. Also author of *How to Keep Your Money and Freedom.*

WORK IN PROGRESS: An autobiography; *Happiness Is a Warm HSL,* a collection of cartoons from "International Harry Schultz Letter."

SIDELIGHTS: Although based in Europe, Harry D. Schultz travels constantly, writing from every continent. He was listed in the *Guinness Book of World Records,* 1981, 1982, and 1983 editions, as the world's highest-paid investment consultant, at $2,000 per hour.

BIOGRAPHICAL/CRITICAL SOURCES: Barron's, October 23, 1967, November 27, 1967; *News of the World,* March 17, 1968.

*   *   *

SCHUMAN, Patricia Glass   1943-

PERSONAL: Born March, 15, 1943, in New York, N.Y.; daughter of Milton and Shirley (Goodman) Glass; married Alan B. Schuman, August 30, 1964 (divorced, 1973). *Education:* University of Cincinnati, A.B., 1963; Columbia University, M.L.S., 1966. *Religion:* Jewish. *Home:* 77 Fulton St., New York, N.Y. 10038.

CAREER: Brooklyn Public Library, Brooklyn, N.Y., librarian trainee, 1963-65; teacher of library in high school in New York City, 1966; New York City Community College of the City University of New York, New York City, assistant professor and acquisitions librarian, 1967-70; R. R. Bowker Co., New York City, associate editor of *School Library Journal,* 1970-73, senior acquisitions editor in book editorial department, 1973-76; Neal-Schuman Publishers, New York City, president, 1976—. Visiting lecturer, Columbia University, 1980—.

MEMBER: American Library Association (member of council, 1972-80), Special Libraries Association, Women's National Book Association, Social Responsibilities Round Table (co-ordinator, 1971), New York Library Association.

AWARDS, HONORS: Fannie Simon Award for a distinguished contribution to publishing and librarianship, Special Libraries Association, 1983.

WRITINGS: Materials for Occupational Education: An Annotated Source Guide, Bowker, 1971, 2nd edition, Neal-Schuman, 1983; *Social Responsibility and Libraries,* Bowker, 1976; *Library Users and Meeting Personal Needs: AWHCLIS Discussion Guide,* National Commission of Libraries and Information Service, 1979.

(Contributor) *What Else You Can Do with a Library Degree,* Neal-Schuman, 1980; (contributor) *New Options for Librarians: Finding a Job in a Related Field,* Neal-Schuman, 1984. Contributor to library journals.

*   *   *

SCHWAB, Peter   1940-

PERSONAL: Born November 15, 1940, in New York, N.Y.; son of Henry (a businessman) and Hilda (Hess) Schwab. *Education:* Fairleigh Dickinson University, B.A., 1962; New School for Social Research, M.A., 1966, Ph.D., 1969. *Residence:* New York, N.Y. *Office:* Department of Political Science, State University of New York, Purchase, N.Y. 10577.

CAREER: Adelphi University, Garden City, N.Y., instructor, 1966-69, assistant professor of political science, 1969-71; State University of New York College at Purchase, assistant professor, 1971-73, associate professor, 1973-80, professor of political science, 1980—, chair, division of social science, 1983—. Lecturer, American Museum of Natural History.

AWARDS, HONORS: Fulbright-Hays grant for research in Ethiopia, 1968; State University of New York research grant, 1972-73, 1974-75.

WRITINGS: (With George Frangos) *Greece under the Junta,* Facts on File, 1970; (editor) *Biafra,* Facts on File, 1971; (editor) *Ethiopia and Haile Selassie,* Facts on File, 1972; *Decision Making in Ethiopia,* Fairleigh Dickinson University Press, 1972; (with J. Lee Shneidman) *John F. Kennedy,* Twayne, 1973; *Is America Necessary?,* West Publishing, 1976; *Human Rights: Cultural and Ideological Perspectives,* Praeger, 1979; *Haile Selassie: Ethiopia's Lion of Judah,* Nelson-Hall, 1979; (contributor) *Marxist Governments—A World Survey,* Macmillan, 1979; *Toward a Human Rights Framework,* Praeger, 1981; *Marxist Regimes: Ethiopia,* Pinter, 1984.

Contributor to *Encyclopedia Americana, Yearbook on International Communism.* Contributor to *African Development, Journal Geneve Afrique, African Affairs, Plural Societies,* and *Journal of Modern African Studies.* Book review editor, *Transnational Perspectives.*

SIDELIGHTS: Peter Schwab has traveled in Asia, Europe, most of Africa, and the Carribean. He told *CA* that he "writes for the simple reason that it will aid society, and it will live beyond me."

*   *   *

SCOFIELD, Jonathan
See LEVINSON, Leonard

*   *   *

SCOTT, Johnie Harold   1946-

PERSONAL: Born May 8, 1946, in Cheyenne, Wyo.; son of Johnie Security (a laborer) and Mattie Lee (Livingston) Scott; married Joyce La Verne Hurdle (a music teacher), November 21, 1967; married Bessie Irene Mosley (a human services professional), June 14, 1975; children: Tadd Onomowale, Cicely Amber, Cheslea Jenine, Charmaine Imani. *Education:* Attended Harvard University, 1964-65, and East Los Angeles Junior College, 1965-66; Stanford University, B.A., 1970, M.A., 1972; Ph.D. candidate, University of Southern California, 1981—. *Politics:* Democrat. *Religion:* Baptist. *Resi-*

dence: Lake View Terrace, Calif. *Office:* Charles R. Drew Postgraduate Medical School, 1621 East 120th St., Los Angeles, Calif. 90059.

CAREER: Frederick Douglass House Foundation, Los Angeles, Calif., national coordinator of project development, 1966; Stanford University, Stanford, Calif., teacher in Cinema Arts Workshop, Department of Afro-American Studies, 1967-72, artistic director and producer, Black Theatre Productions, 1967-70; *Newsweek,* San Francisco, Calif., editorial intern, 1969-70; *Time,* San Francisco, correspondent, 1972-73; former director of affairs, Afro-West: Theatre of the Black Arts; Watts Health Foundation, Los Angeles, health information officer, 1972-78; Charles R. Drew Postgraduate Medical School, Los Angeles, public relations officer, 1978—.

Accredited Public Relations designation, Public Relations Society of America, 1980. Filmmaker for Midpeninsula Urban Coalition, Fair Housing Campaign, 1970-71; film director and member of board of directors, Human Pespectives, Inc., Woodside, Calif., 1971—. Program coordinator, Watts Writers Workshop Career Academy, Los Angeles, 1970—; member of board of directors, University of the Streets (educational program for residents of Lower East Side), New York, N.Y., 1971—. Member of arts committee, Urban Arts Foundation, Palo Alto, Calif., 1970—; special assistant, Watts Community Housing Corp.; administative assistant to Assemblyman Leon Ralph, California State Legislature. Consultant on minority group history, Opportunities Industrialization Center West, Menlo Park, Calif.

MEMBER: International Association of Business Communicators, Public Relations Society of America, American Medical Writers Association, American Film Institute (charter member), Greater Los Angeles Press Club, Alpha Phi Alpha.

AWARDS, HONORS: "Emmy" award nomination from Academy of Television Arts and Sciences, 1966, for "The Angry Voices of Watts"; scholarship to intern as director of film, "Across 110th Street," Academy of Motion Picture Arts and Sciences, 1971-72; Best Story Award, Greater Los Angeles Press Club, 1975, for "Best Story—Problems of Daily Living."

WRITINGS: "The Angry Voices of Watts" (television documentary), produced by National Broadcasting Company in 1966; "The New Voices of Watts" (television documentary), National Broadcasting Company, 1968; "David" (3-act play), commissioned by Los Angeles Festival of Performing Arts, 1969; "Brothers Where Are You?" (television documentary), Randall Youth Foundation, 1972; (editor) *Children of the Promised Land* (anthology), Bal News Service, 1981.

Contributor: Budd Schulberg, editor, *From the Ashes: Voices of Watts,* New American Library, 1966; J. Anthony Lukas, *Don't Shoot! We Are Your Children,* Random House, 1971.

Contributor of poetry to anthologies, including *The New Black Poetry,* edited by Clarence Major, International Publishers, 1967, *We Speak as Liberators: Young Black Poets,* edited by Orde Coombs, Dial, 1969, *Brilliant Corners,* edited by Bob O'Meally and Richard Grant, Stanford University Press, 1967-71, and *A Rock against the Wind,* edited by Lindsay Patterson, Dodd, 1973.

Contributor of poems to *Time, Los Angeles Magazine, Antioch Review, Black on Black* (Stanford University), and *Stanford Alumni Almanac;* contributor of essays to *Harper's, Pageant,*

Western Review (University of New Mexico), *New Lady,* and *Stanford Alumni Almanac.*

WORK IN PROGRESS: A novel, based upon experiences of a trauma center in the heart of a major urban ghetto.

SIDELIGHTS: Johnie Harold Scott told *CA:* "I don't think there's any question but that my being a Black American who was raised in one of the major Black urban communities—Watts—has served as the primary factor in my own career development. This dates back to senior high school for me where I was able, by virtue of a Hearst Newspaper Syndicate-sponsored program for aspiring journalists, to write a weekly sports column in the Los Angeles *Herald-Examiner.* Two years later, as a result of the Watts riots of 1965, I became one of the original founding members of the Watts Writers Workshop along with author-screenwriter Budd Schulberg, which opened many opportunities as a professional writer of the Black Experience in America. It was right after the Watts riots that I re-entered school, this time at Stanford University where I majored as an undergraduate in creative writing (Honors English) and later, in graduate school, in mass communications.

"I do not seek to limit myself to solely being a writer of books. My concern to reach the modern audience includes those who are not book-literate (i.e., the underserved and indigent) which accordingly means I have a real interest in theatre and electronic media (radio plays, television, film). I would hope that what I have to say will not only entertain, but that it will be informative and uplifting as well. The best way to describe my work habits when writing is that I become very immersed in the project and cull from newspapers, interviews, libraries, and the imagination those elements which will help tell the story or dramatize the point. In serving as the editor for *Children of the Promised Land*—an anthology of writing produced by recovering drug abusers in one of the largest drug rehabilitation programs in the inner city of Los Angeles—I conceptualized and led a twenty-week writers workshop which was aimed at helping these people learn how to express themselves through writing. The Modern Language Association has translated at least one of my articles into a foreign language. I [wrote], directed and produced a one-hour documentary on the problems facing urban streetgangs in Los Angeles entitled 'Brothers Where Are You?' in 1972, for the Randall Youth Foundation, through the United Way of America. The project I am currently working on—a broad scale look at how violence impacts on the lives of inner city dwellers with particular heroes, if you will, being the security force at a major acute care hospital (loosely modeled on the Martin Luther King, Jr./Charles R. Drew Medical Center here in south-central Los Angeles)—is being approached with definite intentions of a book as well as a feature film.

"The best advice I would give to aspiring writers is to read prolifically and widely, and to write as frequently as possible without 'falling in love' with what is written. Be open to being edited and, in fact, seek out a good editor. By the same token, I have been influenced by many other writers of whom only a few would include James Baldwin, Alice Walker, Ralph Ellison, Harold Cruse, Eugene O'Neill, Bertolt Brecht, Henrik Ibsen, Stephen King, Peter Straub, Budd Schulberg. The influences range from their commitment to intellectual honesty in writing to attention insofar as craftsmanship is concerned to a sincere desire to communicate a message to others.

"I'm excited at the contemporary scene, especially writers such as Alice Walker, Stephen King, Arthur Clarke—from which you might gather or infer that I like the creative approach to writing; I like people who employ their imagination but also do not mind doing research.''

BIOGRAPHICAL/CRITICAL SOURCES: New Yorker, August, 1966; *New York Times,* December 11, 1966, December 12, 1966; J. Anthony Lukas, *Don't Shoot! We Are Your Children,* Random House, 1971.

*   *   *

SCRIABINE, Helen (Gorstrine) 1906-

PERSONAL: Born February 13, 1906, in Dvinsk, Russia (now Soviet Union); came to the United States in 1950, naturalized in 1955; daughter of Aleksander and Nadeschda (Poznanskaya) Gorstkina; children: Alexander Scriabine. *Education:* Technirum, Russia, B.A., 1923; University of Leningrad, M.A. (with honors), 1941; Syracuse University, Ph.D., 1962. *Home:* 28 West Park Rd., Iowa City, Iowa 52240. *Office:* Department of Russian Language and Literature, University of Iowa, Iowa City, Iowa 52240.

CAREER: Teacher in Soviet Union before coming to the United States; Air Force Language School, Syracuse, N.Y., deputy chief instructor in Russian, 1950-53; University of Iowa, Iowa City, assistant professor, 1960-66, professor of Russian language and literature, 1966-74. Summer teacher at Columbia University, 1962, Middlebury College, 1964, and Institute of Soviet Study, Munich, Germany, 1966-71. *Member:* Modern Language Association of America.

WRITINGS: (With Oppenheimer) *Russian Grammar,* Lucas Brothers, 1962; *Les Faux Dieux: Essai sur l'humour, Michel Zostchenko et Marcel Ayme,* two volumes, Mercure de France, 1963; (with Koschenova) *History of Russian Literature,* Lucas Brothers, 1963; (editor) *Pushkin Stories, Lermontov Stories, Checkov Stories,* Lucas Brothers, 1964; *V Blokade,* Bashkiezev (Munich), 1964, translation by Norman Luxenburg published as *Siege and Survival: The Odyssey of a Leningrader,* Southern Illinois University Press, 1971; (editor) *Short Stories by Pushkin, Lermontov and Dostoevsky,* Harper, 1965.

Leningrader Tagebuch: Aufzeichnungen aus d. Kreigsjahren, 1941-1945, Biederstein-Verlag, 1972; (contributor) *Historical and Literary Perspectives: Essays and Studies in Honor of Albert Douglas Menot,* Coronado Press, 1973; *Godyi Skitanii,* Les Cinq Continents (Paris), 1975; *Piat Vstrech,* Logos (Munich), 1975; *After Leningrad,* Southern Illinois University Press, 1978; *The Allies on the Rhine,* Southern Illinois University Press, 1980; *Detstvo: Iunost'v Tsarskoi Russii i v Sovietskom Soiuze,* Almanach (Los Angeles), 1980. Contributor to Russian journals and to *Books Abroad.*

WORK IN PROGRESS: A book on living in the United States.

AVOCATIONAL INTERESTS: Travel.

*   *   *

SCRIVEN, Michael (John) 1928-

PERSONAL: Born March 28, 1928, in Beaulieu, Hampshire, England; son of Victor Reginald and Hilda (Grice) Scriven; married Mary Anne Warren, 1970. *Education:* University of Melbourne, B.A., 1948, M.A., 1950; Oxford University, D.Phil., 1956. *Politics:* Independent. *Religion:* Atheist. *Home:* 415 Drakes View Dr., Inverness, Calif. 94956. *Office:* University of San Francisco, 2130 Fulton St., San Francisco, Calif. 94117.

CAREER: University of Minnesota, Minneapolis, instructor in philosophy, 1952-55, research associate in philosophy of science, 1955-56; Swarthmore College, Swarthmore, Pa., assistant professor of philosophy, 1956-60; Indiana University at Bloomington, professor of the history and philosophy of science, 1960-66; University of California, Berkeley, professor of philosophy, 1966-78; University of San Francisco, San Francisco, Calif., professor of philosophy, 1978—. Fellow, Center for Advanced Study in the Behavioral Sciences, 1962-63; Alfred North Whitehead Fellow, Harvard University, 1970-71. Summer teaching at New School for Social Research, 1959, and Wesleyan University, 1961, 1962; visiting affiliate of Department of Education, University of Western Australia. *Member:* American Philosophical Association, Mind Association, Parapsychological Association.

WRITINGS: (Editor with Herbert Feigl) *Foundations of Science and the Concepts of Psychology and Psychoanalysis,* University of Minnesota Press, 1956; *Applied Logic,* Behavioral Research Laboratories, 1964; *Primary Philosophy,* McGraw, 1966; (editor with W. J. Moore and Eugene P. Wigner) *Symmetries and Reflections,* Indiana University Press, 1967; *Evaluating Higher Education in California,* California Legislature, 1973; *Evaluation: A Study Guide for Educational Administrators,* National Ed.D. Program for Educational Leaders, 1974; *Reasoning,* McGraw, 1976; *Evaluation Thesaurus,* 2nd edition, Edgepress, 1980, 3rd edition, 1981; *The Logic of Evaluation,* 2nd edition, Edgepress, 1980; (with Barbara G. Davis and Susan Thomas) *The Evaluation of Composition Instruction,* Edgepress, 1981; *Evaluating Word Processing,* Edgepress, 1983; *Word Magic: Evaluating and Selecting Word Processing,* 1983; (with Steven Manus) *How to Buy a Word Processor,* Alfred Publishing, 1983. Author of cassettes, ''Evaluation Skills,'' American Research Association, c. 1974, and ''Speaking of Educational Evaluation: Trends in Education,'' McGraw, 1974. Contributor of more than 200 articles and reviews to journals.

WORK IN PROGRESS: Ed Tech, for Edgepress.

AVOCATIONAL INTERESTS: Parapsychology, sports cars, social reform.

*   *   *

SEARA VAZQUEZ, M(odesto) 1931-

PERSONAL: Born September 11, 1931, in Allariz, Spain; son of Aser (an industrialist) and Herculina (Vazquez Calvino) Seara Pavon; married Rita Bertha Helene Michelmann de Seara, November 29, 1960. *Education:* Consejo Superior de Investigaciones Cientificas (Instituto Jaime Balmes), diploma in sociology, 1954; Sociedad Espanola de Estudios Internacionales y Coloniales, diploma in international politics, 1955; Universidad de Madrid, Bach. of Laws, 1955; University of Paris, Doctor of International Law, 1959. *Home:* Cerro dos Conejos 26, Mexico City, 21, Mexico. *Office:* Institute of Comparative Law, Universidad Nacional Autonoma de Mexico, Mexico City, 20, Mexico.

CAREER: Universidad Nacional Autonoma de Mexico, Mexico City, professor of international law in the National School of Political Sciences and the School of Laws, beginning 1961, research fellow in the Institute of Comparative Law, beginning 1961, professor of international organization in the National School of Political Sciences, beginning 1962, professor of international politics, beginning 1963, coordinator of Seminar on International Trade, 1964. Participated in Space Law Colloquium (London, 1959, Washington, 1961), International

Congress on Comparative Law (Hamburg, 1962), and many other congresses on international law. Visiting professor at University of Utah, 1965-66, and University of Caracas, 1966; director of Seminar on World Order, University of Bogota, 1966.

MEMBER: Sociedad Espanola de Estudios Internacionales y Coloniales, Sociedad Astronomica de Espana y America, London Institute of World Affairs.

WRITINGS: The Functional Regulation of Extra-Atmospheric Space (English language), Springer Verlag, 1960; *Introduction al derecho internacional cosmico,* Universidad Nacional Autonoma de Mexico, 1961, published as *Cosmic International Law,* Wayne State University Press, 1965; *Manual de derecho internacional publico,* Pormaca, 1964, 5th edition published as *Derecho internacional publico,* Editorial Porrua, 1976; *Sintesis del derecho internacional publico,* Universidad Nacional Autonoma de Mexico, 1965; *Del Congreso de Viena a la paz de Versalles,* Universidad Nacional Autonoma de Mexico, 1969; *Paz y conflicto en la sociedad internacional: Articulos,* Universidad Nacional Autonoma de Mexico, 1969; *La politica exterior de Mexico: la practica de Mexico en la derecho internacional,* Editorial Esfinge, 1969.

La paz precaria: de Versalles a Danzig, Universidad Nacional Autonoma de Mexico, 1970; *Tratado general de la organizacion international,* Fondo de Cultura Economica, 1974; *La Sociedad democratica,* Universidad Nacional Autonoma de Mexico, 1976. Contributor of articles to *Revista de Ciencias Politicas y Sociales* (Mexico), *Il Diritto Aereo* (Italy), *Annuaire Francais de Droit International* (France), and other professional journals.

WORK IN PROGRESS: El derecho internacional publico segun la jursprudencia de la corte internacional de justicia.

SIDELIGHTS: M. Seara Vazquez speaks English, French, Portuguese, German, and Russian.

BIOGRAPHICAL/CRITICAL SOURCES: El Alcazar (Madrid), May 8, 1959, June 6, 1959; *Le Figaro Litteraire,* May 9, 1959; *El Noticiero Universal* (Barcelona), June 14, 1959; *A B C* (Madrid), June 25, 1959.†

*   *   *

SEGAL, Ronald (Michael) 1932-

PERSONAL: Born July 14, 1932, in Cape Town, South Africa; son of Leon (a managing director) and Mary (Charney) Segal; married Susan Wolff, July 17, 1962; children: Oliver, Miriam, Emily. *Education:* University of Cape Town, B.A., 1951; Trinity College, Cambridge, B.A. (with honors), 1954; University of Virginia, graduate study, 1955-56. *Home:* The Old Manor House, Manor Rd., Walton-on-Thames, Surrey, England.

CAREER: National Union of South African Students, director of faculty and cultural studies, 1951-52; *Africa South: An International Journal* (quarterly), Cape Town, South Africa, founder, 1956, publisher and editor, 1956-60; went into exile in England where he published and edited *Africa South in Exile,* 1960-61; Penguin Books Ltd., London, England, general editor of "Penguin African Library," 1961—. Convenor at International Conference on Economic Sanctions against South Africa, London, 1964, and International Conference on South West Africa, Oxford, England, 1966.

WRITINGS: The Tokolosh (novel), Sheed, 1960; *Political Africa: A Who's Who of Personalities and Parties,* George Ste-

vens, 1961; *African Profiles,* Penguin, 1962; *Into Exile,* McGraw, 1963; *The Anguish of India,* Stein & Day, 1965 (published in England as *The Crisis of India,* J. Cape, 1965); *The Race War: The World-Wide Clash of White and Non-White,* J. Cape, 1966, Viking, 1967; (editor with Ruth First) *South-West Africa: Travesty of Trust,* Deutsch, 1967; *America's Receding Future,* Weidenfeld & Nicolson, 1968, published as *Americans: A Conflict of Creed and Reality,* Viking, 1969; *The Struggle against History,* Weidenfeld & Nicolson, 1971, Bantam, 1973; *Whose Jerusalem?: The Conflicts of Israel,* Bantam, 1973; *The Decline and Fall of the American Dollar,* Bantam, 1974; *Leon Trotsky: A Biography,* Pantheon, 1979 (published in England as *The Tragedy of Leon Trotsky,* Hutchinson, 1979); (with Michael Kidron) *The State of the World Atlas,* Simon & Shuster, 1981.

SIDELIGHTS: In 1959, because of anti-government politics, Ronald Segal was banned from all gatherings in South Africa. He has been in exile in England since that time.

Segal's "*The State of the World Atlas* is . . . an occasion of wit and an act of subversion," writes John Leonard of the *New York Times.* Using charts and maps, this book illustrates "the bad dreams of the modern world, [which are] given color and shape and submitted to a grid that can be grasped instantaneously. This ingenious atlas belongs, if not in every home, then certainly in every school and oval office," concludes Leonard.

Although Richard Pipes of the *New York Times Book Review* and Alec Nove of *Times Literary Supplement* criticize Segal for using inadequate background for *Leon Trotsky: A Biography,* Nove calls the book "a competent and readable survey of Trotsky's life," and Pipes emphasizes that the book is "well written." Robert Kirsch writes in the *Los Angeles Times Book Review* that *Leon Trotsky: A Biography* is an "impressive biography and assessment" of the Russian revolutionary.

BIOGRAPHICAL/CRITICAL SOURCES: Times Literary Supplement, September 24, 1971, December 7, 1979; *New York Times Book Review,* December 29, 1979; *Los Angeles Times Book Review,* April 6, 1980; *New York Times,* February 24, 1981.

*   *   *

SEIDE, Diane 1930-
(Diane Seidner)

PERSONAL: Born June 15, 1930, in New York, N.Y.; daughter of Alvin (a salesman) and Sylvia (an artist; maiden name, Kessler) Seide; married Joseph Seidner, May 28, 1960 (divorced January, 1971); children: Michael David, Sabrina Jennifer. *Education:* Attended Ithaca College, 1948-50; Adelphi University, B.S., 1953; also attended New School for Social Research. *Home:* 11 Waverly Place, New York, N.Y. 10003.

CAREER: Registered nurse; St. Vincent's Hospital, New York City, head nurse of psychiatry, 1957-58; Mount Sinai Hospital, New York City, instructor in nursing and delivery room head nurse, 1958-59; worked as free-lance writer and editor, 1959-71; St. Luke's Hospital, New York City, head nurse, 1971-72; *Parents' Magazine,* New York City, associate editor, 1973; writer, 1973—; currently psychiatric nursing coordinator, St. Claren's Hospital, New York City.

WRITINGS: (Under name Diane Seidner) *Young Nurse in New York* (young adult), Dial, 1967; *Careers in Medical Science,* Thomas Nelson, 1972, revised edition published as *Careers in*

Health Services, Lodestar Books, 1982; *Looking Good: Your Everything Guide to Beauty, Health, and Modeling* (young adult), Thomas Nelson, 1977; (with Mark Traynor) *Mark Traynor's Beauty Book,* illustrations by Charles Bisaquino, Doubleday, 1980. Author, with Minna Kubie, of *Organic Beverages,* Bantam; also author of novels under pseudonyms. Contributor of articles to *Parents' Magazine* and other periodicals. Associate editor, *R.N.,* 1960.

WORK IN PROGRESS: Careers in Nursing, for Lodestar; a novel about the mental health care system.

*   *   *

SEIDNER, Diane
   See SEIDE, Diane

*   *   *

SELZER, Richard   1928-

PERSONAL: Born June 24, 1928, in Troy, N.Y.; son of Julius Louis (a family doctor) and Gertrude (Schneider) Selzer; married Janet White, February, 1955; children: Jonathan, Lawrence, Gretchen. *Education:* Union College, Schenectady, N.Y., B.S., 1948; Albany Medical College, M.D., 1953; postdoctoral study, Yale University, 1957-60. *Home:* 6 Saint Ronan Ter., New Haven, Conn. 06511. *Agent:* Georges Borchardt Inc., 136 East 57th St., New York, N.Y. 10022.

CAREER: Private practice in general surgery, 1960—. Yale University, associate professor of surgery in Medical School, fellow of Ezra Stiles College. *Military service:* U.S. Army, 1955-57.

AWARDS, HONORS: National Magazine Award from Columbia University School of Journalism, 1975, for essays published in *Esquire;* honorary degrees from Union College, Georgetown University, Albany Medical College, and Medical College of Pennsylvania.

WRITINGS: Rituals of Surgery (short stories), Harper's Magazine Press, 1974; *Mortal Lessons* (essays), Simon & Schuster, 1977; *Confessions of a Knife* (essays), Simon & Schuster, 1979; *Letters to a Young Doctor* (essays and fiction), Simon & Schuster, 1982. Contributor to popular magazines, including *Harper's, Esquire, Redbook, Mademoiselle, American Review,* and *Antaeus.*

WORK IN PROGRESS: Essays, memoirs, and short stories.

SIDELIGHTS: Richard Selzer draws upon his experience as a surgeon in his writing, both for the discipline it requires and for material. His stories and essays lead the reader through hospital wards, illuminating the world of medicine and surgery. Selzer's writing ranges from detailed descriptions of the human anatomy and operating techniques to discussions of patients' reactions to sickness and impending death. In the *New York Times Book Review,* Fitzhugh Mullan writes of Selzer's work, "His marvelous insight and potent imagery make his tales of surgery and medicine both works of art and splendid tools of instruction."

Selzer first attracted serious literary attention with his second book *Mortal Lessons.* These essays, which J. F. Watkins in the *Times Literary Supplement* calls "prose poems," open the human body to view. Examining the hair, skin, bones, liver, stomach, kidneys, and bladder, Selzer maintains that this visceral side of medicine has its own unique beauty. *Newsweek's*

Peter S. Prescott, however, finds the essays "grisly anecdotes" and contends that Selzer "aims to shock." On the other hand, *Time's* Peter Stoler writes that Selzer's portrayal of the dark side of medicine "forces physicians to think abut the morality of medicine." He adds, "*Mortal Lessons* will not make any surgeon a better technician; but it just might make him a healer."

Selzer's *Confessions of a Knife,* another collection of essays, presents striking examples of what the surgeon encounters in his work. In "Racoon," a woman suffering pain after an operation on her abdomen seeks relief by tearing open her stitches and reaching into her gut. In "Sarcophagus," a tumor weakened aorta crumbles as Selzer works unsuccessfully to stop the rush of blood; the surgeon shares his failure with the reader. *New York Times* critic Christopher Lehmann-Haupt writes of *Confessions:* "There may be some beauty in the way Dr. Selzer writes about these encounters with sickness and death, but to me the art of them seems gratuitous. It is quite enough that such things simply happen." Yet other reviewers commend Selzer for refusing to touch up the unpleasantries of his profession. As Henry McDonald writes in the *Washington Post Book World,* Selzer reveals the dexterity of a surgeon when handling the complicated dichotomies he encounters: the physical and the mental, joy and pain, life and death. McDonald points out, "In all such pairs of opposites, Selzer refuses to settle for abstractions but probes deep within their single, sensuous source." In a *New York Times Book Review* article, Lawrence Shainberg finds that Selzer's representation of pain, failure, and death "forces the reader to confront and endure his terror, and acknowledge his own vulnerability." As Elizabeth Peer states in *Newsweek,* "By dwelling on the mechanics of death, [Selzer] celebrates life."

Letters to a Young Doctor, the fourth of Selzer's books, contains both essays and short fiction. Based on his own early experience in medicine, the book is written as a series of letters of advice to a young surgeon. In one piece, "Imelda," Selzer relates the story of a medical tour through Central America on which he accompanied a plastic surgeon. An attempt to correct the cleft lip of a beautiful young girl ends tragically when she dies under anesthesia. Selzer awakens the next day to find that during the night the surgeon had returned to the corpse and corrected the deformity. Anna Fels sees in *Letters to a Young Doctor* the author's "need to grapple physically with the grotesque." In a *Nation* article, Fels states, "Selzer is one of the few medical writers who take a hard look at the actual subjects of medicine: disease, deformity and the human body in all its frailties."

Although a number of reviewers criticize Selzer's overly embellished prose style, David Black in the *Washington Post* points out: "When he forgets to be fancy, Selzer becomes a writer of great force. When he is colloquial, his prose is superior. And his anecdotes tend to be . . . dramatic." Concludes *Los Angeles Times* critic Elaine Kendall, "No one writes about the practice of medicine with Selzer's unique combination of mystery and wonder."

BIOGRAPHICAL/CRITICAL SOURCES: New York Times Book Review, January 9, 1977, September 2, 1979, August 29, 1982; *Time,* January 24, 1977; *Newsweek,* January 24, 1977, September 3, 1979; *Saturday Review,* August 4, 1979; *Washington Post Book World,* August 5, 1979; *Chicago Tribune Book World,* August 26, 1979; *New York Times,* August 27, 1979, September 28, 1979; *Times Literary Supplement,* May 29, 1981; *Washington Post,* August 14, 1982; *Los Angeles Times,* August

27, 1982; *Nation,* October 9, 1982; *Detroit News,* January 9, 1983.

* * *

SEMMLER, Clement (William) 1914-

PERSONAL: Born December 23, 1914, in Mercunda, South Australia, Australia; son of John Frederick and Marie (Kleinig) Semmler; married Catherine Wilson, December 20, 1974; children: (former marriage) Jacqueline, Peter, (current marriage) Imogen. *Education:* University of Adelaide, B.A., 1936, M.A., 1938. *Address:* The Croft, St. Clair St., Bowral, New South Wales 2576, Australia.

CAREER: Australian Broadcasting Commission, Sydney, New South Wales, supervisor of youth education for South Australia, 1942-46, assistant director of variety, 1947-48, assistant controller of programs, 1948-60, assistant general manager for programs, 1960-64, deputy general manager, 1965-77. Member of Advisory Committee on the Humanities, National Library of Australia Council; deputy president of Library Council of New South Wales; member of advisory committee, Flinders University of South Australia Drama Centre and New South Wales Arts; member of Canberra Theatre Trust; member of Council of Sydney College of Advanced Education; chairman of Council of Alexander Mackie College of Advanced Education; chairman of board of City Art Institute of New South Wales. *Member:* University Club (Sydney). *Awards, honors:* D.Litt., University of New England (Australia), 1968; Officer, Order of the British Empire, 1970, for services to Australian literature.

WRITINGS: For the Uncanny Man: Essays on James Joyce and Others, F. W. Cheshire, 1963; (editor with Derek Whitelock) *Literary Australia,* F. W. Cheshire, 1965; *Barcroft Boake—Poet of the Stockwhip,* Oxford University Press, 1965; *A. B. "Banjo" Paterson,* Oxford University Press, 1965, 2nd edition, 1972; (editor and author of introduction) *Stories of the Riverina,* Angus & Robertson, 1965; *Kenneth Slessor,* Longmans, Green and British Council, 1966, 2nd edition, 1969; (editor) *Coast to Coast, 1965-1966* (Australian short stories), Angus & Robertson, 1966; *The Banjo of the Bush: The Life and Times of A. B. Paterson,* Landsdowne Press, 1966, 4th edition, University of Queensland Press, 1984; (editor and author of introduction) *Twentieth Century Australian Literary Criticism,* Oxford University Press, 1967; *A. B. Paterson—Great Australian,* Oxford University Press, 1967; (editor and author of introduction) *The World of Banjo Paterson,* Angus & Robertson, 1967.

The Art of Brian James and Other Essays on Australian Literature, University of Queensland Press, 1972; *Douglas Stewart,* Twayne, 1974, 2nd edition, Angus & Robertson, 1977; (contributor) G. Dutton, editor, *Australian Literature,* Penguin, 1976; *The Australian Broadcasting Commission: Aunt Sally and Sacred Cow,* Melbourne University Press, 1981; (editor and author of introduction) *A Frank Hardy Swag,* Harper, 1982. Contributor to literary journals. Literary reviewer, *Sydney Morning Herald, Brisbane Courier Mail, Australian Book Review,* and *Quadrant;* media critic, *Sydney Morning Herald* and *The Bulletin;* editorial consultant, *Poetry Australia.*

WORK IN PROGRESS: Editing *The War Diaries of Kenneth Slessor.*

AVOCATIONAL INTERESTS: Jazz music (regarded as Australian authority on jazz), golf, gardening.

SETHI, Narendra Kumar 1935-

PERSONAL: Born July 12, 1935, in India; son of Seth Nemichandji (a businessman) and Laxmi Devi (Luhadiya) Sethi; married Kiran Jain (an executive), April 24, 1956; children: Madhu Milind, Manoj Milind, Michelle. *Education:* Agra University, B.A., 1953, M.A., 1955; Calcutta University, M.A., 1956; New York University, M.B.A., 1961, Ph.D., 1962. *Politics:* None. *Religion:* Jain. *Home:* 194 Greenham S., Forest Hills, N.Y. 11375. *Office:* Department of Management, St. John's University, Jamaica, N.Y. 11439.

CAREER: St. John's University, Jamaica, N.Y., associate professor, 1966-69, professor of management, 1969—, chairman of department, 1969-72. Partner, Binodiram Balchand & Co.

MEMBER: Indian Forum for the Professions (president), Academy of Management, Institute for Decision Sciences, Association for International Business Education, Indore Management Association, Malwa Chamber of Commerce.

AWARDS, HONORS: Shell Company assistance grant, 1969-70; Shiram award, 1974; BAZME-ADAB awards, 1982, 1983; New York Asian-American Lions Club award, 1984.

WRITINGS: The Word Is Split, Writers' Workshop (Calcutta), 1961; *Shabda Ki Chalna,* Malvika Prakashan, 1961; *Hindu Proverbs,* Peter Pauper, 1962; *Song Lines of a Day,* Writers' Workshop (Calcutta), 1965; *A Bibliography of Indian Management,* Popular Prakashan, 1966; (contributor) S. B. Prasad, editor, *Management in International Perspective,* Appleton, 1966; *The Setting of Administrative Management in India,* St. John's University Press, 1969.

Management Perspectives, [Bombay], 1973; *Environmental Management,* [The Hague], 1973; *Managerial Dynamics,* [New Delhi], 1979; *Managerial Mirage,* [New Delhi], 1982; *Operations Management,* [New Delhi], 1984. Contributor of about one hundred and fifty articles to management and economic journals in the United States and India.

WORK IN PROGRESS: Three books, *A Managerial Critique of Public Relations, Mary Parker Follett: A Historical and Comparative Study of Her Contribution to Management, A Bibliography of Public Relations in Management.*

* * *

SEYMOUR, Whitney North, Jr. 1923-

PERSONAL: Born July 7, 1923, in Huntington, W.Va.; son of Whitney North (a lawyer) and Lola (Vickers) Seymour; married Catryna Ten Eyck (a writer and artist), November 16, 1951; children: Tryntje (daughter), Gabriel (daughter). *Education:* Princeton University, B.A. (magna cum laude), 1947; Yale University, LL.B., 1950. *Politics:* Republican. *Religion:* Episcopalian. *Home:* 290 West 4th St., New York, N.Y. 10014. *Office:* 100 Park Ave., New York, N.Y. 10017.

CAREER: Admitted to the Bar of New York State, 1950; Simpson, Thacher & Bartlett (law firm), New York City, associate, 1950-53; assistant U.S. attorney for southern district of New York, 1953-56; Simpson, Thacher & Bartlett, associate, 1956-59; New York State Commission of Governmental Operations, New York City, chief counsel, 1959-60; chief counsel for Special Unit of New York State Commission of Investigation, 1960-61; Simpson, Thacher & Bartlett, partner, 1961-70; New York state senator in Albany, 1966-68; U.S. attorney for southern district of New York, 1970-73; Simpson, Thacher & Bartlett, partner, 1973-83; Brown & Seymour (law firm), New York City, partner, 1983—. Co-founder of Natural Resources Defense Council, South Street Seaport Museum, National Citizens for Public Libraries, and Public Libraries Research and Education Fund. Co-chairman, Citizens against PACs; member of boards of civic groups, including Literacy Volunteers of New York. *Military service:* U.S. Army, Artillery; served in Pacific theater; became captain.

MEMBER: Phi Beta Kappa, Phi Delta Phi, "various bar associations."

AWARDS, HONORS: LL.D. from New York Law School, 1972.

WRITINGS: (Editor) *Small Urban Spaces: The Philosophy, Design, Sociology, and Politics of Vest-Pocket Parks and Other Small Urban Open Spaces,* New York University Press, 1969; *The Young Die Quietly: The Narcotics Problem in America,* Morrow, 1972; *Why Justice Fails,* Morrow, 1973; *United States Attorney,* Morrow, 1975; *Fighting for Public Libraries,* Doubleday, 1979; *Making a Difference,* Morrow, 1984. Contributor to magazines.

SIDELIGHTS: When Whitney North Seymour, Jr., was assistant U.S. attorney for the southern district of New York, he participated as chief appellate attorney in the prosecution of Frank Costello. Later, as a state senator, he became involved in legislation on housing, then returned to investigating and prosecuting federal crimes in the areas of narcotics, white-collar crime, and official corruption, and also became interested in civil enforcement actions in the fields of the environment, civil rights, and consumer fraud.

He writes: "I view writing for publication as an opportunity to achieve public awareness of contemporary problems and needs I have seen as a lawyer, public official, and concerned citizen. I hope my books have helped produce some constructive change, and have provided encouragement to younger people to get out and *do* something about things they believe are wrong."

* * *

SHARMA, Partap 1939-

PERSONAL: Born December 12, 1939, in Lahore, India (now Pakistan); son of Baij Nath (a civil engineer and farmer) and Dayawati (Pandit) Sharma; married Susan Amanda Pick, October 21, 1971; children: Kiran Namrita, Tara Natasha. *Education:* St. Xavier's College, Bombay, India, B.A. (with honors), 1959. *Politics:* "Democratic, anti-censorship, but no political party." *Religion:* Hindu. *Home:* 1 Goolestan, 34 Bhulabhai Desai Rd., Bombay 400 026, India. *Office:* Flat 5B, Block 6, Shyam Nivas, Bhulabhai Desai Rd., Bombay 400 026, India. *Agent:* Olivar Swan, Collier Associates, 875 Avenue of the Americas, Suite 1003, New York, N.Y. 10001.

CAREER: Actor, director, and writer. Indian National Theatre, Bombay, playwright and director of English drama, 1961—. Chief free-lance commentator for newsreels and documentaries produced by Films Division (Bombay), 1960—, also producer-director; host of "What's the Good Word?," a program for Television Centre (Bombay), 1975-76; actor in Hindi feature films.

MEMBER: Cine Artistes Association, Radio Advertisers and Producers Association of India, Commentators Guild, National

Centre for the Performing Arts, Films Division Film Study Group, Club Mahabaleshwar, Amateur Riders Club, Academy of Martial Arts.

AWARDS, HONORS: Silver Gazelle from the President of India, 1971, for lead role in feature film "Phir Bhi" (title means "Even Then"); national award for best Hindi film of the year for "Phir Bhi"; first prize from RAPA, 1976, for best voice in radio-spots; All-India Excellence Award, 1982, for directing audio-visual on karate entitled "The Empty Hand."

WRITINGS: The Surangini Tales (juvenile), Harcourt, 1973; *Dog Detective Ranjha* (juvenile), Macmillan, 1977; *The Little Master of the Elephant* (juvenile), Macmillan, 1984; *Top Dog* (juvenile), Andre Deutsch, 1985.

Plays: "Bars Invisible" (three-act), first produced in Bombay at Indian National Theatre, June 10, 1961; "The Word" (three-act), first produced in Bombay at Bombay Arts Festival, March 26, 1966; *A Touch of Brightness* (three-act; first produced on the West End at Royal Court Theatre, March 5, 1967), Grove, 1967; "The Professor Has a Warcry" (five-act), first produced in Bombay at Impermanent Theatre, January 15, 1970.

Documentary films; all self-directed: "The Framework of Famine," 1967; "The Flickering Flame," 1974; "Kamli," 1976.

Work represented in anthologies, including *Twenty-Five Years of Indian Independence,* edited by Jag Mohan, Vikas, 1973; *Young Winter's Tales 5,* edited by M. R. Hodgkin, Macmillan (London), 1974; *Aspects of Indian Literature,* edited by Suresh Kohli, Vikas, 1975; *Young Winter's Tales 8,* edited by Hodgkin, Macmillan, 1978. Contributor of stories and articles to magazines.

WORK IN PROGRESS: Days of the Turban and two other novels, a trilogy touching on contemporary events in India.

SIDELIGHTS: Partap Sharma comments: "Stories are perhaps a way of making more coherent and comprehensible the bewildering complexity of the world. I learn and discover as I write and I try to share what I have understood. This began with me when I was a child, before I could read, and when I needed to deduce a story to explain the pictures in a book. But that is just the technique; the aim is to uncover an aspect of the truth. The truth isn't always palatable. Two of my documentaries and a play have been banned. The High Court reversed the ban on the play; it is now a text in three Indian universities."

* * *

SHAW, Charles R(aymond) 1921-

PERSONAL: Born February 28, 1921, in Indianapolis, Ind.; son of Thomas O. (a merchant) and Hilda (Rodenbeck) Shaw; married Margery Schlamp, May 31, 1942 (divorced); children: Barbara Rae. *Education:* Attended Hanover College, 1938-41; New York University, M.D., 1946. *Office:* Department of Biology, M.D. Anderson Hospital and Tumor Institute, University of Texas Health Science Center at Houston, Houston, Tex. 77025.

CAREER: Certified psychiatrist. Cornell University, Ithaca, N.Y., resident in internal medicine at infirmary, 1947-49, assistant professor of medical nutrition, 1949-51; University of Michigan, Neuropsychiatric Institute, Ann Arbor, resident psychiatrist, 1953-56; Hawthorn Center, Northville, Mich., child psychiatrist, 1956-67; University of Texas Health Science Center at Houston, M. D. Anderson Hospital and Tumor Institute, professor of biology and chief of medical genetics section, 1967—, associate pediatrician, associate professor of pediatrics, and clinical associate professor of psychiatry, 1975—. *Military service:* U.S. Army, 1943-45. U.S. Air Force, 1951-53; became captain.

MEMBER: American Psychiatric Association, Genetics Society of America, American Society of Human Genetics, American Association for Cancer Research.

WRITINGS: The Psychiatric Disorders of Childhood, Appleton-Century-Crofts, 1966, 2nd edition, 1971; *When Your Child Needs Help,* Morrow, 1972; *When You Need Help with Cancer,* Morrow, 1973; (editor with A. Clark Griffin) *Carcinogens: Identification and Mechanisms of Action,* Raven Press, 1979; (editor) *Prevention of Occupational Cancer,* CRC Press, 1981. Former editor of *Biochemical Genetics.*

WORK IN PROGRESS: An autobiographical novel, *Cancer Breakthrough.*

SIDELIGHTS: Charles R. Shaw once told *CA:* "Writing is strictly a sideline as I'm busy and active in cancer research. [I] moved into this field about 1962, a defector from psychiatry. My novel [in progress] is a personal account of a successful effort in cancer research, with emphasis on personalities and the effects of success and failure in research."

AVOCATIONAL INTERESTS: Flying airplanes.†

*   *   *

SHELBOURNE, Cecily
   See GOODWIN, Suzanne

*   *   *

SHELDON, Scott
   See WALLMANN, Jeffrey M(iner)

*   *   *

SHERMAN, Arnold   1932-

PERSONAL: Born May 27, 1932, in New York, N.Y.; son of Joseph (a button salesman) and Gladys Sherman; married Mary Lucille Harris, 1952; children: Michele, Jonathan, Laura. *Education:* Attended Brooklyn College (now Brooklyn College of the City University of New York). *Religion:* Jewish. *Home:* Moshav Michmoret, Israel. *Office:* Technion—Israel Institute of Technology, Haifa, Israel.

CAREER: Aviation Week, New York, N.Y., news editor, 1957-63; Israel Aircraft Industries, Lod, Israel, public relations director, 1963-65; El Al-Israel Airlines, Lod, vice-president of public relations, 1965-82; Technion—Israel Institute of Technology, Haifa, Israel, executive vice-president, 1983—. *Military service:* U.S. Army, 1951-52. Israeli Army, 1967—.

WRITINGS: Impaled on a Cactus Bush: An American Family in Israel, Sabra Books, 1970; *In the Bunkers of Sinai,* Sabra Books, 1971; *El Al: The Story of an Airline,* Vallentine, Mitchell, 1973; *Lightning in the Skies,* Bitan, 1973; *When God Judged and Men Died,* Bantam, 1973; *The Druse,* Bazak, 1974; *The Pomeranz Connection,* Stone, 1976; *Israel on Ten to Fifteen Dollars a Day,* Frommer, 1976; *Blue Sky, Red Sea,* Edanim, 1977; *Dream of Rohamim,* Bitan, 1977; *The Ship,* Semana, 1978; *Wings of Icarus,* Bitan, 1979; *Splintered Cedar,* Bitan, 1980; *Israel High Technology,* Semana, 1984; *Going My Way,*

Semana, 1984. Also author of *Impaled on a Rhino's Horn,* Bitan. Contributor to American and Israeli periodicals.

WORK IN PROGRESS: A book on the formation of the Israel Air Force.

SIDELIGHTS: Arnold Sherman lived in Paris for one year and in Mallorca for a year. In 1971 he went on safari in East Africa.

*   *   *

SHIRAKAWA, Yoshikazu   1935-

PERSONAL: Born January 28, 1935, in Kawanoe City, Japan; son of Shigeru (a company executive) and Shina (Ishamura) Shirakawa; married Kazuko Miyamoto (a president of a Japanese dancing school); children: Eri. *Education:* Nihon University, B.A., 1957. *Home:* 2-12-15, Takanawa, Minato-ku, Tokyo 108, Japan. *Agent:* Image Bank, 633 Third Ave., New York, N.Y. 10017.

CAREER: Nippon Broadcasting System, Literature and Art Division, Tokyo, Japan, producer, 1957-58; Fuji Telecasting Company, Tokyo, chief cameraman, 1958-60; free-lance photographer, 1960—. Special lecturer, Japan Photographic Academy, 1967—; chief instructor and chairman of the board of directors, Kanto Photo Technique Academy, 1974—. Work has been exhibited at fourteen one-man shows, including Konishiroku Gallery, Tokyo, 1957, Nikon Salon, Tokyo, 1970, "The Seat of the Gods" exhibition in ten major Japanese cities, 1971-73, and "Eternal America" exhibition in thirteen Japanese cities, 1975-77.

MEMBER: Japan Professional Photographers' Society (director, 1967—), Japanese Alpine Club, Nikakai Association of Artists.

AWARDS, HONORS: Annual Minister of Health and Welfare awards, 1956-61; Special Prize at National Park Photo Contest, 1960; Nika Prize at 53rd Nika Exhibition, 1968; Annual Award of the Photographic Society of Japan, 1970; 13th Art Prize from the Mainichi Newspapers, 1972; Minister of Education Award, 22nd Fine Art Grand Prix, 1972; Photographer of the Year award, American Society of Magazine Photographers, 1981.

*WRITINGS—*In English: *Arupusu,* Kodansha, 1969, translation by J. Maxwell Brownjohn published as *The Alps,* Abrams, 1975; *Himaraya,* Shogakukan, 1971, translation by Thomas I. Elleott published as *The Himalayas,* Abrams, 1973; *America Tairiku,* Kodansha (Tokyo), 1975, translation by T. Uetsuhara published as *Eternal America,* Kodansha (New York), 1975.

Technical books: *Roshutsu no kimetaka* (title means "Exposure and Its Determination"), Ikeda Shoten, 1955; *Camera no Chishiki to utsushi-kata* (title means "Camera and How to Use It"), Ikeda Shoten, 1955; *Sangaku-shashin no giho* (title means "Mountain Photography"), Rikogakusha, 1973.

Photography books: *Shiroi Yama* (title means "White Mountains"), Hobundo, 1960; *Yama* (title means "Mountains"), Chikuma Shobo, 1971; *Kami-gami no za* (title means "The Seats of the Gods"), Asahi Newspapers, 1971; *Shinyaku seisho no sekai* (title means "World of the New Testament"), Shogakukan, 1978; *Showa Shashin Zenshigoto/series No. 2, Yoshikazu Shirakawa* (title means "All Photographic Work of Showa Era/series No. 2"), Asahi Newspapers, 1982; *Shirakawa Yoshikazu Sangaku Shashin Zenshu* (title means "Collection of Mountains Photographs by Yoshikazu Shirakawa), Shogakukan, 1982; *The China Continent*, two volumes, Shogakukan, 1984.

WORK IN PROGRESS: A book of photography, *Kyuyaku seisho no sekai* (title means "World of the Old Testament"), for Shogakukan.

SIDELIGHTS: Yoshikazu Shirakawa told *CA:* "Over a period of sixteen years, I have made photographic trips to 130 of the world's countries, seeing with my own eyes, I believe, nearly all of nature's wonderful creations and developing a worldwide point of view. I have photographed from the ground and from the air, my flights having numbered in the thousands, and feel that I am accustomed to seeing nature as a macrocosm.

"To speak of the 'mysteries' and 'wonders' of nature is easy, but I wonder how many people have felt the meaning of those words. How many people have actually experienced those mysteries and those wonders? Very few, I imagine. I feel fortunate in believing that I am one of the few, and it is my earnest wish to pass on to all my deep impressions and barely imaginable experiences. I would like all people to discover anew this earth of ours. It is my fervent desire to show the way to a revitalization of humanity through the pictures I have taken.

"Our age cries, as no other period in the history of mankind has, for the rekindling of the human conscience. Space scientists, medical scientists have taken great strides and made great contributions to mankind; technological advances pile up at a dizzying rate. Yet there is domestic unrest, there are wars between nations, and even in times of peace we are ruining our environment. Day by day our earth is being destroyed, and I have had the fear that in doing my work I may inadvertently have added a stroke to the blueprint of a plan that would make the earth desertic, uninhabitable.

"Recovery of Humanity through rediscovery of the earth is my lifelong theme. *The Alps, Himalayas, Eternal America,* are now in book form. In the future, I want to look at Antarctica, the Andes and Patagonia, fjords, one hundred famous mountains of the world and the Japanese Alps. My life work was planned thirteen years ago; I do not know whether I can accomplish my aim. My hope is to introduce to the world the not yet unraveled mysteries of nature. If through my photographs people were to rediscover this earth of ours, my joy could know no bounds."

BIOGRAPHICAL/CRITICAL SOURCES: New York Times, December 2, 1973; *Wall Street Journal,* December 5, 1973, December 3, 1975; *Washington Post,* December 9, 1973; *Newsweek,* December 17, 1973; *Time,* December 17, 1973, December 22, 1975; *Los Angeles Times,* December 8, 1974, December 7, 1975.

*   *   *

SHULMAN, Morton 1925-

PERSONAL: Born April 2, 1925, in Toronto, Ontario, Canada; son of David (a salesman) and Nettie (Wintrope) Shulman; married Gloria Bossin, May 30, 1950; children: Dianne, Geoffrey. *Education:* University of Toronto, M.D., 1948. *Religion:* Jewish. *Home:* 66 Russell Hill Rd., Toronto, Ontario, Canada. *Office:* 378 Roncesvalles Ave., Toronto, Ontario, Canada M6R 2M7.

CAREER: General practitioner of medicine, Toronto, Ontario, 1950—. Chief coroner of Toronto, 1963-67; member of Provincial Parliament of Ontario, 1967-75. President of Guardian

Morton Shulman Precious Metals, Inc., and Guardian Investment Management. Host of weekly television show, 1975-83; lecturer on investing.

WRITINGS: Anyone Can Make a Million, McGraw, 1967, revised edition published as *Anyone Can Still Make a Million,* Stein & Day, 1973; *The Billion Dollar Windfall,* Morrow, 1969; *Coroner,* Fitzhenry & Whiteside, 1975; *Anyone Can Make Big Money Buying Art,* Macmillan, 1977; *Member of the Legislature,* Fitzhenry & Whiteside, 1979; *How to Invest Your Money and Profit from Inflation,* Hurtig, 1979, Ballantine, 1981. Also author of weekly column for *Toronto Sun;* lead writer for *Moneyletter.*

SIDELIGHTS: Canadian doctor, investor, politician, and bestselling writer Morton Shulman "is somewhat more than the mind-on-the-street can grasp all at once," according to Edith Hills Coogler in an *Atlanta Journal and Constitution* article. "His careers in medicine and the stock market all started . . . when he was an intern. 'I got married,'" Shulman told Coogler "'and her cousin advised us to take our $400 and invest it. We lost nearly all of it in penny stocks. . . .' Even now, years afterward, he is somewhat less than enthusiastic about penny stocks.

"But in 1962, he treated his loss like a challenge. 'I started again, and it was a new issue market. And I made mistakes, but it didn't cost me money. In six months I made $25,000. . . . That was exciting. Before long, I could have quit medicine, but I love medicine; it is my way of life. I am still practicing in Toronto every morning, and I am still into the stock market, but that is just a hobby.'"

Another of Shulman's "hobbies" is writing. He has written about his experiences as Toronto's chief coroner in *Coroner;* about his stint as a member of Ontario's Provincial Parliament in *Member of the Legislature;* and about investment strategies in *Anyone Can Make a Million, The Billion Dollar Windfall, Anyone Can Make Big Money Buying Art,* and *How to Invest Your Money and Profit from Inflation.*

In *How to Invest Your Money and Profit from Inflation,* says reviewer James K. Glassman in a *Washington Post Book World* article, "it isn't Shulman's advice that makes this such a good book. It's the way he tells his story. . . . He is relentlessly personal. Shulman has made a fortune, and he shows how he did it. He's so brash, so obnoxious that he's actually endearing. . . . One has to admire Shulman's crass, backslapping, risk-taking style. In an age in which taste counts for so much, he readily admits he doesn't have any—and proves it on any page. As a result, every page is a joy to read."

AVOCATIONAL INTERESTS: Fine wines, collecting fifteenth- and sixteenth-century watches and clocks.

BIOGRAPHICAL/CRITICAL SOURCES: Atlanta Journal and Constitution, September 16, 1973; *Authors in the News,* Volume I, Gale, 1976; *Washington Post Book World,* April 11, 1980; *New Republic,* June 21, 1980; *New York Times,* March 10, 1981.

*   *   *

SHURKIN, Joel N. 1938-

PERSONAL: Born June 12, 1938, in Orange, N.J.; son of Bernard and Selma Shurkin; married Lorna Greene (a writer), July 4, 1966 (divorced); children: Jonathan G., Michael R. *Education:* Emory University, B.A., 1960; Temple University, graduate study, 1960-62. *Religion:* Jewish. *Home:* 2727 Midtown Ct. #23, Palo Alto, Calif. 94303. *Agent:* Mitchell J. Hamilburg Agency, 292 South La Cienega Blvd., Suite 212, Beverly Hills, Calif. 90211. *Office:* News & Publication Service, Santa Teresa St., Stanford University, Stanford, Calif. 94305.

CAREER: Newark Star-Ledger, Newark, N.J., reporter, 1962-63; reporter, United Press International, 1963-68; Reuters, New York, N.Y., reporter, 1968-72; *Philadelphia Inquirer,* Philadelphia, Pa., science writer, 1972-79; Stanford University, Stanford, Calif., instructor in communications, 1980—.

MEMBER: National Association of Science Writers.

AWARDS, HONORS: Aviation-Space Writers awards, 1974 and 1976; shared Pulitzer Prize, 1979; best children's science book award, National Association of Science Teachers, 1979.

WRITINGS: Update, Report on Planet Earth, Westminster, 1976; (co-author) *Helix,* Norton, 1978; *Jupiter: The Star that Failed,* Westminster, 1979; *Invisible Fire,* Norton, 1979; *Engines of the Mind: A History of the Computer,* Norton, 1984.

*   *   *

SILLIPHANT, Stirling (Dale) 1918-

PERSONAL: Born January 16, 1918, in Detroit, Mich.; son of Leigh Lemuel (a sales director) and Ethel May (Noaker) Silliphant; married Tiana Du Long (an actress), July 4, 1974; children: Stirling, Dayle, Loren (deceased). *Education:* University of Southern California, B.A. (magna cum laude), 1938.

CAREER: Walt Disney Studios, Burbank, Calif., publicist, 1938-41; Twentieth Century-Fox Film Corp., New York, N.Y., publicist, 1942, publicity director, 1946-53; screenwriter and independent producer in Hollywood, Calif., 1953—. President, Pingree Productions. *Military service:* U.S. Navy, 1942-46.

MEMBER: California Yacht Club, Phi Beta Kappa.

AWARDS, HONORS: Academy Award ("Oscar") from Academy of Motion Pictures Arts and Sciences, Edgar Award from Mystery Writers of America, and Golden Globe Award from Hollywood Foreign Press Association, all 1968, for screenplay "In the Heat of the Night"; Golden Globe Award, 1969, for screenplay "Charly"; Image Award from National Association for the Advancement of Colored People (NAACP), 1972, for production of "Shaft"; box office writer of year award from National Association of Theater Owners, 1974.

WRITINGS: Maracaibo, Farrar, Straus, 1955; (with Rachel Maddux) *Fiction into Film,* University of Tennessee Press, 1970; *Steel Tiger,* Ballantine, 1983; *Bronze Bell,* Ballantine, 1985.

Screenplays: "Five Against the House," Columbia, 1955; "Huk!", United Artists, 1956; "Nightfall," Columbia, 1957; "Damn Citizen," Universal, 1958; "The Line Up," Columbia, 1958; "Village of the Damned," Metro-Goldwyn-Mayer, 1960; "The Slender Thread," Paramount, 1965; "In the Heat of the Night," United Artists, 1967; "Charly," Cinerama, 1968; "Marlowe," Metro-Goldwyn-Mayer, 1969; "A Walk in the Spring Rain," Columbia, 1970; "The Liberation of L. B. Jones," Columbia, 1970; "Murphy's War," Paramount, 1971; "The New Centurians," Columbia, 1972; "The Poseidon Adventure," Twentieth Century-Fox Film Corp., 1972; "Shaft in Africa," Metro-Goldwyn-Mayer, 1973; "The Tow-

ering Inferno," Twentieth Century-Fox Film Corp., 1974; "Killer Elite," United Artists, 1974; "The Enforcer," Warner Bros., 1976; "The Swarm," Warner Bros., 1977; "Telefon," Metro-Goldwyn-Mayer, 1977.

Teleplays: (And creator) "Route 66" series, Columbia Broadcasting System (CBS), 1960-64; (and creator) "Naked City" series, American Broadcasting Co. (ABC), 1960-63; (and creator) "Longstreet" series, ABC, 1972-74; "Golden Gate," ABC, September 25, 1981. Author of mini-series, "Pearl," ABC, "Space," CBS, and "Mussolini," National Broadcasting Corp. (NBC), and of Movie of the Week, "Fly Away Home," ABC. Also contributor of teleplays to "Chrysler Theatre," "Schlitz Play-house," "Suspicion," "Alfred Hitchcock Presents," "G. E. Theatre," and "CBS Playhouse."

WORK IN PROGRESS: Dust Child, a novel, for Ballantine.

SIDELIGHTS: Stirling Silliphant was working as the Eastern publicity manager for Twentieth Century-Fox in 1950 when he heard that a rival studio was looking for a script for Joan Crawford. Hoping to supply that script, he wrote "Maracaibo." It was flatly rejected by the studio, but Silliphant reworked it into a novel, and, when published, his first book received excellent reviews. "Characterized by both taut and poingant writing, *Maracaibo* is off-beat adventure handled in a gripping off-beat way," writes Rex Lardner in the *New York Times.* Ironically, film rights to the book were later purchased by Paramount, but when Silliphant applied for the job of screenwriter for that project, he was turned down.

Silliphant's next taste of screenwriting came while producing "The Joe Louis Story" in 1953. Unhappy with the script, he rewrote several sections of it. He told Catherine A. Peters in the *Chicago Tribune:* "When I saw the film, the only scenes I liked in it were the ones I had written. I said, 'Hey, maybe I'm a scriptwriter.'" Encouraged by his work on "The Joe Louis Story," he bought the rights to a story by Jack Finney, "Five Against the House," wrote a screenplay based on that story, and produced the film. "Five Against the House" was praised by A. H. Weiler in the *New York Times* as a "suspenseful diversion" with "crisp, idiomatic and truly comic dialogue and a story line that suffers only from surface characterizations." Silliphant followed this success by writing and producing what Peters terms a trio of "film-noir classics": "Nightfall," "Damn Citizen," and "The Lineup."

In 1959 Silliphant turned to television, creating and writing most of the scripts for two classic series, "Route 66" and "Naked City." "Route 66" chronicled the adventures of two American drifters driving a Corvette; "Naked City" was a documentary-style police show set in New York. "Those were probably the most exciting, absorbing four years of my life," Silliphant told Peters. "I lived on the road, traveled all over the U.S. looking for ideas. Then I'd go to New York to work on 'Naked City.' That's how I learned to meet deadlines. We'd have crews waiting for pages from my typewriter. Never missed a deadline." The high productivity demanded by television gave Silliphant an increased feeling of autonomy as a writer. "There's not as much time or money to waste [as in films] and so the writer's vision comes through stronger. I'm a defender of television and what can be done on it," he told Stuller.

When the programs were cancelled, Silliphant returned to screenwriting. His 1967 film "In the Heat of the Night" won an Academy Award for best screenplay. Later work included a string of disaster films for producer Irwin Allen: "The Poseidon Adventure,'' ''The Towering Inferno,'' ''When Time Ran Out,'' and ''The Swarm.'' Though generally dismissed by critics, these films were successes at the box office, and Silliphant was much in demand. ''When producers call and want you to write a script from an idea, or write a screenplay from a novel, then you tend to feel satisfied, successful, wanted and admired. More than money, writing films was an ego thing. I could have been secure, at the top of my field, and gone on writing movies until the day I died. But I was not growing and developing,'' Silliphant told Stuller. Therefore, the writer returned to fiction with the 1983 publication of *Steel Tiger,* the first in a planned series of twelve novels detailing the adventures of John Locke, soldier of fortune. ''The characters in this novel are lively and eccentric, . . . and the plot's complex action is fast paced,'' a *Publisher's Weekly* reviewer wrote of *Steel Tiger.*

''Once you leave [Hollywood], the studios often won't let you back in,'' Silliphant told Stuller. Despite this and the fact that writing the novels ''has represented a major financial change,'' it is something the author says he ''had to do . . . I have some freedom and am finally released from committee- and group-thinking. . . . Most writing is pretty automatic for me. I like the emotional preparation of research; that's perhaps the best part. But in all 85,000 to 90,000 words of *Steel Tiger,* there are only about 5,000 words that are to me a mystery. Where I read back and feel a kind of magic, that third wind where you're in another place. . . . Those passages are what make you want to keep writing.''

BIOGRAPHICAL/CRITICAL SOURCES: New York Times, March 13, 1955, June 22, 1955, January 24, 1957, September 24, 1968, October 23, 1969, January 18, 1970, July 2, 1971, August 4, 1972, December 13, 1972, January 14, 1973, June 21, 1973, December 20, 1974, December 18, 1975, April 12, 1976, December 23, 1976, December 17, 1977, July 23, 1978, January 19, 1979, March 29, 1980; *Christian Science Monitor,* July 9, 1969; *Newsweek,* January 31, 1972; *Women's Wear Daily,* December 18, 1974; *New Yorker,* December 20, 1974; *New York Post,* January 6, 1975; *Time,* January 6, 1975; *Chicago Tribune,* April 3, 1980, August 23, 1983; *Publisher's Weekly,* April 29, 1983; *Writer's Digest,* March, 1984.

* * *

SILVER, Ruth
See CHEW, Ruth

* * *

SILVERSTEIN, Josef 1922-

PERSONAL: Born May 15, 1922, in Los Angeles, Calif.; son of Frank and Betty (Heymanson) Silverstein; married Marilyn Cooper, June 20, 1954; children: Frank Stephen, Gordon Alan. *Education:* University of California, Los Angeles, B.A. (with honors), 1952; Cornell University, Ph.D., 1960. *Politics:* Democrat. *Religion:* Jewish. *Home:* 93 Overbrook Dr., Princeton, N.J. 08540. *Office:* Department of Political Science, Rutgers University, New Brunswick, N.J. 08903.

CAREER: U.S. Merchant Marine, 1942-53; became second officer listed; Wesleyan University, Middletown, Conn., assistant professor of political science, 1958-64; Rutgers University, New Brunswick, N.J., professor of political science, 1967—, chairman of department, 1977-80. Fulbright lecturer, Burma, 1961-62 and Malaysia, 1967-68. Director of Institute of Southeast Asian Studies, Singapore, 1970-72.

MEMBER: Association for Asian Studies, American Political Science Association, American Association of University Professors.

WRITINGS: (Contributor) G. M. Kahin, editor, *Government and Politics of Southeast Asia,* Cornell University Press, 1959, revised edition, 1964; (editor and contributor) *Southeast Asia in World War II: Four Essays,* Yale University Southeast Asian Studies, 1966; (contributor) S. Lipset and P. Altbach, editors, *Students in Revolt,* Houghton, 1969.

(Editor and author of introduction) *The Political Legacy of Aung San,* Southeast Asia Program, Cornell University, 1972; (editor and author of introduction) *The Future of Burma in Perspective: A Symposium,* Center for International Studies, Ohio University, 1974; (contributor) R. M. Smith, editor, *Southeast Asia: Documents of Political Development and Change,* Cornell University Press, 1974; *Burma: Military Rule and the Politics of Stagnation,* Cornell University Press, 1977; *Burmese Politics: The Dilemma of National Unity,* Rutgers University Press, 1980. Author of ''Asia, the One and the Many,'' 20 programs produced on National Broadcasting Co. television, 1967.

WORK IN PROGRESS: New Directions in the Relations of Southeast Asian Nations; Political Ideas and Leadership in Southeast Asia.

SIDELIGHTS: Josef Silverstein told *CA:* ''My writings center around the common theme of national unity and the development of a national mentality in an area where people too often think of themselves first as members of a religious group, second a linguistic group and lastly as members of a nation state. While most of my writings have centered on Burma, I have sought to broaden my scope by examining common questions in neighboring states. Lately, I have been studying the impact of international law and new legal concepts on the region of Southeast Asia.

''It pleases me that some of my writings have been translated into Burmese and Indonesian so that scholars and layman alike in the region can read what I have written and thereby broaden the dialogue I have enjoyed with Asians who know me both personally and through my writings.''

* * *

SIMMONS, Blake
See WALLMANN, Jeffrey M(iner)

* * *

SIMPSON, Harriette
See ARNOW, Harriette (Louisa Simpson)

* * *

SIMPSON, R(onald) A(lbert) 1929-

PERSONAL: Born February 1, 1929, in Melbourne, Australia; son of Herbert Albert (a cooper) and Louise (Rigg) Simpson; married Shirley Athale Pamela Bowles (a research officer), August 27, 1955; children: Meredith, Warwick. *Education:* Melbourne Teachers' College, certificate, 1951; Royal Melbourne Institute of Technology, diploma of art, 1967. *Politics:* None. *Religion:* None. *Home:* 29 Omama Rd., Murrumbeena, Melbourne, Victoria 3163, Australia. *Office:* Chisholm Institute of Technology, 900 Dandenong Rd., Melbourne, Victoria 3145, Australia.

CAREER: Worked as a primary school teacher in Melbourne, Australia, and in England, 1951-57; art teacher in secondary schools in Melbourne, 1958-61; Department of Education, Melbourne, sub-editor, 1962-67; Chisholm Institute of Technology, Melbourne, senior lecturer and lecturer in fine arts, 1968—. Liaison officer, Adelaide Festival of Arts, 1980.

MEMBER: Australian Society of Authors.

AWARDS, HONORS: Australia Council Literature Board special grant to travel, 1977.

WRITINGS—Poetry: *The Walk along the Beach,* Edwards & Shaw, 1960; *This Real Pompeii,* Jacaranda Press, 1964; *After the Assassination,* Jacaranda Press, 1968; *Diver,* University of Queensland Press, 1972; *Poems from Murrumbeena,* University of Queensland Press, 1976; *The Forbidden City,* Edwards & Shaw, 1979; *Poem from "The Age,"* Hyland House, 1979; *Selected Poems,* University of Queensland Press, 1981.

Contributor of literary criticism to periodicals, including *Age* (Melbourne), *Quadrant,* and *The Bulletin.* Poetry editor, *The Bulletin,* 1963-65, and *The Age,* 1969—.

WORK IN PROGRESS: Words for a Journey, a book of poems.

SIDELIGHTS: R. A. Simpson told *CA:* "I feel, and hope, my poetry has moved from preoccupations with formal neatness toward a kind of poetry that is more flexible. I have worked toward experimental regions where language is meant to be stripped of its essentials: 'Student,' 'Diver,' 'Hardiman's Progress' are poems in which I have tried to be more truthful—perhaps an impossibility: artists are not merely 'strippers,' because they must know what to conceal. However, this is the Stripper Age. I want my poetry to be far more interesting in terms of form. I have always thought of myself as being a visual writer—that is, a person who finds satisfaction in the image: my experiments in 'concrete poetry' were by-products of this.

"During the sixties and seventies I tried to achieve more flexible ways, forms in poetry: For a while I was interested in prose poems. Too many of the poems in *Walk Along the Beach* now strike me as being flat, mannered, and merely dull. There were forty-five poems in that collection, and these days about fifteen of them seem worthwhile to me; but I'm probably being too optimistic here.

"The book of poems I am now working on is a continuation of the poems in the 'Later Poems' section of my *Selected Poems.* I have been labelled a 'portraitist' poet, but this is only one side of my work. Although I structured my *Selected Poems* so that the opening section leads the reader into a number of semi-portraits to be found throughout the volume, I have always been interested in the lyrical and satirical, as well as being interested in the possibilities of surrealism. All these aspects are culminating in my recent work."

Simpson's manuscripts and personal papers, and his 1977 report on a visit to England and the United States, are housed in the National Library, Canberra.

*   *   *

SINCLAIR, Andrew (Annandale) 1935-

PERSONAL: Born January 21, 1935, in Oxford, England; son of Stanley Charles (in the British Colonial Service) and Hilary (a writer; maiden name, Nash-Webber) Sinclair; married Marianne Alexandre, 1960 (divorced); married Miranda Seymour,

October 18, 1972 (divorced June 6, 1984); married Sonia Melchett (a writer), July 25, 1984; children: (first marriage) Timon Alexandre; (second marriage) Merlin George. *Education:* Cambridge University, B.A. (double first honors in history), Trinity College, 1958, Ph.D., Churchill College, 1963. *Home:* 16 Tite St., London SW3 4HZ, England. *Agent:* Gillon Aitkens, 17 South Eaton Pl., London SW1W 9ER, England.

CAREER: Cambridge University, Churchill College, Cambridge, England, founding fellow and director of historical studies, 1961-63; University of London, University College, London, England, lecturer in American history, 1965-67; managing director, Lorrimer Publishing, London, 1967-84, and Timon Films, 1969-84; Raleigh Promotions Ltd., London, chairman of operations, 1984-88. Writer and filmmaker. *Military service:* British Army, Coldstream Guards, 1953-55; became lieutenant.

MEMBER: Association of Cinematograph and Television Technicians, Royal Society of Literature (fellow), Society of American Historians (fellow).

AWARDS, HONORS: Commonwealth fellow, Harvard University, 1959-61; American Council of Learned Societies fellow, 1963-65; Somerset Maugham Literary Prize, 1967, for *The Emancipation of the American Woman;* Venice Film Festival award, 1971, and Cannes Film Festival prize, 1972, both for "Under Milk Wood."

WRITINGS—Fiction; novels, except as indicated: *The Breaking of Bumbo* (also see below), Simon & Schuster, 1959; *My Friend Judas* (also see below), Faber, 1959, Simon & Schuster, 1961; *The Project,* Simon & Schuster, 1960; *The Paradise Bum,* Atheneum, 1963 (published in England as *The Hallelujah Bum,* Faber, 1963); *The Raker,* Atheneum, 1964; *Gog,* Macmillan, 1967; *Magog,* Harper, 1972; *The Surrey Cat,* M. Joseph, 1976, published as *Cat,* Sphere, 1977; *Inkydoo, the Wild Boy* (children's story), Abelard (London), 1976, published as *Carina and the Wild Boy,* Beaver/Hamlyn, 1977; *A Patriot for Hire,* M. Joseph, 1978, published as *Sea of the Dead,* Sphere, 1981; *The Facts in the Case of E. A. Poe,* Holt, 1980; *Beau Bumbo,* Weidenfeld & Nicolson, 1985.

Nonfiction: *The Era of Excess,* introduction by Richard Hofstadter, Atlantic-Little, Brown, 1962, published as *The Era of Excess: A Social History of the Prohibition Movement,* Harper, 1964; *The Available Man: The Life behind the Masks of Warren Gamaliel Harding,* Macmillan, 1965; *The Better Half: The Emancipation of the American Woman,* Harper, 1965, published as *The Emancipation of the American Woman,* 1966, reprinted under original title, Greenwood Press, 1981; *A Concise History of the United States,* Viking, 1967; (author of introduction) Homer, *The Iliad,* translated by W. H. D. Rouse, Heron Books, 1969; *The Last of the Best: The Aristocracy of Europe in the Twentieth Century,* Macmillan, 1969.

Che Guevara, Viking, 1970 (published in England as *Guevara,* Fontana, 1970); *Dylan Thomas: No Man More Magical,* Holt, 1975 (published in England as *Dylan Thomas: Poet of His People,* M. Joseph, 1975); *The Savage: A History of Misunderstanding,* Weidenfeld & Nicolson, 1977; *Jack: A Biography of Jack London,* Harper, 1977; *John Ford,* Dial, 1979.

Corsair: The Life of J. Pierpont Morgan, Little, Brown, 1981; (editor) Jack London, *The Call of the Wild, White Fang, and Other Stories,* introduction by James Dickey, Penguin, 1981; *The Other Victoria: The Princess Royal and the Great Game of Europe,* Weidenfeld & Nicolson, 1981; (with Ladislas Farago) *Royal Web*, McGraw, 1982; *Sir Walter Raleigh and the Age of Discovery*, Penguin, 1984.

Plays: "My Friend Judas" (adapted from author's novel of same title), first produced in London at Arts Theatre, October 21, 1959; (adapter) Dylan Thomas, *Adventures in the Skin Trade* (first produced at Hampstead Theatre Club, March 7, 1965; produced in Washington, D.C., at Washington Theatre Club, February 25, 1970), Dent, 1967, New Directions, 1968; "The Blue Angel" (adapted from screenplay of Josef von Sternberg's film of same title), first produced in Liverpool, England, at Liverpool Playhouse, October 1, 1983.

Screenplays: "Before Winter Comes" (based on Frederick L. Keefe's short story "The Interpreter"), Columbia, 1969; "The Breaking of Bumbo" (based on author's novel of same title), directed by Sinclair, Associated British Pictures Corp., 1970; *Under Milk Wood* (based on Dylan Thomas's play of same title; directed by Sinclair; produced by Timon Films, 1971), Simon & Schuster, 1972; "Malachi's Cove," Timon Films, 1973.

Television scripts: "The Voyage of the Beagle," CBS Films, 1970; "Martin Eden," RAI, 1981.

Translator: *Selections from the Greek Anthology*, Weidenfeld & Nicolson, 1967, Macmillan, 1968; (with Carlos P. Hanserv) *Bolivian Diary: Ernesto Che Guevara*, Lorrimer, 1968; (with Marianne Alexandre) Jean Renoir, *La Grande Illusion*, Lorrimer, 1968; *Masterworks of the French Cinema*, Lorrimer, 1974.

Contributor to *Atlantic, Harper's, Observer, Guardian, Spectator, New Statesman*, and other periodicals and newspapers.

WORK IN PROGRESS: King Ludd, a sequel to *Gog* and *Magog*, which Sinclair plans to revise and re-issue as a trilogy; *The Red and the Blue*.

SIDELIGHTS: Among Andrew Sinclair's most imaginative works are the allegorical novels *Gog* and its sequel, *Magog*. A blend of fiction, history, and myth, the books examine Great Britain's past and present through the eyes of half-brothers Gog and Magog, names that evoke the twin giants of British legend whose statues stood guard over London's Guildhall until they were destroyed by German bombs in 1940. As Richard Freedman explains in the *Saturday Review*, Sinclair's modern versions of these age-old figures "symbolize the best and worst people and events from ancient Albion to Labourite Britain."

In the first novel, which begins just after the end of World War II, a seven-foot-tall man is washed ashore on the coast of Scotland, naked and suffering from amnesia. After a brief convalescence, the man—who remembers only that his name is Gog—sets out for London, hoping to learn more about his identity and, therefore, his past. The rest of the novel chronicles his many adventures as he journeys south. In the picaresque tradition, Gog meets a variety of fictional, historical, and mythological characters along the way. Some display concern and offer him assistance and advice; others (including his own wife and half-brother) regard him as "the perfect victim" and derive much pleasure from making him suffer. By the end of the novel, the one-time innocent has developed a less idealistic, more pragmatic attitude toward life, one that acknowledges the existence of evil and corruption and the need for each person to fight his or her own battles.

In their evaluations of *Gog*, critics have tended to rate it in one of two ways: as an unsuccessful attempt at sophisticated satire or as a highly ambitious and imaginative product of genius. An adherent of the former view is *New Statesman* reviewer Kenith Trodd, who characterizes *Gog* as "a series of funny production numbers: droll, but the laughs are hollow where they need to be edgy; the wrong sort of punch." Frank McGuinness also believes *Gog* lacks the proper sort of "punch." Writing in *London Magazine*, McGuinness declares that the book exhibits "perhaps more satirical pretensions than the author's talent for ribald and extravagant inventiveness can finally support. . . . The truth is that if the novel is not without distinction as a study of a mind hovering between sanity and madness, its satirical aims are lost in a welter of scholarly clowning, crude farce and the sort of glib cynicism that is so often mistaken for cold, hard-headed intellectualism."

A similar opinion is expressed by J. D. Scott in the *New York Times Book Review*. "Mr. Sinclair has too much talent to fail to make an impression," the critic begins. "But the impression is confused by too much frenetic action, and softened by long lapses into flat, sometimes merely clever, sometimes merely banal, prose. *Gog* is a monument of myth and slapstick, violence and parody, drama-of-evil and custard-pie comedy. Like some great Gothic folly seen through the mist, it fails to communicate its meaning."

On the other side of the discussion are those reviewers who regard *Gog* as excitingly original and entertaining. Though he thinks the novel is "much too long," Roger Sale comments in the *Hudson Review* that "the end is rich and satisfying, a book the likes of which I have not seen in a long time." In his study *The Situation of the Novel*, Bernard Bergonzi praises Sinclair's "extraordinary imaginative exuberance" and terms *Gog* "an intensely personal book, whose approach could not be followed by writers who do not share Sinclair's preoccupations, knowledge and temperament." Even more enthusiastic is critic Philip Callow, who asserts in *Books and Bookmen*: "[*Gog*] sears and scalds, it's the vision of a cold, planetary eye, and somehow it all founders in the end, goes mad like a cancer and finally smashes in a blind fury of destruction. I'm still reeling. I think there's genius in it."

Rachel Trickett more or less agrees with this assessment of *Gog*, stating in the *Yale Review* that it is "most extraordinary and ambitious. . . . A mixture of traditional genres, the allegory, the romance, and the picaresque tale, it is at once realistic and a fantasy, didactic and mythical, precise and comprehensive. Sinclair complains that most reviewers have misunderstood it, but he can hardly be surprised; it attempts so much. . . . The love of life and a compulsive literary energy are what make *Gog* so impressive a book. . . . Confusion and carelessness are its worst faults, but its inclusiveness is also its strength. Self-indulgent and undisciplined, it nevertheless shows a clumsy but powerful genius which can only leave one astonished, occasionally repelled, but consistently grateful for so much imaginative vigor and breadth."

Magog, the sequel to *Gog*, examines many of the same social, political, and moral issues from the point of view of Gog's half-brother and spiritual opposite—Magog, the "symbol of power, authority, centralization, the tyranny of material success and fashion," as Trickett describes him. Like *Gog*, *Magog* begins in 1945, just after the end of the war. Sinclair portrays his title character as a young civil servant whose promising career with the government comes to an abrupt end when an investigation reveals the extent of his dishonest dealings. Despite this apparent setback, Magog moves on to successively more powerful positions as head of a film production company, an urban developer, and, finally, master of a new college at Cambridge. The focus of the book is on these various stages in Magog's career and on what *Dictionary of Literary Biography* writer Judith Vincent refers to as his ultimate realization "that his material success is hollow and that an inevitably changing order must deprive him of power."

Reviewers have greeted *Magog* with somewhat less enthusiasm than *Gog.* "Gobbling great hunks of time, a vast *dramatis personae;* tossing off puns, inside jokes, bits of mythology; insisting that the life of a man and of an empire have much in common, [*Magog*] trivializes all it touches," declares Patricia Meyer Spacks in the *Hudson Review.* "It's funny sometimes, sometimes even sad, but the lack of sharp authorial perspective makes it seem purposeless."

Commenting in the *New York Times Book Review,* Anthony Thwaite remarks that *Magog* "suffers, as sequels are apt to do, from the disabilities of its predecessor: lumbering in its episodic movement, spotty in its characterization, arbitrary in its action, and megalomaniac in its overview. . . . This book is not an epic, whatever its author's purpose may have been. Nor, despite its blurb, is it a 'wonderfully sardonic morality tale.' Sinclair's juggled universe bears little resemblance to any known world, no matter how hard he tries to reinforce everything with documentary and travelogue. *Magog* is a febrile, self-indulgent, opinionated and finally rather squalidly boring fling at the picaresque."

Unlike their colleagues, reviewers from the *Times Literary Supplement* and *Books and Bookmen* temper their criticism with praise. The *Times Literary Supplement* critic, for example, believes that "too many events" make *Magog* read like "a first-draft synopsis of a twelve-volume novel series, full of bright ideas, sharp comments and ambitions not yet realized." Nevertheless, the critic adds, "Sinclair is always interesting and convincing about [the] details of high life, which he treats with disdain." Oswell Blakeston also has some positive observations, particularly regarding the author's "ear for civil service dialogue." In general, says Blakeston in *Books and Bookmen,* this makes for "a splendid beginning" to the novel. "But then, alas, [Sinclair] plunges into farce," the critic continues. "[And] after one has laughed at a well-aimed poisoned dart of brilliant criticism, it's hard to accept the old custard pie as a devastating weapon."

Kenn Stitt and Lee T. Lemon are among those whose praise for *Magog* is almost without qualification. In a *New Statesman* article, Stitt describes the novel as "a rich and complex book, mirroring the complexities of the world it is set in, its strands intricately and carefully interwoven." Though he finds the theme somewhat trite, Lemon observes in *Prairie Schooner* that the author "does a fine job of showing the reader the peculiar anguish of the successful but hollow man [and] the intricacies of power." Like several other critics, he also finds that Sinclair "has a talent for the memorable turn of phrase." In short, concludes the reviewer, *Magog* "just might be one of the best novels of the past few years"—even better than *Gog.* "The earlier book was a stumbling romp through the history and mythology of the British Isles," says Lemon. "But *Magog* is a different book. Magog . . . is not hindered by his brother [Gog's] ponderous memories. He is a kind of gadfly of meaningless change. . . . By the end of the novel, Magog the manipulator has learned that time brings new and shrewder manipulators, and that one does not have to manipulate for the things which give satisfaction."

In a letter to *CA,* Sinclair comments on the ideas that inspired *Gog* and *Magog* and explains how *King Ludd* will complete the trilogy: "*Gog* is based on Eliot's principle that time past and present and future are all the same. It also attempts to bring alive the legendary and mystical history of Britain as seen in the struggle of the people against the power of the government, of London, of King Ludd's town. There is no resolution to the fight of Gog against Magog, of the land against the city, of the ruled against the ruler, but in that fight lies the spirit and the glory of Albion, whatever it may be. *Magog*'s world is the machinations of power, and how its misuse drove Britain down after the end of the Second World War. *King Ludd* will deal with England from the time of the Luddites opposing the industrial revolution through the neurosis of the 1930s to the odd conflicts of today, where the descendants of the Tolpuddle martyrs now have their unions and use the workers' power to oppress the rest. When brother fights brother, Magog and King Ludd will always rule."

BIOGRAPHICAL/CRITICAL SOURCES—Books: Bernard Bergonzi, *The Situation of the Novel,* University of Pittsburgh Press, 1970; *Contemporary Literary Criticism,* Gale, Volume II, 1974, Volume XIV, 1980; Robert K. Morris, editor, *Old Lines, New Forces: Essays on the Contemporary British Novel, 1960-1970,* Fairleigh Dickinson University Press, 1976; *Dictionary of Literary Biography,* Volume XIV: *British Novelists since 1960,* Gale, 1982.

Periodicals: *New York Times Book Review,* January 22, 1967, September 10, 1967, October 8, 1967, July 2, 1972, October 12, 1980; *Books and Bookmen,* May, 1967, June, 1967, June, 1972; *London Magazine,* June, 1967; *Times Literary Supplement,* June 8, 1967, July 13, 1967, May 5, 1970, June 26, 1981; *New Statesman,* June 9, 1967, May 5, 1972; *Observer Review,* June 11, 1967, January 11, 1970; *Drama,* summer, 1967; *Time,* September 1, 1967; *Saturday Review,* September 16, 1967; *Book World,* September 24, 1967; *Best Sellers,* October 1, 1967; *Hudson Review,* winter, 1967, autumn, 1972; *Listener,* April 4, 1968; *Yale Review,* spring, 1968; *Variety,* January 15, 1969; *Spectator,* April 25, 1969; *Punch,* January 20, 1970; *Prairie Schooner,* spring, 1974; *Chicago Tribune Book World,* April 1, 1979, October 5, 1981; *Los Angeles Times,* April 7, 1981; *New York Times,* April 21, 1981; *Washington Post,* April 30, 1981; *Times* (London), January 21, 1982.

—Sketch by Deborah A. Straub

*   *   *

SINCLAIR, Grace
    See WALLMANN, Jeffrey M(iner)

*   *   *

SINCLAIR, James
    See STAPLES, Reginald Thomas

*   *   *

SINGER, Armand Edwards   1914-

PERSONAL: Born November 30, 1914, in Detroit, Mich.; son of Elvin Satori (a grand opera singer and teacher of voice) and Fredericka (Edwards) Singer; married Mary White (a teacher), August 8, 1940; children: Fredericka Ann Schmidt. *Education:* Amherst College, A.B., 1935; Duke University, M.A., 1939, Ph.D., 1944; Sorbonne, University of Paris, diploma, 1939;

Indiana University, postdoctoral study, 1964. *Politics:* Republican. *Religion:* Protestant. *Home:* 248 Grandview Ave., Morgantown, W.Va. 26505. *Office:* 205-C Chitwood Hall, West Virginia University, Morgantown, W.Va. 26506.

CAREER: Duke University, Durham, N.C., part-time instructor in Spanish and French, 1938-40; West Virginia University, Morgantown, instructor, 1940-47, assistant professor, 1947-55, associate professor, 1955-60, professor of Romance languages, 1960-80, professor emeritus, 1980—, chairman of humanities program, 1963-72, chairman of integrated studies, 1963, acting chairman, department of religion and program for the humanities, 1973, and director of colloquiums on modern literature, 1976-80, 1985. Member of board of directors, Community Concert, Morgantown, 1956-61, and Humanities Foundation of West Virginia, 1981—.

MEMBER: Modern Language Association of America (member of National Delegate Assembly, 1975-77), American Association of Teachers of French, American Association of Teachers of Spanish and Portuguese, Modern Language Teachers Association, South Atlantic Modern Language Association (member of executive committee, 1972-74), West Virginia Association for the Humanities (president, 1980-81), Phi Beta Kappa.

WRITINGS: A Bibliography of the Don Juan Theme: Versions and Criticism, West Virginia University Press, 1954, revised edition published as *The Don Juan Theme, A Bibliography: Versions and Criticisms,* 1965, 3rd edition (with Robert Karpiak), 1985; (author and editor with wife, Mary W. Singer, Frank S. White, and R. Ryland White) *Four Score and Ten,* R. R. White, 1964; (editor and translator with John F. Stasny) *Humanities I: Anthology of Readings,* West Virginia University, 1966; (editor and translator with Stasny) *Humanities II: Anthology of Readings,* West Virginia University, 1967.

Paul Bourget, Twayne, 1976; (contributor) Brigitte Wittmann, editor, *Don Juan: Darstellung und Deutung,* Wissenschaftliche Buchgesellschaft, 1976; (editor-in-chief) *West Virginia George Sand Conference Papers,* Department of Foreign Languages, West Virginia University, 1981; (editor and contributor) *Essays on the Literature of Mountaineering,* West Virginia University Press, 1982.

Contributor of articles to *Columbia Dictionary of Modern European Literature.* Contributor of over one hundred articles and reviews to *Modern Language Journal, Modern Language Notes, West Virginia Philological Papers, Hispania, Nieman Reports, Comparative Literature Studies, Hispanic Review, Laurel Review, South Atlantic Bulletin, National Parks Magazine, Erasmus, American Philatelic Congress Yearbook* and other publications. *West Virginia University Philological Papers,* editor, 1948-50, 1952-54, editor-in-chief, 1950-52, 1954—.

WORK IN PROGRESS: A book on postal stationery of Nepal, with Frank Vignola and Walter Hellrigl; a book of limericks; a catalog of Himalayan mountaineering covers.

SIDELIGHTS: Armand Edwards Singer told *CA:* "Writing is an excruciatingly difficult activity. How often do most of us find the exact word, the fresh, definitive phrase to describe a point of view, an event, a person, a scene? Which is, of course, what keeps us in harness—that endless search—whether we are a Flaubert, composing masterpieces, or just hacks, explaining French past participles or the intricacies of Nepalese philately."

AVOCATIONAL INTERESTS: Photography, travel, philately, mountain climbing, carpentry.

*   *   *

SISTER MAURA
See EICHNER, Maura

*   *   *

SKEDGELL, Marian Jay 1921-

PERSONAL: Surname sounds like "schedule"; born February 22, 1921, in Chicago, Ill.; daughter of William (a printer) and Ann (Steinberg) Castleman; married Ralph E. Skedgell (a merchandising executive), November 9, 1946 (died December, 1977); children: John Alexander, Nicholas George, Kristen Lee. *Education:* University of Chicago, M.A., 1941. *Politics:* Democrat. *Religion:* Congregationalist. *Office:* E. P. Dutton & Co., 2 Park Avenue, New York, N.Y. 10016.

CAREER: Editorial assistant, University of Chicago Press, Chicago, Ill., 1940-42, and Viking Press, New York City, 1943-47; Alfred A. Knopf, Inc. (publishers), New York City, copy editor, 1961-62; E. P. Dutton & Co. (publishers), New York City, beginning 1962, production editor, 1962-64, editorial director of Sunrise Books, 1973-77, senior editor, beginning 1977; free-lance editor and writer, 1964—. Teacher of writing and English literature, Rockland Foundation, West Nyack, N.Y., St. John Fisher College, Rochester, N.Y. Member of board of directors, Roxbury Land Trust.

MEMBER: Authors League of America, P.E.N., Editors Lunch.

AWARDS, HONORS: John Billings Fiske Poetry Prize for "The Return," 1941; Fund for the Republic Award for television script, "Boden's Grave," 1955.

WRITINGS: The Day of the Waxing Moon, Doubleday, 1965; (editor) Jean Ende and Clifford Earl, *Buy It Right!,* Dutton, 1974; (editor) Miriam Hecht, *Dropping Back In: How to Complete Your College Education Quickly and Economically,* Dutton, 1982.

Author of two plays, "Broken Record" and "The Game Preserve," of pageant, "On the Way," for Girl Scouts National Jamboree, 1956, and of television scripts. Contributor to *Poetry, Dyn, Time,* and *New Leader.*

AVOCATIONAL INTERESTS: Music, politics (as a spectator sport).†

*   *   *

SKIPPER, G. C. 1939-

PERSONAL: Born March 22, 1939, in Ozark, Ala.; son of G. C. (a railroad worker) and Ada (Price) Skipper; married Dorothy Wright (a secretary), March 26, 1960; children: Richard Craig, Lisa Ann. *Education:* University of Alabama, B.A., 1961. *Home:* 2344 Pleasant Ave., Glenside, Pa. 19038. *Office:* Al Paul Lefton Co., Philadelphia, Pa. 19106.

CAREER: Huntsville Times, Huntsville, Ala., reporter and columnist, 1961-65; United Airlines, Chicago, Ill., public relations agent, 1966-70; *Travel Weekly,* Chicago, Midwest news bureau chief, 1970-72; Hitchcock Publishing Co., Wheaton, Ill., executive editor, 1973-76; Al Paul Lefton Co., Philadelphia, Pa., currently vice-president of public relations. Has also worked as folk and rock pianist.

WRITINGS—Books for children and young adults, except as indicated; published by Childrens Press, except as indicated: *And the Angels Rage* (adult novel), Touchstone Publishing, 1972; *The Ghost in the Church,* 1976; *A Night in the Attic,* 1977; *The Ghost at Manor House,* 1978.

Death of Hitler, 1981; *Goering and the Luftwaffe,* 1981; *Mussolini: Death of a Dictator,* 1981; *Battle of Britain,* 1981; *Battle of the Atlantic,* 1981; *Battle of Stalingrad,* 1981; *Battle of Leyte Gulf,* 1981; *Battle of the Coral Sea,* 1981; *Battle of Midway,* 1981; *Invasion of Sicily,* 1981; *Fall of the Fox: Rommel,* 1981; *Submarines in the Pacific,* 1981; *MacArthur and the Philippines,* 1982; *Invasion of Poland,* 1983; *D-Day,* 1983; *Pearl Harbor,* 1984.

Former editor of *Motor Service* magazine.

WORK IN PROGRESS: Southbound, a novel; *The Silent Struggle,* a nonfiction book; *Triad Summer,* a novel.

SIDELIGHTS: G. C. Skipper writes: "I've known since I was twelve years old that I not only wanted to write, but *had* to write. Some have labeled this obsession 'talent,' but in reality it's more like a disease. As to the reason why, I'm still trying to figure that out. Insanity helps a whole lot and if you keep your insanity you'll be okay. The worst thing in the world for a writer is to become a 'well-rounded individual.' Writers, I guess, are an egotistical lot—they'd have to be to think they've got anything to say, much less believe people want to hear it. Whew!

"I grew up in Alabama, in the deep South, and I've seen how ridiculous other areas of the country have been in imagining what 'the South' is 'really like.' Now, like country music, suddenly it's 'in' to be Southern—and the worst thing in the world is a Professional Southerner. I believe all creativity springs out of an individual or a section of the country that has known defeat. The South is the only area of the United States that has been defeated. I think that accounts, at least partially, for the Faulkners, the Weltys, the Jacksons, et cetera, et cetera. New York is getting there, too, in its own unique way—hence, the Mailers. In other words all this man-it's-a-rough-miserable-world-type-stuff is good fodder to sprout writers. Outside playing God, I think creativity—in this case in writing—is one of the most honorable, honest contributions Man can make. If it's really good, it survives everything. Any other profession, say a thousand years from now, will look just downright silly—if I can paraphrase Hemingway.

"There's only a handful of good writers around today, hidden among the mass of academic phonies. I mean good in the creative sense of Hemingway, Faulkner and Fitzgerald. Maybe these writers are hidden because the selling of fiction has been reduced to computerized marketing exercised by publishers. Yeah, I know all us word merchants can't be Hemingway and all editors can't be Max Perkins—but it sure would be refreshing to see a novel make it on merit rather than hype. There is a need now in the United States—not for entertainment (there's plenty of that)—but for literature. I'd like to contribute my limited amount to filling that gap."

*   *   *

SLAATTE, Howard A(lexander)   1919-

PERSONAL: Surname is pronounced *Slah*-te; born October 18, 1919, in Evanston, Ill.; son of Iver T. (a clergyman) and Ester Elina (Larsen) Slaatte; married Mildred Gegenheimer, June 20, 1952; children: Elaine (Mrs. Tu Van Tran), Mark Edwin, Paul

Andrew. *Education:* Kendall College, A.A., 1940; University of North Dakota, B.A. (cum laude), 1942, graduate study, 1941-42; Drew University, B.D. (cum laude), 1945, Ph.D., 1956; Oxford University, graduate study, 1949-50. *Home:* 407 Grand Blvd., Huntington, W.Va. 25705. *Office:* Department of Philosophy, Marshall University, Huntington, W.Va. 25701.

CAREER: Co-pastor of Bethelship Methodist Church in Brooklyn, N.Y., 1942-45; minister of education at Methodist churches in New Jersey and Long Island, N.Y., 1945-49; pastor of Methodist churches, Detroit Conference, Detroit, Mich., 1950-56; Temple University, Philadelphia, Pa., associate professor of systematic theology, 1956-60; McMurry College, Abilene, Tex., visiting professor, 1960-63, professor of philosophy, 1963-65; Marshall University, Huntington, W.Va., professor of philosophy, 1965—, chairman of department, 1966—. Member of West Virginia Conference of United Methodist Church, 1966—.

MEMBER: American Philosophical Society, American Academy of Religion, American Ontoanalytical Society, West Virginia Philosophical Society (president, 1966-67, 1983-84).

AWARDS, HONORS: Pilling traveling fellow from Drew University to Oxford University, 1949-50; alumni award, Kendall College, 1964; grants from National Science Foundation, 1965, 1971, and Marshall University, 1977, 1978.

WRITINGS—Published by University Press of America, except as indicated: *Time and Its End,* Vantage, 1962; *Fire in the Brand,* Exposition, 1963; *The Pertinence of the Paradox,* Humanities, 1968; *The Paradox of Existentialist Theology,* Humanities, 1971; *Modern Science and the Human Condition,* Intelman, 1974; *The Arminian Arm of Theology,* 1977; *The Dogma of Immaculate Conception,* 1979.

Discovering Your Real Self, 1980; *The Seven Ecumenical Councils,* 1980; *The Creativity of Consciousness,* 1983; *Martin Heidegger's Philosophy,* 1984. Contributor to philosophy and theology journals.

WORK IN PROGRESS: Time, Existence, and Destiny and *Modern Philosophies of Religion.*

AVOCATIONAL INTERESTS: Singing (as baritone soloist and in operettas), collecting limestone fossils, drama, sports.

*   *   *

SMITH, Elton E(dward)   1915-

PERSONAL: Born November 9, 1915, in New York, N.Y.; son of Elton Herbert (a theater owner-manager) and Christina (a member of the Abbey Players; maiden name Conway) Smith; married Esther Marian Greenwell (a professor), October 17, 1942; children: Elton Greenwell, Esther Ruth, Stephen Lloyd. *Education:* New York University, B.S., 1937; Andover Newton Theological School and Harvard University, S.T.M., 1940; Syracuse University, M.A., 1958, Ph.D., 1961. *Residence:* Lutz, Fla. *Office:* English Department, University of South Florida, Tampa, Fla. 33620.

CAREER: Baptist minister; pastor of churches in Massachusetts, Oregon, New York, and Florida, 1940—; University of South Florida, Tampa, professor of English, Bible, and humanities, 1961—. Fulbright-Hays senior lecturer, University of Algiers, 1969-70, and Mohammed V. University, Rabat, Morocco, 1974-75; visiting professor, University of Paris. Outside reader, University of Florida, and Case Western Reserve University. Moderator, weekly television show "Quest," 1965-

69, 1970-74. Baritone soloist, appearing in lieder and oratorio concerts in Oregon and New York; member and director of community theatres. Member of Chambers of Commerce, Oregon. *Member:* Modern Language Association of America, American Association of University Professors, Conference on Christianity and Literature, South Atlantic Modern Language Association. *Awards, honors:* D.D. from Linfield College; named faculty lecturer, University of South Florida.

WRITINGS: The Two Voices: A Tennyson Study, University of Nebraska Press, 1964; (with wife, Esther G. Smith) *William Godwin: A Critical Study,* Twayne, 1965; *Louis MacNeice,* Twayne, 1970; *The Angry Young Men of the Thirties: Day Lewis, Spender, MacNeice, Auden,* Southern Illinois University Press, 1975, revised edition, 1976; *Charles Reade,* G. K. Hall, 1977, Prior Associated Publishers, 1978. Contributor of articles and reviews to journals, including *Victorian Newsletter, Western Humanities Review,* and *Victorian Poetry.*

WORK IN PROGRESS: City of Daffodils, a novel set in Algiers; *Foster Child,* a novel showing the development of a child in five foster homes; an article on British proletarian poets; research on Tennyson's utopia.

BIOGRAPHICAL/CRITICAL SOURCES: Ledger (Lakeland, Fla.), December 1, 1964; *Tribune* (Tampa, Fla.), January 31, 1965, April 23, 1966; *Times* (Tampa, Fla.), February 22, 1965; *South Atlantic Quarterly,* autumn, 1965, May, 1974, November, 1975, November, 1976; *Western Humanities Review,* autumn, 1965; *Modern Language Review,* April, 1966.

*   *   *

SMYLIE, James H(utchinson)   1925-

PERSONAL: Born October 20, 1925, in Huntington, W.Va.; son of Theodore Shaw (a minister) and Mildred (Hutchinson) Smylie; married Elizabeth Roblee, November 23, 1961; children: Mark Andrew, Margaret Elizabeth, Mary Catherine. *Education:* Washington University, St. Louis, Mo., B.A., 1946; Princeton Theological Seminary, B.D., 1949, Th.M., 1950, Ph.D., 1958. *Office:* Union Theological Seminary in Virginia, 3401 Brook Rd., Richmond, Va. 23227.

CAREER: Ordained clergyman of United Presbyterian Church in the U.S.A., 1949; member, National Capital Union Presbytery. First Presbyterian Church, St. Louis, Mo., assistant minister, 1950-52; Princeton Theological Seminary, Princeton, N.J., instructor, 1956-59, assistant professor of church history, 1959-62, director of studies, 1960-62; Union Theological Seminary in Virginia, Richmond, alumni visiting professor, 1962-64, associate professor, 1964-67, professor of American church history, 1967—. Visiting professor at Pittsburgh Theological Seminary, 1964, 1975, Perkins School of Theology, summer, 1966, Virginia Commonwealth University, 1968, Sweetbriar College, 1974, and Vancouver School of Theology, 1976. Bibliographer and consultant for *American Quarterly.*

MEMBER: American Historical Association, American Studies Association, American Catholic Historical Association, Presbyterian Historical Society, American Society of Church History (secretary, 1963-74), Organization of American Historians, American Academy of Religion, Society for the Scientific Study of Religion, Association for the Study of Afro-American Life and History, American Association of University Professors, Southern Historical Association.

WRITINGS: Into All the World, John Knox, 1965; *A Cloud of Witnesses,* John Knox, 1965. Also editor of *Presbyterians and*

the American Revolution: A Documentary Account, 1974, Presbyterians and the American Revolution: An Interpretive Account, 1976, and Presbyterians and Biblical Authority, 1981.

Contributor: Daniel Callahan, editor, *The Secular City Debate,* Macmillan, 1966; Elwyn Smith, editor, *The Religion of the Republic,* Fortress, 1971; Max J. Skidmore, editor, *Word Politics: Essays on Language and Politics,* J. E. Freel and Associates, 1972; Michael P. Hamilton and Nancy S. Montgomery, editors, *The Ordination of Women, Pro and Con,* Morehouse, 1975; Robert Rue Parsonage, editor, *Church Related Higher Education,* Judson, 1978; Dean R. Hoge and David A. Roozen, editors, *Understanding Church Growth and Decline, 1950-1978,* Pilgrim Press, 1979; Hugh T. Kerr, editor, *Protestantism: A Concise Survey of Protestantism and Its Influence on American Religious and Social Traditions,* Barrons, 1979. Also contributor to *The Church's Ministry in Higher Education,* edited by John H. Westerhoff, 1978, *Virginia Presbyterians in American Life: Hanover Presbytery, 1755-1980,* 1982, and *Die Religion in Geschichte und Gegenwart.*

Contributor to *Encyclopaedia Britannica, Encyclopedia Americana, Dictionary of Western Churches, Westminster Dictionary of Church History,* and *Encyclopedic Dictionary of Religion.* Contributor of articles to journals, including *New South, Theological Education, Harvard Theological Review, Princeton Seminary Bulletin, Christianity Today,* and *American Review.* Editor, *Journal of Presbyterian History,* 1968—; member of editorial council, *Theology Today.*

*   *   *

SNOOK, I(van) A(ugustine)   1933-

PERSONAL: Born March 27, 1933, in New Zealand; son of John Thomas (a shopkeeper) and Mary Monica (Granger) Snook; married Josephine Carde (a speech therapist), January 16, 1965; children: Kathryn, John, David. *Education:* University of Canterbury, B.A., 1962, M.A., 1965; University of Illinois, Ph.D., 1968. *Home:* Aokautere Dr., R.D. 1, Palmerston North, New Zealand. *Office:* Department of Education, Massey University, Palmerston North, New Zealand.

CAREER: Teacher at school in Christchurch, New Zealand, 1961-65; University of Canterbury, Christchurch, New Zealand, lecturer, 1968-71, senior lecturer, 1972-76, reader in education, 1977-80; Massey University, Palmerston North, New Zealand, professor of education, 1981—.

WRITINGS: (With H. S. Broudy, R. D. Szoke, and M. J. Parsons) *Philosophy of Education,* University of Illinois Press, 1967; *Indoctrination and Education,* Routledge & Kegan Paul, 1972; *Concepts of Indoctrination,* Routledge & Kegan Paul, 1972; (with Colin McGeorge) *More Than Talk,* New Zealand Department of Education, 1977; (with Colin Lankshear) *Education and Rights,* Melbourne University Press, 1978; (with McGeorge) *Church, State, and New Zealand Education,* Price Milburn, 1981. Associate editor of *New Zealand Journal of Educational Studies.*

WORK IN PROGRESS: Contributing to *The Politics of Education in New Zealand* and to *The Development of New Zealand Culture.*

*   *   *

SNYDER, Anne   1922-

PERSONAL: Born October 3, 1922, in Boston, Mass.; daughter of Nathan (a manufacturer of key blanks) and Marsha (Borochowitz) Reisner; married Louis Snyder (a plant manager), June 15, 1941; children: Sherri Snyder Stevens, Mari-Beth Snyder Bergman, Nathalie. *Education:* Attended El Camino College, Valley College, University of California, Los Angeles, University of Portland, and Maren Elwood College of Writing, Los Angeles. *Home:* 20713 Exhibit Ct., Woodland Hills, Calif. 91367. *Agent:* Henriette Neatour, Bill Berger Associates, Inc., 444 East 58th St., New York, N.Y. 10022.

CAREER: Television writer and author. Teacher of creative writing for Gifted Children's Association of San Fernando Valley, 1970-76, and at Los Angeles Valley College, Pierce College, and California State University, Northridge. Member of literary advisory board, CompCare Publications.

MEMBER: P.E.N. International, Society of Children's Book Writers, Authors Guild, Authors League of America, Women's National Book Association, Writers Guild of America, West, Southern California Council on Literature for Children and Young People.

AWARDS, HONORS: Child Study Association of America selected *50,000 Names for Jeff* as one of the ten best children's books of 1969; *First Step* received the top juvenile award from Friends of American Writers and special honors from National Council of Christians and Jews, both 1976.

WRITINGS—Novels for juveniles and young adults, except as indicated; published by Holt, except as indicated: *50,000 Names for Jeff*, 1969; *Nobody's Family*, 1975; *First Step*, 1975; *My Name Is Davy—I'm an Alcoholic* (also see below), 1977; *Kids and Drinking* (nonfiction), CompCare Publications, 1977; *The Old Man and the Mule*, 1978; *Goodbye, Paper Doll*, New American Library, 1980.

With Louis Pelletier; young adult novels; published by New American Library: *Counter Play*, 1981; *Two Point Zero*, 1982; *Nobody's Brother*, 1982; *The Best That Money Can Buy*, 1983; *You Want To Be What?*, 1984.

Screenplays: "Women—Alive and Well," produced by PMA Association, 1977; "My Name Is Davy—I'm an Alcoholic" (based on book of same title), NBC-TV, in production.

Also author of documentary screenplay, "New Beginnings," 1977. Author of two "Family Robinson" screenplays for Australian Production Co. Contributor of concepts and scripts to television programs, including "Sign-On Show" (teen daily series), "General Hospital" (daytime soap opera), "Hollywood Squares" (game show), "Lucille Ball Show" (comedy series), and "CBS Repertoire Theatre." Author of script and lyrics for an Ice Capades routine, of lyrics for a recording by vocalist Nancy Ames, and of comedy material for the "Jules Feifer Review."

WORK IN PROGRESS: A series of books; a new programming concept for Children's Television Workshop; a television series; an animated cartoon television series.

SIDELIGHTS: Anne Snyder's work for young adult readers confronts the issues with which many of today's teenagers must contend. She tells *CA* that she is regarded as a bibliotherapeutic specialist and as such enjoys writing "about the everyday problems young people face today." Both *First Step* and *My Name Is Davy—I'm an Alcoholic* explore alcohol abuse and how it affects personal relationships. *First Step*, which has been adapted for television, sketches a picture of life with a mother who "drinks a little." Snyder's protagonist, a high school girl, is

typical of "the twenty-one million kids trapped in alcoholic homes," the author says. The title character in *My Name is Davy*, however, is "trapped" by his own addiction to liquor. The story traces the lonely teenager's descent into alcohol dependence by focusing on Davy's need to feel popular and maintain his relationship with his girlfriend, Maxi. While both *First Step* and *Davy* are fictional accounts, Snyder's *Kids and Drinking* documents the true stories of grade school children who are hooked on alcohol. Often used in schools, the book presents what Snyder hopes is "realistic but hopeful information." The author examines another teenage psychological and physical problem, *anorexia nervosa*, in *Goodbye, Paper Doll*. In this work, a popular, intelligent seventeen-year-old refuses to heed warnings by her doctor and family and, in an effort to remain "paper thin," begins to starve herself.

With Louis Pelletier, Snyder also has written novels that examine values and personal choice in today's society. The authors examine homosexuality in *Counter Play*, the effect of divorce on kids and the handicap of stuttering in *Nobody's Brother*, the consequences of living on overextended credit in *The Best That Money Can Buy*, and the sometimes subtle implications of cheating in *Two Point Zero*. In the latter, according to Annie Gottlieb in the *New York Times Book Review*, "the authors show that the reasons for 'cheating' aren't simple." Concludes the critic: "The serious treatment of this challenging issue, a natural for classroom debate, doesn't quite mesh with the book's sprightly preppy tone. . . . Nonetheless, there's suspense . . . and a happy ending."

My Name Is Davy—I'm an Alcoholic has been translated into Danish and Finnish.

AVOCATIONAL INTERESTS: Pen pals.

MEDIA ADAPTATIONS: "She Drinks a Little," a screenplay based on *First Step*, was produced by ABC-TV; *Nobody's Brother* has been purchased by Orion for a television movie; *Counter Play, Two Point Zero,* and *Goodbye, Paper Doll* have been optioned for television movies.

BIOGRAPHICAL/CRITICAL SOURCES: New York Times Book Review, April 25, 1982.

*   *   *

SNYDER, Solomon H(albert)   1938-

PERSONAL: Born December 26, 1938, in Washington, D.C.; son of Samuel Simon (a systems analyst) and Patricia (Yakerson) Snyder; married Elaine Borko, June 10, 1962; children: Judith Rhea, Deborah Lynn. *Education:* Georgetown University, M.D. (cum laude), 1962. *Politics:* Democrat. *Religion:* Jewish. *Home:* 2300 West Rogers Ave., Baltimore, Md. 21209. *Office:* Department of Neuroscience, School of Medicine, Johns Hopkins University, 725 North Wolfe St., Baltimore, Md. 21205.

CAREER: Kaiser Foundation Hospital, San Francisco, Calif., intern, 1962-63; National Institute of Mental Health, Bethesda, Md., research associate, 1963-65; Johns Hopkins University, Baltimore, Md., resident in psychiatry in university hospital, 1965-68, School of Medicine, assistant professor, 1966-68, associate professor, 1968-70, professor, 1970-77, distinguished professor of psychiatry and pharmacology, 1977—. *Military service:* U.S. Public Health Service, 1963-65; served as senior surgeon.

MEMBER: National Academy of Sciences, American College of Neuropsychopharmacology (fellow), Psychiatric Research

Society, Society for Neuroscience, American Society of Biological Chemists, American Society for Pharmacology and Experimental Therapeutics, American Psychiatric Association.

AWARDS, HONORS: Outstanding Scientist Award, Maryland Academy of Sciences, 1969; John Jacob Abel Award, American Pharmacology Society, 1970; A. E. Bennett Award, Society for Biological Psychiatry, 1970; Hofheimer Prize, American Psychiatric Association, 1972; Gaddum Award, British Pharmacology Society, 1974; Daniel Efron Award, American College of Neuropsychopharmacology, 1974; F. O. Schmitt Award in Neurosciences, Massachusetts Institute of Technology, 1975; Nicholas Giarman Lecture Award, Yale University, 1975; Rennebohm Award, University of Wisconsin, 1976; Salmon Award, 1977; Stanley Dean Award, American College of Psychiatrists, 1978; Harvey Lecture Award, 1978; Albert Lasker Award, 1978; Wolf Award, 1983.

WRITINGS: Uses of Marijuana, Oxford University Press, 1971; *Madness and the Brain,* McGraw, 1974 (published in England as *Drugs, Madness, and the Brain,* Hart-Davis, 1975); (with others) *Opiate Receptor Mechanisms: Neurochemical and Neurophysiological Processes in Opiate Drug Action and Addiction,* MIT Press, 1975; *The Troubled Mind: A Guide to Release from Distress,* McGraw, 1976; *Biological Aspects of Mental Disorder,* Oxford University Press, 1980.

Editor: *Perspectives in Neuropharmacology,* Oxford University Press, 1972; (with Earl Usdin) *Frontiers in Cathecholamine Research: Proceedings,* Pergamon, 1973; (with Leslie L. Iversen and Susan D. Iversen) *Handbook of Psychopharmacology,* Plenum, 1975, Volume II: *Principles of Receptor Research,* Volume IV, Section 1: *Amino Acid Neurotransmitters;* (with James A. Ferrendelli and Bruce S. McEwen) *Neurotransmitters, Hormones, and Receptors: Novel Approaches,* Society for Neuroscience, 1976.

Also editor of papers of the third International Catecholamine Symposium, 1973. Member of editorial board, *Journal of Neurochemistry.*

WORK IN PROGRESS: Laboratory research in psychopharmacology and neurotransmitters.

SIDELIGHTS: Solomon H. Snyder told *CA* he is "interested in linking psychiatry and basic information on the chemistry of the brain. [I am] also eager to explicate for the general public new scientific studies of brain function and drug action." *Avocational interests:* Playing classical guitar.

BIOGRAPHICAL/CRITICAL SOURCES: Washington Post, February 1, 1974; *New York Times,* April 7, 1981.

*   *   *

SOCHEN, June   1937-

PERSONAL: Born November 26, 1937, in Chicago, Ill.; daughter of Sam (a grocer) and Ruth (Finkelstein) Sochen. *Education:* University of Chicago, B.A., 1958; Northwestern University, M.A., 1960, Ph.D., 1967. *Home:* 6238 North Harding Ave., Chicago, Ill. 60659. *Office:* Department of History, Northeastern Illinois University, Chicago, Ill. 60625.

CAREER: Northeastern Illinois University, Chicago, instructor, 1964-67, assistant professor, 1967-69, associate professor, 1969-72, professor of history, 1972—.

MEMBER: American Historical Association, American Studies Association.

AWARDS, HONORS: National Endowment for the Humanities grant, 1971.

WRITINGS: (Editor) *The Black Man and the American Dream: 1900-1930,* Quadrangle, 1971; (editor) *The New Feminism in Twentieth-Century America,* Heath, 1971; *The Unbridgeable Gap: Blacks and Their Quest for the American Dream,* Rand McNally, 1972; *The New Woman: Feminism in Greenwich Village, 1910-1920,* Quadrangle, 1972; (editor with Duke Frederick and William Howenstine) *Destroy to Create: Interaction with the Environment,* Dryden, 1972; *Movers and Shakers: American Women Thinkers and Activists, 1900-1970,* Quadrangle, 1973; *Herstory: A Woman's View of American History,* Alfred Publishing, 1974, 2nd edition, 1981.

(Contributor) Martin Jackson and John O'Connor, editors, *American History/American Film,* Ungar, 1979; *Consecrate Every Day: The Public Lives of Jewish American Women, 1880-1980,* State University of New York Press, 1981; (contributor) Daniel Walden, editor, *Studies in American Jewish Literature,* State University of New York Press, 1983; (contributor) Sarah Blacher Cohen, editor, *From Hester Street to Hollywood,* Indiana University Press, 1983.

WORK IN PROGRESS: The Eclectic American: A Study in Twentieth-Century U.S. Cultural History.

AVOCATIONAL INTERESTS: Reading, tennis, writing fiction.

*   *   *

SOLDO, John J(oseph)   1945-

PERSONAL: Born May 16, 1945, in Brooklyn, N.Y.; son of Victor (a carpenter) and Mildred (a seamstress; maiden name, Ferrari) Soldo; married Martha Schwink, August 22, 1968 (divorced, April, 1971). *Education:* Fordham University, B.A. (magna cum laude), 1966; Harvard University, M.A., 1968, Ph.D., 1972; additional graduate study at King's College, Cambridge, 1969. *Politics:* "Middle." *Religion:* Roman Catholic. *Home:* 238 Ave. U, Brooklyn, N.Y. 11223.

CAREER: Wells College, Aurora, N.Y., assistant professor of English, 1971-72; City University of New York, New York City, assistant professor of English at Bronx Community College and Kingsborough Community College, 1972-73; Columbia University, New York City, assistant professor of English, 1973-77; free-lance writer, 1977-78; Eastern New Mexico University, Portales, associate professor, 1978-84, chairman of department of languages and literature, 1978-82; free-lance writer, 1984—. *Member:* Modern Language Association of America, American Studies Association, Society for Values in Higher Education, Poets and Writers, New Mexico State Poetry Society, New York Poetry Forum. *Awards, honors:* Award for poetry from Academy des Beaux Arts, 1976.

WRITINGS: Delano in America and Other Early Poems, Pearl Press, 1974; *The Tempering of T. S. Eliot,* UMI Research Press, 1983; *Odes and Cycles,* Mosaic Press, 1984; *In an Arid Clime,* Jelm Mountain, 1984; *Studies,* Overtone Press, 1984; *Now Old with My Youth,* Quality Publications, 1984.

Plays: "Delano's Destiny" (poetic drama), first produced in Santa Fe, N.M., at St. John's College, August, 1970; "Delano in America" (with music, mime, and dance), first produced in New York City at St. Paul's Chapel, April, 1974; "Waves Clapping Like Angels" (one-act), first produced in New York City at Glines Theatrer, October, 1978.

Work represented in *Americana Anthology.* Contributor of poems, articles, and reviews to magazines, including *NewsArt, Margins, New Earth,* and *Columbia Review.*

WORK IN PROGRESS: The High Roller, a novel; *Stocks and Blonds,* a music book, with lyrics; books of poems, including *Sonnets for Our Risorgimento, Mirrors for the Harmony of Sex, Passage to Philia* (dramatic poem), *Without Masks,* and *The Kingdom.*

SIDELIGHTS: John J. Soldo told *CA* he "began writing poetry again while living in England during 1969-70. Being in a different culture and living in the country provided a great stimulus."

*   *   *

SOLTIS, Jonas F(rancis)   1931-

PERSONAL: Born June 11, 1931, in Norwalk, Conn.; son of Jonas J., Jr. (a realtor) and Margaret (Soltes) Soltis; married Nancy Schaal (a teacher), September 10, 1955; children: Susan Soltis Shaw, Robin Lee. *Education:* University of Connecticut, B.A. (with honors), 1956; Wesleyan University, M.A.T., 1958; Harvard University, Ed.D., 1964. *Home:* 436 Palmer Ave., Teaneck, N.J. 07666. *Office:* Division of Philosophy and Social Sciences, Teachers College, Columbia University, New York, N.Y. 10027.

CAREER: University of Connecticut, Waterbury, instructor in history and philosophy, 1958-60; Wesleyan University, Middletown, Conn., instructor in education, 1962-64; Columbia University, Teachers College, New York, N.Y., professor of philosophy and education, 1964-79, William Heard Kilpatrick Professor of Philosophy and Education, 1979—, director of Division of Instruction, 1971-75, director of Division of Philosophy and the Social Sciences, 1977-79. Consultant to the Addison-Wesley Publishing Company, Reading, Mass., 1965-68. *Military service:* U.S. Air Force, 1950-54.

MEMBER: Philosophy of Education Society (president, 1975), American Philosophical Association, National Society for the Study of Education, American Educational Research Association, John Dewey Society, Phi Beta Kappa, Phi Delta Kappa.

AWARDS, HONORS: U.S. Office of Education post-doctoral fellowship in education research, 1968-69.

WRITINGS: Seeing, Knowing, and Believing, Allen & Unwin, 1966; *Introduction to the Analysis of Educational Concepts,* Addison-Wesley, 1968, 2nd edition, 1978; (editor with B. Chazan) *Moral Education,* Teachers College Press, 1974; (editor) *Philosophy of Education since Mid-Century,* Teachers College Press, 1980; (editor) *Philosophy and Education,* National Society for the Study of Education/University of Chicago Press, 1981; (with Kenneth A. Strike) *The Ethics of Teaching,* Teachers College Press, 1984; (with D. C. Phillips) *Learning Theories,* Teachers College Press, 1985; (with Walter Feinberg) *School and Society,* Teachers College Press, 1985.

Editor, "Problems in Education" series, 1970, and "Thinking about Education" series, 1984, both published by Teachers College Press. Editor, *Teachers College Record,* 1984—; member of editorial board, *Educational Theory,* 1968-70, *Educational Philosophy and Theory,* 1969—, and *Studies in Philosophy and Education,* 1971-75.

WORK IN PROGRESS: Curriculum and Aims, with D. F. Walker, publication by Teachers College Press expected in 1986; *Approaches to Teaching,* with Gary Fenstermacher, publication by Teachers College Press expected in 1986.

*   *   *

SORKIN, Alan Lowell   1941-

PERSONAL: Born November 2, 1941, in Baltimore, Md.; son of Martin and Sally (Steinberg) Sorkin; married Sylvia Jean Smardo, September 9, 1967; children: David Lowell, Suzanne Elizabeth. *Education:* Johns Hopkins University, B.A. (with honors), 1963, M.A., 1964, Ph.D., 1966. *Politics:* Republican. *Religion:* Lutheran. *Home:* 9110 Ramblebrook Rd., Baltimore, Md. 21236. *Office:* Department of Economics, University of Maryland Baltimore County, 5401 Wilkens Ave., Baltimore, Md. 21228.

CAREER: Bureau of Labor Statistics, Washington, D.C., economist, summers, 1963-64; Research Analysis Corp., McLean, Va., economic analyst, 1966-67; Brookings Institution, Washington, D.C., research associate in economics, 1967-69; Johns Hopkins University, Baltimore, Md., assistant professor, 1969-72, associate professor of international health and economics, 1972-74; University of Maryland Baltimore County, Baltimore, professor of economics and chairman of department, 1974—. Lecturer at Goucher College and George Washington University, 1966-67; part-time professor of health economics, University of Maryland Medical School, 1974—.

MEMBER: American Economic Association, Phi Beta Kappa.

WRITINGS: American Indians and Federal Aid, Brookings Institution, 1971; (with others) *Health and Economic Development: An Annotated, Indexed Bibliography,* Department of International Health, Johns Hopkins University, 1972; *Education, Unemployment and Economic Growth,* Heath Lexington, 1974; *Health Economics: An Introduction,* Heath Lexington, 1975, 2nd revised edition, 1984; *Health Economics for Developing Nations,* Heath Lexington, 1976; *Health Manpower: An Economic Perspective,* Heath Lexington, 1977; *The Urban American Indian,* Heath Lexington, 1978; *The Economics of the Postal Service,* Heath Lexington, 1980; *Economic Aspects of Natural Hazards,* Heath Lexington, 1982.

Contributor of more than thirty articles and reviews to education and social science journals, including *Journal of Negro Education, Growth and Change: A Journal of Regional Development, Social Forces, College and University, Monthly Labor Review, American Journal of Economics and Sociology, Journal of Economic Studies, Journal of Economic Literature,* and *Journal of Health Administration Education.*

WORK IN PROGRESS: Research on correlates of declining birth rates in Punjab; a monograph on the economic aspects of health manpower; a study of the economic and social position of American Indians living in cities.

*   *   *

SORRENTINO, Gilbert   1929-

PERSONAL: Born April 27, 1919, in Brooklyn, N.Y.; son of August E. and Ann Marie (Davis) Sorrentino; married Elsene Wiessner (divorced); married Vivian Victoria Ortiz; children: Jesse, Delia, Christopher. *Education:* Attended Brooklyn College (now Brooklyn College of the City University of New York), 1950-51, and 1955-57. *Agent:* Mel Berger, William Morris Agency, Inc., 1350 Avenue of the Americas, New York, N.Y. 10019. *Office:* Department of English, Stanford University, Stanford, Calif. 94305.

CAREER: "At least twenty-five jobs of all sorts," 1947-65; Neon (magazine), New York City, editor and publisher, 1956-60; Grove Press, New York City, editor, 1965-70; teacher at Columbia University, 1965, Aspen Writers Workshop, 1967, Sarah Lawrence College, 1971-72, and New School for Social Research, 1976-79; University of Scranton, Scranton, Penn., Edwin S. Quain Professor of Literature, 1979; Stanford University, Stanford, Calif., professor of English, 1982—. Military service: U.S. Army, 1951-53; served in medical corps.

MEMBER: P.E.N. American Center.

AWARDS, HONORS: Guggenheim fellow, 1973-74; Samuel S. Fels Award in Fiction, 1974, for short story "Catechism": Creative Artists Public Service grant, 1974-75; Ariadne Foundation grant, 1975; National Endowment for the Arts grant, 1975-76, 1978-79; John Dos Passos Prize, 1981.

WRITINGS: Flawless Play Restored: The Masque of Fungo, Black Sparrow Press, 1974; (translator) Sulpiciae Elegidia/Elegiacs of Sulpicia: Gilbert Sorrentino Versions, Perishable Press, 1977; Something Said: Essays, North Point Press, 1984.

Poetry: The Darkness Surrounds Us, Jargon Books, 1960; Black and White, Totem Press/Corinth, 1964; The Perfect Fiction, Norton, 1968; Corrosive Sublimate, Black Sparrow Press, 1971; A Dozen Oranges, Black Sparrow Press, 1976; White Sail, Black Sparrow Press, 1977; The Orangery, University of Texas Press, 1977; Selected Poems: 1958-1980, Black Sparrow Press, 1981; Splendide-Hotel, Dalkey Archive Press, 1984.

Novels: The Sky Changes, Hill & Wang, 1966; Steelwork, Pantheon, 1970; Imaginative Qualities of Actual Things, Pantheon, 1971; Splendide-Hotel, New Directions Publishing, 1973; Mulligan Stew, Grove, 1979; Aberration of Starlight, Random House, 1980; Crystal Vision, North Point Press, 1981; Blue Pastoral, North Point Press, 1983.

Work appears in anthologies, including: The New American Poetry, 1945-1960, edited by Donald Allen, Grove, 1960; Poesia Americana del '900, Guanda, 1963; The New Writing in the U.S.A., Penguin, 1967.

Contributor to Nation, New York Times, Esquire, Partisan Review, TriQuarterly, Harper's, Poetry, and other publications. Book editor, Kulchur, 1961-63.

SIDELIGHTS: Gilbert Sorrentino has earned critical praise for his highly innovative fiction. The structures of his novels are of particular importance because Sorrentino holds that form is more important than content. "Form not only determines content," he says to Charles Trueheart in Publishers Weekly, "but form invents content." Accordingly, all of Sorrentino's novels are structured in unique ways. "His is a voice," writes William Mattathias Robins in the Dictionary of Literary Biography, "that consistently and with ever-increasing originality stands out from the literary chorus."

Sorrentino's first novel, The Sky Changes, concerns an unhappy married couple who journey across America seeking a way to keep their marriage together. Richard Elman, writing in the Review of Contemporary Fiction, states that he knows "of few works . . . which are so subtle, and touching, in depicting the pain of being mismatched." Each chapter of the novel is named for a town the couple visits on their journey and relates the events which occur in that town. Sorrentino's narrative ignores time sequence in favor of spatial continuity. He states in the Grosseteste Review: "The past, the present, the future are mixed together in order to show very clearly that

there is really no past that is worse than the present and there is no future that will be better than the present." Sorrentino also presents his next novel, Steelwork, out of chronological order. Concerned with the sites and characters of his Brooklyn childhood, it is "an utterly different, quite original method of narration. . . ," writes Shaun O'Connell of the Nation. "[The novel] is made up of ninety-six separate but interlocking dramatic vignettes, scenes which, in their arrangement within the novel, scramble chronology." Jerome Klinkowitz, writing in Literary Disruptions: The Making of a Post-Contemporary American Fiction, finds Steelwork's narrative structure to be appropriate to its theme. "The subject is change," Klinkowitz writes, "and the book's form comes to terms with this reality, grasped imaginatively."

In Imaginative Qualities of Actual Things, Sorrentino satirizes the New York avant-garde art world of the 1960s, a world in which he had played a part. "While each chapter is largely devoted to one of eight characters," writes John O'Brien in the Dictionary of Literary Biography, "the novel proceeds by way of digression, anecdote, asides, and itemizations, all filtered through a narrator whose rage and urbane wit mix into a strangely compassionate yet unsentimental treatment of these meretricious, sometimes gifted artists." Paul Theroux of the Washington Post Book World finds Sorrentino's satire effective, but believes that the author unconsciously echoes what he attacks. "Few people are able to write as well as Sorrentino does here of literary posturing," Theroux observes, "but the trouble is that the book assumes an elaborate posture of its own, and so does the narrator, . . . ; the book contains many of the affectations it condemns." In contrast to this view, Klinkowitz sees Imaginative Qualities as "Sorrentino's most fully realized expression of the novelist's proper role. Throughout he fights against the poor writing and misguided aesthetics that characterizes so much of recent conventional fiction." O'Brien believes that "the technical achievements in this novel opened up a world of possibilities for future novels." These possibilities were partly explored by Sorrentino in his next novel, Splendide-Hotel, a short book consisting of 26 sections, each section based on a letter of the alphabet. By structuring his novel around the alphabet, Sharon Fawcett writes in Open Letter, Sorrentino turns Splendide-Hotel into "a defense of Poetry, radically so, in that it returns to the primary construct of words to get at primary meanings, images." Klinkowitz, writing in the Village Voice, sees this alphabetic structure as a method to make the reader deliberately aware of the novel as writing. It "keeps us right on the pages, like a painter keeps us on the canvas," he explains. "All Gilbert Sorrentino's work refuses to be bland meta-fiction," Klinkowitz concludes, "recounting in second-order terms a story about another reality. It is instead something made and placed in the world, standing for nothing but itself."

Perhaps Sorrentino's most acclaimed novel is Mulligan Stew, a book O'Brien calls "literally a synthesis of almost everything Sorrentino had read and written in the past twenty-five years." The novel is such a tour de force that John Leonard of the New York Times believes there "is a very real question as to whether avant-garde fiction can survive Gilbert Sorrentino's new novel." Drawing elements from a wide range of popular and serious literature, Mulligan Stew parodies its components. "A work of true comic genius," Allen Lacy calls the novel in Books and Art, "[Mulligan Stew] not only entertains and engages the intelligent reader, but also manages to shed light on the processes of literary creation, on the making of bad novels as well as good ones." Similarly, Malcolm Bradbury observes in his review of the book for the *New York Times Book Review* that *Mulligan Stew* "is a neo-Joycean concoction, spawning invention, delighting in lists, inventing languages, animating the endlessly comic fact that every sentence we write may generate its opposite, every structure of significance we create risks being parodied to the point of insignificance, every generative element in any story can move in an infinitude of directions. 'Mulligan Stew' mocks the act of creation. It also thrives on it, turning itself into an abundant and extravagently decorated display of the pleasures of the imagination.''

O'Brien believes that Sorrentino established himself as a "major comic writer" with *Mulligan Stew*. "It contains some of the best parodies since S. J. Perelman at his most manic," Michael Dirda of the *Washington Post Book World* states, "and perhaps the most corrosive satire of the literary scene since early Aldous Huxley. This is a novel with all the stops pulled out, Gilbert Sorrentino's masterpiece.'' Kenneth John Atchity, reviewing the novel for the *Los Angeles Times Book Review,* also calls it a "masterpiece.'' He goes on to describe it as a "singular event in the history of wit and imagination. . . . 'Mulligan Stew' is the end of the self-reflexive novel: Sorrentino brains the genre against the walls of prose. As we watch, we become accomplices, laughing at the murder—because it is a ritual, comic suicide—with a mixture of horror and relief. It's as though Sorrentino, broom and dustpan in hand, has swept into one large steamer trunk—or one pot of Mulligan stew—all the literary leftovers from the past quarter-century.'' According to Stuart Dybek, writing in the *Detroit News, Mulligan Stew* "catapulted Gil Sorrentino's reputation out of the literary underground. In great abundance, it [demonstrates] Sorrentino's collection of modernist techniques and devices as well as his special gift, the ability to blend them in the service of lucidity rather than mystification.''

In his next novel, *Aberration of Starlight,* Sorrentino tells his story in four separate narratives, each told by one of the principal characters. Set on the New Jersey coast during the Depression, the story concerns a divorcee, her ten-year-old son, and her father who meet an unsavory man during their vacation. "It's the kind of plot," Dybek writes, "that could easily become melodrama in the hands of a less acid writer than Sorrentino.'' "Neither nostalgic nor sentimental," writes O'Brien, "the novel sets down the tone and temper of the times as they are reflected in and act upon the four major characters.'' John Morse of *Chicago Review* sees *Aberration of Starlight* as a quite different novel from *Mulligan Stew*. "In contrast, . . . [it] is disciplined in length and form, modest in ambition, and downright decorous in tone," he states. "[Having] railed against all literary conventions in *Mulligan Stew,* Sorrentino has now settled down to write a warm and sensitive story.'' Writing in the *New York Review of Books,* Josh Rubins also sees a great difference between the two books. After rejecting the possibility that Sorrentino may again be writing parody, Rubins states that *Aberration* is really about five characters—the four characters in the story and Sorrentino himself. "But if *Aberration of Starlight* does indeed tell a story of five characters," he writes, "offering more of the traditional novelistic values . . . than Sorrentino has allowed himself in years, it is also his most 'experimental' fiction yet, in the sense that an experiment is something whose outcome you don't know in advance.'' Rubins concludes that the dazzling techniques of *Mulligan Stew* have been used in *Aberration* in a quieter and more reflective manner.

In *Crystal Vision,* Sorrentino deals with some of the same characters and situations from his Brooklyn childhood that were

first introduced in *Steelwork*. The novel, writes Larry Kart of the *Chicago Tribune Book World,* "makes extreme demands on the reader's attention and offers correspondingly extreme rewards.'' Composed almost exclusively of dialogue, the novel's 78 chapters relate the conversations of "a central group of six to eight voices," Thomas LeClair explains in the *Washington Post Book World,* "and perhaps 20 peripheral figures. Setting is only mentioned; Vogler's store and Pat's tavern are auditory, not visual, space.'' Through this constant conversation Sorrentino again comments on the nature of literature. "Stories pack *Crystal Vision,*" writes Valentine Cunningham in the *Times Literary Supplement*. ". . . Stories . . . can magic almost anything into existence.'' But despite the power of stories, they are also seen to be inherently inaccurate, little more than lies. When the character Georgie Huckle tries to materialize women through the power of his story-telling, he fails. "*Crystal Vision* impresses finally," Cunningham believes, "for daunting even its own zests on the horrifying prospect of nothing happening but make-believe.'' "Sorrentino's endless attack on 'literature,'" Kart believes, "rises here to scarifying heights.''

Blue Pastoral is "an anatomy of language," John O'Brien writes in the *Washington Post Book World*. He explains: "Each chapter appears to be an exercise in how language is abused, tortured, and made senseless.'' The language of political speeches, pop songs, advertising, academic journals, and popular magazines are all satirized. One chapter consists of sentences taken from country songs, both real and imagined. "In the end," O'Brien states, "the language and the mechanics of writing become completely unhinged. The last chapter appears to consist of phrases drawn from the rest of the book, now strangely combined. . . . Language has gone mad.'' Joel Conarroe, writing in the *New York Times Book Review,* finds *Blue Pastoral* "a wild and crazy book, lavishly inventive, full of surprises, sometimes exasperating, often exhilerating.'' In *Blue Pastoral,* O'Brien believes, Sorrentino "has made and shaped a work whose brilliance—in this case comic brilliance—is awesome, pure, and perfectly executed.''

"In recent years," Elman writes in his evaluation of Sorrentino's career, "[Sorrentino] seems to wish his readers to share in the fiction of language, pure and abstract, as his most elementary concern, and only means of knowing. I believe this is a persona that should be contemplated for what it is: the means by which an artist of great seriousness, and talent, and ability, has shaped the pain of experience to animate language and show the limitations by which we live, and the dramatic breaks, and small startling changes, and terrible betrayals.''

CA INTERVIEW

Gilbert Sorrentino answered *CA*'s questions by mail in June, 1984.

CA: You've named Ezra Pound, Robert Creeley, and William Carlos Williams as your big literary heroes. Who were the earlier influences, the ones who made you care more about writing than any other kind of life you might have gone into?

SORRENTINO: Given the fact that my attitude toward writing is that it is, for better or worse, an end in itself, and "powers" nothing in the actual world, it seems odd that the writers who moved me at about age eighteen were novelists of social protest—James T. Farrell, Theodore Dreiser, and John Steinbeck, and soon after, the Dos Passos of *Manhattan Transfer* and

U.S.A., which latter I still think is one of the formally great novels of the century. I was quite taken with the seediness of the worlds that they inscribed, and thought I saw the same sort of wretchedness in my own small parcel of this country.

CA: Black and White, White Sail, the orange poems in The Orangery, *"Blue Serge Gavotte" in* Blue Pastoral *are only a few of the more obvious examples of how color figures in your work. Did you, while you were keeping company with the artists who gravitated to New York in the 1950s and 1960s, ever consider becoming a painter yourself?*

SORRENTINO: I never considered it, since I have no visual talents. Colors in my work are, in essence, words that evoke, for me, "private" colors—and many other things.

CA: Music also has been important in your life and your writing. Do you play an instrument now, listen to music while you write, or enjoy music in some other very personal and regular way?

SORRENTINO: I wanted, when I was seventeen, to be a jazz musician, a tenor saxophonist to be precise, and studied, if that's the word, for a time. I thought that there could be no joy so great as playing jazz. I still think, I am convinced, that the composition of an improvised solo of, say, fifteen or twenty choruses, is without equal in terms of creativity. I have heard solos that are literally breathtaking—Monk, Rollins, Parker, Coleman, etc., unerringly building these incredible *things* that are sublime *the first time.* At present, I listen to music (not while I write): jazz of all kinds, but mostly that of "my" era—bop, hard bop, early free jazz; baroque, Mozart, classical modernists, rock, blues, and pop singers who sing the music of the great pop writers of "the golden age," e.g., Harold Arlen, Rodgers and Hart, Cole Porter, Kern, Gershwin, Arthur Schwartz, Noel Coward, etc., etc.

CA: Some of your books are especially handsome, quite literally—well designed, made of fine materials, and put together to stay. Have you had a hand in the making of them beyond the writing stage?

SORRENTINO: No hand, *per se,* but I've suggested jacket designs for, among others, *The Sky Changes* and *Steelwork.*

CA: Did seeing fiction from the editing end at Grove Press from 1965 to 1970 have much direct impact on your own writing?

SORRENTINO: Not at all. The only way that a writer can edit is to remove himself from the writing that he's working on as much as he can. The really good thing about my own editorial work at Grove was that the manuscripts that needed heavy editing (sometimes virtual rewrites) were always nonfiction manuscripts; they were of themselves remote from my fictional problems of the time. Grove's fiction list needed the lightest editing, sometimes only copy-editing. What, for instance, was an editor to say about works by Beckett, Ionesco, Robbe-Grillet, etc.? These writers know what they're doing. To edit them is an absurdity: "Well, Mr. Beckett, we like this *Molloy,* but don't you think it would be of more interest to the reader if we knew a little more about his childhood? I mean, somehow I can't *care* about him, you know what I mean?"

CA: Your writing—particularly the fiction—has attracted a lot of academic interest and been the subject of what seemed to

me as I was reading it like pounds of critical writing. How do you feel about all this analysis of your work?

SORRENTINO: It doesn't bother me in the least. Some of it is good, some bad, and some unbelievable. On the whole, it's better than the reviews of my work.

CA: One of the devices of your fiction—and a great joy for your readers—is the list, sometimes going on for pages and often very funny. The list of book titles and authors from Mulligan Stew *comes to my mind especially. Do you make lists for the fun of it and keep them around waiting for a place to crop up in a novel, or are they usually made up to fit a specific point you've written to?*

SORRENTINO: Made up to fit the structure or to add to it.

CA: Your novels usually have an intricate structure. How much is outlined—either in your mind or on paper—before you start to write?

SORRENTINO: I try to "draw the plans," so to speak, for all my novels before I begin to write, and then I usually work piecemeal; that is, I often work on what I know will be the end of the book before I "begin" the book. The plans, however, are flexible, to allow for changes in attitude and sudden ideas that I realize enhance my vision of what the overall work will look like. But I never write blindly, and have always had problems in understanding what writers mean when they talk about characters "striking out on their own." My characters do what I tell them to do. They are my property and they are totally unreal.

CA: Though you don't usually "tell stories" in the traditional sense, do you enjoy reading the work of any writers who do?

SORRENTINO: I do. Certain detective writers—Hammett, Chandler, Macdonald; Henry James; Dickens; Poe and Hawthorne and Melville, etc. etc.

CA: What publications do you read for short fiction, poetry, and criticism?

SORRENTINO: The *Review of Contemporary Fiction, Mississippi Review, Conjunctions, Modern Literature,* and some others. There are also many magazines that I read "in" when I see that the work of a writer I admire is included. I rarely, if ever, read magazines that feature nothing but poetry; it is all terribly depressing, unless it is just that I grow blind to young poets. I have a hard enough time keeping up with the work of my contemporaries.

CA: Is there anywhere you're aware of now the kind of camaraderie and common purpose among writers that helped get Neon *and* Kulchur *going? Any kind of "underground" or anti-Establishment stirring?*

SORRENTINO: I know of none, but I suspect that they must be there. Any I would know of, or be involved with, at the age of fifty-five, would be the wrong one, surely. Groups such as these are for the young.

CA: How well does teaching mesh with writing for you?

SORRENTINO: It gives me no intellectual problems. As always, and as with any job at all, teaching takes time away from writing. One must eat.

CA: Have your writing and your writing habits been much affected by being in California, being away from New York City?

SORRENTINO: I can't notice any change at all. My writing comes out of an imagined world that has existed for many years in my head. "Locale" has nothing to do with my books; that is, *where* I am affects them not at all.

CA: How do you find you're best able to help students in your writing courses? What are their most difficult problems in getting started as writers?

SORRENTINO: Dealing with structure is most helpful to them, or so I've found. "Editorial" assistance ("Don't you think that this dialogue goes on a little too long?") is, I find, useless, and makes students think of publishing—which they should avoid until they stop being students. The most difficult problem is working steadily and avoiding a conception of their writing as an "assignment" to be graded. All writing courses should be on a PASS/FAIL basis. The second common problem is to get over a sense of competition and the third is to stop thinking about what is still, I fear, called the "content" of a given piece. Form determines content.

CA: Are there works in progress or future plans that you'd like to talk about?

SORRENTINO: No.

CA: Is there any kind of writing you haven't done that you'd like to try?

SORRENTINO: No.

CA: Will your readers ever see any of the early autobiographical novel you wrote and then hid away somewhere? Is there any chance you'll at least mine it for material to make something else from?

SORRENTINO: No, but I "use" everything.

BIOGRAPHICAL/CRITICAL SOURCES—Books: David Ossmann, *The Sullen Art*, Corinth Books, 1963; Donald Phelps, *Covering Ground: Essays for Now*, Corinth Books, 1969; Jerome Klinkowitz, *Literary Disruptions: The Making of a Post-Contemporary American Fiction*, University of Illinois Press, 1975; *Contemporary Literary Criticism*, Volume III, 1975, Volume VII, 1977, Volume XIV, 1980, Volume XXII, 1982; Klinkowitz, *The Life of Fiction*, University of Illinois Press, 1977; *Dictionary of Literary Biography*, Volume V: *American Poets since World War II*, Gale, 1980; *Dictionary of Literary Biography Yearbook: 1980*, Gale, 1981.

Periodicals: *Nation*, October 14, 1961, June 21, 1971, August 21, 1972; *Washington Post Book World*, November 7, 1971, June 17, 1979, August 31, 1980, August 2, 1981, December 20, 1981, May 22, 1983; *Modern Occasions*, winter, 1972; *New York Times Book Review*, July 2, 1972, May 24, 1979, August 26, 1979, August 10, 1980, November 8, 1981, June 19, 1983; *Parnassus*, fall/winter, 1972; *Grosseteste Review*, Volume 6, numbers 1-4, 1973; *Village Voice*, November 22, 1973, May 28, 1979; *Hudson Review*, autumn, 1974; *Vort*, fall, 1974; *Antioch Review*, Volume 34, numbers 1-2, 1975; *American Poetry Review*, January-February, 1979; *New York Times*, May 24, 1979; *Los Angeles Times Book Review*, July

8, 1979; *New York Review of Books*, July 19, 1979, December 18, 1980; *Books and Art*, July 23, 1979.

Times Literary Supplement, May 2, 1980, July 10, 1981, December 4, 1981, January 29, 1982; *Saturday Review*, August, 1980; *Atlantic*, August, 1980; *Detroit News*, August 24, 1980; *Chicago Tribune Book World*, September 28, 1980, February 14, 1982; *Chicago Review*, autumn, 1980; *Review of Contemporary Fiction*, spring, 1981; *Extrapolation*, summer, 1981; *Times* (London), June 18, 1981; *Publishers Weekly*, May 27, 1983.

—*Sketch by Thomas Wiloch*

—*Interview by Jean W. Ross*

*   *   *

SOUTHERN, Eileen   1920-

PERSONAL: Born February 19, 1920, in Minneapolis, Minn.; daughter of Walter Wade (a teacher) and Lilla (Gibson) Jackson; married Joseph Southern (a college professor), August 22, 1942; children: April, Edward. *Education:* University of Chicago, B.A., 1940, M.A., 1941; New York University, Ph.D., 1961; studied piano at Chicago Musical College, Boston University, and Juilliard School. *Home:* 115-05 179th St., St. Albans, N.Y. 11434. *Office:* Department of Music, Harvard University, Cambridge, Mass. 02138.

CAREER: Concert pianist, 1940—; Prairie View State Normal and Industrial College (now Prairie View A&M University), Prairie View, Tex., instructor in music, 1941-42; Southern University, Baton Rouge, La., assistant professor of music, 1943-45; Claflin College, Orangeburg, S.C., instructor in music, 1947-49; Southern University, assistant professor of music, 1949-51; secondary school music teacher in public schools of New York, N.Y., 1954-60; Brooklyn College of the City University of New York, Brooklyn, N.Y., instructor, 1960-64, assistant professor of music, 1964-68; York College of the City University of New York, Jamaica, N.Y., associate professor, 1968-71, professor of music, 1972-75; Harvard University, Cambridge, Mass., professor of music and Afro-American studies, 1976—. Active in Girl Scouts of America, 1954-63.

MEMBER: International Musicological Society, American Musicological Society (member of board of directors, 1973-75), Association for the Study of Negro Life and History, Music Library Association, Renaissance Society, Authors Guild, National Association for the Advancement of Colored People, National Association of Negro Business and Professional Women's Clubs, Phi Beta Kappa, Alpha Kappa Alpha, Mu Sigma, Young Women's Christian Association (chairperson of management committee for Queens chapter, 1970-73).

AWARDS, HONORS: Citation from Voice of America for activities in promoting black music and culture; achievement award from National Association of Negro Musicians, 1971; award from American Society of Composers, Authors, and Publishers, 1973, for *The Music of Black Americans: A History*.

WRITINGS: The Buxheim Organ Book, Institute of Medieval Music, 1963; (contributor) Jan LaRue, editor, *Aspects of Medieval and Renaissance Music*, Norton, 1966; (contributor) Dominique-Rene de Lerma, editor, *Black Music in Our Culture*, Kent State University Press, 1970; *The Music of Black Americans: A History*, Norton, 1971, revised edition, 1983; (editor) *Readings in Black American Music*, Norton, 1971, revised edition, 1983; *Anonymous Pieces in the Ms. El Escorial*

IV. a.24, American Institute of Musicology, 1981; *Biographical Dictionary of Afro-American and African Musicians*, Greenwood Press, 1982. Contributor to encyclopedias and to scholarly journals. Founder and editor, *The Black Perspective in Music*, 1973—.

WORK IN PROGRESS: Computer-Assisted Index of Anonymous Chansons of the Mid-Fifteenth Century.

BIOGRAPHICAL/CRITICAL SOURCES: New York Post, July 22, 1971.

*   *   *

SPARTACUS, Deutero
    See FANTHORPE, R(obert) Lionel

*   *   *

SPIEL, Hilde (Maria)   1911-

PERSONAL: Born October 19, 1911, in Vienna, Austria; daughter of Hugo F. (a scientist) and Marie (Gutfeld) Spiel; married Peter de Mendelssohn (a writer), October 30, 1936; married second husband, Hans Flesch Edler von Brunningen (a writer), February 7, 1971; children: (first marriage) Christine, Anthony Felix. *Education:* Vienna University, Doctor of Philosophy (with honors), 1936. *Politics:* Independent. *Religion:* Roman Catholic. *Home:* Cottagegasse 65/II/3, Vienna XIX, Austria. *Agent:* Dagmar Henne, Seestrasse 6, Munich, Germany.

CAREER: Writer. Has worked in broadcasting, mainly for Norddeutscher Rundfunk, RIAS Berlin and Bayerischer Rundfunk.

MEMBER: P.E.N. (general secretary for Austria, 1966-72; vice-president, 1972), International Writers in Prision Committee, German Academy for Language and Literature, Vienna Concordia, Bavarian Academy.

AWARDS, HONORS: Julius Reich Prize (Vienna), 1933, for *Kati auf der Bruecke;* honorary professorship, awarded by president of Austrian Republic; Cross of Merit, first class, awarded by president of Federal Republic of Germany, 1962; Salzburg Critic Prize; Austrian Cross for Arts and Literature, 1972; prize, City of Vienna, 1976.

WRITINGS: Kati auf der Bruecke (novel), Paul Zsolnay, 1933; *Verwirrung am Wolfgangsee* (novel), R. A. Hoeger, 1935, reissued with slight alterations as *Sommer am Wolfgangsee*, Rowohlt, 1961; *Flute and Drums* (novel), Hutchinson, 1939.

Der Park und die Wildnis, zur Situation der neueren englischen Literatur (essays), C. H. Beck, 1953; (author of text) Elisabeth Niggemeyer, *London: Stadt, Menschen, Augenblicke* (book of illustrations), Sueddeutscher, 1956; *Sir Laurence Olivier*, Rembrandt, 1958.

Welt im Widerschein (essays), C. H. Beck, 1960; (compiler and author of introduction) *England erzaehlt: Achtzehn Erzaehlungen*, S. Fischer, 1960; *The Darkened Room* (novel), Methuen, 1961; *Fanny von Arnstein oder Die Emanzipation: Ein Frauenleben an der Zeitenwende, 1758-1818* (biography), S. Fischer, 1962; (editor and author of commentary and documentation) Shakespeare, *Koenig Richard III*, Ullstein, 1964; (editor and author of introduction) *Der Wiener Kongress in Augenzeugenberichten*, Karl Rauch, 1965, 3rd edition, 1966, translation by Richard H. Weber published as *The Congress of Vienna: An Eyewitness Account*, Chilton, 1968; (author of

introduction) Franz Vogler, *Verliebt in Doebling: Die Doerfer unter dem Himmel* (book of illustrations), Jugend und Volk, 1965; *Lisas Zimmer* (novel), Nymphenburger, 1965; *Rueckkehr nach Wien* (diary), Nymphenburger, 1968; (translator with Otto Breicha and Georg Eisler) *Ver Sacrum: Neue Hefte fuer Kunst und Literatur*, Jugend und Volk, 1969.

(Editor) *Wien/Spektrum einer Stadt*, Nymphenburger, 1971; *Staedte und Menschen*, Jugend und Volk, 1972; (editor) *Die Zeitgenossische Literatur Oesterreichs*, Kindler, 1976; *Kleine Schritte*, Edition Spangenberg, 1976. Also author of *Mirko und Franca, Die Fruechte des Wohlstands*, and *In meinem Garten*, all published by Nymphenburger. Contributor to *New Statesman, Times Literary Supplement, Guardian, Frankfurter Allgemeine Zeitung, Monat, Weltwoche, Sueddeutsche Zeitung*, and other periodical publications.

*   *   *

SPINOSSIMUS
    See WHITE, William, Jr.

*   *   *

STABLER, Arthur P(hillips)   1919-

PERSONAL: Born April 23, 1919, in Sandy Spring, Md.; son of Frederic and Mary (Phillips) Stabler; married Jane Gamble, April 26, 1944 (divorced, 1974); married Nancy Nadas, June 25, 1975; children: (first marriage) Frederic, Jennifer. *Education:* University of Pennsylvania, B.A., 1941, M.A., 1947; University of Virginia, Ph.D., 1958. *Politics:* Liberal. *Home:* 10 Esplanade, Pacific Grove, Calif. 93950.

CAREER: Bowdoin College, Brunswick, Me., instructor in French, 1947-49; University of Virginia, Charlottesville, instructor in French, 1949-51, 1956-58; Denison University, Granville, Ohio, instructor in French and German, 1952-56; North Texas State College (now University), Denton, assistant professor of French and German, 1958-59; Lake Erie College, Painesville, Ohio, associate professor of foreign languages and director of language skills, 1959-61; University of Massachusetts—Amherst, associate professor of French, 1961-62; Washington State University, Pullman, associate professor, 1962-65, professor of foreign languages and literatures, 1966-82; Carmel (Calif.) School District Adult Program, French teacher, 1984—. *Military service:* U.S. Army, Infantry, 1943-46. U.S. Army Reserve, 1951-66; military intelligence; became captain.

MEMBER: Modern Language Association of America, American Association of Teachers of French, Renaissance Society of America, Philological Association of the Pacific Coast, Western Shakespeare Seminar, Phi Beta Kappa.

AWARDS, HONORS: Medal of Alliance Francaise, 1940; Fulbright scholar at University of Grenoble, 1951-52; grants from National Endowment for the Humanities, 1979, and Social Sciences and Humanities Research Council of Canada, 1984, to research *Andre Thevet on North America*.

WRITINGS: The Legend of Marguerite de Roberval, Washington State University Press, 1972; *Four French Renaissance Plays*, Washington State University Press, 1978; (with Roger Schlesinger) *Andre Thevet on North America*, McGill-Queens University Press, 1985. Contributor to *The Americas*, 1985.

Also contributor to Modern Language Association publications, *Studies in Philology, Shakespeare Studies, Etudes Anglaises, Etudes rabelaisiennes, Bibliotheque d'Humanisme et

Renaissance, and other journals. Contributing editor, *Shakespeare Newsletter,* 1973-82.

WORK IN PROGRESS: A "Great American novel."

AVOCATIONAL INTERESTS: Gardening.

BIOGRAPHICAL/CRITICAL SOURCES: Shakespeare Newsletter, December, 1972; *New England Quarterly,* June, 1973.

* * *

STAHL, O(scar) Glenn 1910-

PERSONAL: Born April 30, 1910, in Evansville, Ind.; son of Oscar A. (a business executive) and Mayme (Wittmer) Stahl; married Marie Jane Rueter, June 26, 1934; children: Elaine Marie (Mrs. Gerhard W. Leo), Alan G. *Education:* Evansville College (now University of Evansville), B.A., 1931; University of Wisconsin, M.A., 1933; New York University, Ph.D., 1936. *Politics:* Independent. *Religion:* Presbyterian. *Home and office:* 3600 North Piedmont St., Arlington, Va. 22207.

CAREER: Tennessee Valley Authority, Washington, D.C., personnel worker, 1935-41; Federal Security Agency (now Department of Health, Education and Welfare), Washington, D.C., chief of classification and deputy director of personnel, 1941-48, director of personnel, 1948-51; Federal Personnel Council, Washington, D.C., executive vice-chairman, 1951-54; U.S. Civil Service Commission, Washington, D.C., director of bureau of policies and standards, 1955-69; International Personnel Management Association, Washington, D.C., Washington representative, 1971-73, special consultant, 1973-76; Public Administration Service-Governmental Affairs Institute, Washington, D.C., special consultant, 1973-75.

Faculty member at New York University, 1933-35, University of Tennessee, 1939, and the graduate school of the U.S. Department of Agriculture, 1949-49; adjunct professor of public administration at American University, 1949-69. Visiting lecturer at Florida State University, University of Southern California, University of Chicago, Dartmouth College, University of Virginia, University of Wisconsin, Princeton University, Karachi University, New Delhi University, Tribhuvan University, Nova University, University of Denver, University of Pittsburgh, George Mason University, and Mississippi State University. A representative of the United States at international conferences in Ethiopia, Costa Rica, Ireland, the Soviet Union, Austria, Germany, and Venezuela; United Nations technical advisor to Venezuela, 1958 and 1972; Ford Foundation consultant to India and Nepal 1968, 1969, and 1971, and to Pakistan, 1974; Agency for International Development advisor to Pakistan, 1969, 1971. Member of Arlington County School Board, 1948-50; president of Arlington Committee to Preserve Public Schools, 1958-61.

MEMBER: International Personnel Management Association (member of executive council, 1951-54; president, 1965-66), American Political Science Association, American Society for Public Administration.

AWARDS, HONORS: U.S. Civil Service Commission distinguished service award, 1960; Stockberger Award from Society for Personnel Administration, 1961; Career Service Award of National Civil Service League, 1967; honorary life membership in International Personnel Management Association, 1968; University of Evansville, medal of honor, 1981, and LL.D., 1984.

WRITINGS: Training Career Public Servants for the City of New York, New York University Press, 1936; (with William E. Mosher and J. Donald Kingsley) *Public Personnel Administration,* 3rd edition (Stahl was not associated with earlier editions), Harper, 1950, 4th edition (sole author), 1956, 8th edition, 1983; *The Personnel Job of Government Managers,* International Personnel Management Association, 1971; (coeditor) *Police Personnel Administration,* Police Foundation, 1974; (editor) *Improving Public Services,* International Conference on Improving Public Management and Performance, 1979; *Frontier Mother,* Christopher, 1979.

Contributor of over ninety articles to journals. Editor of *Personnel Administration,* 1945-55.

SIDELIGHTS: O. Glenn Stahl's *Public Personnel Administration* has been published in Spanish and Japanese.

* * *

STAINBACK, Susan Bray 1947-

PERSONAL: Born May 22, 1947, in Baltimore, Md.; daughter of William DeVaughn (an optician) and Cleo (Selig) Bray; married William Clarence Stainback (a university professor), December 16, 1967. *Education:* Radford College, B.S., 1968; University of Virginia, M.Ed., 1971, Ed.D., 1973. *Religion:* Catholic. *Home:* 2922 Minnetonka Dr., Cedar Falls, Iowa 50613. *Office:* Department of Special Education, University of Northern Iowa, Cedar Falls, Iowa 50614.

CAREER: Albemarle County (Va.) public schools, teacher of intermediate age educable mentally retarded students, 1968-70; held part-time positions as consultative specialist, behavior modification consultant, research assistant, and research associate at various school systems in Virginia, 1971-73; Hope Haven Children's Hospital, Jacksonville, Fla., educational and behavioral specialist, 1973-74; University of Northern Iowa, Cedar Falls, assistant professor, 1974-78, associate professor of special education, 1978-79; Florida Atlantic University, Center of Excellence, Boca Raton, associate professor, 1979-80; University of Northern Iowa, associate professor, 1980-83, professor of special education, 1983—. Visiting lecturer in special education, University of Virginia, summer, 1973. Consultant to numerous national, state, and local organizations. *Member:* American Association for the Severely and Profoundly Handicapped, Council for Exceptional Children, Council for Children with Behavioral Disorders, Teacher Educators in Severe Behavior Disorders.

WRITINGS: (With J. S. Payne, R. A. Payne, and husband, William Clarence Stainback) *Establishing a Token Economy in the Classroom,* C. E. Merrill, 1973; (with W. C. Stainback) *Classroom Discipline: A Positive Approach,* C. C Thomas, 1974; (with Harriet Healy) *The Severely Motorically Impaired Child,* C. C Thomas, 1980; (with W. C. Stainback) *Educating Children with Severe Maladaptive Behavior,* Grune, 1980; (with Harriet Healy) *Teaching Eating Skills,* C. C Thomas, 1983; (with W. C. Stainback) *Integrating Students with Severe Handicaps into Regular Schools,* Council for Exceptional Children, 1984.

Also author, with W. C. Stainback, of monograph on background music in the educational setting, 1974. Contributor, with W. C. Stainback, of chapters to numerous textbooks and of more than sixty articles to professional publications, including *Virginia Journal of Education, Education and Training of the Mentally Retarded, Exceptional Children, Journal of*

Abnormal Child Psychology, Teacher Educator, Journal for the Association of the Severely Handicapped, and *Behavioral Disorders.* Consulting editor of numerous journals, including *Journal for the Association of the Severely Handicapped, Education and Training of the Mentally Retarded, Education Review, Journal of Education and Treatment of Children, Behavioral Disorders,* and *Teaching Exceptional Children;* assistant editor, *Education Review,* 1970-71.

WORK IN PROGRESS: Research activities with W. C. Stainback regarding interaction behaviors of the handicapped; a book with W. C. Stainback on methodological considerations in qualitative research.

SIDELIGHTS: Susan Bray Stainback told *CA:* "In education, writing activities provide a great deal of personal satisfaction. They provide an opportunity to contribute ideas and varying perspectives as well as keep in touch with the work of other professionals in a critical, ever-changing field. They also provide for me personally an opportunity to work closely with my husband in attempting to produce a product we can both be proud of, though never allowing either of us to become stagnant in our profession or our friendship."

AVOCATIONAL INTERESTS: Summer lake retreat, family, friends, animals.

* * *

STAINBACK, William (Clarence) 1943-

PERSONAL: Born April 13, 1943, in Emporia, Va.; son of Willard T. and Maybelle (Moore) Stainback; married Susan Bray (a professor of education), December 16, 1967. *Education:* Atlantic Christian College, B.S., 1966; Radford College, M.S., 1967; University of Virginia, Ed.D., 1971. *Politics:* Democrat. *Home:* 2922 Minnetonka Dr., Cedar Falls, Iowa 50613. *Office:* Department of Special Education, University of Northern Iowa, Cedar Falls, Iowa 50613.

CAREER: Virginia State College (now Virginia State University), Petersburg, assistant professor of special education, 1971-73; University of Florida, Gainesville, assistant professor of special education, 1973-74; University of Northern Iowa, Cedar Falls, professor of special education, 1974—. *Member:* American Association for the Education of the Severely and Profoundly Handicapped, Council for Exceptional Children.

WRITINGS—All with wife, Susan Bray Stainback: (And with J. S. Payne and R. A. Payne) *Establishing a Token Economy in the Classroom,* C. E. Merrill, 1973; *Classroom Discipline: A Positive Approach,* C. C Thomas, 1975; *Educating Children with Severe Maladaptive Behavior,* Grune, 1980; *Integrating Students with Severe Handicaps into Regular Schools,* Council for Exceptional Children, 1984. Contributor to *Exceptional Children* and *Journal of the Association for the Severely Handicapped.*

* * *

STALVEY, Lois Mark 1925-

PERSONAL: Born August 22, 1925, in Milwaukee, Wis.; daughter of Aloyisius Leo and Gertrude Katherine (Wolf) Mark; married Conrad J. Stawski, November 13, 1943; married Bennett Stalvey, Jr. (a government executive), May 14, 1955 (divorced, 1977); children: (second marriage) Bennett III, Noah Wolf, Sarah Lois. *Education:* Attended public schools in Milwaukee, Wis. *Politics:* Democrat. *Religion:* "Protestant-Ag-

nostic." *Home and office:* 580 Mountain Shadows Dr., Sedona, Ariz. 86336. *Agent:* Harold Ober Associates, Inc., 40 East 49th St., New York, N.Y. 10017.

CAREER: Lois Mark & Associates (advertising firm), Milwaukee, Wis., president, 1946-54; McCann-Erickson (advertising firm), Chicago, Ill., television and radio writer and producer, 1954-55. Instructor in creative writing and news reporting at Community College of Philadelphia; visiting professor and author-in-residence at Northern Arizona University, summers, beginning 1984. Lecturer at colleges and civic groups nationally. Consultant, Ramsdell-Buckley, 1962-70. State advisory committee member, U.S. Civil Rights Commission, 1965-71.

MEMBER: Authors Guild, Authors League of America.

AWARDS, HONORS: Erma Proetz Award, 1949; Philadelphia Human Relations Commission Award, 1971; Delta Kappa Gama educator award, 1975, for *Getting Ready: The Education of a White Family in Inner-City Schools.*

WRITINGS: The Education of a WASP, Morrow, 1970; *Getting Ready: The Education of a White Family in Inner-City Schools,* Morrow, 1974; *The Education of an Ordinary Woman* (autobiography), Atheneum, 1982. Contributor to *Reader's Digest, Woman's Day, Family Circle, Good Housekeeping,* and other periodicals. Book reviewer, *St. Louis Post Dispatch,* 1970—.

WORK IN PROGRESS: A novel entitled *Goodbye, Dear;* a volume of short stories.

SIDELIGHTS: Reviewing Lois Mark Stalvey's *The Education of an Ordinary Woman,* Anne Wittels comments in the *Los Angeles Times* that "Stalvey's life is not open to argument." Unhappy in childhood, the author became an overachiever in high school. Working as an advertising copywriter for the Gimbels department store after graduation, Stalvey realized that if she attended college she probably would end up, four years later, applying for the type of job she already held. Instead, she stayed on at Gimbels and married her first husband, an Air Force cadet, during her late teens. When he went overseas, she continued to write ad copy. By age 21 she had opened her own agency, Lois Mark & Associates.

The conclusions Stalvey draws from her experiences, Wittels believes, are open to argument. "The carp is with her Queen Bee approach to success," the critic explains. "Despite all her extraordinary achievements, she resolutely insists she is an ordinary woman. . . . Stalvey obdurately assumes everyone shares her courage, energy, intelligence, luck, strength, talent—and chutzpah." Wittels maintains that the author makes no allowances for prejudice and discrimination against women in today's job market.

The Education of a WASP relates Stalvey's family's experience as part of an integrated Philadelphia neighborhood. A *Saturday Review* critic calls the book "often poignant, always precise and explicit," adding that it "is a book for all colors." The author further explores the topics of prejudice and discrimination in *Getting Ready: The Education of a White Family in Inner City Schools.* In the book, "written in simple, straightforward prose, we watch [the author's] three children, 'Spike,' Noah and Sarah, grow up from nursery school through high school in the increasingly black city schools of Philadelphia," explains Rosemary R. Ruether in *New Republic.* "What the Stalveys discover is that, no matter how much the middle-class white family tries to share the experiences of blacks, it remains protected, not only by its unconscious racial myopias, but by the automatic caste privileges that white middle-class children continue to enjoy, even in a largely black inner-city school.''

Stalvey told *CA* that ''at last'' she has arranged the ''perfect writer's life: the serenity of a small Arizona town in which to work and summers of sharing my experiences with students. The teaching assuages the isolation of writing and the writing benefits from three months of interaction with students. Also, after three books based on fact, my 'creative attic' seems to be cleared out. With great excitement, I am now totally involved in dealing with the truths of fiction.''

BIOGRAPHICAL/CRITICAL SOURCES: Washington Post, June 6, 1970; *Best Sellers,* July 1, 1970; *Saturday Review,* November 14, 1970; *St. Louis Post-Dispatch,* April 9, 1974; *New Republic,* April 20, 1974; *Time,* April 22, 1974; Lois Mark Stalvey, *The Education of an Ordinary Woman,* Atheneum, 1982; *Library Journal,* February 15, 1982; *Los Angeles Times,* April 15, 1982.

* * *

STAPLES, Reginald Thomas 1911-
(Howard Bridges, James Sinclair, Robert Tyler Stevens)

PERSONAL: Born November 26, 1911, in London, England; son of William George (a naval officer) and Mary Jane (Brady) Staples; married Florence Anne Hume (a company director), June 12, 1937; children: Jeffery Charles, *Education:* Attended secondary school in London, England. *Politics:* ''Distrust modern politics. Distrust all politicians even more.'' *Religion:* Anglican. *Home:* 52 Dome Hill, Caterham, Surrey CR3 6EB, England. *Agent:* Sheila Watson, 26 Charing Cross Rd., London WC2, England. *Office:* Vista Sports Ltd., Sydenham Rd., Croydon, Surrey, England.

CAREER: Winemaker's apprentice at Pedro Domecq (winemaking firm), 1928-30; worked in office for Blue Star Shipping Co., 1930-40, 1946-50; assistant editor for Home Publishing Co., 1950-53; Staples & Hancock Ltd., founder, 1953, director, 1953-66; managing director of Town & Country Studios Ltd. (commercial photographers), 1966—. Chairman of board of directors of Fullerton & Lloyd Ltd. (magazine publishers), 1953—, and of Vista Sports Ltd., 1970—. *Military service:* British Army, Royal Artillery, 1940-46; served in the Middle East; became sergeant.

MEMBER: Brevet Flying Club.

WRITINGS—All historical novels; under pseudonym James Sinclair: *Warrior Queen* (the story of Boadicea), Souvenir Press, 1977; *Canis the Warrior,* Souvenir Press, 1979.

Under pseudonym Robert Tyler Stevens: *The Summer Day Is Done,* Doubleday, 1976; *Flight from Bucharest,* Souvenir Press, 1977; *Appointment in Sarajevo,* Souvenir Press, 1978; *Women of Texas,* Souvenir Press, 1979; *The Fields of Yesterday,* Hamlyn, 1982; *Shadows in the Afternoon,* Hamlyn, 1983; *The Hostage,* Hamlyn, in press.

WORK IN PROGRESS: The Woman in Berlin and *The Cottage,* both under the pseudonym Robert Tyler Stevens.

SIDELIGHTS: Reginald Thomas Staples told *CA:* ''My spare time pleasure—writing. Wrote millions of words of rubbish over a period of many years. Came down from the mountain of garbage five years ago to apply myself more seriously. Still wrote rubbish but it read better. *Woman* magazine had a rush of blood and accepted *The Summer Day Is Done* for serialisa-

tion, giving it press and television coverage. Same magazine has [since] serialised *Appointment in Sarajevo,* story based on the assassination of Franz Ferdinand in 1914, and *The Fields of Yesterday.*

''Currently working on *The Woman in Berlin,* a story featuring the mysterious nature of events relating to 'Anastasia' in 1925. Am also, currently, wondering how long it will take publishers to achieve what they seem set on, to offer the reading public two kinds of books only—the hyped novels and the autobiographies of discarded mistresses.''

AVOCATIONAL INTERESTS: ''Spare time pursuits—squash, tennis, badminton, hockey, soccer, cricket, golf. Gave them all up in turn, except golf and tennis, to save myself dropping dead while life was still beautiful.''

* * *

STEEL, Tex
See ROSS, W(illiam) E(dward) D(aniel)

* * *

STEIN, Susan M. 1942-

PERSONAL: Born April 5, 1942, in Springfield, Mass.; daughter of Edward Joseph (an accountant) and Fannie (a syndicated columnist; maiden name Emerick) Gleeson; married Charles H. Stein (a teacher), August 17, 1963; children: Edward J., Margaret D., Paul C. *Education:* St. Louis University, B.S., 1962, M.A., 1964; also attended Creighton University, 1967, 1975-76, and University of Nebraska at Omaha, 1970. *Religion:* Roman Catholic. *Home:* 9834 Ruggles St., Omaha, Neb. 68134.

CAREER: University of Missouri—St. Louis, instructor in English, 1964-66; University of Nebraska, Lincoln, instructor in English, 1967-68; University of Nebraska at Omaha, instructor in English, 1974-75; Creighton University, Omaha, instructor in English and education, 1975-76; Brownell-Talbot School, Omaha, teacher of English, 1976-83, chairman of department, 1978-83; Creighton Preparatory School, Omaha, college teacher of English, 1983—. Consultant in business writing, 1982—.

MEMBER: Nebraska Writers Guild.

WRITINGS: (With Sarah T. Lottick) *Three, Four, Open the Door: Creative Fun for Young Children,* Follett, 1971; *Effective Writing,* Farm Credit Banks Eighth District, 1984. Author of a weekly humor column, Omaha *World Herald,* 1973—. Contributor to regional periodicals and newspapers.

WORK IN PROGRESS: A collection of humorous writings.

SIDELIGHTS: Susan M. Stein offers this advice on writing a humorous column: ''Jot down phrases keynoting your week. This can include events, overheard remarks, something you've read; usually something that's happened to you personally will do. Then start writing on one of these phrases. Don't worry about opening sentences; they invariably get rewritten. Try to have a sharp, zingy introduction and then tie the conclusion to it. Keep the conclusion upbeat. Avoid the mawkish and the maudlin. Shun the role of the doomsayer; be an observer. Poke fun at yourself but remember the audience will identify with you, so don't play the complete idiot. Be concrete and specific and, after the first draft, start pruning, simplifying. Go for short sentences and short words. The happy part about being a humorist is knowing that each crisis—such as the dishwasher flooding all over the kitchen floor in the midst of a formal dinner—is at least fodder for a column.''

*   *   *

STEINBERG, Danny D(avid Charles)   1931-

PERSONAL: Born August 10, 1931, in Toronto, Ontario, Canada; son of William and Rose (Davis) Steinberg; married Miho Tanaka (a university professor), November 2, 1962; children: Kimio (son). *Education:* University of British Columbia, B.A., 1960; University of Hawaii, M.A., 1964, Ph.D., 1966. *Home:* 4-419-2 Ikebukuro, Hata Ikebukuro Haitsu, Toshima-ku, Tokyo 171, Japan. *Office:* Rikkyo University, Nishi Ikebukuro Toshima-ku, Tokyo 171, Japan.

CAREER: University of Illinois at Urbana-Champaign, Institute of Communications Research, postdoctoral fellow, 1967-69; University of Hawaii, Honolulu, assistant professor, 1969-72, associate professor, 1973-79, professor of English as a second language, 1980-82; Rikkyo University, Tokyo, Japan, professor, 1983—.

MEMBER: American Psychological Association, Japan Psychological Association.

AWARDS, HONORS: University of Hawaii Research Council grant, 1969, 1970, 1971; U.S. Office of Education grant, 1971, 1980.

WRITINGS: (Editor with L. Jakobovits and contributor) *Semantics: An Interdisciplinary Reader in Philosophy, Linguistics, and Psychology,* Cambridge University Press, 1971; *Psycholinguistics: Language, Mind and World,* Longman, 1982. Contributor to *Journal of Experimental Psychology, Journal of Verbal Learning and Verbal Behavior, American Journal of Psychology,* and *Japanese Journal of Educational Psychology.*

*   *   *

STEINER, Peter O(tto)   1922-

PERSONAL: Born July 9, 1922, in New York, N.Y.; son of Otto Davidson and Ruth (Wurzburger) Steiner; married Ruth Riggs, December 20, 1947 (divorced, 1967); married Patricia Owen, June 2, 1968; children: (first marriage) Alison Ruth, David Denison. *Education:* Oberlin College, A.B. (magna cum laude), 1943; Harvard University, M.A., 1949, Ph.D., 1950. *Office:* Literature, Science and the Arts Bldg., University of Michigan, Ann Arbor, Mich. 48109.

CAREER: University of California, Berkeley, instructor, 1949-50, assistant professor of economics, 1950-57; University of Wisconsin—Madison, associate professor, 1957-59, professor of economics, 1959-68; University of Michigan, Ann Arbor, professor of economics and law, 1968—, chairman of department of economics, 1971-74, dean of College of Literature, Science, and the Arts, 1981—. Visiting professor, University of Nairobi, 1974-75. *Military service:* U.S. Naval Reserve, 1944-46; became lieutenant. *Member:* American Economic Association, American Statistical Association, American Association of University Professors (president, 1976-78). *Awards, honors:* Social Science Research Council faculty research fellow, 1956-59; Guggenheim fellow, 1960-61; Ford Foundation faculty research fellow, 1965-66.

WRITINGS: (With William Goldner) *Productivity,* University of California Press, 1952; *An Introduction to the Analysis of Time Series,* Rinehart, 1956; (with Robert Dorfman) *The Economic Status of the Aged,* University of California Press, 1957;

(with Richard G. Lipsey) *Economics,* Harper, 1966, 7th edition, 1984; *On the Process of Planning,* Center of Economic Planning and Research, 1968; *Public Expenditure Budgeting,* Studies of Government Finance, Brookings Institution, 1969; (with Blinder, Solow, Break, and Netzer) *The Economics of Public Finance,* Brookings Institution, 1974; *Mergers: Motives, Effects, Policies,* University of Michigan Press, 1975; *Workable Competition in the Radio Broadcasting Industry,* Arno Press, 1979.

Contributor: Wilma Donahue and Clark Tibbits, editors, *The New Frontiers of Aging,* University of Michigan Press, 1957; *The Price Statistics of the Federal Government,* National Bureau of Economic Research, 1961; S. C. Smith and E. N. Castle, editors, *Water Resource Development,* Iowa State University Press, 1964; John Meyer, editor, *Transportation Economics,* Columbia University Press, 1965; Allen V. Kneese and Smith, editors, *Water Research,* Johns Hopkins Press, 1966; Paul MacAvoy, editor, *The Crisis of the Regulatory Commissions,* Norton, 1970; Harry M. Trebing, editor, *Essays on Public Utility Pricing and Regulation,* Institute of Public Utilities, Michigan State University, 1971; *The Economics of Public Finance,* Studies of Government Finance, Brookings Institution, 1974. Contributor of more than fifty articles and reviews to economics and law journals.

BIOGRAPHICAL/CRITICAL SOURCES: University Bookman, winter, 1968.

*   *   *

STEINER, Wendy   1949-

PERSONAL: Born March 20, 1949, in Winnipeg, Manitoba, Canada; came to the United States in 1970; daughter of William Harrison (an educational psychologist) and Ida (Abramson) Lucow; married Peter Steiner (a professor of Slavic language and literature), February 2, 1973. *Education:* McGill University, B.A., 1970; Yale University, M.Phil., 1972, Ph.D., 1974. *Home:* 4817 Trinity Pl., Philadelphia, Pa. 19143. *Office:* Department of English, University of Pennsylvania, Philadelphia, Pa. 19104.

CAREER: Yale University, New Haven, Conn., assistant professor of English, 1974-76; University of Michigan, Ann Arbor, assistant professor of English, 1976-79; University of Pennsylvania, Philadelphia, assistant professor, 1979-82, professor of English, 1982—. Member of several committees; lecturer.

MEMBER: Academy of Literary Studies, Modern Language Association of America, Semiotic Society of America (member of executive board, 1978-80).

AWARDS, HONORS: Woodrow Wilson fellowship, 1970-71; doctoral fellowships, Yale University, 1970-74, and Canada Council, 1971-74; Rackham research fellowship, University of Michigan, 1977; Josephine Nevins Keale fellowship, University of Michigan, 1978-79; National Endowment for the Humanities research stipend, 1980; research fellowship, University of Pennsylvania, 1981.

WRITINGS: (Translator from the French) Jan Mukarovsky, *Structure, Sign and Function,* Yale University Press, 1977; *Exact Resemblance to Exact Resemblance: The Literary Portraiture of Gertrude Stein,* Yale University Press, 1978; (translator from the Czech with husband, Peter Steiner) *Selected Writings of Roman Jakobson,* Volume V, Mouton, 1979.

(Editor) *The Sign in Music and Literature,* Texas University Press, 1981; (editor) *Image and Code,* Michigan Studies in the Humanities, 1981; (translator from the French) Sergej Karcevskii, *The Prague School: Selected Writings, 1929-1946,* Texas University Press, 1982; *The Colors of Rhetoric: Problems in the Relation between Modern Literature and Painting,* University of Chicago Press, 1982; (author of introduction) Gertrude Stein, *Lectures in America,* Beacon Press, 1985.

Contributor: (With P. Steiner) Jan Mukarovsky, *On Poetic Language,* [Lisse, Netherlands], 1976; R. W. Baily and others, editors, *The Sign: Semiotics around the World,* Michigan Studies in the Humanities, 1978; Andre Helbo, editor, *Le Champ semiologique,* Le Creuset (Brussels, Belgium), 1979; John Odmark, editor, *Linguistic and Literary Studies in Eastern Europe,* Walter Benjamins, 1979; Karl Menges and Daniel Rancour-Laferriere, editors, *Axia,* Akademischer Verlag Stuttgart, 1981; Miroslav Cervenka and others, editors, *The Structure of the Literary Process,* John Benjamins, 1982. Contributor to journals, including *New Literary History, Critical Inquiry, Semiotica,* and *Yale University Library Gazette.*

WORK IN PROGRESS: Storied Pictures: Narrativity in Literature and Painting; contributing to Volume V of *The Cambridge History of American Literature;* contributing to *Columbia Literary History of the United States.*

SIDELIGHTS: Wendy Steiner told *CA:* "Gertrude Stein interested me as a problem in criticism because she strikes everyone intuitively as crucial to modernism, yet defies conventional literary-critical explanation. She seemed a perfect case—and a very deserving one—to examine in the light of structuralist and semiotic methodology, and I have been amply rewarded for this attention with surprising insights into Stein, modern literature in general, and the very methodologies that I was so interested in applying. Out of this work has come my current preoccupation with the relation between modern painting and literature, for Stein and cubism were closely connected. This new topic, involving concrete poetry, nonsense in the two arts, William Carlos Williams and Brueghel, imagism, vorticism, and other modern schools, will be my next full-length study."

*   *   *

STEPHENS, Edna Buell   1903-

PERSONAL: Born June 15, 1903, in Spiro, Okla.; daughter of Charles Ross and Beulah (Hickman) Stephens. *Education:* University of Arkansas, B.A., 1927, M.A., 1933, Ph.D., 1961; University of Colorado, graduate study, 1939, 1954; University of North Carolina, graduate study, 1946-48; attended International Summer School, Meyerhofen, Austria, 1951. *Politics:* Liberal Democrat. *Religion:* Methodist. *Home:* 2616 Tanglewood St., Commerce, Tex. 75428.

CAREER: Teacher in public schools of New Mexico, 1927-31; John Brown University, Siloam Springs, Ark., instructor in Spanish, 1933-37; teacher in public schools in Arkansas, 1938-39; teacher in public schools in Texas, 1939-42; U.S. Office of Censorship, El Paso, Tex., deputy assistant censor of Spanish, 1942-45; El Paso High School, El Paso, teacher, 1945-49; Frank Phillips College, Borger, Texas, instructor in English, 1949-61; East Texas State University, Commerce, 1961—, professor of English, 1968-73, professor emeritus, 1973—.

MEMBER: American Association of University Women (president of Commerce Branch, 1975-76), South Central Modern Language Association, Texas Association of College Teachers, Sigma Tau Delta, Delta Kappa Gamma (treasurer, 1962-64).

AWARDS, HONORS: East Texas State University research grant, 1970, for research on the Haiku and Zen in Hawaiian and Japanese libraries.

WRITINGS: John Gould Fletcher, Twayne, 1967; (contributor) Wolfgang Bernard Fleischman, editor, *Encyclopedia of World Literature in the 20th Century,* Ungar, 1967; *Plum Petals, and Other Poems,* privately printed, 1971; (contributor) John A. Garroty and Edward T. James, editors, *Dictionary of American Biography,* Scribner, 1974; (contributor) *Dictionary of Literary Biography,* Volume IV: *American Writers in Paris, 1920-1939,* Gale, 1980; *Songs of Four Seasons,* privately printed, 1981.

Contributor of poems to *Southwest Review, Kaleidoscope, Florida Magazine of Verse, Backroads,* and *Forthcoming;* contributor of book reviews to El Paso *Times;* contributor of article to *Kappa Delta Gamma Bulletin.* Former book review editor, *Ozark American;* editor, *Texas Bulletin,* American Association of University Women, 1948.

WORK IN PROGRESS: A book of poetry; *Influence of Zen Buddhism on American Poetry.*

SIDELIGHTS: Edna Buell Stephens writes *CA* that her "major interests include modern poetry, the haiku, language study, Zen Buddhism, Oriental art and philosophy (especially Chinese and Japanese), politics, gardening, ecology. I have done research in Hawaii and Japan, including at the East-West Center, Hamilton Library, and Sinclair Library at the University of Hawaii, the University of Tokyo Library, National Diet Library (Tokyo), and University of Kyoto Library. A travel enthusiast, I have made several trips to Europe, one to Canada, many to Mexico. In 1978, I was a member of one of the first groups permitted to tour the People's Republic of China."

She indicates that she considers "it important to my career that from early childhood I was read great poetry, and that I was brought up in the country. Influences on my poetry have included Auden, Gerard Manley Hopkins, Housman, Anglo-Saxon poetry. Readers have found a Whitman influence. All of these poets have in their work expressed a sense of wonder, a love of words, and, perhaps with the exception of Whitman, a feeling for form, usually traditional. To me, the best poetry, besides having meaning, also makes use of music, metaphor, imagery, rhyme of some kind. A good poem conveys to its reader a happy sense of discovery."

*   *   *

STERN, Ellen Norman   1927-

PERSONAL: Born July 10, 1927, in Hannover, Germany; came to United States in 1939, naturalized in 1945; daughter of Leo and Gertrude (Salomon) Norman; married Harold H. Stern (a self-employed sales representative), October 7, 1956; children: Lawrence Norman, Michael Bruce. *Education:* University of Louisville, B.A., 1950. *Politics:* Democrat. *Religion:* Jewish. *Home:* 135 Anbury Lane, Willow Grove, Pa. 19090.

CAREER: Writer. Production assistant for station WAVE-TV, Louisville, Ky., 1950-55; National Broadcasting Corp., New York City, production assistant, 1955-57; Children's Aid Society, New York City, secretary to director of Foster Home Department, 1957-59.

WRITINGS: Embattled Justice: The Story of Louis Dembitz Brandeis (juvenile), Jewish Publication Society, 1971; *Dreamer in the Desert: A Profile of Nelson Glueck*, Ktav, 1980; *Elie Wiesel: Witness for Life*, Ktav, 1982. Contributor of stories and articles to *Louisville Courier-Journal, Philadelphia Bulletin, Reconstructionist Views, Jewish Digest*, and *World Over*.

SIDELIGHTS: Ellen Norman Stern comments: "Even at this stage of my life I still have heroes: the people whose lives and accomplishments contribute to the welfare of mankind. I enjoy writing about them. Each one, whether the subject of a story or a book, has given a new dimension to my own life. I find that I enter a whole new world every time I work on a story or a book. I learn things I did not know before, and see things in a new light. Gaining this new knowledge is the biggest bonus of my writing. The lessons I learn result in stories and, for me, writing those stories is the happiest part of my life."

AVOCATIONAL INTERESTS: Historical subjects.

* * *

STEVEN, Hugh 1931-

PERSONAL: Born March 21, 1931, in Vancouver, British Columbia, Canada; son of David and Mable (Knowles) Steven; married Norma Van Boeyen (an editor, writer, and typist), May 5, 1951; children: Wendy, Dave, Lee, Karen. *Education:* Attended Summer Institute of Linguistics, 1956, University of Oklahoma, 1967, and Regent College, 1969. *Religion:* Protestant. *Home:* 1309 North Linwood Ave., Santa Ana, Calif. 92701. *Office:* Wycliffe Bible Translators, Inc., Huntington Beach, Calif. 92648.

CAREER: Woodward Stores Ltd., Vancouver, British Columbia, junior manager, 1949-56; Wycliffe Bible Translators, Inc., Huntington Beach, Calif., buyer and administrator in public relations in Mexico, 1956-67, regional secretary and writer in Chicago, Ill., 1968-69, author-at-large, 1970—, work has taken him to South Pacific, Latin America, Africa, Europe, and Vietnam.

AWARDS, HONORS: Night of the Long Knives was named one of ten outstanding children's books of 1972 by the National Association of Christian Schools.

WRITINGS: Manuel, Revell, 1970; *You Eat Bananas*, Regal Books (Ventura, Calif.), 1971; (with James C. Hefley) *Miracles in Mexico*, Moody, 1972; *Night of the Long Knives* (juvenile), Regal Books, 1972; *The Reproducers*, Regal Books, 1972; (with Cornell Capa) *Language and Faith*, Wycliffe Bible Translators, Inc., 1972; *The Measure of Greatness*, Revell, 1973; *It Takes Time to Love*, Wycliffe Bible Translators, Inc., 1974; *Kim*, Harvest, 1975; *They Dared to Be Different*, Harvest, 1976, revised edition, Wycliffe Bible Translators, Inc., 1983; *To the Ends of the Earth*, Christian Herald Publishers, 1978; *The Man with the Noisy Heart*, Moody, 1979; *Danger in the Blue Lagoon*, Good Life Productions, 1979.

Never Touch a Tiger, Thomas Nelson, 1980; (with wife, Norma Steven) *Tolo, the Volcano's Son*, Wycliffe Bible Translators, Inc., 1981; *Good Broth to Warm Our Bones*, Crossway, 1982; (with N. Steven) *Pass the Word*, Wycliffe Bible Translators, Inc., 1984; *A Thousand Trails: Personal Journal of William Cameron Townsend*, Volume I: *1917-1919*, CREDO Publishing (Langley, British Columbia), 1984. Contributor of more than two hundred articles to Christian denominational magazines, including *World Vision* and *Christian Herald.* Contributing editor, *In Other Words*.

WORK IN PROGRESS: Volume II of William Cameron Townsend's journal, *1920-1945*; a biography of Joanne Shetler, linguist and Bible translator in the Philippines; a young adult adventure story set in Alaska.

SIDELIGHTS: Hugh Steven told *CA:* "From my earliest memory I was captive to the story. I loved authors like Jack London, Charles Dickens, Robert Louis Stevenson, Rudyard Kipling, and more. It was narrative and fairy tales that satisfied my childhood longing for adventure, for exploration and the need to know. Like food, shelter, love, and acceptance, stories are an essential part of human need. I had food and shelter as a child but felt bereft of love and acceptance. It was through stories that I discovered windows and doorways to adventure and knowing, and it was through God's storybook, the Bible, that I found in Jesus Christ love, acceptance, and relief from deep feelings of rejection.

"When I began to feel an itch to write (historical biography), I was motivated to explore the lives of those who had found meaning to life through a personal love relationship with God through Jesus Christ, and whose motives, actions, and thoughts were based upon God's Word as revealed in the Bible. Thus, most of the stories I write are about people who spend their lives living and working with ethnic minority groups in isolated corners of the world. They are Bible translators, the Mother Teresas of this world who perform daily quiet acts of heroism.

"In a word, I look for the transcendental purposes or meaning to life as acted out in the lives of ordinary people. Often these people, without knowing it, are mirrors of a greater reality—a practical extension of the words of Jesus Christ: 'A new commandment I give you. Love one another. As I have loved you, so you must love one another.'"

* * *

STEVENS, Robert Tyler
See STAPLES, Reginald Thomas

* * *

STEVENSON, J. P.
See HALDANE-STEVENSON, James Patrick

* * *

STEVENSON, James Patrick
See HALDANE-STEVENSON, James Patrick

* * *

STEWIG, John Warren 1937-

PERSONAL: Born January 7, 1937, in Waukesha, Wis.; son of John G. and Marguerite W. Stewig. *Education:* University of Wisconsin, Madison, B.S., 1958, M.S., 1962, Ph.D., 1967. *Religion:* Episcopalian. *Home:* 2908 North Stowell Ave., Milwaukee, Wis. 53211. *Office:* University of Wisconsin, 393 Enderis Hall, Milwaukee, Wis. 53201.

CAREER: Elementary school teacher in Monona Grove, Wis., 1958-64; Purdue University, West Lafayette, Ind., assistant professor, 1967-72, associate professor of curriculum and instruction, 1972-77; University of Wisconsin—Milwaukee, professor of language arts, 1977—. Faculty member and workshop leader at colleges and universities in the United States and Canada, including Indiana University, School of the Ozarks, and University of Victoria; speaker at schools and professional gatherings. Worked as music teacher at a hospital school for school-age patients. Member of Wisconsin Statewide Literacy Assessment Advisory Committee, 1974; member of advisory board of Madison Cooperative Children's Book Center, 1974-78.

MEMBER: International Reading Association, Association for Childhood Education International, National Council of Teachers of English (president, 1982-83), Wisconsin Council of Teachers of English (member of board of directors, 1977-79; president, 1980-81), Milwaukee Association for the Education of Young Children, English Association of Greater Milwaukee (member of board of directors, 1973-81).

AWARDS, HONORS: Grant from U.S. Office of Education, 1973.

WRITINGS: Spontaneous Drama: A Language Art, C. E. Merrill, 1973; *Exploring Language With Children,* C. E. Merrill, 1974; *Read to Write: Using Literature as a Springboard to Children's Composition,* Hawthorn, 1975, 2nd edition, Holt, 1980; *Children's Language Acquisition,* Department of Public Instruction (Madison, Wis.), 1976; *Sending Messages* (juvenile), Houghton, 1978; (editor with Sam L. Sebesta, and contributor) *Using Literature in the Elementary Classroom* (monograph), National Council of Teachers of English, 1978.

Children and Literature, Rand McNally, 1980; *Teaching Language Arts in Early Childhood,* Holt, 1982; *Exploring Language Arts in the Elementary Classroom,* Holt, 1983; *Informal Drama in the Elementary Language Arts Program,* Teachers College Press, 1983.

Contributor: Joe L. Frost, editor, *The Elementary School: Principles and Problems,* Houghton, 1969; Martha King and others, editors, *The Language Arts in the Elementary School: A Forum for Focus,* National Council of Teachers of English, 1973; Linda Western, editor, *Children's Literature,* Extension, University of Wisconsin—Madison, 1975; Walter Petty and Patrick Flynn, editors, *Creative Dramatics in the Language Arts Classroom,* State University of New York at Buffalo, 1976; Bernice Cullinan and others, editors, *Literature for the Young Child,* National Council of Teachers of English, 1977; Claire Ashby-Doris, editor, *The Interrelationships of the Arts in Reading,* Collegium Book, 1979; Gay Su Pinnell, editor, *Discovering Language with Children,* National Council of Teachers of English, 1980.

Contributor of more than forty articles and reviews to language arts, library, and theater journals. Editor of column, "Instructional Strategies," in *Elementary English,* 1972-73; member of editorial boards, *Childhood Education,* 1972-74, *The Advocate,* 1973—.

SIDELIGHTS: John Warren Stewig told *CA:* "Scholars have shown through research what perceptive teachers have observed for years: children come to school with impressive abilities to use language. The school's task is to help them improve the natural language skills they already possess. This has to be done apart from traditional, analytic/evaluative exercises which have pervaded the curriculum for too long. My writing for teachers is concerned with this common theme: there are imaginative ways to enhance children's language, without forsaking the structure and sequence which creative approaches too often ignore.

"I have written about each of the language arts: listening, speaking, reading and writing. A particular interest has been showing teachers how to make creative drama integral to all of these language arts. My focus is on providing imaginative

activities, set within a framework (rationale) which would help teachers understand why the activities are crucial for children. Too frequently creativity is seen as complete freedom: nothing could be further from the truth. I have written at length about how to use the language of writers for children, and children's own language, to plan curricula that are responsive to children's needs, and challenging in ways too often left untapped. One effort was *Sending Messages,* a juvenile title, which helps children understand some ways adults use language in society. To be truly literate, we need to understand the processes involved as adults use language. This book speaks to children on their level about this rather complex activity."

BIOGRAPHICAL/CRITICAL SOURCES: Wesley Shibles, *Metaphor: An Annotated Bibliography and History,* Language Press, 1971.

*   *   *

STILLMAN, Richard J. 1917-

PERSONAL: Born February 20, 1917, in Lansing, Mich.; married Ellen Darlene Slater; children: Richard II, Thomas, Ellen. *Education:* University of Southern California, B.S., 1938; Harvard University, graduate study, 1938-39; Command & General Staff School, graduated, 1943; Syracuse University, M.S., 1950, Ph.D., 1955; Army War College, graduated, 1960; North Atlantic Treaty Organization Defense College, graduated, 1961. *Home and office:* 2311 Oriole St., Lake Oaks, New Orleans, La. 70122.

CAREER: U.S. Army, 1938-65, platoon leader in infantry, 1939-40, and member of War Department General Staff, 1941-42, commissioned in regular army as 2nd lieutenant of infantry, 1942, promoted to major, 1942, lieutenant colonel, 1944, and colonel, 1955, retired as colonel; Ohio University, Athens, 1965-67, became professor of business administration, director of Center for Economic Opportunity, and director of management programs; University of New Orleans, New Orleans, La., professor of management, 1967-82, professor emeritus, 1982—.

Held command and staff positions in Europe, the Far East, and the U.S.A., 1942-65; during World War II served in operations section of Third Army, and as secretary of General Staff to General Patton, 1944-45; U.S. Military Academy, West Point, N.Y., member of staff and faculty, 1952-55; commanded 20th Infantry and Reserve Forces Act regiment, 1956-57; faculty member, NATO Defense College, 1961-63; office of the Secretary of Defense, assistant division chief, Policy Division and Chief Strategic Studies Branch, International Security Affairs, 1963-65.

MEMBER: Financial Management Association, American Finance Association, Academy of Management, Army-Navy Country Club.

AWARDS, HONORS—Military: Legion of Merit Bronze Star, Luxembourg Order of the Crown, Paratrooper Badge, War Department and Department of Defense Badges. Civilian: Scouters Award, Boy Scouts of America, 1955; Naval Institute Award, 1966, for essay "The Pentagon's Whiz Kids."

WRITINGS: U.S. Infantry: Queen of Battle, F. Watts, 1965; (with Florette Henri) *Bitter Victory,* Doubleday, 1970; *Guide to Personal Finance: A Lifetime Program of Money Management,* Prentice-Hall, 1972, 4th edition, 1984; *Do It Yourself Contracting to Build Your Own Home: A Managerial Approach,* Chilton, 1974, 2nd edition, 1981; *Personal Finance Guide and Workbook: A Managerial Approach to Successful*

Household Recordkeeping, Pelican, 1977; *Moneywise*, Prentice-Hall, 1978.

More for Your Money: Personal Finance Techniques to Cope with Inflation and the Energy Shortage, Prentice-Hall, 1980; *Your Personal Financial Planner*, Prentice-Hall, 1981; *Small Business Management: How to Start and Stay in Business*, Little, Brown, 1983.

Also author of a poster entitled "Dow Jones Industrial Average: 1896-Present (with Stillman's Significant Political, Military, Technological and Economic Events)," 1984. Contributor of more than forty articles to professional journals.

WORK IN PROGRESS: How to Use Your Personal Computer to Manage Your Personal Finances, with John Page, for Prentice-Hall; *Dow Jones Industrial Average*, for Dow Jones/Irwin; *How to Budget Wisely*, for the Pentagon Federal Credit Union.

SIDELIGHTS: Richard J. Stillman told *CA:* "I began writing articles for military publications while in the service. It provided an opportunity to express my thoughts on subjects dear to my heart. My second career in academia offered an even greater opportunity in view of the publish or perish philosophy. Presently I am devoting full time to writing—a third career that began as a hobby thirty years ago. I am working longer hours but I find immense satisfaction in helping others profit from my experience in my areas of expertise. Writing has required me to use my time wisely. It can be done almost anywhere—so long as you can put pen (typewriter/word processor) to paper. I find those interminably long waits at doctors offices and airports ideal. Air travel also permits much good work."

BIOGRAPHICAL/CRITICAL SOURCES: O. N. Bradley, *A Soldier's Story*, Holt, 1951; *Monterey Peninsula Herald*, March 21, 1956; *Detroit News*, February 22, 1957; Ladislas Farago, *Patton: Ordeal and Triumph*, Helene Obolensky, 1963; *New York Times*, May 29, 1966; *New Orleans Magazine*, November, 1972; *Times Picayune/States-Item* (New Orleans), July 8, 1984.

*   *   *

STIVENS, Dal(las George)   1911-

PERSONAL: Born December 31, 1911, in Blayney, Australia; son of Francis Harold and Jane (Abbott) Stivens; married Mary Burke, 1939 (died, 1941); married Winifred Wright, September 22, 1945 (divorced, 1977); children: Katrin, Christopher. *Education:* Attended Barker College, Hornsby, New South Wales, Australia, 1927-28. *Politics:* Liberal. *Religion:* Agnostic. *Home:* 5 Middle Harbor Rd., Lindfield, New South Wales, Australia 2070.

CAREER: Writer. Served in Australian Department of Information, 1944-50; Australia House, London, England, press officer, 1949-50. Commonwealth Literature Fund lecturer at University of Adelaide, 1963. Chairman of literary committee of Captain Cook Bicentenary Celebrations, 1969-70. Member of New South Wales advisory committee of Australian Broadcasting Commission, 1970-73. Painter; has exhibited his work in galleries and institutions, including James Cook University and John Curtin House. *Military service:* Australian Army, 1943-44; served in Education Service.

MEMBER: P.E.N., Australian Society of Authors (founder, 1962; foundation president, 1963-64; vice-president, 1964 and 1966; president, 1967-73).

AWARDS, HONORS: Commonwealth Literary Fund fellowship, 1951, 1962, 1970; Miles Franklin Award for best Australian novel, 1970, for *A Horse of Air;* Patrick White Award, 1981, for a body of work contributing to Australian literature.

WRITINGS: (With Barbara Jeffries) *A Guide to Book Contracts*, Australian Society of Authors, 1957; (editor) *Coast to Coast: Australian Stories, 1957-58;* Angus & Robertson, 1959; *The Incredible Egg* (natural history), Weybright & Talley, 1974; *The Portable Dal Stivens* (anthology), Queensland University Press, 1984.

Novels: *Jimmy Brockett*, Britannicus Liber, 1951; *The Wide Arch*, Angus & Robertson, 1958; *Three Persons Make a Tiger*, Cheshire, 1968; *A Horse of Air*, Angus & Robertson, 1970; *The Bushranger*, Collins, 1979.

Short story collections; published by Angus & Robertson, except as indicated: *The Tramp and Other Stories*, Macmillian, 1936; *The Courtship of Uncle Henry*, Reed & Harris, 1946; *The Gambling Ghost and Other Stories*, 1953; *Ironbark Bill*, 1955; *The Scholarly Mouse and Other Tales*, 1957; *Selected Stories, 1936-1968*, 1970; *The Unicorn and Other Tales*, Wild & Woolley, 1976; *The Demon Bowler and Other Cricket Stories*, Outback Press, 1981.

Contributor to natural history periodicals, including *Wildlife, Pacific Discovery, Animal Kingdom*, and *Natural History*.

WORK IN PROGRESS: Book of drawings with text; a novel, short stories, paintings, and drawings.

SIDELIGHTS: Asked if he would describe himself as a regional writer, Stivens told *CA:* "Not really. Some works are regional in that the setting is Australian. But much of my writing—particularly the fables—have no regional setting. In the past a prominent Australian critic called me cosmopolitan."

AVOCATIONAL INTERESTS: Theater, natural history, travel, art, music.

*   *   *

STOCK, R(obert) D(ouglas)   1941-

PERSONAL: Born December 2, 1941, in Akron, Ohio; son of Robert P. (a chemical engineer) and Barbara (Broughton) Stock; married Barbara Jergovich, 1975. *Education:* Kent State University, B.A., 1963; Princeton University, M.A., 1965, Ph.D., 1967. *Politics:* Conservative. *Religion:* Episcopalian. *Home:* 1925 Van Dorn St., Lincoln, Neb. 68502. *Office:* Department of English, University of Nebraska, 304 Andrews Hall, Lincoln, Neb. 68588.

CAREER: University of Nebraska, Lincoln, assistant professor, 1967-72, associate professor, 1972-77, professor of English, 1977—.

MEMBER: Modern Language Association of America, American Society for Eighteenth-Century Studies.

WRITINGS: Samuel Johnson and Neoclassical Dramatic Theory, University of Nebraska Press, 1973; *Samuel Johnson's Literary Criticism*, University of Nebraska Press, 1974; *The New Humanists in Nebraska*, University of Nebraska Press, 1979; *The Holy and the Daemonic from Sir Thomas Browne to William Blake*, Princeton University Press, 1982.

WORK IN PROGRESS: The Flutes of Dionysus: Daemonic Enthrallment in Literature.

SIDELIGHTS: R. D. Stock told *CA:* "I have been especially interested in studying the decline in modern society of the 'enchanted view,' or a sense of the numinous—a phenomenon remarked by such diverse thinkers as Carl Jung, Emile Durkheim, Robert Nisbet. As a writer, consequently, I have been much occupied with the eighteenth century, when the decay of those feelings first became evident in a forcible way, and with those writers since who have endeavored through their philosophical and imaginative works to revive a sense of the supernatural world, or at least to retard the secularizing and trivializing forces of modernism. 'Emancipation' is a word celebrated by many contemporary writers, but the emancipation I should like to observe is from the trite and dogmatic materialism to which many of them, it seems, subscribe."

BIOGRAPHICAL/CRITICAL SOURCES: Choice, December, 1973; *Times Literary Supplement,* September 24, 1982; *Sewanee Review,* July, 1983; *Criticism,* winter, 1983.

*   *   *

STOOKEY, Robert W(ilson) 1917-

PERSONAL: Born July 20, 1917, in Maquoketa, Iowa; son of Robert Marshall (a teacher) and Beatrice (Wilson) Stookey; married Louise Auch, April 6, 1946. *Education:* Sorbonne, University of Paris, diploma, 1938; University of Nebraska, B.A., 1938, M.A., 1940; University of Texas, Ph.D., 1972. *Politics:* Liberal. *Religion:* Presbyterian. *Home:* 3304 White Pine Dr., Austin, Tex. 78757. *Office:* Center for Middle Eastern Studies, University of Texas, Austin, Tex. 78712.

CAREER: U.S. Foreign Service, Washington, D.C., third secretary and vice consul in Tangier, Morocco, 1946-49, vice consul in Nairobi, Kenya, 1949-52, second secretary in Ankara, Turkey, 1952-53, involved in Arabic language and area training in Washington, D.C. and in Beirut, Lebanon, 1953-55, principal officer in Basra, Iraq, 1955-57, regional affairs officer in Cairo, Egypt, 1957-59, Department of State, foreign relations officer, 1959-61, and officer in charge of Sudan affairs, 1963-66, charge d'affaires in Taizz, Yemen, 1961-63, supervisory political officer in Jidda, Sauda Arabia, 1966-68; retired from U.S. Government service, 1968; University of Texas at Austin, research associate at Center for Middle Eastern Studies, 1973—. Fulbright-Hays senior research scholar in Yemen, 1973. *Military service:* U.S. Army, Field Artillery, 1941-46; became major; received Bronze Star.

WRITINGS: America and the Arab States: An Uneasy Encounter, Wiley, 1975; (with James A. Bill) *Politics and Petroleum: The Middle East and the United States,* King's Court Communications, 1975, new edition published as *With or Without Oil: The Middle East and the United States,* 1979; *Yemen: The Politics of the Yemen Arab Republic,* Westview Press, 1978; (translator) Jacques Berque, *Cultural Expression in Arab Society Today,* University of Texas Press, 1978; (contributor) P. Edward Haley and Lewis W. Snider, editors, *Lebanon in Crisis: Participants and Issues,* Syracuse University Press, 1979.

(Contributor) Michael Curtis, editor, *Religion and Politics in the Middle East,* Westview, 1981; *South Yemen: A Marxist Republic in Arabia,* Westview, 1982; (editor and contributor) *The Arabian Peninsula: Zone of Ferment,* Hoover Institution, 1984. Contributor to Middle East journals.

WORK IN PROGRESS: Editing, with William Roger Lewis, a book entitled *The End of the Palestine Mandate,* for University of Texas Press; with Kenneth R. Bain, preparing a second edition of *America and the Arab States,* for Knopf.

SIDELIGHTS: Robert W. Stookey told *CA:* "The privilege I have had of studying Middle Eastern politics both from within as an active participant, and from the sidelines as a scholar, is a precious one given to rather few. We Americans have critically important interests in this part of the world, and can safeguard them only through wise policies rooted in sympathetic understanding by our public of the peoples of ths turbulent and disconcerting region. In our relations with the Middle East we have blundered into some booby traps in the past; if my writing helps us to avoid some of those that lie ahead, my labor will be amply rewarded.'

Reviewing *America and the Arab States: An Uneasy Encounter,* Alan Howton described the book as "excellent." He wrote in *Middle East Journal* that its "outstanding quality is balance," especially with respect to the Arab-Israeli conflict.

BIOGRAPHICAL/CRITICAL SOURCES: Middle East Journal, Volume 30, number 3, 1976.

*   *   *

STOWERS, Carlton 1942-

PERSONAL: Born April 14, 1942, in Brownwood, Tex.; son of Ira (in sales) and Fay (a secretary; maiden name, Stephenson) Stowers; married Betty Darby, October 7, 1962 (marriage ended); married Lynne Livingston, November 30, 1975 (marriage ended); married Pat Cruce, March 2, 1981; children: Anson, Ashley. *Education:* Attended University of Texas, 1961-63. *Religion:* Episcopalian. *Home:* 1015 Randy Rd., Cedar Hill, Tex. 75104.

CAREER: Associated with *Amarillo Daily News,* Amarillo, Tex., 1966-69, and *Lubbock Avalanche Journal,* Lubbock, Tex., 1970-73; free-lance writer, 1974-76; *Dallas Morning News,* Dallas, Tex., sportswriter and columnist, 1976-81; affiliated with *Dallas Cowboys Weekly,* 1981—. Writer and associate producer of weekly television series "Countdown to '84," USA Cable network.

MEMBER: Professional Football Writers Association, Texas Sportswriters Association.

AWARDS, HONORS: State awards for newspaper journalism include citations from Texas Headliners Club, Texas Sportswriters Association, Texas UPI Editors Association.

WRITINGS: The Randy Matson Story, Tafnews, 1971; *Spirit,* Berkley, 1973; (with Wilbur Evans) *Champions,* Strode, 1978; *The Overcomers,* Word Books, 1978; (with Trent Jones) *Where the Rainbows Wait,* Playboy Press, 1978; (editor) *Happy Trails to You* (autobiography of Roy Rogers and Dale Evans), Word Books, 1979.

Journey to Triumph, Taylor Publishing, 1982; *The Unsinkable Titanic Thompson,* Eakin Press, 1982; *Dallas Cowboys Bluebook III,* Taylor Publishing, 1982; *Friday Night Heroes,* Eakin Press, 1983; *Partners in Blue,* Taylor Publishing, 1983; *Dallas Cowboys Bluebook IV,* Taylor Publishing 1983; (with Billy Olson) *Reaching Higher,* Word Books, 1984; *The Dallas Cowboys: The First 25 Years,* with a foreword by James Michener, Taylor Publishing, 1984; *The Cowboys Chronicles,* Eakin Press, 1984.

Contributor to magazines, including *Good Housekeeping, Sports Illustrated, TV Guide, Inside Sports,* and *People.*

WORK IN PROGRESS: A book on Christian athletes; the true story of a Texas murder case.

SIDELIGHTS: Carlton Stowers told *CA:* "The greatest enjoyment I receive from my work is the variety of projects I'm involved in. A newspaper background has provided me with the kind of work habits necessary to work swiftly and on more than one project at a time. In recent years I've dealt more attention to nonfiction books and have also found that television writing provides me a welcome respite from the long narrative of print journalism on occasion. I'm fortunate that a variety of subjects interest me, therefore I don't devote my efforts to a particular field even though I continue to do a considerable amount of sportswriting."

*   *   *

STRICKER, George   1936-

PERSONAL: Born November 6, 1936, in Bronx, N.Y.; son of Irving (an office manager) and Diana (Coopersmith) Stricker; married Joan Levy, January 16, 1960; children: Jocelyn, Geoffrey. *Education:* University of Chicago, A.B., 1956; University of Rochester, Ph.D., 1960. *Home:* 134 Wooleys Lane, Great Neck, N.Y. 11023. *Office:* Institute of Advanced Psychological Studies, Adelphi University, Garden City, N.Y. 11530.

CAREER: University of Rochester, Rochester, N.Y., assistant lecturer, 1959-60, assistant professor of psychology, 1960-61; Goucher College, Baltimore, Md., assistant professor of psychology, 1961-63; Adelphi University, Garden City, N.Y., assistant professor, 1963-65, associate professor, 1965-70, professor of psychology, 1970—, assistant dean of Institute of Advanced Psychological Studies, 1966-84, dean, 1984—. Private practice as clinical psychologist, 1963—. Clinical psychologist at Rochester State Hospital, 1959-60, Atascadero State Hospital, 1960, Sheppard and Enoch Pratt Hospital, 1962-63, and Nassau County Drug Abuse and Addiction Commission, 1969-71. Clinical assistant professor, Cornell University Medical College, 1966-68. Senior research scientist, New York State Narcotics Addiction Control Commission, 1968-70; member of Commissioner's Task Force on Professional Education in Psychology, New York state, 1974—.

Consultant, State of California, 1960-61, Eastman Dental Center, 1962-70, Beth Ha Gan School, 1966-68, Episcopal Church, 1967-68, and Queens-Nassau Mental Health Center, 1968-84. Chairman, national advisory panel of the American Psychological Association to the CHAMPUS project; vice-chairman of New York State Board of Psychology, 1976-85; diplomate in clinical psychology, American Board of Professional Psychology, 1975; distinguished practitioner in psychology, National Academies of Practice.

MEMBER: American Psychological Association (fellow), Association for the Advancement of Psychology, Society for Projective Techniques and Personality Assessment (fellow; treasurer, 1975-80; president, 1982-84), American Association of University Professors, Eastern Psychological Association, New York State Psychological Association (past president), Nassau County Psychological Association, Sigma Xi.

AWARDS, HONORS: U.S. Public Health Service postdoctoral research fellow, 1960-61; U.S. Office of Education research grant, 1963-64; co-recipient of Frank Ritter Award, Rochester Academy of Medicine, 1965, for paper, "Audio Analgesic Effects"; National Institute of Mental Health grant, 1966-68; National Institute of Law Enforcement and Criminal Justice grant, 1969-71.

WRITINGS: The Experimental Induction of Mood, Office of Naval Research, 1961; (with Melvin Zax) *Patterns of Psychopathology*, Macmillan, 1964; (with Zax) *The Study of Abnormal Behavior*, Macmillan, 1964, 3rd edition, 1974; *Students' Views of the College Environment*, U.S. Office of Education, 1965; (contributor) L. Kingsley, editor, *Selected Papers on Psychotherapy*, Adelphi University, 1968; (contributor) G. D. Goldman and D. S. Milman, editors, *Modern Woman*, C. C Thomas, 1969.

(With M. R. Goldfried and I. B. Weiner) *Rorschach Handbook of Clinical and Research Applications*, Prentice-Hall, 1971; (editor with M. Merbaum) *Search for Human Understanding*, Holt, 1971, 2nd edition, 1975; (with F. Weiss) *Kicking It*, Pyramid Publications, 1971; (editor with Goldman) *Practical Problems of a Private Psychotherapeutic Practice*, C. C Thomas, 1972, 2nd edition, Jason Aronson, 1981; (editor with Merbaum) *Growth of Personal Awareness*, Holt, 1973; (contributor) Goldman and Milman, editors, *The Neuosis of Our Time: Acting Out*, C. C Thomas, 1973; (contributor) Goldman and Milman, editors, *Psychoanalytic Psychotherapy*, Addison-Wesley, 1978; (contributor) H. Goldstein, editor, *Readings in Dyslexia*, Speal Learning Corp., 1978.

(Contributor) A. G. Awad, H. B. Durost, and W. O. McCormick, editors, *Evaluation of Quality of Care in Psychiatry*, Pergamon, 1980; (contributor) Goldman and Milman, editors, *Addiction: Theory and Treatment*, Kendall/Hunt, 1980; (editor with B. B. Wolman) *Handbook of Developmental Psychology*, Prentice-Hall, 1982; (contributor) M. Rosenbaum, editor, *Ethics and Values in Psychotherapy: A Guidebook*, Free Press, 1982; (with M. N. Fisher) *Intimacy*, Plenum, in press; (with R. Keisner) *The Implications of Non-Clinical Research for Clinical Practice*, Plenum, in press.

General editor, "Bison Books in Clinical Psychology" series, University of Nebraska Press, 1979-81; co-editor, *International Encyclopedia of Psychiatry, Psychology, Psychoanalysis, and Neurology*. Contributor to *Proceedings of the 73rd Annual Convention of the American Psychological Association*, 1965. Also contributor to *Journal of Social Psychology, Dental Progress, New York State Dental Association, Psychological Reports, Journal of Clinical Psychology, Psychological Review, Journal of Personality, Medical Care, American Psychoanalyst*, and other professional journals. Consulting editor, *Journal of Personality Assessment*, 1976-85, *Professional Psychology*, 1979—, and *Journal of Urban Psychiatry*, 1979—; guest editor, *Professional Psychology*, 1982.

*   *   *

STROEYER, Poul   1923-

PERSONAL: Born July 13, 1923, in Copenhagen, Denmark; son of Peter Stroeyer Pedersen and Olga Esbensen; married Solveig Lauritzen, August 20, 1947; children: Poul, Jr., Pia Marianne, Per-Erik. *Education:* Educated in Copenhagen, Denmark. *Home:* Ymervaegen 18, 182 63 Djursholm, Sweden.

CAREER: Writer; illustrator; cartoonist. Political cartoons, illustrations, and paintings have been exhibited in European countries, Canada, and Japan; paintings are represented in Swedish museums.

MEMBER: Association of Illustrators (Sweden), Organization of Artists (Sweden), Union of Authors (Sweden), Association of Journalists (Sweden).

AWARDS, HONORS: German Children's Book prize, 1961, for *PP and His Big Horn;* Elsa Beskowplaketten, 1967, for children's books.

WRITINGS—All self-illustrated: *Bubus jungletur* (juvenile; title means "Bubus's Trip in the Jungle"), Wilhelm Hansen, 1948; *Stroeyers dagbook* (title means "Stroeyer's Daybook"; also see below), Almqvist & Wiksell, published annually, 1954—; *PP och hans stora horn* (juvenile; title means "PP and His Big Horn"), Almqvist & Wiksell, 1966; *Bytt aer bytt* (juvenile), Almqvist & Wiksell, 1960, translation by Maria Cimino published as *It's a Deal,* McDowell, Obolensky; *Utan ord* (title means "Without Words"), Almqvist & Wiksell, 1963.

PP fixar allt (juvenile; title means "PP Fixes Everything"), Askild & Kaernekull, 1972; *Guld, Groenland och Transsib* (title means "Gold, Greenland and Transsib"), Almqvist & Wiksell, 1974; *Foelj pilen PP* (juvenile; title means "Follow the Arrow, PP"), Askild & Kaernekull, 1979; *Tre decennier* (title means "Three Decades"), Mariebergs Foerlag, 1980; *Stroeyers Skissbok fraen Paris* (title means "Stroeyer's Sketchbook from Paris"), Mariebergs Foerlag, 1982.

Illustrator; juveniles: Sven Ingvar, *Alla tiders Joje,* Raben & Sjoegren, 1950; Lennart Hellsing, *Summa summarum,* Raben & Sjoegren, 1950; Hellsing, *Den kraangliga kraakan,* Raben & Sjoegren, 1953, translation by Nancy and Edward Maze published as *The Cantankerous Crow,* Astor-Honor, 1962; Ingemar Hasselblad, *Agusta aaker ut,* O. Eklund, 1954; Gunnar Brolund, *Grabben paa maanen,* O. Eklund, 1954; Margit Holmberg, *Tre smaa skoeldpaddor,* O. Eklund, 1954; Hellsing, *Den flygande trumman,* Raben & Sjoegren, 1954; Hellsing, *Krakel Spektakel-boken,* Raben & Sjoegren, 1959.

Hellsing, *ABC,* Raben & Sjoegren, 1961; Olle Holmberg, *Sotarpojken och prinsessan,* Bo Cavefors, 1964; *Sjoeroevarbok,* Raben & Sjoegren, 1965, translation by William J. Smith published as *The Pirate Book,* Delacorte, 1972; Hellsing, *Boken om Bagar Bengtsson,* Raben & Sjoegren, 1966; Hellsing, *Boken om Kasper,* Raben & Sjoegren, 1971; Hellsing, *Haer dansar herr gurka,* Raben & Sjoegren, 1977; Hellsing, *Gaes med kraes,* Raben & Sjoegren, 1981.

Illustrator; for adults: Gallie Akerhielm, *Konsten att tjusa mannen,* Wahlstroem & Widstrand, 1950; Edward Clausen and Knud Lundberg, *Aet, drick och var smaert,* Raben & Sjoegren, 1951; Clausen and Lundberg, *Mat som goer Er smaert,* Raben & Sjoegren, 1951; Clausen and Lundberg, *Baettre nerver—baettre humoer,* Raben & Sjoegren, 1953; Chic Sale, *The Specialist,* Forum, 1953; Torsten Ehrenmark, *Petmoijs besyaerligheter,* Lindqvists Foerlag, 1953; Cello, *Lika vaenligt somvanligt,* Gebers, 1953; Mark Spade, *Fagotter paa loepande band* (title means "How to Run a Bassoon Factory"), Forum, 1954; Ehrenmark, *Foer soemnloesa dagar,* Lindqvists Foerlag, 1954; Cello, *Saa, skoerda och saa vidare,* Gebers, 1954.

Ehrenmark, *Petmoijs petitesser,* Lindqvists Foerlag, 1955; Cello, *Foerlaat en yngling,* Gebers, 1955; Herman Stolpe, *Boecker paa oede oe,* KFs Bokfoerlag, 1956; Axel Wallengren, *Falstaf Fakirs vitterlek,* Gebers, 1956; Cello, *Skum paa ytan,* Gebers, 1956; Stig Jaerrel, *Lapp pae luckan,* Wahlstroem & Widstrand, 1957; Cello, *Det gamla spelet om en far,* Gebers, 1957; Lundberg, *Fin form paa laett saett,* Raben & Sjoegren, 1958; Clausen and Lundberg, *Spis, drik og bliv sund,* Branner og Korch, 1958; Lundberg, *Bedre examen-lettere,* Branner og Korch, 1958; Cello, *Med pegasen i botten,* Gebers, 1958; Clausen, *Pengene*

og livet, Branner og Korch, 1959; Cello, *Laett faerdiga stycken,* Gebers, 1959.

Bertil Gillqvist, *Saelj med Bertil Gillqvist,* Forum, 1960; Cello, *Bara foer lust,* Gebers, 1961; Cello, *Familjens flintis,* Gebers, 1962; Clausen, *Pengar aer inte allt,* Sparfraemjandets Foerlag, 1963; Cello, *En hoeg repriser till hoegre priser,* Gebers, 1963; Goeran Smith, *Service,* Prisma, 1964; Cello, *Aarsberaettelse,* Gebers, 1964; Cello, *Cellos glada ark,* Gebers, 1965; Cello, *Stora jubelboken,* Gebers, 1966; Axel Johansson, *Faafaengens kemi,* AV Carlsons, 1966; Ehrenmark, *Aarets Ehrenmark,* Aahlen & Aakerlunds Foerlag, published annually, 1966—; Cello, *Valsen gaar,* Gebers, 1967; Cello, *Cellos lilla lila,* Gebers, 1968; Cello, *Cellos godbitar,* Gebers, 1969.

Cello, *Bland tomtar och troll,* Gebers, 1970; Bertil Dahlgren, *Laerarens lilla groena,* Tempus Foerlag, 1970; Maj-Britt Baehrendtz, *Roer paa dig,* LTs Foerlag, 1970; Ehrenmark, *En smoergaasaetares bekaennelser,* Askild & Kaernekull, 1970; Cello, *Rapport fraan kaasoergaarden,* Gebers, 1971; Cello, *Till min egen lilla skatt,* Gebers, 1972; Ning-tsu Malmqvist, *Att aeta med pinnar i Sverige,* Forum, 1972.

Creator of a daily political cartoon, "Stroeyers dagbok" (title means "Stroeyer's Daybook"), in *Dagens Nyheter* (a daily newspaper), Stockholm. Also author of television scripts. Contributor of articles to *Dagens Nyheter.*

SIDELIGHTS: Poul Stroeyer wrote and illustrated his first children's book in one day, when he was twenty years old. It was published four years later. "Luckily," he told *CA,* "I lived in Sweden at that time and was therefore spared the awful experience of reading the reviews, with the exception of one which my parents forwarded to me from Denmark. This particular review stated—if my memory does not fail me—that 'the drawings are better than the text.' I felt that the reviewer had been very kind, since I had expected the verdict that the text was even worse than the drawings.

"In any event, I decided to abstain from writing the text of children's books and instead be content with illustrating them. It was not until 1956 that I dared to try a second time and now I write in Swedish, my acquired language. This book, *PP and His Big Horn,* later appeared in Germany where it was awarded the German Children's Book prize."

Stroeyer's books have been translated into Danish, German, English, and Japanese. He has traveled to approximately seventy countries.

*   *   *

STRUNG, Norman 1941-
(Asouff Barkee, Conrad Miller, Bart Yaeger)

PERSONAL: Born October 21, 1941, in New York, N.Y.; son of August (a banker) and Marion (Hoffmann) Strung; married Priscilla Hoerschgen, October, 1963. *Education:* Montana State University, B.S., 1963; attended University of Montana, 1963-64. *Politics:* "Three-quarters Democrat, one-quarter unpredictable." *Religion:* "Pantheist." *Home:* Cottonwood Canyon, Bozeman, Mont. 59715.

CAREER: Free-lance writer. Has worked as a clamdigger, carpenter, and a licensed hunting and fishing guide. Instructor in English, Montana State University, Bozeman, 1964-67. Consultant, Hunting and Fishing Library and Fish America Foundation.

MEMBER: Outdoor Writers Association of America (member of board of directors, 1972-75, 1978-81; president, 1984-85), American Society of Journalists and Authors, Authors League of America, Rocky Mountain Outdoor Writers.

WRITINGS: (With Dan Morris) *The Fisherman's Almanac,* Macmillan, 1970; (with Morris) *Family Fun Around the Water,* Cowles, 1970; *The Hunter's Almanac,* Macmillan, 1971; *Camping in Comfort,* Lippincott, 1971; (contributor) Dan and Inez Morris, editors, *The Complete Outdoor Cookbook,* Hawthorn, 1971; *Deer Hunting,* Lippincott, 1974; *Misty Mornings and Moonless Nights: A Waterfowler's Guide,* Macmillan, 1974.

(Editor) *Communicating the Outdoor Experience,* Outdoor Writers Association of America, 1975; (with Sam Curtis and Earl Perry) *Whitewater!,* Macmillan, 1975; *An Encyclopedia of Knives,* Lippincott, 1976; *The Complete Hunter's Catalog,* Lippincott, 1977; *To Catch a Trout,* Stein & Day, 1979; *Fishing the Headwaters of the Missouri,* Mountain Press, 1981; *The Art of Hunting,* Hunting and Fishing Library, 1984.

Contributor, occasionally under pseudonyms Bart Yaeger and Asouff Barkee, to national magazines, including *Field & Stream, Boys' Life, Fishing World, Gray's Sporting Journal, Small Boat Journal,* and Petersen's *Hunting.* Outdoor editor, *Mechanix Illustrated;* associate editor, *Field and Stream.*

SIDELIGHTS: Norman Strung told *CA:* "You can trace all these things to the tap root of independence. I am a writer because a writer is the most independent of beings; independent of thought, action, income and lifestyle, ultimately, with only himself to blame for success or failure. The word 'freelance' is one of the most accurate in our language. But that root feeds a tree with many branches. I must recognize a love of language and the printed word; its ability to communicate with uncommon grace victories and defeats and love and beauty. To influence, to converse, to shape thoughts, to put myself on paper and have the me that is in works worthy enough to be read by another human being. If for some reason I ceased to write professionally, I would write an awful lot of letters. Then, somewhere near the tip of the tree, greens my 'specialty,' outdoor writing. It is too easy to say that I am an outdoor writer because I love the outdoors because they are the only place where you really have a place in life. But that is the theme . . . or philosophy if you will . . . that nourishes my writing and my life."

*   *   *

STUART, Irving R.   1916-

PERSONAL: Born March 15, 1916, in New York, N.Y.; son of Simon and Lena Stuart; married Helen G. Sheffield (a teacher), June 28, 1941. *Education:* City College (now City College of the City University of New York), B.S.S., 1938, M.S., 1948; New York University, Ph.D., 1951. *Residence:* White Plains, N.Y. *Office:* Department of Psychology, Herbert H. Lehman College of the City University of New York, Bronx, N.Y. 10468.

CAREER: Clinical psychologist; Herbert H. Lehman College of the City University of New York, Bronx, N.Y., assistant professor, 1954-65, associate professor, 1965-71, professor of psychology, 1971—. *Military service:* U.S. Army, 1943-46.

MEMBER: International Council of Psychology, American Psychological Association, Interamerican Society of Psychology.

WRITINGS—Published by Van Nostrand, except as indicated: (Editor with L. E. Abt) *Children of Separation and Divorce,* Grossman, 1972; (editor with Abt) *Interracial Marriage,* Grossman, 1973; (editor with Abt) *Social Psychology and Discretionary Law,* 1978; (editor with Abt) *Children of Separation and Divorce: Management and Treatment,* 1981; (editor with Abt) *The Newer Therapies,* 1982; (editor with C. F. Wells) *Pregnancy in Adolescence: Needs, Problems and Management,* 1982; (editor with Wells) *Self-Destructive Behavior in Children and Adolescents,* 1983; (editor with Joanne G. Greer) *The Sexual Aggressor: Current Perspectives on Treatment,* 1983; (editor with Greer) *Victims of Sexual Aggression: Treatment of Children, Women, and Men,* 1984.

Contributor to *Journal of Social Psychology, Journal of Aesthetic Education,* and *International Journal of Social Psychiatry.*

*   *   *

SULLIVAN, Sheila   1927-
(Sheila Bathurst)

PERSONAL: Born January 29, 1927, in Malaya; daughter of Henry (a civil servant) and Georgina (a psychologist; maiden name, McCormick) Bathurst; married David Sullivan (a barrister), August 16, 1952 (divorced, 1978); children: Oriel, Tessa, Jocelyn. *Education:* Oxford University, M.A. (with honors), 1948. *Politics:* Social Democratic Party. *Religion:* None. *Home:* 69 North End Rd., London NW11, England. *Agent:* Curtis Brown Ltd., 168 Regents St., London W1R 5TA, England.

CAREER: Oxford University Press, Oxford, England, member of publicity and editorial staffs, 1948-51; French Lycee de Londres, London, England, teacher of English, 1952-55; freelance writer and editor, 1955—.

MEMBER: P.E.N., Friends of the Earth.

WRITINGS: (Under name Sheila Bathurst) *The Blind Beggar's Daughter* (children's opera libretto), Novello, 1951; (editor) *Critics on Chaucer,* Allen & Unwin, 1971; (editor) *Critics on T. S. Eliot,* Allen & Unwin, 1972; *Summer Rising* (novel), Weidenfeld & Nicolson, 1975; (contributor and illustrations editor) Margaret Drabble, editor, *The Genius of Thomas Hardy,* Weidenfeld & Nicolson, 1976; *Notes on Sterne's "Sentimental Journey,"* Longman, 1984; *"The Sweeniad" by Myra Buttle,* Allen & Unwin, 1984.

WORK IN PROGRESS: A novel; critical and editorial work.

*   *   *

SUTHERLAND, Margaret   1941-

PERSONAL: Born September 16, 1941, in Auckland, New Zealand; daughter of William Charles and Dorothy Genevieve (Bolton) Mansfield; married Alan Sutherland (a business consultant), December 12, 1959; children: Roger Anthony, Claire Frances, David Alan. *Education:* Educated in Auckland, New Zealand. *Religion:* "Subud." *Home:* 346 Huia Rd., Titirangi, Auckland, New Zealand.

CAREER: Writer, 1968—.

AWARDS, HONORS: Literary fellow at Auckland University, 1981; New Zealand Government's Scholarship in Letters, 1984.

WRITINGS: The Fledgling (novel), Heinemann, 1974; *Hello, I'm Karen* (juvenile), Methuen, 1974, Coward, 1976; *The Love*

Contract (novel), Heinemann, 1976; *Getting Through* (stories), Heinemann, 1977; *Dark Places, Deep Regions* (stories) Stemmer House, 1980; (contributor) *The Oxford Anthology of New Zealand Writing since 1945*, Oxford University Press, 1983; *The Fringe of Heaven* (novel), Stemmer House, 1984.

WORK IN PROGRESS: A short-story collection.

SIDELIGHTS: Margaret Sutherland writes: "I used to admire writers with a kind of projected yearning, I suppose. Now I am one, I have only one piece of advice to anyone with that sense of latent talent. Believe very little about the trials, difficulties, and loneliness of a writer's life. These are nonsense. I have never heard of a job without its times of trial, but let us not forget those other times, of concentration, sureness, surprise at the creative flash, satisfaction at the sustained craftsmanship, puzzlement at the source and particular direction of theme, gratitude for the expression of a gift. Writing is a delightful form of invention. It asks for very little outlay of equipment and money, is wonderfully portable and needs no special qualifications. It requires space. Create that space and writing will come and fill it. It is the best teacher of patience I have personally met with. It has required me to get over self-pity, a sense of inferiority, a fear of rejection, laziness, a tendency towards the second-best effort, and a desire to manipulate material for effect instead of waiting, watching, listening. I can compare it to nothing except life itself! It is the result of my living and, as the work slowly takes shape, it can teach me what is important to me, where I am off the track and what is actually real to me."

*   *   *

SUTTON, Larry M(atthew) 1931-

PERSONAL: Born February 24, 1931, in Winter Haven, Fla.; son of Clarence F. (a businessman) and Irma L. (Ashley) Sutton; married Margalo Ann Roller (a teacher), October 18, 1951; children: Debra, Jeffrey, Hollee, Jodi. *Education:* Florida Southern College, B.S., 1954; University of Florida, M.Ed., 1965. *Home:* 1000 West Lake Martha Dr., Winter Haven, Fla. 33880. *Office:* Department of English, Polk Junior College, Winter Haven, Fla. 33880.

CAREER: Ward's Nursery, Avon Park, Fla., production manager, 1959-64; Polk Junior College, Winter Haven, Fla., professor of English, 1965—. Director, American Red Cross, Winter Haven chapter, 1972. *Military service:* U.S. Army, 1949-51; became sergeant; received three battle stars.

MEMBER: Modern Language Association of America, Florida Association of Junior Colleges, Florida Council of Teachers of English.

WRITINGS: (With Maurice Sutton and R. W. Puckett) *College English: A Beginning*, Holbrook, 1969; (with M. Sutton and Puckett) *A Simple Rhetoric*, Holbrook, 1969; (with Puckett and Dion Brown) *Journeys: An Introduction to Literature*, Holbrook, 1970; *Taildraggers High*, Farrar, Straus, 1985.

Books for young people; illustrated by Pat Blumer; published by Carolrhoda Books: *The Mystery of the Late News Report*, 1981; *The Mystery of the Blue Champ*, 1981; *Ghost Plane over Hartley Field*, 1981; *The Case of the Trick Note*, 1981; *The Case of the Smiley Faces*, 1981.

Contributor to *Walt Whitman Journal*, *Real West*, and other publications.

WORK IN PROGRESS: A novel set in Florida's Ten Thousand Islands, which focuses on the lives of fishermen from the viewpoint of a fifteen-year-old boy.

SIDELIGHTS: Larry M. Sutton told *CA:* "For a long time after getting out of the army, my main writing interest lay in serious adult novels depicting the drama of people affected by war. These stories weren't all 'war' stories. Most were intended to show how absurdly war affects people and how our new, young heroes tended to mock the lingering romantic tradition associated with war. But most of these long works, except for spinoff stories or articles, never saw the light of publication. My attic grew heavy.

"Lately I've become interested in writing for and about children; this seems to give me a new zest for writing and I have stories and books going into print.

"For settings, I'm interested in the wilderness or other adventurous places such as airports. This apparently stems from my childhood spent mostly alone in the backwoods of Florida. Above all I want these stories to be interesting, with swift rising action, a good climax. If they also happen to say something 'uplifting,' that's for the better; and I hope they do. . . .

"About writing in general, I have this comment: It's hard for many readers to understand how something which appears so simple after it's written—such as a good, exciting story—could be so hard to write. But the writer's job isn't over when he visualizes interesting settings and begins to feel the emotions of his characters; he must then 'show' these items to his readers so that they can judge if character X is lazy or heroic or caught in a bad situation. It would be much easier for a writer to 'explain.' But explaining is not the writer's job; he must *show* or *dramatize* (and it's much easier to *explain* than it is to *show*). This showing, so that readers can make their own inferences, is what good writing is all about. It calls for hours of work, of revision, in order to find the right words that evoke the proper impression in the reader."

*   *   *

SWANSON, Gustav A(dolph) 1910-

PERSONAL: Born February 13, 1910, in Minn.; son of Gustaf Alfred (an electrician) and Pauline Hagman Swanson; married Evadene Burris (a writer), April 11, 1936; children: Hildegarde Swanson Morgan, Evadene Swanson Gale, Arthur B. *Education:* University of Minnesota, B.S., 1930, M.A., 1932, Ph.D., 1937. *Politics:* Independent. *Home:* 1404 West Lake, Fort Collins, Colo. 80521. *Office:* Department of Fishery and Wildlife, Colorado State University, Fort Collins, Colo. 80523.

CAREER: University of Minnesota, Minneapolis, assistant professor, 1937-41, associate professor of wildlife management, 1942-44; U.S. Department of the Interior, Fish and Wildlife Service, Washington, D.C., biologist and chief of Division of Wildlife Research, 1946-48; Cornell University, Ithaca, N.Y., professor of conservation, 1948-66, head of department, 1948-66, executive director of Laboratory of Ornithology, 1958-61; Colorado State University, Fort Collins, professor of wildlife biology and head of department of fishery and wildlife biology, 1966-75, professor emeritus, 1975—. Visiting professor, Montana State University, New Mexico State University, Texas A&M University, University of Alaska, and University of Minnesota. Member of board on agriculture and renewable resources, National Academy of Sciences/National Research Council, 1974-77; chairman of Environmental Task Force, Ft.

Collins, Colorado Designing Today, 1973-77. Consultant to New York State Joint Legislative Committee on Natural Resources and to National Wildlife Federation and Nature Conservancy (England).

MEMBER: International Association of Fish and Wildlife Agencies, American Ornithologists Union, American Association for the Advancement of Science (fellow), American Institute of Biological Sciences, National Audubon Society (member of board of directors, 1950-56; president of Fort Collins, Colo. chapter, 1979-80), American Society of Mammalogists, National Wildlife Federation, Wildlife Society (honorary member; president, 1954-55), Wilson Ornithological Society (treasurer, 1938-42).

AWARDS, HONORS: Fulbright fellow in Denmark, 1961-62, and at University of New England (Australia), 1968; fellow of Rochester Museum, 1956; Aldo Leopold Memorial Medal from Wildlife Society, 1973; named Outstanding Department Head, Colorado State University, 1974.

WRITINGS: (With Thaddeus Surber and T. S. Roberts) *Mammals of Minnesota*, Minnesota Department of Conservation, 1945; (editor) *The Use and Effects of Pesticides*, New York Joint Committee on Natural Resources, 1963; (with Theodore Shields and others) *Fish and Wildlife Resources on the Public Lands*, Colorado State University, 1969; (editor with Eugene Decker) *Wildlife and the Environment*, Colorado State University, 1973; (with D. R. Allardice, G. E. Radosevich, K. E. Koebel) *Water Law in Relation to Environmental Quality*, Colorado State University, 1974; (with R. A. Ryder) *Conservation and Management of Nongame Birds*, Colorado State University, 1978, revised edition, 1983; (editor) *The Mitigation Symposium*, Forest Service, U.S. Department of Agriculture, 1979. Also contributor to *Wildlife in America*, edited by Howard Brokaw, 1978. Contributor to scientific journals. Editor of *Journal of Wildlife Management*, 1949-53.

SIDELIGHTS: Swanson comments: "I have been interested in wildlife, especially birds, and natural history all my life, and count it good fortune to have been able to have a career in this general area, which has also served as my hobby."

BIOGRAPHICAL/CRITICAL SOURCES: Journal of Wildlife Management, Volume XXXVII, number 3, 1973.

SYDNEY, C.
See TRALINS, S(andor) Robert

* * *

SYNAN, (Harold) Vinson 1934-

PERSONAL: Born December 1, 1934, in Hopewell, Va.; son of Joseph Alexander (a minister) and Minnis (Perdue) Synan; married Carol Lee Fuqua, August 13, 1960; children: Mary Carol, Virginia Lee, Vinson, Jr., Joseph Alexander III. *Education:* Emmanuel Junior College, diploma, 1955; University of Richmond, B.A., 1958; University of Georgia, M.A., 1964, Ph.D., 1967. *Politics:* Republican. *Office:* Director of Evangelism, Pentecostal Holiness Church, Franklin Springs, Ga. 30639.

CAREER: Pentecostal Holiness minister and historian; teacher in senior high schools in Prince George County, Va., 1960-61, and Chesterfield County, Va., 1961-62; Emmanuel College, Franklin Springs, Ga., instructor, 1962-75, chairperson of Division of Social and Behavioral Sciences, 1967-75; Pentecostal Holiness Church, Franklin Springs, currently director of evangelism.

MEMBER: American Historical Society, Southern Historical Society, Society for Pentecostal Studies (founding member; general secretary; president, 1973-74).

WRITINGS: El Movimiento Pentecostal, Enrique Chavez (Chile), 1967; *Emmanuel College: The First Fifty Years*, North Washington Press, 1968; *The Holiness-Penetecostal Movement in the United States*, Eerdmans, 1971; *The Old Time Power*, Advocate Press, 1973; *Charismatic Bridges*, Servant Publications, 1974; (editor) *Aspects of Pentecostal-Charismatic Origins*, Logos International, 1975; *Azusa Street*, Logos International, 1976; *In the Latter Days*, Servant Publications, 1984.

Also author of document of affiliation between Pentecostal Holiness Church (U.S.) and Pentecostal Methodist Church (Chile).

BIOGRAPHICAL/CRITICAL SOURCES: Pentecostal Holiness Advocate (Franklin Springs, Ga.), January 1, 1972.

T

TAINES, Beatrice (Green) 1923-

PERSONAL: Born June 12, 1923, in New York, N.Y.; daughter of Joseph H. (a businessman) and Ruth (Cohen) Green; married Robert Taines (a physician), June 12, 1944; children: Carla, Peter, Andrew, Sarah. *Education:* Hunter College (now of the City University of New York), A.B., 1944; University of California, Berkeley, M.A., 1959, M.J., 1972; John F. Kennedy University School of Law, J.D., 1979. *Home and office:* 3185 Walnut Blvd., Walnut Creek, Calif. 94596.

CAREER: Admitted to State Bar of California, 1979. U.S. Office of War Information, New York, N.Y., news editor, 1944-46; free-lance writer, 1946-48; Diablo Valley College, Pleasant Hill, Calif., instructor in journalism, 1961—; Office of the State Public Defender, San Francisco, Calif., law clerk, 1979, Court of Appeal, San Francisco, law clerk, 1980; Superior Court, Contra Costa County, Martinex, Calif., civil research attorney, 1980-81; private practice of appellate law, Walnut Creek, Calif. 1981—. Lecturer; has made numerous appearances on local radio and television programs. Member of California State School Library Standards Committee. Past chairman of Concord Arts Festival; member of local cultural commission; member of Contra Costa Grand Jury.

MEMBER: American Federation of Teachers, Faculty Association of California Community Colleges, Diablo Valley College Senate.

AWARDS, HONORS: U.S. Office of Education fellowship, 1972; National Endowment for the Humanities fellowship, 1974-75; named Outstanding Educator of America, 1975.

WRITINGS: (With William Sparke) *Doublespeak: Language for Sale,* Harper, 1975; *Woman of Valor, Man of Honor,* Harper, 1975; (contributor) Sparke, editor, *Prisms: A Self Reader,* Harper, 1975; *Help Help: A Brief Guide to College Reading and Writing,* Diablo Valley College, 1976; *What Can You Say about Movies?,* Diablo Valley College, 1979; *Depth,* Prima Facie Press, 1981; *Read On, Write On,* Insight International, 1981.

Author of "Issue Spotting: A Guide for Law Students" series, for Prima Facie Press: *Criminal Law,* 1980; *Torts,* 1981; *Contracts,* 1981; *Civil Procedure,* 1982; *Real Property,* 1983; *Constitutional Law,* 1984; *Criminal Procedure,* 1984. Contributor

to professional journals and popular magazines, including *Liberty, Woman,* and *Mademoiselle.*

SIDELIGHTS: Beatrice Taines comments: "I teach public relations and magazine article writing; many of my students have published work written in the latter course. I initiated a new course in doublespeak at my college. Students in the class analyze deceptive uses of language and visuals in public affairs, advertising, and literature, as communicated through all media.

"My law practice is limited to appeals that involve extensive legal research and the writing of massive briefs."

AVOCATIONAL INTERESTS: Travel—Taines has been to England, Spain, Australia, Japan, New Guinea, Israel, Hong Kong, Romania, Scandinavia, Greece, France,, and Egypt.

*   *   *

TAKAHASHI, Yasundo 1912-

PERSONAL: Born June 12, 1912, in Nagoya-shi, Japan; son of Sakunosuke (an artist) and Teruko (Umemura) Takahashi; married Kuwaki Kusunoki, April 9, 1940; children: Yuri (Mrs. J. Canfield). *Education:* University of Tokyo, B.S., 1935, Ph.D., 1946. *Home:* 135 York Ave., Kensington, Calif. 94708.

CAREER: Japanese National Railways, Tokyo, Japan, design engineer, 1935-37; Yokohama Technical College, Yokohama, Japan, professor of mechanical engineering, 1937-40; Nagoya University, Nagoya, Japan, professor of mechanical engineering, 1940-44; University of Tokyo, Tokyo, professor of mechanical engineering, 1944-58; University of California, Berkeley, professor of mechanical engineering, 1958-79, professor emeritus, 1979—; professor at Toyohashi University, Japan, 1979-81; senior consultant, Mikuni Berkeley Research and Development, 1981—.

Visiting professor at University of Grenoble, 1965 and 1970, Tokyo Institute of Technology, 1965 and 1970, National Polytechnic Institute, Mexico, 1972, University of La Plata, Argentina, 1973, and Keio-University, Japan, 1977.

MEMBER: Japan Society of Instrument and Control Engineering (honorary member), Instrument Society of America, American Society of Mechanical Engineers (fellow).

AWARDS, HONORS: Fulbright scholar at Massachusetts Institute of Technology, 1954-55; Doctor Honoris Causa, National Polytechnic Institute of Grenoble, 1978.

WRITINGS: Theory of Automatic Control, Iwanami, 1954, revised edition, 1959; *Automatic Control System Design Manual,* Kyoritsu, 1954, revised edition, 1970; *Systems and Control,* Iwanami, 1968, revised edition, 1978; (with D. Auslander and M. J. Rabins) *Control,* Addison-Wesley, 1970; *Theory of Dynamic Systems via Computer,* Kagakugijutsu-sha, 1971; (with Auslander and Rabins) *Introducing Systems and Control,* McGraw, 1974; *Control System Computation via Personal Computer,* Ohm Co., 1982; *Digital Control,* Iwanami, 1985.

Editor emeritus of *Journal of Dynamic Systems, Measurement, and Control* of American Society of Mechanical Engineers.

WORK IN PROGRESS: Computer-Aided Instruction Software on Dynamic Systems and Control.

SIDELIGHTS: Yasundo Takahashi told *CA* that "making educational software for personal computers is a new form of textbook writing with expanded dimension."

* * *

TALBERT, Charles H(arold)   1934-

PERSONAL: Born March 19, 1934, in Jackson, Miss.; son of Carl E. (a minister) and Audrey (Hale) Talbert; married Betty Weaver, June 30, 1961; children: Caroline O'Neil, Charles Richard. *Education:* Howard College (now Samford University), B.A., 1956; Southern Baptist Theological Seminary, B.D., 1959; Vanderbilt University, Ph.D., 1963. *Politics:* Democrat. *Religion:* Baptist. *Home:* 3091 Prytania Rd., Winston-Salem, N.C. 27106. *Office:* Box 7212, Wake Forest University, Winston-Salem, N.C. 27109.

CAREER: Wake Forest University, Winston-Salem, N.C., assistant professor, 1963-68, associate professor, 1969-74, professor of religious studies, 1974—.

MEMBER: Society of Biblical Literature, Society for New Testament Studies, Catholic Biblical Association, Society for Values in Higher Education, National Association of Baptist Professors of Religion.

AWARDS, HONORS: Cooperative Program in Humanities fellowship, 1968-69; Society for Religion in Higher Education fellowship, 1971-72; Reynolds research leave, 1979.

WRITINGS: Luke and the Gnostics, Abingdon, 1966; *Reimarus: Fragments,* Fortress, 1970; *Literary Patterns, Theological Themes, and the Genre of Luke-Acts,* Scholars Press, 1974; *What Is a Gospel?,* Fortress, 1977; (editor) *Perspectives on Luke-Acts,* Association of Baptist Professors of Religion, 1978; *Reading Luke,* Crossroad Publishing, 1982; *Luke-Acts: New Perspectives from the Society of Biblical Literature Seminar,* Crossroad Publishing, 1983; *Acts: Knox Preaching Guides,* John Knox, 1984.

Member of editorial board, *Journal of Biblical Literature,* 1981-83. Editor of dissertation series, National Association of Baptist Professors of Religion, 1981-83, and Society of Biblical Literature, 1984-86.

WORK IN PROGRESS: Two books of Biblical commentary.

SIDELIGHTS: Charles Talbert's book *Literary Patterns, Theological Themes, and the Genre of Luke-Acts* has been translated into Japanese. Talbert is competent in Hebrew, Greek, Latin, French, German, and Italian.

TALBOT, Gordon (Gray)   1928-

PERSONAL: Born June 17, 1928, in Utica, N.Y.; son of Clio Earl and Jane (Arnold) Talbot; married Janet Tuttle, August 20, 1949 (died July 3, 1977); married Katherine Colby, October 20, 1979; children: (first marriage) David, Carol. *Education:* Houghton College, B.A., 1949; Nyack College, Th.B., 1951; Wheaton College, Wheaton, Ill., M.A., 1956; New York University, Ph.D., 1968. *Politics:* Republican. *Office address:* RFD 2, Box 622, Union, Me. 04862.

CAREER: Pastor of Christian and Missionary Alliance church in Batavia, N.Y., 1952-54; Bryan College, Dayton, Tenn., instructor in Christian education, 1955-57; Houghton College, Houghton, N.Y., instructor in Christian education, 1957-60; director of Christian education for a Baptist church in Des Moines, Iowa, 1960-63; Detroit Bible College, Detroit, Mich., professor of Christian education, 1963-70, chairman of department, 1964-70; Canadian Bible College, Regina, Saskatchewan, professor of Christian education, 1970-71; free-lance curriculum writer in Houghton, 1971-75; Winnipeg Bible College, Otterburne, Manitoba, professor of Christian education, 1975-76; Christian Schools, Inc., Glen Cove, Me., president, 1976-78; curriculum writer in Houghton, South Hamilton, Mass., and Union, Me., 1978—. Co-owner of Shore Village Book Shoppe, Rockland, Me., 1983—.

WRITINGS: The Breakdown of Authority, Revell, 1976; *How to Study Your Bible,* Back to the Bible Broadcast Correspondence School, 1976; *Overcoming Materialism,* Herald Press, 1977; *A Study of the Book of Genesis,* Christian Publications, 1981. Contributor of about two hundred articles to religious periodicals.

* * *

TARR, Joel A(rthur)   1934-

PERSONAL: Born May 8, 1934, in Jersey City, N.J.; married Arlene Green, 1956 (deceased); married Tova Brafman, 1978; children: (first marriage) Michael, Joanna; (second marriage) Maya, Ilana. *Education:* Rutgers University, B.S. (with high honors), 1956, M.A., 1957; Northwestern University, Ph.D., 1963. *Office:* Program in Technology and Society, Carnegie-Mellon University, Pittsburgh, Pa. 15213.

CAREER: Northwestern University, Evanston, Ill., instructor in history, 1959-61; Long Beach State College (now California State University, Long Beach), Long Beach, Calif., instructor, 1961-63, assistant professor of American history, 1963-66; University of California, Santa Barbara, visiting assistant professor of American history, 1966-67; Carnegie-Mellon University, Pittsburgh, Pa., assistant professor, 1967-70, associate professor, 1970-76, professor of history, technology, and urban affairs, 1976-78, professor of history and public policy, 1978—, director of Program in Technology and Humanities, 1975—, co-director of Ph.D. program in applied history and social science, 1977—. President of Public Works Historical Society, 1982-83.

MEMBER: Society for the History of Technology, American Association for the Advancement of Science, Sigma Xi.

AWARDS, HONORS: American Philosophical Society grants, 1964, 1966; Scaife Fellow, Carnegie-Mellon University, 1967-69; National Foundation for the Humanities junior fellow, 1969-70; National Science Foundation awards, 1975, 1978, 1983;

awards or grants from Andrew W. Mellon Foundation, 1975 and 1980, Exxon Foundation, 1980, and NOAA, 1982.

WRITINGS: A Study in Boss Politics: William Lorimer of Chicago, University of Illinois Press, 1971; (contributor) Bruce Stave, editor, *Urban Bosses, Machines, and Progressive Reformers,* Heath, 1971; (contributor) Alexander Callow, editor, *American Urban History,* 2nd edition (Tarr was not associated with earlier edition), Oxford University Press, 1973; (consulting editor) *Living in Urban America,* Holt, 1974; (editor) *Patterns in City Growth,* Scott, Foresman, 1975; (contributor) James P. Walsh, editor, *The Irish: America's Political Class,* Arno, 1976; (contributor) Robert P. Sutton, editor, *The Prairie State,* Eerdmans, 1976; (editor) *Retrospective Technology Assessment,* San Francisco Press, 1977; *Transportation Innovation and Changing Spatial Patterns in Pittsburgh, 1850-1934: Essays in Public Works History,* Public Works Historical Society, 1978.

(Contributor with S. Stewman) *Public-Private Partnerships in American Cities,* Lexington Books, 1982; (contributor with K. Koons) Mark Rose and George Daniels, editors, *Energy and Transport: Historical Perspectives on Policy Issues,* Sage Publications, 1982; (contributor) Royce Hanson, editor, *Perspectives on Urban Infrastructure,* National Academy of Sciences, 1984.

Also contributor to *Records of the Columbia Historical Society,* edited by J. Kirkpatrick Flack, 1984. Contributor of more than fifty articles to professional journals, including *Agricultural History, American Heritage, Business History, Civil Engineering, Journal of Social History,* and *Technology & Culture;* contributor of over fifty reviews to professional journals and national publications.

WORK IN PROGRESS: Long-Term Pollution Trends in East Coast Estuaries; History of Industrial Waste Disposal.

SIDELIGHTS: Joel A. Tarr writes: "My interest for the past few years has been in the interface between technology and society, particularly the city and technology and technology and the environment. In addition to this area, I have been attempting to use history as a means to shed light upon present day technology-society problems and to aid in anticipating technology impacts."

*   *   *

TATE, Robin
    See FANTHORPE, R(obert) Lionel

*   *   *

TAYLOR, Michael J. H.   1949-

PERSONAL: Born December 6, 1949, in Middlesex, England; son of John W. R. and Doris A. Taylor; married wife, Isobel, June, 1974. *Education:* Attended secondary school in Surbiton, England. *Home:* 51 Higher Dr., Banstead, Surrey, England.

CAREER: Writer.

WRITINGS—Published by MacDonald & Jane's: (With father, John W. R. Taylor, and Kenneth Munson) *Jane's Pocket Book of Military Transport and Training Aircraft,* 1974; (with Munson and J.W.R. Taylor) *Jane's Pocket Book of Commercial Transport Aircraft,* 1974; (with Munson and J.W.R. Taylor) *Jane's Pocket Book of Light Aircraft,* 1974; *Jane's Pocket Book of Research and Experimental Aircraft,* 1976; *Jane's Pocket*

Book of Homebuilt Aircraft, 1977. Also contributor, *All the World's Aircraft.*

Published by Jane's Publishing Co.: *Jane's Encyclopedia of Aviation,* 1980; *Fantastic Flying Machines,* 1981; *Planemakers—Boeing,* 1982; *Milestones of Flight,* 1983; *Planemakers—Shorts,* 1984. Also author, *Giants in the Sky.*

Other publishers: (With J.W.R. Taylor) *Helicopters of the World,* Ian Allen, 1976; (with J.W.R. Taylor) *Missiles of the World,* revised edition, Ian Allen, 1976; (with David Mondey and J.W.R. Taylor) *The Guiness Book of Air Facts and Feasts,* revised edition, Guiness, 1977, new edition, 1984; *Warplanes of the World, 1919-39,* Ian Allen, 1981; *Jet Fighters,* Biron Books, 1982; *Jet Bombers,* Biron Books, 1983; *Commercial Aircraft,* Optimum Books, 1983; *Fighter Aircraft,* Optimum Books, 1983.

Editor of *Aircraft Illustrated,* 1976-77, and of *Jane's Aviation Review.*

*   *   *

TERRY, Margaret
    See DUNNAHOO, Terry

*   *   *

TERZANI, Tiziano   1938-

PERSONAL: Born September 14, 1938, in Florence, Italy; son of Gerardo (an artisan) Terzani; married Angela Staude (a writer); children: Folco, Saskia. *Education:* University of Pisa, Ph.D., 1961; Columbia University, M.I.A., 1969. *Politics:* "Left wing in capitalist countries, right wing in Communist countries." *Address:* Via San Carlo 7, Florence, Italy. *Agent:* Agenzia Letteraria Internazionale, Via Manzoni 41, I-20121 Milan, Italy. *Office: Der Spiegel,* 2 Kennedy Ter., Hong Kong.

CAREER: Lawyer in Florence, Italy, 1962-63; businessman, 1963-67; *Der Spiegel,* Hamburg, West Germany, correspondent in Singapore, 1971-75, Hong Kong, 1975-80, Peking, 1980-84, Hong Kong, 1984—.

WRITINGS: Pelle di Leopardo (title means "Leopard Skin"), Feltrinelli, 1973; *Giai Phong!: The Fall and Liberation of Saigon,* St. Martin's, 1976; *Cambodian Holocaust,* Rowohlt, 1981; *Freunder unter chinesen,* Rowohlt, 1984.

WORK IN PROGRESS: A novel on China.

SIDELIGHTS: Tiziano Terzani writes: "I am a journalist and I don't see what else I could be. If I was born rich a century ago I would have traveled the world and written letters to my friends. I am doing just that and I am getting paid for it."

*   *   *

TEZLA, Albert   1915-

PERSONAL: Born December 13, 1915, in South Bend, Ind.; son of Michael and Lucia (Szenasi) Tezla; married Olive Anna Fox (a psychiatric nurse), July 26, 1941; children: Michael William, Kathy Elaine. *Education:* University of Chicago, B.A., 1941, M.A., 1947, Ph.D., 1952. *Home:* 5412 London Rd., Duluth, Minn. 55804.

CAREER: Employed during his early career as shipping clerk, lathe operator, and secondary teacher; Indiana University, South Bend, instructor in English literature in Extension Division, 1946-48; University of Minnesota, Duluth, instructor, 1949-

53, assistant professor, 1953-56, associate professor, 1956-61, professor of English, 1961-83, professor emeritus, 1983—. Columbia University, visiting professor of Hungarian literature, 1966, visiting scholar, 1975. *Military service:* U.S. Navy, 1942-46; became lieutenant; received Purple Heart and Commendation Medal.

MEMBER: International Association of Hungarian Studies (member of executive committee).

AWARDS, HONORS: Faculty-staff award from University of Minnesota Student Association, 1958, for contributions to student life outside the classroom; Fulbright research fellow in Vienna, 1959-60; American Council of Learned Societies grants, 1961, 1968; Inter-University Committee research fellow in Budapest, 1963-64; Outstanding Teacher Award, University of Minnesota Student Association, Duluth, 1965; commemorative medal from Institute of Cultural Relations (Budapest), 1970, for contributions to the knowledge of Hungarian culture in the United States; International Research and Exchanges Board research fellowship, 1978; National Endowment for the Humanities research grant, 1978-81; award from ARTISJUS, Agence Litteraire, Theatrale et de Musique (Budapest), 1982, for translations of Hungarian literature.

WRITINGS: An Introductory Bibliography to the Study of Hungarian Literature, Harvard University Press, 1964; (contributor) *East Central Europe: A Guide to Basic Publications,* University of Chicago Press, 1969; *Hungarian Authors: A Bibliographical Handbook,* Belknap Press, 1970.

(Editor and contributor) *Ocean at the Window: Hungarian Prose and Poetry since 1945,* University of Minnesota Press, 1981; (contributor) Paul Varnai, editor, *Hungarian Short Stories,* Exile Editions (Toronto), 1983; (contributor) *William Rose Benet: The Reader's Encyclopedia,* Crowell, 1984; (contributor) *World Authors Today, 1975-1980,* H. W. Wilson, 1985; (contributor) *Thirty-Three Hungarian Short Stories,* Corvina Publishing House (Budapest), 1985; *Ferenc Santa: The Fifth Seal and Selected Short Stories,* Corvina Publishing House, 1985; (with daughter, Kathy Elaine Tezla) *Valahol tul, meseorszagban; magyarok Amerikaban, 1895-1920: Somewhere in a Distant Fabled Land,* Europa (Budapest), in press.

Also contributor to *Academic American Encyclopedia,* Arete Publications, 1980. Contributor to *New Hungarian Quarterly, Valosag,* and other periodicals.

WORK IN PROGRESS: The Hazardous Quest: Hungarian Immigrants in the United States, 1895-1920; Four Plays by New Hungarian Playwrights; The Selected Writings of Ivan Mandy; A History of Hungarian Literature since 1945.

SIDELIGHTS: The University of Minnesota, Duluth, has established the Albert Tezla Scholar/Teacher Award in honor of the author. The award recognizes "faculty members who excel in bringing to the classroom a teaching style that emphasizes the worth of research," Tezla told *CA.*

*   *   *

THANET, Neil
    See FANTHORPE, R(obert) Lionel

*   *   *

THIHER, Allen   1941-

PERSONAL: Surname rhymes with "fire"; born April 4, 1941, in Fort Worth, Tex.; son of Ottah A. (a salesman) and Helen (Massy) Thiher. *Education:* University of Texas, B.A., 1963; University of Wisconsin, M.A., 1964, Ph.D., 1968. *Home:* 105 Meadow Lane, Columbia, Mo. 65201. *Office:* Department of Romance Languages, 27 Arts and Science Building, University of Missouri, Columbia, Mo. 65211.

CAREER: Duke University, Durham, N.C., assistant professor of French, 1967-69; Middlebury College, Middlebury, Vt., assistant professor of French, 1969-76; University of Missouri—Columbia, associate professor 1976-81, professor of French, 1982—.

MEMBER: Modern Language Association of America, American Association of Teachers of French, American Association of University Professors, Phi Beta Kappa.

AWARDS, HONORS: University of Wisconsin fellowships, 1963-66; Fulbright scholarship, 1966-67; Middlebury College faculty research grant, 1971; Shell Foundation grant, 1973; Guggenheim fellowship, 1976-77; University of Missouri, summer research fellowship, 1978, travel grants, 1979 and 1981, and Chancellor's Award for outstanding research in the humanities and the arts, 1981.

WRITINGS: Celine: The Novel as Delirium, Rutgers University Press, 1972; *The Cinematic Muse: Critical Studies in the History of French Cinema,* University of Missouri Press, 1979; (contributor) *Actes du Colloque international d'Oxford,* Societe des etudes celiniennes, 1981; (contributor) Morris Beja, S. E. Gontarski, and Pierre Astier, editors, *Samuel Beckett: Humanistic Perspectives,* Ohio State University Press, 1983; *Words in Reflection: Modern Language Theory and Postmodern Fiction,* University of Chicago Press, 1984; *Raymond Queneau,* Twayne, in press.

Also contributor to a volume on Franz Kafka, published by Indiana University Press. Contributor of book reviews and essays to journals, including *Modern Fiction, Modern Drama, PMLA, Philological Quarterly, Romance Notes, Literature/Film Quarterly, Dada/Surrealism, Kentucky Quarterly of Romance Studies,* and *Boundary 2.*

*   *   *

THOMPSON, Paul   1943-

PERSONAL: Born November 23, 1943, in Hitchin, England; son of Philip John and Doris (Swann) Thompson; married Janet Catriona (employed by British Broadcasting Corp.), May 8, 1965 (divorced January 10, 1980); married Veronique Bernard (an actress and theatre director), February 14, 1981; children: (first marriage) Karen Nicola. *Education:* Attended school in Hitchin, England. *Politics:* Socialist. *Home:* 24, Carlton Hill, London N.W.8, England. *Agent:* Michael Imison, Dr. Jan van Loewen Ltd., 21 Kingly St., London W1R 5LB, England.

CAREER: Professional actor, 1964-76; theatre director, 1971—; Morley College, London, England, director of Theatre School, 1974—. Acting tutor at Royal Academy of Dramatic Arts, 1978—; playwriting tutor at City Literary Institute and Antioch International, 1978—. Writer-in-residence, National Theatre, 1977-79, and Royal Shakespeare Co., 1977.

AWARDS, HONORS: Arts Council bursary, 1976.

WRITINGS—Musical plays: The Children's Crusade (first produced in London at National Youth Theatre, September, 1973), Heinemann, 1975; *The Motor Show* (first produced in Dagenham, England, at Leys Hall, March, 1974; produced in London at Half Moon Theatre, April, 1974), Pluto Press, 1975; *By Common Consent* (first produced at National Youth Theatre, September 9, 1974; also see below), Heinemann, 1976; *The Lorenzaccio Story* (first produced by Royal Shakespeare Co. in Stratford-upon-Avon, England, at The Other Place, July 4, 1977), Pluto Press, 1978.

Author of filmscript, "By Common Consent" (based on his musical play of the same title), British Broadcasting Corp. Television, 1975; contributor to filmscript, "Lion of the Desert," Falcon Film Productions, 1979. Also author of adaptation, Vampilov, *Last Summer in Chulimsk*, Birmingham Repertory Theatre, 1984.

WORK IN PROGRESS: Research for a play and for a feature film.

SIDELIGHTS: Paul Thompson has directed productions at numerous theatres, including King's Head Theatre, Soho Poly, Almost Free Theatre, and Royal Academy of Dramatic Arts.

*   *   *

THOMPSON, Thomas 1933-1982

PERSONAL: Born October 3, 1933, in Fort Worth, Tex.; died of cancer, October 29, 1982, in Los Angeles, Calif.; son of Clarence (a teacher) and Ruth (a high school principal) Thompson; married Joyce Alford, 1958 (divorced, 1969); children: Kirk M., Scott M. *Education:* University of Texas, B.A., 1955. *Residence:* Los Angeles, Calif. *Agent:* Robert Lantz, 114 East 55th St., New York, N.Y. 10022.

CAREER: Houston Press, Houston, Tex., reporter, beginning 1955, city editor, 1957-61; *Life,* New York, N.Y., 1961-72, worked as assistant editor, staff writer, entertainment editor, and Paris bureau chief; writer, 1972-82. Teacher of writing at University of Southern California and other institutions.

AWARDS, HONORS: National Headliner Award for investigative reporting and Sigma Delta Chi national medallion for work appearing in *Life;* Edgar Allan Poe Award from Mystery Writers of America, 1977, for *Blood and Money.*

WRITINGS—Nonfiction, except as indicated: *Hearts: Of Surgeons and Transplants, Miracles and Disasters along the Cardiac Frontier,* McCall Publishing, 1971; *Richie: The Ultimate Tragedy between One Decent Man and the Son He Loved,* Saturday Review Press, 1973; *Lost!,* Atheneum, 1975 (published in England as *Hell and High Water,* Deutsch, 1975); *Blood and Money,* Doubleday, 1976; *Serpentine,* Doubleday, 1979; *Celebrity* (novel), Doubleday, 1982. Also author of script for television movie "Callie and Son," 1981.

Contributor of several hundred articles to national magazines, including *McCall's, Ladies' Home Journal, New York Times, New Times, Cosmopolitan, New York,* and *New West.*

WORK IN PROGRESS: A novel and a nonfiction book, both for Doubleday.

SIDELIGHTS: A best-selling author of what the *Chicago Tribune's* Eric Zorn once described as "chronicles of blood, lust, money, betrayal, murder, jealousy, drugs and greed," Thomas Thompson began his writing career as a journalist in his native Texas. His first job after graduating from college was with the *Houston Press,* where, at the age of twenty-three, he became the youngest city editor of a major metropolitan U.S. newspaper. After spending six years in Houston, Thompson left for New York to join the staff of *Life* magazine. There he soon

established himself as a disciplined reporter who completed his work quickly and thoroughly and, as some of his colleagues recalled, with a certain Texas-style panache.

When *Life* ceased publication in 1972, Thompson decided the time was right to give free-lance writing a try. Making Los Angeles his new home base ("I was worn out by New York," he told a reporter for the *New York Times Book Review*), he produced two books in rapid succession—*Hearts,* an account of the rivalry between doctors Michael DeBakey and Denton Cooley, and *Richie,* the story of a Long Island man who killed his drug-addicted son after the teenager attacked him with a knife. Both were expanded versions of highly-praised articles that had originally appeared in *Life.*

It was in 1969 and 1970, while in Houston doing some research for *Hearts,* that Thompson first heard the story that would eventually inspire his nonfiction blockbuster *Blood and Money.* In February, 1969, thirty-eight-year-old Houston socialite Joan Robinson Hill died suddenly after a brief, mysterious illness. The adored only child of self-made Texas oil millionaire Ash Robinson, Joan was at the time of her death unhappily married to her third husband, plastic surgeon John Hill. Ash Robinson, who harbored an intense hatred for his son-in-law, pressured authorities to investigate the possibility that Hill had murdered Joan. At his own expense, Robinson arranged for renowned New York medical examiner Dr. Milton Helpern to perform a second autopsy on the woman's body. Though the autopsy did not reveal an exact cause of death, it did indicate that Joan had received inadequate care during her illness. As a result, Hill was charged with criminal negligence—murder by omission.

The trial that followed, one of the most sensational in Houston's history, saw Hill's second wife (a woman he married shortly after Joan's death) testify that he had admitted poisoning Joan with an injection from a hypodermic filled with a culture grown from human excrement. But other accusations she made proved to be so biased and unsubstantiated that the judge in the case declared a mistrial.

Before Hill could be retried for his wife's murder, however, he himself was murdered by an apparent robber who was in turn shot and killed by a policeman while resisting arrest. The gunman's girlfriend later insisted that Ash Robinson had paid her boyfriend $5000 to kill John Hill; she and another woman charged as accomplices in Hill's murder were eventually tried and sent to prison. Because he could not definitely be linked to any crime, Ash Robinson remained a free man—free to spend his last days "brooding about several wrecked lives and the man he hated most," as Newgate Callendar reports in the *New York Times Book Review.*

Fascinated by the mystery surrounding Joan Robinson Hill's death and the colorful cast of stereotypical Texas characters implicated in the case, Thompson soon became convinced he could write a book on the story. He spent about eighteen months in Houston conducting interviews, transcribing notes and tapes, and reading court transcripts and other pertinent documents. "I used nothing unless I was able to double check it," the author told *Publishers Weekly* writer Barbara Bannon.

As far as readers and critics were concerned, Thompson's long hours of research were well worth the effort. "Thomas Thompson has done a terrific job on this gaudy story, which can hardly be surpassed for crass opulence, crude energy and morbid fascination," declared Walter Clemons in his *Newsweek* review of *Blood and Money.* "Texas bragging has over the years become a notorious bore. But they do murders down there better than anywhere else, and *Blood and Money* is an absolute spellbinder.''

Callendar found the massive, detailed book similar in many ways to Truman Capote's *In Cold Blood*. Though he felt that Thompson was not Capote's stylistic match, the critic nevertheless called *Blood and Money* ''an amazing story.'' Continued Callendar: ''The case had more than its share of bizarre episodes, and Thompson has made the most of these without sensationalizing them. He has also thrown in some titallating material about the amazing moneyed Texans and their way of life. Thus the book has a bit of social commentary in it. It ends inconclusively because there is no clear ending. . . . But it is a story with panoramic sweep. Thompson, a good, investigative reporter, has, one feels, presented it fairly, dispassionately and skillfully.''

The *New York Times*'s Christopher Lehmann-Haupt observed that ''there comes a point about a third of the way into [*Blood and Money*] when the excitement of the narrative seems to ease a bit'' as John Hill goes on trial for murdering his wife. ''Not that this would be the worst thing in the world that could happen to the reader,'' continued the critic. ''We have already had enough action, mystery, passion and gore to fill up most true-crime dramas of the sort that *Blood and Money* is successfully trying to be. . . . But one needn't have worried, as it turns out, the excitement has barely begun. . . . We are [soon] off on another narrative roller-coaster, with even steeper dips and climbs through Texas society, even sharper hairpin turns around questions of probability and motive. . . . At the end, when one looks back, the first third of *Blood and Money* seems comparatively placid.'' In short, concluded Lehmann-Haupt, *Blood and Money* is ''a thoroughly absorbing epic of revenge. It has, as they say, everything—from gossip to grisliness, from savagery to suspense. There may even be a lesson in it somewhere; but as long as the plot keeps twisting . . . who cares?''

Blood and Money was still climbing the best-seller lists when Thompson began the research for his next book, *Serpentine*. The idea for *Serpentine* came from a brief newspaper article Thompson read that reported on the capture in New Delhi of murder suspect Charles Sobhraj. According to the authorities, thirty-five-year-old Sobhraj, a psychopathic con man of Indian and Vietnamese extraction, had made a career out of befriending unwary Western tourists in the Far East, then drugging, robbing, and occasionally murdering them—often by setting them on fire after they were unconscious or too groggy to resist. Intrigued by the potential story he saw in Sobhraj's life and crimes, Thompson convinced his publisher to finance an exploratory trip to India. While there, the author had the opportunity to meet with Sobhraj and Marie-Andree Leclerc, a French-Canadian secretary whose obsession with the charming murderer led her to become his chief accomplice. ''When I saw Sobhraj, probably the most fascinating man I've ever met, and this plain girl, I began to wonder how they got together,'' Thompson told Tony Chiu of the *New York Times Book Review*. ''And what caused their lives to collide with those of their many victims.'' Attempting to find the answers to these and other questions, Thompson stayed in Asia for two years, tracing Sobhraj's brutal career from one country to another.

In an *America* review of *Serpentine*, Thomas M. Gannon praised Thompson's ''prodigious personal research'' and declared him to be ''a reporter of special competence.'' Gannon predicted commercial success for the book based on the author's ''generally skillful handling of the lurid subject matter, coupled with the reading public's apparently endless fascination with bizarre criminal behavior.'' *Washington Post Book World* reviewer Ross Thomas also used the word ''lurid'' to describe *Serpentine*, but he deemed the story ''eminently satisfying if your taste runs to the works and deeds of perfectly wicked villains.''

Commenting in the *New York Times Book Review*, Tom Buckley suggested that *Serpentine* might be somewhat *too* lurid. Though he cited among the book's virtues ''Thompson's exhaustive research into the background of Sobhraj and his supposed victims, his evocation of the exotic locales in which he operated . . . , and his descriptions of the operations of criminal justice systems on the other side of the world,'' Buckley nevertheless felt that the plethora of detail ultimately lessens *Serpentine*'s impact. What happens, maintained the critic, is that Sobhraj soon becomes ''so unrelievably loathesome that readers are likely to tire of his adventures well before the story is over.''

Laurence I. Barrett agreed in a *Time* review that Thompson had a tendency to get bogged down ''in an excess of disorienting detail'' during the course of his ''pounding story of larceny and murder from Hong Kong to Paris.'' ''Still,'' the critic concluded, ''*Serpentine* should hold readers' attention in coils of intrigue, twists of coincidence, and burlesque failures of police in seven countries, the grit of a few civilians outraged enough to play vigilante and the final caper that trips the outlaw. If the book has a message it is that travelers should avoid more than the water in places like Delhi, Bangkok, Kabul and Katmandu.''

After the success of *Blood and Money* and *Serpentine*, Thompson began to receive many offers to do additional true-life crime books, including works on the Patty Hearst kidnapping, the Jonestown massacre in Guyana, and the Hillside Strangler murders in California. But by this time, his enthusiasm for the genre had waned considerably. ''I had a feeling I'd gone about as far as I could go in nonfiction after *Serpentine*,'' Thompson remarked to *Publishers Weekly* writer Wendy Smith. ''It was an enormous project, and I was tired and sick after it was finished. . . . I don't want to do that any more; I'm not interested in major crimes that have been steamrollered by the media.''

Instead, Thompson decided to pursue a new goal—completing his first novel. Curious about what he once termed in the *New York Times Book Review* as ''the most appalling condition people can achieve,'' the author set out to examine the notion of celebrity. ''Celebrity is something Americans invented, like jazz or chop suey,'' Thompson explained to Smith. ''Europeans have royalty, but we had to create people to look up to and admire. Over the years at *Life* I'd written about many celebrities, and I wanted to write a novel exploring why anyone would *want* to be famous.''

The novel, appropriately entitled *Celebrity,* opens with a mystery. A shooting—perpetrator, victims, and motive unknown—leaves one man dead, another critically injured, and a third charged with murder. Through flashbacks, the author then proceeds to introduce the reader to his three protagonists. Friends since childhood, the three—Kleber Cantrell, Mack Crawford, and T. J. Luther—are involved in a rape and apparent murder on the eve of their graduation from high school in 1950. Pledging to remain silent about the crime, the young men go their separate ways, each one seeking his own road to fame and fortune. Cantrell becomes a Pulitzer Prize-winning journalist and successful screenwriter, Crawford a college football hero and Hollywood star, and Luther (following several years spent as a hoodlum and con artist) a charismatic right-wing evangelist and cult leader. Their twenty-fifth class reunion draws them back to their hometown of Fort Worth and, eventually, to the fatal rendezvous described at the beginning of the novel. In a final courtroom scene, the identities of the killer, his victim, and the wounded witness are at last revealed, as are some critical details concerning the long-ago rape and the events that led up to the shooting. Still another murder occurs, this time in the courtroom itself, before the author brings his tale to a close.

For the most part, reviewers found *Celebrity* less entertaining than Thompson's nonfiction works, citing its length (561 pages in the hardcover edition) and the plot's tendency to strain believability to the limit as major drawbacks. A *West Coast Review of Books* critic, for example, wrote that despite the "fascinatingly fleshed" main characters in *Celebrity*, the end of the novel leaves us "somewhat less than satisfied because we have come such a long way in our immersion into the beings of 'the three princes' that the simple tying up of loose and even ambivalent strands seems manipulative."

Writing in the *New York Times Book Review*, Mel Watkins maintained that "the credibility of both the characters and the plot are undermined by Mr. Thompson's vacillation between a straightforward, almost journalistic view of his characters' interaction with actual people and real incidents of the 50's and 60's and an ironic perspective from which he lightly pokes fun at people and events. . . . [As a result, *Celebrity* becomes] an offbeat, mock-suspense tale. While arresting at times, it is finally desultory and a bit long-winded."

John Erlichman, commenting in the *Washington Post Book World*, also wished the novel had unfolded at a faster pace and that Thompson had been less coy about revealing crucial plot details. During the course of the story, said the critic, "Thompson has hinted, he's told us just enough to make us wonder. . . . But he's been so cute about it that, rather than build the suspense, he's worn us all out and we've long ago quit caring. If we'd known right at the top that one of the three old pals killed another, it wouldn't have hurt the story. In fact, I'd have been willing to wade through the remaining thickets of . . . prose to find out who did what to whom. As it is written, I decided it probably wasn't worth the effort."

Detroit News reviewer Robin Watson disagreed with these assessments of *Celebrity*. "In an incredibly well-paced novel, Thompson pulls out his surprises right up to the very end," declared Watson. "For the reader, it means a joyous process of discovery. Despite the book's suspense, skimming for quick answers is unthinkable. And the rich colloquialism of its language, the consistency of its metaphor, the probing exploration of ideas and the genuinely human characters who live out its true-to-Texas larger-than-life successes and tragedies separate *Celebrity* from mere trendy trash."

Though it did not receive widespread critical acclaim, *Celebrity* was greeted with enthusiasm by the reading public. It remained on national best-seller lists for six months after its publication in early 1982; by the end of the year, more than 110,000 hardcover copies had been sold.

In April, 1982, shortly after *Celebrity*'s release, Thomas Thompson talked with *Los Angeles Times* reporter Paul Rosenfeld about his future plans. No longer worried about a recurrence of the writer's block that plagued him while he was attempting to complete his first novel, Thompson was already at work on two new projects, both of which promised to result

in characteristically massive tomes. "As I get older," Thompson observed, "I keep writing bigger and bigger books. And I regret it. It's just that I want to give the reader . . . more." When asked how much more, the author had a ready reply: "James Agee died in a taxicab with forty ideas in his pocket. Forty good ideas. Isn't that a worthwhile goal?"

Less than six months later, Thompson learned he was terminally ill with liver cancer; doctors attributed the development of the disease to a case of hepatitis he had contracted in India while doing research for *Serpentine*. He died on October 29, 1982, only a few weeks after the diagnosis. His passing elicited the following tribute in *People* from longtime friend and former *Life* magazine colleague Richard B. Stolley: "'You want to be good or famous?' the cynical editor asks his young reporter in the [television] miniseries 'Celebrity.' 'When you decide, let me know.' Tommy Thompson never had to decide. As journalist and author, he was both. . . . He had seen too much misery and death around the globe to be totally selfish about his own mortality [when he discovered his condition was hopeless]. . . . 'Dick,' he said [to me], 'you and I have already lived better, more exciting lives than most of the rest of the world.' It was surely true of Tommy. He lived with a breadth that ordinary people never achieve."

MEDIA ADAPTATIONS: Richie was produced as a made-for-television movie and *Celebrity* was adapted as a three-part television miniseries. Both aired on the National Broadcasting Company network.

AVOCATIONAL INTERESTS: Tennis, gardening, walking on the beach, "planning ski trips to St. Moritz which never seem to come off."

BIOGRAPHICAL/CRITICAL SOURCES: Newsweek, June 4, 1973, October 4, 1976; *Washington Post Book World,* June 17, 1973, November 11, 1979, April 11, 1982; *New York Times Book Review,* July 15, 1973, October 3, 1976, October 21, 1979, December 23, 1979, May 9, 1982; *Publishers Weekly,* September 6, 1976, October 3, 1977, April 10, 1981, October 23, 1981; *New York Times,* September 20, 1976, October 13, 1981; *West Coast Review of Books,* January, 1977, May, 1982; *Washington Post,* October 24, 1979; *America,* November 24, 1979; *Time,* December 17, 1979; *Los Angeles Times,* April 24, 1982; *Detroit News,* May 9, 1982; *People,* June 7, 1982, February 20, 1984; *Chicago Tribune,* February 12, 1984.

OBITUARIES: Los Angeles Times, October 30, 1982; *Washington Post,* October 30, 1982; *New York Times,* October 31, 1982; *Newsweek,* November 8, 1982; *Time,* November 8, 1982; *Publishers Weekly,* November 12, 1982.†

—*Sketch by Deborah A. Straub*

*   *   *

THORNBURG, Hershel D(ean) 1936-

PERSONAL: Born October 27, 1936, in Wichita, Kan.; son of Ellis E. and Beulah (Morrison) Thornburg; married Glenda Zimmerman, August 10, 1957; married second wife, Ellen Branson (a dental hygienist), January 26, 1968; children: (first marriage) Marcia, Marchel; (second marriage) Konried, Kristen. *Education:* Friends University, B.A., 1959; Wichita State University, M.Ed., 1966; University of Oklahoma, Ed.D., 1967. *Home:* 1201 East Calle Elena, Tucson, Ariz. 85718. *Office:* Department of Educational Psychology, College of Education, University of Arizona, Tucson, Ariz. 85721.

CAREER: Wichita Public Schools, Wichita, Kan., teacher and principal, 1960-65; University of Oklahoma, Norman, instructor in educational psychology, 1966-67; University of Arizona, Tucson, 1967—, began as associate professor of education, currently professor of educational psychology, head of department, 1983—.

MEMBER: American Psychological Association, American Educational Research Association, American Society for Preventive Dentistry, Society for Adolescent Medicine, National Society for the Study of Education, American School Health Association, National Council of Family Relations, Western Psychological Association, Rocky Mountain Psychological Association, Southwestern Psychological Association, Phi Delta Kappa.

WRITINGS: Sex Education in the Public Schools, Arizona Education Association, 1969; An Investigation of Attitudes among Potential Dropouts from Minority Groups during Their Freshman Year in High School, U.S. Office of Education, 1971; (editor and contributor) Contemporary Adolescence: Readings, Brooks-Cole, 1971, 2nd edition, 1975; Child Development, W. C. Brown, 1973; School Learning and Instruction, Brooks-Cole, 1973; School of Learning, Brooks-Cole, 1973; (editor and contributor) School Learning and Instruction: Readings, Brooks-Cole, 1973; Psychological Behavior of the Preadolescent Child, W. C. Brown, 1973; Adolescent Development, W. C. Brown, 1973; (editor) Preadolescent Development, University of Arizona Press, 1974.

Development in Adolescence, Brooks-Cole, 1975; Contemporary Adolescence, Brooks-Cole, 1975; You and Your Adolescent, H.E.L.P. Books, 1977; Punt, Pop: A Male Sex Role Manual, H.E.L.P. Books, 1977; The Preteen Years, H.E.L.P. Books, 1978; Youth: Transition Years, H.E.L.P. Books, 1978; The Bubblegum Years: Sticking with Kids from 9-13, H.E.L.P. Books, 1979; Introduction to Educational Psychology, West Publishing, 1984.

Contributor to Arizona Teacher, Journal of School Health, College Student Survey, Sexual Behavior, Psychology in the Schools, Adolescence, and other professional journals.

WORK IN PROGRESS: Introduction to Education; Introduction to Health Education; Life Span Development; articles on early adolescents, adolescents, adolescent health care, and instructional design.

SIDELIGHTS: Hershel D. Thornburg told CA: "My primary research and writing interest now is the continued development of an adequate instructional theory which will better describe the functions of the classroom teacher. Several research studies designed to confirm many of my theoretical concepts are now under way."

He added: "I am very excited about the emergence of the new field of early adolescent development. My personal writing and research in the field has yielded me great insights into the developmental nature of individuals between ten and fourteen years of age. I anticipate that this age range will become the new problem area for parents, teachers and social service workers in the future. It is as if these individuals are picking up today where adolescents of twenty years ago left off. As founder and editor of the Journal of Early Adolescence, I am able to see progression in the field and find it to be most exciting."

THORPE, Trebor
    See FANTHORPE, R(obert) Lionel

*   *   *

THORPE, Trevor
    See FANTHORPE, R(obert) Lionel

*   *   *

TIGER, Lionel   1937-

PERSONAL: Born February 5, 1937, in Montreal, Quebec, Canada; son of Martin and Lillian (Schneider) Tiger; married Virginia Conner (a professor and writer), August 19, 1964; children: Sebastian. Education: McGill University, B.A., 1957, M.A., 1959; University of London, Ph.D., 1962. Agent: Lynn Nesbit, International Creative Management, 40 W. 57th St., New York, N.Y. 10019. Office: Department of Anthropology, Douglass College, Rutgers University, New Brunswick, N.J. 08903.

CAREER: University of British Columbia, Vancouver, lecturer in political sociology, 1963, assistant professor of sociology, 1963-68; Rutgers University, New Brunswick, N.J., Livingston College, associate professor of anthropology, 1968-70, Graduate School, associate professor of anthropology, 1970-72, Douglass College, professor of anthropology, 1972—, director of graduate programs in anthropology, 1970-72. Visiting lecturer, Western Washington State College, 1963; member of lecture series in nursing education, Vancouver General Hospital, 1964-65; program chairman, Committee on African Studies in Canada, 1965; consultant and leader of agent training programs, Department of Indian Affairs, Vancouver, 1968; Guggenheim Foundation, consulting research director, 1972—, co-principal investigator of program in socio-biology, 1972-83.

MEMBER: P.E.N. (United States executive board secretary, beginning 1981), American Anthropological Association (fellow), Royal Anthropological Institute (fellow), Canadian Sociology/Anthropology Association, American Sociological Association (fellow), American Association for the Advancement of Science, Society for the Study of Evolution (fellow), Association for the Study of Animal Behaviour.

AWARDS, HONORS: Chester McNaughton Prize for Creative Writing, 1956. Grants and fellowships include: Ford Foundation Foreign Area Training Fellowship, 1962; Canada Council Summer Research Grant, 1965; Guggenheim fellowship, 1968; Canada Council-Killan Bequest Awards for Inter-Disciplinary Research, 1968, 1969-70.

WRITINGS: (With C. W. Eliot, K. D. Maegele, M. Prang, and M. W. Steinberg) Discipline and Discovery, University of British Columbia, 1966; Men in Groups, Random House, 1969; (with Robin Fox) The Imperial Animal, Holt, 1971; Women in the Kibbutz, Harcourt, 1975; (editor) Female Hierarchies, Aldine, 1978; Optimism: The Biology of Hope, Simon & Schuster, 1979.

Contributor: Horace Miner, editor, The City in Modern Africa, Praeger, 1967; C. McAuliffe, editor, Re-action, Boyd & Fraser, 1971; Duane Quiatt, editor, Primates on Primates, Burgess, 1972; Perry and Seidler, editors, Contemporary Society: An Introduction to Social Science, Harper, 1972; Sandberg, editor, Order and Diversity, Wiley, 1973; Fox, editor, Somatic Factors and Social Behavior, Malaby Press, 1975; Chagnon and

Irons, editors, *Biology and Social Organization,* Duxbury, 1979; Steklis and Kling, editors, *Hormones, Drugs, and Social Behavior among Primates,* SP Medical and Scientific Books, 1983.

Author of over one hundred papers on sociology and anthropology presented at professional meetings and symposiums. Contributor to *Encyclopedia Americana;* also contributor of articles and book reviews to journals in his field. Member of editorial board, *Journal of African Studies in Canada,* 1966-68, *Social Science Information,* 1975—, and *Ethology and Sociobiology.*

SIDELIGHTS: "I am saying that making optimistic symbols and anticipating optimistic outcomes of undecided situations is as much a part of human nature, of the human biology, as are the shape of the body, the growth of children, and the zest of sexual pleasure," Lionel Tiger writes in *Optimism: The Biology of Hope.* "This optimism," he continues, "is related to our general confidence in social arrangements which a mammal with a lengthy phase of dependence will develop, but also with a kind of cognitive overdrive associated with our past as a hunting primate. When we acquired our huge cerebral cortex, this elaborate organ started producing an ever more complex and imaginative stock of optimistic schemes and varying plausible adventures. Neither the consciousness of mortality nor a cold sense of human frailty depresses the belief in desirable futures."

Writing in the *New York Times,* Anatole Broyard calls Tiger's book "a marriage of virtuoso scholarship and highly sophisticated romantic speculation about the nature and condition of our species. Whether you are persuaded by it or not, 'Optimism' is a brilliant raid on contemporary thinking in biology, anthropology and sociology."

BIOGRAPHICAL/CRITICAL SOURCES: New York Times, June 18, 1969, May 2, 1979; *Life,* June 20, 1969; *Newsweek,* July 7, 1969; *New York,* July 7, 1969; *Statesman,* July 18, 1969; *Book World,* July 20, 1969, October 12, 1969; *Spectator,* January 10, 1970; *Canadian Forum,* February, 1970; *Commonweal,* March 20, 1970; *L'Express,* March 8-14, 1971; *Observer,* June 24, 1979; Lionel Tiger, *Optimism: The Biology of Hope,* Simon & Schuster, 1979.

*   *   *

TOBIAS, Andrew P. 1947-

PERSONAL: Born April 20, 1947, in New York, N.Y.; son of Seth D. (chairman of an advertising agency) and Audrey J. (president of a national service organization) Tobias. *Education:* Harvard University, B.A. (cum laude), 1968, M.B.A., 1972. *Residence:* New York, N.Y. *Agent:* Sterling Lord Agency, 660 Madison Ave., New York, N.Y. 10021.

CAREER: Writer. Harvard Student Agencies, Inc., Cambridge, Mass., president, 1967-68; National Student Marketing Corp., New York, N.Y., vice-president, 1968-70.

AWARDS, HONORS: Gerald Loeb award, 1984.

WRITINGS: (Editor) *How to Earn (a Lot of) Money in College,* Harvard Student Agencies, Inc., 1968; (with Arnold Bortz and Caspar Weinberger) *The Ivy League Guidebook,* Macmillan, 1968; *Honor Grades on Fifteen Hours a Week,* Collier, 1969; *The Funny Money Game,* Playboy Press, 1971; *Fire and Ice: The Story of Charles Revson,* Morrow, 1974; *The Only Investment Guide You'll Ever Need,* Harcourt, 1977; *Getting By*

on $100,000 a Year (and Other Sad Tales) (Book of the Month Club alternate selection; dual main selection of Fortune Book Club), Simon & Schuster, 1980; *The Invisible Bankers: Everything the Insurance Industry Never Wanted You to Know* (Book of the Month Club, Fortune Book Club, and Conservative Book Club selection), Simon & Schuster, 1982; *Money Angles,* Simon & Schuster, 1984; *Managing Your Money* (computer program), Micro Education Corp. of America, 1984.

Contributor to national magazines, including *Playboy, Esquire, New York Magazine, Parade,* and *Fortune.* Contributing editor, *New York Magazine,* 1972-76, and *Esquire,* 1977-1984.

SIDELIGHTS: Andrew Tobias "is a member of the irreverent new breed of business writer, who can wade fearlessly into the most abstruse financial transaction and emerge with an account of what happened that reads like *The Ipcress File,*" writes Anne Chamberlin in the *Washington Post Book World.* A graduate of Harvard College and the Harvard Business School, Tobias began writing when he was still an undergraduate. His tongue-in-cheek guide to surviving the college grind, *Honor Grades on Fifteen Hours a Week,* gave him the chance to make people laugh and helped him formulate the breezy but informed approach that has become his trademark.

Tobias's first real business book, *The Funny Money Game,* appeared in 1971—the same year he severed his head-spinning association with the National Student Marketing Corporation and enrolled as a graduate student at Harvard. The book chronicles the meteoric rise and fall of this expansion-oriented conglomerate from an insider's point of view. In his next project, Tobias turns from the profile of a corporation to the profile of a quintessential business personality, Charles Revson, the cosmetics magnate. Though Revson was despised by many of his business associates, *Fire and Ice: The Story of Charles Revson* tries to present a balanced picture. "Tobias does his level best to separate the true from the merely vengeful, seeking confirmation or modification where he can, but not letting the lack of it stand in the way of including a good story," *New York Times* reviewer Richard R. Lingeman notes. "His seine catches a lot of the muck, which should please gossip fans who like theirs down and dirty. Yet he clings to a seriousness of purpose on the whole and is fair, with a sympathetic bias toward Revson."

Both *Fire and Ice* and Tobias's subsequent book, *The Only Investment Guide You'll Ever Need,* were best-sellers, and his promotional tours across the United States not only boosted his sales but put him in touch with his readers. He once joked to *Publishers Weekly* interviewer Stella Dong that he "writes to satisfy two constituencies—'my mother' and 'the business people who want to be talked to by someone who understands their problems.'" Then, on a more serious note, he explained that his writing "has to make sense and be fun to read for the average person. The challenge is to do that without being wrong or oversimplifying the subject."

His most challenging subject to date has been his investigation of the American insurance industry—a behemoth so complex that Tobias believes even some of its agents do not fully understand its nature. His book, *The Invisible Bankers: Everything the Insurance Industry Never Wanted You to Know* took five years to complete, far longer than Tobias had anticipated. "I'd like to tell you that I bugged the office of the president of a major insurance company or that I had secret meetings in dark parking lots with some incredible Deep Throat source," he told Stella Dong. "But actually I spent most of my time poring over industry reports with titles like 'Best's Aggregates and Averages.' If I told you more your eyes would glaze over.''

Because his subject was so inherently boring, Tobias drew raves for his engaging approach. *Publishers Weekly* describes him as ''a genius who can transform a billion dull dollars into a million loud laughs,'' and Peter Passell commends his ''ability to transform a dense analysis of insurance into a good read,'' in the *New York Times Book Review*. Using anecdotes and informative trivia to enliven his report, Tobias unearths what Passell calls ''the venality and sloth of an industry only marginally accountable to the public.''

Tobias not only lambasts the present system, he also makes suggestions for improvement. ''He proposes subjecting insurers to Federal oversight because the state regulators who now govern them are too closely allied with the industry,'' explains Susan Dentzer in *Newsweek*. Under ideal conditions, full disclosure would also be required so that ''how much insurers would likely pay out in claims, or interest on a given insurance policy would be printed at the beginning to encourage price-cutting and comparison shopping,'' continues Dentzer. And, finally, Tobias advocates a nationwide system of no-fault automobile coverage ''to get more money to the victims of auto accidents and less to lawyers waging liability suits or insurance agents selling the coverage,'' Dentzer explains.

Some of Tobias's suggestions strike industry experts as being over-simplified. The retired chairman of one insurance company, for example, agreed with many of Tobias's points, but dismissed his ideas for reform as ''utopian.'' And *Washington Post Book World* reviewer, Ronald Kessler, expresses a desire for more evidence and suggests that ''the book fails repeatedly to support its points with specific examples or documentation.'' But Christopher Lehmann-Haupt of the *New York Times* assesses Tobias's approach differently: ''The real reason he has softened his muckraking—the real reason his book maintains its good-humored tone throughout and steadfastly avoids any hair-tearing or screeching—is because muckraking is so much more effective when done that way.''

BIOGRAPHICAL/CRITICAL SOURCES: New York Times, April 21, 1968, August 25, 1976, February 22, 1978, May 21, 1978, August 31, 1980, February 18, 1982; *Saturday Review*, October 16, 1971, September, 1980; *Wall Street Journal*, December 20, 1971, December 8, 1976; *Publishers Weekly*, July 11, 1980, December 18, 1981, January 22, 1982; *Washington Post Book World*, August 24, 1980, February 14, 1982; *Newsweek*, March 1, 1982; *New York Times Book Review*, March 14, 1982; *Los Angeles Times Book Review*, April 4, 1982; *New York Magazine*, March 12, 1984.

—*Sketch by Donna Olendorf*

*   *   *

TODSICHER, J(ohn) Edgar 1926-

PERSONAL: Born December 26, 1926, in Yahoo, Kan.; son of Andrew Jackson (an itinerant preacher) and Thelma (Thanatogenes) Todsicher; married Inocencia B. Engkopf, June 26, 1944 (divorced, 1972); married Amelia Whitbread, July 4, 1973 (divorced, 1975); married Nancy Snake Bear (a souvenir retailer), June 25, 1976; children: (first marriage) John Wayne, Carrie Nation (Mrs. Gerry C. Mander), Bob Jones, Aimee Semple, Mercury and Apollo (twin sons; deceased), Richard Spiro; (second marriage) Cosmo Milhous; (third marriage) Joyce Loud Snake. *Education:* Attended God's Peace and Power Baptist Seminary, 1944; Gopher Junction Community College,

A.A., 1947; also studied Kranshaw Correspondence Course in salesmanship, 1949, and attended Betsy Barnes Business College, Gopher Junction, 1951. *Politics:* ''Liberty.'' *Religion:* ''Native Pantheism.'' *Home:* 221 Lewiston Rd., Grosse Pointe Farms, Mich. 48236. *Office:* Todsicher-Bear Wild West Novelty Products, 17 Cowpoke Dr., St. Clair Shores, Mich. 48080.

CAREER: Employed as door-to-door vacuum cleaner salesman in Haggard County, Kan., 1950-51; Heep Collection Agency, St. Louis, Mo., collector, 1952-56; Eddie Scheister's Used Parts and Service (used car dealer), St. Louis, Mo., salesman, 1956-59, in charge of training salesmen, 1959-62; Sado & Miasma Life Insurance, Inc., Grand Rapids, Mich., broker, 1963-69; Caveat Emptor Life Insurance, Detroit, Mich., founder and president, 1969-76; Todsicher-Bear Wild West Novelty Products, St. Clair Shores, Mich., vice-president, 1976—. Organizer of evangelical meetings for Amazing Grace Baptist Union throughout southern U.S., 1952-62; founder and treasurer of Metropolitan Church of True Believers, Detroit, Mich.; founding member of Great Spirit Church, Detroit, Mich., 1976. *Military service:* U.S. Army, chaplain's assistant, 1947-49.

MEMBER: Western Merchants and Clothiers Association, Rhinestone Guild, Saddle Tramps, Native American Souvenir Association, Historical Americana Retail-Wholesalers.

AWARDS, HONORS: Sons of Business award, 1968, for outstanding service to the life insurance community; George Lincoln Rockwell Memorial award, Sweet Jesus Press, 1970, for ''True-Belief'' series; Pearly Bridle award, Fancy Duds Association, 1980, for *Plains Tuxedos: A History of Fringed Leather Attire;* award of merit, Western Merchants and Clothiers Association, 1980.

WRITINGS: The Christian Car Salesman: Moral Merchandising (booklet), Betsy Barnes Business Press, 1958; (with father, Andrew Jackson Todsicher) *Armageddon Trilogy,* Schweinkopf Publishers, Book 1: *Armageddon and You,* 1959, Book 2: *Armageddon Revisited,* 1961, Book 3: *Son of Armageddon,* 1961; *Redemption in Our Time: How Life Insurance Can Save America,* Palm Tree Press, 1975; *Life Insurance and the Hereafter: How You Can Collect on Your Own Policy,* Palm Tree Press, 1975.

From Right to Left: One Man's Personal and Political Odyssey through the American Socio-Political Landscape, New Discovery Publications, 1976; *Buying Back Manhattan: American Souvenirs as a Force to Be Reckoned with in the National Marketplace,* Todsicher-Bear Books, 1979; *Plains Tuxedos: A History of Fringed Leather Attire,* Todsicher-Bear Books, 1980; *Marketing Western Products: A Guide to Manufacturing and Distribution,* Western Merchants and Clothiers Association, 1981.

''True Belief'' series, all published by Sweet Jesus Press: *The First Book of True Believers,* 1964; *Total Immersion and True Belief,* 1964; *True Belief and Your Children,* 1965; *True Belief and the Evils of Fluoridation,* 1966; *True Belief and Communism,* 1966; *True Belief and LSD,* 1967; *True Belief and Perversion,* 1967; *True Belief and Woman's Place,* 1968; *True Belief and Your Operation,* 1970; *The Moon Walk and True Belief,* 1970; *True Belief and America's Deteriorating Morals,* 1971; *True Belief and the Necessity of Repealing the Nineteenth Amendment,* 1972; *True Belief and Your Divorce,* 1972; *True Belief and Salvation through Remarriage,* 1973; *True Belief and the Evils of Sex Education,* 1974.

WORK IN PROGRESS: Selling America Back to the Americans: A Brief History of Western Souvenirs, for Todsicher-Bear books.

SIDELIGHTS: J. Edgar Todsicher told *CA:* "In 1976 I met and married Nancy Snake Bear, an event which effectively ended my long personal obsession with the nightmare netherworld of right-wing extremist politics and religious fundamentalism. Together Nancy Snake and I founded Wild West Novelty Products, a firm dedicated to helping Americans discover their roots through the acquisition of authentic souvenir reproductions of items from our country's great past. History has shown us that social enlightenment is primarily the product of simple economics. By selling back to Americans what was once theirs in the past, we can achieve not only profound social awareness but a high degree of economic fulfillment as well. Thus, with a good conscience, we can reap the vast benefits of the Free Enterprise system while at the same time contributing to social justice and better culture."

AVOCATIONAL INTERESTS: The stock market, inventing Native American costumes.

BIOGRAPHICAL/CRITICAL SOURCES: Seymour Slarom, *A Christian Interpretation of "The Armageddon Trilogy,"* Sweet Jesus Press, 1963; *Supremacist Quarterly,* spring, 1968; *Yahoo* (Kan.) *Herald,* November 17, 1970; *Garment Marketing Newsletter,* December, 1980.

*   *   *

TOOLE, Rex
    See TRALINS, S(andor) Robert

*   *   *

TORRO, Pel
    See FANTHORPE, R(obert) Lionel

*   *   *

TOWNSEND, Mark
    See WALLMANN, Jeffrey M(iner)

*   *   *

TRACY, Leland
    See TRALINS, S(andor) Robert

*   *   *

TRAINOR, Richard
    See TRALINS, S(andor) Robert

*   *   *

TRALINS, Bob
    See TRALINS, S(andor) Robert

*   *   *

TRALINS, Robert S.
    See TRALINS, S(andor) Robert

TRALINS, S(andor) Robert   1926-
    (Bob Tralins, Robert S. Tralins; pseudonyms: Ray Z. Bixby, Norman A. King, Alfred D. Laurance, Keith Miles, Sean O'Shea, Rex O'Toole, C. Sydney, Rex Toole, Leland Tracy, Richard Trainor, Ruy Traube, Dorothy Verdon)

PERSONAL: Born April 28, 1926, in Baltimore, Md.; son of Emanuel (a shipbuilder) and Rose (Miller) Tralins; married Sonya Lee Mandel; children: Myles J., Alan H. *Education:* Attended Eastern College (now University of Baltimore), 1946-48.

CAREER: Writer. *Military service:* U.S. Marine Corps Reserve, 1943-45.

WRITINGS: How to Be a Power Closer in Selling, Prentice-Hall, 1960; *Dynamic Selling,* Prentice-Hall, 1961; *Torrid Island,* Novel Books, 1961; *Pleasure Was My Business* (autobiography of Madam Sherry [pseudonym of Ruth Barnes] as told to Tralins), Lyle Stuart, 1961; *Caesar's Bench,* Tuxedo Books, 1961; *Law of Lust,* Tuxedo Books, 1961; *Congo Lust,* Tuxedo Books, 1961; *Naked Hills,* Tuxedo Books, 1961.

Hillbilly Nymph, Tuxedo Books, 1962; *Freak Woman,* Novel Books, 1962; *Nymphokick,* Merit Books, 1962; *Four Queens,* Novel Books, 1962; *Seductress,* Novel Books, 1962; *Female Rapist,* Novel Books, 1962; *Love Goddess,* Novel Books, 1962; *Primitive Orgy,* Novel Books, 1962; *Passion Potion,* Novel Books, 1962; *Hired Nymph,* Novel Books, 1962; *Office Girl,* Novel Books, 1962; *Four Wild Dames,* Novel Books, 1962; *Seduction Salon,* Novel Books, 1962; *International Girl,* Novel Books, 1962; *Barechested Beauty,* Novel Books, 1962; *Smuggler's Mistress,* Novel Books, 1962; *Jazzman in Nudetown,* Bedside Books, 1963; *Orgy of Terror,* Novel Books, 1963; *Freak Lover,* Novel Books, 1963; *Colossal Carnality,* Novel Books, 1963; *Love Experiment,* Novel Books, 1963.

The Ultimate Passion, Novel Books, 1964; *Experiment in Desire,* Novel Books, 1964; *Love Worshiper,* Novel Books, 1964; *Erotic Play,* Novel Books, 1964; *Goddess of Raw Passion,* Novel Books, 1964; *Donna Is Different,* Novel Books, 1964; *The One and Only Jean,* Novel Books, 1964; *Rites of the Half-Women,* Novel Books, 1965; *Squaresville Jag,* Belmont Books, 1965; (with Dr. Michael M. Gilbert) *Twenty-one Abnormal Sex Cases,* Paperback Library, 1965; *They Make Her Beg,* Novel Books, 1965.

Beyond Human Understanding: Strange Events, Ace Books, 1966; *The Miss from S.I.S.,* Belmont Books, 1966; *The Chic Chick Spy,* Belmont Books, 1966; *The Cosmozoids,* Belmont Books, 1966; *The Ring-a-Ding UFO's,* Belmont Books, 1966; *Strange Events Beyond Human Knowledge,* Avon Books, 1967; *Cairo Madam,* Paperback Library, 1968; *Clairvoyant Strangers,* Popular Library, 1968; *Weird People of the Unknown,* Popular Library, 1969; *Children of the Supernatural,* Lancer, 1969; *Fetishism,* Paperback Library, 1969; *Runaway Slave,* Lancer, 1969; *Slave's Revenge,* Lancer, 1969; *Panther John,* Lancer, 1969.

Supernatural Strangers, Popular Library, 1970; *The Hidden Spectre,* Avon, 1970; *ESP Forewarnings,* Popular Library, 1970; *Clairvoyant Women,* Popular Library, 1970; *Clairvoyance in Women,* Lancer, 1971; *Supernatural Warnings,* Popular Library, 1972; *Ghoul Lover,* Popular Library, 1973; *Android Armageddon,* Pinnacle Books, 1974; *Buried Alive,* Merit

Publications, 1977; (author of introduction) *Psychic Women*, 3rd edition, Merit Publications, 1977; *Chains*, New English Library, 1981.

Author of screenplay "Illegal Tender," 1975; also author of *Death Before Dishonor*, 1962, *Captain O'Six*, 1962, *Artist Swinger*, 1963, *Devil's Hook*, 1963, *The Smugglers*, 1964, *The Pirates*, 1964, *Gunrunner*, 1964, *Slave King*, 1965, *Sexual Fetish*, 1966, *Gomer Pyle, USMC*, 1966, *Dragnet '67*, 1966, *Remember to Die*, 1966, (under pseudonym Dorothy Verdon) *First Try*, 1966, (under pseudonym Leland Tracy) *Song of Africa*, 1968, (under pseudonym Richard Trainor) *Yum-Yum Girl*, 1968, *Black Brute*, 1969, *The Mind Code*, 1969, *ESP Forewarnings*, 1969, *Black Pirate*, 1970, *The Hidden Spectre*, 1970, and (under pseudonym Alfred D. Laurance) *Homer Pickle the Greatest*, 1971.

Under pseudonym Ray Z. Bixby: *The Rites of Lust*, Softcover Library, 1967.

Under pseudonym Norman A. King: *French Leave*, Midwood, 1967; *Turn Your House into a Money Factory*, Morrow/Quill, 1982. Also author of *So Cold, So Cruel*, 1966, *Hide and Seek*, 1966, and *The Flyers*, 1967.

Under pseudonym Keith Miles: *Dragon's Teeth*, Popular Library, 1973.

Under pseudonym Sean O'Shea: *Whisper*, Softcover Library, 1965; *What a Way to Go*, Belmont Books, 1966; *Sex Variations in Voyeurism*, Award Books, 1967; *Psychokick*, Lancer Books, 1967; *Operation Boudoir*, Belmont Books, 1967; *Win with Sin*, Belmont Books, 1967; *The Nymph Island Affair*, Belmont Books, 1967; *The Invasion of Nymphs*, Belmont Books, 1967; *Topless Kitties*, Belmont Books, 1968.

Under pseudonymm Rex O'Toole: *Cheating and Infidelity in America*, Belmont Books, 1968. Also author of *Remember to Die*, 1967, *Variations in Exhibitionism*, 1967, *Confessions of an Exhibitionist*, 1968, and *Gigolos*, 1969.

Under pseudonym C. Sydney; all published by Midwood Books: *Lure of Luxury*, 1966; *Trick or Treat*, 1966; *Sin Point*, 1966; *Hideaway Lane*, 1966; *Ripe and Ready*, 1966; *Lost and Found*, 1966; *Executive Wife*, 1967; *Take Me Out in Trade*, 1967. Also author of *Stay until Morning*, 1966, *The Higher the Price*, 1966, *The Love Business*, 1966, *Office Swinger*, 1966, and *Give and Take*, 1967.

Under pseudonym Rex Toole: *Soft Sell*, Bee-Line Books, 1967; *Nymphet Syndrome*, Award Books, 1967.

Under pseudonym Ruy Traube: *The Seduction Art*, Belmont Books, 1967; *Uninhibited*, Belmont Books, 1968; *Memoirs of a Beach Boy Lover*, Lancer, 1969.

SIDELIGHTS: S. Robert Tralins told *CA:* "[I am] reverting to the writing of serious, long length fiction." He adds: "[I have] been moving in this direction for twenty years."

BIOGRAPHICAL/CRITICAL SOURCES: Los Angeles Times Book Review, November 11, 1982.†

*   *   *

TRASK, Jonathan
   See LEVINSON, Leonard

*   *   *

TRAUBE, Ruy
   See TRALINS, S(andor) Robert

TREE, Cornelia
   See NICHOLS, Nina (Marianna) da Vinci

*   *   *

TREFOUSSE, Hans Louis   1921-

PERSONAL: Surname is pronounced "Trayfus"; born December 18, 1921, in Frankfurt, Germany; came to the United States in 1936, naturalized in 1943; son of George L. (a physician) and Elizabeth (Albersheim) Trefousse; married Rashelle Friedlander (a teacher), January 26, 1947; children: Roger Philip. *Education:* City College (now City College of the City University of New York), B.A., 1942; Columbia University, M.A., 1947, Ph.D., 1950. *Politics:* Democrat. *Religion:* Jewish. *Home:* 22 Shore Acres Rd., Staten Island, N.Y. 10305. *Office:* Department of History, Brooklyn College of the City University of New York, Brooklyn, N.Y. 11210.

CAREER: Adelphi College, Garden City, N.Y., instructor in history, 1949-50; City University of New York, Brooklyn College, Brooklyn, N.Y., instructor, 1950-57, assistant professor, 1958-60, associate professor, 1961-65, professor of history, 1966—, Graduate School and University Center, New York, N.Y., associate professor, 1962-65, professor of history, 1965—. Visiting professor at University of Wisconsin—Milwaukee, 1959, 1968, University of Minnesota, 1963, and Johns Hopkins University, 1964. Editorial advisor, Twayne Publishers. *Military service:* U.S. Army, 1942-45; became captain; received Bronze Star with oak-leaf cluster and Purple Heart. U.S. Army Reserve, 1945—; present rank, lieutenant colonel.

MEMBER: American Historical Association, Organization of American Historians, Reserve Officers Association of the United States, New York Historical Society. *Awards, honors:* Distinguished teaching award, Brooklyn College (now Brooklyn College of the City University of New York), 1960; Guggenheim fellow, 1977-78; American Council of Learned Societies grant, 1984.

WRITINGS: Germany and American Neutrality, 1939-1941, A. B. Bookman, 1951; *Ben Butler: The South Called Him Beast*, Twayne, 1957; (editor) *What Happened at Pearl Harbor?*, Twayne, 1958; (author of preface and introductory notes) Gideon Welles, *Civil War and Reconstruction*, Twayne, 1959; (author of preface and introductory notes) Welles, *Lincoln's Administration*, Twayne, 1960; *Benjamin Franklin Wade: Radical Republican from Ohio*, Twayne, 1963; (editor) *The Cold War*, Putnam, 1965; *The Radical Republicans: Lincoln's Vanguard for Racial Justice*, Knopf, 1969.

(Editor) *Background for Radical Reconstruction*, Little, Brown, 1970; (editor) *The Causes of the Civil War*, Holt, 1971; *Reconstruction: America's First Effort at Racial Democracy*, Van Nostrand, 1971; *Impeachment of a President: Andrew Johnson, the Blacks, and Reconstruction*, University of Tennessee Press, 1975; *Lincoln's Decision for Emancipation*, Lippincott, 1975; (editor) *Toward a New View of America: Essays in Honor of Arthur C. Cole*, Burt Franklin, 1977; (editor with Abraham S. Eisenstadt and Ari Hoogenboom) *Before Watergate: Problems of Corruption in American Society*, Brooklyn College Press, 1978; (editor) *Germany and America: Essays on International Relations*, Brooklyn College Press, 1980; *Carl Schurz: A Biography*, University of Tennessee Press, 1982; *Pearl Harbor: The Continuing Controversy*, Robert E. Krieger, 1982.

Editor of "Statesmen and Rulers of the World" series, Twayne, 1966-76. Contributor to *Encyclopaedia Britannica* and to periodicals, including *Far Eastern Quarterly, Antioch Review, Mississippi Valley Historical Review,* and *Civil War History.*

WORK IN PROGRESS: A biography of Andrew Johnson.

BIOGRAPHICAL/CRITICAL SOURCES: Book World, January 12, 1969.

* * *

TRENT, Olaf
See FANTHORPE, R(obert) Lionel

* * *

TUERCK, David G(eorge) 1941-

PERSONAL: Surname is pronounced "Teerk"; born February 11, 1941, in Belleville, Ill.; son of George N. (a musician) and Bertha (Brandmeyer) Tuerck; married Gay Herzog, June 2, 1962; children: John. *Education:* George Washington University, A.B., 1962, A.M., 1964; University of Virginia, Ph.D., 1966. *Politics:* Republican. *Religion:* United Church of Christ.

CAREER: University of Illinois at Chicago Circle, assistant professor of economics, 1966-70; California State College, Bakersfield, associate professor of economics, beginning 1970.

MEMBER: American Economic Association, Southern Economic Association, Omicron Delta Epsilon.

WRITINGS: (With Leland B. Yeager) *Trade Policy and the Price System,* International Textbook, 1966; (with Yeager) *Foreign Trade and U.S. Policy: The Case for Free International Trade,* Praeger, 1976; (editor with Patrick M. Boarman) *World Monetary Disorder: National Policies vs. International Imperatives,* Praeger, 1976; (editor) *The Political Economy of Advertising,* American Enterprise Institute for Public Policy Research, 1978.

WORK IN PROGRESS: Public finance (some legal aspects) and international economics.

AVOCATIONAL INTERESTS: Music.†

* * *

TURNBULL, Bob 1936-

PERSONAL: Born November 21, 1936, in San Diego, Calif.; son of Bob III (a historian and teacher) and Amorita (an optometrist; maiden name Treganza) Turnbull; married Julie Elizabeth James (a 1970 Orange Bowl princess and singer), October 8, 1970; married Yvonne Marie Gourlie (a nutritionist), March 9, 1979; children: (first marriage) Bob Kekoakalani. *Education:* Pacific Western University, M.A., 1977, Ph.D., 1978; attended Air War College and Army War College. *Politics:* Independent. *Office address:* Sonrise Seminars, P.O. Box 1350, Tustin, Calif. 92681.

CAREER: Actor in Hollywood, Calif., 1957-68, with roles in over forty television programs, including "Hawaii Five-O," "Petticoat Junction," "General Hospital," "My Three Sons," "Man from UNCLE," and "The Fugitive," and in eleven films, including "Tora, Tora, Tora," "Camelot," "Spartacus," "The Story of Ruth," and "The Absent-Minded Professor"; Waikiki Beach Chaplaincy (non-denominational ministry offering beach and hotel worship services and beach and street evangelism), Honolulu, Hawaii, founder and president,

1968-80; Continental Broadcasting Network, Virginia Beach, Va., exercise specialist for "USam" television program and actor on "Another Life" daytime drama, 1980-82; KYMS Radio, Orange County, Calif., host of "Music . . . and More" variety program, 1983—. President of Sonrise Seminars, 1983—.

Chaplain of Honolulu Police Department; weekly speaker for "Sun and Soul Talk," a worship service held on the beach of the Hilton Hawaiian Village Hotel. Founder of HOTLINE, Honolulu's twenty-four-hour telephone counseling service; founder and publisher of *Hawaii Free Paper.* Host of three radio programs in Hawaii; narrator of two records, *The Husband and Wife Game* and *The Apostle.* Volunteer assistant football coach, University of Hawaii. Member of national advisory board, American Security Council.

MEMBER: International 700 Club, National Association of Evangelicals, Fellowship of Christian Athletes, Academy of Motion Picture Arts and Sciences, Screen Actors Guild, American Federation of Television and Radio Artists, Thalians. *Awards, honors:* Angel award, Religion in Media, for "Free to be Fit" radio/cassette series; named Man of the Year by Waikiki Junior Chamber of Commerce; honorary co-director, National Association of Christian Singles.

WRITINGS: (Contributor) Ralph Benner and M. J. Clements, *The Young Actor's Guide to Hollywood,* McCann-Erickson, 1962; *Will the Old Bob Turnbull Please Drop Dead,* David C. Cook, 1970, published as *Hawaiian Soul,* Bible Voice, 1978; *Calling Angel One,* Bible Voice, 1975; *Deliver Me from Garbage,* Revell, 1978; *How to Handle Your Hassles and Hurts,* Bible Voice, 1979; *Free to Be Fit,* Bethany House, 1982. Also author of cassette program, "Free to Be Fit," and of religious tracts, *Christ Told the Truth,* American Tract Society, 1964, and *New Christian? Big Deal!,* Good News Publishers, 1966.

BIOGRAPHICAL/CRITICAL SOURCES: Robert Stone, *God Has a Man in Waikiki,* Revell, 1972, published as *God's Man for Waikiki,* Bible Voice, 1978.

* * *

TURNER, Ann W(arren) 1945-

PERSONAL: Born December 10, 1945, in Northampton, Mass.; daughter of Richard Bigelow (a printer) and Marian (an artist; maiden name, Gray) Warren; married Richard E. Turner (a teacher), June 3, 1967. *Education:* Attended University of Manchester, 1965-66; Bates College, B.A., 1967; University of Massachusetts, M.A.T., 1968. *Politics:* Liberal Democrat. *Religion:* Protestant. *Home and office:* Briar Hill Rd., Williamsburg, Mass. 01036. *Agent:* Marilyn Marlow, Curtis Brown Ltd., 575 Madison Ave., New York, N.Y. 10022.

CAREER: High school English teacher in Great Barrington, Mass., 1968-69; writer, 1969—. Assistant house manager at a home for young women with drug problems; telephone operator for Northampton Hotline (crisis intervention center), 1973-75.

AWARDS, HONORS: First prize from *Atlantic Monthly* college creative writing contest, 1967, for "Athinai"; American Library Association notable book Citation, 1980, for *A Hunter Comes Home.*

WRITINGS: Vultures (nonfiction for children), McKay, 1973; *Houses for the Dead* (study of death in several cultures), McKay, 1976; *A Hunter Comes Home* (novel for children), Crown, 1980; *The Way Home* (novel for children), Crown, 1982; *Tickle*

a Pickle (poems for children), Four Winds, 1984; *House in a Hill* (poem), Macmillan, 1985. Also author of *Rituals of Birth* (nonfiction).

WORK IN PROGRESS: A novel, *Matilda's Revenge; Street Talk*, poems.

SIDELIGHTS: Ann W. Turner writes: "My upbringing influenced my writing. Possibly because my liberal family was somewhat 'different' from the New Englanders of our town, I grew up being interested in different peoples and cultures. Living in the country and having an artist for a mother gave me a certain way of seeing, an eye for beauty and interest in what others might think ugly or dull; dead weeds, old men and women, fat ladies at the beach, ancient and venerable crows, and vultures. I still live in the country, draw nourishment from it, and write about the seasons in my journal.

"I am concerned with the things that make each culture individual, and the traits that hold us together. To understand ourselves now, I feel we must know the Eskimos, the Aborigines, the ancient Chinese, and Paleolithic man. We are that strange tribe in the jungle; we are the people so old that only their bones and amulets are left. In strange and beautiful ways we are the same, yet different. That is what I write of, and will probably continue writing of for a long, long time."

BIOGRAPHICAL/CRITICAL SOURCES: Daily Hampshire Gazette, October 21, 1976.

*   *   *

TURNER, Graham   1932-

PERSONAL: Born September 8, 1932, in Macclesfield, Cheshire, England; son of Fred and Annie Gertrude (Bradbury) Turner; married Jean Staton Forster, July 25, 1962; children: Patrick Henry, Rachel Elizabeth, Hannah Lucy. *Education:* Attended Christ Church, Oxford, 1950-53, and Stanford University, 1953-54. *Religion:* Christian. *Home:* Wootton House, Wootton Boars Hill, Oxford, England. *Agent:* Hilary Rubinstein, A. P. Watt Ltd., 26/28 Bedford Row, London WC1R 4HL, England.

CAREER: Free-lance writer and broadcaster. Reporter for *The Scotsman,* Edinburgh, Scotland, 1958-61, *Sunday Times,* London, England, 1961-63, and British Broadcasting Corp., London, 1963-65; British Broadcasting Corp., economics correspondent, 1965-70. *Military service:* Royal Air Force, 1955-58; served as education officer.

WRITINGS: The Car Makers, Eyre & Spottiswoode, 1963, revised edition, Penguin, 1964; (with John Pearson) *The Persuasion Industry,* Eyre & Spottiswoode, 1965; *The North Country,* Eyre & Spottiswoode, 1967; *Business in Britain,* Little, Brown, 1969, revised edition, Penguin, 1971; *The Leyland Papers,* Eyre & Spottiswoode, 1971; *Towards a New Philosophy for Industry and Society,* Ashridge Management College, 1972; *More than Conquerers,* Hodder & Stoughton, 1976. Contributor to *Encounter, Observer,* and *Listener.*

BIOGRAPHICAL/CRITICAL SOURCES: Listener, June 15, 1967; *Times Literary Supplement,* November 2, 1967.

*   *   *

TURNER, Jonathan H.   1942-

PERSONAL: Born September 7, 1942, in Oakland, Calif.; son of John Hugh (a developer) and Maries R. (Rubell) Turner; married Susan Hainge, September 7, 1967 (divorced, 1971); married Sandra Leer, November 24, 1971; children: Patricia, Donna, Kenneth. *Education:* University of California, Santa Barbara, B.A., 1965; Cornell University, M.A., 1966, Ph.D., 1968. *Politics:* Democrat. *Home:* 2935 Chillon Way, Laguna Beach, Calif. 92651. *Office:* Department of Sociology, University of California, Riverside, Calif. 92502.

CAREER: University of Hawaii, Honolulu, assistant professor of sociology, 1968-69; University of California, Riverside, assistant professor, 1969-72, associate professor, 1972-77, professor of sociology, 1977—.

MEMBER: American Sociological Association, Pacific Sociological Association.

WRITINGS: Patterns of Social Organization, McGraw, 1972; *American Society: Problems of Structure,* Harper, 1972; *The Structure of Sociological Theory,* Dorsey, 1974, 2nd edition, 1978; *Privilege and Poverty in America,* Goodyear Publishing, 1976; *Social Problems in America,* Harper, 1977; *Sociology: Studying the Human System,* Goodyear Publishing, 1978; *Functionalism,* Cummings, 1978.

The Emergence of Sociological Theory, Dorsey, 1981; *Societal Stratification: A Theoretical Analysis,* Columbia University Press, 1984; *Oppression: A Socio-History of Black-White Relations,* Nelson-Hall, 1984; *American Dilemmas,* Columbia University Press, 1985; *Sociology: A Student Handbook,* Random House, 1985; *Sociology: The Science of Human Organization,* Nelson-Hall, 1985; *Herbert Spencer: Toward a Renewed Appreciation,* Sage Publications, 1985.

*   *   *

TWEDT, Dik Warren   1920-

PERSONAL: Born December 30, 1920, in Minneapolis, Minn.; married; two children. *Education:* University of Minnesota, B.A. (magna cum laude), 1941; Northwestern University, M.S.J., 1948, Ph.D., 1951. *Home:* 57 Bellerive Acres, St. Louis, Mo. 63121. *Office:* School of Business Administration, University of Missouri, 8001 Natural Bridge Rd., St. Louis, Mo. 63121.

CAREER: Precision Hone Co. (automotive tool company), Detroit, Mich., vice-president and general manager, 1941-42; Time Inc., New York, N.Y., public relations and agency supervisor, 1942-46; Clissold Publishing Co., Chicago, Ill., assistant promotion manager, 1946-51; Young & Rubicam, Inc. (advertising agency), Chicago, manager of experimental research, 1951-52; manager of experimental research and supervisor on several accounts, Needham, Louis, & Brorby, Inc. (marketing consultants), 1952-56; Kenyon & Eckhardt, Inc. (advertising agency), Chicago, research director and plan board chairman, 1956-57; Leo Burnett Co. (advertising agency), Chicago, senior account executive, 1957-60; Faison & Twedt, Inc. (marketing consultants), Chicago, president, 1960-62; Batten, Barton, Durstine & Osborn, Inc. (advertising agency), Chicago, vice-president of marketing services and plan board chairman, 1962-63; Oscar Mayer & Co. (food company), Madison, Wis., director of marketing planning and research, 1963-71; U.S. Postal Service, Washington, D.C., executive director, 1972; University of Missouri—St. Louis, professor of marketing and psychology, 1972—.

Diplomate of American Board of Professional Psychology, 1956; licensed psychologist in Illinois, 1959, Wisconsin, 1965, and Missouri, 1978. Member of editorial review board, American Marketing Association, 1963—.

MEMBER: Advertising Research Foundation (general conference chairman, 1966), American Association of Public Opinion Research, American Marketing Association (business manager, 1958-63; president, Chicago chapter, 1960; national vice-president, 1962; member of census advisory committee, 1968-72; president, St. Louis chapter, 1980), American Psychological Association (fellow, 1958—; president of consumer division, 1962), American Standards Association (chairman, Task Force on Standard Geographic Units, 1956-67), American Statistical Association, Sigma Delta Chi.

WRITINGS: (With Harry Deane Wolfe) *Essentials of the Promotional Mix,* Appleton-Century-Crofts, 1970; *Modern Marketing,* Random, 1975; *Personality and Marketing,* American Marketing Association, 1979; (contributor) *Handbook of Modern Marketing,* McGraw, 1984; *Survey of Marketing Research,* American Marketing Association, 1984.

Contributor to *Encyclopedia of the Social Sciences.* Contributor to numerous marketing and psychology journals, including *Journal of Applied Psychology, Harvard Business Review, Journal of Marketing, Annual Review of Psychology, Business Management, Marketing Management, Food Product Development,* and *Marketing Insights.*

*   *   *

TYSON, Joseph B(lake)   1928-

PERSONAL: Born August 30, 1928, in Charlotte, N.C.; son of Joseph B. (a construction worker) and Lucy (Lewis) Tyson; married Margaret Helms, June 12, 1954; children: Linda S. *Education:* Duke University, A.B., 1950, B.D., 1953; Union Theological Seminary, New York, N.Y., S.T.M., 1955, Ph.D., 1959. *Religion:* Methodist. *Home:* 8636 Capri Dr., Dallas, Tex. 75238. *Office:* Department of Religious Studies, Southern Methodist University, Dallas, Tex. 75275.

CAREER: Southern Methodist University, Dallas, Tex., instructor, 1958-60, assistant professor, 1960-65, associate professor, 1965-74, professor of religious studies, 1974—, director, Center for the Study of Religion in the Greco-Roman world, 1983—, head of department, 1965-75.

MEMBER: American Academy of Religion (president of southwestern region, 1968-69), Society of Biblical Literature, Studiorum Novi Testamenti Societas.

WRITINGS: A Study of Early Christianity, Macmillan, 1973; *Synoptic Abstract,* Biblical Research Associates, 1978; (contributor) W. O. Walter, editor, *The Relationships among the Gospels,* Trinity University Press, 1978; (contributor) W. R. Farmer, editor, *New Synoptic Studies,* Mencor University Press, 1983; *The New Testament and Early Christianity,* Macmillan, 1984. Contributor of articles to *Journal of Biblical Literature, Novem Testamentum,* and *New Testament Studies.*

WORK IN PROGRESS: Research in early Christianity and its relationship to Judiasm; *Luke and the Death of Jesus.*

U

UPHOFF, Walter H. 1913-

PERSONAL: Born February 28, 1913, in Sheboygan County, Wis.; son of Emil Theodore (a farmer) and Anna Eva Helena (Hameister) Uphoff; married Mary Jo Weiler, August 10, 1938; children: Norman Thomas, Eugene John, Charles Maynard, Walter Collins. *Education:* University of Wisconsin, B.S., 1934, Ph.M., 1935, graduate study, 1949-50. *Politics:* Social Democrat. *Religion:* Society of Friends (Quaker). *Home:* Route 1, Oregon, Wis. 53575. *Office:* New Frontiers Center, Oregon, Wis. 53575.

CAREER: Instructor in workers education in Wisconsin for Works Progress Administration, 1935-37; University of Wisconsin School for Workers, Madison, instructor, 1937-38; Farm Security Administration, Lincoln, Neb., regional education adviser, 1938-39; curriculum supervisor, Wisconsin Workers Education Program, 1939-40; farmer-labor relations representative, Wisconsin Federation of Labor, 1940-41; Fellowship Farm Co-op, manager in Oregon and Wisconsin, 1941-50; University of Minnesota, Minneapolis, research associate, Industrial Relations Center, 1951-53, assistant professor, 1953-61, associate professor of industrial relations and head of labor education, 1961-63; University of Colorado, Boulder, professor of economics and director of labor education, 1963-76, professor emeritus, 1976—; New Frontiers Center, Oregon, Wis., president, 1979—. Lecturer at universities, community organizations, and on radio and television programs. Wisconsin Association of Cooperatives, board member, 1946-58, secretary, 1948-52. Socialist candidate for U.S. senator from Wisconsin (Norman Thomas ticket), 1944, and for governor of Wisconsin, 1946 and 1948. Consultant to Alan Neuman Productions and Postscript Productions.

MEMBER: International Institute of Integral Human Studies, American Society for Psychical Research, Spiritual Frontiers Fellowship, ESP Research Associates Foundation (board member), Verein fuer Tonbandstimmenforschung (Germany). *Awards, honors:* Fulbright senior research grant, University of Cologne, 1958-59.

WRITINGS: The Kohler Strike: Its Socio-Economic Causes and Effects, privately printed, 1933; *Kohler on Strike: Thirty Years of Conflict,* Beacon Press, 1966, updated paperback edition, 1967; (editor) *Prepaid Group Practice Health Plans,* Center for Labor Education and Research, University of Colorado,

1968; (contributor) Harold Sherman, *You Can Communicate with the Unseen World,* Fawcett, 1974; (contributor) Sherman, *The Dead Are Alive,* Amherst Press, 1981.

With wife, Mary Jo Uphoff: *New Psychic Frontiers: Your Key to New Worlds,* Smythe, 1975, 3rd edition, New Frontiers Center, 1980; *Mind over Matter: Masuaki Kiyota's PK Feats with Metal and Film,* New Frontiers Center, 1980; *Group Health: An American Success Story in Prepaid Health Care,* Dillon Press, 1980.

Capital Times, Madison, Wis., former columnist on farmer-labor relations and author of column, "Co-op Corner," currently co-author of column, "Beyond the Five Senses." Contributor to *Funk & Wagnalls Yearbook,* 1964-66; contributor of articles on parapsychological research to *Psychic Researcher, Esotera, Pursuit, Fate, Probe the Unknown, New Realities,* and *Allgemeine Zeitschrift fuer Parapsychologie.*

SIDELIGHTS: Walter H. Uphoff has made fifteen trips to Europe, one to the Far East, and one around the world. His earlier trips related to trade union and political developments; the last twelve trips have concerned research in parapsychology.

Uphoff told *CA:* "It is becoming increasingly obvious that traditional views of life and the universe are inadequate to explain broader dimensions of reality. An open-minded approach to political and economic systems and to inter-personal and international relations can be enhanced as we learn more about psychic and non-material aspects of life."

BIOGRAPHICAL/CRITICAL SOURCES: Colorado Alumnus, May, 1964.

* * *

UROFSKY, Melvin I. 1939-

PERSONAL: Born February 7, 1939, in New York, N.Y.; son of Philip and Sylvia (Passow) Urofsky; married Susan Linda Miller (the deputy secretary of administration for Commonwealth of Virginia), August 27, 1961; children: Philip Eric, Robert Ian. *Education:* Columbia University, A.B., 1961, M.A., 1962, Ph.D., 1968; University of Virginia, J.D., 1984. *Politics:* "Democratic-Independent." *Religion:* Jewish. *Home:* 1500 Careybrook Dr., Richmond, Va. 23233. *Office:* Department of History, Virginia Commonwealth University, Richmond, Va. 23284.

CAREER: New York State Employment Service, New York City, interviewer, 1962; Robert Saudek Associates, New York City, researcher, 1963; Ohio State University, Columbus, instructor in history, 1964-67; State University of New York at Albany, assistant professor of history and education, 1967-70, assistant dean for innovative education, 1970-72, lecturer in history in Allen Center, 1972-74; Virginia Commonwealth University, Richmond, 1974—, currently professor of history. Chairman, Zionist Academic Council, 1976-79. Consultant to Institute for the Advancement of Urban Education.

MEMBER: Organization of American Historians, American Zionist Federation (member of national board and executive committee; co-chairman of Commission on Zionist Ideology), American Jewish Historical Society (chairman, 1980-83), Richmond Oral History Association (founder; president).

AWARDS, HONORS: National Endowment for the Humanities, grants for editing Louis D. Brandeis letters, 1967-74 and 1984-86, senior fellowship, 1976-77; American Council of Learned Societies grants-in-aid, 1972, 1978; Jewish Book Council Kaplun Award, 1976.

WRITINGS: Big Steel and the Wilson Administration: A Study in Business-Government Relations, Ohio State University Press, 1969; (editor) *Why Teachers Strike: Teachers' Rights and Community Control,* Doubleday-Anchor, 1970; (editor with David W. Levy) *Letters of Louis D. Brandeis,* State University of New York Press, Volume I: *Urban Reformer, 1870-1907,* 1971, Volume II: *People's Attorney, 1907-1912,* 1972, Volume III: *Progressive and Zionist, 1913-15,* 1973, Volume IV: *Mr. Justice Brandeis, 1916-1921,* 1975, Volume V: *Elder Statesman, 1922-41,* 1978; *A Mind of One Piece: Brandeis and American Reform,* Scribner, 1971; (editor) *Perspectives on Urban America,* Doubleday, 1973; *American Zionism from Herzl to the Holocaust,* Doubleday, 1975; *We Are One! American Jewry and Israel,* Doubleday, 1978; *Essays on American Zionism,* Herzl Press, 1978; *Louis D. Brandeis and the Progressive Tradition,* Little, Brown, 1980; *A Voice That Spoke for Justice: The Life and Times of Stephen S. Wise,* State University of New York Press, 1981. Contributor of numerous articles to scholarly journals and popular periodicals. Member of editorial board, *Midstream,* 1978—.

WORK IN PROGRESS: A constitutional history of the United States.

SIDELIGHTS: Melvin I. Urofsky's *Louis D. Brandeis and the Progressive Tradition* "is not a full-blown biography moving into the inner person of a truly great man," states Philip Allan Friedman in the *Los Angeles Times.* "Rather, it is a fine study . . . of Brandeis' crusading public career—as the people's defender against the 'curse of bigness' in business, as the great dissenter along with Justice Holmes on the highest court of the land, and as the leader of the American Zionist Organization." Opposing monopolies and working for wage-earners' rights, Brandeis became a top adviser to President Woodrow Wilson, a Supreme Court justice, and a renowned professor of law. Credited with upgrading the teaching of law "by popularizing the case-study method," according to Friedman, Brandeis often researched cases independently while serving on the bench. In addition to writing the biography of Brandeis, Urofsky, with David W. Levy, has edited and published Brandeis letters spanning more than seventy years.

BIOGRAPHICAL/CRITICAL SOURCES: Los Angeles Times, February 12, 1981.

V

VALENS, Evans G.

HOME: 280 Rose Ave., Mill Valley, Calif. 94941.

CAREER: Writer. Producer and director of series for National Educational Television, including "The Atom," "The Elements," "Virus," and "The Measure of Man."

AWARDS, HONORS: Edison Award for best science book for youth, for *Elements of the Universe.*

WRITINGS: Me and Frumpet, illustrated with photographs by the author, Dutton, 1958; (with Glenn T. Seaborg) *Elements of the Universe,* Dutton, 1958; (with Wendell M. Stanley) *Viruses and the Nature of Life,* Dutton, 1961; *Wingfin and Topple,* illustrations by Clement Hurd, World, 1962; *Wildfire,* illustrations by Clement Hurd, World, 1963; *The Number of Things: Pythagoras, Geometry and Humming Strings,* Dutton, 1964; *Magnet,* illustrated with photographs by Berenice Abbot, World, 1964.

Motion, illustrated with photographs by Berenice Abbott, World, 1965; *A Long Way Up: The Story of Jill Kinmont,* Harper, 1966, revised edition published as *The Other Side of the Mountain,* Warner Books, 1976 (published in Japan as *Window to the Sky); Cybernaut* (poem), Viking, 1968; *The Attractive Universe: Gravity and the Shape of Space,* illustrated with photographs by Berenice Abbot, World, 1969; (with Ernst G. Beier) *People-Reading,* Stein & Day, 1975; *The Other Side of the Mountain: Part II,* Warner Books, 1978.

Television plays: "The Silver Lieutenant," KPIX-TV, 1954; "The Red Myth" (seven-part series), National Educational Television, 1957; "IGY: The International Geophysical Year" (ten-part series), National Broadcasting Corp., 1957. Also author of seven half-hour shows for "Johns Hopkins File Seven," ABC-TV, 1957, and of narration for "Moonwalk One."

WORK IN PROGRESS: Did You Hear the Bird Singing in the Forest?, a biography of a deaf orphan; a nonfiction book on the nature of dreaming and the unconscious.

SIDELIGHTS: Evans G. Valens told *CA:* "Late in 1957 [the National Broadcasting Corp.] aired a series of live television shows about the International Geophysical Year. . . . In our imagination, with the help of star backgrounds, a six-foot relief model of Earth and a meticulously sculptured nineteen-inch moon, we backed off into space and surveyed our planet with fresh eyes. Sputnik had been up three weeks. The view was a surprise, like hearing your own voice for the first time. It was exciting to see the planet whole, and it was humbling to realize how neatly man is trapped, like color in an apple, within the skin.

"Eight years later I began writing again about the earth in space . . . also about the force that holds it in orbit and the problems, psychological as well as technical, of getting away from it and back to it again. Since the material refused to fit into a single frame, the end result was two books—a long poem, *Cybernaut,* and a straight, expository 'science book,' *The Attractive Universe: Gravity and the Shape of Space.* The two books were written concurrently, and they borrowed constantly from each other. Ideas and images often began in one book and jumped to the other, seemingly for reasons of their own. The image of a man launching himself (by legpower) into orbit around an asteroid would not fit in the poem, but it grew to become a chapter in *The Attractive Universe.* On the other hand, my original example of weightlessness in the gravity book moved over to the poem as 'I am a child rope-jumping / Trapped in that free moment / When the rope snaps dust / And child is on the sky.'

"The moral of all this? A reminder that science, as well as art, has to do with discovering, feeling, experiencing, sensing, realizing. And that neither art nor science has any intention of remaining in its proper pigeonhole. Both are sensitive to promising analogies, both are concerned with seeing beyond the surface and getting at the root of things."

MEDIA ADAPTATIONS: The Other Side of the Mountain and *The Other Side of the Mountain: Part II* have been filmed as motion pictures.

*   *   *

van der KROEF, Justus M(aria)   1925-

PERSONAL: Born October 30, 1925, in Djakarta, Indonesia; naturalized U.S. citizen; son of Hendrik L. (a naval officer) and Maria (van Lokven) van der Kroef; married Orell Joan Ellison (a librarian), 1955; children: Adrian Hendrik, Sri Orell. *Education:* Millsaps College, B.A., 1944; University of North Carolina, M.A., 1947; Columbia University, Ph.D., 1953. *Politics:* Conservative. *Religion:* Presbyterian. *Home:* 165 Linden Ave., Bridgeport, Conn. 06602. *Office:* Department of

Political Science, University of Bridgeport, Bridgeport, Conn. 06602.

CAREER: Michigan State University, East Lansing, instructor in history, 1948-52, assistant professor of foreign studies, 1952-55; University of Bridgeport, Bridgeport, Conn., associate professor, 1959-65, professor of political science, 1965-68, C. A. Dana Professor of Political Science, 1968—, chairman of department, 1965—. Research associate, Institute of Strategic Studies, Islamabad, Pakistan, 1981—. Visiting professor, Nanyang University, 1963-64, University of the Philippines, 1966, and University of British Columbia, 1974. Editorial director, Communications Research Services. Member of national advisory board, Charles Edison Memorial Youth Fund, 1972—. *Military service:* Royal Netherlands Marine Corps, 1944-45.

MEMBER: American Political Science Association, University Professors for Academic Order (national president, 1971-72), American-Asian Educational Exchange (director, 1968—).

AWARDS, HONORS: Senior fellow of Research Institute on Communist Affairs (Columbia University), 1965-66; post-doctoral fellow, University of Queensland (Australia) 1968-69; Mellon Foundation research fellowship, 1983.

WRITINGS: Indonesia in the Modern World, William Heinman, Volume I, 1954, Volume II, 1956; *The West New Guinea Dispute,* Institute of Pacific Relations, 1958; *Indonesian Social Evolution: Some Psychological Considerations,* van der Peet, 1958; *The Communist Party of Indonesia: Its History, Program and Tactics,* University of British Columbia Press, 1965; *Communism in Malaysia and Singapore: A Contemporary Survey,* Nijhoff, 1967.

Indonesia after Sukarno, University of British Columbia Press, 1971; *The Lives of SEATO,* Institute of Southeast Asian Studies (Singapore), 1976; *Communism in Southeast Asia,* University of California Press, 1980; *Kampuchea: The Endless Tug of War,* University of Maryland Law School, 1982.

Contributor of 300 articles to scholarly journals in the United States and abroad. Member of editorial advisory board, *Journal of Asian Affairs,* 1975—, and *World Affairs,* 1976—; associate editor, *Asian Thought and Society,* 1976—.

WORK IN PROGRESS: The Association of Southeast Asian Nations: Search for Security.

SIDELIGHTS: Justus M. van der Kroef writes *CA:* "Reading and writing about Southeast Asia, visiting and researching in the area, have been the heart of my life. No pleasure in my life has compared to the gathering together of (hopefully new) facts and insights about this part of the world where I was born, and then to make these facts and insights come together in a piece of writing. I consider myself to have been extraordinarily fortunate to have been able to do this for all of my adult life. I would not have wanted it any other way."

*   *   *

Van DORNE, R.
   See WALLMANN, Jeffrey M(iner)

*   *   *

van FRAASSEN, Bastiaan Cornelis

EDUCATION: University of Alberta, B.A. (with honors), 1963; University of Pittsburgh, M.A., 1964, Ph.D., 1966. *Office:* Department of Philosophy, Princeton University, Princeton, N.J. 08554.

CAREER: Yale University, New Haven, Conn., assistant professor, 1966-68, associate professor of philosophy, 1968-69; University of Toronto, Toronto, Ontario, associate professor, 1969, professor of philosophy, 1971-81; University of Southern California, Los Angeles, professor of philosophy, 1976-81; Princeton University, Princeton, N.J., professor of philosophy, 1982—. Visiting professor, Indiana University, 1968-69.

AWARDS, HONORS: Guggenheim fellowship, 1970-71.

WRITINGS: Introduction to the Philosophy of Time and Space, Random House, 1970; *Formal Semantics and Logic,* Macmillan, 1971; (with Karel Lambert) *Derivation and Counterexample,* Dickinson, 1972; *The Scientific Image,* Clarendon Press/ Oxford University Press, 1980. Contributor of articles to technical journals.

WORK IN PROGRESS: Research on philosophy of science and logic.

SIDELIGHTS: Bastiaan Cornelis van Fraassen "is a stylish and witty writer, and wears his mathematical and scientific learning lightly," according to *Times Literary Supplement* reviewer Christopher Peacocke, who says van Fraassen's *The Scientific Image* "would make an excellent introduction to the philosophical issues clustering around scientific realism for undergraduates if set in conjunction with the recent realist literature."

BIOGRAPHICAL/CRITICAL SOURCES: Times Literary Supplement, January 30, 1981.

*   *   *

VANGELISTI, Paul 1945-

PERSONAL: Born September 17, 1945, in San Francisco, Calif.; son of Nicholas Thomas (an accountant) and Josephine (a saleswoman; maiden name, Zangani) Vangelisti; married Margaret Dryden, December 31, 1966 (divorced, 1980); children: Tristan, Simone. *Education:* University of San Francisco, B.A., 1967; graduate study at Trinity College, Dublin, 1967-68; University of Southern California, M.A., 1971, doctoral study, 1972. *Home:* 3132 Berkeley Circle, Los Angeles, Calif. 90026. *Office:* Otis Art Institute of Parsons School of Design, 2401 Wilshire Blvd., Los Angeles, Calif. 90057.

CAREER: San Francisco Department of Recreation and Parks, San Francisco, Calif., recreation director, 1967-68; University of Southern California, Los Angeles, assistant instructor in English, 1968-72; *Hollywood Reporter,* Hollywood, Calif., assignment editor, 1972-73; KPFK-Radio, North Hollywood, Calif., cultural affairs director, 1974-82; part-time instructor at colleges in Los Angeles, 1980—; Otis Art Institute of Parsons School of Design, Los Angeles, instructor, 1984—.

WRITINGS—Poetry; published by Red Hill, except as indicated: *Communion,* 1970; *Air,* 1973; *Tender Continent,* Chatterton's Bookstore, 1974; *Pearl Harbor,* Isthmus, 1975; *Il tenero continente* (bilingual; title means "The Tender Continent"), Edizioni Geiger, 1975; *The Extravagant Room,* 1976; *Two by Two,* 1977; *Remembering the Movies,* 1977; *Another You,* 1980; *Un grammo d'oro,* Cervo Volante (Rome), 1981; *Ora blu,* Telai del Bernini (Modena), 1981; *Abandoned Latitudes,* 1983; *Rime,* 1983.

Editor: (With Charles Bukowski) *Anthology of Los Angeles Poets,* 1973; *Specimen 73* (catalog and anthology), Pasadena Museum, 1973; (and translator with Milne Holton) *New Polish*

Poetry, University of Pittsburgh Press, 1978; (with Adriano Spatola and translator) *Italian Poetry, 1960-1980: From Neo to Post Avant-Garde*, 1982.

Translator: *Sixteen Poems of Vittorio Sereni*, 1971; Spatola, *Mayakovskiiiiiiij*, 1975; Giulia Niccolai, *Substitutions*, 1975; Corrado Costa, *Our Positions*, 1975; Rocco Scotellaro, *The Sky with Its Mouth Wide-Open*, 1976; Franco Beltrametti, *Another Earthquake*, 1977; Antonio Porta, *As If It Were a Rhythm*, 1978; (with Carol Lettieri) Mohammed Dib, *Omneros*, 1978; Spatola, *Various Devices*, 1978; Costa, *The Complete Films*, 1983. Co-editor of *Invisible City*.

* * *

van RJNDT, Philippe 1950-
(Philip Michaels)

PERSONAL: Born July 12, 1950, in Montreal, Quebec, Canada; son of Pieter and Helena (Trubetskoy) van Rjndt. *Education:* McGill University, B.A., M.A.; attended Sorbonne, University of Paris, 1971-72. *Politics:* "Pragmatic—believe in the powers behind the throne." *Religion:* None. *Residence:* Toronto, Ontario, Canada. *Agent:* Henry Morrison, 58 West Tenth St., New York, N.Y. 10011.

CAREER: Novelist and screenwriter.

*WRITINGS—*All novels: *The Tetramachus Collection*, Putnam, 1976; *Blueprint*, Putnam, 1977; *The Trial of Adolf Hitler*, Summit Books, 1978; (under pseudonym Philip Michaels) *Grail*, Avon, 1982; *Samaritan*, Dial, 1983; (under pseudonym Philip Michaels) *Come, Follow Me*, Avon, 1983.

WORK IN PROGRESS: Preparing a film adaptation of *The Tetramachus Collection*.

SIDELIGHTS: Philippe van Rjndt told *CA:* "I consider myself truly fortunate in being able to do what I want, hopefully do it better with each successive book and live in a comfortable style.

"Although my primary interest is, and probably always will be, international politics and history, I have moved into different genres whenever a theme or story was sufficiently intriguing. *Grail* and *Come, Follow Me* were occult thrillers whose form was better suited to the kind of story I had to tell.

"Given the economic realities of publishing today, I feel it behooves an author to know as much as he or she can about the 'business' side of books. The author can no longer isolate himself from the packaging and marketing of his books, especially if [they're] fiction.

"In spite of the vicissitudes of the career I can think of none better. So often my research has led me into areas I never thought I would touch. As a result the writer never stops learning and exploring. This process of discovery may well be what the craft is all about."

While van Rjndt speaks openly of his career as a writer of novels, *Publishers Weekly* correspondent Beverly Slopen points out that "there are few facts in the life story of Philippe van Rjndt which can be easily verified. . . . Everything . . . about the man is cast in mystery." First of all, notes Slopen, "there is the matter of his name which he assumed [in 1974]. . . . It is not just a pseudonym but a complete identity. . . . When asked his real name, he replies emphatically, 'Nobody has that. I have become Philippe van Rjndt. It's who I am.'"

Furthermore, says Slopen, "what he does reveal about his life . . . is a tale possibly stranger than his fictions and possibly true. He claims to have been a spy for an independent intelligence organization based in Geneva which served as 'a go-between for the two rival intelligence agencies for the U.S. and Soviet Union.' And this when he was a mere lad between the ages of 17 and 23."

When asked about his relative youth as a spy, van Rjndt believes he "wasn't too young. I did elementary intelligence work, basically in the analysis of newspapers, radio and journals."

Most of van Rjndt's novels are based on stories of international crime, politics, and intrigue. His reviewers often note the high degree of authenticity of his fiction, which may or may not be a result of his earlier career in intelligence. Of his first novel *The Tetramachus Collection*, for example, Newgate Callendar writes in a *New York Times Book Review* article that "the basic idea [of the book] is staggering, and van Rjndt has done a great deal of research. . . . He writes from fierce indignation, and *The Tetramachus Collection* is an unusual piece of work."

Similarly, Stanley Ellin remarks on *Samaritan* in the *New York Times Book Review*, saying that what makes this novel "extraordinary is that the outrageous and horrifying events . . . become much more credible than the fictional doings in the usual thriller. Philippe van Rjndt's mastery of his complex narrative, his convincing descriptions of Warsaw, Moscow, New York, Rome and Amsterdam and, above all, his obviously passionate commitment to political morality and his faith in human decency add up to a stunning and often moving experience."

AVOCATIONAL INTERESTS: Scuba diving.

BIOGRAPHICAL/CRITICAL SOURCES: New York Times Book Review, December 19, 1976, October 2, 1977, February 13, 1983; *Publishers Weekly*, November 13, 1978; *Washington Post*, January 30, 1979.

* * *

Van WEDDINGEN, Marthe 1924-
(Claire Dumas)

PERSONAL: Born July 12, 1924, in Herck-la-Ville, Belgium; daughter of Emile (a lawyer) and Germaine (Strauven) Van Weddingen. *Education:* Free University of Brussels, received degree in law. *Politics:* None. *Religion:* None. *Home and office:* 22 Rue Tonduti de l'Escarene, 06000 Nice, France.

CAREER: Solicitor in law courts in Brussels, Belgium, 1955-69; writer, 1975—.

AWARDS, HONORS: Prix de l'Ete from the city of Cannes, France, 1975, for *L'Herbe chaude*.

*WRITINGS—*Under pseudonym Claire Dumas: *L'Herbe chaude* (novel), Grasset, 1975, translation by Jennifer Malkin published as *The Stranger*, Ballantine, 1977; *Un Ete d'orages* (novel; title means "A Stormy Summer"), Grasset, 1978; *Une Femme Perdue*, Grasset, 1983; *Les Inconditionnels* (novel), Grasset, 1985.

Author of radio play, "Banlieue" (title means "Suburb"), aired on French radio, September 23, 1978, and play, "Le Jeu," 1984.

SIDELIGHTS: Marthe Van Weddingen told *CA:* "Writing has always been essential to me. I think I can't live happily without reading and writing. Even as a child I wrote a lot: diaries, letters, short stories. During my career as a solicitor I was short of free time, but as soon as I came to live in the south of France, a very peaceful place, I wrote again and, for the first time, thought about being published.

"I was a career woman and now I live in Nice without working. This gives me, I think, a particular view on the two kinds of lives women can have: working or staying at home. The [first] two novels I wrote, and the play as well, reflect this experience.

"I want to write novels about love, friendship, nature, solitude, disillusionment and fright; about women, what they are, and what they are trying to be; about men and the lives of couples. I want to write about obsessions, happiness, personal life, liberty, death, and truth. I don't care about religion or politics. I care about human beings and animals, about nature and the sun, about life—what it is and what it could be—and about our duties and powers with respect to ourselves, our happiness, and our personal values and liberty.

"I believe in imagination. The first fight—and the delight!—of a writer is to create a world that doesn't exist, and that readers will recognize and accept as real.

"I enjoyed the fact that *L'Herbe chaude* was adapted for French television (September 27, 1978). It was a very rich experience for me. I also took great interest in the writing of the radio play 'Banlieue.' It is a totally different kind of writing. I enjoyed it. I enjoyed writing 'Le Jeu,' and I hope it will be acted [onstage].''

*   *   *

VARGISH, Thomas   1939-

PERSONAL: Born February 13, 1939, in Granville, N.Y.; son of Andrew (a college teacher) and Frieda (Baer) Vargish; married Linden K. C. Foo (a research technician), June 8, 1963 (divorced, 1975); married Elizabeth Deeds Ermarth (a university professor), October 27, 1977; children: (first marriage) Nicholas. *Education:* Columbia University, B.A., 1960; Merton College, Oxford, M.A., 1963; Princeton University, Ph.D., 1965. *Politics:* Democrat. *Home:* 2430 Pickwick Rd., Baltimore, Md. 21207. *Office:* Department of English, University of Maryland, Baltimore County, Catonsville, Md. 21228.

CAREER: Dartmouth College, Hanover, N.H., assistant professor, 1965-70, associate professor, 1970-75, professor of English, 1975-83; University of Maryland, Baltimore County, professor of English, 1983—.

AWARDS, HONORS: Rhodes scholarship, 1960; Woodrow Wilson fellowship (honorary), 1960; Guggenheim fellowship, 1972.

WRITINGS: Newman: The Contemplation of Mind, Oxford University Press, 1970; *The Providential Aesthetic in Victorian Fiction,* University Press of Virginia, 1985. Contributor to *P.M.L.A.* and *Studies in the Novel.*

WORK IN PROGRESS: A book on the theory of relativity in its cultural contexts.

*   *   *

VASIL, R(aj) K(umar)   1931-

PERSONAL: Born July 1, 1931, in Amritsar, India; son of Lal Chand and Pushpa Vasil; married Deepa Chopra, January 25, 1957; children: Anamika, Latika. *Education:* Lucknow Uni-

versity, India, M.A., 1953, Ph.D., 1957; University of Malaya, Malaysia, Ph.D., 1967. *Office:* Political Science Department, Victoria University, Wellington, New Zealand.

CAREER: Asia Publishing House, Bombay, India, editor, 1959-60; Jadavpur University, Calcutta, India, lecturer in international relations, 1960-67; Victoria University, Wellington, New Zealand, reader in political science, 1967—. Visiting professor, University of California, Santa Cruz.

WRITINGS: Politics in a Plural Society: A Study of Non-Communal Political Parties in Malaysia, Oxford University Press, 1971; *The Malaysian General Election of 1969,* Oxford University Press, 1972; *Public Service Unionism,* Times Books, 1979; *Ethnic Politics in Malaysia,* Radiant Publishers, 1980; *Politics in Bi-Racial Societies: The Third World Experience,* Vikas, 1984; *Governing Singapore,* Eastern Universities Press, 1984.

WORK IN PROGRESS: Politics in ASEAN Countries: A Comparative Analysis.

*   *   *

VERDON, Dorothy
See TRALINS, S(andor) Robert

*   *   *

VICHAS, Robert P.   1933-

PERSONAL: Surname is pronounced *Vick*-us; born October 26, 1933; son of Peter (a businessman) and Idalene (Cooper) Vichas; married Dolores M. Flores Castellon, June 26, 1965. *Education:* Louisiana State University, B.S., 1965; University of the Americas, Mexico City, Mexico, M.A., 1966; University of Florida, Ph.D. and Certificate in Latin American Studies, 1967; Institut Universitaire de Hautes Etudes Internationales, Geneva, Switzerland, Diplome, 1972; University of Pennsylvania, certificate in international business, 1983. *Home address:* P.O. Box 6129, Norfolk, Va. 23508. *Office:* Old Dominion University, 5215 Hampton Blvd., Norfolk, Va. 23508.

CAREER: Sales manager, Capitol Service, Inc., 1952; in business, 1953-57; Dunn & Bradstreet, Inc., New York, N.Y., financial analyst, 1957-63; East Carolina University, Greenville, N.C., assistant professor of economics and finance, 1967-68; West Georgia College, Carrollton, associate professor of economics and director of Latin American studies, 1968-72; director and vice-president, Executive Management Consultants, Inc., 1969-71; director of research and fund manager, American Commodities Exchange, 1972-73; Northwood Institute, Midland, Mich., lecturer, 1974-75; University of Connecticut, Storrs, professor of business policy and strategy, 1977-81; Old Dominion University, Norfolk, Va., professor of strategic management, 1981—. Fulbright-Hays lecturer in economics and business, University Jose Simeon Canas, San Salvador, 1970; visiting professor of business, Interamerican University and Catholic University of Puerto Rico, 1975-76. Consultant in commodities futures, 1973-76.

MEMBER: Academy of International Management, Business Association for Latin American Studies (executive secretary, 1983—), United Commercial Travelers, Institute of Management and Marketing (New Delhi; honorary fellow), Rocky Mountain Council for Latin American Studies (member of executive committee), Order of the Cross Society (board member and officer, 1975—), Aircraft Owners and Pilots Association,

Beta Gamma Sigma. *Awards, honors:* Ford Foundation grant for research in Nicaragua; grants for study, research, or travel from West Georgia Foundation, Center for Constructive Alternatives, Foundation for Economic Education, and Old Dominion University.

WRITINGS: (Editor with W. Glenn Moore and contributor) *Coeval Economics: A Book of Readings,* McCutchan, 1970; *Getting Rich in Commodities, Currencies, or Coins,* Arlington House, 1975; (contributor) V. Orval Watts, editor, *Politics vs. Prosperity,* Pendell, 1976; (contributor) Doria Bonham-Yeaman, editor, *Developing Global Strategies,* Universidad de Navarra, 1982.

Published by Prentice-Hall: *Handbook of Financial Mathematics, Formulas, and Tables,* 1979; *Handbook of Annotated Financial Forms,* 1981; *Complete Handbook of Profitable Marketing Research Techniques,* 1982; *New Encyclopedic Dictionary of Systems and Procedures,* 1983; *The Bible's Message for Living in a Free Society Today,* 1985; *Financial Officers' Handbook of Forms,* 1985.

Contributor to conference proceedings in India, Mexico, Puerto Rico, and the United States. Contributor of articles and reviews to periodicals, including *Human Events, Marketing Times, Journal of Management Studies, American Economic Review, Ideas Sobre la Libertad,* and *Choice.* Associate editor, *The Envoy,* 1983—.

WORK IN PROGRESS: An encyclopedia of financial forms, solutions, tools, and shortcuts, for Prentice-Hall; a casebook for strategic managers; a revision of *Handbook of Financial Mathematics, Formulas, and Tables;* a research project on aviation safety.

AVOCATIONAL INTERESTS: Aviation (received aviation certificate from Tidewater Community College).

* * *

VOIGT, David Quentin 1926-

PERSONAL: Born August 9, 1926, in Reading, Pa.; son of Henry William (a professor of English) and Ethel Helena (Osmond) Voigt; married Virginia Louise Erb (an elementary teacher), December 27, 1951; children: David Jonathan, Mark William. *Education:* Albright College, B.S., 1948; Columbia University, M.A., 1949; Syracuse University, Ph.D., 1962. *Politics:* Democrat. *Religion:* Protestant. *Home:* 112 A Mifflin Blvd., Reading, Pa. 19607. *Office:* Department of Sociology, Albright College, Reading, Pa. 19603.

CAREER: Albright College, Reading, Pa., associate professor, 1964-72, professor of sociology and anthropology, 1972—. Adjunct professor of anthropology and sociology at Franklin and Marshall College, 1970-71. Coach of Brookline Colts (baseball team), Reading, 1972—. *Military service:* U.S. Army Air Forces, 1944-46; U.S. Air Force Reserve, beginning 1947; retired as major.

MEMBER: American Sociology Association (fellow), American Anthropological Association (fellow), Society for American Baseball Research (former president), North American Society for Sports History, Northeastern Anthropological Association, Eastern Sociological Association, Pennsylvania Sociology Society (secretary-treasusurer, 1966-68; president, 1970-72).

AWARDS, HONORS: Lindback Award for Distinguished Teaching, 1974; Albright College Distinguished Alumnus Award, 1977.

WRITINGS: American Baseball: From Gentleman's Sport to Commissioner System, University of Oklahoma Press, 1966; *American Baseball: From the Commissioners to Continental Expansion,* University of Oklahoma Press, 1970; *America's Leisure Revolution: Essays in the Sociology of Leisure and Sport,* Albright College Printing Office, 1970, new edition, 1974; *A Little League Journal,* Bowling Green University Press, 1974; *America through Baseball,* Nelson-Hall, 1976.

(Contributor) *National Pastime,* Society of American Baseball Research, 1982; *American Baseball: From Postwar Recovery to the Electronic Age,* Pennsylvania State University Press, 1983; (contributor) Janet C. Harris and Roberta Park, editors, *Play, Games and Sports in Cultural Contexts,* Human Kinetics, 1983; (contributor) Ray Browne, editor, *Forbidden Fruits: Taboos and Tabooism in Culture,* Popular Press, 1984.

Contributor to *Dictionary of American Biography.* Contributor of articles to *New England Quarterly, Abraham Lincoln Quarterly, Journal of Popular Culture, Journal of Leisure Research, Journal of Sports History, Journal of the Society for American Baseball Research,* and historical journals.

WORK IN PROGRESS: American Baseball: A Concise History, for Pennsylvania State University Press.

SIDELIGHTS: David Quentin Voigt told *CA:* "My research and writing [have] been geared to the idea that organized sport furnishes a mirror for viewing the processes of American societal development and change."

AVOCATIONAL INTERESTS: Manager of little league and junior league teams, and of the "Mifflin Codgers," an aging men's softball team.

* * *

von HIRSCH, Andrew 1934-

PERSONAL: Born July 16, 1934, in Zurich, Switzerland; came to the United States in 1941, naturalized citizen, 1947; son of Baron Donald (a diplomat) and Katherine (a language pathologist; maiden name, Bachert) von Hirsch. *Education:* Harvard University, A.B., 1956, LL.B., 1960. *Office:* Graduate School of Criminal Justice, Rutgers University, 15 Washington St., Newark, N.J. 07102.

CAREER: Attorney in private practice in New York, N.Y., 1961-63; staff lawyer for various government agencies in New York, 1964-69; legislative counsel to U.S. Senator Charles E. Goodell, in Washington, D.C., 1969-70; Committee for the Study of Incarceration, Washington, D.C., executive director, 1971-74; State University of New York at Albany, visiting associate professor of criminal justice, 1974-75; Rutgers University, Graduate School of Criminal Justice, Newark, N.J. professor of criminal justice, 1975—. Visiting professor, law faculty, Uppsala University, Sweden, 1985.

WRITINGS: Doing Justice: The Choice of Punishments, Hill & Wang, 1976; (with Kathleen Hanrahan) *The Question of Parole: Retention, Reform or Abolition?,* Ballinger, 1979; (editor with Hyman Gross) *Sentencing,* Oxford University Press, 1981; *Past or Future Crimes,* Rutgers University Press, 1985. Contributor to criminology journals.

WORK IN PROGRESS: Continuing research on sentencing reform, especially issues of fairness and justice in sentencing.

W

WALKENSTEIN, Eileen 1923-

PERSONAL: Born November 2, 1923, in Philadelphia, Pa.; daughter of Ben (a musician and paperhanger) and Ethel (Teplitsky) Walkenstein; married David Biser, August, 1957 (deceased); children: Daniel, Tara, Seth, Merissa. *Education:* University of Pennsylvania, B.A., 1946; Woman's Medical College, M.D., 1950. *Home:* 1100 Greenwood Ave., Wyncote, Pa. 19095.

CAREER: Kingsbridge Veterans Administration Hospital, Bronx, N.Y., resident in psychiatry, 1951-54; private practice in psychiatry in New York, N.Y., 1954-64, Los Angeles, Calif., 1964-68, and Miami Beach, Fla., 1968-74; conducted workshops at growth centers in London, England, Paris, France, and Rome, Florence, and Naples, Italy, 1974-76; writer, 1976—. Teacher of courses in poetry and creativity.

WRITINGS: Beyond the Couch, Crown, 1973; *Shrunk to Fit,* Coventure Ltd., 1976; *Don't Shrink to Fit!,* Grove, 1976; *Fat Chance,* Pilgrim Press, 1982; *Your Inner Therapist,* Westminster, 1983.

Author, producer, and director of video film "Beyond the Couch." Contributor to *American Journal of Psychiatry.* Contributing editor of *Voices: Art and Science of Psychotherapy.*

WORK IN PROGRESS: Nucleus Therapy: Pursuit of the Unicorn; Reconnecting—You Must Go Home Again; and a third book, tentatively entitled *Body Electric.*

SIDELIGHTS: Eileen Walkenstein, according to David Boadella in *Energy and Character: The Journal of Bioenergetic Research,* is "a pedestal-breaker, a shatterer of idols, a human voice crying against the wilderness of expertise in which she was trained, and against which in order to stay alive and in order to help people who came to her for help to become alive, she had to rebel."

What she produced in her book *Beyond the Couch* Boadella describes as "immense energy which will infuriate authoritarians everywhere." Walkenstein admits, "I am tactless, straightforward, and non-dainty in my language. The book is a vernacular, non-technical expression of my feelings in relation to the dehumanization of the human animal and the processes in America, especially American medicine, and more particularly in American psychiatry and psychoanalysis, which help create the human vegetable and uncreate the man.

"In our culture we are fast becoming robots or vegetables, losing touch even with our own tears, losing contact with our innards, leaving our marionette heads to bob and bow to someone else's strings (purse strings? . . . power strings?). My book is my small attempt to put a finger in the dike of this technological-head-robotizing current that threatens to flood us all. I am not only a monomaniac but a multiple one at that! It is my own passion play!"

"Although the book is a great shout for life, there is also deep wisdom in it," Boadella writes. "At a time when, with the advent of primal therapy, there is great emphasis on the need to yell out one's pain, she offers a simple reminder to those who scream easily: 'if you're a screamer, things are going out of you all the time and you're not allowing anything to come in—spend some time letting things come in—let your breath come in; keep your mouth shut and let others' words come in; look with your eyes and let the others' eyes come in—this trip will take you toward greater contact than is possible in any of your yells. Listen to silence instead of the sound of your own probably blaming, accusatory voice. If you listen intently enough, you'll hear your body singing to its animal rhythm, which your yells have been blotting out.'"

BIOGRAPHICAL/CRITICAL SOURCES: Energy and Character: The Journal of Bioenergetic Research, May, 1973.

*　　*　　*

WALKER, Peter N. 1936-
(Andrew Arncliffe, Christopher Coram, Tom Ferris, Nicholas Rhea)

PERSONAL: Born May 18, 1936, in Glaisdale, North Yorkshire, England; son of Norman Walker (an insurance agent) and Eva Mary Rhea Walker (a teacher); married Rhoda Mary Smith (a shorthand typist), January 10, 1959; children: Janet, Andrew, Patricia, Sarah. *Education:* Educated in England. *Religion:* Roman Catholic. *Home:* Arncliffe House, Ampleforth, York Y06 4DA, England. *Agent:* Laurence Pollinger, 18, Maddox Street, London W1R 0EU, England.

CAREER: Writer; former police officer. Lecturer at law and police training schools. *Military service:* Royal Air Force, 1954-56; became corporal. *Member:* Crime Writers' Association (England), Society of Authors, Writers Guild, Nottingham

Writers' Club (vice-president), Yorkshire Dialect Society (member of council). *Awards, honors:* Second prize from Queen's Police Gold Medal Essay Competition, 1967.

WRITINGS—Published by R. Hale, except as indicated: *Carnaby and the Goalbreakers,* 1967; *Carnaby and the Hijackers,* 1967; *Carnaby and the Assassins,* 1968; *Carnaby and the Conspirators,* 1969; (under pseudonym Tom Ferris) *Espionage for a Lady,* 1969; *Carnaby and the Saboteurs,* 1970; *Fatal Accident,* 1970; *Panda One on Duty,* 1971; *Carnaby and the Eliminators,* 1971; *Special Duty,* 1971; *Carnaby and the Demonstrators,* 1972; *Panda One Investigates,* 1972; *Identification Parade,* 1972; *Illustrated History of Punishment,* David & Charles, 1973; *Major Incident,* 1974; *The Dovingsby Death,* 1975; *Murder by the Lake,* 1975; *Carnaby and the Kidnappers,* 1976; *The MacIntyre Plot,* 1976; *Missing from Home,* 1977; *Witchcraft for Panda One,* 1978; *Target Criminal,* 1978; *Carnaby and the Counterfeiters,* 1980; *The Carlton Plot,* 1980; *Siege for Panda One,* 1981; *Teenage Cop,* 1982; *Carnaby and the Campaigners,* 1984; *Robber in a Mole Trap,* 1984.

Under pseudonym Christopher Coram: *A Call to Danger,* 1968; *A Call to Die,* 1969; *Death in Ptarmigan Forest,* 1970; *Murder beneath the Trees,* 1979; *Prisoner on the Dam,* 1982.

Under pseudonym Nicholas Rhea: *Constable on the Hill,* 1979; *Constable on the Prowl,* 1980; *Constable around the Village,* 1981; *Constable across the Moors,* 1982; *Constable in the Dale,* 1983.

Author of weekly column, "Countryman's Diary," in *Darlington Times* and *Stockton Times.* Contributor of articles on folklore and rural matters (generally under pseudonym Nicholas Rhea) to periodicals; contributor to police publications. Founder and former editor, *Police Box.*

WORK IN PROGRESS: More crime novels; nonfiction.

* * *

WALLACE, David Rains 1945-

PERSONAL: Born August 10, 1945, in Charlottesville, Va.; son of Sebon Rains (a psychologist) and Sarah (Hahn) Wallace; married Elizabeth Ann Kendall (an artist), July 3, 1975. *Education:* Wesleyan University, Middletown, Conn., B.A. (cum laude), 1967; graduate study at Columbia University, 1967-68; Mills College, M.A., 1974. *Politics:* Democrat. *Home address:* P.O. Box 517, Covelo, Calif. 95428.

CAREER: Metropolitan Park District of Columbus and Franklin County, Columbus, Ohio, public information specialist, 1974-78; free-lance writer, 1978—.

MEMBER: Wilderness Society, Sierra Club, Nature Conservancy.

AWARDS, HONORS: Silver Medal, Californiana category, Commonwealth Club of California, 1979, for *The Dark Range: A Naturalist's Night Notebook* and 1984, for *The Klamath Knot: Explorations of Myth and Evolution;* Ohioana Award, science category, 1981, for *Idle Weeds: The Life of a Sandstone Ridge;* John Burroughs Medal for Nature Writing, 1984, for *The Klamath Knot: Explorations of Myth and Evolution.*

WRITINGS—All published by Sierra Books: *The Dark Range: A Naturalist's Night Notebook,* illustrations by Roger Bayless, 1978; *Idle Weeds: The Life of a Sandstone Ridge,* 1980; *The Klamath Knot: Explorations of Myth and Evolution,* 1983; *The Wilder Shore,* 1984; *The Turquoise Dragon,* 1985.

Contributor to conservation journals and newspapers, including *New York Times Book Review, Sierra, Wilderness, Country Journal,* and *Ohio Sierran.*

WORK IN PROGRESS: Bulow Hammock.

SIDELIGHTS: David Rains Wallace told *CA:* "My writing arises from a fascination with this planet—its climate, waters, rocks, soils, plants, and animals. I want to awaken readers to the fact that we remain a part of the biosphere, that we cannot destroy it without destroying ourselves."

Wallace's regard for nature is reflected in *The Klamath Knot: Explorations of Myth and Evolution,* in which he explores a unique tract of wilderness along the California-Oregon border. Commenting on Wallace's work, Clifford D. May writes in the *New York Times Book Review,* "He spins intriguing scientific tales and tosses out some delightful tidbits of arcana." A *Publishers Weekly* reviewer adds, "This is a rare and imaginative introduction to a wilderness that links past and present; Wallace belongs to the first rank of science writers."

BIOGRAPHICAL/CRITICAL SOURCES: San Francisco Bay Guardian, November 9, 1978; *Cleveland Plain Dealer,* November 17, 1980; *Publishers Weekly,* December 3, 1982; *Wall Street Journal,* February 14, 1983; *Washington Post Book World,* March 13, 1983; *Philadelphia Enquirer,* July 17, 1983.

* * *

WALLACE-CRABBE, Chris(topher Keith) 1934-

PERSONAL: Born May 6, 1934, in Richmond, Victoria, Australia; son of Kenneth Eyre (a journalist) and Phyllis Vera May (a pianist; maiden name, Cock) Wallace-Crabbe; married Marianne Sophie Feil; children: Ben, Georgia, Toby. *Education:* University of Melbourne, B.A., 1956, M.A., 1963. *Politics:* Socialist. *Religion:* Agnostic. *Home:* 121 Victoria St., Fitzroy, Victoria 3065, Australia. *Office:* Department of English, University of Melbourne, Parkville, Victoria 3052, Australia.

CAREER: Royal Mint, Melbourne, Victoria, Australia, junior technical officer, 1951-52; journalist in Victoria, Australia, 1953-54; Gas & Fuel Corp., Melbourne, clerical officer, 1954-55; Haileybury College, Brighton, Victoria, Australia, teacher, 1957-58; University of Melbourne, Parkville, Victoria, Australia, senior lecturer in English, 1968-76, reader in English, 1976—. Visiting fellow at University of Exeter, 1973; visiting senior member of Oxford University, 1983-84. *Military service:* Royal Australian Air Force, 1952-53.

MEMBER: Australian Academy of the Humanities.

AWARDS, HONORS: Harkness fellow at Yale University, 1965-67; Farmer's Prize for Poetry, 1969.

WRITINGS: (Editor) *The Australian Nationalists,* Oxford University Press, 1971; *Act in the Noon* (verse), Cotswold Press, 1975; (editor) *The Golden Apples of the Sun: Twentieth-Century Australian Poetry,* Melbourne University Press, 1980; *Splinters* (novel), Rigby, 1981; *The Amorous Cannibal* (verse), Oxford University Press, 1985.

All published by Angus & Robertson: *The Music of Division* (verse), 1959; *In Light and Darkness* (verse), 1963; (editor) *Six Voices,* 1963, revised edition, 1974; *The Rebel General* (verse), 1967; *Where the Wind Came* (verse), 1971; *Selected Poems,* 1973; *Melbourne or the Bush: Essays on Literature and Society,* 1974; *The Foundation of Joy* (verse), 1976; *The Emotions Are Not Skilled Workers* (verse), 1980.

WORK IN PROGRESS: "A series of poems on mental structures and psychological guises, and a speculative book on the gestures that make up autobiography."

SIDELIGHTS: Chris Wallace-Crabbe told *CA:* "My writing has for some time been influenced by modern Italian poetry, and by the visual arts, so that Florence became a natural place to stay and work in 1978. While there, I was not only able to make progress with the main projects which I had in hand, but also to translate some of the poetry of Eugenio Montale. It seems to me that submitting oneself to the pressures of a foreign culture for some time can creatively inform and reinforce that rootedness in home-soil which is for me an essential part of one's writing. What is more, a good deal of modern Italian poetry takes the live landscape as its prime source of metaphors in ways that have immense relevance for an Australian poet. Further details about my own cultural sources will be found in *Melbourne or the Bush.*

"The interaction between psychology and politics is a continuing concern of mine, as is the imaginative quality of psychoanalytic speculation. Our myths are bits of psychic machinery."

AVOCATIONAL INTERESTS: Visual arts, team sports, body surfing.

BIOGRAPHICAL/CRITICAL SOURCES: Westerly, Volume I, 1969; *Meanjin,* Volume XXIX, 1970; Geoffrey Dutton, editor, *The Literature of Australia,* 2nd edition, Penguin Books, 1976; *Times Literary Supplement,* January 30, 1981, February 5, 1982.

*   *   *

WALLER, J(ames) Irvin   1944-

PERSONAL: Born July 24, 1944, in England; naturalized Canadian citizen; son of George (a Lord Justice of appeal) and C. M. Waller; married; wife's name Myriam; children: two. *Education:* Cambridge University, B.A., 1965, diploma in criminology, 1966, Ph.D., 1973. *Home:* 9, Guertin, Aylmer, Quebec J9H 4W5, Canada.

CAREER: University of Toronto, Toronto, Ontario, senior research assistant at Centre of Criminology, 1966-69, research associate, 1969; Cambridge University, Cambridge, England, Laidlaw Research Fellow at Institute of Criminology, 1969-70; University of Toronto, research associate at Centre of Criminology, 1970-73, senior research associate, 1973, assistant professor, 1972-73, associate professor of law, 1973; Ministry of the Solicitor General, Ottawa, Ontario, director of Research Division, 1974, director general, beginning 1974. Conducted research at University of Abidjan, 1973.

MEMBER: Ontario Association of Criminology and Corrections (director, 1971—), John Howard Society (Toronto; director, 1973—).

WRITINGS: (Contributor) D. J. West, editor, *The Future of Parole,* Duckworth, 1972; (contributor) Edward Sagarin and Donal E. J. McNamara, editors, *Corrections: Problems of Punishment and Rehabilitation,* Praeger, 1973; *Men Released from Prison* (monograph), University of Toronto Press, 1974; (with J. K. Hugessen, J. A. Phelps, and R. G. Gervais) *Report of the Task Force on Release of Inmates,* Information Canada, 1974; (contributor with Janet Chan) L. Wilkins and D. Glazer, editors, *Correctional Institutions,* 2nd edition, Lippincott, 1976; (contributor) Emilio C. Viano, editor, *Victims and Society,*

Visage Press, 1976; (with Norman Okihiro) *Burglary: The Victim and the Public,* Canadian Studies in Criminology, 1978. Contributor to professional journals.

WORK IN PROGRESS: Editing *Selected Readings for the National Conference on the Disposition of Offenders in Canada,* with John Edwards.

SIDELIGHTS: J. Irvin Waller's main concerns have been parole and release experiences, parole supervisor role studies, and research on burglary and the public. He has conducted study tours of prison and after-care systems in Czechoslovakia, Poland, Belgium, and the Netherlands, as well as in England and the United States.†

*   *   *

WALLMANN, Jeffrey M(iner)   1941-
(Phyllis Baxter, Nick Carter, Tom Cutter, Leon DaSilva, Amanda Hart Douglass, Wesley Ellis, Helga Goering, Carlotta Graham, Milton Granby, Donald Heflin, Peter Jensen, Margaret Maitland, Matthew Miner, Richard Mountbatten, Rick Renault, John Reskind, Jackson Robard, Grant Roberts, Gregory St. Germain, Bill Saxon, Scott Sheldon, Blake Simmons, Grace Sinclair, Mark Townsend, R. Van Dorne, Carole Wilson; William Jeffrey, a joint pseudonym)

PERSONAL: Born December 5, 1941, in Seattle, Wash.; son of George Rudolph (an architect) and Elizabeth (a teacher; maiden name, Biggs) Wallmann; married Helga Eikefet (a translator), December 1, 1974. *Education:* Portland State University, B.S., 1962. *Home:* 3163 West 13th Pl., Eugene, Ore. 97402. *Agent:* Richard Curtis, 164 East 64th St., Suite 1, New York, N.Y. 10021.

CAREER: Dale Systems, New York, N.Y., private investigator, 1962-63; Dohrmann Co., San Francisco, Calif., assistant buyer, manager, and public money bidder, 1964-66; manufacturer's representative in electronics industry in San Francisco area, 1966-69; Salgscentralen Skribent AS, TransEuropean, Cinelux Universal, and London Films International, public relations director in Spain, Germany, Scandinavia, and France, 1970-75; *Riviera Life,* editor-in-chief in Monaco, 1975-77; full-time novelist, 1978—. Public relations-marketing consultant, 1978—.

MEMBER: Mystery Writers of America, Science Fiction Writers of America, Western Writers of America, Crime Writers Association, National Association of Realtors, Sons of Norway, Loyal Order of Moose.

WRITINGS: The Spiral Web, Signet, 1969; (under pseudonym Carlotta Graham) *Prowl Car Girl,* Filandia, 1973; *Judas Cross,* Random House, 1974; *Clean Sweep,* Barrie & Jenkins, 1976, Avon, 1977; (under pseudonym Scott Sheldon) *The Ikon,* Futura Publishing, 1977; (under pseudonym Amanda Hart Douglass) *Jamaica,* Leisure Books, 1978; *Deathtrek,* Belmont-Tower, 1980; *Brand of the Damned,* Leisure Books, 1981; *Blood and Passion,* Belmont-Tower, 1981; *The Manipulator,* Avon, 1982; (with Tom Jeier) *Return to Canta Lupe,* Doubleday, 1983; *Business Basic for Bunglers,* Soft Gold, 1984; (with Jeier) *The Celluloid Kid,* Doubleday, 1984; (under pseudonym Tom Cutter) *Tracker #5,* Avon, 1984; *The Chugalug Nude,* Heyne, 1985; *Durango Dust-Up,* Heyne, 1985; (with Jeier) *Montezuma's Revenge,* Doubleday, 1985; (with Jeier) *Lead Poison,* Heyne, 1985.

All published by Tiberon: (Under pseudonym Richard Mount-batten) *Spell of the Beast*, 1969; (under pseudonym R. Van Dorne) *The Desolate Cove*, 1970; (under pseudonym Carole Wilson) *Karen and Mother*, 1971; (under pseudonym Grace Sinclair) *Mother's Share*, 1971; (under pseudonym Phyllis Baxter) *Homework at Teacher's*, 1972; (under pseudonym Helga Goering) *Piano Teacher*, 1973; (under pseudonym Blake Simmons) *Faculty Advisor*, 1973; (under pseudonym Milton Granby) *The Lady Dentist*, 1973; (under pseudonym Donald Heflin) *Teacher's Exposure*, 1973.

Under pseudonym Nick Carter; all published by Award: *Hour of the Wolf*, 1973; *Ice Trap Terror*, 1974.

Under pseudonym Leon DaSilva; all published by Belmont-Tower: *Green Hell* (nonfiction), 1976; *Angolan Breakout* (nonfiction), 1976.

Under pseudonym Wesley Ellis; all published by Jove: *Lone Star on the Treachery Trail*, 1982; *Lone Star and the Hardrock Payoff*, 1983; *Lone Star and the Gold Raiders*, 1983; *Lone Star and the Mexican Standoff*, 1983; *Lone Star on the Owlhoot Trail*, 1984; *Lone Star and the Hangrope Heritage*, 1984; *Lone Star and the Riverboat Gamblers*, 1984; *Lone Star and the Moon Trail Feud*, 1984; *Lone Star and the Rancho Diablo*, 1985; *Lone Star and the California Oil War*, 1985.

Under pseudonym Peter Jensen; all published by Liverpool: *A Mother's Love*, 1969; *The Virgin Couple*, 1970; *Her Honor the Judge*, 1970; *Ravished*, 1971; *Father and Son*, 1971.

Under pseudonym John Reskind; all published by Tiberon: *The Unholy Master*, 1969; *Parksburg Saga* (six volumes), 1970; *Caesar Conquers*, 1972; *Caesar's Revenge*, 1972; *Caesar Comes Home*, 1972; *The Senator's Secretary*, 1974.

Under pseudonym Jackson Robard; all published by Tiberon: *Gang Initiation*, 1971; *Present for Teacher*, 1972; *Teacher's Lounge*, 1972.

Under pseudonym Grant Roberts; all published by Liverpool: *The Reluctant Couple*, 1969; *Wayward Wives*, 1970; *Rajah*, 1971.

Under pseudonym Bill Saxon; all published by Tiberon: *The Terrorists*, 1972; *Junkyard Rape*, 1973.

Under pseudonym Mark Townsend; all published by Tiberon: *White Captive*, 1969; *Teenage Teaser*, 1973.

With Bill Pronzini, under joint pseudonym William Jeffrey: *Duel at Gold Buttes*, Leisure Books, 1982; *Border Fever*, Leisure Books, 1983; *Day of the Moon*, R. Hale, 1983.

Contributor to numerous anthologies. Contributor of fiction and nonfiction articles, often under pseudonyms, to various magazines, including *Argosy*, *Ellery Queen's Mystery Magazine*, *Alfred Hitchcock's Mystery Magazine*, *Mike Shayne's Mystery Magazine*, *Zane Grey Western*, *Venture*, *Shipping Register and Shipbuilder*, *Oui*, and *TV Guide*.

WORK IN PROGRESS: Sigma One, Abbatoir, The Blockbuster, The Conniver, and other novels; nonfiction books and articles.

SIDELIGHTS: In attempting to compile a list of his books, Wallmann encounters the difficulties of a prolific writer who uses a variety of pseudonyms and writes in several genres, often for original paperback publication, and frequently for smaller houses which are less than efficient in keeping records.

Wallmann writes: "Going strictly by income derived (the only way to go!), I've sold more than one hundred novels and over fifty novelettes, short stories and articles since 1969. Also to my credit are eleven book translations, and I've been translated into six languages.

"I have also been anthologized. In addition to the book publishers listed above, I have been published by the Playboy Press, and by science fiction, mystery, and western magazines, some oddball men's magazines and a few short-lived magazines like *Coven 13*. Plus, as I mentioned, anthologies including *Best Detective Stories of the Year* and Random House's Alfred Hitchcock series.

"The hardcover stuff under my own name is easy to list, and for that matter so are most of the pure contract jobs done under pseudonyms or house names like 'Nick Carter.' But, over the years, some of my paperpulp has been published under names and titles chosen by the companies after they've accepted my manuscripts, and even I don't know how they end up. It's hard enough to get marginal publishers to send author's copies—living in France made it downright impossible. So it's a bit of a shock to browse through a second-hand bookshop in New York City and come up with something I had written as *Enemy Legion* by Matthew Miner appearing in print as *White Captive* by Mark Townsend. This is especially true in what is referred to as 'ephemeral' writing. And I'm not sure anyone would *want* to know about all this stuff."

*   *   *

WALLS, David Stuart   1941-

PERSONAL: Born October 21, 1941, in Chicago, Ill.; son of John Archer and Elizabeth (Smith) Walls; married Lucia V. Gattone, November 25, 1971; children: Jesse Michael. *Education:* University of California, Berkeley, B.A., 1964; University of Kentucky, M.A., 1972, Ph.D., 1978. *Home:* 943 McFarlane Ave., Sebastopol, Calif. 95472. *Office:* Office of Sponsored Programs, Sonoma State University, Rohnert Park, Calif. 94928.

CAREER: U.S. Department of Health, Education, and Welfare, Washington, D.C., management intern, 1964-65; Office of Economic Opportunity, Washington, D.C., administrative assistant, 1965-66; Appalachian Volunteers, Inc., Prestonsburg, Ky., field coordinator, 1966-69, director, 1969-70; Berea College, Berea, Ky., part-time instructor, 1970; University of Kentucky, College of Social Professions, Lexington, assistant professor, 1974-81, associate director of Appalachian Center, 1977-81; Sonoma State University, Rohnert Park, Calif., director of Office of Sponsored Programs, 1982—, vice-president and manager of Academic Foundation, 1982—. Member, National Council of University Research Administrators.

MEMBER: Society of Research Administrators.

WRITINGS: (Editor with John B. Stephenson) *Appalachia in the Sixties: Decade of Reawakening*, University Press of Kentucky, 1972; (contributor) J. W. Williamson, editor, *An Appalachian Symposium*, Appalachian State University Press, 1977; (contributor) Helen M. Lewis and others, editors, *Colonialism in Modern America: The Appalachian Case*, Appalachian Consortium Press, 1978.

(Contributor) Scott G. McNall, editor, *Theoretical Perspectives in Sociology*, St. Martin's, 1979; (senior author) *A Baseline Assessment of Coal Industry Structure*, Ohio River Basin Energy Study and U.S. Environmental Protection Agency, 1979; (contributor with Dwight B. Billings) *Harvard Encyclopedia of American Ethnic Groups*, Harvard University Press, 1980.

Member of editorial board, *Appalachian Journal,* 1979—.

WORK IN PROGRESS: Research on non-profit organizations in the United States.

*   *   *

WALLS, Dwayne E(stes)   1932-

PERSONAL: Born May 16, 1932, in Morganton, N.C.; son of William Roy (a clergyman) and Dora (Buchanan) Walls; married Judith Michaels (a teacher), September 20, 1958; children: Helen Elizabeth, Dwayne E., Jr. *Education:* Attended Lenoir Rhyne College, 1950, 1953-54, and University of North Carolina, 1953-57. *Politics:* Democrat. *Religion:* Protestant. *Home address:* Route 3, Box 415, Pittsboro, N.C. 27312. *Agent:* Sterling Lord Agency, 660 Madison Ave., New York, N.Y. 10021. *Office:* University of North Carolina, School of Journalism, Chapel Hill, N.C. 27415.

CAREER: University of North Carolina, Chapel Hill, news bureau writer, 1954-55, alumni association editorial assistant, 1955-56; *Durham Sun,* Durham, N.C., staff writer, 1956-57; *Durham Morning Herald,* Durham, staff writer, 1957-59; *Chapel Hill Weekly,* Chapel Hill, N.C., news editor, 1959-61; *Charlotte Observer,* Charlotte, N.C., staff writer, 1961-71; free-lance writer, 1971—; Duke University, Durham, part-time research associate, 1972-73; Southern Regional Council, Atlanta, Ga., program officer, 1973-75; North Carolina State University at Raleigh, lecturer in journalism, 1977-79; currently lecturer in journalism at University of North Carolina, Chapel Hill. *Military service:* U.S. Air Force, 1951-53.

AWARDS, HONORS: George Polk Memorial award; Sidney Hillman Foundation award; American Political Science Award for Excellence in Public Affairs Reporting; three awards from the National Conference of Christians and Jews; five awards from the North Carolina Press Association; two awards from Atlanta chapter of Sigma Delta Chi; fellowships from National Endowment for the Humanities, American Political Science Association, Ford Foundation, and Louis M. Rabinowitz Foundation.

WRITINGS: Fayette County, Tennessee: Tragedy and Confrontation, Southern Regional Council, 1969; *The Klan: Collapsed and Dormant,* Race Relations Information Center, 1970; *The Chickenbone Special,* Harcourt, 1971; (editor) *Amazing Disgrace,* South Carolina Council on Human Relations, 1972; *The Kidwells,* Carolina Academic Press, 1983. Contributor to *Editor and Publisher* and *Saturday Review.*

WORK IN PROGRESS: The Culture of Poverty in an East Tennessee Coal Field.

*   *   *

WARSH
See WARSHAW, Jerry

*   *   *

WARSHAW, Jerry   1929-
(Warsh)

PERSONAL: Born June 12, 1929, in Chicago, Ill.; son of Julius (a display designer) and Jeanette (Seamans) Warshaw; married Joyce Milash (a free-lance writer), May 1, 1960; children: Elizabeth. *Education:* Attended Chicago Academy of Fine Arts, 1947-49, Illinois Institute of Design, 1954-55, and Art Institute

of Chicago, 1955-56. *Politics:* "Moderate Liberal Independent Democrat, etc." *Religion:* "Non-Active Jewish." *Home and office:* 748 Hinman Ave., Evanston, Ill. 60202.

CAREER: American Adventure Comic Strip, Bennington, Vt., art assistant, 1950-51; Cartoonist's Studio, Chicago, Ill., illustrator, 1951, 1953-55; O'Grady-Payne Studio, Chicago, illustrator, 1958-59; Visual Arts Studio, Chicago, illustrator, 1965-70; free-lance illustrator, 1970—. Art consultant and designer, Illinois Sesquicentennial Commission, 1965-69. *Military service:* U.S. Army, 1951-53.

MEMBER: Society of Typographic Arts, Illinois State Historical Society, Chicago Historical Society (life member), Chicago Press Club, Art Institute of Chicago, Civil War Round Table of Chicago (former president), Evanston Historical Society, Children's Reading Round Table of Chicago (vice-president, 1972-73; former president).

AWARDS, HONORS: Award of merit for art direction for designing and illustrating the *Illinois Intelligencer* (Sesquicentennial Commission newspaper); award of honor for design of official seal and flag, Illinois Sesquicentennial Commission, 1969; award for design of official seal, Illinois Constitutional Convention, 1971; *Catholic Magazine* Artist of the Year, 1977.

WRITINGS—Self-illustrated: *The I Can't Draw Book,* Albert Whitman, 1971; *The Funny Drawing Book,* edited by Caroline Rubin, Albert Whitman, 1977; *Draw Yourself a Zoo,* Scholastic Book Services, 1979.

Illustrator: Jule Krisvoy, *New Games to Play,* Follett, 1968; Florence Heide and Sylvia Van Clief, *The New Neighbor,* Follett, 1971; David L. Harrison, *The Case of Og the Missing Frog,* Rand McNally, 1972; W. Burmeister, *The Long View of Lincoln,* Longview Books, 1975; Joel Rothman, *How to Play the Drums,* Albert Whitman, 1977; Burton Albert, Jr., *More Codes for Kids,* Albert Whitman, 1979.

C. B. Labrid, *Princess Priscilla's Problem,* Children's Press, 1980; Pegreen Snow, *Mrs. Periwinkle's Groceries,* Children's Press, 1981; Catherine Petrie, *Joshua James Likes Trucks,* Children's Press, 1982; Nancy Polette, *Tangles,* Book Lures, 1983; Polette, *The Thinker's Mother Goose,* Book Lures, 1983.

All written by Ann Bishop; published by Albert Whitman, except as indicated: *Hey Riddle Riddle,* 1968; *Riddle Red Riddle,* 1969; *Noah Riddle,* 1970; *The Riddle-iculous Rid-Alphabet Book,* 1971; *Chicken Riddle,* 1972; *Merry-Go-Riddle,* 1973; *The Ella Fanny Elephant Riddle Book,* 1974; *Wild Bill Hiccup's Riddle Book,* 1975; *Oh, Riddlesticks,* 1976; *The Riddle Ages,* 1977; *Annie O'Kay's Riddle Roundup,* Elsevier/Nelson, 1981; *Cleo Catra's Riddle Book,* Elsevier/Nelson, 1981; *Hello, Mr. Chips!,* Lodestar/Dutton, 1982.

Also illustrator of textbooks for Rand McNally, Scott, Foresman, Sadlier, Economy Co., Benefic, Combined Motivations, and Science Research Associates Reading Program.

WORK IN PROGRESS: Gilbert and Sullivan for Fun; The Big and Little Animal Book; a collection of cartoons from *Marriage* magazine, *The Family Room; Draw Yourself a Circus; The Teachers Drawing Book.*

SIDELIGHTS: Jerry Warshaw told *CA:* "Recently, because of my two drawing books, I've been giving talks to schools and libraries. I have found these to be quite rewarding. My basic theme is simply to introduce and encourage confidence in drawing, by emphasizing observation, imagination, simplicity, and experimentation. I am teaching children how to think—not how to draw—and teaching them to not be afraid of putting something on paper. My talk includes a lot of verbal interplay with the students. I have also conducted several sessions of an eight-week course for ages five through thirteen called 'The Drawing Group' wherein we test our powers of observation and imagination.''

AVOCATIONAL INTERESTS: Civil War, sports cars, model railroads, photography, film, and theatre.

BIOGRAPHICAL/CRITICAL SOURCES: Chicago Sun Times, February 27, 1972; *St. Louis Post Dispatch,* July 10, 1973, March 10, 1977.

* * *

WATKINS, T(homas) H(enry)   1936-

PERSONAL: Born March 29, 1936, in Loma Linda, Calif.; son of Thomas F. (a mailer) and Orel (Roller) Watkins; married Elaine Otakie, January 26, 1957 (divorced); married Ellen J. Parker, June 12, 1976; children: (first marriage) Lisa Lynn, Kevin Blair. *Education:* Attended San Bernardino Valley College, 1954-56; University of Redlands, B.A., 1958; San Francisco State College (now University), graduate study, 1963-64. *Politics:* Democrat. *Religion:* ''Former Catholic, now militantly ecumenical Christian.'' *Home:* 2226 Decatur Pl. N.W., Washington, D.C. 20008. *Office:* The Wilderness Society, 1901 Pennsylvania Ave. N.W., Washington, D.C. 20006.

CAREER: American West Publishing Co., Palo Alto, Calif., managing editor, 1966-69, editor, 1969-70, associate editor, 1970-76; *American Heritage* (magazine), New York, N.Y., member of board of editors, 1976-79, senior editor, 1979-82; *Wilderness* (magazine), Washington, D.C., editor, 1982—.

WRITINGS: San Francisco in Color, Hastings House, 1968; (with Roger R. Olmsted) *Here Today: San Francisco's Architectural Heritage,* San Francisco Chronicle, 1968; (with others) *The Grand Colorado: The Story of a River and Its Canyons,* American West, 1969.

California in Color: An Essay on the Paradox of Plenty, Hastings House, 1970; (with others) *The Water Hustlers,* Sierra Club, 1971; *Gold and Silver in the West: The Illustrated History of an American Dream,* American West, 1971; *California: An Illustrated History,* American West, 1973; *On the Shore of the Sundown Sea,* Sierra Club, 1973; *Mark Twain's Mississippi: The Pictorial History of America's Greatest River,* American West, 1974.

(With Charles S. Watson, Jr.) *The Lands No One Knows: America and the Public Domain,* Sierra Club, 1975; *John Muir's America,* illustrated with photographs by DeWitt Jones, American West, 1976; (with Olmsted) *Mirror of the Dream: An Illustrated History of San Francisco,* Scrimshaw Press, 1976; *Taken by the Wind: Vanishing Architecture of the West,* illustrated with photographs by Ronald Woodall, New York Graphic Society, 1977.

Gold Country, illustrated with photographs by Stanly Truman, California Historical Society, 1982; (author of introduction) John Wesley Powell, *Lands of the Arid Region of the United States,* new edition, Harvard Common Press, 1983. Contributor of more than 200 articles to numerous periodicals.

WORK IN PROGRESS: A biography of Harold L. Ickes, Secretary of the Interior from 1933 to 1946.

SIDELIGHTS: T. H. Watkins writes that ''some people call me an historian, some a journalist, some an environmentalist—

they're all wrong. I'd prefer to think of myself *first* as a writer—a writer who happens to work in all these areas, as well as anything else which presents itself. I'm in love with words, with the sound and muscularity of phrases. . . . At the same time, I cannot deny a profound dependence upon the historical view, for it seems to me that it provides the essential key to understanding—and understanding is the only shield we have against fate and all its consequences.

''I learned this essential fact, among other things, from the one writer who has influenced my work, such as it is, more than any other: Wallace Stegner, the novelist and historian who needs no encomiums from me to place him at or very near the head of the small list of this century's major American writers.''

BIOGRAPHICAL/CRITICAL SOURCES: New York Times Book Review, December 14, 1969, December 18, 1977.

* * *

WATT, Donald Cameron
   See CAMERON WATT, Donald

* * *

WEAVER, Mateman
   See GREENE, A(lvin) C(arl)

* * *

WEBER, David J.   1940-

PERSONAL: Born December 20, 1940, in Buffalo, N.Y.; son of Theodore C. (an appliance dealer) and Frances J. Weber; married Carol S. Bryant (a teacher), June 16, 1962; children: Scott David, Amy Carol. *Education:* State University of New York College at Fredonia, B.S., 1962; University of New Mexico, M.A., 1964, Ph.D., 1967. *Home:* 6292 Mercedes, Dallas, Tex. 75214. *Office:* Department of History, Southern Methodist University, Dallas, Tex. 75275.

CAREER: San Diego State University, San Diego, Calif., assistant professor, 1967-70, associate professor, 1970-73, professor of history, 1973-76; Southern Methodist University, Dallas, Tex., professor of history, 1976—, chairman of department, 1979—. Fulbright lecturer, University of Costa Rica, 1970. Danforth associate, 1973—. Member of board of editors, Southern Methodist University Press, 1983—. Member of advisory board, Texas Humanities Center, 1980-83; member of National Council of Advisors, Institute of the American West, 1983—.

MEMBER: American Historical Association, Conference on Latin American History, Organization of American Historians, Western History Association.

AWARDS, HONORS: The Taos Trappers: The Fur Trade in the Far Southwest, 1540-1846 was named best book on Southwest history by Border States Regional Library Association, 1970-71; Outstanding Educator of America award, 1973; National Endowment for the Humanities fellow, 1974-75; *Foreigners in Their Native Land: Historical Roots of the Mexican Americans* was selected as one of the outstanding academic books on the history of North America by *Choice,* 1974-75; American Philosophical Society grant, summer, 1975; Huntington Library fellow, summer, 1975; American Council of Learned Societies fellow, spring, 1980; Herbert E. Bolton Award in Spanish Borderlands History, *Western Historical Quarterly,* for article "The Failure of a Frontier Institution. . ."; *The Mexican Frontier, 1821-1846: The American Southwest under Mexico* received awards from Westerners International, Border States Regional Library Association, Sons of the Texas Republic, and Texas Institute of Letters.

WRITINGS: (Editor and translator) *The Extranjeros: Selected Documents from the Mexican Side of the Santa Fe Trail, 1825-1828,* Stagecoach Press, 1967; (editor) Albert Pike, *Prose Sketches and Poems Written in the Western Country (with Additional Stories),* Calvin Horn, 1967; (editor) David H. Coyner, *The Lost Trappers,* University of New Mexico Press, 1970; *The Taos Trappers: The Fur Trade in the Far Southwest, 1540-1846,* University of Oklahoma Press, 1971; *Foreigners in Their Native Land: Historical Roots of the Mexican Americans,* University of New Mexico Press, 1973.

(Editor) *El Mexico Perdido: Ensayos sobre el antiguo norte de Mexico, 1540-1821,* Secretaria de Education Publica, 1976; (editor) *Northern Mexico on the Eve of the United States Invasion: Rare Imprints Concerning California, Arizona, New Mexico and Texas, 1821-1846,* Arno, 1976; (editor with Duane L. Smith) *Fortunes Are for the Few: Letters of a Forty-niner by Charles William Churchill,* San Diego Historical Society, 1977; (editor) *New Spain's Far Northern Frontier: Essays on Spain in the American Southwest, 1540-1821,* University of New Mexico Press, 1979; *The Mexican Frontier, 1821-1846: The American Southwest under Mexico,* University of New Mexico Press, 1982; (editor and translator with Conchita Hassell Winn) *Troubles in Texas, 1832: A Tejano Viewpoint from San Antonio,* Wind River Press, 1983; *Richard H. Kern: Expeditionary Artist in the American Southwest, 1848-1853,* University of New Mexico Press, 1985.

Co-editor of "Histories of the American Frontier" series. Contributor to several volumes of *The Mountain Men and the Fur Trade of the Far West,* edited by LeRoy R. Hafen, 1966-72; contributor of over eighty articles and reviews to historical journals. Member of board of editorial consultants and book review editor of *Journal of San Diego History,* 1971-76; member of board of editorial consultants, *New Mexico Historical Review,* 1977—, *Meyibo,* 1977—, and *California Historical Quarterly,* 1980—; member of board of editors, *Western Historical Quarterly,* 1975-80, and *Southwest Review,* 1983—.

WORK IN PROGRESS: A study of Spanish activity in the American West, 1529-1821; another book.

* * *

WEBSTER, Frederick E., Jr. 1937-

PERSONAL: Born October 22, 1937, in Auburn, N.Y.; son of Frederick E. (a merchant) and Evelyn (Dudden) Webster; married Mary Alice Powers, December 27, 1957; children: Lynn Marie, Mark Andrew, Lisa Ann. *Education:* Dartmouth College, A.B., 1959, M.B.A. (with distinction), 1960; Stanford University, Ph.D., 1964. *Religion:* Episcopalian. *Home:* Deer Run Farm, Etna, N.H. *Office:* Amos Tuck School of Business Administration, Dartmouth College, Hanover, N.H. 03755.

CAREER: Stanford University, Stanford, Calif., acting instructor in marketing, 1963-64; Columbia University, New York, N.Y., assistant professor of marketing, 1964-65; Dartmouth College, Amos Tuck School of Business Administration, Hanover, N.H., assistant professor, 1965-68, associate professor, 1968-72, professor of business administration, 1972-79, E. B.

Osborn Professor of Marketing, 1979—, associate dean, 1976-83. Has taught in management development programs in the United States and abroad, including University of the Witwatersrand, 1968-69, Cambridge University, 1971, and Centre d'Etudes Industrielles, Geneva, Switzerland, 1972—. Director of Vermont Public Radio, CPM, Inc., and of Vermont Log Buildings, Inc.; trustee, Alice Peck Day Memorial Hospital, and Marketing Science Institute. *Member:* American Marketing Association.

WRITINGS: (Editor) *New Directions in Marketing,* American Marketing Association, 1965; (editor with Kenneth R. Davis, and contributor) *Readings in Sales Force Management,* Ronald, 1968; (with Davis) *Sales Force Management: Text and Cases,* Ronald, 1968; *Marketing Communication: Modern Promotional Strategy,* Ronald, 1971; (with Yoram Wind) *Organizational Buying Behavior,* Prentice-Hall, 1972; *Social Aspects of Marketing,* Prentice-Hall, 1973; *Marketing for Managers,* Harper, 1974; *Field Sales Management,* Wiley, 1983; *Industrial Marketing Strategy,* revised edition, Wiley, 1984; (with Davis and Boyd) *Marketing Management Casebook,* Irwin, 4th edition, 1984.

Contributor: James Bearden, editor, *Personal Selling: Behavioral Science Readings and Cases,* Wiley, 1967; Ralph L. Day, editor, *Concepts for Modern Marketing,* International Textbook, 1968; Robert F. Gwinner and Edward M. Smith, editors, *Sales Strategy: Cases and Readings,* Appleton, 1969; Bernard Morin, editor, *Marketing in a Changing World,* American Marketing Association, 1969; S. H. Britt, editor, *Consumer Behavior in Theory and in Action,* Wiley, 1970; J. A. Barnhill, editor, *Sales Management: Contemporary Perspectives,* Scott, Foresman, 1970; S. Neelamegham, editor, *Marketing Management and the Indian Economy,* Vikas Publications, 1970; R. L. Day and T. E. Ness, editors, *Marketing Models: Behavioral Science Applications,* International Textbook, 1971.

Editor of Wiley's "Marketing Management" series. Contributor of articles and reviews to marketing journals. Member of editorial board, *Journal of Marketing.*

WORK IN PROGRESS: Research in marketing and corporate strategies, industrial buyer behavior, field sales management, and marketing performance appraisal.

AVOCATIONAL INTERESTS: Downhill and cross-country skiing, squash, fishing.

* * *

WEBSTER, Jan 1924-

PERSONAL: Born August 10, 1924, in Blantyre, Scotland; daughter of William (a grocer) and Maggie (a nurse; maiden name, Henderson) McCallum; married Andrew Webster (a newspaper editor), August 10, 1946; children: Lyn Margaret, Stephen William. *Education:* Attended Hamilton Academy, 1938-40. *Politics:* "Uncommitted." *Religion:* Presbyterian. *Home:* 5 Methley St., London, SE11 4AL, England.

CAREER: Border Mail, Kelso, Scotland, journalist, 1941; Kemsley Newspapers, Glasgow, Scotland, journalist in Glasgow, 1942-46, and London, 1946-48; free-lance journalist, 1948-60, and fiction writer, 1948—.

WRITINGS: Colliers Row (novel), Lippincott, 1977; *Saturday City,* St. Martins, 1979; *Beggarman's Country,* St. Martins, 1979; *Due South,* Thorpe, 1983.

SIDELIGHTS: Jan Webster writes: "Chiefly, my aim is to present the Scots, not as the pawky, kilt-wearing, haggis-eating figures of popular conception, but as the thrusting, exciting, ambitious 'repressed romantics' (this last according to Welshman Richard Burton!) they really are. No tiny nation as contributed so much to the world, and it is time Scotland stepped out from England's shadow to enjoy a cultural Renaissance."

BIOGRAPHICAL/CRITICAL SOURCES: Weekend Scotsman, March 19, 1977; *Croydon Advertiser,* April 29, 1977; *Times Literary Supplement,* March 5, 1982.

*   *   *

WEIDENBAUM, Murray L(ew)   1927-

PERSONAL: Born February 10, 1927, in Bronx, N.Y.; son of David and Rose (Warshaw) Weidenbaum; married Phyllis Green, June 13, 1954; children: Susan, James, Laurie. *Education:* City College (now City College of the City University of New York), B.B.A., 1948; Columbia University, M.A., 1949; Princeton University, M.P.A., 1954, Ph.D., 1958. *Politics:* Republican. *Religion:* Jewish. *Home:* 709 South Skinker, St. Louis, Mo. 63105. *Office:* Center for the Study of American Business, Washington University, St. Louis, Mo. 63130.

CAREER: State of New York, Department of Labor, New York, N.Y., research economist, 1948-49; U.S. Bureau of the Budget, Executive Office of the President, Washington, D.C., fiscal economist, 1949-57; General Dynamics Corp., Convair Division, Fort Worth, Tex., economist, 1957-58; Boeing Co., Seattle, Wash., corporate economist, 1958-63; Stanford Research Institute, Stanford, Calif., senior economist, 1963-64; Washington University, St. Louis, Mo., associate professor, 1964-66, professor of economics, 1966—, chairman of department, 1966-69, 1971-74, director of Center for the Study of American Business, 1975-81.

Royer Visiting Professor, University of California, Berkeley, 1972. Member of business research advisory council, U.S. Department of Labor, and of committee on government operations and expenditures, U.S. Chamber of Commerce, 1959-63; chairman of subcommittee on military and international budgets, 1960-63; executive secretary of Presidential Committee on the Economic Impact of Defense and Disarmament, 1964; director of economic research program, National Aeronautics and Space Administration, 1964-69; member of committee on science, technology and regional growth, National Academy of Sciences, 1967-68; assistant secretary of the treasury, U.S. Department of the Treasury, Washington, D.C., 1969-71; chairman of President's Council of Economic Advisors, 1981-82. Consultant to U.S. Department of State, Congressional Joint Economic Committee, and other government bodies; member of board of economists of *Time. Military service:* U.S. Army, 1945.

MEMBER: National Economists Club (member of board of governors), American Economic Association, American Statistical Association, Cosmos Club (Washington, D.C.). *Awards, honors:* Distinguished Writers Award, Georgetown University, 1971; elected to Free Market Hall of Fame, 1983; recipient of Alexander Hamilton Medal.

WRITINGS: Federal Budgeting: The Choice of Government Programs, American Enterprise Institute for Public Policy Research, 1964; *Prospects for Reallocating Public Resources: A Study in Federal-State Fiscal Relations,* American Enterprise Institute for Public Policy Research, 1967; *Prospects for the*

American Economy during the Post-Vietnam Period, Department of Economics, Washington University (St. Louis), 1967; *The Modern Public Sector: New Ways of Doing the Government's Business,* Basic Books, 1969; *Matching Needs and Resources: Reforming the Federal Budget,* American Enterprise Institute for Public Policy Research, 1973; *Economics of Peace Time Defense,* Praeger, 1974; *Government-Mandated Price Increases,* American Enterprise Institute for Public Policy Research, 1975; *Government Credit Subsidies for Energy Development,* American Enterprise Institute for Public Policy Research, 1976; *Business, Government, and the Public,* Prentice-Hall, 1977, 2nd edition, 1981; *The Future of Business Regulation,* Amacon, 1980.

Also author of numerous studies published by Washington University, Stanford Research Institute, and American Enterprise Institute for Public Policy Research. Regular columnist, *Christian Science Monitor;* former columnist for Los Angeles Times Syndicate, and *Washington Report.* Contributor to economic journals and popular periodicals, including *Saturday Review, Business Week, Fortune,* and *Wall Street Journal.* Co-editor, *Regulation.*

WORK IN PROGRESS: Government Power and Business Performance.

*   *   *

WEIL, Roman L(ee)   1940-
(Eli Worman)

PERSONAL: Surname is pronounced "Weel"; born May 22, 1940, in Montgomery, Ala.; son of Roman Lee (an attorney) and Charlotte (Alexander) Weil; married Cherie Buresh (a librarian), December 18, 1963; children: Alexis Cherie, Charles Alexander Roman, Lacey Lorraine. *Education:* Yale University, B.A., 1962; Carnegie-Mellon University, M.S.I.A., 1965, Ph.D., 1966. *Home:* 950 Sheridan Rd., Evanston, Ill. 60202. *Office:* Graduate School of Business, University of Chicago, 1101 East 58th St., Chicago, Ill. 60637.

CAREER: Carnegie-Mellon University, Pittsburgh, Pa., instructor in mathematics and economics, 1963-65; University of Chicago, Chicago, Ill., instructor, 1965-66, assistant professor, 1966-70, associate professor of management and information sciences, 1970-74, instructor and assistant professor of mathematical economics in Graduate School of Business, 1965-70; Georgia Institute of Technology, Atlanta, Mills B. Lane Professor of Industrial Management, 1974-76; University of Chicago, professor of accounting, 1976—, director of Institute of Professional Accounting, 1978—. Visiting associate professor of industrial administration, Carnegie-Mellon University, 1971-72; visiting professor of accounting, Stanford University, 1984. Certified Public Accountant, 1973. Member of advisory committee on replacement cost implementation, Securities and Exchange Commission, 1976-78. Consultant, Jewel Tea Co., 1965-66, Beverly Bank, 1969-70, Department of Health, Education, and Welfare, United States Public Health Service, 1972; also consultant to International Business Machines, Levi-Strauss, Pillsbury, Sidley & Austin, Marmon Group, and several others.

MEMBER: American Accounting Association, American Institute of Certified Public Accountants, National Association of Accountants, American Economic Association, Econometric Society, Institute of Management Sciences, Illinois Society of Certified Public Accountants.

AWARDS, HONORS: National Science Foundation grant, 1967-79; Graham and Dodd Scroll from Financial Analysts Federation, 1975, for "Inflation Accounting: What Will General Price Level Adjusted Income Statements Show?"

WRITINGS: (With Sidney Davidson, James S. Schindler, and Clyde P. Stickney, under own name and under the pseudonym Eli Worman) *Accounting: The Language of Business,* Thomas Horton, 1974, 6th edition, 1984; (with Davidson and Schindler) *Fundamentals of Accounting,* 5th edition (Weil was not associated with previous editions), Dryden, 1975; (with Davidson and Stickney) *Inflation Accounting: A Guide for the Accountant and the Financial Analyst,* McGraw, 1976; (editor with Robert F. Vancil and contributor) *Replacement Cost Accounting: Readings on Concepts, Uses, and Methods,* Thomas Horton, 1976; (with Davison, Schindler, and Stickney) *Financial Accounting: An Introduction to Concepts, Methods, and Uses,* Dryden, 1976, 4th edition, 1985.

(With Davidson and others) *Financial Reporting by State and Local Government Units,* Center for Management of Public and Non-Profit Enterprise of the University of Chicago, 1977; (editor with Davidson and contributor) *Handbook of Modern Accounting,* 2nd edition (Weil was not associated with first edition), McGraw, 1977, 3rd edition, 1983; (editor with Davidson and contributor) *Handbook of Cost Accounting,* McGraw, 1978; (with Davidson, Stickney, and Schindler) *Managerial Accounting: An Introduction to Concepts, Methods, and Uses,* Dryden, 1978, 2nd edition, 1985; (with Davidson and Stickney) *Intermediate Accounting,* Dryden, 1980, 4th edition, 1984.

Contributor: Ralph Willoughby, editor, *Sparse Matrices and Their Applications,* IBM Data Processing, 1969; J. M. Lishan and D. T. Crary, editors, *Investment Process,* International Textbook Co., 1970; H. Raupach, E. Fels, and E. Boettcher, editors, *Jahrbuch der Wirtschaft Osteuropas,* Gunter Olzog Verlag, 1970; E. J. Elton and M. J. Gruber, editors, *Security Evaluation and Portfolio Analysis,* Prentice-Hall, 1972; Largay and Livingston, editors, *Accounting for Changing Prices,* Wiley, 1976; H. Aaron, editor, *Inflation and Income Tax,* Brookings Institution, 1976; William S. Eastman, Jr., editor, *Inflation Accounting/Indexing and Stock Behavior,* Faulkner, Dawkins, & Sullivan, 1976; R. Henry and O. Moeschlin, editors, *Mathematical Economics and Game Theory,* Springer-Verlag, 1977.

Contributor to journals, including *Financial Analysts Journal, Journal of Legal Studies, Accounting Review, Econometrica, Journal of Business, Management Science* and *Journal of Finance.* Associate editor, *Managment Science,* 1970-76, *Accounting Review,* 1975-78, and *Financial Analysts Journal,* 1981—; departmental editor, *Communications of the Association for Computing Machinery,* 1971-73; editor, 25th anniversary issue of *Communications of the Association for Computing Machinery,* July, 1972.

WORK IN PROGRESS: Various articles for journals.

*   *   *

WEISHEIT, Eldon 1933-

PERSONAL: Born January 13, 1933, in Clayton, Ill.; son of Harry (a farmer) and Edna (Gamm) Weisheit; married Carolyn Pomerenke (a teacher), August 15, 1954; children: Dirk, Timothy, Wesley. *Education:* Concordia Theological Seminary, Springfield, Ill. (now Fort Wayne, Ind.), completed six-year program, 1962. *Politics:* "Independent Democrat." *Home:* 700 South Kolb Rd., Tucson, Ariz. 85710.

CAREER: Ordained to Lutheran ministry, 1962; Trinity Lutheran Church, McComb, Miss., pastor, 1962-65; Lutheran Church of the Epiphany, Montgomery, Ala., pastor, 1965-71; *Lutheran Witness,* St. Louis, Mo., associate editor, 1971-75; Trinity Lutheran Church, Roselle, Ill., pastor, 1976-77; Fountain of Life Lutheran Church, Tucson, Ariz., senior pastor, 1977—. Former member of board of governors, Concordia Historical Institute; member of children's script committee, Lutheran Television; vice-president of English District of Lutheran Church, Missouri Synod.

WRITINGS—Published by Concordia, except as indicated: *Sixty-One Worship Talks for Children,* 1968; *Sixty-One Gospel Talks for Children,* 1969; *Excuse Me, Sir,* 1971; *The Preacher's Yellow Pants,* 1973; *The Zeal of His House* (a history of the Missouri Synod of the Lutheran Church), 1973; *Moving,* 1974; "To the Kid in the Pew" series (chapel talks), three books, 1974-76; *Should I Have an Abortion?,* 1976; *Abortion: Resources for Pastoral Counseling,* 1976; *A Sermon Is More Than Words,* 1977; *The Gospel for Kids,* Volume I, 1977, Volume II, 1978, Volume III, 1979; *The Gospel for Little Kids,* 1980; *God's Promise for Children,* Augsburg, Volume I, 1980, Volume II, 1981, Volume III, 1982; *Psalms for Children,* Volume I, Augsburg, 1983.

Also author of scripts for radio programs, including "The Lutheran Hour," "Day by Day with Jesus," and "Portals of Prayer." Contributor to "Augsburg Sermons." Regular contributor to *Lutheran Witness;* contributor of poetry to *This Day* and *Christian Century;* contributor to *Concordia Pulpit, Lutheran Standard,* and *My Devotions.* Editor, *Advance* (magazine), 1972-75.

WORK IN PROGRESS: Worship Is an Active Verb.

SIDELIGHTS: Eldon Weisheit told *CA:* "I am now completing a twelve-year program of writing a children's sermon for each of the four lessons in the three-year lectionary used by most Christian churches in the U.S. I had planned to hang up the typewriter after this project was done. However, the Bible study involved and the method of communication used has opened many new doors for me. I am now doing twelve to fifteen workshops a year on related subjects and may continue writing as a way of recording and expanding my work in the parish ministry."

AVOCATIONAL INTERESTS: Jogging: "I did 2,800 miles the year I turned 50."

BIOGRAPHICAL/CRITICAL SOURCES: Lutheran Witness, September, 1970.

*   *   *

WELCH, Claude E(merson), Jr. 1939-

PERSONAL: Born June 12, 1939, in Boston, Mass.; son of Claude Emerson (a surgeon) and Phyllis (Paton) Welch; married Nancy Edwards, June 19, 1961 (died May 9, 1979); married Jeannette Ludwig, June 13, 1981; children: (first marriage) Elisabeth, Sarah Jane, Martha, Christopher. *Education:* Harvard University, B.A., 1961; St. Antony's College, Oxford, D.Phil., 1964. *Politics:* Democratic. *Religion:* Protestant. *Home:* 120 Burroughs Dr., Buffalo, N.Y. 14226. *Office:* 685 Baldy Hall, State University of New York, Buffalo, N.Y. 14260.

CAREER: State University of New York at Buffalo, assistant professor, 1964-68, associate professor, 1968-72, professor of political science, 1972—, dean of Division of Undergraduate

Studies, 1967-70, associate vice-president for academic affairs, 1976-80, chairman of department, 1980-83.

MEMBER: African Studies Association (fellow), Inter-University Seminar on Armed Forces and Society, Phi Beta Kappa.

WRITINGS: Dream of Unity, Cornell University Press, 1966; (editor) *Political Modernization,* Duxbury, 1967, revised edition, 1971; (editor) *Soldier and State in Africa,* Northwestern University, 1970; (editor with Mavis Bunker Taintor) *Revolution and Political Change,* Duxbury, 1972; (with Arthur Smith) *Military Role and Rule.* Duxbury, 1974; (editor) *Civilian Control of the Military,* State University of New York Press, 1976; (editor with Alan Smith) *Peasants in Africa,* Crossroads Press, 1978; *Anatomy of Rebellion,* State University of New York Press, 1980.

WORK IN PROGRESS: A book on military disengagement from politics, *No Farewell to Arms?*

SIDELIGHTS: Claude E. Welch, Jr. told *CA:* "How does political violence affect developing countries? What are major contrasts among rebellions, revolutions, and coups d'etat? What roles do armed forces play in removing civilian governments, in ruling, or in disengaging from direct political roles? These are the issues with which I've wrestled since the mid-1960s. My current research, focused on Africa and Latin America, involves determining the conditions under which—if at all—'successful' returns to the barracks can be, and have been, achieved. In short, I focus on the Third World as an interested, concerned American citizen, anxious that the opportunity for peaceful development be found beyond our shores."

* * *

WELLS, Ronald Vale   1913-

PERSONAL: Born August 16, 1913, in Cleveland, Ohio; son of Earl Harold (an educator and lawyer) and Irene (Leffler) Wells; married Patricia Woodburne, June 20, 1938; children: David Woodburne, Robert Vale. *Education:* Attended Iowa State University, 1931-33; Denison University, A.B., 1935; Crozer Theological Seminary, B.D., 1938; Columbia University, Ph.D., 1942. *Home and office address:* Box 255 Kelly Rd., East Chatham, N.Y. 12060.

CAREER: Minister of American Baptist churches in Somerville, N.J., 1938-42, Bridgeport, Conn., 1942-47, and Ames, Iowa, 1947-52; American Baptist Convention, Board of Education, New York City, associate executive secretary, 1952-62; Crozer Theological Seminary, Chester, Pa., president, 1962-70; Sioux Falls College, Sioux Falls, S.D., president, 1970-74; vice-president for educational affairs, Crozer-Chester Medical Center, 1974-76; United Presbyterian Church, Major Mission Fund, New York City, director and fund counselor, 1976-79; senior consultant with Marts and Lundy Financial Development Consultants, 1980—. *Awards, honors:* D.D., Denison University, 1959, Colby College, 1961, Brown University, 1962, Bucknell University, 1969; L.L.D., Franklin College, 1960; H.L.D., Widener College, 1970.

WRITINGS: Three Christian Transcendentalists, Columbia University Press, 1943, revised edition, Octagon, 1972; *Spiritual Disciplines for Everyday Living,* Character Research, 1982. Contributor to *Journal of Pastoral Care* and *Christian Ministry.*

SIDELIGHTS: Ronald Vale Wells told *CA* that *Spiritual Disciplines for Everyday Living* took forty years to write. Thirty-five years ago, editors at Harper and Row urged Wells to

publish material on the "eight spiritual disciplines [that] are the heart of the book." Wells "kept writing, researching and speaking at conferences about . . . these disciplines. But most important of all," he notes, "they were . . . disciplines by which I lived my life as educator, administrator, fund raiser, minister, and counselor."

"Finally in 1965 there came the opportunity to offer a graduate seminar with the material I had gathered," explains Wells. Successful at five graduate theological seminaries, the seminar provided Wells a chance to see how his "insights about each discipline could be of great benefit to all who were seeking a much more creative life-style in dealing with major issues in personal living and human relations."

"I wrote the book in the hope that it would prove to be helpful to a wider constituency than those in my own immediate circle of friends and colleagues in education, administration, and the ministry," the author states. "Why did the writing take so long? Partly because my research of necessity had to be piecemeal, and the living experience came clear . . . over these forty years." A chance meeting on a flight from New York to St. Louis brought Wells into contact with Penny Colman, an editor "whose interests and expertise were in this very field [of disciplines by which to live]." She became his editor, and "under her firm, honestly critical but always encouraging prodding," Wells finished the book. "At this time," the author adds, "we are exploring the possibility of a one-hour pilot program for educational television."

* * *

WEST, Bill
See WEST, William G.

* * *

WEST, William G.   1930-
(Bill West)

PERSONAL: Born May 24, 1930, in Paducah, Tex.; son of Kade and Ruth (Grayum) West; married Ann Radnor, June 12, 1976. *Education:* Baylor University, B.A., 1951; Southwestern Baptist Seminary, B.D., 1954, Th.D., 1957. *Home:* 21318 Park Willow, Katy, Tex. 77450. *Office address:* Box 218551, Houston, Tex. 77218.

CAREER: Ordained Southern Baptist minister, 1951; student pastor, 1954-57; First Baptist Church, Okmulgee, Okla., 1957-65; River Oaks Baptist Church, Houston, Tex., pastor, beginning 1965; professional speaker and president of West & Associates, Houston, Tex. Former trustee and associate professor, Houston Baptist University.

WRITINGS—Published by Phoenix Books, except as indicated: *Free to Be Me,* Word Books, 1971; *How to Survive Stress,* 1980; *The Platform to Success,* 1982; *Successful Supervision Step by Step,* 1982.

AVOCATIONAL INTERESTS: Cycling, photography, canoeing, hiking.

* * *

WESTWOOD, Gordon
See SCHOFIELD, Michael

WHEATCROFT, John   1925-

PERSONAL: Born July 24, 1925, in Philadelphia, Pa.; son of Allen Stewart (a clergyman) and Laura (Daniel) Wheatcroft; married Joan Osborne, November 10, 1950; children: Allen, David, Rachel. *Education:* Attended Temple University, 1942, 1946-48; Bucknell University, B.A., 1949; Rutgers University, M.A., 1950, Ph.D., 1960. *Home:* 55 South 8th St., Lewisburg, Pa. 17837. *Office:* Department of English, Bucknell University, Lewisburg, Pa. 17837.

CAREER: University of Kansas, Lawrence, instructor in English, 1950-52; Bucknell University, Lewisburg, Pa., instructor, 1952-57, assistant professor, 1957-62, associate professor, 1962-66, professor, 1966, presidential professor of English, 1978—. Distinguished visiting professor, University of Montana, Missoula, 1969. *Military service:* U.S. Navy, 1943-46. *Member:* Poetry Society of America.

AWARDS, HONORS: Lindback award for distinguished teaching, 1964; Alcoa Playwriting Award and National Educational Television Award, 1967, for "Ofoti"; Yaddo resident fellow, 1972; MacDowell Colony resident fellow, 1974.

WRITINGS: Death of a Clown (poems), Thomas Yoseloff, Inc., 1964; *Prodigal Son* (poems), Thomas Yoseloff, Inc., 1967; *Ofoti* (play; first produced by National Educational Television, 1966; produced by Public Broadcasting Service, 1984), A. S. Barnes, 1970; *Edie Tells* (novel), A. S. Barnes, 1975; *A Voice from the Hump* (poems), A. S. Barnes, 1977; *Ordering Demons* (poems), Cornwall Books, 1981; *Catherine, Her Book* (novel), Cornwall Books, 1983. Contributor of poetry to *Harper's Bazaar, Ladies' Home Journal, Mademoiselle, New York Times, New York Herald Tribune,* and other magazines and newspapers.

WORK IN PROGRESS: A collection of stories, *Slow Exposures;* a novel, *The Beholder's Eye.*

*   *   *

WHEELER, Helen Rippier

EDUCATION: Junior College of the Packer Collegiate Institute, A.A., 1946; Barnard College, B.A., 1950; Columbia University, M.S., 1951, Ed.D., 1964; University of Chicago, M.A., 1954. *Home:* 2701 Durant Ave., No. 14, Berkeley, Calif. 94704.

CAREER: Hicksville Public Library, Hicksville, N.Y., library director, 1951-53; University of Chicago, Chicago, Ill., staff member of Laboratory School, and part-time foreign student adviser, 1953-55; teacher-librarian in a Chicago high school, 1955-56; Columbia University, Teachers College, New York, N.Y., staff member of Agnes Russell Center, 1956-58; City Colleges of Chicago, Chicago, library director and audio-visual coordinator, 1958-62; Columbia University, Latin American specialist, 1962-64; Drexel Institute of Technology (now Drexel University), Philadelphia, Pa., adjunct assistant professor, 1964-65; University of Hawaii, Honolulu, associate professor, 1965-66; Indiana State University, Terre Haute, associate professor, 1966-68; St. John's University, Jamaica, N.Y., associate professor, 1968-69; consultant and writer, 1969-71; Louisiana State University, Baton Rouge, associate professor, 1971-73; consultant and writer, 1973—. Member of staff, National Society for the Study of Education, 1953-55.

MEMBER: International House Association, American Library Association, Association of College and Research Libraries, American Association of Community and Junior Colleges, American Association of University Professors, American Association for Affirmative Action, Association of Feminist Consultants, National Women's Studies Association, Women's Institute for the Freedom of the Press, National Organization for Women, American Association of University Women, Women Library Workers, Women Educators, California Society of Librarians, California Clearinghouse on Library Instruction, Social Responsibilities Round Table.

WRITINGS: (Contributor) Charles Trinkner, *Better Libraries Make Better Schools,* Shoe String, 1962; (contributor) Florence Lee, *Principles and Practices of Teaching in Secondary Schools,* McKay, 1964; *The Community College Library: A Plan for Action,* Shoe String, 1965; *A Basic Book Collection for the Community College Library,* Shoe String, 1968; *Womanhood Media,* Scarecrow, 1972, supplement, 1975; *Learning the Library: A Skills and Concepts Series* (multimedia kit), Educational Activities, 1975; *Library Reference Information: How to Locate and Use It* (multimedia kit), Educational Activities, 1979.

(Contributor) Dana Densmore, editor, *Syllabus Sourcebook on Media and Women,* Women's Institute for Freedom of the Press, 1980; (contributor) James Danky and Sanford Berman, editors, *Alternative Library Literature, 1982-1983: A Biennial Anthology,* Oryx, 1984; (contributor) *The Women's Annual, 1983: The Year in Review,* G. K. Hall, 1984. Contributor to periodicals, including *Journal of Library History, Women Studies Abstracts, Library Journal, Choice,* and *Mensa Bulletin.*

SIDELIGHTS: Helen Rippier Wheeler is proficient in Spanish; she has travelled extensively.

*   *   *

WHEELOCK, John Hall   1886-1978

PERSONAL: Born 1886, in Far Rockaway, Long Island, N.Y.; died March 22, 1978, in New York, N.Y.; son of William Efner and Emily Charlotte (Hall) Wheelock; married Phyllis E. De Kay, August 25, 1940. *Education:* Harvard University, A.B., 1908; graduate study at University of Goettingen, 1909, and University of Berlin, 1910. *Home:* 350 East 57th St., New York, N.Y. 10022.

CAREER: Charles Scribner's Sons, New York, N.Y., bookstore employee, 1911-26, editor, 1926-47, editor in chief, 1947-57, director and secretary, 1932-42, treasurer, 1942-46, assistant treasurer and assistant secretary, 1946-57. Honorary consultant in American letters to Library of Congress.

MEMBER: American Academy of Arts and Letters, Poetry Society of America (vice-president, 1944-46), National Institute of Arts and Letters (vice-president), Academy of American Poets (chancellor, 1947-71; honorary fellow, 1974-78), Phi Beta Kappa.

AWARDS, HONORS: Golden Rose, New England Poetry Society, 1937; Ridgely Torrence Memorial Award, 1956, and Borestone Mountain Poetry Award, 1957, both for *Poems Old and New;* Bollingen Prize, 1962; Signet Society Medal, Harvard University, 1965, for distinguished achievement in the arts; Gold Medal, Poetry Society of America, 1972, for notable achievement in poetry; Dr. Humane Letters, Otterbein College.

WRITINGS—Poetry: (With Van Wyck Brooks) *Verses by Two Undergraduates,* privately printed, 1905; *Human Fantasy,*

Sherman, French, 1911; *Beloved Adventure*, Sherman, French, 1912; *Love and Liberation*, Sherman, French, 1913; *Dust and Light*, Scribner, 1919; *The Black Panther*, Scribner, 1922; *The Bright Doom*, Scribner, 1927; *Collected Poems, 1911-1936*, Scribner, 1936; *Poems Old and New*, Scribner, 1956; *The Gardener and Other Poems*, Scribner, 1961; *Dear Men and Women: New Poems*, Scribner, 1966; *By Daylight and in Dream: New and Collected Poems, 1904-1970*, Scribner, 1970; *In Love and Song: Poems*, Scribner, 1971; *This Blessed Earth: New and Selected Poems 1927-1977*, Scribner, 1978; *Afternoon: Amagansett Beach*, Dandelion Press/Eakins, 1978.

Other books: *Alan Seeger: Poet of the Foreign Legion* (essay), Scribner, 1918; *A Bibliography of Theodore Roosevelt*, Scribner, 1920; (translator) *Happily Ever After* (fairy tales), Scribner, 1939; (compiler, editor, and author of introduction) *The Face of a Nation: Poetical Passages from the Writings of Thomas Wolfe*, Scribner, 1939; (editor and author of introduction) *Editor to Author: The Letters of Maxwell E. Perkins*, Scribner, 1950, reprinted, Berg, 1977; *What Is Poetry?*, Scribner, 1963. Editor, *Poets of Today, Volumes I-VIII*, Scribner, 1954-61. Contributor to *Dictionary of American History*, Scribner, 1940, and to numerous periodicals.

SIDELIGHTS: John Hall Wheelock was an editor and poet who began writing in his early teens and continued until his death at age 92. He published his first book of poems with Van Wyck Brooks when they were both undergraduates at Harvard. Although he and Brooks hired on together at Funk & Wagnalls to work on the *New Standard Dictionary*, Wheelock was reportedly not the master at working out definitions that Brooks was, and he was soon discharged. It was then that Wheelock began his long association with Charles Scribner's Sons, starting out in the Scribner Bookstore and working his way up to editor-in-chief, a position he held until 1957, when he retired.

A traditionalist whose skill improved with age, Wheelock began by imitating such nineteenth century poets as Swinburne and Wordsworth, but later in life developed his own distinctive style. According to Henry Taylor in the *Sewanee Review*, Wheelock's "improvement [was] especially remarkable when we realize that no radical shift occurred in thematic or formal preoccupations. The later poems [grew] naturally out of the earlier ones, pursuing the same themes of love, death, and the tragic nature of life; they move in the same traditional forms. But their voice is distinctively Wheelock's own."

Successful not only as a poet but also as an editor, Wheelock developed the *Poets of Today* series, which combined the work of three previously unpublished poets in a single hardbound volume that attracted more critical notice than slim separate volumes would have done. Among those he introduced were James Dickey, Louis Simpson, and Joseph Langland. The success of the series gave him great satisfaction and he was apparently pleased with his endeavors, saying "All my choices turned out well."

BIOGRAPHICAL/CRITICAL SOURCES: James Nelson, editor, *Wisdom*, Norton, 1958; *New York Times Book Review*, September 24, 1961, February 2, 1964, December 10, 1978; *Saturday Review*, November 4, 1961; *Christian Science Monitor*, December 14, 1961; *New Yorker*, April 14, 1962; *Book Week*, October 27, 1963; *Sewanee Review*, summer, 1971; *South Atlantic Quarterly*, spring, 1973; *Contemporary Literary Criticism*, Volume XIV, Gale, 1980.

OBITUARIES: New York Times, March 23, 1978; *Washington Post*, March 24, 1978; *Newsweek*, April 3, 1978; *Time*, April 3, 1978.†

WHITE, Lawrence J. 1943-

PERSONAL: Born June 1, 1943, in New York, N.Y. *Education:* Harvard University, A.B. (summa cum laude), 1964, Ph.D., 1969; London School of Economics, M.Sc., 1965. *Home:* 110 Bleecker St., Apt. 21-B, New York, N.Y. 10012. *Office:* Graduate School of Business Administration, New York University, 90 Trinity Pl., New York, N.Y. 10006.

CAREER: Harvard University, Development Advisory Service, Cambridge, Mass., development adviser to governments of Pakistan and Indonesia, 1969-70; Princeton University, Princeton, N.J., assistant professor of economics, 1970-76; New York University, Graduate School of Business Administration, New York, N.Y., associate professor of economics, 1976-78; U.S. Council of Economic Advisers, Washington, D.C., senior staff economist, 1978-79; New York University, Graduate School of Business Administration, professor of economics, 1979—; U.S. Department of Justice, Antitrust Division, Washington, D.C., chief economist, 1982-83.

MEMBER: American Economic Association.

WRITINGS: The Automobile Industry since 1945, Harvard University Press, 1971; *Industrial Concentration and Economic Power in Pakistan*, Princeton University Press, 1974; *Reforming Regulation: Processes and Problems*, Prentice-Hall, 1981; (editor with M. Keenan and contributor) *Mergers and Acquisitions: Current Problems in Perspective*, Lexington Books, 1982; *The Regulation of Air Pollutant Emissions from Motor Vehicles*, American Enterprise Institute for Public Policy Research, 1982; *The Public Library in the 1980s: The Problems of Choice*, Lexington Books, 1983.

Contributor: (With E. E. Bailey) W. G. Shepherd and T. G. Gies, editors, *Regulation in Further Perspective*, Ballinger, 1974; R. E. Canes and M. J. Roberts, editors, *Regulating the Product*, Ballinger, 1975; S. M. Goldfeld and R. E. Quandt, editors, *Studies in Non-Linear Estimation*, Ballinger, 1976; W. Adams, editor, *The Structure of American Industry*, 5th edition, Macmillan, 1977, 6th edition, 1982; (with E. S. Mills) A. F. Friedlaender, editor, *Approaches to Controlling Air Pollution*, M.I.T. Press, 1978.

D. H. Ginsburg and W. J. Abernathy, editors, *Government, Technology, and the Future of the Automobile*, McGraw, 1980; R. R. Nelson, editor, *Government and Technical Progress: A Cross-Industry Analysis*, Pergamon, 1982; P. B. Downing and K. Hauf, editors, *International Comparisons in Implementing Pollution Laws*, Kluwer-Nijhoff, 1983.

North American editor, *Journal of Industrial Economics*, 1984—.

WORK IN PROGRESS: Research on antitrust policy, financial regulation, and the ocean shipping industry.

*   *   *

WHITE, William, Jr. 1934-
(Spinossimus)

PERSONAL: Born June 8, 1934, in Philadelphia, Pa.; adopted son of William (an accountant and auditor) and Ruth (McCaughan) White; married Sara Jane Shute (a nurse), September 8, 1956; children: Rebecca, Sara, William III, James M., Elizabeth, Margaret. *Education:* Haverford College, B.S., 1956; Westminster Theological Seminary, B.D., 1961, Th.M., 1963;

Dropsie College for Hebrew and Cognate Learning (now Dropsie University), Ph.D., 1968. *Politics:* Christian-Social democrat. *Religion:* Presbyterian (Reformed). *Home:* 2272 Patty Lane, Warrington, Pa. 18976. *Office:* Box 638, Warrington, Pa. 18976.

CAREER: Employed during his early career as mailman, hospital orderly, gas pumper, and mill hand; affiliated with U.S. Civil Service, Glenside, Pa., 1956-63; Temple University, Philadelphia, Pa., instructor in ancient history, 1964-68; Ellen Cushing Junior College, Bryn Mawr, Pa., assistant professor of biology and physics, 1966-68; East Carolina University, Greenville, N.C., assistant professor of history, 1968-70; Philadelphia College of Textiles and Science, Philadelphia, professor of history, 1970-71; North American Publishing Co., Philadelphia, editorial director, 1971-73; Old Testament editor, Thomas Nelson, Inc., 1976—; publisher, Franklin Institute Press, 1976-81; state publisher, Commonwealth of Pennsylvania, 1982—. Writer for radio and television. Publisher of *Cancer Therapy Abstracts, Carcinogenesis Abstracts, Nutrition and Cancer,* and *International Bulletin of Magnetic Resonance.* Emergency Care Research Institute, senior medical writer, 1972-74, managing editor, 1972-75. Consultant to numerous private and government organizations, including Auerbach Corp. and Data Communications.

MEMBER: American Association for the Advancement of Science, American Historical Association, Mensa, Intertel, Tyndale House (Oxford, England). *Awards, honors:* National Endowment for the Humanities grant for study in Israel, 1968; fellow of International Committee for Chemical Research (Japan), 1969-70.

WRITINGS: (Editor and translator) *A Babylonian Anthology,* Morris Press, 1966; (contributor) Stephen Benko and John J. O'Rourke, *The Catacombs and the Colosseum,* Judson, 1970; (editor and contributor) *The North American Reference Encyclopedia of Women's Liberation,* North American Publishing, 1972; (editor with F. Little) *The North American Reference Encyclopedia of Ecology and Pollution,* North American Publishing, 1972; (contributor) *The Law and the Prophets,* Presbyterian & Reformed, 1973; (editor with R. Albano) *North American Symposium on Drugs and Drug Abuse,* North American Publishing, 1974.

(Contributor) *The New Zondervan Pictorial Bible Encyclopedia,* five volumes, Zondervan, 1975; (with D. Estrada) *The First New Testament,* Thomas Nelson, 1978; *Van Til: Defender of the Faith* (biography), Thomas Nelson, 1979; (co-editor) *The New King James Bible,* Thomas Nelson, 1979; (editor with J. I. Packer and M. C. Tenney) *The Bible Almanac,* Thomas Nelson, 1980; (contributor) *Theological Wordbook of the Old Testament,* two volumes, Moody, 1980; (contributor) *The New International Dictionary of Biblical Archaeology,* Zondervan, 1983; *Laser Printing: The Fundamentals,* Carnegie Press, 1983; *Theological and Grammatical Phrasebook of the Bible,* Moody, 1984; (co-editor) *Nelson's Expository Dictionary of Biblical Words,* Thomas Nelson, 1984; *Close-up Photography,* Eastman Kodak, 1984; (editor) *A Laboratory Handbook of Photomacrography,* Focal Press, 1985.

Juveniles—All self-illustrated; all published by Sterling: *A Frog Is Born,* 1972; *A Turtle Is Born,* 1973; *The Guppy: Its Life Cycle,* 1974; *The Siamese Fighting Fish: Its Life Cycle,* 1975; *An Earthworm Is Born,* 1975; *The Angelfish: Its Life Cycle,* 1975; (with Sara Jane White) *A Terrarium in Your Home,* 1976; *The Edge of the Pond,* 1976; *Forest and Garden,* 1976; *The Cycle of the Seasons,* 1977; *The American Chameleon,* 1977;

Edge of the Ocean, 1977; *A Mosquito Is Born,* 1981. Also author, with White, of *The Housefly,* 1981.

Contributor of more than one thousand articles to periodicals, including *Vanguard of Canada, Christian Scholar's Review, Westminster Theological Journal, Industrial Research, Photographic Applications in Science and Medicine,* and *Mikroskopion.* Associate editor, *Data Processing Magazine;* managing editor, *Health Devices;* editor, *Engineering* and *Science and Technology News.*

WORK IN PROGRESS: Electronic Technical Publishing (ETP/STP); Subminiature Photographic Techniques, for Focal Press; *A Grammatical and Exegetical Bible Sentence Book;* editing *The Parents Desk Reference of Christian Parenting,* for Zondervan, and *Jesus Christ: His Life and Times,* for Thomas Nelson.

SIDELIGHTS: William White, Jr., told *CA:* "As an author with a radical-Christian philosophy of science, I have tried to innovate the use of the latest tools and methods in the biomedical field for use in juvenile books on science. I have utilized the light microscope, micromanipulation, photomacroscopy and scanning electron microscopy in illustrating explanations of growth-edge scientific ideas for young readers. This is done by using familiar life forms—turtles, lizards, exotic fishes, as the vehicle for demonstrating basic ideas in physiology, biochemistry, ethology, biophysics and ecology." He adds that he has recently advanced his "efforts into biological and nonbiological systems. Of special interest has been the problem of coding of parallel relational information from language to language and from biotic system to biotic system. Recent work has centered on Computer Graphics (CG) and Iconic Database Management Systems (DBMS)."

AVOCATIONAL INTERESTS: Literature (particularly Japanese, Chinese and Russian), microbiology, biotechnology, ichthyology and herpetology.

*   *   *

WICK, Carter
   See WILCOX, Collin

*   *   *

WIDEMAN, John Edgar   1941-

PERSONAL: Born June 14, 1941, in Washington, D.C.; married Judith Ann Goldman; children: Daniel Jerome, Jacob Edgar, Jamila Ann. *Education:* University of Pennsylvania, B.A., 1963; New College, Oxford, B.Phil., 1966. *Office:* Department of English, University of Wyoming, Laramie, Wyo. 82070.

CAREER: Howard University, Washington, D.C., teacher of American literature, summer, 1965; University of Pennsylvania, Philadelphia, 1966-74, began as instructor, professor of English, 1974, director of Afro-American studies program, 1971-73; University of Wyoming, Laramie, professor of English, 1975—. Made state department lecture tour of Europe and the Near East, 1976; Phi Beta Kappa lecturer, 1976; visiting writer and lecturer at numerous colleges and universities; has also served as administrator/teacher in a curriculum planning, teacher-training institute sponsored by National Defense Education Act. Assistant basketball coach, University of Pennsylvania, 1968-72. National Humanities Faculty consultant in numerous states; consultant to secondary schools across the country, 1968—.

MEMBER: National Humanities Faculty, Association of American Rhodes Scholars (member of board of directors and of state and national selection committees), Phi Beta Kappa.

AWARDS, HONORS: Received creative writing prize, University of Pennsylvania; Rhodes Scholar, Oxford University, 1963; Thouron fellow, Oxford University, 1963-66; Kent fellow, University of Iowa, 1966, to attend creative writing workshop; named member of Philadelphia Big Five Basketball Hall of Fame, 1974; Young Humanist fellow, 1975—; P.E.N./ Faulkner Award for fiction, 1984, for *Sent for You Yesterday.*

WRITINGS—Novels, except as indicated: *A Glance Away,* Harcourt, 1967; *Hurry Home,* Harcourt, 1970; *The Lynchers,* Harcourt, 1973; *Damballah* (short stories), Avon, 1981; *Hiding Place,* Avon, 1981; *Sent for You Yesterday,* Avon, 1983; *Brothers and Keepers* (memoirs), Holt, 1984. Contributor of articles, short stories, book reviews, and poetry to periodicals, including *Negro Digest, Black World, American Scholar, Gentleman's Quarterly, New York Times Book Review,* and *Washington Post Book World.*

WORK IN PROGRESS: A novel.

SIDELIGHTS: John Edgar Wideman has been hailed by Don Strachen in the *Los Angeles Times Book Review* as "the black Faulkner, the softcover Shakespeare." Such praise is not uncommon for this author, whose novel *Sent for You Yesterday* was selected as the 1984 P.E.N./Faulkner Award winner over works by Bernard Malamud, Cynthia Ozick, and William Kennedy. Wideman attended Oxford University in 1963 on a Rhodes scholarship, earned a degree in eighteenth-century literature, and later accepted a fellowship at the prestigious University of Iowa's Writers' Workshop. Yet this "artist with whom any reader who admires ambitious fiction must sooner or later reckon," as the *New York Times* calls him, began his college career not as a writer, but as a basketball star. "I always wanted to play pro basketball—ever since I saw a ball and learned you could make money at it," he told Curt Suplee in the *Washington Post.* Recruited by the University of Pennsylvania for its team, Wideman first attended that school as a psychology major, attracted by the "mystical insight" he told Suplee that he thought the study would yield. When "it turned out to be rats" and clinical experiments, Wideman changed his major to English, while continuing to be mainly concerned with basketball. He played well enough to earn a place in the Philadelphia Big Five Basketball Hall of Fame, but, he told Suplee, as his time at the University drew to a close, "I knew I wasn't going to be able to get into the NBA [National Basketball Association]. What was left?" The Rhodes scholarship answered that question. Wideman began to concentrate on his writing rather than sports and did so with such success that his first novel, *A Glance Away,* was published just a year after he earned his degree from Oxford.

The story of a day in the life of a drug addict, *A Glance Away* reflects the harsh realities that Wideman saw and experienced during his youth in Pittsburgh's ghetto, Homewood. And, though the author has lived in Laramie, Wyoming, since 1975, later novels also described black urban experiences. He explained to Suplee, "My particular imagination has always worked well in a kind of exile. It fits the insider-outside view I've always had. It helps to write away from the center of the action."

Wideman's highly literate style is in sharp contrast to his gritty subject matter, and while reviews of his books have been generally favorable from the start of his writing career, some critics initially expressed the opinion that such a formal style was not appropriate for his stories of street life. For example, Anatole Broyard praises *The Lynchers* in his *New York Times* review, stating: "Though we have heard the themes and variations of violence before in black writing, 'The Lynchers' touches us in a more personal way, for John Edgar Wideman has a weapon more powerful than any knife or gun. His weapon is art. Eloquence is his arsenal, his arms cache. His prose, at its best, is a black panther, coiled to spring." But Broyard goes on to say that the book is not flawless: "Far from it. Mr. Wideman ripples too many muscles in his writing, often cannot seem to decide whether to show or snow us. . . . [He] is wordy, and 'The Lynchers' is as shaky in its structure as some of the buildings his characters inhabit. But he can *write,* and you come away from his book with the feeling that he is, as they say, very close to getting it all together." In the *New York Times,* John Leonard comments on the extensive use of literary devices in *The Lynchers:* "Flashback, flashforward, first person, third person, journals, identity exchange, interior monologue, dreams (historical and personal), puns, epiphanies [are all used]. At times the devices seem a thicket through which one must hack one's weary way toward meanings arbitrarily obscure, a vegetable indulgence. But John Edgar Wideman is up to much more than storytelling. . . . He is capable of moving from ghetto language to Joyce with a flip of the page."

Saturday Review critic David Littlejohn agrees that Wideman's novels are very complex, and in his review of *Hurry Home* he criticizes those who would judge this author as a storyteller: "Reviewers . . . are probably more responsible than anyone else for the common delusion that a novel is somehow contained in its discernible, realistic plot. . . . *Hurry Home* is primarily an experience, not a plot: an experience of words, dense, private, exploratory, and non-progressive." Littlejohn describes *Hurry Home* as a retelling of an American myth, that of "the lonely search through the Old World" for a sense of cultural heritage, which "has been the pattern of a hundred thousand young Americans' lives and novels." According to Littlejohn, Wideman's version is "spare and eccentric, highly stylized, circling, allusive, antichronological, far more consciously symbolic than most versions, than the usual self-indulgent and romantic works of this genre—and hence both more rewarding and more difficult of access." Reviewing the same book in the *New York Times Book Review,* Joseph Goodman states: "Many of its pages are packed with psychological insight, and nearly all reveal Mr. Wideman's formidable command of the techniques of fiction. Moreover, the theme is a profound one—the quest for a substantive sense of self. . . . The prose, paratactic and rich with puns, flows as freely as thought itself, giving us . . . Joycean echoes. . . . It is a dazzling display. . . . We can have nothing but admiration for Mr. Wideman's talent."

Enthusiastic reviews such as these established Wideman's reputation in the literary world as a major talent. When his fourth and fifth books—*Damballah,* a collection of short stories, and *Hiding Place,* a novel—were issued originally as paperbacks, some critics, such as John Leonard and Mel Watkins, reacted with indignation. Leonard's *New York Times* review uses extensive quotes from the books to demonstrate Wideman's virtuosity, and states, "That [these] two new books will fall apart after a second reading is a scandal." Watkins's *New York Times Book Review* article on the two books, which were published simultaneously, has special praise for the short-story volume, and ends with a sentiment much like Leonard's on the books' binding. He writes: "In freeing his voice from the confines of the novel form, [Wideman] has written what is possibly his most impressive work. . . . Each story moves far beyond the primary event on which it is focused. The prose is labyrinthine—events and details merge and overlap. . . . Like [Jean] Toomer, Mr. Wideman has used a narrative laced with myth, superstition and dream sequences to create an elaborate poetic portrait of the lives of ordinary black people. And also like Toomer, he has written tales that can stand on their own, but that assume much greater impact collectively. The individual 'parts' or stories, as disparate as they may initially seem, form a vivid and coherent montage of black life over a period of five generations. . . . These books once again demonstrate that John Wideman is one of America's premier writers of fiction. That they were published originally in paperback perhaps suggests that he is also one of our most underrated writers.'' Actually, it was the author himself who had decided to bring the books out as original paperbacks. His reasons were philosophical and pragmatic. ''I spend an enormous amount of time and energy writing and I want to write good books, but I also want people to read them,'' he explained to Edwin McDowell in the *New York Times*. Wideman's first three novels had been slow sellers ''in spite of enormously positive reviews,'' he told Suplee, and it was his hope that the affordability of paperbacks would help give him a wider readership, particularly among ''the people and the world I was writing about. A $15.95 novel had nothing to do with that world.''

Damballah and *Hiding Place* had both been set in Homewood, Wideman's early home, and in 1983 he published a third book with the same setting, *Sent for You Yesterday*. Critics were enthusiastic. ''In this hypnotic and deeply lyrical novel, Mr. Wideman again returns to the ghetto where he was raised and transforms it into a magical location infused with poetry and pathos,'' writes Alan Cheuse in the *New York Times Book Review*. ''The narration here makes it clear that both as a molder of language and a builder of plots, Mr. Wideman has come into his full powers,'' he continues. ''He has the gift of making 'ordinary' folks memorable. . . . Mr. Wideman establishes a mythological and symbolic link between character and landscape, language and plot, that in the hands of a less visionary writer might be little more than stale sociology.'' States Garett Epps in the *Washington Post Book World*, ''Wideman has a fluent command of the American language, written and spoken, and a fierce, loving vision of the people he writes about. Like Faulkner's, Wideman's prose fiction is vivid and demanding—shuttling unpredictably between places, narrators and times, dwelling for a paragraph on the surface of things, then sneaking a key event into a clause that springs on the reader like a booby trap. . . . *Sent for You Yesterday* is a book to be savored, read slowly again and again.''

When he ventured into nonfiction for the first time with his book *Brothers and Keepers,* Wideman continued to draw inspiration from the same source, Homewood. In this book, Wideman comes to terms with his brother Robby, younger by ten years, whose life was influenced by the street, its drugs and its crime. The author writes, ''Even as I manufactured fiction from the events of my brother's life, from the history of the family that had nurtured us both, I knew something of a different order remained to be extricated. The fiction writer was a man with a real brother behind real bars [serving a life sentence in a Pennsylvania penitentiary].'' In his review in the *Washington Post Book World*, Jonathan Yardley calls *Brothers and Keepers* ''the elder Wideman's effort to understand what happened, to confess and examine his own sense of guilt about his brother's fate (and his own).'' The result, according to the reviewer, is ''a depiction of the inexorably widening chasm

that divides middle-class black Americans from the black underclass.'' Wideman's personal experience, adds Yardley, also reveals that for the black person ''moving out of the ghetto into the white world is a process that requires excruciating compromises, sacrifices and denials, that leaves the person who makes the journey truly at home in neither the world he has entered nor the world he has left.''

Wideman has, however, made a home for himself in literary circles, and at the same time has learned from his experience to handle his success. When *Sent for You Yesterday* won the P.E.N./Faulkner Award—the only major literary award in this country to be judged, administered and largely funded by writers—Wideman told Suplee he felt ''warmth. That's what I felt. Starting at the toes and filling up. A gradual recognition that it could be real.'' Still, the author maintained that if such an honor ''doesn't happen again for a long time—or never happens again—it really doesn't matter,'' because he ''learned more and more that the process itself was important, learned to take my satisfaction from the writing'' during the years of comparative obscurity. ''I'm an old jock,'' he explained. ''So I've kind of trained myself to be low-key. Sometimes the crowd screams, sometimes the crowd doesn't scream.''

BIOGRAPHICAL/CRITICAL SOURCES: Journal of Negro History, January, 1963; *Negro Digest,* May, 1963; *New York Times Book Review,* September 10, 1967, April 19, 1970, April 29, 1973, April 11, 1982, May 15, 1983; *American Scholar,* autumn, 1967; *Saturday Review,* October 21, 1967, May 2, 1970; *New York Times,* April 2, 1970, May 15, 1973, November 27, 1981, May 16, 1984; *Newsweek,* May 7, 1970; John O'Brien, editor, *Interviews with Black Writers,* Liveright, 1973; *Shenandoah,* winter, 1974; *Michigan Quarterly Review,* winter, 1975; *Contemporary Literary Criticism,* Volume V, Gale, 1976; *Los Angeles Times Book Review,* April 17, 1983; *Washington Post Book World,* July 3, 1983, October 21, 1984; *Washington Post,* May 10, 1984, May 12, 1984.

—*Sketch by Joan E. Marecki*

*   *   *

WIENER, Joel H.   1937-

PERSONAL: Born August 23, 1937, in New York, N.Y.; son of Philip Wiener; married Suzanne Wolff (a reading teacher), September 4, 1961; children: Paul, Deborah, Jane. *Education:* New York University, B.A., 1959; graduate study at University of Glasgow, 1961-63; Cornell University, Ph.D., 1965. *Home:* 267 Glen Court, Teaneck, N.J. 07666. *Office:* Department of History, City College of the City University of New York, Convent Ave. and 133rd St., New York, N.Y. 10031.

CAREER: Skidmore College, Saratoga Springs, N.Y., assistant professor of history, 1964-66; City College of the City University of New York, New York, N.Y., associate professor, 1966-76, professor of history, 1977—, chairman of department, 1981—. Visiting lecturer, University of York, 1971-73; member of conference on British Studies. *Member:* Royal History Society (fellow), Research Society for Victorian Periodicals (president, 1983-85), American Historical Association.

WRITINGS: The War of the Unstamped, Cornell University Press, 1969; *A Descriptive Finding List of Unstamped British Periodicals: 1830-1836,* Oxford University Press, 1970; (editor) *Great Britain: Foreign Policy and the Span of Empire, 1689-1970,* four volumes, McGraw, 1972; *Great Britain: The Lion at Home,* four volumes, Bowker, 1974; (contributor) J.

Don Vann and Rosemary T. VanArsdel, editors, *Victorian Periodicals: A Guide to Research,* Modern Library Association of America, 1978; *Radicalism and Freethought in Nineteenth-Century Britain,* Greenwood Press, 1983; (editor) *Innovators and Preachers: The Role of the Editor in Victorian Britain,* Greenwood Press, 1985.

WORK IN PROGRESS: A history of the Victorian editor.

AVOCATIONAL INTERESTS: Films, theater, opera.

* * *

WIGAL, Donald 1933-

PERSONAL: Surname is pronounced Why-*gal;* born January 16, 1933, in Indianapolis, Ind.; son of Wayne Wendell and Mary Louise (Eder) Wigal. *Education:* University of Dayton, B.S., 1955; Dominican House of Studies, River Forest, Ill., certificate in theology, 1961; University of Notre Dame, M.A., 1965; Columbia Pacific University, Ph.D., 1980; University of the State of New York Regents External Degree Program, permanent secondary education certificate, 1981. *Home:* 4 Park Ave., New York, N.Y. 10016. *Agent:* World Wide Licensing, 29 East 21st St., New York, N.Y. 10010. *Office address:* Institute for Independent Studies, Alternative Research, P.O. Box 432, New York, N.Y. 10156.

CAREER: Member of the Marianists (Catholic religious order), 1951-68; University of Dayton, Dayton, Ohio, instructor in music, theology, and art, 1962-68; Grey Advertising, New York City, librarian and market researcher, 1968-71; World Horizon Films, Osining, N.Y., director, 1972; Dell Publishing Co., New York City, executive editor of special markets, 1972-76; president, Alternative Works Inc., 1976-78; Lakewood Books, Clearwater, Fla., executive editor, 1978—; affiliated with Institute for Independent Studies (subsidiary of Alternative Research), New York City, 1980—. Instructor at Antioch College, 1965; guest instructor at Xavier University, 1967, and Mary Rogers College, 1968; mentor at Columbia Pacific University, 1982—.

MEMBER: American Society of Composers, Authors and Publishers, American Society of Journalists and Authors, Editorial Freelancers Association, Williams Club.

WRITINGS: (With Sharon Feyen) *Screen Experience: An Approach to Film,* Pflaum, 1968; (editor) *Drug Education,* William Sadlier, 1970; *The Winter Games,* Pfizer Chemical, 1970; (editor) *Filmmaking for Children,* Pflaum, 1971; *Conoco: The First One Hundred Years,* Dell, 1975; *Crossword Lover's Book of Lists,* Lakewood Books, 1977; *Biorhythms: Your Cycles in Life,* Q Publications, 1978; *Personal Energy,* Profile Books, 1978; *Fun-to-Find Puzzles,* four books, Lakewood Books, 1979.

General Knowledge, Coleco, 1980; *Soap Opera Trivia,* S. S. & B., 1980; *1001 Questions and Answers on the Bible,* Coleco, 1981; *TV Trivia,* S. S. & B., 1981; *Supertrivia Mania,* Coleco, 1982; *Word Streamers* (puzzle book), Lakewood Books, 1982; *Fascinating Facts about Animals,* Coleco, 1982; (contributor of songs) Carolyn Hardesty, *Baby Fitness,* Lakewood Books, 1983.

Cookbooks; published by Lakewood Books, except as indicated: *Love Your Kitchen,* Dell, 1975; *The Great Potato,* 1980; *Breads You Can Bake,* 1981; *Sodium Counter and Diet,* 1982; *Quick and Easy Salads,* 1984.

With Charles Murphy; all published by Herder & Herder in 1970: *A Sense of Life, A Presence of Love, A Way of Community, A Vision of Hope.*

Compiler of index: *A History of Theater,* Ungar, 1972; *Academic American Encyclopedia,* Areta, 1980; (with Diana Pons) *The Pet Encyclopedia,* Thomas Nelson, 1981; (with Pons) *The New York Times Encyclopedia of Film,* New York Times, 1984. Also compiler of about one hundred indexes for various universities and publishers, including seven of the volumes in the "Readers Index to the Twentieth Century Views," Prentice-Hall, 1972.

Author of promotional material for Kellogg's, Eastern Airlines, and other companies; also author of technical writings, including over six hundred abstracts assigned under a government contract, for Plenum, 1982-83. Author, under twenty pseudonyms, of twenty romantic short stories for Hyman; contributor of short stories to textbooks, including *Teaching Teens* and *Effective English.* Creator of about four hundred puzzles and word games, including "Pencil Hunt" and "Original Puzzles and Games," for popular magazines. Contributor of about fifty articles to journals and religious magazines; contributor of articles on video approaches to personal fitness in *Pre-Recorded Video* and *Video Buyer's Guide,* both 1983.

SIDELIGHTS: Donald Wigal told *CA:* "Professionals rarely admit that they chose their career because of anything less than a call by some driving creative force. It is somehow an admission of frailty or limited talent to admit that one's choice was one of survival, or even one of finding the least resistance.

"I thought I had only a few choices before me when I was considering writing and editing as a career. I could continue to be a teacher, musician, theologian or researcher. But, for me, teaching and especially teaching theology in the 1960s was becoming too political. And teaching the theology of organized religion became less and less relevant. At the same time I was not a polished musician who could make a living performing. Composing music, even when driven by nearly uncontrollable urges, was a luxury more than a means of survival. Researching seemed creative and productive only when coupled with writing. Finally, editing seemed to be the pragmatic compromise by which I could make a living, be creative, and still stay in touch (through writing) with theology, music, art, and even indirect teaching.

"Years before making this choice, I had written columns in my high school paper about popular music. I remember that initial thrill of seeing a few of my words reach the printed page without too much editing. I remember also being complimented, especially for a phrase which the editor had inserted. I recall, after another such humiliation . . . , I resolved to print and distribute my own newspaper. Reading the life of Benjamin Franklin convinced me that self-publishing was the only way to really communicate one's unedited thoughts. After trying a few little essays on my own I soon realized how necessary an editor was. The blend of editing and writing was beginning to be attractive and has been ever since.

"Now, thirty-five years later, I can see both sides of that infamous fence between editors and writers. On the one side, as an editor of mass market lines of non-fiction and fiction, I receive about one thousand unsolicited manuscripts a year. Yet I recall only two titles out of the past one hundred seventy-five which came to me over the transom. The most frequent mistake authors make is to submit material which is unrelated to the house's publishing pattern and history; trade titles are submitted as mass market, impulse titles as serious studies, and so forth in various combinations of inappropriateness. The daily exercise of answering such queries is a discipline which helps me see the other side of the fence, the writer's view of publishing. This is a daily and dramatic reminder of the importance of reaching the target market through the best medium. Or, as the journalists say, 'Know what you want to say; know to whom you want it said; say what you want to say to whom you want it said.' It took me a few years to realize that those are three steps, not one simultaneous impulse.

"Writing helps editing, of course, but in some ways not so obvious. The application to publishing of an old cliche results in the suggestion that 'those who can't write, edit.' But, the reverse is rarely proposed. I find the two disciplines are complimentary, both philosophically and pragmatically. They call upon different kinds of creativeness and require an ever refreshing blend of give and take; they are the yang and yin of publishing, and I could not give up one for the other.

"Similarly, I find that the disciplined writing of fiction or puzzle-making helps the creation of non-fiction. . . . Even the interdisciplines of music and words seem to blend at times when I least expect it, causing a lyrical phrase to pop up amid a software review and, contrastingly, some subtle complex reference somehow influences a simple melodic line. Maybe the need to survive forces this openness, but whatever work there is to be done, I always try to like what I do, rather than just do what I like. Editing and writing seem to be constantly changing roles in their body-soul existence as I give them what I can and receive much more in return. I hope other writers have experienced the joys of editing, and other editors have enjoyed the fulfillment which can come from writing. I need them both and they seem at times to need me."

BIOGRAPHICAL/CRITICAL SOURCES: C. J. Puotinen, *Career Astrology: Counseling for the Nineteen Eighties,* Ninth Sign, 1980; *Indianapolis Star,* July 25, 1981.

*   *   *

WIK, Reynold M. 1910-

PERSONAL: Born March 19, 1910, in Norbeck, S.D.; son of Nicholas (in business) and Emma (a teacher; maiden name, Olson) Wik; married Helen Bryan (a librarian and teacher), August 22, 1942; children: Denis Peter. *Education:* Sioux Falls College, B.A., 1936; University of Minnesota, M.A., 1940, Ph.D., 1949; further graduate study at Harvard University, 1940, University of Chicago, 1941, and Indiana University, 1941-42. *Politics:* Liberal. *Religion:* Baptist. *Home:* 4641 Meldon Ave., Oakland, Calif. 94619.

CAREER: High school teacher of history in Cresbard, S.D., 1936-37, Parker, S.D., 1937-39, Minot, N.D., 1939-41, and Pontiac, Mich., 1942-43; Minot State Teachers College (now Minot State College), Minot, assistant professor of history, 1943-45; University of Minnesota, Minneapolis, instructor in history, 1945-46; Northern Iowa University, Cedar Falls, instructor in history, 1946-47; Bethel College and Seminary, St. Paul, Minn., professor of history, 1947-51; Mills College, Oakland, Calif., May Treat Morrison Professor of History, 1951-75; Sioux Falls College, Sioux Falls, S.D., professor of history, 1976-84. Fulbright lecturer at Free University of Berlin, 1955-56; lecturer at University of California, Berkeley, 1964; visiting distinguished lecturer at Boise State University, 1974, and Georgetown College (Georgetown, Ky.), 1978. Public lecturer on the history of technology. Member of board of trustees of Sioux Falls College, 1972-81. Consultant to galleries and museums.

MEMBER: Society for the History of Technology (past member of advisory council; member of executive council, 1962-65),

Agricultural History Society (member of executive committee, 1961-64; president, 1981); American Studies Association (northern California president, 1967-69), Association of American Historians, Pacific Historical Association (member of executive council, 1960-64).

AWARDS, HONORS: Albert J. Beveridge Memorial Prize from American Historical Association, 1950, for *Steam Power on the American Farm;* Guggenheim fellow, 1958-59; Ford Foundation grant, 1954; Social Science Research Council grant, 1956; American Philosophical Society grant, 1964; National Academy of Sciences grant for Japan, 1974; D.H.L. from Sioux Falls College, 1974; National Endowment for the Humanities grant, 1977.

WRITINGS: Steam Power on the American Farm, University of Pennsylvania Press, 1953; (contributor) David Van Tassel and Michael Hall, editors, *Science and Society in the United States,* Dorsey, 1966; (contributor) Melvin Kranzberg and Carroll Pursell, editors, *Technology in Western Civilization,* Volume II, Oxford University Press, 1967.

Henry Ford and Grass-Roots America, University of Michigan Press, 1972; (contributor) Richard Lowitt and Joseph Wall, editors, *Interpreting Twentieth-Century America: A Reader,* Crowell, 1973; (contributor) Kranzberg and William Davenport, editors, *Technology and Culture,* Schocken, 1973; (contributor) Nicholas Corts and Patrick Gerster, editors, *Myths and the American Experience,* Volume II, Glencoe, 1978; John Burke and M. Eakin, editors, *Technology and Change,* Boyd & Fraser, 1979.

(Contributor) David L. Lewis and Laurence Goldstein, editors, *The Automobile and American Culture,* University of Michigan Press, 1983; *Benjamin Holt and the Invention of the Caterpillar Tractor,* American Society of Agricultural Engineers, 1984. Contributor of more than fifty articles and reviews to science, agriculture, and history journals, and newspapers. Advisory editor of *Technology and Culture,* 1958—.

WORK IN PROGRESS: The Radio and Social Change in America.

SIDELIGHTS: Reynold M. Wik wrote to *CA:* "Since I was raised on a farm in Faluk County, South Dakota, I learned to operate farm machinery. My father, Nicholas, owned a large Reeves steam traction engine which he used for plowing and threshing grain, and I used to observe this engine as a young lad on the farm. After entering the teaching profession and doing historical research, it was natural for me to make a study of rural technology in America. As a result, I wrote *Steam Power on the American Farm,* which has remained the definitive work describing the application of steam power to agriculture.

"Subsequently, I did research in the archives of the Ford Motor Company in Dearborn, Michigan, where I read thousands of letters written to Henry Ford, most of them from rural Americans. Out of this research emerged the book, *Henry Ford and Grass-Roots America,* an account of the Model T car and Henry Ford's life-long interest in American agriculture.

"In 1974, I began research on the invention of the Caterpillar track-type tractor which was developed by Benjamin Holt of Stockton, California. Since this invention became the father of the military tank of World War I and the bulldozer of World War II, and the modern snowmobile, it is of paramount importance in the history of technology. This work completes what I like to call the 'Wik Trilogy'—three works depicting the evolution of the farm steam engine, the Model T car, and the Caterpillar tractor.

"My interests tend to focus on the average working man and his reactions to his own experiences in using new machines of great economic importance. These machines eliminated the 'Man With the Hoe,' and emancipated millions from back-breaking manual labor. These pioneers are, in my opinion, real heroes."

AVOCATIONAL INTERESTS: Travel, photography, restoring old Ford automobiles.

*   *   *

WILBOURN, Carole C(ecile)   1940-

PERSONAL: Born March 19, 1940, in New York, N.Y.; daughter of Gus and Harriet (Greenwald) Engel; married David Lee Wilbourn, September 13, 1965 (divorced, 1970); married Paul D. Rowan (a veterinarian), October 2, 1978 (divorced, 1982). *Education:* New York University, B.S., 1965. *Office:* Cat Practice, 230 West 13th St., New York, N.Y. 10011.

CAREER: Cat therapist. Cat Practice, New York, N.Y., co-founder, 1973, and currently consulting associate; makes house calls to cats with emotional and behavioral problems; Humane Society counselor. Plans parties for cats. Previously worked as substitute teacher in public high schools, and as Playboy bunny, 1965-73; also participated in various humane activities, including work on a telephone information service about cats.

WRITINGS: Cats Prefer It This Way, Coward, 1976; *The Inner Cat,* Stein & Day, 1978; *Cat Talk,* Macmillan, 1979; *Cats on the Couch,* Macmillan, 1982. Author of monthly column in *Cat Fancy.* Contributor of articles to *Ladies Home Journal* and *Cosmopolitan.*

WORK IN PROGRESS: Another book about cats, for McGraw.

SIDELIGHTS: Carole C. Wilbourn, in her practice of feline psychotherapy, has treated more than 7,000 cats. She told *CA* that she "was very interested in cats and their welfare and want people to understand their cats better." Wilbourn and her partner, Dr. Paul D. Rowan, told Bill Hayward in *Cat People:* "When cats were a god image for the Egyptians, it really was because what they were looking for was a whole sense of self-awareness. It was a time when the training of people in that culture was to strive toward a total awareness of all their powers as a person. Because cats were so good at it, they served as models."

In an interview with *Us* magazine, Wilbourn revealed some of her professional observations: "[Cats are] affected by pleasure, by pain, by sadness, just like people. . . . Cats get emotional. They really depend and act on the feelings they pick up from their humans. . . . If the human's head is messed up, the cat stands a good chance of being in bad shape, too." What's the best thing that you can do for your cat? Wilbourn advised that you make sure that your cat is aware that you love him.

AVOCATIONAL INTERESTS: Psychology, ballet, aerobic dance, jogging, and bicycling.

BIOGRAPHICAL/CRITICAL SOURCES: Us, September 19, 1978; Bill Hayward, *Cat People,* Doubleday, 1978.

*   *   *

WILBUR, James B(enjamin) III   1924-

PERSONAL: Born February 21, 1924, in Hartford, Conn.; son of James Benjamin (an industrialist) and Martha (Shekosky) Wilbur; married Margie Ann Mattmiller (an educator), July 9, 1949; children: James Benjamin IV, Ann Elizabeth. *Education:* University of Kentucky, A.B., 1948; graduate study at Harvard University, 1948-49; Columbia University, M.A., 1951, Ph.D., 1954. *Home:* 22 West View Crescent, Geneseo, N.Y. 14454. *Office:* Department of Philosophy, State University of New York College, Geneseo, N.Y. 14454.

CAREER: Adelphi University, Long Island, N.Y., assistant professor, 1954-59, associate professor philosophy, 1959-64, head of department, 1954-64; University of Akron, Akron, Ohio, professor of philosophy and head of department, 1964-68; State University of New York College at Geneseo, professor of philosophy, 1968—, head of department, 1968-78. Visiting professor at University of Kent, Canterbury, England, 1971. Member of board of advisors, Empire State College of the State University of New York, Saratoga Springs, N.Y., 1971-75. Founder and director of Conferences on Value Inquiry, 1967—. *Military service:* U.S. Army, 1942-45.

MEMBER: American Philosophical Association, American Association of University Professors, American Society of Value-Inquiry (secretary-treasurer, 1970-72; president, 1973), Long Island Philosophy Society (founder, 1964), Creighton Club (president, 1970-72), Rochester Oratorio Society. *Awards, honors:* National Endowment for the Humanities grant, 1981-82; AACSB Western Electric Fund award, 1983.

WRITINGS: (With Harold Allen) *The Worlds of Plato and Aristotle,* American Book Co., 1962, revised edition, Prometheus Books, 1979; (with Allen) *The Worlds of Hume and Kant,* American Book Co., 1965, revised edition, Prometheus Books, 1982; (editor and contributor with B. Magnus) *Cartesian Essays,* Nijhoff, 1969; (editor with Erwin Laszlo) *Value in Philosophy and Social Science,* Gordon & Breach, 1970; (editor with Laszlo) *Human Values and Natural Science,* Gordon & Breach, 1970; (editor with Laszlo) *Human Values and the Mind of Man,* Gordon & Breach, 1971; (editor and contributor) *Spinoza's Metaphysics,* Van Gorcum, 1976; (with Allen) *The Worlds of the Early Greek Philosophers,* Prometheus Books, 1979.

Editor of monographs; all published by State University of New York College at Geneseo: (With Laszlo) *The Dynamics of Value Change,* 1978; *Human Values and Economic Activity,* 1978; (with Laszlo) *Value and the Arts,* 1979; *The Life Sciences and Human Value,* 1979; *Human Value and the Law,* 1980; *Ethics and Management,* 1981; *Ethics and the Market Place: An Exercise in Bridge-Building; or, On the Slopes of the Interface,* 1982; *Integrating Ethics into Business Education,* 1984; (and contributor) *The Integration of Ethics into Business Education: Essays on the S.U.N.Y. College at Geneseo Experience,* 1984.

Contributor to *Proceedings of the Second Conference on Business Ethics,* 1982, and to *Proceedings of the Seventh Conference on Business Ethics,* in press. Executive editor of *Journal of Value Inquiry,* 1967—; guest editor of *Journal of Business Ethics,* 1982, 1984.

WORK IN PROGRESS: Studies in Kant's ethics; *The Foundations of Corporate Responsibility; The Worlds of the Hellenistic Philosophers,* with Allen, for Prometheus Books.

AVOCATIONAL INTERESTS: Golf.

*   *   *

WILCOX, Collin   1924-
(Carter Wick)

PERSONAL: Born September 21, 1924, in Detroit, Mich.; son

of Harlan C. and Lucille (Spangler) Wilcox; married Beverly Buchman, December 23, 1954 (divorced, 1964); children: Christopher, Jeffrey. *Education:* Antioch College, A.B., 1948. *Politics:* Democrat. *Religion:* None. *Home:* 4174 26th St., San Francisco, Calif. 94131. *Agent:* Blassingame, McCauley & Wood, 432 Park Ave. S., New York, N.Y. 10016.

CAREER: Writer. Advertising copywriter in San Francisco, Calif., 1948-50; teacher of art at Town School, San Francisco, 1950-53; partner in Amthor & Co. (furniture store), San Francisco, 1953-55; owner of lamp firm, San Francisco, 1955-71, designing and manufacturing lamps and other decorative items for the home. *Military service:* U.S. Army, 1943.

MEMBER: Mystery Writers of America, Sierra Club, Aircraft Owners and Pilots Association.

WRITINGS: The Black Door, Dodd, 1967; *The Third Figure,* Dodd, 1968; (under pseudonym Carter Wick) *The Faceless Man,* Saturday Review Press, 1975; *The Third Victim,* Dell, 1976; (with Bill Pronzini) *Twospot,* Putnam, 1978; *Spellbinder,* Fawcett, 1981; (under pseudonym Carter Wick) *Dark House, Dark Road,* Raven House, 1982.

All published by Random House: *The Lonely Hunter,* 1969; *The Disappearance,* 1970; *Dead Aim,* 1971; *Hiding Place,* 1972; *Long Way Down,* 1973; *Aftershock,* 1975; *Doctor, Lawyer,* 1977; *The Watcher,* 1978; *Power Plays,* 1979; *Mankiller,* 1980; *Stalking Horse,* 1982.

WORK IN PROGRESS: Two books, *Swallow's Fall* and *The Magdalena Decision.*

SIDELIGHTS: Collin Wilcox's police procedural novels, which take place in the complex urban setting of San Francisco, feature the exploits of homicide lieutenant Frank Hastings, a former football player for the Detroit Lions. Of his work Wilcox writes: "I'm a partisan of the mystery/suspense genre; I think it offers a framework for serious commentary on contemporary life. I like living in San Francisco; I think it's an exciting, vital city that still retains some of it's frontier excitement beneath an aura of new world sophistication. I also think that, for better or worse, San Francisco leads where other American cities follow, an important plus for a writer."

AVOCATIONAL INTERESTS: Bridge, cycling, flying.

BIOGRAPHICAL/CRITICAL SOURCES: San Francisco Chronicle, May 21, 1967.

*   *   *

WILCOX, Dennis L.   1941-

PERSONAL: Born March 31, 1941, in Rapid City, S.D.; son of Herbert Dennis (a banker) and Star (Polhemus) Wilcox; married Marianne Milstead (a dietitian), May 24, 1969. *Education:* University of Denver, B.A., 1963; University of Iowa, M.A., 1966; University of Missouri, Ph.D., 1974. *Politics:* Liberal Republican. *Religion:* Episcopalian. *Home:* 1740 Marina Way, San Jose, Calif. 95125. *Office:* Department of Journalism and Mass Communications, San Jose State University, San Jose, Calif. 95114.

CAREER: Grand Junction Daily Sentinel, Grand Junction, Colo., reporter, 1963-64; Ohio State University, Columbus, editor of university publications, 1965-67; Ketchum, Inc. (fund development counsel), Pittsburgh, Pa., public relations associate, 1968-71; Chapman College, World Campus Afloat, Orange, Calif., public information officer and instructor, 1971-74; San

Jose State University, San Jose, Calif., professor and head of public relations degree program, 1974—. Visiting professor, University of Colorado Semester at Sea Program, 1978, and Rhodes University, South Africa, 1982; faculty associate, East-West Center, Honolulu, 1982.

MEMBER: International Association of Business Communicators, Public Relations Society of America, Association for Education in Journalism, San Francisco Public Relations Round Table.

WRITINGS: English Language Dailies Abroad, Gale, 1967; *Mass Media in Black Africa: Philosophy and Control,* Praeger, 1975; (consulting editor) Lawrence Nolte, *Fundamentals of Public Relations,* Pergamon, 1979.

(Contributor) George T. Kurian, *World Encyclopedia of the Press,* Facts on File, 1982; (contributor) Jane Curry and Joan Dassin, editors, *Press Control around the World,* Praeger, 1982; (co-author) *Effective Publicity: How to Reach the Public,* Wiley, 1984; (co-author) *Public Relations Strategies and Tactics,* Harper, 1985. Contributor of articles on public relations and international communications to various periodicals.

WORK IN PROGRESS: Ethics in organizational communications, satellite communications, and African press.

*   *   *

WILKERSON, Cynthia
See LEVINSON, Leonard

*   *   *

WILKINSON, Paul   1937-

PERSONAL: Born May 9, 1937, in Harrow, Middlesex, England; son of Walter Ross and Joan Rosemary Wilkinson; married Susan Flook (a medical social worker); children: Rachel, John, Charles. *Education:* University of Wales College at Swansea, B.A., 1959, M.A., 1968. *Office:* Department of Politics, University of Aberdeen, Old Aberdeen AB9 2UB, Scotland.

CAREER: University of Wales, University College, Cardiff, assistant lecturer, 1966-68, lecturer, 1968-75, senior lecturer in politics, beginning 1975; University of Aberdeen, Old Aberdeen, Scotland, reader in politics, 1978, professor of international relations, 1979—. Member, Scottish Advisory Committee of Independent Broadcasting Authority. *Military service:* Royal Air Force, 1959-65.

MEMBER: International Institute for Strategic Studies, Royal United Services Institute for Defense Studies, Royal Institute of International Affairs, British International Studies Association, Political Studies Association.

WRITINGS: Social Movement, Praeger, 1971; *Political Terrorism,* Halsted, 1974; *Terrorism versus Liberal Democracy: The Problems of Response,* Institute for the Study of Conflict, 1976; *Terrorism and the Liberal State,* Macmillan (England), 1977, New York University Press, 1978; (editor and contributor) *Terrorism: Theory and Practice,* Westview Press, 1978; *Terrorism: International Dimensions,* Institute for the Study of Conflict, 1979.

The New Fascists, Grant McIntyre (England), 1981, revised and enlarged edition, Pan Books, 1983; (editor and contributor) *British Perspectives on Terrorism,* Allen & Unwin, 1981. Editor of *Key Concepts in International Relations* series, Allen & Unwin, 1984—.

Contributor to political science journals, including *World Today*, and newspapers. Editorial adviser, *Contemporary Review;* member of editorial board, *Terrorism: An International Journal*.

WORK IN PROGRESS: Rules of War; research on international terrorism; a work on liberal democratic theory, with special reference to international relations.

SIDELIGHTS: Paul Wilkinson writes: "I am best known for my studies of terrorism and civil violence. Writing from the perspective of liberal democratic philosophy, I have consistently and passionately condemned terrorism as an unmitigated evil. I believe that terrorist violence is inherently morally unjustifiable because it involves the murder and maiming of the innocent. Whatever terrorists may say, there are always alternative forms of protest, opposition and resistance available which do not necessitate the deliberate and systematic murder of the innocent.

"The major preoccupations of my recent work have been the protection of the life and rights of the innocent, and the design of policies and measures at both national and international levels to defeat terrorism in ways fully compatible with liberal democracy and the rule of law. I am currently engaged in a major study of the efforts to revise and extend the humanitarian laws of war, the problems of their enforcement in major armed conflicts, and the longer-term problems of reforming the international system."

AVOCATIONAL INTERESTS: Modern poetry, modern painting, walking.

BIOGRAPHICAL/CRITICAL SOURCES: Terrorism: An International Journal, Volume I, number 2, 1978; A. Schmid, *Political Terrorism: A Guide to Concepts and Literature*, 1983.

*　　*　　*

WILLIAMS, Robert C. 1938-

PERSONAL: Born October 14, 1938, in Boston, Mass.; son of Charles Regan (a public health official) and Dorothy (Chadwell) Williams; married Ann Kingman (a biology assistant), August 27, 1960; children: Peter, Margaret, Katharine. *Education:* Wesleyan University, Middletown, Conn., B.A., 1960; Harvard University, A.M., 1962, Ph.D., 1966. *Home:* 428 Melville Ave., University City, Mo. 63130. *Office:* History Department, Washington University, St. Louis, Mo. 63130.

CAREER: Williams College, Williamstown, Mass., assistant professor of history, 1965-70, assistant to the provost, 1968-70; Washington University, St. Louis, Mo., 1970—, began as associate professor, currently professor of history and dean. *Member:* American Association for the Advancement of Slavic Studies (president, Central Slavic Conference, 1970-71), Phi Beta Kappa, Sigma Xi. *Awards, honors:* Woodrow Wilson fellowship, 1960; Kennan fellow, 1976-77.

WRITINGS: Culture in Exile: Russian Emigres in Germany, 1881-1941, Cornell University Press, 1972; *Artists in Revolution: Portraits of the Russian Avant-garde, 1905-1925*, Indiana University Press, 1977; *The Culture Exchange: Russian Art and American Money, 1900-1940*, Harvard University Press, 1980; *Crisis Contained: The Department of Energy at Three Mile Island*, Southern Illinois University Press, 1982; *The American Atom*, University of Pennsylvania Press, 1984. Contributor of articles to *Yale Review, Slavic Review, Journal of History of Ideas.* Editor of *Berkshire Review*, 1967-70, and *Kritika*, 1968.

WORK IN PROGRESS: The Klaus Fuchs Case: Science, Secrecy, and Security in the Nuclear Age.

SIDELIGHTS: Though he is the author of a number of studies of Russian society, Robert C. Williams' *The Culture Exchange: Russian Art and American Money* has received particular attention from critics for its revealing portrayal of the strange relationship between Soviet government officials and wealthy American art collectors that existed in the first half of the twentieth century. "Drawn from both Russian and American sources," writes James R. Mellow in the *New York Times Book Review*, "and from well-publicized tax trials and less accessible Government records that reveal the shadier aspects of the subject, 'Russian Art and American Money' is a detailed, scholarly account of the once-secret transactions by which the treasures of the Romanovs (imperial porcelains, Russian silver, Faberge jewelry, from the collection of Csar Nicholas II) and some of the greatest masterpieces in the history of art (Rembrandts, Raphaels, Titians and Van Eycks stripped from the walls of Russian museums) became the property of American millionaires." These transactions occurred, according to Mellow, because "Following the Revolution of 1917, much of Russia's artistic patrimony . . . had its price. From Lenin and Trotsky to Stalin and his Five-Year Plans, the Soviet effort to sell valuable paintings and sculptures, the nationalized wealth of the Russian nobility—to 'turn diamonds into tractors,' as one Russian official put it—became standard practice in the financing of the new regime and its technological programs."

Among the wealthy Americans who took advantage of the Russian need for foreign currency were Andrew Mellon and Armand Hammer. The former was responsible for the largest of these exchanges of art for cash in 1930-31, when, according to Norman Stone in the *Times Literary Supplement*, he "acquired twenty-one masterpieces of European art from the Hermitage collection. He paid $6,654,053 for a set which included Rembrandt's 'Polish Nobleman' and 'Woman Holding a Pink', Veronese's 'Finding of Moses', [and] Velazquez's 'Innocent X.' The Mellon sale alone made up one third of the value of Soviet exports to America in that year. Soviet sales of works of art, to finance the country's industrialization, brought in 4,600,000 roubles in 1929, 6,300,000 in 1930, 2,700,000 in 1931, 1,900,000 in 1932." Stone concludes: "This is the depressing story which Robert Williams has told. He does not draw a moral from his tale, but he tells it with conviction."

BIOGRAPHICAL/CRITICAL SOURCES: Yale Review, Autumn, 1978; *New York Times Book Review*, March 9, 1980; *Times Literary Supplement*, March 28, 1980; *National Review*, July 11, 1980.

*　　*　　*

WILLIAMS, Rose
See ROSS, W(illiam) E(dward) D(aniel)

*　　*　　*

WILLIE, Charles V(ert) 1927-

PERSONAL: Born October 8, 1927, in Dallas, Tex.; son of Louis (a former Pullman porter and real estate broker) and Carrie (Sykes) Willie; married Mary Sue Conklin (an organist, singing teacher, and choir director), March 31, 1962; children: Sarah Susannah, Martin Charles, James Theodore. *Education:* Morehouse College, B.A., 1948; Atlanta University, M.A., 1949; Syracuse University, Ph.D., 1957. *Religion:* Episcopalian. *Office:* 457 Gutman Library, Graduate School of Education, Harvard University, Cambridge, Mass. 02138.

CAREER: Syracuse University, Syracuse, N.Y., instructor, 1952-60, assistant professor, 1960-64, associate professor, 1964-68, professor of sociology 1968-74, chairman of department, 1967-71, vice-president of student affairs, 1972-74; Harvard University, Cambridge, Mass., currently professor of education and urban studies. Research sociologist, New York State Mental Health Commission, 1951-52; instructor in sociology at State University of New York Upstate Medical Center, 1955-60; research director of Washington, D.C. Project, President's Committee on Juvenile Delinquency and Youth Crime, 1962-64; lecturer in sociology at the Medical School, Harvard University, 1966-67; vice-president of House of Deputies, Episcopal Church General Convention, 1970-73.

MEMBER: Social Science Research Council (member of board of directors, 1969-74), Social and Behavioral Sciences Assembly of the National Research Council, American Sociological Society (fellow), Society for the Study of Social Problems, American Public Health Association, Eastern Sociological Society (president, 1974-75), Phi Beta Kappa.

AWARDS, HONORS: Health Information Foundation research grant, 1958-60, State University of New York Upstate Medical Center; National Science Foundation conference grant, Syracuse University, 1967-68; faculty service award from National University Extension Association, 1967; Ford Foundation research grant, 1969-71, for study of black students at white colleges; Falk Medical Fund conference grant, 1970-71; D.H.L., Yale University, 1972; D.D., General Seminary, 1974; M.A., Harvard University, 1974; Distinguished Alumnus Award, Syracuse University, 1974; National Institute of Mental Health grant, 1976-77; Danforth Foundation grant, 1982; Spence Foundation grant, 1983; Lee-Founders Award, Society for the Study of Social Problems.

WRITINGS: Church Action in the World, Morehouse, 1969; (editor) *The Family Life of Black People,* C. E. Merrill, 1970; (with Arline McCord) *Black Students at White Colleges,* Praeger, 1972; (with Jerome Beker) *Race Mixing in the Public Schools,* Praeger, 1973; (editor with Bernard Kramer and Betram Brown) *Racism and Mental Health,* University of Pittsburgh Press, 1973. *Oreo: A Perspective on Race and Marginal Men and Women,* Parameter Press, 1975; *A New Look at Black Families,* General Hall, 1976, 2nd edition, 1981; (editor) *Black-Brown-White Relations: Race Relations in the 1970's,* Transaction Books, 1977; (editor with Ronald R. Edmonds) *Black Colleges in America,* Teachers College Press, 1978; *The Sociology of Urban Education: Desegregation and Integration,* Lexington Books, 1978; *The Caste and Class Controversy,* General Hall, 1980; *The Ivory and Ebony Towers,* Lexington Books, 1981; (with Susan Greenblatt) *Community Politics and Educational Change,* Longman, 1981; *School Desegregation Plans that Work,* Greenwood Press, 1983.

Contributor to *Psychology Today, American Sociological Review, American Journal of Public Health, Journal of Negro Education, Professional Geographer,* and *Review of Religious Research.*

*   *   *

WILSON, Carole
    See WALLMANN, Jeffrey M(iner)

WILSON, Larman C. 1930-

PERSONAL: Born April 20, 1930, in Lincoln, Neb.; son of Curtis M. and Naomi J. (a professor; maiden name, Gilbert) Wilson; married Olga Jurevitch, September 5, 1959; children: Natalia Ann, Katherine Teresa. *Education:* Attended University of Minnesota, 1950; Chadron State College, B.A., 1952; University of Florida, graduate study, 1954; University of Maryland, M.A., 1957, Ph.D., 1964. *Religion:* Protestant. *Home:* 4843 Chevy Chase Blvd., Chevy Chase, Md. 20815. *Office:* School of International Service, American University, Washington, D.C. 20016.

CAREER: University of Maryland, College Park, lecturer in political science and economics in Atlantic Division of Overseas Program in Bermuda, Labrador, Newfoundland, Iceland, and Greenland, 1957-59, lecturer in political science, 1961-64; U.S. Naval Academy, Annapolis, Md., assistant professor of political science, 1964-68; American University, Washington, D.C., associate professor, 1968-74, professor of international relations, 1974—, associate dean, 1982-84. President, Inter-American Council, 1973-74. Consultant on international law, development in developing countries, the Dominican Republic, the Caribbean, Central America, and Mexico.

MEMBER: American Political Science Association, American Society of International Law, International Studies Association, Latin American Studies Association, American Association of University Professors.

AWARDS, HONORS: Organization of American States fellowship to Tercer Curso de Derecho Internacional (Brazil), 1976.

WRITINGS: (With D. S. Hitt) *A Selected Bibliography of the Dominican Republic: A Century after the Restoration of Independence,* Center for Research in Social Systems, 1968; (with E. Chang-Rodriguez and others) *The Lingering Crisis: A Case Study of the Dominican Republic,* Las Americas Publishing, 1969; (with G. P. Atkins) *The United States and the Trujillo Regime,* Rutgers University Press, 1972; (with H. E. Davis and others) *Latin American Foreign Policies,* Johns Hopkins University Press, 1975; *The Inter-American System and Its Future,* Organization of American States, 1979; (with R. Millett, W. M. Will, and others) *The Restless Caribbean,* Praeger, 1979; (with D. C. Piper, R. J. Terchek, and others) *Interaction: Foreign Policy and Public Policy,* American Enterprise Institute for Public Policy Research, 1983. Contributor to journals of international affairs and Latin American studies.

*   *   *

WILSON, Robley (Conant), Jr. 1930-

PERSONAL: Born June 15, 1930, in Brunswick, Maine; son of Robley Conant (a teacher) and Dorothy (Stimpson) Wilson; married Charlotte Lehon, August 20, 1955; children: Stephen, Philip. *Education:* Bowdoin College, B.A., 1957; Indiana University, graduate study, 1960; University of Iowa, M.F.A., 1968. *Home address:* P.O. Box 527, Cedar Falls, Iowa 50613. *Office:* Department of English, University of Northern Iowa, Cedar Falls, Iowa 50614.

CAREER: Valparaiso University, Valparaiso, Ind., instructor in English and Russian, 1958-63; University of Northern Iowa, Cedar Falls, assistant professor, 1968-70, associate professor, 1970-75, professor of English, 1975—. Has given readings and lectures at colleges and universities all over the United

States. *Military service:* U.S. Air Force, 1951-55; became staff sergeant. *Awards, honors:* Drue Heinz Literature Prize, 1982, for *Dancing for Men;* Guggenheim fellow, 1983-84.

WRITINGS: All That Lovemaking (poems), Country Print, 1961; (editor with Stephen Minot) *Three Stances of Modern Fiction: A Critical Anthology,* Winthrop Publishing, 1972; *Returning to the Body* (poetry chapbook), Juniper Press, 1977; *The Pleasures of Manhood* (stories), University of Illinois Press, 1977; *Living Alone* (fictions), Fiction International, 1978; *Dancing for Men* (stories), University of Pittsburgh Press, 1982.

Poems and stories anthologized in ten collections, including *All Our Secrets Are the Same,* Norton; *Three Genres,* Prentice-Hall; *Interpreting Literature,* Holt. Contributor of poems and stories to literary journals and popular magazines, including *Antaeus, Atlantic, Esquire, Nation,* and *New Yorker.* Editor of *North American Review,* 1969—.

SIDELIGHTS: With the publication of *Dancing for Men,* Robley Wilson, Jr., "may climb out into the world of recognized authors, those whose names are mentioned in lists and are used as illustrations," predicts Anatole Broyard in the *New York Times.* Although judged "uneven in execution" by Malcolm Boyd, the critic admits in the *Los Angeles Times Book Review* that Wilson's work nonetheless is "stunningly original," "significant," and "daring." Often focusing on the relationships between men and women, the stories in *Dancing for Men* feature people who find it difficult to resolve their need for privacy and their urge to express individualism with being intimately involved with another person. "The characters break out of their habits, their adjustments, their preconceptions, for a while," Broyard explains, "and then [they] get back in as if they had never been there before." The stories illuminate both the static and the ever-changing aspects of personality and relationships.

Of the book's eleven stories, Broyard writes, the seven best "are the sort of pieces that talk to each of us, murmur, whisper and shout at us, too." Adds Susan Osborn, commenting in the *Village Voice Literary Supplement:* "[The author] is a superior writer who understands how to make the most of subconscious associations. . . . Connected incidents seem at first not to relate. But as we read on, we realize that while they may perplex our intelligence, they make a kind of irrefutable subconscious sense." Although she feels Wilson's presentation of women frequently discloses the male characters'—or the author's—misogyny, Osborn in the end states that "there is no doubt that Wilson is a superb writer. At times, his syntactical adjustments make for lovely, poetic sentences . . . , his images are keen, and he is often possessed of a great psychological acuity."

BIOGRAPHICAL/CRITICAL SOURCES: Village Voice Literary Supplement, December 12, 1982; *New York Times,* February 4, 1983; *Los Angeles Times Book Review,* March 6, 1983.

*   *   *

WINGLER, Hans M(aria) 1920-

PERSONAL: Born January 5, 1920, in Constance, Germany; son of Hans (a merchant) and Gertrud (Lange) Wingler; married Hedwig Tax (a writer of essays on philosophy), November 20, 1969; children: (first marriage) Lothar, Angelika; (present marriage) Johannes. *Education:* Studied history of art and archaeology at University of Frankfurt and University of Vienna. *Home:* Heerstrasse 68, D-1000 Berlin 19, West Germany. *Of-*

fice: Bauhaus-Archive, Klingelhoeferstrasse 14, Berlin 30, West Germany.

CAREER: University of Frankfurt, Frankfurt am Main, Germany, assistant at Institute of Art History, 1945-49; Harvard University, Cambridge, Mass., research fellow at Busch-Reisinger Museum, 1957-58; art critic and scholar, 1957—; Bauhaus-Archive, director in Darmstadt, West Germany, 1960-71, director in Berlin, West Germany, 1971—. Lecturer at Illinois Institute of Technology, University of Amsterdam, and at other schools and museums in Europe and South America.

MEMBER: International Institute of Architecture (Bologna, Italy; honorary member), Association Internationale des Critiques d'Art, International Commission of Museums, Deutscher Werkbund (honorary member).

AWARDS, HONORS: Award of the Republic of Austria, 1956, for *Oskar Kokoschka: Das Werk des Malers;* Dr. phil.h.c., Technical University, Munich, West Germany.

WRITINGS: Oskar Kokoschka: Das Werk des Malers, Galerie Welz, 1956, translation by Frank S. C. Budgen and others published as *Oskar Kokoschka: The Work of the Painter,* Faber (London), 1958; *Kokoschka-Fibel,* Galerie Welz, 1957, translation by Peter George published as *Introduction to Kokoschka,* Thames & Hudson, 1958; (with Friedrich Welz) *Oskar Kokoschka: Das Druckgraphische Werk,* Verlag Welz, Volume I, 1975, Volume II, 1981.

Editor: (And author of foreword) *Die Bruecke: Kunst im Aufbruch,* Buchheim-Verlag, 1954; *Ernst Ludwig Kirchner: Holzschnitte,* Buchheim-Verlag, 1954; *Oskar Kokoschka: Kuenstler und Poeten,* Buchheim-Verlag, 1954; *Der Blaue Reiter,* Buchheim-Verlag, 1954; (and author of introduction) *Der Sturm,* Buchheim-Verlag, 1955; (and author of epilogue) Johann von Goethe, *Walpurgisnacht,* Buchheim-Verlag, 1955; *Oskar Kokoschka: Schriften, 1907-1955,* Langen-Mueller, 1956; *Oskar Kokoschka: Ein Lebensbild in zeitgenoessischen Dokumenten,* Langen-Mueller, 1956, enlarged paperback edition published as *Oskar Kokoschka: Ein Lebensbild,* Ullstein, 1966; *Wie sie einander sahen: Moderne Maler im Urteil ihrer Gefaehrten,* Langen-Mueller, 1957; Ludwig Meidner, *Hymnen und Laesterungen,* Langen-Mueller, 1959; *Oskar Kokoschka: Die traeumenden Knaben und andere Dichtungen* (booklet), Galerie Welz, 1959.

Das Bauhaus, 1919-1933: Weimar, Dessau, Berlin, Rasch, 1962, enlarged edition published as *Das Bauhaus, 1919-1933: Weimar, Dessau, Berlin und die Nachfolge in Chicago seit 1937,* Rasch, 1968, translation by Wolfgang Jabs and Basil Gilbert, edited by Joseph Stein, published as *The Bauhaus: Weimar, Dessau, Berlin, Chicago,* M.I.T. Press, 1969; *Die Kunstschulreform 1900-1933,* Mann, 1977.

All published by Kupferberg: *Die Mappenwerke "Neue europaeische Graphik,"* 1965, translation by Gerald Onn published as *Graphic Work from the Bauhaus,* New York Graphic Society, 1969; Walter Gropius, *Die neue Architektur und das Bauhaus,* 1965; Paul Klee, *Paedagogisches Skizzenbuch,* 1965; Oskar Schlemmer, Laszlo Moholy-Nagy and Farkas Molnar, *Die Buehne im Bauhaus,* 1965; Theo van Doesburg, *Grundbegriffe der neuen gestaltenden Kunst,* 1966; Gottfried Semper, *Wissenschaft, Industrie und Kunst,* 1966; Gropius, *Apollo in der Demokratie,* 1967; Ludwig Hilberseimer, *Berliner Architektur der Zwanziger Jahre,* 1967; Moholy-Nagy, *Malerei, Fotografie, Film,* 1967; Moholy-Nagy, *Von Material zu Architektur,* 1968; Schlemmer, *Der Mensch,* 1969; Gyorgy Kepes, *Die Sprache des Sehens,* 1970; Serge Chermayeff and Christopher Alexander, *Gemeinschaft und Privatbereich*, 1971; Piet Mondrian, *Neue Gestaltung*, 1974; Gropius, *Bauhausbauten Dessau*, 1974; J. J. P. Oud, *Hollandische Architektur*, 1976; Albert Gleizes, *Kubismus*, 1980; Kasimir Malewitsch, *Die gegenstandslose Welt*, 1980; Gropius, *Internationale Architektur*, 1981; Gropius, *Neue Arbeiten der Bauhauswerkstaetten*, 1981.

Editor of various Bauhaus-Archive publications and a Bauhaus catalogue. Contributor to *Encyclopaedia Britannica*, *Kindlers Malerei-Lexikon*, and other collections.

SIDELIGHTS: Hans M. Wingler's *The Bauhaus: Weimar, Dessau, Berlin, Chicago* "is probably the most compendious anthology of documents ever devoted to a single episode in the modern movement," writes Hilton Kramer in the *New York Times Book Review*. The director of the Bauhaus-Archive, Wingler has, in this book, assembled a record of the design school, including manifestos, essays, newspapers, letters, illustrations, and photographs. A *Times Literary Supplement* reviewer comments that this "fascinating and invaluable collection, presented with a minimum of editorial comment" will help clarify current views of the Bauhaus.

BIOGRAPHICAL/CRITICAL SOURCES: Times Literary Supplement, September 13, 1963, April 16, 1970; *Spectator*, August 9, 1967; *New York Times Book Review*, September 28, 1969; *New Republic*, October 11, 1969; *Newsweek*, December 15, 1969; *New York Review of Books*, January 1, 1970; *Commentary*, March, 1970.

*   *   *

WINNER, Irene P(ortis)   1923-

PERSONAL: Born April 7, 1923, in Chicago, Ill.; daughter of Henry Roy (a businessman) and Jane (Oransky) Portis; married Thomas G. Winner (a university professor), September 25, 1942; children: Ellen, Lucy Franziska. *Education:* Radcliffe College, B.A., 1943; Columbia University, M.A., 1953; University of North Carolina, Ph.D., 1967. *Home:* 19 Garden St., Cambridge, Mass. 02138.

CAREER: Office of War Information-Office of Strategic Services, Washington, D.C., research analyst, 1943-46; Wayne State University, Detroit, Mich., visiting instructor in anthropology, 1962-63; Brown University, Providence, R.I., research associate in office of provost, 1968-71; Ossabaw Island Project, Ossabaw Island, Ga., fellow, 1971; Tufts University, Medford, Mass., visiting lecturer in anthropology, 1972, 1974, 1975; Brown University, research fellow, 1973; Emmanuel College, Boston, Mass., associate professor of anthropology, 1975-79; Brown University, currently adjunct associate professor of semiotics. Visiting professor in semiotics, University of Urbino, Italy, 1982; lecturer in anthropology, Lesley College, 1982. Senior research associate, Center for Philosophy and History of Science, Boston University; associate, Center for Philosophy of Education, Harvard University, 1983—.

MEMBER: International Association for Semiotic study, American Anthropological Association (fellow), Society for Applied Anthropology (fellow), American Ethnological Society, Current Anthropology (associate), Semiotic Society of America, American Association for the Advancement of Science, American Association for the Advancement of Slavic Studies, Council on Anthropology and Education, Society for the Anthropology of Visual Communication, American Association for Southeast European Studies, Society for Slovene Studies (member of executive council), Northeastern Anthro-

pological Association, Anthropological Society of Washington.

AWARDS, HONORS: Wenner-Gren Foundation fellowship in Yugoslavia, 1964-65; American Council of Learned Societies and Social Science Research Council grant for research in Eastern Europe, 1972-73.

WRITINGS: A Slovenian Village: Zerovnica, Brown University Press, 1971; (editor with Jean Riniker-Sebeok) *Semiotics of Culture*, Mouton, 1979; (editor) *The Dynamics of East European Ethnicity Outside of Eastern Europe*, Schenkman, 1983; *The Peasant and the City in Eastern Europe*, Schenkman, 1984.

Also author of monograph "Semiotics of Culture: The State of the Art," Toronto Semiotic Circle Monographs, 1982. Contributor to *Central Asian Review*, *East Central Europe*, *Canadian-American Slavic Studies*, *Current Anthropology*, *American Anthropologist*, *Sociologija Sela*, *Semiotica*, and *Etnografia Polska*. Co-editor, *American Journal of Semiotics*, 1980-84; member of editorial board, *East Central Europe* and *Southeastern Europe*.

WORK IN PROGRESS: Research on semiotics of culture and on Slovene ethnicity in the United States.

*   *   *

WINTER, Gordon   1912-

PERSONAL: Born May 17, 1912, in London, England; son of Arthur (a company director) and Ottilie Winter; married Mary Jackson, October 22, 1939 (divorced, 1943); married Elspeth Kerr Bone (a business executive), November 6, 1948; children: William, Andrew, Lucinda. *Education:* Attended Camberley Staff College, 1943. *Politics:* Conservative. *Religion:* Church of England. *Home:* Noble Tree End, Hildenborough, Kent, England. *Office: Country Life*, Kings Reach Tower, Stamford St., London S.E. 1, England.

CAREER: British Broadcasting Corp., London, England, staff member, 1937-57; *Country Life*, London, chief assistant editor, 1957-77, consultant editor, 1977—. Member of board of directors of Lighthouse Books, 1947-53. *Military service:* British Army, Royal Artillery, 1936-45; became lieutenant colonel.

MEMBER: Royal Ocean Racing Club, London Rowing Club, Leander Club.

WRITINGS: The Horseman's Week-End Book, Seeley Service, 1936; (with wife, Elspeth Winter) *Ourselves in Canada*, Seeley Service, 1958; *A Country Camera, 1844-1914: Rural Life as Depicted in Photographs from the Early Days of Photography to the Outbreak of the First World War*, Country Life, 1966, Gale, 1971; *Past Positive: London's Social History Recorded in Photographs*, Chatto & Windus, 1971, published as *A Cockney Camera: London's Social History Recorded in Photographs*, Penguin (Harmondsworth, England), 1975.

The Golden Years 1903-1913: A Pictorial Survey of the Most Interesting Decade in English History, Recorded in Contemporary Photographs and Drawings, David & Charles, 1975; *The Country Life Picture Book of Britain*, Country Life, 1978; *How the Countryside Was Made*, Dinosaur Publications, 1980; *The Country Life Picture Book of the Thames*, Country Life, 1982; *The Country Life Picture Book of Royal London*, Country Life, 1983.

Also author of material for radio and television. Member of editorial staff of *Field*, 1932—, and *Listener*, 1937-39; director of *Fortnightly Review,* 1938-53; editorial consultant to *Country Landowner,* 1983—.

WORK IN PROGRESS: A book commissioned by the Granada Group.

SIDELIGHTS: Gordon Winter comments: "The principal activity of my lifetime and of my writings has been the defence of the beauty of the countryside of the United Kingdom, which I regard as the source of inspiration for our English civilisation. The weekly magazine, *Country Life,* reflects all my personal interests.

"Since 1978 I have devoted much time to devising and organising the *Country Life* Farming and Wildlife Award, given annually to the British farmer who has done most, in that year, to encourage wildlife on his farm, within the constraints of successful commercial farming."

* * *

WITHINGTON, William Adriance 1924-

PERSONAL: Born February 17, 1924, in Honolulu, Hawaii; son of Frederic Burnham (a minister) and Margaret (Adriance) Withington; married Anne Tonon, September 1, 1955; children: Robert Adriance, Sally. *Education:* Harvard University, A.B., 1946; Northwestern University, M.A., 1948, Ph.D., 1955. *Office:* Department of Geography, University of Kentucky, Lexington, Ky. 40506.

CAREER: George Washington University, Washington, D.C., instructor, 1948-51, assistant professor of geography, 1951-52; University of Kentucky, Lexington, instructor, 1955-56, assistant professor, 1956-63, associate professor of geography, 1963—. Visiting professor of geography at Nommensen University (Indonesia), 1957-59, California State College at Hayward (now University), summer, 1970; lecturer at University of London, Brussels Center for Southeast Asian Studies, and University of Heidelberg, summer, 1968. Senior planner, Boston City Planning Board, 1955; co-chairman of Lexington-Fayette County Committee on Religion and Human Rights, 1964-65; Lexington-Fayette County Urban League, initial board member, 1965-66; member of Southeast Asia Development Advisory Group, 1968-72; consultant on Southeast Asia to International Development Research Centre, Ottawa, Canada, winter, 1971-72.

MEMBER: Association of American Geographers, Association for Asian Studies, American Geographical Society, Kentucky Academy of Science (chairman, geography section, 1972, 1983), Sigma Xi.

WRITINGS: (With Margaret Fisher Hertel) *Southeast Asia,* Fideler, 1963, revised edition published as *Asia: Man in Southeast Asia,* 1978, new revised edition published under original title, Fideler, 1984; (with Hertel) *Asia with Focus on Southeast Asia,* Fideler, 1964, revised edition, 1968; (contributor) Paul Griffin, editor, *Geography of Population,* Fearon, 1969; (contributor) Ashok Dutt, editor, *Southeast Asia: Land of Contrast,* Kendall/Hunt, 1974, revised edition, Westview, 1984; *Atlas of Sumatra,* privately printed, 1978; *Kentucky in Maps,* Franklin Geographical Society, 1980.

Contributor to *American Peoples' Encyclopedia, Encyclopedia Americana, Geographical Abstracts, Focus, Revue de Sud-Est Asiatique et de l'Extreme-Orient, Journal of Geography, Annals of the Association of American Geographers, Tijdschrift voor Economische en Sociale Geographe, Pacific Viewpoint,*

Journal of Tropical Geography, Indonesia Circle, Sumatra Research Bulletin, Geographic Review, and *Kentucky Study Series.*

WORK IN PROGRESS: Evolution of Kentucky's Lake Landscape: 1925-Present; Dynamics of Name Changes in Sumatra Indonesia: Administrative Areas and Selected Cities; a revised edition of *Kentucky in Maps.*

* * *

WOESSNER, Warren (Dexter) 1944-

PERSONAL: Born May 31, 1944, in New Brunswick, N.J.; son of Warren Wendling (a chemist) and Flora (Dexter) Woessner; married Joyce Howe (a University of Wisconsin state employee), April 17, 1971; married Carol Lipetz (an attorney), April 30, 1983. *Education:* Cornell University, A.B., 1966; University of Wisconsin—Madison, Ph.D., 1971, J.D., 1981. *Home:* 1253 West Minnehaha Pkwy., Minneapolis, Minn. 55419. *Office:* Merchant & Gould, 801 Nicollet Mall, Minneapolis, Minn. 55406.

CAREER: University of Wisconsin—Madison, research associate in School of Pharmacy, 1971-72; Miles Laboratories, Madison, senior research scientist, 1972-81; Kenyon & Kenyon, New York, N.Y., patent attorney, 1981-83; Merchant & Gould, Minneapolis, Minn., patent attorney, 1983—.

MEMBER: American Bar Association, American Chemical Society.

AWARDS, HONORS: Memorial Union Creative Writing Contest award, University of Wisconsin—Madison, 1967, 1968, 1969, and 1970; National Endowment for the Arts creative writing fellowship, 1974; Wisconsin Arts Board fellowship in creative writing, 1975 and 1976.

WRITINGS—All poetry: *The Forest and the Trees,* Quixote Press, 1968; *The Rivers Return,* Gunrunner Press, 1969; *Inroads,* Modine Gunch Press, 1970; *Landing,* Ithaca House, 1974; *Lost Highway,* Poetry Texas, 1977; *No Hiding Place,* Spoon River Press, 1979. Contributor to *Poetry, Poetry Northwest, Nation, Hanging Loose, Ironwood,* and other periodicals. Senior editor, *Abraxas* (poetry magazine).

WORK IN PROGRESS: A collection of poetry, *Storm Lines;* more poetry and criticism.

AVOCATIONAL INTERESTS: Ornithology, photography, travel.

* * *

WOLFF, Miles 1945-

PERSONAL: Born December 30, 1945, in Baltimore, Md.; son of Miles Hoffman (a newspaper editor) and Anna (Webster) Wolff; married Michelle Guimond, 1983. *Education:* Johns Hopkins University, A.B., 1965; University of Virginia, M.A., 1967. *Home:* 1700 Rosedale Ave., Durham N.C. 27707.

CAREER: Savannah Braves Baseball Club, Savannah, Ga., general manager, 1971-73; Anderson Mets Baseball Club, Anderson, S.C., general manager, 1974; Jacksonville Suns Baseball Club, Jacksonville, Fla., general manager, 1975; Richmond Braves Baseball Club, Richmond, Va., play-by-play announcer, 1977; Durham Bulls Baseball Club, Durham, N.C., president, 1980—; Utica Blue Sox Baseball Club, Utica, N.Y., president, 1982; publisher of *Baseball America,* for American Sports Publishing, Inc., 1982—. *Military service:* U.S. Navy, 1967-70; became lieutenant.

WRITINGS: Lunch at the Five and Ten, Stein & Day, 1970; *Season of the Owl* (novel), Stein & Day, 1980.

WORK IN PROGRESS: The Cockatrice, a contemporary fantasy.

SIDELIGHTS: Miles Wolff comments: "Most of my time is spent trying to get our newspaper, *Baseball America,* on its feet and running various minor league enterprises, chiefly the Durham Bulls."

*   *   *

WOLFF, Sonia
See LEVITIN, Sonia (Wolff)

*   *   *

WOLKSTEIN, Diane   1942-

PERSONAL: Born November 11, 1942, in New York, N.Y.; daughter of Harry W. (a certified public accountant) and Ruth (Barenbaum) Wolkstein; married Benjamin Zucker (a gem merchant), September 7, 1969; children: Rachel. *Education:* Smith College, B.A., 1964; studied pantomime in Paris, 1964-65; Bank Street College of Education, M.A., 1967. *Religion:* Jewish. *Home:* 28 Bank St., New York, N.Y. 10014.

CAREER: Hostess of weekly radio show, "Stories from Many Lands with Diane Wolkstein," WNYC-Radio, New York City, 1967—. Featured storyteller at numerous gatherings; instructor in storytelling and children's literature, Bank Street College, New York City, 1970—; leader of storytelling workshops for librarians and teachers. Teacher of mythology, Sarah Lawrence College, 1984.

AWARDS, HONORS: Honorable mention, New York Academy of Sciences, 1972, for *8,000 Stones;* Lithgow-Osborne fellowship, 1976, 1977; American Institute of Graphic Arts award, 1977, for *The Red Lion: A Persian Sufi Tale;* American Library Association notable book citation, 1978, for *The Magic Orange Tree and Other Haitian Folk Tales,* and 1979, for *White Wave: A Tao Tale;* recipient of Marshall grant.

WRITINGS: 8,000 Stones, Doubleday, 1972; *The Cool Ride in the Sky: A Black-American Folk Tale* (Xerox Book Club selection), Knopf, 1973; *The Visit,* Knopf, 1974; *Squirrel's Song: A Hopi-Indian Story,* Knopf, 1975; *Lazy Stories,* Seabury, 1976; *The Red Lion: A Persian Sufi Tale,* Crowell, 1977; *The Magic Orange Tree and Other Haitian Folk Tales,* Knopf, 1978; *White Wave: A Tao Tale,* Crowell, 1979; *The Banza: A Haitian Folk Tale,* Dial, 1980; (with Samuel Noah Kramer) *Inanna, Queen of Heaven and Earth: Her Stories and Hymns from Sumer,* Harper, 1983; *The Magic Wings,* Dutton, 1983.

Recordings: "Tales of the Hopi Indians," Spoken Arts, 1972; "California Fairy Tales," Spoken Arts, 1974; "The Cool Ride in the Sky," Miller-Brody, 1975; "Eskimo Stories: Tales of Magic," Spoken Arts, 1976; "Hans Christian Andersen in Central Park," Weston Woods, 1981; "Psyche and Eros," Cloudstone Productions, 1984. Contributor of articles to periodicals, including *School Library Journal, Wilson Library Bulletin, Parabola,* and *Quadrant.*

SIDELIGHTS: Her storytelling career has taken Diane Wolkstein from the John Masefield Storytelling Festival in Toronto, Canada, in 1972, to the Fifth National Association for the Preservation of Storytelling Festival in Jonesboro, Tennessee, in 1977. On two separate occasions, she has told stories to Queen Margareta of Denmark and to Princess Benedikta.

AVOCATIONAL INTERESTS: Travel.

BIOGRAPHICAL/CRITICAL SOURCES: New York Times Book Review, September 25, 1983.

*   *   *

WONNACOTT, Ronald J(ohnston)   1930-

PERSONAL: Born September 11, 1930, in London, Ontario, Canada; son of Gordon (a teacher) and Muriel (Johnston) Wonnacott; married Eloise Howlett, September 11, 1954; children: Douglas, Robert, Cathy Anne. *Education:* University of Western Ontario, B.A., 1955; Harvard University, A.M., 1957, Ph.D., 1959. *Religion:* United Church of Canada. *Home:* 171 Wychwood Park, London, Ontario, Canada. *Office:* Department of Economics, University of Western Ontario, London, Ontario, Canada N6A 3K7.

CAREER: University of Western Ontario, London, assistant professor, 1958-61, associate professor, 1961-64, professor of economics, 1964—, chairman of department, 1969-72. Visiting associate professor, University of Minnesota, 1961-62. Consultant to Stanford Research Institute, Resources for the Future, Economic Council of Canada, and other groups. *Military service:* Royal Canadian Naval Reserve, 1951-55; became lieutenant.

MEMBER: Canadian Economics Association (president, 1981-82), Royal Society of Canada (fellow), American Economic Association, Econometric Society.

WRITINGS: Canadian-American Dependence: An Interindustry Analysis of Production and Prices, North-Holland Publishing, 1961; (with Grant L. Reuber) *The Cost of Capital in Canada,* Resources for the Future, 1961; *Manufacturing Costs and the Comparative Advantage of United States Regions,* University of Minnesota, 1963; (with brother, Paul Wonnacott) *Free Trade between the U.S. and Canada,* Harvard University Press, 1967; (with David E. Bond) *Trade Liberalization and the Canadian Furniture Industry,* University of Toronto Press, 1968; (with P. Wonnacott) *U.S.-Canadian Free Trade,* Canadian-American Committee, 1968; (with brother, Thomas Wonnacott) *Introductory Statistics,* Wiley, 1969, 4th edition, in press; (with T. Wonnacott) *Econometrics,* Wiley, 1970; (with T. Wonnacott) *Introductory Statistics for Business and Economics,* Wiley, 1972, 3rd edition, in press; *Canada's Trade Options,* Economic Council of Canada, 1975; (with P. Wonnacott) *Economics,* McGraw, 1979, 2nd edition, 1982; (with T. Wonnacott) *Regression,* Wiley, 1981; (with T. Wonnacott) *Statistics: Discovering Its Power,* Wiley, 1982. Contributor to economics journals.

AVOCATIONAL INTERESTS: Golf, skiing, tennis.

*   *   *

WONNACOTT, Thomas H(erbert)   1935-

PERSONAL: Born November 29, 1935, in London, Ontario, Canada; son of Gordon (a teacher) and Muriel (Johnston) Wonnacott; divorced; children: Rebecca, Cecilia, Daniel. *Education:* University of Western Ontario, B.A., 1957; Princeton University, Ph.D., 1963. *Politics:* "Moderate; vote issues, not parties." *Religion:* Unitarian Universalist. *Residence:* London, Ontario, Canada. *Office:* University of Western Ontario, London, Ontario, Canada N6A 3K7.

CAREER: Wesleyan University, Middletown, Conn., assistant professor of mathematics, 1961-65; University of Western Ontario, London, associate professor of mathematics, 1966—. Visiting professor, Duke University, 1965-66; visiting research associate, University of California, Berkeley, 1972-73.

MEMBER: American Statistical Association.

WRITINGS—With brother, Ronald J. Wonnacott, except as indicated: *Introductory Statistics*, Wiley, 1969, 4th edition, in press; *Econometrics*, Wiley, 1970; *Introductory Statistics for Business and Economics*, Wiley, 1972, 3rd edition, in press; (sole author) *Calculus*, Wiley, 1977; *Regression*, Wiley, 1981; *Statistics: Discovering Its Power*, Wiley, 1982.

WORK IN PROGRESS: Research in mathematical social sciences and medicine; more books on statistics.

SIDELIGHTS: Thomas H. Wonnacott wrote *CA:* "I love teaching, and writing textbooks is just a natural outgrowth of that."

Wonnacott's work has been translated into Japanese, Italian, and Portuguese.

AVOCATIONAL INTERESTS: Folk dancing, touch football, music, farming, skiing.

* * *

WOOD, Phyllis Anderson 1923-

PERSONAL: Born October 24, 1923, in Palo Alto, Calif.; daughter of Carl Arthur (a high school principal) and Beulah (Davidson) Anderson; married Roger Holmes Wood (a certified financial planner), December 26, 1947; children: Stephen Holmes, David Anderson, Martha Helen, Elizabeth Satterlee. *Education:* University of California, Berkeley, A.B., 1944; Stanford University, teaching certificate, 1946; San Francisco State University, M.A., 1977. *Religion:* Presbyterian. *Home:* 65 Capay Circle, South San Francisco, Calif. 94080.

CAREER: Teacher of speech, drama, and English in high schools in California, 1944-49; Jefferson High School District, Daly City, Calif., teacher of reading and basic English skills, 1965—. *Member:* International Reading Association, National Council of Teachers of English, Authors Guild, Authors League of America, California Writers Club. *Awards, honors:* Helen Keating Ott Award, Church and Synagogue Library Association, 1981.

WRITINGS—For young adults, except as indicated; published by Westminster, except as indicated: *Andy*, 1971, published as *The Night Summer Began*, Scholastic Book Services, 1976; *Your Bird Is Here, Tom Thompson*, 1972; *I've Missed a Sunset or Three*, 1973; *Song of the Shaggy Canary*, 1974; *A Five-Color Buick and a Blue-Eyed Cat* (Junior Literary Guild selection), 1975; *I Think This Is Where We Came In*, 1976; *Win Me and You Lose* (Junior Literary Guild selection), 1977; *The Novels of Phyllis Anderson Wood: A Teacher's Guide*, New American Library, 1977; *Get a Little Lost, Tia*, 1978; *This Time Count Me In*, 1980; *Pass Me a Pine Cone* (Junior Literary Guild selection), 1980; *Meet Me in the Park, Angie*, 1983.

WORK IN PROGRESS: Challenges in Remedial English, a textbook.

SIDELIGHTS: Phyllis Anderson Wood told *CA:* "I began writing for young adults because as a teacher of high school reading classes I was continually hampered by the lack of books that appealed to students who hadn't yet formed a reading habit. For the past seven years, through the publication of eight novels, my students have been both my soundest critics and my warmest fans. Having had to decide, initially, whether I would write to please the students or the critics, and having opted for the students' enthusiasm, I now am pleased to be getting positive support from both groups."

* * *

WOODS, P. F.
See BAYLEY, Barrington J(ohn)

* * *

WOOLLEY, A(lban) E(dward, Jr.) 1926-

PERSONAL: Born September 26, 1926, in El Dorado, Ark.; son of Alban Edward (a printer) and Ira (Sawyer) Woolley; married Dorothy Caroline McInnis, June 6, 1952 (divorced February, 1964); married Dorothy Ellen Riley, November 24, 1964 (divorced April, 1977); married Maisie Pennington, September, 1984; children: (first marriage) Wendy, Mike, Jill; (second marriage) Amy, Ben, Daniel. *Education:* Attended Louisiana State University; Goddard College, B.A., 1969, M.A., 1971; Kensington University, Ph.D., 1979. *Religion:* Methodist. *Home:* 803 Edgemoor Rd., Cherry Hill, N.J. 08034. *Office address:* P.O. Box 4152, Cherry Hill, N.J. 08034.

CAREER: State University of New York College at New Paltz, associate professor of art and photography, 1958-61; free-lance magazine writer, 1961-67; New York Regional Educational Center, New Paltz, associate director, 1967-68; *Pageant* (magazine), New York, N.Y., photography editor, 1969-71; *Today's Health* (magazine), Chicago, Ill., managing editor, 1971-73; *PSA Journal*, Philadelphia, Pa., editor in chief, 1979-81; *Lab World* (magazine), Philadelphia, editor and publisher, 1981-82; Woolley Publications, Inc., Cherry Hill, N.J., president, 1984—. Has had twenty one-man photographic exhibitions; other photographs are displayed in permanent collections at Museum of Modern Art, Dartmouth College, State University of New York, Louisiana Art Commission, and Louisiana State University. Democratic candidate for New York State Senate, 1968.

MEMBER: Photographic Society of America, American Society of Magazine Photographers, National Press Photographers Association, Society of Education Photographers, Rotary Club.

AWARDS, HONORS: Named photographer of the year by Louisiana Art Commission, 1953-54; Jessie H. Neal award for editorial excellence, 1978, 1980; gold medals for photojournalism in exhibitions in Port Huron, Mich., Chicago, Ill., San Francisco, Calif., and Wichita, Kan.; silver medal for photojournalist of the year, 1984.

WRITINGS—All self-illustrated: *Night Photography*, Greenberg, 1955; *Photographic Films and Their Uses*, Chilton, 1959; *Outdoor Four Seasons Photography*, Chilton, 1960; *Photographic Print Quality*, Chilton, 1961; *Creative 35mm Techniques*, A. S. Barnes, 1962, revised edition, Hastings House, 1970; *Photographic Lighting*, A. S. Barnes, 1963, revised edition, Hastings House, 1970; *Traveling with Your Camera*, A. S. Barnes, 1964, revised edition, Hastings House, 1971.

Camera Journalism, A. S. Barnes, 1965; *Persia/Iran*, Amphoto, 1965; *35mm Nudes*, Amphoto, 1966; (with John Dyson) *Our Historic Hudson*, James B. Adler, 1968; *Besler Topcon Unirex/Auto 100*, Amphoto, 1972; *Photography: A Practical and Creative Introduction*, McGraw, 1972; *Expressions: Eleanor on Her Life*, Woolley Publications, 1984.

Contributor of stories and articles to major magazines and newspapers, including *Look, Saturday Evening Post, Time, Sports Illustrated, New York Times,* and *Parade.* Editor-at-large, *Contemporary Photographer;* editor, *Journal of International Physicians;* contributing editor, *Photographic Trade News.*

WORK IN PROGRESS: Sally and Company, a novel; *Images of Africa,* for Decker.

AVOCATIONAL INTERESTS: Travel, sports, antiques.

*   *   *

WORMAN, Eli
   See WEIL, Roman L(ee)

*   *   *

WRIGHT, H(ugh) Elliott 1937-

PERSONAL: Born November 20, 1937, in Athens, Ala.; son of Hugh E. (a clergyman) and Angeline (Shannon) Wright; married Juanita Bass (a minister), December 30, 1963. *Education:* Birmingham-Southern College, A.B., 1959; Vanderbilt University, B.D., 1962, D.Min., 1967; graduate study, Harvard University, 1962-63. *Politics:* Democrat. *Home:* 4761 Henry Hudson Pkwy., Bronx, N.Y. 10471. *Office:* National Conference of Christians and Jews, 71 Fifth Ave., New York, N.Y. 10003.

CAREER: Ordained minister of United Methodist Church-Tennessee Annual Conference, 1962; youth director in Nashville, Tenn., 1961-62, and Belmont, Mass., 1962-63; pastor in Baxter, Tenn., 1963-64; Tennessee Heart Association, Nashville, field secretary, 1964-65; associate pastor in Nashville, 1965-66; pastor in Brentwood, Tenn., 1966-67; Religious News Service, New York City, Protestant-Orthodox editor, 1967-75; free-lance writer and consultant, 1975-80; National Conference of Christians and Jews, New York City, coordinator of Project on Church, State and Taxation, 1981-83, vice-president for program, 1983—. Editorial assistant, *Motive,* 1965-67; host, "Challenge to Faith" program, WOR-Radio, 1973-75. Pastoral associate, Riverdale Presbyterian Church, Bronx, N.Y., 1974—. Consultant to religious and educational organizations, including Auburn Theological Seminary, Hartford Seminary Foundation, 1972, 1976-78, and United Methodist Board of Global Ministries, 1975-78.

MEMBER: Authors Guild, Authors League of America, Religion Newswriters Association, United Presbyterian Men, Phi Beta Kappa, Alpha Tau Omega, Alpha Psi Omega, Eta Sigma Phi, Sigma Delta Chi.

AWARDS, HONORS: Founders Medal, Vanderbilt University, 1962; Shepherd Prize, Vanderbilt University, 1962; Religious Heritage of America Award in Journalism, 1972.

WRITINGS: (With R. S. Lecky) *Can These Bones Live? The Failure of Church Renewal,* Sheed, 1969; (editor with Lecky) *Black Manifesto: Religion, Racism, and Reparation,* Sheed, 1969; (with R. W. Lynn) *The Big Little School: Two Hundred Years of the Sunday School,* Harper, 1971, 2nd edition, Religious Education Press/Abingdon, 1980; *Go Free,* Friendship Press, 1973; (with wife, Juanita B. Wright) *The Challenge of Mission,* United Methodist Board of Global Ministries, 1973; (with Howard Butt) *At the Edge of Hope: Christian Laity in Paradox,* Seabury, 1978; (with Douglas McGaw) *A Tale of*

Two Congregations, Hartford Seminary Foundation, 1980; *Holy Company: Christian Heroes and Heroines,* Macmillan, 1980.

Also author of a viewers' guide to "Six American Families" television series, 1977. Ghost writer, including one major autobiography. Contributor to *New York Times, Washington Post,* and to religious journals, including *Christian Century* and *National Catholic Reporter.*

WORK IN PROGRESS: Research on church-state relations.

*   *   *

WYNAR, Lubomyr R(oman) 1932-

PERSONAL: Born January 2, 1932, in Lvov, U.S.S.R.; came to the United States in 1955, naturalized citizen, 1960; son of Ivan (a professor) and Eufrosina (a teacher; maiden name, Doryk) Wynar; married Anna T. Kuzmych (a sociologist), July 15, 1962; children: Natalia. *Education:* Attended University of Munich, 1949-51; Ukrainian Free University, M.A., 1955, Ph.D., 1957; Western Reserve University (now Case Western Reserve University), M.S.L.S., 1959. *Home:* 4984 Pheasant Ave., Ravenna, Ohio 44266. *Office:* School of Library Science, Kent State University, Kent, Ohio 44242.

CAREER: Case Institute of Technology (now Case Western Reserve University), Cleveland, Ohio, instructor in bibliography and periodicals librarian, 1959-62; University of Colorado, Boulder, assistant professor of library science and head of Social Sciences Library, 1962-65; Bowling Green State University, Bowling Green, Ohio, assistant professor and director of Bibliographical Research Center, 1966-68, associate professor of library administration and assistant director of libraries, 1968-69; Kent State University, Kent, Ohio, professor of library science and ethnic studies, 1969—, director of Center for the Study of Ethnic Publication, 1971—. Faculty member at University of Denver, summers, 1961, 1963-65. Research associate at John Carroll University, 1962-76. President of Intercollegiate Council on Ethnic Studies in Ohio, 1978-83.

MEMBER: American Historical Association, American Library Association (chairman of Slavic and East European section, 1971-73, 1980-81), American Association for the Advancement of Slavic Studies, Association for the Study of Nationalities (vice-president, 1977-79), Association of Ukrainian American University Professors (president, 1982—), Ukrainian Free Academy of Arts and Sciences in the United States (chairman of Commission on Immigration, 1969—), Ukrainian Historical Association (president, 1982—), Shevchenko Scientific Society (vice-president of Historical and Philosophical Division, 1973-80), Ohio Library Association, Colorado Library Association. *Awards, honors: Encyclopedia Directory of Ethnic Newspapers and Periodicals* was named best reference book of 1972 by American Library Association; grant from U.S. Office of Education, 1977-78.

WRITINGS: Andrew Voynarovsky: A Historical Study, Verlag Logos, 1961; *A History of Early Ukrainian Printing, 1491-1600,* Graduate School of Library Science, University of Denver, 1962; *S. Harrison Thomson: A Bio-Bibliography,* Library, University of Colorado, 1963; *History: A Bibliographical Guide,* Library, University of Colorado, 1963; *Prince Dmytro Vyshnevetskyi,* Ukrainian Academy of Arts and Sciences, 1965; *Ukrainian Kozaks and the Vatican in 1594,* Ukrainian Historical Association, 1965; *Guide to Reference Materials in Political Science,* Colorado Bibliographical Institute, Volume I, 1966, Volume II, 1968; *The Early Years of Michael Hrush-*

evsky, 1866-1894, Ukrainian Historical Association, 1967; *American Political Parties*, Libraries Unlimited, 1969.

Michael Hrushevsky and the Shevchenko Scientific Society, 1895-1930, Ukrainian Historical Association, 1971; *Ethnic Groups in Ohio*, Ethnic Heritage Program, Cleveland State University, 1975; (editor) *Habsburgs and Zaporozhian Cossacks*, Ukrainian Academic Press, 1975; *Encyclopedia Directory of Ethnic Organizations in the United States*, Libraries Unlimited, 1975; (with wife, Anna Wynar) *Encyclopedia Directory of Ethnic Newspapers and Periodicals*, Libraries Unlimited, 1976; (with Lois Butlar) *Building Ethnic Collections*, Libraries Unlimited, 1977; (with Marjorie Murfin) *Reference Services*, Libraries Unlimited, 1977; *Guide to Ethnic Museums, Archives and Libraries in the United States*, Center for Ethnic Studies, Kent State University, 1978.

Ethnic Films and Filmstrip Guide for Libraries and Media Centers: A Selective Filmography, Libraries Unlimited, 1980; *Slavic Ethnic Libraries, Museums and Archives in the United States*, American Library Association, 1980; (editor) *Atlas Istorii Ukrainy* (title means "Historical Atlas of Ukraine"), Ukrainian Historical Association, 1981; *Michael Hrushevsky's Autobiography of 1926*, Ukrainian Historical Association, 1982; *Dmytro Doroshenko: 1882-1951*, Ukrainian Historical Association, 1983.

Managing editor of "Bio-Bibliographical Series" and editor of "Social Science Reference Services" for University of Colorado Library, 1963-65. Contributor of more than two hundred articles and reviews to academic journals. Editor of *Ukrainian Historian*, 1964—; founder and editor of *Ethnic Forum*, 1980—. Section editor of ethnic studies in *American Reference Books Annual*, 1974—.

WORK IN PROGRESS: Slavic Press in the United States; Reference and Information Services; Guide to Ethnic Reference Materials; Michael Hrushevsky: Bio-Bibliography.

SIDELIGHTS: Lubomyr R. Wynar writes that his main interests are history, library science, ethnic studies, and bibliography. "I was initially trained as a historian in the area of East European history, with an emphasis on Ukrainian political, cultural, and social history of the sixteenth through the eighteenth centuries. Later, when I completed my studies in library science, I continued to be actively involved in both, researching various topics in Ukrainian historiography, primarily because this area of East European history has been rather neglected by American historians.

"As a librarian and library science educator, I have always recognized the important role that the library can play in providing services to American ethnic communities. In this respect librarians and information specialists should not only be able to recognize the special needs of the various ethnic groups within their communities, but must also be aware of voluminous amounts of ethnic materials published by such groups within this country. This literature, ranging from periodicals to newspapers, greatly impacts the American ethnic readership, and as such cannot be ignored by institutions whose primary role lies in information dissemination to all elements within society. The journal *Ethnic Forum*, which I initiated and am presently editing, is just one attempt to bring together ethnicity and librarianship."

* * *

WYNN-JONES, Michael 1941-

PERSONAL: Born September 17, 1941, in Pentre, Wales; son of Edward (a priest) and Dilys (a teacher; maiden name, Spenser) Wynn-Jones; married Delia Smith (a culinary journalist and television broadcaster), September, 1971. *Education:* Worcester College, Oxford, B.A. (with honors), 1964. *Home address:* Stowmarket, Suffolk, England.

CAREER: Nova, London, England, assistant editor, 1965-68; *Daily Mirror*, London, deputy editor, 1969-70; *Spectator*, London, associate editor, 1970-71; editorial consultant and writer, 1971—.

MEMBER: Royal Automobile Club (honorary historian).

AWARDS, HONORS: Frank Luther Mott Award, 1976, for *The Cartoon History of the American Revolution*.

WRITINGS: The Cartoon History of Britain, Macmillan, 1971; *Lloyds of London*, Hastings House, 1973; *A Newspaper History of the World*, Morrow, 1974; *The Cartoon History of the American Revolution*, Putnam, 1976; *The World One Hundred Years Ago*, Mackay, 1976; *Deadline Disaster*, Regnery, 1976; *The Cartoon History of the Monarchy*, Macmillan, 1977; *The People's Jubilee*, Metheun, 1977; *George Cruikshank: His Life and London*, Macmillan, 1978; *The Derby: The Story of the World's Greatest Horse Race*, Croom Helm, 1979; *One Hundred Years on the Road*, McGraw, 1982.

Contributor to British publications, including *Radio Times* and *Observer*. Editor, *Twentieth Century*, 1966-71, and *Pell Mell and Woodcote*, 1981—.

WORK IN PROGRESS: A study of nineteenth-century cartoonists for publication by John Murray.

SIDELIGHTS: Michael Wynn-Jones comments, "Basically my interest is in *visual* history; e.g., political cartoons, newspapers, photographs, etc., which I try to use as primary historical sources." *Avocational interests:* Cricket, travel, food and wine.

Y

YAEGER, Bart
See STRUNG, Norman

* * *

YEATES, Maurice 1938-

PERSONAL: Born May 24, 1938, in England; son of Lewis Yeates; married Marilynn Snelbaker (a lecturer), 1962; children: Maurine, Harry. *Education:* University of Reading, B.A. (honors), 1960; Northwestern University, M.A., 1961, Ph.D., 1963. *Office:* Department of Geography, Queen's University, Kingston, Ontario, Canada.

CAREER: Queen's University, Kingston, Ontario, assistant professor, 1965-68, associate professor, 1968-70, professor of geography, 1970—, head of department, 1973-79, dean of School of Graduate Studies and Research, 1979-84. Consultant to Canadian government ministries and departments.

MEMBER: Royal Society of Canada (fellow), Canadian Association of Geographers, American Association of Geographers, Regional Science Association.

AWARDS, HONORS: American Association of Geographers, 20th International Geographical Congress participation award, 1964; Canada Council leave award, 1971-72, 1978-79, 1984-85; Canadian Association of Geographers award, 1982.

WRITINGS: (With E. J. Taaffe and B. J. Garner) *The Peripheral Journey to Work: A Geographic Consideration,* Northwestern University Press, 1963; (with R. S. Thoman and E. C. Conkling) *The Geography of Economic Activity,* McGraw, 1967; *An Introduction to Quantitative Analysis in Economic Geography,* McGraw, 1967.

(With P. E. Lloyd) *The Impact of Industrial Incentives,* Queen's Printer, 1970; (with Garner) *The North American City,* Harper, 1971, 3rd edition, 1980; *An Introduction to Quantitative Analysis in Human Geography,* McGraw, 1973; *Main Street,* Macmillan, 1975; (with Conkling) *Man's Economic Environment,* McGraw, 1976; *North American Urban Patterns,* Wiley, 1980.

WORK IN PROGRESS: Land in Main Street; The Urban Consequences of Core/Periphery Developments in the Canadian Economy.

SIDELIGHTS: Maurice Yeates told *CA* that he has "now had at least one jog in thirty different North American cities."

* * *

YOLTON, John W(illiam) 1921-

PERSONAL: Born November 10, 1921, in Birmingham, Ala.; son of Robert Elgene (an engineer) and Ella Maud (Holmes) Yolton; married Jean Mary Sebastian (a librarian), September 5, 1945; children: Karin Frances (Mrs. Bryant Griffith), Pamela Holmes (Mrs. Derek A. Smith). *Education:* University of Cincinnati, B.A., 1945, M.A., 1946; University of California, Berkeley, graduate study, 1946-50; Balliol College, Oxford, D.Phil., 1952. *Religion:* None. *Home:* 39 Wakefield Ln., Piscataway, N.J. 08854. *Office:* Milledoler Hall, Rutgers College, New Brunswick, N.J. 08903.

CAREER: Johns Hopkins University, Baltimore, Md., visiting lecturer in philosophy, 1952-53; Princeton University, Princeton, N.J., assistant professor and bicentennial preceptor, 1953-57; Kenyon College, Gambier, Ohio, associate professor of philosophy, 1957-61; University of Maryland, College Park, professor of philosophy, 1961-63; York University, Downsview, Ontario, professor of philosophy, 1963-78, chairman of department, 1963-72, acting president, 1973-74; Rutgers University, New Brunswick, N.J., dean of Rutgers College and professor of philosophy, 1978—.

MEMBER: American Philosophical Association, Canadian Philosophical Association, Mind Association, American Society for Eighteenth-Century Studies.

AWARDS, HONORS: Fulbright fellow at Oxford University, 1950-52; Leonard Nelson Foundation prize, 1959.

WRITINGS: John Locke and the Way of Ideas, Clarendon Press, 1956; *Philosophy of Science of A. S. Eddington,* Nijhoff, 1960; (editor) *Locke's Essay Concerning Human Understanding,* Dent, 1961, revised edition, 1965; *Thinking and Perceiving,* Open Court, 1962; *Theory of Knowledge,* Macmillan, 1965; *Metaphysical Analysis,* University of Toronto Press, 1967; (editor) *John Locke: Problems and Perspectives,* Cambridge University Press, 1969.

Locke and the Compass of Human Understanding, Cambridge University Press, 1970; *Locke and Education*, Random House, 1971; (author of introduction and commentary) John Locke, *The Locke Reader*, Cambridge University Press, 1977; *Thinking Matter*, University of Minnesota Press, 1983; *Perceptual Acquaintance from Descartes to Reid*, University of Minnesota Press, 1984; *John Locke: A Study of His Thought*, B. H. Blackwell, 1985; (with wife, Jean S. Yolton) *John Locke: A Reference Guide*, G. K. Hall, 1985.

Editor, *Studies in Eighteenth-Century Culture*, 1984—; member of editorial board, Clarendon edition of the "Works of John Locke," 1972— (chairman of editorial board, 1983—); member of advisory editorial board, "Collected Papers of Bertrand Russell," 1975— (chairman of advisory editorial board, 1983—).

WORK IN PROGRESS: A critical edition of Locke's *Some Thoughts Concerning Education*, with J. S. Yolton; research in seventeenth- and eighteenth-century continental philosophy.

*   *   *

YOUNG, Thomas Daniel   1919-

PERSONAL: Born October 22, 1919, in Louisville, Miss.; son of William A. (a physician) and Lula (Wright) Young; married Arlease Lewis, December 21, 1941; children: Thomas Daniel, Jr., Terry Lewis, Kyle David. *Education:* University of Southern Mississippi, B.A., 1941; University of Mississippi, M.A., 1948; Vanderbilt University, Ph.D., 1950. *Religion:* Methodist. *Home:* 857 Highland Crest, Nashville, Tenn. 37205. *Office:* Department of English, Vanderbilt University, Nashville, Tenn. 37203.

CAREER: University of Mississippi, University, instructor in English, 1946-48; Mississippi Southern College (now University of Southern Mississippi), Hattiesburg, assistant professor, 1950-51, professor of English and chairman of department, 1951-57, acting dean, Basic College, 1954-55; Delta State College, Cleveland, Miss., professor of English and dean, 1957-61; Vanderbilt University, Nashville, Tenn., dean of admissions, 1961-64, professor of English and chairman, 1964-72, Gertrude Conaway Vanderbilt Professor of English, 1972—. *Military service:* U.S. Army Air Forces, 1942-45.

MEMBER: Modern Language Association of America, South Atlantic Modern Language Association, (chairman of American literature section, 1970).

WRITINGS: (With F. C. Watkins) *The Literature of the South*, Scott, Foresman, 1952, revised edition, 1968; (with M. T. Inge) *Donald Davidson: An Essay and a Bibliography*, Vanderbilt University Press, 1965; (with Ronald Fine) *American Literature: A Critical Survey*, American Book Co., 1968; (contributor) *American Writers*, Scribner, 1968; (editor) *John Crowe Ransom: Critical Essay and a Bibliography*, Louisiana State University, 1968.

John Crowe Ransom: An Introduction, Steck, 1970; (with Inge) *Donald Davidson*, Twayne, 1971; (editor) *The Literary Correspondence of Allen Tate and Donald Davidson*, University of Georgia Press, 1975; *Gentleman in a Dustcoat: A Biography of John Crowe Ransom*, Louisiana State University Press, 1976; (author of introduction) Allen Tate, *The Fathers and Other*

Fiction, Louisiana State University, 1977; (editor) *The New Criticism and After*, University Press of Virginia, 1977.

(Editor) *The Man of Letters in America: The Correspondence of Allen Tate and John Peale Bishop*, University of Kentucky Press, 1980; *The Past in the Present: A Thematic Study of Modern American Fiction*, Louisiana State University Press, 1981; *Tennessee Writers*, University of Tennessee Press, 1981; *Waking Their Neighbors Up: The Agrarians Fifty Years After*, University of Georgia Press, 1982; *John Crowe Ransom: An Annotated Bibliography*, Garland, 1983; (editor with John Hindle) *Selected Essays of John Crowe Ransom*, Louisiana State University Press, 1983; (co-editor) *Selected Letters of John Crowe Ransom*, Louisiana State University Press, 1984. Contributor of articles to *Modern Fiction Studies*, *Sewanee Review*, *Mississippi Quarterly*, *Southern Review*, and other journals.

WORK IN PROGRESS: Co-editing a study of Southern literature, for Louisiana State University Press.

SIDELIGHTS: Thomas Daniel Young has devoted much of his writing career to the study of John Crowe Ransom, one of the more eminent poets and scholars of the early twentieth century. *Gentleman in a Dustcoat: A Biography of John Crowe Ransom*, one of Young's works, has been labeled "the definitive biography" of the poet by a *Choice* critic. Of a later book, *Selected Essays of John Crowe Ransom*, which Young edited with John Hindle, Donald Davie of the *New York Times Book Review* notes: "[The editors'] selection . . . is made to show how Ransom steadily built up and then maintained a coherent philosophical position."

BIOGRAPHICAL/CRITICAL SOURCES: Georgia Review, spring, 1967, spring, 1969; *New Republic*, February 12, 1977; *Antioch Review*, spring, 1977; *Christian Century*, April 27, 1977; *Choice*, June, 1977; *Sewanee Review*, July 1977; *Times Literary Supplement*, March 26, 1982; *New York Times Book Review*, May 20, 1984.

*   *   *

YOUNGBLOOD, Ronald F.   1931-

PERSONAL: Born August 10, 1931, in Chicago, Ill.; son of William C. (a banker) and Ethel (Arenz) Youngblood; married Carolyn Johnson, August 16, 1952; children: Glenn, Wendy. *Education:* Valparaiso University, B.A., 1952; Fuller Theological Seminary, B.D., 1955; Dropsie College for Hebrew and Cognate Learning (now Dropsie University), Ph.D., 1961. *Religion:* Baptist. *Office:* Bethel Theological Seminary West, 4747 College Ave., San Diego, Calif. 92115.

CAREER: Bethel Theological Seminary, St. Paul, Minn., assistant professor, 1961-65, associate professor, 1965-70, professor of Old Testament, 1970-78; Wheaton Graduate School, Wheaton, Ill., professor, 1978-81, associate dean, 1978-80, dean, 1980-81; Trinity Evangelical Divinity School, Deerfield, Ill., professor, 1981-82; Bethel Theological Seminary West, San Diego, Calif., professor, 1982—. Has spent four summers in Europe as translator-editor of the New International Version of the Old Testament, sponsored by International Bible Society. *Member:* Society of Biblical Literature, Evangelical Theological Society, Near East Archaeological Society (member of board).

WRITINGS: Great Themes of the Old Testament, Harvest Publishing, 1968, revised edition published as *The Heart of the Old Testament*, Baker Book, 1971; *Special Day Sermons*, Baker Book, 1973; *Faith of Our Fathers*, Regal Books, 1976; *How It All Began*, Regal Books, 1980; *Exodus*, Moody, 1983; (editor with Morris Inch) *The Living and Active Word of God*, Eisenbrauns, 1983; *Themes from Isaiah*, Regal Books, 1983.

Contributor of articles to *Journal of Biblical Literature, Bulletin of American Schools of Oriental Research, Journal of the Evangelical Theological Society*, and *Jewish Quarterly Review*. Editor, *Journal of the Evangelical Theological Society*.

WORK IN PROGRESS: Commentaries on Judges, 1 and 2 Samuel, Proverbs, and 1 and 2 Kings; a survey of the Old Testament.

SIDELIGHTS: Ronald F. Youngblood is fluent in Hebrew and has made nine trips to the Middle East.

Z

ZAMPAGLIONE, Gerardo 1917-

PERSONAL: Born November 18, 1917, in Rome, Italy; son of Arturo and Alessandra (Quagliotti) Zampaglione; married Anna Spataro, February, 1951; children: Arturo, Giuseppe. *Education:* University of Rome, degree in law, 1939, degree in political science, 1945. *Religion:* Roman Catholic. *Home:* Via P.S. Mancini 12, 00196 Rome, Italy. *Office:* Italian Consulate General, 3 Raja Santosh Rd., Calcutta, India.

CAREER: Worked as journalist, 1945-48; official of Italian senate, 1948; Italian Ministry of Foreign Affairs, Rome, member of staff, 1949-51, Italian consul in Toronto, Ontario, 1951-53, and Stuttgart, West Germany, 1953-58; Council of Ministers of the European Communities, Brussels, Belgium, director general, 1961-73; Italian ambassador to Kuwait, 1974-77, Pakistan, 1977-79, Switzerland, 1979-80, and Indonesia, 1980-83; Italian Consul General in Calcutta, India, beginning 1983. *Military service:* Italian Army, 1940-45; became captain.

WRITINGS: Italy, Benn, 1956; *Diritto consolare* (title means "Consular Law"), two volumes, Stamperia Nazionale, 1956, 2nd edition, 1970; *Breve storia dell' integrazione europa* (title means "Short History of European Unity"), Edizioni Cinque Lune, 1957, 2nd edition, 1958; *L'Idea della pace nel mondo antico,* Edizioni ERI-RAI, 1967, translation by Richard Dunn published as *The Idea of Peace in Antiquity,* University of Notre Dame Press, 1973; *Storia del Kuwait* (title means "History of Kuwait"), Edizioni ERI-RAI, 1978; *Una politica estera per l'Europa Unita* (title means "A Foreign Policy for United Europe"), Edizioni Cinque Lune, 1978; *L'Europa e gli organismi comunitari* (title means "Europe and the Community Institutions"), Edizioni ERI-RAI, 1979. Contributor of articles on peace and pacifism, the political and economic unity of Europe, and consular law and practice to magazines.

WORK IN PROGRESS: A history of Italians in Illawarra, New South Wales, Australia.

SIDELIGHTS: Gerardo Zampaglione writes: "I am confident that European unity will perhaps be the greatest achievement of our era. Its political, economic, and social implications will in fact be so far reaching that all countries of the world will be affected by it.

"Having served for over eleven years in the capacity of director general for general affairs of the Council of Ministers of the European Communities, I have collected first-hand experience and evidence that European unity is not only desirable but also possible. As a matter of fact it is the most practicable and feasible way to defend democracy, of giving the world stability, security, and of raising the standard of living of all human beings. European unity will also be a guarantee for peace. The moment when Europe will be one, having abolished borders which generally lack moral and economic justification because they are simply the result of past antagonism and wars, it will be possible to solve, in spirit of brotherly cooperation, the problems of poverty, distress, and underdevelopment which are the origin of wars.

"This explains why, side by side with the problems of European unity, I have during my lifetime also been interested in pacifism in general and ways and means to enforce lasting peace among nations of the world. I have consequently tried to investigate if peace was just an ideal and a hope of our times and if it was not deeply rooted in the past of humanity and in the speculations of ancient philosophers, reformers, theologians, etc. It has been as a consequence of this research that I have written my essay on the 'History of Peace in Antiquity.' I have now in mind to pursue this research with reference to medieval and modern times and to the Eastern societies and to their trends of thought and historic traditions.

"My book *Diritto consolare* (Consular Law) is today considered the standard book for the Italian Consular Service and is adopted as such by the Italian Diplomatic and Consular Representatives."

*   *   *

ZEIGFREID, Karl
See FANTHORPE, R(obert) Lionel

*   *   *

ZERMAN, Melvyn Bernard 1930-

PERSONAL: Born July 10, 1930, in New York, N.Y.; son of Abraham (in real estate) and Ida (Belsky) Zirman; married Miriam Baron, September 14, 1952; children: Andrew, Jared, Lenore. *Education:* University of Michigan, B.A., 1952; Columbia University, M.A., 1953. *Politics:* Democrat. *Religion:* Jewish. *Home:* 110-37 68th St., Forest Hills, N.Y. 11375. *Office:* Random House, Inc., 201 East 50th St., New York, N.Y. 10022.

CAREER: Harper & Row Publishers, Inc., New York City, assistant to sales manager, 1959-64, sales department office manager, 1964-67, assistant director of sales, 1968-70, trade sales manager, 1970-77, administrative sales manager, 1977-79; Random House, Inc., New York City, administrative sales manager, 1979—; writer.

AWARDS, HONORS: Freedom Foundation Award, 1981, for *Beyond a Reasonable Doubt: Inside the American Jury System.*

WRITINGS—Nonfiction: *Call the Final Witness,* Harper, 1977; *Beyond a Reasonable Doubt: Inside the American Jury System* (for young adults), Crowell, 1981.

WORK IN PROGRESS: A book for young adults.

SIDELIGHTS: Call the Final Witness is Melvyn Bernard Zerman's account of the trial of Ricky Mathes, a Queens, N.Y. teenager who in 1977 was accused—and eventually acquitted—of the fatal shooting of a salesman. The author was a member of the jury that decided the youth's fate; Zerman's book, according to Tim Wicker in a *New York Times Book Review* article, "tells us a great deal about Ricky Mathes and his life on the streets and in the schools of New York; about Riker's Island, where he was incarcerated for 11 months; and about [the] criminal justice system."

The Mathes case was unique because "indisputable proof seemed to have been presented—*three* eyewitnesses . . . identified the youth as the murderer," notes Wicker. "But by the time a determined defense had cross-examined the witnesses as to all the circumstances in which they had supposedly seen Mathes, as well as the discrepancies in their accounts of their own movements, [the jury was] confronted with the agony of judgement rather than the certainty of truth." And while the author presents a criminal justice system that seems based on arbitrariness and even discriminatory practices, Zerman shows that "when the doors finally close on a jury, its 12 members are face to face with the most harrowing of tasks—to determine the fate, perhaps even the life or death, of a fellow human being," Wicker writes. "It is a task for which few can ever be well-equipped, or eager, but which might fall on any citizen at any time. . . . [The author] makes clear the racial prejudice that threatened Ricky Mathes and how Mathes's defiant demeanor on the witness stand tended to reinforce the prejudice."

"We all recognized," states Zerman in *Call the Final Witness,* "that more was being demanded of us—in the way of wisdom, if nothing else—than had often—perhaps ever—been demanded of us before. . . . If a person, whatever his background, knows that much is expected of him—no less than helping to determine the course of someone else's life—in all probability that person will strive with all his capability to be wise and compassionate, to stretch himself beyond his foibles and his prejudices. One thing you can be sure of: he will not forget that the stakes are high."

BIOGRAPHICAL/CRITICAL SOURCES: Melvyn Bernard Zerman, *Call the Final Witness,* Harper, 1977; *New York Times Book Review,* May 1, 1977, July 19, 1981.

*   *   *

ZIADEH, Farhat Jacob 1917-

PERSONAL: Born April 8, 1917, in Ramallah, Jordan; son of Jacob (a merchant) and Nimeh (Farah) Ziadeh; married Suad Salem, July 24, 1949; children: Shireen, Susan, Rhonda, Deena, Reema. *Education:* American University of Beirut, B.A., 1937; University of London, LL.B., 1940. *Religion:* Greek Orthodox. *Home:* 3919 48th Ave. N.E., Seattle, Wash. 98105.

CAREER: Princeton University, Princeton, N.J., instructor in Arabic, 1943-45; called to the Bar, Lincoln's Inn, London, England, 1946; magistrate, government of Palestine, 1947-48; Princeton University, lecturer, 1948-54, assistant professor, 1954-58, associate professor of Arabic and Islamics, 1958-66; University of Washington, Seattle, professor of Near Eastern studies, 1966-82, adjunct professor of law, 1978—, chairman of department of Near Eastern languages and literature, 1970-82, director of Near East Center, School of International Studies, 1975-82; Consortium of American Universities, director of Center of Arabic Studies Abroad, American University, Cairo, Egypt, 1983—.

MEMBER: American Oriental Society, American Association of Teachers of Arabic (former president), Middle East Studies Association of North America (member of board of directors, 1969-71; president, 1979-80).

WRITINGS: (With I. Freiji) *History of the American People,* (in Arabic) Princeton University Press, 1946; *Arabic Primer,* Princeton University Press, 1949; (with R. Bayly Winder) *An Introduction to Modern Arabic,* Princeton University Press, 1957.

(Editor and translator) S. Mahmassani, *The Philosophy of Jurisprudence in Islam,* E. J. Brill, 1961; *A Reader in Modern Literary Arabic,* Princeton University Press, 1964; *Lawyers: The Rule of Law and Liberalism in Modern Egypt,* Hoover Institution, Stanford University, 1968; (editor and author of introduction) al-Khassaf, *Adab al-Qadi,* American University of Cairo Press, 1979; *Law of Property in the Arab World: Real Rights in Egypt, Iraq, Jordan, Lebanon and Syria,* Graham & Trotman, 1979.

SIDELIGHTS: Farhat Jacob Ziadeh told *CA:* "Arabic culture and civilization are among the world's greatest. I see my career as contributing in a small way to the integration of Arabic culture in world culture."